ALSO BY MAEVE BINCHY

Fiction

Light a Penny Candle
Echoes
The Lilac Bus
Firefly Summer
Silver Wedding
Circle of Friends
The Copper Beech
The Glass Lake
Evening Class
Tara Road
Scarlet Feather
Quentins
Nights of Rain and Stars
Whitethorn Woods
Heart and Soul
Minding Frankie
A Week in Winter
Chestnut Street

Nonfiction

Aches & Pains
The Maeve Binchy Writers' Club

Maeve's Times

Maeve Binchy

Maeve's Times

In Her Own Words

EDITED BY RÓISÍN INGLE

INTRODUCTION BY
Gordon Snell

Alfred A. Knopf · New York · 2014

THIS IS A BORZOI BOOK PUBLISHED BY ALFRED A. KNOPF

 Published in the United States by Alfred A. Knopf, a division of Random House LLC, New York, a Penguin Random House company.

Originally published in Ireland by Hachette Books Ireland, a division of Hachette U.K. Ltd., London, in 2013.

www.aaknopf.com

The material in this work first appeared in *The Irish Times.*

Library of Congress Cataloging-in-Publication Data
Binchy, Maeve.
[Essays. Selections]
Maeve's times : in her own words / Maeve Binchy ; edited by Róisín Ingle ; [introduction by Gordon Snell].—First edition.
pages cm
Selected essays are published in The Irish times over fifty years.
ISBN 978-0-385-35345-8 (hardcover)—
ISBN 978-0-385-35346-5 (eBook)
I. Ingle, Róisín editor of compilation. II. Irish times (Dublin, Ireland : 1874) III. Title.
PR6052.I7728A6 2014
824'.914—dc23 2014001284

Jacket illustration by William Low
Jacket design by Stephanie Ross

Manufactured in the United States of America

First United States Edition

Note on Maeve Binchy and *The Irish Times*

Maeve Binchy was appointed Women's Editor of *The Irish Times* in October 1968. As a young teacher she had loved both her job and her holiday travels, and had been a favourite contributor since her first travel letter, sent in by her father, was published a few years earlier. On her appointment the then News Editor, the late Donal Foley, declared, 'Won't she be great crack to work with? And she's a brilliant writer!' Both proved true over a career which lasted the best part of fifty years.

Maeve wrote for and edited the daily 'Women First' page until 1973, when she transferred to the London office as a columnist, feature writer and reporter, balancing the day job with her rapidly growing career as a writer of fiction and drama. When Maeve resigned from the staff of *The Irish Times* in the 1980s, she retained her close association with the paper as a regular contributor. Maeve and her husband, Gordon Snell, moved back to Ireland in the early eighties.

Contents

TWO NEWS REPORTS

EIGHTIES

Introduction

From her earliest childhood, Maeve loved stories – and wanted to be part of them. When her father started to read her some tale of two children wandering through a wood, she asked at once, 'Where was I?'

He would say patiently, 'You were sitting in a tree beside the path.' And with Maeve happily located, the story could go on.

When she grew up and became a storyteller herself, she made her readers feel that, like little Maeve in the tree, they were on the scene, among the action and the characters. She did the same in her journalism, writing with on-the-spot directness of the people and events she met with.

It was her father's enthusiasm that led to Maeve becoming a journalist in the first place. As a teacher she used her long holidays to travel all over the world, on cargo ships, cheap flights, trains and hitch-hiking. She worked in school and holiday camps, on a kibbutz, and as a tourist guide, in North America, the Middle East and Asia.

Her father sent some of her long, lively letters home to the newspapers, who published them as articles. That was the start of her career as a columnist – a job she kept doing happily even after she had become a celebrated novelist.

Whether she was observing a couple having an angry but icily polite disagreement, or feeling the panic – including her own – brought on by the trials of air travel, or watching the outlandish fantasies of the fashion industry, she had a unique eye and ear for the quirks, intensities and absurdities of human behaviour.

No wonder her readers were delighted with her – for she told it all with the eagerness and enthusiasm of someone who says: 'Just wait till I tell you what happened . . .' and goes on to tell an enthralling and often hilarious tale.

She brought the same directness to her many serious reports for the paper – on the bombs in London and other cities, the capsized ferry disaster, and the savage war in Cyprus.

Maeve followed the advice she often gave to aspiring writers – to write as you speak. Her view of the world and the people in it was the same in her writing as it was in her life: she was compassionate and perceptive, she treated everyone with the same considerate interest, and her humour was uproarious but never sneering or cruel.

Her capacity for friendship seemed limitless, and hundreds of people from all over the world, who never knew her, have written to say that they thought of her as a friend.

I can almost hear her say, 'That's enough of that! You make me sound like some kind of saint!' Indeed as a schoolgirl, sainthood was a role she considered aiming for, but decided against – partly on the grounds that it could involve martyrdom, but really because it just wasn't her style.

We must all be glad she took on the roles she did, as teacher, writer and friend to so many – and I above all feel specially lucky that we met, and spent so many happy and loving years together.

When I read these articles, stories and reports from *The Irish Times*, I hear her voice and feel she is back with us again, in all the vivacious joy she created around her. In these words, and in her many novels, short stories, plays and films, Maeve lives on – and always will.

Gordon Snell

SIXTIES

School Outing

29 October 1964

Oddly enough, the horror of a school outing is not the responsibility of looking after other people's children in alien surroundings, nor is it the noise and possibility of them getting out of hand. The real problem is wondering whether they are going to be bored. The outing is so eagerly anticipated, and so much discussed, that it has to be an anti-climax – unless there are a few unexpected delights, like a teacher getting stuck in a hedge, or half of the sixth years being left behind in a chip shop, or someone getting involved with a man.

Of course, the real disaster is collecting the money. How often have I collected 38 times 18s and spent it three times over before the day came when the man in CIÉ had to be paid?

Then there is the likelihood of someone getting sick; far from being able to minister to such unfortunates, I start to get sick myself, which undoubtedly heightens the awfulness for everyone involved. In all the years of hot bus journeys and twisty bends on the roads, and 12-year-olds eating four pounds of sweets in between bags of chips and bottles of Coca-Cola, no one has ever gotten sick, but I can never believe my luck will hold.

We went to Wales recently and to date this was by far the best outing. From the children's point of view it was going to a foreign country – there would be Customs and foot-and-mouth spray on the way home. There would be new, strange Woolworths to investigate, there was a chance to see both the mail boat and the ferry, since we went out by the former and came home by the latter. They could even send postcards to people saying 'spending a little while in Wales' without elaborating that the little while was five hours. There was also Caernarfon Castle, the *raison d'être* of the whole visit, but no one gave that much thought.

From a teacher's point of view, it also had everything to recommend it. It didn't leave at a ridiculous hour in the morning; in fact we only left Dún Laoghaire at eleven-thirty a.m. Once you got them on the boat there was really nothing that could happen to them except the obvious and if that did happen someone would be bound to notice and stop the ship. Exploring the boat took most of the first hour, settling on a place for the mammoth eating of sandwiches brought us up to about two o'clock. Then there was an hour of everyone rubbing themselves with Nivea cream. After this the Welsh coast was sighted and approved of, and we got on to land and into a bus in a matter of minutes.

The bus is a must. Firstly there is nothing whatsoever to do in Holyhead, and if you just bring them out to Bangor to swim, there is all that nightmare of counting them the whole time. Anyway, if they spend the day on a beach, someone is bound to say that they should have saved the 37s and gone to Dollymount. But the bus is very cunning indeed, and anyway, if you have a soul at all, you would want them to see Caernarfon and this is not really feasible without your own bus.

The bus driver was called Fred. He looked as if he might be offended if the children sang in the bus, so I hoped they wouldn't, but I didn't like to forbid it because that sort of singing is all part of the Outing anyway. However, they were quite sensitive about the whole thing, and every time he pointed out an RAF camp, or rock climbers on the mountains, they would pause respectfully in the middle of some terrible song about 'I'm the son of the Hickory Hollow tramp' and listen with interest.

There was enormous and unfeigned interest in the village with the longest name in the world. Pencils and notebooks were out and the bus had to stay beside the signpost until everyone copied down Llanfairpwllgwyngyllgogerychwyrndrobwllllantysiliogogogoch.

Fred, because he could not only spell it, but could also pronounce it, became the hero of the hour.

We only had an hour-and-a-quarter in Caernarfon, so my dissertation from the battlements had to be shorter than I would have liked. But I could see that the lure of the foreign Woolworths and the alien sweets would outweigh too much chat about Edward I and the Welsh Barons, and the one thing you do realise as a teacher is your limitations.

A horror story of the previous week – when apparently a Dublin boys' school had missed the boat home because the bus arrived back too late – so impressed me that I encouraged Fred to speed through the setting sun back to Holyhead; we may have had to forego a few slate quarries on the way, but not even a diamond mine would have seemed worth the risk of having to sleep in a bus with forty schoolgirls and face their parents the next day.

From motives of economy we had an enormous and unladylike feed of fish and chips in a Holyhead café, then, fragrant with vinegar, we got onto the ferry. The children went out on deck, I went to the bar. Later a deputation came in with faces of doom.

'You're wanted on deck, Miss Binchy,' they announced to the whole bar, and everyone assumed it was probably by the police. I assumed, with even greater fear and certainty, that someone had been sick. In fact, it was only to settle an argument about the Wicklow mountains, which had just come purplishly into view.

For 37s each (only 18s 6d for everyone under 15) plus a sum of £11 for the hire of Fred and his bus, it was a marvellous day. The trouble is, it went so successfully that they are now talking confidently in terms of a trip to France.

Just Plane Bores

13 September 1968

The dangers of getting stuck with a bore in a plane considerably outweigh the other hazards of plane travel. There is no comforting insurance policy against this, however, for what actuary could possibly relate the risks to any practical premium?

I often hear people saying that they sat beside a frightfully interesting chap on a plane, but I just don't believe it. The only people I sit beside are people who read the safety regulations with an intensity that could only come from certainty of disaster. One woman even asked my advice when she came to the bit about removing false teeth during a forced landing.

'Do you think I should take out my crown filling?' she asked me anxiously.

Sometimes, I must admit, I escape these relatively harmless people and I sit beside know-alls, people who wince when the engine sounds change, people who have known better lines, faster jets, classier meals and more certain likelihood of reaching one's destination.

I never met anyone remotely interesting in a plane but I have seen interesting people. I sat behind Kirk Douglas once, and I sat across the aisle from a couple who had the most terrible argument that ended in their throwing drinks at each other and me. I heard a girl complain to the hostess on a flight to New York that Aer Lingus must have lost all sense of shame to let men and women use the same toilets. I was once on a plane where I was the only passenger and sat in a Kafkaesque silence surrounded by empty seats. Risk of boredom at the hands of a passenger was minimal certainly, but it's not usually practical to fly solo, so most of us are stuck with the plane bores for all our flying years.

People have a habit of confiding terrible secrets in planes. They tell things that would in a less rarefied atmosphere remain much more wisely unsaid. A man who told me that he was smuggling 15 watches made me so nervous that I was the one blushing, stammering and hesitating at the airport, and was eventually and very reasonably searched after the performance, while the smuggler ticked his way unconcernedly to the airport bus.

The last time I was coming back from Israel my neighbour sobbed the whole way from Tel Aviv to London, choking out explanations about how badly she had behaved all the summer; she'd never broken the Sabbath she said until she went to Israel, she'd always eaten kosher until she went to Jerusalem. The irony of it. She wept, and I nearly wept with her, but of course when we got to London Airport she had recovered and I was the one who couldn't bear to meet her father's eye as he stood there with his long black beard, he who'd always kept the Sabbath and eaten kosher all his life.

If people are not telling you about their operations, their bank balances, the highly unsatisfactory state of their marriages or how they were cheated by hoteliers, travel agents and the entire population of whatever country you happen to be leaving, then they are inclined to interrogate you about the most intimate details of your life.

'How can a schoolteacher afford to go to Hong Kong for the summer holidays?' rasped a terrible Australian, who was going to be my neighbour for the next 20 hours.

There is no fully satisfactory answer to a question like that, and as I was already afraid that my bank manager could well be waiting on the tarmac in Dublin with the same words on his lips, I couldn't say anything convincing in reply. The Aussie became sour at my refusal to be frank and began a tirade against all Europeans, who were a miserable bankrupt lot altogether – he had no further fodder for this in my uncalled-for explorations.

Europeans always sneered at Australians, he went on, they thought Australians had nothing but beer and going to the beach and sheep stations – he went on, and on, and on. Singapore, Calcutta, Beirut, Vienna – all came and went and we were still talking about the outback and the Aborigines. We were making maps on our plastic trays of food and letting the ice cream be Queensland and the salt be Perth. We nearly came to blows about the hors d'oeuvres. I said it should be Adelaide, he said it was Melbourne and since it was his continent, I let it be Melbourne. But the whole journey was exhausting and I thought longingly of the wonderful journey out which took five weeks, and there was an adventure every single day and nearly 600 people on the ship.

Shortly after this marathon flight I decided that the fault was certainly mine. No one else seemed to have such bad luck and when I read Helen Gurley Brown's book *Sex and the Single Girl* I knew it must be my fault. Planes, she said, are wonderful places for picking up Grade A men. The more international and exciting the flight, the better your chances would be. I had an unworthy suspicion that even the vibrant H. G. Brown would not have made much of old Waltzing Matilda and his White Australia policy, his wallabies and his test match. However, I decided to follow her instructions on the very next flight.

According to *Sex and the Single Girl*, you should get a seat fairly near the front of the plane (if that's how you get into the plane; presumably if it's one of the ones where you climb in through the tail, you should sit near the back). Then leave a great big handbag on the seat beside you. At the approach of other women or Grade Z men you leave the bag there, but when a Grade A man approaches you whip the bag from the seat and stare straight ahead.

Once the Grade A man is installed you must establish contact by fumbling over your safety belt and the intention is to entangle yourself and the man in a knot from which with much tinkling laughter you both extricate yourselves, and such splendid rapport having been made he offers you a refined cocktail once you are airborne, and things progress from there.

I'll say this for *S and the SG*, the beginning part works like a dream. A man like Marlon Brando sat down beside me; the belt business was a fiasco because he started to fumble with his belt at the same time, and whatever way we seemed to do it we had to call the air hostess to disentangle us from the muddle. She took so long that I thought she was going to send for an acetylene torch. Anyway calm was restored and we were airborne. All around us people were clicking cigarette lighters and ordering refined cocktails, but the false Marlon Brando was staring straight ahead. It turned out that he was absolutely terrified of flying; all that business about the safety belt was the last straw and he seemed on the verge of having a very loud and serious fit. Determined to avoid this at all costs, I bought him a Scotch, the worst possible thing I should have done apparently, but it calmed him and he went to sleep almost at once on my shoulder.

Now the journey from London to Gibraltar is very short, and although it is undoubtedly good for the morale to have a handsome man asleep in my arms – I smiled pityingly at all the people who passed by, who had no man at all – it did present grave problems when we got to the Rock. He just wouldn't wake up. One of the hostesses thought he was dead but the other said he was just unconscious so I had to stay around for what was going to be either a revival or an inquest. I missed my bus to Malaga, I had to deal with Marlon Brando's business partner who fortunately came to collect him, there was much face slapping, and 'wake up Pete old man'. Nobody believed me when I said he was afraid of flying but everyone agreed that to feed a highly strung man like Pete Scotch whiskey was a most foolish and suspect course of action.

So whenever I hear about the excitement and glamour of air travel I'm inclined to be a little cynical and I look forward to the day when we'll have either single rows of seats, or compulsory films that must be watched in silence by the whole plane load, or better still, the sort of club car, Pullman lounges that you see in American films, where you can talk to everyone. Until then, we'll just continue to belt ourselves in two by two or three by three and bore each other to death at altitudes of thousands of feet, flying hundreds of miles an hour all round the world.

But Does Anybody Care?

1 January 1969

Perhaps it matters to you that Hull is 226 miles from Brighton and that there are 40 poles (or perches) to the rood. I feel that if you had started out on the road to Hull you'd have a roadmap or the signposts anyway, and if for some extraordinary reason you were lying down on the ground measuring things in roods and perches, it would all be written on the measuring tape.

Anyone going back to Oxford this month *knows* that the Hilary Term starts on January 19th and no one else will be at a disadvantage by not knowing; and since neither the March nor September eclipses of the sun will be visible from Greenwich, why torment us by telling us about them?

I must say that I find it very disagreeable indeed to open my diary on New Year's Day and find pages of advice about poisoning, shock and wounds. Choking, in particular, is very loathsome.

Would anyone remember 'to dislodge obstruction, bend head and shoulders forward and in case of small child, hold upside down then thump between shoulder blades' – just because the eye happened to light on this one day when looking for a telephone number?

The advice is not all that practical, either. Severe Case of Cramp usually sets in when you are standing in a bus, and you can't very well 'take hold of foot and turn toes firmly upward until spasm has passed'. And in the case of poisoning by mouth, how on earth are most people to neutralise acid poisoning by administering *chalk*?

This year's diary seems loath to leave any space at all for what I hope will be my own memorable activities, so full is it of ridiculous information. Sandwiched between the telephone number you should call in Upavon if you want the weather forecast and a useless page giving the equivalent American and Continental clothes sizings (but admitting sadly that it is always best to try on the article before buying it) there is a type of Bon Viveur guide to wine, compiled by the Wine and Food Society. Everything gets a mark from 0 to 7; 0 equals 'no good' and 7 'the best', it says simply. Apart from the interesting historical question it raises for the amateur – who must wonder whether it was drought or storms or strikes in the vineyard that made 1956 a poor starter – surely no one is going to take it seriously, and whip it out for consultation while the wine waiter hovers?

Then there is the page marked 'my car' with all kinds of spaces for numbers of boot key, of ignition key, of chassis and insurance policy. To my mind, the type of person who would fill all this in is also the type who keeps a leather-bound log book in the glove compartment with the same details lovingly inscribed. He probably calls the car 'she' and knows everything by heart anyway.

Yet into this whole field of bushels and pecks, centigrade and Fahrenheit, Lammas Day being August 1st and the sun rising at 9.05 a.m. next Saturday, Queen Elizabeth the Queen Mother being born on August 4th, 1900, and Ramadan facing us on November 22nd, has come a new challenge – the Special Interest diary. Not only the schoolboy, the businessman and the lady are catered for now, but a whole range of unlikely diarists from the filmgoer to the gardener, the photographer, the motorcyclist, the electrical engineer and the handyman.

It certainly seems more reasonable to gear a diary to someone's job or hobby than to assume that everyone in the world is going to be interested in the Golden Number, the Dominical Letters and the Epact, whatever the Epact may be. Last year it was nought, and this year they forgot it, thankfully, in my particular diary.

Still, the specialised diaries have problems of their own. Would you rather carry around pages of advice about planting and pruning, or handy hints on slapping crows' feet away from your eyes? You'll have to make up your mind whether you are a lady first or a gardening enthusiast, or else buy two diaries. Perhaps they might organise detachable pages of information and you could make up personal diaries for your friends out of all of them: for the golfer – businessman – Catholic – music radio ham, for example. It has endless possibilities.

The main idea of a diary, in case you have lost sight of it, is to provide some open space. From years of catastrophe with the page-a-day ones, I've now settled for a week between two pages, so that Sunday is always on the top left-hand corner. In the excitement of all those empty pages you think that you can fill a page a day easily, but by January 11th the whole thing has become impractical. Pages glare at you in empty accusation, two pages stick together and you completely forget to do something that you'd written in in red ink – there are pitfalls all the way with the page-a-day kind, unless you are aged 14 and have something to say to yourself.

What do people write in diaries anyway? I remember seeing a television programme quite a long time ago, about children's diaries, and the kind of things they put in them. Apparently there was a relentless litany of 'Got up, got dressed, went to school', broken only by the triumphant but shaky hand of the mumps or measles victim: 'Didn't get up, didn't go to school.' They seemed to be obsessed with what the teachers wore; whether or not they liked them was quite immaterial to the interest in professional garb. Very few children's diaries carried on in February. I can never quite regard mine as just an appointment book, and I feel a terrible urge to put in happenings and comments. I know it is both foolish and dangerous, particularly for someone who loses a diary so regularly.

But after I discovered that in my indiscreet days I entered for Saturday, July 27th, 1963: 'This was one of the best days in my life,' and now I can't remember why, I thought that whatever the risk, names and places must be brought back again.

Actually, if you do put a bit of your life into your diary you are much more likely to get it back when you lose it than if you just list letters to write and how you spent your money. I'm sure it's not the fact that I have written 'Large financial reward for finder' on mine that makes people post it to me or ring me and arrange a personal delivery, because no one except an unpleasant schoolboy ever accepted the reward. I even telephoned the police in Pearse Street once to say that I'd left it in a phone box in Westmoreland Street, and could they ever ask any Garda who was passing to look and see was it there? As if this was the most normal request for Gardaí in that area, they agreed and I collected it, red-faced, from the station next day.

I'd even thought of bringing my diary to the Income Tax Commission in support of an appeal if necessary, but it's probably just as well that it hasn't been, yet. Even though there is lots of evidence of legitimate spending that no one would have had the energy to fake, there are all the other things as well which might take from the seriousness of the situation.

So, like the man who made his money not out of the mustard eaten but by what people leave on their plates, diary publishers never really care whether or not we are faithful in our New Year's resolve to record the happenings of 1969. Until they invent diaries that come in shorter editions at more frequent intervals, they have nothing to worry about. While disclaiming any responsibility for errors, they can continue to blind us with information which we mentally note as certain to be useful while we leap through it, looking for the cheerful space about whom to notify in case of accident.

A Turkish Bath

12 May 1969

I didn't believe that anything could cost only £1 in The Dorchester, it is not the kind of place that you expect to get much change from a fiver even if you were buying a drink. But they were right, the Turkish bath is only £1 and if you lose all sense of proportion and decide to have a massage as well it comes to £2.

The porter nodded understandingly and approvingly when I asked him for directions to the Place; he didn't quite say that he thought it an excellent idea on my part, but he certainly implied that it was a much wiser way of using The Dorchester than joining the ladies who were having morning coffee and sticky cakes in the lounge.

Down a carpeted stairs to a receptionist who takes your name and hands you to a further receptionist in a white coat. 'Do I pay now?' I asked ignorantly, but this was all brushed aside with embarrassment, and indeed it *was* foolish, I suppose, to think that they have to take the money from you on the way in. Few people would have the courage to leave by a back entrance minus their clothes just to avoid paying £1. I was shown to a cubicle, given a key to a great big chest and asked to deposit not only my valuables, but also my clothes in this, given a huge white towel that would have swamped Finn MacCool, a pair of rubber sandals that wouldn't have fitted Madame Butterfly and led towards the Room.

The Room looked like something from a film set. There were about two dozen armchairs dotted around, all covered with snow-white towels. There was an alarming notice that said SILENCE in huge letters, and there was one occupant that looked as if she were dead in one of the chairs. The assistant led me to a chair, and said that I should stay there for about ten minutes before going into the heat. As I was already wondering if my heart had stopped beating from the temperature we were in, I asked was this not the heat, but she said disapprovingly that this was just the warm room and went away.

I sat nervously and self-consciously in the towel-covered chair. There wasn't a move from the corpse in the other one, and just as I was going to call the assistant and report the first fatal casualty of the day, it moved and said languidly, 'You should have brought something to read you know, it would make you more relaxed, and you would sweat more.' The possibility of going back to the newsstand in the foyer garbed as I was did not recommend itself, so we called the assistant and asked for some reading matter that would help me to relax and sweat. She brought the *Daily Mirror*.

In no time at all it was time to move from what was called euphemistically the warm room, towards the Heat. The Heat was a tiled room with slotted benches around it, a bit like what I think a men's lavatory might look like. Suddenly the warm room seemed cool as a mountain stream. The corpse hadn't come with me, so I prepared to meet new friends. There was again one occupant, the thinnest woman I have ever seen in my life, wrapped from armpit to knee, not in a nice clinical towel, but in a red rubber sheet. The notice SILENCE was there again, but I thought I would die if I didn't know why she was wearing the sheet, so I risked it. 'It's better for sweating,' she said definitively, 'much better.'

It turned out she liked talking, so we agreed to waive the rules until someone else came in. She went there every week, when she came up to London to do the shopping. Sometimes she stayed for three hours and didn't ever get around to the shopping, but it didn't matter because most things could be delivered, even these days. She was surprised I hadn't thought of bringing a rubber sheet. It was great for getting all the impurities out of the body; she looked reflectively up into the clouds of steam, as if she could see them wafting away. I looked nervously, too, wondering where they would land.

We were joined by two chubby American teenagers, who didn't want to have a Turkish bath at all, but their mother had been appalled at how thin everyone was in England, and since they were staying at the hotel she had sent them down to the Heat for the morning. Momma was at this moment probably eating spoonfuls of something fantastic in Fortnum & Masons, they grumbled. They wanted to be outside seeing London. One of them complained that she was taking creative writing at school, and she wanted to have something to write about when she got back.

'You could always write about this,' I said helpfully.

'Who'd wanna read about this?' she said reasonably.

It was all-change time again soon. A woman wearing a black bathing suit came in and called me by name to follow her. 'Good luck,' said the Yanks gloomily. We went into a place resembling a clean abattoir with trestle tables and many taps and drains. I thought in my stupidity that this was the massage, but in fact it was what is known as the rub down, and incidentally is included in the £1.

The rub down consisted of the woman in the bathing togs asking me to lie naked on a trestle table while she took what could only have been a pot scourer and scrubbed every inch of me. I was afraid to look at anywhere she rubbed twice in case seven layers of skin would have disappeared forever. Then she took what must have been a giant shaving brush and lather and washed it all over again. Then there was a hose of warm water, which was nice, but lastly I had to stand up and be hosed with cold water, which was not nice. I was led back to my cubicle and told that the masseuse would come for me shortly, but to have a little nap.

What seemed like two days later, when I woke from the deepest sleep I have ever known, the masseuse was there; on with the mad sandals and the huge towel, and off to a part of the building where there was a swimming pool surrounded by cubicles that looked like well-equipped stables. 'Swim about a little, but don't talk,' I was told, which seemed an unnecessary caution, since there was no one to talk to, but perhaps some people, a little unnerved by all that scouring and heat, *do* in fact talk to themselves.

The solitary silent and stark naked swim being over, and I can't think when I felt so foolish in my whole life, we went into one of the stables, and I had the best massage possible. I can't remember what the woman's name was, though I did write it down at the time, but you couldn't miss her. She had been there for years, apparently, and is very much in demand. I only got her by accident.

On questioning, I told her how much I earned, why I was in London, whether I was in love, the state of the Irish economy, what I thought of Enoch Powell and advised her where to go on her holidays. She told me what she earned, the famous people she had massaged, a very exciting story about a film star, 'no names mentioned, of course', how the type of person had changed over the years in The Dorchester, and that I should have a massage every day, and never eat again in my life. We had a lovely time and I was very sorry when the hour was up.

Back to the cubicle again, yet another deep sleep, a cup of tea, three cigarettes, and I got dressed. Taking the money at the door seemed to be a severe embarrassment to the receptionist, but we managed it, and I left The Dorchester three hours after I had gone in, feeling better than I have ever felt in my life. All the cares and woes of the Ideal Homes Exhibition were long forgotten, I had lost three pounds in weight and only two in money. It's about the best value in London.

Life as a Waitress

30 June 1969

The worst thing about life as a waitress was the Out door; it was only rivalled by the In door. One small miscalculation with either and you were on the floor with a tray of broken everything. If it happened in the dining room, the Wing Commanders and the Flight Lieutenants were so mortified that they all looked away and pretended it hadn't happened. If the crash came in the kitchen, there was more help, but considerably more abuse as well. The head waiter would repeat for the hundredth time that these damn students were more trouble than help, and the evil man who brought the vegetables would remind everyone of the time some unfortunate from St Andrew's had got his foot caught in the dishwasher and the washing up had to be done by hand for three weeks.

I was there for eight weeks, eight years ago, and I earned £10 a week and my keep. My keep must have been worth another ten, because we all ate huge meals both before and after the meal we were serving, and lived in palatial rooms, where we demanded new releases for the record player every week. We were miles from the nearest town, which was good, as there was no chance of spending all the Big Money we earned, and there were a hundred ways, most of them respectable, of increasing one's wages.

The greatest problem after the doors was the Catering Manager, who had an unfortunate phrase: 'I'm not a church-going man myself, but I know what's what.'

This was invariably said when the occasion least called for it, and we were all puzzled by its significance. He said it to me when I arrived, and as I had done nothing yet except stammer that I would work very hard, it was rather a blow. He followed it up by warning me sternly that the men didn't *marry* the waitresses and said that I might laugh now, but many of my countrywomen were laughing on the other side of their faces at the expense of the National Health. It was not an auspicious start.

But I soon got quite good at it all. There were all kinds of new things to learn, like how to carry seven plates without spilling the gravy and not resting three of them on my chest. There was no little crook in my wrist to balance them like everyone else seemed to have, but I practised and found that if you put everything on top of each other regardless and gave them a quick wipe before putting them down it was the best. All the rest of the waitresses wore powder-blue nylon overalls, but there wasn't one that would fit me and allow me to appear in public. So I wore a dignified restrained navy dress of my own, and everyone thought I was the manageress, and made complaints about 50-year-old waitresses who had been there all their working lives. I accepted these complaints regally and did nothing about them.

It was very hard not to join in people's conversations. I was severely reprimanded for contradicting a student, who said he had landed beautifully that morning on the airstrip. When I told him very truthfully that everyone in two miles' radius had thrown themselves on the ground at his approach, there was consternation.

'You must know what's what,' said the Catering Manager disapprovingly. 'I hope I won't have to mention this again.'

There was a lot of dishonesty in the kitchen, which was as pointless as it was professional. Everyone was well paid and reasonably happy, but the stealing seemed to be a way of life. There were three dustbins, but one of them wasn't a real dustbin. Every time we used a dozen bottles of tomato juice or a dozen anything, in fact, one bottle was put in the false dustbin and a mysterious man came every week and sold it all. We got about £1 14s each from the profits, and I was warned sternly that if I didn't like it I was to shut up about it, because there had been a bit of trouble one year over a student. He had behaved foolishly, and instead of giving the money to a charity like any normal well-heeled student should have done, he wrote a series of letters to everyone, including the Catering Manager, who had been very upset, and this was partly responsible for his strange attitudes and limited vocabulary ever since.

I learned, among other things, that you must never send a knife or fork back because it is dirty. This only resulted in extreme indignation, plus class and racist remarks about it being far from clean forks that the clientèle were reared. The usual method of cleaning the offending fork was to rub it in the under-chef's hair. His oily head gave it an unparalleled shine, and the complainer ate his dinner, happy to have scored a point, with a piece of cutlery that shone with brilliance, oil and dandruff.

I hated the way we were told to recommend the food that was going off in the kitchen. At a briefing council before lunch we would be told that kidney stew wouldn't last another hour; it was to be proffered, suggested and even brought in error to anyone who looked as if they might eat it. It was a nightmare to ask those innocent boys, whose stomachs were already turning over at the thought of flying that afternoon, to eat something that we in the kitchen had rejected automatically. The pink blancmange was about the most revolting of all, and I think the only Reserved Sin I ever committed knowingly was to tell a weedy-looking Scot that blancmange was the best thing known to man for building muscles, and he would wolf it down obediently every day.

Sometimes I went for a flight in an aeroplane. The students and air people (the ones who never married the waitresses) were occasionally at their wits' end for entertainment, and when all else failed would fly me to Cambridge for afternoon tea. They thought it was very jolly of me to be a waitress, and hoped that our economy would recover sufficiently to let me get work at home soon. I made up terrible lying stories about having worked in Kilburn, but moving to the country to meet a nicer class of person, and they were delighted with me.

One of the respectable ways of earning more money was to work in the bar at night. I did this once with disastrous results. You got £3 for the four and a half hours, and, since my only other diversions were having my hair permed into what looked like a Brillo soap pad by the other waitresses, I thought the bar seemed a great plan. I must be the only person who ever lost over £5 by having to work there.

Firstly, I didn't understand about the tips. When people said 'have a drink yourself' I beamed with pleasure and gratitude, and refused every drink virtuously on the grounds that I was a bit busy. I never thought of putting two shillings into a glass jar on the shelf, which was what they meant me to do. Then I didn't know how to work the automatic stopper on the spirit bottles, and a whole bottle of Gordon's gin flowed down the sink. Worse still, I couldn't keep up with the washing of glasses and had to send a fevered message to the evil vegetable man, who charged me 30 shillings to help with the washing up.

There was a most attractive-looking Welshman whom I fancied greatly, and even though he wouldn't marry waitresses, the Catering Manager had said yet *again* when he saw me getting out of a helicopter with him, I had great hopes. However, I lost him completely the night I worked in the bar. He wanted to arrange some very complicated deal about drinking that night with 'the old man'. Whenever *he* bought a drink it was to be a small one, and if by any chance the old man bought one it was to be a large one. I totally misunderstood his intentions and thought simply that he wanted to get the 'old man' drunk for some fell purpose. Actually, of course, he just wanted to get drunk himself at the expense of the old man, and when I made the obvious mistake he became very sour. He came into the kitchen next day and fingered the meat cleaver thoughtfully. 'I thought you were clever,' he said, and I never saw him again.

There was a sex maniac in charge of the cooking; he was called Pio, and was like a stage Italian. In the middle of most confusing orders, when I would call, 'Pio, could you give me two liver and bacon and three cottage pies,' he would put on a vulpine smile and roar, 'I geev to you if you geev to me,' and everyone would laugh as I rushed out the In door and back in the Out door, in sheer fright.

But, still, I think I liked it. I liked John, the sad Irish waiter, and I liked Julie, who was described by everyone as a tramp, as they gave her cigarettes and leaned forward breathlessly to hear her latest adventures. I liked all the food, and the fact that I saved £73 in eight weeks, which I never did before or since. I learned a great deal about Life, and, more important, I learned never, no matter how great the temptation, to send back a dirty fork. Not every under-chef might have such hygienic hair as the one I knew.

Back to School

21 August 1969

I have been so long on the other side of the classroom that I almost forget what going back to school was like for the pupils. To me it was always a hectic rush in from the dawn flight or the mailboat, and a total disbelief that the long hot summer had really become a matter of timetables, homework, corrections, schedules and textbooks once again. If I got through the first day without remembering that I had left my suitcase at Milan or that I had lost the address of some sinisterly handsome Yugoslav, it was a miracle. I never had the least sympathy for the unfortunates in front of me. All that came the second day of term when we had more or less settled in.

But then I didn't have to deal with four-year-olds. All my kids were jaded, yawning sophisticates of 14 and upwards. I had to divulge only the new and terrible text of Livy we would be attacking, and try to pretend that this one was better than the others because Hannibal would be sliding up and down the Alps instead of having endless parleys with everyone at the foot of the mountains. I had to tell them that Otto and Henry the Fowler were really swinging people once you got to know them, and to utter a few hollow remarks about clean sheets and new leaves and all being forgotten since last term. I could never have coped with four-year-olds.

I would see them arriving up to the school door, little hands clutched in the nervous hands of nervous parents. I would see the faces pucker up, the hostility, the forced cheer on everyone's part, and wonder yet again was there any possible way to make the First Day any less harrowing for everyone concerned. About 20 minutes before school began the first howl would be heard from a cloakroom. It may have been caused by some perfectly reasonable cause like not being able to change one's shoes or Mummy saying something idiotic like 'Don't cry now' to a perfectly happy child, but there it would come anyway, and like brucellosis it's catching. 'Why is he howling?' was the immediate thought that flashed around everyone's mind, 'this place must be howlworthy in some way,' and then everyone would start.

There was one mother that I really admired. She had about five children at the school, and from the time they were three years old, those children were used to the place. They would come in and deliver elder brothers and sisters, they would come and collect them again in the afternoons. They knew when others didn't know that school was not a place where one would be abandoned forever with a brand new school bag one day by a weeping mother. When this mother had a chance she left her three-year-old casually for an hour in the back of the tinies' classroom anyway, and said, 'Get on with your colouring book, I want to talk to the headmistress.' They were all so well adjusted it was almost frightening.

Then there was the mother I couldn't bear. She came in like Maria Callas one morning and asked to see all the lavatories. Then she asked to be introduced to all the other children by name, then she took her own frightened offspring out of a car, and with more pomp and ceremony than all the doings in Caernarfon she marched the unfortunate boy into the classroom.

'These are your new friends, Johnny,' she intoned as you might address the life convicts of Cell Block B. 'You are going to have a lovely time playing with them all'; she held the traditional handkerchief to her eyes and left under severe emotional strain. The kindergarten teacher said that it took Johnny six months to get over the shock of it all.

If mothers only realised that going to school is not the severe break for the child as it is for themselves, a great deal of unnecessary trouble could be spared. It is obviously a great milestone for a mother if the only child ceases to be under her feet for the whole day, and is plunged into a new environment for the very first time. But it is only hard for the child if all this tension is built up beforehand. I don't think it's a good thing for everyone from Grandmother to the milkman to say how big a day it is for the little darling to be going off to school. The little darling might be tempted to believe that it is. I don't think it's wise to make too much fuss about a new school uniform, since the trappings and paraphernalia can become an obsession. A five-year-old is not a good recipient of a long emotional lecture from both mother and father about how much they expect from this giant step.

What *is* a good idea for parents is to maintain a steady and informed interest in their children's work and play during school-days. This will be a hundred times more valuable than regarding the first day as something like a Royal Command Performance and then forgetting the whole thing for evermore. The happiest children I taught were the ones whose parents knew and cared what the actual school day was like. Not necessarily the busybodies, in fact not at all the busybodies now that I come to think of it. The children would often complain that their parents were fascinated by all their efforts when they were at the stage of making pot hooks, but lost interest once it came to conjugating verbs.

'Well what *can* we do?' said one gloomy mother to whom I mentioned this with my sledgehammer tact. 'Am I to spend the whole day with *Teach Yourself Physics* propped up on the eye-level grill, so that we can all speak the same jargon?'

Parents should try to remember their children's friends, their teachers, their activities. They should listen when the children talk. It is all a matter of sustained interest rather than initial histrionics. I remember sitting behind a child aged about nine and her mother on a bus. The child was talking enthusiastically about Miss O'Connor.

'That's the maths teacher?' yawned Mama.

'NO, I told you it's the history teacher,' said the child.

'I didn't know you were doing history,' said Mother. 'Will you really need another pair of shoes this term, you've had three this year already.'

I thought it was very depressing, not because we teachers want to be enshrined between pictures of popes and American presidents in every child's home, but because parents should care.

There are 20 books to be written on how parents and teachers can do so much for the children by cooperating in spirit as well as in crashingly boring PTA meetings. One of the first steps is to get to know each other. So next week, when you take your four-year-old's little hot hand and lead him up the steps of his new school, or encourage your 14-year-old to his new senior school, try to get to know the teachers. Forget all that amateur psychology about children reacting to new surroundings and remember all that good old-fashioned idea about your friendly local teacher being a real live human being. If bank managers are busy portraying themselves as normal decent souls, we teachers will have to start the same process. Only the trouble is that we don't have the money for all that advertising.

Thinking About Underwear Down Under

10 September 1969

At some stage in everyone's life someone said that you must always wear nice underthings in case you were knocked down by a bus and had to be taken to a casualty ward. I was so frightened by this that I bought new sets of everything and then defeated the whole object by staying well clear of buses. Still, there is a great deal of truth in the statement that you feel much better if everything is snow white and lace-covered from the skin out. I have spoken long and loud before about how difficult this is for anyone who is not a Stock Size, because there is an international conspiracy that large ladies should wear gunmetal underwear decorated and relieved only by huge rolls of elastic and what they call slimming panels. But even so, there are people who can buy attractive underthings and don't, on the very dubious grounds that they aren't going to be seen.

I asked a few doctors who have seen women at their most defenceless to comment on our record as regards underwear, but they seem to be what we never really thought they were – totally unconcerned with it all. One said that the only thing he really objected to was nothing at all to do with underwear, it was drainpipe trousers. If you have something wrong with a knee or a calf you have to remove the pants entirely, causing enormous embarrassment to patient and further delay to doctor. Another said that people who come to be examined should realise that not only the part you consider to be affected may be looked at, but also a great deal more. He will never forget the mortification of someone who showed him a lily-white foot to be perused about a swollen ankle, but when he asked to see the other one for comparison it was almost covered in moss. He suggested a good bath as the solution, and was surprised that more people hadn't thought of this before.

I don't believe all this nonsense about not wearing nylon underwear because it doesn't absorb sweat. I think it is a lot worse to have all the fabrics that do absorb sweat, and have to be treated like precious fabrics from the Orient as a result. At least nylon knows the pace of modern life, it can be washed, it doesn't ask to be ironed, and it will be there winking at you in the morning ready to be worn again. It can be dyed a nice bright colour if the original white gets grey, and most of all it doesn't complain. It costs a bit less than all these prestige fabrics, and they actually manage to make it in a few nice colours and designs. No one who has seen nylon should ever be pitied if they end up on an operating table feeling foolish in long, hairy combinations that belonged to their eldest brother.

But the real joy of living when we do is, of course, the invention of tights. Years ago at the pantomime I saw a Principal Boy in these and thought they would be the end to all problems, and now eventually everyone has come around to agreeing with me. They are more expensive in that if one leg or the middle goes, you are economically minus two legs, but there are all kinds of cunning things you can do about this, like hacking off the good leg and wearing it in the old traditional way with the old traditional apparatus. It means that you must remember to buy all your pantyhose in the same colour, but that shouldn't be too much for any of us fashion-conscious people, should it?

The joy of being able to cross your legs without seven minutes' judicious edging to the front of your chair and back again, and much surreptitious feeling to make sure that acres of thigh are not visible, has to be known to be believed. The sheer delight of knowing that you need never again hunt for an Irish threepence to put in your suspender when the terrible little knob has worked its way down to the sole of your foot, is one worth having. The days you feel too fragile to wrestle with a corset, for want of a better term, are no longer with us since the invention of tights. If we could only get the makers to invent something which is both sheer and long-lasting, we could be said to have arrived in the perfect society. As it stands, one can often be in the lovely position of having to choose between something that looks like a stocking and lasts three days, or something that will last but looks like a surgical bandage.

Men are always being asked their views on women's underwear and they never say anything useful, so I just wouldn't give them all the chance here in the office. Men always profess to like blacks and scarlets and things, but like their wives to wear broderie anglaise from head to toe until they look as if they had just wandered off the film set of *Oklahoma*.

Women were loath to talk about the whole subject, which may or may not be healthy, but one great thread of uniformity ran through what everyone said. We are all in favour of wearing things that have a double purpose, like bra-slips, or panty-girdles or any other hyphenated garments that save effort in the mornings. Whereas we all used to wear one bra, one girdle, one slip, one pair of pants and two stockings (no one admitted to wearing vests), which was a total of six garments, now this *can* be cut down to a bra-slip and a pair of pantyhose, which is two. The national average is probably three or four. It is all more labour-saving and comfortable somehow, in these busy days.

On the topic of pretty underthings, everyone said that if all things were equal, which they aren't, they would indeed choose the attractive lacey flowered ones. But there is a big problem here. Anything that has any remedial nature manages to sacrifice beauty somewhere along the conveyor belt. The bra that holds you in or pads you out is not necessarily or at all the bra that has little rosebuds and pink lace. The girdles that look alluring could let you bulge alarmingly.

But is anyone ever satisfied with their own shape anyway? As someone put it, there is always one unanswerable question, in the words of the old song:

'Which would you rather
Or rather would you be
Legs to the oxter
Or stomach to the knee?'

The Nonsense of Etiquette

30 October 1969

The real immorality in life is to pretend that etiquette matters. It is the kind of pretence that brings a whole trail of neurosis and misery, as well as creating an artificial society of poseurs. The worst type of columnist is the one who orders her readers to follow the waiter under pain of death, rather than do the normal thing and let the unfortunate man who brought her to the restaurant crash his way through the tables.

These etiquette fiends do not answer a great need in the country; they create it. I do not accept for one moment that anyone feels more secure and able to face life once they have been definitely forbidden to say 'pleased to meet you'. The happiness of knowing how to say 'How do you do?' is a very ephemeral joy, and the amount of security that a nervous, socially aspiring woman can get from a paperback book on how it's done, or a weekly nightmarish sermon in a magazine, seems very dubious.

Of course there are legions of people who will not agree. They will say that it is all very well for those who are born to it to scorn etiquette and social ease; that a duchess has the right and the aplomb to tear her meat apart with bare hands in a restaurant if she chooses. But this is only perpetuating the whole terrible conspiracy.

There is no such thing in Ireland as being born knowing how to eat oysters or how to address an abbot in speech and on the envelope, or whether you should hunt for a fishbone that is certain to kill you in ten seconds with a fork or with your fist. Nobody will need to know all these things. Telling people how this must or must not be done is going to conjure up a world of decision-making, where the wrong choice in a heavily charged moment is going to mean instant disgrace, and months of recrimination.

I don't know how to eat mussels. I am neither proud nor ashamed of this, and if ever I wanted to order them in a restaurant I would ask the waiter or a neighbour how to attack them only if I thought that what seemed the obvious way would reduce everyone to helpless laughter or nausea. If I were on my own eating them, I think I would try some way that managed to get them out of the shell and into my mouth without covering myself and the table with sauce. But what a world it would be if I felt I had to slink into bookshops, and look up 'Eating' under the letter M when I thought there was a chance they might be placed suddenly and viciously before me.

The only real rule in etiquette is to realise that times change, manners change and that there are no absolutes. And even if there were absolutes, what would it matter? What will happen to the hostess who serves to the right and takes away from the left, or whichever is the wrong thing to do? Does she really think it matters? Is there anyone in the world who could produce one single reason for it mattering except a whole lot of claptrap based on what someone somewhere decided had been the Only Way to do it since the court of Louis XIV?

When schools offer classes in etiquette, parents often bray with delight and think that here, at last, is something that will stand to their daughters in years to come. But my heart sinks when I hear of them, and I envisage some undoubtedly impeccable lady telling the girls how to word invitations for dinner parties, when the most probable type of entertainment they will have to organise is beer and spaghetti on a Saturday night. I know of one real and documented occasion when a nun told the pupils in the Confirmation class that one girl was not being asked to take the Temperance pledge because she would have many demanding occasions in her social life when she left school where she would have to drink, and all the parents crowed their approval of this wisdom. They should have been outraged that the nun had made a class distinction at the age of 12 between this child, who was of a better home and a lovelier family, and the rest.

I wonder if Emily Post's marathon guide to every possible situation that could rear its head to harass a human will help the situation or just make it worse.

Will everybody sit up in bed laughing themselves sick at the etiquette of gloves and napkin? Will they be depressed to think that in 1922 women went out in droves to buy this ludicrous tome, which eventually ran through 99 printings and sold four million copies? Most frightening of all, will any reader who pays £2 10s for the new edition, brought out, I assume, as a giant laugh at this stage, take one word of what Emily wrote seriously? More than any other book that has appeared recently, I would love to know its sales today. I would be fascinated to know who buys it and why I got it to review, but if I had seen it in someone's house I certainly would have bought it. At least two people I showed it to are ordering copies.

It is well over 600 pages of utter and complete nonsense, but it is compulsive reading. There is drama in every line, from the gentle warning not to refer to a bell as a 'tintinnabulary summons' or a cow's tail as 'bovine continuation', to the wording of engraved pew cards for weddings.

Emily Post was everyone's ideal woman in the twenties. Americans bought her book without question as soon as there was to be a wedding in the house. She was a Baltimore Beauty herself, which of course gave her the right to speak; her wedding to Edwin M. Post Jnr in Tuxedo Park was one of the year's social events. As Edwin became more and more important in Wall Street, Emily became more and more obsessed with table settings and the duties of a chaperone.

It is easy to be wise after the event, and I know very little about either of them, but I do feel that it must have been quite predictable that the social event of 1892 should have ended in the Divorce Court of 1906.

Then Emily got down to business seriously, and told the world that if a wedding present had to be delayed through illness or disaster, a note should be written At Once to explain the delay and announce that the gift was on its way. She decided that people must have maids with low voices and that children in nice families should have visiting cards which they leave at parties bearing their name and Chez Maman instead of an address.

She goes completely berserk in the chapter about issuing invitations by telephone. Messages should always follow a prescribed form, apparently: 'Is this Lennox 0000? Would you please ask Mr and Mrs Smith if they will dine with Mrs Grantham Jones next Tuesday, the tenth, at eight o'clock? Mrs Jones' number is Plaza one-two, ring two.'

I am afraid I cannot understand from the book how this message should be communicated. Is it from Mrs Jones' butler to Mrs Smith's butler? It would appear to be, because the answer is also in the third person. Even the most personal phone calls seem to have official starts, middles and ends, while the behaviour of engaged couples towards each other has to be seen to be believed.

There is a chapter on how to get people to talk to each other at meals. That is really called the Turning of the Table. I attacked it with enormous interest, thinking it was some form of spiritualism patronised by Good Society, but didn't it turn out to be a whole set of directions on which way your face was meant to be turned after the fish course! I am copying directly from the book at this stage: 'The turning of the table is accomplished by the hostess who merely turns from the gentleman (on her left probably) with whom she has been talking during the soup and fish course to the one on her right. As she turns, the lady to whom the "right" gentleman has been talking turns to the gentleman further on, and in a moment everyone at the table is talking to a new neighbour.'

But what in the name of God are they all going to say? Emily really falls down on this. What could you possibly say, out of the blue, to a man on your right when the starting gun has been fired by the hostess turning? Or perhaps you aren't meant to say anything. She has a stern chapter on people who talk too much. I find myself caught between fascination, horror and sheer disbelief. Could anyone have cared, I wonder, and then I remember that four million people went out, presumably sober, and bought the book, and it fills me with rage.

It is due to the Emily Posts, the Amy Vanderbilts and their successors that you have unfortunates writing urgently to magazines saying that they must know by return of post whether to call the bride and bridegroom at a wedding next Saturday 'The happy couple' or 'Mary and Jimmy', when they have to make a speech. No punishment is great enough for anyone who made them feel it mattered a damn.

SEVENTIES

The World's Greatest Lies About Women

16 June 1970

1. Men like fat, cuddly women. They do, to laugh with and at, but not to fall in love with, behave extravagantly towards and join in matrimony with. If your role is that of sister, playmate and confidante, be as fat and cuddly as possible. If you hoped for anything more adventurous, get thin.

2. Men like women without make-up. They don't. They like extremely well and carefully made-up women whose skin has that expensive cultured look which comes from three hours at the dressing table. A woman who is really without make-up would frighten them to death. They regard blotches as eczema, and uneven colouring as a sign of tertiary syphilis.

3. Men like women in midi-length clothes. Not in Ireland yet, they don't. A maxi was fine during the winter for a young second arts student, and only when worn over the briefest of midi skirts so that everyone got the best of both worlds. They are afraid that their girlfriend's midi might be mistaken for someone else's leftover skirt, or worse still for a foolish attempt to be ahead of fashion, which is considerably more sinister than being behind it.

4. Everyone looks better in summer than in winter. Completely untrue. Everyone has more courage in summer, that's all. In winter you wouldn't dare to show veiny legs that had undergone a half-hearted attempt at instant tanning, and wear sleeveless dresses that showed the most ageing part of the body – the flesh on the top of the arms. For all those who turn that mythical brown, thousands more go red, or freckled, or that attractive shade of peel that can be a menace to anyone who sits beside you. Winter is safer, much.

5. Pregnant women are beautiful. They are, if they are sitting in a Chanel dress with a white collar framing an unworried face, thinking beautiful thoughts about a wonderful and miraculous event that is going to change everyone's lives. They are considerably less than beautiful if they are wearing their sister-in-law's maternity dress, elastic stockings, bemoaning the fact that they can't drink gin, and wondering how on earth they are going to afford another child.

6. It doesn't matter if you aren't beautiful. You are quite right, it doesn't matter a damn to anyone else, but it matters quite a lot to you.

Baby Blue

24 December 1971

My first evening dress was baby blue, and it had a great panel of blue velvet down the front, because my cousin who actually owned the dress was six inches thinner everywhere than I was. It had two short puff sleeves, and a belt which it was decided that I should not wear. It was made from some kind of good taffeta, and had, in its original condition, what was known as a good cut.

It was borrowed and altered in great haste, because a precocious classmate had decided to have a formal party. A formal party meant that the entire class turned up looking idiotic and she had to provide 23 idiotic men as well.

I was so excited when the blue evening dress arrived back from the dressmaker. It didn't matter, we all agreed, that the baby blue inset was a totally different colour from the baby blue dress. It gave it contrast and eye-appeal, a kind next-door neighbour said, and we were delighted with it. I telephoned the mother of the cousin and said it was going to be a great success. She was enormously gratified.

I got my hair permed on the day of the formal party, which now many years later I can agree was a great mistake. It would have been wiser to have had the perm six months previously and to allow it to grow out. However, there is nothing like the Aborigine look to give you confidence if you were once a girl with straight hair, and my younger sister who hadn't recognised me when I came to the door said that I looked 40, and I thought that was good too. It would have been terrible to look 16, which was what we all were.

I had bought new underwear in case the taxi crashed on the way to the formal party and I ended up on the operating table; and I became very angry with another young sister who said I looked better in my blue knickers than I did in the dress. Cheap jealousy, I thought, and with all that puppy fat and navy school knicker plus awful school belted tunic as her only covering, how could she be expected to have any judgment at all?

Against everyone's advice I invested in a pair of diamante earrings, cost 1s 3d old money in Woolworths; they had an inset of baby blue also, and I thought that this was the last word in coordination. I wore them for three days before the event, and ignored the fact that great ulcerous sores were forming on my earlobes. Practice, I thought, would solve that.

The formal party started at nine p.m. I was ready at six, and looked so beautiful that I thought it would be unfair to the rest of the girls. How could they compete? The riot of baby blue had descended to the shoes as well, and in those days, shoe dyeing wasn't all it is these days. By seven p.m. my legs had turned blue up to the knee. It didn't matter, said my father kindly, unless, of course, they do the can-can these days. Panic set in, and I removed shoes, stockings and scrubbed my legs to their original purple, and the shoes to their off-white. To hell with coordination, I wasn't going to let people think I had painted myself with woad.

By eight p.m. I pitied my drab parents and my pathetic family, who were not glitter and stardust as I was. They were tolerant to the degree of not commenting on my swollen ears, which now couldn't take the diamante clips and luxuriated with the innovation of sticking-plaster painted blue. They told me that I looked lovely, and that I would be the belle of the ball. I knew it already, but it was nice to have it confirmed.

There is no use in dwelling on the formal party. Nobody danced with me at all, except in the Paul Jones, and nobody said I looked well. Everyone else had blouses and long skirts which cost a fraction of what the alterations on my cousin's evening dress had set me back. Everyone else looked normal, I looked like a mad blue balloon.

I decided I would burn it that night when I got home, in the garden in a bonfire. Then I thought that would wake my parents and make them distressed that I hadn't been the belle of the ball after all, so I set off down the road to burn it on the railway bank of Dalkey station. Then I remembered the bye-laws, and having to walk home in my underwear, which the baby had rightly said looked better than the dress, so I decided to hell with it all, I would just tear it up tomorrow, at dawn.

But the next day, didn't a boy, a real live boy who had danced with me during one of the Paul Joneses, ring up and say that he was giving a formal party next week, and would I come? The social whirl was beginning, I thought, and in the grey light of morning the dress didn't look too bad on the back of a chair.

And there wasn't time to get a skirt and blouse and look normal like everyone else, and I checked around and not everybody had been invited to his formal party; in fact only three of us had. So I rang the mother of the cousin again, and she was embarrassingly gratified this time, and I decided to allow my ears to cure and not wear any earrings, and to let the perm grow out, and to avoid dyed shoes.

And a whole winter season of idiotic parties began, at which I formally decided I was the belle of the ball even though I hardly got danced with at all, and I know I am a stupid cow, but I still have the dress, and I am never going to give it away, set fire to it on the railway bank or use it as a duster.

Women Are Fools – Mary
7 May 1973

Mary's father died on her 21st birthday, when she had been celebrating not only the key of the door but an honours BA. She missed him in a mild guilty sort of way because she never knew him too well. All those years at boarding school, then at university, she hadn't brought friends home much because there was nothing to do, she thought, in the small country town, and her friends would be bored.

She had a sister years and years older who was a nun in America, and got leave to come over for the funeral, and two brothers, one who was courting, and one who was only a schoolboy.

She didn't know her mother too well when she was 21, but now at 29 she knows her only too well, and doesn't like what she knows. Or so she says.

The mother sold the house in the country town and came to Dublin. It would be handier, she said. Mary could live with her while doing the HDip. The courting son was married and living in Dublin in a year and the schoolboy son could go to a good school in Dublin. It was all a great idea said the mother, and Mary thought it would be cheaper certainly and it had been a bit lonely sometimes in Dublin on her own, and at least she would get good meals and have someone to talk to at weekends.

She forgot what it was like to be living at home again. A home where her mother always said, 'If your poor father were only here he would . . .', and he would always be doing or saying something so unlikely that Mary grew to resent the phrase, and the inevitable accusations that she didn't respect the memory of her father began.

Mary got a job easily enough teaching in Dublin. It was a large convent school, and it was in this that I met her, because our school had a debating competition with hers and her pupils beat mine, and annoyed as I was because I thought my kids were better, I liked their teachers, who seemed kind of interested in the whole idea of giving them self-confidence and not teaching them typical debating phrases off by heart. So we went and had a coffee after we put our various charges on buses and sent them home with dire warnings about not getting distracted by chip shops en route.

She told me that she didn't really like teaching, and wanted something abroad, that she found it difficult to find a sort of 'set' in Dublin now that she had left college. People were all scattered, and at school who on earth did you meet except the nuns, the other teachers, the children and the parents? I knew it only too well, but assured her that it sort of evolved. She was bored by her married friends, she said, they all seemed so complacent. I said mine weren't because they were all poor and didn't have much to be complacent about. We thought a bit about how to get a job for her abroad, and about how dreadful it was that the only kind of men you'd want to go out with were all married already.

Again I met her and this time she said she was going to start going to dances again; she told me a bit about her whining mother, who always went on about her missing her chances, and Mary wondered aloud even more whiningly to me and her mother where on God's name were the chances?

The first Chance came at a dance hall where Mary spent a really appalling night. The dancers who weren't her pupils were elderly nurses in cardigans, she said; the men were either children or ageing, dribbling drunks. One man in the room seemed to be neither a drunk of 50 nor a child of 15; at the second last dance, he eyed Mary and they jived away until the national anthem.

She had nothing in common with him, but he took her home, and when he said that he'd give her a ring next week he actually did. And Mary was delighted that she had a fellow, although it has to be said she did talk about him as you would about a worn-out carpet sweeper that someone had given you when they had bought a new electrical thing. She was grateful but not totally satisfied with her lot.

Her mother wanted to know all about him, who his people were, and didn't like the sound of he works in Aer Lingus or Guinnesses or CIÉ or wherever it was, because his job was never defined there. So Mary didn't bring him home, they went to the pictures a lot, and necked in the back of his car out at Burma Road in the nice car park built just for that purpose, and he gave her a handbag for her birthday, and he didn't ask her home either which was a relief because Mary didn't feel bad about her not doing the same, and just as she was getting ready to buy him a cashmere sweater for his birthday some Good Friend managed to tell her that it wasn't his difficult mother he didn't want her to meet, it was his difficult wife.

We agreed over a lunch one day that it had been a horrible shock, a great relief that she hadn't been really interested in him and an even greater relief that Mary hadn't given in to all his frightful sexual demands. That was the biggest bonus of all.

Her next Chance came when I introduced her to a professional bachelor, professional in the sense of always being determined to remain a bachelor. We were sure he wasn't married, but I was equally sure he never would marry. It lasted about three months, dinner in little restaurants where you could dance, theatres.

I don't think he made any frightful sexual demands, if so they weren't mentioned, but she brought him home often, and he got very uneasy about the best china being brought out and Mary's mother saying that she would leave you young people alone and vanishing, so he asked me to help him unload her which was a lousy rotten thing to do and I said he was to do it himself, the weak fool, and the weak fool just stopped ringing her, and her heart was broken, because school was getting more and more boring and mother was more and more trying and Mary had really thought that This might be It.

She met a man in a pub shortly afterwards while waiting for a girlfriend. He invited them both to a party, and there was a lot of drink and messing, Mary said, but it was better than nothing, and he and his gang had parties nearly every weekend up in Rathmines, where they all lived in bedsitters or flats, and it was getting harder and harder for Mary to take a taxi out nine miles home afterwards, so she got into the habit of staying with her friend Brenda in town. Mother would be a bit sour, but at least not suspicious, and indeed at this stage she had nothing to be suspicious about because Mary *was* staying with Brenda and they would both have glasses of milk and discuss the talent at the party and wonder which one of the lads they should try and settle for.

And then she fell in love. Yes, that's what it was; she really found someone she loved much more than herself, and someone she couldn't live without. I didn't see her at all during this great period, but everyone who knew her said he was a total bastard, had got one of these funny divorces, because he had a load of money and a small luxurious flat that he actually called a 'pad' somewhere in Fashionable Dublin Four, and this was even further from Mary's home than ever, and so Brenda was being used as a very real excuse this time.

Brenda had a phone, and if Mary's mother rang, as she often did, Brenda would say, 'Hold on a minute, she's in the bath,' and then ring Mary at the pad and tell her to ring her mother quick, for God's sake.

I met them once and I agree he was very, very attractive and charming. He had a certain smoothness which I didn't like, but then put that down to prejudice because I had heard he was a smooth bastard from people who are kind of right about these things. But that night when I was eating a very quick meal before going to the theatre, and was by myself, they asked me to join them, and he did have something very warm about him; he seemed to be interested in her, and pleasantly interested in whatever I had to say too. He talked a bit about 'my little nipper' and explained that he was divorced, so there didn't seem to be any great deception or anything involved. Mary said her mother was going on a coach tour soon and that she and the guy would be having a party in his pad and I must come. The relevancy of the coach tour didn't strike me for the moment until I remembered that naturally her mother thought she was staying with Brenda four to five nights a week. He said it had been very, very nice to meet me, which I thought was a bit overdoing it; it might have been nice enough, but since I was shovelling food into my mouth and looking at my watch, it could hardly have been very, very nice. Still, people talk different ways.

And act different ways, too.

He never suggested marriage to Mary, though she was quite willing to go to England and get married there, or in the registry office here, but apparently whenever she brought it up he said that the Irish laws were funny, and even though he did have a Mexican divorce or whatever it was, there was always the possibility that one could be prosecuted for bigamy here. Not likely, he said, because the courts hate doing it, it makes them look ridiculous, but possible. He would, however, like Mary to move in with him.

And Mary loved him so much and her mother was still so unaware of his existence, and Brenda was leaving town to go to London, that there really were problems.

'Could you tell her the truth?' I asked foolishly, because really it was a foolish question.

All right, so Mary was 26, she was entitled to do whatever she liked; she certainly didn't love her mother enough to be deeply upset about hurting her. But then mothers are mothers and I can't believe that four years ago a woman in her fifties would like her daughter to move in with a divorced man. I couldn't believe for a moment that Mary's mother, who was practically a law unto herself, would countenance it for a minute.

Selfishly I thanked heaven that I lived in Dalkey and there was no fear that Mary could ask me to pretend I was living with her, because there is no way you could say Dalkey was nearer her work than her own house was. What did the man say? Oh well, he said, it was up to her to arrange things and she was so desperately afraid that she'd lose him, and he did so need someone to get his shirts cleaned, and cook his supper, she couldn't leave and there would have to be a way.

The way, when found, was so ludicrous and financially disastrous you will find it hard to believe.

Mary told her mother that she was going to do an evening course and would have to take a room in town. She rented a bedsitter and paid £6 a week for it, brought in some of her things. She now had clothes and possessions in three houses, her mother's, her man's and her new totally unused and useless bedsitter. Every Tuesday, which was her half day, she would bring in some more things from the pad to the bedsitter and ask her mother to tea. Mother was getting older, sadder and sourer. She couldn't understand why Mary was paying £3 to her old home, £6 to a landlord, when she had a perfectly good home of her own, and, said the mother sinisterly, perfect freedom to entertain all her friends there. The house was now too big for Mother. Tuesdays took on the nature of a nightmare.

Then there were the weekends. Mother couldn't understand that Mary had suddenly joined An Óige and was going on winter and summer hikes, when she didn't seem to know a thing about the organisation nor anyone in it.

I don't know Mary very well, remember, but I think that the man loved her a lot. He certainly made her very happy and apart from all the deceptions at home and the effort and the covering up and trying not to meet people that might conceivably split on them, it was a good, happy relationship.

For nearly a year.

The man, it appeared, was a little mean. Mary was only taking home £22 a week from her teaching, and nine of that was gone on two other sets of accommodation already. He expected her to pay for half their housekeeping and he liked living well. He bought her nice presents of course, but Mary was getting into debt. He had pictures of his nippers all over the pad; and none of Mary. She thought that was a bit hard, but the price you pay for this kind of setup. He had to go to business dinners, and naturally couldn't bring her along. So she spent long evenings looking at television, wondering what time he would come home. And she couldn't ask her friends in because it wasn't her place. So she would go out to a coin box phone occasionally and ring her mother, pretending she was phoning from the hall of the place she was meant to be living in, and her mother would have some other complaint. And she often went to the cinema on her own.

Then the doubts began. Was it a simple magazine case of letting herself go, did he find her less attractive now, had she moved in too easily, why were there so many business dinners now and hardly any at all six months ago? Was there someone else?

It couldn't be that he was lonely for the children because his ex-wife had remarried and the children were living with her in Switzerland. He didn't even have to send her alimony because this time, she had married a near millionaire. He never spoke of her at all, or why they had separated. Mary had never asked.

The summer holidays were coming up, and to get over the guilt feelings about Mother, Mary decided to get herself further in debt and take the two of them to Majorca. She wrote every day to tell him how she loved and missed him. He didn't write at all, because her mother would probably ask who the letters were from. She admired his tact in not writing.

Eventually the 14 days were over, and for appearances Mary stayed the night in her mother's home, and then looked in at her false flat to make sure it hadn't been broken into, and happily trotted up to the pad.

He wouldn't be home for ages, so she could make a great dinner. There was washing up in the sink, two of everything; he must have had Freddy to a meal. There was new talcum, and perfume in the bathroom, but they weren't presents, they were half used. It couldn't have been Freddy, he doesn't use Blue Grass.

The door opened and the Man came in, finding Mary sadly looking at a white dressing-gown on the back of the door. He had been coming back to clear up the evidence. They looked at each other, according to her own tale, for five minutes without saying anything, and then he had to say something and mercifully for Mary he didn't say, 'I can explain everything.'

What he did say was, 'Well, I suppose it had to end sometime.'

She doesn't know why he took someone else in, she doesn't know who the other person is or was, or if they are still there. She just knew that life was over. She packed there and then, borrowing one of his suitcases, and saying, 'Is this record yours or mine?' He stood stonily, and she never spoke to him again. That was three years ago.

Then Mary became known in the current attractive jargon of our times as 'an easy lay'. She moved properly into what was her false flat and made it her real flat. She got drunk and told her mother all about the Man, her mother forbade her to come back again and told the priest, and Mary told her to keep to her lonely bitter ways, and hasn't seen her mother properly for three years except at frosty Christmas lunches.

She had a short affair, which by her standards now means a relationship that lasts a month or two, with the father of one of her pupils, and was sacked from the school. She got another job in a provincial town for a while, but didn't even need to be sacked from that one because her poker playing, drinking and sleeping with the commercial travellers at the hotel made her a town name in three months.

I met her at the races there a few weeks ago. I didn't know her at first, but we met in the bar where I had lost my purse and it had been retrieved by an honest barman. She looked a little lost, and offered me a drink. I had people searching other corners of the race course for my purse so had to refuse but asked her to ring me during the Easter holidays, which she did.

She is pregnant; she hasn't a clue in the world who the father might be. You name him, it could be that person. It's now too late for an abortion, she thinks, she doesn't even damn know. She supposes she'll have it, and get it adopted. Would I know where she could do that? I would.

She also had a sort of half idea of keeping it, would I know how she could get help to do that? I would. What did I think about it all?

Well, what on earth could I think, except that life is unfair as I think more and more these days, and wonder was it ever meant to be fair? It's unfair on Mary's child who isn't wanted, it's unfair on Mary's mother who has no husband, and a daughter a nun in America, and a married son, and an emigrated son, and a daughter who is going to be a Public Disgrace. And it's unfair on Mary because she had no strength, and she has this belief that a lot of women have that they don't control their own lives. That they are somehow blown along by fate.

And I said that perhaps a child would give her something to live for, and someone to love. But I knew when saying it that she would have loved it to be His child, the only man she ever cared about, not the child of a number of people who stopped the loneliness of the night for her by coming home to her flat.

And I also know that a teacher will not be able to rear a child alone, and that Mary's mother won't help. And I know that if Mary is going to carry on the way she is at the moment, she won't be much of a mother or a teacher anyway. And so I gave her the addresses that we have listed in our little green note book, and hoped that the professionals will help her, and I rang Ally and Cherish about her, and said that she would be contacting them, and they said certainly they would do all they could for her. And I know they will, but I don't know that Mary will do all she can for herself, because she has that kind of hopeless beaten look, which has nothing to do with being pregnant and unmarried, it was there before. It has a lot to do with expecting life to be beautiful and easy like it is for everyone else and bitterly disappointed when it isn't. And that's why we are all such fools.

Women Are Fools – Lorraine

8 May 1973

Lorraine was at UCD with me in the late fifties and when everyone was wearing ten of those ridiculous stiff petticoats, Lorraine wore 20. She was in digs with a motherly kind of woman who liked her because Lorraine was obsessed with clothes and would lend Mrs whoever-she-was her good handbag in exchange for a blouse or one of her son's long sweaters, which were all the rage then too.

I didn't know her very well at this stage and always thought of her as one of those who used to be back combing their hair in front of the mirror in the Ladies' Reading Room, as it was called.

When we went to dances in '86' or in the Four Courts where the Solicitors' Apprentices used to run a very great kind of hop, Lorraine always danced with this fellow called Martin who was good-looking and quiet and did Commerce. It was assumed, again in the language of the time, that they were doing a line.

The year we were all meant to be studying for our degree, I got to know Lorraine better because nobody was studying at all. We had all taken holiday jobs on the grounds that if we got away from the distractions and the barbecues at White Rock and all that sort of thing there would be more chance of getting some work done.

I was teaching in St Leonard's-on-Sea, and by chance Lorraine was there too, working in a library in nearby Hastings, so we used to meet a bit and talk. I was mainly worried in case I was teaching the pupils rubbish, and that I would fail my BA because I didn't know one word, line or fact of American history. Lorraine was worried because she was always giving out books to people who looked like professional book thieves and she was hoping that her hard-to-get policy with Martin was going to pay off.

We had hours and days of Martin as we sat on the beach, me with American history books, Lorraine with unopened old English tomes. It *had* been the right thing, hadn't it, to pretend that one wasn't available? It would make him more interested, wouldn't it? There was no danger he'd meet someone else at home, was there? Reassurances from me, struggling with names I had never heard of and battles I hadn't known had taken place. Positively the right thing.

In August when everyone really *was* studying, I heard that they were engaged and would be married immediately after graduation. It seemed the most remarkable and romantic thing in the world, a triumph for all that Angela MacNamara advice about not giving your favours too easily, and not being too easy to get. She was just 20, he was her first and only boyfriend.

The rest of us went on sourly to do our HDip. Martin got a job in the Civil Service. Lorraine got a hopeless kind of job as someone's personal secretary.

Then she was coyly pregnant, and they had to leave their flat and I used to meet them at the odd party and it was always whine, whine, whine about the price of houses, and the not knowing whether to knit things in pink or in blue, and we found them a bit of a drag. We who had so much else to live for, like trying to find a teaching job in Dublin and/or a boyfriend.

And again by chance they got a house next door to a great friend of mine, so I kept coming across her for years afterwards. My friend had advised her to knit everything in white; it would be safer, and she had been delighted with that idea and kept out of everyone's way knitting until the girl was born, and a boy was born a year later and another girl after that.

This brings us to about 1964 and Lorraine and Martin had a new whine: it was about family planning. They just couldn't afford any more children, and you just had to sneeze and Lorraine got pregnant, and they were both very good Catholics and really wasn't it all terribly unfair? They had discussed it with Father Peter who had been very understanding and said that they should see a good doctor about the rhythm method, and with Father Brian who hadn't been a bit understanding and said that God never brought a life into the world that He didn't want, and there was never a mouth that He couldn't feed. And we were all so helpful to Lorraine and Martin and said yes, isn't Father Brian right? Look at the thousands who die of starvation, God just didn't want those apparently. And they became bewildered and didn't talk about it so much, which was what we wanted.

Martin was doing all right in his job, he was promoted and went back to college to do a post-graduate degree as a sort of part-time release. Lorraine just learned a bit of dressmaking and they went to the odd dance and my friend minded their three babies for them and they seemed just like any other married couple with a little too much money and a little too high aspiration in life.

I got the shock of my life when I saw Lorraine extremely drunk at a party about four years ago. She was simply incapable of standing up, so with the loyalty of the American-style old alumnae, a few of us got her out of it and brought her to the nearest house and sobered her up, with coffee, lots of it. Nobody could find Martin at the party.

He wasn't there. He was minding the children but Lorraine had decided she was sick of everything and of him being so dull and not wanting to go anywhere and she was still attractive for God's sake and she had no one to talk to all day, and he at least had his friends in the office, and all he wanted to do was to look at the telly and make love. And he had got round some priest, who said that if the doctor said she should take the Pill, then it was all right, and now she was taking the Pill and she and Martin would go to hell when they died. And she felt such a hypocrite at Mass every Sunday and it wasn't fair. She hadn't been to Communion for two years and she sobbed after we had all said something soothing about 'If the priest says it's all right. . . .'

So Lorraine said that wasn't the point, *she* didn't believe it was all right, it was just that Martin was a glutton for sex, and he had told it all to the priest in some dishonest way, she knew that. And perhaps the priest was one of those who were leaving. Priests were getting married all round the place, and you didn't know who you were talking to these days, and the whole Church seemed to be very confused.

More important than the Church being confused, in the short term we thought, was how to get her home to Martin sober and without explanation. She said she didn't give a damn what he thought, he was a man who never thought about anything anyway.

Pure *Woman's Own*, we felt, as someone with a car deposited her on her doorstep and weakly drove away before she got out her key.

And then I began seeing her everywhere, smartly dressed and laughing, and not drunk, but drinking, at press receptions that I had to go to because of work or coming out of smart bars that I wouldn't go into because of what they charge for drink, justifying it on the decor and the fact they give you peanuts. She was always being photographed at the races 'seen exchanging a joke', and I caught a glimpse of her in a sports car with a fellow who is known for describing in detail every encounter he ever has with a female.

The children were nine, eight and seven when I came across Martin in a country hotel with a woman who was not Lorraine. Two days of pretending not to see him, and rushing out of lounges as he came in, and eventually he said, 'I don't suppose you'll tell.' Which annoyed me to hell for two reasons.

The arrogant Edwardian assumption that the gent is allowed have his little fling and little floozy and that everyone will stand by him, and the other assumption that I might be on the phone to Dublin already saying, 'Lorraine, dear, I think you ought to know. . . .' I was just sad, the way anyone would be sad, and for some reason all her religious confusions came back to me, and I knew with a kind of instinct that she was not being unfaithful to him in the literal sense but was trying desperately to have a good time and be part of what she thought was a glamorous world, a world she missed by marrying so young, a world that confused her because its values weren't the ones she had learned in a country town, a convent school, a motherly digs and one summer abroad working in a library in Hastings.

You know the way it works. I wasn't back in Dublin two days when I met her.

'I believe you ran into Martin on a business trip,' she said.

Dishonest, mistrustful clown, I thought, and agreed that I had been talking to him for a few minutes. Had I time for coffee, she wondered? Oh God, I might as well hear it now. I might as well start saying I didn't know who he was with, whether all men were sex fiends and brutes or not. It was now or sometime. Right, we'll go to Bewley's.

But I was all wrong, couldn't have been more wrong, in fact. She wanted a chat just. The children were all so well, she was on the committee of this and that and could we ever give a little publicity to their flag day, and now that everybody was interpreting Humanae Vitae so liberally and all these cardinals were saying it as well, she felt fine, and she went to Communion regularly. She was a member of a little group that did spiritual reading and met once a fortnight to discuss it with each other and a priest who knew a lot more than they did.

She had stopped running around. It was all so silly, really, these parties and nightclubs, people thought you were there for One

Thing. And now that Martin was so busy and had to take so many business trips she spent much more time with the kids. Everything was going so well it was a pity that I had never married. Oh yes, I agreed, but I keep trying.

That pleased her. Martin wouldn't be at home next weekend either but when he was, they'd have a little dinner party and he could bring along some single men, and you'd never know. I wondered did Martin know any single men; but said it would be lovely, and she was right you know, you never did know. We parted very happily.

Martin's next affair was so public that the children even heard about it at school.

Now Martin's latest really was a tramp. It's hard to give that description to anyone, but this girl was the end. She went with anyone who could give her a good time, she didn't know the meaning of love and she didn't care about families or people. She was out for her pretty little self.

Lorraine eventually got one of those 'I think you ought to know' calls. It was only a matter of time, I suppose, but it was terrible the way it hit her.

She didn't start any of the devious tricks of winning him back. She didn't go and have a silly perm and wear glamorous nightgowns, she just decided that it was all over and assessed the whole situation over a lonely cup of instant coffee in the kitchen one morning. If he was having fun, well so would she.

She picked on the most unlikely man in the world. A quiet, rather inarticulate man who had a fairly happy home life, and she just set herself at him. He had vague connections with libraries and publishing so she played up all she knew about the pathetic little holiday job she had a hundred years ago it seems, and assumed an interest in all his work. It took six weeks, they tell me, before he gave in. Then they started hiring rooms for the afternoon in Dublin hotels, and she just felt she was getting back at Martin, and he felt desperately worried in case someone might tell his wife.

'Pure playboy' we decided at this stage, because you see no one was very fond of Lorraine, and no one could understand her motives. It went on for about a year. If anyone thought anything I suppose it was about how dreadful it must have been for the children. Mummy with a worried man, Daddy with an out-and-out chancer. But anyway none of us had enough courage or interest to say Stop.

And it stopped when the out-and-out chancer found someone else richer, freer and more fun. And Martin wanted a bit of home life and it just wasn't around. And about six months later the quiet, inarticulate man took a job about a thousand miles from here, to get out of the situation, and brought his fairly happy wife with him, and there they were. Mutually suspicious, and deeply unhappy.

To this day I don't know what Martin does with his life. I don't really care because I never got to know him, but I care a bit, I suppose, because I see what a failure he and Lorraine made of the whole thing, the whole business that was meant to be sickness and health, in good times and bad times. I just see what had happened to her at the age of 32.

She is probably the best-known easy lay in Dublin. You only have to be nice to her, if you are a man, and she will get a little drunk and a little emotional, and say that God was very unfair when He made the world, and go home to bed with you.

It didn't come home to me until a few months ago when a friend, a good friend of mine, said he had got himself stupidly involved with a very clinging woman, and she kept ringing him indiscreetly at his office. He was trying to get out of it, but she seemed so dependent and she seemed to have nothing to live for, and she was deeply religious, and guilty, and he wondered what the hell he should do.

I knew it was Lorraine because I had seen them talking in a pub one day and knew that this is a village, not a capital city, and that it was the latest of her 'involvements'. All right, what should I do, women are fools. Should I go out to her house and say this guy has a good job and a good wife and stop bothering him? Should I tell him to choke her off, and have her eventual breakdown on my neck? Should I ask Martin out to dinner and say, 'You're both young still, can't you make a new start?'

I did one thing. I had a party and asked a priest, and got him talking to Lorraine. I eavesdropped every few minutes and they seemed to be getting on fine. He was saying things like 'Your teenage children will need you now more than ever' and she was saying, 'I know, I know, but I feel so dishonest and neglectful, how can I ever re-establish something?' And I felt like some kind of Solomon. That evening anyway.

But she didn't stop her way of life. As I write she is involved with a boy, and I mean boy, of 22 who keeps ringing me and saying things like 'That brute of a husband ill-treats her and how do you get an annulment in this country?' And I don't know what to say.

And last week she rang me up and said that she would be very grateful if I could ask someone what that priest meant on television when he said that Marriage was dead when Love was dead, and could I tell her about all that old thing about annulment costing a lot of money. Was that true these days?

'Why don't you just go and live in England for a bit and get a divorce?' I asked, tough but practical.

'It has to be an annulment or nothing,' she said.

It appeared that God would sanction an annulment and just about everything else, but not a horrible secular thing like a divorce.

'Oh God, Lorraine,' I said, 'you are a fool.'

And I know she'll never speak to me again.

Women Are Fools – Sandy

9 May 1973

Sandy read Exodus when she was 18, about the same time as I did, but she read it in Yorkshire, and had married Johnny by the time she got to Israel. She believed that life was very commercial and rat race–ish in London and that in the orange groves and the purity of Israeli kibbutz life, they could really be both themselves and part of a greater movement. Johnny was easy going, he looked into the practicalities of the thing, and he decided that they would try it for a year or two anyway. He could always get a job in engineering again when they came back to London; it didn't seem like a New Life, but if Sandy was so determined, there could be nothing lost. They bought eight good books on teaching yourself Hebrew, they bored a lot of their friends with talk of going to a new land and a new life. They packed their two tiny children into a plane and went to the kibbutz.

I saw them the day they arrived, pale and blonde and starry-eyed. They handed the two little boys over to the Children's House and were given a bungalow to live in. They were told, as I had been, that the kibbutz could make no promises, if they were going to stay forever it would have to be by a vote from all the members. But then they didn't have to spell it out so much for me, because I was going in September anyway, back to teaching. There were no problems in my case.

And indeed there seemed to be none in Sandy's either. That

summer she became tanned and happy, she worked with me in the chicken house for a few weeks, we used to take day-old chicks and inject them against something, and we both cried the day that I choked one by mistake, because I held it too tightly, and Sandy was so soft that she buried it, instead of throwing it into the dustbin like the rest of them would have done.

Johnny was working on the dam, we had all learned passable Hebrew, but Johnny was better because nobody at his end spoke any English at all.

Their children were very happy. They were three and one, and the three-year-old was saying things in Hebrew to Sandy in one month, which excited her very much. She and Johnny were with them for five hours every day from two in the afternoon until seven, when they would put the baby to bed, and send little Tom to his tea. Nobody ever mentioned to any of us or to the children that we were any different to anyone else because we weren't Jewish. We never thought about it ourselves anyway.

And the long hot summer wore on and I was changed to making yoghurt from six a.m. until two instead of being in the chicken house, and Sandy was out picking grapes and got even browner and healthier, and she had a funny, happy smile, and a way of saying 'Shalom' to everyone with a grin that should have made us realise her happiness wasn't going to last. But then why should it? I mean, what was wrong with the setup? They were a young couple in love and idealistic, and getting on well with everyone. Sandy didn't look a fool at all. Compared to all her other friends, the working wives that she had left behind in London, she was in a paradise; no money worries, no health worries, near the sea, part of a commune.

They weren't my *best friends* there, but I missed them and thought about them a lot when I went home. No one is much good at letter writing on a kibbutz, and apart from a New Year's card I never heard from them. The following summer when I got off the bus for my three months visit, they were all there, as usual; nothing seemed to have changed. Miriam was still the cynical wit, David the fellow who got things done. Some of the older men and women with Polish names that I never got to know well threw their arms around me and said that I was one of the few summer visitors who ever returned. Sandy and Johnny were so good at Hebrew now that they could hardly bring themselves to talk in English, they said! They were terribly happy; a year and three months had gone by and no one had said anything about a vote. They were obviously there for life. Why didn't I go up to Tel Aviv for a month, marry someone and bring him back to the kibbutz? Life was so perfect.

And it was. No yoghurt making, no chickens, I was allowed to bring the kids for swims, if I could prove that I could shout, in Hebrew, all right and useful phrases like 'Come in at once' or 'Nobody out further than their waists'. Sandy's little boy Tommy was there and he literally couldn't speak a word of English. He was golden and had lots of friends.

One evening I was listening to the record player I had borrowed from a nice old Hungarian, who said that he now knew all the records in the library, and I could have the player until they got a few new ones. There were a lot of crickets outside competing with the music, and the laughter of a very young army group of boys and girls of about 18 who had been billeted on the kibbutz for a month and we all found them a terrible nuisance.

Sandy knocked at the door, and she didn't seem happy at all and there was very little of that fey glow. 'I'm pregnant,' she said.

Now what is so bad about a happily married woman having a third baby, you might wonder? The words didn't strike the terror into me that they have when other people have said them. But then of course I remembered the kibbutz rule, two children and no more. There was every kind of birth control available free and medical help as well, as regards a choice. Anyone who miscalculated had to go to Tel Aviv and have an abortion, there were simply no exceptions. There was no shame about the abortion either in the community, people just laughed and said how stupid of you. But Sandy was really grey with worry. She would like another little Tommy or Frank. She didn't know after all if they were going to be allowed to stay there forever. Should she have the child and go? If she had the child, there was no way she could stay, we both knew that. We decided to ask David, he knew the answer to everything.

David asked us in for coffee, he asked his wife to go off somewhere for an hour and she good-humouredly agreed. He said that in fact there had been a vote about allowing Sandy and Johnny to stay and that out of 300 people 287 had said yes. So they didn't bother telling this to the two of them because they might go around wondering who the other 13 were and it might make them feel edgy. Go ahead and have the abortion, said David, there's no fear.

I went to Tel Aviv on the bus with her. We found the doctor.

'Silly girl,' he said kindly. 'Sit up in the chair here.'

'Now?' screamed Sandy and I together in horror. We thought you went to bed for a day or two and got injections and tranquilisers and pep talks and anaesthetics and days to recover.

'Now,' said the doctor.

A nurse came into the room. She was young and pretty, she was kind, she spoke English, which was a great help to me anyway. She said the doctor had done five that morning and would do another 11 before leaving. There was simply nothing to it. Sandy could go home to the kibbutz that night; there was just no problem. Her friend, who had had one done yesterday, was working again this afternoon. It's all a matter of coming in time, like Sandy had; please stop getting excited now.

Sandy begged me not to leave. She told the doctor I was her sister. So I held her hand throughout and looked out the window and thought perhaps life is tougher here, and maybe Sandy after a year here would be tougher, and I would selfishly wipe it all out of my mind, and perhaps I could be tough too. And in 20 minutes Sandy was lying, wrapped in a rug, in a sort of waiting room, and the nice nurse brought her a cup of tea as she was coming round from one of those anaesthetics you get to have your teeth out. And the nice nurse reminded us that we could only use the waiting room for an hour.

I got a taxi and brought Sandy to a hotel. I telephoned the kibbutz and told them a lie, said we had missed the bus and that we would be back tomorrow. I said to tell Johnny that Sandy was fine.

'Well of course she is,' said whoever answered the phone, but whoever it was did tell Johnny anyway.

All night we sat and smoked, and she told me about her life in England and her wealthy parents in Yorkshire who hadn't wanted her to marry Johnny but softened a bit when he got a good engineering job, and how she believed that only in Israel could you be really decent.

But now she had this awful feeling that it wasn't a decent thing to do to kill an unborn child, and she wondered for the fiftieth time would it have been a boy or a girl.

The doctor had said casually, 'It's not possible to know at this stage, Sandy, do stop worrying, will you?'

And we went off on the bumpy bus next morning, and I deposited her at her bungalow, and Johnny came back from the dam and thanked me for going with her and asked me with his eyes would she be all right, and I kept nodding, and trying to put it all out of my mind.

And the second long hot summer went on and though Sandy

had lost what I fancifully thought had been the glow, she seemed fine. And we worked together one week at the potato-peeling machine, which was such a lousy job you only got it one week a year, and we had plenty of time to talk; she never mentioned the event again, and with great relief neither did I.

The way they work things on a kibbutz is often by rotating the horrible jobs with the good ones, so that even if you are a specialist like Johnny was and are needed on the dam you have to take your turn in the kitchen as well. There is no status, which is what Sandy loved about everything, and at the end of August when it was Johnny's turn to work in the kitchen, he was also in charge of the money, which had to be paid out to some delivery man who came once a week. Nobody in a kibbutz sees or touches money, their meals, drinks, clothes, accommodation, and cigarettes even, are all free. So Johnny got the £45 from the kibbutz secretary and left it on the window under a big jug of orange juice to wait until this man would come to be paid. In a kibbutz £45 in cash would probably be like a thousand, because it just isn't used or seen.

When the delivery man knocked at the door, the money wasn't there. Johnny was disturbed, but not greatly so; someone must have taken it away for safer keeping. But a huge search was mounted and no one could find it. There was no question of the delivery man having snatched it because he hadn't even come in the kitchen door.

Suddenly the whole atmosphere changed. Suddenly there was suspicion. In the 28 years since the kibbutz had been in existence, nothing like this had ever happened before. Johnny was scarlet with horror and Sandy was white with concern. They begged to have their bungalow searched and poor Johnny tried to account for his movements like an Agatha Christie villain, saying, 'Well I moved from the window to the dish-washing machine and then I went to see how the fish were frying and then. . . .' The kibbutz secretary had given another £45 to the bemused delivery man, who thought that all kibbutz dwellers were mad anyway.

Sandy went around saying to everyone very reasonably but also very repetitively, 'What would we want with £45 anyway, supposing we were the kind of people who would steal?'

Everyone shrugged, some more sympathetically than others, but they all, we all, said it was a great mystery, all right, and money didn't fly off a window sill. I tried to tell her it would die down like rows did in a school or an office, but she was deeply disturbed and kept saying it was a plot. It was one of the 13 who didn't want them to stay. She went to David's house day and night to ask him who the 13 were, and he begged both Johnny and myself to keep her quiet, she was upsetting the even tenor of their ways. Then Sandy would come to *my* room at all hours and beg me to realise that they were under suspicion and that the kids would hear about it, and really hadn't they a right to know who the people were that didn't want them to stay. And why couldn't we call in the police, or the army or someone with a lie detector.

One evening about a week later, when it all had far from died down like in an office or a school, Sandy stood up during dinner and became hysterical. She shouted and cried and said that she wasn't a thief and her husband wasn't a thief, and everyone was treating them as if they were. She then said, as I dreaded, 'It's just because we're not Jewish, because we're different, that you've picked on us. We aren't the same as you, that's what it all boils down to. It's a question of race. We're different.'

David stood up too. He had a calm voice and was a leader in every possible sphere of their life in that community. He spoke very gently. 'Sandy, that's not so. You, yourself, said you felt the same as we did, you wanted to build a new land, you wanted to live near and on the land, and you wanted to share. The day you and Johnny asked to be members of our commune you said you weren't doing it for atonement about Hitler or anything. I asked you not to look at the numbers on people's arms from concentration camps because you just *might* begin to feel different. You assured me that you felt one of us and we made you members. The fact is that Johnny "lost" £45 and that never happened here before and so people are upset.'

Six hundred eyes stared at them both, for what seemed an hour. Sandy spat at David and left the room, Johnny followed. They spent two days telephoning London getting £100 which Sandy threw on the floor of the kibbutz secretary's office, and they packed one small grip bag and their two startled children on to the bus. They wouldn't say goodbye to anyone.

Terrible, unforgivable, tragic were the words people used as the bus went away in a shower of dust and hot smoke. Every single person was upset; it was too small and parochial for people to be above judgment and comment. They wondered aloud at Sandy's bitterness, had it been latent there all the time, at whether she believed Johnny might have taken the money. They wondered why she had been so keen to come in the first place, they wondered could the abortion have unhinged her, they asked me to remember everything she had said to me. They really cared what was going to happen to her. Not so much about Johnny, he was sort of adaptable, they thought.

At dinner the night after they went, there was a terrible argument at one table with people screaming and shouting in Hebrew. I couldn't understand a word of it, so great and frightening was the intensity. An old man was being hustled out the door, a nice old man, he used to work in the chicken place with me one year and help me with holding them so they would feel comfortable. He was crying, and his whole face was distorted. It took me an hour to find out what had happened; he had suddenly put his hand into his pocket and taken out £45, and said something like, 'Now that the hypocritical Goi have gone, here's the money; I have no secrets, and I don't steal from my own.' Instead of being congratulated, as the old man thought he would be, he was turned on by everyone. His shouts about what the Goi had done to his wife and children and everyone he knew in Treblinka were ignored, his rage that the Christians, especially the English Christians, had stood by in 1948 and let seven Arab states attack the new pathetic Jewish homeland, went unheard. He was marched to David's house, where David was minding Malka, his quiet wife, sick with a kind of flu and a kind of depression over Sandy and Johnny's terrible exit.

David wasted no time. He tried to find out had they left the country. No, they were booked for the following morning, someone in the airlines told him eventually. He took a motorbike and went miles through the night to find their hotel; he didn't, but he was at Lod Airport before they arrived. That much we knew as we waited in the hot day. David will bring them back, it will all be made up, we told each other. The other poor man is sick, he will be taken away to hospital. Johnny and Sandy will understand; they will come back. We didn't really believe it.

David came back alone with a scar on his face. Sandy had hit him in the departure lounge with her handbag. She and Johnny and the two toddlers had got on the plane to London. They had said, David told a few people, that Treblinka hadn't been half hard enough for the old man.

It was a sad summer.

I wrote to them, and said I was often in London and that if ever they would like to meet me, we could talk about other things, not Israel. I heard nothing for two years, so after two letters I left it.

Two years later I got a letter from Johnny, he said he had just heard me on a radio programme and thought he'd like to meet me for a meal sometime I was in London. We arranged a place, and I asked, with some kind of unexpected sensitivity, first about the children. They were fine. I wouldn't know Tommy now, he was a little man; and Frank was a real character. I asked about his job and he about mine, we talked about the cost of holidays, and whether Snowdon would have been a good photographer anyway or had made it because of Margaret. When we started talking about the scampi we were eating I couldn't bear it any more.

'Where's Sandy?' I asked very quickly, hoping that the best he would say was that she was a bit depressed and didn't want to meet anyone with associations with the unhappy incidents. I thought the worst he might say was they had parted, because he seemed to be talking about the kids as if they were his sole responsibility. Nothing prepared me for his equally quick answer.

'She's in jail,' he said.

When they had got back to England her parents had been no help. They had told everyone that their crazy little daughter and son-in-law had done their stint out in the sun for the Israelis and had now seen sense and come home again. Sandy then turned against her mother. They had rented a flat in London and he got a job; Sandy seemed cheerful, for a while. They decided to have another child and somehow she wasn't getting pregnant. She went for an examination and was told that the abortion had done something which would not only prevent her having children, but might lead to a hysterectomy. Johnny was vague; I think he suspected that Sandy made it up, because he said pleadingly either you have a hysterectomy or you don't, isn't that right? I didn't know.

And then Sandy had lost all control. One day she had gone to Stamford Hill, Golders Green, and a couple of other areas where Jews lived in numbers. She had thrown stones in windows of jewellers, of places with Jewish names, of synagogues when she could find one. She had hired a motor scooter, and got away each time before she was caught. It was evening before the police came and found her with a bagful of stones on the pillion of the scooter, heading off again and laughing.

Of course he had got her psychiatric help. She was in a very nice place for a month, and convinced everyone, himself included, that it had been a wild aberration. She had seemed so ashamed of herself and asked everyone nervously was she going mad, and promised that she would make up the damage she had done so sincerely that she had fooled even the psychiatrist.

She was on the probation act or under it or whatever you are, and Johnny had to give up work for a couple of months and go cap in hand, he said, to her father for money to look after her. She read a lot, and wouldn't talk about it, and refused a psychoanalyst, and then six weeks later took a fire shovel and broke three windows again of Jewish shops, and said so coldly in court that she was perfectly sane, but just wanted to equal an old score, that this time the Law was a bit suspicious of her, and it was all at the time when people were beating up Pakistanis. Poor Johnny's face was more bewildered than when the £45 had disappeared.

She chose jail, and she said she would do it again when she came out. So they had better keep her there a long time. Her psychiatrist said she wasn't fit to be imprisoned.

He had begged everyone to let him state the facts and the history, but Sandy was so cold, so full of hate, so full of the Enoch Powell phraseology that really the Law had no option. She had been in prison now for two months with four more, two if her behaviour was good, but she said that if they were going to release her early she would shout out more anti-Semitic things and be kept in.

The psychiatrist, who was fuming because she was in jail at all, said that he would get her into a good place and they would cure her, but Johnny didn't believe they ever would. He wanted to know about the kibbutz, had I been back? I had. Did the tomato scheme work? Did the dam still go peculiar? Was the food any better? Had they made a profit yet on the chickens? Did Ari and Miriam get a divorce? Nothing about himself and Sandy, it might have been a book that he had read, and been interrupted in. He wanted to know how the serial was continuing.

'They are always asking do I see you,' I said diffidently. 'They want news of you terribly.'

'Well you'll have plenty to tell them this year,' he said bitterly.

Pageantry and Splendour at Westminster for the Royal Wedding

15 November 1973

The ushers were simply delighted to see me. 'Splendid,' they said, 'absolutely splendid. Let's have a little look. Oh, yes, seat number 17 this way. Super view, and just beside the telly, too. Super!' They could have been brothers of my dearest friend, instead of members of Mark Phillips' regiment examining the press ticket, which had cost £23.

Westminster Abbey was lit up like an operating theatre; the light from the chandeliers was only like candlelight compared to the television lights. Well, since 500 million people, including the Irish, were meant to be looking in, I suppose you had to have it bright enough to see something. There was plenty to see from the top of a scaffolding over the north transept. Grace Kelly staring into space, looking like she always looked, kind of immaculate.

Rainier has aged a bit oddly and looks like Marlon Brando in *The Godfather*. Harold Wilson, all smiles and straightening his tie, his wife looking as if she were about to compose the final poem on the occasion. Jeremy Thorpe was all giggles and jauntiness, Heath looked like a waxwork.

Anthony Barber looked suitably preoccupied, as well he might, with a State-of-Emergency going on outside the Abbey doors, and Whitelaw looked as if it was his first day off in two years. There were a lot of people whose faces I thought I knew, but it was no help asking for advice on either side. The man from the *Manchester Evening News* seemed to be writing an extended version of *War and Peace* in a notebook and on my right an agency reporter was transcribing a file of cuttings.

And then the royals started to arrive. We could see them on the television set – which was six inches from me – leaving Buckingham Palace in their chariots, and like characters stepping out of a film, they suddenly turned up a hundred feet below our seats. The Queen Mother looked the way she has ever looked – aged 56 and benign. The Queen looked thin and unhappy in a harsh blue outfit. Princess Margaret looked like a lighting devil with a cross face and an extraordinary hideous coat, which may have been some multi-coloured fur. But then was there ever an animal or even a selection of animals that would have been given such a coat by Nature.

The Phillips' parents looked sick with nerves; nobody in the place was hating it as much as they were. Mother Phillips nearly tore her gloves to shreds, father Phillips let his invitation fall and it struck me as odd that the groom's parents should have had to carry an invitation at all. The son and heir stood smiling and resplendent in scarlet, dimpling and smiling, and you felt that if all else failed and he doesn't become a brigadier or something in six months, he will have a great living in toothpaste commercials.

The Dean of Westminster, who is a very civilised, cheerful sort of man, was sort of happy about it all, and so was the Archbishop of Canterbury. They beamed all round them and extracted a few return grins from the nervous-looking lot in the VIP seats. The choirboys looked suitably angelic and uncomfortable in their ruffs. One of them got his fingers caught behind his neck and had to have it released.

The trumpeters were noble and rallying, and the Beefeaters were traditionally beefy. Everything was as it should be in fact, as we waited for the bride.

About three seconds after the glass coach had left Buckingham Palace with Anne and her father we were all handed two pages of strictly embargoed details about the wedding dress: it would have threatened national security to have had it before, apparently. Journalists all around me were devouring it and rewriting the details of seed pearls and 1,000 threads of 20-denier silk to every inch of the garment. When she arrived at the door of the Abbey there was a bit of excitement about arranging the train and adjusting the tiara, and the bride looked as edgy as if it were the Badminton Horse Trials and she was waiting for the bell to gallop off.

Up at the altar all the royals looked out as eagerly and anxiously as if they thought the Duke of Edinburgh and his only daughter might have dropped off for a pint on the way. The Queen actually smiled when they got into sight and Mark gave a matinee-idol shy, rueful smile. Princess Margaret read her programme of the wedding service as if it were the latest Agatha Christie that she had promised to finish before lunchtime.

The Duke of Edinburgh went and sat beside his wife and mother-in-law and seemed to have a far greater control over his sword than did Prince Charles, who carried his as if it were an umbrella. I was waiting for half his relatives to have their legs amputated but there must have been some kind of plastic top on it because nobody seemed to be maimed or anything when they were leaving.

The service went as planned and the young voices were clear and loud, as everyone remarked approvingly afterwards, no coyness or nervous stutters. There were a lot of hymns, and I saw the Queen singing her head off, but gloomily, and the Phillips parents sang, too, nervously on their side.

Then off they galloped down the aisle and it was over. And do I mean over! There was no hooley in the palace or anything; the party had been on Monday night. The people who had got all dressed up went home, I suppose. The bridal couple had about nine hours of photographs, and all the people who had been camping on the street packed their spirit stoves into plastic bags and went off for lunch.

It was a superbly organised show, with all the actors playing their parts perfectly, timing and all. Everyone who had a role kept to it: the Duchess of Kent looked sweet and pure English girlhood; Princess Alexandra managed to give the odd vaguely tomboyish grin which she thinks is expected. The Duke of Edinburgh and Lord Snowdon looked as self-effacing as Mark Phillips is beginning to look already. The ushers saw us out, thrilled that we had been able to get there and hoping earnestly that we had a good view of everything. The evening papers were already on the streets with early photographs. 'The Snow White Princess!' screamed one headline, as if the readers had expected the bride to wear scarlet jodhpurs.

It was a very well-produced show, no one could deny that, but then the actors are getting slightly above Equity rates.

How to Speak Proper

27 May 1974

I was particularly fond of the word 'antithesis' and used to drag it into all kinds of conversations, until I noticed people smiling at the way I pronounced it. Apparently there was something unusual about the 'th' bit, which made me red with rage since the English are totally unable to speak their own language and insist on talking about the Shar of Persiar, and having a good idear about something, and wondering what's going to happen next in Eirer.

It was with a vicious joy that I discovered that the BBC had a pronunciation unit no less, a section which defined the correct way to use words, where to lay the emphasis and, most importantly, how to deal with unfamiliar places and people's names. Armed with recent examples of their horrifying mispronunciations I went off to investigate it, sure that I would give them a few helpful hints and set them straight on it all. It wasn't only the infamous Drogg-heeda, and the multifarious pronunciations of Charlie Haughey's name at a time gone by, but it was words like 'Sinai' which I was certain they had got wrong.

Mrs Hazel Wright wouldn't give an inch on Sinai. Not a centimetre. Yes, she knew I'd been there, so had the hundreds of others who objected to it being pronounced Sign-e-eye. But still she had done her work and this was what had come of it. In Hebrew and many Arabic languages the A and the I were both lone vowels, in rapid speech it was pronounced Sign-e-eye. Look at the file, look at the research. But since you could never be doctrinaire about language, it was quite possible that this pronunciation might change. They were not pedants, they didn't want to impose a pronunciation, in a few months they might agree that common usage had sanctioned it and then it would be Sign-Eye, as I wanted.

They were not stuffy in the pronunciation unit, she said firmly. And indeed stuffy they are not. They have a huge metal filing index with over 100,000 entries. As soon as a word is queried or thought worth querying, a little card is filled out on it, with the whole history of the investigations and a summary of the findings. Sometimes, of course, a place or a person comes into the news so rapidly that they don't have time to find out how it should be pronounced. But they usually have it right in a few hours. 'Like some Northern Ireland names,' I said, thinking of the time that poor Henry Kelly had been going to bed in Belfast satisfied that he covered the main stories of the day. He turned on the two a.m. news and heard that there had been great trouble in Collisland, a place of which he had never heard. Frantic, he checked around and was told to go back to sleep; they meant Coal island and he had done the story hours earlier.

Mrs Wright agreed. Scottish, Welsh and Irish names were difficult to pronounce to a southern English ear and voice. If they had to be pronounced without recourse to any advice people usually tried to say them as they were written, which, she agreed, was not only unwise but which had too many bad precedents. 'When you think that the English have a name like Featherstonehaugh and are capable of pronouncing it in at least five ways including Fanshaw and Feesonhay it's ridiculous that we should expect others to go by spelling alone. But we don't really, you know. We go to great trouble to try and get it right, and sometimes it's not as easy as you think.'

In the case of an Irish place name the following procedure is used. Firstly they go to their enormous index to see is it included. A great many names are there already. Asked to pick one at random, I chose 'Magherafelt'. There were four pages of notes on it, beginning with the report of a BBC overseas reporter who said that when he was there during the war, local people had called it

Maarafelt, and going on to various contradictions of this all dated and documented. There were reasons for accepting or rejecting the Macherafelt pronunciation, and an eventual conclusion as to how it should be uttered. Suppose the name did not appear in the index? Mrs Wright and her assistants would telephone the Irish Embassy in London. There was a girl in the library there, Dympna Coughlan, who went to great trouble to tell them how it was pronounced. If she didn't know or gave a couple of alternatives they would ring their man in Dublin or Belfast or wherever and ask him to enquire around a bit and see what was the accepted usage; sometimes they rang Brigid Kilfeather in RTÉ who would help them. I wouldn't believe all the trouble they had had with Seán Mac Stíofáin's name. Honestly, everyone they asked gave them a different variation.

Were the biggest files on Irish names then? Not at all. You had to remember how many countries they were dealing with, especially through the Overseas Service at Bush House. Actually if I wanted to see the biggest file it was on the word 'Nyasaland'. It went on for over 16 pages, coming up with the final conclusion that it should be pronounced Nee not Nye. The biggest problem was that they had to remember they were speaking in English and since English people didn't call Paris 'Paree' they had to concentrate on what would be the accepted English pronunciation of the word. They weren't monitors or spies in the pronunciation unit. They didn't listen to broadcasts and ring up a speaker and pounce on him for saying the word incorrectly. They don't have time for one thing, and that's not their job for another. It's funny that an organisation like the BBC which was for so many years considered rightly or wrongly the great authority on how to talk nicely should in fact have just a small section where people apply if they want to know how to pronounce a difficult word. Certainly Mrs Wright, who is an honours graduate in modern languages and who has phonetic training, is very capable of dealing with anything that occurs, and many things that don't occur. Every morning they send around a list of words which they think might be needed during the day, like 'Ma'alot' in Israel or 'Potchefestroom' in South Africa.

It all began, this care and emphasis on pronunciation, as long ago as 1926, when an advisory committee on spoken English was set up under the chairmanship of the then poet laureate Robert Bridges, and it went on gently, I would imagine, discussing things in an academic way until 1939 when the war meant an end to all such committees. Shaw was on the team with them and gave a lot of good and memorable advice, although he is once meant to have said that it would have been a hell of a lot better if they had a few London taxi drivers and less lords and ladies on it. The woman who had done all the donkey work on the committee was Miss Elizabeth Miller, whose name is still a legend in the BBC. She took over the pronunciation business for the whole Corporation. Hers are the main body of the notes in the files and Mrs Wright pays tribute to the way she worked almost unsung and quite obviously had to fight long battles over almost every word for many years. Miss Miller retired two years ago but the standards she set in policy still remain, and are strenuously supported by those who have come after her.

I found some of the items in the pronunciation handbook utterly comic, like the paragraph that deals with local educated usage, which is established 'by consulting the vicar of the parish, the town hall, or the police'. How could you seriously ask the police or the vicar how to pronounce a place? 'I don't agree with you at all,' said Hazel Wright, 'you can't ask the first person you meet or take a name out of a phone book to define how a place is pronounced. Vicars and policemen have often been a long time in the area, they meet a lot of people by the nature of their work, they get a good average idea of how the majority of the people pronounce the place and that's what we need.' It is interesting to note that the BBC these days is more anxious to avoid being patronising than to sound posh. For example, they don't try too hard to get local accent or pronunciation and emphasis in case it looks as if they are trying unsuccessfully to take off the accents of the people who are strangers to them. The British say *post* office. In Ireland we accent the second word; a reporter in Ireland would not conform to this because it would look odd and sound odder.

They try too not to be too accurate. This came up over the recent football match. There is no adjective 'Argentinian'. In fact, the word you should use is 'Argentine' to describe the team. But the pronunciation unit did not recommend this as it sounded a little too hair-splitting and liable to be misunderstood by the majority of the audience. If I thought that the BBC pronunciation unit was rather over-documented, said Hazel Wright, I should have a look at the way the French go about it. Almost every day she receives their documentation and it is incredibly detailed and indeed much more dictatorial. It is also extraordinarily charming since every manifesto about the wrong pronunciation of consonants before vowels ends with a little quote from the famous. I examined a few. 'I've been speaking prose for forty years and didn't know it' Molière. Or: 'A knowledge of words is a knowledge of things' Plato. The French do things with style, thinks Mrs Wright. Who wouldn't like to do things with more style if there were more of them, and more time? She doesn't want to order people what to say but to be able to give exhaustive reasons for any particular pronunciation she suggests. Her rooms are surrounded with reference books as well as files. The phone hardly stopped ringing with people wanting to know how to pronounce things.

'Life would be very simple for us if we didn't have news,' she says. 'You see we could get the correct pronunciation of any word correctly in a day or two, but somehow that isn't the way a radio and television service works. It has to know at once or not at all.'

Who Sent This Postcard?

2 September 1974

It arrived the other day. A nice postcard of Paris. On the back was this message: 'Everything arranged this end. Have finished the book finally. Paris as lovely as it always was. Hope everything fine with you now. Love John.'

This is the greatest mystery that has ever occurred in my life. What has he arranged at his end, for God's sake? Is it a hotel room, a bank robbery, an interview with the President? Who is he? I checked the Johns I know. The ones in *The Irish Times* are still working away at their desks and are arranging nothing in Paris.

I know a travel agent called John, who told me gloomily that he couldn't afford to go to Paris to arrange anything. I rang a John who works in the hotel business and had a ridiculous shouted conversation with him about bed nights and tourist receipts, but he hasn't been to Paris for five years and doesn't think he'll ever see it again. Then what could the book be, is it one he has written or just one he has read? I suppose I can watch the book lists for a year or two in case John Somebody published something, but suppose he was just wading through *War and Peace*? I'm delighted Paris is as lovely as it always was, but is there an implication that we once saw it together? I was never in that city with anyone called John, never. There were no moonlight walks by the Seine holding the hand of a John. He must mean that it was as lovely as he separately and I separately had always found it. Why shouldn't everything be fine with me? Now or any other time. What wasn't fine? It's terrible to try and think of the things that haven't been fine, you just become very neurotic. Could he be somebody I met when I fell down all those stairs and had to be taken breathing oxygen to a hospital? That was the last time that things weren't fine. Or was he around when I lost my diary with every address, phone number and piece of information I will need for the rest of my life?

Oh to hell with him; anyone who has the arrogance to sign himself John and expect to be recognised doesn't deserve a moment's thought. But why can't I sleep worrying about what he has arranged at his end. And what damn book has he finished? And why did he spell my name right if I don't know him, and why couldn't he have sent a postcard to somebody else?

Holiday Romance

6 November 1974

If you go to the Club Méditerranée on your own, you have to share a hut or a bungalow with someone else. One time, when I was in Turkey, I shared with a girl called Francine. She was very, very beautiful; she examined all my clothes with a lack of interest, went through the three pieces of make-up I had with disappointment, asked me rather humiliatingly did Irish women not care about being chic, and finally, deciding that I would be no threat to her, became my best friend for three weeks.

Francine was an air hostess. She was recovering from a serious operation, the details of which I tried to shut out but it seemed to be bits of stomach being untied from where they were and tied to other bits. She was also recovering from a broken heart, had borrowed £200 from a friend for clothes and was going to have a marvellous time, and return to Paris looking magnificent and possibly with a new remedy for the broken heart in tow.

We had an unspoken arrangement about not meeting during the day. Because Francine would spend the morning on the beach miles away from everyone, sunbathing nude. She would have three green figs for her lunch, which was insanity since the food was included in the price and was magnificent. She would spend the afternoon in the 'Hammam,' or Turkish bath, and emerge after about three hours looking lovely.

Dinner time was when she would cast around for men to hunt. For the first week there was little interesting to catch. She would discuss the conquests flatly when we went to bed. 'No, the Italian lawyer was very boring. I wish I could have found him suitable, because he is from a very wealthy family, but no.' And a most handsome lounge lizardish sort of person who paid her constant attention was dismissed petulantly. 'You see, he is a great nuisance. Other men do not come and talk to me while he is there, and he is a very stupid and very vain little man.'

I left her to go off and do a strenuous six-day excursion in the valley of Goreme. It meant crawling through rock-hewn churches, climbing what looked like the face of the Eiger. Filthy and out of breath, I would return to our central Turkish base each evening for a quick wash and a night of cheap wine, wondering vaguely how Francine was making out with the checklist of possibles she had drawn up. There seemed nobody likely for me to bring back to her on the outing. They were all filthy as I was, and seemed to have no interest in anything except rock-hewn churches, which I guessed might not be Francine's secret passion.

In fact, they were a pretty dull lot, the men on that trip, and the dullest of all was a surgeon with a pipe which made him totally inarticulate in any language. He had a difficult 18-year-old son behaving like a 12-year-old, full of sulks and shoulder shrugging and boredom which drove us all mad. The surgeon said to me once that he couldn't continue talking with me unless I would learn to pronounce the French word 'suspendu' correctly, because it made his teeth water to hear the way I did say it. That kind of thing can either be a challenge or a pain in the face. It was a pain in the face. On our return to the main camp, Francine looked even more beautiful but a bit cheesed off on the quest for the grail. Men there had been in plenty presenting themselves, but they were all of inferior intelligence. Since Francine was not exactly Einstein, this seemed odd but interesting. I wondered hesitantly should she go out and look for friends during the day instead of waiting until dinner time. I had found some playmates of my own out in fishing boats and at barbecues. No, said Francine purposefully, that would not do at all. You would meet a rough sort of person that way. And how could you judge their manners and their style if you didn't meet them at dinner?

The next night I introduced her to Christian, the sour doctor. I thought it would be a conversation of ten seconds' duration, and was surprised to see them half an hour later chatting away. That night she sat with him at dinner and was very, very late back to our bungalow. She turned on the lights, handed me a cigarette and, clasping my hand, said, 'You are a genius; he's perfect, just perfect.'

To be woken from sleep to such enthusiasm is startling, but the more I thought of the strange doctor and the magnificent-looking romance-seeking Francine, the more I began to think it was one of those dreams where you imagine that your younger brother is married to Catherine the Great and you wonder what to do about it.

It was no dream. The 24-year-old Francine and the 50ish Christian were inseparable for the rest of the holiday. She would wake me every night to tell me the details, which were very, very boring, and mainly involved her strategy in not giving him all he would naturally as a man want, because it was wiser to wait until they were married.

One night, despairing to be woken to the same story, I said that perhaps he might not want all that men might naturally want on account of sharing a bungalow with his 18-year-old son, and she said I had a lot to learn. The son, who was called Claude, became even more painful as time went on, and was sitting shrugging and yawning every time I was dragged to join them all for a drink. He was interested in no subject and one day in desperation I asked him what he would like best to happen that afternoon.

He said, 'I would like that stupid girl to leave my father alone and find some cowboy to divert her. My father is very easily swayed.'

Oh drama, drama. I couldn't bear to leave them not knowing what was going to happen though I didn't really like any of them enough to be on anyone's side.

But the months went by and the time I could afford to go to Paris came eventually. I wrote to Francine and said it would be nice to meet for lunch. On the way to the restaurant I expected she would have difficulty in remembering what Christian's name was. He seemed to be such an unlikely life partner. But there he was, the two of them smiling, and a bit of diamond flashing. They had just become engaged; would I come to their wedding? They insisted on giving me a ticket as a present, because I had introduced them, remember? Well, I was polite for a bit. They would have met anyway; it wasn't fair to take a ticket. And then, of course, I gave in as we had all known I would.

It was an extraordinary wedding. The town hall one day, a church the next, two great feasts, lots of congratulation, everybody on both sides of the family assuring me of the good work I had done. If ever there was a couple so right for each other it was Christian and Francine. The sour Claude had become less shruggy. He said it was better for his father not to have a lonely old age. I swore to become a deep and intimate friend of the whole family, and we exchanged Christmas cards for about three years as an assurance that this is what indeed I was.

Then I had a party, a party all of my own in Paris. It sounds very grand, and in fact I thought I would never get a chance to write about it. It was in fact 12 people invited to my hotel bedroom to have some duty-free Irish whiskey, which I had smuggled in. I invited Christian and Francine among the guests. Maybe you know already what was going to happen, but I hadn't a clue, and it staggered me for weeks. Francine arrived, but with her glum stepson Claude, less glum and deeply protective to the extent of embracing his stepmother in the most unacceptable manner, as the French would say.

Francine dragged me aside, telling me that I looked a bit better than before but not much. I should have my eyebrows done professionally and perhaps red hair what with being Irish. 'Where's Christian?' I squeaked, knowing I was going to hear something strange.

'Oh well, you know it was never very wise, when there is such an age difference and everything. He has gone to live in Switzerland. He is a very famous surgeon there now in a clinic, he is very happy. This man is interested really only in his work. You do understand and I would die in Switzerland. All those dull, clean, plain people. I would die outside Paris. He knows that, he writes from time to time. He did a very famous operation and it was in the papers.'

I'm really not able for all this sort of thing at all you know, despite my pretensions, and my voice was like some kind of puppet by the time I managed to get out the words, 'And what about Claude?'

'Oh, isn't he marvellous? You are a genius, he is just perfect.

Everybody would have such a happy holiday romance if they only went on a holiday with you. I can never thank you enough.'

I Was a Winter Sport

21 November 1974

I knew that I would probably fall, but I didn't expect to fall coming out of the railway station. Crowds of elegant Germans in posh ski wear tramped over me, a few British looked embarrassed and then looked away, an Italian man bent down and told me that it happened to the best of us and went away without picking me up. When the station was empty three porters got me to my feet and begged me not to take the next train home. Madame would be skiing like a bird, they assured me, and like a fool I believed them, and slid and crawled my way to the hotel.

It was full of sweat and heat, and pipes gurgling, and basements with people throwing skis around like darts, and radiant faces talking about the south piste, and worried brows discussing ski bindings. There was registration for the nursery school and a lot of hot rum, and a view from the bedroom like the best Christmas card ever and a very deep, slightly bruised sleep.

Next day, hot chocolate, plenty of buns to keep up the strength, into the ski pants that looked great in Dublin and cost a week's salary. Beside everything else on the patio they looked like fancy dress. On with about four sweaters, in case I got frostbite and a jar of cream rubbed into my face in case there was sunstroke going around as well. Left, right, left, right, and we marched to the foothills of a crag.

The ski instructor was called Mike, and nobody fell in love with him. In three languages he told us how to put on our skis, which were waiting in battered splendour on the snow. A man fell over just bending down to pick them up, and I was so sympathetic that I rushed to help him up and fell on top of him, which was a bad start, since Mike said in three languages again that there would be time for that sort of thing later, could we concentrate on getting the skis on now please. We extricated ourselves, and a nice 12-year-old tied on both our skis for us.

It was the most awkward thing I have ever done. Each foot seemed to weigh a ton and to be 20 feet long. It was impossible to point oneself anywhere without doing damage to someone else and one woman became quite hysterical because she found herself sliding sideways with gathering speed and couldn't stop. Mike had to go and head her off before she went into a wall at a hundred miles an hour and that caused a lot of alarm in those of us who stood rooted to the ground. Skiing sideways was a new horror we hadn't thought of.

He put us in two circles like a Paul Jones and we were asked to walk around to get used to the feel of the things. The space between each walker increased to huge distances because everybody seemed to be sticking a ski into the bottom of the person in front, and you couldn't turn around to protest because you fell over at once if you moved in any direction except purposefully forward. So there were great oaths in many languages, as we marched gloomily around the churned-up snow dragging these fiendish appendages.

Just when I was wondering would it be time for the après ski to begin, Mike said that it was now nine-thirty a.m. and that we should all have the feel of the skis, so would we please follow him and we would learn walking on a slope. A small gradient, he explained, in case the nursery school became frightened by the word 'slope'.

It looked like the wrong face of the Eiger when we had to climb it, and the scene began to be like one of those dreams where you try to move but find yourself constantly in the same place. Worse really, because in those dreams you are at least vertical, there is no sense of constantly hitting the ground. The Falling Man and The Hysterical Woman and a Twitchy Swede and I spent most of our time clutching each other and dragging each other down again. About ten of the group seemed to have mastered it and were scaling the small gradient as if they had been born to such things.

'Cheats,' said The Falling Man. 'I've read about those kind, they know all about skiing. They only join nursery classes to look good and improve their egos.'

'I think I'm going sideways again,' screamed The Hysterical Woman, and we all plunged out to rescue her, knocking her to the ground in the effort.

'The rarified air is doing nothing for my heart, he is beating too rapidly,' said The Twitching Swede. So The Falling Man gave him a nip of brandy, thinking that this might slow it down.

Mike skied back to us in a show-off way from the front of the group. He rolled his eyes to heaven. 'Drinking is bad,' he said in many languages.

We were all sitting in the snow drinking The Falling Man's brandy at this stage, and if ever spirits are said to be medicinal it was in this case. Mike thought, however, it was loose living. 'I will take that,' he said like a school prefect and confiscated The Falling Man's flask. We watched it disappearing like you would a life raft, but were too mute with fear to do anything except agree. Drinking was bad, we admitted humbly and repentantly.

Mike dragged us all to our feet, and pushed us towards the ascent again. It was a sorry progress. The Swedish heart was beating much too rapidly, hysteria was coming on strong with The Nervous Lady, The Falling Man and myself dragged ourselves painfully towards the summit, and Mike whizzed around us like a butterfly telling us always first in German, then in Italian and finally in English that we mustn't lift our feet so high, and finally we made it to the group who were on top of the hill. 'Now comes the interesting part,' said Mike.

Great, I thought, about to take off my skis and run back to the hotel, it's time for lunch. Not at all. The interesting part was apparently the exercises. The limbering up, the bending and stretching. The kind of thing in fact that I used to tell terrible lies in school to avoid, and here I was on a glass mountain abroad, at great cost, trapped and unable to get out of them. It went on until my body cried out with the agony of it all, and I wondered what would happen if I said I felt faint.

I tried it. 'You are out of condition,' said Mike. 'Keep bending, it will make you less faint and more fit.'

I don't remember coming back to the hotel, but I gather we stumped and spiked our way down, falling, and knocking down others, and the good ones in the group were beginning to be released from the rest of us and to have two beginners' classes: one for good beginners and one for bad beginners. I went to bed immediately, and didn't wake until the next morning, which was roughly 18 hours' sleep.

We kept it up for three days, the bad beginners. We were joined by a fifth bad beginner who was an elderly Brazilian learning to ski secretly so that he could accompany his young wife on her winter sporting holidays. The third day he agreed that he didn't mind if she made off with every ski instructor in Europe. He wasn't going to join the game. We assured him that if they were all like the dreaded Mike, he would have no competition at all, she'd only be screaming to get back to him and to Rio.

This cheered him so greatly he decided to hire a sleigh one day and take us on a tour. So we climbed in with rugs and flasks and great goodwill and roared past the good beginners and Mike, who were walking around in circles practising an elementary turn, and we had a beautiful day in a forest where there was no cracking ice, and you could walk in powdery snow without falling at all. The next day we advised the Brazilian to write to his wife saying he was passing through a posh ski resort but the snow didn't seem to be good. We advised this because he was becoming morose and guilty and wondering what she was thinking; he was the kind of man who sends telegrams rather than letters, and that night he had one back from her saying she loved him, so he took us all to a great log cabin and we kept drinking her health all night.

And The Falling Man taught us to play canasta, so we sat all day out on the terrace and got great suntans playing cards. And the Swede, who had stopped twitching, said that his heart felt much better and he had gone and discovered a very cheap place where they had schnitzel and salad so we wouldn't get fat. The Hysterical Woman had become as calm as the Mona Lisa. She asked us to take pictures of her in various ski poses, and we did, and in return she gave us a great recipe for cheesecake, and we went to the kitchen of the hotel and tried it one day when everyone else was out doing elementary bends and falling and breaking their limbs. I told them all about proportional representation, which is a great party piece for foreigners, and wrote down how it worked, with explanations of quotas, first counts, eliminations, distribution and transfers. They loved it and said that the whole trip had been worthwhile for this alone.

And then the week was up, and we avoided Mike's eye and went to the station, where nobody fell and the porters remembered me and said that it was always the same, people came nervously but they left being able to ski like birds.

Keeping Faith with My Dear, Dear Dublin

5 February 1975

A friend of mine who emigrated some years ago used to drive me mad when she came back to Dublin for holidays. Firstly her accent had changed and had overtones of Chelsea, then she was using phrases that the natives do not know, like 'Isn't that a pretty little house?' 'That was naughty of you to buy me a large drink.' Having lived perfectly happy for 20 years in Dublin, she suddenly saw all its faults and filth on her return. The streets had become covered with litter, she would say how terrible to see children begging, all the lovely buildings were being knocked down, wasn't it odd that you found Irishmen always drinking in pubs without their wives, and wasn't it amazing to see so many people outside churches on Sundays?

I determined that I would never behave like a returned emigrant and at least nobody has detected the slightest change in the way I speak – only, I suppose, surprise that I still speak so much after exposure to the more taciturn British. But I am making the same kind of mistakes, the little tell-tale things that show you have been living in another world, and it's worrying.

Like the phone, I can't believe that you have to pay fourpence. I simply can't take it in, and it looks absurd to come back from a telephone in my own home town saying, 'It doesn't work and I did put the tuppence in.' I had forgotten you couldn't get beer in a restaurant, which is idiotic since I spent at least two years shouting in the paper that the licensing laws should be changed.

The minimum fare on the bus startled me so much that I thought the conductor didn't understand I only wanted to go four stops. My first gin and tonic of the weekend nearly knocked me out after the pathetic drop in the bottom of the glass that goes as an English measure. I had brought people home grand cheap little velvet jumpers you can get in Marks and Spencers and thought they would be ecstatic with them. The ecstasy was dimmed by the fact that you can buy the same ones here and everyone had already bought half a dozen.

At least half a dozen men I know have nice long, clean hair when they used to tell me that they hated their sons having the same thing not two years ago; at least 20 women who used to have a great line in chat about their deep freeze and their au pairs have joined some kind of helpful thrusting organisations and are helping and thrusting all round the place. People ask me did I hear about things like us having a new President, and Ireland beating England at the international, and I begin to wonder where they think I am and who I work for.

Nobody at all speaks about doom, nobody has mentioned that we should be hoarding food, or putting money into building societies or taking it out of building societies. Things seem to be as dear, if not dearer, than in London, salaries don't seem to have jumped accordingly and yet everyone thinks we'll be fine once the warm weather comes.

Food seems to be extraordinarily expensive, and so do clothes, but nowhere do I hear great cries about how hard it is to live, to manage to eat, to dress or to get by. They ask me is Britain breaking up, which is a bit difficult to answer because I have no idea, they don't seem to be worried about Ireland breaking up and think that it will all be grand once the fine weather comes.

Nobody mercifully has had one conversation about the drop in share prices or the rise in them or whatever, which is great because even though the people I meet in England don't have any shares either they always seem a bit worried about other people's and the consequent ill-health of the nation if they go below a certain figure.

Out in Killiney I saw people walking Afghan hounds which, I feel, must be a sign of prosperity, but I am assured that it's just the same person with the same hound that I keep seeing. A few people who should have done it years ago are talking about medical check-ups, and cholesterol, and increasing their subscription to the voluntary health, but that is probably a sign of nothing except that we are all getting older and more worn out. I took two taxis and both taxi drivers knew me but didn't know I had been away, they just thought I had got mean about taking taxis. You can get telephone messages in pubs, and leave your suitcase in restaurants again, which is lovely, and you can meet 20 people in the space of a morning just by walking about, which is lovelier still. You can't say a word about anyone because either they or their best friend are sitting at the next table.

I hear the most outrageous and utterly unfounded stories about people that nobody has checked out but everybody accepts and then forgets. Half my friends disappeared suddenly out of Dublin to go to the Merriman School, which I get a feeling seems to be occurring every six weeks. I can't even talk about films like *The Front Page* because they're here already. I thought they were joking me when I had to pay 7p to post a letter. England nearly rose in rebellion when it went up to 4½p not long ago.

It's wonderful to be able to go and see everyone again without undertaking mammoth journeys across a huge city, and even better when everyone will agree to come into Bowes pub to see me, instead of having to arrange rendezvous places halfway between me and them, as you would in London. You can cash a cheque in lots of places without hunting for your credit card, and I got over the fact that cigarettes were so much dearer because the woman in the shop was so nice and told me that they were ruining my health, she remembered when I had rosy cheeks and wasn't bent double whooping and wheezing over the counter.

I can take up any conversation where I left it off a month or two ago. I didn't have to explain about the IRA to anyone and everyone kept asking me when I was going back.

The Couple Who Behaved Perfectly

7 January 1976

She had a lot of very good skirts and some really expensive soft twinsets. She knew how to knot a scarf around her throat so that it didn't look like a bandage. She would read the *Daily Mail* at breakfast while he read the *Daily Telegraph*; their dog waited obediently out in the hall since animals were welcome but not in the dining room. She had nice bright awake eyes and looked as if she might want to have a chat as they ate scrambled eggs and toast, but in her circle she had probably learned early that men aren't communicative at that hour. So she would look out the window a bit at the seagulls over the harbour, and at the life of the village getting under way, and say nothing.

Every morning he said the same thing when the last cup of coffee had been drained and his mouth carefully wiped for danger of a last lurking crumb. With a rattle of the newspaper, and with the air of a man who has put up with ladies being late and slow and unpredictable all his life he would say, 'Right, if you're ready, we might as well push off, what?'

She had always been ready at least ten minutes ahead of him. But a bright little smile would come on cue and she would say, 'Yes. Why not, I'm ready now, I think.'

And smiling at the waitress with the friendly but not familiar smile that those who are at ease in country houses or good hotels always have, they would walk from the dining room, pick up the dog's lead and stroll down the street to their car. It was very like them, their car – good, expensive, well-kept but not showy.

I used to wonder what they talked about as they settled in and fastened their seat belts. Would they have planned their sightseeing the night before, or would he say, 'I thought we might go and look at that headland that Charles and Antonia told us about, what?'

Or were they in fact not real at all? Were they part of a gang of jewel thieves and once in the car would he say, 'Great stuff, Tiger Lil, we had them fooled again this morning, let's get to Diamond Harry's place and get hold of last night's haul.'

There seemed to be no way of knowing at all.

Or there wasn't until one night when the hotel dining room was more crowded than usual and we all had to push our tables slightly closer together. They were in the habit of exchanging a few sentences over the evening meal so this was a marvellous opportunity to hear what they actually said.

She always wore something dark and understated for dinner, if understated means that it wasn't covered with jewels or cut to the navel. He would wear a dark suit and tie, the tweedy morning look wouldn't have been at all suitable. They had a sherry each before their meal and he would spend a considerable amount of time discussing with the wine waiter the half bottle of the wine they had nightly. Whatever it was she would sip, and think and sip again and say, 'Lovely, really very good.'

That much I had noticed when they were far away. I had thought that if he had ordered methylated spirits with the same formality she would have sipped it and given the same reply.

From close up he looked slightly younger and she slightly more tired than I had thought. They debated whether to have whitebait or the pâté with very logical reasoning, like having had pâté at lunch but not really knowing whether a whole plate of whitebait might not be too heavy a starter. I felt sure that they were not a real married couple on a holiday at all. They had to be a pair of actors brought in from a professional company to lend the hotel some style and character. Nobody could invent and mean dialogue like theirs unless it had been intended for the stage.

'I think the tide is coming in again, dear, do you?'

'No, actually, I think it's going out.'

'But it seems to be further into the harbour than it was at lunchtime.'

'Oh really? It probably came in further and then started to go out. Tides do, you know.'

'I don't want to disagree with you, dear, but it's further in now than it was when I was dressing, it's up higher on the pier.'

'Yes, I'm sure it may be, dear, but that doesn't mean that it can't be going out now, does it?'

'But you haven't even looked, dear.'

'Then how can you expect me to make any judgment at all, dear?'

It was riveting stuff.

When the wine ritual was over, and the main course eaten, they had their usual microscopic piece of Stilton. And here the pattern changed.

'I think we might have two vintage ports,' he said to the wine waiter without consulting her.

'How splendid, port!' she said politely, in tones that you knew meant she would have said How Splendid if he'd ordered a glass of arsenic.

When the port arrived, he raised his glass and said in the same studied tones, 'It hasn't worked at all, of course.'

'I'm not sure what you mean,' she said.

'The holiday, the getting away, the behaving normally. It hasn't worked, it's just as bad as being at home.'

By this stage I was so interested I was practically sitting in their laps all the while, pretending to read, of course, the greatest cover an eavesdropper can ever have. But they were far too honourable to have suspected that anyone would be so unsporting as to listen to someone else's private conversation, so I was safe.

'I don't know,' she said, considering. 'It has been very pleasant really. We have been lucky with the weather, and we've been most comfortable here. No, I've enjoyed it, dear, a lot actually. I'm sorry if you haven't.'

'I'm not talking about the holiday,' he said, and there were no dears or whats in his conversation now, he was quite different to his normal self.

'I don't want to disagree with you, but you just said this very minute that the holiday hadn't worked for you. . . .'

'Please don't try and throw words at me to prevent me finishing what I'm trying to say. I said that it's all been a waste of money and time and we might as well never have come. I can't think why I allowed myself be talked into it at all. I knew from the moment that you suggested it that it was insane . . . and that we can't . . . can't . . .' He ran out of fluency.

'Dearest, you're not going to say "we can't go on like this", are you? It would be too much. I think I'd get a fit of hysterics.'

He grinned. 'I was going to say it, and I tried to change half way but couldn't think of anything else that began with "we can't",' he said, and again they looked like a happy couple exchanging a pleasantry.

There was a bit of a pause.

I decided that he was having an affair with someone else, and wanted a divorce, and that she had said let's have a quiet week away from everything and make no hasty decisions, and then we'll sit down and talk about it in a civilised manner. I was very sorry for her, because she looked nice and kind, and probably loved doing the flowers and taking healthy walks with that nice brushed dog, and gardening, and hanging up hunting prints so that they got the light. And now when he left her she would have a very lonely time, and she was undoubtedly very dependent on him and devoted to him, which passes for love with a lot of people.

I was sorry too that the nice week in the beautiful countryside and in the village with the magical little harbour hadn't worked for her.

The pause ended.

'You're not making it easy for me, you know,' he said, twisting his glass of port around in his fingers. 'You could make it much easier, you know, if you'd only allow us to talk about things. I don't think all this coolness is healthy, I really don't. Why don't you cry or show some emotion like women do?'

'My dear, I've said over and over again I haven't the least idea what other women do. They never discuss it with me, and indeed if I knew I don't suppose for a moment that I would want to copy it, just to fit in with some kind of convention. You should be very grateful that I am being so calm, it should surely help you.'

I don't know, I thought to myself, I think he hates it. Men like him would expect a woman to cling and weep, not just let him go without discussing it, but then why had she insisted on coming on a holiday with him? It was very confusing.

'After 15 years nobody has a right to be so calm,' he said. 'I seriously do think you are having some kind of depression or nervous trouble. Why don't you let me make an appointment for you to see someone? Old Harris has all the best contacts, and you could talk to somebody very sympathetic, somebody who's the best in his field, what? It wouldn't be like going to a psychiatrist because you were, you know, not quite . . . it would be more like having a discussion with somebody trained who could tell us why you want to do this.'

'Dear, listen to me just one last time, I've told you and I am not telling you again. I am leaving. On the first of next month I am going. The house will be perfect, the decorators are finished already. I am not taking any of the jewellery or furs, they will be put into storage. I want to take Nelson, but if you want him very much then he must stay with you. I will let you have evidence of adultery immediately I have left, and the divorce action will be undefended. I will ask for no alimony, I want nothing at all, least of all a scene.'

'But, for God's sake, why? And who are you going to? I'll know sooner or later when I get this evidence of adultery, as you call it. You can't have had time to have any adultery. It's ridiculous.'

'Could you keep your voice down, please, dear? There will be no discussion whatsoever. I really didn't expect to have to say this so often. You have always behaved perfectly to me, and I think that I am behaving perfectly to you now. You looked very tired and overworked, so after I gave you my news I was concerned that you might become ill. That's why I suggested that we have this holiday, insisted on it, as you describe it. I was right, you look ever so much better now, all the rest and the good food and the change. I knew it would do you good.'

And then wiping away any crumbs of cheese, she stood up and said, 'Right, if you're ready we might as well push off, what? And perhaps we could take Nelson for a walk around the harbour before we go to bed.'

A Snatch at Some Happiness

5 February 1976

She had been married for 10 months and she found it odd that this sense of doom lay like a big heavy meal on her chest. She couldn't explain all that to the doctor, of course, because she had already told him she felt a bit off when she went three months before to find out if she were pregnant. He had examined her blood pressure, her heart and taken a blood test, and he told her she was as fit as a fiddle.

And there was no reason she should feel a sense of doom. Andy was kind to her and he said he loved her often which she liked hearing, and she believed. The girls at work were envious of her because she was always rushing out at lunch hour to buy their evening meal, and they thought that was a lovely secure thing to be doing. They had a flat which got lots of sunlight, and had a bit of a garden. They often had people in for spaghetti on a Friday or a Saturday. They were saving £48 a month between them; putting it into a building society so that they would be able to get a deposit on a house when the Time Came.

She thought a lot about the Time Coming, and was very disappointed each month to realise that there was little hope of the excitement of wondering, hoping, getting tests done and discovering that she was pregnant. In her mind she never thought much beyond the pregnancy and the birth.

She never thought about what it would be like to have a child around the place, she just thought about having a child.

It was Andy's mother who started to make things seem more urgent. Six months married and not a sign of anything yet, was the kind of throwaway line she could manage to include into every conversation. She was a grandmother five times over, it wasn't any of her damn business whether there was a sign of anything or not. How dare people be so personal and offensive, they wouldn't dream of telling you that you had a poor sense of dress, or bad teeth, but they felt they could comment on the most intimate side of your life, with a kind of coarse ribaldry that they would never use in any other context.

Then it was the man she worked for. He was wondering, he had said to his wife the night before, if his nice secretary had been looking a bit pale recently. Now he was a married man, and he had four children, and she must have no hesitation in telling him if she thought there was a little one on the way. Women needed rest at the beginning and he would only be too glad to let her have a few days off if she needed them. His eyes seemed piggy to her rather than kind, and she thought again how appalling it was that this man who never even addressed her by her first name should feel free to comment on the possibility of a life growing or not growing in her body.

It was when her sister came back from America and oohed and aahed over the flat, over Andy and over the wedding pictures and presents that the weight on her chest got very heavy indeed. Her sister had a way of looking at her with an upwards downwards glance, a look that said starkly, Is she? Isn't she? Her sister managed to say at every meal that one of the greatest regrets in her own successful life had been that she had never had children. She used to talk about it to Andy at night sometimes. Would he like a child? Of course he would, eventually. Maybe three; an only child would be spoiled and lonely, and two might dislike each other and that would be bad luck on them. Three seemed a safer number. He spoke about it in the same way he spoke of maybe bringing all his golf clubs to Spain for a fortnight and staying in Marbella, playing 36 holes a day. As a nice but unlikely event.

And one weekend when she was shopping she saw two very pregnant women at the supermarket shelves, and they seemed smug and complacent, and knowing it all, and having it all, and she realised that what they had was the ultimate recognition of their role. And she felt very cheated and stood for a long time with her wire basket empty thinking that it had always been the same, at school she had never won the prizes, been on the first teams, been chosen to speak in debates. Even though she had been just as good as those who had got these things.

Not long after that she saw a baby in a pram outside a shop. It looked very small and very peaceful. It had a little red face but not a cross little face, its hand was under its little chin and it wore a furry bonnet. She put out her own hand and touched its face; it opened its eyes and smiled.

Minutes later an untidy-looking girl rushed out and started putting parcels on to the pram. She explained that the baby was a girl and she was four weeks old. Yes, she had a lovely smile but some people said those things weren't smiles at all, it only meant the baby had wind. She was no trouble, she slept for hours and hours, and she was great fun to play with. Her name was Amanda, and she was never going to let her be called Mandy, it must be the whole name.

So she went home and thought about Amanda who was great fun to play with and who, of course, had a smile, not wind, and wondered about her sleeping there peacefully in a pram, and decided that the pram would be nice near the window where the sunlight could come in. And that Amanda would like a row of coloured beads on her pram, not a lot of untidy parcels. And she thought about Amanda's hair for a long time and wondered if she had dark strands or blonde strands under that furry bonnet, and wondered did her toes have the same grip as her fingers, which was something someone had once told her about a baby.

The next day she left work as usual at lunchtime but, instead of going into the supermarket to buy the things for dinner for Andy and herself, she just went up to a pram where there was a sleeping baby, bigger than Amanda, no furry bonnet but a little pink hat. As if she had been doing it all her life, she kicked the brake free underneath the pram and wheeled it away. She didn't look around to see was anyone watching her, she didn't look into the shop to see would the mother come out, she just pushed the pram home and she went by different ways, she chose lanes and alleys through the city, not the main streets, she didn't feel like talking to anyone about Amanda yet. She just walked deliberately down lane after lane smiling into the pram.

She stopped at a chemist, bought a bottle, a tin of baby milk powder, a packet of disposable nappies, a tin of baby talcum powder, a shampoo that said it wouldn't hurt a baby's eyes. The man in the chemist said that the baby was a fine little fellow and she looked at him coldly and said it was a girl and her name was Amanda. The chemist man said apologetically that it was hard to tell when they were that wrapped up.

And then she went home and parked the pram by the window where the early afternoon sunlight came in on the pram, and touched the pink knitted bonnet. And the baby didn't wake up for a while so she didn't think it needed to be changed but she left the nappies nearby just in case, and she made up the bottle as it said you should on the side of the tin. And the sun went down so that the light was a bit pink like the bonnet.

And then Andy's key turned in the lock and everything changed. It seemed to be a series of questions and Oh my Gods, and whys and telephone calls to the police, and the police arriving in a car with a woman who had a scarlet face from crying, and her husband who was shouting, and a doctor, and an injection, and a bit of sleep. And there were days of people saying no action would be taken, and people asking her had she had infertility tests, and had she considered adoption, and did Andy refuse to let her have a child.

And all the time she was very calm because there was very little to say. She left her job, even though they told her she was always welcome back and her boss said that she was a woman born to be a mother and one day she would have a little one of her own. And the doctor told her that there was nothing wrong with either herself or Andy and, of course, they would probably have a baby in time. And they told her she was very lucky that the Law was so kind that no action was being taken, and she went to see a kind, wise man twice a week and told him about her childhood, and he gave her tablets which took some of the pain and the feeling of having a heavy meal off her chest.

Vanity of Vanity, All Is Vanity

23 February 1976

No it is *not* my first Communion picture, it was taken on a cold Tuesday morning last November. I got it taken because I'm such an honest poor old thing that I didn't want to be using a picture that was four years old.

Normally, I'd just look at the photographer with a desperate intensity and hope it would all be over quickly and I could get on with my life, but this time I'd been reading a surfeit of these articles about women who decline and go to pieces in their mid-thirties, so I decided I would go to a hairdresser and have a lovely memento of myself looking at my best. I also had a sneaking, ageing hope that someone I don't know at all might fancy me from afar and cut out the picture and put it over his lonely fireplace.

The hairdresser was very excited when I told her that I wanted to look nice for a photograph. 'Is it for a pen friend?' she asked interestedly. 'We get a lot of requests for pen-friend photography.'

When I told her it was for a newspaper she brought the whole salon around to discuss it. Kiss curls, wigs, streaks, colouring, perms and plaits were discussed and eventually she did it like a mad magician all coming up to a conical point, and they all said it was very slimming, and I went home in horror and washed it all out with a hungry detergent.

I had also read that if you wore something soft and flattering around the neck it did marvels for you. I contemplated soft flattering things like an angora scarf. But somehow it looked like one of those halters people wear when they have been in a car accident. And I tried a necklace and it looked like one of these before and after things, where so and so used to wear cheap shoddy trinkets until we taught her how to dress, so I just put on a blouse backwards because the back of it looked soft and flattering and I pinned it all together at the back where no one would see.

Then I went off to a photographer.

Liam White is a professional photographer who earns his living taking pictures of things and people. Over 10 cups of coffee in his house I told him that I would like something soft and gentle that would let readers know what a lovely mind and heart I had, and that if it wouldn't cost a fortune I'd like the lines under my eyes touched up a bit.

Liam White said that touching pictures up did cost a fortune and, if I was being honest at showing myself at my real age, wouldn't it be a bit hypocritical having the eyes touched up? I said that if it was expensive we'd better leave it. And I sat and smiled at him soppily for about 15 minutes and never felt so foolish in my whole life.

Then he sent me the pictures and I was delighted with them, and I thought I would buy lots of big heavy silver frames and put the pictures in them and give them to people for their pianos with my name scrawled across the bottom left. And for a mad moment I thought that maybe a restaurant might like one, with a kind of a message like 'Thanks for all the lovely portions of No. 67 and the bottles of number 154.'

And then it appeared in the paper and people keep writing in and telling me that I am a disappointment to them, and why produce this old photograph taken during my teens, and since when have I become so vain that I have taken to having pictures retouched. A man who said he had always mildly fancied me from afar was now totally turned off and would fancy Nell McCafferty instead.

Well, to hell with the begrudgers. I don't see any of you lot who write in showing me your own photographs. That's the way I look when I'm nice and clean and tidy and that's the picture I'm going to use. And the only reason I'm making any fuss about it all is that if readers only knew how the men in this paper react when having their photographs taken there would be less fuss about my poor effort. I've been up in the photographers' department while fellow journalists have been recorded on celluloid or whatever it is. I've seen all the worried looking in mirrors, the careful tousling of the hair so that it will look natural, the wondering whether we look better with glasses or without them. Is the finger better on the left side of the chin or the right side? Do we look more urgent if we are on a telephone or not? Men have been known to tear up old pictures they don't like in case it might ever be used by accident, even in an obituary.

And then I knew a man who had all his teeth cleaned and filed and polished for a television appearance and who was most dissatisfied with his smile when he saw it on the screen. He actually wrote in to the head of engineering and wanted to know if they could improve their lighting techniques so that his teeth would look more brilliant during the next appearance.

And I once interviewed a man about a nice healthy manly outdoor sport and asked a photographer to take his picture. The healthy outdoor manly man behaved like Maria Callas over the whole thing and refused to let a line be printed until he had seen proofs of the picture, and even then he wanted it done all over again to the point where I told him that I had forgotten what I had interviewed him about now, and he wrote six distressed letters about me to people of importance and made my life miserable.

And I took a nice holiday snap of about six of us once sharing a joke and looking happy. One of the men looked a bit fat because of the way he was sitting. (In fact, without being too sensitive about it, he had a great beer belly for all to see.) When the snap was being handed around to recall happy, sunny days his face clouded over in rage. Could he have a look at the negative, he asked all in an icy calm voice.

Unsuspectingly, I handed it to him and he tore it up with the print so that nobody could ever again think of him with a paunch.

At a wedding recently there was more fuss getting combs for the bridegroom and best man in case they might look dishevelled than there was arranging the bride for the loveliest day of her life. It looked like a scene from some American comedy where everybody was in some kind of drag. And a man who is normally very well balanced and normal showed me 36 contact proofs of pictures to choose the best one. What was it wanted for? An old boys' school annual actually. The fact that the people who knew him knew what he looked like and the others didn't matter was something he couldn't grasp.

So I'm not going to become upset when people ring up with abuse, and write me these patronising letters. I know that I am young and simple and pleasant looking and that the day I got that picture taken I was all of these things plus very clean and tidy and wearing a blouse backwards.

A Nice, Traditional, Normal Sort of Patrick's Day

22 March 1976

I've spent years with people asking me what a normal St Patrick's Day is like in Ireland, but I've no way of knowing. I've never had a normal St Patrick's Day in my life. When I was about eight I remember a St Patrick's Day with us all wearing shamrock coming from Mass, and two great discoveries that I made. One that St Patrick's Day didn't count as Lent and I could eat sweets, which was an unexpected ecstasy. I also remember asking my mother as we walked back from the church how were children born, and she told me casually. I felt enormously sorry for her having such delusions about it all and confided to my father that she seemed to have got things very confused. He said that he didn't know but there was probably some truth in what she had said. I abandoned the whole idea of it being in any way accurate for about a year.

Then there was a St Patrick's Day at school when I was in my religious maniac stage and I insisted on coming in and helping the boarders to sing the Mass in case I was needed there more than in the parish church. And a nice nun allowed me to check that all the statues of the national saints were properly garlanded with flowers and I went home happy that up there Patrick was having a good day and didn't feel foolish in front of Peter or Francis or any of the other lads.

And there was a time at college when we had a St Patrick's night barbecue on the beach and we all had to bring a pound of sausages and a bottle of wine, and I didn't drink in those times and brought a bottle of orange for myself as well, which fell and broke as we were going down the cliffs and people said thank God it hadn't been the wine. I remember sitting there parched and singing 'Lazy River' which was having one of its ninetieth revivals at the time, and there was an awful incident where somebody went off with my best friend's boyfriend and she cried and cried, and we decided to punish this other girl, and somebody actually cut off her ponytail, which was an appalling thing to do when you think back on it.

There was a time when I was teaching that I actually forgot about St Patrick's Day and went into the school as usual. The town seemed unusually quiet and the bus unusually late, but since I was marking children's exercise books at the last minute as usual, this didn't occur to me as anything odd. In the school I felt that punctuality had reached a new low and was prepared to speak to the headmistress about it. It was only when I couldn't find her that I realised what day it was, and as I went gloomily to the dog show, I thought back on life and younger days of giving up sweets and decorating statues and I realised that growing up meant less deep feelings.

But the following year there were plenty of deep feelings. Some distant and pleasant American cousins announced they were coming to Ireland. Letter followed letter about all the fun they were going to have, all the great scenes they were going to join, the fantastic welcome they were going to get. Mystified, we reread the letters again and again. Could they be talking about the place we all knew?

They were coming so far and making such an effort we would have to do something. My mother refused to dye the potatoes green. Utterly. But, we kept wailing, they write about looking forward to the green potatoes, it wouldn't hurt us to make them green just once. My father refused to call himself O'Binchy for the occasion, and hang a harp outside the gate. I was beginning to think of dressing up in some kind of uniform to go out on the tarmac at Dublin Airport piping a melancholy tune. It was all solved for us by their plane being delayed. They didn't get here until the next day.

They had a great time at New York Airport, they said, lots of green beer and songs and entertainment. But they were of course heart-broken that they had missed what they kept calling The Real Thing.

And I spent a St Patrick's Day once in a hotel by the sea where I had gone to think about things and have a rest. And it was such a beautiful day I decided to go and walk along the beach to a deserted place and contemplate a swim. The sun was beating down, there wasn't a soul about, so I went into the sea alone and naked and swam about thinking about things and delighted with myself. From nowhere came an elderly couple who parked themselves beside my clothes. Suspicious that they might be about to steal everything I owned, I scrutinised them from the water. Not at all, they were people I knew slightly from Dublin who had heard from the hotelier that I was there. Kindly, they thought they would come along and have a chat with me in case I was lonely and all by myself. I contemplated the problem out in the sea. I was too sophisticated to say, 'You must turn your backs now because I have nothing on.' I wasn't sophisticated enough to walk out stark naked.

But then I couldn't stay in the sea forever. A hopeless kind of shouting match took place. 'I don't seem to have any bathing togs on,' I shouted idiotically.

'What?' they shouted.

'I didn't know I was going to meet anyone, I haven't any clothes on,' I screamed.

'What? Do you want your clothes? We'll mind your clothes,' they shouted.

'Perhaps if you went along the beach I'll join you later,' I yelled.

'Not at all, we'll wait here, glad to have a rest,' they called.

I had to do it. Yelling and screeching to alert them of what would be emerging from the water, I raced out of the sea and dived on my coat. Neither of them raised an eyebrow.

'It must have been cold,' said the 80-year-old husband.

'You should have brought a towel anyway,' said the 75-year-old wife, disapproving at my lack of care about my health. Stunned, I walked back to the hotel with them and played poker with them all afternoon.

There was a St Patrick's Day when I had to interview a famous person because he couldn't find any other free time, and I went to his hotel room as arranged. He thought I was part of the hotel staff and said to me wearily, 'I suppose you'd better send up a bottle of whiskey or something, I have some idiot woman from some paper coming to do an interview and I suppose she drinks like a fish like all of them.'

And two years ago I was in a hotel in Morocco with two girl-friends and we spent our National Feast day having a row with the hotel manager about the price of everything, and the fact that we had veal for breakfast, lunch and dinner. In between bouts of the row we would go out and sit in the boiling sun and say that it was all grand because everyone would be being drowned and bored at home and perhaps we were better here than there.

And last year I was standing amazed in New York at what looked like a million people dancing and skipping down Fifth Avenue, and the whole city went mad for 12 hours, and I wondered were there any words at all to try and describe it, or would people think I was just exaggerating as usual.

So what about last Wednesday?

With a history of abnormal St Patrick's Days, I waited its dawning with some interest. It began with a flight from Dublin to London. British Airways gave the passengers shamrocks, which was nice, and distracted me until the plane was off the ground.

I had also remembered the number of the seat which has room for long legs and that was good. I can't tell it to you actually, because it's a bit of special information you pick up from long, harrowing travel and nobody should be allowed to have it too easily.

And when I got to London there was a message for me on the board, which is something I love because it looks so important in front of all the other passengers. Actually it was only from a friend who had passed through the night before and who knows I love getting messages. It said 'Happy St Patrick's Day' but I nodded over it wisely for a bit, hoping that people would think it was about some major management decision that I would have to make in the next hour.

And all had changed utterly in London since I left.

Harold Wilson had gone, Princess Margaret's marriage had gone. Some lovely mustard seed that I had planted on my window sill had gone mad and only grown in one corner of its cheap little plastic tray, where it looked like all the seeds had jumped on top of each other instead of growing in nice normal lines.

But it was a normal working day, with people going about their work and forgetting about St Patrick, which was sad. I went to a businessy sort of lunch where the chairman did say at the end of it, 'and now not forgetting what day it is I ask you all to stand and drink a toast. . . .' so I thought this was great. But the toast was to the company which had been 25 years in business and not to poor St Patrick who has been in business for a hell of a lot longer.

And on the bus I met a man wearing a shamrock, too, and he and I had a great chat about St Patrick and what a shame it was that he wasn't more highly thought of everywhere.

And then the man went on and said that the real rot set in when some scholar in Ireland had done a bit of investigation and decided that there might be more than one St Patrick, but since the scholar was my uncle I kept quiet on that point.

And in the evening Córas Tráchtála had a little party where they invited mainly foreign people who had done business with Ireland or helped Irish exports or something.

And amid the roar of conversation and goodwill three different people said to me that it must be lonely to be over in London and not having a nice, normal St Patrick's Day at home.

The Day We Nearly Wrote a Sex Book

4 October 1976

I was nearly the co-author of a best-selling pornographic book, and sometimes when I stand in the rain waiting for a non-existent bus and unable to afford the taxis that come by empty and warm and comfortable, I think that it was very feeble of me not to have gone ahead with the project. I don't even have the moral comfort of knowing that I refused riches for all kinds of pure and upright reasons, it was just sheer cowardice that stopped me in the end – that and the laziness and inertia of all my friends.

A few years ago, struck by yet another blow like an increase in the price of fags or drink or huge telephone bills or something, ten of us sat grumbling in a pub on a Saturday night. The usual remedies to the taxing economic situation were discussed and dismissed. Making gin in the bath. Yes fine, but how did you do it? And it would mean you couldn't wash, you might be very drunk, but very dirty as a result. And there was a thought that people had gone blind or mad from it during prohibition.

And there was rolling your own cigarettes. Fine, but it took so long, and all the tobacco kept falling out, and it didn't taste as nice, and somebody had burned all their eyelashes off by forgetting to put any tobacco at all into the paper and just lighting the outside.

Phones? Well you could stop using them, and there was the widely held belief that if you started making suspicious conversations down them they would be tapped, and when your phone is tapped apparently it can't be cut off even if you never pay your bill at all.

But what we were really after was some big quick money, and we hit on the idea of writing a porn book between us. With ten of us, that would only be 3,000 words each, which is nothing. A 30,000-word novel full of sex, it would have to make us a fortune, and it wouldn't take us a week to write. So carried away with the sheer brilliance of it, we wrote out an outline plan. It was going to be the story of an innocent young American girl who came to Ireland to see the land of her ancestors. She was choosing Ireland because she was fed up with all the immorality in the United States and wanted to be somewhere good and pure. Our boon was going to be the tale of her disillusionment.

We were each 'to do a chapter on the kind of thing we knew best'. A sudden silence fell on the group at that stage. What did we mean 'the thing we knew best'? A great unwillingness to admit that we knew 'anything best' came over us and there was a lot of shuffling and the outline plan looked as if it were to be abandoned at birth. Then somebody bought a round of drinks and the price of them shocked us into action again. Why didn't we each describe the kind of ordinary life we knew best, and do a chapter of that, adding all kinds of torrid sexual overtones to it, so that it would be a book of merit as well as hardcore porn? That suited everyone and we divided it up happily.

There was an American in our midst and he was to write chapter one, 'Magnolia Leaves America'. He was to write about the filth and perversion that was making life unbearable for her there. He asked anxiously how deeply did he have to go into the filth and perversion, because he had lived in a small town, and probably didn't know in detail the great degrees of all that went on in big cities. Nonsense, we told him, all small towns in America are much, much worse than Peyton Place, use your imagination.

Chapter two, 'Magnolia Arrives in Ireland', was to be written by the man who had once worked in a summer job in Aer Lingus. He could do all the steamy scenes aboard the plane. He too started backtracking a bit and said that he had worked on the ground and he wasn't sure that he would have all the sex scenes aboard the plane absolutely accurate. That didn't matter at all, we told him firmly, he must draw on his background of working in an airline, otherwise he couldn't be in on it at all. Hastily and greedily he agreed that there must be something wildly sexual going on on most flights and he'd check it all out.

Because I was writing about tourism in those days I was asked to write chapter three, 'Magnolia Checks into Her Hotel'. Very easy chapter that, they said, hotels are full of vice and corruption, and I knew a lot of hotel managers, I'd do the thing in an hour. I bleated that most of the hotel managers I met used to talk to me more about getting tourists and getting better grading with Bord Fáilte than about the lust and licentiousness of their staff and clients, but I was assured that I had got an easy number and if I didn't take it I'd be given something more difficult, so I took it.

'Magnolia Looks for a Job' was to be done by a girl who worked in an insurance office, and she was told that she was lucky too because nobody else would have the access she did to what went on behind filing cabinets. She said that in her office the worst thing that ever went on behind a filing cabinet was that she went there alone sometimes to eat a chocolate biscuit so that the other girls wouldn't tell her she was greedy, and we said she's got to liven it up a bit.

Chapter five, 'Magnolia Has a Night Out', was to be written by a sort of glamorous man who always says I was at this place last night or the other place and the joint was swinging. He looked a little troubled when we said this was to be the most pornographic chapter of all to retain the readers' corrupt interest. 'Why do I have to write the most important chapter?' he whinged. 'Because you are a very good writer and you know all the joints that swing,' we said firmly and he was a bit pleased though still troubled and agreed to do it.

Chapter six, 'Magnolia Goes to the Dáil', was to be written by a reporter who sometimes does Dáil reporting. He said that you don't get much training for lusty arousing kind of descriptive pieces when you are just taking down what the TDs are saying but we said nonsense. He didn't have to make Magnolia go through the whole business of getting elected, just have her as a simple-minded tourist coming in and asking to visit the Irish Parliament the way people do, and then sort of go on with the usual. 'But I think the usual kind of thing is that they come in and sit in the gallery and then go home,' he said in a nit-picking way and was advised he'd better make it a hell of a lot racier than that.

Chapter seven, 'Magnolia Takes Up Sport', was to be written by a journalist who works on the sports pages of a newspaper. 'What sport?' he asked. Any sport, we said. Anything at all from watching greyhound racing to playing squash. His brief was so nice and vague that we all felt he was getting off too lightly, but he kept saying that we didn't understand how difficult his wife would prove if ever any of this was made public and we all said nonsense that we'd all get into appalling trouble with someone if it did, we would have a great pseudonym, and just divide the half million quid or whatever we earned into ten parts. We'd use a post office box number for all the correspondence about it, and all the dealings about the film rights and everything.

'Magnolia on Stage' would be chapter eight and an actress was going to write that. She was the most cheerful about it and said she'd have all kinds of terrible things happening to Magnolia in her dressing room, and in the wings, but particularly at the party on the first night of the play. So that was very trouble-free and we all thought deep silent thoughts about the private life of the actress which we had assumed to be blameless and even rather dull up to this.

Chapter nine, 'Magnolia in High Finance', was the lot of a man who had always claimed that he had made a bit of money on stocks and shares in his time. He was appalled at his task. 'Have you ever seen the stock exchange?' he begged. 'You couldn't write anything vaguely pornographic about it, it's ridiculous.'

We advised him to think of the money he'd be losing by opting out and he said he'd rack his brains.

The final chapter, 'Magnolia Leaves Again', was to be written by a teacher because she had absolutely refused to write anything whatsoever concerning the school she taught in. We told her that the nuns were unlikely to be buying cellophane-wrapped porn and would never read it, and the book would be banned in Ireland anyway. But she said no, the nuns found out everything you did, and she wasn't going to be sacked and pronounced unhireable for the rest of her life, no matter how many millions she earned from the film rights of the book. Grudgingly she said she'd do the bit where Magnolia was sitting alone in her flat with the door barred against rapists and perverts and would write the big crisis part about Magnolia saying that wicked though the United States were they were like cloisters compared to Ireland. The book would end with her getting on a boat to America, not wanting to risk the horrors of chapter one and whatever had happened to her on the plane. And everyone went home happy with their instructions and promising to meet with the completed chapter next Saturday.

The only pornographic book I had at home was *Fanny Hill* and I read it again and again but there was nothing about hotels in it, so I rang a friend in London and asked her to send me something particularly foul from some seedy bookshop, and she kept asking me had I gone mad and said she wouldn't dream of doing it for me until she knew why. I said it was a secret and I was sworn not to tell anyone and she said that everyone seemed to be going off their heads in Dublin. By a great stroke of good luck I was sent to London for two days myself and I went into a terrible shop where I was the only woman and a small evil man kept asking me not to finger the books unless I was going to buy them. I humbly told him that I wanted something about sex in hotels and he became more benign and said he'd see what he could do. I stood for what seemed like a fortnight in the shop until he came back with a book called *Hot Honeymoon Hotel* which cost £2. I was too embarrassed to check it with him so I paid him and ran. It was an amazing book certainly, but it was mainly photographs, that kind with so many limbs in them it's like a puzzle in a child's book and you'd have to colour them in to see which arm or leg belonged to whom. It made me very uneasy, and I kept thinking how awful it would be if I dropped dead on the street while I had it in my handbag and people would think that this was my normal reading matter.

Anyway I copied down a few useful phrases out of it in a sort of code for myself and I left the book in a litter bin at Heathrow Airport where someone must have got a nice surprise later on, and came home to write the chapter. It took me about 14 hours to write and I kept wondering who would want to read it, but then the memory of *Hot Honeymoon Hotel* and its price tag of £2 came back and I persevered. Ten nice neat pages of typing with 300 words each on them. I put it in an envelope on the Saturday and wondered had the other nine found it as difficult as I had or were they all deep down much more experienced and sophisticated. Almost everybody was there, and I was waiting for someone to call the meeting to order. Nobody had envelopes or typescripts on the table or anything. I supposed like myself they were keeping them out of sight.

The chat went on, and on, and on, and nobody mentioned putting all the chapters together and sort of editing out any discrepancies. And finally I couldn't bear it any more and said, 'Well, did we all find the porn-writing difficult?' And somebody looked at me blankly and said 'porn-writing?' That was the damn sportswriter who had all the sports in the world to choose from. I knew his fear of his wife was too great, I knew it and the girl in the insurance company said, 'It was all a joke, wasn't it?' A bit nervously and hopefully I thought. And the man who had worked for a bit in Aer Lingus gave a sigh of pure relief and said, 'Oh yes, of course it was a joke.' And the others all ratted, so I ratted too and said naturally I was only joking, and went up to the ladies and tore up 'Magnolia Checks into Her Hotel' into little pieces and burned it in an ashtray and gave up my chance of being a millionaire.

A Week of Self-Improvement

11 October 1976

During the weekend I made the mistake of reading one of those magazines written by a new brand of unreal woman. These are the dames who are on their third and finally happy marriage, who behave like an angelic drama mum to his children, her children and their children, who earn £9,000 a year in some dynamic career, run a boutique and a charity shop in their spare time, give dinner parties, look magnificent, travel all over the world with pigskin luggage and 21-year-old male admirers, and still find time in their bionic hearts to advise the rest of us how to live our lives.

One of these hard-faced Hannahs suggested that I and the other million fools who would be hanging on her words should try a week of self-improvement. We would be astonished, she pontificated, at how much more alive we would feel. No, we were to make no excuses, everyone had a lunch hour, hadn't they? We were to forswear lunch and start improving ourselves instead. We would thank her later.

Monday: *Learn a new skill: yoga? calligraphy? a language?*

Well determined and all as I was to test this dame's theory, the lotus position was something that I didn't see fitting happily into my life. Slow, beautiful handwriting was for monks in the eighth century, not for journalists in the twentieth. Fast, accurate typewriting would be a much more intelligent thing to do. But since I taught myself to type despairingly eight years ago and worked out a great hit and miss system which involves five fingers out of the 10 that I have, and means that it's mainly readable, I don't think I'd learn anything from someone who tried to force me to do hard things like use all the fingers and not look at the keys. It had better be a language. So on Monday, yet again I took up Italian. I love it, of course, the only trouble is that I'm never able to remember a word of it, or create a sentence in it. But there was no excuse.

The Inner London Education Authority has provided classes in a place off Fleet Street which is actually 54 paces from my office. They have lunchtime Italian classes on a Monday. It would be nice and familiar anyway, I thought, all that '*Ecco il Maestro*' and '*Come sta? Bene grazie, e Lei?*' In fact I was really looking forward to the familiar business of getting as far as lesson four in yet another instant and painless way to master the language. There were 12 of us in the class. We sized each other up as playmates for the year; I thought they looked very good value. We all told each other eagerly that our ambition was to be able to sit in the middle of a huge Italian group, exchanging jokes and shouting and realising that everyone else wasn't fighting just because they were shouting.

The teacher came in, she was splendid. She looked about 80, and was full of extravagant gestures, and delighted to meet us all. She was actually so nice and beaming and full of charm that she looked like a stage Italian mama sent over by Central Casting. And we all thundered out '*Ecco la classe, ecco il libro, ecco il maestro*', terribly happily with her, and this time – perhaps this time – I might stick to it. She was so damn nice, and she believed that we were all doing splendidly. I mingled with my classmates afterwards, because the awful article had said I would make friends of my own age and different sexes when learning a new skill. But they were harder working than I, and they kept talking about putting the definite pronoun before words like studenta and porta, and weren't at all into asking me to marry them or have a brief and brittle affair. But perhaps that will come later, I thought happily and put a few definite pronouns in with the best.

Tuesday: *Brighten yourself up, have a facial.*

The Italian class had been such a success that I ploughed ahead with all the rest of the advice. Indeed brightening myself up would be a fine thought, I decided, having examined myself in a magnifying mirror for the first time since I was a teenager, and it wasn't a joyous experience.

'Do you want the full facial, the mini facial, the city skin breather, or just a cleanse and make-up?' asked the voice from the big store.

'How much is the full?' I asked humbly.

'Well it would depend, Madam, it could be as little as £4 depending on what you want done.'

But I wanted them to tell me what I wanted done; I dithered for a while.

'Of course if you wanted eyelashes tinted, facial hair removed, unsightly blemishes covered up, skin peeling, and vapour masks, it would all add up,' the voice said.

This made my crumbling brain come to a decision. 'I'll have the mini facial,' I said firmly and went along at lunchtime to have it.

It was horror from the word go. I longed for the self-improvement of '*ecco il maestro*'. Instead I had 'Good heavens, we do need a little work here, don't we? Did you say you only booked for the mini facial? Ah, well, we'll see what we can do.'

I spent an hour and £2.80 fighting off offers to tear off my eyebrows, refusing to pay another 60p to have my face hoovered with some electric vacuum cleaner that had come in that week from America, and denying utterly that I wanted my ears pierced, even though there had been some mistake and a piercing girl came into the cubicle with what she called sleepers saying that cubicle eight had ordered them.

The beautician was nice but single-minded. She saw a course of treatments for my face, she saw them every week, the full not the mini variety. She saw herself selling me creams to plump out tissues and to beat back lines, she saw a rich heavy night cream, and a light nongreasy day cream. She saw much more than just Brightening Myself Up, which was what I saw. I regard it as the major achievement of the week that I was grown up enough not to see any of these things with her, and be able to leave with the lying promise that I would think about what she said. I didn't look any brighter at all, and I will *never* think about what she said. It's too dispiriting.

Wednesday: *Help other people, it will make you feel good inside.*

It seemed an odd if not selfish reason to help other people, but maybe these hard, brittle women phrase things oddly. Perhaps it was just a ploy to get us out there doing something instead of just talking about it. I rang an old people's home and asked could I help them serve lunch, they said they'd be delighted and off I went.

I was in the room where they served the wheelchair lunch, which meant gathering everyone together and assembling them around the table. You had to tie bibs around people, long plastic ones which practically covered the whole chair. I thought this was very undignified and said that I was sorry to the old man that I was tying into his bib first.

'Not at all,' he said. 'I'd much prefer a pinny, the old hands aren't what they used to be, and all this convenience food, you know, it slips off the fork. Much prefer to be well covered up.'

They were having soup, and then bacon casserole and mash, and then stewed apricots and custard.

'Why aren't you wearing a uniform?' asked one old lady to me as I was passing her food.

'They didn't have one to fit me,' I said.

'People are getting much fatter nowadays,' she said thoughtfully and not in any way insultingly. 'I suppose it's the lack of exercise, and so much food available and everything since the last war.'

She told me about her son who was married to a very fat selfish woman, which was odd since fat people are meant to be jolly, but her daughter-in-law was sour and selfish, and she had three sour fat grandchildren. It was a sad thing to end up having been responsible for three sour grandchildren.

'Perhaps they'll get thinner,' I said hopefully.

'But will they get less sour?' she wondered, and there was no answer to that.

I was helping to clean up, and an old man told me not to, that only people who couldn't speak English cleaned up. I thought this was a wrong theory, but he said it was very sensible, people who could speak English talked to the guests, the others who would like to talk to them but couldn't cleaned up.

So I went to talk to him and he told me he was 91 and very happy. He had been so lucky to get into this home, because there were three television sets, and three sitting rooms, so you could watch whatever channel you liked, and that this was the kind of thing that really made a home successful, and he got £2 of his pension into his hand every week, and was saving it up to buy a nice West Indian nurse a Christmas present, because she had been great to him, and she kept promising to take him back to Trinidad with her, even though they both knew it was a joke.

And then they were all having a little doze, and they would have afternoon tea at four when other helpers would come in and serve it to them at their chairs. I don't think it really made me feel good inside but it made me a lot less afraid of being old.

Thursday: *Brighten up your office, we work better in bright surroundings.*

This was actually taken out of my hands because the office was full to the gills of workmen brightening it up for me. The London Editor had cunningly arranged that the Conservative Party Conference should be taking place in Brighton, as far away as possible from 85 Fleet Street while this chaos was going on, so I had to deal with it alone.

Well, deal with it? It was a matter of getting down on all fours and crawling under my own desk to be able to sit at it. Then I was trapped in a corner, while Alf and Bert walked backwards and forwards across it foot in typewriter and bottom on telephone, both cheerfully apologising and saying they hoped they weren't disturbing me. Every time the phone rang they both took out pneumatic drills, and made exaggerated dentist noises about a foot from my ear, and anyone who telephoned me on Thursday may well be justified in thinking that I had gone mad.

I managed a few calls by putting my head and the phone in a drawer. But when I got it out again, Alf had piled four chairs on my desk, and Bert had moved the filing cabinet over to block the door. They had both left in search of some electricians and so I missed the coffee trolley when it passed the door and I missed going out to a nice wine and cheese reception, but at least there were no drills going and nobody pacing backwards and forwards on my desk so I got a bit of work done.

And then they came back and they told me that this job was going to take a bit longer than I thought and than they thought and they started drilling again. And I picked up the potted plant that was going to brighten up my office for me and I left silently with it under my arm and went to a library not far away and read three books that I had to review.

I felt a bit guilty because it was a Christian Science Reading Room and I apologised for not reading anything about Christian Science but the woman said it didn't matter, I could read whatever I liked, so I hid the titles from her and read away until it got dark.

Friday: *Shake yourself out of your old routine. Do something you would never normally do.*

The trouble here is that I don't have an old routine. Nearly every day I do something that I wouldn't normally do, there's no normal. But I'm still not glittering and action-packed like these new women that upset me so much.

I must try to think of something really unusual to do at lunchtime.

I've seen all the lunchtime plays that I want to, and then that couldn't be called unusual. I've never been up to the top of the post office tower, but it's a dull day and would I see anything? There is a lunchtime cookery class I believe somewhere, but then that's too like Monday and learning a new skill. Eventually I thought of something. I'd take a walk. I would go and explore parts of the city I had never seen. This would be helpful about opening my mind and broadening my horizons, not to mention flattening my feet.

I set off happily and marched down towards the City, to the stockbrokers and the banks and the money houses, looking fearfully upwards in case I'd be hit by falling bodies of speculators. But nothing like that happened. I just got a bit weary plodding on through these caverns of streets, when suddenly a door opened, and two men, locked in what looked like a very un-Londonish embrace, hurtled out. Still groping each other, they fell on to the ground and rolled lovingly towards the traffic. Taxis and buses were now practically standing up on their hind legs to avoid them, and there was an enormous amount of excitement. So near me were they that they actually knocked my handbag out of my hand, so I had to join them more or less in order to get it back.

I was extremely embarrassed by the whole thing, kneeling beside them on the edge of the footpath saying, 'Excuse me . . . I'm sorry . . . you seem to have . . .'

Then I made the appalling discovery that they were not murmuring endearments to each other at all, they actually were trying to kill each other.

'I'll get you,' one was panting.

'Lying bastard,' the other was huffing.

I grabbed my bag and explained to all the onlookers that it was really mine, one of those long, boring explanations that make you seem guilty when you are really innocent. 'You see I don't know either of them,' I explained to a stunned crowd. 'You see, I was just passing by and they kind of knocked my handbag . . . it is mine, you see, it has all my things in it. . . .'

Nobody believed me; they were as amazed by me and my speech as they were by the men pounding each other in the gutter.

There are policemen when you need them, and two approached, the crowd was waved on. I moved off too and the two men were stood up, dusted down, and forced to give some explanation of their behaviour. I took a taxi back to the office, which cost 90p, and decided that if I had been asked to explain my part in the whole business and had said that it was all part of a week of self-improvement, well you might never have heard from me again.

Violet

25 June 1977

Violet rang yesterday with the bad news that she is coming to London for a week. When I think of the 164 people I would love to be coming to London for a week, I wonder why it has to be Violet. She's not a friend, she has no friends, she has contacts. It's me in London, and Hilary in Galway, and Helen in Cork, and Ruth in Paris, and Sheila in Belfast. Sheila had to take a week off to recover last autumn.

Violet's visits are very upsetting. If she was really horrible, it would be possible to say that you didn't want to see her ever again, to say that life was too short, and put down the phone. But she is only accidentally horrible, and that's why we all get sucked into these appalling arrangements, and end up hating her and hating ourselves as a result.

I was wondering if you could book me a hotel. Nothing too fancy, something rather quiet and nice.

Oh, that's going to be easy for a start. In London, in July, in Jubilee Year? If I knew how to find something rather quiet and nice, I could set up in business immediately and make a fortune. But I am not going to ask her to stay. I'm not. I'm not. It would be an abuse of hospitality. When she went to stay with Helen in Cork, Helen had scrubbed the house from top to bottom and Violet still managed to imply that she would get scurvy from it. She actually bought some spray thing and cleaned Helen's windows. She came to a meal here once and said, 'Aren't cleaning ladies unreliable?' which left me in a rage for two months, because it was an innocent remark designed to wound and hurt.

So a hotel it has to be, three hours of phoning and cajoling, and asking people do they know anywhere, and then taking the stick afterwards because it'll turn out to be full of foreigners, far from taxis or have a shower that doesn't work.

And I wonder if you could book me a couple of seats for some good shows. I mean, you're there on the spot, you'd know how it works.

I won't. I'll give her the name of a friend in a theatre-booking agency, and shift the lot on to him. I don't care if she has to pay 30 pence more a ticket, I'm not going to have anything like last time. 'Well, I suppose it was interesting. But very shouty, don't you think, and rather vulgar. I'm not prim and proper, and I think you should call a spade a spade, but honestly what was the point of it all? I suppose when you live here, you see things differently.'

And there was the harmless musical I had suggested. 'Well, I'm sure the children would have loved it. Very colourful and everything. But not quite what one comes to London to see.'

I'll want to pick your brains about shopping. I'm going to buy a complete summer wardrobe when I'm there.

If you want to know all the latest places, I don't even know the earliest places. I will not spend five minutes going into boutiques with idiotic names, and trying to recall what colour people are wearing this season. I don't know what shape of toe shoes have, and there are many other things I want to know before that piece of info. Violet's last visit gave me nightmares. 'I think you must have made a mistake in the name, I looked through everything, and honestly they were all a year old. Nothing new at all. And between ourselves just a little bit tatty, no cut, nor any style. You must have mixed it up with somewhere else or it must have changed hands.'

I had been told authoritatively that it was the smartest and most expensive shop in London. This year I'll be honest, I'll tell her I know only Marks and Spencers and food shops and off-licences, and newsagents. She'll think I have gone mad, but better to have her think that.

I thought I'd telephone Barbara and we could all meet for a meal, I'm sure she'd have us out to the house like last time. I'm dying to see what they've done with it now.

I'm surprised it hasn't had swastikas painted all over it by now. Barbara's fascist husband deserves them more than most. I'll never forget the evening there during Violet's last visit. I went to the bathroom so often to avoid jumping at him and hitting him that they all thought I had some intestinal disease. Barbara herself had been all right, but muted, and we had lots of nice chat about how he wouldn't let a Trade Unionist Commie under his roof, wanted military service for all the layabouts who wouldn't work even if there was work, and said that their launderette smelled of curry these days, because of all those blacks who would be much happier at home anyway, better weather and nice simple village life for them.

A meal with Barbara and her husband – oh that would be a lovely thing.

And I'm dying to catch up on all the gossip. There's lots to tell you from here . . . but not over the phone.

Violet, you're wrong. You could say anything over the phone. If half the Special Branch and the whole of Dublin were listening in, you could tell it all, and we'd be deafened with the clicks of everyone hanging up.

'Frank and Mary, you remember them, oh you must know them, well they spent a fortune on a tumble dryer, a fortune, which is ridiculous, Frank sends all his shirts to the laundry and Mary, well we all know how Mary looks, there's no need to be unkind. I can't imagine why their ordinary spin dryer wouldn't have done them. We went to this new place for dinner the other night. Everyone goes there now, it was full of people one knows. Who? Well, that actress was there, or is she an actress? She's on television maybe, very attractive in a brassy sort of way. She was there. I can't understand how you don't know David Frost. I mean, he lives mainly in London, doesn't he? I'd have thought you'd have met him by now. My sister-in-law's friend met him at a party a few years ago, and she'd only been in London a few months. Still, as you say, it's a big place.'

And I have one tiny favour to ask you. You know that ponyskin coat Gerald gave me for the last baby? Well, it needs to be cleaned, and there's a marvellous place in London, but – and this is the problem – it takes two weeks, so if I could give you the ticket and a cheque then the next time you're coming over . . .

Not again, not again. Finding somewhere in some street that not even taxi drivers have heard of, carrying it draped in tissue and polythene over my arm, trying to remember not to leave it in some pub, or I'll spend next year's salary replacing it. Dealing with security people about it, explaining to the Customs that it isn't mine, it wouldn't fit me, I wouldn't wear it if it did, that it was bought in Dublin, that I'm not a ponyskin smuggler from way back. I had to do all that with some sequinned thing she had once, and what was worse, everyone told me that it could have been cleaned perfectly well in Dublin. I'm not going to do it. I'm allergic to fur, I'm against animals being made into coats, my memory has crumbled. I'd lose it. Get someone else, Violet, get someone else. Remember what happened to poor Hilary. She was months getting hand-knit sweaters to her from Connemara and then bringing them back to women to reknit them because the shoulders weren't right.

Listen, this is very confidential. I was thinking of getting a sort of check-up while I'm there. It seems a waste to be in London where you can have all these cervical smears and breast examinations just by going to a Family Planning place. Could you ring up and make an appointment for me, I'm sure you'd know how to do all that, and it's much less messy than having it done here.

What do I do? 'Hello, is that the Family Planning? There's a tourist coming over for a week. She'd like a medical examination, please. No, I don't think she wants any advice about family planning, I think she has that under control. It's just the free medical she'd like. Yes, she could have it done in Ireland. Yes, they do have proper medical services there. No, it wouldn't cost her anything, but she doesn't like hanging about. I'm not sure why; it might be that it interferes with bridge or golf or shopping, depending on what day it is, I suppose. No, I don't think for a moment that she would regard this as an abuse of your services.'

What I don't want is to be any trouble to you. I know you lead such a busy life.

How can she manage to make a busy life sound something kind of underground and sordid? I get the feeling that she thinks I do several shifts a week as a Madam in a brothel, and this is why I am too tired to know about boutiques and posh dry-cleaning. Last time she was in Paris, she thought that Ruth was 'rushing about too much'. It was said with overtones that Ruth might have been rushing from one playboy's pad to another. Ruth, in fact, had been driven to such hysteria by Violet's relentless journey to jewellers and furriers that she had invented a heavy social life and gone to see six films by herself in a row, just to get out of the shopping expeditions. I could leave London for a week, but apart from being defeatist, cowardly and unkind it wouldn't really make anything any better. There would be a dozen horrors waiting for me on my return, parcels delivered to my house or left in the office to readdress and post; tickets, dockets, vouchers, goods to be exchanged. No, it's better to stay and face it and tell her, in controlled tones, what can and cannot be done.

In rational moments I tell myself that she is not evil, that she must be lonely running around from contact to contact exhausting us all, buying hundreds of pounds' worth of clothes, sending excited postcards to her rather glum husband and her neighbours. And I wonder why her visit fills me with such dread, when I know she can't be trying to put me down or upset me continually. That she only does these things by accident. But then, I can hear her voice saying, 'You must show me what you bought in Australia' and I'll take out the boomerang and the didgeridoo, and the huge bottle-opener shaped like a kangaroo. Violet will laugh indulgently and say, 'What funny rubbishy things, but show me what you really bought.'

Anna's Abortion

9 July 1977

Anna loved Michael. She was sure of it. Michael was sure of it. Anna knew that she should take the pill, she used to take it two years ago when she loved Stephen, but this time . . . well it made you fat, it was embarrassing asking the family doctor for it, it might give you varicose veins, and who knows what it could be doing to your insides.

Anna was very organised. She used to put little crosses in her diary when she expected her period; it didn't happen on May 1st, but Anna had read lots of magazine articles, so she wasn't worried at all. Anxiety could delay it, and she had loads of anxiety.

Her father wasn't well at all. He was only 60 but he was behaving like a man of 90. He was thinking of giving up his large business, he was complaining of pains and aches. Life at home, when she went there every month or so, was far from great; that made her anxious.

Michael made her anxious too, sometimes. He kept saying he liked his independence but if ever he could settle down with anyone, it would be her; he begged her not to rush him. Anna thought that was very honest. She never rushed him at all. Then on May 28th–May 29th this year, a long sunny weekend, Anna realised she had missed her second period, and she couldn't put it down to anxiety any more. So she did what she had once heard that people did, she took a sample of urine and brought it to Holles Street Hospital with a fee attached to it, and called the next day for a result.

Anna knew that they didn't normally give out results to patients, so she pretended that a doctor had asked her to leave the specimen in, because he was on holiday, and there had been no problem. No problem until the report said 'positive', and then there was every problem.

Her family would die. Yes, she knew that lots of girls had told their parents, and the parents had surprised them by taking it all very well. Her parents were different, they wouldn't surprise her at all. They had been appalled when a cousin had got married in a hurry four years ago. They would take nothing well. Her mother would say she was putting nails in her father's coffin. There was no question of telling the family.

She had also heard that fellows took this kind of thing well too, that they did all kinds of cliché things. They rose to responsibilities, they loved the idea of fatherhood, they found that this cemented relationships, they said they were pleased and proud. Michael wouldn't feel anything like that, he would flee from responsibilities, he would hate and deny the idea of parenthood. He would feel that this had cracked the idea of a relationship wide open.

So Anna decided that she would have an abortion. On Wednesday, June 1st, she rang a friend of hers in London – a girl she met maybe once a year, but who was nonetheless a friend. She told her the tale, she listened to the ten minutes' abuse about how could she have been so silly, and wasn't she 26 years of age, and didn't she know that these things could have happened.

Eventually the friend, whose name was Marianne, said she thought that abortion was wrong and that there might be an argument for it being called murder.

Anna said she had faced that argument and had rejected it, and what she wanted was not so much moralising as just the name of a doctor, an ordinary GP, and an introduction, because she didn't want to go through the time-wasting business of establishing an address in London and pretending to be on somebody's panel.

The doctor's name and address was found quite simply. It was Marianne's doctor, who had done three things for Marianne in seven years, two prescriptions for antibiotics and one ear syringe.

Marianne rang him and said a friend of hers who was pregnant wanted to visit him, and it would be a great favour if he could see her and discuss termination of pregnancy. Dr Smith said fine, tell her to come to surgery.

So on Monday, June 6th, Anna queued up with all the other patients, and when it was her turn, Dr Smith gave her a quick examination, confirmed that she was pregnant, and asked her to sit down and discuss it for a few minutes. This surprised Anna because she thought English doctors just wheeled you in and out.

Dr Smith said, 'Why do you want a termination?'

Anna said, 'You wouldn't have time to hear the whole story, the waiting room is full of people.'

Dr Smith said, 'You had to wait until I talked to other people; they'll wait until I talk to you.'

So Anna told him the bones of the story. She said that she could never support a child on her own, she couldn't give a child the love and attention it should have, that Michael would feel trapped, and wouldn't want any part of it.

She explained about her parents who lived in a small country town, and how they would be disgraced if the baby was acknowledged, and how she couldn't really hide it from them even if she wanted it, which she didn't.

Dr Smith listened to her, and produced a form which he had to fill in in order to get her a termination of pregnancy. He explained that it was very difficult to get an abortion, or termination as he kept calling it, on the National Health if you were not a resident in some area paying a regular contribution in the form of a stamp. People didn't like doing terminations, he said kindly, not that there was anything terrible about it. It was just that it was sort of anti-medicine, in a way. It had nothing to do with creation or curing, or healing; it seemed to have something a little bit to do with destroying.

Anna was upset to hear this. She didn't like the word 'destroy'. She thought that since it was permitted by law, people did it all the time.

Not all the time, Dr Smith thought. In fact, he knew several London hospitals which restricted terminations to four a week, even though the demand might be much higher.

'So where do the others go?' asked Anna.

'That's why we are filling in this form,' said Dr Smith. 'Presumably you have enough money?'

'Presumably,' said Anna coldly.

'I don't make any money out of it,' said Dr Smith, equally coldly.

He telephoned a gynaecologist, Mr Brown, and made an appointment for the next day at three p.m. 'Be there at two-thirty,' he said. 'You will have to discuss the arrangements with his secretary and she will tell you how much it costs. You'll have to pay tomorrow afternoon, and in cash, not in a cheque. I think it will be £150 to £170. That will include everything – nursing home, anaesthetist, operation, meals, the lot.'

Anna wondered aloud why it had to be in cash. She thought abortions were legal in Britain; it smelled of the back street and the charlatan to pay somebody in five-pound notes.

'It's certainly not back-street,' said Dr Smith. 'It's Wimpole Street, off Harley Street. It's not a charlatan either, he is a highly respected surgeon. There's nothing dirty or shoddy about it, he'll send you to the Welbeck or the Wellington or the Harley Street, or any of the best places. It's all legal; these are first-class nursing homes. You won't think that they are anything but luxury and highly professional when you go there. Only a very small number of the patients are there for terminations, other people are having appendix or gallbladders done.'

Anna was still worried about having to pay in cash.

Dr Smith had no explanation. 'It's just the way they do it. These men find that people are seldom grateful for their surgery and care, and that often they don't pay afterwards. So they insist on keeping everything businesslike, that's all.'

Next day at two-thirty, Anna went to Mr Brown's consulting rooms in Wimpole Street. His secretary looked like Jane Fonda and spoke like a deb, on a bad day. 'Let's be practical,' she said nauseatingly.

'Here's the damage, would you like to pay me now?' It was £173.50. 'You get a super lunch,' said the awful deb, consolingly.

'It's a bit dear for lunch,' said Anna.

'It's not only for lunch,' said the awful deb wisely.

Mr Brown was very elegant-looking. He had well-manicured hands, Anna noticed. He had that kind of half-grey hair that only wealthy people had; poorer people were grey at random, rich people were grey at the edges. It was all to do with expensive barbers.

Mr Brown examined her again. Not that he didn't trust the word of her eminent GP, he said winsomely, but one had to be sure for oneself.

He confirmed that she was indeed seven to eight weeks pregnant; how wise of her to come in such good time, so many women are very silly about all this. She didn't have any doubts, no? Good, good.

Anna sat there wondering how much he earned. She knew a little about property and salaries. He must have to pay out at least £7,000 a year for the rooms and secretary. He probably took home at least another seven thousand to support the wife in the pearls with the Irish wolfhound, in the picture on the desk. He was probably taxed on an estimated £20,000. He probably earned a conservative £30,000.

He asked her to be at the nursing home, fasting, at nine next morning. Just bring overnight things, nothing to worry about. Simple at this early stage, she'd have forgotten about it in July. But why not get herself fixed up with some kind of protection while she was in Britain; they didn't have such things in Éire, did they?

Anna went back to Marianne's flat, and looked at telly, and refused to talk about it. Marianne was relieved. Marianne thought it was killing, and she wanted to put it out of her mind forever, but she didn't want to hurt Anna.

Next morning, Wednesday, June 8th, Anna arrived by taxi at a nursing home in Putney. It was a lovely Georgian house, or three Georgian houses knocked into one. It had thick pile carpets and tasteful pictures, and recent magazines in the waiting room. At nine-fifteen a.m. she was in a bed in a bright sunny room.

It was a room for two. The other girl was a little drowsy; she had her pre-med, the injection to make her sleepy. She said her name was Sandra, she was Australian, and that her brother-in-law was coming to see her at lunchtime. She said that this was her second termination, and there was nothing to it. Anna wished she looked more cheerful, but then Sandra was very sleepy, so she decided to forget it.

Someone came and listened to her chest. A bossy Irish nurse gave her a hospital gown instead of her own nice nightdress, which she had bought for the occasion.

'Keep that for when you're back home again,' the nurse said. 'You don't want it ruined on you.'

That alarmed Anna, but she was determined to keep her mouth shut, and not to ask questions or tell tales herself. She thought the only way to go through this was with some kind of appearance of dignity.

Then she got her pre-med, and she felt drowsy and she thought about Michael for a bit. She had told him she was going to London for a week to stay with Marianne and that had pleased him. He had said it would cheer her up, she had seemed moody of late. She wondered if Michael would have liked a son or a daughter, and if they would have made good, laughing parents for a child. Her own parents had always been very gloomy; Michael's had been so old that they were like grandparents. By the time they brought the trolley in to take her to the theatre, she wondered should she have told Michael and given him a choice. But it was too late now.

In the theatre, she smiled up at Mr Brown, and he smiled down at her.

'You get your money's worth in terms of civility,' she said.

'The Irish have a great charm,' he said. And then she was asleep.

She remembers them helping her back into bed, but she went to sleep very quickly again.

She woke and they were doing an examination.

'All fine,' said the bossy Irish nurse. 'What would you like for lunch?'

Anna said she'd like something light, and she got an omelette and salad and sauté potatoes, with a crème caramel and a silver pot of coffee. Sandra was awake and eating steak and beans to build her strength up. 'It wasn't bad now, was it?' she asked cheerfully.

For the first time, Anna thought about it. She felt no pain, no discomfort, nothing. It was like coming around from the anaesthetic when you had a tooth out. No, she agreed, it wasn't bad.

Sandra's brother-in-law came in, and had a whispered conversation with her. It seemed mainly hostile; it seemed to be all about some lie Sandra had told a friend of his, he couldn't understand why girls told lies. Men didn't tell lies.

When he had gone, Sandra explained that she had been having an affair with her brother-in-law's boss, and she had got pregnant. Her brother-in-law was so anxious to keep his boss's respect that he had paid for the abortion. But he had made Sandra swear to keep it secret. People were so stupid about things, Sandra thought.

Nobody came to see Anna, and the day seemed long. She had afternoon tea, and she had grilled sole for dinner. She paid an extra £3 to have a television in the room, and she and Sandra looked at a few programmes because it was better than talking.

The Irish nurse came in to know if they wanted her to order taxis in the morning. They would get another examination at seven-thirty and then they should be packed and on their way.

Their beds would be taken again by nine-fifteen tomorrow.

'You sound very disapproving of it,' said Anna suddenly.

'No, I'm not,' said the nurse. 'It's not my business to approve or disapprove. I just think someone who's educated like you are should have been able to avoid it.'

'If we all avoided it, how would you earn a living?' asked Anna furiously.

'Somewhere where we didn't behave as if we were working in a posh execution yard,' said the nurse.

'I bet you don't tell them at home that this is where you're working,' said Anna.

'I'd tell them sooner than you'd tell them where you're visiting,' said the nurse.

Anna apologised; she said she was upset, she didn't mean to shout.

'That's all right,' said the nurse. 'I'm upset a lot of the time, I only shout some of the time.'

And she gave them sleeping tablets, and the two girls fell asleep.

Next morning it was all flurry. They were woken at seven, asked to wash in readiness for Mr Brown. He came in and behind screens gave each of them a quick examination and quick smile. All was fine, absolutely fine.

And so on Thursday, June 9th, at nine o'clock Anna went to Marianne's flat just before Marianne left for work. She said she'd like to stay the day, but would go home that night. Marianne felt guilty that she hadn't done more. 'Stay and we'll have dinner together, anyway,' she urged.

But when she got back from work Anna was gone, leaving a nice thank-you note. Anna went back to work next morning. She didn't want to sit at home thinking about it. They were surprised to see her in the office, but she said that London was so tiring she couldn't stick it any more.

That's all a month ago; she still sees Michael a few nights a week. He still thinks that an involvement of any more permanent nature would change everything and take away the magic. And Anna agrees; it would be awful to take away the magic.

Idiotic Queues

15 November 1978

All over London there were long, idiotic queues outside bakeries and even in supermarkets because of the bread strike. The English are mad about queuing, mad about it. At the slightest hint of there being more than three people anywhere, a queue will form. I think it reminds them of the camaraderie during the war when it really was necessary to stand in great long lines for food, any food. Because the queues you see nowadays are senseless. There's not a serious shortage of bread at all and, even if there were, aren't there other things, not necessarily cake, which people could eat?

The bread strike is, as people say, crumbling. In as much as anyone can understand what was happening it seems that at least a third of the workforce has passed pickets, and most shops have at least some bread every day. But the happy lines of queues are talking in blockade terms and have put on their siege mentality again.

'I've heard they have some in Islington,' says an old man. 'Now I have to get one for the lady in number six, and one for the sisters in number eight and one for my next-door neighbour, but if you like I'll try and get you one, too.'

It's a sort of game of triumphing over desperate odds and beating the system and ganging together. I'm hopeless altogether at it, because even though I like a 400-calorie hunk of bread and butter as much as the next glutton, I can't believe that you'd have to queue for it. Anyway, there's grand Indian bread, little packets of six flat oval things and they're lovely if you heat them up. At 30p a packet they're a bit dearer ounce for ounce than ordinary bread, but not that much.

I suggested to a queue fanatic that she buy this instead of standing on her old legs for an hour in the November winds. No. That wouldn't do at all. Indian bread would taste of curry and have a foreign smell. No it didn't, I said. It was like that flat Greek bread, it was exactly the same as our bread but it just had no yeast or baking powder in it. Her face fell in disappointment. She had been looking forward to the queuing, it would be a happy communal event. People would establish a common bond through groaning about workers who are never satisfied these days.

And in the little shops which sell sandwiches and plastic cups of coffee to workers at this end of town, which is office worker land, the bread hunt is on.

'Chubbies sandwich bar has real bread,' said an over-excited girl in the lift. 'I'm going up to get four cheese sandwiches, then I'll take the cheese out and we'll have proper bread at home.'

Some offices were even doing a shift system, with office workers replacing each other in the queues when lunch-hour was over for the one who had been standing there.

'What do you think is the best way to hoard bread?' I heard a woman asking someone quite seriously. 'I never understood what was so wrong with Mrs Thatcher hoarding things that time. People made such a silly fuss about it all but I think she was quite right. It's only sensible to stockpile if these Marxists are going to stop us getting our daily bread.'

Her friend suggested that she remove everything from her fridge and hoard it there. Another eavesdropper suggested to me that he'd like to tell her where to hoard it.

Bathroom Joggers

9 December 1978

It is well known, of course, that joggers are mad, but when they jog in the torrents of rain you'd wonder should they be put away. All along the road this morning you could see them when the driving rain cleared a bit, steaming and glowing and giving themselves pneumonia as well as coronary arrest. Sometimes one jogs onto a bus, which is particularly bad news. I hate to see someone breathing unnaturally, like people do at the Olympic Games. I hate to see a grown man in a pair of pyjamas that he calls a tracksuit unable to gasp out his destination, and most of all I hate the aura of virtue that comes off him with the steam.

So it is with some pleasure that I see a new Christmas gift launched today by the Campari Sports Equipment Company for a mere £70. It's a sort of a home jogger which takes the offensive sight of public jogging off the streets. The 'Fun-Run', as it is misleadingly called, looks like a bathroom scales, and you keep running on it like mad and it clocks up how many miles you've gone, all the while you never have to leave your bathroom. It comes complete with heart-stopping charts and graphs showing you that you are past your prime if you are over 25 anyway, but with proper racing on old 'Fun Run' you might stagger along living some passable kind of life even after that age. It also gives you 14 danger signals to look out for if you jog. I'm glad they've got around to admitting that jogging had, in fact, some built-in hazards, though I think nobody admitted it until joggers started to drop dead like flies in parks all over the world.

Anyway, these danger signals include extreme fatigue, it says, and your fingernails turning purple. So Campari suggest that you should do warming-up exercises before you start hurtling off on the machine – things like limbering up your back and shoulder muscles apparently. And they stress you shouldn't do it if you feel exhausted. Naturally they don't want to be deafened with the clump of falling bathroom joggers keeling over dead on their 'Fun-Runs'. I was a bit disappointed when I asked what a 'Fun-Run' looked like. I thought it would be like that long rubber moving pavement that the bionic woman trains on when she has to do something a bit demanding, but no, it's just exactly like a scales except, instead of telling your weight, it tells you how far you've run.

The more your silly old knees keep coming up, the more theoretical three-feet steps you have taken. And an alternative Christmas jogging present if you can't manage a 'Fun-Run' would be the Runner's Diary. It's a huge thing like those impressive padded diaries with all the hours written in which executives have on their desks for women graduates to fill in for them. Anyway, the Runner's Diary is seething with information about running being the road to understanding and contentment and health. It has dreadful diets for each day of the year, calorie charts, spaces to put in how much you ran, which are good spaces, and how much you ate, which are bad spaces, and advice about breathing from the stomach rather than the chest and moving your legs from the hips not the knees.

It's altogether a very unsettling and unpleasant diary, which is obviously going to sell enormously well and delight the jogging recipients before their fingernails turn purple.

Happy Hypochondria
28 May 1979

I am a very nervous person about my own health; when I get a headache I wonder if it is meningitis, when I have a twinge in my stomach I wonder has my liver finally packed it in. If I get the smallest cut I watch the tiny drops of blood in horror in case I have haemophilia and will bleed to death there and then.

For years and years I tried to disguise this terror, and put a big brave face on it. I would try desperately to be casual when they were taking blood pressure, searching in the face of whoever was wrapping the terrible bit of canvas around my arm for some sign that I was finished. 'I suppose that's nice and normal,' I would say in what I thought was a healthy, uncaring voice, but inside my heart would be thumping in great booms of terror and my eyes were wild for reassurance.

I used to read magazines in doctors' waiting rooms until the words became a red blur of misery in front of me. Everyone else looked so uncaring about their bodies as they sat there genuinely absorbed in some out-of-date colour supplement, while I'd be afraid to glance at the horoscopes in case Gemini was missing, or it would say that I should make the most of the short bit of time I had left.

If ever I got a spot I thought it was a harbinger of a skin disease that would peel back all the covering on me and expose veins and muscles. A piece of grit in my eye and I was wondering about Moshe Dayan and whether he left the patch on or took it off at night.

But all the time I hid this hypochondria from the world, because I thought grown-ups were meant to be brave and uncaring about themselves and their illnesses. The impassive faces around me in terrifying places like an outpatient ward, this must be the norm.

But now I've changed. Now I admit I'm terrified, and it's much, much better. You have to persuade people that you're not joking, because some of these hard-boiled medics actually think it's unlikely that you could be weeping with nerves inwardly. They think it's a fairly pleasant thing to come up against the medical profession and that we should be pleased rather than fearful.

I began to Come Out as a Bad Patient with the dentist. A gentle softspoken Englishman who had never as he said himself met my type of person before. I explained to him that I was probably more nervous of dentists than anything in the world except flying, and could he show me his hands to ensure that he had no hidden weapons on them. He did this and I relaxed a fraction.

We had a depressing discussion about my teeth and I managed to jump out from under his arms and nearly knocked both of us on the floor.

'Why did you do that?' he said sadly, putting on his glasses again.

'I thought you were going to pounce,' I said. 'I'm very nervous.'

He said he'd have to look at them.

'Could you look at them without instruments?' I asked.

He couldn't. He needed a mirror and a pickaxe. He promised me that he couldn't take out teeth suddenly with a mirror and a pickaxe so I'd be safe.

Since then life with this dentist has been easy. He explains everything, he shows me his hands and lets me examine the pockets in his white coat. He doesn't say 'Aha' any more because it terrifies me. He explains why it wouldn't be a good idea to have a card with me at all times saying 'I am a nervous person. In case of an accident, if I am unconscious, please remove all my teeth so that I won't ever have to worry about fillings and injections again.' He says that is not the act of a nervous person, it's the act of an insane person and I mustn't do it.

Now that he knows I'm nervous and self-dramatising, the whole relationship is on an honest basis. It's the same with the doctor. I told him that I was possibly the most nervous person he would ever meet in his whole career.

'Nonsense,' he said, 'a nice big cheerful person like you, nervous. Ridiculous.'

I argued this with him logically. Indeed I was very nice and very big and cheerful but that didn't mean I couldn't be nervous as well. The things weren't mutually exclusive. Why should he accept that a small, horrible, depressed person was nervous and I wasn't? It floored him.

'You don't look nervous,' he came back with a bit weakly.

So I was very glad that I had told him. Now I remind him each time I see him that I'm nervous in case he's forgotten.

'I know,' he said the last time, shaking his head. 'I know you think you're nervous, I've written it in your file. I'm not to use long words. I'm not to say "Aha" and I'm not to assume that you're brave.'

Life would be a lot more comforting for everyone, doctors and patients alike, if people admitted that they were very frightened when they are. You don't get a sudden strength from pretending to be brave, you just get treated like a brave person, while if you admit humbly to being appallingly feeble about things the chances are you'll get someone to be kind and gentle to you when they would have been brisk otherwise.

There's strength in unity, and if all of us cowards come out openly and honestly they'll have to take us seriously. They can't laugh us all out of the waiting rooms and the hospital beds, can they?

The Man in South Anne Street
6 June 1979

The man in the phone box in South Anne Street was like a lighting devil. First he had lost his five pence, then he had lost his second five pence, and the box was full of litter and bad smells, and the walls were daubed with things, and, God, could things get any worse he asked rhetorically into the air and at myself. They could. At that precise moment a blast of electioneering nearly lifted us bodily out of the street, and the man's face turned such a frightening colour I thought he was choking. I tried to remember what you did when people choked and since it didn't come back to me immediately I was about to contact a competent-looking person but he recovered. It was Stress, he told me, Stress and Fury brought on by living in this country.

The pubs in Anne Street weren't open, mercifully, or I might be there still with him on the self-deluding pretext that I was actually interviewing him and getting an insight into how Stress-Filled Dubliners lived. As it was we just leaned up against the wall of the deserted post office and calmed each other down.

It was the electioneering that had finished him off. Send Your Best to Europe. Was he the only person who found that funny? If we were sending the Best to Europe, what were we keeping for ourselves? The second best? The worst? Answer him that. I said I didn't think that was the way they meant it. They meant more that if you were sending people to Europe you should imagine that you were sending great people. It was a measure of how important you thought Europe was. What he thought Europe was could not be printed. In fact it should hardly be said, I told him disapprovingly. Well, he couldn't help that. That's what he thought about it. Send our best. He'd like to send the lot, actually, and not only to Europe, further. What did I as a normal, ordinary woman think about Ireland these days? Wasn't I ashamed of my life to be living in such a madhouse? I said that I was sort of only half here, and half there and all round the place. He said he knew how I felt. I explained that I meant that I lived in England. His eyes went piggy with envy.

'You live in England?' he said like you might say to someone, 'You mean you eat as much as you like and you don't get fat?'

I explained that I did mainly.

'That would be lovely,' he said, calming down like the way a child forgets a tantrum when the thought of something pleasant is put into his mind.

'But it's lovely here,' I said with the fierce possessive love I feel for Dublin which I would never have admitted until a few years ago.

'In England,' he said, as one who spoke in a dream, 'you can post a letter. You can go out to a post office and buy a stamp, a postal order, send a telegram. You can ring up and get information, and directory enquiries. You can get petrol. They empty rubbish bins. And they're having no European elections to dement themselves further.'

Oh, but they are, I told him. They're definitely having European elections. In fact, I am meant to be there now writing about them.

Nothing could have displeased him more. People who wrote about the European elections were almost worse than anyone else in the whole sorry business. It was bad enough having to join up with a lot of foreigners in a meaningless sort of group to make the farmers richer than they already were and butter dearer than it already was. It was bad enough having to change our money system from what it used to be and to what everyone knew it was to desperate, complicated things which varied every day, and nobody could change for you in any bank in the world because nobody knew what it was any more. It was bad enough to live in a country which slowly collapses, and that was becoming a living joke, but people who wrote about these things only encouraged the decline.

I got fed up with him. I had been sorry for him about the phone box. I had lost two shillings in it myself and there was a rotten smell in it, but I felt he was taking things too far to deny any enthusiasm for Europe. 'What would cheer you up?' I said to him in a schoolmistress sort of way.

Before he could tell me, a girl with a nice, friendly face approached us with election literature for the Labour Party. The man studied it, his colour beginning to mount again. 'I hate people with double-barrel names,' he said about Jane Dillon-Byrne.

'At least they're good names,' I said. 'It's not Fossington-Fossington or Chomondly-Chomondly.'

'The trouble about people like you is that you see good in everything,' he said, and he tore the leaflet into a thousand pieces and increased the litter in the city.

A Magic Meeting

Published in My First Book *by Maeve Binchy* (Irish Times, *1976)*

'Hello, don't I know you from somewhere?'

It's always happening to Audrey Hepburn, but this guy was no Cary Grant either, so I decided that it happens to us ordinary people too.

'I don't know, do you?'

'Well I think I do, you look sort of familiar, like someone I would know, if you know what I mean.'

I looked windswept and wet, but then perhaps he was used to wet climates.

'I'm not desperately sure, I know a lot of people,' I said. Why did I say that? It sounds like boasting, it sounds idiotic. I rush on to say something that will take the harm out of it. 'I mean I'm from Dublin,' I gushed, 'and everyone in Dublin knows a lot of people.'

'I've never been to Dublin,' he said.

'You should, you should,' I said. Bord Fáilte would have been proud of me and taken me to their Baggot Street bosom instead of shying away from me every time I meet them individually or collectively.

'Dublin is lovely, especially in May. I always think May is the best month.'

'Do you?' he said, 'I thought it would have been appalling in May.'

'It's not,' I said, thinking that the magic meeting was palling a bit.

'But I do know you,' he said. 'I have a distinct memory of talking to you for hours and hours sometime. Can't you remember where it was?'

'I can't,' I said, biting back the next boastful thing I was going to say, which was that it could have been anywhere because I go so many places.

'We talked about tax evasion,' he said, happiness dawning on his face.

Now that's something I never talk about, because, honestly, I have nothing at all to say on the subject. Not, of course, that this would necessarily strike it from the topics I discuss, but it's something that would bore me rigid. People saying, 'You should claim for the light and heating of the room where you work,' or 'You write me a cheque and I'll write you a cheque.'

It's too wildly beyond anything I could grasp.

'Were you for it or against it?' I asked jovially.

'I was neither,' he said, 'but you were very well up in it all.'

This was taking a bad turn. He couldn't be some spy sent out from the tax office in Dublin to hound me down in a London street and get me to admit everything? There's nothing to admit, for God's sake, except that I pay too much PAYE because I can't understand the forms.

'I don't think I know anything about it at all,' I said, trembling with guilt, and reddening and prepared to hand myself over.

'I'm rarely wrong about these things,' he said. 'I have a memory of you smoking a cheroot and saying you had a scheme which would mean that you would never pay tax again.'

'I don't smoke cheroots,' I cried desperately.

'You were about to give them up at the time,' he said. 'I suppose you didn't, though, it seemed to be causing you some pain.'

Cary Grant was never like this. In one of his pick-ups he would have remembered my eyes, or the song that they were playing at the time, we would have gone to a wine bar or a skiing chalet to discuss it. We would have fallen hopelessly in love. Cary would never have droned on about cheroots and tax evasion. I said what I should have said at the outset.

'I think that you must be mixing me up with someone else.'

A look of desperation came into his eyes. He was obviously for some reason determined to keep me there, which was flattering. He seemed to need to know me so badly, I almost relented. Perhaps he was just gauche and hadn't seen enough Cary Grant films, perhaps he was a rough diamond. Perhaps as the women's magazines are always saying, he was the strong, worthy type, few words, those few foolish, but worth a million of your other kind of man.

'Well, I met someone like you somewhere,' he said firmly. 'And I have an hour to kill and I was wondering would you like to come and have a hamburger so that we can think where it was. Oh, come on. You look as if you have nothing to do either.'

'You could read the evening paper,' I said, because I am so extremely kind I would never hurt anyone's feelings. I wouldn't tell him to get lost, that he was an offensive bore.

'I've read the evening paper,' he said.

I was silent.

'Well, make up your mind,' he said. 'It's starting to rain, do we have a hamburger or don't we? It's stupid standing here getting wet.'

All right, all right, in years to come you'll tell me I missed my big chance, that I could have developed an interest in smoking small black cigars and evading taxes even if it meant understanding them first in order to evade them. Perhaps we could have been sitting in his baronial hall with 28 guests and telling them the funny way we met all those years ago.

Perhaps you are right, and I was wrong, but I said, 'I hate people talking about "killing time". There's very little of it left, we shouldn't kill what there is. I'm afraid I must go on home. Thank you for the offer all the same.'

As I squelched off in the rain, he shouted, 'You were always too bloody intense, I remember that about you. Go back to your cheroots and your tax forms, I don't care.'

Oh Trevor Howard and Cary Grant, why did you have to louse up our lives making us think that chance meetings were great?

Do It Honestly or Not at All

Published in My First Book *by Maeve Binchy* (Irish Times, *1976*)

I got a pen and paper and did the whole thing very systematically. It was on a train going to Ipswich and the man opposite me was doing it also, writing sneaky figures in the margin. Occasionally we would put our hands around the page like children at school who didn't want anyone to see how they were getting on. At first it looked pretty good.

Age group between 31 and 39, which is grand and vague, means that I should live until I was 77.

Place where you live. Greater London nowadays, so that's another year, 78.

I suppose journalism is laughingly called 'professional job'. It isn't 'skilled' in my case, and with all the modesty in the world I think it doesn't fit into their classification for 'unskilled' so I add another two years, 80.

How do friends and relations describe you? Fortunately you never hear most of their descriptions. Calm is not an adjective I have ever heard about myself in any of its variations like always, or usually, or even moderately. On the other hand, people are inclined to say things like 'hopelessly overwrought again'. So to be honest define that as moderately tense, and subtract one year. Back to 79.

Single and under 40 I am, so it's down another two years. Why? Why? But actuaries must know their job is to know what weakens people. 77.

I knew it was coming – the cigarettes. I think I smoke 40, but I know I have to go into the third packet, so it's age 67 now.

Drink. What's an average day? Well if it was the previous Thursday . . . no forget that. If it were this particular Sunday there would be no drink at all. Come on, be honest, it works out at what they revoltingly call 'six tots' a day. I know, I know, but either do the thing honestly or not at all. Subtract five. 62.

Exercise. Run six miles a day? Are these actuaries *insane*?

Let's see. It's about three minutes to the bus, and about one minute from the bus to the tube. And about 30 seconds when you get off the tube. The same going home. Come off it. No exercise. Subtract five years, 57.

Weight. By the worst luck ever, hadn't I weighed myself at Liverpool Street Station while waiting for the train. Otherwise I might have fooled myself a bit. No, the truth was just over two stone overweight. That was half an hour ago, there was no reason to believe that I had got thinner since then. Subtract six years. 51.

Now what's 'often ill', for God's sake? Does it mean all the time, some of the time? When you take the other alternatives, I suppose it *is* often. All that business about the gall bladder, and the limp I had where they were going to have me shot in the office unless I went to a doctor and had it cleared up. I get a lot of headaches . . . stop whining and feeling sorry for yourself. Subtract two years you silly hypochondriac and shut up. 49.

False teeth? Now this is embarrassing. I *have* one false tooth. Is it right to take the thing literally? They said teeth (plural), didn't they? But the principle is that one fang is gone. It didn't fall out by itself from age or being diseased, it was sort of assisted out in an incident. Still it's gone. Subtract three years. 46.

So, no plans for how I can spend the seventies, the sixties or even the fifties. It'll all be over at 46. I read that line about it not being scientific again and again. The man opposite me was doubled with laughter. He's going to live until he's 73, why shouldn't he laugh? He said I had been too harsh with myself about the false tooth as we did it again to check. I said he had been too indulgent with himself about his weight. He said that it was being dramatic to call myself 'moderately tense'. I said he was being insanely optimistic calling himself 'always calm'.

We both agreed that it was a very foolish and frightening exercise, that it didn't take anything into account like family history or ill health, like whether you had children or not, like whether your skilled job was steeplejack or draughtsman. It didn't bother to investigate whether you had money worries, came from a family of long-livers, or had your home in a war zone. The man said that it was rather unfair that he got extra years for not smoking and drinking. I said that perhaps when he got to 73 he could take up both feverishly on borrowed time. He then worked out his boss's life expectancy and was disappointed to find that was 85.

Anyway, according to the actuaries, you may not have to read me for much longer.

TWO NEWS REPORTS

Though she may be best known and remembered for her features and regular weekly columns, Maeve Binchy was also a skilled news journalist. The following are excerpts from just two major stories she covered from the London office.

Hope and Bitter Memories

24 July 1974

In the third week of July 1974 a Greek military junta backed a coup in Cyprus, prompting Turkey to retaliate with an invasion. Maeve Binchy had just returned from a holiday in Cyprus, and was asked to go back to report on the conflict. She has described this as the proudest moment of her career, because despite total isolation and terrible conditions, she got a story into The Irish Times *every day.*

Don't talk to any Cypriot about Geneva. Geneva is not on fire. What will Mr Callaghan and Dr Waldheim do about the sons and brothers who are dead? Will this high-power conference bring love and peace and co-existence with the men who are shooting at you to kill tonight, they ask. Are we all expected to live like dear friends after this week?

And not every country has known a military coup and a foreign invasion in one week. Tonight I talked to the Turkish Cypriot refugees, who sat spooning meat from tins and crying in the dark field where they wait to hear more news of their fellow Turks.

And the news they hear is not good. They know that whole villages have been wiped out. There are too few Turks here for comfort, they say. Where are the women, and the children from that little village and that little sector of the town?

An old man whose wife had been killed in a mountainous Turkish village near Platea told me that he had been saved by God, not Allah.

He was a Maronite. His poor wife was in heaven now. It was too terrible to tell, he said, but he told it with tears streaming down his old, brown face. They had a small shop, some Greeks in the next village, young and drunken, had come there late one night, ages ago, like three weeks previously, and demanded food. The old man said they were not open. The young thugs had put stones through the windows, and said they would be dead. Back they came on Saturday. Shouting and screaming that it was now war, they had worn uniforms; they came into his shop, to this one only, and shot his wife.

Another Turkish man confirmed his story. He said that they had been able to get lorries and get to the base quickly. They buried the old man's wife in the garden and said prayers and then drove past before any other villagers could be massacred.

They know nothing, nothing about what is happening outside, only that Ankara Radio tells them first it has come to help the Turkish Cypriots establish their rights, and now that these rights have been established. It must be strange, harsh news to hear when you sit spooning out tinned meat, and thinking of your wife buried in the garden.

But there is not general despondency among the Turks, not even those whose villages have been attacked. At last Turkey has really come, and the intense pride that this gives them will be some solace when it is all over and the problems of normal life begin again. Turkey promised to come before and didn't. Now it actually arrived and it will show the Greek Cypriots that the island is not all theirs, that a decent democratic way of life for all Turkish people will be maintained henceforward.

And in a strange way they have some reason for this wild belief, because their status, however personally disturbing, must be collectively improved when the bargains are being made, when the law-makers are yet again drawing up the rules.

I asked them did they not regret that the Turks had only landed in two areas of the Island, thus exposing the scattered villagers to risk. 'President Ecevit is sad tonight in Ankara,' said one young woman, who was a teacher in her town. 'He did not want so many Turkish Cypriots to be attacked but what could he do? He had to land somewhere. He could hardly drop a hundred men into each village. These are the sacrifices we must make.'

She went on to describe the sacrifices they had made. They had been a minority with titular representation.

Oh yes, it looked good at the beginning, they had been given Vice-Presidentship and positions for a small Turkish National Guard. They were second citizens in every way, except one, she said proudly. 'We are half of Cyprus. Even though our population is not half nor even a quarter, they must consider us one half of the population, and the Greeks the other when any decisions are made. That is what they never understood, but now that Turkey has shown real support and not forgotten us, things will be different.'

It all seemed so clear and so right that the Turks should be the victims in this mad war that I found myself agreeing with her from the heart. And the heart can change in a short walk through the section where the Greek Cypriot refugees are spooning meat out of tins.

There was an old Greek woman who thinks that her three sons are dead. Someone explained to me that she had not stopped wailing since Saturday morning when she was taken by friends to Dhekelia. They were in Kyrenia. They must be dead. Everyone is dead in Kyrenia. She was being looked after by a woman of about 40, her daughter-in-law, who refused to believe anyone was dead. The Turks had been pushed back into the sea. She had heard it all day on the radio.

An old Greek man thought that Cyprus would have to be partitioned sooner or later. Why not give the Turks Kyrenia since they had captured it anyway? Move the rest of the Turks in there, and let them feel happy with their harbour looking over at Turkey if that was what they wanted.

And what will happen to them all? The mixed villages will have to go, for a start. When the whole truth of this week's fighting comes out it will be shown that many of the killings were to settle old scores, feuds and hatreds growing and festering in tight communities where the fear of fear grew and grew. Partition has never worked well anywhere else, as we all know, but it might be the only solution.

Numbed Dover Waits for Lists of the Dead

9 March 1987

On 6 March 1987, the Herald of Free Enterprise *ferry on the Cross Channel route capsized near the Belgian port of Zeebrugge in a disaster which killed 253 crew and passengers. When reporters were cordoned off from the site, Maeve quietly bought a ferry ticket so she could access the passenger terminal to talk to passengers and relatives. This is her report from Dover.*

There was a fine coat of snow over the Cliffs of Dover making them whiter than ever at the weekend. The flag was at half-mast on Dover Castle . . . the town, which has always claimed to be the largest passenger port in the world, had a heavy feel about it as the reality seemed to sink in.

One of the FEs was not coming home. There are eight of the Townsend Thoresen ships called *Free Enterprise*, and, just as Sealink vessels are known by affectionate nicknames or initials, the Free Enterprises were always the FEs, and they were always considered unsinkable. All day long the local radio station broadcast the telephone numbers for enquiries, but stressed that there really wasn't very much more information.

From Friday to Sunday, distraught relatives moved in a maddened circle from Dover to Maidstone where the police headquarters had been set up, on to Gatwick where some survivors had been flown in, then back to Dover where 30 surviving crew members had returned unexpectedly on another ferry.

The horror of the first published lists was that nobody was utterly certain whether this was a list of known dead or known living. So to hear a name read from a list could have meant the best or the worst.

In Enterprise House, the company's Dover headquarters, the staff were red-eyed with lack of sleep and tears shed for friends and for the very fact of the catastrophes . . . families sat in little clusters on the benches of the big departure hall, they followed the staff with their eyes and whenever a telephone rang on a desk, a small crowd would gather immediately, just in case.

Wearily, the ferry staff faced television teams and made statements. 'I have been asked to say that the Kent Police will answer any questions from now on.'

'Well what have we all been doing here for God's sake?' asked a man, distraught for news of his son.

'I don't know, I'm terribly sorry, but we realise that the lists are incomplete . . .'

The man, whose face was so drawn it looked like a skull, clutched at her hand. 'If you do know, I'd prefer to hear it now. I don't want his mother to go on hoping.'

The tired girl from the ferries swore that she did not know. She pressed several ten-pence pieces into his hand so that he could ring the police in Maidstone. 'I'm sorry,' she said again.

'I know you're sorry. He was only 19,' the man said.

A woman who was waiting for her sister-in-law to come back from this Continental shopping trip said that they might all be better off at home, looking at their televisions. A Salvation Army woman gave her more tea and sat down beside her on the bench.

'Tell me about your sister-in-law. What did she go to buy?' she asked.

'She might be drowned,' the woman was frightened to talk about her in case it might bring bad luck.

'But we don't know that. Tell me what did she go to buy?'

'Well she said there wasn't all that much in Zeebrugge and she would go on to this place called Knokke-Heist that was nearby. What will happen to her children if she's gone?'

'Don't think about that yet. The Lord will help, tell me about this place where she went shopping . . .'

Around the terminal building the crowds came and went as if by looking at that cold, grey sea they could somehow make it more likely that people had been taken from it the previous Friday night. And all around the Eastern Dock there were the distressingly inappropriate advertisements saying that the Continent is nearer than you think and perhaps the saddest of all, the big signs: 'They're here, the new big value luxury ferries.'

It was the endless waiting that was so hard to watch, even as an outsider. People passive in the never-never land of not being sure a full day and a half after the tragedy.

Gently, the police, the ferry officials and clergymen explained that there had been such a panic; nobody was too sure of what names were given and what names were taken. These English-sounding names would be unfamiliar to Flemish and French speakers. . . .

And in the town which has so strenuously opposed the building of a Channel tunnel, people said that it would be a crime if this disaster were to lead to the public believing that a tunnel was the only way to cross the sea.

Quietly, and without the usual excitement and fuss of people going on their holidays, the passengers filed on and off the rows of ferryboats in the harbour. And in a wet, cold, sad Dover, the ships sailed in and out under the white cliffs. The seagulls called as they always did but through the sleet and in the silence they seemed as sad as funeral bells.

EIGHTIES

The Right to Die in Your Own Home

17 February 1980

My neighbour in London has lived for 81 years in her house. She came there when she was five. Before that she lived in a cobbled mews where her father was a coachman but he lost his position because the family he worked for decided to go over to the horseless carriage. The mews where she once lived changed hands for three quarters of a million pounds not long ago.

They liked the new house when they came there in 1909 and had five nice peaceful years before the First World War. She remembers when that war ended in 1918 and all the excitement and the men coming back. And she worked in a big firm which gave a celebration party where George Robey sang. Every lady who worked in the firm was allowed to invite a gentleman and every gentleman a lady – the night is as clear to her as if it had been last week.

Much clearer, actually. Last week wasn't all clear.

Her sight is so bad these days that she dare not even boil a kettle in case she burns herself, so another neighbour, a woman from further up the road, comes in and makes her breakfast, her lunch and her tea. The State, through the welfare services, gives an allowance for this, called an Attendance Allowance, of £27 a week.

This is a fairly regular procedure now in London, where there is a real need for it. A lot of elderly people have no relations nearby, the very nature of big city living means they have few close friends.

Britain is a very ageing society, the contrast between there and here is extraordinary. Here the parks are filled with children, in London they are filled with the old. In Dublin you hold a supermarket door open for a mother with a pram, in London for an elderly couple with a basket on wheels.

The health cuts have meant that a serious attempt is being made to keep old people out of residential care. On a purely factual and financial level it has been worked out that it is much dearer to put a person in a home permanently than it is to provide what are called back-up services. Attendance allowances are a part of the back-up. The State also provides a Home Help twice a week for two hours on each occasion, and a bath attendant once a week to assist in washing. The Home Helps often say that they are more needed to assist as company than as cleaners, and that sometimes they are followed around by the people whose houses they are trying to clean. The need for conversation is greater than for vacuuming.

The bath attendants say that very often they are told that the old person 'doesn't feel like a bath today'. It's too cold or they're too tired or whatever. It's not a police state, they say, they can't drag the person upstairs and insist on cleaning them.

So back-up services and a fair amount of people calling in and taking an interest have meant that this neighbour has been able to live in her home reasonably well for the past few years, since her sight and hearing and mobility have all so disimproved. She has resisted sheltered accommodation, rightly saying that where could be more sheltered than where she is? A house whose every floorboard and stair step has been familiar for eight decades. And people will find her, she says, if she has a fall. She has given the keys to people who will come and look for her if she doesn't answer the phone.

She didn't answer the phone last week. Her bed was empty when I went in. She was lying underneath it, unable to get up. There were no bones broken, so she couldn't be taken to hospital. The police, who now work the ambulances because of the strike, helped to carry her downstairs and settle her in a chair.

Snow white and shocked from who knows how many hours like that, she was determined to be cheerful. Part of the generation that doesn't like to worry the doctor, she agreed under duress to let him call. He is a determined man, he said she must go into hospital to be looked at, and because casualty departments will admit an ambulance with an old person if it comes with a doctor's referral, she was taken to Charing Cross Hospital in Fulham.

And that's where she is today, while they try to decide whether she will be able to manage at home any more. The last time she had a fall they built an extra rail on the stairs; the time before that they arranged a commode.

People have shaken their heads darkly and said, 'Thatcher's Britain!' They say the old lady is not able to look after herself and there shouldn't be all this cheeseparing and pussyfooting about, people like that should be given good residential care in their last years, they worked hard enough for it during their time.

But I'm not sure. I don't think it's as simple as that. I can see that, alarming as it might be to neighbours who are at the moment relatively mobile, an old woman might like to live and die in a house where she has been since the year Lloyd George tried and failed to bring in the People's Budget and Bleriot tried and achieved the first flight from Calais to Dover.

Yet, when I see her all clean and pink in a hospital bed with nurses around and company and no fear of falling and lying through the long hours of the night alone on a floor, then I think she must stay in care. She doesn't get frightened of burglars when she's in hospital.

She doesn't find her heart thumping in fright when someone knocks on a door after seven in the evening, thinking that it's muggers like she reads about in the local papers. And there is an argument that says since she can't really enjoy her own home maybe she should go into something more organised.

But there's another argument which says we only have one crack at life and if you protest so strongly that you want to be in your own place, regardless of falls and knocked-over tables and things not being as clean as they used to be, then that's where you should be.

And that is actually what Thatcher's Britain is trying to do for old people . . . keep them in their homes.

It doesn't, of course, give nearly enough in resources. You get the feeling that the Prime Minister wants a return to old-fashioned values of neighbourliness and concern, because the government doesn't have to pay for such things. And yet to my intense annoyance I can't disagree with her. I only wish I had her sense of certainty about everything. It would be great to know which bed my neighbour should sleep in tonight, and know it was the right place for her.

When Beckett Met Binchy

14 May 1980

Beckett looks 54, not 74; he looks like a Frenchman, not an Irishman, and he certainly looks more like a man about to go off and do a day's hard manual work rather than direct one of his own plays for a cast which looks on him as a messiah come to rehearsal.

He has spikey hair which looks as if he had just washed it or had made an unsuccessful attempt to do a Brylcreem job on it and given up halfway through. He has long narrow fingers, and the lines around his eyes go out in a fan, from years of smiling rather than years of intense brooding.

He is in London to direct the San Quentin Workshop production of *Endgame* and *Krapp's Last Tape* for Dublin's Peacock Theatre. It will open in Dublin on May 26th. Beckett has become very involved with this San Quentin group since the early sixties when he heard what was happening in the big American Jail.

One of the convicts, Rick Cluchey, who was serving what might have been a life sentence for a kidnap and robbery but which turned out to be only 11 years, persuaded the authorities to let the prisoners do Beckett plays and they performed them in a studio theatre in what used to be the prison's gallows room.

The plays made such an impact on the prisoners, who immediately saw similarities between the imprisonment felt by Beckett's characters and themselves, that they were repeated over and over. The word got out and it even got as far as Beckett in Europe.

Nowadays, Cluchey and Beckett are friends, something that the convict in San Quentin would have thought impossible. Cluchey and his wife, Teresita Garcia-Suro, have called their two young children after Beckett and his wife, Suzanne.

Rick Cluchey knows nearly every word that Beckett has written but when he is in a position of actor with Beckett as director, he says he tries to forget everything he ever thought himself, tries to strip his mind and memory of actors' tricks and his own interpretations, and just wait like a blank sheet of paper for Beckett to tell him what to do.

This is what was happening down at the Riverside Studios in London where they were getting the rather minimal set ready for a rehearsal of *Endgame*. They needed a chair for Hamm to sit in, a ladder for Clov to run up and down, and a dustbin for Nagg. Nell, the other dustbin inhabitant, hadn't arrived yet (she is Teresita and was coming over from America the next day), so this day Beckett played Nell.

He was endlessly finicky and pernickety about the height and shape of the props, he ran up and down Clov's ladder a dozen times to see was it the right kind of ladder, and if it gave Clov space to turn around and deliver his lines.

He sat in Hamm's chair another dozen times raising it and lowering it so that it would be at the right angle when Clov came over to whisper in his ear. I thought I was going to die with irritation and impatience but the American actors, Bud Thorpe, Alan Mandell and Rick Cluchey, hung on every instruction and rushed to carry it out.

Douglas Kennedy from the Peacock Theatre in Dublin sat with his notebook, taking heed of all the requirements that would be needed in Dublin. Finally, Beckett got down to words.

The main thing you'd notice is that he thinks the play is a song, or a long rhythmic poem. He can hear the rhythm, he can hear it quite clearly in his head and his work as a director is to get the actors to hear it too. That's why he goes over and over each line, saying it not all that much differently to the actor (in fact you'd have to strain to hear the difference), but it has a beat the way he says it and, once that beat is caught by the actors, it sounds quite different.

He stands there in front of them, mouthing the lines they say word perfect in his own play, up to the pauses and the half pauses, quite confident that this conversation between wretched imprisoned people is almost the obvious definition of the human condition. He doesn't ever apologise for his own work, excuse it or say, 'What I'm trying to say here is this . . .'

In fact, it seems to stand there beside him, this play, as if it was an important statement, and he is just helping the actors to unveil it.

Beckett is courteous, he never raises his voice. 'Bud, may I suggest something here?' he says to a young American actor, Bud Thorpe, who thinks that, when he has grandchildren, they'll never believe this, not in a million years.

'Alan, Alan, take the rhythm. You have to knock on the bin, the rhythm comes in the knocks, it sets the speed for the conversation. Come, no, I'll get into my bin.'

And Beckett sits down beside Alan Mandell to play the loving scene between the two dustbin-imprisoned folk who can only remember, wish and regret. Mandell says he'll never forget it to his dying day.

He has ludicrous energy, Beckett. When the actors, all decades younger than him, were tiring, needing a break, a coffee, he was still as fresh as when he started, the tones, the rhythms were running through him; his spare body, in its almost traditional uniform of two thin polo-necked sweaters, moved from side to side of the stage, bending, crouching, stretching. Even I, sitting silently on my chair, began to feel weary and wish he'd stop for a few minutes.

He did. He lit another of the small cheroots he smoked and came over to me. I looked behind me nervously, assuming he was going to talk to someone else.

It had been a very firm arrangement. I could watch but not talk. Write but not interview. I assumed he was going to ask me to leave.

He introduced himself to me as formally as if I might have had no idea who he was and assumed he was someone who came in off the street to direct the play. He asked how *The Irish Times* was getting on and I gave him the usual loyal craven tale about it being the best newspaper in the world. He only saw it from time to time, he said, but he seemed to go along with my opinion of its excellence.

'I remember it more in the days of Bertie Smyllie,' he said. 'Did you know him?'

'No, but I believe he was a bit of a personality,' I said, helpfully wishing that, when Beckett had decided to talk to me, I could find something entertaining to say to him.

'My memory of him was that he ran his newspaper from the pubs and that there were circles around him, listening to what he wanted to do and running away to do it. He used to drink in the Palace. Is the Pearl still there?'

'No, it's been bought by the bank,' I said.

'The bank,' said Beckett thoughtfully. 'The bank. How extraordinary.'

It seemed to upset him deeply. I wondered should I tell him about all the alternative drinking places we had found, but I decided that he was more brought down by the notion of the bank owning the Pearl than the actual deprivation of the drink in it.

'And I believe the Ballast Office clock has gone,' he said gloomily. I agreed and hoped that he might hit on something that was still there in Dublin. 'How do people know what time it is?' he asked.

'I think they sort of strain and look down the river at the Custom House,' I said.

'It's the wrong angle,' he said.

He was silent then, and I wondered was he really concerned about the people not knowing what time it was, or had he gone off on a different train of thought.

'Will you come to Dublin yourself to see this?' I asked.

'Not this time, no, I shan't be coming this time,' he said.

His accent is sibilant French with a lot of Dublin in it. Not as lispy as Seán MacBride but not unlike it, either. I was afraid I had given him a bum steer by letting him dwell on the Ballast Office and the Pearl.

'There's a lot of it left, you know,' I said.

He smiled. 'I'm sure there is, but I must get back to France and Germany . . . that's where my work is. . . .'

'What are you working on next?' I asked him.

'A television play, it will be done for German television in Stuttgart. I like Stuttgart, not the town itself, it's down in a hole, a deep hole, but I like when you go up on the hills outside Stuttgart. And I like the people there that I work with . . . I am looking forward to it.'

'Does it have a name?' I wondered.

'No name, and no dialogue, no words.'

'That's a pity,' I said.

After a morning of listening to his words, I could have done with more. Anyway, I'm rigid enough to think that a play should have words, for God's sake.

He saw this on my face, and he smiled a bit. 'It will be very satisfactory,' he assured me. 'It's all movement, activity, percussion, cohesion. . . .'

'Why do you like working with the people in Germany on this sort of thing?' I asked, the tinge of jealousy evident in my tone.

'Oh, they understand, we understand the rhythm of it . . .' he said.

He picked up the issue of *The Irish Times* that was on my lap, and looked at it for a while, not really reading, more remembering.

He had liked Alec Newman, he said, a very gentle man. He had admired Myles na Gopaleen and laughed so much at everything he had written but had been a bit disappointed when he met him because he had expected too much. There were a lot of things he thought of about Dublin from time to time. Niall Montgomery. Had I known him? He was a good man.

He decided that those young actors had had enough rest. He went back to them. They took up at a part of the play where Hamm has to say, 'This is not much fun.' Rick Cluchey as Hamm said his line, giving it all the weight it deserved. 'I think,' said Beckett, 'I think that it would be dangerous to have any pause at all after that line. We don't want to give people time to agree with you. You must move and reply to him before the audience start to agree with him.'

And Beckett laughed and lit another cheroot and settled in for hours' more work.

Fit for a Queen

23 May 1980

I met this woman at a party and she was quite drunk and had tears of vodka pouring down her face as she decided she was going to confide her biggest secret to me.

She had her bras and corsets made for her specially at a place in the West End, which also made bras for the Queen.

She told me that I'd love it, that it would become quite an addiction, that I'd never be able to buy an ordinary bra again without wincing and feeling third rate. She said I should go the next day and see them myself.

With difficulty she was restrained from taking off her dress there and then to show me their handiwork and I assured her I would check them out. She wrote the name on my cheque book, in my diary and, to my annoyance, all over some letters that I was going to post to other people. Then, happy that she had done her duty, she passed out.

I needed a new bra. It's never what I would call heady excitement going to buy clothes of any kind if you aren't a Stock Size, so I thought I might investigate the royal corsetières.

I hoped they wouldn't be snooty and put me down. It's bad enough to be put down when you're dressed. Naked, it's intolerable. They live in South Molton Street, and you have to make an appointment. The place was faded genteel, lots of elegant-looking wraps and robes about the place and Christmas cards from the royal family; and discretion hung heavily over the whole place like ectoplasm.

The lady, whose name was Daphne, was crisp and welcoming.

She seemed quite confident that the outcome was going to be a spectacular success. She looked like the kind of person that would never discuss money in a million years.

There are a few advantages about being more or less grown up. When I was younger I would have sat there tortured wondering how much the damn thing cost; nowadays life is too short.

'How much will it cost?' I asked, brazen as hell.

'About £30. It depends on how much fitting we have to do,' she said.

It sounded a great deal of money, but then foul ones on which nobody has lavished any attention at all are about £18 in sickly pink and even more if they're any colour you might wear. I decided to live dangerously and have one built for me.

'That's fine,' I said.

'We'll call Madame,' she said.

Madame was tiny and from somewhere in Europe that gave her an accent which sounded as if she had come out the door of Central Casting. She was petite and charming, and she said ooh la la, twice. She had a tape measure around her neck, she had pins in her mouth. Together we marched in to the fitting room.

First she would make a model, she said, and when we got the model right she would make the bra. It would be like a kind of masterplan, she would work from it. It would be as good as having me there.

I got a feeling of rising panic. Surely she wasn't going to cover me in putty or plaster of Paris so that she'd remember my shape.

I stood there unhappily, with my arms crossed modestly over my bosom.

'Oh, maybe you should just make it . . . sort of largish,' I said vaguely, looking around fearfully for whatever they were going to pour over me.

By this stage she had taken out a grand harmless-looking thing which was like two huge steel horseshoes covered in fur and kind of white cotton. She fixed it onto me and we scooped bits of me into it and I was delighted.

'Oh, it's great,' I said happily. 'I'll take it.'

With enormous patience she explained that this wasn't it. This was just what she was going to work from, the real thing wouldn't be dull old cotton, it would be satin and lace.

I felt very foolish but Madame didn't mind at all. She buzzed around me like a butterfly, nipping here and folding there and raising and lowering. I felt like the prow of a ship. I was delighted with myself.

Then she said she was satisfied and I got out of it with very bad grace and put on what I had come in with which was very humble by comparison, and we made another appointment.

I offered to pay a deposit and Daphne said that was super, but you got the feeling that if I hadn't they'd still have gone ahead and made it. On the stairs I met a woman who stood back to let me pass and I noticed she had a bosom like the nose cone of a plane. She had obviously been there already and was coming back for another fix.

A week later I went back full of confidence. This time Madame produced a confection of satin and little roses and lace. It would make your heart soar to look at it. I quite understood why the vodka-soaked woman felt the urge to take off her dress and display hers.

A frown on Madame's face, a few more little pulls and pushes, she buzzed and Daphne came in and purred and I moved in a stately way around the fitting room, and begged to be allowed to take it just as it was, but they said nonsense, the whole notion of having a bra made was so that it could be fitted. They said it would be ready on Thursday.

And it was. A final fitting . . . an enormous amount of mutual congratulation. No pressure whatsoever to buy anything else. I wrote a cheque for the remainder and they waved away the banker's card. In the privacy and peace of a corsetières, they assume a lady is a lady and not a bounder.

It is possibly the most cheering garment I ever bought. It is firm to the point of being like reinforced steel. It's so comfortable that it's like wearing a cushion around the bosom. It will look fantastic if I'm knocked down by a bus.

I don't know if it actually does anything for men in the sense of an infrastructure, which is what bras are meant to be about . . . but I know that if there's another revolution and I'm told to burn it, I'll abandon the sisters before I'd let it go.

Contraceptive Conversation

16 February 1981

Today I had an argument with a stranger, a real live argument with a woman I'd never met before as we waited at a bus stop for what seemed a considerable length of time.

'Very depressing kind of day,' she said.

'Grey,' I agreed. 'But it might cheer up later.'

'Nothing much to be cheerful about, though, is there? Look at the papers,' she said.

Obligingly I looked at the front page of *The Irish Times*. Compared to some days, I thought the news was fairly neutral. 'Do you mean Mike Gibson not playing rugby for Ireland any more?' I asked, not quite seeing anything that would cause gloom.

'Never heard of him,' she said.

It couldn't be the heady excitement of will we, won't we about the EMS; she was hardly brought down by the fact that the RUC may have been kidnapping Father Hugh Murphy, since he was safe and well; the talks were continuing in an RTÉ dispute, but that wasn't enough to lay anyone low. No, it had to be Haughey and the Contraceptive Bill.

'Do you mean about having to have a doctor's prescription?' I asked.

'Indeed I do,' she said.

'Well I suppose it does make us look very foolish trying to legislate for everyone else's morality and pass the buck to the doctors,' I said cheerfully. 'But then I'm a fairly optimistic person, and I'd prefer to regard it as a step in the right direction.'

There was a stony silence. I wondered had she heard me. After all, she was the one who started the conversation. 'So, even though it's a bit of a joke, it's not all that bad,' I said, keeping things going as I thought.

'Is that your view?' she said.

'Well it's not a very thought-out view,' I backtracked. 'But it's a kind of instant reaction, if you know what I mean.'

'You approve of all that sort of thing,' she said in a kind of hiss.

'Oh yes, I think people have the right to buy contraceptives,' I said, wishing somebody else would come along and stand at the bus stop and shout 'good girl yourself' at me.

'And you'd like to see them in public places,' she said, eyes glinting madly.

'Well not in parks or concert halls or places like that. But on shelves in chemists, certainly. Then, if people want to buy them they can and if they don't, nobody's forcing them to.' I thought I had summed up the case rather well.

'On shelves so that everyone can see them,' she said, horrified.

'Well they're in packets,' I said, 'with kind of discreet names on them. They don't leap up off counters and affront you.'

'And how might you know all this?' she asked.

'Well I've seen them in chemists in London,' I said defensively.

'If they're so discreet, how did you know what they were?' she asked, tellingly.

'Well, you'd sort of know. I mean people have to know where they are, for God's sake. I mean they shouldn't have to go playing hide and seek around the chemist's with the assistant saying warmer and colder.'

The woman wasn't at all amused. 'I'm sure you know where they are because you buy them,' she said.

I began to wonder why it is increasingly less likely that I ever have a normal conversation with anyone. 'I once bought a huge amount,' I said reminiscently. 'As a kind of favour to a lot of people. They knew I was going to be in London, and they kept asking me to bring some home.'

She was fixed on me with horror. All her life she knew she would meet someone as wicked as this, and now it had happened.

'I didn't know what kind to get or what the names of them were, so I asked for four dozen of their best contraceptives and a receipt. They looked at me with great interest.'

'I'm not surprised,' said the woman.

'But imagine smuggling them all in for people, and not making any profit on them and not even . . . you know . . . well, getting any value out of them myself as it were.'

She stared ahead, two red spots on her cheeks, and mercifully the bus came. She waited to see if I went upstairs or downstairs so she could travel on a different deck.

The Happy Couple

29 July 1981

It would be impossible for you to know the amount of goodwill there is directed towards the royal couple unless you were here in London. For a month, the shops and buildings all along the wedding route have been smartening themselves up. There isn't a space that doesn't have the faces of the young couple decorated with flags and coats of arms and loyal greetings.

Men and women who have sparse and drab weddings themselves, people who had no honeymoons, even those who don't have a proper home to live in, let alone a palace, are out on the streets cheering and laughing and wishing Charles and Diana a happy wedding day. It's a combination of a lot of things. It's going to be a great spectacle; everyone feels like a festival; it's a day off but, most important, people think they know Charles and Diana now and what they know, they like. The couple are very, very popular.

Hundreds of thousands of ordinary people in Britain have been feeling a real concern for Prince Charles, and worrying about his lonely life. They read endless descriptions of the evenings he spent at home and how he is secretly a family man at heart. Now, they are overjoyed that he has fallen in love and is having a fairytale wedding to a beautiful girl.

Hundreds and thousands of girls all over the country are identifying like mad with Lady Diana, whom they see as one of themselves but a bit posher. They will never marry a prince and have carriages and horses and fanfares and the works but she is doing it for them, in a way. In fact, it is touching to see how little envy and how much genuine enthusiasm there is around the place.

Charles has always been very well liked in England. He was educated, if not exactly like an ordinary person, at least like an ordinary upper-class person, which gave him some kind of touch with reality. He was trained in the various armed forces and learned how to do all kinds of things like deep-sea diving and flying a helicopter and playing a cello. He also had to learn about meeting total strangers and expressing an interest in whatever it was that had to have an interest shown in it. At this, he has been very good. He decided somewhere back along the line that if he was going to have to do it, he might as well do it properly, so instead of saying 'how fascinating', he says, 'what is this, how does it work, what's it for?'

He is always courteous and able to send himself up. When he went through that stage of falling off every horse he sat on, he laughed at himself, and he even asked one of his aides to buy the disrespectful mug which has his ears sticking out as handles. He doesn't yawn and look at his watch like his father does, nor does he look as tense and strained as his mother sometimes does. Very few people envy him his wealth or his estates. Hardly anyone envies him his job. He is a Good Guy.

Lady Diana is the living proof that men don't respect you if you give in to them, and that princes certainly won't marry you if there's even a question that you might have given in to anyone at any stage.

Lady Diana Spencer has had a hard few months and if she can stand up to this, she is thought to be able for whatever else is in store. After all, very few brides have to go through the embarrassment of having their uncle announce proudly that they are virgins. Lord Fermoy, the brother of Lady Diana's mother, made this statement, 'My niece has no past.' She has had to have a gynaecological examination to ensure that she is capable of bearing children, she has had to move in with her husband's grandmother in order to get a crash course on how to behave like a royal. She has been instructed to keep her mouth shut, to say nothing in public. She has been asked to lose weight and to lose some of her old friends because they are not suitable any more. To be the future Queen Diana is exciting but there are a lot of hard things to be done on the way.

But Diana Spencer is very popular too, not just because she is young and pretty. She has the kind of background that people like to read about. Old noble family, young princes as playmates when she was a toddler, nice exclusive girls' schools, Riddlesworth then West Heath and then a smart Finishing School in Switzerland where she learned to ski and speak a little French.

She had a lot of unhappiness, the kind that everyone can sympathise with; being the child of a broken marriage and because she wasn't very intellectual, she didn't try for A Levels. Instead, she asked her father if he could buy her a flat in London and she would get a job. Her father bought her a flat for £100,000 and she asked three friends to share it, they paid her the rent each month and very shortly after they moved in, she got a job helping at a kindergarten school which had been set up by two friends of hers.

She never did a season, or came out as a deb. She wasn't a girl who went to smart nightclubs like Wedgies or Tokyo Joe's. Perhaps because of her own lack of home life she tried to make her flat into a home. She and Virginia and Carolyn and Ann lived like other debbie girls who liked shopping at Harrods and having little supper parties but they were quieter than most and spent a lot of evenings looking at television.

The telephone directory is hardly big enough for the list of names that Prince Charles was going to marry at one time or another, but very few of these are among his close friends nowadays. Only Lady Jane Wellesley remains from the old flames, and she doesn't count because she was always meant to be more interested in her work than marrying the Prince of Wales.

Another lady called Lady Tryon is a close friend. She is Australian and Charles calls her Kanga and takes her advice about everything, it is said . . . including the suitability of the new bride.

He has a hard core of male friends including Nicholas Soames, Lord Tryon, Lord Vestey and Lord Romsey . . . they are thought to be secure in their circle and don't fear that marriage will take the prince away from them completely.

For Diana, it may be different. Even though she was able to give her flatmates a phone number of the Palace at Clarence House and begged them to ring her up for chats, they keep finding that she's in the middle of this or that and it is frowned on to interrupt her. The flatmates have been so discreet and refused very tempting bribes to tell their stories about life with Lady Di that it is believed they may well be rewarded by being allowed to remain friends. The trouble is, of course, that they are not quite upper class enough . . . but if they behave nicely it may be overlooked.

It's easy to know all this kind of gossip and speculation about Charles and Diana. In fact in the London of the last month, it would be difficult not to know it. There is a determination to celebrate and indulge and even wallow in it all. People want to read the same old stories over and over – how he proposed, what she said, what he thought, what they said then. . . . They are like children wanting to hear the same fairytales over and over. And the best bit of the fairytale is today, which is why hundreds of thousands of men, women and children have been up all night to share in it, to be a part of a world where princes are strong and kind and princesses are young and beautiful and virtuous and if you position yourself rightly you might get a wave or a smile from them.

Encounters at the Airport

7 November 1981

At the shop in London Airport, there was a young man studying the display of postcards. Then he went to a section which had simply big words on the front like THANK YOU and I LOVE YOU. His eyes went up and down the shelves until he found what he wanted, and he bought 12 of the one that said 'SORRY'.

He was tall and fair-haired and blameless looking. I haven't had a wink of sleep wondering what he did. Two women on the plane were discussing a friend they had seen in London who had got amazingly slim.

'Unnaturally slim, I'd call it,' said the one with the velvet beret.

'You wouldn't even call it slim, it's downright thin,' said the fur hat.

'Fashionably thin is one thing, but this is verging on the bony,' said the Beret.

'Yes, the face is getting kind of gaunt,' said the Hat.

At that point the air hostess passed with the coffees.

'Two vodka and tonics, please,' said the Beret.

The air hostess broke the news that ordinary people aren't allowed to buy drink on planes any more; you have to call yourself Executive and pay a fortune and sit in the front, and they'll pour drink on you free. The Hat and the Beret received this news glumly, as indeed have we all in our time. But they thought back to their slim friend.

'Probably just as well,' said the Hat.

'Maybe it was meant as an omen,' said the Beret.

As we waited for the luggage to come out, my mind was a red blur of relief that we had landed and filled with resolutions never to go up there into those skies again. Dublin Airport is grand about luggage trolleys these days; there were dozens of them where you could see them, unlike a lot of places where they hide them behind huge cardboard walls. A woman and daughter who were having a hard time relating to each other were leaning on a trolley.

'There, now, the bank's open in the airport on a Sunday. Wouldn't that be a handy thing to know?'

'Why would it be handy?' asked the girl.

'If you wanted to cash a cheque, you could come out here.'

'God,' said the girl, 'twenty-four miles to cash a cheque, God.'

Mothers are slow to take offence at tones and dismissiveness. This woman chattered on about how the cases would soon be out and then they'd be on their way, and how grand it was to be home and how great it had been to be away. The girl grunted and eyed the crowd in a hopeless quest for an Airport Encounter with a young man who would whisk her away to less tedious chat.

'When all's said and done, I think it's best to fly by plane.' The mother looked pleased that she had come to this decision.

'Aw, God,' said the girl, 'what else would we fly by but a plane? Seagull?'

Out in the place where people wait to meet the Arriving Passengers, a family was peering nervously as there seemed to be no sign of their son.

'Is there anyone else left?' his mother asked me.

'There are a few people fighting with the Customs men,' I said with my terrific sense of humour, which was like a lead balloon.

The family went ashen at the thought of it.

'I meant talking to Customs men,' I said humbly.

That still didn't please them; what could he be talking to the Customs men for?

'Perhaps he bought presents,' said the father.

The mother's face registered a belief that he had been carrying a potato sack full of cocaine. 'Please God he's not in any trouble,' she said.

I went around and hid behind a pillar so that I could see what happened. In a minute he came out, and the family nearly fainted communally with relief.

'What did they want, what were they looking for?' demanded the father.

'Did they find anything?' begged the mother.

The unfortunate boy had been to the lavatory, had made a phone call, and his case had come off last anyway. He had walked innocently past the Customs men, he had nothing only one bottle of gin as a present anyway. What was all the fuss? What, indeed? I tiptoed away.

At the phones, which look like Space Age things with us all clustered around what seemed like a big squat tree with telephones growing on it, there was a man flushed and triumphant. 'I don't know what the country's coming to,' he said happily. 'I've got on to Wexford in no time, no crossed lines, nobody bit the nose off me. Maybe it's the end of the world.'

Up in the Clouds with Charlie Haughey
4 February 1982

Charlie Haughey got up at seven-thirty a.m. yesterday morning and had a cup of tea. Later on he had another cup of tea and a third. That's his breakfast, not only during the campaign but always. 'I don't bother with breakfast,' he says fastidiously, as if those who do are somehow gross.

By eight o'clock he was washed and dressed and ready for the economic advisers who were going to prepare him for the morning's press conference. He emerged ready for anything. He likes to look presentable, he says, he knows that people often judge by appearances, and he doesn't find it a waste of time to have to keep himself looking Milan.

He thinks that if you are in the public eye you owe it to people to look well. He often remembers Seán Lemass telling them all in the old days that people are entitled to seeing you looking your best. 'Seán Lemass's great phrase was "who did your haircut?",' not just to Charlie but to all of them.

Charlie's own hair is very silvery and well groomed these days. If he hadn't taken his father-in-law's advice literally he has certainly taken the spirit of it. Did he give it a lot of attention?

'Well, Maureen Foley of Clontarf has always kept it in order for me. She's made me look respectable for the past while, and then for the debate my son Ciaran's girlfriend did it. She's qualified as a hairdresser so she had a go for that night.'

Was he pleased with the debate?

'Very. It's hard to know,' he says, 'how much the general public will be swayed by two men talking to each other,' but he thinks it was civilised and that they covered a fair amount of ground.

He had no complaints about Brian Farrell. He was a very professional chairman and he didn't favour either one of them. Was it nerve-racking? It was undoubtedly stress-creating. He had cleared the previous day to have a proper rest and time on his own or with just a few advisers to clear his mind and to marshal his thoughts. Did he sleep at all during the day waiting for the debate? Not really, a couple of snoozes but not going to bed and drawing the covers over him and going in to a deep sleep. Nothing as deliberate as that.

After the debate he had come home and there had been a crowd in and yes indeed they had talked about it. No they had not played it over on the video; they remembered the bits they wanted to talk about. Were people over-flattering to him, did he think, in fear of inferring his wrath? He smiled beatifically. Wrath? He seemed not to have heard of such a possibility. But seriously he said he did hear the bad as well as the good and his family in particular were all very frank with him.

There'll be no fear that he would live in an ivory tower out in Kinsealy. He had a busy day yesterday, not too much time to sit and brood over what the papers said about the confrontation. He is sunnier about the papers this time round. He thinks they have managed to dilute some of the more extravagant plunges at the jugular. He has always felt and still believes that there is a kind of media fog about things like elections, where everyone in papers and on the radio believes their own preferences.

Just look how wrong they all were about the divorce referendum, to take just one example. But he agreed that he's getting an easier passage this time. People are not hostile. 'Perhaps they've just got used to me,' he said. 'I've been around so long now they know I don't eat babies.'

Or indeed much else. Charlie Haughey wasn't planning on having any lunch. He doesn't bother with lunch on the campaign, he says, in the same way that he dismisses breakfast. But it's because he's never anxious to break the momentum.

It's a delay, a diversion, a bit of a waste of time to have to go and sit down for lunch somewhere. A cup of tea out of his hand would be enough for him. A sandwich if he was pushed. We drove from Kinsealy into the Berkeley Court Hotel in Ballsbridge, his mind now clear about what he would say at the press conference to launch the plan for an international financial services centre in Dublin.

At the hotel handlers and television teams and people in good suits who had all had their hair cut stood around. The lights, the thumping music played low but insistently, the television screens and the paraphernalia of a press conference were all underway. After eleven he would go to the helicopter pad in Vincent's Hospital and fly to Limerick, and then to Listowel. No, nobody was in trouble, just trying to get around and see everyone, that's all.

There didn't have to be a reason to go to places, a base party reason. Take today, for example. He'd be up in Killybegs this morning to launch their fisheries policy document and there was no question of looking for extra seats up there. No, it was quite possible to go to places for real reasons. Charlie Haughey had planned to be back in his home while it was still daylight and he would spend the rest of the evening in his own constituency.

He loves walking around the constituency with people saying hello to him, and telling him about the real issues of the election, about wanting a bit of hope and about how Charlie would give it to them. He thinks about that when he wakes up and that makes it easy to get up in the mornings.

Election Brings Life to an Ageing Society

3 June 1983

For many old people, the huge rosettes and the bright young people coming to rap on their doors is a welcome chance to meet people. They haven't had people taking such an interest in them since the last election when the circus came around as well. The arguments about youth unemployment are almost meaningless on some streets where teenagers don't play and babies don't cry to each other from prams. In many parts of Britain, an ageing society, almost everyone on the electoral roll is on the pension as well.

They ask about the cost of living and the Tories tell them that four years ago inflation raged at 18 per cent, but now thanks to careful management it is down to 4.5 per cent. This simply is the best guarantee that they can afford to live. If they say, well it's still difficult to live, the answer is, imagine what it would have been like if inflation had been allowed to continue.

The Labour candidate will tell them that fuel costs have been forced up behind their backs and that Labour will cut these. Labour will freeze council and all rents for at least a year. Labour will insulate their houses.

The Alliance says one of the great wrongs pensioners suffer from is that they have to pay fixed charges for gas, electricity and telephone. All these fixed charges would go under an Alliance government.

Old people ask the candidates too about reducing the retirement age. In Britain, men retire at 65 and women at 60, and there has been increasing interest in a younger retirement age for men both from management and workers. So if a household asks the canvassers what the policies on retirement are, they will get these answers:

The Conservatives say that to reduce the retirement age would cost £2,500 million and is hard to promise. The Tories also say that they are against compulsory retirement at any age.

Labour says that its aim is a common retirement age of 60, and that if returned it will endeavour to get this organised, but it will first raise the pensions before it does anything else.

The Alliance has no very strong views, but says that it should all be more flexible.

A matter which worries many pensioners is the earnings rule. This means that if you earn any more than £57 a week and are in receipt of the pension, that pension will be reduced in line with your earnings. Many older people who feel capable of working on for several years after official retirement age resent this rule greatly.

The Conservatives say that it was their party which raised the earnings rule to £57 from a lower figure and they hope to take the top level away altogether eventually. Labour says that it doesn't intend to do anything about it at once since it's a matter that only affects a small number of the country's pensioners anyhow. The Alliance is in agreement with the Conservatives on this matter.

So far, no specific campaign has been spearheaded towards the elderly. The granny vote has not been isolated as an area of winning support. It is presumed that the elderly in society will follow very much the general view on matters to do with defence and the economy, and will share the opinions left or right on a normal statistical basis. But there are some matters, like the cost of living, law and order, and housing, where you would imagine that more specific attempts might have been made to woo this considerable section of the electorate. There's nothing to stop you being a floating voter at any age. Pensioners do not always vote according to the habits of a lifetime.

Maeve's Operation: The Whole Story

8 October 1983

First I'm afraid you have to have a little of the background. Since July, I haven't been able to straighten my right leg. This is of no consequence when you're sitting down or lying down which I seem to do a lot of, but in the odd bits where you have to walk from one place to another it is very harassing. Not to put it too finely, it means you can't walk.

I have arthritis in the other leg and so I thought gloomily that it must be spreading, like a rumour, or like one of those nice Russian vines that cover a wall in no time. But this knee took on terrible proportions, and by the time I found it easier for people to pour my gin and tonic into a saucer and let me at it on all fours like a big kitten I considered the wonderful Art of Medicine and went to a doctor who was very nice and said it seemed unmerciful to her and she sent me to a specialist.

I can't tell you all these people's names because it would be advertising, but suffice to say the country is filled with kind, sympathetic GPs and serious, efficient orthopaedic surgeons.

We had a merry month in August which involved great things like heat treatment which were really nice and didn't work and cortisone injections in the knee which were desperate and didn't work. 'Will these make my neck swell up?' I asked anxiously. I'm chubby enough already without gaining a lot of innocent fat from a knee treatment. It wouldn't, I was told. Then because we were all getting puzzled and I was like Quasimodo on two sticks now and I was wondering would I have to be fitted with a collar on my neck and led around . . . I went for an arthrogram.

Now I know I'm a long time coming to the hospital bit but

honestly if you've never had an arthrogram you'd need to know about them. They call them X-rays. And you go like a simpleton to the X-ray department of a hospital to have one. I thought it was a great name for a start: arthrogram, like something out of *Minder* or a telegram from Guinnesses.

By this time the scene had shifted back to London but I feel sure that the beauty and joy of an arthrogram is pretty much the same no matter what part of the world you're in. First it was in an operating theatre, second it took nearly two hours, third it involved a series of injections of dyes to point up little-known facets of the knee and lastly it had something straight from a James Bond film: they blow your knee up with gas like a balloon and X-ray it in its expanded state. I was nearly demented at this stage and trying to make conversation with people who seemed to be surrounding the operating table in increasing numbers. I saw a pile of papier-mâché hats and wondered did those who have to be exposed to radiation a lot wear hats as well.

'Do you often wear those hats?' I asked a tiny girl from Trinidad.

'They're sick bowls,' she said.

'Are you very uncomfortable?' the polite English radiologist asked kindly.

It was a ludicrous question. I tried to single out the most agonising thing about it all. 'There's some awful bit of machinery underneath my knee sticking into it,' I said, thinking it was probably a wrench or a hammer that someone had left there by mistake.

'That's my hand,' said the radiologist.

Ashen, I came out of it all and carried the pictures around my neck on a string until I got home. Remember I was now walking on two sticks and it's not easy to carry things and the arthrogram was not something I would repeat just because I lost the snaps. The snaps and myself flew back to Dublin and the serious but brilliant orthopaedic surgeon looked at them.

'Nothing,' he said after five minutes.

'Was there no film in the camera?' I said, tears in my eyes, ready to go back and bludgeon them all to death in that hospital with their own sick bowls.

'No, perfect pictures, just reveal nothing at all,' he said.

I waited for it . . . my poor big heart thumping, I waited and he said it.

'We'd better open you up.'

When the world settled down from the thunderous roar of terror that filled my ears, I heard myself saying in a high-pitched voice of total panic, 'Well, if that's it, then I suppose that's it. Let me look at my diary.'

I couldn't even see my diary. I just agreed like a big lamb to what he said, and a date was fixed. And I went to Admissions and an admission date was organised and then there was no getting out of it. I looked at the knee very dismally. What could it be, I asked myself in lay person's terms. Maybe my leg had just gone crooked to punish me for all my loudness and showing off. I was going to suggest this to the surgeon, but brilliant and serious he was, a person able to cope with an impish, ageing sense of humour he was not, so I said nothing.

I packed five books and a typewriter and 144 sheets of paper, and a manual on how to take up calligraphy and several tomes about evergreens so that I'd be an expert on them when I came out. I remembered to take some nightdresses and a wash bag too, but only at the last moment so I had to carry them in a plastic bag.

I put on my ingratiating face when I met the nurses on Floor Three of St Vincent's Private Hospital. 'I'll be a model patient,' I said. 'I'll be no trouble.'

Two of them remembered me from the gall bladder incident over a decade ago. 'She'll be a monster,' they said.

'I've got much calmer and older and more fearful since then,' I said.

They were possibly the kindest bunch of women I ever met in my life anywhere, and I'm not only saying that because one day I suppose I'll have to go back to them, to get a new hip, but they were kind. There wasn't one of them I could find fault with and let me tell you after a day or two I was ready to find fault with anything that moved. But not the nurses ever. Night and day cheerful and reassuring and they didn't even laugh at the typewriter and the books that just sat there untouched for two and a half weeks. They know we like to come to hospital with our illusions. I suppose there's a name for the operation. I didn't ask. I was so weakened by the memory of the arthrogram. I wanted no more definitions; anyway, a kind, efficient and nameless anaesthetist came the night before to tell me about it, and I closed my ears so that I wouldn't hear a single word while maintaining what I hoped was a look of alert interest on my face.

'Is there anything you'd like to ask?' he said politely.

'Might I die of a heart attack without your noticing what with being a bit on the plump side?' I asked.

'No,' he said.

They'd notice and stop me dying of a heart attack. They had a machine that told them that sort of thing. I lay in the dark and thought about people who have much worse things and wondered how they could bear them and I thought of all the bravery in the world. And big, sad tears came down my face. The night nurse who can hear silent tears at a hundred yards came in.

'I know you won't believe me. I was caring about other people,' I said.

'I know you were, aren't you a grand, kind thing,' she said.

And I told her that I now understood immediately why men married their nurses and if things had been different I would propose to her there and then, and we both said wasn't it great that I only had a silly old knee and not something awful and I went to sleep while she was talking to me.

They gave you three Valium next day to space you out and so of course I didn't know where I was but I was very, very happy. Unfortunately what often happens is that the schedule takes longer than they think. Some operation they think is simple turns out to be long and complicated then the lovely floaty Valium wears off and you know only too well where you are. And you can't keep asking to be topped up because that would be bad for you to tank you out of your mind.

So I remember the journey on the trolley passing ordinary people doing ordinary things. They had washed, or scrubbed I think it's called, my right knee so much I thought it wasn't going to survive it.

'I must admit I don't normally wash my knees that much,' I said humbly in case my own native filth was responsible for all the pain and we could now call the whole thing off, and put the pain in my leg down to common dirt.

They explained that they didn't either but this was to make it nice and sterile. Then they put gauze on it and a sort of red flag. I didn't like the red flag.

'Is that so he'll know which one to do?' I said in mounting panic, every story about people amputating the wrong limbs coming back to me in a line.

No, apparently, it was to keep it warm and sterile, they said. I wonder, but anyway it's not something you'd fault them on. And then to be honest I really don't remember much more. I have to rely on other people for what went on.

They say I asked the serious surgeon how old he was, which I might well have because it was something I had been speculating about. And he had said, 'guess' and I had guessed right, which had pleased the semi-conscious me enormously and horrified the acolytes who wouldn't have dreamed of asking a consultant surgeon anything at all. And apparently I had forgotten all about my knee and wouldn't listen when they tried to tell me what was wrong with it. Instead of listening I paid flowery compliments to everyone I met. 'How very courteous of you to come in and see me,' I said to one greatly loved sister who had been sitting there like a lamb waiting till I woke up. I used to say this to her graciously each time I woke up. She must have loved her vigil. When my other greatly loved sister came in I said it was extraordinarily courteous of her to have taken so much time off work even though this was the middle of the night and she'd had to fly home early from a conference in order to receive this level of conversation.

I had refused to allow my husband to come anywhere near me for the whole business, because he had a big broadcasting job in London that day and I couldn't have borne to think of him sitting in the corridor not understanding nuns and holy pictures and maybe thinking that I'd snuffed it. But I made an ill-timed attempt to ring him. He had been on the phone many times and quite unlike myself now knew what was wrong with me.

'Isn't it great?' he said.

'Isn't it great?' I said, miffed. My voice sounded as if I had drunk an entire bottle of some spirituous liquor ten minutes previously.

'But isn't it great what they found?' he said, happily determined not to be put off by this sporting drunk ready to fight with her shadow.

'I don't think they found anything,' I slurred. 'I forgot to ask.'

'You were full of Foreign Bodies. They got them all out,' he said happily.

'I think Gordon is very drunk,' I said, and hung up. Fortunately the angelic sisters got him back on the line and then I agreed to look at a jar full of ridiculous things, bits of bone, bits of cartilage, like the kind of jar a child might take home from a day on the beach.

'They were never in my knee,' I said. And then I looked at them with pride. Not everyone goes round carrying that kind of stuff in a knee; it reminded me of space debris. I was delighted with it, and then to be honest all was semi-oblivion for a couple of days.

I had no visitors only family and nurses so I felt safe in saying I love you to everyone who approached my bed. The paper lady was surprised but tolerant. And then came the dull bit, the bit where you think you're well but you keel over if you get out of bed, where you ache for visitors but after five minutes the room is spinning and you want to go to sleep. And in the end the only thing you yearn for is television.

And you won't believe this but just as I was sitting up and saying I'm going to have a whole night of telly and I won't look at one documentary or one serious analysis, I'll look at rubbish until they come and tuck me up, the entire television reception disappeared from the place. I joke you not – Thursday, Friday, Saturday, Sunday, Monday, we lay like mad bats in our beds, no Gaybo, no *Gone with the Wind*, no *Three Days of the Condor* that I once queued for an hour and a half in Fulham to see. I was purple with rage. Oh there were explanations, none of them made any sense to invalids. I wondered would I get a rebellion going and get us all to march on our crutches up to Phoenix Relays or to sister somebody and beat them all about the heads. You have no idea how awful it is lying there when you think you're going to have *Remington Steele* and instead you have your own thoughts. A fearsome fury descended on me and I staggered out of bed and tried to push the television out into the corridor. A nun tried to restrain me. She had been explaining yet again why the hospital had been five days without television. I wouldn't listen.

'Excuse me,' I said, filled with this new excessive politeness which seems to have been injected with the anaesthetic. 'I am moving this out to the corridor; if I do not have a room with a television, why do we keep up the pretence that I have?'

They told me people would fall over it in the corridor so instead I hung my dressing gown over it and went to sleep in a monstrous sulk.

I started to walk round the room. My leg was nearly straight. I had a frightening series of encounters with what calls itself the physiotherapy department but is actually a troupe of circus trapeze artists and acrobats who got stranded in Vincent's. They think you can lift your heel while you keep the back of your knee flat on the bed or the ground. Try it. No one can do it. They can do it of course because they are all the Flying Firenzes or something in real life and are just doing physio as a power trip. They also were one nicer than the other . . . and in the days when I was like a weasel with no television and no concentration, I couldn't even finish the *Evening Herald* . . . I couldn't find a fault with a physio. And then they said I could go.

I had heard awful stories that the bill was pinned by a dagger to your chest when you woke up from the operation but this was not so. It wasn't mentioned until the last day and delivered discreetly. And the nurses of the Third Floor all came and said goodbye and lyingly told Gordon that I had been as good as gold, which he didn't believe for two seconds, and in an odd way I knew I'd miss them, and I hoped whoever would be sleeping in my room that night would get well and strong like I did. And I cried to think of the people who hadn't been as lucky as I was with just Foreign Bodies.

Then I cheered up again and was the life and soul of the car until I saw Dalkey, when I started to bawl again, and most people there must think I have a wretchedly unhappy home life.

And then I came back to London which is where I am meant to be living though as people often say to me you'd never know it. And I asked Aer Lingus would they mind me having a wheelchair because that's a long haul on a weak leg uphill when you get off the lurching bus. They said there was no problem, and honestly, not that I'd wish a day's illness or incapacity on anyone, a wheelchair is your only man at an airport.

First a car into the gate, not a lurching bus, and then a great fellow called Joe who was from Limerick and off we went. Joe said that he'd have to take a bit of a run at the ramp if I didn't mind. Mind? I adored it. Imagine racing up past executives and eager, earnest walkers. I was crazed with power. I waved like the Queen Mother at everyone I knew and everyone I didn't, the latter being much the larger percentage. In fact I would have happily done a tour of all the terminals but the luggage arrived and Joe wheeled me to a taxi and Gordon packed in all the unread books and the typewriter and the tomes of evergreens and *The Art of Calligraphy* and soon we were home.

You know when you listen to hospital requests the way all the messages seem to be a bit samey, the thanks is so fulsome and it's always said in exactly the same words. Now I know why. There are no other words to express the relief and gratitude and amazement at the skill and kindness of people who were total strangers a couple of weeks ago, people who will hold your hand in the night and wash the back of your neck and root around for hours in a big silly knee full of Foreign Bodies. I hope they get satisfaction in their work. I really do. Because they give it. In spades.

Keeping Cruise off the Roads Is New Priority

16 November 1983

'They would have been more interested in the arrival of the New Beaujolais than the cruise missiles if it hadn't been for us,' said Laura, who has been at Greenham Common for 13 months. She spoke with tears of frustration in her eyes. The peace women have been outsmarted by the US Starlifters, which touched down while the protesters were either asleep or at the other side of the airfield.

The first missiles had arrived just before nine a.m. on Monday when the women were leaving their little tents to organise breakfast. Yesterday had been widely rumoured as Arrival Day and the women had been planning a serious rehearsal of what form their protest would take. So it was with disbelief and horror that they realised about noon that the long crates which had been slid out of the back of the Starlifter had been taken under heavy guard straight to the nuclear shelters. In fact, Cruise had arrived while they slept.

Trying desperately to rally, the women insisted that the missiles might be in the base but they would never come out. Greenham is intended to be only a storage depot for cruise missiles and they could not be fired from there, claim the women. The plans to settle the missiles in various other parts of the British countryside will now be the main focus of their attention.

'We could never have stopped planes and helicopters,' said Lynn Jones, a long-time resident. 'But we are not going to let them travel down our roads.'

Their candlelit vigil on Monday night was joined by many more supporters and when yesterday dawned cold and wet, the women were ready but on the wrong side of the airfield. This time the Galaxy aircraft and another Starlifter flew in accompanied by US military helicopters and guarded by British Army forces on the ground. Objects covered in tarpaulin and believed to be the actual warheads for the missiles were unloaded swiftly. Suddenly the singing and protesting women hundreds of yards away realised what was happening and ran for that corner of the fence, but too late to see the actual unloading of the weapons for which they have been waiting for over two years.

Two of the women who have been at Greenham since the beginning were sobbing openly. The two long winters, the lost springs and summers seemed to be in vain. They stood looking emptily from afar at the now unloaded planes. Their misery was like a long howl in the November afternoon.

But others reassured them and gradually got their spirits up again. So the missiles were in, but how could they get out? How could they get to their destinations if there was a massive campaign of civil disobedience? Suppose you had thousands of private cars blocking the cruise convoys? Suppose you had hundreds of pedestrians on the zebra crossings? Suppose even that you dug up the roads? It might be a crime of sorts digging up the roads with pneumatic drills, but it wasn't killing people or blowing them to Kingdom Come.

Arms linked, tears dried, they rallied. They told the press that they were still winning because they had brought the matter to the front of people's minds, and kept it there. The polls showed many more people objecting to the missiles now than there were in June during the election campaign. Even those who were for the missiles were jumpy about who had authority to fire them.

'Ronald Reagan played into our hands by being such a silly twit about Grenada,' said one tired, debby-looking girl, trying to wrest some good news from the crumbling day.

They barred the main gate again and lay down in front of it and cheered as young policemen first cautioned and then arrested over 120 of them. They don't mind appearing in court over and over just so long as they keep it all at the front of people's minds.

'At least they didn't come quietly,' said the peace women proudly as they settled down to guard the few possessions of their colleagues, who had gone off in the dark under arrest but also under the camera lights of television crews from all over the world.

Develop Your Own Style

30 November 1983

The only useful advice I ever got about writing was to write as you talk. I talk a bit too quickly and certainly too much, so that's the way I write as well. I don't know how it works for silent, thoughtful people who only speak when they have something to say. I imagine it should work rather well. Whatever they write would be worth reading. This is not artistic or literary advice, it is practical and down-to-earth . . . and if you are having difficulty beginning something . . . an article, a short story, a novel or a play . . . ask yourself, 'What am I trying to say?' Then say it aloud and nine times out of 10 you'll have your first sentence. And once your first sentence is written down in front of you it's much, much easier to do the next one, and so on.

Unfortunately at school when we learn English we have to take on board a great number of words, expressions and forms of speech which are not used in everyday communication. This is necessary,

I think, in order to fill up the gaps in vocabulary. It would be ridiculous to leave school with whole sections of the English language unknown to us just in order to clear the mind for easy communication. The language is rich so it's important to know the huge range of words and their shades of meaning. But, and it's a very large but, the trouble is that just because we do have to learn so many complicated and elaborate words we are inclined to overuse them. Not in speech, mind you, unless you happen to be a very pompous and mannered talker, but certainly in writing.

Time and again, I read short stories from young people – and oddly girls are the worst offenders – which are so choked up with words and phrases which they would never in a million years use in conversation that it makes the story itself unreadable.

An example: 'Untimely fingers of frost in what should have been the season of mists and mellow fruitfulness nipped Ann O'Leary as with furrowed mien she proceeded from the domestic portals and directed her steps to the main thoroughfare.'

She was trying to say, 'It was a cold autumn day when a worried-looking Ann O'Leary left her house. . . .' or something like that.

Now I don't know why we should think that the more disguises and padding we put on a thought the more respectable it becomes. It must be a throw-back to the days when we crammed as many words and allusions into a school essay in order to let the English teacher know that we were at least aware of them. Fine if that's what you're about, letting an examiner know that you absorbed a barrel full of vocabulary. But if you are trying to tell a story simply . . . or get an idea or a picture out of your mind and into someone else's, then it needs to be a lot more simple, a lot less cluttered. In fact a lot more like the way you speak.

Last year in Waterford I was making this point and a girl in one of the groups asked me a question which I couldn't answer. She said that if she was really to write as she spoke, it would be full of schoolgirl slang and local idiom and phrases that were currently fashionable but might be out of favour soon. Is that the way she should write, she wanted to know, because that was the way she talked? I've thought about it a lot since. She was right of course, her own school-speak was probably as unsuitable for getting her thoughts across to people outside her immediate circle as would be the awful essay-style crowded prose and jargon. Yet it would have more truth in it, and more honest attempt to say something simply. And as she grew to be aware what was in fact just the artificial group-talk that we all use at different times of our lives . . . she could discard it in favour of a direct and uncluttered style.

It's not easy to do at once, not if you have been used to writing as a vehicle for other people's thoughts and expressions. But once you start it becomes easier and easier and you will wonder how you could ever have begun a tale with some showy sentence full of words and hiding what you meant to say. It's a bit easier also to hide the real you, and what you feel if you use the disguise of other people's language. It's somehow safer to say 'within the hallowed walls of this esteemed place of learning' instead of saying 'here at school' because the first one has a kind of sardonic ring to it . . . the second is more naked.

You could begin with a diary. Just telling it like it is. No high-sounding phrases, no wishing to impress, because in a diary you are writing to yourself. You could say what it's like now in the winter of '83, what you feel, what you think about. Nobody will read it but you. But when you've done a page or two go back over it with a red pen and hunt ruthlessly for phrases and words that are not your own, for things that would be foolish and fussy if said aloud.

I think that's the best way to approach creative writing. To realise that it is creative, and you are the one creating it. Don't be content with other people's words, use your own. Don't worry about style, if you speak like yourself for long enough the style will be there. It will be *your* style. You will be writing like yourself. You will have found your own voice.

One Eye on Bargains, One Eye on Alsatians

9 January 1984

A cold, bright morning, and a small crowd stands outside Harrods studying the free store map which the management wisely distributes at sales.

This saves endless hours of questioning, and helps the bargain hunters to work out a flight path from the main door to Fine China in the centre of the second floor, where a Wedgwood dinner service is reduced from £1,226 to £613.

Others were planning a quick gallop up the escalators to the Fur Rooms on the first floor, over on the corner where Brompton Road joins Hans Crescent – one floor above the spot where a bomb killed six people and wounded 90 last month.

There is nothing to show what happened here in December. No wreath, no flowers, no message scrawled in hurt or rage on any wall. Not even the broken windows. The whole menswear department has been fully repaired and was trading normally during the sale.

But there are no cars parked now in the side roads, and even a private car dropping somebody off at the door has barely time for the passenger to get out before it is waved on.

And all around stand policemen and policewomen, either

speaking softly into the little radios which they wear fixed to their lapels, or just looking on with watchful eyes and a hand lightly laid on the collar of equally vigilant Alsatian dogs.

Lots of other men seem to be on the lookout too. These are plain-clothes Special Branch officers and members of the Anti-Terrorist Squad. They say that some of the people inside the store who might look like assistant manager or floor supervisor are in fact Special Branch as well.

The sale began officially on Friday morning, with the usual overnight campers pitching their tents early on Thursday evening. Some are paid to go and queue for bargains. One boy was paid £100, to get a television and video set which had been reduced from £1,000 to £500. He said that the fellow who paid him would still be able to sell the goods at a profit after that, so it was worth it to everyone. Including Harrods, presumably, who have the reputation of offering really gigantic bargains.

The store's managing director and chairman, Mr Aleck Craddock, said that the people who normally shopped in Harrods had no intention of staying away because of the bomb. In fact, he thought it had made them more determined than ever to come and buy. He announced that since the bombs, trading had not decreased at all, in fact it was 14 per cent up on the same period last year.

On the same factual note, Mr Craddock continued to express his belief that the store would be able to announce record takings of £25 million over the three-week sales period. More than 250,000 people attended the opening day. But not everyone is able to show such a calm and unruffled front.

Some of the 5,000-plus staff are very unhappy and distressed and don't mind admitting it. A woman in the china department said that on Friday there had been a great deal of noise and crashing about while people literally struggled over bargains, breaking crockery and china. She said her nerves got very bad and she had to sit down for a long time. She kept thinking that the bombers had come back to finish them off.

A young woman told me that if I went past the Staff Only door, I would see that the corridors were lined with messages of sympathy to the staff from the public – people had written from everywhere to say how terrible it was. A lot of people had wanted to send sympathy to the families of those people who had been killed or injured, but they didn't know where to write so they just wrote to Harrods. There were some letters from Ireland also, people writing to say that the Irish were upset too.

Some of the staff thought that these should be put up on a wall where the public could see them and realise the support that people gave the store, but the powers that be said no, that would be a bad idea. It would keep reminding people of the terrible thing that had happened, and really, it was best for people to forget and get on with living.

The crowds on Saturday morning seemed less than usual for the first Saturday of the sale, which is after all the first day that ordinary people who work Monday to Friday can get to it. There wasn't the stampede and throng that has been known and some of the staff were relieved to be able to breathe a little more easily than they expected. The tight security was adding to what was the normal tension of the country's biggest sale. But the big, silent police presence was obviously a great comfort to the shoppers, some of whom approached a little uneasily, one eye on the bargains and one eye on the big Alsatian dogs straining at their leads.

A Tipperary Robin Hood

7 December 1985

Twelve Christmases ago, when I had just come to live in Hammersmith, I was shocked at a notice which went in everyone's door telling them to look out for signs of old people who might be dead in bedsitters upstairs. They gave handy hints such as not having heard them move around, or milk bottles piling up outside the door. Then you were to say to yourself: aha, there must be a dead person in there. The notion that in bedsitter-land you wouldn't know who lived in the same house, or how frail they might be, was very hard to accept.

I think things have got much better. Social workers, who have got such a bad time over the deaths of children released from care back to families who were violent, also have the care of the elderly and it's not always easy.

There's a very cheerful social worker who has her hands full with the area round where I live. I'm not sure what her title or job strictly is, because they call her the Welfare, the Town Hall, the woman from the madhouse, Old Nosey Parker, the Labour, the Social Services, the Warder, the Warden and the Minder.

They are half-afraid of her in case she will change their lives in some unacceptable way, like giving them a Home Help or putting them into sheltered accommodation. They are half-afraid that she isn't doing enough for them and that there might be free coal or another £2 a week if they play their cards right.

She is a marvellous woman, from Tipperary, and she is probably a saint. In her car she always has a dozen hand-knitted shawls. She gets the people in a local home to knit them; she pretends she has knitted them herself, so the old women with thin, shivering shoulders will take them because they think they're a genuine gift. She tells me she has hours of paperwork getting the money for the bloody wool and knitting needles, and she has to disguise it very deeply because they won't pass anything irregular or allow any hint of charity to come from public funds.

She has boxes of packet soup – she says she thinks she's turning into an oxtail by now, she has so much of it. She tells them it was a free sample and why don't they try it; she gets in, puts on the kettle and they all sip a mug of it and nod and say possibly, but she knows they will never stir themselves to buy it, so next week or next visit she will have another so-called free offer.

She picks up a lot of odd newspapers, anywhere – in restaurants, bus shelters. Sometimes she just swipes them from her own office. In some of the houses she visits, she thinks they would like a daily paper but it's a bit of an extravagance, so she casually says, 'I've finished with this' and sees it pounced on eagerly. They read out bits about the royals and Joan Collins to her, and she knows it was right to give them a few stories to think about.

She says that isolation is the real killer and that many old people just turn their faces to the wall and die in the winter from no disease, from no hypothermia; just from no will to go on.

Her priority is to keep them warm this winter, to explain that gas and electricity will NOT be cut off, that there are always funds from some public purse to meet a heating bill. It's hard to get that into the heads of people who have been brought up thrifty and in fear of authority which will punish them if they use two bars of the fire.

She thinks that the social services in England are basically very good and mean well; they have to cope with great cuts in funding, and every year there seems to be more to do and less resources to do it with. It's no use trying to explain this to Thatcher's government, it doesn't listen. Not to reasoned appeals, not to strikes, not to emotional demonstration.

She thinks it's better to get on with it; you keep more people warm by wrapping them up in shawls and giving them soup than you do by signing petitions and marching to Westminster. A lot of her colleagues disagree. They say she comes from a background where charity was acceptable, where people EXPECTED the Little Sisters, the Vincent de Paul and a dozen others to help. In the Welfare State, people don't have that system. They pay taxes all their working lives so that they can be looked after when the time comes.

So more and more she has to disguise her kindness in case it be defined by anyone as charity. She thinks that if she ruled the world she wouldn't give them a pension at all, she would give them free heating, get a certain amount of food delivered to their doors each day with a newspaper.

They should have vouchers for clothes, and there should be a law saying they all had to go out and eat lunch in a centre each day. That way they would meet other people. And all the pet-food manufacturers should be forced to give those tins they advertise totally free to pensioners, so that there would be no question of spending everything on the tortoiseshell cat called Margaret Rose and forgetting to buy any food for the cat's owner.

But then she sighs and says that's only ludicrous, you can't play God. And she's off again with a dozen small umbrellas. She bought them at £1 each from a man, without asking him which lorry they fell off. She will give them here and there, with some tale about having ordered too many in the office and the company refusing to take them back.

She thinks that a lot of the elderly get drenched when they go out and the damp goes into their bones. She'll probably never get the money through for 12 black-economy umbrellas, but it's not a fortune. She shrugs, the Tipperary Robin Hood who is the very acceptable face of the Welfare and the human side of bureaucracy, in a city which fears that its old people will die of cold this winter but hasn't the machinery to prevent it.

Maeve on Margaret Thatcher

19 June 1986

In February 1975, all kinds of women rubbed hands with glee that our girl or indeed any girl had become leader of the Conservative Party. Four years later when she made it to 10 Downing Street there was still an almost tribal pleasure amongst women to think that one of the sex had finally got there.

Now as she sails towards her 61st birthday in the autumn with the firm intention of trying for a third term of office, the gosh-imagine-a-woman-Prime-Minister excitement has worn off.

What has replaced it? Most women think that Margaret Thatcher is a mixed blessing. She has done one great thing, which is to take the giggle out of female political leaders. It is impossible to remember that newsreaders could hardly keep a straight face seven years ago when referring to 'The Prime Minister and her husband'. The very phrase 'Madam Prime Minister' was always said with such heavy inverted commas at that time that nobody believed it could ever be anything except a laboured joke. In the House of Commons the irony with which friend and foe larded their voices when saying 'The Right Honourable Lady' was like very bad stand-up comedy.

Now there is no irony. Madam Prime Minister has gone into the vocabulary with much greater ease than say the word 'chairperson'. In fact, there are some who feel that there had never been anything except a Madam Prime Minister in charge of the country. She has done that, but she is not a woman's folk hero, she is not a role model for her sex. When people praise Thatcher, and many, many do every day, they praise her not at all for anything to do with being a woman. And perhaps that is her greatest achievement. She has almost single-handedly banished the notion that it is somehow unusual or special for a woman to be able to do anything. For that, if for nothing else, women in the future may thank her.

A woman barrister who knew her at Lincoln's Inn in the early fifties says, 'I cannot take her seriously as leader of the country because I remember her so well 30 years ago. She was fearfully impatient, quick yes, and bright but if everyone else doesn't understand every single thing immediately she goes spare. I can't think how she manages the Cabinet meetings. Just to discuss a case with her in the old days had us all in a frazzle. She was very hard-working, and you would never know that she had twin toddlers at home. She always said she had a good nanny and, unlike any other mother, literally never seemed to give the children a thought during the day. Perhaps I'm just being a bit bitchy saying that about her. But it seemed to us then a little unnatural. I'm not just saying it because she's Prime Minister.'

A woman social worker says that Thatcher has a genuine and utterly sincere crusading attitude towards equal rights for women at work and that she will pursue this very vigorously but in exactly the same way and at the same time as she will pursue policies against work shirking which she imagines she sees everywhere and regulations preventing local councils giving support to those they consider needy.

The trouble about Thatcher is that she gives with one hand to women and she takes away with the other. She's fine for the hard-working single-minded woman who wants to be an entrepreneur and who is somehow in some magic way able to get her children satisfactorily looked after all day. She is not so fine for the woman with three children who goes to the post office each week to collect her benefits. That woman is going to find the hospital giving her less under Thatcher and the schools giving less to her children.

If you are a woman like Thatcher yourself, you do well. But times don't move as speedily as she does, and most of the people who are like her are actually men. She is disciplined in a way that most busy people, men and women, would love to be disciplined even if they would abhor the manner and the message. A woman television executive who has seen her on several television programmes speaks of her with something like awe. 'She comes in here, her make-up is perfect, I mean it's not just good make-up, she has had a proper professional television make-up at home or in the office or in the car. I don't know where. Nor do I know how she gets the time. So it means that she doesn't have to spend any time at all being made up here and that gives her a certain importance. All the men are being powdered and toned down and she is sitting there calm as anything pretending to be interested in how we run a television station.

'She may be dying for a drink, but she won't have one, nor a sandwich or anything and we bring out nice ones when she's on. She says, "No, thank you," she doesn't eat between meals, and you know that in her whole life she never has, any more than she ever went to bed with her make-up on.

'She will just smile at you coldly if you praise her and you realise that she has little time for anyone, like 99 per cent of the world, who are human enough to have a Scotch and a sandwich either before or after an important television programme.'

She just doesn't rate people who aren't as strong as she is. A woman publisher who has refused several books on the Thatcher enigma, on the grounds that no one knows yet what it is, says that she thinks the Prime Minister's much-vaunted courage within her own party is a distinct disservice to the cause of women rather than giving women something to crow about.

'Look here, we get a woman Prime Minister, who got in by turning on the guy who gave her all the honours and preferments. Sure I know that's politics, but it's also a characteristic that is often attributed to women, disloyalty, spitefulness.

'Then when she's in, what does she do? It's like the mad queen in *Alice in Wonderland*, Off With Their Heads. Stevas, Ian Gilmour, Jim Prior, Francis Pym, Cecil Parkinson, anyone who looks crooked at her or who has a bit on the side. Now if a man did that, we'd be up in arms and so we should about her too. She's making it harder and harder for any party to elect a woman again, they'll have their worst fears about bossy women confirmed in this administration. She may have the distinct achievement of being the first and the last woman Prime Minister of this country.'

A buyer in one of the big London stores says that Mrs Thatcher must have sat down carefully with a stylist and chosen her clothes with exactly the same care that she chose her War Cabinet. 'There's never anything really smart but there's rarely anything quite terrible either. She's dressing as Mrs Middle England. Do you remember that time during an election broadcast when David Dimbleby got so excited he called her Mrs Finchley and the name stuck, well that's the way she dresses, middle-aged businesswoman from Finchley. Spot on. And you do know that she's got four of every outfit, so that she always looks spanking clean but not too extravagant. She must have 10 of that blue houndstooth suit she wears with the blouse and floppy bow tie neck. I must have seen it on her a hundred times and it always looks as if it comes straight from the dry cleaners which it possibly has. And they did a great job on her hair and make-up as well as her voice. She looked quite mad at her wedding and in the early days. I wish all the 60-year-old women who come in here could get the same kind of right-on-the-button advice as she's got.'

She does not appear to have close women friends, but she has very little time for any friends. And she does seem to get on very well with her husband. She said in a revealing remark that it was great to have one person who would stand by you and understand what you were trying to do, even when nobody else seemed to. That was a touching reference to the much-mocked Denis Thatcher, who is now legendary for his hopes that the wife will give up the job and that they can retire to snifters and golf. But the wife hasn't given any indication of doing anything of the sort. In fact when she was going through a bad patch 15 years ago and had the nickname Milk Snatcher on account of proposals about taking away junior school free milk, her husband advised her to get shut of the lot of it and leave public life. She is said to have told him that she'd see them in hell first, before she would quit. It would be the same now.

A woman who worked with her in the Ministry of Education and always spoke highly of her said that she thought the remark about 'at least one person who will stand by you' was a very sad one indeed. She didn't find it human and showing the tender side of Margaret Thatcher. She thought it showed the hard and empty side. 'Most women have a friend or many friends who will be loyal to them, believe the best and put the most optimistic slant on what you do. It's a sad comment on Margaret, that after all her years and doing what she believes is right, that she only has her husband. She makes no mention of her children. And her children are not close to her and now they realise she was never close to them. It's a frightful object lesson of the loneliness of power-seeking. I hope she doesn't put all women off trying to succeed in any field.'

There's a shop not far from where I live where the daughter of the family is extremely bright and has ambitions to do law. She gets little help from the family, who want her to get behind the counter as quick as she can, marry a bloke who'll bring a few quid into the place and drop these notions about being a barrister. 'We aren't people like that, we're greengrocers,' they tell her, as if this was the last word on the subject.

'But look at Mrs Thatcher,' the girl was unwise enough to say. 'Her father was a grocer in Lincolnshire, and look at her.'

'Yeah, look at her,' they all say, and heads shake and somehow she feels that no real battle has been won for her by the woman Prime Minister.

No Fags, No Food – It's No Fun Being Fergie

21 July 1986

When Sarah Ferguson wakes up this morning in the house of her fiancé's grandmother, she won't just stretch, reach for a cigarette, have a cup of coffee and toast and wonder what to do with her day, like many another horsey Sloane will do. Heavens no!

Sarah was put off the fags long ago when royal nuptials seemed likely and she wasn't allowed to have the normal pound of sweets a day that every reformed smoker needs for three months, because they said she was already a bit pudgy for a princess. Look at Diana, please, and learn. One newspaper set a cameraman on her at Ascot just to count the chocs she ate; then the paper delivered a diatribe against her greed. Another paper sent a spy to Madame Tussaud's to measure the hips of the wax model of Sarah and came up with a guess of 42 inches. No, there will be no breakfast today.

And she won't need to wonder what she will do when she gets up. Her timetable, hour by hour, has been handed out to press people the world over. She will read with everyone else that she has already packed for the honeymoon and that she has taken all the telephone calls that she is going to have time to take from friends wishing her well.

This morning there is yet another rehearsal at Westminster Abbey. So far these have been less than glorious. The adults have all been rooted to the ground with nerves and the children quite wild with excitement. There has been face-pulling and even punch-ups about carrying the train. This morning is the last try. The Archbishop and staff of Westminster Abbey are not the kind of showbiz folk who believe that a disastrous dress rehearsal makes a stunning first night.

Then it's back to Clarence House and a lunch party. Among the guests will be Sarah's mother, who will go into history for having asked innocently where else *could* one meet one's husband except at polo. Considering that she herself met two husbands at polo and that one of them is an Argentine, it might have been wiser to sing very low of the sport. Sarah's stepmother will also be there. The two ladies get on very well in public and all niceties are observed, but the crack is not judged to be mighty.

Then there's a rest of an hour – hardly to ingest lunch, since Sarah Ferguson hasn't been let near a plate of food in weeks, but to calm her down and dress her up for the next outings: a champagne reception at the Guards' Polo Club and dinner at Windsor Castle.

Her future mother-in-law and father-in-law will be at both dos and so will Charles and Diana. Andrew will probably be allowed to have a drink and might even be given something to eat. The public hasn't developed any dangerous anxiety about the width of his waist yet.

The full guest list for both these glittering functions has not been made available yet to the press, but perhaps Sarah Ferguson knows whether the question mark over Nancy Reagan's name has been removed and whether she will have another delight ahead of her . . . earnest conversation with America's first lady.

The timetable suggests that it will be early to bed tonight for the future princess. Which indeed is to be devoutly hoped for. With a glass of nice, warm, fat-free milk, two super-strength Mogadons which would fell an ox, and a very few minutes' last-minute wonderings, could it all possibly be ever worthwhile?

It Was One of Those Custard Heart Days

22 November 1986

'In five weeks' time it will be all over,' said the woman with the neatly zipped tartan shopping bag on wheels. She was full of triumph at having worked it out. 'All over and done with,' she said, in case any of us thought that Christmas might linger on a bit this year and trickle through until February. Her mouth was a thin line of satisfaction at having tamed the prospect of any festivity. She cast a gloom over everyone shopping in the late-night grocery.

It was one of my custard heart days. Sometimes I'm like a weasel with these killjoy people. But maybe she had a sad life. It could be that her husband had died during the year, or that her daughter had got married to someone they didn't like and there had been a row.

Perhaps she had come from a home where they didn't ever celebrate Christmas much, or even something horrible could have happened at Christmas time and every year it came back to her. In one of my rare fits of kindness I smiled and said that it was true that there was a lot of fuss made about Christmas all right.

The Lord punishes the insincere. I didn't mean it at all. I was only saying it to please her. It was the wrong thing to do. I had misread her signs totally.

'Well that's as may be,' she sniffed at me disapprovingly. 'And I'm the first to say live and let live. But I think it's a pity when folk can't have one short season of the year when they spread a little goodwill.' She looked me up and down sadly. 'I daresay that you have your own reasons for hating Christmas and I wouldn't presume to intrude and ask what they are. But perhaps I might say this, if you and the other people who hate Christmas were to think of the innocent little children who enjoy it, and the old people who have parties in the centre, and comedians and personalities giving their time free to dress up as Santa Claus in hospitals, then you might think a bit more warmly about it.'

Well, what would you have done? Tell her that you were lying in the first place, pretend to be converted to her bossy, cliché-ridden view of the world? Go deaf and wander off in the other direction? Abandon the wire shopping basket and run out of the late-night grocery? Wave at a mythical friend? Nod sagely with the all-purpose and meaningless cockney response, 'Well this is it. Isn't it?'

I was rescued. A man with the most bad-tempered face I have ever seen outside a cartoon came pounding in to the late-night grocery. He headed straight for the woman with the unctuous views and the tartan shopper on wheels.

'May I just ask you one question? Just one? Did you come in here for a conversation session with total strangers or was it possibly, as you claimed, for the shopping? I only ask because I have two traffic wardens up my arse outside, I've been round the block twice and we've missed ten minutes of *Sportsnight* already.'

I could see why she wanted a little goodwill in her life: both of them working late, London traffic being like a mediaeval view of hell, crowds, queues, short tempers. I looked at what she had bought as it was being checked out and she packed it neatly into the shopping basket on wheels which was totally unnecessary since she had a husband and car outside the door. She had a lot of cat food, three kinds of cleaning stuff and wire wool and big black plastic bags. She had one lamb chop, two apples and a tube of indigestion tablets. It seemed a poor haul for someone whose mate was missing *Sportsnight*, and I keep hoping that they do have a cat.

❦

I have a friend who works in a bookshop and who is constantly amazed by the things people buy as Christmas presents. Men buy *Cooking for Idiots* and expect to get a tinkle of female laughter when the paper is ripped off it on the day. Women buy *The Duffer's Golf Guide* . . . and expect a similarly delighted response.

My friend, who hasn't the same wish to enter into other people's lives as I do – and has certainly not the time, sitting at a busy till in a large bookshop – says she arranges gift wrapping or personalised red Christmas bags for books without blinking an eye at the lack of wisdom involved in the choice. Until this week.

A nice young man, blond hair falling into his eyes, eager to a fault, hesitant and cursed with that over-apologetic manner which some people wrongly think is politeness, approached her. He wanted to know about this service called Post-A-Book, which means that you pay the shop for the postage, address the envelope, and they'll send it off for you.

The book was addressed to a woman, and he signed a card with what was presumably his own name since he paid with a credit card and it was the same name as on the card. 'Merry Christmas Darling, Love from Harry,' he wrote, and put it in with the book.

The book was called *A Guide to Better Sex* and the subheading said that it was a manual for those who found that the fizz had gone out of sex and who noticed that things were not as they used to be in the first heady days of their relationship.

Even the sight of a queue forming up behind the eager young man didn't stop my friend from making a last-ditch stand.

'It's a bit technical, this book, I believe,' she began.

'Oh yes, so it says,' the young man said happily.

'I wonder, is it a suitable Christmas present? It's more a thing someone might buy for herself or himself, or sort of after a bit of a chat, you know?' She was desperate now.

'No.' He was firm. 'No, I think she'd like it, and I'm sending it early because . . . well, she'll have plenty of time to read it in advance. Before the Christmas holidays, you see. . . .' he said with the open, trusting face of the fool that he was.

The Man Who Set Up Office in the Ladies

13 December 1986

I went into the ladies' cloakroom of a hotel and a man sat peaceably at a sort of dressing table. The place where you are meant to be a woman and sit combing your hair and adjusting your make-up. The man had his briefcase beside him and he was fairly absorbed in some kind of paperwork.

He certainly wasn't doing anyone any harm, and I often think that the distinction is fairly arbitrary anyway in cloakrooms. After all, single-sex facilities are available on the Continent and I've never been in a private house where they made a distinction, except in one place in Australia where they had 'Blokes' and 'Sheilas' written on the doors.

It was a perfectly comfortable place to sit: chair, desk and even a mirror to examine himself in if he had any doubts about self-image. He wasn't taking up too much space, it was easy to sit beside him and adjust your make-up. It was just a small bit unsettling to know what exactly he was doing there.

This was an Irish provincial town, the man must surely have known the ladies who were coming in and out to what was after all their designated area. He had the air of a man who had been there some time. His ashtray had several butts in it. He was a man who had settled in.

There was a box of tissues on the table which he called on occasionally for a nose blow. He seemed quite oblivious of the lavatory flushing and hand washing going on a few yards away from him, admittedly round a corner. This part of the cloakroom was in sort of an alcove. I knew it would be on my mind forever if I didn't find out. He would join the other unsolved mysteries, like the man who wore a hair roller with an otherwise conservative city gent image; like the Christmas card I get every year signed SLUG; like the man who used to come into *The Irish Times* every day to buy yesterday's paper but not today's. He said it was because he didn't actually take it, he wasn't an *Irish Times* reader but people were always mentioning something in it that he wanted to follow up, which was why he bought the previous day's.

My head is too full of these confusing things. 'Damp old day out,' I said to him.

'Is it?' he looked up politely. 'It was all right when I came in, but of course it's very changeable this time of year.'

'Have you been here for a while?' I asked, heading off a lengthy and generalised weather conversation.

'Oh yes, a fair bit, I have to meet someone, but there's no sign of him; still, I suppose it's the traffic, getting out of Dublin is a nightmare these days.'

He was going to meet another male in the ladies' cloakroom of the hotel. This could not be usual practice.

'Why do you decide to meet here?' I asked, with all the subtlety of my trade.

'It's sort of half way between us,' he said agreeably. 'Rather than have either of us drive 100 miles, we both drive 50, harder on him of course because he's got to get out of Dublin, as I said.'

'And do you always choose this place?'

He seemed so . . . helpful. I was sure he'd tell me.

'No, funnily, we usually go to the other hotel, but someone told us that there was more privacy here, you can have a chat without being disturbed. It's the divil to get service though, I'll tell you that. I've been here over an hour and nobody's come to take my order.'

I looked at him fixedly for a few moments. 'They mightn't think you were ordering in here, you know, people don't usually.'

He looked around him mildly. 'Why not, do you think?'

'I think that they'd never imagine anyone in the ladies' cloakroom might want coffee and sandwiches brought in,' I said.

'The what?'

I repeated it.

He stood up like a man who had been shot in the back in a film and was about to stagger all over the set before collapsing. 'I don't believe you,' he said.

I showed him round the corner, where two women were washing their hands, I showed him a line of cubicles and machines on the wall that seemed to prove conclusively where we were. His colour was very bad and I wished, as I always wish, that I had left well alone, and let him sit there all week if necessary rather than bringing on this distress.

'Mother of God,' he croaked. 'Is this where I've been all afternoon?'

'Didn't you notice?' I asked.

'I thought there was a lot of hair combing going on beside me and that women were getting a bit casual about doing up their faces in public. What am I going to do?' He looked utterly wretched.

I told him that since none of these fiercely combing and titivating women had complained about him to the management, it seemed to prove that there was no harm done, and that women were becoming generally more relaxed about things, which had to be good.

He wanted none of my philosophising. He had bundled all his papers into the briefcase and was looking at me as his saviour. 'Would you have a look out to see?' he begged.

'I wouldn't know your friend, why don't you go out yourself?' I said. 'I'll come with you if you like.'

I thought he needed somebody to lean on, he sounded so frail. 'No, I mean look out in case anybody sees me coming out of the . . . er . . . the Ladies,' he said.

I checked that the coast was clear. It seemed fairly academic, since anyone who had been in had already seen him. But perhaps he was more afraid of being seen by his own sex.

He straightened his tie and thanked me again. He assured me

that he was not a mirthless man and he would see the humour of this. Not now, at this very moment, but eventually. I don't know when he saw the humour of it, but not I think when he found his friend, who was sitting impatiently on his third pot of coffee.

'What in the name of God happened to you?' the friend said. 'I've been on to your office, on to your home. I nearly had the guards out for you.'

The man recently released from the Ladies lowered his voice.

'We'll have a brandy,' he said.

'Was it the car? Did you hit anything?'

'No.'

'Is it your heart, any chest pains, any pins and needles in your arm?'

'No.'

'It's nothing to do with the firm, no redundancies or anything?'

The man who had been waiting all afternoon looked anxious.

'No, would you get us a drink, I've been all afternoon in the ladies' lavatory.'

'Were you being sick?'

'No, I was waiting for you.'

'I'll get the brandy fast,' said the man who had been waiting. 'I'll go up to the bar and get it myself.'

A Royal Romance Spelling Danger from the Start

9 November 1987

Things look bad when the popular papers have started to ask solemn questions of Harold Brooks Baker, who is the publisher of *Burke's Peerage*. Suppose the royal couple wanted a divorce . . . he is asked in awed whisper . . . just suppose. Then would it cause constitutional crises beyond the wildest imaginings? Even more frightening, Harold Brooks Baker says not at all, no worries, or words to that effect. The heir has been provided, not only the heir but the spare. A divorce would be sad but that's all. Nothing would teeter, nothing would crumble. Diana would be called Diana, Princess of Wales, not The Princess of Wales. The problem would be if Charles wanted a new wife and wished to create her Queen. Brows furrow a little over that knotty problem, but they clear again when everyone realises what a good chap Charles is, and they know he wouldn't do anything silly to rock the boat, nothing unwise that would remind a nation of his mother's uncle and all the hoo-ha 50 years ago.

Charles is a luckless fellow in many ways. He will be 40 on Saturday, he has known since childhood what his role would be but never how hard it would turn out to be because he couldn't have seen how the world would change. When he was 16 his country was full of respect still for royalty, and there were decent attitudes like letting the young royals alone and giving them their privacy and not insulting them too much because they couldn't answer back. But the world changed all round him and nobody told him how and if he should change. His mother thought there was no way that things should change, his father was never very interested in him since he didn't like that terrible school where they all run up and down in their vests and knickers and it's called endurance or character building.

Charles means so well and tries so much that sometimes it would break your heart. He visits deprived inner cities and is taken on tours of areas where the very lucky have some desperate jobs in sweatshops and the rest have no jobs at all. His face forces itself into a look of concern. He says earnestly to the swarm of reporters and photographers that are like a permanent fog around him that one must do something, that one is so admiring of what has been done already but that one must never cease from doing more. His accent separates him, as does his attitude and his whole background, but there is something about him that saves him. Nobody is going to call him a stupid, unfeeling berk, because he genuinely seems to care. Like he cares about getting the *Mary Rose* up from the bottom of the sea, and like he cares about giving his views on architecture and like he cares about shooting small birds at Balmoral or taking swipes with a sort of upmarket pickaxe at a ball from the back of a polo pony. When he straightens his tie nervously, when he admits that he talks to the plants and flowers in his estates, when he makes leaden attempts at humour, you'd be on his side rather than against him. Who else do you know coming up to a fortieth birthday who had so much and yet was able to do so little with it?

Diana, Princess of Wales is in many ways a luckless girl too. She was so shy when she faced the first barrage of press at her engagement ceremonies that her throat closed over and she literally couldn't speak. She was warned that it would be a goldfish bowl, but how could she have known just how many sides and how clear the glass? She did in many ways everything that the country wanted of her and did it so well that she is probably responsible for the whole royal industry all by herself. She was so beautiful for one thing, and none of the rest of the royals ever were, so she was the centre of attention.

She lost weight, she gained confidence, she learned style. The Sloane woolies and wellies went their way and the designer clothes came in, she was always ready to show a bit of bosom and a bit of thigh. The ranks of photographers following her trebled. But how could she have known that it was a dangerous game? When she was in a secret island, very pregnant and thinking she was alone, the papers sent cameramen to hang from trees and pass by in boats with long-distance lenses on their cameras.

She could be excused for thinking she was very important. If she read the newspapers and even believed a tenth of what they said about her then she would have had every reason for thinking that she was very important and powerful indeed.

The people, and not only the British people but the people everywhere, including Ireland, of course, loved a bit of romance and a lovely role model. Even though there were always aspects about the royal romance that spelled danger from the word go. The world believed that it was love at first sight, a strong prince and a beautiful shy girl becoming a fairytale princess, because that is what the world had always wanted to believe in one shape or another. It literally created that belief, and the popular papers and magazines were there to play back to the public exactly what was being demanded. In a secular and permissive society it should have seemed absurd that the strong prince had to marry a virgin but that was literally what had to be. Diana's uncle in embarrassed tones told a world that should have been equally embarrassed to hear the information that this was indeed the case. Everywhere it seemed like a reward for being a good girl. Look at what happens, you get to marry the prince if you don't give away that which is more precious than jewels. If anyone had paused to think about a girl 13 years younger than Charles, a girl with no real education let alone the strange sort of education that prepares you for being a royal . . . then it was obvious that there would be difficulties. If anyone had stopped to think about a decent, well-meaning guy who had no interest in pop music and who knew only women who found backgrounds into which to blend, then it should have been clear that there would be problems.

But nobody wanted to see the problems. And everyone was so relieved, the world had a fairytale wedding, the Queen of England really and truly believes that the succession is very important, as you and I might believe if we had gone through all that anointing and sceptre and Commonwealth routine. Princess Anne, whose own marriage was far from successful, got the spotlight taken off her and turned into a reasonable person with a serious interest in raising money for children in need. Princess Margaret, also relieved that she was out of the firing line for having the odd cigarette in public, was delighted with it too. The Queen Mother, whose smile goes right round her face and who likes happy endings, thought that it had all turned out fine.

But the public appetite is never fully fed. Professor Anthony Clare has said that the people have created a romantic fairytale which, like all fairytales, should have ended at the point where the prince and princess have arrived at the altar. Perhaps even it might have been allowed to continue until the two blond little boys came on the scene and the family were seen in the sunset in one of their palace homes.

The appetite has been whetted by glimpses inside Charles and Diana's home, respectful and pseudo-relaxed interviews trying to show that they are just like everyone else, which of course they can't be because everyone else doesn't have small armies camped outside their homes wondering when and if they will speak to each other, smile at each other, or hold hands again.

They may hate each other by now, or it may in fact have been the mildest row that caused them to spend some weeks apart. Loves and marriages have survived separations of weeks and months even. But few other people have such huge pressure on them to have a public reconciliation. What other couple had to go through the hurt and upset with the eyes of literally the whole world on them?

The German visit was yet one more charade: Diana re-launches the mini skirt, wears a sultan's gift of diamonds, Charles straightens his tie and says what a pretty colonel in chief she is, news bulletins report that they are seen talking to each other, the world sighs with relief.

But meanwhile the Queen of England walks with her dogs and knows she cannot yet retire as she'd like to, and the princess's divorced aunt and separated sister wonder what all the fuss is about. And maybe 10 times an hour newspapers ring Harold Brooks Baker of Burke's Peerage and he assures them that a divorced Charles could indeed become king. Unthinkable a while ago but not unconstitutional, he insists. And the world becomes a less safe place for a lot of people.

Making a Spectacle of Myself

8 October 1988

It happened at the Abbey Theatre a few weeks ago. The print on the programme had got all small and fuzzed around the bits where it told you what plays the actors and actresses had been in before. I was disappointed for them and felt they deserved better from the management. To my surprise the woman in front of me was reading bits out of it to her husband; I thought she must have got a clearer copy and asked could I have a loan of hers. To my surprise, by the time she had handed it to me, her copy had become small and fuzzed too. Sadly, I gave it back. 'I think it's the eyes,' I said to her in a doom-laden voice.

'Well, why don't you put on your glasses?' she asked, reasonably.

But she wasn't to know that it was my pride and joy, the ability to read the small print on bye-laws before others could see the noticeboard itself, the slight hint of envy and disbelief around one that one with so dissolute a lifestyle didn't need to fumble in a handbag or reach for a string around the neck in order to look at snaps or read the fine print of a menu in a dark restaurant. I, who used to read in the twilight when others wouldn't be able to find the book if they put it down for a minute, now I was going to have to get glasses.

Naturally, like every major event, I made a drama and a production out of it. I had no intention of going quietly into the dark night of spectacle-wearing. Nor was I going to delay. The very next day, when the plane landed me back in London, I made an appointment to see an ophthalmic surgeon. The receptionist and I consulted our Filofaxes. No, not early in the morning, she said, he would be operating.

'Operating?' I shouted down the phone in such a fright that strong men and women trying to reclaim their baggage from the carousels stopped short to know what was going on.

'Well, yes,' she said nervously.

'I don't think I want that kind of an eye doctor,' I said firmly. 'I want one that will either say tut tut, it's just that you're a bit tired and it will be fine when you've had a nice long rest, or else give me something that will bring out the cheekbones in my face and make me see everything again.'

There was a silence. You could see her wondering whether this appointment should be written into his book, whether this encounter was to be encouraged.

'Who exactly recommended you to us?' she asked, in one of those tones that frighten me to death and bring on a huge sense of middle-aged respectability.

'Fearfully sorry,' I said. 'Where were we? Yes, indeed, eleven-thirty would be fine.'

They had property magazines only in the waiting room. A woman with a hat and gloves asked me was it my first time.

'You'll like him,' she said positively. 'Great soap and water man, of course, says a lot of the problem is caused by all these creams and scrubs and grains and peeling.'

I felt a wave of nausea. Nobody had ever told me anything about any of these things in the care of the eye. And I had always thought you should keep soap and water out of your eyes. It turned out, of course, that the waiting room served several specialists. Hers was a dermatologist. There were other doctors in the building that might have been more alarming – she could have told me that he always suggested a bypass or a hysterectomy. I was calm by the time I was called.

It was like a dentist's chair without the instruments. You kept looking at things and answering lovely bright-child questions like whether you see more green than red. Then there was the sort of cartoon-style 'can you read the bottom line?' bit and a few drops in the eye and a reassuring pat and the news that I was luckier than most people, the average age for it was 44 to 46. I had lasted a few years longer. This made me feel like a champion. I thought of going down to the Savoy Theatre and having a word with Mickey Rooney, who is there in a song-and-dance musical and talking about us old survivors. It was the only doctor's surgery that I left without the customary instructions to have lost three stone the next time I came in. I told him that, praisingly. I said he shone amongst fellow medics in his attitude. He said diplomatically that he was sure his fellow medics were very right in whatever they advised, but it had no adverse effect on the sight.

'Probably helps it,' I said cheerfully and went off in search of a place to get the specs. I told the girl I wanted something showy. She found the description too vague.

'If you could tell me what kind of showy, like do the glasses of any personality appeal to you?'

I thought for a little and decided I wanted them like Edna Everage's, not exactly like hers, but in that area. The optician was regretful. They didn't do that kind of range.

'Huge, then, like dinner plates,' I said. I wasn't going for half moons or something restrained. We tried on every pair in the shop, and to my annoyance the ones that met with the most approval from everyone, including myself peering at them in a mirror, were extremely discreet ones with mainly colourless frames around the eyes and a bit of blue on the bits that go over the ear. They look very dull on the table, and I can't really see them properly on my face because they're not meant for looking at faces in mirrors – they're meant for books and papers and theatre programmes and telephone directories.

I can see all kinds of things with them, including a sort of numbering on my typewriter showing you how many spaces you've gone. I never knew it was there, and apparently that is the explanation for all those irregular sort of paragraphs over the years.

There is only one puzzlement. The glasses have a name on them. It's written in small letters inside one of those bits that goes over your ear. I suppose in posher spectacles it would be a Designer Label. But what it seems to say is 'Happy Pouff. Paris France'. I've asked other people who can read it with their own glasses on to check this out, and indeed this would appear to be the name. Maybe everyone has awful silly names written on the inside of their glasses on the grounds that the poor weak-eyed people wearing them won't be able to read them. It would be worth finding out.

Madam Is Paying?

Published in Maeve's Diary (Irish Times, *1980s)*

Today I took a man to lunch. It's something I have done many times before in my life, and hope to do again. It's not something that makes me feel aggressive, butch or dominant. It doesn't seem to emasculate and weaken the men who have been taken to lunch either. Never did I feel I should be groping under the table, fumbling to get past his knees, to hand him the fiver or the tenner. Never did I think the table should be booked in his name.

Today was a beauty, however. I had booked a table for two for one o'clock. I arrived on the dot and gave my name.

'Mr Binchy's table is this way, madam. I don't think he's arrived yet.'

I said nothing. Sometimes, it's not worth the whole business of explanations, especially when it wasn't going to change anything. I mean, I was getting to the right table. I ordered a gin and tonic while waiting.

The waiter looked mildly disapproving. He felt there was an outside chance that the man who had booked the table might hit the waiter across the face for having let a female guest order a drink on her own. He brought it along, grudgingly.

The man I was taking to lunch rushed in, apologetically. He

is an engaging-looking American, who has written a book about Californian way-out lifestyles and meaningful relationships. He is, I think, about 60 or 65. His main emotion was shame at being five minutes late. The waiter hovered about in a worried way.

'I have brought your guest an aperitif, Mr Binchy,' he said to the American author, fearfully. The American looked back at him fearfully. Was this some terrible plot? Would he have to pay for the meal? Was I passing him off as my husband or my father? He was filled with unease.

'What will you have, I'm paying,' I said firmly, and he ordered a highball, with a marginal air of relaxing.

All through the meal it went on. He got the menu with the prices, I didn't; he was shown the wine list, I was ignored; the tray of cigars was brought to him at the coffee stage, even though we had both made it perfectly clear to this dumb, chauvinist waiter that I was the one who was in charge of the lunch.

Then came the bill. You must remember that this man and I had been discussing the whole role of female assertiveness in a West Coast marriage. We had agreed that patterns had changed beyond recognition because of the women's movement nowadays, women no longer saw marriage in its traditional role of giving security or stability.

Over the cheese we had marvelled at how much had happened in how short a time. And there stood the waiter, discreetly trying to catch the American's attention so that he could present him with the piece of paper which couldn't possibly be shown to a woman.

'I'm in the lucky position of being invited to lunch,' the American said engagingly, waving over to me as if to indicate that funds unlimited were available at my side of the table.

The waiter stood still.

'Madam is paying?' he asked in a voice full of doom.

'That's right,' I said cheerfully, getting out my chequebook.

'By cheque,' he said defeatedly.

'Oh, they let women have them these days,' I said with an attempt to cheer him up.

As an attempt it failed. He took my cheque and cheque card like a butler in a film might pick up a tousled gypsy child to remove it from his lordship's eyes.

There was no service charge included so I left a 10 per cent tip, which is, I think, what people do. He looked at the money as if it were the worst humiliation he had ever undergone. I was desperately tempted to snatch it back, since I had got no service, I had only got a patronising sneer throughout. But then, that would have given him further fuel about women if I had taken the money back. So, even though I didn't feel like it, I grinned at him and thanked him for the nice meal. And though he certainly didn't feel like it, he grinned back, and said it had been nice to see me and hoped he would see me again.

As we came out into the cold sunshine, the American author looked back thoughtfully at the restaurant and shook his head.

'It'll be some while before he'll let it all hang out with an assertively laid-back female,' he said, disappointed that the time was changing so slowly after all.

NINETIES

Even the Presidents Are Getting Younger

1 December 1990

It's one thing to notice the guards getting younger, to look over people's shoulders at their passports and realise they were born the year you left teaching but truly it's a bit hard to become older than the President of Ireland *and* the Prime Minister of Britain all in one month. Only the comforting lined face of George Bush gives me any hope that there are some elderly folk out there trying to run things. I keep expecting some fresh-faced boy that I taught up to First Communion class to emerge as the Pope.

It's not something that will darken my brow for the rest of my natural or anything, it's just that these things seem to come all at once. A letter in flawless English from a Dutch student who is doing a thesis on Irish women asked me would I talk to her about what I and all my friends felt the day we got the vote. A girl's school having a sale of work wondered could I donate any mementoes of the old days like a fan or a dance card so that people could get the flavour. A kindly and we hope short-sighted woman told a whole bookshop that she remembered me climbing through the window of the nurses' home in Vincent's in 1935.

A child doing a school essay asked me for advice. They had been asked to imagine that they had been alive the day decimal currency was introduced in Ireland. He wondered what the place had been like then. It was tempting to draw a picture of gas lamps, and cobbled streets and coaches rattling by but since a lot of the teachers probably wouldn't remember it either, there was no point in being ironical – the child might have got a low mark and been deemed stupid.

I told him the truth about that day, and that it happened to be a day that a deeply unsatisfactory romance of mine was over, and like everyone in such a situation I was On the Verge.

One cross word from anyone and the floodgates would open. Determined to begin a new life full of sharp, clear decisions and snappy dialogue, I got on the bus. Everyone else was saying 'a shilling', which was the fare. In a voice that could cut through steel, I asked for 'five pence please'.

The conductor may have been having a crisis of his own. He looked at me without much pleasure. 'If there's one thing I hate it's a smart alec,' he said. I looked at him in disbelief and then I began to cry; the bus was racked with sobs, and heaving and whooping. Every single passenger took my side, they had no idea what it was about, but he had grossly offended me, a paying passenger, trying to coordinate with all these instructions about trying to Think Decimal. Scant thanks you got for thinking decimal, only dog's abuse from public officials. They were going to take his number and report him for upsetting the poor woman who was only struggling like the rest of the population to cope with what we all knew would be our ruination and our downfall. I was now terribly sorry for the conductor and trying to get people not to report him, which only made me look nicer and him look even more foul.

New passengers getting on were told of the horror of it. By now he was meant to have called me a smart arse, he had shouted at me, he had frightened me, he wouldn't hear the end of this. Oh no.

No fare was taken from me in either the old or new money, and I staggered off the bus eventually red eyed and thanking my loyal supporters. They all waved at me out the window as the bus pulled away, some of them made fists of solidarity, and the unfortunate conductor ashen with fright was trying to cover his badge number.

The child said it was interesting but probably not what the teacher had in mind. Sadly I agreed, these kind of tales are never what the teacher had in mind.

I would like to thank the seven readers who wrote in saying that they agreed with me about working at home and the nightmarish difficulty of actually starting the damn thing when everything else on earth seems more interesting.

One woman listening to the radio when she should have been working heard an item about bees, and went out and bought two hives. She has a lot of stings, very little honey, a fascination with bees and no income from her real work, she tells me. I would also like to thank the 23 readers who wrote to correct me about the previous Governor General of Canada being a woman, not a man. I was going to say it was just a little test, or I'm glad you're all awake, but it might have looked as if I were flailing on the ropes so I didn't say it.

And if you are reading this in Canada tomorrow night as you might well be, it's because a couple called Kevin and Meta Hannafin of the Irish Newspaper and Book Distributors bring in national, provincial and Sunday papers. At eight o'clock on a Sunday night you can get them, and they have to wait until Wednesday in Chicago, the Hannafins say with some pride.

I would particularly like to thank the reader who said that there was a message on her telephone answering machine asking how to get rid of fleas from a cat or dog's cushion. The person hadn't said who they were but it sounded like my voice and the kind of thing I would ask. Since I hadn't left a number, she wrote to me at the paper and the answer was to stuff the cushion with dried ferns. Ferns are said to frighten off fleas. She gave no address to save me the bother of getting in touch again.

Again? If she thinks I rang her and left this request on her machine then surely I should know her address. I have a friend who always says, 'Let it pass, let it pass.' How can you let something as mystifying as that pass? But then there could be something about some people which actually goes out and attracts the confusing, the incomprehensible and the downright barking. It has nothing to do with being loud and extrovert and claiming to enjoy unexpected experiences.

One of the quietest and most demure authors I know got a postcard the other day from a boy, man maybe . . . saying, 'My grandmother says you know everything; how is CWRW, the Welsh word for beer, pronounced? Trusting you can oblige.'

The flattery was very pleasing; someone's grandmother thought she knew everything . . . Of course she did no work that morning looking through dictionaries and Books of Unusual Facts. She eventually had to ring a newspaper in Wales and found that the answer was Koo Roo. The whole thing took forever but she felt it was somehow more satisfying than finishing the chapter that was already a week late.

And I agree, it's so much better being thought a person who leaves messages about fleas on the answering machines of strangers or someone who knows how to pronounce beer in Welsh than to be thought capable of nothing.

I heard two students talking glumly about their mothers. One apparently obsessed, day and night, about the house. The other was in a worse state. 'She just sits and looks in front of her as if all her brain cells were dead,' the daughter said sadly. 'Of course she will be 50 at Christmas; what's left for her when you come to think of it?'

My Theodora Story

6 April 1991

Last week, when I was writing about sauces in a restaurant, I felt the familiar sense of fear that Theodora might read it and tell me that even now at this late stage I had still learned nothing about cookery terms.

But last Saturday the pages were full of appreciation and memories of Theodora FitzGibbon, and I remembered my own Theodora story and how she had said I must always tell it after she was dead, since it reflected huge credit on her and George and none at all on me.

I *think* I was the one who hired Theodora on a regular basis for *The Irish Times*. The more famous she became, the more often I say that it was I who found her. Anyway, when I became women's editor in 1968, knowing nothing about fashion and cookery, it was great to have that side of things handled by experts. In the beginning she used to discuss recipes with me, but the feeling of talking to a brick wall must have overcome her, because she eventually gave up. One inkling of my limitations may have come when she typed out a recipe that included one to one and a half pounds of split peas. The way it was written, a 1 and then another 1 and a ½, made me think it must have been eleven and a half pounds that she meant, and I amended her copy accordingly.

It was around that time that she decided to take control of her own column, and sometimes her husband, George Morrison, would send us a picture to go with the piece that Theodora wrote. I loved it when he did, but it was always just a little bonus.

So there was this day when it came to getting the cookery page ready and it was one of the days that George hadn't sent an illustration. The recipes were for various ways of cooking veal. Of course, because I wasn't well organised there was no time to ask the *Irish Times* photography department to set up a nice, relevant picture, so I looked through what I always called my Emergency Cookery Pictures File. These were things that had come from various sources, you know, pots of marmalade beside oranges, and picnic hampers. Nothing seemed very suitable until I saw a nice, vague-looking picture of a casserole with a lot of spoons and servers and forks sticking out of it. It wasn't the *best* but it would do, I told myself. A swift caption was typed by me: 'Tasty veal casserole, excellent for a winter evening.' And with the totally undeserved feeling of a job well done, I took the train out to Dalkey at the end of the day.

My father and I were looking at the nine o'clock news on television when I saw something that made me deeply uneasy. I saw Dr Christiaan Barnard, the heart transplant surgeon, getting off a plane somewhere after yet another successful operation, and I knew suddenly where I had seen that picture before. It was in fact a picture of open-heart surgery. What I had taken to be forks and servers were in fact clamps and forceps.

I telephoned the paper and asked them to hold the cookery page. As a request at ten past nine at night, it was poorly received. I was asked why, and the explanation was met with disbelief.

'I think you had better get in here as quickly as possible,' said the editor in a voice that I knew was holding on by only a thread.

We had no car, so I started to run the nine miles from Dalkey to Dublin purple-faced, panic-stricken. An unknown man with a car gave me a lift, and when he heard my errand he abandoned his car in the traffic in D'Olier Street and came in with me, a total stranger, saying he had to see; he loved to know how other people coped in a crisis.

Grimly, I discovered, very grimly. They stood around my desk searching hopelessly for any alternative picture; not having unearthed the Emergency Cookery Pictures File, they found only a cache of Kit Kat wrappers and a bundle of magazines of much lower brow than I would have liked it known I read.

The replacement picture had to be of the same size. There was now no time to enlarge or reduce anything that emerged from the file. Eventually I found one, an egg in an egg cup . . . I think it was a picture from an advertising agency trying to show the charms of some china.

Underneath the picture, and under the grim glance of Top People, I typed out, 'Why be content with a boiled egg on a winter's evening when you could have all these tasty veal recipes?'

Theodora was on the phone bright and early.

'You didn't exactly kill yourself getting an illustration,' she said to me frostily.

But she was delighted with the explanation of the terrible happenings the night before. She said she had lived a colourful life and it would have been entertaining to have added a prosecution for cannibalism to her other achievements. She seemed to regret my last-minute discovery and heroic dash to save us all from turning out a cookery page that would have been a collector's item.

She said almost wistfully that it would have been something that would make people remember her . . . as if there were a chance that any of us will ever forget Theodora.

Heading for the Hustings

4 April 1992

Even though a heavy cloud of greyness is hanging over the British election, there's still a whiff of intrigue about it all. I'm excited already at the thought of going to the press conferences and looking them all straight in their weary eyes and seeing how they're bearing up.

And it also reminds me of the great happiness of going back to school knowing that a hated teacher has gone, you can hardly dare to believe it. She won't be there in the hound's-tooth suit baying at the back of the hall, turning with reptilian cunning to the cowering ministers on either side saying those dreaded words, 'I think that's one for you, Home Secretary, or Chancellor,' addressing any number of men whose nervous systems and political futures she unsettled over the years.

I have no nostalgia for those Thatcher days when the sun always shone and we were sure of a good row story every outing.

I think the place is far better without her, and for once she may have done the wisest thing by leaving town. Because she sure as hell did everything else wrong a year and a half ago when she was leaving. She waited to be booted out, she patted the head of the little grey boy who was to be her successor and she even chose the wrong little grey boy to be her puppet because he cleared his throat and found his own voice and lived perfectly well without her.

She should have gone six months earlier and sat watching them running around like headless rabbits tearing each other to bits.

That's what I would have done. I would have sat there with a false smile playing around my chops saying that I was absolutely certain that they'd all manage *much* better without me.

And then I would have laughed all the way to the Thatcher Institute listening to a chorus of world opinion trilling that everything would have been perfectly fine if only I'd stayed.

But then she's not the only politician who stayed too long in these islands. It seems to go with the territory.

What is beyond comprehension is how a woman who loved free enterprise and what she called the cut and thrust of the marketplace could have made such a monumental cock-up of writing and selling her memoirs. She was months dillying and dallying and allowing everything that could possibly be said in her book be said elsewhere. She was said to be taking the advice of her son, someone whom she had rarely consulted on anything during his whole existence.

A forthright, if inelegant, American publisher said she should have done the deal when she was red hot or not at all. She should have held an auction, promised to name names, say that she was going to right wrongs, avenge grievances, and possibly describe some of the frostiness of Her Majesty the Queen during their weekly conferences.

If she had done this, her asking price in dollars and sterling could have gone through the roof, the publisher lamented sadly.

She would not be human if she did not feel some small satisfaction at the way the boys in the nursery are messing it all up now that Nanny has been sacked. She would not be normal if she did not take a small *frisson* of pleasure from the polls. But had she only gone in time, she could have been regarded forever as the Monarchy in Exile, and she could have had her ego massaged until she lived to be a hundred.

But she's gone, and though her shadow hangs over the country she ruled for so long with such certainty and so little self-doubt, she will not be a consideration this time round.

It can hardly be a presidential-style election since the candidates trail so little glory. Just from my brief four hours a day spent watching the campaign on television, they all seem to me to be in pretty poor shape. John Major has almost blended into the background, they're afraid to photograph him against anything except primary colours. Neil Kinnock is as white as a sheet and as hoarse as a crow, Paddy Ashdown's famous lopsided smile seems to be held on with putty, and they are all moving into the most important week of their lives.

It will be very exciting to get back to it all. To see them again, lining up each morning striving for the newsbites, the one phrase of burning sincerity that will catch every news bulletin, the one lashing out against the other side in a phrase that 20 script-writers worked on all night. I will sit with the press corps, the lay analysts who try to spot victory or defeat in the red-eyed faces on the platform. And I'll walk through the streets of Hammersmith, one of the safer Labour seats in London but with pockets of bright blue resistance in the most unlikely places.

There are a few times in life when Irish journalists are greatly in demand among the British media, usually to explain the Third Secret of Fatima, or the artists' tax-free exemption scheme. But at general elections, people always want us to explain proportional representation in case it might ever become a real issue.

And this time, for the first time, it just might.

Please Don't Forget to Write

2 January 1993

There's a great advantage in being grown up. You don't have to swim if it's pouring rain. You can sit and look at the others being dragged in – to get value, or because they've come all this distance, or just because it's Christmas morning.

I'm a great believer in not doing things just for some ritualistic principle; or that's what I said as hot tropical rain lashed down on Bondi Beach.

The people in the next car were not so lucky. They didn't have the Inner Zen that would enable them to sit there and drink the ice-cold champagne anyway. They also had three screaming sons with bodyboards who wanted to be in that surf at once. 'They'll be trampled on – the place is full of Poms,' said the mother anxiously.

'Piss off, Poms,' screamed the children in excitement, quoting a graffito seen on every Qantas advertisement: a polite way of registering disapproval of British Airways buying a stake in the national airline.

People were setting up little camps on the beach in the rain which everyone knew would pass soon. They were planting Canadian, Greek and Italian flags in the sand.

'Where's ours?' asked one little boy.

'It's *all* ours,' said his father, shivering in his bathing trunks.

That pleased the elder two. The youngest one was interested in a well-developed lady shaking the drops off her bosom as she came out of the tide.

'That lady lost her bra,' he said, looking at her with deep interest and some sympathy.

'Not all she lost, I'd say,' his father said.

'She's still got the bottom bit.' The boy was a stickler for accuracy.

'For the moment.' The man looked knowledgeable about such things.

'Perhaps, Brian, you might take your son out to the sea, which is the reason we came here, rather than embark on any further instruction, sensitive as it may be, on the Facts of Life.'

It would have been interesting to know how their Christmas Day went on, but then wouldn't you want to follow almost everyone home? Like the two men in their braces and hats on the back of their heads, sitting on the Promenade in Bondi, saying to each other sagely, 'Better to stay out of the house. Women don't like *people* in a house when they're cooking.'

Or the girl all dressed up to meet the boy's family who asked, 'Is there anything I shouldn't talk about?'

'Communism,' said the boy.

'Right.' She took it on board with a puzzled expression. I felt she should have enquired further but the young probably know what they're at.

Our own Christmas was fine thank you and, apart from chickening out on the swim, went as forecast. There was a moment though when the soft, warm night air came in the open windows and the lights of Sydney Harbour twinkled beyond the gently moving curtains when one of our number asked, 'Do you think that with four people out of five fast asleep during the video we could say that a democratic decision might be to turn it off?' And we all woke up angrily, denied having dozed at all and fought to keep awake to the end.

❦

And then came the Sales. The biggest one is in Grace Brothers, where they had the usual attractions of televisions at $50 and washing machines at $70 to get the crowds in. These special bargains were called 'Doorbusters', a name they'll probably drop now, since the crowds actually did break the doors down in eagerness to get at them, and glass was everywhere, wounding a lot of the shoppers. But still the buses and cars and even the ferry boats are weighed down with huge parcels, brightly coloured sheets and duvet covers, huge terracotta pots for the garden, deck chairs, garden lights – all the luxuries for summer living.

At a party I met a woman who asked me could I tell her absolutely honestly whether I thought she had a mad face. With total honesty I told her that I did not, and wondered why. She said that for the second year in succession she had been photographed for the newspapers as a sort of face in the crowd to illustrate Sales Frenzy. Once had been bad enough but twice was something that would make you think.

At the same party I asked someone who the man was that had just walked in.

'Someone whose face I had hoped never to have looked upon in what remains of my life,' said my informant, who told me the newcomer's enormities and how he had wrecked the particular part of the media he worked in. I heard of his sleazy way with women, his betrayals of trust, his sailing close to the wind financially and that he owned a Rottweiler. By the time I was introduced to him there was nothing he could say to redeem himself.

'I'm not surprised you like Sydney,' he said. 'On a gossip level it's just like Dublin.'

And of course he is absolutely right. I just hadn't realised it before.

I feel as if I have always lived here. The neighbourhood is so familiar now. There's not a day that you'd leave the house without meeting someone you know. On the road where I live I meet Siobhan McHugh and her marvellous baby Declan; in the Dry

Dock pub they know our table; in Manjits Indian restaurant they bring the poppadums and chutney before we sit down. In the hairdresser opposite the police station – which calls itself 'The Crop Shop Opposite the Cop Shop' – they'd remember you after one visit and make you feel like a friend. In Ralph's delicatessen, they keep hoping I'm going to emigrate there; they like the reckless abandon with which I buy food. There are three gorgeous cats where we live and sometimes I go into Heavy Petting to consider gifts for them, and they are full of advice.

Fireworks over the harbour for New Year, everyone out in the warm night air, windows open and the old or the children waving at the festivities.

And before going to bed we all light those green coils that smell slightly like incense and burn through the night, killing, we hope, any mozzies that come in the open doors. And the cats sleep peacefully out of doors on the warm wood shavings that are ground cover, and there's a wonderful yellow plant called Kangaroo Paw that is all lit up in the dawn at about six o'clock when it's bright enough to read in bed but there's no anxiety-related pressure to get up just because you're awake.

And tonight it's off to the Sydney Opera House for the gala opening of *Lughnasa*.

It's over four months since we left Ireland but thanks to the friends, colleagues and family who have been so great about keeping in touch it doesn't seem anything like that.

It *truly* has been so good to get letters from home that I have resolved for 1993 to write to the Irish abroad. We may seem overconfident, as if we almost preferred where we are to where we were. But the truth is that we are all desperate to hear from home.

Casually Elegant Meets the Mob

9 January 1993

You never know exactly what they mean about dressing up in Australia. We spent a couple of nights in a resort called Terrigal, in a smart kind of hotel where they left a note in each room saying that guests would probably appreciate some advice about Dress Codes. Fearfully we read that the Executive Lounge was Casually Elegant in the evenings, and Smartly Casual in the mornings. They defined Smartly Casual as meaning no bathrobes or swimwear, which left the field fairly open.

But it was confusing because Casually Elegant in the Key Largo Lounge meant No Runners. What could they want in La Mer, the gourmet dining room? The instructions were Elegant Resort Wear. I put on all my jewellery and a lot of eyeshadow and hoped that would compensate for the ordinary summer dress. Gordon bought a tie.

Everyone assumed we were the cabaret. Elegant Resort is taken to mean open-necked shirts, shorts – and one woman was definitely barefoot, but she had cunningly draped tinsel around her legs so that it looked like exotic twinkling Roman sandals.

So back in Sydney at the opening night of *Dancing at Lughnasa* you wouldn't know *what* they were going to wear for a glitzy night out, and there was the usual rainbow of clothes: little black dresses and pearls; great Hawaiian-type shirts over psychedelic shorts; marvellous beaded and brocade-type Asian jackets. They came in from the warm night air around the harbour to the cool air-conditioned Opera House.

In the row just in front of us a line of people came in, all the men dressed in smart dark suits. I speculated about them happily – they might be coming from a funeral, or possibly serious negotiations within the Mob. Then one of them, who was Martin Burke, the Irish Ambassador, introduced me to another of them, who was Paul Keating, the Prime Minister of Australia, and that sorted out who they were.

There's huge rivalry between Melbourne and Sydney, so Martin Burke had to go to the play's opening in both cities, which he said was no hardship at all. I explained the Cork–Dublin thing to Paul Keating in case it was something he would ever need to know and he listened gravely, adding that if you lived in Australia and didn't live in Sydney you were merely camping out.

The night was a huge success and there was one unexpected laugh in the script: when Gerry the Welsh Romeo describes his kind of dancing as 'Strictly Ballroom' there was a cheer. Australians are as proud of the success of this film as they have been of anything for years, and love to know that it's showing in cities all over the world.

There was a reception afterwards where I realised from the photographers that the gorgeous woman sitting beside us who was about one inch wide was in fact Judy Davis the film star, and I was having a great, happy conversation with a man called Michael Bailey who worked in television. We were getting along fine until someone whispered to me that he read the weather forecast and my brow darkened.

'I don't make it up, I'm not a Met Man. I only read it,' he pleaded.

But the magic was gone. The Australian weather forecast is as helpful as our own; it says things like sunshine mixed with showers or showers mixed with sunshine and everyone thinks that this is useful.

They are so conscious of equality in this land I was horrified to see an advertisement on television for one of the January sales. It was for a women's dress shop called Katie's. And the ad was a male voice over scenes of empty office desks saying that no female employees could be expected to show up for work until Katie's sale was over.

It was so uncharacteristically sexist in a land which is making great strides against the old macho Ocker image of beer-swilling Australian men liking women to be in the kitchen, the bed or at the filing cabinet, I wondered whether to ring up and complain; but then I decided that was being tiresome. It's not my country. It was late at night. I didn't know the number of the television station.

But enough people *did* ring up. The very next day there was an announcement saying that the advertisement had been withdrawn because it had unconsciously given offence.

The managing director of the company bleated a bit and said that there had been women involved in the advertising agency which dreamed up the account – which was a bit of a last-ditch flail I thought – and he kept referring to the *ladies* who had phoned in telling the store that they wouldn't shop there unless the ad was removed. He said that of course he hadn't intended to imply that *ladies* would put shopping before work. He realised that it might have been unwise to have had a male voice, implying that employers were male and employees were all *ladies*. I know nothing about the shop, but everyone says that it's not a question of any publicity being good publicity; the whole thing did it nothing but harm.

And now for the clear-up. How can seven weeks have gone in this little house when it only feels as if we had just arrived? Where did all the stuff come from? It was lean and spare when we came into it.

There are going to be endless trips to various recycling areas before we leave. I hated throwing out the cards that came the whole way from the other side of the earth, but to carry them back again? That way madness lies.

And now everything has a sense of being the last time. The

last lunch out in Bondi on the balcony of Ravesi's watching the world go by. The last sneaking into a five o'clock movie on a wet afternoon, with a choice of maybe 20 in the huge George Street cinemas. The last breakfast in the garden watched by three solemn cats wondering why we like mangoes so much. The last drive out to Long Nose Point to see the ferries cross the harbour. The last night out with friends.

And this morning we will be moving backwards out of the little house, cleaning as we go – just as I remember doing so many years ago in Ballybunion when it was a matter of honour to leave the lodge in just as good shape as you found it.

And then it will be time to go to the airport, with yet another bag added to the luggage, faces rounder and redder than when we arrived here, and check-in at Departures.

I'm not expecting the destination to give you any great sense of pleasure as the winds blow and the rains fall, but the ticket actually says Bali.

Someone's got to do it.

They'll Never Let Her Go

4 December 1993

Of course it won't be goodbye. The public will never let her go, the girl who lived her whole adult life in front of their eyes; the awkward, blushing, stammering Sloane whose main and possibly only qualification for marrying the prince was that she was a virgin.

Daughter of a broken marriage, step-daughter of Raine who could have been sent down by Central Casting to play the wicked stepmother, step-granddaughter of the marvellous, batty old Barbara Cartland, who could out-hat and out-pink the Queen Mother any day and who had written nine million novels about gels keeping their virginity and landing nice princes as a result. And daughter of the burbling, confused old Earl of Spencer, who barely made it up the aisle with her, who was seen taking photographs of the crowds who were taking photographs of his daughter.

In addition to her purity, she had all the right credentials, including her Julie Andrewsesque job as sort of nanny-like teacher to lovely little posh children. . . . She was awkward, shruggy and young when she was introduced to the cameras and the horrific lifestyle that was to follow.

Then the world watched her change. She lost her puppy fat, she stopped wearing woolly cardigans, she showed her bosom and her legs. She smiled at people because she realised that they *liked* it rather than thinking they might sometimes *deserve* it, as her mother-in-law and sister-in-law had always done.

And when she saw how much they liked it, she did it more and more. She smiled upwards at photographers, laughed and threw back her head, and it wasn't long before she was on the cover of every magazine that wanted to increase its sales by a minimum of 40 per cent.

Diana sold papers, magazines and books. So many that the market couldn't keep up with the demand. There is no way they are going to let her go now, no matter how many messages, coded or otherwise, come from Buckingham Palace.

For years people have followed the Diana story. They went through her eating disorders with her. Mothers whose daughters had anorexia or bulimia watched her anxiously, willing her to get better, to become happier, so that their daughter would too, thinking that it was all more understandable somehow if a lovely princess could endure such an illness.

Diana made motherhood fashionable too. They waited out on the streets for news of her babies. They stood cheering as she left hospital with the little boys. Nobody could say you were just a breeding machine if you looked at the youthful Diana running with her sons held by the hand.

Then they saw her marriage grow cold and sad. And everyone who had a bad marriage, or even a row within a good marriage, felt better somehow when they saw that such problems and sorrows could even befall the charming princess.

They suffered with her over the humiliation of the Camilla tapes. Whether she loved Charles or not, it was degrading to have the intimate conversation of a husband and mistress broadcast and published all over the world. . . . And the evidence of previous cover-ups, of friends who had been false friends, made ordinary British people feel weak with sympathy for Diana – for Diana who had done nobody any harm, but who had brought warmth and charm to the endless round of royal duties, for Diana who had picked up children and cuddled them instead of waving at them royally, for Diana who had sat on the beds of dying AIDS patients and held their hands. She was pilloried in the gutter press and called an associate of sodomites when she did this, but she had taken no notice and altered her schedule not at all.

Then the accusations came that she was running a rival court.

Almost all the press and most of the public thought 'good luck to her' . . . but there was a fear that the monarchy might not survive such antics. So, bit by bit, heavy pressure was put on Charles to get involved and to get on with things and to make his voice heard.

Charles couldn't compete with Diana in looks, which was not his fault and it was very unfair of the Diana supporters to mock his appearance. He couldn't compete in terms of charm either, because he was literally brought up to believe that he was special, important and different, and descended from lines of that stuff, and couldn't just behave ordinarily. It's a nightmare for him to try to be ordinary.

But what he did was to have an affair – and then did nothing about it when it became public knowledge. He should have apologised to everyone involved and tried to make a go of his marriage instead of being aloof and glum. Or else he should have apologised to everyone, abdicated in advance, married Camilla and got a divorce as everyone else of his nationality, religion and class would have done.

Instead he has played a wounded nobleman whose camp is trying desperately to build him up into some kind of king material.

Diana hasn't put an elegant foot wrong in most people's opinion. If she has to cut down on her public duties, there are many who will see this as part of a bad-tempered, weaselish palace conspiracy.

They will all regret that there's a possibility we may be seeing less of her and more of the other. The other hasn't nearly as much to recommend him.

They are sorry they won't see her crowned queen. But they are not going to say goodbye to a girl who seemed to do everything according to the dream. Ordinary people are still going to want Diana on the cover for a long time to come.

There Is No Excuse

26 March 1994

I regard people who say they'll meet you at eight p.m. and then turn up at eight-thirty as liars. I had a colleague years ago in my teaching days who used to smile and say that she was *always* late, as if it were something outside her control, like having freckles or a Gemini star sign. At first I went through agonies thinking she had been mown down by a bus. After that I would arrange to meet her, not on the corner of a street or at the cinema, but in a café where at least I could sit down while waiting. After that I stopped meeting her. There were too many main features beginning at five-twenty missed, too many buses gone, too many houses where I had to be part of an apology for an unpunctuality that was none of my making.

She lives in another country now and I met someone who had been to see her. Just as nice as ever, apparently, just as good company. Much loved by her children but treated as a dotty old lady who can't be relied on. She would never turn up to pick them up from school, so they just adapted to doing their homework in the school yard. So she is still at it, thinking she can say one thing and do another, and everyone will forgive her because she is unpunctual the way other people are left-handed or colour-blind.

Of course she got away with it because people are so astounded by the unpunctual that they forgive them and allow them to roam the world as ordinary people instead of as the liars they are. It's our fault for putting up with it in every walk of life and I advise people to declare war on the unpunctual. It's no longer acceptable to consider it an attractive, laid-back, national characteristic. It is in fact a lazy, self-indulgent, discourteous way of going on. Already there are a lot of signs that people do not accept it as charming.

I remember a time when the curtain never went up on time in a Dublin theatre because, as the theory went, the Irish were all so busy being witty and wonderful and entertaining in bars they couldn't do anything as pen-pushing, meticulous and prosaic as coming in and being seated before eight o'clock. But enough protests from those who objected to people shuffling in late to performances has led to their not being admitted until the first interval, and it's very interesting to see how that has concentrated the ability to get to the place before the lights go out.

Staff of Aer Lingus don't think it's charming and witty to leave late because their wonderful free-spirited clients can't be hurried, and likewise with trains, the DART and the buses. Religious services don't take account of some quirk in the national psyche by having Mass at around eleven or Matins at approximately ten. Races, football matches, television programmes start on time. Why should business appointments and social engagements be let off this hook? And yet this week I was talking to an American publisher on the phone who said that she was expecting an Irish author in her office but he was 40 minutes late. She laughed good-naturedly and even though she was 3,000 miles away I could see her shrug forgivingly. 'Oh well, that's the Irish for you!' she said, as if somehow it explained something. To me it explained nothing.

As a race we are not naturally discourteous. In fact, if anything, we wish to please a bit too much. That's part of our national image. So where does this unpunctuality come into the stereotype? Has it something to do with being feckless and free and not seeing ourselves ever as a slave to any time-servers or time-keepers? It's a bit fancy and I don't think that it's at all part of what we are.

Not turning up at the time you promised seems quite out of character and if we do it, it must be because it has been considered acceptable for too long. If nobody were to wait for the latecomer, then things would surely change. If the unpunctual were to be left looking forlorn and foolish when they had ratted on their promise, then people would keep better time. We shouldn't go on saying that it's perfectly all right and, nonsense, they mustn't worry, and really it was quite pleasant waiting here alone wondering was it the right day, the right place, or the right time. We should never again say to latecomers that they're in perfect time when the meal is stuck to the roof of the oven and the other guests are legless with pre-dinner drinks.

Sit in any restaurant, bar or hotel foyer and listen while people greet each other. 'I'm very sorry. The traffic was terrible.' 'I'm sorry for being late. I couldn't get parking. . . .' 'I'm sorry. Are you here long? I wasn't sure whether you said one or half past. . . .' 'I'm sorry, but better late than never.' I wouldn't forgive any of these things. In a city, people with eyes in their heads *know* that the traffic is terrible; they can see it. Unless they have been living for a while on the planet Mars, they're aware that it's impossible to park. If they couldn't remember whether you said one or half past, that shows *great* interest in the meeting in the first place. And as for better late than never, I'm not convinced.

Fear of Falling Off the Wagon

23 April 1994

A very agreeable, social sort of man, he says he won't come to Ireland for this particular gathering because he couldn't bear all the flak he will get about not taking a drink. He remembers Ireland in the old days, he says, when you brailled your way from the early Bloody Mary to the lunchtime pints and everyone was defined by the amount they could put away, while abstainers were mocked as Holy Joes, Cute Hoors or possibly Not Real Men.

Not the place for a man four years into a different way of life, he says. Why draw it on himself? He's not afraid that he'll weaken or anything; it's just that he couldn't take all the explanations, the defensive attitude he will have to adopt, the rationalising, the assuring people that he doesn't object to their lifestyle, it's just that his own is not the same. He's been here before, he says; he knows of what he speaks. No, life is too short to take on that hassle. He's going to miss the reunion.

I advise him to think again and ask a few people, as well as myself, before he pleads an excuse not to meet classmates who were great pals in the years gone by. He may be very pleasantly surprised. The Ireland of his student days, 20 odd years ago, which he revisited 10 years ago, is not today's Ireland, regarding attitudes to drink.

He will not find people calling him Matt Talbot or Father Mathew if he asks for mineral water. They will not ask for an explanation, nor will they want one. And best of all, they will not turn red, watery eyes on him and sob into their own drinks about how they wished they had his strength. There are lots of nice pink livers in Ireland.

Ah, but Maeve was always one to see what she wanted to see, he says. I would like him to come and meet his fellow students so I could be expected to create a rose-tinted world for him, where people are mature and wise and tolerant. This is not what he hears.

Right, I tell him, this is what I hear and see and notice. I notice that pubs, which love selling soft drinks anyway and always thrived on the mixers because they constitute almost pure profit, not attracting any tax, now have a whole rake of alcohol-free beers and low-alcohol lagers, and they are being wooed senseless by the various mineral-water manufacturers, dying to get their particular shade of bottle and label in.

Publicans, who used to collapse like a Bateman cartoon if anyone asked for coffee, now want to know if you want decaf or cappuccino. In recent years, I cannot have heard a barman make a joke about serving a Real Man a non-alcoholic drink. I haven't seen a sigh, or heard a groan. I have never heard an explanation about someone being a Pioneer, it being Lent, or the breathalyser, or the price of gargle being offered. Maybe I don't go to enough macho bars but I do go to a reasonable cross-section and in recent times I have never heard anyone being challenged after ordering the drink of his or her choice.

I agree that years ago the order would go, 'Four pints, two gin-and-tonics, three large Paddies and a Cidona for your man!' Your man was thereby marked as being outside the tribe. Nowadays it's just as often the reverse; it could be a round of white wine and soda and many varieties of non- or low-alcohol drinks and someone saying apologetically, 'Do you mind if I have a short, it has been a bad day?'

Like smoking. People don't say they've given up apologetically. The apology is from the one who asks for the ashtray. I told the man who thinks that attitudes are frozen that when I gave up smoking I was afraid to answer the telephone in case I had to have a cigarette before I spoke; I was so unused to the experience of one without the other. Not a good example, he says. The phone wouldn't take me by the throat and say I was no fun without a cigarette – go on, have just one.

But I told him that he was guilty of over-dramatising himself. Everyone he will meet at his reunion will have read the bad news about how many units are safe per week. Some of them, admittedly, may have decided to take no notice, but they will know about them, they will not think he is wearing a hair shirt and chains around his middle if he doesn't lower a bottle of sherry at the reception. Some of his colleagues and friends will have read the tests under the heading 'Are you an alcoholic?' and by question three realised that they should be in treatment. Some will have done something; some will have said these questionnaires are run by some backlash pressure group. But they will have read them. There will be colleagues who have had friends die of drink-related illnesses, or passed over for promotion because of being a bit unreliable in that department.

He will discover that the liquid lunch is no longer a permanent feature of Irish middle-class life in the mainstream, as it might have been when he left. Not an eyebrow is raised if a captain of industry or a politician or even a successful journalist asks for a glass of water; heads will not wag. They will not say that's what has him where he is, either for good or evil. It's just one more choice people make. Like having no car and walking to work can be as high in the pecking order as having a car the size of a house. I advise him to give it a lash.

The profession that he is in has changed. Its ideas of machismo have altered greatly and not just because his colleagues have become middle-aged. New attitudes are all the more apparent among the younger generation. He may not find Ireland an entirely pluralist society but at least he will find his countrymen and women broad-minded enough to know that we owe no explanations for what forms of pleasure or madness we deny ourselves. And he will also have a great time.

Getting It Right at the End

14 May 1994

Years ago, there was a different code. You went to see a friend who was terminally ill and you looked into the eyes which would not see for much longer and you swore that the person had never looked better. You could see a terrific improvement since the last visit, and it would be no time before everybody was as right as rain again. The more hearty and jovial the protestation, the better you thought the whole thing had gone. At least you felt you had handled the performance as it should have been done, and you were hugely relieved that nobody's guard had broken down and there had been no danger of anyone saying anything important about life and the leaving of it.

We don't know what they felt about it, the people who were at the receiving end of all this histrionic pretence that everything was normal. It might have been some consolation to them, but surely they saw through it. In the dark hours of the night, they must have wondered why there was no communication left between friends who had once talked about everything. Just when they needed real conversation most, they got reassurance, platitudes and, in fact, lies and this from friends who used to sit up until dawn to discuss the meaning of the universe, the future of art, and the likelihood of getting someone you fancied to fancy you. Why should it turn to 'Ho ho ho, and aren't you looking well today?' It was because the well could not bear to admit the thought that the rest of the world was not well. So what do you do if a friend is terminally ill? You do not want to go in with a face like the tombstone they know is not far away. You might not wish to bring up unaccustomed spiritual reading, likely aphorisms or new thinking on reincarnation.

Last year I had a friend who was given three months to live, and I asked him to tell me what were the best things people could do and what were the worst. He said that the very worst thing to do was to send a Get Well card, one with bunny rabbits crying into spotted handkerchiefs and saying, 'Sorry to hear you are not so well.' He used to look at these cards blankly and knew that they were the conditioned response and automatic reflex of people who meant desperately well, but who had to hide behind totally inappropriate greeting cards. He wanted to reply on another card, saying, 'I'm trying, God damn it.' But he didn't. And he didn't because he knew that the idiotic bits of card with hospital beds and sexy nurses and thermometers and bad puns hid the real message of sympathy and huge distress. He said that he really didn't like people urging him to get another opinion and saying that it couldn't do any harm. It would do harm, he thought, because it would waste time, the one thing there wasn't much of left. He preferred people to call it cancer if they spoke of it at all, rather than use some euphemism, and he also wished that he didn't have to spend so much time thanking people politely for their suggestions of healing crystals, prayers Never Known to Fail, or the laying on of hands by someone who lived half a continent away.

Those of us who knew him well and asked him how he wanted to do it were told. He wanted to remember the good, laugh at the funny, hear all the gossip, and try to be as normal as possible. Even though he could no longer eat, he wanted to come to restaurants with us and didn't want to see anyone wince when he told the waiter he was on a diet. He said that three months was a terrific bit of notice to get. You could make all kinds of arrangements, ask people to take a book from your collection, burn incriminating letters, heal old enmities, and send postcards to people you admired. Once upon a time he had thought it would be good to die in his sleep or in a car crash. Something instantaneous. But there was a sense of time borrowed about this three-month sentence. Without being in the slightest maudlin, he said it was something we should all be lucky to get.

He said that he didn't really like bunches of flowers, there was too much of the sick room and even the funeral parlour about them arriving in great quantities. But what he really liked was a rake of stamped postcards or a couple of colourful tracksuits which he could wear around the house, and a few videos to watch at night. He didn't like letters telling him that lots of people had conquered this and surely he would too. But neither did he like the letters saying that he had a good innings and that, at 60, he had done everything. He wanted to be the judge of that. But he did love to hear from the many people he had known during his life, saying briefly that they had heard about his diagnosis and that they were sorry. Letters that then went on to say things he could hold on to, things about time well spent, marvellous places seen, and memories that would live forever. All this brought a smile to his face and made the tapestry richer and less laced with regret. He said that if at all possible, he would like there to be no tears, but he knew this was hard, and he didn't mind unnaturally bright eyes, because he knew this was a sign of grief felt but bravely fought back. He could understand why some people hadn't the guts to come and see him, but he wished they had.

It has taken me a year to get the courage to write down his advice to those who want to do their best for friends who are about to die. A year in which I have never ceased to admire his bravery and honesty and to believe that there may be a lot of it around if we could recognise it. We planted a rose tree, a Super Star, in his memory, and at last I feel the strength to pass on his advice to those who might learn from it.

For Tired Read Terrible

25 June 1994

It was a lovely sunny day on Bloomsday and I was sitting in the hallway of the Joyce Centre in Dublin, delighted with myself. Why wouldn't I be? I was watching all the comings and goings, the people dressed up, the American tourists, the faces I hadn't seen for years. I was waiting to do an interview and was given a glass of lager to pass the time. Not many people would be having as good a time on a Thursday afternoon at one-thirty, I said to myself.

And then a woman came in whom I used to know years ago, when we were young teachers. She was a very positive person then, I remember. She used to take her pupils on great trips to France, which they never forgot. She had amazing projects in her classroom, and she used to go around with a box on the back of her bicycle asking people who had gardens if she could have cuttings, and then she used to get the kids to plant them around the schoolyard.

She was a leader in everything, the first to give up smoking, the first to organise lunches where people were asked to contribute the price of a meal for the hungry, the first I knew to go to America for the summer and work as a camp counsellor. I had nothing but good memories of her.

She seemed glad to see me too, but then her face fell. 'You look desperately tired,' she said sympathetically. 'Are you all right?'

Well, the sun went out of the day and the fun went out of the Joyce Centre and the taste went out of the glass of lager and the sense of being as free as a bird went out the window.

Tired is not a good thing to be told you look. Tired is terrible. And the really infuriating thing is that I was not tired, I had been in bed nice and early the night before. And I was tidy. Tired can often mean that you look like a tramp, but no, I had gotten all dressed up, complete with white collar, to be interviewed. And I wasn't sweating or collapsing up flights of stairs. I was sitting calm as anything in the hall.

And if I was 25 years older than when we last met, so was she.

So, stupid as this may seem, I looked upset. I must have bitten my lip or may have looked as if I was going to burst into tears, because she said at once that she was sorry, and wanted to know what she had said.

'I'm not tired,' I said, like a big baby.

She tried to explain that tired was okay. We were entitled to be tired. By God, we had earned the right to it. We worked hard, we had done so much. It would be an insult if we *weren't* tired.

She was backtracking, trying to dig herself out of it, I said.

No way, she insisted, and wasn't I the touchy one trying to read other words into a perfectly acceptable observation, and more meanings than were implied in an expression of concern?

But what was she going to do about my tiredness? Suppose I had admitted it? Just suppose I had agreed that I was flattened by fatigue and had been waiting for someone to come in that door to identify it. What was her cure? Had she ginseng or Mother's Little Helpers in her handbag? Did she have a personal fitness trainer, a protein diet, a Seventh Son or shares in a health farm?

We argued it away good-naturedly, as we had always argued in years gone by. She had always been a woman of strong views, a characteristic I admire. I have even remembered many of her maxims, such as 'Avoid restaurants that have strolling musicians', 'Never play cards with a man named Doc' and 'Don't resign before lunch'.

But what's the point of telling someone that they look tired, even if you don't mean it as a euphemism for old, ugly, unkempt or rapidly going downhill? Was it a kind of sympathetic come-on . . . expecting an answer along the lines of Nobody Knows the Trouble I've Seen?

She was spirited about it. And she nearly won the argument.

Would I prefer, she wondered, if we were all to turn into those dinkleberries who greet each other with an effusion of insincere compliments: 'Oooh, you look marvellous' and 'Oooh, you've lost loads of weight and honestly, I never saw you looking better, what have you been doing?' The greetings and the compliments becoming like a ritual dance where the vain and the self-centred rake through a form of words, wondering if there is a 'marvellous' too few or an expression of astonishment not heightened enough. Surely we haven't reached this stage?

But then, when she said tired, did she mean that as some sort of shorthand, to be a jovial punch on the shoulders between old mates, a kind of bonding between the worn out?

She thought about it.

She thinks she meant that she liked me from the old days, and it was good to see me again, and when she came upon me I had a serious expression on my face as I had been talking to a woman about her late husband and maybe she remembered me roaring about, not sitting down. And in a sense, she didn't want to be one of those people who always said twitter twitter things and assumed other people had lives that were free of care. And on reflection, she said, now that we had argued the thing down to the bone, she would never as long as she lived tell another human being that they looked tired again.

Traveller's Tales – The Call of the Check-In Desk

3 September 1994

Two years ago I went around the world, heading west into the sun all the time, and I loved every bit of it, except the two and a half days in Las Vegas and the memory of an unmerciful row in Los Angeles Airport. Looking back, I don't know how we did it. If it's Monday it must be Arizona, if it's oysters at five pence each, it must be Auckland, if it's police horses with red tinsel necklaces, it must be Christmas Eve in Sydney. If it's people playing tinkling music and wearing flowers in their hair, it must be Bali. And this for two people who normally sit with two small cats looking at the television at night, or else in other people's houses, staring mystified at bridge hands and wondering how many points you need to respond to a call of 'one diamond'.

So now the urge has come again: the call of the check-in desk, the unpacking in strange hotel rooms, the day tour of a new city, the heat in October, the factor 15 sun lotion in November, the postcards home, meeting friends in far-off lands, the sense of something new going to happen every day, the writing of a weekly travel diary, of working out what possible time it could be at home if I wanted to ring the family or friends. I want to read newspapers again in different countries, obsessed with different issues, utterly unaware of our concerns. I'm looking forward to celebrating other people's festivals and thanksgivings, lamenting their political systems and weeping over their ludicrous weather forecasts, where Met men and women look into the entrails and forecast, in different accents, sunny periods with some showers or showery periods with some sun and get paid salaries for doing this.

I don't have four and a half months to examine the world this time, only about half as long, in fact. But I met a marvellous couple last week in County Clare, who told me they were doing the entire cosmos in three weeks and they found it a satisfactory kind of undertaking. The secret is having early nights everywhere, they confided, and drinking a lot of fluids – mainly bottled water – and not going to any country where the people were in any way hostile to your people.

Boastfully I mentioned that I was in the habit of touring the cosmos myself, and they wanted to know my secrets. These were different secrets; they had nothing to do with early nights, bottled water and wondering whether anyone would be hostile to my people. They had a lot to do with only meeting people you wanted to meet, seeing things you thought you would like rather than you should like, late nights and much bottled wine. I told them happily about packing half-a-dozen Ella Fitzgerald and Liam O'Flynn tapes – great for evenings far away – about bringing a small torch, having nothing that needed ironing and always going to airports an hour early to keep the blood pressure down. They looked at me steadily and thanked me for sharing this with them.

Younger friends wondered why would I visit a lot of the same places again when there were so many new places left to see. It's hard to explain that if a dozen Australian sunrises are good, then two dozen are better, if laughing all night with great friends thousands of miles away was good in 1992, it should be just as good in 1994, and would not be long enough this time either. Last time I missed a general election, which was heart-breaking, but good friends sent faxes with essential information like the results of each count in Dún Laoghaire/Rathdown – good deeds like that will never be forgotten.

I have four weeks before I go, and now that I'm not in the business of dishing out advice any more, I'd love to receive some –

if you have any ideas about travelling light or making things easier in some way, it would be great to hear from you. Nothing about travelling irons please, or sheets of tissue paper to make sure the creases fall out. No hints about putting jewellery in hotel safes; this would fall on deaf ears. I had four great dresses made by a friend of mine, who is actually a rather important person in costume design in a theatre. I gave her one dress as a sample, and asked her if she could find an assistant or a student who would make four like it, the only requirements being no discussion about it, no fittings and no ironing. She said she had to make them herself because she spent her working life telling others that you must discuss everything down to the bone, have a fitting twice a day and never use these horrible synthetic fabrics, but have everything natural and crushable. Her entire credibility would have been shot to pieces if it were known that she had a friend with such base requirements.

But out there, somewhere, there are people with marvellous ideas, like the journalist who told me that when you bought books abroad you should send them home by surface mail, which costs hardly anything and then they arrive as a lovely surprise weeks later when you'd forgotten about them. A photographer who told me that if I wanted great holiday snaps, I should look first at the main postcards of wherever I was and go to where they were taken, since these were the guys who had figured out the best angle to take the shot. And since there should be a pool of brilliant travellers' ideas, I'll publish some of the ones that appeal to me most.

Last time I went looking at the cosmos I swore I would be better informed when I went to examine it again; I would know intelligent things about the places I was going to visit. But, somehow, two years passed by and I never got informed. I greatly look forward to hearing any advice which might be put into practice during my second crack at the cosmos.

Love's Last Day Out

11 February 1995

The last Thursday of every month, their mother came to Dublin for an outing. There was a day excursion fare and if you got to the station nice and early you got a great seat on the train. Then, at what she still called Kingsbridge, one of her daughters met her. This was Jenny, the daughter who didn't go out to work. They would meet Nuala, the daughter who did go out to work, at lunchtime.

It was a wonderful routine, never broken over the years, except when one of Jenny's babies was inconveniently born in the last week of a month and once when their mother had a chest infection. The outing took the same form always. Jenny would drive down the quays, and her mother would cluck at the changes she saw on every visit. It had all been altered, the implication being for the worse, but they knew it wasn't since last month or last year; their mother was thinking of 30 or 40 years ago, when the world was young.

Jenny would then park and her mother would sigh at the way so many people brought their cars into town for no reason at all. And then they would head for Brown Thomases. It was always said in the plural; if you said it in the singular it meant you didn't know it. It was like people who said St Stephen's Green. The tour took two hours, never less. In fact, Jenny thought that had the time been available it might have taken all day. Her mother stood at the front door and sighed with pleasure. Everything that lay ahead was like a wonderland. In a changing world this place remained as it always was, a temple of comfort and luxury.

They would start at the cosmetics counters. Mother knew a lot of the elegant women who demonstrated and sold the various fragrances and creams. Well, she didn't really know them but she remembered them from visit to visit. 'When I was here last month you were telling me about this new firming cream for the throat,' she might say to one. They were invariably helpful and interested and often gave her a spray of something new and very sophisticated that had just come in. Years ago there had been a very nice woman called Caroline Mahon who mother had got to know. She had wept and sent a letter to the store when she read of Caroline's death in the paper. But all these girls were very helpful and took all the time in the world. Which, as Jenny said grimly, was more than duty required since her mother's face, with its dusting of face powder and merest touch of lipstick, was not going to be an arena on which the great cosmetic wars of the world could be fought and won.

Then they went to look at scarves and ribbons and particularly at the kind of ribbon comb attachments that someone going to a glittering evening do might wear in her hair. Mother had short grey hair, hidden on the day of the outing by a hat. She never wore these hair ornaments but she fingered them, lovingly clucking over the prices, but saying that of course if you had the right dress then these ribbons could set it off and make the whole thing into a coordinated outfit that would be very striking. And then they might go to the cookery shop where they would examine whole ranges of coloured cookware and mother would discuss 12-place settings and easy-care napkins.

They would try on jackets, a nice jacket. A nice jacket paid for itself a hundred times over, she would tell the salespeople. And as they would nod and agree, she would see the price and cluck that it was steep but then you were paying for the cut. 'And the material,' the assistant might say. 'Pure wool.' 'And the name,' mother would say and put the jacket back on its hanger.

The tour almost always ended in the bed linen department downstairs. Real down was debated, the kind of goose that had delivered up the feathers for the duvet was identified, queen size and king size beds were clucked over; in the old days there had been just a double bed. Mother nearly always bought a pillowcase, it was wrapped carefully in the distinctive bag of the store and she would leave reluctantly for lunch with Nuala.

Since mother did not walk far, lunch was in Dawson Street or Wicklow Street. It was a nightmare for Nuala, who worked on the southside. She gave up trying to find lunchtime parking and took a taxi instead, arranging for another taxi to pick her up an hour and a half later. This meant nearly two and a half hours away from the office, unheard of in the place where she worked, but Nuala said that not to have it for her mother's outing was unthinkable. She worked longer hours to compensate and always felt slightly guilty about it.

At lunch mother would talk about the tragedy of growing old on your own without knowing love and a family. Nuala would clench her teeth and smile ever more brightly as she said in a tinny voice that one never knew what was around the corner. And, at the age of 43, with the same relationship, of which her mother knew nothing, she found it harder and harder to play this role. Then it would be Jenny's turn, what a pity the children had done such odd things, gone to Australia with no job and no plans, didn't write letters to their gran, were never there when she came to the house. Jenny smiled and shrugged and said that was the way it was, and what could you do?

The sisters' eyes met across the table. Twelve times a year they felt united by this huge resentment of the mother they both loved. Then Nuala's taxi would come and she would go, and it was always too soon and nothing had been said and she worked too hard and perhaps that's why she hadn't settled down like a normal person. And then Jenny would get the car and take mother home for afternoon tea, never sure whether she wanted one of her children to be there and possibly bring up an argument about the Church, or whether it was better to face into an empty house. And she would put Mother on the train. All the way to the station and as they boarded the train, Jenny's mother talked about the great visit to Brown Thomases. It was a tragedy that it was going to change into that Marks and Spencers.

Last month at lunch she told Jenny and Nuala that she might cease these outings to Dublin. After all, with no lovely visit to Brown Thomases what was the point? Her two daughters looked at her blankly. Nuala began a useless attack, saying that the place had always been a bastion for the rich and privileged and that it was absurd to say it was for ordinary people. Jenny, trying to be a peacemaker, said that BT's would be across the street and that everything would be just the same. But their mother would not be consoled, without any idea that she was writing off over 20 years of being welcomed warmly to Dublin by her two girls. As far as she was concerned it had been maybe 250 visits to an escapist paradise.

She was 71, too old to have the shining, glittery toy snatched away from her. Too innocent to hide from her children that the disappointment was so great it had clouded her judgment and her love for her family.

A Walk on the Wild Side

25 February 1995

It was usually with a group of friends in those days and they would all make sure to buy a different Sunday newspaper so they could go and have a drink afterwards and read four papers instead of one. It was very companionable then but of course nobody had time to do anything like that now; they were all in marriages or relationships varying from uxorious to deeply unsatisfactory and they would corpse themselves laughing if she were to suggest anything as ludicrous as walking down the pier on a cold Sunday and going to have a few jars.

Nowadays they asked each other to dinner parties, at infrequent intervals, to drinks mornings or to charity dos; the days of sharing newspapers and glasses of lager were long gone. So, if she were to go down the pier, she would go alone. But it might look odd if she met someone she knew, which was part of the purpose of the trip, so she borrowed a dog from a neighbour. She could always say it was a keep-fit exercise. The dog was less fit than herself and seemed to have had enough after a few steps. But she dragged him along behind her. She noticed that everyone else seemed to be following behind bounding hounds who were straining at leashes – she had obviously taken the wrong breed. This was a sleep-by-the-fire-and-wait-for-bits-of-roast-beef-after-lunch kind of dog.

She had dressed quite carefully: a smart jacket with a white shirt coming out over it; dark pants and boots; no handbag or anything prissy like that; hair wind-blown but not messy. If she met anyone from the past she would look fine. She would also have her explanation – her husband was at the golf club for a special competition so she was released from making Sunday lunch and she thought she would blow away the cobwebs. It was mainly true. It was a bit true. And anyway, one of the great things about growing older is that you know people don't care about your circumstances all that much.

After 10 minutes she met a man she hadn't seen since they were students. He looked in very poor shape, she thought, and she could hardly believe that he must be the same age as she was.

'Are you at the same game as myself?' he asked her hopefully.

'What game is that?' She felt she might be. A game that involved beating back loneliness, trying to banish the growing feeling that life had not turned out as she had hoped it would.

'Waiting for the pubs to open?' he said, as if it were obvious.

She didn't want to have a drink with him, his story was bound to have been worse than her own. 'No, no, purely exercise,' she said, and bounded on.

He had been such a firebrand at college; they all thought he would have been a politician. She would not allow herself to be brought down by him, he was not someone she had been fond of, there was no room in her heart to feel sorry about acquaintances, people she half knew. She had enough things she really did care about. She met a couple with their teenage children. The children were polite and shook hands; the parents were holding each other's gloved hands as they shivered in the sea breeze. They told her she was looking terrific and they laughed at the lazy dog who had been so delighted with the pause for chat that he had fallen fast asleep at their feet. Their praise sort of made up for the fact that they were happy and together on a Sunday and holding hands still and that their children would bother to go out walking with them and be courteous enough to greet someone who was introduced.

And she met another couple she knew, walking together in animated conversation. They stopped to exclaim briefly how healthy and young she looked. They went back to their argument, which was about *Riverdance* and whether people were building all kinds of fantasies and wish fulfilment on it, or whether people who said that were just a shower of begrudgers. They seemed pleased to see her and each hoped to recruit her to their own side of the argument. They assumed she had been to the Point and shared the experience.

She felt nonplussed as she walked on. Imagine, people thought that she had the kind of marriage which involved joint outings to something like that, which she would have loved. It must have been two decades since she had been in a lively discussion with him about anything except the latest crisis concerning the children, or the fact that he hadn't come in for a lunch or dinner that she had prepared. And everywhere she looked, it seemed that they walked the pier as if it was the gangway into the Ark, they went two-by-two, unless they were accompanied by eager, happy children who seemed perfectly content in the company of their parents. The single people that she did see were young, determined and obviously going somewhere.

Perhaps this had not been such a good idea. Then she met the man in the anorak. About 50-ish, hands in pockets, nice friendly face. He was carrying a small exhausted Pekinese in his arms.

'At least yours is on his feet,' he said, nodding at her exhausted charge who was gasping for air and for mercy beside her.

'He'd be a bit heavier to carry than yours,' she said. And they were friends.

They decided to turn back. They walked companionably back to the mainland, laughing over things like dogs having no stamina. And it was the most normal thing in the world to go and have a drink. When the boy came to the table, the man in the anorak said he hadn't a penny on him. It would have been nicer if he had been just a little bit apologetic and said that by some amazing chance he had come out without his wallet. But he didn't; he just said he had no money. So she bought him a pint and a gin and tonic for herself and then another pint and another gin and tonic.

They talked about the football match and Northern Ireland and the new plans for Dún Laoghaire, and Joe Duffy on RTÉ and the divorce referendum and Bishop Casey and the DART and then it was time for the pub to close. And he said that maybe he might see her on the pier next Sunday if she was a regular. And they woke the sleeping dogs and went their ways without exchanging names or family circumstances.

All week she had been wondering if she would walk the pier again. There were so many things to put on one side of the scales. Including the knowledge that it's always women who feel low and unappreciated, who walk blindly into the most ludicrous situations. And would she be buying him pints all her life? But there was a bit of ballast on the other side too. It's a long time since she had a proper chat on a Sunday and a bit of fresh air and, in a sense, it all depends on the weather tomorrow.

Peter Panic Attack

6 January 1996

The Messer will be 59 in February, into his sixtieth year he said on the phone, mystified as if it had suddenly crept up on him unfairly from behind.

It had been a long time now, 10 years maybe since I had talked to him; he sounded just the same, like he had sounded in UCD a long, long time ago.

He was calling from London on New Year's Eve. He was on standby for a flight to Dublin, and had suddenly thought it would be great to see the New Year in with the old gang.

The Messer sounded so enthusiastic about the people of the past that you would get carried along with it and think they were all there waiting to gather in Neary's. He spoke about them as if we were all still in duffle coats in Earlsfort Terrace. He spoke of people who would be spending New Year's Eve with their grandchildren, people who had lived abroad for 30 years, people who had become recluses and disappeared from anyone's lives. He asked warmly after two men who had died, and seemed shocked by the news. He must have known, he must have.

I remember telling him about one myself 10 years ago, and the other was so well known even the Messer would have read about it. And yet you couldn't feel enraged with him; he was so grieved, and said such warm and appreciative things about them both, remembering the good and the positive.

And after all he had been abroad.

He only came home rarely, on spur of the moment goodwill visits expecting to find everything frozen in a time warp of 35 years ago, a perpetual student life where people would assume he had only been away for a matter of weeks.

And where was he staying: in Dublin?

The question was always asked to the Messer with some trepidation, but even as it was asked you remembered the hollow nature of the request. The Messer always said that he was fine, and he would get fixed up, he never asked straight out for a bed for the night. He knew that the offer of a bed was increasingly refused as the years went by, because it was never for the night; it was for many nights and usually involved other people coming and going and irritation turning into conflict and guilt, huge, huge guilt, because the Messer was a decent person and none of this ever seemed to be his fault. Directly.

But somehow, even though he said he was fine and would get fixed up he never was fine and never did get fixed up, and someone always had to look after him because nobody could be so awful to him as to walk out and leave him there, or so patronising as to give him the price of a hotel room.

So what happened over the years was that you'd try to second guess the Messer, arranging to meet him somewhere in the city centre for a specific time in the middle of the day before things got to the stage that he would come home with you, being firm about your own commitments while assuring him that you were enormously enthusiastic about seeing him again, which was actually true.

His life is lived entirely in the past; he has painted the edges of everything we lived through then with heavy silver, and sees it all through the rosiest of spectacles.

He never remembers any incident that reflects anyone in a poor light, yet he makes us all uneasy because we have felt that time has marched on. Maybe we are all dull and middle-aged and middle class and the Messer who is older than any of us is the gilded youth, the Peter Pan who somehow kept the faith when the rest of us lost our wish to be free spirits.

We even pretend in his presence, people who meet rarely and casually. For his sake we let it be thought that we are all together the whole time and resist asking each other questions that would prove us to be near strangers.

The Messer gives little information about his own life: there was a wife and son a long time ago, and then another wife, and a long-time companion and someone in Prague who might or might not have been a wife. But they are never brought along to meet the friends of his golden youth – they are spoken of vaguely and benignly but with a slight raising of the shoulders, a near shrug, as if their responses and unpredictability are beyond the Messer's comprehension.

Work seems too dangerous a topic to bring up. Certainly it's not something that the Messer would introduce into the conversation.

He is interested in an astounded sort of way to hear what the people of his generation did with their degrees or often without them. His own was never conferred, because it was never given, 'too many' confusions and mix-ups and situations at the time.

And there are pen pictures of cities far away, all of them great places in their own way but none of them a patch on Dublin, which of course is greatly pleasing and flattering – but doesn't hold water.

If Dublin is so great . . . why isn't the Messer here all the time?

Anyway, as a standby he got on a plane. Of course he did. Quite possibly a passenger with a ticket may have ceded a seat to him. That's the kind of person he is, charming and helpless and bewildered and good-natured.

And because it was a No Room at the Inn situation on New Year's Eve he just wandered around the Old Haunts as he calls them looking for ghosts, waiting for the crowd to turn up. You just could not ask the Messer to anyone else's house, too many years of people in floods of tears, fights in kitchens, the wrong thing being said over dinner tables, unlikely candidates being found in bed with the Messer or even more unlikely candidates being tight-lipped and furious because they were not in bed with him.

All those promises made and broken, all those cars over the years having to drive 30 miles in the rain to collect some late arriving friends that the Messer had assured of a welcome.

And as the clock struck 12 and those of us who had sort of grown up in our different ways celebrated in various parts of the forest I would say a lot of us thought briefly of the Messer and wondered for a little instant had we been selfish to exclude a man who thought so well of us all, and who had written a memory book in which we all had starring roles.

But I looked around my gathering and felt deeply grateful that he wasn't there, unwittingly upsetting all the good-natured people I was with, starting a political argument with one, an affair with another and with the sure knowledge that somewhere out there a crowd of Other People were hovering, waiting to join us.

The Messer rang from Shannon Airport last night. He was on standby for a flight out.

He had a great time in Dublin, but when had he not? God, wasn't it a fantastic city; no, he hadn't run into anyone from The Old Gang, they had all been tied up or out of town but he had gone to some of the Old Haunts.

And he had met a gorgeous girl celebrating her twenty-first birthday, and she had said to join them and they all went on and on, to pasta in one place and really lovely people, and then a nightclub. Imagine Dublin full of nightclubs! And then they had plenty of room in their place so he stayed, which was just as well because the poor girl had this awful row with her boyfriend on New Year's Eve as it happened, and it was good that she had an older, wiser man to pick up the pieces, and a lot of their friends were going to the west so he went along too and it had all been great and he was so glad he had just acted on impulse and come to Ireland for the New Year.

'Do you ever do anything on impulse these days?' he asked me.

'Can I write about you?' I said suddenly.

He said he'd love it and then his coins ran out.

He won't be back for many years, he may never read it. None of what he calls the Old Gang has an address for him, we never had. We must never feel guilty about him, never ever again.

Fortunes have been invested by pharmaceutical companies

seeking the secret of eternal youth, and we happened to meet a man called the Messer who found it all by himself.

He didn't grow up, simply because he didn't want to . . . maybe it's as simple as that.

Little Person! Tiny Person!

13 January 1996

At the hairdresser sat a woman who was, to my mind, the client from hell. But what do I know? They seemed to love her and fawn over her.

'I'm going to have an entirely new style,' she said.

'Right, now do you want it close to your face?'

'No, no, not close to my face.'

'Away from your face then?'

'No, not away from my face.'

I wanted to fly from my chair in my protective gown and take her by the throat. But they were interested; it was, after all, a challenge and they decided to call another stylist for a consultation.

The other stylist appeared and the woman who neither wanted her hair close to her face nor away from it gave a screech that froze everyone in the salon.

'But you've lost so much weight. You've lost stones and stones. Little person! Tiny person! How did you do it?'

'Well, it's not all that much and I . . .' She didn't get an inning.

'But you're a tiny person; you used to be a huge, huge person. Remember those great jowls you had? Real jowls, they were darling, and look at you now. A little person. How super, no jowls. Don't ever let it creep on again, will you?'

I thought about it for a long time. Would the little person, the tiny jowl-less person, like all this praise? Was it the reward for the diet, the self-control, the exercise? Or might she resent the spotlight and the attention of 30 people beaming on her and the memory of an earlier, more hideous self being brayed all over the salon? It was a mystery.

And I was so glad that I am not in hairdressing. It would be so easy to let that scissors slip.

Fighting February

10 February 1996

A hairdresser told me people do desperate things to their heads in February. They are so fed up of life being cold or wet or dark or whatever, they make reckless decisions and get the lot lopped off, or the colour changed radically to counteract a pallid face.

They sit discontentedly in their chairs before and after the transformation and even though it's not good for business, she would often suggest to them that they do something else, rather than a revolution with their hair which they might spend a year regretting and growing back to the proper shape or returning to the proper colour.

'Like what?' a gloomy woman said to her last year.

It was a puzzlement but the hairdresser was a woman of courage. 'You could go to line dancing,' she suggested. And the gloomy woman did.

And on the very first night, she met a man in the line as they were dancing whom she liked much better than her husband. And he tilted his hat forward and talked in a nice jokey country and western style. The gloomy woman seemed to be cheering up by the hour.

Her husband just looked up from the paper when she came home in the evenings and he said they were all cracked to be doing that sort of thing, and there was someone, somewhere making big money out of eejits buying fringed skirts and laced boots.

The children were grown up, but still mystified when they heard their mother was leaving home and moving in with the man from line dancing; their father was philosophical.

'She was always that way in February,' he said. 'It was a kind of a thing with her. It was as if she thought the good weather would never come again.'

Apparently, he shook his head about it, accepting it as inevitable, just one more of the many bad hands that life dealt. His wife walking out on him.

Whether there might also have been something wrong with their lifestyle was something he never paused to speculate about in the following months, when the good weather had come back but his wife was still with the man who tilted his hat.

The hairdresser said to me that from now on she's keeping quiet: if someone wants a head shaved to the bone in February, she'll do it. But I said no, the gloomy woman was somehow waiting for that man in the line dance. The hairdresser must not feel responsible, she must go on interfering in people's lives. Doing that is just proof that we are alive.

❦

This friend of a friend, also an anti-February person, gives a St Valentine's Day party every year. The simple rule that nobody who is officially or emotionally attached can attend. The theory was you wouldn't have lovebirds canoodling and making you sick, or old staid married couples nodding and patronising everyone to death. No, this was to be a gathering where the mind-set of everyone was unencumbered – her phrase, and a fairly horrible one, it has to be said.

Anyway, it turned out to be a fine gathering over the years as the group changed from being twentysomething to thirtysomething, and a new decade is approaching.

Some people have dropped out because of getting involved and attached, which presumably was what a lot of it was about.

Some have moved from one state to another and back.

Everyone brings a bottle of good wine and they can ask to include new blood as well. If these people are unattached and come along bearing the requisite bottle, that's considered great too.

But last year two deceivers were at the party. Men who were certainly committed officially, and as far as their wives believed, committed emotionally as well. Dublin is a small city; they were unmasked at an early stage. Now a shadow hangs over this party.

Everyone had thought it was for real. Now, you might just as well go to a nightclub, they all say.

One of the parents at a school I know has a cookery class in her home. She has children round each Tuesday in February and they all bring their own ingredients. They are boys and girls and they all sit and watch her do it first; then she gives them boards, dishes and part of the kitchen table each and they do it themselves.

They have made gingerbread, pizzas, cheesecake and pancakes. That was last year's repertoire.

The children and their parents would have been happy for it to go on all year, but the woman said no, it was only February, in order to beat the blues.

I said I didn't know children felt low in February.

'Who said anything about them feeling low?' she asked. She was doing it to raise her own spirits.

❦

There are two men I know in Dublin who have hardly noticed February for the past 20 years.

February is quite simply the time they put their heads down and make money. They'll dig your garden, cut things back mercilessly, they'll teach your children to drive in your car, take your rubbish to the dump, they'll collect dry cleaning, stack trolleys in supermarkets, clean windows and cars, clear out garages and attics. I know they offer their services to drive drunks home, and I suspect they also drive other people's hackney cabs.

This is all on top of their day jobs, which could be described as office work.

They have regular clients; they strike a rate and work almost around the clock. But only for this one month of the year.

Why only February?

It's the month before March, stupid. And March is when you go to Cheltenham. Do you know nothing?

❦

Since I left teaching and got more or less in control of my own life, I always tried to have a holiday in February. The sun on your shoulders seems to do you twice as much good in the month when you know it's going to be dark when you wake and dark while you're still at the keyboard. So today, I should be in South Africa.

I have the highest of hopes about the sun, despite the telephone interview I did for a radio station there. I was burbling on about how much I was looking forward to the heat, and the talk show host said I should bring my umbrella, which I thought was a weak but good-natured weather joke, so I laughed immoderately.

Apparently it wasn't a joke at all; the rain was bucketing down outside the studio. She was giving me practical advice.

I tell you this so that you will not hate me for having gone to the sun yet again.

She Didn't Do So Badly

8 June 1996

Forty years ago this week I did my Leaving Certificate. The biggest, laziest, youngest girl in the class, my head was full of lollipop music that summer. I think my whole life must have related to it since I have no other memories at all of the time all my revision was done to the tune of 'The Man from Laramie', and 'Hernando's Hideaway'. If I kept the record player really low in the bedroom I was allowed to play it but they could apparently hear it everywhere so I used to sit on the floor beside it reading my North and Hillard and rapping out the words.

'With ask, command, advise and strive. *By ut* translate infinitive.' It went almost magically to the Johnston Brothers' version of Hernando. Try it. And you could sing the prime ministers of Britain to 'Cherry Pink and Apple Blossom White' too, if you had a mind to.

It was too late to put anything to the tune of 'Rock Around the Clock', because we knew the real words too well and it wouldn't work trying to put in the French verbs that were conjugated with *être* or whatever had to be sealed into the brain in those last weeks and days.

There was a thing in trigonometry, the proof of a sine or a cosine I think, it went beautifully to 'It's Almost Tomorrow', and in fact I liked it better at the time than the Dreamweavers' version. But some songs were sacred. There were a lot of things I could have sung to 'Memories Are Made of This' but I didn't want to destroy the sound of Dean Martin's lovely velvet voice by listing the terms of the various Land Acts or Home Rule bills. And of all the songs that summer, it was the one I loved best.

I was terrified that somehow I mightn't have any memories. That life would pass by and I wouldn't have enough fresh and tender kisses to look back on, not to mention stolen nights of bliss. I was dying for a stolen night of bliss. It was the only thing that kept my head down to do any study at all. Whatever chances there might be of getting together a stolen night of bliss if you had the Leaving, if you hadn't, then there wouldn't be any chance whatsoever.

I remember that I got a small piece of steak with my tea when the others would just have sausages. My father and I, the workers, would get steak. It was meant to give me great energy for all the studying I was doing but in fact, of course, it only made me feel guilty.

The great surge of energy only went into dancing 'Mambo Italiano' round the bedroom to myself wondering did I look like Rosemary Clooney and singing 'Rock and Roll Waltz' in what I thought was a terrific take off of Kay Starr. The steak fed my delusions that I would in fact be a performer and that the Leaving Cert was not only not essential, it might even hold me back.

But I was the eldest of the family so there was more than usual depending on this result. They would get some kind of inkling from my score whether the show was on the road, or if they had been fooling themselves and we were all as thick as planks.

So I decided regretfully that I would have to get it to keep the peace, and to reassure them. And once it was got I could go off on stolen nights of bliss and be 'discovered'.

I would be an Educated Rock Star and when Dickie Valentine

would lead me on stage with him to do a reprise of 'The Finger of Suspicion', pointing at me all the while, no one need ever know that I had got my Leaving Cert, I could just keep quiet about it.

I suppose it all proves I wasn't nearly old enough to leave school or indeed to be allowed out anywhere if these were my views. I am trying to be honest, but 'discovery' is definitely what must have been uppermost in my mind that May and June. Suez hadn't happened, Hungary hadn't happened; Ronnie Delaney's Olympics were later. I sure as hell wasn't thinking about knowledge for the sake of it or an academic career, just scrape in, do law, be a judge or something until I was discovered. I thought a lot about Grace Kelly and Prince Rainier and a bit about Khrushchev and atheistic communism, but much, much more about someone, hopefully Tony Bennett, who was going to 'Take My Hand' because I was a 'Stranger in Paradise'.

I remember the first day of the Leaving Cert and there being some idiotic row at school about whether we should wear our uniforms or not. There was a View that said we should, it would sort of straighten us up, make us realise that this was all work and part of the studying process. There was another more liberal View which won in the end that it didn't matter if we went in our vests and knickers as long as we tried to write down what we had been learning for over a decade.

We would meet girls and even fellows from other schools on the way home and compare the questions. You didn't really want to talk to anyone who hadn't done it. We all hated showing the papers to the teachers and our parents.

The poor teachers would say, 'Well at least you knew that, didn't you?' stabbing at something and you wouldn't remember whether you had known it or not.

And at home the exam papers were always spread out on the kitchen table and studied by everyone. Even Smokey the disdainful cat used to come and look at them as if he could have got through them with no worries. And they assumed I would have done brilliantly in English.

'Aren't you always telling long, rambling stories about things, the essay would have been no trouble to you,' my mother said proudly.

'And those are grand straightforward questions about Shakespeare,' my father said approvingly. They were indeed, but only for people like himself who had read and understood it all. Not so straightforward for those who had tried desperately to set the Tomorrow and Tomorrow and Tomorrow speech to the tune of she wears red feathers and a hula hula skirt. And none of them were any good at Maths or Irish so that had to be an unknown quantity, and I did a lot of dealing with the Almighty about good behaviour and putting Stolen Nights of Bliss on hold for the foreseeable future if I got the exam.

And then there was an endless, endless summer waiting. I think the sun shone every day but Met Éireann, of course, will tell me that it never came out at all.

And then there was the day the results came. We were in Ballybunion, and we had a Fuller's cake for tea and I was allowed to eat two of the four solid chocolate drops on top myself. And compared to all the Einsteins in Kerry, of course, my Two Honours were a poor thing. And only a Pass in English. Imagine!

Still it was worthy of being celebrated. And it was. In style.

I wish they knew that of all their children, I was to be the least educated of all. But Two Honours in those days served fine to start me off for the rest of my life.

And of course if I had it all over again I would have worked harder, read more, opened my mind, made them prouder of me. But that's only what I think now as I look back on a summer that seems like the other day.

Curmudgeons of Summer

9 July 1996

'I don't like summer myself. Personally,' said the girl in the pale pink shorts and the dark pink halter top. She was eating a huge ice cream cone and waiting in the crowds to see the USS *JFK* come into view in Dún Laoghaire.

She looked like an advertisement for summer, with her shiny hair, her 97 small, healthy teeth, her light suntan and her air of well-being.

'I know,' said her friend, who was no use as a friend. She had said 'I know' to people for all of her 18 years and you could tell she would do so forever. 'I know what you mean.'

The girl who didn't like summer, personally, was at least a person of views; she was prepared to elaborate on her stance.

'You see the thing about summer is that you expect so much from it,' she said earnestly. 'Every time you open the papers or turn on the television there's someone saying, "Here comes summer," and you get all excited and then nothing much happens at all.'

'Oh, I know,' said the other one.

Socrates had a friend like that, didn't he, when he was writing the Dialogues, some dumbo who said 'Assuredly' every two pages or so.

Deeply depressing, I would have thought, and wouldn't have crossed the road to meet the guy again. But look at it this way: they remained mates, at least until the end of the book, so people might just appreciate that kind of attitude in other people. Anyway, the girl who didn't like summer, personally, seemed perfectly pleased with the response.

'Like they're always saying that the deep dark days of winter are behind us – I love winter.'

'Oh, winter's great,' said the other.

'And you could stay in bed on a winter morning without being demented by the birds, they've all gone down to the Mediterranean or died or something in winter, you'd get a bit of peace.'

'The birds are brutal,' said her friend.

'You know where you are in winter, you're cold and wet and you know that's what it's going to be, you haven't a clue where you are in summer.'

'Not a clue.'

'It could be pouring rain or roasting the skin off of you, and what's there to do anyway?'

'Tell me about it,' said the other.

They were both gorgeous-looking, and getting many admiring looks from what I would have thought were fine young fellows as they stood scantily clothed, staring with dulled eyes out at the *JFK*.

The girl in the two shades of pink finished her ice cream and licked her fingers.

'You know another thing about summer, you end up eating 300 calories of this stuff without realising you're even doing it.'

The other one nodded until her head nearly fell off.

'You're right,' she said. 'You're too right.'

I didn't wish the pink girl a more sunny attitude, or a sense of priorities. I was sorry that she didn't have anyone to disagree with her and to sing some song in praise of summertime. I wished her a better friend.

❦

The woman polishing her brasses was dying for a chat. 'It's a nightmare trying to keep the house right in summer,' she said. I told her she was doing a great job of it. But no, apparently the bright light of summer was the enemy. You could shine and shine and some smear always showed up. But the very worst thing was the way the bit of brass polish comes off on the door, well, that kind of thing goes unnoticed in winter, but at this time of the year it's a nightmare.

I thought to myself that a nightmare was putting it a bit strongly, and though a lot of people have very exacting standards about housekeeping, there's a question of going too far.

'You see there should be some method which means that you only clean the brass and not the door,' she said. What I should have said of course was, 'I know, this is what you're up against.' Why do I never realise that this is the right thing to say almost all the time?

But I said that there was a woman who lived near us in London who had little cardboard shields cut out and she used to lay them over the knocker and the letter box and just clean within them so that the brass polish didn't get on the door.

Well, if I had found the Holy Grail or the Missing Link she couldn't have been more interested. And was it heavy cardboard and did you stick it onto the door, or just hold it, and imagine my doing that. She'd never have thought it about me, just goes to show how wrong you can be about people. She was going to go in and make one immediately, and would a cornflake packet be strong enough, or should it be something sturdy and what did I use myself?

I was purple in the face trying to tell her that I had never done it, but she didn't believe me. If you had a wonderful hint like that, then of course you'd use it. I had transformed her summer for her, she said. But don't you like summer anyway, I pleaded.

I wished she did, but in fact she didn't. The sofa covers faded, the net curtains looked grimy after three days, you realised how much of the place needed painting. One good thing about winter, she said mysteriously, was that everyone was in the same boat.

There's this couple who have been given the loan of a mobile home for a week. They were delighted because they thought they could have one last real family holiday before the kids grew up and wanted to go off on their own. There's only one problem. The children think they are grown up and have planned to go off on their own already. They're 15 and 16, for heaven's sake. What would they be doing going on a holiday with their parents?

A holiday is what it says it is, it's time off to enjoy yourself, to be free to do what you want. The mobile home would be like home, but even more uncomfortable. You'd have to be in for meals and clear up after them and you wouldn't be allowed go anywhere.

Now they don't quite say it like this, but that's the drift.

And they don't buy the idea of it being one last holiday either. You can be absolutely certain that come next year there'll be one more 'last holiday', and so on until they are old and grey.

The kind thing to do is to cut it now and let the parents realise that it's not on packing Scrabble and a family-size Nivea Creme any more.

I know I'm a softy, but I wish there could have been a compromise. That the children could have come to the mobile home for just a weekend. That way things wouldn't have looked so bleak for good, warm people whose only crime was to want to enjoy the summer.

The Fall

19 October 1996

Years ago, before I knew that people called things by different names, we knew an American person named Martha and she used to talk a lot about the fall. I didn't know it was autumn for ages because she had so many other marvellous expressions and dramas in her life that the thought of a huge upcoming fall off a roof or a wall or something was only too likely. After all, her father had lost all his money in the Crash, and we thought it was a car crash and asked why he didn't go back to the scene where the crash had happened and look for it. And when she talked about little cookies we thought she meant small people in chefs' outfits.

I call her a person, not a girl or a woman, because we thought she was oldish, almost bordering on being an adult. She was the cousin of a neighbour and she came to spend four weeks' vacation every year. She used to clean the house from top to bottom as payment for her keep. She talked about Jell-o and turnpikes and trashcans and how her uncle used to take the paddle to his sons if they behaved badly.

Mostly we didn't know what she was talking about, but she seemed to treat us as equals, which was great. It was a time when it was much more important that people were of goodwill and occasionally had candy to offer than that we understood what they were talking about. We were always pleased when Martha arrived, and we listened, bewildered, to some of the things she said.

Like, back home she worked for a tightwad who ran an old folks' home, and her brother hoped to hang out his shingle and her sister had saved for a muskrat coat. And always she said she wished she could stay in Ireland for the fall. She would love to see just one fall in this part of the world. It would be wonderful what with there being so much greenery already.

I didn't ask anyone about it because, to be honest, I got the impression that the grown-ups thought Martha was a bit soft in the head and I didn't want to let her down and I thought it was odd to look forward to and be wistful about seeing a fall of any sort. And I had no idea what greenery had to do with anything.

And the years went on and her uncle's wife died and he didn't see any need to drag the unfortunate Martha back to be a skivvy in the house. Those were his words. His late wife had always referred to it as giving the girl a holiday. But anyway, Martha didn't come. And sometimes she sent us the funnies from American newspapers – Blondie and Dagwood and things – and we got a lot of the jokes in them.

And one day some years later her uncle said that some people were just born for trouble, and that Martha had all the hallmarks of that kind of person. It wasn't bad enough that her father had lost all his money on some cracked stocks and shares, her brother had been forbidden to practise law because of some misunderstanding, her sister had left home without a forwarding address. Martha's mother was in a decline, so they had arranged that the mother go in to the home where Martha worked – no wages for Martha, but then no fees for the mother.

I was about 14 then.

'It's not fair,' I said.

Martha's uncle said that in his opinion life was rarely fair.

Martha didn't remember what age we were or else she thought we'd still like the funnies, and when I was about 16, I actually got her address and wrote to thank her. She wrote back to tell me she was in love.

And this was fantastic. Firstly nobody talked much about love, no one old like in their twenties, which Martha was, and she told me that his name was James and his aunt was a patient in the home and that when his aunt died James would be very rich and they would get married. And I was very excited by this and asked what kind of things James said, and Martha rather innocently wrote and told me and I told them to the girls at school.

And Martha said that when she and James got married they would come to Ireland for a honeymoon – they would come for the fall. I knew what the fall was now but I didn't rate it much in those days. I wrote and told her that she shouldn't bother, the summer was nicer, and of course she wouldn't have to clean her dead aunt's house now. I even said that she had been very good to do all that years ago. And she wrote an odd letter saying that she looked back on those days like heaven, the work was so much easier than here in the old people's home. She would love to leave but of course there was her mother to support there, and then James coming in twice a week to see his aunt.

I always thought she was a nurse there but she was a lowly cleaner, she explained. She said that she had never claimed to be anything else. She asked for a picture of Ireland in the fall.

We didn't have colour films in our cameras in 1956 and our garden looked desperate anyway, and my mother said why wouldn't I take a snap of it when there was something to see instead of everything straggling and dying. I found a wet-looking picture postcard which looked as if it were taken in Famine times and sent it to Martha. She didn't reply and then we lost touch.

And when I was 20 and saw the colours of my first fall in New England I remembered Martha and wrote to the old people's home that the tightwad had run. I didn't know his actual name, but a woman wrote back and said that Martha didn't work there any more, adding that the management had entirely changed.

And I felt somehow that Martha had been annoyed with me for sending her that horrible postcard so I wrote again and wondered did they know where she was, because I wanted to send her a proper picture of Ireland.

And the woman wrote to say Martha was in a penitentiary, she and a young man had been convicted of the unlawful killing of the young man's aunt. . . . It had always been thought that Martha was very much under the young man's influence.

Martha's mother had died shortly after it, her brother had been in some kind of trouble and there was no trace of her sister.

Her uncle in Dublin is long dead.

Martha would be 65 now.

It's not her real name, but if she were out there and on the internet? Maybe.

On this lovely autumn day when the fall in Ireland never looked better, I would love to find her, and to take her back to see it just once. I don't want to hear about James. I don't imagine she sees much of him.

There are greater coincidences in the world than that I should find her and show her the Irish autumn she wanted so much to see.

Let's Talk Gridlock

30 November 1996

When I went to live in London in the early 1970s I used to be knocked backwards by the amount of traffic-conversation that preceded every gathering. If you went to someone's house for dinner you were expected to give an account of how you hacked your way through the jungle to get there, as if the place was some kind of forest clearing in Borneo instead of a suburban house in Ealing, and in turn you had to listen to everyone else's story.

I decided it was a ritual, like the way a dog often turns round a lot before settling down; London people had to tell you where they left the M4 and how they had skirted round the back of Paddington. Then, when it had all been said, you could talk about real things.

It was very boring and I used to thank the Lord that in Dublin there would never be endless traffic stories like this because there weren't a dozen alternative ways of getting from one place to another; you sort of went on the main road. So we could start the real conversation immediately, I thought. We were ahead of the game.

Wrong.

They're here.

And if you want to unleash them on yourself, just mention the three words Traffic Management Plan and you'll get worse than you would believe possible.

And the really bad part about it is that there's no real solution except to leave three hours earlier than you need for everything, like in the middle of the night. And buy tapes with sounds of water rippling over the little rocks, things that will calm you down, and keep saying 'ohm, ohm' and try to loosen your grip on the wheel if you see bones coming through white flesh on your knuckles.

That, and the knowledge that you are not alone, may help.

Listen to the conversations all round you, know that everyone else is in the same position. Get solidarity and comfort from realising that the city has come to a standstill for everyone, not just for you. Listen, listen and calm down.

In a restaurant, a couple waits for their host. He arrives in the door with a face like thunder, nearly taking the door of the restaurant, the waiter, and the people at two tables with him in his path to his own table. He starts dragging off his wet overcoat, his gloves; his face is purpling up by the moment.

'Jesus Christ' are the first words he gets out, and the place is treated to a description of how he waited for 20 minutes at one set of traffic lights, and 10 at the next and there was no parking and there were wardens and guards like spare parts at a wedding, walking round leering at people, and *Jesus Christ!*, again bawled at the top of his voice.

The startled couple, who had been waiting for him more than half an hour, lied and said they had only been there for five minutes: the crumbs of 10 bread rolls proved them to be dishonest.

'Can I take your coat?' the waiter asked, politely.

'Look, I don't need any hassle today, let me tell you.'

The waiter moves nervously away. The man who owns the restaurant arrives to take the coat, which is thrown half on a chair, half on the floor, with the gloves and a scarf and the man looks as if he's about to strip down to the buff unless somebody stops him and calms him down.

'A nice drink, perhaps?' The owner cannot find the right word. There are no right words.

'Nor do I want to be patronised,' cries the purple man in a choking voice that terrifies the wits out of his two lunch guests, who had wrongly thought they were going to have a nice meal out.

❦

On the bus, the woman got up three times to ask the bus driver was there no way he could go any faster. The first two times he explained politely that there wasn't. The third time there was a slight edge to his voice when he asked had she any suggestions. Like maybe ploughing through the solid line of traffic ahead of him? Or revving up seriously and taking the bus into a flight path 10 feet above the line of trucks, cars and buses below?

There were tears in her eyes.

'I'm sorry,' she said, and went back to her seat.

People were kind and came up with suggestions. Could she get off the bus and walk? No, she walked with a stick, she wouldn't be any quicker.

What about a taxi?

Wouldn't it be the same snail's pace?

Yes, but at least the taxi driver could take a different route. People will understand if you're late, they told her, everyone's late these days. It just can't be helped. Everyone understands.

The woman could not be consoled. It was an appointment with the bank. Everything depended on their getting this overdraft. The bank had a feeling that they had been unreliable in the past.

We all had the feeling that she might have been – the tears of mascara didn't make her look like a good risk.

The bus was silent thinking about banks. Someone gave her a tissue and someone else loaned her a mobile phone. She made a poor job of explaining the traffic situation. None of us had any hope for the loan.

A boy stood at the bus stop – like everyone else he had been waiting forever as things went slowly by, grim-faced people from an adult world staring unhappily ahead.

'Did you have a nice day at school?' asked an old lady anxious for a conversation – any conversation – to pass the time. The bus was 200 yards away, it might take 15 minutes to get to us.

'No,' he said.

'Why was that, dear?'

'The bus was late getting there and the teacher said how was it that the rest of the class got in, and I said they had fathers with cars and they all got up at six o'clock in the morning and I was told not to give cheek.'

'Yes, well,' she said.

'And then we all got late to the football pitch because the bus didn't come and there was no football, and now the bus hasn't come and I'm going to be late home and they're going to say how is it that I'm the only one late home, and none of them go out but if I said that I'd be giving cheek again.'

'It's a hard life,' the old lady said.

'It's a shit life,' said the boy, ending the friendship between them.

Outside a solicitor's office. An awkward meeting, two one-time friends have fallen out, a business is being wound-up, there are still areas of disagreement about some outstanding debts.

'Let's try to get this done in as civilised a way as possible,' says one of them.

'Yeah, well it would be easier to be civilised if your bloody lawyer had turned up.'

'He's stuck in traffic, his secretary said.'

'Secretary? Gargoyle, more like. Where's she coming from not letting us smoke in the building, for God's sake?'

They stood glumly in the rain smoking while traffic inched by.

Once they had cursed the traffic to the pit of hell, and counted the number of cars that had only one person each in them, there wasn't much to talk about. So they inhaled. And they talked about the old days, when they were starting out.

When the solicitor arrived yelping about gridlock and the car scrappage scheme and nobody caring and cities coming to a standstill, the two men were looking at each other as normal human beings. One of the few success stories of the Christmas traffic.

'They've Gone and Dumped Portillo . . .'

3 May 1997

As soon as the sun started to shine in London it was as if someone had shouted 'Strip'. They stood half naked outside the pubs, pints in hands and faces upturned to the hot sky. In the parks they lay out on rugs in shorts and bikinis, their skin glistening with oil. They had dragged tables and chairs out into front gardens and people without gardens draped themselves over steps and footpaths. It was only the first day of May but there was terrific heat in the sun – and those who live in a city of nearly 12 million people will take any opportunity at all that might suggest closing their eyes and pretending it's Midsummer's Day.

And even at the polling station in a west London school there was a holiday air. A woman with sunglasses on her head, two small children by the hand, came to the gate of the little school.

'Don't talk to anyone at all, just look at all the lovely pictures the other children have drawn while Mummy votes,' she said.

'I want to vote,' said the five-year-old.

'Not now, darling, later . . . look at the nice pictures on the wall.'

'You never let me vote.'

The seven-year-old was examining the artwork. 'These are no good. Our school is better,' he pronounced.

'Shush, darling, they're doing their best, it's a very little school.'

'It's a *normous* school,' said the child.

'I meant they don't have all the marvellous classrooms and lots of good teachers like your school does.'

'It's an awful school, Mummy, why are you voting here?'

'It's where we vote, darling, now *do* look after Charles.'

'I *want* to vote,' said Charles in the querulous tones that he may still have in 13 years' time when he is allowed to vote.

'Charles, darling, just a little patience for Mummy then we buy mangoes and ice-cream, all go to Grandmother's garden for a lovely, lovely visit.'

'I hate Grandmother,' said Charles.

Most people smiled tolerantly at each other as if to acknowledge that children always speak their minds.

'I bet she hates you, too,' said an old unshaven man bent over a stick, a bottle of ginger wine peeping from his pocket.

It did the trick and silenced Charles and his discontented elder brother. They stood fearfully in the small, run-down school, worrying about what the future might hold for them.

In the restaurant the waitress said that she was doing her own poll. She asked every single person who came in which way they had voted and amazingly as soon as they had got over the shock of breaching the secret ballot, they all told her.

'It's going to be a landslide,' she said cheerfully to the owner as she bustled through the In door and the Out door of the kitchen.

'You wish,' said the dour owner, who had worked out with two accountants and a man from a money house that he would be marginally better off if the Tories won, but that the country was going down the tubes no matter who won.

'Aren't you excited?' the waitress asked him.

'Takes a lot more than a bit of unscientific research bothering the customers to make me excited,' he said.

'It's not unscientific, we get them from every walk of life here.'

'I'll bet my whole week's wages Labour gets in with a majority of over 160,' she said.

'Your week's wages? Don't be so foolish, woman.' It was easy winnings but he didn't want to bankrupt the staff at the same time. She was determined, however. She asked three customers to be witnesses to the deal. Even those of us who were not regulars could telephone and make sure that he would honour the bet if she won – or lost.

'Don't be specific about the majority,' people warned her. But she was a confident, New Dawn Woman. She wouldn't reduce it – 160 or more, she said – and went on serving tables, her face full of smiles.

I rang the place yesterday to check the situation. Apparently they had all stayed up most of the night watching the television. When the majority topped 160 the waitress had bought champagne.

'Fine bloody socialist she turned out to be,' said the owner glumly. A hangover, a lost bet, the wrong government in power – it was not a good Friday.

'Did you tell her that?' I wondered.

He had, of course, several times during the night but as she poured the champagne she had said that this was what it was all about, champagne for everyone, not just the fat cats.

'Fine bloody grip on reality she has,' the owner added, as he bid me farewell.

A woman who works in a factory reports that they all began the day yesterday by dancing round in a conga line singing 'They've gone and dumped Portillo . . . They've gone and dumped Portillo . . . da da da da da.' And it proved so catchy that even the supervisors and management side of things thought it was funny and sang it too.

The phrase got into people's heads and at lunchtime when they went to the pub they started it again and this time the whole pub joined in.

'What's Portillo done to them?' the barman asked.

'He looks like a prat,' said a man at the bar.

'Not fair to judge the poor fellow by his face,' said the barman.

'He talks like a prat.'

'Oh well, then,' said the barman, as the pub danced on.

Mrs Perfect

13 December 1997

Mrs Perfect got married in May 1970 and to this day she has never forgiven Charlie Haughey for upstaging her at the wedding. The guests talked of nothing but the arms-smuggling charges that had just been announced. She felt nobody gave her even a passing glance as she walked up and down the aisle. Their wedding seemed only like a supporting act to the dramas that were going on elsewhere. She was 25 years old, she looked wonderful – she can show you the wedding pictures to prove it – but they were more interested in Blaney and Haughey that day.

She knew that you have to work at marriage – her mother told her that long, long ago. Let nobody tell you that running a home was easy, her mother had always said; it involved ceaseless vigilance and planning.

So Mrs Perfect had done exactly that, and never more so than at Christmas.

Hers was going to be the Christmas that would be remembered by everyone. Planning began in early summer, when she would start the present list. Her gifts were never extravagant but very thoughtful.

If you ever said to Mrs Perfect that you liked chutney, she would write it down, and she would cross-reference this on her chutney list.

She made two summer shopping trips to the North, where many things were much cheaper, and she never travelled without her list, plus the list of what she had given for the past five years.

She knew how dangerously easy it would be to give the same person an aromatic herb pillow year after year if you didn't keep proper records.

All her Christmas cards are sent on December 6th; she books her Christmas Eve hair appointment in November to make sure she gets the right time. The turkey, ham and spiced beef are ordered weeks in advance and the shopping list, the Christmas countdown and two stuffing recipes are photocopied and pasted to the back of a cupboard door by the beginning of the month.

She knows a place where you can get a non-shedding tree, and bought it long before the rush so that she could get the right shape.

The lights have been tested, a candle bought for the window, a holly wreath for the door.

The fridge and the freezer are filled with things that can be brought out instantly for unexpected guests, though there seems to be fewer of those than there once were.

Still, it's good to be prepared.

The children have all left home now, so you would think it would be less pressurised than it used to be. But Mrs Perfect laughs at this notion. It's worse than ever, she says: you have to remember all their in-laws – a tin of mince pies here, a potted plant there. Not that in-laws is the right word, more like common-law in-laws. None of them married, all in what people call 'relationships' and not a sign of a grandchild from anyone.

Mrs Perfect says it doesn't look at all good at the bridge club, where she has no pictures to show. You can't show snaps of your gorgeous home – only grubby faces of little toddlers are acceptable, followed by screeches from the others saying that you don't look old enough to be a granny.

No brownie points for having made the cakes and the puddings in November, tippexed-out the changes of address in the Christmas card list book, polished the brasses and decorated the house within an inch of its life.

They have a drinks party about two weeks before Christmas and Mrs Perfect used to love the way people oohed and aahed over the way the house was already festive and decorated.

People groaned and said they hadn't even begun their shopping yet and everything was so rushed and there was so much to do and the Christmas season started earlier and earlier, preventing them from doing anything at all. She used to think this was just a way of going on, a style of speaking, until she noticed that it was quite possibly true. She saw neighbours dragging home a tree on

Christmas Eve, and she would get the same, guilty poinsettia from apologetic friends who said it was so hard to think of anything but at least this would be colourful.

Mrs Perfect had been thinking of their presents for at least six months. Wasn't it odd that other people didn't do the same?

It's hard to know who to talk to about it. Mrs Perfect's considerably less than perfect husband isn't around all that much. He seems very delighted with his comfortable, well-run home. Well, she thinks he is. But honestly, it's hard to know. Things have changed, probably, from the way they were in her own mother's day when you were judged by how you ran a house.

Nowadays, people possibly had different goals, but it was complicated trying to work out what they were.

Mrs Perfect's husband told her to stop fussing round like an old hen when she said something totally innocent like how they need to get up at six o'clock on Christmas morning to have everything ready.

She had actually said it so that he wouldn't come home at all hours from a do like he did last Christmas Eve.

That's when he snapped at her and called her an old hen. He said the children were in headlong flight from her because she made such an almighty fuss over everything. All people wanted to do at Christmas was get on with it, for heaven's sake. Why couldn't she take that on board?

He had apologised, of course, for his outburst, and said it was harsh of him, particularly when she went to so much trouble and wore herself out for everyone else. All he had been trying to say was that a tin of soup would do people fine rather than weeks of boiling bones. He hadn't meant to sound bad-tempered.

And of course Mrs Perfect had forgiven him, her mother always said that men hate a woman who sulks.

But it is worrying her.

None of her four children and their 'partners', as they call them, is going to be with her for Christmas Day this year. Is this pure chance, or the way things happen, or is it more sinister? Does she fuss them all to death?

At the Christmas drinks party this week she wondered were people annoyed with her and even slightly pitying rather than impressed with her perfect home.

Who moved the goalposts?

And when were they moved?

Mrs Perfect thinks we should have been told.

Death in Kilburn

19 December 1997

The response to 'Death in Kilburn' was such that Maeve made it the basis of a play, Deeply Regretted By. *First produced as a television drama by RTÉ, the play won a Jacob's Award that year, the award for best script at the Prague TV Festival, and was chosen to represent Ireland at the Prix Italia and the New York TV Festival.*

Patrick went into hospital on December 1st. He was sure he would be well home for Christmas, because it was only a light form of pneumonia, they told him. Modern drugs cured that kind of thing easily.

They didn't cure Patrick. He died on Wednesday, 7th, without very much pain.

Stella was negotiating about the Christmas turkey when the news came from the hospital. She couldn't believe it, she kept thinking that it was a huge hospital and they must have made a mistake.

She asked the priest to come with her to the hospital. He was a nice new priest who had come to the area a couple of years before, he wasn't attached to the parish church, he worked in welfare.

Father O'Brien went to the hospital with Stella and he asked all the right questions. It was a viral pneumonia, it hadn't responded to antibiotics. Nothing could have been done, his coming into hospital had just meant that he died with less discomfort and he had aids to his breathing up to the very end. They were very sorry and they gave Father O'Brien and Stella cups of coffee out of a machine without asking them to pay for them. They told them to sit there as long as they liked.

Stella said they had better send telegrams to his mother and his brothers in the west of Ireland, and Father O'Brien brought her back to his office to do this. They gave his office number as somewhere to ring, because Stella and Patrick didn't have a phone.

She went home by herself to tell the children when they got back from school. They had four children, and they all came home around four p.m. She bought a cake for tea because she thought it would cheer them up, and then she decided that it was too festive, the children would think they were celebrating or something, so she brought it back to the shop and they gave her the 65p back.

On Thursday December 8th, the feast of the Immaculate Conception, the children were off school anyway. They sat around in the house while a neighbour made cups of tea for Stella and told her that she should thank her maker every hour of the day that Patrick hadn't been on The Lump like so many other men, and that there would be something to feed his wife and children now that he was gone.

Stella agreed mechanically, felt a sense of cold all through her stomach. She still thought that Father O'Brien might run in the door with his face all smiles, saying that it was a mistake, that it was another Patrick who had died of this thing that drugs couldn't cure.

But Father O'Brien was having a very different kind of conversation. Two men had arrived in his little office. They were Patrick's brothers, they had got the night boat over and come up on the train to Euston. It was their first time in London.

They hoped Father O'Brien would understand why they had come and appreciate the urgency of what they were doing. They were bringing Patrick's body back with them to the west. They had been given the name of an Irish undertaker who arranged funerals across the channel and they were going to see him now.

'But he's lived all his life here,' said Father O'Brien. 'Won't he want to be buried here where his wife and children can visit his grave?'

'No,' said the older brother. 'He'd want to be buried in the parish church at home, where his wife and seven children can visit the grave.'

Oh dear God, thought Father O'Brien to himself. Here we go. 'Well I think you'll have to discuss this with Stella,' he began.

'We don't know anything about Stella,' said the brothers.

'I'll take you to Stella's house,' said Father O'Brien firmly.

The brothers agreed reluctantly that if it would avoid trouble they supposed they'd better go.

Father O'Brien got someone to look after his telephone and they walked off past the shops that were all lit up with Christmas lights and plastic holly sprigs. Father O'Brien got rid of the children and the neighbours and sat through the worst conversation of his 15 years as a priest.

Somehow anything he had to take before was easier than watching a woman realise she had been deceived for years, seeing the peeling back of layer after layer, realising that on five occasions when Patrick had gone home alone to see his old mother he had managed to conceive another child.

He could barely look at Stella's face when the halting, inarticulate sentences came out of the brothers, each one filling in a dossier of deceit and weakness and double dealing.

'What's she like . . . your sister-in-law?' Stella said eventually.

'"Like"?' Well she's a grand girl, Maureen. I mean she's had a hard life what with Patrick having to work over here and all, and not being able to get home except the once every summer.'

'But we were married in a church,' said poor Stella. 'We must be really married, mustn't we, Father?'

There was a throat-clearing silence and Father O'Brien started to talk about God understanding, and Stella being truly married in the sight of God, and nobody being able to make hard and fast judgments about anything, and his voice petered out a bit.

The brothers were even more restless than Father O'Brien. With some kind of instinct that he still doesn't know how he discovered, he suggested that he take them for a pint because the pubs had just opened, and that he would come back and talk to Stella later.

He settled them in the corner and listened. The story was simple, Patrick's funeral had to be at home, otherwise it was not a funeral. Otherwise his whole life cycle would have no meaning. It would be like being lost at sea not to be brought home to rest.

And that Englishwoman couldn't possibly come home with him and behave as a wife. They had nothing against the poor creature, it was obvious there had been some misunderstanding, but Father could see, couldn't he, how much scandal there would be if she came the whole way over in black and brought her children with her, it would be flying in the eyes of God.

Father O'Brien's pint tasted awful.

And then there was the mother to think of, she had worked her fingers to the bone for the family, she was 83 now, they couldn't have a common-law Englishwoman turning up at the Mass, now surely that was reasonable enough, wasn't it?

Stella was sitting where he had left her. She couldn't have moved from the table, and the door was on the latch the way he had left.

'Maybe there's a case for what they want to do?' he began.

'Sure,' said Stella.

'It has nothing to do with the rules or laws or what the neighbours think, maybe there's just a case for letting him go back there to rest. It will give a lot of other people a lot of peace. . . .'

'Oh yes, that's true,' said Stella.

'And we can have a proper Mass for him here, too, you know,' said Father O'Brien desperately.

'That would be lovely,' said Stella.

'I've got to go back and tell them if you agree,' he said glumly.

'What do you think is best?' she asked sadly.

'Well, I don't think anything is best, it all looks terrible and bitter, and I feel hopeless, but if you ask me what I want, I want Patrick to be buried here with you and his family all there to say goodbye.

'If you ask me what would bring the greatest happiness to the greater number then I think that you should let him be buried in Ireland.'

'It's a bit hypocritical, isn't it, Father? Up to this morning you regarded us as a good Catholic family, part of your flock. Now suddenly I am an "outsider", a woman living in sin, someone who can't go to a funeral in Holy Catholic Ireland in case I give scandal.

'I suppose the children are bastards as well. Everything that went before is all written off.'

'There's nobody who could say one word against you, Stella,' he began.

'Except that my husband was really my fancy man, and I can't go to his funeral, myself and the four love children stay here while the wailing and the drinking and the praising and the caterwauling goes on in the west of Ireland, isn't that right?'

'It's not like that.'

'It is like that. And someone would say what a great man he was and how hard it is that emigration causes the break-up of families for so many people. . . . I'm not English, Father, I was born here but my parents were Irish, and know about funerals, I've heard them talk about them.'

'No one said life was fair,' he said. 'It's been very cruel to you this Christmas.'

'Tell them they can have him,' she said. She didn't come to the door, she wanted no Mass in Kilburn.

The brothers arranged with the undertaker and the body was taken to London Airport and flown to Shannon and driven up the west coast and two weeks before Christmas on a cold Sunday afternoon Patrick was buried in a churchyard a mile from the house where he was born.

Saved by the Wiles of Cupid

14 February 1998

Of course their names are not Sean and Maire, but they *are* from the south-west of Ireland and they are out in Cape Town on a holiday.

And when they arrived at their hotel they were asked did they want to make a booking for St Valentine's Day. Special dinner.

'Ah, we'll sort that out later,' said Sean.

After all, it was January 24th – three full weeks before the saint's feast day. This was serious advance planning that was being called for.

'Touting for extra business, looking for a quick buck,' Sean said to Maire on that first night. 'That'll be it, believe me.'

And Maire said 'fine', and that's all she said.

The hotel didn't tout for business in any other way. It let them bring wine into their room, it pointed out a cheap laundromat, it let them make sandwiches out of the breakfast buffet.

But the following Saturday it asked them again, 'Made your plans for St Valentine's Day?' And Sean, who by this stage had got a suntan and was thinking in rands, not punts, thanked them politely but said there was no real rush.

And then they began to read the papers.

Page after page showed the restaurants that are completely booked up for February 14th. They watched the talk shows at night on television, heated debates . . . is it all too much this Valentine fuss, or is it wonderful and symbolic?

Does it mean that 364 days a year your loved one does *not* think about you, but that's OK if there's one day that the loved one *does* made a fuss?

The flower shops all over town have had huge warning notices up urging people not to leave it until the last minute. The South African phone service, Telekom, has huge ads showing empty flower buckets outside florists, and giving the grim reminder 'Phone First'.

Everything seemed to be referring to the day. Slimming machines were offered at 10 per cent off if you ordered them before The Day. Building societies were offering 16 per cent Home Loans on any love nest where the paperwork was done in time for St Valentine. There were so many heart-shaped Valentine balloons, paper flowers, teddy bears, gold-wrapped chocolates, satin and sequinned offerings in the newsagent's that Sean and Maire could barely find a picture of Table Mountain to send to annoy the folks back home in the rain.

Saturday night would be their last night. Sean did not want to be wandering the streets of Cape Town, his nose pressed against windows where lovers or pretend-lovers were toasting each other in sparkling wine at £2 a bottle and them unable to get anywhere to sit down.

He booked.

'All right, yes, a Valentine special,' he said awkwardly. He had never sent a Valentine to Maire. Not in 39 years of marriage. It wasn't the way for them, or their kind. They were people who worked hard and got on with it.

Not fancy words and poems and flowers.

Irishmen of his class, his age, didn't go in for that sort of thing. That was for romantic-novelists, card manufacturers, flower sellers, confectioners, restaurant owners. They were the people who made the money out of it. Didn't Maire *know* he was fond of her? They had been married nearly 40 years, raised a family. You don't have to say these things with lots of red and white decorations for them to become real, Sean believes. And had Maire ever sent him a Valentine's Day card, did he think?

Well, in the past when the children were at a silly age she might have thrown an old Valentine on the table and they all had a laugh and wondered who it might be from. . . .

And I asked Maire on her own would she have liked Valentines at all over the years, and she said she would of course – like any human. But Sean wasn't made that way and it would be like asking for people to do something completely against their nature. He was a good man to her. He'd give her money to buy one for herself if he thought she was fussing over it.

But oddly, for the first time he was looking around him out there where waitresses and shopkeepers and barbers and deck-chair attendants were all talking about the feast day. He had actually said to her that maybe sending a card was a cultural thing – like wearing shamrock on St Patrick's Day. So she wouldn't be surprised if the man she fell in love with in 1958 when Mick Delahunty's band was playing might well buy her a card this year. It wouldn't continue at home, but it was different in the southern hemisphere.

And love is in the air all over the place, not only for the Feast Day. This week Nelson Mandela's handsome face smiles out of every paper as he clasps the hand of Graça Machel, widow of the Mozambican President. He has now spoken publicly of his love for her, how they talk every day on the telephone and how she has changed his life. Commentators on all sides seem to be full of indulgence and delight about it all, even though weddings have not actually been mentioned. Even Archbishop Desmond Tutu harrumphs only mildly about it and though he has to point out to the President about being a role model for young people, there has not as yet been any serious thundering from pulpits.

And then there's the other marvellous love story that's all over the papers. The tale of David and Caroline Dickie. He is 80, she is 70. They only met recently at a party in England and confided to each other that their children were plotting to put them into old people's homes against their wills. So they came out on a holiday to South Africa and got married.

According to the way it's told here, their children *still* don't know. David is English and used to work in Kenya. Caroline is originally Irish, a teacher, and used to work in Zambia. They both look radiant, barefoot on a sandy beach under a caption saying 'Saved By The Wedding Bells'.

They are going back to England to face the music today, and if I had the energy and the time I'd find them and go with them myself just to see the St Valentine's Day surprise a lot of people are going to get when they find out.

Just Don't Ask

14 March 1998

When we were young teachers a wise woman told us that we should never ask the children to tell the class what they did for Easter or Christmas or Confirmation or St Patrick's Day.

Don't ask, she said, because it will turn out that some of them did nothing at all or – worse still – had a really awful time. Nothing points up the inequality of people's lives more starkly than asking innocent children to tell you how they spent what was meant to be a festival.

But once I forgot this and asked them what they did for the National Day.

There was the usual chorus of visiting granny and going to watch the parade and having lunch in a hotel from the lucky ones.

And then there was a child who said they spent the whole day looking for a vet's that might be open because their dog had got hurted.

And I asked what had happened to hurt the dog.

Later you get a sense of what not to ask, but you don't have it when you're 22 and eager to be nice to the children and encourage them to tell stories.

It was a tale of a brother who had been away at sea coming home unexpectedly and his not liking the fact that Mammy's friend was living in the house and breaking a chair, and the dog got frightened and ran under the table whining.

And there had been a fight between the girl's brother and her Mammy's friend, and the dog hadn't understood so he jumped at the brother not realising who he was and to save himself her brother had picked up a bread knife and the dog was badly hurted.

And we all sat in that classroom as the horror of someone else's St Patrick's Day came through to us.

And I remember her voice going on about it not being too bad in the end because eventually she and her sister brought the dog to a hospital – a hospital for people – and someone there knew a vet nearby, so they carried the dog to his house and he stitched the cut in the shoulder and the dog would limp always on his front left paw and he had a bit of a cough but he was not going to die which they thought he might when they saw all the blood.

I wonder do any of the other pupils remember her telling that story? She is dead now, so I can tell it without hurting her.

She left school without any real education or exams, nothing much at home to encourage her, and she married when she was 19 – to a very nice fellow apparently, and they had a grand marriage until she died at the age of 38, some complications after a routine operation.

I'm sure that during the years of her happy marriage she didn't keep thinking back to that terrible St Patrick's Day in 1962 when she and her little sister carried a big dog covered in blood all around Dublin and eventually going to a hospital for people.

Maybe even the sadness and fright of the Domestic Incident had long died down in her mind.

Not in mine.

I think of it every St Patrick's Day when I see the Special Menus advertised in hotels, when I hear the oompah-oompah of a band. Not because I want to superimpose on everyone else's happiness the image of those two frightened little girls whose dog always coughed and walked with a limp as a result of the day's events.

I suppose it's just to remind us not to assume.

It certainly cemented the lesson that the wise old teacher had taught us, and now that I'm not in the classroom any more it hasn't lost its relevance. I strongly believe that you don't do thoughtless, cheerful vox pops to people about feast days.

In spite of the greeting cards, the streamers, the cheerleaders and the festivities, a startling number of people may have remarkably little to celebrate.

And all this came to mind because I met a glowing young girl with a tape recorder who was doing a series of ad-lib recordings in a shopping mall for a radio programme.

She thrust her microphone at passers-by and with a huge infectious grin she asked every one of them, 'What will *YOU* be doing on St Patrick's Day?' Her tone expected a reaction of riotous excitement, fun, happy families and carnival time.

In my earshot she met a man who would be going to see his wife up in the hospital as usual.

She met a woman who said she was going to stay in bed all day with the sheet up to her chin because she was demented with all the demands her children were making.

She met an elderly woman who said she wouldn't be doing much because she had been broken into and robbed.

In one way I wished the gorgeous girl with the microphone might realise that not everybody on this windy day was gearing up to a party-party spirit. That she was unearthing more despair than hope.

But then as a co-worker I was sort of sorry for her. I know what it's like when people won't say what you want them to, when they refuse to behave like a crowd sent down by Central Casting who are mouthing exactly what you want to hear.

But finally she met another gorgeous young girl like herself.

'I'm a *SINBAD*, I'll be cruising Temple Bar,' said the interviewee, which seemed to satisfy the girl with the microphone perfectly.

But not me.

'Excuse me,' I said, coming out of hiding from my lurking position. 'What's a *SINBAD*?'

Apparently it's a Single Income No Boyfriend, Absolutely Desperate.

But then everyone knew that, didn't they?

Bleach Sniffers on My Desk

18 April 1998

It had been a good day and when I saw a little ant run across my desk I thought to myself, in a rare fit of Buddhist kindness, that the poor little fellow hadn't much of a life, really. The desk must have seemed endless to him and he didn't know what awful dangers, such as myself, were lurking nearby. So I picked him up on a postcard and carried him out to the garden and put him in a big pot that contains a fuchsia. There, now he would have grand things to eat – old fuchsia leaves, earth grubs, much nicer than a dull old desk.

Feeling very proud of myself and full of virtue, I went back to work and discovered 12 more ants crawling up the screen of the word processor.

Suddenly we had a distinct change of policy.

No more mercy dashes to the potted fuchsia.

The ants were too many and too insistent and in the wrong place. I went for the Parozone and a J-cloth, and having nearly asphyxiated myself I looked at the surface to see had I dealt with them as quickly and efficiently as I believed.

The ants loved the Parozone. They reeled a bit at first – as we all might with a first, strong gin and tonic – but they obviously took to it greatly, and sent out a message for their friends to come and join them. The other ants heard somehow that the good times were rolling on my desk and they arrived eager to share the delicious taste of bleach.

The day looked a lot less good somehow and I withdrew a bit to consider my position. Now, I don't like them. We're not meant to like things with six legs and antennae. Nobody enjoys seeing things much smaller than us scuttling around the place, particularly around our place.

And it was actually a question of numbers. One ant was all right but this amount was not. And I had the feeling the ant which had been carried outside had long said farewell to the fuchsia leaves and had come back to join the bleach sniffers. And of course there's the huge guilt feeling: this must mean I have a filthy house. Why else were crawling insects marching towards it? Quite obviously it's a place that any infestation would love to settle in.

This was doubly distressing because I was expecting a colleague to arrive from London and we were going to be spending some six hours at this desk going through a manuscript page by page.

The thought of having to beat the ants off with a ruler before we could even read the thing was not something I wanted to contemplate. Nor did I fancy what might be reported about the standards of hygiene in modern Dalkey.

Sitting well back from the desk full of reeling, happy ants, I reached cautiously for the telephone to ring Éanna Ní Lamhna, of RTÉ's nature-programme fame, who would be the right person. She would know what was politically correct about ants without being foolishly sentimental and asking me to give them muesli for their breakfast or anything. But there was only her answering machine. In times of stress nowadays I have a big mug of tea and turn on the radio. So, having examined the mug very carefully for fear of drinking a dozen ants accidentally, I turned on RTÉ.

A huge ant discussion was taking place. I looked at the radio beadily for a bit. People are always imagining they hear voices on the radio talking to them: it's a fairly common paranoia apparently. But I listened very carefully and they really were talking about ants.

And wonderful, healing words came out of the little radio: 'It doesn't mean your house is dirty.' The man said it twice. I could have leaped into the radio and hugged him. Apparently it's just that people have patios near their houses more nowadays, and grouting between tiles. Yes, yes, I was saying, looking out at the roof garden with its tiles, all this is true. The ants are just looking for food, that's why they come indoors, the calming voice said. Yes, well. That's as may be. But you'd wonder why can't they eat the grouting and the things outside where nature intended them to be? This point was not properly dealt with, I felt.

Anyway, they moved on to a pest person, and the pest person said that there were indeed far more inquiries about ants at the moment, a lot of people had been inquiring. Anxious even.

Well, that makes you feel better. Up to a point. At least the house isn't dirty. It has been said on the radio, so it must be true. And there's somehow comfort in knowing that they've got into other people's places.

But not huge comfort.

Remember the Hitchcock film *The Birds*? It wasn't that much help to know that they were in everyone else's house pecking their eyes out, too.

There's always a really good, kind person on these programmes and he came on and said that ants were fantastic little creatures and hugely helpful in the ecosystem. They ate dead insects and they aerated the soil.

Yes, well. I looked at them marching up and down the screen of the laptop and forced myself to think well of them. Even if I could carry them all out, would I be able to motivate them to eat dead insects and aerate the soil?

The kind man was saying that possibly the best thing to do was to make sure they didn't get in in the first place and more or less ignore them if they did.

But then I thought of the six hours of work at this desk that lay ahead, and I took a magnifying glass and looked at an ant carefully and whipped myself up with hatred for their species. And I went out and bought ant-killer. The ant-killer was full of warnings. First it said, 'Use only as an insecticide,' which was a staggering instruction. What did they expect people to use it as? A deodorant? To ice a cake?

Then it said that you should wear rubber gloves and keep it miles from any electrical equipment and never let any of it get into the air, only on to skirting boards and window frames.

They'd obviously never come across an infested desk because there were further warnings about not putting it near furniture or matt surfaces. And that it would be detrimental to pond life and must be kept far, far from anywhere animals might feed.

And just at that point the two cats came in, knowing that all was not well, and that *The Little Book of Calm* was badly needed. And the moment I thought of them licking this murderously poisonous stuff and lying dead beside the ants, all eight paws rigid in the air, my decision was made. I carried the ant-killer to the garden shed and all the pages that had to be gone through downstairs to the dining-room table. At the moment, an ant-free zone.

Talking to Various Ships Passing in the Night

18 July 1998

It's a crime to be lonely. Nobody might ever have discovered, it could have gone on for years, this harmless little scheme of Nora going out to the airport two or three times a week.

She went there because she was lonely, because it's easy to talk to people at airports, there's an atmosphere of excitement and energy and people going to places, and coming home.

Much better anyway than sitting looking at the four walls of your house.

And it's not all just looking at the people going off to their different flights, you can browse in the bookshop there, have a snack, get your hair done even.

Sometimes she would get talking to families with children.

Nora liked that, she'd ask them where they were going and what they thought it was going to be like.

One little boy said he'd send her a postcard, but Nora didn't mind when he didn't. There was too much to do in Disneyland.

There's a kind of system about striking up conversations, she says. Like there's no point at all trying to talk to anyone who has a mobile phone, they're only dying to use it to make a call or else waiting for it to ring.

People on their own with briefcases are not likely to want to chat. And anyone rooting in a bag looking for tickets or passport is a bad starter, they're too fussed to concentrate on a nice conversation with a stranger.

Nora has had some of her best chats with people going on package tours, especially bus tours. Women wearing badges with the name of the coach tour company were particularly approachable.

Some of them had never travelled abroad before and were a little anxious. Nora would reassure them and say that these companies were great, they looked after everyone and nobody would get lost.

She has patted down a lot of those who were nervous about a trip to Lourdes or a Five Capitals in Seven Days tour.

Nora, who has been abroad only rarely herself, is well able to head their anxieties off at the pass. Oh yes, the buses do stop several times and indeed everyone in these hotels speaks English and there's great shopping where they'll give you the price in pounds as well as in foreign currency.

She waves them off, feeling that in a way they almost are friends.

No, they don't ask her too much about where she's going herself; it's odd that, but people aren't all that interested. She doesn't tell them packs of lies and make up mythical journeys. She doesn't need to.

If they do press her, she says she's just on a little hop across the water this time, and they let it go.

Nora is a mine of information for travellers. She's nearly as good as the personnel in uniform.

She can tell you which gate your flight leaves from, where the letter box is, the nearest ladies' cloakroom.

She often carries paper clips which are a good way of constructing a makeshift lock on a suitcase. Someone showed her once, and it was too good a hint not to pass on. It would delay a thief anyway and that's what matters, Nora would explain sagely – and people were always very grateful.

She often talked to Americans who had been here on a holiday and they told her about their trip. One of them had even given Nora an address in case she was ever in Seattle.

Then she might take the escalator down from Departures and go to sit in Arrivals for a while.

It's very easy to talk to people there, particularly when flights have been delayed. That's a great opportunity.

She got talking to a woman once who was waiting to meet a cousin from America. A very nice person, they had a lot in common, Nora said. The woman liked the same television programmes, and was about the same age. She didn't live far away either.

She would have been a fine friend. But Nora didn't like to push things.

It was so easy for people to reject you, keep you out of their lives. It was hurtful when it happened.

Nora didn't see any point in going out of her way to attract it. This woman had a life of her own, a cousin from America, plans for the summer.

The woman had asked who Nora was meeting and Nora had been vague.

Oh, the flight wasn't due until much later, she said, and somehow that covered it. No need to say who was coming or who wasn't.

The woman had said that she too was a compulsively early person. They really could have become friends.

But then she might have found out that Nora was a person who went out to Dublin Airport not to meet anyone but just for something to do, and once this was revealed she would be seen in a different light.

Odd is what people called it. Odd and sad. The people who knew.

And they were many now because two people had said casually to Nora's niece that they had seen her aunt at the airport. Her niece was always saying Auntie Nora should develop some hobbies, get out more, meet people.

The niece, a busybody of the highest order, had interrogated Nora.

Nora was never good at lying, she couldn't think up a story that would sound convincing. So she told the truth.

And now they are all frowning and tutting.

Her sister, who lives in the country, came up to see her and tried to persuade her to go to the doctor so that he could give her a little something for her nerves. She said there was no shame in it these days.

But Nora says there's nothing wrong with her nerves.

And her nephew, who is in social work, says he can get her accepted for one morning a week in a day centre. Even though, strictly speaking, she's too young, not quite 70. A lot of the people will be quite frail and in wheelchairs but still it would be company and something to look forward to. Wouldn't it?

Her brother's wife, always one for the tart word, apparently said that Nora was lucky to have so much time on her hands. If she had raised a family and had to look after a man, a house, a brood of children, she wouldn't have these problems.

Nora would love to have had a man, a house and a brood of children, but things didn't work out that way.

The bossy niece said that surely she must have some friends, neighbours, people she knew?

And it's very hard to explain to the young and confident that other people have their own lives and they close their front doors on you when they go back to them.

And Nora has only her little flat, which sort of chokes her if she's in it too long on her own.

She wasn't complaining about being lonely, she says. Nora never mentioned it to anyone really.

It was a thing people didn't understand, it seemed that you must be some horrible person if you didn't get on like a house on fire with your neighbours and have 100 people you used to know at work rushing in and out of your house.

It's as if everyone is afraid of lonely people, if they reach out to the lonely who knows where it would end?

So she didn't tell anyone, she just went to a busy, exciting place and talked to a variety of ships that were passing in the night. That's how she saw it.

Not doing anyone any harm, filling her days nicely.

But now it seems this is odd and sad, normal people don't do things like that.

From now on Nora must be watched. Carefully.

Sweet Dreams

25 July 1998

There's this good-tempered man called John, whose boss insulted him deeply at the end of May. His boss said, quite casually and without malice, that poor old John was way beyond being computer literate and though not exactly a dinosaur in the quill-pen league couldn't be expected to know a spreadsheet from a search engine.

John has August off and he has plans. He is a 51-year-old married man with two children. Normally they take a house by the seaside but the children were getting bored with it, so this year they are not packing the buckets and spades. His wife is going to take in three foreign students for the month. His sons, mollified by the fact that there are going to be drop-dead gorgeous Mediterranean girls, are going to hang around and help them integrate.

John is going to do an intensive, four-week computer course. It will cost exactly the same as renting the holiday home. John will eat less, drink less, spend far less than if he were in a resort. Ahead of him lies that glorious day in the first week in September when he will be so much on top of things that the man who called him Poor Old John will wilt in his soft Gucci shoes and be henceforth riddled with great self-doubt about his powers of judgment. It's a vision that will sustain John throughout concentrated hours of taskbars, title bars and toolbars instead of the kind of bars he was normally used to in August.

It will be the most satisfying summer ever.

Maria is 26 and this summer she is going to spend her summer holiday finding a husband. She knows how it's done. You just turn up looking well where there are loads of fellows. Not in a pub when they're all drunk. Not in a disco or a club when it would be dead easy to get a fellow for the night but not at all easy to get a husband. It had to be planned scientifically.

You don't want to waste time on tourists, visitors, handsome fellows passing through looking for one-night stands. You go where there will be a glut of marriageable men. She has studied lists of conferences, golf classics, race meetings, yachting events. She knows where they will be and she will be there. With a cover story.

She is here on a short vacation with her mother and she has come to the hotel. Mother will be distracted elsewhere with friends but will be constantly expected on the scene. This way Maria doesn't look like she's there to pick people up. She won't be taken for a Working Girl cruising the provincial hotels sending out wrong, if exciting, signals to professional men in their late thirties. Her quarry.

Her mother will turn up full of apologies later on in the evening when friendships have been made but before they can be expected to be cemented in bed or anything.

But could this possibly work and why would her mother go along with it? Maria shrugs. How else do you think her mother ever found Maria's father all those years ago? And it was much harder back in the 1960s than it is nowadays.

Ronnie, who is 12, got third prize in a local photography competition. The prize was a book token for £10. But more important, he got a certificate and he has had this certificate laminated and wears it around his neck on a cord.

He lives near a well-known beauty spot in an area very much visited by tourists. Ronnie noticed that people coming to see the sights always wanted their whole family to be included in the shot. They would offer strangers their camera with detailed and complicated instructions of what to press.

How much better to have a semi-professional like himself involved. He stands nearby, hovering silently, ready for the opportunity.

'I'm in the business of photography myself,' he will say to a group as if they had actually asked a 12-year-old boy his line of work. He will indicate the certificate hanging around his neck like a press pass as proof of his great skills.

People usually nod gravely at this, there's not much else they can do.

'So if you'd like me to include you all in a snap I know the best place for you to stand and I charge £1 per session.'

He will produce for inspection a pound coin of his own in case any of them might be confused about the currency. They normally enquire about the nature and extent of a session. Ronnie says that it would include up to half a dozen shots with any of the cameras of the group in question. Much more often than not, they agree. They admire his enterprise, his sheer gall.

And it is a help to have someone who doesn't keep bleating about what should they look through and what should they press.

He has been watched beadily since mid-June by a woman who runs a nearby craft shop. She still can't make up her mind about Ronnie. He's certainly putting in the hours and making the most of his summer. It's just that with no overheads at all, he can take in £50 on a good day. That's rather a lot for a 12-year-old boy, she thinks. In fact, it's astronomical.

But she has no proof that he'll spend it foolishly or that earning this fortune in a wet summer will somehow lead him into organised crime, so she still can't blow the whistle on him.

❦

And what about myself, off on sort-of holidays until the start of September – what will I do? I know what I think I'll do, of course, walk my legs off, read the 36 books listed in a spiral-bound notebook, master the internet, deal with all the letters in the in-basket, learn to cook with yeast, visit at least six parts of Ireland I've never been to, identify and plant a yellow flower that has been driving me mad in other peoples' gardens for years, write postcards of praise to people I admire, teach the cats some kind of trick, any trick, so that people will think they are brighter than they are, label the videos, learn to park in something smaller than a football pitch.

But then maybe I won't do any of those things.

The whole essence of anyone's summer holiday is that it is always based on some kind of dream.

Staving Off the Senior Moments

17 October 1998

There was a time when I used to give advice, serious advice, on travel pages, about what to take with you on a trip. I never took any notice of the advice myself in those days, since as long as you had the bottle of gin, the 200 ciggies and the portable typewriter everything else was only icing on the cake.

I used to look with scorn at all the people in airports fussing about their matching luggage, their eyes scanning the carousel in case one piece had gone missing. I was always half hoping mine would go missing and I might get the compensation. It did once, in New York, and instead of buying a nightdress and a change of underwear I bought a desperately expensive bubble bath and a bottle of champagne and even now, 35 years later, I remember it all with pure pleasure.

No such freedoms these days. If I should lose the case that has all my work in it, I may as well give up on the future.

If I lost the case with the garments, it would be serious. Being a large person, I can't easily get things in shops that will fit me. I have to speak at various functions and they might not take too well to my wearing the same outfit for six weeks. So I have joined the ranks of those who look anxiously until the two brightly coloured, glaring suitcases come out of the innards of a plane.

Tomorrow night I will be unpacking them in a hotel that looks out on the Pacific Ocean.

In the old days I used to pack in 10 minutes. The old days are gone. I'm ashamed to say it has taken a week to pack.

I got a clipboard – not just a piece of paper but a serious clipboard – and I listed all the items. I felt somehow powerful and in control as I wrote down things such as: Sellotape; torch; Velcro rollers; corkscrew; good black dress.

There was a time when I used to think only the insane would make lists like this, but alas I have travelled to too many places and found myself disappointed with the contents of the two glaring cases when I arrived. Like the time I took six pairs of shoes, six T-shirts and no skirts whatsoever to South Africa.

So I realised it was time for the clipboard. It's not that anyone is getting old or forgetful or anything. Lord, no. What people like myself have nowadays is what the Americans call a 'senior moment'. It's a wonderful phrase and one I have taken up enthusiastically. It takes the whole harm out of being bewildered.

Tomorrow night, when I am unpacking the glaring suitcases in a faraway place, I don't want any surprises. But if it were only a matter of what you took with you for six weeks it would be reasonable enough; sadly, it's also a matter of what you leave behind you.

There will be other people staying in the house here while we are gone, so it's not a matter of ramming awful things into a cupboard and saying that it can all be dealt with in December. It means a visit to the dump, which always frightens me because I assume everyone there is getting rid of dismembered bodies and that they think I am doing the same. And a visit in what might, hopefully, be off-peak hour to the bottle bank and the paper bank – rain forests of newspapers and magazines unread going back to be pulped somewhere. And taking out all the things from the press where the table napkins are, in case I might have hidden some cheese there to stop me eating it.

And one of the things I love to do, in what a psychiatrist friend calls my pathetically over-documented life, is stick my snaps in an album. I don't feel right until I'm up to date with this. So it involves getting out all the pictures since summer, and oohing and aahing over a trip to the Isle of Man, and to Schull, and to the Merriman Summer School, and to get an honorary degree in Queen's, and to visit Dickson's Nurseries in Newtownards, and a party in London, and a magical day at the National Ploughing Championships which I think I enjoyed more than anything else this year.

Sorting out all that takes time.

And there are the letters to write which I will not take with me and carry around the world as I have done so often: instead, I will stay up late and write them before I go.

And I won't worry that the cats will miss us because cats have their own agenda and they will think whoever is here is us really, just as long as the bowl of food is put out and someone tells them they are wonderful.

And it doesn't really matter that we will be in some places where it is snowing and others where the sun will be splitting the stones.

And as usual, Gordon is calm and has his own clipboard to humour me and tries to head off too many 'senior moments' by reminding me to take my laptop computer, which I nearly forgot.

I read once in an etiquette book that if you are about to travel, you should take out an advertisement in a quality paper and tell society of your plans. So in a way, that's what I am doing.

2000s

Mr Gageby . . .

3 July 2004

There is a dangerous tendency of thinking your own time was the best, and there were no days like your days. Journalists fall into this trap more easily than anyone else. It's as if we want people to know what stirring times we lived through, what dramas our newsroom saw and what near-misses we had, and what amazing never-to-be-equalled camaraderie we all shared.

All over Ireland this week there will be people telling such tales of Douglas Gageby's time.

And even as I write his name I feel forward.

I never called him anything except Mr Gageby.

I met him when I was a 27-year-old schoolteacher in Dublin, sharing a dream with half the country that maybe I could write if someone would let me.

Even when I nearly caught up with him in age and we were friends, when he asked me to call him Douglas, I could never do it. He was too important.

At the job interview where he asked what I would do if I were to run the Woman's Page, I suggested that we relegate Fashion to one day, Cookery to another, and then get on with what people would be interested in on the other four days.

He asked mildly what I thought people might be interested in, and I blinded him with my views.

'Of course, she's never worked a day in her life in a newspaper,' he said to Donal Foley, the news editor.

'She has to learn somewhere,' Donal said, and Mr Gageby nodded and said that was fair enough.

So who wouldn't love someone who took such a mad risk?

My memory of those days was that he seemed to be forever in his office.

Day and night.

That wasn't possible because we knew he had a great family life, he often talked about his children, and he always talked about his wife, Dorothy.

He was invited everywhere, but he was never a great one for going to receptions or dinners, except the Military History Society of Ireland which he was very keen on.

He was handsome, he was confident at work, he was happy in his home life, he was courageous and he was dragging the paper into modern times.

No wonder so many of us were mad about him.

He had, of course, a short fuse.

There is nobody who doesn't have a Mr Gageby experience of some kind. Like when he would bellow his annoyance at something that appeared in Yesterday's paper.

There was never such a thing as Today's paper, there was the one we had written Yesterday which, according to him, was full of faults and mistakes and unbelievable oversights, or Tomorrow's, which was going to be spectacular and we would stick everyone else to the ground with our stories, insights and backgrounds.

I have seen Mr Gageby incandescent with rage about a sports writer who said that a match was a nip-and-tuck affair and gave no further detail, and a financial journalist who said the AGM of some company was predictable, but hadn't explained what had been predicted.

He has been white-faced over someone who missed the one big row that week in the Senate, or called the ceremony that happens in England the Trooping OF the Colour when there should be no OF in it, apparently. And somebody invariably got it wrong, and somebody else invariably let it past.

I have been at the receiving end when the Woman's Page had a series of apologies in it.

We regret that when we said 11½ pounds of split peas, we actually meant 1 to 1½ pounds of split peas.

We regret that when we said this dress in Richard Alan's cost £20, we actually meant it cost £200.

We regret we have given the wrong number of the Gay Switchboard, the wrong score in the All-Ireland.

His eyes were narrow. I wondered how I had ever thought he was handsome.

'Your page is a laughing stock,' he said. 'With the possible exception of the *Straits Times* in Malaysia, I have never seen a worse Features page.'

My face was scarlet for 48 hours. I contemplated emigrating.

Next week it was forgotten and we could breathe again.

But, by God, how he stood up for us, all of us.

He never gossiped about one to another, and he fought our enemies and people who said we were less than great.

He said that we reported what we saw.

Even when his back was against the wall over what we had reported or misreported.

We knew we would not be sold down the river.

And I know he had hard times in Stephen's Green clubs when some of us were a bit light-hearted about the British royal family.

And though I lived my whole life slightly in awe of him, it was not of his doing. He was warm and friendly and interested in the lives of all his workforce.

When I took all my courage in hand and invited him to lunch with us, he said he would come if we had one course, and that he really liked sardines with lemon juice. He may, of course, have been protecting himself and Dorothy against botulism, since they knew only too well some of my limitations through the cookery page and my misunderstandings of presenting food.

If you were going to lunch with someone who had used a picture of open-heart surgery to illustrate veal casseroles, perhaps you, too, might have asked for sardines.

But we lunched happily summer after summer, alternately in their house and ours.

And it was wonderful to be in the presence of a couple who loved each other and never felt they had to hide this from anyone else.

I would have liked them to live forever as part of all of our lives.

But they didn't, and I hope their family will always know how many of us got a great and exciting start in our writing lives under his editorship.

And how proud we were to be part of the time when he took our newspaper out of the shadows and into the light.

Every time I think of Mr Gageby, I straighten myself up a little and hope to try and do him some kind of credit somewhere along the line.

Another World for the Price of a Cup of Coffee

30 October 2004

You would get the smell half a street away, coffee like it never smelled at home. And the fresh-from-the-oven cakes and buns, six of them on a plate ready and waiting for you on the table.

Long before the days of self-service, the waitresses would come and serve you, always with a few words about the world we lived in. Like the rain maybe, or the sales, or Peggy Dell playing the piano in a furniture shop across the road, or the marriage of Princess Grace, or the hardy souls who swam all the year round in our cold seas.

And then they would leave you to your own chat, going off to talk on other topics at other tables.

Bewley's was filled with characters and we would talk about them for a bit before settling down to our own chat. There used to be a woman with a handsome, ravaged face and wild and curly hair, wearing a matted fur coat with not much underneath it. There was a rumour that she was a wealthy person and that someone had left Bewley's a sum of money to make sure she was fed every day, which she always was, with great kindness and charm.

There was an old man whose coat was tied with a rope, who always complained that the tea was cold. The thin, slightly stooped waitress would feel the side of the teapot and assure him that it would roast the hand off you, so then he would grudgingly drink it.

There were men with sheaves of papers covered in figures, adding and subtracting; there were well-known poets and writers and actors. Real celebrities were there, such as Maureen Potter at one table or Eamonn Andrews at another, and everyone would just nod at them, delighted to be sharing the same aromatic air – but we would never go up and disturb them.

When I was a student we could make one cup of coffee last an hour and a half and, like everyone else, we felt a slight guilt in case this sowed the seeds of the eventual decline of Bewley's fortunes. But we had to make it last because nobody wanted to leave the warm, happy coffee and sugar-flavoured fug and go out into the cold, rain-filled streets. And nobody had the price of another cup of coffee.

I look back on hours and hours of conversation then, about communism, about how to starch petticoats, about who would be on the committee of the L & H debating society. And about how, when we were old and rich, we would come back from overseas and buy a whole plate of cakes and have three coffees each. It was the 1950s then, and we all assumed we would have to go away to get a job, and a lot of us did.

Then, when I was a young teacher, I would bring the pupils' exercise books and correct them in Bewley's. History essay after history essay, more coffee, more cigarettes to keep me going, and the waitresses would be most sympathetic.

'You lot earn your money,' one of them said to me. I thought she earned hers much harder, clearing up marble table after marble table of slopped coffee and crumbs, but there was never a complaint.

Sometimes, when I didn't even have time to go in, I would stand and watch the windows and wallow in the smell. The amazing sight of beans jumping, being ground just for our pleasure – it was very heady. And then we all bought our first coffee-makers there and were surprised that it didn't taste quite as good at home.

When I joined *The Irish Times* there was Bewley's right opposite us at a time when it was slightly easier to cross the road than it is now. And there were many long discussions there too. Things that were too private to be discussed in the Pearl bar or in Bowes but which needed the solidarity of the marble table and the almond bun.

Like what? I don't know. Love, hope, disappointment, press freedom, whether we had better coverage of something than the other papers, elections, sports, and what readers really wanted and whether or not we should try to give it to them.

In those days the budget extended to more than one promised cup of coffee. But when the bill was being totted up the waitress would ask, 'How many almond buns?'

The number would be admitted.

'And did you have butter with them?' she would inquire, in the kindly but firm way that a priest might have asked you, 'did you take pleasure in it?' a long time ago.

Oh yes, we always had butter with the almond buns. Like we always loved going in to sink down and forget the outside world in Bewley's, and like we sang carols outside it for many Christmases, and like we always felt safe there and at home.

It was all things to all people and we are allowed to be sentimental and sad that a little bit of everybody's past has gone and that we can't conjure it up any more just for the price of a cup of coffee.

'One Up for the Cardigans'

12 February 2005

The news programme announces the engagement in the little minimarket where people are doing their morning shopping. The younger people ignore it, as they continue to root around looking for extra complimentary CDs among the magazines or to lick bits of frozen yoghurt from the outside of the cartons. . . .

The older people are more interested.

'That will be a relief to Her Majesty,' says the woman with a basket full of lentils for herself and choice cuts for her cat. 'Her poor Majesty was exhausted trying to turn the other way; now it will all be above board.'

'A lot of bloody nonsense,' says the man in the cloth cap with the north of England accent, who buys tins of pilchards and oven chips and nothing else. 'Pair of them were perfectly all right living over the brush like half the country; he's only marrying her because they're asking questions about how much of our money he spends on her anyway.'

And the large, comfortable woman who sits like a wise old bird at the checkout is very pleased.

'It's one up for the cardigans,' she says. 'I knew the day would come when a woman as shabby as myself would marry a prince.'

I lived here in these London streets in 1981 when Charles was getting married for the first time, and the atmosphere was electric. The playboy prince was going to settle down, and he had found a nice virgin girl to marry. Yet, at his engagement press conference, when asked was he in love, he had said rather ominously, 'Yes, whatever that means.'

But the country had gone mad with an innocent pleasure. It was July 1981, and there was a huge fireworks display in Hyde Park the night before the wedding. There were street parties, and I was almost afraid to tell people I was talking to on the tube to St Paul's that I had an invitation to the do in my handbag. They might have killed for it. And I say 'the people that I talked to' because for a day or two London forgot its introversion and everyone spoke to everyone else. It was like the day the Pope had come to Dublin two years previously.

It was something that was of its time and will never happen in the same way again. There's no excitement about Charles and Camilla in the streets of west London this time around. No spontaneous flags and bunting, no lump in the throat empathising with the happy event.

The past 24 years have seen too much murky water flow under too many bridges. The little virgin bride shed all her shyness and puppy fat and became one of the world's most beautiful women, and Charles, who had never loved her remotely, behaved as badly as any pantomime villain. The disastrous royal marriage was lived out in public, with other parties briefing the media about the rights and wrongs of the situation. The couple's two little boys struggled on, surrounded by butlers, nannies and nonspeaking relatives.

Princess Diana, who at one stage held all the cards because she was *nice* to people and full of charm, lost out in the end in every possible way. Charles, who became more arrogant and mutinous with every passing year, made little attempt to hide his relationship and now seems, oddly, to have won. It looks now as if he is being rewarded: he is getting the marriage he should have had 35 years ago when Camilla was certainly up for it but when he dithered and couldn't make a decision.

It's not a love story that immediately sets the bells ringing or promises to get to the heart of the nation. But never underestimate the power of the media. About 20 minutes after the usual messed-up announcement from Clarence House, a statement that left so many questions unanswered and showed a complete lack of planning and preparation, all the television channels had wheeled in the ageing royal-watchers. They were brought out of mothballs and dusted down and wound up to go. I know what I'm talking about; I was one of them.

Queen Elizabeth II has four children. I was at three of their weddings and I didn't bring any of them much luck. Only Prince Edward's first marriage has survived, and Princess Anne's second marriage.

I am sure Charles and Camilla, who have had each other out on approval for some time, will make a go of it. And truly, most people of goodwill will wish them happiness, as you would to anyone who has had a troubled journey in romance.

But it's such a different scene this time around. I wonder whether Charles, in his very narrow world, knows this. It's hard for any of us to know what other people think and how they live and what their values are. But it must be harder for the Prince of Wales, surrounded as he is by sycophants and by people who grew up in the same strange enclosed world as himself, where journalists are called 'reptiles' and where there are the People Who Matter and then the rest of the world, which doesn't matter a bit. He must think he is a scream, because I have seen the awful, fawning, servile press, really worse than reptiles, laughing hysterically if he makes a stupid joke. Why would he *not* think that his forthcoming wedding should be on the same scale as the last one? He has no loving family to lean on.

His parents never went to visit him when he was at that terrible school, Gordonstoun. Do you know anyone who was *never* visited at boarding school by their parents? He was completely out of touch with the life his first bride wanted to live, and there was nobody to advise him, except in the ways of protocol, history and tradition, which could be summed up as 'wives must learn'. He was singularly unlucky in that his wife never did.

His polo-playing friends told him that Diana was a loony tune and that his best bet was to invite Camilla to their house parties. Then, somewhere along the line, somebody taped his intimate conversation with Camilla years ago and broadcast it to the world. That was the only day I felt really sorry for Charles. I could have wept for his sheer embarrassment as I saw him on television straightening his cuffs and going to see his mother, who was after all the queen of the country that was rocking to his bizarre sexual fantasies. Strange as they were, they *were* his and Camilla's own business.

So the man who will presumably one day be king may not have a clue how his future subjects think of him and his wedding.

For a start, most of the broadcasts and breaking news and interviews focused on the issue of what poor Camilla would be called. She would not *dare* to call herself Princess of Wales, would she? She couldn't ever be queen, could she? And eventually, two hours later, Charles's expensive spin doctors and PR people issued a statement defining what the woman would or would not be called.

Then there were hours of debate about whether a civil ceremony would be a proper marriage for a head of the Church, or whether a church wedding would be worse. Then they debated whether Charles was only marrying Camilla now because the House of Commons Public Accounts Committee might uncover something too damaging about what he had spent on the lady. Or because the results of the second inquest into Princess Diana's death were to be published, possibly throwing up even more bad publicity about the royal family. Or because the Archbishop of Canterbury said that they should regularise their situation.

And as if all this wasn't bad enough for a couple planning their wedding, it was said that the Labour party was incandescent with rage because Charles and Camilla's plans were messing up the timing of the next election.

I am basically a big custard heart. I don't know these people at all. I've watched them for three decades, notebook in hand, but I don't know them or know anybody who knows them. But I am interested in their love story. I think Charles is arrogant and selfish, but the roots of that lie in his upbringing. I think Camilla is basically a decent and horsey cardigan who loves Charles and is prepared to go through all this (like she has gone through so much already) from the sheer accident of falling in love with him. And really, I don't think she cares *what* she is called. She isn't even trying to be 'queen of hearts', and it must be painful and hurtful when she is compared to her beautiful, warm, but deeply unhappy predecessor.

The young have no interest in the affairs and doings of such elderly people. The Diana activists may feel that somehow Camilla triumphed in the end, and perhaps they will dislike her for that. I can't be the only person in the world who doesn't think hereditary monarchy is a good idea but who still does genuinely wish these two confused middle-aged people a great wedding day and a good time together.

My Part in the Movies

17 September 2005

They say that handing over your story to film-makers is like sending your first child to school. The book, like the child, still belongs to you in a sort of a way, but it's not the same way. Now there's a different life, with a lot of other people involved. But a child can't stay at home forever, and a book is better when it gets a further life, so I am always delighted when someone thinks that one of my stories is good enough to make into a movie.

I know, of course, that not everything will fit in. *Tara Road* is a long story, with many characters, so some have to go if we are to make sense of it in an hour and a half of cinema. I don't write the scripts myself; I have tried, but I'm not good at it. I prefer to tell a story in big, swooping terms, pausing to tell you what someone's thinking about, worrying over, hoping for. You can't do that in a screenplay. It's very brief, with lots of short sentences and plenty of white space on the page. That's not my scene at all.

You have to suggest things in a screenplay, so the director and actors can take it up and make sense of it. I find it much easier to tell things. So I have great respect for those who can write a script and then for the others who can turn a short screenplay, of about 100 pages, into a whole film.

The author has no say in casting, finding locations or choosing music. So you wait with an eager face to see what they will do. It's as much a surprise for the writer as it is for the audience.

Sometimes people have very unhappy times watching their beloved book transfer to the movies, but I enjoyed it all so much and had such good times on the set that I thought I would share it with you.

I have been lucky before. I enjoyed so much the filming of *Circle of Friends*, with Minnie Driver and Chris O'Donnell, the television version of *Echoes*, with Geraldine James, and the TV movie of *The Lilac Bus*. But *Tara Road* has long been one of my favourite stories. It's about two women who exchange homes and, in doing so, find more than a place to spend two months and lick their wounds: they discover redemption.

Many years ago we exchanged our London property for a house in Sydney, and it was a great experience. *Tara Road* is not our story, because nothing would be duller than reading about two happily married, settled couples, which is what we and they were. Still, it was fascinating living in their home, knowing their secrets and realising that they knew ours. They had no corkscrew; we had no cereal bowls. By the time I left their house, with its wonderful bottlebrush trees and exotic birds on the garden fence, I felt I knew them more than I knew neighbours of 20 years at home. And so I wrote the story.

I can't remember what I thought my characters Ria and Marilyn looked like, because all I can see are the beautiful, strong, sensitive faces of Olivia Williams and Andie MacDowell registering hope and grief and triumph when it is called for. I don't think I ever saw in my mind's eye all the other characters, either. I just had a feeling for them, and now they are brought to life for me: the strong-willed Mona, played by Brenda Fricker; the elegant and faithless Rosemary, played by Maria Doyle Kennedy; the sexy, feckless Danny, played by Iain Glen; the handsome Stephen Rea, playing Colm, the restaurant owner; and the children, who behave just like Ria's children would have behaved. I will never see any of them in any other way.

As for the house, I had a road in mind in Dublin for which I made up the name Tara Road. The film company asked where I was thinking of, and I told them. It wouldn't work, they said, as it was much too narrow. They would hold up traffic with their huge generators and all the crew. So the location people went out and found another house to film it in, which is perfect. It's almost as if it had been built for it, exactly the kind of road I had in mind, with those big, high-ceilinged rooms where Ria had been once so happy, then so lonely; where Marilyn tried to look for peace and found half of Dublin passing through to interrupt her.

So I approached the filming with great optimism. I have always known that film-makers hate the author around the place. They always fear that he or she is going to say that it wasn't at all like that. We are looked at with fear and mistrust. Yet it isn't human to expect us to stay away, especially when it's being filmed down the road. So I asked politely if my husband, Gordon, and I could come along and watch. Quietly. I stressed the word.

And that's what we did. We peeped in at the huge Tara Road house, the apartment where Bernadette lived; we watched astounded while our marvellous local fishmonger's was changed into a US delicatessen over a bank holiday weekend. We were very polite to Gillies MacKinnon, the director, and to his camera and sound people; we admired all the actors and told them they were just the part.

Eventually they realised we were just ageing groupies, loving everything and therefore no trouble. And they sensed that Gordon and I were dying for little walk-on parts. So it was arranged that we were going to play Martini drinkers in Colm's restaurant.

I wish I could tell you how excited we were. We went to bed early the night before, because the limo came for us at seven a.m. Then we went to make-up. We didn't have to go to costume, because they asked us to wear anything of our own that was not black or navy. For some reason now forgotten, I wore lilac. Then it was time for our scene. We would be sitting on high chairs at the bar in Colm's restaurant. Stephen Rea was to serve us with two triangular Martini glasses, each with an olive in it. We were to say nothing aloud but to mouth thank-you words at him.

Just before they said 'Lights, camera, action' I said to Gordon that I could murder this Martini. I felt we had been up for hours. He said he wouldn't hold his breath about its being a real Martini, but I am an eternal optimist. I said we should look at the way there was condensation on the glass; they wouldn't have gone to all that trouble to chill a glass of water.

'It's twenty past nine in the morning,' Gordon said.

He was right. It was water.

I ate the olive resentfully. Each time during the three takes. Then the camera moves inexplicably from us to the stars. But we are there. You wouldn't want to blink or look down to choose a sweet or anything, or you would miss us, but we are part of it.

In the last cut I saw of the film we are still there, sipping delicately, mouthing our thanks and, in my case, wondering why on earth I wore lilac, which is the most enlarging colour in the spectrum.

It's a terrific, moving and touching film. We have all had losses in our lives, we have all loved foolishly and been lonely. The film tells very clearly, as the book tried to do, that the solution is in our own hands, that we have to make ourselves better. There is no cavalry waiting on a cliff to rescue us. We have to do it for ourselves.

Marilyn and Ria do that on the screen as much as they did in the book, played by two wonderful actors who, with the rest of my cast, told this story as well as I could have hoped and better. I was lonely when the film crew packed up and went away, as they do. But at least we have the book, and the movie is out there to be seen as well.

Striking a Pose for My Country

25 October 2005

When the National Gallery of Ireland first suggested it, I had the very real fear that it might be some terrible practical joke. That it could be a *Candid Camera* style television programme watching people making fools of themselves by accepting huge honours like that and then having to bluster their way out of it.

But they seemed serious. So I was utterly delighted and waited for the artist to arrive.

She was Maeve McCarthy and had been at the same school as I had, though admittedly a quarter of a century later. We talked animatedly about loved figures and less-than-loved figures in the place, and had a great bond.

I had looked her up and seen how successful she was, as well as all the competitions she had won. She had painted a self-portrait which everyone had said was very good, but in real life she was good-looking, and the self-portrait had made her look a lot less attractive than she was. If she's so tough on herself, I thought, what is she going to do to a subject? And I sort of hinted that.

But she explained that there were various conventions about a self-portrait, which I thought was all very well in theory but going to be a bit tough on me if she was into too much gritty realism. Still, we were into it now.

She told me the bad news was that she couldn't paint from photographs, but the good news was that I didn't have to sit still. I could move about and talk and drink mugs of tea and everything.

So I was busy then trying to look for nice bits of our house to be painted in – near the one good piece of furniture maybe, with some tasteful glass arranged on it?

She said she would like to prowl about the place looking for a setting and could I just get on with my life so that she could observe me?

So I chose a day when Gordon would be out and I got on with life, trying to ignore her. For a whole morning I yacked away on the phone, typed with my four-finger typing, looked things up in the dictionary, stroked the cat who had settled in the 'Action This Day' basket, and had a script conference about a project with Jean Pasley where McCarthy was most helpful and came up with some good ideas.

After a day of prowling she had chosen the location. It was to be upstairs in our study where you can see Dalkey Castle in the background over the roof. And she wanted Gordon to sit in on the roof terrace – sort of out of sight but with his legs in the picture. His legs? Yes, just his presence around the place apparently, and he would be reading *The Irish Times*. What? Product placement? No, you would only get a hint that it was *The Irish Times*. Right. Right.

So we had the first sitting; there was some discussion about the colour I would wear, and eventually I settled on blue. Maeve McCarthy set up her easel and I sat down nervously and waited for it to begin.

We talked about everything under the sun – life, death, hopes, disappointments, friends, family, travel. And then the sitting was over.

I had heard you must not look at your own portrait until it is finished. But she shrugged. Of course I could look at it, she said.

Interestingly, there was no face.

Lots of Dalkey Castle, and the roof, and the desk I was sitting at, and big, blue shoulders, but no face.

I managed to say nothing. After the fourth sitting, when there was still no face – only pixelation like they put in a newspaper to hide the face of the Accused or the Suspect – I thought I would mention it.

'Oh I won't do your face,' she said, at which I felt dizzy and wondered had I entirely misunderstood the whole thing.

'Not until much later,' she added to my relief, and the blood returned slowly to my veins.

After the sixth sitting, still no face as such. She asked me if I liked the picture. We were such friends now, I had to be honest. 'I spend over €20 each time you come getting my hair done and it doesn't really show. I wonder does the hair look a bit flattened in the portrait?' I said nervously.

'You're very lucky you didn't have Gwen John painting you – she made subjects put Vaseline all over their heads so that she could see the shape of the skull,' Maeve McCarthy said unsympathetically.

And then the pixelation went and I saw my face, and the lovely picture of our cats, and a picture of our friends on the wall, and a mug of tea with Nighthawks on it. And best of all the reassuring presence of Gordon outside the window, reading a paper, which could be *The Irish Times*. And then it was all over.

Maeve McCarthy packed up her easel and her brushes and her little jars of whatever it was and left.

And I missed her like mad.

She made it all very painless, she was great company and I am as pleased as anything that it was done.

It is a huge honour to be chosen by the national gallery of your own land to hang in its halls, and to be lent a talented portrait painter for a summer of friendship and insights.

I will of course be hovering a lot about the gallery for some time pretending I have come to see something else, or that I am taking some overseas visitors for a tour. But really I will be there to make sure they don't take it down.

Ten Things You Must Never Say to Anyone with Arthritis

30 January 2009

1. 'Cheer up, nobody ever died of arthritis.' This statement is, oddly, not cheering at all. We have dark, broody feelings that if people did die of arthritis there might have been huge, well-funded research projects over the last few decades, which could have come up with a cure.

2. 'It's just a sign of old age, it will come to us all.' No, it's not a sign of old age. Even toddlers can get arthritis, and some old people never get a twinge of it. The very worst phrase you can use is 'Haven't you had a good innings?'

3. Remember that marvellous radio series about disabilities called *Does He Take Sugar?* The message of that title means you should never ask, in the hearing of someone with arthritis, 'Do you think she'll be able to manage the stairs?' Arthritis can make us many things, but it certainly doesn't make us deaf.

4. Avoid mentioning magic cures, as anyone with arthritis will already have heard of vinegars, honey, mussels, berry teas, and so on. We will probably have tried them too. It is dispiriting to be told of someone else who was once bent double but now climbs mountains before breakfast.

5. Don't ever say, 'That walking stick is very ageing – I wouldn't use it if I were you.' Did you think we thought

of the stick as a fashion accessory? Of course we know it's hardly rejuvenating to be seen bent over a stick, but when the alternative is a knee or a hip that could let us down, or pitch us into the traffic, then the stick is a great help. It is sad when people give us the impression that it makes us look 100 years old. At least we are getting out there, and that should be praised and encouraged.

6. Never let the phrase 'a touch of arthritis' pass your lips. You don't say someone has a touch of diabetes or a touch of asthma. It is denying sympathy and concern for people who have a painful and ever-present condition to minimise it to just 'a touch'.

7. Don't suggest a healthy walk to blow away the cobwebs. People whose joints are unreliable don't want to get further proof of this when they are halfway down the pier. Unless you are a physiotherapist, don't impose exercise on others.

8. Don't tell arthritis sufferers to go and live in a hot, dry climate like Arizona. We know it might be easier on the joints, but some of us are very happy here with family and friends, and we don't want to be packed off like remittance men.

9. One time you shouldn't stay silent is when your favourite restaurants, theatres or galleries are difficult to access for a friend with arthritis. Before you turn your back on them, be sure to tell the owners or proprietors exactly why you will not be making a booking. You can be very polite and praising ('I hear such good things about your place'), but after the flattery should come the reason for regret ('Can I

just confirm that there isn't a lift and that the cloakrooms are up or down a flight of stairs?'). If enough people were to do this, it would not take long to improve facilities. If we don't tell the offenders, how will they know there's a problem?

10. Don't ever say, sadly, how tragic it is that nothing has been done for poor arthritis sufferers. Plenty is being done. Just contact Arthritis Ireland, or phone its new helpline. Then you will have an idea of how much is happening and you can be a true and informed friend rather than a false and frightening one.

What's It Like to Have a House Full of Film Crew? Let Me Tell You All About It

24 December 2010

Well, I did say from the very start that there was a problem. There was no extreme poverty in the tale, no family discord, no feuds, no emigration. Nothing to hang a good story on. But they said they knew all that and they still wanted to go ahead.

So Gordon and I had a working party on it and listed the arguments for and against. Against doing the whole thing were the fact that the story was too tame to hold people's interest and the fact that I love talking so much that once I get started I can't be stopped. And in favour of it was that it would be good to have something that would confound my enemies, but we couldn't think of any enemies we wanted to confound, so that one didn't really work. But also in favour of it was that we know Noel Pearson, whose company would be making it, and we knew it wouldn't be a dull and glum sort of thing.

I checked with my sister and brother to see whether they would be horrified by it all, and they said nonsense and I should go ahead. So I said yes, because I'm as easily flattered as the next person, and I thought it would be great to be made much of and for people to arrange flattering lighting and tell me they were ready for my close-up. And of course this was all at the end of the summer, when autumn seemed miles away.

But, the way things do, the day arrived. I met the director, Sinéad O'Brien; I actually knew her mother and her father and her grandmother. I wondered mildly was she old enough to be directing documentaries, but she assured me she was, so we got that out of the way early on.

And then, bit by bit, I met everyone else, the cameramen and the sound recordists, all of them cheerful, charming and hugely apologetic about the amount of gear they had to bring into the house. We were apologising equally for the smallness of the house, as we would reverse into the bathroom, climb over what seemed like gigantic metal trunks, and negotiate floors covered with thick cables.

The lights were so bright you could see everybody's nose hair and any other imperfection in the skin; but there was Make-Up to deal with that. There were never fewer than 12 people around, each one knowing exactly their role. Archives would be taking out my papers, borrowed on a daily basis from UCD library, and getting out old scrapbooks that I had totally forgotten. Continuity was making sure I was wearing the same dress to continue a conversation as I had been wearing to begin it the day before – people with clipboards who knew far more about me than I knew about myself.

When I would say vaguely that something happened back in the 1960s or 1970s, they would actually know the date.

A gloom-ridden acquaintance told me I would be demented from making them all tea. I want to put on record that no cup of tea was ever brewed in this house for the crew.

Magically, trays of sandwiches or little cakes appeared from Dalkey's cafés and food shops; cartons of good coffee were always available.

If they had been doing a documentary with a more able-bodied person there could have been great shots of me striding along the beach at White Rock or climbing Killiney Hill. I could have been down at Dalkey Island, talking to the porpoises and the seals.

But this wasn't on.

I find moving about very hard these days, so it all had to be done at home. I caught sight of myself on a monitor one day and almost forgot to talk, because I was in a kind of torpor, wondering why I hadn't gone on that diet I thought I was going to try, a diet that apparently puts hollows in your cheeks and makes your neck long and thin. I had even cut it out of a newspaper and filed it away carefully in a yellow file called 'Action This Day' last August and forgotten about it totally.

But otherwise I just talked and talked until I felt there wasn't one more word to say.

Any question I was asked I answered at immense length. I exhausted myself and them.

They reassured me and said that once the editor had got at it these monologues would look much more acceptable.

I dearly hope this is so.

Then I would hear tales of the days they interviewed other people: family, friends and colleagues. It wasn't that I was worried would these people tell any Awful Secrets, because, honestly, there aren't any Awful Secrets, but I hated them having to say nice things on order.

I wasn't allowed anywhere near all this filming, quite rightly, and I even had to leave the house when Gordon, my husband, was being interviewed, because they didn't want me staring at him beadily, willing him to say how wonderful I was and am.

And it all became a pleasant and entirely unreal routine.

Even the cats got used to the film people being here and came out of hiding to take part once they realised that there was no threat to their existence and that these people left every evening having tidied up the house to a much better degree than they had found it in.

And then it was over, from our point of view anyway, and I sort of missed the huge vans drawing up outside the door, disgorging crates of equipment, and cheerful young people fitting things together and making cameras and lighting out of them as if they were children with building bricks. We used to look around our room that used to have 12 people in it, each one at some task, and now there was only us finishing breakfast, and the cats looking faintly bored that no cabaret was being put on for them today.

And then there came the whole dread feeling of self-doubt. Why had I brought this on us? We were fine as we were. What if people who had been interviewed were on the cutting-room floor? How could I ever meet their eye again? Nothing is any help. One man who tried to calm me down said that nobody will watch it anyway, because they'll all be asleep or drunk at that time on Christmas Day. Somehow that was not as reassuring as he had intended it to be.

Another friend said that it would be undemanding and that was the key word I must remember. Once people had got through a family meal and had all eaten far too much to digest, then something totally bland and undemanding was what they were looking for. And somehow that didn't entirely cheer me up either.

So what *did* I want? I suppose I wanted to acknowledge how lucky I had been in my life and that I had been dealt a great hand of cards. I didn't want it to sound smug or self-satisfied. That's not the way it feels inside, and I hope it doesn't come over like that. I suppose I wanted to thank my family and friends and all the great people I've met along the way – tell them how much I love them.

I didn't say it like that when I was faced with the lights and the cameras. But that's what I meant.

Will and Kate Show Is Testament to Abiding Allure of the Royals

30 April 2011

Well, everyone mellows a bit in 40 years. The edges blur. You see more innocence and hope and harmless lunacy than arrogance and triumphalism. It was a day when two people got married and two billion other people watched them. It was a day when millions dressed up, got over-excited and partied to celebrate young love.

And it wasn't all in England. A man from Eircom who came to sort out the broken-down broadband said that every house he had visited was glued to a television. It was on in the bank and the customers dawdled so that they could see more.

The streets and shops in Dalkey were emptier than on any other Friday. There were many households where ladies gathered, each wearing a hat and carrying a bottle. And why not? It was not a question of wanting to be English, nothing to do with losing our identity, changing our allegiance. It was all about watching a big, glittery show. A well-choreographed parade. With fine horses and gold carriages and flags and marching bands. If that's how you look at it then it's a morning well spent.

The best bit is that we know the cast. The Duke of Edinburgh, who always looks irritated and as if he's on the verge of imploding, looked just the same. But he is going to be 90 next birthday. He has a silly sort of sword, which would be handy to lean on, but he never uses it even though it's hanging from his waist. He walks upright on his own. Queen Elizabeth is 85 and well able to climb into a glass coach and leap out of it without assistance. These are sturdy people; Ruritania doesn't seem to have affected their stamina.

It was so different watching a royal wedding from my own home. For years, I have been going to Westminster Abbey or St Paul's Cathedral and climbing almighty scaffolding to get to a seat on the top of a specially constructed press section. I was at Prince William's parents' wedding and his aunt Anne's and his uncle Andrew's. Not a good fairy at the feast, I fear I brought them no luck. All three marriages ended in divorce.

In a way I wish I had been in London. I miss the magic of the English losing all their reserve, their fear of having a conversation with you in case you might go home with them. Street parties are so much the opposite of the British way of life, which is based on people keeping themselves to themselves. And yet when they did sit down they loved the chance to get to know their neighbours. I remember with great affection those parties at trestle tables with beer and cider and something roasted on a spit.

But hey, what do I know really? Everything's changed since I started being a royal wedding watcher in 1973. For William and Kate's wedding the guests arrived in buses as if they were going to a football match. Years back it was a long line of Bentleys. There was constant reference to the fact that the couple had lived together already for some years. At the time of Diana's wedding her uncle had to tell the world that she was a virgin. At those long-ago marriages Elton John and his partner David would not have been ushered politely into the Abbey. Nor would there have been a rake of red hats – one token Catholic would have covered it.

Of course it's not perfect. Hereditary power is never a good thing. But it's a lot better in a few decades than it used to be. Yes, they still made her change her name to Catherine. They didn't invite poor Fergie, who would have loved a day out. They left Tony Blair off the list. Tony who saved their bacon when Diana died.

But in the end, the bride was beautiful, the groom was handsome, the little pages and flower girls were adorable. It all went like clockwork. The somewhat tarnished image of royalty was forgotten for a day anyway.

Woody Allen always has a useful phrase. And when asked in a movie whether he was mellow, he replied, 'I'm so mellow I'm almost rotten.'

I know what he means. It's not a bad place to be.

POSTSCRIPT

'I Don't Have Any Regrets About Any Roads I Didn't Take . . .'

In conversation with Joanne Hunt, 3 July 2012

The great thing about getting older is that you become more mellow. Things aren't as black and white and you become much more tolerant. You can see the good in things much more easily, rather than getting enraged as you used to do when you were young.

I am much more understanding of people than I used to be when I was young – people were either villainous or wonderful. They were painted in very bright colours. The bad side of it, and there is a corollary to everything, is that when we get older, we fuss more. I used to despise people who fussed.

If I was going on a holiday, I'd just fling a few things into a suitcase and race out to the airport and not talk about it. Nowadays, if I'm going anywhere, the smallest journey, it has to be planned like the Normandy landing.

The relaxing bit is that you don't get as het up and annoyed and take offence as much as you used to.

Another good thing is that you value your friends more as you get older: you're not in any kind of competitive relationship with them any more, wishing to succeed or show off, or impress others.

You value people just for themselves. Unfortunately, as you get older, your friends die. It's that cliché of being afraid to look at the Christmas card list each year because of the people that have gone from it – that is a very sad and depressing thing.

I'm almost afraid to look at photos of my wedding now because so many people have died who were at it. You can't believe they are not all there in some part of the forest, still enjoying themselves.

I have more time certainly . . . and I'm more interested in everything. I'm interested in what other people are interested in, much more. However, you don't have enough energy to do things. It would be lovely to have the energy to do all the things I'm interested in now.

I think it's a balance: nobody has everything at the same time. When you are young, you have time and energy but you don't have any money.

When you get a job, you have energy and money but you don't have time.

And when you are older, you have time and you have money but you don't have enough energy. Nobody has all three together.

I think, as you get older, you do fewer unexpected things. You wouldn't head off somewhere not knowing how you were going to come back again. It's like going out to the middle of a frozen lake: you're always plotting your journey home before you set out somewhere.

I've found growing older most extraordinary. I thought inside you'd change and you'd start thinking like an old person, but I don't think inside I've changed at all. I've just become slightly more tolerant of everybody, which has to be good.

The best is Brenda Fricker's remark that when people of her age meet now they have something called 'the organ recital' where they go through all the organs that are not working. I think that's so funny.

So health is a nuisance and I was talking to a friend of mine and she said, 'Do you remember when we used to have conversations that didn't begin "When I was at the doctor . . ."?'

What did we do with our time when we weren't at the doctor? It does take up a disproportionate amount of your time, just the business of maintenance and keeping yourself together.

There are lots of things I wish I had done more of – studied harder, read more and been nicer and all those things – but I don't have any regrets about any roads I didn't take. Everything went well and I think that's been a help because I can look back, and I do get great pleasure out of looking back.

I get just as much of a laugh out of thinking of funny things from the old days as if they were last week.

I've been very lucky and I have a happy old age with good family and friends still around.

Editor's Acknowledgments

What struck me when I began trawling through the archives was the fact that Maeve arrived at *The Irish Times* in 1964 with a fully evolved writing voice. Whether writing about royalty or reporting from a warzone, her incomparable style was there from the beginning – intelligent, incisive, warm, conversational and witty. She was a one-off in the newspaper world which made selecting the pieces for *Maeve's Times* a real joy.

I was given invaluable help on this project by Maeve's great friend and colleague Mary Maher, who acted as Editorial Consultant. I'm also grateful for the help of Maeve's agent and friend Christine Green and Maeve's husband, Gordon Snell. Thanks to all of you.

At *The Irish Times*, thanks to deputy editor Denis Staunton who gave me this lovely job and to Irene Stevenson, librarian and Maeve fan, who was a constant support. Thanks for putting up with my endless requests, Irene.

The unflappable Ciara Considine at Hachette Books Ireland pulled it all together beautifully – thanks a million, Ciara. Love and gratitude are also due to my mother, Ann Ingle, she knows why.

Finally, thanks to my journalistic hero Maeve Binchy for five decades of stunning service to *The Irish Times*. What a woman.

Róisín Ingle, *The Irish Times*

A Note About the Author

Maeve Binchy is the author of numerous best-selling books, including her most recent novels, *A Week in Winter, Minding Frankie, Heart and Soul* and *Whitethorn Woods,* in addition to *Night of Rain and Stars, Quentins, Scarlet Feather, Circle of Friends,* and *Tara Road,* which was an Oprah's Book Club selection. She has written for *Gourmet; O, The Oprah Magazine; Modern Maturity;* and *Good Housekeeping,* among other publications. She died in July 2012 at the age of seventy-two.

A Note on the Type

This book was set in Adobe Garamond. Designed for the Adobe Corporation by Robert Slimbach, the fonts are based on types first cut by Claude Garamond (ca. 1480–1561). Garamond was a pupil of Geoffroy Tory and is believed to have followed the Venetian models, although he introduced a number of important differences, and it is to him that we owe the letter we now know as "old style."

Typeset by Scribe,
Philadelphia, Pennsylvania

Printed and bound by Berryville Graphics,
Berryville, Virginia

B L A C K S
N
Ephesus
Antioch
Damascus
A N
S E A
Jerusalem
Alexandria
E LOWENSTEIN

THE INTERPRETER'S BIBLE

THE INTERPRETER'S BIBLE

IN TWELVE VOLUMES

VOLUME

I. General Articles on the Bible; General Articles on the Old Testament; Genesis; Exodus

II. Leviticus; Numbers; Deuteronomy; Joshua; Judges; Ruth; Samuel

III. Kings; Chronicles; Ezra; Nehemiah; Esther; Job

IV. Psalms; Proverbs

V. Ecclesiastes; Song of Songs; Isaiah; Jeremiah

VI. Lamentations; Ezekiel; Daniel; Hosea; Joel; Amos; Obadiah; Jonah; Micah; Nahum; Habakkuk; Zephaniah; Haggai; Zechariah; Malachi

VII. General Articles on the New Testament; Matthew; Mark

VIII. Luke; John

IX. Acts; Romans

X. Corinthians; Galatians; Ephesians

XI. Philippians; Colossians; Thessalonians; Timothy; Titus; Philemon; Hebrews

XII. James; Peter; John; Jude; Revelation; Index

VOLUME X

The First Epistle to the CORINTHIANS

The Second Epistle to the CORINTHIANS

The Epistle to the GALATIANS

The Epistle to the EPHESIANS

THE INTERPRETER'S BIBLE

The Holy Scriptures

IN THE KING JAMES AND REVISED STANDARD VERSIONS
WITH GENERAL ARTICLES AND
INTRODUCTION, EXEGESIS, EXPOSITION
FOR EACH BOOK OF THE BIBLE

IN TWELVE VOLUMES

VOLUME
X

Ἐν ἀρχῇ ἦν ὁ λόγος

NEW YORK *Abingdon-Cokesbury Press* NASHVILLE

Library of Congress Catalog Card Number: 51-12276

B

SET UP, PRINTED, AND BOUND BY THE PARTHENON PRESS, AT NASHVILLE, TENNESSEE, UNITED STATES OF AMERICA

ABBREVIATIONS AND EXPLANATIONS

Abbreviations

Canonical books and bibliographical terms are abbreviated according to common usage

Amer. Trans. — *The Bible, An American Translation,* Old Testament, ed. J. M. P. Smith
Apoc.—Apocrypha
Aq.—Aquila
ASV—American Standard Version (1901)
Barn.—Epistle of Barnabas
Clem.—Clement
C.T.—Consonantal Text
Did.—Didache
Ecclus.—Ecclesiasticus
ERV—English Revised Version (1881-85)
Exeg.—Exegesis
Expos.—Exposition
Goodspeed—*The Bible, An American Translation,* New Testament and Apocrypha, tr. Edgar J. Goodspeed
Herm. Vis., etc.—The Shepherd of Hermas: Visions, Mandates, Similitudes
Ign. Eph., etc.—Epistles of Ignatius to the Ephesians, Magnesians, Trallians, Romans, Philadelphians, Smyrnaeans, and Polycarp
KJV—King James Version (1611)
LXX—Septuagint
Macc.—Maccabees
Moffatt—*The Bible, A New Translation,* by James Moffatt
M.T.—Masoretic Text
N.T.—New Testament
O.T.—Old Testament
Polyc. Phil.—Epistle of Polycarp to the Philippians
Pseudep.—Pseudepigrapha
Pss. Sol.—Psalms of Solomon
RSV—Revised Standard Version (1946-52)
Samar.—Samaritan recension
Symm.—Symmachus
Targ.—Targum
Test. Reuben, etc.—Testament of Reuben, and others of the Twelve Patriarchs
Theod.—Theodotion
Tob.—Tobit
Vulg.—Vulgate
Weymouth—*The New Testament in Modern Speech,* by Richard Francis Weymouth
Wisd. Sol.—Wisdom of Solomon

Quotations and References

Boldface type in Exegesis and Exposition indicates a quotation from either the King James or the Revised Standard Version of the passage under discussion. The two versions are distinguished only when attention is called to a difference between them. Readings of other versions are not in boldface type and are regularly identified.

In scripture references a letter (*a, b,* etc.) appended to a verse number indicates a clause within the verse; an additional Greek letter indicates a subdivision within the clause. When no book is named, the book under discussion is understood.

Arabic numbers connected by colons, as in scripture references, indicate chapters and verses in deuterocanonical and noncanonical works. For other ancient writings roman numbers indicate major divisions, arabic numbers subdivisions, these being connected by periods. For modern works a roman number and an arabic number connected by a comma indicate volume and page. Bibliographical data on a contemporary work cited by a writer may be found by consulting the first reference to the work by that writer (or the bibliography, if the writer has included one).

Greek Transliterations

α = a	ε = e	ι = i	ν = n	ρ = r	φ = ph
β = b	ζ = z	κ = k	ξ = x	σ(ς) = s	χ = ch
γ = g	η = ē	λ = l	ο = o	τ = t	ψ = ps
δ = d	θ = th	μ = m	π = p	υ = u, y	ω = ō

Hebrew and Aramaic Transliterations

I. HEBREW ALPHABET

א = ʼ	ה = h	ט = ṭ	מ(ם) = m	פ(ף) = p, ph	שׁ = s, sh
ב = b, bh	ו = w	י = y	נ(ן) = n	צ(ץ) = ç	ת = t, th
ג = g, gh	ז = z	כ(ך) = k, kh	ס = ṣ	ק = q	
ד = d, dh	ח = ḥ	ל = l	ע = ʻ	ר = r	

II. MASORETIC POINTING

Pure-long	Tone-long	Short	Composite *shᵉwa*
◌ָ = â	◌ָ = ā	◌ַ = a	◌ֲ = ᵃ
◌ֵ = ê	◌ֵ = ē	◌ֶ = e	◌ֱ = ᵉ
◌ִ *or* ◌ִי = î		◌ִ = i	
וֹ *or* ◌ֹ = ô	◌ֹ = ō	◌ָ = o	◌ֳ = ᵒ
וּ = û		◌ֻ = u	

NOTE: (*a*) The *páthaḥ* furtive is transliterated as a *ḥaṭeph-páthaḥ*. (*b*) The simple *shᵉwa,* when vocal, is transliterated ᵉ. (*c*) The tonic accent, which is indicated only when it occurs on a syllable other than the last, is transliterated by an acute accent over the vowel.

TABLE OF CONTENTS

VOLUME X

THE FIRST EPISTLE TO THE CORINTHIANS

THE SECOND EPISTLE TO THE CORINTHIANS

THE EPISTLE TO THE GALATIANS

THE EPISTLE TO THE EPHESIANS

MAPS

The First Epistle to the

CORINTHIANS

Introduction and Exegesis by CLARENCE T. CRAIG

Exposition by JOHN SHORT

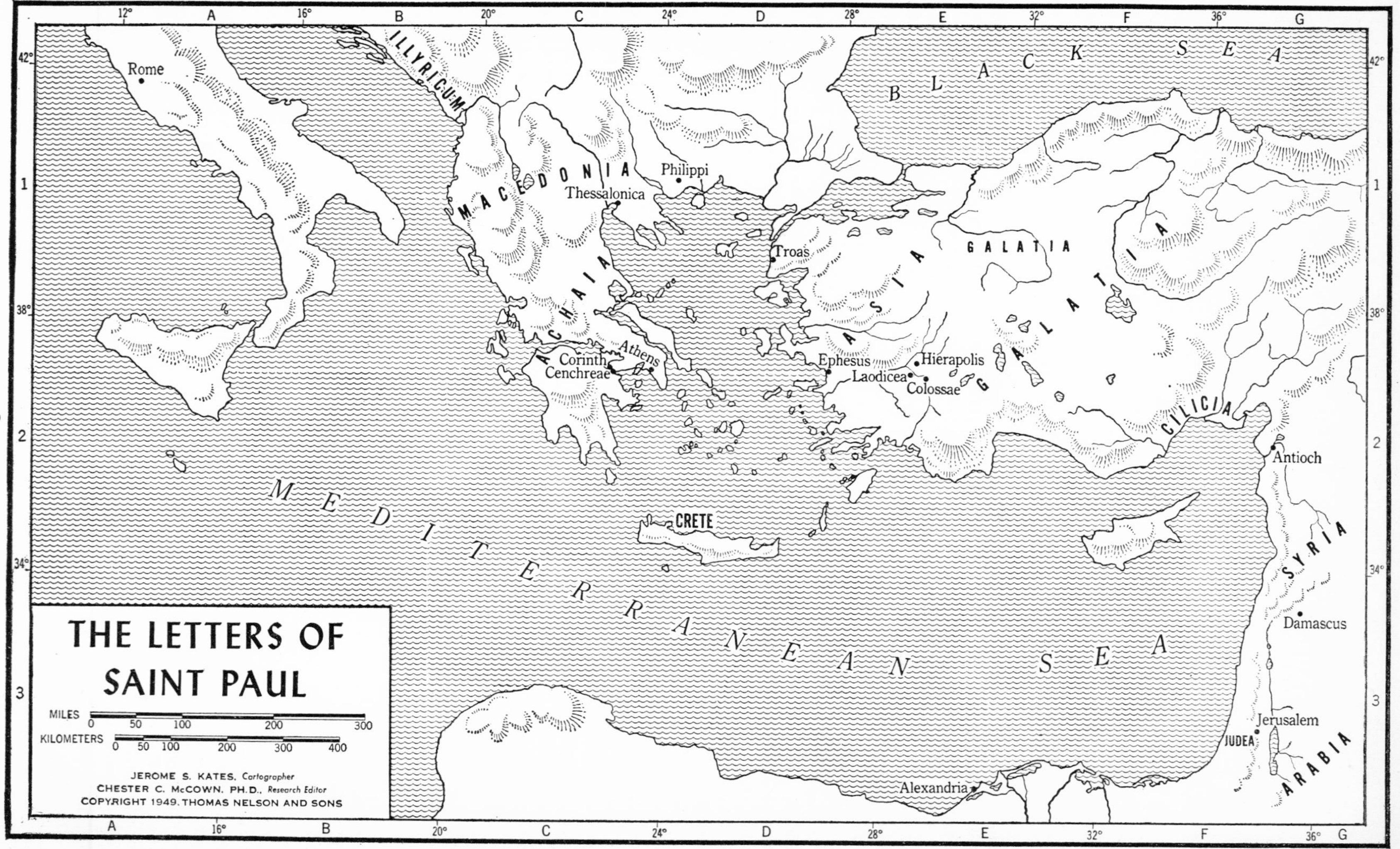
THE LETTERS OF SAINT PAUL
MILES 0 50 100 200 300
KILOMETERS 0 50 100 200 300 400
JEROME S. KATES, Cartographer
CHESTER C. McCOWN, PH.D., Research Editor
COPYRIGHT 1949, THOMAS NELSON AND SONS
BLACK SEA
MEDITERRANEAN SEA
Rome
ILLYRICUM
MACEDONIA
Thessalonica
Philippi
ACHAIA
Corinth
Cenchreae
Athens
CRETE
Troas
ASIA
Ephesus
Laodicea
Colossae
Hierapolis
GALATIA
CILICIA
Antioch
SYRIA
Damascus
Jerusalem
JUDEA
ARABIA
Alexandria

I CORINTHIANS

INTRODUCTION

The community to which Paul wrote lived in Corinth, the capital of Achaia; but this Corinth was not the same Greek city which had headed the Achaean League during the Hellenistic period. That city had been destroyed by Lucius Mummius in 146 B.C.,[1] and for one hundred years its ruins were not rebuilt, although even during that time of desolation the famous Isthmian games had continued. The city was refounded, probably under Julius Caesar, as a Roman colony and was settled at first by former soldiers. This may explain why Corinth had the only amphitheater in Greece. Many of the names connected with Corinth in the New Testament, like Crispus, Titius Justus, and Fortunatus, are Roman. More of the early inscriptions are in Latin than in any other language. Soon, however, many Greeks and Orientals joined in the building of the cosmopolitan city which included in its population many Jews. The excavations, conducted slowly since 1896 under the American School of Classical Studies at Athens, have laid bare many of the important landmarks.[2] They can be identified through the full description which Pausanias wrote a century after Paul's time.

I. Corinth in the Time of Paul

Ancient Corinth was about eight miles from Cenchreae (Acts 18:18; Rom. 16:1) on the Gulf of Saros and nearly two miles from Lechaeum, the port on the western sea on the Gulf of Corinth. It quickly won strategic commercial importance because of its location on the highroad of commerce from the East to the West. Since mariners considered it dangerous to round Cape Malea, the southern promontory of Greece, vessels were often dragged on rollers across the narrow isthmus just north of Corinth, or cargoes were transferred from one port to the other. Hence, the city was a natural stopping point for sea captains and merchants during transshipment. Under Nero (66-67) an attempt was made to cut a canal across the isthmus, but the successful completion of this enterprise awaited the nineteenth century. According to all ancient testimony, Corinth was the wealthiest and most important city in Greece at this time. It was not the philosophical center that Athens continued to be, but it was the capital of the Roman province of Achaia and ranked with Ephesus and Antioch as a commercial center. Estimates of its population run as high as 600,000, including its two ports.

The most prominent physical feature of the city is Acrocorinth, a steep promontory which rises abruptly to a height of eighteen hundred feet. Because of the isolation of this peak it commands a magnificent panoramic view of the mountains of the Peloponnesos to the south and those of central Greece to the north. Paul must have climbed it often and received a new stimulus to forward the world conquest of the gospel. Doubtless in his ascent he avoided the temples of Isis, of Necessity, and of Demeter. On the summit stood the famous temple of Aphrodite, symbolic of the domination of the city by licentious impulses. This precipitous mountain provided protection for the city on one side. The walls on the other sides were six miles in circumference, and the road to Lechaeum was also lined with parallel walls so that the city could have access to the sea even during a siege.

At the center of the city stood the market place, with its bronze statue of Athena and the temple of Apollo, which today is the most prominent ruin from antiquity. Near by stood the fountain of Pirene, which was believed to be connected with the fountain by that name on Acrocorinth. Pirene was, according to legend, "a woman who became a spring because of her tears shed in lamentation for her son Cenchrias,

1 Pausanias *Description of Greece* II. 2.

2 Rhys Carpenter, *Ancient Corinth, A Guide to the Excavations* (2nd ed.; Athens: American School of Classical Studies, 1933).

who was unintentionally killed by Artemis."[3] Naturally, Poseidon was the chief god of Corinth, but there were altars to Hermes, Artemis, Zeus, Apollo, Dionysus, Heracles, and a host of others. Yet it was difficult for these to compete in popularity with Aphrodite, who had "a thousand temple-slaves, courtesans, whom both men and women had dedicated to the goddess."[4] With such attractions it is easy to understand the rise of the proverb among Mediterranean seamen, "Not for every man is the voyage to Corinth."

Paul's work was confessedly among the lower classes (1:26-31). The individuals whom he names may have been among the few who were wealthy or wise, but freedmen and slaves surely comprised the majority of his converts. The bronze workers, potters, shopkeepers, and dock hands drawn to the new faith were joined by few of the powerful and well born. As in the great commercial centers of all times, Corinth knew a great cleft between the rich and the poor. Yet we must never suppose that the slaves were all ignorant toilers. Some were more intelligent than their masters and occupied responsible posts as clerks and administrators.

Less information has come to us from Corinth than from many other places about the private associations or *thiasoi*.[5] Yet religious societies devoted to the worship of popular deities undoubtedly existed and provided for many some measure of preparation for membership in a Christian church. In contrast to the official cult they satisfied the need for fellowship among the uprooted urban proletariat. The Isis cult was especially popular, extending religious equality to women. The likenesses and differences compared with a Christian church will appear throughout the letter. The table of the Lord Jesus should not be attended by those who persisted in the religious meals of Dionysus, Serapis, and other deities.

Two events connected with Paul's stay at Corinth have contact with the general history of the time. We are told that Priscilla and Aquila came to Corinth because of the expulsion of the Jews from Rome under Claudius (Acts 18:2).[6] The most probable date for this event, based on later information in Orosius, is A.D. 49. In Acts 18:12 we read of Gallio being made proconsul of Achaia. This was the Lucius Junius Annaeus Gallio, who was a brother of Seneca, the famous philosopher and a tutor of Nero. An inscription has been found at Delphi which dates his proconsulship within very narrow limits. Deissmann calculated that Gallio came to office on July 1, A.D. 51.[7] Some students of ancient history hold that the date implied by the inscription is a year later. We cannot be sure that Gallio held office for only one year or that the author of Acts had exact information concerning the relative time of the incident in relation to Paul's ministry at Corinth. But the two lines of evidence converge in pointing toward the spring of A.D. 50 as the time of Paul's arrival and the fall of A.D. 51 as the date of his departure.

II. Founding of the Church

Paul was the first Christian missionary to Greece of whom we have any record. The impetus to go west had come following the struggle over the admission of Gentiles to the church. At Jerusalem (Gal. 2:1-10) he had won the victory over those demanding the circumcision of Gentile converts. But in the discussion over the necessity of obedience to Torah, understanding had not been reached on the problem of table-fellowship between Jewish and Gentile believers. This issue arose later at Antioch, and on this point Paul was not supported by Barnabas, his fellow missionary (Gal. 2:11-14). Apparently the apostle did not carry the day in the church there, for from that time on Antioch is no longer his base.

Taking Silvanus as his partner and young Timothy as assistant, Paul went out to preach his law-free gospel in regions yet untouched by missionaries of Christ. After visiting the communities founded earlier in Phrygia and Lycaonia, he went "through the region of Phrygia and Galatia" (Acts 16:6). For some unexplained reason the provinces of Asia and Bithynia were not open to them. Though Acts says nothing about the founding of churches in northern Galatia, it is altogether probable that they were established during this time. But the ultimate destination turned out to be Europe. Strong communities of believers were established in Philippi, Thessalonica, and Beroea.

The first attempt in Achaia proved to be a failure. Acts reports a few converts at Athens (Acts 17:34), but there is no indication of the development of a church there. It proved otherwise at Corinth. In this cosmopolitan city Paul got a strong foothold. We are told that he stayed more than eighteen months, longer than in any other city except Ephesus. Though the relations of Paul with this church did not prove so happy

[3] Pausanias, *op. cit.*, II. 3. 2.

[4] *The Geography of Strabo* VIII. 6. 20.

[5] Franz Poland, *Geschichte des Griechischen Vereinswesen* (Leipzig: B. G. Teubner, 1909).

[6] Referred to in Suetonius *Life of the Deified Claudius* 25. 4.

[7] One of the fullest discussions of the inscription is in Adolf Deissmann, *Paul* (2nd ed.; London: Hodder & Stoughton, 1926), Appendix 1, pp. 261-86.

as with Philippi, Corinth became one of the most important centers of the early church. With that city Paul had his most extensive correspondence. From that place at least three letters were written, I and II Thessalonians and Romans.

Though Silvanus and Timothy were not with him at the outset, Paul quickly found two other collaborators. Priscilla and Aquila had come originally from Pontus and were among the Jews whom Claudius expelled from Rome. Paul was drawn to this couple by ties of economic interests and by ties of belief. In 4:12 and 9:18 the apostle states that he supported himself during his missionary campaigns, but it is only from Acts 18:3 that we learn that his trade was that of tentmaker. Nothing is said in Acts of the baptism of this couple by Paul, and in I Cor. 16:15 it is specifically said that the household of Stephanas were the first converts in Achaia. Hence we must conclude that Aquila and his wife had become Christians at Rome. It is highly probable that those of "the Way" reached Rome not many years after the crucifixion of Jesus. The reference in Suetonius may be interpreted to mean that it was controversy over the messiahship of Jesus which led to the temporary expulsion of Jews from Rome.

In presenting the work of Paul at Corinth, Acts indicates the same pattern as in other cities. He begins in the synagogue, proclaiming to the Jews that the Messiah for whom they had looked was Jesus. We are not told how long the apostle was able to continue this preaching. I Corinthians shows no evidence of ties with the synagogue; yet there is no reason to deny that the apostle got his foothold in this way. Though most of the Jews opposed and reviled him, it was among the god-fearers—the devout Gentiles attracted to Jewish monotheism but unwilling to become proselytes—that Paul found his most fertile soil for the seed of the Word. Yet two of the rulers of the synagogue were won to Christ, Crispus and later Sosthenes.

We have almost no concrete information concerning the eighteen months of missionary work. Instead of describing methods of evangelizing the Greeks, ways of instructing the converts, or problems of community organization, "Luke" recounts for us only a word of encouragement which the apostle received from the Lord (Acts 18:9-10). Though he had an interest in Paul's lodgings (Acts 18:7), he does not tell us where the "many people" met for their worship. Acts affords no background for understanding the type of problem with which I Corinthians deals. All that "Luke" has to describe is the Jewish opposition which led to the bringing of Paul before the proconsul Gallio. That official refused to consider the charges when he realized that they did not involve violation of Roman law, but only of Jewish customs. The incident corroborates other evidence of the privilege of the Jews in regulating their own communities according to the precepts of the Torah. It is not clear why the Jews should have turned on their own leader Sosthenes (Acts 18:16). Probably he is the same as the one mentioned in the address of I Corinthians. Did he join the church in reaction against this violence, or did it occur because the Jews realized that he had protected Paul before Gallio out of interest in the new faith?

There is no need to discuss in detail the travels of Paul in the immediately succeeding months. Priscilla and Aquila were to remove their residence to Ephesus at the same time. Naturally they sailed from the eastern port of Cenchreae. Had Paul expected to return to Syria permanently, and was it the experience in the synagogue which led him to plan to make Ephesus the center of a new missionary campaign? Did Paul reach Jerusalem on this trip, as the Western and koine texts of Acts 18:21 suggest? Is it correct to place the apostolic conference in the midst of the Ephesian ministry, as some do? Why should Paul have made such a long trip, for which Acts suggests no adequate motivation? Is the vow mentioned in Acts 18:18 confused with the vow in 21:24? Fortunately the solution of these problems is not essential for the background of I Corinthians, but to raise them is a reminder of the limitations of our knowledge concerning Paul's career at this time.

Apollos is introduced in Acts 18:24 and he does figure in the Corinthian situation. This Alexandrian had some kind of belief in Jesus on his arrival at Ephesus. His talents of eloquence and fervency could be of great value in the church, and his knowledge of the Old Testament gave him power in confuting the Jews. Though he "taught accurately the things concerning Jesus," it is said that he "knew only the baptism of John." Does that mean that he had been converted in a community which did not practice baptism in the name of Jesus? The difficulty of accepting any such theory lies in the fact that in contrast to the "disciples," with whom Paul later came into contact (Acts 19:1-7), it is not said that Apollos was baptized. Priscilla and Aquila corrected his faith by "expounding to him the way of God more accurately." It is clear from I Corinthians that Paul had full confidence in the reliability of Apollos' message. The incident underlines again what great gaps there are in our knowledge of the spread of Christianity in the first generation.

For Paul's Ephesian ministry "Luke's" information was even more fragmentary and disjointed than usual. That ministry was in many ways the climax of the apostle's missionary work, and at the same time a period of intense opposition. Only a few anecdotes are recorded and they afford but slight illumination of the two-and-a-half-year ministry (Acts 19:8, 10). It was toward the close of this time that our letter was written, but the situation must be reconstructed entirely from the internal evidence which it furnishes.

III. Occasion for the Letter

The intervening events affecting the relations between Paul and the church at Corinth may be tabulated under five headings:

(*a*) Apollos had had a successful period of evangelism in Corinth, but was now back in Ephesus (16:12). He sends greetings to his friends but states that he cannot return at this time. Clearly the Alexandrian missionary had a following which was devoted to him, people for whom Paul was only a name.

(*b*) Since there were some who affirmed, "I belong to Cephas" (1:12), the most natural explanation is that Peter himself had visited the church. The only alternative is that Palestinian Christians had come in his name and were citing his authority. Men whom Paul looked upon as ministers of the old covenant (II Cor. 3:1 ff.) came with letters of introduction at some time before the writing of II Corinthians. This probably took place later than the writing of I Corinthians and indicates part of the cause for the further deterioration of relationships with the church. From Gal. 2:11-14 we may assume that Cephas and his representatives stood closer to the Torah than did Paul. Those drawn to this leadership were apparently the ones most distrustful of Paul's apostleship.

(*c*) A letter had been sent by Paul, to which reference is made in 5:9. This had called for dissociation from immoral people, ethical separation from the ways of the world. The demand had apparently been purposely misunderstood in order to excuse failure to comply. It is highly probable that we have a fragment of this in II Cor. 6:14–7:1. Some of the more stringent sections of I Corinthians have also been assigned to this precanonical letter by interpreters who deny the integrity of our letter.

(*d*) The reply from the church had apparently been brought by some of the leaders at Corinth. Stephanas, Fortunatus, and Achaicus are mentioned in 16:15-18. They would provide a personal source of information concerning developments at Corinth. This letter of the Corinthians asked concerning various problems of marriage (7:1), concerning meat sacrificed to idols (8:1), concerning spiritual gifts (12:1), concerning the contribution for the saints (16:1), and possibly concerning Apollos (16:12). It is not specifically indicated where Paul learned about the case of incest (5:1-5), the legal disputes (6:1-6), the various expressions of freedom (11:2-16), the disorders at the Lord's Supper (11:17-34), and the denial of the resurrection (15:1-58).

(*e*) We are told, however, that it is Chloe's people (probably slaves) who had informed Paul about the party divisions (1:11 ff.). They may also have been the informants on some of the other issues as well. It is a probable hypothesis that they were not returning to Corinth; else Paul would hardly have subjected them to revenge at the hands of those whom he attacks.

Unquestionably the situation at Corinth was too complex and many-sided to be dealt with easily in a single letter. The recognition of this has led to various theories of partition. Johannes Weiss, whose commentary is still an outstanding contribution to the understanding of the letter, supports the following division:[8]

(*a*) The precanonical letter referred to in 5:9 contained II Cor. 6:14–7:1; I Cor. 10:1-23; 6:12-20; 11:2-34; and possibly 16:7-8, 20.

(*b*) Paul's answer to the letter brought from Corinth contained I Cor. 7–9; 10:24–11:1; 12:1–16:6, and possibly 16:16-19.

(*c*) A third letter dealing with factions included I Cor. 1:1–6:11, and 16:10-14, 22-24.

Maurice Goguel follows the same general scheme but with some differences in the distribution of material.[9] His division is as follows:

(*a*) II Cor. 6:14–7:1; I Cor. 6:12-20; 10:1-22.

(*b*) I Cor. 5:1–6:11; 7:1–8:13; 10:23–14:40; 15:1-58; 16:1-9, 12.

(*c*) I Cor. 1:10–4:21; 9:1-27; 16:10-11.

Such partition theories are not to be dismissed as ridiculous, for there is nothing inherently improbable in the idea that selections from various letters which Paul wrote to the church were transcribed on two rolls. Particularly would this be true if the Pauline corpus had its origin in Corinth, a theory for which there is much more to be said than is now usually recognized. If our letter is a scribal compilation from three different letters, we must pay high tribute to the man whose skill has woven them together into so well-constructed a whole. The outline will show that no letter has a more clearly developed sequence. It seems

[8] See details in *The History of Primitive Christianity* (New York: Wilson-Erickson, 1937), I, 356-57.

[9] *Introduction au Nouveau Testament,* "Les épîtres pauliniennes" (Paris: Ernest Leroux, 1926), IV [2], 72-86.

much more probable that this is due rather to the mind of Paul than to the skill of a later scribe. This commentary will assume the general integrity of the letter, and that Paul deals with the different situations in one and the same document. The possibility of certain glosses must not be excluded, though none of the cases is altogether convincing. The passages will be dealt with in the Exegesis.

IV. The Divisions at Corinth

I Corinthians was written to a divided church. This is apparent from the very first section of the letter, where Paul condemns the party strife which had led to the slogans, "I belong to Paul," and so forth. Reasons are given in the Exegesis for recognizing only three definite parties, the personal adherents of Paul, Apollos, and Cephas. Likewise, it is pointed out that it was not from the Apollos party that the most serious trouble had come, but from the local leadership of the Cephas party. Yet Paul is primarily opposing the spirit which animates all the parties. He is not so much supporting his own adherents as condemning all who would put men where Christ alone should stand.

It is plausible to suspect that those who elevated "wisdom" were primarily followers of Apollos. Presumably the Cephas party took a more conservative attitude toward Jewish practices, but we are not told either of these things specifically, and it is presumptuous to draw up an elaborate characterization which would be the product of imagination and conjecture.

Yet we cannot dodge certain questions if an earnest attempt is to be made to understand this letter. It should be clear to any attentive reader that also on the issues discussed in chs. 5–15 the Corinthians were by no means united. What were the further points of difference, and how far do the issues coincide with the bases of division in 1:11–4:21? We may put aside the matter of lawsuits among Christians (6:1-6). That would be an individual rather than a party matter, except in so far as the propriety of participating in the civil institutions of society was concerned. Likewise, it may well be that the divisions at the Lord's Supper (11:18) were social and personal in character and reflected no major contrasts of conviction. But even social groupings tend to follow the lines of belief and inner convictions. As a matter of fact, it is in the later chapters that we get the clearest picture of the salient points of cleavage within the community. This picture must be analyzed before we can have any adequate understanding of the nature of the divisions.

(*a*) First, we see clear evidence of the presence of a libertine attitude. Some members of the community were saying, "All things are lawful" (6:12). By that they meant that sexual conduct was as morally indifferent as eating. Among these we should probably look for the supporters of the man guilty of incest (5:1-5). Paul may have ascribed to this group a more consistent practice of their theory than was actually the case, but clearly there were defenders of decidedly loose sexual standards. On the other hand, there were ascetics who were rejecting marriage completely (7:36-38). Despite his sympathy for this position in practice, Paul could not accept the theoretical basis for it in the sinfulness of marriage. Here was a division where neither group could be equated with the followers of either Apollos or Cephas. The problem arose from the background of the converts rather than from the emphases of their new teachers.

(*b*) Again, we find various emancipation tendencies within the community. The apostle's advice to slaves (7:17-24) need not presuppose an active movement to secure freedom, but certainly many of the women were in revolt against the subordination traditional among Eastern Jews (11:2-16). It would be quite unfair to assume that these women made common cause with the Gnostic-libertines. They were hardly siding with either Apollos or Cephas against Paul. They were converts who interpreted Christian freedom in ways that Paul felt to be unjustified.

(*c*) Emancipation from food laws presented a still further issue. Here we may postulate that it was the Gnostic group which drew the conclusion from the fact that idols had no real existence. Therefore food offered to idols could be no different from other food, and "all things are lawful" (10:23). Opposed to them were those with a weak conscience (8:10) for whom idol meat had emotional associations too strong to be shaken off so quickly. Obviously these were not former Jews still under the influence of kosher regulations but former Gentiles since they had hitherto been "accustomed to idols" (8:7). The adherents of Apollos and Cephas fit neither of these groups. It is a division in terms of varied reactions to the new faith against the old background.

(*d*) A fourth division was created by the emphasis upon the ecstatic speaking with tongues. Usually this development at Corinth has been ascribed to the orgiastic religious heritage of Greek converts. T. W. Manson suggests on the contrary that it was due to the Palestinian influence of the Cephas party.[10] He thinks that

[10] "St. Paul in Ephesus, The Corinthian Correspondence," *Bulletin of the John Rylands Library,* XXVI (1941), 101-20.

the problem arose after Paul's departure; and, at the time he was writing, the church was not yet surfeited with this type of ecstacy. Stress on speaking in tongues was a demand which was being made by the Cephas party as the essential demonstration of possession by the Spirit (Acts 2:1-12). This theory is much less convincing than the view that among local ecstatics an exaggerated regard for the gift of tongues had arisen. These people may have been found primarily among the Gnostic-libertines, but that identification has no certainty. Those who suffered from a sense of inferiority because their gifts were less spectacular may well have included people from all the parties mentioned in chs. 1–4. The self-styled "spiritual" have much in common with the Gnostics of chs 1–2, but we do not know that they comprised a fixed grouping, and they are not to be identified with the followers of Apollos or of Cephas.

(*e*) We meet a further division in the denial of the resurrection of the dead (ch. 15). Who were the members of the community who rejected this? Certainly they had not been prompted by the teachings of Cephas or Apollos. What kind of converts were they if they held to the materialistic view that death ends all? What kind of hope did they cherish? The most satisfactory answer is that they held to such a depreciation of matter that their hope lay in an immortality of the soul which involved no type of resurrection body. For them redemption meant deliverance *from* the body rather than a resurrection. Paul hardly does justice to their view in his argument any more than theological opponents of other times have allowed the positions they were attacking to appear in their strongest form. Nevertheless he was contending for the original form of the faith against changes due to Gnostic assumptions. The Exegesis will make clear what concessions Paul made to this position in regard to the nature of the resurrection body; but for him as a Jew, "body" was indispensable to personality.

It should be apparent from this brief survey that though the party cries on behalf of various missionaries created an unwholesome situation calling for reproof and correction, this was not the most serious aspect of division. There were Gnostic spiritualists who drew libertine conclusions from their emancipation. Here lay the most dangerous peril to the sound development of the church. Were these, then, the Christ party for whom Paul's argument in 1:13 ff. presents so little basis? How could Paul charge the Corinthians with dividing Christ and putting men where only he should stand if one of the parties was appealing to Christ? In 3:22 Paul says that *all* of the leaders belong to the church, but Christ is not one of the series. Rather, all of them, leaders and converts alike, belong to Christ. Yet despite the fact that Paul's words lend so little support to the idea of a Christ party, attempts to find evidence for its existence have continued.

Many earlier writers identified this party as an extreme Judaistic party farther to the right than the followers of Cephas. That relic from the theories of the Tübingen school is today almost universally discarded. Circumcision and extreme legalism were never issues at Corinth to the extent that they were in Galatia. Far more can be said for the contention that the Christ party was a Gnostic-spiritualist group who opposed dependence on any apostle since they received their revelations direct from Christ.[11] They stood at the opposite pole from the Judaizers; they would cut off the new faith from its historic roots and open the floodgates to individual mystic experience.

A somewhat similar theory is set forth by Manson (*op. cit.*). He holds that the Christ party was composed of believers in "God, freedom, and immortality"; they stood for a philosophical monotheism, emancipation from puritanical restrictions, and opposition to belief in a coming resurrection. Undoubtedly these trends were present in the church at Corinth. Yet Manson has not made as plausible a case as Schlatter that these people who adopted the slogan, "I belong to Christ," comprised a group parallel to the Cephas, Apollos, and Paul parties. The beliefs described were dangerous tendencies in the church, but they had little or nothing to do with the personal factions opposed in chs. 1–4.

We may conclude therefore that it is setting a false alternative to ask whether there were three or four parties at Corinth. There were various types of division which followed different patterns. Some were social divisions which appeared at the Lord's table; some were based on allegiance to the particular missionary who had converted them; others were concerned with Gnostic-spiritual positions, and may have represented trends rather than clear-cut party divisions. Such was the divided state of the church to which the apostle wrote to consolidate his authority and set forth the implications of Christian faith which seemed essential to him.

V. Main Themes of the Letter

I Corinthians is not a doctrinal letter in the sense that Romans and Galatians are. It con-

[11] See Wilhelm Lütgert, *Freiheitspredigt und Schwarmgeister in Korinth* (Gütersloh: C. Bertelsmann, 1908); Adolf Schlatter, *Paulus, der Bote Jesu* (Stuttgart: Calwer, 1934).

tains no organized presentation of the Christian faith. It deals primarily with ethical and practical questions. The letter does not raise the issue of the relationship to Judaism so much as of the contacts with the Hellenistic world. The heathen background of the readers is apparent throughout, but the letter also poses the problem of the degree to which Paul himself had been influenced from Hellenism. The exaggerated theories of Bousset, Reitzenstein,[12] and others find less favor today. In fact, in the swing of the pendulum it has actually been contended that at every point the rabbinical influence was paramount with the apostle.[13] Such an extreme position is not warranted any more than its opposite. Paul interprets the gospel from the standpoint of a Hellenistic Jew. His Judaism had not been Hellenized to the same degrees as that of Philo. The underlying assumptions of his thinking still involved the eschatological doctrine of the two ages. Yet despite the dominant messianism, we must expect to find some influence from the world of his time. As a missionary who sought to "become all things to all men" (9:22), he could hardly fail to adapt his presentation to the background of his Greek converts.

Despite the fact that I Corinthians does not contain a systematic presentation of the gospel, every part of the letter deals with some aspect of it. Though Christ is the center of the message, its beginning and end are found in God our Father (1:3). He is the ultimate source of creation (8:6) and the supreme end for all (15:28). He is the only true God (8:4-6), the one who sustains the world of nature (3:6) and providentially ordains the affairs of men (4:9; 7:7; 12:6). Yet men have not known God through their wisdom (1:21). Only in Christ has there come a saving revelation of the One upon whom their lives depend. It is not men who have found God; he chose them (1:27) and in Christ Jesus made up all that they lack. To these God reveals his mysteries through the Spirit (2:10; 4:1). Men may be fellow workmen for God (3:9) but their dependence is on his faithfulness (1:9), the One who is a refuge in the time of severest temptation (10:13) and who gives the victory through Jesus Christ (15:57). Hence, there can be no ground for boasting (1:31). Nevertheless, he is the Judge (4:5; 5:13) who expects the keeping of his commandments (7:19).

[12] W. Bousset, *Kyrios Christos* (Göttingen: Vandenhoeck & Ruprecht, 1913); R. Reitzenstein, *Die hellenistischen Mysterienreligionen* (3rd ed.; Leipzig: B. G. Teubner, 1927).

[13] W. D. Davies, *Paul and Rabbinic Judaism* (London: Society for Promoting Christian Knowledge, 1948).

God in his grace has provided deliverance through the Lord Jesus Christ (1:4). In no other letter does Paul give so full a picture of what Christ meant to him. It is clear that Jesus was a person who lived in history, for he had brothers (9:5), was a teacher (7:10; 9:14), suffered betrayal (11:23), died on a cross (1:18; 15:3), and was buried. Yet he was not simply an earthly figure. All things had come into existence through him (8:6); he had been the Rock from which the Israelites drank in the wilderness (10:4). We might assume that a pre-existent being would necessarily be eternal, but Paul does not take that for granted. God raised him from the dead (15:4), confirming him as Christ and Lord. Paul, however, uses "Christ" not as a title, but as a second name for Jesus, and he does not hesitate to apply the term "Lord" to the earthly, as well as to the exalted, Jesus. This Christ will soon come (1:7; 4:5) to complete the conquest of the God-opposing powers, for through him the new age of redemption has come.

The objective aspects of this redemption, as they are related to the defeat of the "rulers of this age" (2:6), victory over sin in the flesh, and the abrogation of the law, are not developed in this letter. Paul only affirms that Christ "died for our sins in accordance with the scriptures" (15:3). This was the "word of the cross" (1:18), which might be foolishness in the eyes of the world and the children of this age, but was in fact the power of God. Yet if it had not been for the Resurrection, men would still be in their sins (15:17). By Jesus' death and resurrection they had been redeemed from slavery to sin (6:20; 7:23). Men shared in this redemption by becoming "in Christ." This meant a union with him which was so complete that the believer was nothing less than a member of the body of Christ (6:15; 12:12). Those who were in him were therefore certain of being raised at his coming (15:22). They were already living in the new age by the power of the Spirit which Christ bestowed. The Messiah and his people comprised one body. To be "in Christ" was *both* an eschatological and a mystical fact; it is impossible to separate the two aspects of the apostle's experience.

There are also two answers concerning how men became part of the body of Christ. "Faith" or believing is undoubtedly one (1:21; 2:5; 3:5; 14:22; 16:13). Paul does not name propositions to which credence must be given; faith is rather acceptance of the salvation which God has provided in Christ. The other answer is "baptism" by which believers are made into one body (12:13). Since it was baptism into Christ, this sacrament did not depend for validity upon administration by an apostle (1:17). Preaching was a higher function than baptizing. Furthermore, there was no automatic guarantee in baptism (10:2), any more than faith was certain to be permanent. After preaching to others, Paul himself might be disqualified (9:27). But faith and baptism jointly brought union with the body of Christ.

Our letter does not deal primarily with these fundamentals but with the life in the Spirit which should flow from this experience of redemption. Deliverance from sin was the *fact* which the apostle proclaimed in Christ. But sad experience had led him to realize the necessity of expressing this in the imperative rather than the indicative mood. Paul believed that the new life in the Spirit was supernatural in character, but this did not mean that it was supramoral. The Spirit was given to build up the church in love. If that did not take place, one should doubt the presence of the Holy Spirit (3:3).

Paul recognized that the gifts of the Spirit were extremely varied (12:4-11). The community was already endowed with the marks of the messianic time. Some had gifts of utterance, others of healing and service, others of administration, and still others delighted in ecstatic outbursts of speaking in tongues. This was not speech which was intelligible to men but a heavenly language known only to God. Paul insisted that it should be reserved for God unless an interpreter was present to translate it into the language of men (14:13-19, 28). Paul did not depreciate Spirit-filled utterance, but it should be prophecy which builds up the community rather than words which no one can understand (14:3-4). To those who were turning the service of worship into a display of private endowments, Paul would bring the social test; *public* worship must serve the common good (14:12).

The apostle does not use the phrase "fruit of the Spirit" (Gal. 5:22) in this letter, but in almost every chapter he elevates love as the true mark of the new life. A factious church does not fully possess the Spirit, for it is so obviously lacking in love (3:3). Love alone builds up (8:1), and without it the exercise of freedom is dangerous. Love is superior to all other gifts (13:2) and abides when all others cease (13:8). Therefore, all things should be done in love (16:14). It is the guiding principle in facing the moral dilemmas of life.

There were many problems with which the apostle had to help his converts deal. Surprisingly little attention is given to economic questions, for with his foreshortened horizon Paul had no thought of a responsibility to Christianize the economic order. He could even counsel slaves to stay as they were (7:20). Of course dishonesty is to be reproved; but rather than fight for justice a man should forgo his rights (6:7-8). Such detachment from economic interests is inextricably related to the expectation that they will soon be living and reigning with Christ (6:2).

On questions of sexual conduct Paul has much more to say. The Jewish revulsion against the licentiousness of the heathen world is accentuated by his own quite unJewish exaltation of celibacy (7:1, 7). This was strengthened by his belief in the imminence of the Parousia, but it is hardly to be explained exclusively on that ground (7:26). There were Jewish sectarians like the Essenes who went even further than Paul. The Exegesis will show that in 5:1-5 Paul was more strict than the official rabbinical opinion. Possibly the loose standards defended by antinomians (6:12-13) led the apostle to stiffen his position even more against the first approach of immorality.

Among the majority in the church there was no defense of recognized immorality; there was sincere inquiry about the proper standards relative to marriage. Paul does not content himself with saying that everyone is to be guided by the Spirit as he sees fit, provided that it accords with the principle of love. He gives very specific counsels, and moves far in the direction of legislating for the community. He believed firmly that celibacy is to be preferred and that in the urgency of the time marriage is a hindrance to undivided attention to the work of the Lord (7:32-35). Nevertheless, marriage is not a sin, and married couples should not separate but give the partner what is due (7:3-5). Divorce is excluded unless sought by the unbelieving partner, in which case it is to be granted (7:10-12). No contamination is involved in living with an unbelieving husband (7:14). Yet widows and virgins, if they marry at all, should marry only in the Lord (7:39).

In this section, as elsewhere in the letter, it is impossible to avoid the question of the nature of biblical revelation. Are Paul's recommendations really a permanent word of God? The question rises again when he discusses the obligation of women to wear a veil when praying and prophesying (11:2-16) and when he forbids women to speak in church (14:34-36). It is hardly sufficient to dismiss the question with the phrase "situation-conditioned." By what criterion can one determine which advices of Paul are conditioned by the times and which have permanent validity? What Paul has to say elsewhere in criticism of the "works of the law" should apply to any legalistic view of his advices. He sincerely believed that he had the

Spirit of God (7:40) when he wrote. But that judgment must itself be spiritually judged.

Another theme related to life in the Spirit is that of Christian freedom. In the case of the Galatians, Paul needed to urge his readers to stand fast in their freedom (5:1). In the case of the Corinthians, Paul had to urge the limitations which should govern the exercise of freedom. Food offered to idols was the subject affording the occasion for this discussion (8: 1 ff.). Paul agrees that there is nothing inherently wrong in eating meat sacrificed to idols (8:8) except where there is an idol feast in a heathen temple (10:21). There, possession by demons became a parallel possibility to possession by the Holy Spirit. But out of love for the weak brother who cannot forget the old associations, a man should not let his liberty become a stumbling block to others (8:9). In his work as an apostle, Paul was constantly called upon to forgo rights in the interest of others (9:1-23). Incidentally, it is surprising how often the apostle holds himself up as a model for his converts to imitate (4:17; 11:1; 14:19). The sum of Paul's advice is that freedom must always be limited by love for the brethren. It does not mean emancipation from all restraints, but liberation from the bondage to legalism in order that love may find the best way to serve.

This letter affords the fullest portrayal of Christian worship which has come down to us from the first century. The central act lay in the celebration of the Lord's Supper. This was a genuine meal, apparently held in the evening, and one in which gluttony and drunkenness had appeared (11:18-22). In two separate connections (10:16-22; 11:23-34) Paul discusses the significance of the meal which had its type in the supernatural food which the Israelites received in the wilderness (10:3-4). That comparison shows that the sacramental meal did not automatically guarantee salvation (11:29). The meal served to commemorate the acts and words of Jesus in the night on which he was betrayed (11:23); it provided a participation in the body and blood of Christ who was present as the host at the table (10:16); and it looked forward to his coming again for the messianic banquet (11:26). The only Eucharistic sacrifice which Paul knows is the offering of the food. Nothing is said about the conduct of the service being in the hands of any particular officials. The disorders involved a common responsibility. All of Paul's readers should feel obligated to help in correcting them.

In addition to the community meal there is evidently a service of the word, to which anyone might come (14:23). There is nothing to indicate whether it followed the meal or took place at another time. In this service also disorders had arisen through the exhibitions of speaking in tongues. Since God was not a God of confusion (14:33), Paul prescribed regulations that would assure orderly procedure (14:40). Not more than three should speak in tongues and then only if there was an interpreter (14:27-28). Beyond that, every member was free to speak according to his gift. Prophets stood next to the apostles (12:28), but even they must not insist on speaking at length if others desired a chance (14:30). Paul describes a very democratic assembly where there is not one pastor instructing his flock, but where a Spirit-filled group engage in mutual edification.

The last theme which is extensively treated is that of the Resurrection. This letter gives the earliest and most important witness to the resurrection of Jesus. Paul's account shows that the Resurrection was not reported in the form of a "story," as the Crucifixion was, but was rather a "proclamation" (15:3-8). The appearances of the risen Christ to chosen witnesses served only to substantiate scripture in showing the truth of a fact—the act of God in raising Jesus—central to the message of salvation (15:14). This event is the basis for the coming resurrection of believers. The resurrection body, however, is not the same as the one that is laid away (15:35 ff.). Not only is it impossible for flesh and blood to inherit the kingdom of God (15:50), but it is also true that if we are to bear the image of the man of heaven, we shall have a spiritual body like his body of glory.

Paul believed that he was living in the narrow isthmus of time between Christ's resurrection and the final coming in judgment. Then the believers who were living would be clothed in their spiritual bodies (15:51); the dead in Christ would be raised (15:23); and they would rule with him (6:2) until he should destroy every other rule, authority, and power (15:24). When all things had been put in subjection to him, the end would come and he would hand over the rule so that God might be everything to everyone (15:28).

This is not the place to discuss the relationship of these eschatological expectations to the hopes expressed in his later letters. Did Paul radically change his mind in this respect soon after the writing of I Corinthians? Probably not; but that question belongs to the interpretation of II Corinthians. In either case, however, a difficult problem is raised concerning biblical authority. If Paul realized that he had been mistaken and changed his view, what authority does his first teaching have, even though it is contained in Scripture? If he did not change his view, how can the form of his hope still be valid for us in view of the fact that the coming of Christ has been delayed more than nineteen hundred years? These are questions for Christian theology rather than for biblical interpretation. Of one thing we may be sure: Paul did not believe that man was by nature immortal. Participation in the life of the age to come depended on God's act of raising the dead.

VI. Outline of the Letter

I. Introduction (1:1-9)
  A. Address and salutation (1:1-3)
  B. Thanksgiving (1:4-9)
II. The problem of factions (1:10–4:21)
  A. Statement of the problem (1:10-12)
  B. Argument against factions (1:13–3:23)
    1. They put men in the place of Christ (1:13-17)
    2. The wisdom of men and the foolishness of God (1:18–2:5)
      a) The word of the Cross not a new wisdom (1:18-25)
      b) The membership of the Corinthian community (1:26-31)
      c) The manner of Paul's entrance into Corinth (2:1-5)
    3. The true wisdom is not possessed by the factious (2:6–3:4)
      a) God's own wisdom (2:6-9)
      b) A gift through the Spirit (2:10-16)
      c) Factions reveal the absence of the Spirit (3:1-4)
    4. The apostles are not rivals but fellow workers (3:5-23)
      a) Fellow workers together (3:5-9)
      b) Various materials in the temple of God (3:10-17)
      c) All things belong to them (3:18-23)
  C. Concluding considerations (4:1-21)
    1. The real measure of judgment (4:1-5)
    2. The lowliness of the apostles (4:6-13)
    3. Personal appeal (4:14-21)
III. Moral standards of the Christian life (5:1–7:40)
  A. Problems of sex and property (5:1–6:20)
    1. The case of incest (5:1-5)
    2. The purity of the community (5:6-8)
    3. Separation from the world (5:9-13)
    4. Legal cases (6:1-8)
    5. Standards of the kingdom (6:9-11)
    6. Chastity among members of the body of Christ (6:12-20)
  B. Problems of marriage and celibacy (7:1-40)
    1. General principle (7:1-7)
    2. Advices to special groups (7:8-16)
    3. Maintenance of the *status quo* (7:17-24)
    4. Reasons for avoiding marriage (7:25-35)
    5. Advice to ascetic couples (7:36-38)
    6. Advice to widows (7:39-40)
IV. Christian freedom (8:1–11:1)
  A. Food offered to idols (8:1-13)
    1. Contrast between knowledge and love (8:1-3)
    2. The contents of knowledge (8:4-6)
    3. The attitude toward the weaker brother (8:7-13)
  B. Paul's own renunciation of rights (9:1-23)
    1. The privileges of an apostle (9:1-6)
    2. The apostolic right to financial support (9:7-14)
    3. Renunciation for others (9:15-23)
  C. The peril of the strong (9:24–10:22)
    1. The need for self-discipline (9:24-27)
    2. The warning example of the wilderness generation (10:1-13)
    3. The table of the Lord and the table of demons (10:14-22)
  D. Concluding statement of principles (10:23–11:1)
V. Christian worship (11:2–14:40)
  A. The veiling of women (11:2-16)
  B. The Lord's Supper (11:17-34)
    1. The conduct of the meal (11:17-22)
    2. The tradition about the Last Supper (11:23-26)
    3. Dangers in the celebration (11:27-34)
  C. The use of spiritual gifts (12:1–14:40)
    1. Many gifts of the one Spirit (12:1-31*a*)
      a) Recognition of the Spirit of God (12:1-3)
      b) The manifold gifts of the Spirit (12:4-11)
      c) The body and its members (12:12-26)
      d) The apostolic ministry (12:27-31*a*)
    2. The way of love (12:31*b*–13:13)
      a) The superiority of love (13:1-3)
      b) The nature of love (13:4-7)
      c) The permanence of love (13:8-13)
    3. The service of the word (14:1-40)
      a) Contrast of prophecy and tongues (14:1-12)
      b) The comparative value of these gifts (14:13-25)
      c) The Corinthian order of worship (14:26-33)
      d) Closing injunctions to obstinate groups (14:34-40)
VI. The resurrection of the dead (15:1-58)
  A. The resurrection of Jesus (15:1-19)
    1. The tradition concerning the fact (15:1-11)
    2. The significance of his resurrection (15:12-19)
  B. The eschatological drama (15:20-34)
    1. The order of events (15:20-28)
    2. *Ad hominem* rebuttal (15:29-34)
  C. The resurrection body (15:35-50)
    1. Various types of body (15:35-41)
    2. A spiritual body (15:42-50)
  D. The Christian's confidence (15:51-58)
VII. Personal matters (16:1-24)
  A. The contribution for the saints (16:1-4)
  B. Travel plans (16:5-12)
  C. Exhortations, greetings, and benediction (16:13-24)

VII. Date and Early Use

I Corinthians was written from Ephesus or some point near that city (16:8). The coming of Timothy to Corinth is announced (4:17; 16:10), but apparently he was not to be the bearer of the letter and would take a longer route. Since Paul announces the termination of his stay in Asia, it is usually assumed that the letter was written during his last months there. From 5:7 it is concluded that Paul wrote at the paschal season, intending to stay in Ephesus until Pentecost, and then travel through Macedonia and come to Corinth to spend the winter (16:5-6).

We know from II Corinthians, however, that the deterioration of relations with the church led to significant changes in plans. He paid the Corinthian Christians a visit very shortly (II Cor. 2:1) and on his return wrote them a letter "out of much affliction and anguish of heart and with many tears" (II Cor. 2:4), which is not to be identified with any of the extant correspondence. Our II Corinthians was written from Macedonia after Titus had succeeded in bringing about reconciliation with the church and had met the apostle there with the good news.

Can all of these events and this extensive travel be compressed in the short period of six months, or must we postulate a longer time? Jülicher and others have assumed that I Corinthians was written nearer the middle of Paul's stay in Ephesus. Because of "the wide door for effective work" (16:9) Paul stayed longer than he intended when he wrote I Corinthians, and approximately eighteen months separated the writing of the two letters. In that case I Corinthians was written in A.D. 54 and II Corinthians in 55. Manson does not think that 5:7 has any bearing on date and holds that this letter was written in the fall, about twelve months before the writing of II Corinthians. It is not impossible, however, to hold to the usual view, for travel was more frequent and rapid in the ancient world than we sometimes suppose. This would mean that I Corinthians was written in the spring of A.D. 55.

It is unnecessary to discuss the authenticity of the letter. It has been denied only by fanciful scholars who have looked upon all the Pauline correspondence as falsifications from the second century. No letter has better external testimony than this one. Forty years later the church of Rome sent a letter to Corinth which we know as I Clement. There (47:1) the readers are exhorted to "take up the epistle of the blessed Paul the apostle." I Clement contains at least half a dozen quotations and definite allusions to I Corinthians. Ignatius (*ca.* A.D. 110) has no actual quotations from I Corinthians but re-echoes its language so many times that his acquaintance with it is certain. Specific quotations are met again in Justin Martyr (*Dialogue with Trypho* 33) and Athenagoras (*On the Resurrection of the Dead* 18). Irenaeus quotes from almost every chapter, and Tertullian and Clement use it in the same way. It is unnecessary to cite exhaustive evidence, for it is well established that a corpus of Pauline letters circulated widely by the first half of the second century and contained our letter (see Vol. IX, Intro. to Romans). In fact, the corpus may have been collected at Corinth itself.

VIII. Selected Bibliography

For the understanding of I Corinthians the interpreter must draw upon the entire literature concerning the apostolic age, for the problems with which the book deals have so many ramifications. To enumerate books on the Spirit, the Resurrection, New Testament ethics, the relations to the Hellenistic environment, and so forth, would call for the duplication of other bibliographies in this Commentary. On I Corinthians itself the following are among the most useful titles:

ALLO, E. B. *Saint Paul première épître aux Corinthiens.* Paris: J. Gabalda, 1934.

FINDLAY, G. G. "St. Paul's First Epistle to the Corinthians," in Nicoll, W. R., ed. *The Expositor's Greek Testament.* London: Hodder & Stoughton, 1910.

GOUDGE, H. L. *The First Epistle to the Corinthians* ("Westminster Commentaries"). 4th ed. London: Methuen & Co., 1915.

HÉRING, JEAN. *La première épitre de Saint Paul aux Corinthiens.* Paris: Delachaux & Nieselé, 1949.

LAKE, KIRSOPP. *The Earlier Epistles of St. Paul.* London: Rivingtons, 1911.

LIETZMANN, HANS. *An die Korinther I-II* ("Handbuch zum Neuen Testament"). Ed. W. G. Kümmel. 4th ed. Tübingen: J. C. B. Mohr, 1949.

MOFFATT, JAMES. *The First Epistle of Paul to the Corinthians* ("Moffatt New Testament Commentary"). New York: Harper & Bros., 1938.

PARRY, R. ST. JOHN. *The First Epistle of Paul the Apostle to the Corinthians* ("Cambridge Bible"). Cambridge: Cambridge University Press, 1916.

PLUMMER, ALFRED, and ROBERTSON, ARCHIBALD, *A Critical and Exegetical Commentary on the First Epistle of St. Paul to the Corinthians* ("International Critical Commentary"). New York: Charles Scribner's Sons, 1911.

WEISS, JOHANNES. *Der erste Korintherbrief.* Göttingen: Vandenhoeck & Ruprecht, 1910.

I CORINTHIANS

TEXT, EXEGESIS, AND EXPOSITION

1 Paul, called *to be* an apostle of Jesus Christ through the will of God, and Sosthenes *our* brother,

1 Paul, called by the will of God to be an apostle of Christ Jesus, and our brother Sos'the-nes,

---

I. Introduction (1:1-9)

A. Address and Salutation (1:1-3)

In every civilization fixed patterns develop for the most common forms of intercourse. The contemporary paypri show that the salutations in Paul's letters are patterned after the custom of his time; yet his individuality shines through in almost every clause. The RSV emphasizes the three parts of the address by presenting in separate paragraphs the author, the recipients, and the greeting.

1:1. Since Paul will be defending his apostleship in the letter, he begins by emphasizing his calling by Christ Jesus. Whatever takes place through Jesus Christ is in accordance with **the will of God.** Only in Romans does Paul elsewhere use the word

---

1:1. *Paul, Called by the Will of God to Be an Apostle of Christ Jesus.*—What a picture these words evoke of the dauntless pioneer of the Christian faith to the Gentile world. We shall understand the impact of the apostle, not only on his earliest readers, but also on ourselves, if we keep it in our minds as we read this letter to the church in Corinth. Paul is sitting in the house of friends in Ephesus, and with a heavy heart he is studying the various reports that lie before him. His reply, like most letters written by sensitive, sanguine souls, is a revealing document: it helps us understand the apostle who, perhaps more than any other, understood and so marvelously interpreted for all subsequent generations the mind of his Master, Jesus Christ. Sometimes we hear the ring of denunciation, sometimes we almost feel the beat of a loving heart, sometimes we can almost see the tears that stream down his face as he pleads for better things from Christian believers. Like many such letters written by such people, it can, without any sense of contradiction, rise to heights of stern invective, and yet pass immediately into a flood of tenderness. Only deeply sensitive spirits can be so strongly and profoundly stirred.

In what C. G. Montefiore described as "the tragic encounter" between Jesus and the Pharisees that culminated in the climax of the Cross, it seemed as if the gospel of God's liberating love, so greatly revealed in Jesus Christ, had been utterly defeated. Not even the raptures of the disciples convinced of the resurrection of their Master by irrefragable evidence had given that glorious vindication historical significance, so far as the Pharisees and the outside world were concerned. Everything that Paul represented in his character as "a Hebrew born of Hebrews; as to the law a Pharisee" (Phil. 3:5) still stood untouched. But Paul had been conquered by the despised Nazarene. In that conquest the love and the power revealed in the risen Christ played their victorious part. Henceforth Paul is Christ's man, his "bondslave," rejoicing in a bondage which, to adopt the apostle's flair for paradoxical statements of Christian truth, had brought him into unimagined liberty. He is wholly Christ's. As he puts it in his Epistle to the Galatians, "I have been crucified with Christ; it is no longer I who live, but Christ who lives in me; and the life I now live in the flesh I live by faith in the Son of God, who loved me and gave himself for me" (Gal. 2:20).

In such words we have the key to Paul's personality, to his tremendous sense of mission, and to the secret of his impact upon men. It is this intensely felt personal experience of Jesus Christ, the tremendous grip upon him of the

"called" in this connection. Sosthenes is probably the head of the Jewish synagogue who, according to Acts 18:17, was beaten before Gallio's tribunal. The mention of his name is not to add authority to the letter; it is perhaps a polite compliment to a person well known to the readers; or it may be that Sosthenes was serving as amanuensis (Rom. 16:22). Paul is writing personally but also authoritatively as an apostle.

Master, that lies in and behind his profound sense of vocation. With such concentration of experience and purpose little wonder that he has had no equals throughout the centuries as the inspired interpreter of the teaching of Jesus. He did not know everything, and his consummate common sense would have prevented him from even contemplating such a claim, but he could speak with great confidence, and he could and did convey to those who heard him speak an impression of unassailable sources of spiritual strength.

Such is a brief sketch of the experience that lies behind the apostle's thought and his words as he writes to the church in Corinth. The evangelist who is depicted for us in the Acts of the Apostles pursuing his great missionary journeys is never far away; the teacher of the great Christian doctrines who is so obvious in the mighty Epistle to the Romans is close at hand; but it is the pastor we see, as we look at Paul with his heavy heart, and yet with hopefulness, dealing with the situation as reported to him by Stephanas, Fortunatus, and Achaicus. To that task he brings all the inspiration of his experience, all the authority of his status as an apostle, and all his unique understanding of the great gospel to which he is committed.

But he wants to make sure that there will be no mistake about that authority or status. The situation is such that some enforcement of his position is required. He insists, and the point is important, that he is **called by the will of God to be an apostle of Christ Jesus.** These words suggest the apostle's acceptance of the divine initiative in the matter of his call. For Paul, as for the other disciples, only much more dramatically and forcefully in his case, the words of the Master are startlingly true, "You did not choose me, but I chose you and appointed you that you should go and bear fruit and that your fruit should abide" (John 15:16). Apostleship is sealed by acceptance of the call God sends. But with Paul the matter goes much deeper; the initiative of God went so far as to create in his mind a sense of inescapable vocation. The other apostles had been drawn to the Master as particles of steel are drawn to a magnet, but Paul had "kicked against the pricks" (Acts 9:5); he had been arrested in his headlong course as though something or someone, greater and more powerful than himself, had taken hold of him, claimed him, set him aside, trained and prepared and fashioned him as an instrument to be used for the furtherance of mighty purposes. Being the sort of man he was, once he became convinced of the nature of the power that had gripped him, he gave himself to it with glad abandonment. He will not have his status challenged.

When this epistle fails in its purpose, and another stronger letter has to be written, he still has to assert his apostolic authority which gives him the right to deal with the situation (II Cor. 11–12). These experiences give him equal status with the other members of the apostolic band, but it is this deeper experience, the call of God through Christ, referred to in so many different ways throughout his epistles, that is the adequate criterion of his status and vocation. "We are ambassadors for Christ, God making his appeal through us. We beseech you on behalf of Christ, be reconciled to God" (II Cor. 5:20). Could any assertion of apostolic authority or status go further? An ambassador is a representative man: he represents his king in foreign courts. As such he takes precedence according to the status of his nation. An ambassador is one in whom the king repeats himself. Not for one moment does Paul ever lose sight of his status. The strength and tenacity with which he holds to it are conveyed in the strength of the language he uses. The mark of a deeply felt, calm, assured authority is on every syllable he writes. His sense of vocation gives him a feeling of cosmic support in all his experiences and in all he seeks to accomplish. Here lies the deeper secret of his dauntless spirit and courage. This is why one is compelled to believe so much of what he says.

Surely in a world that is constantly in need of the authentic marks of spiritual leadership and of the stamp of authority that lies on truth firmly possessed, the apostle's experience holds a continuing validity and inspiration for ourselves. There is, to those who can hear and sustain it, a call of God to high vocation. He chooses his instruments, and when they respond to his call he possesses and uses them in accordance with his purpose. Such have their own place in the apostolic succession quite apart from any special ecclesiastical organization to which they may belong. Here, as in other matters, "the wind blows where it wills, . . . so it is with every one who is born of the Spirit" (John 3:8). True, there are differences of gifts and voca-

2 Unto the church of God which is at Corinth, to them that are sanctified in

2 To the church of God which is at Corinth, to those sanctified in Christ Jesus, called to be saints together with all

---

2. The readers are **the church of God which is at Corinth.** The word ἐκκλησία could be used for any kind of assembly (Acts 19:32, 39). The religious connection came from its use in the LXX to translate *qāhāl,* the people of God. Paul uses the term more often than any other N.T. writer, twenty-two times in this one letter. In other books, like I Peter, the idea is present, but not this term; and Paul strikingly avoids it in Rom. 1–15. He goes back and forth from the singular to the plural with surprising freedom. The one church was located in many places and he could refer to these congregations either as churches or "the church." Paul does not yet know the word "Christian"; the common designation of believers was the **saints** (Rom. 1:7; II Cor. 1:1; Phil. 1:1; Col. 1:2). The Greek word translated **consecrated** comes from the same root. This did not have a specifically moral significance, as will be seen from Paul's references to the lives of some of these people. But the members of the church had been set apart for God by a divine calling (7:20-21). Jesus distinguished between the "called" and the "chosen," between those to whom the invitation was extended and those who responded (Matt. 22:14). For Paul the **called** are the "chosen."

---

tion: the apostle deals with these later on in his letter (12:4-11; see also Eph. 4:11-13). This is one of the doctrines that receive further explication in the apostle's discussion of the unity of the fellowship and the organic relationship of the parts to the whole, and it is one of the great saving truths that the church of Jesus Christ must recover if it is to speak a convincing and redeeming word.

Let every adequate safeguard be taken by the organized fellowship of the church to test the spirit and so secure the authentic work of the Christian ministry in all its varied aspects. Paul underwent thorough preparation before embarking on his great missionary work (Gal. 1:11-24). Training, meditation, and self-discipline are necessary, and these imply the resources of the organized church; but let no regulation be enacted or applied that quenches such a "call" when it comes to one whom God has chosen for the fulfillment of his purposes.

On the other hand, let no one lightly enter into the work of the ordained ministry of Christ if such a compelling sense of call is lacking. Would not the work of the church be furthered and inspired if its ministry were more strongly marked by that sense of apostolic calling and vocation which Paul could not escape? Being "apprehended of Christ" he could do no other. It might be that the world's famine, a hunger for something more than bread that perishes, and for more than water that quenches physical thirst, a hunger and thirst for a sure, compelling, convincing, authoritative word of God, would be met and satisfied, could all those who feel inclined to serve their fellows by way of the ministry of Christ take an example from the great apostle, even as he himself took his example from Jesus Christ (4:15-16; 11:1). Then the ringing, convincing note of apostolic authority would sound again throughout the world, awakening spiritual reverberations in human hearts.

And our brother Sosthenes: Perhaps this is the Sosthenes to whom reference is made in Acts 18:17. Maybe he became a convert to Christianity. In any case, he is now numbered among the apostle's friends. Paul, ever responsive to the understanding and kindliness of people who gathered around him and who gave him hospitality, courteously associates him with this letter to Corinth. It adds, as do the lists of names appended to his other epistles, the touch of historicity; but too little is known of Sosthenes for anything definite to be said.

2. ***To the Church of God Which Is at Corinth.***—By this phrase Paul means the "ecclesia" of God, a word that recalls the general assembly of free citizens who governed the common life of the Greek city-states (see Exeg.). This "commonwealth of God," as it has been called, is an organized community of people who share a common experience of Jesus Christ, and who are united in love, faith, and loyalty to him and to one another in the bonds of fellowship and service. For Paul the church is the living embodiment of the spirit of the Master. It is his continued incarnation in the world, and its function is to propagate his gospel and to perpetuate and spread his spirit among men until they leaven the life of the whole world.

We can be certain that the membership of the church in Corinth was drawn principally from what might be termed the lower strata of society. Doubtless there were rich citizens, and

Christ Jesus, called *to be* saints, with all that in every place call upon the name of Jesus Christ our Lord, both theirs and ours:

those who in every place call on the name of our Lord Jesus Christ, both their Lord and ours:

From the punctuation of the KJV one might conclude that the letter was also addressed to **all those who in every place call on the name of our Lord Jesus Christ.** That would make it a general epistle, which it manifestly is not. Hence, some commentators excise this as one of the catholicizing glosses which they find scattered throughout the letter (4:17; 7:17; 11:16; 14:33). It is held that these were added by the collector of the Pauline corpus to indicate that the injunctions of Paul in this very personal letter applied also in all of the churches. It is more probable, however, that Paul himself used the appeal to the other communities to bring this very independent congregation into line. The Corinthians do not stand alone in their cult relation to the Lord (cf. Rom. 10:13; Phil. 2:11; Acts 9:14). To **call on the name of our Lord** was the mark of all believers everywhere, and his rule extends over all. The phrase means to confess his lordship rather than to pray to him. Grammatically **theirs** and **ours** might better go with **place** than with **Lord,** but the idea is essentially the same in any case.

---

some well-educated persons in the fellowship. But mostly they would be drawn from the varied types of working people who throng a great seaport, and probably also included some freedmen and slaves. The little community in Corinth could scarcely fail to be affected by the nature of the environment in which its life was set, and the pressure of that environment was very real and very strong. Some of the problems dealt with have their source here. Most of these problems and the questions set for Paul to answer in the report from the church were common to all the churches that were established in Asia Minor. With some of these we shall deal later.

Meantime, let the foregoing suffice to enable us to depict the type of people Paul has in mind when he addresses his letter to the **church of God which is at Corinth.** These are the people **consecrated in Christ Jesus, called to be saints together with all those who in every place call on the name of our Lord Jesus Christ.**

Notice that not all are called to be apostles. That, as we have seen, involves special qualities and duties and status, but all who are members of the church are **called to be saints** (see Exeg.). Again, it is God who takes the initiative: always has it been so.

The Bible is the record of a twofold quest: man's quest for God, and God's quest for man. It tells how they seek for one another, how, through man's folly and ignorance and sin, they often miss one another. Yet it tells also how, through the unceasing activity and long-suffering of God, they gradually get nearer to one another. God constantly pursues that quest. Through events, through inspired men and women, through prophet and priest he draws nearer and nearer as man develops the capacity to recognize, receive, and respond to him. Then at last in the God-man, Jesus Christ, they meet and are one. This is the perfect atonement. The quest is pursued from then until our own times through Christ's continuing presence in the midst, and in the life of the people who have heard God's call to them through Jesus Christ, and who have gladly responded to it.

Such are **called to be saints,** i.e., called to be God's people and to bear their witness to what God requires from them. Christ's indwelling Spirit sanctifies them, molds and shapes and makes them into God's people. It is Christ whose presence is the life of the church, i.e., of all those in the fellowship of the church who call upon his name, for his name implies his spirit imparted to such as are willing by faith to appropriate that gift of grace. In so far as in sincerity and truth his people do respond to him, so does his church fulfill its function of spreading his truth and perpetuating his spirit. Paul, in terms of this call of God to his people, links the local community, in its function as a fellowship, **with all those who in every place call on the name of our Lord Jesus Christ.**

If this prologue to the epistle may be described as an overture, then here is a suggestion of one of the dominant themes which are later to be more fully developed. Meantime, we do well to keep in our minds the sketch that has been drawn of the church in Corinth. These are the people who are **called to be saints,** to be Christ's folk, manifesting his spirit. They are drawn from every type. Christ needs them all if he is to accomplish his redemptive purpose. When man sets to work, his processes tend to fall into grooves of routine; when the Spirit of God is at work, he uses all the infinite

3 Grace *be* unto you, and peace, from God our Father, and *from* the Lord Jesus Christ.

4 I thank my God always on your behalf, for the grace of God which is given you by Jesus Christ;

3 Grace to you and peace from God our Father and the Lord Jesus Christ.

4 I give thanks to God[a] always for you because of the grace of God which was

[a] Other ancient authorities read *my God.*

3. In his customary salutation Paul unites two terms for the divine gift and two sources of this gift. **Grace** is unmerited goodness which men do not deserve. **Peace** is the Semitic term for God's salvation. Paul does not mean that God is the source of one and Christ of the other. Both come from the Father and from the Lord. Paul never employs "Son" for Christ in a salutation, though in other parts of his letters the word often occurs. The exact relationship of the Father and the Lord is not discussed, but there will be indications of Paul's position later in the letter.

B. Thanksgiving (1:4-9)

4. A thanksgiving normally follows the salutation, and in this case it is at best slightly ironical. Paul expresses thanks for some of the manifestations in the community

variety of his creation, in which not even two blades of grass are alike. There is a place in the fellowship of the church and its service for the meekest, mildest, least considered person who is of its number. The man of one talent is as important in the eyes of God as the man with ten. He can make his contribution. In any case, the Master, though he is glad and willing to have the services of those who are greatly talented in the fulfillment of his purposes, never makes a fuss over them when they come to him. He does make a great deal of a cup of cold water given in his name. We are all called to be saints, however humble and lowly we may be. Great services may indicate our talents, but small services indicate the depth of our consecration, and Christ wants that (Matt. 10:42).

3. ***Grace to You and Peace from God Our Father and the Lord Jesus Christ.***—Again we have the suggestion of a theme that is to be developed and made explicit later on in the epistle. Church life in Corinth was defective both in grace and peace. Two of the marks of a genuinely Christian church are unity and love, both of which are spiritual in origin. These were conspicuously missing from church life in Corinth. Later on Paul develops these two themes at great length and with great power. Meantime, he indicates clearly that to a faith which is willing to receive and appropriate them they are the gift of God, mediated through Jesus Christ (vs. 4). Grace and peace are words that have a great place in Paul's writings.[1] This brief note must here suffice in view of more detailed exposition elsewhere.

There is no "higher gift than grace," as John Henry Newman would seem to suggest in his well-known hymn, "Praise to the Holiest in the height." Grace is the very nature of God himself, freely expressed in his self-giving love for man, and in all that he has undertaken for man's full redemption. God is grace, and his graciousness is revealed in Jesus Christ whom here Paul associated with God. Grace is boundless and free and endless in the variety of gifts it bestows and inspires. Grace is conditioned solely by man's need and capacity and willingness to receive it, to accept it, and to proceed on it. The grace of God could not be more concretely depicted than in that suggestive passage in the book of Revelation, where the Spirit of Christ is described as knocking and waiting for entrance into the human soul (Rev. 3:20).

And peace. That too is the gift of God (see Exeg.). The gift of peace was in our Lord's last will and testament for his followers. The church in Corinth, so divided in its membership, is in need of this peace and the sense of well-being it brings.

Peace is born of a consciousness of power which is available to us for all the needs and demands of daily life. It is something more than a "frame of mind," or a "mood," or an "atmosphere." Peace is the outcome of a deep and confident awareness of spiritual reserves that have their source in One who is above us, yet whose Spirit is unceasingly at work in the lives of those who give him hospitality. It is a gift that such spiritual hospitality enables us to experience for ourselves, and, as we shall see, it is above all the fruit of that tree whose roots are the Christian relationships of life.

4-9. ***I Give Thanks to God Always for You.***—These verses form a complete section in them-

[1] James Moffatt, *Grace in the New Testament* (New York: Ray Long & Richard R. Smith, 1932).

5 That in every thing ye are enriched by him, in all utterance, and *in* all knowledge;

6 Even as the testimony of Christ was confirmed in you:

7 So that ye come behind in no gift; waiting for the coming of our Lord Jesus Christ:

8 Who shall also confirm you unto the end, *that ye may be* blameless in the day of our Lord Jesus Christ.

given you in Christ Jesus, 5 that in every
way you were enriched in him with all
speech and all knowledge — 6 even as the
testimony to Christ was confirmed among
you — 7 so that you are not lacking in
any spiritual gift, as you wait for the revealing of our Lord Jesus Christ; 8 who
will sustain you to the end, guiltless in the

---

about which he will be very critical in the body of the letter. The love of Paul for his converts is shown by his prayers for them, to which he makes frequent reference (Rom. 1:8; Phil. 1:3; I Thess. 1:2; Philem. 4; Col. 1:9 (see J. A. Bain, *The Prayers of the Apostle Paul* [London: Lutterworth Press, 1937]). The grace of God is not thought of as a general divine characteristic, but is linked with a specific event, the coming of Christ. At this point, however, contemporary interpretations of Paul divide sharply. We meet here for the second time in four verses Paul's formula **in Christ** (ἐν Χριστῷ). Many interpreters follow Deissmann in understanding this in a mystical sense and believe that the preposition expresses a locative meaning. Christ is the sphere in which the believer lives, where God's grace is experienced. Others, such as Lohmeyer and Bultmann, insist that it is inaccurate to speak of a Christ-mysticism in Paul. To be **in Christ** is to be in the new eschatological situation brought about by the death and resurrection of Christ. Grace was given through that historic event. The two interpretations need not be looked upon as mutually exclusive but as two poles of Paul's thought. Eschatological orientation does not rule out the most intimate mystical fellowship. Throughout the thanksgiving we see the importance of Jesus. The name appears ten times in vss. 1-10. Christ is usually joined, no longer as a title but as a second name. He is God's Son and our Lord (1:9).

5-9. The thanksgiving is chiefly eloquent for what it omits. Possibly the Corinthians had boasted in their letter of their eloquence and their knowledge. Soon Paul will criticize their **knowledge** (1:18–2:5; 8:1-3) and their speaking in tongues (chs. 12–14). For the time being he simply admits that they are not lacking in **any spiritual gift** (χαρίσματι). These gifts had served as confirmation of the testimony to Christ. In vss. 6 and 8 Paul uses specifically legal language. The KJV appears to take Χριστοῦ in vs. 6 as a genitive of source, the testimony which Christ brought. The RSV understands it as the testimony borne by the community to him and 2:1 supports this interpretation. The word **confirmed** (βεβαιόω) was a technical term in business law (Rom. 15:8; II Cor. 1:21; Phil. 1:7; Col. 2:7 (see A. Deissmann, *Bible Studies* [Edinburgh: T. & T. Clark, 1901], pp. 104-9). It is

---

selves, in which the apostle with consummate tact and wonderful Christian spirit is still preparing his readers for what is to follow. There is much to censure and to condemn, but the situation is not one of unrelieved gloom. The apostle's preaching of the gospel to these people, and his sojourn among them, had not been without some solid results. The night is dark, but there are still some stars in the sky. He will not discourage them by dealing with the situation as if it were altogether without its redeeming features. The foundation may be slender, but there is enough of it on which to begin the rebuilding of the Christian life of the community (see Exeg. on Paul's irony).

He lists some of the gifts of the Spirit, to which reference will be made more fully later on (see Exeg.). These Corinthians may have had the defects of their qualities, but the qualities are real, a gift of ready wit, though perhaps given to much fruitless disputation, a delight in exploring all kinds of questions, and a real insight into many important matters. These natural gifts and capacities had been deepened, cleansed, and enriched by the sanctifying power of the Spirit of Christ, so that the Corinthian church was richly endowed. Christian graces are natural endowments and capacities offered in surrender to Christ in the very act of acceptance of the full salvation he provides.

9 God *is* faithful, by whom ye were called
unto the fellowship of his Son Jesus Christ
our Lord.

10 Now I beseech you, brethren, by the
name of our Lord Jesus Christ, that ye all
speak the same thing, and *that* there be no
divisions among you; but *that* ye be perfectly joined together in the same mind and
in the same judgment.

day of our Lord Jesus Christ. **9** God is faithful, by whom you were called into the
fellowship of his Son, Jesus Christ our Lord.

10 I appeal to you, brethren, by the
name of our Lord Jesus Christ, that all of
you agree and that there be no dissensions
among you, but that you be united in the

---

uncertain whether the confirmation is **in** their hearts (KJV) or **among** them (RSV). The ultimate question does not concern their *gifts* but their *guilt.* The Parousia or coming of the Lord will bring the judgment; the "day of the LORD" of the O.T. (Amos 5:18) is now the day of Christ (Phil. 1:6, 10; I Thess. 3:13; 5:23). His coming is the ultimate revealing—a word used of eschatological events as well as teaching about them (ἀποκάλυψις). The word means literally to "unveil"; only in the future is Christ fully unveiled, for in his earthly life the glory had been hidden. Grammatically it is Christ who sustains according to vs. 8, while appeal is made to the faithfulness of God in vs. 9. Paul can speak of either as the author of salvation. It is instructive that his ultimate appeal is to the faithfulness of God (10:13; I Thess. 5:24). Faith means trust in the one who is faithful (Rom. 3:3). Salvation by faith is really salvation by the faithfulness of God.

II. The Problem of Factions (1:10–4:21)

A. Statement of the Problem (1:10-12)

10-12. Paul takes up first of all the problem of factions. When he appeals to the Corinthians to **speak the same thing,** he means of course that he wants them to agree in purpose as well as in words. The term σχίσματα means lit., "rents" or "rifts." These have divided the Corinthian community into factions so that the members are no longer of a common mind. It may be that Paul names the source of his information in order to absolve Sosthenes and Stephanas (16:15) and the other messengers of the church. **Chloe's people** were probably slaves. We may assume that they were not returning to Corinth, where revenge might be taken for their talebearing.

The divisions about which Paul was complaining were not primarily theological but personal. We shall see that there were different emphases in the interpretation of the

---

Even so is the effectiveness of the gospel confirmed in their daily experience (vs. 6). Our natural capacities are enlarged and deepened, and life itself is made more abundant, as we give ourselves, all that we are and possess, to him who gave himself for us. To be a genuine Christian is the most natural thing in the world: not to be a Christian the most unnatural. In life's enrichment they had received ample token of the effective grace of Jesus Christ, **so that you are not lacking in any spiritual gift.** Moreover, what he has begun, given the faithful response of his followers, he will bring to perfect fulfillment (vs. 8). They can rely upon the undeviating faithfulness of God whose initiative has called them **into the fellowship of his Son, Jesus Christ our Lord.**

10-17. ***Party Feeling Runs High.***—Greetings and thanksgivings ended, Paul plunges at once with direct intensity into one of the outstanding problems connected with the Corinthian church. Chloe, obviously a convert to Christianity, probably a convert of Paul, and the first woman to be mentioned in his correspondence, had business connections with the great seaport. Some of her agents had brought sad news of the serious divisions that were disrupting the Christian fellowship in Corinth. **For it has been reported to me by Chloe's people that there is quarrelling among you, my brethren.** The church has divided into various groups and an ugly situation has developed. The Greek temperament, so prone to disputation and faction, was running true to its established type. How difficult it is to resist the pressure of environment and to discipline the often fierce drive of temperament! The spirit of disputation and faction had got into the very life of the church with lamentable consequences.

What is worse, the various factions had

11 For it hath been declared unto me of you, my brethren, by them *which are of the house* of Chloe, that there are contentions among you.

12 Now this I say, that every one of you saith, I am of Paul; and I of Apollos; and I of Cephas; and I of Christ.

same mind and the same judgment. 11 For it
has been reported to me by Chlo′e's people
that there is quarreling among you, my
brethren. 12 What I mean is that each one
of you says, "I belong to Paul," or "I belong to A-pol′los," or "I belong to Ce′phas,"

gospel; but the real cause of dissension lay in allegiance to individual teachers. The first three names require no explanation. It is highly likely that Cephas himself had visited the Corinthian community as well as Paul and Apollos. Converts of these three famous missionaries were so devoted to them that these loyalties brought factions into the church. Possibly the Apollos group exalted "wisdom" (vs. 17 and elsewhere), though that conclusion is not essential to the argument that follows.

But what of the slogan **I belong to Christ?** Was there also a Christ party? Interpreters have not been successful in making a clear case for a fourth party. Some have claimed that the Christ party was composed of the conservative Jewish-Christian wing of the church. But the Judaizing problem is not faced until II Corinthians; there is no probable connection between this passage and II Cor. 10:7. Other scholars have claimed that the Christ party contained spiritualists who admitted the authority of none of the apostles and appealed directly to Christ himself. They depended upon their own revelations and would accept no intermediary. But there is no adequate evidence to show that there was a specific party hostile to all human authority. Undoubtedly some in the community were exercising freedom in dangerous ways, but Paul does not discuss the relation of liberty to love in connection with the problem of factions. It can be concluded therefore that there were only three factions. The sharpest attacks are not made upon some hypothetical "Christ party," but appear to be directed against the followers of Cephas. Paul's relationship with Apollos is always cordial and is used as an example of what the relationship between apostles ought to be.

How then are we to explain the words **I belong to Christ?** Paul does not repeat them in 3:22 nor are they quoted in I Clem. 47:3, where this passage is referred to. Some interpreters take the words as a gloss: an early scribe wrote *his* slogan in the margin,

grouped themselves around the personalities of Paul, of Apollos, and of Peter. Probably the first-named group was composed of those who had been converted under Paul's preaching during his residence in the seaport, and in this mistaken way they were showing their loyalty to him. Others grouped themselves around Apollos, the eloquent and intellectual Alexandrian preacher who had succeeded Paul in the work at Corinth. Probably Peter, who had visited some of the churches, had included a stay in Corinth while on his way to Rome, and had impressed the people there as being the leader of the original band of disciples. It may be that his influence was greatest with the Jewish Christians, to whom he would make a strong appeal, as contrasted with that of Paul, who was now established as the Apostle to the Gentiles, and who was constantly under attack by the Christian-Jewish traditionalists who followed him from place to place. In any case, a third clique had bestowed their personal allegiance upon Peter, and a fourth section, actuated doubtless by a subconscious feeling of spiritual superiority which marked them as the most arrogant of the lot, said in effect, "A plague on all your parties; we belong to Christ!" (See Exeg., vs. 12.) It is also possible that these may have been Jewish Christians of an extreme type known as "Messiah Christians," mainly because of their claim to have actually seen or known the Master in the days of his Galilean ministry.

We must not exaggerate these divisions, lamentable though they were; they are to be regarded as cliques rather than as parties (see Exeg., vs. 10). There is no evidence of schism, nor does there appear to be any great difference of doctrinal opinion. Paul does not seem to have attached too much importance to the badges the various parties wore. He is troubled much more about the bad spirit that is corrupting the life and witness of the church and threatening its unity. For the unity of the ecclesia was of supreme moment to him: he could not endure to see it being undermined by the spirit of embittered faction. He is deeply

13 Is Christ divided? was Paul crucified for you? or were ye baptized in the name of Paul?

or "I belong to Christ." 13 Is Christ divided? Was Paul crucified for you? Or were you

from which it later came into the text. Others suggest that it is Paul's own reply to all parties—he belongs to Christ. Still others claim that a group at Corinth was attempting to stand aloof from the factional strife and affirm its sole allegiance to Christ; but in opposing all "denominations," it inevitably became a separate denomination. Whichever of these theories we adopt, we need not see a clearly defined party.

Paul discusses the problem of these factions through the remainder of chs. 1–4. He brings four accusations against the party spirit: (*a*) Factions give to particular apostles a place which only Christ should occupy (1:13-17). (*b*) Many are looking upon the apostles as teachers of philosophy rather than preachers of the word of the Cross (1:18–2:5). (*c*) The true wisdom which is bestowed by the Spirit of God is not to be had by those of factious spirit (2:6–3:4). (*d*) These divisions represent the apostles as rivals rather than as fellow workers under Christ (3:5-23). Ch. 4 concludes the discussion with various types of personal appeal, for Paul was much too wise a student of human nature to think that logic exclusively determined the conduct of men.

B. Argument Against Factions (1:13–3:23)

1. They Put Men in the Place of Christ (1:13-17)

13. The community might be divided, but it was impossible for Christ to be **divided;** the whole church is his body. No one of his apostles could stand in the position of Christ, for it was by his death and resurrection that the redemption of the world was accomplished.

moved and indignant as he thinks of the great matters so gravely jeopardized by the littleness of men, particularly among those who profess the name of Christ. But his indignation and irony are preceded by intense pleading; surely the right approach to such a situation. **I appeal to you, brethren, by the name of our Lord Jesus Christ, that all of you agree, . . . that you be united in the same mind and the same judgment.**

This threat to the unity of the church, to its mind and spirit and mission, touched Paul, as we have already indicated, on a most sensitive spot. We can estimate its impact upon his mind and program by studying his great missionary manifesto, the Epistle to the Romans. His mind and outlook were deeply influenced by Hebrew and Greek modes of thought. This "Hebrew of the Hebrews" was the inheritor of the tradition of the divine mission of his race and its characteristic institution to the whole world. For him the Jewish people were destined to be "the divine commonwealth" into which other nations might be incorporated and so take their place and play their part in the furtherance of the divine purpose. That is one reason why the Pharisees encompassed sea and land to make converts. We must not underestimate the moral passion of the Judaizing mission of the Jews and its power to sustain high standards and achieve spiritual regeneration (cf. Matt. 23:15). Here is one part of Paul's inheritance. It could not fail profoundly to influence his spirit and his outlook on life.

He was also deeply influenced by Greek, and particularly by Stoic, humanism. The Greeks were great humanists! All the gods in the Greek pantheon are anthropomorphic creations sharing human passions and limitations. If a shepherd is frightened as he watches his sheep on the hillsides of Greece, it is because Pan has looked at him from behind a rock. If a child is swept over a precipice by a tempest, it is because the spirit of the wind wants her to be his playmate. For the ancient Greek there was a dryad in every bush, a naiad in every pool. In such fashion did these old-time Greeks make themselves at home in this strange world.

Paul, who was well acquainted with Greek thought, must have felt the impact of the Stoic refinement of this Greek humanism. No doubt at first the Pharisee in him revolted against the Stoic conception of the fundamental unity of mankind. Stoics taught that God had made of one stock all the nations of the earth, and the time came when Paul had to accept this hard fact (cf. Acts 17:26). His sense of corporate unity and responsibility among mankind is already revealed in his deeply realized consciousness of sin (cf. Rom. 3:9-25). He saw clearly that if ever the grave spiritual condition of humanity was to be changed into something

14 I thank God that I baptized none of you, but Crispus and Gaius;
15 Lest any should say that I had baptized in mine own name.
16 And I baptized also the household of Stephanas: besides, I know not whether I baptized any other.

baptized in the name of Paul?
14 I am thankful[b] that I baptized none of you except Crispus and Ga'ius;
15 lest any one should say that you were baptized in my name.
16 (I did baptize also the household of Steph'a-nas. Beyond that, I do not know

[b] Other ancient authorities read *I thank God.*

Paul uses his own name at this point in order to bring out the fact that he is not criticizing the followers of other apostles any more than his own supporters. He is objecting to any member's imagining that the evangelist through whom he had been converted was the one to whom he owed allegiance. In some of the mystery cults the priest who performed the rites was looked upon as the father of the initiates. Though Paul claimed to be their spiritual father (4:15), converts were baptized not in his name, but in the name of Christ. It is clear that baptism was not yet according to a trinitarian formula (cf. Acts 10:48; etc.).

14-16. Paul goes on to assert that it had not been his practice to baptize at all. He starts out to name the exceptions. **Crispus** is probably the ruler of the synagogue whose conversion is reported in Acts 18:8. **Gaius** must be Paul's host who is mentioned in Rom. 16:23, a letter written from Corinth. We see how casual was Paul's dictating when it was necessary for him to add **Stephanas,** the first fruits of Achaia (16:15), possibly at the

better, something that would fulfill the divine purpose in the creation of mankind, viz., "the revealing of the sons of God" (Rom. 8:19), then God must exert himself to the uttermost. The other works of creation manifest the effortless ease of the divine Creator, but the redemption of man called for something more intense and sustained. Paul, convinced at last that no final distinction between Jew and Gentile could be maintained, saw that deeper unity guaranteed and extended in the establishment of the church of Jesus Christ. The church of Jesus Christ in any one place is a microcosm of what, in the final triumph of God's gracious will, humanity in its entirety is destined to become.

Man is created to be a son of God, and the missionary enterprise of the church is to convey to him a revelation of his high destiny, and to do all it can, at great cost if necessary, to persuade him to accept that destiny. Such was the tremendous and thrilling sense of mission inspiring this "ambassador on behalf of Christ." Such are some of the ideas and convictions that inspire and sustain him in his hazardous missionary journeys. Such is his purpose in the establishment of Christian communities. They are to be the leaven that in the end will leaven the life of the entire world. This great apostle's eyes are on the ends of the earth! The Christian churches are to be centers of unity scattered throughout all the world until the whole of mankind is brought into the unity of the faith and the glorious liberty and abundant hope of the sons of God. And now his high hopes are threatened with disaster by the spirit of partisanship rampant in the church life in Corinth. Little wonder he begins by recalling the members of the community in Corinth to the central issues of the gospel which he had preached and which they had received.

Surely there is a pertinent and continuing relevance in these things. This great goal of a church which includes all mankind, and in which "The kingdom of the world has become the kingdom of our Lord and of his Christ, and he shall reign for ever and ever" (Rev. 11:15), has gripped the imagination and inspired the service of Christian leaders in successive generations. The conversion of the Emperor Constantine seemed to the early Christian fathers to promise the great goal of a Christian world. They set to work to secure that unity of faith and order which would be its spiritual strength, and which would give it cohesion. Thus the church in these first centuries girded itself for the fight against paganism without and heresy within its borders, so waging a war on two fronts. Here lies the deeper reason for the great church councils, and for the writing of the creeds. When the Roman Empire crumbled under the onslaught of the barbarian invaders, it was the Christian church that preserved such unity as was left in the known world. There followed on that era the great conception of the medieval church, a church that sought to be comprehensive, catholic, universal, and eternal, gathering under its vast canopy all the races and nations of the world. The outline of the story of this great

17 For Christ sent me not to baptize, but to preach the gospel: not with wisdom of words, lest the cross of Christ should be made of none effect.

whether I baptized any one else.) 17 For Christ did not send me to baptize but to preach the gospel, and not with eloquent wisdom, lest the cross of Christ be emptied of its power.

---

prompting of his amanuensis. For fear there had been other omissions, Paul adds that he cannot recall any more instances.

17. From this testimony some commentators have drawn the false conclusion that Paul was depreciating baptism. This was farthest from his intention. Faith *and* baptism brought the believer into union with Christ, and thus his representative death became ours. All that Paul means to say is that there is differentiation of function within the church. It was usual for baptisms to be performed by his helpers. He knows nothing of a regulation that the administration of the sacraments was reserved for the highest ministry. To Paul the highest ministry was the preaching of the gospel (12:28). The content and method of this preaching provide us with the transition to the next section.

---

vision, with all its stresses and strains, its strength and its weakness, is told in many books.

> St. Paul's Epistles to the Corinthians show how the attempt to persuade their converts to put away earthly things taxed the patience and energy of the earliest apostles. The task became impossible when every member of any political community which possessed an ecclesiastical organization was supposed to be a follower of Christ. The influence of the Church penetrated social relations through and through, and it is foolish to feel surprise if Christianity suffered in the process. St. Boniface found that the German converts instinctively regarded baptism and the rites of the Church as forms of magic or merely external acts; and his experience has countless parallels throughout the history of the church up to our own day.[2]

Even so does history repeat itself!

But the quest for unity endured even after the disruption of the medieval church at the time of the Reformation and the Counter Reformation. The outlines of a truly ecumenical church are again beginning to emerge. What other institution than the church of Jesus Christ is fitted by its message, by its tradition and essential mission, to say the uniting, healing word to a divided and tragic world? With what mighty impact the gospel of reconciliation could smite the evil things that bedevil mankind if all the members of the Christian church could find grace sufficient to sit down at the same table and sing the same song, having mended the rents made in the seamless robe by the divisions and schisms and denominationalisms of Christian believers! Would not the word of Paul, were he able to stand among us all in the flesh, be the very word of rebuke and exhortation he addressed to the church at Corinth long years ago? **I appeal to you, brethren, by the name of our Lord Jesus Christ, that all of you agree and that there be no dissensions among you, but that you be united in the same mind and the same judgment.**

Before taking the issue further, Paul expresses his thankfulness that apart from Crispus, Gaius, and the household of Stephanas (Rom. 16:23; Acts 18:8; I Cor. 16:15) he had baptized none of them, **lest any one should say that you were baptized in my name.** He had no interest in making his converts Paulinists; he cared only that they should be true followers of Jesus Christ. When he writes further, **For Christ did not send me to baptize but to preach the gospel,** he does not intend to minimize the sacrament of baptism, but implies that it does hold a subordinate place to the preaching of the Cross (see Exeg., vss. 14-16, 17). Here, as in other ways, the great apostle walks closely in the steps of the Master, who subordinated his healing works to the proclamation of his gospel truth. He also wished his hearers to believe in him because of the truth of his message and not because of any miracle that he might perform. Central things should always be given the central place. This is axiomatic with Paul.

There may also have been another thought in his mind. The sacrament of baptism for him was symbolic of death to the old pagan mode of life and of resurrection to the new Christian way (Rom. 6:3-4). But some members of the church in Corinth were very far from manifesting a new way of life, and Paul is thankful that so far as their failure is concerned, he has no personal responsibility. It would be quite in keeping with his habit of getting at the very heart of a problem or situation to insist that

[2] F. M. Powicke, "The Christian Life," in *The Legacy of the Middle Ages,* ed. C. G. Crump and E. F. Jacob (Oxford: Clarendon Press, 1926), p. 31. Used by permission.

18 For the preaching of the cross is to them that perish, foolishness; but unto us which are saved, it is the power of God.

18 For the word of the cross is folly to those who are perishing, but to us who are

2. The Wisdom of Men and the Foolishness of God (1:18–2:5)

a) The Word of the Cross Not a New Wisdom (1:18-25)

It may be that it was the Apollos faction which laid too great stress upon **wisdom.** But it was a natural consequence of any overevaluation of men. There are three steps in Paul's refutation of the emphasis upon wisdom. (*a*) The general proposition that the word of the cross is not a new wisdom (1:18-25); (*b*) this is proved by the nature of the Corinthians' own community (1:26-31); (*c*) it was also shown by the manner of Paul's entrance into Corinth (2:1-5).

18. The Christian message is not an "eloquent wisdom" but the **word of the cross.** Paul elevates the Cross throughout his letters (II Cor. 13:4; Gal. 3:1; 5:11; 6:12, 14;

when people make vows or demonstrate in any such ritual their confession of faith they ought to live up to their promises. But more pressing matters are calling for attention, and to these the apostle now gives his thought.

18-31. ***The Preaching of the Gospel and Human Wisdom.***—Having unburdened himself thus briefly on the subject of baptism, Paul turns to something much nearer to his heart, viz., the sacrament of the word which he had been "engrossed in preaching" while he was in Corinth. To that message he would recall them now, for it is central and fundamental to everything else. Once again we realize the supreme value of this epistle for the light it throws on the life of these early churches. The peculiarity of the Greek temperament is obvious: it was attracted to Christianity more as an intellectual system of beliefs, as we have noted in the partisanship given to Apollos, than as the revelation of a spiritual power that reaches down with redeeming grace to the moral foundations of life. It was more receptive of new ideas than of spiritual and moral ideals, and was more ready to listen to any eloquent rhetorician who had some new philosophy to expound than to make life measure up to the standards of Jesus Christ. Other great leaders besides Paul have found it easier to change people's ideas than to change their sentiments. Judging by the questions to which the apostle addresses himself in his various epistles this outlook of mind and spirit was typical of many of the churches. The deepest need of the members was to be built up in Christian character, and this was to be done by concentrating both intellect and will on God's revelation of himself and his divine purposes in Jesus Christ. The supremacy of Christ had been the burden of Paul's preaching in Corinth. For him Christ was the focus of history, the crown of true philosophy, and the sole adequate criterion of truth and therefore of reality. In a mighty, cosmic-embracing sentence this inspired genius of an apostle sums up the philosophy of creation, and of all human history, when he writes, "God was in Christ reconciling the world to himself" (II Cor. 5:19). This is the key to all Paul's reasoning and entreaty as he addresses himself to the church in Corinth. It was this gospel that with glowing heart he had preached to them and that they had so gladly received.

Little wonder that we detect a note of sheer incredulity as the apostle puts his searing, searching questions to the members of the community. How high they had been raised from their pagan condition: to what abysmal depths they had fallen! Divided as they are by their spirit of partisanship, he recalls for them that wonderful unity they had found, at least for a time, through their faith in Christ. "Is Christ divided?" (Vs. 13.) There is indignation and something amounting almost to horror in the threefold question he presses home to their hearts. How could they even imagine that Christ could be divided, or that Paul could be crucified for them? Was it not in the name of Christ, and not of Paul, that they were baptized? These are the forceful questions that clear away the mists and fogs of faction and disputation and prepare the way for a re-emphasis of the central conviction of the Christian faith.

Let us notice again that this letter, like the others written by the apostle, reflects his gracious mind and spirit. In the section under discussion we catch something more than a glimpse of Paul as a greathearted Christian gentleman. His innate courtesy is seen in the substitution of his own name for that of Peter or Apollos in these questions addressed to his readers. Such is one of the marks of a magnanimous mind. It was the "man in Christ" who writes, "Was Paul crucified for you? Or were you baptized in the name of Paul?" (vs.

Phil. 2:8; 3:18; Col. 1:20; 2:14). He was not thinking of the actual piece of wood. Nor was the **word of the cross** simply the story of the Crucifixion in all its gruesome details. It was the glad news that "God was in Christ reconciling the world to himself" (II Cor. 5:19). It was the message about what this event meant for man's redemption. Paul divides

---

13). Jesus Christ had certainly got deep into the very spirit of this man to make so profound a difference to the fanatical Pharisee and racialist depicted for us in Acts 8–9. A lesser man, or one less deeply versed in the grace of Jesus Christ, might have given way to the temptation to substitute these other names. Here we have a revelation of the courtesy and humility of "the foremost of sinners" (3:4-5; I Tim. 1:15). These references indicate something more than a change of mind: they are the marks of a man who has suffered a great change of heart, and they add force to his expostulations as well as to his pleadings. His is a letter written by one who has prepared himself before he puts his hand to paper. The best and most telling pastoral efforts, whether letters or sermons, are the products of such men and women, those who first prepare themselves. Paul passes that test with honors. How many hours had he spent on his knees before he began to write? What mistakes and needless troubles might be avoided if the apostle in this, as in other things, were to become our example!

Paul was far from being flawless in character. Many a time his hot temper got the better of him. We know that he quarreled with Barnabas over the question whether John Mark should or should not accompany them on a certain missionary journey (Acts 15:36-40). We also read that in certain matters he withstood Peter to his face (Gal. 2:11). It is quite possible that Demas, who forsook the apostle and went back to his own people, being himself a Greek, found Paul's ardent Jewish temperament somewhat trying. Paul had the idiosyncracies of genius. And we know that in his correspondence, when deeply moved, he could use violent, even brutal language (Gal. 5:12); but with all his faults, the predominant impression is one of humility and sensitiveness toward his fellow men. The proud, fanatical Pharisee who set out for Damascus "still breathing threats and murder against the disciples of the Lord" (Acts 9:1) is submerged in Christ, to whom he belongs, and whom he seeks to serve. Troubled and moved as he is, it is the courteous, kindly, considerate Christian gentleman and saint we see as we read these opening passages of his letter to his friends. Such a spirit shines like a great light. Such a life has an abiding significance as an example to all who would walk the way of Christ. It is the sole irrefutable argument for the validity of Christian faith.

To a closer consideration of that gospel which meant so much both for Paul and for his converts, and indeed for the entire human race, we now come. Nothing could be clearer or stronger than his own words that still fall on the ears of imaginative and sensitive readers like the strokes of a hammer on an anvil. **For Jews demand signs and Greeks seek wisdom, but we preach Christ crucified, a stumbling-block to Jews and folly to Gentiles, but to those who are called, both Jews and Greeks, Christ the power of God and the wisdom of God.** These words are the very heart of Paul's message: at its center is the Cross. "Christ crucified," for Paul, is the crowning revelation of God. He is the key to the meaning of the universe, in and through whom God's final and absolute word is spoken. "For us there is one God, the Father, from whom are all things and for whom we exist, and one Lord, Jesus Christ, through whom are all things and through whom we exist" (8:6). With the coming of Jesus the doors of a great new order of life swung widely open on their hinges, and hope was born anew in a world that was seeking for deliverance from the things that were strangling its best life. To that world, and for all subsequent ages, God had come in Christ with a great word of reconciliation. That word must not be allowed through the misunderstandings of Christian people, or the corrupting influence of human wisdom or rhetoric, to become of no effect. With impregnable confidence and abounding hope Paul had proclaimed the gospel message to the people of Corinth, and now he seeks to reinforce them in their faith.

Paul most certainly has in mind the intellectual, social, and moral background of the Corinthian Christians in writing these lines. He knows well that there are certain preconceived ideas of what constitutes "power" and "wisdom," terms that were current in the philosophical discussions of the times. The "power" and "wisdom" of God are to be conceived in a very different way (see Exeg., vs. 18). For Paul, and indeed for all the N.T. writers, the gospel of Christ is a perfect blending of justice and of love. These are its fundamental terms. This is not the place for any disquisition on the nature of sin: the subject is fully dealt with in the other relevant sections of this Commentary. The fact of sin is obvious enough, and the fact that it does create a barrier between man and God, between man and his

the hearers of this message into two groups. Salvation is here looked upon as a present experience rather than as being safe at the judgment. To one group the message is **foolishness;** we would expect that the opposite would be wisdom, but instead of that it is first of all **power.** In the eyes of the world the Cross was a symbol of weakness and

---

fellow men, as well as setting him at variance with himself, is also obvious. God's justice is involved in the imperative necessity to deal with sin, to break its power, and to set its prisoner free. His love is involved in saving the sinner and in reconciling him to his God, to his fellow men, and within himself. The cross of Christ has moving and saving power because in it justice and love are blended in one great and final revelation of God. Love divorced from justice is always in danger of becoming a sentimental thing: justice divorced from love might verge on lack of mercy. God in Christ lays the expiation of man's offense on himself; and the Cross is the eternal revelation of what man's sin means to God. It is the expression of the highest aspect of the spirit known and experienced by man, and also of the greatest uplifting and redeeming power in the universe, viz., the power of vicarious suffering. A true parent's agony when a beloved son or daughter, heedless of all promptings and warnings, pursues reckless and perilous courses is but the faintest reflection of the agony of God in the face of the sin of man. The Cross is the eternal exposure and condemnation of all that crucifies the spirit of Christ and hinders God's beneficent purposes for his creatures in every age. All the motives that make the wounds of Christ bleed in each succeeding generation were represented at Calvary. Pride, arrogance, the sin of the closed mind, apathy and indifference, pseudo culture, cynicism, and disillusioned idealism, the perversion of law and order and of morality itself, military might, and intolerant, narrow-minded goodness, as well as a host of other things, were represented in the various groups of people who conspired to bring Jesus Christ to his cross. The caldron of hatred that seethed at its foot contained all the ingredients that compose the Christ-crucifying spirit rampant at all times, and in some measure in every heart. We are linked by chains of motive to those who crucified Jesus Christ. The words of the old Negro spiritual are pertinent to ourselves, as with Paul we contemplate again the spectacle of the Cross and ponder its cosmic meaning:

Were you there when they crucified my Lord?
Were you there . . . ?

There can be only one answer: it is the prayer of the publican in the parable of Jesus, "God, be merciful to me a sinner!" (Luke 18:9-14). On the Cross, God in Christ takes upon himself the penalty and shame and consequence of man's sin.

And on the Cross, God reveals forever his method of dealing with it. He meets it and seeks to master it by an overwhelming passion of cleansing, redeeming, forgiving love. The riposte of God to the sin of man is to be measured in the first prayer that Christ offered on Calvary, "Father, forgive them; for they know not what they do" (Luke 23:34). The man or woman who can contemplate the Cross, and meditate on its meaning unmoved, is near to being a "lost" soul; "lost" in the sense of the word as used by the Master himself. The gospel of the Cross is the supreme and ultimate revelation of God: the Cross is the crucial element in Christianity. Little wonder that as Paul thinks again of his conversion, of his mission, in the light of the meaning of the Cross, he cannot forbear a gasp of horror as the scene becomes vivid to his intense imagination (2:8). The well-known lines of Isaac Watts's great hymn come back to our minds:

When I survey the wondrous Cross
On which the Prince of Glory died,
My richest gain I count but loss,
And pour contempt on all my pride.

The meaning of the Cross as envisaged by Paul is most certainly the supreme expression of **the power of God.** There God in Christ is exerting himself to the utmost, and at great cost, to bridge the gulf created between him and man by man's sin. No other power in the world had done it: none other has been able to do it. As one theologian has put it, "The atonement was a task fit for the energy of God." Such a reconciliation lies far beyond the power of man. The essence of that reconciliation or atonement is forgiveness. Man sometimes says, in respect of some offense he has committed, "I cannot forgive myself." The reply to that is that he never could. Only the person whom he has wronged could offer forgiveness. On the Cross, in a way totally unexpected though glimpsed by Isaiah in his great conception of "the suffering servant," God achieved his mighty purpose. He did it on his own initiative. None other than himself could have induced him to do it. "For by grace you have been saved through faith; and this is not your own doing, it is the gift of God" (Eph. 2:8). The Cross is the unique

19 For it is written, I will destroy the wisdom of the wise, and will bring to nothing the understanding of the prudent.

20 Where *is* the wise? where *is* the scribe? where *is* the disputer of this world? hath not God made foolish the wisdom of this world?

being saved it is the power of God. 19 For
it is written,

"I will destroy the wisdom of the wise,
and the cleverness of the clever I will
thwart."

20 Where is the wise man? Where is the
scribe? Where is the debater of this age?
Has not God made foolish the wisdom of

---

futility. But the power of God is measured by a different standard. Believers are saved, not by some new intellectual truth, but by the apprehension of a new power.

19-20. Characteristically Paul appeals to scripture, a free combination of Isa. 29:14 with Ps. 33:10. The former passage deals with the emergency when the prophet faced the worldly-wise politicians in the Assyrian crisis. Triumphantly Paul announces the futility, not of his own message, but of the endeavors of the leaders in both Israel and Greece. Both nations had their philosophers or wise men; both had their scribes or men of letters; both had their rhetoricians and debaters. All these belonged to **this age.** The term αἰών stood originally for a long period of time; then it was used to distinguish this age from the next. **World** has for most people a spatial connotation, while Paul was thinking definitely in temporal terms. Yet it was but a short step to a qualitative distinction between the two ages. In the last clause of vs. 20 the word is κόσμος rather than αἰών.

---

and supreme revelation of the power of God; it is the unique blending of justice and love in the supreme expression of vicarious suffering. As such it is God's way of reconciling sinful man to himself, and also to his fellow men. It is the key to the meaning of that vast creative process in the midst of which our lives are set.

Such was the great apostle's message to the Corinthians when he sojourned with them: "When I came to you, brethren, I did not come proclaiming to you the testimony of God in lofty words or wisdom. For I decided to know nothing among you except Jesus Christ and him crucified" (2:1-2). For him the theme is far too great, far too moving, to be the subject of meretricious rhetoric. Such a theme to a sensitive spirit finds its own majestic mode of presentation. True eloquence is not of the schools: it is the offspring of a spirit that is impassioned by some great message that has laid hold of it, possessed it, and made it the instrument through which the message is uttered. Paul was well aware of the depths to which the ancient eloquence of Greece had sunk. Once rhetoric was the study of the noble art of persuasion, and then it was linked to worthy purposes. Its best exponents were statesmen like Pericles or orators like Demosthenes, or the greater Sophist teachers of a bygone era. Now it had become the plaything of itinerant professional entertainers who would use it for any subject however trivial in order to amuse their audiences and bring gain to themselves.

But even on its highest level the gospel is not, as far as Paul is concerned, to be preached **in lofty words.** Nothing is to detract attention from the centrality of the Cross and its saving power. The great cosmic message, of which the cross of Christ is the focus, is to shine, so to speak, by its own light; it is the preacher's main preoccupation just to let it shine. The instruments, whether words or the man himself, as Paul makes clear later on in his letter, are subordinate to the main theme.

18-25. ***The Gospel Contrasted with Human Wisdom.***—Paul now goes on to contrast this gospel of **the word of the cross,** which he has preached like a herald making a proclamation, with human philosophy. Some have suggested that memories of his comparative failure at Athens, where his group of listeners dispersed after he spoke of the resurrection of Jesus, still rankled within him. In Athens the philosophers and their followers, who loved to engage in endless discussion and speculation about all manner of things, were befogged by their own preconceptions. At its best, as expounded by great teachers like Plato and Aristotle, and later by Plotinus and many another, the Greek love of wisdom was a quest for light on the meaning of life, and ultimately for God, whose existence alone, as they divined, gives life and creation its meaning. That is one strand in Plato's great dialogue *The Timaeus.* One can go even further and say that in the writings and teachings of the Greeks there is a *preparatio evangelica* which supplements that of the Hebrew prophets. There was a kind of intellectual craving which stimulated the Greek mind and kept it on the quest. On its highest

21 For after that in the wisdom of God the world by wisdom knew not God, it pleased God by the foolishness of preaching to save them that believe.

the world? 21 For since, in the wisdom of God, the world did not know God through wisdom, it pleased God through the folly of what we preach to save those who be-

21. This verse may be understood in two quite different ways. According to one, **in the wisdom of God** is equivalent to "providentially": God arranged that man's wisdom should fail in attaining knowledge of him. According to the other interpretation, **the wisdom of God** is the immanent beauty and order of creation to which Paul refers in Rom. 1:19-20. Wisdom had been the agent of God in creation (Prov. 8:22-26). F. A. Spencer translates "notwithstanding the wisdom of God" (*The New Testament of Our Lord and Savior Jesus Christ* [New York: The Macmillan Co., 1937], p. 448). Despite the evidences of God in his world, philosophy did not come to a knowledge of God. In that

level, as represented by the best Greek thought, we may say that man's philosophy or wisdom is an impulse Godward. To the Greeks, who were looking for an "intellectual panacea," the gospel of the Cross was folly: it did not satisfy their intellectual cravings.

On Paul's view it is hopeless to attempt to get into touch with the reality of God by philosophy as the Greeks of his day understood it. One might as well approach a rose from the angle of relativity, or the sheer beauty of an Alpine precipice from the angle of the latest theories of physics. Those ancient Greeks, like many of their modern counterparts, were searching for clear-cut definitions. No one has ever yet got into touch with God in terms of his omniscience, or omnipotence, or omnipresence, or infinitude. Definitions can never be translated into living experiences that move the heart, give direction to the will, and transform the human spirit. The reality of falling in love can be revealed only by falling in love, and not by any philosophical analysis of the process. These Greeks, in which term the apostle includes the Gentile world, tried to reach God through their philosophy; and they laughed Paul to scorn. **Greeks seek wisdom, but we preach Christ crucified, . . . folly to the Gentiles.**

The gospel is also contrasted with the theology of the Jews (see Exeg., vss. 19-20). To reinforce and emphasize his argument Paul resorts to the device of paradoxical antithesis. **Has not God made foolish the wisdom of the world? . . . For the foolishness of God is wiser than men, and the weakness of God is stronger than men.** Jewish religious hopes in the days of Paul were based on apocalyptic expectation of a dramatic, catastrophic deliverance from Roman oppressors: they looked for a deliverer who would make the nation supreme among the nations of the world. Part of their deep disappointment in Jesus in the days of his flesh is directly traceable to his refusal to give to the nation military leadership, after the style of the Maccabees. In Paul's day Palestine was like a banked fire. Rome procurators were able to extinguish the licking flames of sporadic, local insurrection; but the banked fire was a different matter. Had Jesus at the height of his popularity but given the word, thousands of swords would have leaped from their scabbards, and Rome might have been hard put to it to contain the eruption of the pent-up religious idealism and fanatical nationalism of the Jews. To a people whose imagination and spirit were fired by such ideas and such apocalyptic hopes the sign of a "Christ crucified" was an unspeakable offense. To them **the word of the cross** was an utterly repellent thing. They would have none of it.

But the word of the Cross has a wisdom and a power of its own, **the power of God and the wisdom of God.** That wisdom and power had been demonstrated among the Corinthian believers (2:4-5). The gospel is not the product of human wisdom. In its quest for the meaning of life and for God, the human mind could never have conceived it. If man's philosophy on its highest level is an impulse Godward, God's philosophy is an impulse manward. Through Jesus Christ and him crucified a new conception of the power and wisdom of God came flooding into the world (see Exeg. on **power** and **wisdom,** vss. 24-25). The ideas of vicarious suffering and of grace were foreign to the modes of thought of the Greco-Roman world, and so remained, as far as philosophy is concerned, for some time. Even for Plotinus the creation of the universe is due to the unconscious overflowing of the Unknown from whom all things have their existence. How far this is from either the Christian conception of grace or the self-sacrifice of "God in Christ" on Calvary's Cross! Yet in the experience of men it is the greatest lifting power in the world. Such folly on God's part transcends all human wisdom, and such weakness, in its transforming effect, far exceeds all human or physical power,

22 For the Jews require a sign, and the Greeks seek after wisdom:
23 But we preach Christ crucified, unto the Jews a stumblingblock, and unto the Greeks foolishness;

lieve. 22 For Jews demand signs and Greeks
seek wisdom, 23 but we preach Christ crucified, a stumbling-block to Jews and folly

judgment Paul was correct. Salvation does not depend upon knowledge but on faith. The KJV would seem unnecessarily to disparage preaching here. What Paul labeled as folly was not the act of preaching but its content, **what we preach.**

22-23. The message seemed foolish because it did not correspond to the desires of men. That Jews sought **signs** is the witness of the Gospels (Mark 8:11-12; John 4:48). Even a miracle-loving church preserved the refusal of Jesus to perform an outward sign to validate his mission. That the Greeks were lovers of philosophy is shown by the zeal with which they later attempted to turn Christianity into a logical system of doctrine. Paul gives no suggestion that the pagans at Corinth had been prepared for his message of the Cross by the various myths of dying and rising gods. To both groups a crucified Messiah was nonsense. Stumbling block (σκάνδαλον) was a favorite word of Matthew for a temptation to sin. Paul connects it (Rom. 9:33) with that which caused Israel to fall. To both Jew and Greek the Cross was aesthetically offensive and an evidence of weakness rather than of strength.

What a marvelous thing it would be if we could recover for ourselves something of the amazing wonder of this new conception of wisdom and power that swam into the realm of human thought during that first century of the Christian Era. Familiarity can induce something akin to contempt even with regard to the holiest things in our Christian faith. How one wishes that modern man might read the N.T., as it were for the first time. "Christ crucified," the power of God! Surely it is a spectacle of weakness, "not so much tragic as pitiful." [3] It spells failure and disaster. How can men put their trust in a God who reveals his power in such fashion? Yet that was Christ's deliberately chosen way of revealing the Father whom he served to the uttermost. The Cross was Christ's way of conquest. It was the last thing he had to offer to the fierce drive of the world, and he broke that drive by exhibiting, even to the death of the Cross, his stainless goodness, his matchless grace, his terrible meekness, and his wonderful love. From that Cross a new force sprang into being, new so far as the understanding of man is concerned, a force of life, love, and goodness that was to cut deep ravines in the history of the world, and that was to capture the minds of men and of nations.

On the Cross Christ revealed **the power of God.** Those who watched him there, and who heard him pray for his crucifiers, felt the power of that life, and passed beyond it to its sources in God. It is the word of the Cross that so far from destroying faith in God or making it difficult has fostered, and strengthened, and spread it.

After all, what ought we to mean by power? Surely the deeper meaning of power is effectiveness in achieving our purposes. To understand the power of God requires that we should first understand the purpose of God. When we know what that purpose is, then we can tell if God is able to give effect to it. We have seen what the inspired writers of the Bible conceive to be the purpose of God. Paul has put it into clear focus for us. It is to achieve "a commonwealth of God," into which all the nations of the earth can be gathered, and in which every single soul, the man with one talent as well as he with ten, can have a part. To change the metaphor, it is to bring all the sheep everywhere into the sheepfold of the great Shepherd of the sheep. It is, in the word of the Master himself, to gather all the peoples of the world into the all-embracing range of "the kingdom of God." That purpose will have been fulfilled when full effect is given to these petitions included in the Lord's Prayer,

> Thy kingdom come,
> Thy will be done,
> On earth as it is in heaven.

The real hope of the world lies in the fulfillment of this purpose. It is achieved as men and women in every age make their individual response to "the high calling of God in Christ Jesus." All they have to do is to hear the gospel, to believe in it, and to respond to it. To achieve this God has concentrated his energies; he has

[3] Kenneth Scott Latourette, *The Unquenchable Light* (New York: Harper & Bros, 1941), p. xi.

24 But unto them which are called, both Jews and Greeks, Christ the power of God, and the wisdom of God.

25 Because the foolishness of God is wiser than men; and the weakness of God is stronger than men.

to Gentiles, 24 but to those who are called, both Jews and Greeks, Christ the power of God and the wisdom of God.
25 For the foolishness of God is wiser than men, and the weakness of God is stronger than men.

24-25. But to those whom God calls from all nations it is both **power** and **wisdom.** It is uncertain whether these words are applied to Christ because of the theme under discussion, or whether they are used in a specific christological sense. Simon Magus had been called "that power of God which is called Great" (Acts 8:10). The wisdom of God was a separate hypostasis in much of the later Jewish literature (Ecclus. 24:9; 51:23; Wisd. Sol. 7:24 ff.; 9:9; etc.). Nevertheless, in the light of the paradox that foolishness is the true wisdom, it would seem precarious to take the terms here as christological titles.

Looking back over the paragraph, we see that it would not be difficult, if this evidence is taken by itself, to interpret Paul as a preacher who belittled all learning. That would be, however, a gross misrepresentation. He himself was a man of real though restricted scholarship. He does not disparage knowledge as such. But he is very certain that it does not bring men to God. That depends upon God's own act of redemption in the cross of Christ. Access to God is not through human philosophy but through the historical revelation in Christ.

---

set himself to win the hearts and minds of men. If he can do it, he has vindicated his power and also his wisdom. He chose the way of self-sacrificial love and vicarious suffering. It is the self-sacrifice and vicarious suffering of God that is epitomized on Calvary's Cross. All other methods have failed to win the allegiance of men to righteousness, to good will, to peace, and to love. The only way left to God was the way he chose. When sin, malice, misunderstanding, and hatred have done their worst, just to go on loving proved to be the way of victory. There is the ultimate quality that is required for love. It must endure the worst and yet remain true to itself; it must sustain the most shattering defeat and still be love. There is no power in heaven or earth like the power of love that suffers to the utmost, is battered, bruised, spat upon, crucified, and yet remains love. In the end the human heart cannot withstand the power of love like that. It is power—spiritual power! It is the power of God and, having regard to his method of achieving his purposes, it is the supreme manifestation of the wisdom of God. In the long run such love is bound to win the victory. Perhaps the scales will fall from the eyes of such as Annas and Caiaphas and Judas Iscariot, and of all who have some resemblance to them in spirit and outlook; and if not here, then hereafter, when judgment has completed its work, as the case may be, they will gaze upon the love they crucified and be beaten, broken, and captured by it. Can God who loves like that, whose will and resources are equal to his great redemptive and creative purposes, finally be defeated in any single soul he has created?

The word of the cross is also **the wisdom of God.** It was the amazing insight of Jesus Christ that made him choose the way of the Cross. He might have chosen the sword. He had only to stamp upon the earth to call into existence an army of fanatical patriots who might have menaced, and perhaps even overthrown, the power of Rome. He rejected it. They would have made him a king. He refused the crown and chose the Cross. He chose it because it was the only way of bringing in his kingdom. It was the only way to win and to purify and to keep the hearts of men. The love rejected on the Cross is the highest wisdom. It haunts the heart and troubles the conscience, and it does lead men and women to the place of repentance and renewal of spirit. That is what the Cross did; that is what it has accomplished ever since. To the mind of man the Cross has often seemed to be the symbol of weakness. Those who stood at its foot would not have prophesied any future at all other than utter oblivion for the man and the cause that were crucified there. But that man is the most significant of all personalities for every age. His message and spirit are the sole message and spirit that can save the world. A scientific civilization, if the world is to escape a doom that always darkly threatens it, needs above all else to be baptized into his spirit and guided and illumined by his truth. The word of the Cross has outlasted Rome and many another empire since Rome's day. It has withstood the rise and fall of strong

26 For ye see your calling, brethren, how that not many wise men after the flesh, not many mighty, not many noble, *are called:*

27 But God hath chosen the foolish things of the world to confound the wise; and God hath chosen the weak things of the world to confound the things which are mighty;

26 For consider your call, brethren; not many of you were wise according to worldly standards, not many were powerful, not many were of noble birth; 27 but God chose what is foolish in the world to shame the wise, God chose what is weak in the world

b) THE MEMBERSHIP OF THE CORINTHIAN COMMUNITY (1:26-31)

26-29. Paul turns from the general discussion of the failure of wisdom to the specific situation in the Corinthian church. If a teacher has a new philosophy to expound, there is only one place for him to go, viz., to the schools. But the Corinthian church bore no resemblance to a Greek academy. Three privileged groups are mentioned, those excelling because of knowledge, power, or family connections. The church did not contain many who shared in any of these advantages, but apparently there were some. Men like those whom Paul names in this letter were hardly "nobodies." But the great majority were slaves and freedmen who had no claim to position in the eyes of the world. In the church it

nations. It has withstood the scrutiny of two thousand years. It still has power to shake the heart and to transform the spirit of him who receives it. "The cross leads the generations on." Again to quote Latourette:

> No other life ever lived on this planet has been so potent in the affairs of men. The most widely spread of the religions of mankind, Christianity, has Jesus as its central figure. . . . From Jesus, through Christianity, have issued impulses which have helped to shape every phase of civilization.[4]

That power and wisdom of God enshrined in **the word of the cross** still pursue us, for his kingdom is not yet won. But "the hound of heaven" is on the track. We cannot escape him. We barricade all the doors of our life as we will, but Christ will wait and knock and plead. In the end the barriers must fall, whether in love or in judgment; for there is a limit to the loneliness man can bear, and the ultimate loneliness is that of the soul bereft of God.

> Yet let him keep the rest,
> But keep them with repining restlessness;
> Let him be rich and weary, that at least,
> If goodness lead him not, yet weariness
> May toss him to my breast.[5]

The word of the Cross is the dominant theme of this epistle, and indeed of all Paul's letters. In them it is explicit or implicit, even in the Epistle to Philemon. It sets the tone and standard for all that is to follow. Like an echoing detonation it sounds right through this letter to the Corinthians, and as we listen to it, the reverberations still retain their ancient power.

26-31. ***God's Chosen Instruments.***— (See Exeg., vss. 26-29.) We get another glimpse of the composition of the church in Corinth through the window of these verses. As we have already noted, the members were drawn in the main from the humbler section of the community. Paul uses the fact to point the contrast between the earthen vessel and the heavenly treasure it contains (II Cor. 4:7), and to reinforce his previous contrast between the wisdom of God and that of man. Obviously God's purpose was to base men's faith not on human cleverness, but on his own self-revelation of power through Jesus Christ. That is why Paul concludes the section with an abbreviated quotation from Jer. 9:23-24. **Therefore, as it is written, "Let him who boasts, boast of the Lord."**

It is neither pride of intellect nor of civic position and prestige that counts in the eyes of God. Such folk are apt to be arrogant and proud of spirit, and are prone to commit the sin of the Pharisees, viz., the sin of the closed mind. It is to the humble-minded and the unsophisticated that the call comes, as it came from the Master himself to the fishermen pulling their nets by the lakeside. The self-sufficient spirit has no place for God. As the apostle warns his readers later in this epistle, lest they fall into the very sin which prevented God's revelation of his purpose from reaching those others whom he has set aside as unworthy to receive it: "What have you that you did not receive? If then you received it, why do you boast as if it were not a gift?" (4:7.)

[4] *Ibid.*, pp. xi-xii.

[5] George Herbert, "The Pulley."

28 And base things of the world, and things which are despised, hath God chosen, *yea,* and things which are not, to bring to nought things that are:
29 That no flesh should glory in his presence.

to shame the strong, 28 God chose what is
low and despised in the world, even things
that are not, to bring to nothing things
that are, 29 so that no human being might

---

was entirely different. There nothing depended upon worldly success; the divine calling alone mattered. As always, Paul assigned the initiative to God. Salvation does not come through what men have done but through what God has done for them. What they have lacked has been made up in Christ. There is as a result no reason for the human boasting which is found among men who are proud of their scholarship, their position, or their descent. It may be that the **things that are not** (τὰ μὴ ὄντα) was a technical philosophical phrase. Paul is attempting to assign a reason where Jesus simply gave humble thanks. "I thank thee . . . that thou hast hidden these things from the wise and understanding and revealed them to babes" (Matt. 11:25; see also Luke 14:21). Paul was influenced in his phraseology, however, more by Jer. 9:23-24, "Let not the wise man glory in his wisdom, let not the mighty man glory in his might, let not the rich man glory in his riches; but let him who glories glory in this, that he understands and knows me." This is the source of the quotation with which the apostle closes the chapter. All natural advantages have been rendered worthless; we are entirely dependent upon God's gift.

30. God is the ultimate source of what believers receive and the gift comes to them "in Christ." Again we are face to face with the alternative as to whether Paul thinks of a mystical dwelling in Christ, or the new eschatological situation brought about by his death and resurrection. Christ is the origin and ground of their new possession. This is described by the inclusive word **wisdom** because of the preceding discussion. Of course it is God's wisdom. This wisdom which is given through Christ is then considered under three aspects: righteousness, consecration, and redemption. These are not successive stages of salvation but different metaphors by which Paul describes the one experience. **Righteousness** is not simply one of the moral virtues but the divine acquittal, or will to save, which Christ has revealed (Rom. 3:21). In I Cor. 6:11 this is the last in the series, where

---

There is a reminiscence here of the first beatitude in the Sermon on the Mount. "Blessed are the poor in spirit, for theirs is the kingdom of heaven" (Matt. 5:3), i.e., blessed are the humble-minded, the teachable ones, for God's Spirit can reign in their hearts. His purposes can be revealed to them and they are enabled thereby to understand. Pride here is given, by implication, first place in the list of deadly sins. On the other hand, humility of spirit is one of the gates that open upon the heavenly kingdom (see Exeg., vs. 30). Through that gate the all-conquering power of God can come flooding into the human heart and give it a spiritual victory over the power of the world.

It did not look like it then, but history has since proved the truth of Paul's prophetic words. These Corinthian Christians, like the first disciples, were insignificant and unimportant people. No one who knew them would have said they represented anything that would be of significance in future ages. Yet the most significant men in the Roman Empire nearly two thousand years ago were the fishermen of Galilee, and the key people in the vast unrolling of the mighty panorama of subsequent history were the members of the Christian community. Despite their weaknesses, their failures, and their stupid wranglings, they were the instruments of a spirit that was to sweep through the empire and through the centuries long after the empire itself had passed away. They were the pioneers in Europe of a new order of life that was to endure to our day. They were to blaze the trails and set up the signposts along which the myriad feet of generations unborn were to travel. They were helping to swing open great new doors of hope through which grateful men and women in every age were to pass into newness of life.

True it is that the prospects did not look good. The spirit of the age was against them. The Greco-Roman culture, represented by statesmen, poets, and philosophers, was against them. They were overshadowed by the vast edifice of a pagan tradition that had existed for long centuries. The religious temper of the Jews was against them, and the might of the

30 But of him are ye in Christ Jesus, who of God is made unto us wisdom, and righteousness, and sanctification, and redemption:
31 That, according as it is written, He that glorieth, let him glory in the Lord.

boast in the presence of God.
30 He is the source of your life in Christ Jesus, whom God made our wisdom, our righteousness and sanctification and redemption;
31 therefore, as it is written, "Let him who boasts, boast of the Lord."

---

again Paul affirms that we are justified in Christ Jesus. **Sanctification** translates the Greek word ἁγιασμός, an important Pauline term. From the same root come the adjective "holy" and the noun "saint." The word has the cult significance of "bringing into nearness to God." Of course this does not take place through man's effort, but through God's work in Christ and the Spirit. Neither here nor in 6:11 does the term stand last in the series, and in no passage in Paul does it describe an advanced state of Christian living. It is simply the opposite of iniquity and uncleanness (Rom. 6:19; I Thess. 4:3, 7). **Redemption** is a figure drawn from the slave market. Deissmann has called attention to the practice of sacral manumission by which ransom money was paid at a temple and the freedman came under the protection of the divinity (*Light from the Ancient East* [2nd ed.; New York: George H. Doran, 1927], pp. 318-31). Though Paul may remind his readers that they were bought with a price (6:20), he never suggests anyone to whom it is paid. For Paul this is only one of the metaphors to symbolize what had been done for men in Christ. Rom. 3:24 also connects redemption with justification. In Rom. 8:23 this involves the transformation of our bodies into bodies of glory. In Col. 1:14 redemption is explained as "the forgiveness of sins."

31. Behind all of these figures which are drawn from various human relationships is the one great fact: God has freely given us in Christ what no man—whether wise or strong—could obtain for himself. Human pride must give way to trusting humility. Our only boast can be in the one who has given so freely.

---

empire itself by the behest of Caesar summoned its energies to destroy them. The book of Revelation is the testament of a crucified church, though every second verse is a banner, stained, as it were, with the blood of Christian saints and martyrs, yet inscribed with the legend "Victory," and waving triumphantly above their heads. Yet by "the word of the cross," the gospel to which they were committed and with which they were entrusted, the early Christians, humble and insignificant people like the Corinthian community, won their resounding victory. History bears its witness to the astonishing fact. Given a humble, teachable, and obedient heart in which to rest and through which to work, there is "a love divine, all loves excelling," and nothing can ever stay its redeeming work.

Times come again and again when Christian people are depressed by the criticism of their contemporaries, and by the apparent meagerness of the contribution they may make in the solution of the tremendous problems of the age. It may seem to them as if their individual life and witness counted for less than nothing, as if any individual life or contribution were like a matchwood boat tossed and flung by gigantic waves which threaten to destroy it each anxious instant. But deeper reading of history and a quiet pondering of some of the great prophetic words of scripture more than help to redress the balance. Great consequences often flow from small causes. Especially is it so if God is involved.

> He has shown strength with his arm,
> he has scattered the proud in the imagination of their hearts,
> he has put down the mighty from their thrones,
> and exalted those of low degree (Luke 1:51-52).

We can take comfort and inspiration to ourselves from these things. **God chose what is foolish in the world to shame the wise, God chose what is weak in the world to shame the strong, God chose what is low and despised in the world, even things that are not, to bring to nothing things that are, so that no human being might boast in the presence of God.** As Wendell Phillips once put it, "One on God's side is a majority."

> He that is down needs fear no fall;
> He that is low, no pride;
> He that is humble ever shall
> Have God to be his guide.

2 And I, brethren, when I came to you, came not with excellency of speech or of wisdom, declaring unto you the testimony of God.

2 For I determined not to know any thing among you, save Jesus Christ, and him crucified.

2 When I came to you, brethren, I did not come proclaiming to you the testimony[c] of God in lofty words or wisdom.
2 For I decided to know nothing among you

[c] Other ancient authorities read *mystery* (or *secret*).

c) The Manner of Paul's Entrance into Corinth (2:1-5)

For a third demonstration of the fact that the message is not a new wisdom, Paul appeals to his own work when he came to Corinth. It has been popular to see in this testimony of Paul a confession concerning his preaching before this time. Having tried philosophy at Athens without success, he then resolved to confine himself to preaching the Cross. Such a conclusion has little ground. First, "Luke" must bear the responsibility for the wording of the address before the Areopagus. It is much closer to the spirit of the Apologists than to the Paul of the letters. There were no witnesses from among Paul's friends. But even if we do assume that Paul gave essentially this address, it would be only another example of his becoming "all things to all men" (9:22). As a matter of fact, however, the Athenian sermon does not omit the Cross. The real sermon, after the bridge to his audience, is in Acts 17:31, where world judgment is proclaimed by the one whom God raised from the dead. Certainly this is one aspect of "the word of the cross" (1:18). Paul had been preaching for more than fifteen years when he reached Corinth; he had already founded churches in several provinces. Are we to suppose that he suddenly modified the gospel to which the Jerusalem pillars had added nothing? (Gal. 2:6.) Had Paul ever depended upon **plausible words of wisdom** since the risen Christ had appeared to him? (Gal. 2:20; 3:1.) No; Paul is simply describing his normal missionary practice.

2:1-2. Paul's sarcasm is not directed against any previous experience of his own, but against the leaders of a faction at Corinth which had exalted wisdom. It is difficult to determine the original text as between **testimony,** which is read in both the KJV and the RSV, and **mystery,** which is read in the RSV mg. Probably the latter is a scribal insertion from vs. 7. Here the **testimony of God** is the "word of the Cross"; but as we shall see, "the mystery" is to be distinguished from this. Paul states his decision negatively, **I decided to know nothing.** Literally speaking, it is impossible by an act of will to discard

So sang the shepherd lad in John Bunyan's great allegory. We may do the same.

2:1-5. ***Paul's Own Practice.***—By a very characteristic reference to his own example, Paul now reinforces his exhortations both with regard to the partisan spirit of the church and with regard to what he has just said about subordinating personalities to the glory of the gospel message. He is able to write as he has done, extolling humility of spirit, because his words are the expression of himself. He is only the messenger, the agent of God, whose importance lies solely in the nature of the message he brings. **For I decided to know nothing among you except Jesus Christ and him crucified.** It is the proclamation that matters, not the herald. That heralds and agents are called upon to deliver such messages is another illustration of the wonderful condescension of God.

Paul can claim to be quite consistent so far as his own practice is concerned. Perhaps with the memory of his somewhat disappointing experience in Athens to guide him, he tells his readers that he had firmly set aside any temptation to be rhetorical (see Exeg.). Nor had he couched the gospel in any context of current philosophy. There is no assumption of superiority; on the contrary, he confesses his nervous trepidation, excusing himself on the ground that he was feeling far from strong when he came to them. But all had conspired to merge the messenger in his message. It was far from his wish that he should impress by his personality: it was his deepest desire that the message should convince by its own inspiring truth. Here as elsewhere he might have written, "I want you to know, brethren, that what has happened to me has really served to advance the gospel" (Phil. 1:12).

He will take up this point again (3:1-9). Meantime, with these oblique references to the unworthy descendants of the great Sophists,

3 And I was with you in weakness, and in fear, and in much trembling.
4 And my speech and my preaching *was* not with enticing words of man's wisdom, but in demonstration of the Spirit and of power:
5 That your faith should not stand in the wisdom of men, but in the power of God.
6 Howbeit we speak wisdom among them that are perfect: yet not the wisdom of this world, nor of the princes of this world, that come to nought:

except Jesus Christ and him crucified. 3 And
I was with you in weakness and in much
fear and trembling; 4 and my speech and
my message were not in plausible words of
wisdom, but in demonstration of the Spirit
and power, 5 that your faith might not rest
in the wisdom of men but in the power of
God.
6 Yet among the mature we do impart
wisdom, although it is not a wisdom of
this age or of the rulers of this age, who

---

knowledge which one actually does possess. In 8:4 it is shown that Paul did not fail to emphasize the monotheistic base of Christian faith, and the Cross could not be separated from the Resurrection (15:3 ff.). Paul is affirming the center of his message, not the whole circumference.

3-4. It does not take great imagination to picture the timidity of a lonely missionary beginning his work in a great commercial city. **Weakness** is not necessarily a reference to his "thorn in the flesh" (II Cor. 12:7), but is in contrast to "the power of God." Elsewhere Paul suggests that his oratorical skill was not of the best (II Cor. 10:10; 11:6). Acts reports at Corinth a heavenly voice to quiet his fears (Acts 18:9). The word translated **demonstration** (ἀπόδειξις) was a technical term of rhetoric. What Paul depended upon was none of these arts but the power of the Spirit. Faith rests not upon persuasive arguments, but upon the work of God in the hearts of men. It is the Spirit which makes faith possible. As we shall see in 12:9, faith is itself a gift of the Spirit. Vs. 4 contains a wild assortment of variants in the Greek text. Surely the KJV is wrong in reading **man's,** but the text adopted in the RSV is not certainly original, for πειθός is not elsewhere found as an adjective. It may be that we should follow the shortest text of all, πειθοῖ σοφίας, which would be translated "persuasion of wisdom." But that reading would not change the real meaning in any way.

3. The True Wisdom Is Not Possessed by the Factious (2:6–3:4)

a) God's Own Wisdom (2:6-9)

Paul now turns to his third argument: God's true wisdom is communicated only by the Spirit. Factions show that the Corinthians do not possess the Spirit in its fullness, and so they cannot expect to have this wisdom. The entire section raises in acute form the problem of Paul's relationship to Hellenistic mystery religions and the possibility of influence by them (see Vol. VII, pp. 89-94). We must view the section as a whole if we are to understand its several parts.

6-9. Who are the **perfect** (KJV), **mature** (RSV)? Those who believe that this section is dominated by ideas from the mysteries think that the word (τέλειοι) should be rendered

---

Paul preserves a kindly and discreet reticence about other Christian teachers who had been less than wise or modest in their presentation of the message. The persuasive power of any preacher of the gospel lies much less in what he says than in what he conveys. This is axiomatic with Paul. His words might be carved on the mantelpiece, or in some such prominent place, in every preacher's study, **My speech and my message were not in plausible words of wisdom, but in demonstration of the Spirit and power, that your faith might not rest in the wisdom of men but in the power of God.**

6-8. *Wisdom in the Gospel.*—The apostle now reinforces his previous argument with regard to wisdom by insisting that there is a higher wisdom which yields real insight into the nature and purposes of God, although it is only comprehensible to those who can be described as spiritually mature (see Exeg., vss.

7 But we speak the wisdom of God in a mystery, *even* the hidden *wisdom,* which God ordained before the world unto our glory;

are doomed to pass away. 7 But we impart a secret and hidden wisdom of God, which God decreed before the ages for our glorifi-

"initiates." The adjective is built on the noun τέλος, "end"; the general meaning therefore is "brought to completion." Absolute perfection is not affirmed of finite human beings. These people are the opposite of "the babes" (3:1; 14:20) ; they are the ones in whom the Spirit has really produced a new life. They are to be identified with the "spiritual" (vs. 15) , and stand in contrast to two other groups: the "natural" (KJV) or "unspiritual man" (RSV) and also to the "carnal" (KJV) or "men of the flesh" (RSV) .

What is the **wisdom** which these, in contrast to the others, are able to receive, the **wisdom of God in a mystery** (KJV) or the **secret and hidden wisdom of God** (RSV) ? Though some interpreters would identify this with "the word of the cross" (1:18) , that seems highly unlikely. It is a wisdom which many of the Corinthians do not have, and yet they have all heard Paul's mission preaching. On the other hand, there is no reason to ascribe to Paul esoteric doctrines reserved for a few special initiates. His mysteries are mysterious in character; nevertheless they are proclaimed to all who can understand them. Three times Paul indicates specific aspects of his mysteries (15:51; Rom. 11:25; Col. 1:26-27) : viz., the coming of the Parousia in that generation so that some will not die, the place of the hardening of the Jews in God's plan of salvation, and the indwelling Christ. Since vs. 9 also describes what the mystery is which God reveals through his Spirit, we are safe in concluding that it involves eschatological aspects of redemption, God's full plan of salvation.

Who are the ἄρχοντες τοῦ αἰῶνος τούτου, the **princes of this world** (KJV) , **rulers of this age** (RSV) , who did not understand this mystery? Often it has been assumed that these were Caiaphas and the Sanhedrin, Pilate and Herod, the religious and political authorities collaborating in the crucifixion of Jesus (Acts 13:27) . But how could they have known the secrets of God's plan of salvation? Clearly we must adopt the interpreta-

6-9) , i.e., to those who are adequately Christian, especially when they forgather in the spirit of Christian fellowship. There is implied in these words a rebuke to the members of the Corinthian church who imagine themselves to be perfectly equipped by the current philosophical and mystery cults of the day to be able to unravel the deepest secrets of God. Doubtless in their intellectual arrogance they criticized Paul's presentation of "the word of the cross" as the gospel which could yield both insight and power with regard to the innermost nature of things. In this connection we must keep in mind that the cosmos-ranging mind of the apostle had found in the revelation of God in Jesus Christ and him crucified a philosophy of creation and of life. It is involved in all his epistles. Paul warns them that such presumption classes them with **the rulers of this age** (see Exeg.) . None of them, with all their Hellenic learning and mystery cults, had really understood God's method of revealing his wisdom and power, **for if they had, they would not have crucified the Lord of glory.** Once again we must realize that for Paul, Jesus Christ and him crucified is the revelation and the revealer of God. All that Jesus Christ was and all that he achieved, by word and deed and spirit, is a revelation of God. From Bethlehem to Nazareth, from Nazareth to all the villages and towns of Galilee, from Galilee to Judea and Jerusalem, from Jerusalem to Gethsemane, from Gethsemane to Calvary, and from Calvary to the Garden of the Resurrection and the Mount of Ascension the word goes forth, "He who has seen me has seen the Father" (John 14:9) . That, too, is axiomatic with Paul: it is a foundation stone of his Christian belief.

Genuine insight into reality is the outcome of reason fructified by revelation. Without revelation there can be neither reason nor reasoning. Reality must reveal itself to make itself known. In a well-known aphorism, included in the preface he wrote for the first published edition of the *Critique of Pure Reason,* Kant says, "Reason without sense is empty: sense without reason is blind." Sense data are essential to understanding, and understanding is necessary if such experience is to have any value for men and women as they seek to adapt themselves to their environment. So is it with this strange, complex Reality amid which our

8 Which none of the princes of this world knew: for had they known *it,* they would not have crucified the Lord of glory.

cation. 8 None of the rulers of this age understood this; for if they had, they would

tion, which goes back to Origen, that these are the angelic rulers who, according to ancient thought, stood behind human agents and were the real causes of historic events. They were the "angels" and "principalities" (Rom. 8:38) who had been defeated on the Cross. Possibly Paul may have shared ideas similar to those in the Ascension of Isaiah 10–11, where the heavenly Christ is not recognized by the powers as he descends through the heavens. Not understanding God's mystery, these principalities and powers had conspired to bring Jesus to his death. In fact, however, this brought his triumph over them (Col. 2:15). These rulers are to be identified with "the elemental spirits of the universe" (Gal. 4:3, 9; Col. 2:8) which are no longer to be served, since the Crucifixion brought the defeat of the "ruler of this world" (John 12:31).

We are now ready to put together these conclusions. Paul does have a secret wisdom for those mature Christians who fully possess the Spirit. It concerns fuller details of God's plan of salvation, which the angelic powers did not know. Since Paul was thinking of **this age** and the age to come, **world** (KJV) is misleading. **Doomed to pass away** renders a present tense; the final defeat of these powers awaits the Parousia (15:25). Then believers will receive their bodies of glory, **our glorification** (I Thess. 2:12; Phil. 3:21; Rom. 5:2; 8:17). Christ is referred to as **the Lord of glory** because he possessed the divine splendor of light (δόξα) and bestowed this glory on men. Paul climaxes his description of this secret wisdom by a presumed appeal to scripture. But where are these words **written?** Origen and Ambrose say that they come from the Secrets of Elias. But would Paul have used his formula for scripture citation to refer to a noncanonical writing? I Clem. 34:8 has the same quotation, but its author might have drawn it from our letter, which he knew well. Later the passage came into the text of the Ascension of Isaiah 11:34, but that could not be Paul's source. Isa. 64:4 comes nearest to the words of our quotation, but if this is Paul's source, he makes a very free adaptation. Paul's final emphasis upon

lives are placed. But much, very much, depends on the receptiveness of the individual. Spiritual wisdom is spiritually discerned. Only those whose minds and hearts are open to receive what God, on his own initiative, is more than willing to give, are likely to receive enlightenment, or be initiated into the eternal **secret and hidden wisdom of God, which God decreed before the ages for our glorification.** Man is slow to learn that God's ways are not our ways, nor are his thoughts our thoughts (Isa. 55:8-9). He tends to be prejudiced in favor of his own unaided capacity to gain insight into the deeper aspects of reality, not understanding that even those aspects of reality he does comprehend are due to the fructifying combination of reason combined with revelation. There are degrees of revelation. The higher degrees are available only to the spiritually mature. Those who suffer from any conceit of knowledge, who are not prepared to sit down in wonder before a new fact, as all the greatest scientists and thinkers do, such wonder as that with which young children regard their world, are unlikely to achieve the kind of understanding for which the apostle pleads. Still less are they likely to understand the eternal significance of the Cross or **the Lord of glory.** "The closed fist can receive nothing," states an old Chinese proverb. Neither can the closed mind or heart. Such people cheat themselves.

Paul is really reinforcing his argument and preparing the way for what is to follow. All these statements are to be linked with his assertion of apostolic authority and the insight that goes with it, as such insight has been sharpened by his own experience. **Among the mature we do impart wisdom, . . . we impart a secret and hidden wisdom of God, which God decreed before the ages for our glorification.** Again, there is the implied rebuke to arrogance; for the revelation of God in "the word of the cross" is very far removed in its emphasis on the self-sacrifice and vicarious suffering of God from the arrogant self-sufficiency of man and his human wisdom. The perfection of human personality lies in our approximation in spirit and outlook to the God who is thus revealed. The creative power of the universe itself, according to one of the major notes in the teaching of the N.T., is aligned with this supreme end (John 3:1-3).

9 But as it is written, Eye hath not seen,
nor ear heard, neither have entered into
the heart of man, the things which God
hath prepared for them that love him.
10 But God hath revealed *them* unto us
by his Spirit: for the Spirit searcheth all
things, yea, the deep things of God.

not have crucified the Lord of glory. 9 But,
as it is written,
"What no eye has seen, nor ear heard,
nor the heart of man conceived,
what God has prepared for those who
love him,"
10 God has revealed to us through the Spirit.
For the Spirit searches everything, even the

love is instructive. The road to the secret wisdom of God is not through some initiation ceremony or philosophical instruction, but through the highest gift of the Spirit, love.

b) A Gift Through the Spirit (2:10-16)

10-12. Paul turns next to the place of the Spirit in imparting this true wisdom. He does not say that the Spirit teaches all things, but that he **searches everything,** or investigates. The only other place where Paul uses the word is in Rom. 8:27, where he speaks of the searching of the hearts of men by God. That activity is an aspect of the omnipresence of the Spirit. Yet we must not make the mistake of confusing Paul's idea of the Spirit, the supernatural gift to believers, and to them only, with the Stoic idea of a reality permeating the entire natural universe. Paul uses the word πνεῦμα in a wide

This secret wisdom of God has been hidden from all previous generations before Christ, presumably because humanity was unable to receive it. Still is it hidden from those who put their faith in human wisdom and also from those whom Paul calls "babes in Christ" (3:1-2). He also states that it is hidden from **the rulers of this age, who are doomed to pass away,** by whom he means "the elemental spirits of the universe" (Gal. 4:3; Eph. 6:12; Rom. 8:38). But in crucifying **the Lord of glory** they overreached themselves, being overwhelmed by the triumph of the Resurrection. As John Masefield has put it in a fancied conversation between Procula, the wife of Pontius Pilate, and Longinus, the centurion who commanded the soldiers on Calvary, "Do you think he is dead?" she asks. "No, lady, I don't." "Then where is he?" "Let loose in the world, lady, where neither Roman nor Jew can stop his truth."[6] **None of the rulers of this age understood this; for if they had, they would not have crucified the Lord of glory.** On that sorrowing note Paul goes on to quote freely what are thought to be the words of one of the postexilic prophets:

No, as it is written,
what no eye has ever seen,
what no ear has ever heard,
What never entered the mind of man,
God has prepared all that for those who love him
(vs. 9 Moffatt).

This rhapsody, written in one of those moments of kindling thought to which Paul is prone, for the encouragement and inspiration of his readers, follows from his explanation of the secret wisdom of God. It is inspired by the apostle's conception of the creative order. Great experiences have been the portion of those who have found new life in Christ, and great expectations for the world that is and that is to come flow from these experiences. This thought doubtless sounded the bugles in the souls of the more sensitive and spiritually minded among the Corinthians. Undoubtedly they have brought similar inspiration for successive generations of Christian folk. They will do as much for us if we can glimpse a few aspects of their meaning.

9-16. ***Great Experiences and Great Expectations.***—These words indicate what his faith in Christ meant for Paul. For him it was a rich, comprehensive word that spelled comfort and confidence and security. But it also meant more. For the apostle, God is such that anything great was liable to happen at any moment to receptive men and women, especially if they were members of a united, devoted Christian fellowship. Wonderful as the past had been—and we must remember always that Paul lived on this side of the crucifixion of Jesus—his life was centered in the living Christ. The range and inspiration of his faith spring from that mighty event. The God who raised Jesus from the dead is equal to any possibility. To a receptive and expectant faith the gates of the future, full of unexpected possibilities, were widely open. How good it is to have a firm grasp of such a faith at all times.

[6] *The Trial of Jesus* (New York: The Macmillan Co., 1925), p. 111.

11 For what man knoweth the things of a man, save the spirit of man which is in him? even so the things of God knoweth no man, but the Spirit of God.

12 Now we have received, not the spirit of the world, but the Spirit which is of God; that we might know the things that are freely given to us of God.

13 Which things also we speak, not in the words which man's wisdom teacheth, but which the Holy Ghost teacheth; comparing spiritual things with spiritual.

depths of God. 11 For what person knows
a man's thoughts except the spirit of the
man which is in him? So also no one comprehends the thoughts of God except the
Spirit of God. 12 Now we have received not
the spirit of the world, but the Spirit which
is from God, that we might understand the
gifts bestowed on us by God. 13 And we
impart this in words not taught by human
wisdom but taught by the Spirit, interpreting spiritual truths to those who possess the Spirit.[d]

[d] Or *interpreting spiritual truths in spiritual language;* or *comparing spiritual things with spiritual.*

---

variety of ways. Sometimes it seems more like an impersonal power. Here it is the self-consciousness of God, by analogy to the human πνεῦμα, which is man's self-consciousness. The passage suggests the possibility of a psychological interpretation of the Trinity, paving the way for Augustine's approach. In these verses the word πνεῦμα is used in more than the usual variety of ways. Paul speaks of **the spirit of man,** the **spirit of the world** (κόσμος not αἰών) and the **Spirit of God.** The English texts attempt to make the distinction clear by the use of capitals for the last. But since the Greek has no such indication, we cannot be sure when Paul means the divine Spirit and when he means simply this faculty of human nature. He nevertheless makes a tremendous claim in this passage. In the bestowal of the Spirit men have received nothing less than God's self-consciousness. Therefore they are able to understand his secret wisdom. The Greek has no noun at this point, simply the participle of the verb χαρίζομαι, which means "to bestow spiritual gifts."

13. When these are passed on to others, it is not in the language of **human wisdom,** but in a teaching **by the Spirit.** Just how this takes place is obscured by the conciseness of Paul's expression and the ambiguity of the words which he uses. The verb συγκρίνω may mean either "compare" (as in II Cor. 10:12) or "interpret" or "combine." Paul uses two

---

From our vantage point, in respect of history and knowledge and time, such a faith is abundantly justified. Christian faith is a maximum faith: it sets no limits to the possibilities where the power and wisdom of God are concerned. How foolish of the Corinthian Christians to be squabbling about unimportant matters when all these rich prospects already guaranteed in their experience are open to them! How pertinent is the same thought for our own day and generation: what a rebuke in particular to all defeatism and pessimism!

For one thing, the illimitable resourcefulness of God is illustrated in the creative process itself: that is part of his handiwork. In the course of unnumbered centuries amazing things have happened in the realm of creativity. Had it been possible for any one of us to stand by, like some "disinterested spectator" of all time and history, having no prevision or knowledge of what was to come, could we have conceived the world we know today in the light of its beginnings? From the primeval gaseous mist, somehow revolving slowly on some immense axis, there have evolved the various aspects of the civilization we know. From inorganic matter humanity has come, cities have been built, arts and sciences have evolved, and where once fierce creatures contended for mastery there are great cities and towns, and villages, and Christian homes. For those whose insight penetrates the surface appearance of things the entire creation is preaching a great sermon on the wisdom and power and unpredictable providence of God.

The same truth is illustrated in the lives and characters of men and women; when God is given an opportunity to deal with a human soul, things that have never been conceived are likely to happen. The unstable Peter is transformed into the solid rock of a man who stoutly defended his Master even though under the threat of death (Acts 4:13, 19-20). The irresponsible Augustine is converted to Christianity and becomes a bishop of the church and a mighty instrument in the shaping of its the-

14 But the natural man receiveth not the things of the Spirit of God: for they are foolishness unto him: neither can he know *them,* because they are spiritually discerned.

14 The unspiritual[e] man does not receive the gifts of the Spirit of God, for they are folly to him, and he is not able to understand them because they are spiritually dis-

[e] Or *natural.*

words for "spiritual"; one is the neuter plural, but since the other is in the dative case, it might be either masculine or neuter. Hence all of the three translations given in the RSV are linguistically possible. There is no consensus among modern interpreters on a choice among them. The reading preferred by the RSV seems best to fit the context, for Paul is discussing how his secret wisdom may be imparted. On the other hand the KJV translation is assumed by Reitzenstein and Lietzmann when they paraphrase, "while we compare with the spiritual gifts and revelations which we already possess the gifts and revelations which we receive" (R. Reitzenstein, *Die hellenistischen Mysterienreligionen* [3rd ed.; Leipzig: B. G. Teubner, 1927], p. 188).

14-16. These verses raise the question of how exactly Paul is using psychological terms. It is not easy to confront the English reader with the problem, for we have no such adjective as "soulish." Basic to the passage is the assumption that "spirit" (πνεῦμα) and "soul" (ψυχή) are antithetic. We can call the man of vs. 15 **spiritual,** but how shall we designate the man of vs. 14? The KJV uses **natural man;** Goodspeed, "material"; the RSV, **unspiritual,** i.e., not having the Spirit (but cf. mg. **natural**). On the other hand, Paul assumes that "spirit" and **mind** (νοῦς) are identical. The citation from Isa. 40:13 induces the change to this terminology. Paul frequently identified **Lord** in the O.T. with Christ. When the apostle closes with the phrase **the mind of Christ,** he is not thinking of the mental faculties with which Jesus was endowed. He means that Spirit which dwelt in Christ, who was himself the Spirit (II Cor. 3:17) and the giver of the Spirit.

Paul will return in 15:44-46 to the same contrast between the "soulish" and the "spiritual." There it is clear that he is arguing from Gen. 2:7, where it is said that Adam was created "a living soul." Christ established a new order of humanity through the

ology. An insipid preacher like John Wesley is transformed into a blazing brand who moves through a dark period of English history like a lighted torch. So does Saul, the fanatical persecutor of the Christian church, become the great Apostle to the Gentiles. Men and women, countless numbers of them, are transformed out of all resemblance to their past selves when a spark of love to God and a grain of faith in him open heart and mind to the inflooding of his Spirit. Surely it is the stimulus and incentive of such a faith that we need now. Let Christian folk everywhere, by their love and devotion, keep the channels open for God, and who can tell what his response might be? It is never wise to prophesy what is likely to happen in history, for one can never tell what individuals will emerge, or what they will do. Perhaps the world has yet to see what God can do through a band of people, or even through the life of one man, utterly devoted to him. Things that have not even been conceived have already been prepared by God for those who love him.

And the truth contained in these lines is illustrated in the events of life. History is in the making, and its shaping forces are the experiences that are conserved not only in the institutions of the human race and of nations, or in the character and personality of individuals, but also in the ideas and ideals, the values and convictions, that lie ahead and beckon man onward. Two thousand years ago Jesus Christ came into the world with his great watchword, "the kingdom of God," the kingdom for which he taught men to pray, and which Paul preached in Corinth and elsewhere with all the passion of his ardent nature. Still the race is working toward its realization. Sometimes it falls back, but if there is any clue in the monumental work of Kenneth Scott Latourette,[7] on the whole there is gain. The Spirit, always ready to reveal God's deepest secrets to those whose spiritual maturity is marked by their love of him, is ceaselessly at work in the world. Surely the highest hopes of men are bound up with that truth. Not even a Cross could stop it. To his disciples in the upper room in Jerusalem, on the night in which he was betrayed, Christ

[7] *A History of the Expansion of Christianity* (New York: Harper & Bros., 1937-45), Vols. VI, VII.

15 But he that is spiritual judgeth all things, yet he himself is judged of no man.
16 For who hath known the mind of the Lord, that he may instruct him? But we have the mind of Christ.

cerned. 15 The spiritual man judges all things, but is himself to be judged by no
one. 16 "For who has known the mind of the Lord so as to instruct him?" But we have the mind of Christ.

Spirit. Jas. 3:15 and Jude 19 show the continued use of the term "soulish" within the church in a decidedly derogatory sense. Normally Paul uses the word **mind** in the neutral sense of our actual faculties which may be devoted either to good or to evil. In Rom. 7:23-25 he contrasts "the law of my mind" with "the law of sin . . . in my members." But in Rom. 1:28 and Col. 2:18, "mind" is connected with radical evil.

How did Paul come to distinguish so sharply between the "soulish" person and the "spiritual"? No such contrast is to be found in Greek philosophy. Appeal has been made to the Hellenistic mysteries and the later Gnostics, where the divine Spirit replaces the human soul. But no evidence has been adduced from texts before the time of Paul to support this hypothesis. The apostle looked upon the Spirit as an added factor. Though he thought that believers had received a truly supernatural endowment, he did not hold that they had been lifted above the possibility of human sin. Individual verses must always be interpreted in the light of Paul's whole thought and on this point he is abundantly clear.

The things of the Spirit (KJV) may be interpreted as the **gifts** (RSV) which are to be discussed in chs. 12–14. Without possessing the Spirit, a man is not in position to understand the Spirit's gifts or to evaluate them. The verb translated **discerned** in vs. 14 and **judges** in vs. 15 is ἀνακρίνω. It means to examine or investigate. Paul does not really mean to lift the spiritual man above the possibility of all judgment at the hands of his fellows. Every page of this letter calls for evaluation by the members of the church of the conduct of one another and for mutual helpfulness. What Paul would exclude is a judgment from wrong premises, as he states again in 4:1-4. When the standard is false, the judgment will be untrue. But if **the spiritual man judges all things** (or all persons?) Paul must think of believers as judging one another. The words **no one** would therefore refer to those who do not possess the endowment for understanding the **gifts of the Spirit.** Paul quotes Isa. 40:13 again in Rom. 11:34. There it is to confess that even he does not understand the mysteries of God. Here it leads to the assurance that the secret wisdom has been made known to those who possess Christ, the Spirit.

---

gave an assurance such as had never before fallen from human lips, "I go to prepare a place for you . . . that where I am, there ye may be also" (John 14:2-3). And again, "So you have sorrow now, but I will see you again and your hearts will rejoice, and no one will take your joy from you" (John 16:22). That goal lies beyond our vision in the realm of the unseen, but here and now we have sufficient tokens to assure us that it is splendid beyond our highest imaginings, and it is the portion of all in whose hearts there flickers a flame of love to God. On the word of the Master, attested by the apostle who entered most deeply into the Master's mind and spirit, we may rest assured. In this letter a great pastor, whose magnificent mind is impassioned by the Christian world view, gives his readers every incentive to abandon themselves to one who came to be their life and joy and peace. Hold fast to faith! Let nothing diminish the flame in our hearts. God's response will outdistance our sublimest imaginings.

Paul concludes his important and significant digression by insisting on the thought that such spiritual things can only be spiritually discerned (see Exeg.). **The unspiritual man does not receive the gifts of the Spirit of God, for they are folly to him, and he is not able to understand them because they are spiritually discerned.** Paul, the disciplined disciple of Christ, and his apostle, speaks with authority here. He has fulfilled the conditions and can end his rhapsody on the note of a great claim. **We have the mind of Christ,** i.e., "Our thoughts are Christ's thoughts" (Moffatt). (But see Exeg.)

3 And I, brethren, could not speak unto you as unto spiritual, but as unto carnal, *even* as unto babes in Christ.

2 I have fed you with milk, and not with meat: for hitherto ye were not able *to bear it,* neither yet now are ye able.

3 But I, brethren, could not address you as spiritual men, but as men of the flesh, as babes in Christ. 2 I fed you with milk, not solid food; for you were not ready for

c) Factions Reveal the Absence of the Spirit (3:1-4)

3:1-4. Paul now comes to the application, and to his own self-defense. Superficially viewed, the passage seems to involve Paul in self-contradiction. He is writing to baptized Christians who received the Spirit through faith and baptism. Yet he accuses them of not having the Spirit. They were not even controlled by "soul" but by **the flesh.** Since **carnal** (KJV) has not maintained general currency, the RSV uses **men of the flesh.** The key to this difficulty is to be found in Paul's chief contribution to the N.T. conception of the Spirit. All early Christians ascribed prophecy, tongues, and miracles to the work of the Spirit. But Paul gives an essentially moral interpretation. Since Christ is the Spirit, the fruits of the Spirit are the chief moral virtues (Gal. 5:22-23). Where those are absent, it must follow that the Spirit is nothing more than a latent possibility. We find this same antinomy in Rom. 8. It is affirmed in Rom. 8:9 that the readers are not in the flesh since the Spirit of God dwells in them. Yet in Rom. 8:12 they are exhorted not to live according to the flesh. Here at Corinth the jealousy and strife which had led to their party cries were marks of a life according to the flesh. The ethical result proves the absence of that by which Paul's wisdom could alone be received.

3:1-17. ***Failure of the Corinthian Community to Enter into the Fullness of This Spiritual Experience.***—Having led his readers to such heights, Paul now follows the example of his Master given to the disciples on the Mount of Transfiguration. Amazed and inspired by their wonderful experience, they wanted to remain there. But at its foot there were men and women in desperate need. To these, with all his helping, healing power, Jesus returned (Matt. 17:1-21). So Paul turns the attention of his readers from the contemplation of the heights to which they might have risen, to a consideration of their own condition and failure to do so. His analysis holds good for similar conditions to this very day.

He is well aware of the high demands involved in any adequate response to the call of Christ. He knows well that these demands, and the great standards they involve, are bound to create tension in the soul and in the Christian community itself. But the very essence of the new faith that has been preached to them is to hold men and women to the highest. In the end that manner of life alone leads to life's fullness and to complete all-round personality. Paul therefore turns again to a consideration of the failure of his converts in Corinth to approximate to this great goal.

There are two main reasons. They are worldly-minded **men of the flesh** (see Exeg.), and the proof of that charge is that there was a spirit of partisanship among them: they were lacking in the elementary moral qualities of consideration, mutual forbearance, sincerity, and above all, humility. **For while there is jealousy and strife among you, are you not of the flesh, and behaving like ordinary men?** The second reason for their failure is that they are spiritually immature: they have not grown up, and as Paul writes they are showing few signs of growth. **I, brethren, could not address you as spiritual men, but . . . as babes in Christ.** They were still unable to digest the more solid food of Christian faith and doctrine. **I fed you with milk, not solid food; for you were not ready for it; and even yet you are not ready, for you are still of the flesh.** In other words, they were still in the infant class, and were showing as yet few signs of progress. It seems that this distinction between "babes" and the more "mature" members of a community is a reminiscence of Paul's classroom days, for apparently in some at least of the Greek schools and academies such a distinction was drawn between the elementary and the more advanced pupils (see Exeg., vss. 1-4).

Their worldly, immature spirit is made obvious by their partisan divisions and wranglings, with all that these imply of lack of a real Christian fellowship of love and faith and service, qualities which are among the essential conditions of growth in spiritual insight into the wisdom of God. This partisanship which was

3 For ye are yet carnal: for whereas *there is* among you envying, and strife, and divisions, are ye not carnal, and walk as men?

4 For while one saith, I am of Paul; and another, I *am* of Apollos; are ye not carnal?

it; and even yet you are not ready, 3 for you
are still of the flesh. For while there is jealousy and strife among you, are you not of the flesh, and behaving like ordinary men?
4 For when one says, "I belong to Paul," and another, "I belong to A-pol'los," are you not merely men?

The immaturity of the converts leads him to use the figure of milk and meat, which the authors of Hebrews (5:12-14) and I Peter (2:2) are later to employ. Philo has a similar application in his tract *On Husbandry* 9: "Seeing that for babes milk is food, but for grown men wheaten bread, there must also be soul-nourishment, such as is milk-like suited to the time of childhood . . . and such as is adapted to grown men." In the present context Paul must mean by **milk,** "the word of the cross" and by **meat,** "the secret and hidden wisdom of God." The Corinthians are not yet ready for any higher teachings so long as their party strife continues. The RSV translates **ordinary men** in order to make clear that the alternative is not that they might have been divine. They were not acting as the sons of God, which they should have become through the Son. Later scribes could not understand why Paul should expect his readers to be other than "men." Hence they changed ἄνθρωποι to σαρκικοί. The KJV is translating that mistaken text with **carnal.** By the word **merely** the RSV attempts to bring out that Paul expects conduct which will reveal the fruit of the Spirit. There should be no place for the strife which is ordinarily found among men in whom the flesh has not been condemned through the power of Christ, the Spirit (Rom. 8:3 ff.).

---

the bane of Greek community life had invaded the church. It was destroying the vitality of the church, and the vigor and challenge of her witness. It was obliterating the vital distinction that should mark the Christian community and its fellowship in contrast with the pagan world. It was the very negation of the beating heart of the church, viz., Christian love. Paul will have much more to say about "love" later on. Meantime, like a great physician of the soul, he puts his finger on the diseased spots and makes the diagnosis clear. Diagnosis precedes the remedy. This is an important matter. Often enough since Paul's day the charge has been leveled against the church that there is not enough difference between those who are members and the average man-in-the-street with whom one can do business, whose character is trustworthy, but who makes no profession of faith and seldom attends church services. The Master requires that there should be a marked difference (Matt. 5:20). The apostle is here underlining his Master's words. The partisans had grouped themselves around the persons of Apollos and Peter and Paul, and perhaps some others. In Paul's view that was an obvious mark of the worldly-mindedness of the community. His references to Apollos are couched in the friendliest vein, but there is a strong suggestion that he has someone else in mind whom in courtesy he does not name, but who seems to be, at least in part, responsible for these regrettable divisions. When Paul is deeply moved, as more than one commentator has remarked, he is all the more inclined to refrain both from invective and personalities. Pity it is that the apostle's example in this respect and in similar circumstance was not more closely followed (4:18; 5:13; II Cor. 2:5; Gal. 5:10).

The further effect of such worldly partisanship is, as it were, to invert the pyramid of Christian faith and gospel teaching, and to balance it precariously on its apex. Paul, and doubtless Apollos and others, had ever been anxious that the messenger should be merged in the message, that the glory should go to God; that the vision of the living Christ should be unshadowed by the interposition of any of his agents, no matter how gifted or impressive either in speech or appearance or both. Partisanship tends to reverse that order, and the result can be only spiritual confusion and ineffective witness to the things of the faith.

Once in Lystra, following on the preaching of Paul and Barnabas, and on the healing of a crippled man, the people had wanted to pay the apostles divine honors, but they would have none of it. They were there as ministers of Christ, as his ambassadors, therefore as representative men, pointing away from themselves to him who was the source of their message (Acts 14:8-18). So is it with the situation in

5 Who then is Paul, and who *is* Apollos, but ministers by whom ye believed, even as the Lord gave to every man?

5 What then is A-pol′los? What is Paul? Servants through whom you believed, as the

4. The Apostles Are Not Rivals but Fellow Workers (3:5-23)

Paul's final argument is to the effect that the factions assume the basic error that the apostles are in competition with each other, when as a matter of fact they are co-workers. He begins with the figure of agriculture, shifts at the end of the first paragraph to the building trade, and that leads him to the specific thought of the church as the temple of God. The final paragraph catches up threads from the entire discussion.

a) Fellow Workers Together (3:5-9)

5. Here, as in 4:6, Paul selects Apollos as the example of the one with whom he stands in the right relationship. Possibly this would not have been equally true with Cephas. But what he wants to say is that *all* apostles are only servants of God. It is not *who* they are but *what* they are that matters. It is clear that διάκονος is not yet a technical term for the office of deacon.

Corinth as Paul sees it. **What then is Apollos? What is Paul? Servants through whom you believed, as the Lord assigned to each.** They are trustees of the gospel, and the essence of trusteeship is to be disinterested. It is the gospel that matters. The messenger may not be merely incidental: he is necessary. Yet no one must confuse the means with the end. "But just as we have been approved by God to be entrusted with the gospel, so we speak, not to please men, but to please God who tests our hearts" (I Thess. 2:4). Paul is quite clear that neither Apollos nor himself is to blame for the cliques that have been formed. They were perfectly content to be the instruments of God's purposes.

Surely this is a note that needs to be constantly reaffirmed with regard to the function of the church and the nature of the ministry. It has been said with a certain degree of truth that there are three classes of people in the world. By far the larger group are content to drift with the tide. It is likely that the majority of the people of the world do not know what they are aiming at. They have no clear-cut consciousness of any supreme end toward the attainment of which all their activities should be directed, and in terms of which they should be co-ordinated. The second and smaller group may be called travelers, for travelers do at least possess a certain sense of direction. They are making for a definite goal, and they have a definite purpose in view. It may not be a goal or purpose that will enable them to stretch and fulfill all the powers of their being. Life may even be organized, as it often is, around such ends as to work destructively for themselves and many others. History, individual and universal, provides many an illustration of this sobering truth. Such lives have direction, but they may be incomplete lives, and often "lost" lives. The third and smallest group may be described as the "representative men and women." They are the people who stand for something bigger than themselves. They stand for great causes, and in their lives they represent these causes. Jesus Christ, the greatest of all representative men, if he may be so described, was the incarnation of his truth. From the angle of the Christian faith this is the highest type of representativeness.

To that supreme issue in the life of the world, involving as it does a challenge to the social trends of the times, Christian preachers, pastors, teachers, and evangelists are called. In that representative service all members of the Christian church have a part, a part that can be played by no other. Wherever we are and wherever we go there ought to be that about us which will enable men and women to describe and explain us, as once they found the explanation of the new atmosphere and spirit that the apostles brought into the streets of Jerusalem, "Now when they saw the boldness of Peter and John, and perceived that they were uneducated, common men, they wondered; and they recognized that they had been with Jesus" (Acts 4:13). Something of that nature must have been in Paul's mind as he wrote his exhortation to the Corinthians bidding them to rid themselves of their unspiritual partisanship. It is a living message still to the church of Jesus Christ all over the world. It is the representative people, especially those who stand for the highest things, that are "the salt of the earth," and "the light of the world" (Matt. 5:13, 14).

5-9. *The Church as a Garden.*—Paul uses two vivid metaphors to emphasize his points and to underline a grave warning. The pictures

6 I have planted, Apollos watered; but God gave the increase.

7 So then neither is he that planteth any thing, neither he that watereth; but God that giveth the increase.

8 Now he that planteth and he that watereth are one: and every man shall receive his own reward according to his own labor.

9 For we are laborers together with God: ye are God's husbandry, *ye are* God's building.

10 According to the grace of God which is given unto me, as a wise master-builder, I have laid the foundation, and another

Lord assigned to each. **6** I planted, A-pol'los
watered, but God gave the growth. **7** So
neither he who plants nor he who waters
is anything, but only God who gives the
growth. **8** He who plants and he who
waters are equal, and each shall receive his
wages according to his labor. **9** For we are
fellow workmen for God[f]; you are God's
field, God's building.

10 According to the commission of God given to me, like a skilled master-builder

[f] Greek *God's fellow workers.*

6-8*a*. Paul had begun the work at Corinth. The use of the term "watering" in connection with Apollos does not mean that he had made no new converts; Paul is simply referring to the second stage in promoting growth. Yet human effort is never the real source of a spiritual result. As in Jesus' parables of growth (Mark 4:26-29), the emphasis lies not on what man has done in sowing, but on that which is outside his power and depends upon God alone. All man's labor would be in vain if God did not cause the seed to grow. It is not necessary to hold that Paul has the parable of the sower in mind (Mark 4:3-9). The planter and **he who waters** are not **one** (KJV) in the sense that they are identical, but in the sense that they have **equal** importance for the final result (RSV). Matthew interpreted the parable of the weeds as meaning that the field was the world (Matt. 13:38). Here it is the church. In Ezek. 36:9 the mountains are to be tilled and sown by God. Jer. 18:9 brings together the two figures of building and planting.

8*b*-9. Though Paul was very sure that all is of grace (Rom. 4:4), **reward** (KJV) or **wages** (RSV) occurs four times in this letter (see vs. 14; 9:17, 18). The word (μισθός) is most characteristic of Matthew, who uses it ten times. The last of these instances is in the parable of the workers in the vineyard (20:1-15), which seeks to make it clear that God is not a paymaster who rewards on the basis of the work done, but one who delights to give to all alike. In this chapter, Paul, the former Pharisee, seems to cling to distinctions of wages, as he also claims a residue of merit in ch. 9. But in neither place is there any thought of earning participation in the age to come.

b) Various Materials in the Temple of God (3:10-17)

10-11. A change of tone comes with the change of figure. The other man who is now building is not named. There was nothing wrong with Apollos' watering of the field, but

---

have life in them. He represents a Christian community as a garden that one preacher or evangelist may plant and another may water, but the true source of its beauty and vitality is God. There is little difference between the planter and the one who tends the garden; they will be rewarded according to their labor (see Exeg., vss. 8*b*-9); but God who employs them is the one who is ultimately responsible both for the garden and its usefulness and beauty. **I planted, Apollos watered, but God gave the growth.** Incidentally, had he drawn out his lovely metaphor a little further, Paul might have added, for doubtless he thought of it, and the thought is fruitful, that a garden would be a monotonous thing were it stocked with only one kind of flower. There is ample room in God's great purpose for every type of personality, and gift, and institution, and for many gardeners. But let it be one garden, planted by God, whose Spirit sustains its life. Perhaps the ecumenical church will one day fulfill that condition.

10-17. *The Church as a Building.*—Paul reinforces his contentions with another vivid metaphor, that of the church of Jesus Christ as a building in which all have a place. He seems to be particularly fond of this illustration, for he

buildeth thereon. But let every man take heed how he buildeth thereupon.

11 For other foundation can no man lay than that is laid, which is Jesus Christ.

12 Now if any man build upon this foundation gold, silver, precious stones, wood, hay, stubble;

I laid a foundation, and another man is
building upon it. Let each man take care
how he builds upon it. 11 For no other
foundation can any one lay than that
which is laid, which is Jesus Christ. 12 Now
if any one builds on the foundation with
gold, silver, precious stones, wood, hay,

---

clearly some defective materials are going into the building. God had commissioned Paul through the act of grace which had made him an apostle. He was **a skilled master-builder** who had laid the right foundation. There could be **no other foundation** for the church than **Jesus Christ.** Why did that need to be stressed to the Corinthian community? Could it be that the leader of the Cephas faction was claiming that Peter was the rock on which the church was built? (Matt. 16:18.) That is quite possible; it sounds as if Paul had such a tradition in mind and that he is strenuously resisting any such idea. Paul himself did not build on foundations laid by other men (Rom. 15:20). Yet he did not oppose that practice in others, as may be seen from his cordial words about Apollos. What aroused his ire was the *kind* of work which had been done. Just as he had opposed Cephas to his face (Gal. 2:11), he did not hesitate to oppose those who apparently claimed his authority at Corinth.

12-15. So long as one thinks of actual building materials, one will look upon the list given by Paul as absurd. Gold and silver ornaments might be used, but who would

---

uses it in a similar way in his Epistle to the Ephesians (2:20-22). His deep concern is that the building itself shall be sound and the materials able to pass the stringent test of judgment fire.

The passage begins after the apostle's high claim for the soundness of his own work, **According to the commission of God given to me, like a skilled master-builder I laid a foundation, and another man is building upon it.** Paul's sensitive conscience, inspired by his high sense of vocation, is satisfied with the gospel foundation which is laid. **For no other foundation can any one lay than that which is laid, which is Jesus Christ.** He is an architect who knows his job and who has done it thoroughly. All this reinforces what he has written before concerning "the word of the gospel," and there is no need for further exposition here. Christ is the great foundation reality of the world and of all life. That being so, no other foundation can be laid. But like a superlative craftsman and artist, the apostle is anxious concerning the type of work and material that those who have succeeded him have put into the building. There has been a friendly reference to Apollos. Now, without resentment, and recognizing that others must take their place and play their part in bringing the building to completion, he utters a grave warning. It is another example of the innate courtesy of the greathearted Christian gentleman that he does not name the person whose work he regards as having very doubtful value. Some have thought that this was an oblique reference to the partisans who had taken Peter as their hero (see Exeg., vss. 10-11); others have thought there are side references to the "Christ party" which Paul gently reproves by implication with the suggestion that all of them belong to Christ (vs. 23). Be that as it may, his emphasis falls on the really important point, the quality of the material that is being put into the edifice (see Exeg., vss. 12-15). That will be put to the test of fire. In so far as it consists of **gold, silver, precious stones,** it will pass the test: in so far as it is composed of **wood, hay, stubble,** the consequence will be utter destruction. There can be no doubt from the context that Paul is using these terms figuratively.

What is less sure is whether he is referring to an apocalyptic and imminent day of judgment,[8] or to the constant test to which spiritual things are put in the everyday life of the times (see Exeg., vss. 12-15). If some recollection of one of the great parables of the Master is in the mind of Paul as he pondered these matters and wrote these words, then the latter implication would also at least have been present to his thought (Matt. 7:24-29; Luke 6:46-49). Life and circumstance apply the judgment test that reveals the quality both of the foundations on which we build and the materials we use. None can escape it. To change the metaphor and to put it into the context of the Master's para-

[8] James Moffatt, *The First Epistle of Paul to the Corinthians* (New York: Harper & Bros., 1938; "The Moffatt New Testament Commentary"), p. 41.

13 Every man's work shall be made manifest: for the day shall declare it, because
it shall be revealed by fire; and the fire
shall try every man's work of what sort it is.
14 If any man's work abide which he
hath built thereupon, he shall receive a
reward.
15 If any man's work shall be burned,
he shall suffer loss: but he himself shall be
saved; yet so as by fire.

stubble — [13] each man's work will become
manifest; for the Day will disclose it, because it will be revealed with fire, and the
fire will test what sort of work each one has
done. [14] If the work which any man has
built on the foundation survives, he will
receive a reward. [15] If any man's work is
burned up, he will suffer loss, though he
himself will be saved, but only as through
fire.

---

put jewels into the structure of a building? (Cf. Rev. 21:18 ff.) Brick, stone, and mortar are not mentioned, and who would seriously think of using hay or stubble? Clearly the application which Paul intends to make has led to the elimination from the figure of all resemblance to real life. Paul has two contrasts in mind. The first is between the worthful and the unworthful, quite apart from whether the materials were ever used in actual buildings. The other is between the fireproof and the inflammable, because before his eyes was the Day of Judgment. Hence, **Day** is capitalized in the RSV (Mal. 4:1; II Thess. 1:10; Heb. 10:25). II Baruch 48:39 shows how it was envisaged: "Therefore a fire will consume their thoughts, and in flame will the meditations of their minds be tried." There are materials which will be unconsumed by the fire (I Pet. 1:7), and others that will be burned (Matt. 7:19). Here, however, the reference is to a testing, not of the converts, but of the work of the teachers. Salvation by grace does not exclude belief in a judgment, even on believers (II Cor. 5:10; Rom. 3:6). Though Paul feels certain of the overthrow of the wrong type of work, he does not hand over his opponent to destruction. This man

---

ble, we all have to face sooner or later the kind of weather that reveals the spiritual and moral foundations of our individual life. If the foundations and the material are good—and security against storm and stress were primary requisites for building in Eastern lands—then the building will stand the test. If not, ruin is the inevitable consequence.

Paul is quite clear in his mind that however and whenever the testing comes, it will come. Therefore let those teachers who have succeeded him in his mission to the Corinthians take heed that their teaching is sound, and that it conforms to the foundation already laid. It will surely be put to the trial: it will be judged. That is a good and sobering thought for all men engaged on any worth-while project to keep in mind. Christianity, as Paul understands and expounds it, is the whole of life, inspired and illumined by the Spirit and purpose of Jesus Christ. All service is his service if it is done in his name, in his spirit, and for his sake. Such a conception of daily work ennobles the task and also the man or woman who performs it. And each one in some way or other is therefore making some kind of contribution to the building up of the church, that world-wide community of Paul's great vision. Let us all take heed how we build. **Each man's work will become manifest; for the Day will disclose it, because it will be revealed with fire, and the fire will test what sort of work each one has done.** Such reflections may have a wider reference than those in the apostle's mind, for obviously he is thinking of the teachers who have succeeded him. One of the great dominant notes of Pauline teaching is the personal responsibility of each individual for his life, and beyond that, the fact that somehow, somewhere, sometime he will have to render his account to God. Milton's great lines, written in indignation against false shepherds and shoddy work, still ring like a tocsin in the ears of those who are disposed to listen.

Blind mouths! that scarce themselves know how to hold
A sheep-hook, or have learn'd aught else the least
That to the faithful herdsman's art belongs!

. . . .

The hungry sheep look up, and are not fed,
But, swoln with wind and the rank mist they draw,
Rot inwardly, and foul contagion spread:
Besides what the grim wolf, with privy paw,
Daily devours apace, and nothing said.
But that two-handed engine at the door
Stands ready to smite once, and smite no more.[1]

The apostle Paul and the poet John Milton, both of whom had a robust sense of man's

[1] "Lycidas,"

16 Know ye not that ye are the temple of God, and *that* the Spirit of God dwelleth in you?

17 If any man defile the temple of God, him shall God destroy; for the temple of God is holy, which *temple* ye are.

18 Let no man deceive himself. If any man among you seemeth to be wise in this world, let him become a fool, that he may be wise.

16 Do you not know that you are God's temple and that God's Spirit dwells in you? 17 If any one destroys God's temple, God will destroy him. For God's temple is holy, and that temple you are.

18 Let no one deceive himself. If any one among you thinks that he is wise in this age, let him become a fool that he may

---

will be saved by this purification. It is not strange that Roman Catholics should appeal to this verse in support of the idea of purgatory. We have already noted how Paul clings to the thought of a reward for the sound effort of the evangelist or teacher. An eschatological faith cannot escape it.

16-17. Thus far Paul has not described the exact character of the building erected on the foundation of Christ. Now the apostle introduces the further thought that it is nothing less than **God's temple** in which his **Spirit dwells.** In Jewish apocalyptic we find the belief that in the last times God would build a temple in which he could dwell (Enoch 91:13; etc.). This eschatological expectation was spiritualized by application to the community of believers (I Pet. 2:5). Therefore, teachers who were tearing down and dividing the church were committing sacrilege. In this figure there is another indication of the oneness of the church. Paul's thought is reached in three steps: God's temple is holy; you are that temple; therefore you must be holy. This prepares the way for the discussion in ch. 5 of moral degradation within the church.

c) All Things Belong to Them (3:18-23)

18-20. It is not at all clear why Paul should suddenly revert to his attack on wisdom (1:20-25). Could it be that the dangerous individual who threatened to destroy God's temple was the local leader of the Apollos faction after all? Once more the readers are

---

moral and spiritual responsibility in the sight of God, had it been possible for them to meet, would have understood one another perfectly.

A further point of interest and value is Paul's belief that it is possible for a teacher of good or exemplary character to be guilty of poor workmanship. The latter will be destroyed, but the teacher will be saved despite the destruction of his work. Grace is here operative. Yet let it be remembered that the achievement of moral quality is bound up with good workmanship. Poor workmanship is often enough an index of defective moral quality. Here as elsewhere the good workman will prepare himself before he starts on his task. Paul is also enough of the Jew, bred in the old tradition of belief that God assigns rewards and punishments for tasks achieved or left undone, to state his belief that though everything is due to the grace of God, yet the good workman will receive due reward. **If the work which any man has built on the foundation survives, he will receive a reward.** It were better left on the higher plane on which the great apostle himself abides, despite these relics of earlier belief, to put in the best work on the great foundation which is Jesus Christ, and find in the resulting satisfaction all the reward that is necessary.

> I gave My life for thee:
> What hast thou given for Me? [2]

The section ends on another series of somber warnings. The church, i.e., the community of Christian believers in Corinth, is God's chosen temple; it is sanctified by the indwelling of his Holy Spirit, and it must be treated as such. Nothing impure or profane must be allowed to violate its sacredness. The spirit of worship, of service, of fellowship and humility must be manifest in its very atmosphere. Just as desecration of a pagan temple in those far-off days carried the heaviest penalties, so will God wreck the man who wrecks his chosen dwelling place. **Do you not know that you are God's temple and that God's Spirit dwells in you? If any one destroys God's temple, God will destroy him. For God's temple is holy, and that**

[2] Frances Ridley Havergal, "I Did This for Thee: What Hast Thou Done for Me?"

19 For the wisdom of this world is foolishness with God: for it is written, He taketh the wise in their own craftiness.
20 And again, The Lord knoweth the thoughts of the wise, that they are vain.
21 Therefore let no man glory in men: for all things are yours;

become wise.
19 For the wisdom of this world is folly with God. For it is written, "He catches the wise in their craftiness,"
20 and again, "The Lord knows that the thoughts of the wise are futile."
21 So let no one boast of men. For all things are

---

reminded of the contrast between the wisdom of men and the foolishness of God. It is Paul's formulation of the paradox that a man must lose his life in order to gain it (Mark 8:35; Matt. 10:39; Luke 17:33). Paul is now addressing the community as a whole rather than specific teachers. They must not be deceived about the way to attain the real wisdom. It is through belief in "the word of the cross." Again we marvel at Paul's ability to reinforce his words with O.T. quotations. In both citations the wicked are oppressing the poor. Ps. 94:11 actually reads "man" instead of "wise." Even apostles could have slips of memory in quoting scripture.

21-22*a*. The Corinthians had been affirming their allegiance to men. This should be reversed. The teachers belonged to them, not they to the teachers. Hence, there was no need to confine themselves to only one. The community should profit from what all had to give. If Paul could have looked down the ages, how he would have extended that list and condemned those who said, "I belong to Luther," or to Calvin, or to Wesley, or to

---

temple you are. Could any appeal for reverence and dignity and a sense of "the holy" in its numinous aspects be more highly pitched? There is nothing men need more than a deeper, stimulating awareness of the greater, more important, much more significant unseen environment in the midst of which all earthly activities and hopes are placed. We need to recover in daily life a sense of the immutable majesty and unfailing providence of God before whose face the generations rise and pass away. Life will be great again as a sense of the sacred infuses all human activities in every field. It is the function of the church, the community of believers, to keep alive and intense in the midst of the world this very element in the essential nature of things. Paul, with all his Jewish sense and tradition of the fitness of things that pertain to the worship of God, in its individual as well as its cosmic setting, is zealous that the church of Christ should maintain the tradition. God's dwelling is sacred: let nothing be done that encroaches upon its essential atmosphere of consecration to him and his holy purposes.

There are two final words. He returns to his general subject and condenses in a few sentences (vss. 18-20) all that he has said about the conceit and pride and arrogance of human wisdom as set against the wisdom of God, and he underlines once more his plea for the humility of the teachable spirit. With his accustomed courtesy and personal humility he associates Apollos and Peter as instruments that had been used of God for the spiritual welfare of the Christian community in Corinth. It is a final plea not to set the instruments in disproportionate relationship to the cause they were sent to serve. "So let no one boast of men" (vs. 21). Then, as so often happens, there is a swift transition of mood, and Paul embarks on one of his great soaring flights of inspired thought and imagination, in which he sees "all things" as being within the gift of God's loving providence to those who by faith in Christ belong to him. There is a legitimate sense of pride, but it is the pride that acknowledges Christ as Lord, and that lays itself at his feet.

21-23. *Paul's Rhapsody.*—From this height of rapture Paul must almost have lost sight of the painful, heartbreaking circumstances in the Corinthian church which first compelled him to put his pen to paper. How much more would he rather have written entirely in this vein. These words indicate the heights and the riches that the gospel of Christ has made available for them and for all mankind. What an inspiring and delivering word it would have been! One can detect the note of impatience in Paul's epistle, as for these few inspired and enraptured moments he swings away from the pettiness of the partisan-riven church of Corinth to contemplation of the heights and depths of the all-inclusive grace of the God revealed in Christ. Maybe the apostle has suddenly recollected a fragment of Stoic philosophy, "All things belong to the truly wise," and seizing upon it he transforms it by putting it into a Christian setting.

22 Whether Paul, or Apollos, or Cephas, or the world, or life, or death, or things present, or things to come; all are yours;
23 And ye are Christ's; and Christ *is* God's.

yours, 22 whether Paul or A-pol'los or Ce'-
phas or the world or life or death or the present or the future, all are yours; 23 and
you are Christ's; and Christ is God's.

Campbell, or to some other great servant of Christ's church. **All . . . are yours.** But Paul did not include any outside the apostolic group, such as Socrates, Plato, Aristotle, or Posidonius. Was that an oversight, or was it intentional? Is that evidence of Paul's ignorance, his narrowness, or of the concentration which Christians at all times should show?

22*b*. Paul passes on from *men* to *things* and *events.* They too are to be taken up into the divine service. The passage has a close resemblance to Rom. 8:38—only there he adds the angelic powers to the servants named here. In Romans, Paul is persuaded that nothing can separate his readers from the love of God. Here, Paul is exhorting them to exercise their rightful lordship over all things. The **world** is referred to, as so often in John, as an enemy power. Life may serve for their sanctification, and death need only be an interlude before the resurrection. All time can serve the purposes of God.

23. All things belong to them, but they do not belong to all these. The teachers are all servants, not masters. The believer knows only one master, Christ. Life should have a

What a tremendous assertion to make. Yet we must seek to understand it if we are to understand the pastoral urgency that is so obvious in his epistle. Is Paul swept off his feet by his emotions as he makes this comprehensive claim? Is he laying too great a burden on our capacity for faith? No! Christian faith for Paul is never qualified. Faith in Christ for him is a maximum faith. He would have agreed with the Scottish philosopher, David Hume, that a limited God has little real value either for philosophy or for religion. Thus he is fond of that inclusive word "all." He will have no carefully qualified assent to the gospel message. He is, as modern psychologists would say, "a man whose reactions are either 'all' or 'none.'" He is the supreme exemplar of splendid believing.

All the marvel and manifold wonder of the world and all its beauty are ours if we have eyes to see and hearts to appreciate them. These are part of God's gift in Jesus Christ to every one of us. The whole of nature becomes to the Christian man a great sacrament that speaks of God, and as we enter more and more deeply into the Master's mind and spirit we share his outlook and catch his gift of looking up. Have more beautiful words ever been written than these: "Consider the lilies of the field, how they grow; they neither toil nor spin; yet I tell you, even Solomon in all his glory was not arrayed like one of these" (Matt. 6:28-29)?

And life's sweet relationships and experiences are also ours in and through Christ. Love of dear ones, tender and precious memories, joys that are hallowed and sorrows that are sanctified by the indwelling Spirit of Jesus Christ are also within the gift of God's grace to those who are his. These and many another gem on life's necklace are ours if we have the spirit and outlook that can possess and turn them to account. Even its challenging experiences are ours; its anxieties, its pains, and its adversities. The great apostle includes every one. In a later epistle to these same people he makes this thought quite plain (II Cor. 6:1-10). This surely is part of what he means when he writes, "With all our affliction, I am overjoyed" (II Cor. 7:4). He was a man who had learned to wrest triumph from his troubles. Christ crucified had taught him that lesson. He is quite clear as to God's purpose for the entire world and for every man, woman, and child in it, and he is certain that every experience of life, no matter what it is, if met in the right spirit, will minister to that great goal. Duty can help us along that path; even the grooves of routine can be transformed into highways that lead to God if filled with the atmosphere of the Master's presence. Suffering can play its part. Christ was perfected by the things which he suffered (Heb. 2:10). Suffering has been the mother of sympathy, pity, compassion, and insight into the needs of others, and all these and many other associated qualities are among what some of the Christian mystics have called the "adornments of the spiritual marriage." Suffering so turned to account can be another great highway that leads us to God.

And—daringly Paul includes it—**death** is ours. A strange inclusion and a challenging thought. Yet this is part of the Christian message. Just as life's beginnings here are full of

4 Let a man so account of us, as of the ministers of Christ, and stewards of the mysteries of God.

2 Moreover it is required in stewards, that a man be found faithful.

4 This is how one should regard us, as servants of Christ and stewards of the mysteries of God. 2 Moreover it is required of stewards that they be found

---

focal loyalty; man's freedom lies in being a slave to Christ. But why should men belong to Christ? The hierarchy is not complete until we add the final term: **Christ is God's.** Paul does not recognize two Gods, but a strict subordination of the Anointed to the One who subjects all things to himself. With all the christocentric language in Paul—"I have been crucified with Christ" (Gal. 2:20) —his thought is ultimately theocentric. Christ has his central place only because it is through Christ that God has reconciled the world to himself (II Cor. 5:19) . Christ is central because he is our way back to God.

C. Concluding Considerations (4:1-21)

1. The Real Measure of Judgment (4:1-5)

4:1-2. Paul has completed his formal criticism of the parties at Corinth. He turns to the responsibilities of the teachers. They are servants of Christ, not subject to the whims of the community. (The word Paul uses here for servant [ὑπηρέτης] is found nowhere else in his letters.) They are **stewards of the mysteries of God** (cf. I Pet. 4:10) , not teachers of the doctrines which men might choose. "Steward" (οἰκονόμος) is a term relatively infrequent in the N.T. outside of Luke 16. He was the manager or administrator of an estate. Faithfulness is the first requirement in a steward for he deals with what belongs to another. The **mysteries** (cf. Matt. 13:11) which Paul was proclaiming were not to be adjusted to the desires of his hearers, for they were not his own. Though the

---

God—how else can we interpret and understand the miracle of birth and life?—so death can be full of God. For Paul and for those who have learned to interpret life in the light of Christ, death is but the forging of the last link in the chain that unites the frail, tossing bark of life to the anchor that is cast within the veil. It is the last rung of the ladder that stretches from earth to heaven for the Christian believer. It is by the grace of God the last sunset on earth of some perfect day for a saint called to the Father's home. W. E. Henley seems to have painted the Christian picture of death in these lovely lines:

> So be my passing!
> My task accomplished and the long day done,
> My wages taken, and in my heart
> Some late lark singing,
> Let me be gathered to the quiet west.
> The sundown splendid and serene,
> Death.[3]

In Christ, writes Paul, death is ours; and then the door opens upon vistas not yet conceived; because, as he has already written, the heart of man cannot conceive them. **All . . . are yours,** but only if we are Christ's for **Christ is God's.**

[3] "Margaritae Sorori," from *Poems,* by W. E. Henley. By permission of the author's representative and Macmillan & Co., publishers.

4:1-21. ***A Plea for Trust and Respect.***—Apostles are servants and stewards of a sacred trust. Now Paul returns to the point raised in the previous chapter, viz., the position of the apostles with regard to the churches, and the respect and trust that are due to them. **This is how one should regard us, as servants of Christ and stewards of the mysteries of God.** He is far from implying that there is any comparison between the gospel with which such stewards are entrusted and the mystery cults that were rife in the empire at that time.[4] All that he is trying to make clear is that his friends and himself seek only to be faithful and disinterested trustees. This is a sensitive point with Paul. We shall see immediately how he had been hurt and stung by irresponsible criticism, although indeed, like the genuine steward and trustee he is, his deeper concern is for the spiritual well-being of the members of the church. Even so is that distinctive quality of true trusteeship, viz., faithfulness, made plain. So also is the note of objectivity clearly sounded. These are the twin marks of all genuine trustees or stewards, especially those who like Paul have been entrusted with the glorious gospel of the blessed God (II Tim. 1:11-12). The greatest teachers understand these things.

[4] T. R. Glover, *The Conflict of Religions in the Early Roman Empire* (London: Methuen & Co., 1919).

3 But with me it is a very small thing that I should be judged of you, or of man's judgment: yea, I judge not mine own self.
4 For I know nothing by myself; yet am I not hereby justified: but he that judgeth me is the Lord.
5 Therefore judge nothing before the time, until the Lord come, who both will bring to light the hidden things of darkness, and will make manifest the counsels of the hearts: and then shall every man have praise of God.

trustworthy. 3 But with me it is a very small thing that I should be judged by you or by any human court. I do not even judge myself. 4 I am not aware of anything against myself, but I am not thereby acquitted. It is the Lord who judges me. 5 Therefore do not pronounce judgment before the time, before the Lord comes, who will bring to light the things now hidden in darkness and will disclose the purposes of the heart. Then every man will receive his commendation from God.

earliest MS, the Chester Beatty papyrus (p^{46}), supports the reading of an imperative verb in vs. 2, the usual text, followed in both the KJV and the RSV, is preferable.

3-5. Standing under this divine responsibility, Paul is quite unmoved by the opinions which the church may hold about him. Throughout vss. 3-4 the word translated **judge** is ἀνακρίνω. This covers the judicial activity of investigation and the weighing of evidence. In order to indicate Paul's shift to the simple verb κρίνω, which means "to come to a verdict," the RSV uses **pronounce judgment.** Paul's words agree with the injunction of Jesus in Matt. 7:1, "Judge not, that you be not judged." Neither teacher would have men be without opinions; but both warn that the final judgment is in the hands of God. Literally, Paul speaks of a "human day" in vs. 3. Since the contrast is with the Day of Judgment when the Lord comes, it is clearer to call it a **human court** (RSV). We are not to conclude that Paul never had any consciousness of wrongdoing, though he does show throughout the letter a supreme self-confidence that his judgment corresponds to the will of God. All he means to assert is that a clear conscience is not enough for anyone. Inner satisfaction does not prove that a person is righteous. Acquittal is in the hands of the Lord at the time (II Cor. 10:18) when all motives and all circumstances are brought into

As Plato puts it again and again in his dialogues, notably in *The Republic,* the essence of any trade or profession is that the artisan or professional man should seek to give the best service he can render. A good shoemaker is one whose interest it is to make good shoes, and a good shepherd is one whose chief interest is the welfare of his flock. Perhaps such ideas are in the apostle's mind as he emphasizes the thought that Peter and Apollos and himself have no other wish than to be humble and faithful servants of Jesus Christ, making known the riches of his gospel of grace to all mankind. As such, proudly, and with a hint of disdain for captious critics in Corinth, he writes that he and his friends are indifferent to both the praise and the blame of men. They are perfectly aware of their responsibility to men as trustees of the gospel (vs. 2), for they also know that they are accountable to God (vss. 3-5). Meantime, they will do that which is right in quiet disregard of the state of public opinion. In any case, all of these matters will be made clear and open by God himself. It is the part of apostles to be faithful in delivering the message: it is the part of their hearers to remember that there is a responsibility in hearing as well as in preaching. When secret things are made plain, the motives of the human heart will be revealed by God (vs. 5).

Here, as so often in the apostle's writings, these guiding principles are valid for all personal relationships if the moral standards of society are to be maintained on a high level. In respect to our social status as "members one of another" we are all in the position of trustees and stewards. There is some service we can render according to such talents or capacities as we may possess, or according to such opportunities as may come our way. Let us offer such service as worthy to be done for its own sake and in the best interest of our fellows, as we are able to form right judgments concerning their interest. We can sound the notes of faithfulness and objectivity. Let captains of commerce and industry consecrate their gifts, not to their own personal gain as their supreme motive, but to the well-being of their fellow men. Let those who serve at the bench or on the land or the sea or in the air perform their service as being worthy of their best efforts for the commonweal. The moral con-

6 And these things, brethren, I have in a figure transferred to myself and *to* Apollos for your sakes; that ye might learn in us not to think *of men* above that which is written, that no one of you be puffed up for one against another.

7 For who maketh thee to differ *from another?* and what hast thou that thou didst not receive? now if thou didst receive *it,* why dost thou glory, as if thou hadst not received *it?*

6 I have applied all this to myself and A-pol'los for your benefit, brethren, that you may learn by us to live according to scripture, that none of you may be puffed up in favor of one against another. 7 For who sees anything different in you? What have you that you did not receive? If then you received it, why do you boast as if it were not a gift?

---

the light. **Acquitted** (RSV) is preferable to **justified** (KJV) as the translation of δικαιόω in a context so definitely legal. Paul can speak of justification as having already taken place, or as still to come at the end. Here, in contrast to Rom. 8:30, he does not hold that the experience of justification at conversion assures acquittal at the Last Judgment. The course of action between will determine. Then the secret things will be made known (Luke 8:17) when God will judge men through Christ Jesus (Rom. 2:16). If every man is to receive some **commendation,** judgment will mean more than a simple division of the sheep from the goats (Matt. 25:31-46). There would appear to be some reward for all.

2. The Lowliness of the Apostles (4:6-13)

6-7. Once more Paul selects the relationship between himself and Apollos as the one by which the Corinthians should be guided. **All this** (RSV) refers to vss. 1-5 rather than back to 3:5-9. The conclusion of the section is that the readers should not be puffed up about *any* teacher. The intervening words, however, present a perplexing and probably insoluble problem. Moffatt simply leaves a blank here assuming some text corruption. Goodspeed renders, "to teach you the old lesson, 'Never go beyond the letter.'" The koine text, translated by the KJV, had an additional verb φρονεῖν, which was translated to **think;** and **of men** was added from the context. Literally, the critical text reads, "That you might learn in us not beyond what is written," with some verb obviously to be supplied. Does "what is written" refer to the letter which Paul is writing, to words of the Lord, or to the O.T.? Since the phrase is the usual formula for scripture, most modern commentators believe that this is what Paul is commending. There were Gnostics and spiritists at Corinth for whom the revelations which they themselves received took

---

sequences and the ensuing satisfaction will be found to outdistance by far any personal material advantages that might accrue as the consequence of less altruistic motives. Thus to live and to serve as Christian stewards and trustees, each in his private station, is to carry the spirit of Christian fellowship into life's common places, tasks, and duties, with redemptive power. Those who so live will also command the trust and respect of their fellow men and the approval of God. Elsewhere in a different connection Paul again emphasizes this thought of man's responsibility to his fellow men and in the sight of God (for a fuller discussion of the general implications of Paul's teaching see pp. 118-122).

6-21. ***Pauline Irony and Pathos.***—This section comprises one of the most celebrated passages of all the epistles of the N.T. (cf. Exeg., vss. 6-7). It is a revealing passage, a kind of window let into the great apostle's heart, and as we look through we can see what a capacity he possesses for deep feeling. Only persons who can be moved to great heights of love and tenderness can be stirred to such strong indignation. Paul's devotion to Jesus Christ is the measure, in a sense, of the fanaticism with which he once sought to destroy the Christian church. He is, to speak colloquially, "a great human" and a most lovable man who is revealed in this passage of his letter, which is notable as well for its literary style as for the emotions it reveals.

It begins wistfully enough, though the undertone of irony is obviously present, with a quiet reproach against the idea of special favorites among preachers and apostles. Such immature and childish preferences can provoke only strife

8 Now ye are full, now ye are rich, ye have reigned as kings without us: and I would to God ye did reign, that we also might reign with you.

9 For I think that God hath set forth us the apostles last, as it were appointed to death: for we are made a spectacle unto the world, and to angels, and to men.

10 We *are* fools for Christ's sake, but ye *are* wise in Christ; we *are* weak, but ye *are* strong; ye *are* honorable, but we *are* despised.

8 Already you are filled! Already you have become rich! Without us you have become kings! And would that you did reign, so that we might share the rule with
you! 9 For I think that God has exhibited us apostles as last of all, like men sentenced to death; because we have become a spectacle to the world, to angels and to men.
10 We are fools for Christ's sake, but you are wise in Christ. We are weak, but you are strong. You are held in honor, but we

---

precedence over the written word; hence the paraphrase of the RSV that they should **live according to scripture.** To those who were complacently assuming superiority Paul denies any distinction. A causative force should be assigned to the verb (διακρίνει), but it is more likely a matter of *giving* distinction to them rather than of seeing it in them (RSV). Even if they do possess gifts, these are bestowed by the Spirit. Therefore no ground for boasting can possibly exist for any individual. He can only be grateful for the gifts which he receives.

8-12*a*. Next Paul employs irony and sarcasm. The Corinthians were behaving as if they thought the kingdom of God had already fully come. They were acting as if they were already reigning with Christ (6:2; Luke 22:29-30; Rev. 20:4). They were mistaking the guarantee which the Spirit bestows for the plentitude of God's salvation. Believers had not yet received their bodies of glory. They were living in that narrow isthmus of time between the resurrection and the parousia of Christ. This was a period when suffering was the lot of true Christians (I Thess. 3:4). It had come to the apostles. Should their Corinthian converts experience so different a fortune? This passage belongs with II Cor. 4:7-10; 6:4-10; 11:23-27; and Rom. 8:35-37 as a catalogue of the sufferings of Paul. He does not write out of bitterness concerning these hardships, but to shame his readers.

Jesus had pronounced woes on the **rich** (cf. Luke 6:24). The blessings which he had promised were not to be fulfilled until the coming of the kingdom. John charged the church of Laodicea with being rich and filled (Rev. 3:17, 21). Kingdom phraseology does not appear frequently in Paul, but the term is found in the climax of this chapter, vs. 20 (see also 6:9-10; 15:24, 50; Gal. 5:21; I Thess. 2:12; II Thess. 1:5). It is with genuine

---

that will break the peace of the church to fragments and help to destroy the spirit of fellowship (vs. 6). In any case, Paul asks with growing indignation who conferred the right on any member of the church to indulge in this criticism which is stinging him into making his stern rebuke. Is it pride of knowledge or insight that has stimulated such to arrogate to themselves the position of critics and judges? Paul will have none of it. **For who sees anything different in you? What have you that you did not receive? If then you received it, why do you boast as if it were not a gift?** Had they any great attainments of their own, against which they might measure the comparative failure of their teachers, they might have the right to speak. But in the absence of such attainments the inference is that it were more fitting at least to keep silent. This passage, with all its implications, might well be studied by some modern critics of the church and its ministers.

Too much is said by irresponsible people about the so-called failure of the church. How do they know the church has failed, if it has failed? Where do such people get their standards? Have they devised or achieved such standards themselves, or are they judging the church by the standards of Christ in his church? If so, they are under the same searching condemnation and stimulus. The prayer of the publican is more likely to be heard in heaven than the self-asserted righteousness, and all it implies of the right to criticize others, of the Pharisee. With mounting indignation Paul sweeps such pretensions violently aside.

Now he begins to write in letters of flame as he draws a passionate contrast between the

11 Even unto this present hour we both hunger, and thirst, and are naked, and are buffeted, and have no certain dwelling place;

12 And labor, working with our own hands: being reviled, we bless; being persecuted, we suffer it:

13 Being defamed, we entreat: we are made as the filth of the world, *and are* the offscouring of all things unto this day.

in disrepute. [11] To the present hour we
hunger and thirst, we are ill-clad and buffeted and homeless, [12] and we labor, working with our own hands. When reviled, we
bless; when persecuted, we endure; [13] when
slandered, we try to conciliate; we have
become, and are now, as the refuse of the
world, the offscouring of all things.

---

poignancy that Paul expresses the wish that this were actually so and that the messianic rule had begun. A passage like this is sufficient refutation of those who minimize the eschatological element in Paul. Though believers were already "in Christ," salvation belonged to the future when he would come in glory. If the apostles are **last of all,** that does not mean that they are really "first" (Matt. 20:16). Paul is thinking either of the captives who bring up the rear of a triumphal procession and will be put to death, or of condemned criminals from the lowest class of society. The word for theater (θέατρον) is used by metonomy for the spectacle given there. Since Paul was a Roman citizen, he would not have been literally thrown into the arena. The apostle is thinking rather of the fury of mobs which he had had to face in the arena of the world. Instead of three groups of observers of the struggle (KJV), it is preferable to find only two (RSV); the **world** is composed both of **angels** (I Pet. 1:12) and of **men** (Heb. 10:33). Paul now reverts to the terms he had used in 1:26-29. He has taken his own injunction of 3:18 to "become a fool." The reference to the **weak** looks ahead to 9:22, where Paul will take his stand beside them. Vs. 11 probably refers primarily to the hardships of travel. Supporting himself by his trade as a tentmaker is viewed here not as in 9:15 but in a very different light (Acts 18:3; 20:34; I Thess. 2:9; II Thess. 3:8). His readers would readily accept this as a hardship, for Greek teachers did not work with their hands.

12*b*-13. The Christian spirit of nonretaliation is described in a beautiful series of antitheses. It is the ideal of Matt. 5:44 ff., Rom. 12:14 ff., and I Pet. 3:9. Not that Paul himself always lived up to it perfectly. He confronted some revilers whom he is not exactly blessing even in this letter. Though the verb παρακαλέω may mean **entreat** (KJV), it is also sometimes used in the sense of **conciliate** (RSV), and that certainly fits the context here. The final phrase of the paragraph may be nothing more than a repetition

---

comfortable, self-satisfied, and complacent Corinthians and the austere, sometimes hard conditions endured by the apostles, and particularly by himself. He lashes his opponents and critics with scorn as he reminds them of the cost to those who had brought them the message of Christ's redeeming grace. He spares them nothing. **Without us you have become kings! And would that you did reign, so that we might share the rule with you! For I think that God has exhibited us apostles as last of all, like men sentenced to death; because we have become a spectacle to the world, to angels and to men.** That is a picture taken from the gladiatorial shows in the Roman arenas, a device that Paul was fond of using to illustrate his points (15:30-32; cf. Exeg.). So the contrast runs on.

But he is not being sarcastic for the mere sake of relieving his feelings. He is contrasting the attitude and circumstances of the Corinthians with the lot of Apollos and himself that they might be moved to a different frame of mind. Is it too much to suggest that he really wants them to think of the Author of their salvation, who, as the writer to the Hebrews puts it, "for the joy that was set before him endured the cross, despising the shame" (Heb. 12:2)? It is the appeal of the Cross, as shared by the apostles who endured so much to bring to the Corinthians the happiness of deliverance from the old ways of life in a world that had grown weary, where only the grief, the worm, and the canker were left, into a great new order where the fruits of splendid living were a joy that had its source above, and a peace passing understanding which the world could neither give nor take away. It is the apostle's

14 I write not these things to shame
you, but as my beloved sons I warn *you.*
15 For though ye have ten thousand instructors in Christ, yet *have ye* not many
fathers: for in Christ Jesus I have begotten
you through the gospel.
16 Wherefore I beseech you, be ye followers of me.

14 I do not write this to make you
ashamed, but to admonish you as my beloved children. 15 For though you have
countless guides in Christ, you do not have
many fathers. For I became your father in
Christ Jesus through the gospel. 16 I urge

---

in extreme form of 1:28—that Paul has taken his place beside the dregs of society. But both of the Greek nouns (i.e., those rendered by RSV **refuse** and **offscouring**) are found in a very particular connection, which is illustrated by Prov. 21:18, where the LXX uses the first to translate the Hebrew word for "ransom." It had been the custom to remove the defilement of a city by a human sacrifice. Since this had to be a freewill offering, usually only those for whom life had become intolerable would offer. Those who believe that Paul is referring to this practice translate by "scapegoat." Since elsewhere (Phil. 2:17) he could apply the figure of sacrifice to himself, the possibility is not to be excluded here. Yet the apostle would never attach the same significance to his own hardships as to the sufferings of Christ.

3. Personal Appeal (4:14-21)

14-16. Despite the disavowal in his words, Paul is definitely trying to shame his readers, as he explicitly affirms elsewhere in the letter (6:5; 15:34). The Corinthians were his children because they were his converts (II Cor. 6:13; Philem. 10; in Gal. 4:19 the comparison is with a mother). In addition to their physical fathers, the converts had a spiritual father "in Christ." The figure is found very widely, and may be illustrated from the story of Rabbi Eleazar's visit to Rabbi Eliezer who lay on his sickbed: "You are more to Israel than a father or mother; they have significance for this world, but the master in this world and the world to come" (Quoted in Strack-Billerbeck, *Kommentar zum N.T. aus Talmud und Midrasch* [München: C. H. Beck, 1926], III, 341). Paul was not being very complimentary when he referred to the other teachers as **guides** (παιδαγωγοί). These were not **instructors** (KJV)—cf. Gal. 3:24, where "schoolmaster" is a quite erroneous translation—but attendants to whom small boys were entrusted in going back and forth to school. These παιδαγωγοί were often quite worthless slaves. They could be changed as

---

appeal to vicarious suffering. As we have seen, it possesses the greatest lifting power in the world: if that appeal fails, what other is likely to avail?

> Love so amazing, so divine,
> Demands my soul, my life, my all.[5]

There follows that swift transition of mood from invective and irony and indignation to tenderness, as the apostle pleads with the Corinthian Christians **as my beloved children.** The metaphor of spiritual fatherhood takes the place of the apostle who asserts his authority and divine commission. After all, it was through his preaching to them that they became converts to Christianity. He looks on them with the same tenderness and compassion and love that a father shows to his children, and he pleads with them to take their example from him, as he takes his own example from his beloved Lord. There lies the deeper aspect of the pastoral relationship. Paul is not only the great theologian of the early Christian church, and the great missionary consumed with desire for the redemption of the world, but the tender pastor on whose great heart there lies "the care of all the churches." Let them imitate children at least in one respect, where there is a true family relationship, and make their father the hero whose example is to be followed with pride and with love.

Finally, to make certain as to all these matters which have been dealt with, and others which are pending, Timothy, Paul's son in the faith, and one who fully understands the apostle's mind, has been sent to recall them to the original teaching, and to remind them of Paul's own example (see Exeg., vss. 17-20). Again Paul

[5] Isaac Watts, "When I survey the wondrous Cross."

17 For this cause have I sent unto you Timotheus, who is my beloved son, and faithful in the Lord, who shall bring you into remembrance of my ways which be in Christ, as I teach every where in every church.

18 Now some are puffed up, as though I would not come to you.

19 But I will come to you shortly, if the Lord will, and will know, not the speech of them which are puffed up, but the power.

20 For the kingdom of God *is* not in word, but in power.

21 What will ye? shall I come unto you with a rod, or in love, and *in* the spirit of meekness?

you, then, be imitators of me. 17 Therefore
I sent[e] to you Timothy, my beloved and
faithful child in the Lord, to remind you
of my ways in Christ, as I teach them
everywhere in every church. 18 Some are
arrogant, as though I were not coming to
you. 19 But I will come to you soon, if the
Lord wills, and I will find out not the talk
of these arrogant people but their power.
20 For the kingdom of God does not consist in talk but in power. 21 What do you
wish? Shall I come to you with a rod, or
with love in a spirit of gentleness?

[e] Or *am sending.*

---

often as one liked, but no one else could take a father's place. Children should take their father as an example (cf. 11:1; I Thess. 1:6; II Thess. 3:9; Gal. 4:12; Phil. 3:17). This ideal of imitation applied not only to the lowliness which Paul has described in 4:10-13, but to all of his "ways in Christ" (vs. 17).

17-20. The sending of Timothy was one more proof of Paul's fatherly love (16:10). Apparently he was not the bearer of the letter, and his arrival was not expected until after it had been read to the community. The Jewish idea of the two ways was early taken up into Christianity (Did. 1:1). Paul speaks of **my ways** just as he does of *my* gospel. But he was not the author of either. It was the way of Christ: *the Way* (Acts 9:2). The arrival of Paul's helper might raise in the minds of **some** of his opponents the question whether Timothy was a substitute for Paul himself. Out of a sense of inferiority did he fear to come? Paul assures them that he **will come,** and very **soon.** The reservation **if the Lord wills** is also found in Jas. 4:15 (cf. Rom. 1:10). It is not Jewish, but was a frequent pagan form of devout recognition of Providence. The arrogance of some in the community refers to vss. 8 ff. Words of reputed wisdom again are contrasted with the **power** of the Spirit (2:4). **The kingdom of God** is not used eschatologically as in vs. 8, but of the present rule, as in Col. 1:13; 4:11; Rom. 14:17.

21. After employing argument, irony, and loving appeal, Paul ends with a threat. He is coming—there will be no mistaking that. With the church itself lies the choice of what will take place at that time. He would like to come in a **spirit of gentleness,** but he

---

suggests plainly that he is aware of the names of those who are mainly responsible for all the trouble. He also knows of their arrogance and pride and has heard of their contemptuous references to him. Let them not presume too far. Paul's tenderness is the tenderness associated not with weakness or gentleness, but with strength. **Some are arrogant, as though I were not coming to you. . . . What do you wish? Shall I come to you with a rod, or with love in a spirit of gentleness?** That, too, is part of the apostolic and prophetic message and spirit.

There is a place for indignation and anger in the Christian witness in the world. Our Lord sometimes was constrained to use words that stung like the Roman lash (Luke 17:2; Mark 3:1-6). But we must note that his anger was never directed against those who had done him a personal wrong: it was ever unselfish anger. Especially was it directed against those who oppressed widows and little children. As has been said, his great gospel is compounded of love and of judgment. Love in isolation from judgment is ever in danger of degenerating into mere sentimentality; judgment isolated from love is in danger of forgetting mercy. In the gospel of Jesus Christ, and particularly in his own life, these two are perfectly blended. Here Paul is little concerned about himself. He is desperately concerned about the spirit and the well-being and the mission of the church he has founded. He will not tolerate any spirit or defect or blemish that threatens its life. His

5 It is reported commonly *that there is* fornication among you, and such fornication as is not so much as named among the Gentiles, that one should have his father's wife.

5 It is actually reported that there is immorality among you, and of a kind that is not found even among pagans; for a man

can apply the **rod** if necessary. This is not a shepherd's staff, but the schoolmaster's whip—and Paul did not believe in sparing the rod in the raising of his children. From the way in which II Corinthians looks back upon painful events, we must conclude that the choice actually fell upon the rod. The factions were, in fact, to go from bad to worse.

III. Moral Standards of the Christian Life (5:1–7:40)

The second main division of the letter deals with ethical problems—with sex and property relations. From the very beginning these have been two of the most difficult realms of life to Christianize. We do not know whether Paul learned of the derelictions within the community from the slaves of Chloe, or from the bearers of the letter from the church. The topic of sex problems is continued in ch. 7, when Paul takes up the questions which that letter raised, beginning with marriage.

A. Problems of Sex and Property (5:1–6:20)

1. The Case of Incest (5:1-5)

5:1. Paul begins with an expression of hot indignation at the moral depths to which he believes the community has fallen. The term ὅλως does not mean that it is **commonly**

very love for the church and for the Head of the church gives force to the indignation he reveals against those who are betraying and destroying the cause. There is need for Christian anger and indignation in the face of the crying social, political, economical, and religious evils of our times. Let it be inspired and kindled, as Paul's was, by our love, like his, for the person of Christ and his cause. Such anger is as safe as it is necessary. As someone has said: "Anger is one of the sinews of the soul; he who lacks it hath a maimed mind."

It would seem from references in II Corinthians that Paul's promised visit actually took place; that there were stormy scenes in which the apostle was insulted and vilified. Little wonder that his experience with the Corinthian church well-nigh broke his heart.

5:1-13. ***The Moral Background.***—This chapter is another window that opens upon the background to the Corinthian scene. By various accounts the moral reputation of Corinth did not stand very high. Wealthy people permitted themselves all kinds of licentiousness, while poor people languished in misery. Generally speaking, there was no very obvious relationship between religious belief and practice and the conduct of ordinary life. Religion tended to be divorced from ethics. In the main, the mystery cults did not require from their devotees any strict regard to a high level of ethical conduct. Doubtless there were, as we know from the writings of the great Greek thinkers of that era and even later, outstanding examples of exemplary character and life in the non-Christian community; but that was largely a matter for the individual to settle for himself. One could acquire a reputation for holiness without equating it with either chastity or morality. As it must have been virtually impossible for the members of the Christian community to avoid all contact with the pagan community, supposing that the desire to avoid it was present, and that is doubtful, we can understand how the pressure of such an environment on the individual Christian believers was likely to make itself felt.

Here lies one of the points of tension between the faith and worship and witness of the church and its pagan environment. From the very first Christianity was an ethical religion. Its ethics are rooted and grounded in its faith and worship. No one can read the Sermon on the Mount without realizing the very high ethical standards, with respect both to inner motive and to outward conduct, as set forth by Jesus to his disciples. And we know that their force is derived from the fact that they were the expression of his own spirit and manner of life. The apostle has already indicated his attitude on these ethical matters (3:16-17).

The roots of this close relationship between worship and morality, so far as Christianity is concerned, run deeply into the past. Paul is as

(KJV) reported, but that **actually** (RSV) they have fallen to this depth and the report of it has reached Paul. The term πορνεία means extramarital intercourse of any kind. The RSV avoids the use of **fornication** on the ground that it is a word not in common use today. **Named** (KJV) comes from the corrupt koine text. The situation to which Paul refers is that of a prominent member of the church who was living with his stepmother. Presumably this man's father was dead, for the relationship is not called adultery. Whether the woman is the man's only wife or this is a case of concubinage is not indicated. The ground for Paul's objection lies in the fact that this relationship violated pagan custom as well as Jewish law.

Marriage to a man's stepmother was forbidden in Lev. 18:8 and carried the death penalty (Lev. 21:11; see also Deut. 22:30; 27:20). This relationship was also forbidden by Roman law. Though Corinthian life did not stand directly under this jurisdiction, its influence would be strong. Presumably this man was a former pagan to whom Jewish law would not apply, and Paul does not claim that Christians were obligated to keep the law. Strack and Billerbeck have made an exhaustive analysis of the early Jewish traditions (Halakah) on the subject, as to whether a proselyte could marry his stepmother (*Kommentar zum N.T. aus Talmud und Midrasch,* III, 343-58). They have shown that there would have been no objection to this marriage on the part of the majority rabbinical opinion. Rabbi Akiba (A.D. 135) held the contrary opinion, though the final Talmudic decision did not sustain him. When a proselyte was received, he was looked upon as a newborn child. A previous marriage would not be taken into consideration. Since only the mother relationship was looked upon as certain among pagans, there would be no objection to a proselyte marrying a woman who had been the wife of his reputed father.

Paul, therefore, is vehemently contending for the point of view which was not finally maintained (in so far as it applied to non-Jews). It may be that the members of the church were aware of this difference of opinion when they supported their fellow member in his marriage. The situation shows that Paul's own sympathy was in the direction of a strict construction in sex regulations. It also provides another instance where the extent of Paul's rabbinical training comes into question. His knowledge of scripture and of Haggadic expansions is clear; it is not apparent that he had been trained in the application of preceptive regulations (Halakah). Paul deals with the question only from the standpoint of the man. Possibly the woman was not a Christian. In any case, it was the man's conduct which was determinative. There is nothing to indicate that Paul's warmth was induced by any personal antagonism—that this was the teacher destroying God's temple (3:16). Nor are we to connect this incident with the case of church discipline with which Paul deals in II Cor. 2:5-11; 7:12. That was a personal affront to Paul, probably during a visit which followed shortly after the writing of I Corinthians. Here Paul is simply defending what seems to him to be the correct moral standard for those who would live according to the Spirit.

---

much moved by his sense of Judaistic tradition as contained in the Law and the Prophets as by his sense of what is fitting in a Christian believer. For him the faith involves moral purity and strong, well-established sentiments of character. How otherwise could the Christian church be a purifying leaven in the life of the world? How otherwise could it fulfill its divine mission of deliverance and redemption and the establishment all over the world of the kingdom of God? By its complacency in overlooking the grave offense with which ch. 5 deals, the church in Corinth is imperiling its very life. We can begin to understand, then, the depth of Paul's shocked indignation and emotion, and also the violence of the action he insists must be taken with regard to the situation. Now let us turn to a more detailed exposition.

1-5. ***Gross Immorality.***—What has aroused and appalled the apostle is **a man . . . living with his father's wife** (see Exeg.). Despite the fact that Paul here contrasts the community unfavorably with pagans, such illicit sexual liaisons were not unknown in the Greco-Roman world, although they were generally reprobated by the better elements in society. The shocking thing is not only the sin itself, and all that it implies of a divorce between religion and morality to the detriment of both,

2 And ye are puffed up, and have not rather mourned, that he that hath done this deed might be taken away from among you.
3 For I verily, as absent in body, but present in spirit, have judged already, as though I were present, *concerning* him that hath so done this deed,

is living with his father's wife. 2 And you are arrogant! Ought you not rather to mourn? Let him who has done this be removed from among you.
3 For though absent in body I am present in spirit, and as if present, I have al-

---

2. But Paul was fully as much concerned about the community's attitude toward this man's conduct as about the sin itself. They were to be a holy community, set apart for God; though they may have been guilty of the grossest sins before being received into the church (6:9-11), such actions were to continue no longer. They should have bemoaned the existence of such conduct and have put out the evildoer. Instead of that, they were **arrogant**—a word (φυσιόω: lit., "to inflate") used in the N.T. only by Paul, always in a derogatory sense; of the seven instances, six occur in this one letter (4:6, 18, 19; 8:1; 13:4). Possibly Paul has been induced to take up this case here because of his allusions to the arrogance of the community at the close of the preceding chapter. There is difference of opinion concerning the proper punctuation of this sentence. The RSV recognizes that ἵνα may introduce a command as well as a final clause (as in KJV). Yet there is no doubt that Paul is calling for drastic action. What was this, and how was it to be determined?

3-5. It is easy to string together an English equivalent for Paul's Greek phrases; it is another thing to be sure of the connections which he really intended. Probably Paul expected that a meeting of the community should be held. Yet it is certain that he was not leaving to their judgment the character of the decision to be taken. In his apostolic authority Paul had already **pronounced judgment** on behalf of the community. When

---

but that the church in Corinth had complacently condoned the offense. There is no evidence of any sense of shame or grief or indignation among the other members of the church (see Exeg., vs. 2). As Paul writes, **And you are arrogant! Ought you not rather to mourn?** It may be that the church in Corinth, like others elsewhere,[6] was suffering from an outbreak of what has been called antinomianism, an ugly name for an ugly sin. The general idea was that professing Christians were exempt from the moral law. Everything, such people contended, depends not on any personal merit but on faith. This is, of course, as Paul's indignant phrases sufficiently indicate in his letters to the Corinthians, a perversion of his teaching. Jude also denounces this perverse attitude to the moral implications of the faith in no uncertain language; and James, who has written in scathing words, makes the Christian attitude quite clear, "What does it profit, my brethren, if a man says he has faith but has not works? Can his faith save him? . . . So faith by itself, if it has no works, is dead" (Jas. 2:14-17).

Perhaps the individual concerned was one of the more wealthy and influential members of the little community, and thus nothing was done to discipline him for his moral laxity. Paul will stop at no drastic measure to end this sorry state of affairs. As ever he is prompt and emphatic in his judgment. **Let him who has done this be removed from among you,** and again, **Drive out the wicked person from among you.**

3-5. ***Discipline.***—The community must purge itself by excommunicating the offender. Here Paul's very language emphasizes his sense of status as an apostle. He assumes that the church meeting has been called and that he himself is present in spirit; with a deep sense of authority and responsibility **in the name of the Lord Jesus** he passes a severe sentence of expulsion on the offender. So long as such a one is permitted to remain among them he imperils the life and witness of the church. The responsibility for his moral lapses cannot be confined to himself: they will bring the entire church into disrepute.

How often that has happened; and how quick the outside world is to condemn the entire community for the fault of one or a few of its members. Of course it is unjust. Of course no sensible or fair-minded person would apply such a test to any other profession. One

[6] James Moffatt, *The General Epistles* (London: Hodder & Stoughton, 1928; "The Moffatt New Testament Commentary"), pp. 216-17.

4 In the name of our Lord Jesus Christ, when ye are gathered together, and my spirit, with the power of our Lord Jesus Christ,

ready pronounced judgment 4 in the name of the Lord Jesus on the man who has done such a thing. When you are assembled, and my spirit is present, with the power

they meet in his physical absence (though he will be spiritually present), they are to ratify the decision which Paul is demanding. The authority of the Lord Jesus is mentioned twice; Paul claims it for his decision and also for the forthcoming meeting of the community (cf. Matt. 18:20). The **power of our Lord Jesus** is probably to be connected with both vss. 4-5. The assembly was held in his name and the verdict has his authority.

To deliver . . . to Satan has been understood by many to mean excommunication. By turning him out of the church they will put him in a sphere where the power of Satan is without limitation, and thus his sins will lead to his death. But since **deliver . . . to Satan for the destruction of the flesh** can only mean **death,** the emphasis lies on that conception (cf. I Tim. 1:20). Paul calls for the invoking of a curse that will bring about the man's death. Whether he thought of a result similar to that in the altercation between Peter and Ananias and Sapphira (Acts 5:5, 10) we cannot say. Paul is said to have invoked blindness on a Jewish magician at Paphos (Acts 13:11). There are many such cases of divine punishment reported in the apocryphal Acts. In Paul's letters we read that Satan caused sickness (II Cor. 12:7; I Thess. 2:18); he was the tempter (7:5) whose seat lay in the flesh, which would be destroyed by his activity. But Satan was powerless in relation to the higher faculty of man (πνεῦμα). The Day of the Lord would bring the resurrection, a new spiritual body, and the possibility of the man's salvation. Though that eventuality is held out, nothing is said about intercession now for the erring member of the community (cf. Jude 22-23; Jas. 5:16). It is natural to compare the disciplinary

might as well condemn a gardener and his roses because one rose is a poor specimen, or the medical or legal profession, or the Christian ministry, because one or two members of these professions have failed to measure up to the standards involved. But the church of Jesus Christ need not expect to receive justice from the world. All the more reason why anything that imperils its witness should meet with prompt and drastic treatment. The cause is a greater thing than the individual who is meant to propagate it.

This is the very spirit in which Paul deals with the situation. As such it is of value to us. There is no sense of personal animosity. Paul's magnanimity is seen again and again in his refusal to allow personal offenses against himself to weigh too heavily with him (cf. Exeg., vss. 3-5). He would be less than human if he were not to feel hurt and disappointed, but he is always ready to condone and to forgive (II Cor. 2:5-11). It is the sacredness of the church and its great mission that concern him. The new moral standards which have been revealed in Jesus Christ, and which in loyalty and love to him Christians ought to accept and manifest as their rule of life, must be safeguarded. Any offense against the community that exists to spread the leaven of these standards must be treated as a matter of the utmost gravity. We must realize that Paul is the inheritor of his own Jewish traditions in this matter. There are precedents in Hebrew history for the exclusion and punishment of those who committed offenses against the nation (Ezra 10:8). This individual has sinned against the good name and witness of the Christian community; at all costs he must be expelled.

Some may think that this is going too far. Is there no place in Paul's thought for the hidden motive which, if understood, might cast a flood of condoning light on the individual concerned and mark him as one who needs help rather than condemnation? What of the temptations that have been resisted? What of the fierce drive of heredity and the tremendous pressure of environment? Is there to be no evidence offered for the defense? Perhaps a Scottish poet will enter a caveat:

> Then gently scan your brother man,
> Still gentler sister woman;
> Tho' they may gang a kennin' wrang,
> To step aside is human.
> One point must still be greatly dark,
> The moving *why* they do it;
> And just as lamely can ye mark
> How far perhaps they rue it.
>
> Who made the heart, 'tis He alone
> Decidedly can try us;

5 To deliver such a one unto Satan for the destruction of the flesh, that the spirit may be saved in the day of the Lord Jesus.

of our Lord Jesus, 5 you are to deliver this man to Satan for the destruction of the flesh, that his spirit may be saved in the day of the Lord Jesus.[f]

[f] Other ancient authorities omit *Jesus*.

procedure here with that outlined in Matt. 18:15-17. We have no means of knowing whether groups or individuals had labored with the man urging him to desist from his sin. But if the man was legally married to his stepmother, could one ask that they be divorced in the light of what Paul has to say in 7:10-12? What form might his repentance have taken? In Matthew the penalty does not go beyond dropping the individual from the membership of the church.

Was Paul insisting upon a wise course of action? Would Jesus have done this, or would he have been more merciful toward the sinful? Is this the love which Paul is later to commend which "bears all things, . . . hopes all things"? We should remember that Paul felt a responsibility for the maintenance of the moral standards of a community which was constantly in danger of being infected by the sexual looseness of the surrounding pagan world. The incident should not be judged apart from the philosophy of the libertines, which Paul will discuss in 6:12-20. Here was an example of acting on the conviction that "all things are lawful for me" (6:12). Though we think of judgment as an exclusively divine prerogative, Paul reminds his readers in 6:2 that they are soon to sit in cosmic judgment. Finally, it is to be remembered that Paul's ultimate objective was to save the man. If it seems a strange method to us, we should reserve harsh criticism of the apostle in the absence of full knowledge of the circumstances.

He knows each chord, its various tone,
  Each spring, its various bias.
Then at the balance let's be mute,
  We never can adjust it;
What's done we partly may compute,
  But know not what's resisted.[7]

But Paul has not lost sight of the possible penitence of the sinner and his restoration to the fold. True enough, the apostle delivers the man to Satan for the destruction of his sensuous nature. That also had its precedents: Paul is the child of his times. With the story of Job and many another instance in his mind, he is of the generally accepted belief that supernatural evil powers are ever on the watch to tempt and to destroy the faithful, even as Job was tried and tested and tempted. How much more would they torment such as were cast out from the fellowship of the church. The consequences might take various forms, such as disease and suffering or even death (see Exeg.). Such ideas were current in those times and are not unknown in Greek mythology. They still exerted a powerful influence in Jewish minds (Luke 13:1-5). Paul and the community in Corinth shared these views. Therefore, invoking his authority as an apostle, and in the sacred name of the Lord Jesus he consigns the man to Satan, that through suffering his spirit may yet be saved in the Day of Judgment. The door is not slammed forever. Given a change of heart, restoration may come. Yet the discipline is essential. The great standards of Christian morality must be sustained. By all means let discipline in the first instance be persuasive in its method of dealing with those who have slipped. Let Christian fellowship and friendship and helpfulness go as far as they possibly can. Above all, let the Master's own method be followed, the method of vicarious suffering. There is no power of moral and spiritual uplift and regeneration equal to it. The cross of Jesus Christ is its supreme expression, the unveiling of the very heart of God. When persuasions fail, however, and men and women are still unmoved by the knowledge that their delinquency and foolishness are causing suffering to others, then they are perilously near to becoming lost souls. Such excommunicate themselves.

There must be a place in the life of the Christian community for spiritual discipline. The point of tension between the standards of Christ and those of the world, even at their best, must be maintained. Only so is spiritual progress possible. Yet let love and the power of vicarious suffering that goes with its deepest expression do their utmost before extreme measures are taken.

[7] Robert Burns, "Address to the Unco Guid, or the Rigidly Righteous."

6 Your glorying *is* not good. Know ye not that a little leaven leaveneth the whole lump?

7 Purge out therefore the old leaven, that ye may be a new lump, as ye are unleavened. For even Christ our passover is sacrificed for us:

6 Your boasting is not good. Do you not know that a little leaven ferments the whole
lump of dough? 7 Cleanse out the old leaven
that you may be fresh dough, as you really are unleavened. For Christ, our paschal

2. The Purity of the Community (5:6-8)

6-8. Here, as always, Paul is thinking of the effect on the whole community. He uses the analogy of yeast or **leaven** by way of illustration. Essentially the same proverb is employed in Gal. 5:9. The activity of yeast forms the basis for one of the parables of Jesus (Luke 13:21) ; it presents a striking contrast between a small beginning and a great ending (Jas. 3:3-5). Paul is not concerned with this incident alone but with the tremendous consequences which it may have for the ideals of the church. It is not the offending member but the laxity of the community which Paul compares with leaven. The figure leads him to draw conclusions for discipline from an allegorical interpretation of the O.T. (Gal. 4:30). The feast of Unleavened Bread was an agricultural festival celebrated during the seven days following Passover. The latter was a primitive nomadic festival, which originally had had no connection with the feast of Unleavened Bread. In Exod. 12:15 ff. we read the instructions for searching the house to remove every trace of leaven. The rules were greatly expanded in the traditions brought together in Pesahim (see Herbert Danby, *The Mishnah* [Oxford: Clarendon Press, 1933], pp. 136 ff.). No grain containing fermentation might be in the house during the festival.

Paul gives this cult requirement a moral application through an elaborate allegorization. **Leaven** is sin; the house is the church; the Christian life is the celebration of the festival (Mark 2:19) ; **unleavened bread** is the righteous living of converts. Conversion and the removal of sin are represented by the **fresh dough.** The Christ who demands this moral transformation and makes possible this renewal is himself the **paschal lamb** who was slain before the opening of the feast. Throughout the entire allegory the apostle mingles affirmation with exhortation. They *are* such a body, but on the other hand, they must *become* it. The contrast between the **old** and **new (fresh,** RSV) does not arise so much from the figure as from the language which Paul customarily used to contrast the former life of converts with that which should flow from the experience of redemption (Rom. 7:6; Col. 3:9 ff.). A somewhat similar allegorization of leaven is to be found in Philo (*On Mating with the Preliminary Studies,* 161 ff.). Plutarch used the comparison of leaven with evil. That it should come to Paul's mind at the time he dictated this letter was probably due to the nearness of the Jewish festival (16:8).

6-13. ***Ethical Implications of the Christian Faith.***—Two important matters are involved here. One is the insistence of the apostle on the ethical implications of the Christian faith. That, as we have seen, was one of the distinctive features of Christianity in general contrast with the pagan cults amid which it was set. There is a very real sense in which this insistence on moral probity and integrity of character was part of the offense of Christianity in the ancient world. Tolerant Rome would have left Christianity untroubled had the church been tolerant of pagan modes of life. But Christianity could never have survived on these terms. The words of the Master rang through the minds of the first Christian apostles and evangelists as they spread the faith abroad: "And if you salute only your brethren, what more are you doing than others? Do not even the Gentiles do the same? You, therefore, must be perfect, as your heavenly Father is perfect" (Matt. 5:47-48). Paul is determined that those who call themselves by the name of Christ shall mean something distinctive by it. Like their Master, they are in the world to set up a standard of moral judgment. It might be said that for Paul the highest compliment that could be paid to him, or to any others among the Christian brethren, would be to make the remark, "These people are followers of Christ." How otherwise could the kingdom spread? What other convincing reason could be given

8 Therefore let us keep the feast, not with old leaven, neither with the leaven of malice and wickedness; but with the unleavened *bread* of sincerity and truth.

9 I wrote unto you in an epistle not to company with fornicators:

lamb, has been sacrificed.
8 Let us, therefore, celebrate the festival, not with the old leaven, the leaven of malice and evil, but with the unleavened bread of sincerity and truth.
9 I wrote to you in my letter not to

The passage contains one of the comparatively few sacrificial allusions in Paul. The discrepancy between Mark and John regarding the date for the death of Jesus cannot be decided by this reference; yet, since the lamb was slain before the meal, it would lend some support to the Johannine assumption that the Last Supper was not a Passover, but that Jesus was slain at the hour when the lambs were being sacrificed in the temple. We should remember, however, that the Passover sacrifice had no connection with the forgiveness of sin. Paul assumes that his Gentile readers will be familiar with the Passover customs. We wish that we knew if the Jewish festivals were continued at this time in Paul's churches. At least the Paul of the Acts of the Apostles was a man who was not indifferent to their celebration (Acts 20:16).

3. Separation from the World (5:9-13)

9-13. This laxity of standards leads Paul to correct the Corinthians' misunderstanding of something he had written in a previous letter. It is not possible to identify the letter with the one he is now writing. It would almost appear as if the Corinthians had purposely misunderstood the meaning of Paul's injunction. When he had called for a separation of the church from the world, he did not expect to be taken so literally. Of course there were immoral people in the society about them, with whom they must have some contacts. There were family, economic, and fraternal ties which could not be completely severed.

---

for the establishment and the propagation of the faith?

9-13. ***Conscious and Unconscious Influence.***—Again it is clearly implied in the apostle's view that members of the church should represent the Christian conscience in their community. They are meant to be, in the great metaphors of Jesus, as "salt" and "light" in the life of the world. These suggest the importance of the conscious and unconscious moral and spiritual influence of good men and women. "Light" may be taken to represent the conscious influence of such people. It contrasts strongly with darkness: it is more obvious than "salt." But if the light becomes dimmed to the extent that it scarcely differs from darkness, then what value can it possess? Conscious influence in this respect calls for rectitude of life. There is always an unseen audience, like that in the jail in Philippi, which was listening to the songs of praise that rang through the midnight from the innermost dungeon where Paul and Silas were incarcerated (Acts 16:25), and unknown to ourselves members of that audience are watching us to see how we comport ourselves in the life and stress of our times. They want to know how we stand up to trouble and temptation, what books we read, what attitude we take toward different types of people, and what the general tenor of our spirit is as we meet the recurrent circumstances of daily life. Many take their cue from us. It is not unimportant in the life of the world as we know it, even as it was not unimportant in Paul's day, how ordinary Christian folk, members of the church of Jesus Christ, conduct themselves. Too easily can we yield to the temptation to think that one's personal influence and example count for little, that they will make little difference to the general trend of the life of our times. They may matter much more than we realize. Difficult as it may be to estimate the contribution of ordinary Christian folk to the life of our times, nonetheless, were it possible—and the indifferent person ought to be thankful it is not—to eliminate every Christian from the common life, the effect would be profound. The consequences might well be devastating.

More than we realize depends on the quiet, constant, consistent witness of the believer in the life of his times and in the circumstances in which he finds himself from day to day. On the other hand, one ill-considered word or deed may well annihilate the conscious influence of a lifetime. That particular tragedy has often happened. Paul's implied plea has a continuing validity for the consistency and purity of Christian witness right through the ages. If there is

10 Yet not altogether with the fornicators of this world, or with the covetous, or extortioners, or with idolaters; for then must ye needs go out of the world.

associate with immoral men; **10** not at all meaning the immoral of this world, or the greedy and robbers, or idolaters, since then you would need to go out of the world.

But **to eat with such** at the community meal and welcome those of notoriously immoral conduct in the church would mean that the church had sunk to the level of the world. Some of the more stringent passages in the canonical form of I Corinthians, and especially II Cor. 6:14–7:1, are frequently assigned to this earlier letter. Probably it dealt only with separation from those guilty of sexual sins. Paul now extends the prohibition to a wider vice catalogue.

anything questionable in the life of a professing member of a fellowship which is meant to be a standard of judgment and a conscience to the community in which it is set, let it be dealt with at once as a deadly menace.

Salt suggests another aspect of Christian witness which is also germane to this section, viz., the power of unconscious influence. None can separate himself from the personal influence of his life. Wherever we go we carry that influence with us. Our conscious influence is an intermittent and spasmodic thing at best, depending upon circumstance and time and place. But unconscious personal influence is continuous, and it exerts a telling effect on those with whom we come into contact. The one guarantee we can have as Christians that our personal influence shall constantly tell for the deepest things of our faith is that, like Paul, we should be indwelt and possessed by the Spirit of Christ. Such lives are as "salt" working unobtrusively but effectively in the life of the community. But as Jesus pointed out, "If salt has lost its taste, how can its saltness be restored? It is no longer good for anything except to be thrown out and trodden under foot by men" (Matt. 5:13). Such considerations in one form or another must have been in the mind of Paul as he dealt with this particular situation in the Corinthian church. Nothing can be permitted to diminish the vigor and power of its Christian witness. The life of the Christian community must be in conformity with the gospel, and the standard there is set by the Master himself.

Paul takes drastic action in expelling the offender because of the peril of his example and influence to the church. He is quite clear in his mind that it is essential because even one disloyal member of the community can bring the whole into disrepute. The life of a Christian community must remain unstained by any kind of compromise with evil or even with doubtful things. What shocked the apostle was the complacency with which the affair had been regarded by the church. He tells the members flatly that there is nothing praiseworthy about their self-confidence: **Your boasting is not good.** Then with a simple parable he drives home his point. A little leaven ferments the whole lump of dough. The inference is that if the leaven is impure, then the dough as a whole will suffer. Here is a principle that holds good in many fields (Eccl. 10:1). A small blemish will destroy a good man's influence. One false note will spoil, at least for the conductor and the more musically sensitive of his audience, the music that the orchestra plays. In the realm of spiritual things this process is intensified. The Christians must do their utmost to be "sincere," i.e., like the specification which old-time sculptors laid down for the marble they ordered, "without flaw"; and their personal integrity must be, as far as possible, unchallengeable. Paul knew that the one irrefutable argument for the reality and freedom and beauty of the Christian life lies less in doctrine and dogma, though obviously these are important, than in consistent Christian living. What holds for the individual is true for the community as a whole. Therefore, **cleanse out the old leaven that you may be fresh dough.** The reference to the Passover would strike a note familiar to Corinthians who were acquainted with Jewish ritual practices.

Then, like the needle of a magnet swinging to the pole, Paul's thought returns to Jesus Christ. These Corinthian Christians had been liberated by "the word of the cross"; by him who, like the Passover lamb, had been offered, though of his own volition, as a sacrifice that they might live. Through acceptance of him as Lord and Savior they had been brought into the great new order of life manifested by him. As he writes in a later letter to the same church, "Therefore, if any one is in Christ, he is a new creation; the old has passed away, behold, the new has come" (II Cor. 5:17). They have been brought into a new, happy, spirit-releasing and delivering knowledge of God; so the spirit of the Christian community, in the light of this generous, unstinted self-giving of God through Christ, should be one of happiness and rejoicing: all fear should be dispelled, and cer-

11 But now I have written unto you not to keep company, if any man that is called a brother be a fornicator, or covetous, or an idolater, or a railer, or a drunkard, or an extortioner; with such a one, no, not to eat.

11 But rather I wrote[f] to you not to associate with any one who bears the name of brother if he is guilty of immorality or greed, or is an idolater, reviler, drunkard, or robber — not even to eat with such a

[f] Or *now I write.*

The use of vice catalogues as a form of moral instruction came to Hellenistic Judaism from the popular philosophy. None is found in rabbinical literature, though they are common in Philo and in such works as the Wisdom of Solomon and IV Maccabees. Rom. 1:26-32 and Col. 3:5-10 afford typical examples in Paul which stress the sins of intention (cf. also Mark 7:22 and Did. 2:1; 5:2). But in this letter Paul is speaking of the *acts* of men with whom one should have no association in the church. The actual terms used are rarely employed elsewhere by Paul.

In all, six types are mentioned in vss. 10-11. All reappear again in 6:9-10, where four others are added. The word πόρνος—**fornicator** (KJV), **immoral** (RSV)—refers to sex offenders in the widest sense of the term. This is placed first in every list because looseness in sex standards presented the biggest peril. Paul does not speak here of the sin of covetousness but of the man who is **covetous.** The apostle had much less to say in

tainly the old shackles of bad habit and sin that had bound them should be cast aside forever. The new relationship is one that should bring not only moral and spiritual regeneration, but a new sensitiveness of moral obligation to God. Once again, their standard and guide is Jesus Christ, who exhibited so perfectly the relationship of complete communion and fellowship with his heavenly Father. In itself this sense of obligation is a condition of abiding joy. Clean living is a joyous, healthy, and natural way of life, natural in the sense that this is what God intended in his creation of us. There can be no real happiness found in pursuance of degenerate modes of life. One's capacity for assimilating new sensations can soon exhaust itself, leaving little but boredom and weariness in its train. As Moffatt puts it in his commentary on this epistle, "Only the clean life can enjoy the festival." Perhaps we shall have to return to the simple joys, to craftsmanship, and to a less sophisticated mode of life if laughter is to return to the human race. So may his church teach the world how to share its Master's joy. Nowhere is it made clearer than in the passage we have just been discussing that one of the great contributions of primitive Christianity to the life of its times, and to all subsequent ages, was the irrevocable union between this consciousness of God's redemptive power in Jesus Christ as experienced by the individual who accepts it, as well as the community that exists to proclaim and manifest it, and a deep sense of moral responsibility both to God and to man. In this connection, as in another relationship, what "God hath joined together let no man put asunder."

9-13. ***Paul Returns to the Special Case Under Review.***—Paul is aware of the pressure of the environment in which the Christian community is placed and in which it must live its life and make its witness. Contact with pagans, whose moral standards and habits are far lower than those prescribed for followers of Jesus Christ, can scarcely be avoided. In fact—as it would appear almost immediately, for Paul has to deal with the problems arising from the situation (ch. 7; see also Exeg. on 6:9)—some members of the church were married to pagan partners. What, as Christians, is to be their attitude to this union? Others were servants and slaves in pagan households and were aware of the vices of their masters and mistresses. Others again had their place in the public or business life of the great seaport and were constantly being invited to the homes of their acquaintances. Nice points of tact and etiquette and courtesy were involved. What is to be done: how ought they, who belong to the new order of life, to act with regard to such circumstances? These were among the questions put to Paul by the friends who brought him a report from the church; and the situation seems to have been general among the churches throughout Asia Minor and even farther afield (Rom. 14). Paul deals in the course of the epistle with the principle involved, and we shall take up these points in the relevant section. Here he recognizes the general situation and lays down one or two rules for the safeguarding of Christian morality. **I wrote to you in my letter not to associate with immoral men; not at all meaning the immoral of this world, or**

12 For what have I to do to judge them also that are without? do not ye judge them that are within?

13 But them that are without God judgeth. Therefore put away from among yourselves that wicked person.

one. 12 For what have I to do with judging outsiders? Is it not those inside the church whom you are to judge? 13 God judges those outside. Drive out the wicked person from among you.

condemnation of **greed** than Jesus, yet the sin appears in all his lists (cf. Rom. 1:29; Col. 3:5; I Thess. 4:6). The reason for stress at this point will appear in 6:5-8, where he alludes to his readers as defrauding each other. The **idolater** will be dealt with in ch. 10. Possibly Paul had in mind the use of charms or fetishes which should bring good luck, as much as the worship of images. **Reviler** may be induced from 4:12, and Paul may have in mind specific attacks upon himself. **Drunkard** anticipates Paul's criticism of the disorders at the Lord's table (11:21). Criticism of intemperance in the use of alcohol occurs infrequently in the ethical advices of the apostle (Rom. 13:13; I Thess. 5:7). It does not appear as a major temptation or sin. The word ἅρπαξ denotes a man who robs by violence; this is hardly understood today from the word **extortioner** (KJV); better, **robber** (RSV). No actual cases are referred to in the letter.

Outsiders is a term often used for nonbelievers (I Thess. 4:12; Col. 4:5; I Tim. 3:7; Mark 4:11). In this chapter Paul is thinking of self-discipline within the community. The fact that in the future believers will share in the judgment (6:2) does not empower them

the greedy and robbers, or idolaters, since then you would need to go out of the world.

But there is a point where one must have strength and courage of conviction and resolutely "draw the line." It may not always be possible to avoid contact with pagans; it is possible to avoid all association with any professing Christian whose mode of life is a reproach to everything the church should represent by way of clean living and high thinking in the general community. To give point to this direction Paul lists certain abuses of character and conduct and directs the church to ostracize those who exhibit such vices. He is quick to add that it is no part of his business as an apostle to pass judgment on those who are outside of the church. That is a matter for God. **Is it not those inside the church whom you are to judge? God judges those outside.** The situation is different with those who are inside the church, and who therefore have certain responsibilities with regard to its witness. That witness must at all costs, in a pagan community, be kept pure and clean and strong.

Some are immoral and sensual and greedy. Obviously Paul is aware that those whom he so brands do indeed associate with pagan cults. That is why he also names them as idolaters. So to indulge themselves is in his eyes a prostitution of the freedom that they have received through their faith in Jesus Christ. Again, there is more than a hint of antinomianism in this passage. Some are drunkards and others are thieves. All of this gives point to the earlier charge, "Your boasting is not good." What is there to be proud of in such a church? Still others have unbridled tongues and are "backbiters" or revilers of their fellow men. How can this pernicious vice be reconciled with the vital spirit of brotherly love which ought to be the characteristic mark of every Christian community? (See Exeg., vss. 10-11.)

There is a place in the Christian fellowship for well-informed, kindly, and constructive judgment and criticism. One who seeks to minister in the things of Christ is more likely to be helped and stimulated by kindly but candid critics than by benevolent friends. But such criticism is far removed from the rank abuse so strongly reprobated by the apostle. He knew what he was writing about because he had suffered from it, though it is characteristic enough that he makes no reference here to his own troubles. Once again, at all cost let the life of the fellowship be kept clean and sweet and wholesome and effective. There is no need, after all, for any member of the Christian fellowship to be associated with pagan cults. Elsewhere Paul, in writing of some who have done so, says, "For many, of whom I have often told you and now tell you even with tears, live as enemies of the cross of Christ" (Phil. 3:18). The highest ethical standards are constantly required of those who call themselves by the name of Christ in any and every age. Whatever is inconsistent with the spirit of Christian love is inconsistent with the Spirit of Christ. If those who offend against this vital principle are impervious to the remonstrances or pleadings of their Christian brethren, what

6 Dare any of you, having a matter against another, go to law before the unjust, and not before the saints?
2 Do ye not know that the saints shall judge the world? and if the world shall be judged by you, are ye unworthy to judge the smallest matters?

6 When one of you has a grievance against a brother, does he dare go to law before the unrighteous instead of the saints? 2 Do you not know that the saints will judge the world? And if the world is to be judged by you, are you incompetent

to begin now. Though Paul does not use any formula of citation, his words calling for the expulsion of unworthy members re-echo a constantly recurring refrain in Deuteronomy (17:7; 19:19; 22:21; 24:7). Judgment should begin within the church itself (I Pet. 4:17).

4. Legal Cases (6:1-8)

The relation of the church to those outside leads to a consideration of the jurisdiction of the courts. If Christians are not to judge outsiders, neither are outsiders to judge them. Part of the background for Paul's advice is found in the privileges which Jews possessed in the Roman Empire in applying their own law (see Jean Juster, *Les Juifs dans l'Empire Romain* [Paris: P. Geuthner, 1914], II, 93-126). The rabbis deduced from Exod. 21:1 that it was unlawful to take a case before idolatrous judges. It was customary to appoint three judges to handle cases among Jews (Strack and Billerbeck, *Kommentar zum N.T. aus Talmud und Midrasch,* III, 364-65). But Paul is not thinking of a permanent legal status for the church; in vivid expectation of the consummation of the divine rule the apostle is pleading that its members begin now to exercise the responsibilities which shall so soon be theirs. The cases referred to do not involve criminal law, but concern property **grievance** (vss. 7-8). The disputes should be settled within the community and not taken before pagan officials for adjudication.

6:1-4. Two terms are used for believers: **brother** and **saints** (see 1:2). The former is used thirty-eight times in this one letter and the latter six. Believers are joined to each other by this intimate tie because together they are set apart for God. They are in contrast to the **unrighteous.** Paul does not mean that no heathen judge was ever just; pagans as such were designated in this way. It is these pagan judges **who are least esteemed by the church** (vs.

part have they in the life of the Christian community? They must not be permitted to destroy or blunt its witness. There is a place for wise, firm, loving discipline in the church. Paul draws the necessary inference, **Drive out the wicked person from among you.**

6:1-8. ***Litigation Between Christians in Pagan Courts.***—Obviously an important principle in the realm of church government has emerged, and it is illustrated in the manner in which Paul deals with these pastoral problems. That principle is no less than the sovereignty of the church within the limits of its own community life. It would be going too far to say that the apostle is establishing the doctrine of the autonomy of the individual church. Clearly he is not, for he does not hesitate to use his own authority as an apostle to insist on certain things being done, and even to threaten, if they are not done, that he will come and do them (4:18-21). But subject to these pastoral rights, as he conceived them, a wide field of sovereignty is left for the local church itself in respect of the relationships between the members.

One instance has already been dealt with. Now the apostle turns to another. **When one of you has a grievance against a brother, does he dare to go to law before the unrighteous instead of the saints?** There is no obvious connection between this particular circumstance and the previous case of gross immorality with which Paul has dealt in strong and scathing terms. The treatment he advises is therefore different. The procedure he lays down, and some of the reasons he gives for it, moreover, have value for our own times. It had apparently come to his notice, perhaps at the instance of Chloe's people, that some members of the community were involved in a dispute about property or finance or perhaps in some breach of contract, and that they had gone to law with one another. This involved arguing the case before pagans who might not have been held in very high respect by the church. Such procedure Paul condemns on three main grounds,

3 Know ye not that we shall judge angels? how much more things that pertain
to this life?
4 If then ye have judgments of things
pertaining to this life, set them to judge
who are least esteemed in the church.
5 I speak to your shame. Is it so, that
there is not a wise man among you? no,

to try trivial cases? 3 Do you not know that
we are to judge angels? How much more,
matters pertaining to this life! 4 If then
you have such cases, why do you lay them
before those who are least esteemed by
the church? 5 I say this to your shame. Can

---

4). The KJV understands that Paul is urging the Corinthians to turn over their disputes to be settled by the lowliest members of the community. That would be sarcasm: let the most insignificant decide the inconsequential! The RSV adopts the view that those who are held in low esteem in the church are not themselves part of that body. They are the heathen judges. Paul asks why the Corinthians should be so inconsistent as to take problems to them which they themselves do not feel competent to decide.

The judgment by the **saints** was to accompany their messianic rule. The **angels** are mentioned as the most important part of the world over which they are to exercise sovereignty under God. This reflects an expectation which was already to be found among the Jews. According to Dan. 7:22, "judgment was given to the saints of the most High" (see also Enoch 1:9; Wisd. Sol. 3:8). That the saints will stand above angels is affirmed in II Baruch 51:12, "There will then be excellency in the righteous surpassing that in the angels." While the fallen angels would be included (Jude 6; II Pet. 2:4), Paul was not thinking exclusively of them. Participation in the messianic rule is not confined to the twelve disciples (Matt. 19:28) or to a select company of the martyrs (Rev. 20:4). It will be the privilege of all those who are baptized in Christ; and this rule will come during the time when he destroys "every rule and every authority and power" (15:24). Yet the apostle never forgets the fact that even believers will face a judgment (II Cor. 5:10).

Paul uses the word κριτήριον in vss. 2 and 4. This means a court of judgment (Jas. 2:6); but in the passage before us almost all modern commentators believe that the word must refer to the **cases** which are tried rather than to the tribunals in which the trials take place. The KJV uses **matters** in vs. 2 but **judgments** in vs. 4. The RSV uses **cases,** though this meaning is not elsewhere confirmed.

5-6. The Corinthians had been boasting of their wisdom. Here was their opportunity to show it. In contrast to 4:14, Paul admits that he wants to shame them because such

---

though in doing so he makes no suggestion that justice will not be dispensed by the courts. Paul's strictures are inspired by deeper, more compelling reasons. Probably too he has in mind the traditional Jewish method of dealing with such disputes among members of the synagogue.

Drawing on prophetic tradition, notably from the prophecy of Dan. 7:22, he argues that since it is the destiny of the Christian saints to judge the world, they ought not to descend to the triviality and absurdity of going to law against one another in the courts of the very pagans they are destined themselves to judge (see Exeg., vs. 3). As prospective judges of the world, they ought surely to be repositories of sufficient wisdom to handle their own affairs with equity. There ought—and the famous Pauline irony breaks through here—to be at least one person among them who might judge in such matters. **Can it be that there is no man among you wise enough to decide between members of the brotherhood, but brother goes to law against brother, and that before unbelievers?** What judge in modern times, in such trivial matters, would seek redress in the courts over which he himself presides? Such is the picture that Paul has in mind as he reminds them of their exalted destiny. There is a hint of Greek thought here, for similar beliefs were held by some of the prevailing cults. Let Christians be conscious of their own high prerogatives and act accordingly.

But there are still deeper reasons and even firmer grounds for the apostle's remonstrance. He develops the Christian argument and lifts the matter to a higher level. Such incidents bring the witness and the fellowship of the church into disrepute among pagans, and harm the spirit of fellowship within the church,

not one that shall be able to judge between
his brethren?
6 But brother goeth to law with brother,
and that before the unbelievers.
7 Now therefore there is utterly a fault
among you, because ye go to law one with
another. Why do ye not rather take wrong?
Why do ye not rather *suffer yourselves to*
be defrauded?
8 Nay, ye do wrong, and defraud, and
that *your* brethren.
9 Know ye not that the unrighteous shall
not inherit the kingdom of God? Be not
deceived: neither fornicators, nor idolaters,

it be that there is no man among you wise
enough to decide between members of the
brotherhood, 6 but brother goes to law
against brother, and that before unbelievers?
7 To have lawsuits at all with one another is defeat for you. Why not rather
suffer wrong? Why not rather be defrauded?
8 But you yourselves wrong and defraud,
and that even your own brethren.
9 Do you not know that the unrighteous
will not inherit the kingdom of God? Do

---

unbrotherly conduct had been displayed in the presence of **unbelievers.** It is unlikely that Paul was thinking of the establishment of regular ecclesiastical courts.

7-8. The real concern of the apostle was not with the administration of justice in courts. He condemns the men who are instigating lawsuits. They have not yet learned the attitude which Jesus enjoined of turning the other cheek when injury had been received (Matt. 5:39; I Pet. 2:23). This was not simply a **fault** (KJV) among them; it was utter **defeat** (RSV; cf. Rom. 11:12). More than that, they were actually defrauding their own brethren. A Christian should always suffer wrong rather than do wrong. Paul was quite indifferent to the question whether any society could ever be based on such an idealistic principle. He is commending the attitude of living above the law, because a man should be concerned with his responsibilities rather than with his rights.

5. Standards of the Kingdom (6:9-11)

9-11. What is the difference between the church and the world if there are **unrighteous** among those who should be saints? For the third time in the chapter (vss. 2, 3, 9) Paul

---

a fellowship which should be firmly based on love and brotherhood and forgiveness. Always at the back of the apostle's mind is the divine mission of the church. While he deals with local cases, he sees clearly the far-reaching implications. If the unity of the peace and fellowship of the church cannot be preserved in the spirit of Christian love and forgiveness, how can it fulfill its mission among the nations of the world? That thought is valid still. There may be matters which concern the church in which the law of the land is involved. Instances will readily recur to all students of church history. There was the case of the disposal of church property, for example, at the time of the disruption of the Presbyterian Church in Scotland. In such cases there is every legitimate reason for taking adequate legal measures. But in the realm of strictly personal affairs, which can and ought to be settled out of court, especially between Christians, much harm can be done to the witness and worship of the church, not only in the eyes of the world, but in its own life, if a different procedure is followed. In this as in other areas Christians should demonstrate their love one for another. We can leave the point for the moment. Later on Paul will write in imperishable words his great conception of the nature of Christian love.

There is a still higher, and final, reason for following a different procedure in matters of dispute and grievance. Paul's thought swings like the needle of a magnet to its spiritual pole, the spirit and the teaching of his Master. How close is the correspondence between Paul's words and the teachings of Jesus (Matt. 5:39-40). The final court of reference for Christian life and conduct is always the teaching and standards of Jesus Christ. **Why not rather suffer wrong? Why not rather be defrauded?** There we catch a gleam of the face of Christ. In the matter of grievances, as in other things, his spirit and teaching are the final court of reference and appeal. Better to lose the case than dim the splendor of the cause.

9-11. ***Plea for All-Round Righteousness.***—Having made his point, Paul now improves the occasion by including a general principle that Christian believers must be distinguished by righteousness of life not only in one or two

nor adulterers, nor effeminate, nor abusers
of themselves with mankind,
10 Nor thieves, nor covetous, nor drunkards, nor revilers, nor extortioners, shall
inherit the kingdom of God.
11 And such were some of you: but ye
are washed, but ye are sanctified, but ye
are justified in the name of the Lord Jesus,
and by the Spirit of our God.

not be deceived; neither the immoral, nor
idolaters, nor adulterers, nor homosexuals,[g]
10 nor thieves, nor the greedy, nor drunkards, nor revilers, nor robbers will inherit
the kingdom of God. 11 And such were
some of you. But you were washed, you
were sanctified, you were justified in the
name of the Lord Jesus Christ and in the
Spirit of our God.

[g] Two Greek words are rendered by this expression.

---

asks, **Do you not know?** The **kingdom of God** is here the eschatological age following the resurrection (15:50). This is the inheritance of those who are in Christ; but it is a kingdom which the immoral will not enter. The Exeg. of 5:11 discussed six of the terms in this vice catalogue. It is striking that Paul should have repeated them all. **Thieves** are now mentioned in addition to **robbers.** The apostle seems to be looking back on his discussion of property quarrels; some of the members had not manifested common honesty. But it is the sex misdemeanors which are most emphasized in anticipation of the discussion with the libertines. **Adulterers** are mentioned only here by Paul. For the two nouns translated in the KJV as **effeminate** and **abusers of themselves with mankind,** the RSV uses simply **homosexuals.** This vice is condemned by the apostle in Rom. 1:27. Its prevalence in the ancient world is witnessed by the moralists of the time. Paul mentions it when writing *from* or *to* Corinth, a city where licentiousness was especially rife. If **some** of the church members had been guilty of practices like these, Paul had certainly drawn his net through the dregs of the city.

No matter how much the apostle stresses the importance of righteousness, he is never led to say that salvation is by works. If men are to enter the kingdom of God, it is not through what they have done but through what God has done for them. This is expressed in three terms which are parallel in substance to those in 1:30. "Redemption" is not mentioned here, though it is involved in the metaphor with which Paul closes the chapter, "you were bought with a price" (vs. 20). **Justified** stands last instead of first, showing once more that the apostle did not think of a chronological sequence of different experiences (for **sanctified** [ἡγιάσθητε] see on 1:30). The new term is **washed,** most appropriate in relation to the moral filth which he has been describing. Obviously Paul is referring to baptism, the experience in which the believer dies to sin (Rom. 6:6) so that sin will no longer reign in him. This transformation has already taken place, yet the letter indicates at the same time how incomplete is the sanctification which these Christians have obtained.

---

respects, but in every way. **Do you not know that the unrighteous will not inherit the kingdom of God?** Again there is more than a reminiscence of the teaching of Jesus. Although Paul states the issue in negative terms, the implication of the higher standard for believers is there. Something far more than the recognized morality of contemporary society, even at its best, is required; far more than a mode that is scarcely distinguishable from pagan immorality (Matt. 5:20). Obviously the apostle is perturbed by the influence of the immoral pagan community upon the lives of the members of the church. He again makes his point crystal clear in his list of particular vices which exclude their perpetrators from any participation in the kingdom of God. There is a special reference to unnatural vice, homosexuality, which though sometimes punished even in pagan communities was in general condoned, but against which Christianity set itself uncompromisingly from the first (see Exeg., vss. 9-10). By their conversion and baptism the Corinthian Christians had made witness to their inward spiritual cleansing by the grace of Christ from all such immoral contamination. Having been cleansed at such cost, they were now no longer their own, but Christ's folk. Such reprehensible conduct was utterly inconsistent both with their experience and with their profession of faith. They were jeopardizing their "standing" before God and their "prospects." How could his Holy Spirit rule in such hearts?

12 All things are lawful unto me, but all things are not expedient: all things are lawful for me, but I will not be brought under the power of any.

13 Meats for the belly, and the belly for meats: but God shall destroy both it and them. Now the body *is* not for fornication, but for the Lord; and the Lord for the body.

14 And God hath both raised up the Lord, and will also raise up us by his own power.

12 "All things are lawful for me," but
not all things are helpful. "All things are
lawful for me," but I will not be enslaved
by anything. 13 "Food is meant for the
stomach and the stomach for food" — and
God will destroy both one and the other.
The body is not meant for immorality,
but for the Lord, and the Lord for the
body. 14 And God raised the Lord and will

6. Chastity Among the Members of the Body of Christ (6:12-20)

Paul now returns to the question of standards of sexual conduct. It is a question which raises the whole issue of the nature of Christian freedom, a subject to be dealt with at length in chs. 8–10. Now that believers have been consecrated, cannot they do as they please? In the style of the diatribe, Paul argues with an imaginary opponent who sets forth the case of the libertines. The RSV puts their slogans in quotation marks in order to make the difference of speakers clear. The subject matter of the paragraph would fit the description of the letter referred to in 5:9, but there is no adequate reason to remove it from the present context.

12-14. Behind the slogan **all things are lawful** is the assumption that physical acts do not affect the inner man. Paul asserts on the contrary two limitations on a Christian's freedom. (*a*) The first is from the social point of view; is the act **helpful** (7:35; 10:23; 12:7) to others? (*b*) The second is from the individual's own point of view; will the act make us slaves to passion and thus destroy freedom itself? Paul knows well that sin can be the most inexorable master (Rom. 6:12). Real freedom lies in the choice of our master. The subject of food is not introduced because Jewish dietary regulations were the subject of controversy. Rather, the Gnostic libertines had used the agreement on the fact that food did not raise a moral issue to support their contention that sexual conduct also had no moral significance. Paul grants that both food and the stomach belong to the transient physical sphere in which there can be no real defilement to man (Mark 7:18-19). But he denies that there is a parallelism and rejects the conclusion that the unregulated satisfaction of sexual desires is simply natural. It is uncertain with which

12-20. ***Christian Liberty Versus Moral License.***—The apostle goes on to emphasize the range and depth of the principle he has just laid down; and his statement still holds good for every Christian believer and for every Christian community. In a series of balanced antithetical sentences he draws a clear distinction between liberty and license, between what is lawful and what, in the highest sense of the word, is not expedient. These, as we shall see presently, are useful, practical distinctions. Had they always been clearly understood and firmly grasped, the persuasiveness of Christian teaching might possibly have been more effective in certain circumstances than has actually been the case.

In effect, when Paul writes **All things are lawful for me,** he is asserting the freedom of the believer, a matter on which, having regard to his previous servitude to the Jewish law, he lays great insistence in his writings. As a Christian he asserts boldly that he may do anything he wishes. One is reminded of the well-known saying of Augustine, "Love God and do as you like!" Paul, however, goes on to say, **But not all things are helpful. Helpful** (RSV) should be taken as suggesting the KJV's **expedient** (see Exeg., vss. 12-14).

In a pagan community it is easy, too easy, as he well knows, for Christian freedom to be travestied. Freedom has not been given through Christ's grace only to succumb to any other appetite, whether it is sexual lust or mere gluttony (vs. 13). Doubtless at the back of Paul's mind there was also the Greek conception of temperance as that virtue is discussed in a book like Plato's *Republic*. There temperance is described as the control of appetite by

15 Know ye not that your bodies are the
members of Christ? shall I then take the
members of Christ, and make *them* the
members of a harlot? God forbid.
16 What! know ye not that he which is
joined to a harlot is one body? for two,
saith he, shall be one flesh.
17 But he that is joined unto the Lord
is one spirit.

also raise us up by his power. 15 Do you not
know that your bodies are members of
Christ? Shall I therefore take the members
of Christ and make them members of a
prostitute? Never! 16 Do you not know
that he who joins himself to a prostitute becomes one body with her? For, as it is written, "The two shall become one."[h] 17 But
he who is united to the Lord becomes one

[h] Greek *one flesh.*

---

clause Paul's reply begins. The real rejoinder opens with the words **the body is not meant for immorality.** The body is not something transient, but will be raised from the dead. For the moment Paul disregards the complete difference between the resurrection body and the earthly body (15:35-38). Apparently he assumes that the defiling of one affects the other. Man is not an immortal soul imprisoned in material substance until death. Paul writes not from the Greek point of view but from the Hebraic, according to which the person is looked upon as a psychosomatic entity. And the whole person belongs to the Lord.

15-17. The closeness of this union with Christ is expressed in terms of the body and its members, a figure which Paul will develop at length in ch. 12. As a result of baptism, the believer's body (i.e., himself) has become nothing less than a part of the body of Christ. That union excludes other unions which are incompatible with it. Sexual intercourse is not a passing physical act, but one that unites two persons in an intimate bond. A man who visits a prostitute **becomes one body with her,** and that act separates him from membership in the body of Christ. Paul's most emphatic negation, μὴ γένοιτο (ten times in Romans), is used here for the only time in this letter. In his revulsion against licentious standards Paul adopts a line of argument which really proves too much. He supports his contention by quoting Gen. 2:24, according to the LXX, which had introduced the word **two.** Its relevance depends on the identification of **body** (σῶμα) and **flesh** (σάρξ). But this O.T. verse dealt with marriage, and it is clear from ch. 7 that Paul did not hold that marriage separates from the body of Christ. Possibly he would have explained that a married couple together became one member of Christ's body; therefore a man must choose between the two unions which are mutually exclusive. It is instructive that Paul does not approach the problem from the standpoint of community health or of respect for personality considered simply on the human plane. The relationship to God through Christ is affected by this self-indulgence and that becomes the point of Paul's criticism. Vs. 17 comes to a curious climax. We would have expected the conclusion that union with Christ makes us one body with him. Possibly the word σάρξ has induced the use of its opposite, πνεῦμα, **spirit.** If we are **united to the Lord,** we will use our freedom quite otherwise than by visiting a prostitute. To have intercourse with the priestesses of Aphrodite meant consecration to the goddess, and exclusion from the body of Christ.

---

reason. In effect, the apostle is pleading for a life disciplined by moral bonds in God's Spirit. Here the word **expedient** (KJV) comes into its own. In that same context of Greek philosophic thought "expedient" implies right purposes or the highest good. The highest good for Christians is recognition of the lordship of Jesus Christ in every aspect of life. That principle governs both liberty and expediency, and these should be tested in its light. Hence he can write, **Shun immorality. . . . You are not your own; you were bought with a price. So glorify God in your body.**

In this connection Paul's use of the term "body" is interesting, though perhaps somewhat ambiguous (see Exeg.). Paul uses "body" in this passage as equivalent to the term "self" or "personality." Neither in the Greek nor in the Hebrew can we find words which convey quite the sense of these two terms as used in modern philosophical or religious thought and writings. Here the apostle, though defending any legitimate conception of Christian freedom, condemns any misconception of it that leads to a debauched life. The fullness of personal life for Paul is that life which is illumined and

18 Flee fornication. Every sin that a man doeth is without the body; but he that committeth fornication sinneth against his own body.

19 What! know ye not that your body is the temple of the Holy Ghost *which is* in you, which ye have of God, and ye are not your own?

20 For ye are bought with a price: therefore glorify God in your body, and in your spirit, which are God's.

spirit with him. **18** Shun immorality. Every
other sin which a man commits is outside
the body; but the immoral man sins against
his own body. **19** Do you not know that
your body is a temple of the Holy Spirit
within you, which you have from God?
You are not your own; **20** you were bought
with a price. So glorify God in your body.

---

18. Only here and at 10:14 does Paul counsel flight from sin. Some temptations are too insidious for anyone to temporize with them. Paul's horror at sexual immorality is shown by his quick generalization, which can hardly be substantiated. Not only such **immorality,** but drunkenness, suicide, and other sins as well affect a man's **own body.** His words indicate also how little he is considering the personality of the woman who submits to a man's lust. If **outside the body** includes a reference to sins of attitude and intention (cf. Rom. 1:29-31), the apostle is ignoring the contention of Jesus that the most serious sin is the "adultery of the eye" (Matt. 5:28).

19-20. Once more (vss. 2, 3, 9, 15, 16) Paul introduces a statement with the query **Do you not know?** In 3:16 the entire community is referred to as the temple in which God's Spirit dwells. Here, every member has that distinction. This requires separation from sin (cf. II Cor. 6:16). The Holy Spirit is not a natural possession of all men but has come through the risen Christ. This connection leads the apostle to allude to the redemptive death of Christ, which he here considers as a ransom (cf. Mark 10:45; I Pet. 1:18-19). Nothing is said about who had received the **price** (7:23). This is simply one of the many metaphors by which the apostle describes Christian deliverance (cf. Gal. 3:13; 4:5; see Exeg. on 1:30). The slave had previously made the deposit in the temple treasury; but when Christ paid our redemption price, he had received nothing from us. If a Corinthian slave was from the time of his manumission the slave of the god, how much more were those in Christ obligated to devote their all to him. To the protest of self-sufficient man, "Cannot I do what I will with my own" (cf. Matt. 20:15), he replies, **You are not your own.** God is glorified not by a verbal cult, but by the presenting of our bodies in worthy deeds (Rom. 12:1). The Godward aspect of worship comes through a life completely dedicated to his service.

---

empowered by the indwelling of the Holy Spirit (vs. 19). Such vices as he denounces menace and destroy this sacred relationship and diminish the worth and value and well-being of the personality. They are therefore to be avoided like a plague by Christian believers. Indulgence in these ways blunts the fine edge of personal life and diminishes one's sensitivity to spiritual realities.

Much of this, if indeed not all of it, is borne out by sociology, particularly as regards prostitution, which Paul equally condemns. While it may be possible to escape, at least for the time being, any physical or physiological consequences, it is not possible to escape the psychological consequences. Prostitution is bound to have adverse psychological effects on the individuals concerned, and in addition, inevitably on the moral and spiritual structure of society. Moreover, as in the apostle's view, any person indulging in such practices merges his "personality" with that of his partner in vice, and defiles thus the very shrine of God to whom alone the "personality" of the believer belongs. Christian freedom is freedom to serve God, and to be so disciplined in Christian standards and habits of living that all such vices as the apostle names and condemns will be eschewed by every believer. Even then the Christian church was waging unremitting warfare against paganism without and heresy within. One of the earliest heresies against which the apostles had to fight was the pernicious idea that Christian liberty implied license. Paul will have none of it. Those who are "called to be saints" are dedicated to the spirit of Christianity. Such conduct

7 Now concerning the things whereof ye wrote unto me: *It is* good for a man not to touch a woman.

2 Nevertheless, *to avoid* fornication, let every man have his own wife, and let every woman have her own husband.

3 Let the husband render unto the wife due benevolence: and likewise also the wife unto the husband.

4 The wife hath not power of her own body, but the husband: and likewise also the husband hath not power of his own body, but the wife.

7 Now concerning the matters about
which you wrote. It is well for a man not
to touch a woman. 2 But because of the
temptation to immorality, each man should
have his own wife and each woman her
own husband. 3 The husband should give
to his wife her conjugal rights, and likewise the wife to her husband. 4 For the
wife does not rule over her own body, but
the husband does; likewise the husband
does not rule over his own body, but the

B. Problems of Marriage and Celibacy (7:1-40)

1. General Principles (7:1-7)

The Corinthians had written a letter making inquiries about marriage (7:1), food offered to idols (8:1), spiritual gifts (12:1), the contribution for the saints (16:1), and possibly about Apollos (16:12). It may be that other topics not introduced by the formula **now concerning** were also on the agenda furnished by the church. This topic of marriage naturally follows the preceding discussion for libertinism and asceticism are twin aberrations in religion. The section 7:36-38 will indicate the presence of the latter tendency. Paul's own point of view inevitably lent encouragement to those who felt that marriage should be repudiated entirely. The whole chapter is dominated, just as are 6:1-8 and 15:51, by the expectation of the imminent Parousia. Responsibility toward children and the generations to come does not enter into the apostle's calculations, for he thought of himself as living not in the first century but in the last century. Marriage was of doubtful wisdom because it might divert from undivided attention to the work of the Lord.

7:1-4. In Gen. 2:18 we read, "It is not good that the man should be alone." Paul thought that the opposite was true, and in this opinion showed himself at variance with the usual Jewish point of view. The rabbis considered that marriage was an unqualified duty for a man. To **touch a woman** is a common biblical euphemism (Gen. 20:6; Prov. 6:29). The apostle is not thinking here of sexual immorality, but of the marriage relation. He exalts celibacy above the married state, but at the same time recognizes that not all can exercise such self-control. He rejects unhesitatingly the view that marriage is a sin. Probably some zealots were insisting upon abstention from marital intercourse. Paul was much too realistic and too sound in judgment to make any such demand, but he does

---

as the apostle condemns is utterly inconsistent with this status. And his convictions need to be reaffirmed by the church in every age.

7:1-16. ***Concerning Marriage.***—Paul now gives his attention to questions that had been sent to him by the church (vs. 1). The first of these has to do with marriage and divorce, and more generally with relationships between the sexes. The Corinthian Christians must have felt the difference between the standards required of them as professing Christians and those of the pagan community of which they were also members. This involved some of them in embarrassing and challenging situations.

The apostle's reply is interesting and instructive. Obviously the marriage relationship did not appeal to him, and he seems to have regarded the more intimate sex relationship with some distaste. He is of the definite opinion that it is better for Christians to follow his personal example and remain unmarried. **It is well for a man not to touch a woman.** But he soon makes it clear that he is giving expression only to his own private opinion (vs. 25; see Exeg., vss. 1-4). Here we note an interesting point. Paul, unlike others in his day and certainly since then, is ever careful not to invoke the authority of Jesus for what he feels is an expression of his own personal point of view. This is a good practice for all Christians to follow. Too

5 Defraud ye not one the other, except *it be* with consent for a time, that ye may give yourselves to fasting and prayer; and come together again, that Satan tempt you not for your incontinency.

6 But I speak this by permission, *and* not of commandment.

7 For I would that all men were even as I myself. But every man hath his proper gift of God, one after this manner, and another after that.

wife does.
5 Do not refuse one another except perhaps by agreement for a season, that you may devote yourselves to prayer; but then come together again, lest Satan tempt you through lack of self-control.
6 I say this by way of concession, not of command.
7 I wish that all were as I myself am. But each has his own special gift from God, one of one kind and one of another.

---

call for mutual consideration. In such an intimate relation one party may not arbitrarily make a decision which may affect so vitally the other partner. Here is an equality of rights which Paul does not recognize in 11:7 ff. To say that **the wife** should **rule over** the husband's **body** contradicts the patriarchal order. It is regrettable that Paul, the bachelor, should have ignored so completely all other aspects of the companionship of married couples and should have written as if marriage were little more than legalized cohabitation.

5-7. That sexual intercourse brought cult impurity was an idea current not only among Jews (Exod. 19:15; Lev. 15:18; etc.) but also among the Greeks. Paul grants that abstention for purposes of worship was permissible provided that it was by common agreement and not the selfish decision of one partner. It must be temporary, however, for otherwise there might be temptation to seek satisfaction outside of marriage. Satan appears as the tempter. But Paul wants to make it plain that none of his directions to married couples are absolute commands. Since he considers celibacy preferable, all of this **is by way of concession.** When he wrote in vs. 2 that **each man should have his own wife,** he had not meant that marriage was obligatory. Paul recognized, however, that continence was **his own special gift** and one which many others had not received. To **wish that all were** like himself was natural but futile. Other men had other gifts which Paul did not

---

often the authority of the Master or of the Holy Spirit is claimed for what turns out to be no more than private opinion or even prejudice. Paul is never willingly guilty of such confusion of thought.

There is, however, something to be said for his point of view. It is true that a celibate order of clergy or ministers or missionaries would to that extent be freed from certain anxieties and preoccupations. This indeed has been the practice of well-known religious orders. But it can be rightly maintained that the marriage relationship involves character-enriching experiences which equip the man of God for his special tasks. How can one who by virtue of his office is denied a normal home understand the special trials and temptations of those whose life is lived within the bounds of that relationship? Paul never really forces this question. More generally, this must be left as a matter for the individual conscience.

While the foregoing represents Paul's own attitude, his advice concerning the marriage relationship is remarkable for its sanity and its modernity. He rejects any suggestion that marriage is sinful (see Exeg., vss. 1-4). Nor does he insist, as some members of the community did, on the value of celibacy in the marriage relationship (vss. 2-3). He concedes that for special reasons married people may practice celibacy, but urges that to avoid any **temptation** they should resume normal married life. He is very frank about the risks and dangers of prolonged abstinence in this matter, for he is only too well aware of the abnormal strain which such an unnatural requirement is liable to place upon human nature. Marriage for Paul is divinely ordained, and therefore not only permissible but honorable. Moreover, within the marriage relationship, involving as it does cohabitation, the two individuals are merged into one personality. Therefore he urges that the marriage should be full and complete in every respect—spiritual, mental, and physical. Therefore he writes, **Do not refuse one another except perhaps by agreement for a season.**

Little comment is needed on these points: the harm that can be caused by enforced abstinence in respect of cohabitation is well known. The consulting rooms of psychiatrists are thronged with people who suffer in various ways as the outcome of sex frustration. Such

8 I say therefore to the unmarried and widows, It is good for them if they abide even as I.

9 But if they cannot contain, let them marry: for it is better to marry than to burn.

10 And unto the married I command, *yet* not I, but the Lord, Let not the wife depart from *her* husband:

8 To the unmarried and the widows I say that it is well for them to remain single as I do. **9** But if they cannot exercise self-control, they should marry. For it is better to marry than to be aflame with passion.

10 To the married I give charge, not I but the Lord, that the wife should not

---

possess. Possibly Aquila could have inserted from the enjoyment of his gift a valuable paragraph on the spiritual values of marriage which would have made this chapter more complete.

2. Advices to Special Groups (7:8-16)

Three important assumptions underlie this chapter. (*a*) The first we have already noted: though marriage is not a sin, celibacy is to be preferred. (*b*) The second now appears: it is the responsibility of the religious leader to give marriage counseling. (*c*) The third is indicated by Paul's counsel: words of Jesus have a place of supreme authority in the guidance of the church. These words are to be clearly distinguished (vss. 10, 12) from the wisest insight of a devoted servant of the Lord. Paul may believe that he has the Spirit of God (vs. 40), but that does not justify ascribing his best judgment to Jesus himself. This passage has an important bearing on our theories of the fidelity of the transmission of the words of Jesus.

8-9. The **unmarried** probably include those who have never been married as well as those separated. **Widows** probably included widowers. Paul will return to their special case in vs. 39, and also deal at length in vss. 25-35 with his reasons for preferring virginity. Here he repeats what he said in vs. 1, **it is well,** but again qualifies it in the same way as in the preceding paragraph. Some have held that Acts 26:10 implies that Paul was a member of the Sanhedrin and therefore must have been a married man. In the light of what he writes here he certainly had no living wife, and from the chapter it is highly unlikely that he ever had been married. To **burn** does not refer to hell fire (Tertullian) but, as in the RSV, to **be aflame with passion.**

10-11. The best-attested saying of Jesus is his repudiation of divorce. It stands both in Mark 10:5-9 and in Q (Luke 16:18) and in this letter, which was written earlier than any of our Gospels. Paul enters into no discussion concerning who is guilty of adultery in the case of remarriage, but he does insist that in the case of those already separated, they should **remain single.** Paul knows nothing of any exception, such as is recognized in

---

abstinence can wither the marriage relationship, especially when a nation is at war and is compelled to segregate great numbers of men and women in unnatural exclusion from one another. To a lesser degree the passionate drive of the sex instinct is liable to become enhanced when legitimate gratification is withheld. The honorableness of Christian marriage is at one and the same time an adequate medium both of expression and of discipline for the full sex life of men and women. It is a tribute to Paul's comprehensive understanding of these things, despite his own predilections, that he writes as frankly and as wholesomely as he does. His underlying concern is that the marriage should be happy and helpful to both partners.

We have taken note of the apostle's preference for the celibate life. This colors the advice he gives to **the unmarried and the widows.** Almost immediately he will elaborate some of his reasons for this. Meantime, we may note that he seems to be strangely insensitive to the happiness he must have witnessed in such a household as that of Aquila and Priscilla. Yet he again recognizes the strength of the sex instinct and advises accordingly, **It is better to marry than to be aflame with passion.** Now he turns to the difficult question of divorce, and here he does invoke the authority of Jesus (Mark 10:5-9; Luke 16:18). This teaching is laid down as a ruling for all the churches. It ought, however, to be kept in mind that Jesus

11 But and if she depart, let her remain
unmarried, or be reconciled to *her* husband: and let not the husband put away
his wife.
12 But to the rest speak I, not the Lord:
If any brother hath a wife that believeth
not, and she be pleased to dwell with him,
let him not put her away.
13 And the woman which hath a husband that believeth not, and if he be
pleased to dwell with her, let her not
leave him.

separate from her husband 11 (but if she
does, let her remain single or else be reconciled to her husband) — and that the husband should not divorce his wife.
12 To the rest I say, not the Lord, that
if any brother has a wife who is an unbeliever, and she consents to live with him,
he should not divorce her. 13 If any woman
has a husband who is an unbeliever, and
he consents to live with her, she should not

Matt. 5:32 and 19:9, "except on the ground of unchastity." This was obviously an addition modifying the unqualified word of Jesus. That a **wife should not separate from her husband** stands close to Mark 10:12, where the right of a wife to divorce her husband is rejected. Though Paul insists that this is a command of **the Lord,** he does not refer to any collection of words of Jesus in his possession. We do not know whether such collections were in circulation or not. That they existed can be no more than a probability. Paul gives no advice regarding Christian marriages beyond the fact that they should continue. It was too late for a married person to decide, with Paul, that celibacy was to be preferred.

12-16. The reader might wonder who **the rest** might be. The apostle at once makes clear that he has in mind mixed marriages, where only one partner was a Christian. Obviously Jesus could have had no occasion to make a pronouncement on that situation. Two principles govern Paul's position: (*a*) First, the indissolubility of a marriage once it has been entered into; the Christian partner is never to take the initiative in seeking a divorce. (*b*) On the other hand, **if the unbelieving partner desires to separate,** the Christian **is not bound.** It is recognized that Christian faith brings new standards of life. A heathen partner should not be compelled to continue under the new circumstances unless he or she is entirely willing to do so. Paul would not sanction Christians marrying nonbelievers any more than Ezra (10:10) would permit Jews to marry Gentile women; but he did not call for the dissolution of such marriages. No cult impurity arose from such a union, for **the unbelieving husband is consecrated through his wife.** Here we see a very primitive and material view of holiness and uncleanness as transmitted by contact. Paul is not thinking of the moral influence of persons on each other, but of the physical

---

had in view the rabbinical law which specified a variety of offenses for which a husband, whose rights were obviously ranked higher than the wife's, could obtain divorce. Paul was undoubtedly influenced by his rabbinical traditions. It is questionable whether under different traditions and customs the same rule would hold. The ambiguity of the position of the various Christian denominations with regard to this vexed question is an index of the diversity of opinion which prevails. Nevertheless, Paul has much to say that is worthy of serious attention and is of real help to all who seek light and guidance on this important subject.

Most probably the question arose in the Corinthian church because of mixed marriages between Christians and pagans (see Exeg., vss. 10-11). If one of the partners to an already existing marriage should become a convert to the new faith, and this had happened over and over again, the question was bound to arise, at least in certain cases, as to whether such a marriage could endure. "Can two walk together, except they be agreed?" (Amos 3:3.) Paul quite definitely says that neither should divorce the other. He holds by the Christian principle of the indissolubility of the marriage bond. In general, he advises against mixed marriages. "Do not be mismated with unbelievers. For what partnership have righteousness and iniquity? Or what fellowship has light with darkness?" (II Cor. 6:14.) But where the relationship already exists the matter is rather different, **the wife should not separate from her husband, . . . the husband should not divorce his wife.** That statement of mutual obligation is clear enough. In other words, and in a modern setting, where people have made certain

14 For the unbelieving husband is sanctified by the wife, and the unbelieving wife is sanctified by the husband: else were your children unclean; but now are they holy.

15 But if the unbelieving depart, let him depart. A brother or a sister is not under bondage in such *cases:* but God hath called us to peace.

divorce him. 14 For the unbelieving husband is consecrated through his wife, and
the unbelieving wife is consecrated through
her husband. Otherwise, your children
would be unclean, but as it is they are holy.
15 But if the unbelieving partner desires to
separate, let it be so; in such a case the
brother or sister is not bound. For God

---

quality of holiness. The children of such a union are **holy.** Nothing is specifically stated about the need to baptize children under these circumstances. Yet O. Cullmann is going quite beyond the evidence when he contends that Paul held the baptism of such a child to be unnecessary since by birth it already belonged to the body of Christ (*Die Tauflehre des Neuen Testaments* [Zürich: Zwingli, 1948], pp. 21, 38).

Paul grounds the permission to separate, if the heathen partner insists, on the fact that **God has called us to peace.** It is doubtful that he would have admitted other things which destroy marital harmony as also justifying the dissolution of the marriage. Instead of developing that theme, he meets the objection of the Christian partner in two rhetorical questions. Some apparently wanted to hold the unbelieving partner in the hope of leading to his conversion. Paul wisely reminds them that there is no certainty of such a result; marriage is not a sphere for missionary work. One might ask why, if an unbelieving husband is already consecrated through the wife, he still needs to be saved. Apparently Paul distinguishes between the absence of contamination, and salvation. One other question remains unsolved. If a believer is divorced by the unbelieving partner, what then? Paul's wish would be that he stay unmarried, but, as in the other situations, that is not made compulsory. Do we have here, then, the one scriptural ground for the remarriage of divorced persons? Some commentators have thought so, but the conclusion rests on very

---

vows they should stand by them at all costs. Should the issue, however, become sharp in the case of a marriage between a believer and a pagan, then the first step in any divorce proceeding should be left to the pagan partner. That attitude, of course, implies Christian forbearance to the utmost on the part of the Christian believer (vss. 12-13; see Exeg., vss. 12-16). Paul's reasons for this standpoint are both interesting and convincing. They spring from his profound sense of the personal unity of the married couple, and also from his belief that the faith and spirit of the Christian partner might transform the relationship for the unbelieving partner. If at all possible, therefore, this bond is not to be broken. In such a marriage the two are truly one; the one cannot stand in a definite relationship to God without involving the other. Hence the conversion of the other is always within the realm of possibility. It is the bounden duty of the believer so to exercise Christian patience and forbearance, and above all, love, that the union may become complete in every aspect of personal life and relationship. **For the unbelieving husband is consecrated through his wife, and the unbelieving wife is consecrated through her husband.** On the other hand, if, despite all the love and forbearance of the believing partner to such a union, the other pushes matters to an extreme issue, then the consequences must be accepted. Peace of mind and spirit is too precious to be disrupted for all time by an unwilling pagan partner to such a union. **But if the unbelieving partner desires to separate, let it be so; in such a case the brother or sister is not bound. For God has called us to peace.** It is obvious that the apostle is seeking to hold the relationship to the highest Christian standards. This involves a bond of love that nothing should be allowed to break. As Christ is the sanctifier of his church, so the Christian partner in a mixed marriage is the channel of sanctification to the pagan partner (Eph. 5:21-33). The fullest possible scope is to be given to the sanctifying power of the Spirit to accomplish his redeeming work. Undoubtedly this calls for sacrifices, perhaps costly sacrifices. Nevertheless, in the interest of the redemptive work of Christ through his church for the people of the world, they are to be made. The story is told of a humble Christian man in the north of England whose marriage was ruined by a wife who fell into dissolute ways. His friends urged him to seek relief

16 For what knowest thou, O wife, whether thou shalt save *thy* husband? or how knowest thou, O man, whether thou shalt save *thy* wife?

17 But as God hath distributed to every man, as the Lord hath called every one, so let him walk. And so ordain I in all churches.

has called us[h] to peace. 16 Wife, how do you know whether you will save your husband? Husband, how do you know whether you will save your wife?

17 Only, let every one lead the life which the Lord has assigned to him, and in which God has called him. This is my rule in all

[h] Other ancient authorities read *you*.

precarious grounds. As at many other points, it is wiser to admit that we do not know what his counsel would have been.

3. Maintenance of the Status Quo (7:17-24)

The advice to "stay as you are" in regard to marriage is now extended to other fields of life, including one's national and economic status. During the Reformation period this section was extremely important for the development of the idea of Christian "calling." Paul himself was not thinking of vocation in terms of a Christian's task in the world, but of a station in life which should not be altered. Unquestionably his words here have lent powerful support to the conservatives of all time who seek to resist social change. They have contended that Christian duty involves staying as you are, and that any attempt to rise involves disobedience toward God. But these champions of Paul's doctrine of "calling" frequently overlook the revolutionary expectations of the apostle. People were to stay as they were because the present age had at best but a few years to last. Present inequalities were already abolished in Christ (Gal. 3:28) ; and when he comes, the old state of affairs will pass away. Unless Paul's vivid eschatological expectation is borne in mind, the reader will grossly misinterpret his intention.

17. There is a predestination which does not relate to final salvation, but to a man's abilities and the station in which he finds himself. The "given" is the "existential situation" which is not of our choosing but is **assigned** to us and against which it is fruitless to rebel. This is a thought to which Paul often returns (12:11; Rom. 12:3; II Cor. 10:13). God is in a sense responsible because no matter how evil the situation may appear, he at least permits it. Paul describes his advice as a **rule in all the churches** (1:2; 4:17; 11:16; 14:33). Christians are not to stir up opposition to the political and economic order, but are to wait patiently for the great overturning which is so near at hand.

---

by way of divorce: she had given him sufficient reason to do so. But he steadfastly refused. "I married her because I loved her from childhood; I promised before God that I would take her to be my wedded wife, for better or for worse, and I shall stand by my vow." Things did not improve. When years later she died, his hands were spread over her still in pity and in love. When men and women, in God's house, in his presence and in the presence of earthly witnesses, make their solemn marriage vows and promise to stand by one another "for better or for worse," they ought to mean what they say. To frame a vow, and to give public adherence to it, is like tying oneself to a stake that is driven into the swirling, spumming stream of time and circumstance. It is meant to prevent us from being swept off our feet and carried away. Fewer marriages would come to shipwreck if people would seek the grace that is freely offered them in Christ. We are invited not only to be patient, to be forbearing, or to endure: we can also pray. It was a wise writer in the Hebrew tradition who penned these words: "Except the Lord build the house, they labor in vain that build it" (Ps. 127:1). Let Christ have his place in the life of the home, and his presence will sanctify the marriage relationships: his grace will enable those who seek and accept it to stand by their vows.

17-24. ***Other Relationships.***—Having established the principle that conversion to Christianity does not involve the rupture of the marriage relationship, Paul now extends it to other aspects of life. His teaching is in the nature of a digression, yet it reinforces everything that he has just written (see Exeg., vs. 17). Someone has said, "Circumstances are the

18 Is any man called being circumcised? let him not become uncircumcised. Is any called in uncircumcision? let him not be circumcised.

19 Circumcision is nothing, and uncircumcision is nothing, but the keeping of the commandments of God.

20 Let every man abide in the same calling wherein he was called.

21 Art thou called *being* a servant? care not for it: but if thou mayest be made free, use *it* rather.

the churches.
18 Was any one at the time of his call already circumcised? Let him not seek to remove the marks of circumcision. Was any one at the time of his call uncircumcised? Let him not seek circumcision.
19 For neither circumcision counts for anything nor uncircumcision, but keeping the commandments of God.
20 Every one should remain in the state in which he was called.
21 Were you a slave when called? Never mind. But if you can gain your freedom,

18. It is unlikely that the Judaistic controversy seriously affected the church at Corinth, or that the **circumcision** of Gentile Christians was an issue. On the other hand, some Jewish Christians may have sought **to remove the marks of circumcision** (I Macc. 1:15). The national customs of the Jews were not to be abandoned simply because of Christian faith unless these interfered with full brotherhood in the community. Though it was faith rather than circumcision which determined the true sons of Abraham, this "seal of righteousness" was expected among those of the Jewish nation. In the light of this verse we realize that Acts is not necessarily unhistorical when it ascribes to Paul a desire to observe many of the distinctly Jewish customs (Acts 20:6, 16; 21:26). He never ceased to be a Jew (9:20; Rom. 9:3).

19. The unimportance of circumcision was a frequent contention of Paul's, but what really matters could be referred to in a variety of ways. In Gal. 6:15 it is "a new creation"; in Gal. 5:6 what matters is "faith working through love"; here it is **keeping the commandments of God.** The new creation is God's work; the other expressions characterize man's response; that love consists in keeping the commandments is also thoroughly Johannine (John 14:15; 15:12; I John 4:21).

20-21. Again Paul reaffirms the principle to stay as you are as he turns to the economic realm for illustration. Usually κλῆσις means "calling" in the sense of invitation to Christian discipleship (1:26). Despite the lack of parallels, it must mean here **state** or "lot." Paul did not work for the emancipation of slaves (3:22). Though he may have hoped for the release of a slave in the particular case of Onesimus (Philem. 21), he sent

shaping hands of God." There is truth in the saying. In that case the Christian is to take his stand and make his witness just where he is. Paul writes, **Let every one lead the life which the Lord has assigned to him, and in which God has called him** (see Exeg.). Perhaps with some reminiscences of anxieties caused him by the Judaizing party, who insisted on the circumcision of pagans who had been converted to Christianity, Paul applies his principle to that rite. Some who had been circumcised, and apparently for some reason were ashamed of it, especially if they stripped themselves for the baths or the games, had sought to remove the telltale marks, much as a man might seek to remove tattoo marks from his skin. Others who had not been circumcised doubtless wondered if, having become Christian, they ought to conform to general practices. Some were slaves and others had achieved freedom, while still others were freeborn. What ought to be their outlook and attitude with regard to the new way of life to which they had been called? What matters most is obedience to **the commandments of God.** That may not be easy: it may on the contrary be difficult. If so, let us remember that the symbol of our faith is a Cross, and that we are invited to bear it for his sake who bore a Cross for us. **You were bought with a price.**

But the principle is valid in other areas as well: it is to determine the attitude of believers to the whole of life. Paul seems to suggest that in practically any set of circumstances one can live a full Christian life. Even slaves may play a worthy part. Perhaps some of these were numbered among the saints of Caesar's household (Phil. 4:22). If they must continue to be enslaved, they can make their witness by endur-

22 For he that is called in the Lord, *being* a servant, is the Lord's freeman: likewise also he that is called, *being* free, is Christ's servant.

23 Ye are bought with a price; be not ye the servants of men.

24 Brethren, let every man, wherein he is called, therein abide with God.

avail yourself of the opportunity. 22 For
he who was called in the Lord as a slave
is a freedman of the Lord. Likewise he
who was free when called is a slave of
Christ. 23 You were bought with a price; do
not become slaves of men. 24 So, brethren,
in whatever state each was called, there
let him remain with God.

---

the slave back to his master so that there might be a purely voluntary decision on the master's part. Here Paul approaches closely the attitude cultivated in Stoicism; but there is a marked difference. Stoicism affirmed that in spite of outer circumstances, the inner freedom of man could and should be maintained. Paul contended that no outer lot could separate a man from Christ (Rom. 8:35). He seemed to think that one could obey God under any economic system. This is true of the slave; but we may not agree that it is equally true of the master. The passage makes it clear, however, that Christianity did not come to the economically dissatisfied as an offer of material betterment. The KJV obscures the real issue by its use throughout of **servant** instead of **slave** (δοῦλος), but in vs. 21*b* it does preserve the ambiguity of the Greek. What is it which the slaves are to **use?** Is it the opportunity to obtain their **freedom** (so the RSV) or is it the condition of slavery which they are to continue to use despite the opportunity to change their status? Because the section deals with staying as you are, many commentators have contended for the latter conclusion. But it is as unlikely that Paul would forbid emancipation as that he would forbid marriage.

22-24. A freedman of the Lord is not one who is free from Christ, but one whom Christ has delivered from bondage to sin (Rom. 6:18, 22; Gal. 5:1). This release is not to autonomy but to a slavery to righteousness and to the heavenly Lord. The free man, judged by social and economic standards, is still **a slave to Christ.** Freedom means service to the master who brings eternal life. Vs. 23 repeats 6:20, where the figure of redemption is explained at greater length. The warning against becoming **slaves of men** may refer to the discussion concerning parties. Church leaders might seek to tyrannize over them, but they had been set free from such bondage. We may wonder whether any Corinthians later turned this phrase against Paul (II Cor. 10:9; 11:20). One new idea is added in the final summarizing (vs. 24). If God has called men in a particular situation, when they remain there they **remain with God.** Fellowship with him is not severed by slavery.

---

ing their lot with Christian fortitude (see Exeg., vss. 21-23). Here the apostle seems to imply that practically any economic system can be made to work for the true benefit of mankind if those engaged in it are Christian in spirit. Those who are free men or who, whether freeborn or enslaved, have been freed from sin by the grace of Christ, are to stand fast in their freedom and turn it to account as the slaves of Christ (vs. 22). As George Matheson sang:

> Make me a captive, Lord,
> And then I shall be free.[7]

This great principle possesses continuing validity. However difficult, there is no legitimate set of circumstances in which we cannot live a full Christian life. The kitchen can become a sanctuary and its service a sacrament acceptable to the Master. The factory can become a church: all the aspects of our economic and political life should be such that we can lift them up to the light of God's countenance and seek his blessing. Let those who teach in schools realize that the cause is holy and its work a divine service. Let professional men in every walk of life add the spirit of Christian friendship to the skill they provide. Each can take a place and play a worthy part. Each can bear his witness in his private station. Christianity is the whole of life illumined, inspired, and permeated by the indwelling Spirit of Christ. Or in Paul's sublime language, **So, brethren, in whatever state each was called, there let him remain with God.**

[7] Used by permission of McClure, Naismith, Brodie & Co.

25 Now concerning virgins I have no commandment of the Lord: yet I give my judgment, as one that hath obtained mercy of the Lord to be faithful.

26 I suppose therefore that this is good for the present distress, *I say*, that *it is* good for a man so to be.

27 Art thou bound unto a wife? seek not to be loosed. Art thou loosed from a wife? seek not a wife.

28 But and if thou marry, thou hast not sinned; and if a virgin marry, she hath not sinned. Nevertheless such shall have trouble in the flesh: but I spare you.

25 Now concerning the unmarried, I
have no command of the Lord, but I give
my opinion as one who by the Lord's mercy
is trustworthy. 26 I think that in view of
the impending[i] distress it is well for a person to remain as he is. 27 Are you bound
to a wife? Do not seek to be free. Are you
free from a wife? Do not seek marriage.
28 But if you marry, you do not sin, and if
a girl marries she does not sin. Yet those
who marry will have worldly troubles, and

[i] Or *present*.

4. Reasons for Avoiding Marriage (7:25-35)

25. The Greek word (παρθένοι), translated **unmarried** (RSV), is literally **virgins** (KJV); but it is clear from what follows that the apostle has in mind the unmarried men as well as the maidens (Rev. 14:4). It may be that these are people who have taken a vow of celibacy. The passage contains the frankest expression of an interim ethic anywhere in the N.T. The apostle's **opinion** is given **in view of the impending distress** (vs. 26) and because **the appointed time has grown very short** (vs. 29) and **the form of this world is passing away** (vs. 31). Since the ground for his advice has not materialized in nineteen centuries, it is difficult to see how anyone can ascribe normative significance to the words. Paul admits that it is not a **command of the Lord.** We may believe that the apostle is **trustworthy** and yet in this particular regard unfortunately mistaken. The word πιστός may mean, however, simply "believer." Paul offers his opinion as a Christian.

26-28. The **distress** does not refer to the sufferings which are the lot of every Christian (4:11; I Thess. 3:3-4), but to the messianic woes which were to precede the end. These were a standing feature of Jewish apocalyptic writings (Assumption of Moses 10:3-6; II Baruch 27:1 ff.; II Esdras 5:1-12; etc.) and appear in all Christian apocalypses as well (Mark 13:5 ff.; Rev. 6; 8–9; etc.). The word ἀνάγκη is used in this sense in Luke 21:23, where the peril to pregnant women is specially noted. **Trouble in the flesh** (KJV) expresses this more literally than **worldly troubles** (RSV). **For a man so to be** (KJV) must in the context mean **remain as he is** (RSV). The point of view throughout the

25-35. ***Advice to the Unmarried.***—Again Paul makes it clear that he is stating his private opinion, though he stresses his sincerity in doing so, in setting forth his reasons for avoiding marriage. Since the age is supposed to be drawing near to its close, and since the event is expected to bring great disorders upon the world, he holds that it is far better for believers to keep life as simple and as free from complications as possible. **I think that in view of the impending distress it is well for a person to remain as he is.** The same thought applies to those who are married and who for one reason or another may be chafing against the bond. According to their state, they should neither seek to be free nor to be married (vs. 27). So far as not only human relationships but also other preoccupations are concerned, in view of **the impending distress,** it were well in Paul's judgment for Christians to cultivate a certain sense of detachment from all worldly concerns (vs. 31). Being thus freed from **all anxieties,** they will be able to "give soul and mind and strength to serve the King of Kings!"

We know that Paul was wrong in his estimate of the nearness of the "end of the age." There are indications in his later epistles that he came to recognize this fact. Nonetheless, believing as he did when he wrote the epistle under consideration, it is a question worthy of thoughtful attention as to whether or not men and women are wise to become involved in a relationship which has "this-worldly" implications only. But the apostle was also guided by higher considerations. These are made plain where he writes, **I want you to be free from all anxieties.** There

29 But this I say, brethren, the time *is* short: it remaineth, that both they that have wives be as though they had none;

30 And they that weep, as though they wept not; and they that rejoice, as though they rejoiced not; and they that buy, as though they possessed not;

31 And they that use this world, as not abusing *it:* for the fashion of this world passeth away.

32 But I would have you without carefulness. He that is unmarried careth for the things that belong to the Lord, how he may please the Lord:

I would spare you that. 29 I mean, brethren, the appointed time has grown very
short; from now on, let those who have
wives live as though they had none, 30 and
those who mourn as though they were not
mourning, and those who rejoice as though
they were not rejoicing, and those who buy
as though they had no goods, 31 and those
who deal with the world as though they
had no dealings with it. For the form of
this world is passing away.
32 I want you to be free from anxieties. The unmarried man is anxious about
the affairs of the Lord, how to please the

chapter is thoroughly consistent. Though marriage is not a sin, it is preferable to stay single. Yet marriage is looked upon as a bondage which is hampering. It does not restrict personal freedom, but interferes with undivided allegiance to the Lord.

29-31. The shortening of the days is referred to in Mark 13:20. The word καιρός is used rather than χρόνος. It is not a matter of extended chronology, but the fateful hour of the divine deliverance. In the brief interval that remains, believers are to be unconcerned with outward affairs. Paul's words have a Stoic sound, but the context of thought is quite different. Paul is not thinking of the maintenance of an unruffled composure at all times. He is concerned with single-minded devotion to the interests of the Lord. But if wives are to be disregarded, how can the husband show the consideration urged in vs. 4? If mourning and rejoicing are alike indifferent, why should one "rejoice with those who rejoice, weep with those who weep" (Rom. 12:15) ? Unconcern for possessions seems more logical and corresponds to the early Christian detachment from the world (Luke 12:16-21) . Some participation in economic life is inevitable (II Thess. 3:12) , but life must not be wrapped up in business. The KJV gives a totally wrong idea in the rendering **abusing it.** Paul is calling for detachment from the world, rather than forbidding its misuse. In Rom. 12:2 Paul uses the verb σχηματίζω when he writes, "Do not be conformed to this world." Here he speaks of the σχῆμα or **form of this world**—the word is κόσμος instead of αἰών. The **world is passing away** (I John 2:17) ; therefore it is the part of wisdom to become as little entangled as possible in its transient affairs.

32-35. With the change of meaning of our English words, **carefulness** and **careth** (KJV) give a quite wrong impression. It is **anxieties** about which the apostle is speaking

is a delightful play in these verses on the double meaning of the word **anxious** (see Exeg., vss. 32-35) . Paul, who had endured much in his ardent desire to fulfill his Christ-given mission, realized the advantages of being a free lance. We can also be certain that the greathearted Christian gentleman did not think it right for him, at any rate, to involve another and a weaker person in the hazards and perils that fell to his lot in his missionary journeyings. He has therefore kept himself free from all such entanglements that he might with greater liberty, and with more opportunity for concentration, pursue his aims; and he commends his own example, as a matter of purely personal preference, to those who would do the same.

The highest motive is also clear in the opinion he delivers on these matters: he has remained unmarried so that his devotion to Jesus Christ and his kingdom may be secure and undivided (vs. 32) . Paul is forever Christ's man. For himself he will allow nothing and no one to supervene in that supreme life of consecration. Naturally enough, what he demands for himself he would request from others. **I say this . . . to promote good order and to secure your undivided devotion to the Lord.**

It is difficult for us to give the apostle our unqualified assent. He is obviously too influenced by his own prejudice in favor of celibacy. Others among the apostles, notably Peter, were married men and they did a splendid piece of

33 But he that is married careth for the things that are of the world, how he may please *his* wife.

34 There is difference *also* between a wife and a virgin. The unmarried woman careth for the things of the Lord, that she may be holy both in body and in spirit: but she that is married careth for the things of the world, how she may please *her* husband.

35 And this I speak for your own profit; not that I may cast a snare upon you, but for that which is comely, and that ye may attend upon the Lord without distraction.

Lord; 33 but the married man is anxious
about worldly affairs, how to please his
wife, 34 and his interests are divided. And
the unmarried woman or girl is anxious
about the affairs of the Lord, how to be
holy in body and spirit; but the married woman is anxious about worldly
affairs, how to please her husband. 35 I say
this for your own benefit, not to lay any
restraint upon you, but to promote good
order and to secure your undivided devotion to the Lord.

(cf. Matt. 6:25 ff.; Phil. 4:6). Clearly he does not mean that they should be **free from** all **anxieties.** Rather, they should be free from all other anxiety except **how to please the Lord.** Paul assumes that marriage is a primary distraction from **the affairs of the Lord.** The endeavor to please one's **wife** or **husband** is supposed to interfere with being **holy in body and spirit.** If this were really so, then should not Paul have agreed that marriage was a sin? Had he observed any such result in Aquila and Prisca? That such dangers might ensue is obvious, but it is hardly the experience of anyone familiar with young people that marriage interferes with service to the Lord. Like so many other good men, Paul is here rationalizing his prejudices. Yet Paul does seek to avoid legislating. His advice is offered for their **benefit** rather than **to lay any restraint** upon them. His one aim is to secure **undivided devotion to the Lord.**

In vs. 34 the MS witnesses vary greatly; the KJV assumes what is known as the Western text (D K O.L., Tertullian, Cyprian, Ambrose, etc.), but it is doubtful that even that text will justify the translation **there is difference also between a wife and a virgin.** Literally it would be: "a wife and a virgin are divided." But preference must be given, as all modern editors recognize, to the reading of B, the Vulg., etc., which connects the verb **divided** with the preceding sentence and inserts the adjective **unmarried** with **women** (γυνή) and omits the word **unmarried** with **girl.** This is the text which is assumed by the RSV. It is the married man **whose interests are divided.** Then the apostle goes on to affirm that there is the same contrast in absorbing interest between the unmarried woman and the one who seeks **to please her husband. Body and spirit** do not refer to separate entities but to two aspects of the one unitary person.

---

work. Paul himself was glad to receive the hospitality of Christian homes. Though his thoughts were concentrated on the risen Lord rather than the Jesus of history, he could not have been unaware of the homely facts of the Master's earthly life and in particular his love of the home. Is not Christianity itself rightly termed a "family" religion? Surely undivided loyalty to Christ and his cause is not incompatible with married life. On the contrary, it can be argued that the personal enrichment that such a relationship can bring is a priceless asset in Christian service. Even if the end of the age were imminent, this would still hold good. As it is, life must go on. Marriage is honorable in all who engage in it, "not unadvisedly or lightly, but reverently and discreetly, and in the fear of God. And it has been consecrated by the faithful keeping of good men and good women in every generation." Granted the single-mindedness of this great apostle in the service of his Master, it is pertinent to reflect that just as his "thorn in the flesh" was a means of grace to him and a mellowing influence on his character, so the experience that marriage at its best can bring might also have enriched his message by giving him deeper, firsthand knowledge of the common lot. Granted, too, the handicaps such a relationship can impose, yet there is truth in the old Norse legend, "The west wind made the Vikings."

36 But if any man think that he behaveth himself uncomely toward his virgin, if she pass the flower of *her* age, and need so require, let him do what he will, he sinneth not: let them marry.

37 Nevertheless he that standeth steadfast in his heart, having no necessity, but hath power over his own will, and hath so decreed in his heart that he will keep his virgin, doeth well.

36 If any one thinks that he is not behaving properly toward his betrothed, if his passions are strong, and it has to be, let him do as he wishes: let them marry—
it is no sin. 37 But whoever is firmly established in his heart, being under no necessity but having his desire under control, and has determined this in his heart, to keep her as his betrothed, he will do

5. Advice to Ascetic Couples (7:36-38)

36-38. In this paragraph also our two translations have entirely different understandings of Paul's meaning. Here the question at issue is not the evaluation of the MS evidence, but rather the meaning of the Greek verb γαμίζω in vs. 38. Its ordinary meaning is **giveth . . . in marriage,** and the KJV interprets the whole section in terms of this assumption. The **man** is a father and **his virgin** is his daughter. Those who support this interpretation say that Paul does not write "father" because in some cases it would be the master of a slave or a guardian or near relative. **Let them marry,** however, involves the introduction of another man hitherto unmentioned. And why should the decision of a father involve such an inner struggle (vs. 37), particularly **if she pass the flower of her age?** One might be led to think that time had taken care of the problem. And who could possibly think that it was a sin for the father to give his daughter in marriage? Clearly this translation gives no acceptable understanding of Paul's meaning.

Everything is simplified the minute it is recognized that in the later Greek the distinction between such verbal forms as γαμέω and γαμίζω had tended to disappear. Clearly Paul means to write **marry.** He is thinking of the dilemma which a young couple face. Some insist that he has in mind nothing more than any engaged couple who might at first have decided to accept Paul's advice and refrain from marriage, and then have found that decision increasingly difficult to maintain. The RSV may be understood thus. It is more probable, however, that Paul is referring to the custom of a young man's taking

36-38. ***Asceticism in Marriage.***—There was also a strongly ascetic element in the Christian community, and it seems to have taken the form of criticism and avoidance of the intimate sex relationship in married life. Indeed, it seems to have looked askance on marriage itself. One custom, which may seem curious to us, was that in which a young man and woman agreed to live together though under vows of celibacy (see Exeg., vs. 36). Paul realizes that some who acted thus were better able to bear the strain than others. Hence his advice to marry or to maintain the relationship as the case may be. In neither set of circumstances is there any sin (vs. 36). **He who marries his betrothed does well; and**—here Paul's prejudice in favor of celibacy is again made plain—**he who refrains from marriage will do better.**

Modern Christian civilization has not in the main followed Paul's advice in this respect. On the contrary, it is a sociological fact that the celibacy imposed by the monastic system right up to the Middle Ages deprived the community of generations of men and women whose endowments of nature and nurture would have been of inestimable value. What reason can we assign to this asceticism in the Corinthian church? It could hardly have stemmed from the rabbinical tradition. Every excess breeds its opposite. The asceticism of some of the cults of those days can be regarded as a protest against the grossness of the period. Perhaps the Gnostic dualism of "spirit" and "matter" had something to do with it. As all matter was conceived to be evil, all contact with matter—and "the flesh" was conceived by some extreme schools as being an aspect of "matter"—was to be made as tenuous as possible in the circumstances. This might be achieved by discipline and mystic devotion. The more devoted Christians in the Corinthian community felt the ascetic appeal most deeply, and doubtless did their utmost to make their opinion acceptable in practice among their Christian brethren. In fact, on the highest level of interpretation their asceticism was a mark of their desire to reveal their devotion to Christ.

38 So then he that giveth *her* in marriage doeth well; but he that giveth *her* not in marriage doeth better.

39 The wife is bound by the law as long as her husband liveth; but if her husband be dead, she is at liberty to be married to whom she will; only in the Lord.

well. 38 So that he who marries his betrothed does well; and he who refrains from marriage will do better.

39 A wife is bound to her husband as long as he lives. If the husband dies, she is free to be married to whom she wishes,

---

a young woman under his protection, and their living together, but under vows of celibacy. Our specific evidence for such a relationship comes from a later time (Herm. Sim. IX 11:1-4), but it seems to be implied here. This translation refers the word ὑπέρακμος to the man rather than the girl. That certainly fits the inner struggle to maintain self-control: **if his passions are strong.** If it is too difficult for them to maintain the celibate vow, it is no sin for them to marry. But Paul does not miss a chance to stress that he looks upon marriage as the less desirable choice.

6. Advice to Widows (7:39-40)

39-40. Widows occupied a special place in the early church. Their support was a benevolent responsibility from an early time (Acts 6:1-6) and soon they constituted a

---

Hence the appeal to Paul for an authoritative ruling on the matter of sex relationships generally and on the marriage relationship in particular. It is possible that since the apostle was unmarried the ascetic element in the church was making a bid for his support of their views.

39-40. ***On the Marriage of Widows.***—The issue is relatively simple. Paul simply applies the principle of the indissolubility of Christian marriage. Husband and wife are bound to one another so long as both are alive. There ought to be no question of divorce between Christian partners. But if one should die—Paul writes with regard to widows who occupied a somewhat special position in the church, but his ruling would hold good with regard to widowers—the other is free to marry a believer (vs. 39). But even so his bias in favor of celibacy leads to the characteristic conclusion that a widow **is happier if she remains as she is.**

There is at least one ambiguity in Paul's teaching concerning marriage and divorce. He does not make it clear whether in case the pagan partner in a mixed marriage seeks and obtains a divorce, the innocent, and by implication Christian partner, is free to remarry. One or two comments may be made on this point. The first is that since strictly Christian vows were probably not involved in any of the instances cited, there can logically be no reference here to the "indissolubility" of the marriage bond. Even so, the moral obligation remains for the Christian partner to maintain the Christian standards as far as possible. No case should ever be based on the circumstance that no specific Christian vows were involved. Paul's ruling still stands. The bond should be maintained: if broken, then let the pagan partner take the first step. But if that step is taken, is it right or just that the innocent party, assuming that the innocent party has honestly and sincerely done everything possible to maintain the relationship, should be obliged to remain single for the rest of his or her life? If it is better to marry than to be harried by the drive of strong instincts and emotions, how can this solution of what can be and often is a pressing problem be denied to the innocent partner? Paul gives no specific guidance on these points.

The one constructive and helpful thing to do is to regard such matters in the spirit of Jesus Christ. He is always Paul's final court of appeal, and his teaching and spirit are our standard of judgment. Jesus was not a lawgiver; his attitude and outlook were prophetic. There is in his teaching neither sanction for divorce nor fanatic opposition to it. His appeal is always to his great law of love, "This is my commandment, that you love one another as I have loved you" (John 15:12). Such love crowns and completes all the relationships of life. But even this great teaching, where divorce is concerned, leaves many questions in a state of ambiguity. Hence there is much confusion, much diversity of opinion in the various Christian churches. One church discountenances all divorce: another permits it in the case of infidelity, but refuses to remarry either the innocent or guilty party. Some churches allow divorce and are willing to remarry the innocent party, while still others in similar circumstances are willing to remarry either party, particularly if the guilty party is truly repentant and honestly seeks to begin married life on a new and better

40 But she is happier if she so abide, after my judgment: and I think also that I have the Spirit of God.

8 Now as touching things offered unto idols, we know that we all have knowledge. Knowledge puffeth up, but charity edifieth.

only in the Lord. 40 But in my judgment she is happier if she remains as she is. And I think that I have the Spirit of God.

8 Now concerning food offered to idols: we know that "all of us possess knowledge." "Knowledge" puffs up, but love

special order (I Tim. 5:3-16). Here the advice is confined to marital status and applies the principles which have been developed throughout the chapter. There should be no divorce at the instigation of a Christian partner; marriage after conversion should be only with believers; such remarriage of a widow is entirely permissible (cf. I Tim. 5:9), though Paul firmly believes that **she is happier if she remains as she is.** Possibly some of the widows were not so sure that he had **the Spirit of God** on this point.

IV. Christian Freedom (8:1–11:1)

A. Food Offered to Idols (8:1-13)

The next question raised by the Corinthians in their letter was **concerning food offered to idols.** The problem had arisen as a result of the attitude taken by certain Gnostics and libertarian members of the community. This was one of the issues on which they had affirmed, "All things are lawful for me" (6:12). Here Paul agrees with their fundamental principles as set forth in 6:13, adhering to the gospel tenet that "there is nothing outside a man which by going into him can defile him" (Mark 7:15). But the use of liberty involves the obligations of love. Though the particular issue of food offered to idols does not arise for people living in Western countries today, the principle bears upon other questions in every civilization. Paul begins the discussion as if it were an issue not yet decided for the Christian conscience in an authoritative way. It is difficult to see how the historicity of Acts 16:4 can be maintained in the face of this passage. There Paul is

foundation of Christian standards and values. There is no clear guidance in the teaching of Jesus (cf. differences of view in Matt. 5:27-32; Mark 10:2-12; Luke 16:18). In the Gospels of Mark and Luke divorce is expressly forbidden; in the Gospel of Matthew an exception is made in the case of infidelity (cf. also Matt. 19:3-9). The truth seems to be that Jesus returned plain answers to plain questions, but laid down no law. What he did was to hold marriage up to the light of God's countenance, as he did with every other legitimate experience and activity. The Christian view is that the relationship is meant to last and the vows are to be kept. No law or regulation is required to achieve this purpose; what matters is that the Christian law of love shall be given full effect, and that the grace of Christ and the indwelling power of the Spirit should sustain his followers in the determination to keep their vows. True love has in it eternal elements. Where the Master gives little specific guidance in the matter of special circumstances, we need hardly expect any from Paul. Sufficient to say that, like his Master, he is concerned to hold all the relationships of life to the highest Christian standards.

More generally, we can be grateful for his teaching. When one thinks of the vast entail of misery and insecurity that the disruption of the home means for the children, if there are children; when one considers the far-reaching effect of the psychological and spiritual repercussions in the minds and lives of the people concerned; when one realizes that what the home is in miniature, so is the nation at large; when one remembers that it is in the home and the family more than in any other institution in the life of a nation that fine quality of character is formed, and that the decay of nations begins in the homes and family life of people who once cherished high regard for these things but who have turned their backs on one of the great master lights that for generations have given guidance to mankind; then one does well to listen to such a summons as we have in this section of Paul's letter to his Christian brethren in Corinth—a summons to high Christian resolve and conduct in this most intimate and tender relationship. The day is ever present for that summons to be uttered and heard. We shall disregard it at our peril.

8:1-13. ***The General Situation.***—Paul is at this point confronted with a different kind of problem: **Now concerning food offered to idols.**

represented as distributing an official decree upon the subject. Here the apostle argues the case on its own merits and appeals to no decision by authoritative officials.

Paul's discussion falls into four main divisions: (*a*) the priority of love over liberty (8:1-13); (*b*) Paul's own renunciation of rights for the good of others (9:1-23); (*c*) the danger even to the strong (9:24–10:22); (*d*) closing assertion of principles in their bearing on private use (10:23–11:1).

It is typical of the apostle that he brings into this discussion important teaching on matters somewhat aside from the main issue. We find assertions of the pre-existence of Christ (8:6; 10:4), teaching about the meaning of the Lord's Supper (10:16-21), and revealing indications of his own attitude toward his ministry (9:19-22).

The section raises the issue of the extent to which a Christian may participate in the heathen society about him. In the younger churches today this problem is more acute; but the teaching is relevant for all who would take discipleship seriously. Wayside shrines before which feasts have been laid out can be seen in south China. Though these expressions of worship will not be found in a city like New York, one may attend there also feasts which are just as difficult to combine with participation at the Lord's table.

1. The Contrast Between Knowledge and Love (8:1-3)

8:1. Clearly Paul is quoting the slogan of a party at Corinth when he writes **all of us possess knowledge.** This gnosis is not the same word as the "wisdom" which was the key word in chs. 1–2, yet both involve the same claim to a superior position due to intellectual

---

A study of his other epistles reveals that this and other kindred problems were general among the churches in Asia Minor and on the European mainland. In the church in Rome the problem was associated with the question of vegetarianism, which was one of the forms the ascetic tendency took in that church, and also with the further question as to whether pagans who had been converted to Christianity were therefore to observe Jewish feast days (Rom. 14:1-6). Here the issue had to do with food which had been consecrated to a pagan deity. Often enough, the meat eaten on various social occasions came from this source—it was part of the animal offered in sacrifice to the deity concerned—and Christians were observed to be present. That was indeed almost inevitable. When a pagan became a Christian he did not therefore break all the bonds of friendship with those who did not, and often enough would be invited to come to their homes and to partake of a meal.[8] Doubtless Jewish influence was involved in the scruples that certain sensitive people held with regard to this matter, for no strict Jew could be induced to touch such food: for him it was contaminated. In any case, the Corinthian situation raised some very serious practical problems; and one is glad it did: glad for the light that is cast upon the life of these primitive Christian churches, and glad for the vital principles of Christian living that were evoked, as well as for new aspects of Paul's amazing personality that were thus revealed. The issue had become important in Corinth; the question whether or not one should eat meat that had been formally consecrated to a pagan deity such as Artemis, the moon goddess and the patron saint of those who enjoyed the pleasures of the hunt, had been elevated into a test of loyalty to Christ and the church.

This in turn had split the church into two groups (see Exeg., vss. 1-13). One group, with which the apostle has strong intellectual and moral sympathies, took the view that idols are nonexistent and that it is therefore absurd to refuse meat which had been formally consecrated to them. **Hence, as to the eating of food offered to idols, we know that "an idol has no real existence," and that "there is no God but one."** This party claimed to be strong minded, enlightened, and free from such foolish prejudices. It had no wish to have its liberty of action compromised by any concession to those who took a different point of view, and its members had little patience, and doubtless much scorn, for the scruples of their opponents.

As we have seen, Paul shared their opinions; but he was very far from sharing their spirit. There was never stouter protagonist of the freedom of the individual conscience than the apostle himself. In his Epistle to the Romans (ch. 14), where he deals with this precise issue, and where he seeks to answer the question implicit in all such inquiries, "How ought we to behave who have been introduced to this wonderful new way of life expressed in the Christian faith?" he almost bluntly says, "When God gave us brains, he meant us to use them!" "Let every one be fully convinced in his own

[8] Moffatt, *I Corinthians*, pp. 101-4.

2 And if any man think that he knoweth any thing, he knoweth nothing yet as he ought to know.

builds up. 2 If any one imagines that he knows something, he does not yet know

---

insight. Paul is more conscious, however, of the limitations of **knowledge.** It may inflate the individual without necessarily serving the community. As in his discussion of "spiritual gifts," he lays primary emphasis on the social effects. Though the word **edifieth** (KJV) has the same root meaning as **builds up,** it has acquired emotional associations not intended by the apostle. He is continuing the figure of construction which had been used in 3:10-14. The KJV unfortunately uses **charity** here, though **love** is used in 4:21; thus it obscures the consistent contrast throughout the passage of **knowledge** and **love.**

2. True knowledge begins in the recognition of our ignorance. Real learning should make men humble rather than conceited. The only fruitful knowledge is that which leads to love.

---

mind" (Rom. 14:5). Paul believed in the right of the Christian individual to exercise his independent judgment on all such questions. But he will not allow the "emancipated" ones to indulge their strength of mind at the expense of those who are ultrasensitive of conscience on such matters. Especially is he against all conceit of knowledge or arrogance of so-called enlightened opinion. There his deliverance on this obsolete question is of value still.

It is probable in the very nature of the situation, remembering the free, independent Greek spirit and the cosmopolitan nature of the great seaport, that the enlightened view was held by the majority in the Corinthian church. Weight of numbers allied to broad, liberal opinion, could all too easily induce a complacent and perhaps arrogant attitude. Again, it was always a temptation peculiar to the Greek temperament to accept the dictum that "knowledge is virtue." Doubtless the emancipated section of the Corinthian Christian community, like some of their modern counterparts, were self-conscious of their strength of mind, liberality of opinion, and force of judgment.

Thus there is something more than a hint of Socratic irony in Paul's strictures concerning "knowledge." Just as Socrates, centuries before, conceived it to be part of his mission to deflate conceit, to expose superficiality in the realm of strongly expressed opinions on all sorts of subjects, and to explode pretensions to knowledge, so Paul, with a hint of irony, criticizes and rebukes those who have adopted toward their more scrupulous brethren a somewhat superior pose. His point is that while there is undoubted moral value in independence and strength of mind and judgment in Christian believers, there is even more to be said for Christian character and love. He sums up his advice in an aphorism, using what seems to have been a favorite expression, **We know that "all of us possess knowledge." "Knowledge" puffs up, but love builds up.**

1-3. *"Knowledge" and "Love."*—We must recognize that Paul is using the term "knowledge" in the somewhat special sense indicated; for it is not universally true that knowledge in the ordinary sense tends to induce a conceited and superior frame of mind (see Exeg., vs. 1). Humility invariably is wedded to knowledge, and the more comprehensive the knowledge of any students of any particular subject may be, usually the more humble minded they are. Those who know most, doubtless, are not ignorant of the importance of what they know or of its implications; the reason for their essential humility of spirit does not lie there: they are conscious that all their knowledge is a mere fragment of what is yet to be known. That is why the truly learned are essentially humble minded. Paul is not thinking of such folk.

He is thinking of the kind of knowledge that is implied in man's personal relationship with God (see Exeg., vs. 3). His trend of thought has Hebrew antecedents. **But if one loves God, one is known by him** (vs. 3). Censoriousness, conceit of knowledge, and the superior attitude, however it may be justified in the circumstances, is incompatible with the spirit of love. When the liberal-minded among the Corinthian Christians took pride in their broad views of the matter under discussion, it was the very limitation of their knowledge that "puffed" them up. How often it is so. When some people learn a little, they imagine that they know a lot. That is why "a little learning is a dangerous thing." Has one not seen that danger, not only in individual and community life, but on the international scale? Had some of those so-called statesmen, who from time to time have so wantonly plunged the world into unparalleled havoc and misery, but known a little more about their own limitations, and a little more

3 But if any man love God, the same is known of him.
4 As concerning therefore the eating of those things that are offered in sacrifice unto idols, we know that an idol *is* nothing in the world, and that *there is* none other God but one.

as he ought to know. 3 But if one loves God, one is known by him.
4 Hence, as to the eating of food offered to idols, we know that "an idol has no real existence," and that "there is no God but one." 5 For although there may be so-

3. Paul concludes his statement with a surprising though characteristic turn. Love is not the road to our knowledge; it is the presupposition of being known by God. Though our earliest papyrus (p^{46}) omits both **God** and **by him,** it is unlikely that these words were absent from the original text. In Gal. 4:9 Paul makes the same contrast between "knowing God" and being "known by him." In 13:12 full knowledge of God belongs to the new age, though we are continually known by him. This idea of the divine initiative roots in the O.T. (Amos 3:2; Jer. 1:5). God had foreknown his people (Rom. 8:29; 11:2). Though believers may not yet know God fully, they may love him in response to his love for them.

2. The Contents of Knowledge (8:4-6)

4. What was the knowledge about food offered to idols which Paul shared with the majority in the Corinthian group? It had two complementary aspects. One could be stated in the language of the Shema which every devout Jew recited daily, **There is no God but one** (cf. Deut. 6:4). The word **other** in the KJV comes from the corrupt Textus

about other people, and about the imponderable elements that have always had a determining voice in the ordering of this mysterious universe in which we live, they might have been purged of their arrogance and conceit, and even have been moved to apply their undoubted powers to constructive rather than destructive purposes. Just as the real cure for little faith is not less faith but more, so the remedy for little knowledge is not less knowledge but more; and with it there ever goes the spirit of humility, **If any one imagines that he knows something, he does not yet know as he ought to know.** Such knowledge "puffs up"!

But love builds up (vs. 1). Paul will have more to say about that later on (see Expos., ch. 13). Meantime, he is content to insist, and it is a favorite theme with him, that love is the really constructive force at work in the world, i.e., love which is inspired by devotion to God, as God has made himself known to men through Jesus Christ. For Paul it is Christian love, *agapē* not *eros,* that yields insight into the nature of God and therefore of reality itself, and that binds the fellowship of Christians together in mutual service and understanding and forbearance. Such love, with the insight it yields, is not a matter of human cleverness; it is, as von Hügel would put it, "given"; it is a matter of revelation. God makes himself known to those who love him, and, as we shall see almost immediately, for Paul love is evoked by the revelation of God's love through Jesus Christ.

Such love is constructive. One may almost say that wherever a truly constructive piece of worth-while work is being done in the world, there the spirit of divine love is active. It may be in the building of a home, or of a genuine fellowship, or of a social community, or of a church, or of a school, or even of institutions devoted to international justice and the peace that is the fruit of such justice; if the spirit of love is present, the effort is in alignment with the nature of things. This is one of the main strands woven into the vast and rich tapestry of Paul's great gospel message. Browning caught the spirit of the constructiveness of Christian love when he wrote:

> Be love your light and trust your guide,
> with these explore my heart!
> No obstacle to trip you then, strike hands
> and souls apart! [9]

For the Christian love that yields true insight, that creates true fellowship, that understands the nature of forbearance, Paul pleads. Such love builds up!

4-6. ***A Confession of Faith.***—Having made this preliminary point by way of preparation for what is to follow, Paul is quite willing to concede that his sympathies lie with those mem-

[9] Ferishtah's Fancies, "Shah Abbas."

5 For though there be that are called
gods, whether in heaven or in earth, (as
there be gods many, and lords many,)
6 But to us *there is but* one God, the
Father, of whom *are* all things, and we in
him; and one Lord Jesus Christ, by whom
are all things, and we by him.

called gods in heaven or on earth — as
indeed there are many "gods" and many
"lords" — 6 yet for us there is one God,
the Father, from whom are all things and
for whom we exist, and one Lord, Jesus
Christ, through whom are all things and
through whom we exist.

Receptus. The complementary truth was that **an idol has no real existence.** The KJV rendering of this half of Paul's statement is distinctly misleading. Paul did not mean that an idol was **nothing in the world.** If by εἴδωλον he meant the statue of the pagan deity, at least that existed. If he meant the deity which it represented, that too had some kind of existence, as Paul goes on to affirm in vs. 5. Various passages in the O.T. made the same assumption (Pss. 82:6; 97:7; 138:1; Job 1:6). If Yahweh was "God of gods" (Deut. 10:17) there must be other entities which bear the name of gods. The RSV translation attempts to express these two sides of Paul's belief, an explicit affirmation of monotheism, and yet admission of the existence of other supernatural beings which some look upon as gods.

5. Paul distinguished between two classes of such beings, **gods** and **lords.** That is unmistakable, though *kyrios* is applied to Yahweh twice as often as *theos* in the LXX, and Paul can use it of God as well as Christ. These lords (Col. 1:16) were rulers over various parts of the world. *Kyrios* is the one to whom a person belongs. The word is used of the master of a slave and of the ruler of his subjects. The Greeks did not often apply the term to their gods, for they did not look upon these deities as creators. It was otherwise in Egypt and the Orient. There it was applied from the first century B.C., especially to Serapis and Isis in Egypt and to Zeus in Syria. It was applied to the Roman emperor first in the reign of Tiberius, but it never became prominent in the imperial cult. It is warmly disputed whether Paul derived his use from the O.T. or whether the terminology arose in contrast to the Hellenistic lords. In 7:10 he applies the term to the earthly Jesus, but more frequently it affirms the dignity and position of the risen and exalted Lord (2:8; Rom. 10:9; II Cor. 4:5; Phil. 2:10).

6. But Paul meant much more than the affirmation of henotheism, the restriction of worship to the God of the Christian faith. In his eyes only one is really God, the Father of all, who is the creator and consummation of all things. So likewise, Jesus Christ was not one Lord among many. He is the only true Lord, one who shares his place with no other because he is the one mediator of creation. Paul chose his prepositions carefully in order to distinguish between God the Father, who is the ultimate source of creation, and Christ, the Lord, **through whom** this activity took place. In Rom. 11:36 Paul applies both

---

bers of the church who are not troubled by scruples over food sanctified to idols, and who, disbelieving in idols, affirm that there is only one true God. But now comes a section of the chapter which is in the nature of a parenthesis; yet it has a definite bearing on what has immediately gone before and what is to follow. It really amounts to a confession of Paul's faith, and therefore marks his general standpoint in dealing with all such problems and situations. We need not look for a systematic exposition of Paul's Christology in the epistle; he is too much concerned with the practical issues: but here he makes his position clear that he regards God as the creator and sustainer of all that has existence, and that his creative, sustaining power is mediated through Jesus Christ (see Exeg., vs. 6). This gives significance to his conception of Jesus as Lord. There is no systematic attempt to identify Jesus with God, yet the spiritual and moral unity between Father and Son is explicitly recognized. For Paul, what Jesus Christ was in time, God is throughout all eternity. His faith in Jesus is bound up with his faith in God, and he is deeply conscious of the debt that all Christian believers owe to Jesus as Lord, and of their profound dependence upon him for their status and preservation. The idea he has in mind is clear: those who have been liberated by faith through the grace of Jesus Christ into a great new experience of life's fullness are in no bondage to idols. **For us there is one**

7 Howbeit *there is* not in every man that knowledge: for some with conscience of the idol unto this hour eat *it* as a thing offered unto an idol; and their conscience being weak is defiled.

7 However, not all possess this knowledge. But some, through being hitherto accustomed to idols, eat food as really offered to an idol; and their conscience,

functions to God alone, but in Col. 1:16 he repeats the affirmation that all things are "through" Christ and "for" Christ.

Some interpreters have sought to exclude the idea of the cosmic mediation of Christ by assigning the whole verse to the Gnostics whom Paul has been quoting. That is unlikely, for it is impossible to deny successfully that Paul believed in the pre-existence of Christ. Though he brings in the cosmological significance of Christ only incidentally in connection with his discussion of other things, this belief clearly belonged to his faith. Redemption could come only through the power which also mediated creation; both the beginning and the end are related to Christ.

It is improbable that we shall ever be in position to explain exactly how Paul came to affirm this pre-existence. Had he ground for belief that Jesus himself had taught it? Was it a development of the Jewish belief in wisdom as the means by which God created? Did it arise through the influence of Greek popular philosophy on a speculative Judaism with which Paul had had contact? Was it due to the influence of Egyptian beliefs that a "Lord" had sway over the world as well as within the cult? It is unlikely that research will ever demonstrate a genealogy satisfactory to all specialists in the field. Because of our very fragmentary evidence from the ancient world, we can know only "in part."

But it is perfectly clear what Paul wants to affirm. Neither Caesar nor Isis is Lord, but only Jesus Christ. When Paul ascribed lordship to Christ, in contrast to later church dogma, he did not mean that Christ was God. Christ was definitely subordinated to God (3:23; 15:28). Paul did not believe in two Gods. He believed in God the Father and in Jesus Christ the Lord. How these were related was a problem which waited upon the theological speculation of a much later time.

3. The Attitude Toward the Weaker Brother (8:7-13)

Paul turns from the knowledge which he shares with his readers to the love which they are not manifesting. Correct intellectual insight is not enough, for Christians are members of a community toward which they have responsibilities. It is striking that Paul did not attempt to educate those who lacked this knowledge, but accused those who were not showing love toward the brethren. He seemed to realize that emotional associations are stronger in controlling the actions of most men than sheer logic. The Gnostics had apparently supposed that by drawing bold conclusions from their new faith they were commending themselves to God. As a matter of fact, they were destroying the weak. When Paul speaks of "weak" and "strong" in Rom. 14:1–15:1 (cf. I Cor. 9:21), the question is of asceticism rather than of contact with idolatry. In each case Paul's appeal is on the same basis, the need for love.

7. The KJV was following inferior MSS when it read **some with conscience of the idol.** Most modern editors read συνήθεια rather than συνείδησις. The former word is the

God the Father, from whom are all things and for whom we exist, and one Lord, Jesus Christ, through whom are all things and through whom we exist. All who by faith have walked in that divine companionship will be guided and marked in their attitude and relationships with their fellows, not by any claim to superiority of knowledge, but by the same spirit of love which has done so much for them. The true effect of such knowledge is revealed by the character of those who possess it. Weaker brethren, for whom Christ also died, are to be dealt with in a spirit of love.

7-13. ***The Christian Attitude to Sensitive Consciences.***—Having thus prepared the way, Paul, like Bunyan's Greatheart, now champions the cause of the weaker brother. There was a minority group in the church who were troubled

8 But meat commendeth us not to God: for neither, if we eat, are we the better; neither, if we eat not, are we the worse.

being weak, is defiled. 8 Food will not commend us to God. We are no worse off if we

basis for the RSV, **through being hitherto accustomed to idols.** All their lives former pagans had assumed that gods partook of the food offered to them. They could not uproot these deep-seated associations in a few months. By a **weak** conscience Paul did not refer to the blurring of a distinction between right and wrong. These people were overscrupulous. Their conscience was weak in the sense that it was inadequately informed by knowledge. The most conscientious people may be moved by quite misguided principles. A conviction of moral obligation is not necessarily accompanied by infallibility of insight into the content of duty.

Paul uses the word **conscience** no less than fourteen times (with six additional in the Pastorals), of which eight occur in this one letter and three more in II Corinthians. All the passages in this letter are found in this discussion of food (vss. 10, 12; 10:25-29). Originally the Greek word had no connection with ethics, but meant "community in knowledge" and then "self-consciousness." It is found in Wisd. Sol. 17:10 and in the popular philosophical writings of the time. Though it is used by Epictetus and Seneca, it is not distinctive of Stoic writers and affords no indication of a particular Stoic influence on Paul. The word does not refer to a guide to conduct but to a "self-consciousness" which follows upon the act and judges it. Paul does not say that the "man" who eats food offered to idols is defiled; it is his **conscience** which is thus affected.

8. In itself food is morally indifferent. At the moment Paul is not necessarily thinking of the kosher regulations of his own people. Did he mean to imply that the eating of pork would create no barrier for reception by God? He certainly would have agreed with the

by scruples of conscience over the question of eating meat which had been formally sanctified to pagan deities, and not all their experience of Christian emancipation could relieve their minds. It would be a mistake to regard them as weak-minded, obstinate, and censorious people who were determined to impose their own ideas on the entire community. Paul himself would have resisted any such attempt. His scathing comments on the Judaizing party that tried to impose Jewish customs and rites, notably circumcision, on Gentile-Christian communities, indicate the strength of his resistance to any such trends in the church. This minority may be regarded as the puritan element in Corinth. They were not so sure as some of their brethren that idols and demonic powers were nonexistent, and in this they found support in the spirit and outlook of the age. In any case, they were against compromise on this particular issue. If we consider the influence of similar people on kindred issues in our own times, we can estimate the effect of this scrupulous section on the life of the church in Corinth. Take such questions as the use and abuse of alcohol, Sunday sport, and the Christian use of the sabbath, as well as pacifism and militancy in time of war. Whether we agree with the puritan element on any or none of these points, no one would seek to deny the value and sincerity of their witness. For them it is a matter of conscience. They have a deep sense of responsibility for their action and for the trend and quality of their personal life. Over and above this, they also have a very wholesome sense of their responsibility in the eyes of God. Such qualities of mind and spirit are not to be lightly regarded. Nor does Paul, though he insists on the right of the private conscience to form its own judgments, lightly disregard them.

But we may come to a deeper understanding of the church situation in Corinth, and the text bears the weight of the inference, if we can visualize a third party in the church, a party not nearly so strong minded as the other two which have been described. Probably the "weaker brethren" is a reference to this third group. **But some, through being hitherto accustomed to idols, eat food as really offered to an idol; and their conscience, being weak, is defiled.** These are not convinced that idols do not exist or that they do not possess certain powers over those who partake of food which comes from the sacrificed animal. They have entered into the fellowship of the Christian faith, but they are also "playing for safety" by occasionally conforming to pagan practices. There are always weaker brethren who try to "run with the hare and hold with the hound." In the O.T. we read much about "the mixed

9 But take heed lest by any means this liberty of yours become a stumblingblock to them that are weak.

10 For if any man see thee which hast knowledge sit at meat in the idol's temple, shall not the conscience of him which is weak be emboldened to eat those things which are offered to idols;

11 And through thy knowledge shall the weak brother perish, for whom Christ died?

do not eat, and no better off if we do. 9 Only
take care lest this liberty of yours somehow become a stumbling-block to the weak.
10 For if any one sees you, a man of knowledge, at table in an idol's temple, might he
not be encouraged, if his conscience is
weak, to eat food offered to idols? 11 And
so by your knowledge this weak man is
destroyed, the brother for whom Christ

---

writer to the Hebrews (13:9) that the heart is not strengthened by food, and he explicitly states in Rom. 14:17 that entrance to the kingdom of God does not depend on dietary practices.

9. In building the temple of God one may use precious stones which will remain. But the conduct of the Gnostics placed a **stumbling-block** in the path of others. The word translated here as **liberty** (ἐξουσία) is not the same as the one used in 10:29 and Gal. 5:1. It is more often rendered as "power" or "authority," but the basic meaning is "capacity to act." Paul may have been induced to use it here because he planned to use it in 9:4, where it is translated "right" (RSV).

10-11. When a Gnostic acts on his conviction that "an idol has no real existence," a man with a **weak conscience** may be encouraged to imitate his conduct. The evil effect will not lie in what he has done, but in his later attitude toward it, when the old emotional

---

multitude" of people who followed the children of Israel from Egypt, and who entered the land after the conquest of Israel by the Assyrians. There is a graphic chapter (II Kings 17) which tells of some of the misadventures of these people. They ascribed their experiences to their failure to adapt themselves to "the manner of the god of the land" to which they had come. Obviously the remedy was to get the priests of Israel to teach them the manner of the god of the land so that he might be placated. This done, the ancient scribe has depicted the resultant situation. "They feared the LORD, and served their own gods." Even thus does life make havoc of logic! Many people try to do that. They call it "making the best of both worlds." Jesus himself was aware of this compromising tendency in human nature and made it quite clear that there are areas where compromise is not to be tolerated. In stern language he warned his hearers, "You cannot serve God and mammon" (Matt. 6:24). These "weaker brethren" doubtless drew comfort for their lapses, despite their twinges of conscience, from the fact that the "enlightened" and strong-minded section of the church, which did not believe in idols, had no scruples about eating such meat.

Paul's attitude to the situation is splendidly characteristic of his broad vision and strength of spirit. As we have noted, he shares the views of those who have no scruples in the matter, and in one more pithy sentence he crystallizes his conviction, **Food will not commend us to God. We are no worse off if we do not eat, and no better off if we do.** Then he aligns himself with those more puritan members of the community to the extent, at least, of asserting strongly that the liberty men find through the faith in Jesus Christ must not be asserted to the extent of confusing and stumbling the weaker brethren. There is a law of liberty and there is a law of love! Where liberty and love cannot walk together in harmonious agreement, then liberty for the Christian must give way to love. **Only take care lest this liberty of yours somehow become a stumbling-block to the weak.** It is possible for the strong-minded, by their indulgence, which does them no harm, to do incalculable harm to a weaker brother. He may even be ruined spiritually (see Exeg., vss. 10-11); and that in Paul's view is a sin both against the "weaker brother" and against Jesus Christ who loved him and who died for him (vs. 11). It is no final argument to say that the weaker brother may be edified or educated by the example of those stronger-minded than himself. As Moffatt[1] points out, there is more than a hint of indignation, which deepens into a note of solemn warning, as he reminds the stronger-minded brethren of the lengths to which Jesus Christ had gone for the redemption of every one of them. Compared with the sacrifice on

[1] *I Corinthians*, pp. 111-13.

12 But when ye sin so against the brethren, and wound their weak conscience, ye sin against Christ.

13 Wherefore, if meat make my brother to offend, I will eat no flesh while the world standeth, lest I make my brother to offend.

9 Am I not an apostle? am I not free? have I not seen Jesus Christ our Lord? are not ye my work in the Lord?

died. 12 Thus, sinning against your brethren and wounding their conscience when
it is weak, you sin against Christ. 13 Therefore, if food is a cause of my brother's falling, I will never eat meat, lest I cause my
brother to fall.

9 Am I not free? Am I not an apostle?
Have I not seen Jesus our Lord? Are

associations may lead to entire loss of faith and a relapse into pagan ways. This cannot be a matter of unconcern for it affects **the brother for whom Christ died.** The death of Christ had a very personal significance (Gal. 2:20).

12. Sin is more than unsocial conduct. We sin against men because of what they are in the sight of God. A sin against brethren in the church is nothing less than a sin against Christ, for Jesus had affirmed, "As you did it to one of the least of these my brethren, you did it to me" (Matt. 25:40, 45).

13. **Make my brother to offend** (KJV) is much too weak to give the force of σκανδαλίζει. This means to "cause him to sin" or **to fall** (RSV). We may offend people without bringing them to disaster. Paul affirmed that **food** is far too unimportant for one to risk such dire consequences because of it. In the light of this possibility love will never insist upon the exercise of such a freedom. Though the phrase used is literally "to the [end of the] age," it is the regular idiom for **never.** In the background of Paul's thought is the strong assertion of Jesus that no sacrifice is too great in order to avoid falling into sin (cf. Mark 9:42-47). The saving of one's self may not be separated from the saving of fellow believers.

B. Paul's Own Renunciation of Rights (9:1-23)

Though it does not directly advance the discussion of the immediate issue, ch. 9 is not on that account to be referred to another of Paul's letters. The section presents an example of his own practice, showing how he had waived admitted rights in the interest of building up the community. Two of these are named: his right to be accompanied by a wife, and his right to be supported by the churches which he served. After all that he had said in ch. 7 about the desirability of the unmarried state, it is not strange that he leaves the first right unamplified. Also, the more he enlarges upon his practice of self-support, the less it appears as a heavy cross for him to bear. Yet in 4:12 he has included it among the hardships which he had to endure.

Calvary, it is a small thing after all to give up this minor indulgence; for what worse off shall any of them be if they refrain from such meat when the integrity and spiritual welfare of the weaker brethren are in jeopardy? Christian liberty is never to be exercised casually. The saving principle is always, even in matters of detail, to walk in the spirit of him who died for us all. Here is one of the apostle's ruling convictions for all the churches. It receives still deeper emphasis in another connection in the Epistle to the Galatians, where among other things he writes, "Bear one another's burdens, and so fulfill the law of Christ" (Gal. 6:2). That may mean shouldering a cross, but the mind of Christ is a cross-bearing mind, and his law is love. Paul adds, as ever, the personal touch. Like his Master, he will require nothing from his Christian brethren that he is not himself prepared to offer. **Therefore, if food is a cause of my brother's falling, I will never eat meat, lest I cause my brother to fall.** And again, in the same connection, "I try to please all men in everything I do, not seeking my own advantage, but that of many, that they may be saved. Be imitators of me, as I am of Christ" (10:33; 11:1).

9:1-27. *Doubts Cast on Paul's Status as an Apostle.*—This chapter marks a change of mood, though as we shall see in a moment, the apostle turns the situation with which he deals to good account as a reinforcement of the pre-

2 If I be not an apostle unto others, yet doubtless I am to you: for the seal of mine apostleship are ye in the Lord.

not you my workmanship in the Lord? 2 If to others I am not an apostle, at least I am to you; for you are the seal of my apostleship in the Lord.

The necessity to preach the gospel leads Paul to widen the perspective until it includes other aspects of his missionary obligation. It involves not only the foregoing of rights, but accommodation to the prejudices and needs of the groups to which he had gone. This will open up the question of the degree to which Paul had become "all things to all men." Does it explain some of the apparently compromising situations in which Acts presents Paul?

Though some interpreters have treated the entire chapter as a unit, the real transition in thought comes with vs. 24. Vs. 23 concludes Paul's discussion of his voluntary restriction of his own liberty. Vs. 24 introduces the next idea: the inherent dangers, even to the strong, which lie in the eating of idol meat under certain circumstances.

1. The Privileges of an Apostle (9:1-6)

9:1. Of course Paul was free, for the heart of his gospel was the liberation which Christ had brought to men who had been enslaved. Of course he was an apostle, for with that claim he had introduced this letter. But these rhetorical questions give him the opportunity to expand on the freedom of an apostle. The first question looks back to ch. 8; the second looks forward to the issues ahead. The inferior texts followed by the KJV have these questions in reverse order. That he *is* an apostle is proved in two ways: (*a*) The risen Christ had appeared to him (Gal. 1:16); the call to this work and the authority for it came directly from the living Lord. Paul employs here the name Jesus. It was not a mythical figure, but the Jesus of history who had appeared to him. The Exeg. of ch. 15 will include a fuller discussion of the appearance to Paul. According to his understanding of apostleship, it was not a ministry which could be communicated by any man to another. (*b*) The second proof lay in the blessing which God had bestowed on his work. Despite the disorders which troubled Paul, the Corinthian community was sufficient demonstration of the fact that God had called him to this task.

2. Those who had not seen the blessings accompanying Paul's ministry might have some reason to doubt his **apostleship.** But it was otherwise with the converts who were the **seal** of his commission. The word **seal** is common in Revelation. Elsewhere Paul uses

---

vious argument where he elevates the law of love above the law of liberty. It is one of the revealing passages in his letters, a kind of literary window through which we get a glimpse of the very soul of this great man. The passage itself is written with deep emotion and also with tender winsomeness, and it depicts for us, as so often Paul's letters do, apparently without his being at all aware of the fact, the man who is overwhelmingly in love with his job as messenger and preacher of the gospel, a gospel which has laid such constraint upon him that he can do no other (vs. 16). It is one of those revealing flashes of autobiography scattered among his writings that reveal a man whose passion is as deep as his vision is high and wide. Paul grows in stature before our eyes as he faces the criticisms, the sneers, and the underhand, subversive movements of his detractors in Corinth, and yet turns their opposition and innuendoes to good account in reinforcing the point at issue.

This is my defense to those who would examine me. Do we not have the right to our food and drink? Do we not have the right to be accompanied by a wife, as the other apostles and the brothers of the Lord and Cephas? There seem to have been at least three points in the critical attitude taken against Paul by certain members of the church, and it is difficult to resist the inference that they were determined for reasons of their own to undermine his influence and his authority and especially his status as an apostle. In the first place, they complained that he declined to accept any maintenance for himself from the church. This is a charge that Paul had to face elsewhere also. "For you remember our labor and toil, brethren; we worked night and day, that we might not burden any of you, while we preached to

3 Mine answer to them that do examine me is this:
4 Have we not power to eat and to drink?
5 Have we not power to lead about a sister, a wife, as well as other apostles, and *as* the brethren of the Lord, and Cephas?

3 This is my defense to those who would
examine me. 4 Do we not have the right to
our food and drink? 5 Do we not have the
right to be accompanied by a wife,[j] as the
other apostles and the brothers of the Lord

[j] Greek *a sister as wife.*

it only in Rom. 4:11, where the sign of circumcision comes afterward as the seal of righteousness which was by faith. The corresponding verb is used in II Cor. 1:22, where it is connected with the gift of the Spirit. Here the conversions have come as a proof of the genuineness of the call which had gone before.

3. Was the apostleship of Paul under attack at Corinth at this time? Certainly that situation was part of the background of II Corinthians (cf. 12:11-12). But had that development arisen as yet? Many interpreters believe that Paul was defending himself here either against a Judaistic wing of the church or against a "spiritual" party. These opponents contended that Paul admitted he was not a real apostle because he did not take support from the church. Paul replies that if he does not exercise this right, it is not because he is unaware of it, or because he thus admits that he is ineligible, but because he chooses to practice this self-abnegation. Such may be the case, but it is difficult to be sure when Paul is replying to attacks, and when he is writing without such motivation. Yet his use of the word **defense** here suggests that he has been attacked.

4. The first right is **to our food and drink** (**power** in the KJV gives a quite erroneous impression). Some believe that the reference is to the fasts—that Paul is claiming the right to disregard such periods. It is much more probable that we should supply the words "at the expense of the community," and see in the verse an initial statement of his chief illustration, his refusal to be supported by the community.

5. Missionaries who traveled in the company of their wives are mentioned in climactic order. Apostles (cf. 15:7) are a larger group than the twelve. We cannot be sure that all

you the gospel of God" (I Thess. 2:9). In the view of his critics this refusal of his to receive any material help cast doubt on his status as an apostle, and they compared him unfavorably with Peter and the other apostles, and—an interesting side light on the growth and development of the early Christian church—with "the brothers of the Lord." Again, they made it a ground of criticism that Paul was unmarried and preferred to travel in company with such as Barnabas or Silas or Luke, while the other apostles undertook their missionary journeys in company with their wives. A third ground of complaint, likely enough, had reference to his liberal views both with regard to food that had been consecrated to idols, and also perhaps with reference to Jewish traditions and customs such as circumcision, and other kindred matters. Perhaps some of the puritan elements in the church can be ranked among the apostle's detractors.

His reply is forthright and strong and is tinged with deep feeling. He is ever sensitive on any point that seems to cast even a shadow of doubt on his full status and authority as an apostle of Jesus Christ. Without wasting time on preliminaries, he plunges right into his defense. **Am I not free? Am I not an apostle? Have I not seen Jesus our Lord? Are not you my workmanship in the Lord?** Using homely illustrations, Paul develops the argument that like the other apostles he is free to receive material maintenance from the churches he serves if he feels inclined to do so. The soldier on active service does not serve his country at his own expense; the keeper of a vineyard is entitled to some of the fruits of his labor, and the herdsman likewise has legitimate rights in respect of the flocks under his care. Paul reinforces his claim by a quotation from scripture (vss. 8-12). At the back of his mind also is the definite rule laid down by Jesus himself (vs. 14). When the seventy were sent out to proclaim the gospel of the kingdom, among other definite instructions the Master included these words, "And remain in the same house, eating and drinking what they provide, for the laborer deserves his wages; do not go from house to house" (Luke 10:7). That ruling was decisive for all the churches.

He argues along two lines. The first is that he also had seen the Lord (vs. 1). There seem to have been those in the church who cast doubt on the full validity of Paul's apostolic status

6 Or I only and Barnabas, have not we power to forbear working?
7 Who goeth a warfare any time at his own charges? who planteth a vineyard, and eateth not of the fruit thereof? or who feedeth a flock, and eateth not of the milk of the flock?
8 Say I these things as a man? or saith not the law the same also?

and Ce'phas? 6 Or is it only Barnabas and I
who have no right to refrain from working
for a living? 7 Who serves as a soldier at
his own expense? Who plants a vineyard without eating any of its fruit? Who tends a flock without getting some of the milk?
8 Do I say this on human authority?

---

of **the brothers of the Lord** were included among these. Elsewhere Paul refers only to James (cf. 15:7; Gal. 1:19). This verse is one important link in the chain of evidence that Jesus was for Paul a strictly historical character. The apostle gives no hint that these were not brothers in the fullest physical sense. **Cephas** is mentioned last because of his party at Corinth. Assuming the identification with Simon Peter, we see the agreement of Paul with Mark on his marital status (Mark 1:30). During the lifetime of Jesus the disciples had "left all" to follow him (Mark 10:28), but apparently this practice had not continued during the time following the resurrection of Jesus.

6. The mention of Barnabas as one who also refrained from living at the expense of the community confirms the language of Acts in referring to both of them as apostles (Acts 14:14). He had accompanied Paul in the evangelization of southern Asia Minor, but the unfortunate break between them (Gal. 2:13) came before the campaigns in Europe. Paul now speaks of his former companion without apparent tension. Since the name of Barnabas does not appear after Acts 15, we have no means of knowing whether he had association with Paul after that time.

2. The Apostolic Right to Financial Support (9:7-14)

In rapid succession Paul offers four arguments in defense of his right: (*a*) It is the custom in daily life (vs. 7); (*b*) it is grounded in scripture (vss. 8-12); (*c*) it is corroborated by temple practice (vs. 13); (*d*) it is the explicit injunction of the Lord himself (vs. 14).

7-8. A **soldier** is not expected to serve at **his own expense;** whatever else a worker in a vineyard or with a flock may earn, he will certainly receive his own keep (cf. Deut. 20:6). These human illustrations are supported by **the law.** Paul appeals, however, to a passage which also deals with these experiences of daily life; but he refuses to believe that Scripture could really be concerned with such mundane matters. Therefore he resorts to allegory in order to extract what seems to him to be a more elevated meaning.

---

on this very ground, viz., that he was not one of the original band of disciples who had been with Jesus in "the days of his flesh." That point has less importance for the modern mind than it obviously possessed then. Many people had seen Jesus in "the days of his flesh"; some had even been attracted to him and had followed him, at least for a season, but that did not then or at any time constitute a call to apostolic status. Paul does not attach undue importance to the point, but for what it is worth he emphasizes his own personal experience (cf. II Cor. 5:16). With the revelation that came to him after travail for a long time in his own soul, Paul, on the high road to Damascus, had received the assurance of his full apostolic authority. He never doubts it, and he will never allow anyone else to do so. Further, he can point to the Corinthians themselves as evidence of his apostolic status. They are the fruit of his cultivating the apostolic ministry, and the living proof of it. **You are the seal of my apostleship in the Lord.**

6-12*a*. *As Apostles, Barnabas and Paul Enjoy the Same Rights and Privileges.*—On all three points already mentioned Paul defends Barnabas and himself. He claims the right, if they so desire it, to be married and to travel with their wives on their missionary journeys or on apostolic visitation (vs. 5). Nor are they denied the right to abstain from the necessity of making material provision for themselves. To make such provision is the duty and privilege of the community to which they are for the time being

9 For it is written in the law of Moses, Thou shalt not muzzle the mouth of the ox that treadeth out the corn. Doth God take care for oxen?

10 Or saith he *it* altogether for our sakes? For our sakes, no doubt, *this* is written: that he that ploweth should plow in hope; and that he that thresheth in hope should be partaker of his hope.

11 If we have sown unto you spiritual things, *is it* a great thing if we shall reap your carnal things?

12 If others be partakers of *this* power over you, *are* not we rather? Nevertheless we have not used this power; but suffer all things, lest we should hinder the gospel of Christ.

Does not the law say the same? 9 For it is
written in the law of Moses, "You shall not
muzzle an ox when it is treading out the
grain." Is it for oxen that God is concerned? 10 Does he not speak entirely for
our sake? It was written for our sake, because the plowman should plow in hope
and the thresher thresh in hope of a share
in the crop. 11 If we have sown spiritual
good among you, is it too much if we reap
your material benefits? 12 If others share
this rightful claim upon you, do not we
still more?

Nevertheless, we have not made use of this right, but we endure anything rather than put an obstacle in the way of the

---

9-12. The humanitarian emphasis of the Deuteronomic code has impressed all modern scholars. Here is a strand of Hebrew legislation which lifts humane considerations above purely cult duties. The reason it gives for sabbath observance is to protect slaves against exploitation. The law is concerned even with the domestic animals who toil for men. But Paul could not realize that God cared for oxen. He thinks that when God forbids muzzling the oxen which turn the treadmill (Deut. 25:4), the passage must refer to ministers of the gospel and their right to be supported. For Paul the O.T. is not a collection of books dealing with concrete historical events and situations. It contains divine oracles to be interpreted by typological and allegorical methods. God spoke, and **it was written,** for the benefit of Paul's generation; and the contents of the scripture concern the issues of his time (cf. 10:11; Rom. 4:23). The apostle can hardly be excused on the ground of the words of Luther, that since oxen cannot read, it must have been written for the sake of men. Paul continues in vs. 10 with an analogy from farm life.

---

attached. **If we have sown spiritual good among you, is it too much if we reap your material benefits? If others share this rightful claim upon you, do not we still more?** And in his opening question, "Am I not free?" the apostle asserts the right of his companion and himself to the exercise of their personal judgment on all ambiguous matters where there is no direct ruling from the Lord. In the case of the Corinthian church he asserts these rights even more firmly than any other apostle might have done, for under Christ he was the founder of that church. Undoubtedly in his mind the Christian ministry has its rights as well as its privileges; and freedom of thought within the range of the gospel with which it is entrusted, the right to marry and to the adequate material maintenance of home life are to be ranked among them. As we have seen, Paul reinforces his statements with quotations from scripture and illustrations drawn from everyday life.

12*b*-23. *Why These Particular Rights Were Not Asserted.*—Paul details with deep feeling and some indignation his reasons for declining to exercise his rights as an apostle. Who is there among preachers of the gospel right up to our own days who has not at some time or other shared his point of view? How one has longed to be free of all necessity for being materially dependent on others so that one could preach the gospel for its own sake! That is the deeper reason in the apostle's mind for the attitude he has taken. He thinks of himself as the **slave** of Jesus Christ **that I might win the more** (vs. 19). A slave has only duties to perform; he can lay no claim to any right or privilege, save such as his master is willing to grant. He regards himself as a trustee, one who has been entrusted with a commission; and in Paul's view the essence of trusteeship is disinterestedness. The commission must be fulfilled for its own sake, and the glad fulfillment of it brings its own reward. Inclination and duty find triumphant coincidence in preaching the message of deliverance that is at the very heart of the gospel. He is absorbed by the necessity to preach. To live and to preach Christ is the master motive of his life. **For necessity is laid upon**

13 Do ye not know that they which minister about holy things live *of the things*
of the temple? and they which wait at the
altar are partakers with the altar?
14 Even so hath the Lord ordained that
they which preach the gospel should live
of the gospel.
15 But I have used none of these things:
neither have I written these things, that it
should be so done unto me: for *it were*

gospel of Christ. 13 Do you not know that
those who are employed in the temple
service get their food from the temple, and
those who serve at the altar share in the
sacrificial offerings? 14 In the same way,
the Lord commanded that those who proclaim the gospel should get their living by
the gospel.
15 But I have made no use of any of
these rights, nor am I writing this to secure

Some take this as a citation from an unknown source which taught that what is true in the raising of food is even more the case in the provision of spiritual food (cf. II Cor. 9:6). But Paul does not restrict his conclusion to that of spiritual reaping on the part of the worker. The missionary deserves a material reward, as the other apostles had claimed, and he too had a right to claim one. When we recall the charges of profiteering and exploitation often leveled at wandering evangelists and church officials, we can understand how this custom in apostolic times might prove an obstacle for suspicious inquirers (cf. II Cor. 11:9; Acts 20:34). The word for **obstacle,** which occurs only here in the N.T., means a "cutting" made in the road to impede an enemy in pursuit.

13. We read in the O.T. (Num. 18:8, 9, 31; Deut. 18:1-4) of the portions of the sacrifices which were reserved for the priests. Naturally, this was also the custom at the pagan temples in Corinth. Though Paul compares his work with that of a priest, he does not mean that he looked upon himself as serving in a specifically priestly capacity.

14. The final authority for Paul is the Lord Jesus. As in 7:10, he cites a word of the Lord to clinch the argument (but cf. Gal. 6:6 and II Thess. 3:9). Paul had none of our Gospels before him, but quotes the substance of Luke 10:7, "The laborer deserves his wages." Did he also know Matt. 10:8, "You received without pay, give without pay"? Matthew distinguishes between pay and the board and room which a missionary might expect (Matt. 10:10).

3. Renunciation for Others (9:15-23)

15-18. It would be easy for his readers to conclude that Paul was laboring this point so long because he wanted them to show belated generosity toward him. The apostle repudiates any such conclusion so emphatically that his sentences lose all proper grammatical construction. This is not apparent from either translation; the KJV follows the

me. Woe to me if I do not preach the gospel! He fulfills himself as he is able to give free vent to the cause for which he has been captured and by which he is possessed. That fulfillment brings rewards with which the exercise of other rights and privileges is not comparable. So impassioned is he by the necessity to proclaim the gospel of Christ, and so moved by his sense of the impending end of the age and the return of the Lord in triumph, that he sets aside all inhibiting factors and prejudices; he forgoes all personal predilections, and carries tolerance and reconciliation to their utmost lengths, that as many as possible may yield to his urgent and intense persuasions and so become convinced believers in Jesus Christ (cf. Exeg., vss. 19-23). **I have become all things to all men, that I might by all means save some.**

No doubt other reasons combined with this supreme reason for declining to exercise his right to material maintenance as an apostle. He must have been aware of the distaste with which some Greeks regarded the Sophists who taught for pay, particularly those who took fees for their teachings in the spheres of ethics and religion. We know that Socrates and Plato and those who shared their views looked with something akin to scorn upon all such professionals. It must be said, as already indicated, that although there is a thrill and a sense of privilege and prestige as well as freedom in undertaking a piece of service, even a life's work, for its own sake and devoid of all material reward, yet there is nothing reprehensible in receiving appropriate emoluments for this service. Paul may have been influenced by the

better for me to die, than that any man should make my glorying void.

16 For though I preach the gospel, I have nothing to glory of: for necessity is laid upon me; yea, woe is unto me, if I preach not the gospel!

17 For if I do this thing willingly, I have a reward: but if against my will, a dispensation *of the gospel* is committed unto me.

18 What is my reward then? *Verily* that, when I preach the gospel, I may make the gospel of Christ without charge, that I abuse not my power in the gospel.

any such provision. For I would rather
die than have any one deprive me of my
ground for boasting. 16 For if I preach the
gospel, that gives me no ground for boasting. For necessity is laid upon me. Woe to
me if I do not preach the gospel! 17 For if
I do this of my own will, I have a reward;
but if not of my own will, I am entrusted
with a commission. 18 What then is my
reward? Just this: that in my preaching I
may make the gospel free of charge, not
making full use of my right in the gospel.

---

koine text which had patched up Paul's grammar, and the RSV constructs an English sentence instead of attempting to reproduce the awkwardness of the better-attested Greek text. Literally Paul wrote, "I would rather die than—no one shall deprive me of my ground for boasting." He had no choice about preaching the gospel. From the day that the risen Christ appeared to him, a divine compulsion had driven him as it had Jeremiah (Jer. 20:9). He could only do his duty (cf. Luke 17:10). Once more the apostle uses his favorite word, **boasting.** There is no ground for that if he preaches the word; a woe falls upon him if he does not do so.

It is not at all certain what Paul means to say in vs. 17. Both of the conditions named cannot be true in his case for they are direct opposites. Since he has just spoken of acting under necessity, it would appear that the first is the unreal situation. But if that is the case, Paul is not using the normal tense for expressing a contrary-to-fact condition. Since, however, he uses the same tense in 15:13, and there it is certainly contrary to fact, we may accept it here and conclude that the following is Paul's idea: "I might have a reward if I were acting of my own free will; but since it is otherwise, I am only entrusted with a commission." The KJV is very misleading with its **dispensation of the gospel.** Some commentators adopt a different punctuation which gives the following, "For if I do this willingly, I have a reward; but if, unwillingly, I am entrusted with a commission, what then is my reward?" In any case, the former Pharisee can secure a reward only by preaching free of charge. His only pay lies in doing it without pay.

---

opinion of these great-minded Greeks who pursued the disinterested quest for knowledge, but clearly he is not prejudiced by it. There is at least one exception to his practice of maintaining himself by the labor of his own hands even while he pursues his apostolic mission (Phil. 4:14-18). The gist of the matter is that teachers, and particularly teachers and preachers of the gospel, should receive enough to relieve them from undue anxiety with regard to material things so that they can give themselves wholeheartedly to their divinely appointed task. They should not receive so much as would give an altogether disproportionate value to the material aspect of their status, and perhaps create a gulf between them and their fellow men. Paul, in being "all things to all men," was following in the steps of his Master, who was alternately blessed and reviled because he was noted as the friend of publicans and sinners. Conscience and circumstances on the part both of the community and of its pastor should in every case be the determining factors in the matter of material benefits. Here as elsewhere, in a time when economic considerations loom large on every horizon, there is guidance to be found in Paul's views and in his practice; particularly in the fact that every consideration is made subservient to the overruling purpose of proclaiming the gospel message to all kinds and conditions of men.

Still other reasons suggest themselves for the apostle's refusal to avail himself of his undoubted rights. His personal integrity is involved. He is prepared to endure anything **rather than put an obstacle in the way of the gospel of Christ** (cf. Acts 20:33-35). It may be that he wished to avoid being a burden to a

19 For though I be free from all *men,* yet have I made myself servant unto all, that I might gain the more.

20 And unto the Jews I became as a Jew, that I might gain the Jews; to them that are under the law, as under the law, that I might gain them that are under the law;

21 To them that are without law, as without law, (being not without law to God, but under the law to Christ,) that I might gain them that are without law.

22 To the weak became I as weak, that I might gain the weak: I am made all things to all *men,* that I might by all means save some.

19 For though I am free from all men,
I have made myself a slave to all, that I
might win the more. 20 To the Jews I became as a Jew, in order to win Jews; to those
under the law I became as one under the
law — though not being myself under the
law — that I might win those under the
law. 21 To those outside the law I became
as one outside the law — not being without
law toward God but under the law of
Christ — that I might win those outside
the law. 22 To the weak I became weak,
that I might win the weak. I have become
all things to all men, that I might by all

19-22. Paul is finished with the specific illustrations from his own life of the renunciation of rights for the good of others. He concludes the section with general principles on the use of freedom. The paragraph is a rhythmic period quite consciously constructed on the chiastic principle (A-19; B-20*a*; C-20*b*; C′-21; B′-22*a*; A′-22*b*). The need to be the slave of all is a restatement of the gospel ethic (Luke 22:25 ff.; Mark 10:43 ff.). Christian freedom involves a new bondage, as Luther developed it in his famous tract on this subject. Throughout this section **win** is used as a technical term of missionary preaching. At the end there is a shift to the stronger verb **save,** but Paul modestly adds **some.** If Acts can be trusted, we may see as illustrations of "becoming as a Jew" the circumcision of Timothy (Acts 16:3), the taking of a vow before his trip to Jerusalem (Acts 18:18), and the paying of the expenses of a Nazirite group (Acts 21:26). There is no occasion to distinguish **those under the law** from **the Jews.** By **the law** Paul certainly meant the Mosaic law. This is simply a restatement to provide a transition to the other situation, accommodation to non-Jews. Paul wants to make it plain that no concession to **Jews** had involved a return to legalism on his part. Though he preached and practiced a law-free gospel, there was a law of Christ to which all were obligated who had been saved by grace through faith (Gal. 6:2). The citation of words of Jesus reveals that Paul found from the Master specific guidance for the practice of love. The **weak** are those referred to in 8:7, 9. Paul becomes **weak** by respecting their conscientious scruples even though he knows that they are mistaken (cf. Rom. 14:1; 15:1; II Cor. 11:29). At every point he has identified himself with others; the gospel cannot be preached except as the missionary takes his place beside those whom he would win.

---

poor church. We must remember that probably there were few really well-to-do members of these early Christian communities. And above all, he was anxious to avoid scandal (vs. 15). No one would ever be able to say, such is part of the legitimate "boasting" of this greathearted and yet passionate apostle, that Paul "lined his own pockets" at the expense of the church he sought to serve. Too many evangelistic campaigns have been shadowed, if not ruined, because to an inordinate extent the missioners have benefited financially from the campaign. Let everything be done in due proportion. Never should there be even a suggestion that the gospel is not **free of charge.** Paul is much more concerned for the full, free impact of the message upon the minds of his hearers, and for the integrity of his conscience, than for material comfort of whatever degree. As he asserts his freedom and his right to receive such benefits as were part of the common lot of all the other apostles, so he also asserts his right, if he is so minded, to dispense with them. **I do it all for the sake of the gospel, that I may share in its blessings.** That is a good example for all Christian workers to follow.

This passage is not altogether a digression, though it does involve a certain change of subject and of mood. Paul was ever concerned that Christians should "stand fast . . . in the liberty

23 And this I do for the gospel's sake, that I might be partaker thereof with *you*.
24 Know ye not that they which run in a race run all, but one receiveth the prize? So run, that ye may obtain.
25 And every man that striveth for the mastery is temperate in all things. Now they *do it* to obtain a corruptible crown; but we an incorruptible.

means save some. 23 I do it all for the sake of the gospel, that I may share in its blessings.
24 Do you not know that in a race all the runners compete, but only one receives the prize? So run that you may obtain it.
25 Every athlete exercises self-control in all things. They do it to receive a perishable

---

23. This verse provides an appropriate transition from Paul's renunciation for the sake of others to self-discipline for his own sake. His entire discussion in 8:1–10:22 follows a chiastic pattern. A—renunciation for the good of others (8:1-13); B—illustrated from Paul's own experience (9:1-22); B′—Paul's own self-discipline (9:24-27), leading to A′—the need for the community to practice self-discipline (10:1-22) for fear that they lose their own salvation. Hence, **for the sake of the gospel** does not in this verse mean "to aid in its proclamation." Paul is moving over to the question of his own participation in its blessings and what he must do to gain his assurance. Sometimes, as in Rom. 8:29-30, he speaks with absolute confidence of his salvation: what God has begun he can be counted upon to carry through to the end. At other times, as in vss. 24-27, Paul speaks from the standpoint of human loyalty and faithfulness: knowing how prone man is to sin, he faces the possibility of ultimate rejection.

C. The Peril of the Strong (9:24–10:22)

1. The Need for Self-discipline (9:24-27)

24-27. This little paragraph is packed with figures from the athletic contests at the Isthmian games. Every pagan Corinthian would be thoroughly familiar with them. Had Paul attended them or would he have approved the witnessing of them by members of his churches? Speculation is futile. As usual, Paul finds it difficult to carry through his figure and he mixes his metaphors badly. He begins with the foot race, where there is only one winner. He wants his readers to run their **race** with the same determination. But he must have quickly realized that in the church all could win **the prize.** That leads him to shift to the rigorous training which all contestants undergo, winner and losers alike. The winner's **prize** is an ivy or pine **wreath** that soon will fade in contrast to the **imperishable** life in the resurrection which awaits believers (cf. 15:53). The figure of a crown is used

---

wherewith Christ hath made us free" (Gal. 5:1). On the matter of eating food which had been consecrated to idols, he was anxious to do two things: to assert and to emphasize this Christ-given liberty, and also to plead for regard for weaker brethren and sensitive consciences. To give effect to the second point he emphasizes the law of love. Just as for love of preaching the gospel he is free to assert or to relinquish his apostolic rights, and chooses the latter course, so are the stronger-minded among the Corinthian Christians, with whom he is really in agreement on the main issue, free to relinquish their right to eat such meat. So does he reinforce his argument from his own example, always a telling point. Hence he closes this section of his letter with a reference to himself.

24-27. ***Need for Sustained Discipline.***—Paul seemingly attended athletic games—a feature of city life in the Greco-Roman world—and is fond of using metaphors drawn from events in the arena. The illustrations he uses are particularly apt because of the religious significance of some of these athletic features. Like his Master, Paul is skilled in his use of vivid and striking illustrations drawn from events that had their place in the life of the people. Here he is making the point that to propagate the gospel, either as a preacher or through the fellowship of the church, is a costly matter. He is prepared to pay the price, and he invites the Corinthian Christians to do the same. Elements in that cost, if the work is to be well done and if the rewards are to be gathered, are sustained training and self-discipline and self-control. The demands of Jesus Christ are high and exacting. His standards are a challenge and reproach to the world. They can never be sustained by desultory or

26 I therefore so run, not as uncertainly;
so fight I, not as one that beateth the air:
27 But I keep under my body, and bring
it into subjection: lest that by any means,
when I have preached to others, I myself
should be a castaway.

wreath, but we an imperishable. 26 Well, I
do not run aimlessly, I do not box as one
beating the air; 27 but I pommel my body
and subdue it, lest after preaching to others
I myself should be disqualified.

---

also in I Pet. 5:4 and Rev. 2:10. This idea leads the apostle to think of another comparison. A runner must know where the finish line is if he is to pursue a straight course. The believer also knows his goal, entrance to the kingdom of God.

At this point Paul shifts from the second person to the first, for he is thinking more specifically of his own struggle. We do not know how rapidly a man of Paul's age could **run,** but he had seen a good deal of "road work" in his missionary campaigning. The sport changes also, and we now find ourselves in the boxing ring, where the movement of Paul's thought becomes even more rapid. Shadowboxing may be good exercise, but it does not defeat an actual opponent. Who is our real opponent? The author of the letter to the Ephesians insists that it is not a human contestant but angelic powers (Eph. 6:12). Here Paul says that it is neither of these; it is his own body (person). No man should blame his failure on another; rather, on his own lack of self-discipline (Phil. 3:12). Paul employs the technical term in pugilism for a knockout blow. But it is delivered to himself.

Now the scene shifts once more and the apostle identifies himself with the herald announcing the results of the games or calling the competitors to their contests. It is the most fitting comparison of all, for the verb used is one of the regular terms for **preaching** the gospel. Paul could visualize the possibility that even a chosen official could be ruled out of the contest. Out of this jumble of figures comes one clear picture—the earnestness of the apostle, who, though he was giving his life for the gospel, realized that he might still be untrue to its demands. The strong must take care on their own account.

---

spasmodic efforts. The Christian life and fellowship are no short, snapshot procedure: they require a long time exposure. Or to revert to Paul's own chosen metaphor, there is in the Christian arena a prize to be won—not as in the stadium where only one prize, and that perishable, is to be had, but a prize for all who attain the goal. "I press on toward the goal for the prize of the upward call of God in Christ Jesus" (Phil. 3:14; cf. Exeg., vss. 24-27). So, just as long training and self-control are needed in the athletic arena if one is to win a race or a boxing contest, similar disciplines are required if excellence is to be achieved in the Christian way of life. Pleasures that make one soft or less sensitive to spiritual things are to be forgone or strictly curtailed. Here again perhaps there is a hint of Greek influence. The virtue of temperance is engendered when the appetites are under the strict control of reason, which for the Greek has the right to rule.

One grows in grace as one gives oneself to study, to meditation, to prayer, to fellowship, and to Christian service, until every aspect of life is governed and permeated by the indwelling Spirit of Jesus Christ. Paul is anxious about a certain slackness in these respects in Corinth. There are values in the ascetic point of view when not pressed to extremes, and there was enough of the Stoic in Paul to enable him to appreciate the astringent element in the moral counsels of the great Stoic teachers.

The Christian life and the Christian cause, not only in the world of Paul's day but in our own, call for moderation and discipline in all things. The preacher cannot do his work effectively unless he is given to serious study of the implications of the gospel in the life of the times, and is bent on making it as effective as he can in its impact on his fellow men. Worship is not worship if conducted in slovenly fashion. It lacks personal force if it is not informed by wide pastoral contacts, and preaching misses its mark if it is not relevant both to the content of the gospel and to the trends of the times, either as an inspiration or challenge or both. Defectiveness or slackness in scholarship in the Christian teacher runs back to defect in moral character. There is point in Paul's advice to Timothy, his "son in the faith": "Set the believers an example in speech and conduct, in love, in faith, in purity. Till I come, attend to the public reading of scripture, to preaching, to teaching. Do not neglect the gift you have. . . .

10 Moreover, brethren, I would not that ye should be ignorant, how that all our fathers were under the cloud, and all passed through the sea;

10 I want you to know, brethren, that our fathers were all under the cloud,

2. The Warning Example of the Wilderness Generation (10:1-13)

The use of the O.T. for preaching illustrations was common in the early church. A little later the letter to the Hebrews will point out the unfaithfulness of the wilderness generation (Heb. 3–4) in contrast to the heroes of faith (Heb. 11). Toward the end of the century another letter addressed to the church of Corinth (I Clement) will be full of O.T. illustrations. Though Paul writes to a predominantly Gentile congregation, he describes the Israelites as **our fathers** because Gentile Christians belong to the "Israel of God." It is amazing how full a knowledge of the O.T. Paul presupposes here on the part of his readers. The passage indicates the prevalence of a typological use of the O.T. in the instruction of converts.

10:1-2. The introductory formula is frequent in Paul (cf. 12:1; II Cor. 1:8; Rom. 1:13; 11:25; I Thess. 4:13). The great act of God's deliverance in the past had been in freeing his people from slavery in Egypt. Before the Israelites entered the Promised Land, there had been a time of trial in the wilderness. God's new act of deliverance had been through the death and resurrection of Christ. Before entrance into the promised land at the parousia of Christ, the new Israel must also pass through a time of testing in the

Practice these duties, devote yourself to them, so that all may see your progress. Take heed to yourself and to your teaching; hold to that, for by so doing you will save yourself and others" (I Tim. 4:12-16). Many a modern Timothy would profit by that advice.

Again, Paul has a right to speak or to write in such terms, for he practices what he prescribes. To the end of his days he practiced the discipline that he enjoins on all the churches. When near the time of his last sacrifice he wrote his second letter to Timothy, we see him revealed as still a student of sacred things: he is still mentally alert to the best thought of his time. "Do your best to come to me soon. . . . When you come, bring the cloak that I left with Carpus at Troas, also the books, and above all the parchments" (II Tim. 4:9, 13). There was not much chance that Paul would be **disqualified.** To the very last all his energies, spiritual, mental, and physical, are concentrated on the one great and all-inclusive purpose, "Necessity is laid upon me. Woe to me if I do not preach the gospel!"

10:1–11:1. ***A Series of Solemn Warnings to the Strong.***—Paul having asserted his status as an apostle and insisted on his right to exercise his own judgment on all matters pertaining to Christian conduct, subject only to the teaching and example of Jesus himself, now returns to the matter under discussion, viz., the eating of meat that has been offered to idols. Some N.T. scholars detect a certain divergence in Paul's treatment of the subject in this chapter (vss. 21-24) from what he has said in ch. 8. There the apostle tolerates the practice and limits it only in terms of the law of love; here he seems to condemn it outright. It has therefore been suggested that this section is part of an earlier letter which has been lost, in which Paul took a more stringent view of the matter. Later reflection has, as it were, induced a mellower, more tolerant attitude on his part. The view here taken is that while this may be so, yet the section is not really inconsistent with anything that has preceded it. The point will be taken up later on.

Meantime, the entire chapter, with its series of warnings, illustrated—as Paul is often wont to do, following on the allusion to his own personal example—from scripture itself (see Exeg.), is written not so much in the interest of the weaker brethren with their sensitive, overscrupulous consciences, as in the interest of the enlightened and strong-minded ones. They are open to certain real dangers in the exercise of the liberty they claim for themselves in the matter of eating meat sanctified to idols. That is why the note of solemn warning runs through the series of illustrations the apostle uses to drive home his point. We must not underestimate the sense of urgency and peril that underlies all that he has written. Very true it is that he is dealing with matters that are far removed from the modern outlook on life. Yet vital principles that have a continuing validity for all subsequent generations are involved. Paul is firmly convinced that idols are

2 And were all baptized unto Moses in the cloud and in the sea;
3 And did all eat the same spiritual meat;

and all passed through the sea, 2 and all
were baptized into Moses in the cloud and
in the sea, 3 and all ate the same super-

heathen world. The pillar of cloud symbolized the guidance of the Lord (Exod. 13:21; 14:19). Though the Israelites had **passed through** the Red Sea, the water had not touched them (Exod. 14:22). Therefore the analogy to baptism was not very close. The real point of connection lay in the act of grace on God's part. As the Israelites had been **under the cloud,** so Christians in their baptism had gone under the water (Rom. 6:3). It is assumed that there was the same connection between this event and **Moses** as between baptism and **Christ. Moses** and **Christ** were the leaders through whom God had accomplished his salvation.

3-4. Paul goes on to point out that the Israelites also had a "type" corresponding to the Lord's Supper. This is the first time in Christian history that the two sacraments are linked together. It is instructive for Paul's understanding of the Eucharist that he does not connect it with Jewish sacrifices, but with the sacred food which God had supplied without priestly mediation. The giving of the "bread from heaven" (Exod. 16:4, 35; Deut. 8:3) is also connected with the Eucharist in John 6:31-34, 49-51. Though the drink is not named, it was originally water; but that should not be pressed to indicate a celebration of the Eucharist with water at this date. At two different places in the O.T. Moses is said to have struck the rock and water flowed out so that the thirsty people might drink. One was at Horeb (Exod. 17:6) and the other in the wilderness of Zin (Num. 20:7-11). Jews at this time had no intimation of the documentary analysis of the Pentateuch; yet they felt that it was necessary to explain such similar incidents at different places. Their deduction was that the **Rock** had **followed** the Israelites. Paul

nonentities; they have no existence whatever. There is only one God: the God and Father of our Lord Jesus Christ. He is sovereign and all-powerful in his universe. But idols most certainly were for Paul and all his enlightened, as well as less enlightened, contemporaries the symbols of demonic powers and forces whose existence was very real and whose influence was very powerful (vss. 19-20). Such ideas can be taken as the text of the sermon, with its series of illustrations and its application, which is preached in this chapter of the epistle. Why is the matter urgent and important, and why do the strong-minded among the Corinthian Christians stand in such danger? The answer is, and it is underlined by the very illustrations Paul uses, that in certain circumstances to partake of such food is to take part in a rite that has definite religious significance, and therefore to establish a definite relationship with the demonic power symbolized by the idol. In other words, in the circumstances that Paul has in mind, the feast has a definite sacramental character. As such it is a direct challenge to Christians and to Christianity. That is a vital point with the apostle. As a consequence, it involves the Christian in inconsistency of spirit, allegiance, and witness. He is prone to the sins of the divided mind, and as James has written in a somewhat different connection, ". . . that person must not suppose that a double-minded man, unstable in all his ways, will receive anything from the Lord" (Jas. 1:7-8). It is then with a deeply felt concern for the spiritual well-being of the church in Corinth that Paul pens this section of his pastoral letter.

1-12. ***A Warning Example from the History of Israel.***—The opening illustration is taken from the record of incidents that occurred during the Exodus from Egypt under the leadership of Moses. The incident itself is "spiritualized," as an earlier generation of preachers would say, and so is used for its allegorical significance as a warning against the abuse of the sacramental grace of God which took some symbolical forms of expression. Paul misses little or nothing in the way of significant detail, and he uses every point with telling effect in pursuance of his purpose. The Exodus, like the Christian gospel itself, was a great deliverance from bondage. It was wrought under God through the medium of Moses, with whom the children of Israel entered into a spiritual relationship, so in a special sense becoming his people. **And all were baptized into Moses in the cloud and in the sea.** They stood, therefore, in a special relationship of allegiance and service and devotion to him, and were subject to his direction and authority. Obviously the apostle has in mind the symbolic significance

4 And did all drink the same spiritual drink; for they drank of that spiritual Rock that followed them: and that Rock was Christ.

5 But with many of them God was not well pleased: for they were overthrown in the wilderness.

6 Now these things were our examples, to the intent we should not lust after evil things, as they also lusted.

7 Neither be ye idolaters, as *were* some of them; as it is written, The people sat down to eat and drink, and rose up to play.

natural[k] food 4 and all drank the same
supernatural[k] drink. For they drank from
the supernatural[k] Rock which followed
them, and the Rock was Christ. 5 Nevertheless with most of them God was not
pleased; for they were overthrown in the
wilderness.
6 Now these things are warnings for us,
not to desire evil as they did. 7 Do not be
idolaters as some of them were; as it is
written, "The people sat down to eat and

[k] Greek *spiritual.*

---

adds a further touch to this midrash in identifying the rock with the Messiah. Philo sometimes connects the rock with *sophia* or wisdom, and sometimes with the logos. As Christ was for Paul the mediator of creation (8:6), he was also the mediator of the blessings recounted in the O.T.

Both **food** and **Rock** are described as **spiritual** (KJV; RSV mg.); that is a misleading English word to convey what Paul had in mind. He does not mean to deny that these were material realities. He means that they transmitted to men the Spirit: the food and the rock were endowed with divine potency. **Supernatural** (RSV) is probably the term which conveys this best to modern readers. Since Christ was identified with the Spirit (II Cor. 3:17), the water which flowed from him brought the Spirit to men (John 7:38-39).

5. The point of these illustrations is clear. The reception of sacraments will not by itself save anyone. Paul emphasizes the fact that all of the Israelites had these benefits, yet **most of them** were destroyed. Despite their sacraments at the present time, the Corinthians may likewise be destroyed. In other words, there is a danger even to the strongest from the heathen influences about them.

6-7. In rapid succession Paul recounts a series of the disasters in the wilderness. Vs. 6 refers specifically to the incident in Num. 11:4-34, where we are told that the Israelites desired the fleshpots of Egypt and were stricken with a plague when they ate quails. Probably Paul uses it only as a superscription for the more pertinent illustrations which follow. The next reference is to the making of the golden calf. The quotation (Exod.

---

of the Christian sacrament of baptism into Christ, which signifies a complete deliverance from the old life of bondage to sin, and the resurrection to a new life through the grace of Christ and the indwelling of the Holy Spirit of God. Doubtless the symbolism of baptism is covered by the passage of the Israelites through the Red Sea (see Exeg., vss. 1-2). Like Christians who have their Eucharist, the Israelites had holy food: they were fed by manna from heaven (vs. 3). They also were refreshed by supernatural drink (vs. 4), for Paul adapts a curious old-time legend that the rock smitten by Moses, from which the water gushed, followed the tribes throughout the course of their desert wanderings. He carries a step further the spiritualizing of this legend by Jewish writers, who see symbolized in the rock the "wisdom of God," by identifying it with Christ.

For they drank from the supernatural Rock which followed them, and the Rock was Christ. There is an underlying emphasis in these opening verses (vss. 1-4) on the wonderful privilege those people enjoyed. *All* were partakers of the divine favor. Yet there was no corresponding realization of the responsibility that ought to accompany such privilege. Someone has said that ingratitude is the meanest sin in the world. The children of Israel were guilty of ingratitude. Privilege without a corresponding sense of responsibility can be a corrupting experience. It has been sternly said, though in a different connection, that privilege minus responsibility has been the mark of the libertine in every age. Sooner or later those who are guilty of such sacrilege feel the reaction of a moral universe. Despite such concrete and vivid tokens of the providence of God, mediated through Moses

8 Neither let us commit fornication, as some of them committed, and fell in one day three and twenty thousand.

9 Neither let us tempt Christ, as some of them also tempted, and were destroyed of serpents.

10 Neither murmur ye, as some of them also murmured, and were destroyed of the destroyer.

11 Now all these things happened unto them for ensamples: and they are written for our admonition, upon whom the ends of the world are come.

drink and rose up to dance." **8** We must not
indulge in immorality as some of them did,
and twenty-three thousand fell in a single
day. **9** We must not put the Lord[l] to the
test, as some of them did and were destroyed by serpents; **10** nor grumble, as
some of them did and were destroyed by
the Destroyer. **11** Now these things happened to them as a warning, but they were
written down for our instruction, upon
whom the end of the ages has come.

[l] Other ancient authorities read *Christ*.

32:6) describes the sacrificial meal and sacred dance in connection with this classic instance of apostasy.

8-10. Throughout Jewish tradition, idolatry and sexual **immorality** are connected (cf. Wisd. Sol. 14:12). This was the case when the Israelite men were enticed by the daughters of Moab (Num. 25:1-9). That Paul's figure is a thousand short of the number given in the O.T. will surprise no one who has tried to quote scripture from memory, but it is fatal to any theory of verbal infallibility. The tempting of the Lord, which was punished by serpent bites, was the complaint of the Israelites that they had neither bread nor water (Num. 21:5-9). Paul alludes to Ps. 78:18 ff. He does not refer to salvation through a serpent lifted up, as in John 3:14. The KJV and RSV mg. translate the koine reading, which has **Christ** instead of **Lord;** though this text is now supported by p^{46}, it is probably a later Christian interpretation. Murmuring or grumbling is almost a theme song in the book of Numbers. Therefore we are probably not to see in the use of the term here a reference to the complaints of Corinthians at Paul's use of apostolic authority. In all of the instances which took place in the wilderness it was God who sent the plague to destroy them (Num. 14:12, 37; 16:41-49; etc.). The increased dualism in Paul is seen when he ascribes it to **the destroyer** (cf. Heb. 11:28).

11. These instances are **warning** examples. The Greek word τύπος has given us "type." These may be of several different kinds. Sometimes in the N.T. the word is used of examples to be emulated (Phil. 3:17; I Thess. 1:7; II Thess. 3:9; I Tim. 4:12; Tit. 2:7; I Pet. 5:3); sometimes it is used of heavenly originals to be copied (Acts 7:44; Heb. 8:5). The noun in vs. 6 and the adverb here (τυπικῶς) are used in a technical expression connected with the typological exegesis of the O.T. (cf. also Rom. 5:14), where the story foreshadows contemporary experience. This usage becomes common in Barnabas and the Shepherd of Hermas. Paul does not deny that these events took place in a literal

---

and in those sacramental ways, those people sinned against God, giving themselves to idolatry and to the lasciviousness that followed it as an inevitable consequence. **Nevertheless with most of them God was not pleased; for they were overthrown in the wilderness** (see Exeg.).

Paul goes on to apply the lesson to the matter under survey. **Now these things are warnings for us, not to desire evil as they did.** The evils and their consequences are listed for the benefit of those to whom this section of the epistle is addressed. The children of Israel played fast and loose with sacramental grace in certain definite respects. They were discontented with the simple but adequate provision made for them by God, and craved for the fleshpots of Egypt, having apparently forgotten the taskmaster's lash and the edict of Pharaoh that they should make bricks without straw. They gave way to idolatry and set up for their worship a golden calf in the desert during the absence of Moses on Sinai's peak, thus violating their allegiance to him, and above all to God. They gave way to moral degradation, i.e., to lascivious practices culminating in immorality (vss. 6-8). They provoked God by doubting his power to provide for them. **We must not put the Lord to the test, as some of them did** (vs. 9). They gave way to a spirit of suspicion, discontent, and grumbling, which is akin to the sin of "murmur-

12 Wherefore let him that thinketh he standeth take heed lest he fall.

13 There hath no temptation taken you but such as is common to man: but God *is* faithful, who will not suffer you to be

12 Therefore let any one who thinks that
he stands take heed lest he fall. 13 No
temptation has overtaken you that is not
common to man. God is faithful, and he
will not let you be tempted beyond your

---

sense, but their real significance lies in the **warning** they provide for those who stand at the end of the age and on the threshhold of the age to come. The use of **world** for αἰών in the KJV is misleading. Paul thinks in terms of the doctrine of two ages (7:29; Heb. 9:26; II Esdras 6:7). The recounting of these experiences was to instruct those who stood in that isthmus of time between the ages. **All** in the KJV comes from the koine text.

12-13. Now Paul returns to his warnings and to general principles in meeting temptations. He is no longer concerned with the effect on others, but with self-protection, even for the Gnostic who feels certain of his salvation. A temptation **common to man** is one which mortals may successfully meet. Despite the paragraph that follows, it is not certain that Paul is contrasting two possible sources of temptation, human and demonic. Though

---

ing" against God, and as a consequence many of them suffered destruction (vs. 10). Paul again reiterates his conviction that these things are recorded as a solemn warning to Christian people, and its urgency is underlined for the Corinthians, who were in danger of giving way to such practices, by the apostle's belief that **the end of the ages** is imminent (vs. 11). **Therefore let any one who thinks that he stands take heed lest he fall** (vs. 12). Though the expectation of an imminent second coming of Christ was beginning to fade when the epistle was written, the warning is given. That somber note is also sounded elsewhere in the N.T., as when the author of II Peter writes, "Since all these things are thus to be dissolved, what sort of persons ought you to be in lives of holiness and godliness, waiting for and hastening the coming of the day of God, because of which the heavens will be kindled and dissolved, and the elements will melt with fire" (II Pet. 3:11-12). In an age of atomic power and bacteriological forms of warfare, not to mention other unspeakable horrors, the urgent representations of both Paul and the writer of the epistle of Peter take on new and significant force. He who runs may read.

13. ***Temptation and Deliverance.***—Then follows a characteristic touch. Paul is never conscious only of the pressure of environment or the fierce drive of one's own passions. He is also deeply aware of the immense reality of divine succor. When the time of testing or trial or temptation comes, the grace of God to overcome it is immediately available to his people. Temptation, in the nature of the case, is inevitable. **No temptation has overtaken you that is not common to man. God is faithful, and he will not let you be tempted beyond your strength, but with the temptation will also provide the way of escape, that you may be able to endure it.**

Whatever the reaction of the modern mind may be to Paul's views on idols and demonic powers and the perils that ensue if anyone partakes of meat that has been sanctified to an idol, what he here writes about temptation and divine succor affects us all. Man is imperfect and therefore is subject to temptation. No one who was wholly perfect could be tempted, even as God cannot be tempted, in the sense that he cannot be the victim of moral seduction to evil ways and practices. There is nothing in the being of God to which such temptation can appeal. Nor could anyone who is wholly evil be tempted; for there would be in such a person, e.g., Satan, no moral element which the appeal for better, finer things could stimulate. It is man, a "son of Adam" and a potential "son of God," fashioned in the divine likeness and for fellowship with God, for co-operation with him in the fulfillment of his divine purposes for his creation, who is subject to the lure of such temptation. There is in man that which responds to the promptings of the Spirit of God, and there is that in him which is lured by evil and unworthy things. He is the child of his environment and of all environing influences, social as well as material; and these, too, are far from perfect. Moreover, the higher he pitches his sense of moral obligation, the sharper the tension between what he is and what he is intended to become. To be fiercely tried and tempted is part of the price he must pay if he would win the fight for true manhood. Sooner or later we all face the test which reveals the moral and spiritual foundations, in their strength or weakness, on which we are building our lives. William James has the same thought in mind when he writes that no one has ever

tempted above that ye are able; but will with the temptation also make a way to escape, that ye may be able to bear *it.*

strength, but with the temptation will also provide the way of escape, that you may be able to endure it.

---

it is not said that God entices to sin, it is affirmed that he permits temptation. That is nearer to the Lord's Prayer, "Lead us not into temptation" (Matt. 6:13), than to the assertion of James that no one is tempted by God (Jas. 1:13). More often Satan appears as the tempter (7:5; II Cor. 2:11; Matt. 4:1; Luke 22:31). The faithfulness of God is a ground of appeal similar to that in James, who cites God's immutability. Some might ask why they should flee from idolatry if God could be depended upon to **provide a way of escape.** Certainly **the way of escape** does not mean that men can be free from temptation, but that they are enabled to stand up under it. If sin is near, so is God. The word for temptation (πειρασμός) is often used for the trials which accompanied the messianic woes (I Pet. 4:12; Rev. 3:10). It is the word employed in Heb. 3:8 for "the day of testing in the wilderness."

---

really graduated in the school of life until he has been well tempted. Even Jesus did not escape fierce temptation, as we know from the vivid and dramatic account given of his temptation in the wilderness. How would he use his God-given powers? That was the nub of the moral and spiritual situation for him. The temptation was to take the easier, more spectacular course. It was rejected because it lowered the standard he had set before himself, and because the stuff of everlastingness was not in it. He shared this experience with us. Temptation is one of the inevitable elements of human life: it is one of the constituent elements. As R. L. Stevenson once put it, it is one of the "crooks of the common lot." But it is not a battle that man is left to fight with his own puny strength or to endure with his own unaided spirit. Divine power is available. Christ's presence is near.

The cultured, Christian Greek scholar who wrote the Epistle to the Hebrews, knowing that a time of fierce trial and temptation for the Christian church was imminent, sought to fortify his brethren against the event by reasserting for them the great convictions of the Christian faith. He knew that when such a test comes, an example is worth more than an argument, and he pointed his readers to the Pioneer of their faith. "For because he himself has suffered and been tempted, he is able to help those who are tempted" (Heb. 2:18). Paul writes in the same spirit of assurance: there is the heartbeat of personal experience in every syllable. God is faithful and will not let anyone be tempted beyond his powers of endurance. This is one of the great sayings of scripture that points in two directions like the signpost at a crossroads. It points on the one hand to a world of chaos and confusion, of moral and spiritual dereliction, and it points on the other hand to a world of divine power and succor and the immediate presence and helpfulness of the Spirit of God. It assures all, since all need the assurance, that interior spiritual resources are available for all who have the faith to appropriate them, and that with the appropriation, ultimately, spiritual victory is gained. This is part of the witness of the saints in every age. It is pertinent for our day and generation and for all generations. When the old habits reassert themselves, when we feel the tug of old associations, when the going is hard and uphill and there seems to be no goal in view, when it seems attractive to follow Demas and to desert the cause of Christ and return to "the world," then God himself will respond to our call and come to our aid if we but look to him. We can endure because God can be trusted. As Moffatt puts it, "Human faithfulness rests upon his faithfulness." [2] It is also part of the privilege and duty of the Christian comradeship in the fellowship of the church —that too is deeply imbedded in Paul's thought —to fulfill the Master's law of love, to bear one another's burdens, and by the contagion, less of our arguments than of our example, to provoke one another to love and to good works. It is often true that our sins are mightier than we can bear. The creative power of Almighty God is manifested as effortless ease in the wondrous working and ramifications of the material universe. But when it came to the task of bridging the gulf between God and man as the consequence of man's sin, even God had to exert himself to the utmost. The Atonement was a work fit for Almighty God! It is not true for any man to say, "My temptations are greater than I can bear." With the temptations, God provides a way of escape that we may be able to endure it. As James puts it, "Blessed is the man who endures trial, for when he has stood the test he will receive the crown of life which

[2] *I Corinthians,* p. 133.

14 Wherefore, my dearly beloved, flee from idolatry.
15 I speak as to wise men; judge ye what I say.
16 The cup of blessing which we bless, is it not the communion of the blood of Christ? The bread which we break, is it not the communion of the body of Christ?

14 Therefore, my beloved, shun the worship of idols. 15 I speak as to sensible men;
judge for yourselves what I say. 16 The cup
of blessing which we bless, is it not a participation[m] in the blood of Christ? The
bread which we break, is it not a participa-

[m] Or *communion.*

3. The Table of the Lord and the Table of Demons (10:14-22)

14. This verse is a transitional sentence which looks back upon the failures of the past and exhorts the readers to avoid such sins in the present. They regard themselves as **wise;** now they have a chance to prove it. The substance of Paul's advice is that they must never participate in idol feasts in pagan temples, for that will mean nothing less than exclusion from the body of Christ. The apostle no longer appeals to Christian love, as in ch. 8. Abstention is a necessary course if association with demons is to be avoided. The difference in point of view in these two passages is undeniable, and it is easy to see why some interpreters want to refer this more stringent section to the precanonical letter described in 5:9. But to assign the passages to different letters does not remove the apparent contradiction in Paul's advice. The difference is due to the different situations about which he is speaking: in one case it is of the private use of meat sacrificed to idols; here it is of participation in sacrificial meals in heathen temples.

As one of the two treatments of the Lord's Supper, this passage has been subjected to the most minute analysis, and heated debates have surrounded its interpretation. Does this section reveal influence upon Paul by the sacramental meals in various mystery cults? Does Paul assume the "eating of the god" and the sacramental realism which appear to lie in John 6:51-59? Our treatment must be confined to the main issues.

16. First, there are two questions which concern the conduct of the meal. (*a*) Paul speaks of **the cup of blessing.** That was the technical term for the third of the cups drunk at the Jewish Passover. Does this substantiate Mark's idea (as opposed to John) that the Last Supper was a Passover? In the light of the phrase used in 11:23, "on the night in

God has promised to those who love him" (Jas. 1:12). Power is available. No one has more power than he believes he has. Trust in God!

14-18. ***An Illustration from the Eucharist.***—Having emphasized his point with an illustration from the O.T., the apostle now reinforces it powerfully with an illustration from the N.T., viz., from the Eucharist or the Lord's Supper. Here we have no detailed exposition of the sacrament; that is to follow in a later section where Paul deals with matters affecting orderliness in the church (but see Exeg., vss. 16, 17). Incidentally the reference indicates that the celebration of the Eucharist was a familiar aspect of the church's worship, so familiar that the use of it as an illustration would be well understood.

The warning against idolatry is reiterated; in Paul's mind the real peril lies there, and is to be guarded against as a deadly sin. At the background of Jewish and Christian thought on this issue lies the view that anything or anyone that takes God's chosen dwelling place in the human spirit is an idol. That is the point of Cowper's well-known hymn, "O for a closer walk with God."

> The dearest idol I have known,
> Whate'er that idol be,
> Help me to tear it from thy throne,
> And worship only thee.

Such idolatry is fatal to Christian faith and service. The peril of it among the Corinthians weighs heavily on the great apostle's heart. Little wonder he writes, **Therefore, my beloved, shun the worship of idols.** Let nothing usurp God's place in the spirit of man, whether the love of money, or ambition, or any other person or thing. Idolatry in the long run spells death to the soul, for that soul is "lost" in Christ's sense of the term when life is organized around the wrong objects of worship. Paul stresses the point by insisting on the analogy between the sacramental character of the Eucharist and the religious significance of any ceremony in pagan temples connected with idols. **The cup of**

17 For we *being* many are one bread, *and* one body: for we are all partakers of that one bread.

tion[m] in the body of Christ? 17 Because there is one loaf, we who are many are one body,

[m] Or *communion.*

which he was betrayed," this conclusion is unlikely, since it is probable that Paul would have identified the night as that of the Passover meal if he could. It is striking, however, that Paul says nothing about a blessing in connection with the bread. Stress is laid rather on the breaking of the bread. (*b*) Why should the cup be mentioned first? This is also the case in the short text of Luke (which ends with Luke 22:19*a*) and in the Didache Eucharistic prayers (Did. 9–10). Appeal has been made to the fact that in pagan meals the cup would precede. Since the other order is witnessed to in ch. 11, it is probable that that is the one which Paul himself preferred and practiced.

The key word in this paragraph is κοινωνία. The KJV translates this and the following genitive as **communion of the blood of Christ.** What is meant by this? "Communion with" someone is clear, but what is "communion of"? In vs. 18 the same stem appears in **partakers of the altar,** and in vs. 20 in **fellowship with devils.** In each case the genitive of some noun follows the word κοινωνός, rather than the preposition "with," as in I John, where it means fellowship with a person. Several monographs have been devoted to this word, and these have shown that "the primary idea . . . is not that of association with another person or other persons but that of participation in something in which others also participate" (J. Y. Campbell, "ΚΟΙΝΩΝΙΑ and Its Cognates in the New Testament," *Journal of Biblical Literature,* LI [1932], 353). Fine distinctions which have been sought between this term and μετέχω cannot be found. The RSV does not hesitate to use **partake** for both. "Sharing" would have been another desirable translation of κοινωνία.

Why does Paul, instead of speaking directly of sharing in Christ, use such a phrase as **participation in the blood of Christ** and **in the body of Christ?** Appeal has been made to the idea that in the Dionysian and Orphic cults there was the actual eating of the god, and it has been held that Paul had in mind such an interpretation of the Christian Eucharist. As demons gain access to us through food which is sacrificed to idols, so Christ comes to us through the cup and the broken bread. But there is no proof that such ideas were prevalent in the first century, and this interpretation breaks down in connection with vs. 18. When the sacrifices in the Jewish temple were eaten by priests and Levites, no one supposed there was any eating of the god. Yet Paul says that they are **partners in the altar.** Conceivably this might refer to the food on the altar, but more likely **altar** is used by metonomy for the God who is worshiped there.

17-20. Others have sought the key to Paul's thought in vs. 17. Though the Greek is obscure, the KJV supplies a connective in a way which can hardly be justified. Some

blessing which we bless, is it not a participation in the blood of Christ? The bread which we break, is it not a participation in the body of Christ? Because there is one loaf, we who are many are one body, for we all partake of the same loaf. The apostle is insisting that to partake of the bread and wine with grateful hearts is to establish and reaffirm our spiritual relationship and fellowship with Jesus Christ. A mystic bond of union with him is acknowledged, and those who partake of this common feast are not only in fellowship with their Lord but with one another. As they receive the bread and wine, so by faith and spiritual intuition they also receive the living Christ into their hearts and lives. All are thus one in him, and through him are in unity of faith and spirit and allegiance and service with one another. This is a brief exposition of Paul's wonderful conception of the church as the body of Christ, which receives fuller exposition later on.

The inference is plain, and Paul leaves the Corinthian Christians to draw it for themselves. In similar fashion Christian believers who participate in ritual feasts in honor of idols are in peril of being drawn into a mystic bond of unity with those who believe in them and who thus honor them. Just as the bread and wine are sacred emblems of the unity of faith and spirit among Christian believers, so meat sanctified to idols and eaten in a ritual feast in some pagan temple is emblematic of a mystical bond between those who partake of it and the idol to whom it was sanctified; or rather, in Paul's view,

18 Behold Israel after the flesh: are not they which eat of the sacrifices partakers of the altar?

19 What say I then? that the idol is any thing, or that which is offered in sacrifice to idols is any thing?

20 But *I say,* that the things which the Gentiles sacrifice, they sacrifice to devils, and not to God: and I would not that ye should have fellowship with devils.

for we all partake of the same loaf.
18 Consider the practice of Israel; are not those who eat the sacrifices partners in the altar?
19 What do I imply then? That food offered to idols is anything, or that an idol is anything?
20 No, I imply that what pagans sacrifice they offer to demons and not to God. I do not want you to be partners with

---

interpret Paul to mean that the members of the church (the body of Christ) are one through their common participation in the same loaf of bread. In other words, the meal is a sacrament of communal fellowship in which their brotherhood is cemented. Though it may be pointed out that their conduct at the Lord's table, as described in ch. 11, is a refutation of such an emphasis, this in itself would not exclude the conception as the ideal for the celebration. Possibly Paul meant that there *ought* to be such a communion with one another. But in the passage before us this is quite a subordinate thought. The conclusion which the apostle draws is not that the Corinthians cannot belong to two fellowships at the same time. Rather, they cannot belong to two Lords, to a demon and to Christ. How then does Paul mean to express this?

The verb **is** (vs. 16) does not express identity, but rather "means" or "effects" or "sets up." **The blood of Christ** does not refer simply to the fluid which coursed through his arteries, but as so often in Paul is a graphic way of referring to Christ's death. **Body** comes of course from the words of the tradition, "This is my body." We must not forget that for Hebraic thought **body** was not simply the physical part of a man but was a word for the whole person. As members of the community partake of the food and drink there is established the closest possible relationship with Christ. He is the host at his table. When food is sacrificed to heathen gods, they participate along with the worshipers. So likewise at the Lord's table, there is a sharing by Christ and by the members of his body. The bond between them is sealed in the common meal. But the bond is severed if a member of the community joins in an idol feast, for that establishes the same kind of partnership with demons.

Paul repeats what he had said in 8:4 about idols, but demons present a different situation. Paul does not deny their existence. He illustrates this with a quotation from

---

the demonic forces or powers of which the idol itself is a symbol (vss. 19-21). The essence of both feasts is a mystic bond of fellowship: on the one hand, that fellowship spells loyalty, devotion, and dedication to Jesus Christ; on the other hand, it spells obedience and devotion to the ideas and doctrines and practices involved in idol worship (see Exeg.). Ideas are dynamic forces. Victor Hugo once said that nothing is so powerful as an idea when its hour has struck. That truth has been illustrated over and over again in history and in life. Great events and personal life have been and are organized around ideas. Ideas incarnate themselves in events and in human lives. Demonic ideas, associated with idol worship, have similar effects. Paul has already illustrated the effects and their consequences in the history of Israel. He trusts his readers to ponder deeply what he has written. **I speak as to sensible men; judge for yourselves what I say.** The point is so important with him, he is so deeply concerned for the spiritual welfare of the church, that he seeks to drive it home still more securely.

18. ***A Further Illustration from the O.T.***—Paul leaves it to his readers' judgment to draw the inference. The ruling thought is that these ritual practices signify a bond of mystic fellowship which may be invisible and yet be very real. Given Paul's background of Jewish ritual practices, especially with regard to the paschal celebrations, the act of eating food laid on the altar signifies union with the god to whom the altar is dedicated.

19-22. ***On the Eating of Meat Consecrated to Idols.***—The consequences are similar with regard to pagan feasts. In these feasts, celebrated in pagan temples, homage is paid to the de-

21 Ye cannot drink the cup of the Lord, and the cup of devils: ye cannot be partakers of the Lord's table, and of the table of devils.

demons. 21 You cannot drink the cup of the Lord and the cup of demons. You cannot partake of the table of the Lord and the

---

the O.T. (Deut. 32:17; Ps. 106:37). Such beings exist and when believers join in pagan festivals they stand in the highest danger. Here speaks the rigorous Paul who called for a sharp break from the surrounding society. "What agreement has the temple of God with idols?" (II Cor. 6:16.) He speaks on behalf of the jealous God of the O.T., who will have none other beside him. In closing, Paul asks the ironical question: Do the Gnostics propose to make their Lord—i.e., Christ—jealous by their conduct in visiting pagan temples? They consider themselves "the strong"; were they really **stronger than he?** (Vs. 22.)

21. Among the papyri found in Egypt are striking parallels to Paul's phrase, **the table of the Lord.** "Chairemon invites you to a meal at the table of the lord Serapis in the Serapeum, tomorrow the fifteenth from nine o'clock onwards" (*Oxyrhynchus Papyrus* CX). Josephus recounts that in the Isis cult one could be invited to the meal of Anubis

---

monic powers associated with the idol. The idols themselves signify nothing that need disturb the Christian believer; but the supernatural agencies which lie behind them and which they represent are for Paul and for his contemporaries a very different matter. To eat food dedicatd to them is to pay homage and to offer allegiance to agencies that are antagonistic to God and to the purposes of God. Paul wishes to make clear to those stronger-minded Corinthian Christians, whom he now has in mind as he writes, that though as Christians they do have very real spiritual privileges, particularly in the matter of communion with the head and life of the church, yet these undoubted privileges must not be abused, nor do they confer any spiritual immunity on those who abuse them. Israel's own failures are a case in point. God is not to be taken for granted and is not to be provoked to wrath. There is a wrath of God as well as a mercy of God. There is justice as well as love. God claims his due even while manifesting to mankind his saving grace. He will not tolerate a divided allegiance. It is both O.T. and N.T. doctrine that men must love God with all their heart and strength and soul and mind. In the long run God has no favors for the casual mind, and if the casual mind goes too far, then, as the writer of the Epistle to the Hebrews puts it "There no longer remains a sacrifice for sins, but a fearful prospect of judgment, and a fury of fire which will consume the adversaries. A man who has violated the law of Moses dies without mercy at the testimony of two or three witnesses. How much worse punishment do you think will be deserved by the man who has spurned the Son of God, and profaned the blood of the covenant by which he was consecrated, and outraged the Spirit of grace?" (Heb. 10:26-29.) Christian devotion must be single-minded and unalloyed. Idolatry is a deadly thing. Wherefore, once again, "Shun the worship of idols." **Shall we provoke the Lord to jealousy? Are we stronger than he?**

Having made these points, Paul goes on to say that an idol is an unreal thing. We can imagine his readers looking at one another and saying, "But isn't Paul contradicting what he has just written earlier in his letter?" (See 8:4.) The apostle is alert to the point. There does seem to be a contradiction between what he wrote then and what he writes now, but it can be shown that in his own mind there was none. He still maintains that an idol is unreal (vs. 19). It is the demonic powers behind it that are the perilous reality (vs. 20). But he goes further than that, and at first sight the apparent contradiction deepens. He states definitely that meat sold in the market place may be eaten with a good conscience (vss. 25-26). How can this be reconciled with what has preceded it? The point is really simple. Paul is drawing a distinction between a ritual feast held in a pagan temple in honor of some pagan deity, in the course of which a libation was offered—a few drops of wine poured out from the cup—in honor of that deity, and a private meal where meat was served that had once been sanctified to the idol in some form or another. It was the ritual feasts which had the definitely religious significance that Paul had in mind. Probably with their elaborate ritual and ceremony they still held a certain fascination for onetime pagans who had become converts to Christianity. Old associations were as apt then as now to be pleasant to the recollection. Moreover, some members of the church in Corinth

22 Do we provoke the Lord to jealousy?
are we stronger than he?
23 All things are lawful for me, but all
things are not expedient: all things are
lawful for me, but all things edify not.

table of demons. 22 Shall we provoke the
Lord to jealousy? Are we stronger than he?
23 "All things are lawful," but not all
things are helpful. "All things are lawful,"

(*Antiquities* XVIII. 3. 4). We do not know what ideas were associated with these meals, and it would be hazardous to attempt to understand Paul from them even if we did. But they do show that **the table of the Lord** would not have been a strange phrase to a convert from paganism. Paul does not conceive of the eating of the god. The living Christ is the host who is present. In partaking of the food the worshipers participate in all that Christ has done for them. Such an intimate association permits a similar partnership with no other.

D. Concluding Statement of Principles (10:23–11:1)

Probably there has been a pause in dictation long enough for Paul to reread his treatment on food sacrificed to idols. He returns now to his general principles and also to the answering of the slogans of his opponents. No longer does he deal with personal danger, but, as in ch. 8, with concern for others. But this shift also corresponds to a change from discussion of meals in heathen temples to those in private houses.

23-24. Paul repeats the slogan of the libertines once more with the same answer he had given in 6:12. To a second quotation he rejoins with the comment he made in 8:1. It is love for the brethren, not the exercise of personal liberty, which builds up the community, and for Paul that is always the central criterion (Rom. 14:19; 15:2). **Wealth**

---

may well have held official positions in civic life and have been expected to attend such feasts and ceremonies. All of this held perilous temptations for such people. Paul therefore writes warningly against participation. There must be no compromise of the Christian conscience with potential evils.

But the question of a simple meal in the private home of a Christian believer, or for that matter, of a pagan friend, is a totally different affair. It seems that often only a portion of the meat consecrated to the idol was specially assigned to it. In certain circumstances, ritual practice being satisfied, the rest of the meat could be disposed of in the usual way to any would-be purchaser in the market place. Despite the fact that it had been formally consecrated to the idol, Paul is of the view that it was quite legitimate, and without offense to the Christian conscience, to purchase and to eat such meat. "For 'the earth is the Lord's, and everything in it' " (vs. 26).

23-30. ***Three Guiding Principles for Christian Conduct.***—Here Paul lays down three principles for the guidance of the Christians in Corinth, in this, as in kindred matters. We notice here another change of emphasis. Hitherto he has been writing to persuade those who are "enlightened" and strong-minded to waive their claims in the interest of those who are scrupulous of conscience and in the interest of weaker brethren who may be "stumbled" by the example of those who "know" that there is no such thing as an idol. Now he writes in his own person and for himself. He has found a new freedom in Jesus Christ, and he is not going to allow that freedom to be trammeled by narrow-minded Jewish prejudices and taboos, either about food which had been consecrated to idols, and which is now offered in the market place for ordinary consumption, or in any other matter that threatens to limit this freedom. **For why should my liberty be determined by another man's scruples? If I partake with thankfulness, why am I denounced because of that for which I give thanks?** His conscience is not in question and, being in good, healthy condition, is not troubling him in the matter (see Exeg., vss. 28-29). Paul is now identifying himself with the strong-minded and enlightened guest. He imaginatively paints just such a scene and set of circumstances where this issue might arise, and even relates the conversation that takes place. He imagines himself, or one of the brethren, having been invited out to dinner, and just as they are about to partake of the food someone says **"This has been offered in sacrifice."** Applying his rules, he limits his liberty by the Christian law of love. He must not upset the scrupulous brother by telling him that his scruples are ridiculous, though in fact they are. The "weaker" brother can be some-

24 Let no man seek his own, but every man another's *wealth*.

25 Whatsoever is sold in the shambles, *that* eat, asking no questions for conscience' sake:

but not all things build up. 24 Let no one seek his own good, but the good of his neighbor. 25 Eat whatever is sold in the meat market without raising any question

(KJV) is very misleading unless understood in the obsolete sense of "welfare." In 13:5 Paul will repeat the description of love that it "does not insist on its own way." Here is an illustration in point. He concludes the discussion with practically the same words (see vs. 33).

25. The word for **meat market** (μάκελλον) had been borrowed from the Latin. **Shambles** (KJV) is not very illuminating to a modern reader. Corinth had been founded as a Roman colony and most of the inscriptions from the first century are in Latin. Among them is one containing the word *macellum;* though the original location is uncertain, the stone almost certainly marked the institution referred to by Paul (see H. J. Cadbury in *Journal of Biblical Literature,* LIII [1934], 134-41). Our clearest idea of *macella* of this time is to be derived from Pompeii. They have been described as "enclosed areas with two-story shops on at least three sides." In addition to meat, other foods such as fish, fruit, and bread were sold. At Pompeii there was a chapel for the imperial cult within the enclosure. This may indicate a religious connection of all foods sold in such an establishment. Certainly most of the meat would have been sacrificed in a temple. Yet Paul does not ask the Corinthians to make any investigation of its source. That would reveal an anxiety unbecoming to a free man of the Lord. Probably **on the ground of conscience** had become a slogan in the controversy (see discussion of the word **conscience** under 8:7). So far Paul is dealing only with what goes on in a man's own home. Of

thing of a nuisance at times. There may even be occasion when for the sake of greater issues he must be disregarded. Some "weaker" brethren are so hedged in by their scruples that if a normal, healthy-minded Christian brother were to have regard to all of them, he would almost need to shuffle off "this mortal coil" and depart these scenes of earth and time. In his effort to avoid upsetting the overscrupulous Paul would never carry his anxiety to the extent of abrogating his liberty or his personal judgment.

The general rule which we noted in beginning this discussion still holds good. In dealing with all these matters God means us to use the brains and the powers of judgment with which he endowed us. Form an estimate of what is helpful and constructive, and above all seek the good of your neighbor rather than your own. The greater good of the greater number must never be lost to sight. To put the matter into a metaphor, let this pyramid be placed firmly on its base; never attempt to balance it precariously on its apex. For the rest, we must seek the full salvation of our fellow men, however weak, and lead them gently into the fullness of the liberty that we ourselves seek to enjoy as followers of Jesus Christ.

23-30. ***Some General Implications of Paul's Teaching Concerning Liberty and Love.***— While the particular problem of food offered to idols as discussed by the apostle has little relevance for us, yet the underlying convictions do possess continuing validity. These convictions are (*a*) our personal responsibility, and (*b*) we must each render an account to God. Not only in the section just discussed but elsewhere (Rom. 14:10-12) such propositions are clearly involved and possess outstanding importance. They are definitely implied in the statement that "sinning against your brethren and wounding their conscience when it is weak, you sin against Christ" (8:12).

(*a*) *The idea of personal responsibility* is central in the Gospels. Moreover, it has been one of the germinative ideas contributed by Christianity to civilization. As such it has evoked revolutionary social and political consequences.[3] Wherever man is in danger of depersonalization as the outcome of political or technical developments, these leading Christian themes ought to be emphasized, for such a process is inimical to his faith in God and therefore to his status as man. As Paul has put it, even the weak man is "the brother for whom Christ died" (8:11).

Moral responsibility is illustrated in history. How otherwise can we adequately account for the rise and fall of civilizations? To every peo-

[3] See A. N. Whitehead, *Adventures of Ideas* (New York: The Macmillan Co., 1933).

26 For the earth *is* the Lord's, and the fulness thereof.

27 If any of them that believe not bid you *to a feast,* and ye be disposed to go; whatsoever is set before you, eat, asking no question for conscience' sake.

28 But if any man say unto you, This is offered in sacrifice unto idols, eat not for his sake that showed it, and for conscience' sake: for the earth *is* the Lord's, and the fulness thereof:

on the ground of conscience. 26 For "the
earth is the Lord's, and everything in it."
27 If one of the unbelievers invites you to
dinner and you are disposed to go, eat
whatever is set before you without raising
any question on the ground of conscience.
28 (But if some one says to you, "This has
been offered in sacrifice," then out of consideration for the man who informed you,

---

course he will repeat a table blessing over the food purchased in the *macellum* (Rom. 14:6). Ps. 24:1, which Paul quotes in vs. 26, was in all probability one of the forms used. There could be no objection to one's partaking of any part of God's good creation for which a proper blessing of the Creator had been spoken.

27-28. But a different situation arises if the Christian is in the home of an unbeliever. Paul is noncommittal on whether the acceptance of such invitations is wise. But if one accepts, there is no reason why one should ask questions about the food. The advice repeats the words of Luke 10:8 where the seventy (-two) are to eat what is set before them. This stands in contrast to Peter's uncertainty at Joppa (Acts 10) and the injunctions of James (Gal. 2:12). A different situation arises, however, if someone expressly calls attention to the fact that this is idol meat. It is not clear whom Paul has in mind. The indefinite **some one** is probably not the host. But since the word is ἱερόθυτος, rather than εἰδωλόθυτος, it is more likely that he is a heathen than that he is a Christian. Yet the reason for pointing out the nature of the food would lie in the belief that a Christian was not expected to eat it with a clear conscience if he knew its character. In this case Paul advises that the Christian guest should refrain from eating the meat.

---

ple is given some master light which indicates its part in the unfolding of God's purposes. So long as it remains faithful to its deepest insights it retains and perhaps even increases its strength and its sense of destiny. When it begins to disregard these divine intimations, something in the spirit of that race begins to die, and sooner or later it is overthrown by another more virile and more single-minded; e.g., only so can we fully explain the fading of "the glory that was Greece," and "the grandeur that was Rome," and many another civilization as well.[4] The deeper meaning of such events is that we live in a moral universe in which mankind reaps what it sows. Paul, possessed as he was of a strong sense of the solidarity of the race and of divine providence, never loses sight of this master conviction.

Moral responsibility is illustrated in individual life. Man is free to choose his course, for God respects the gift that he bestowed. It is not true to say that individuals are the mere victims of heredity and environment, though these are very powerful. None could possibly conceive of any better state than his actual moral and spiritual condition if he were the mere puppet of determining forces. The individual is free to make his moral choice. He can challenge and defy and often overcome heredity and environment. Jesus Christ is the greatest of all personalities because, among many other qualities, there was the power of reaction. When heredity and environment combined to nail him to the Cross, he reacted with such power of redeeming grace that he, and not his crucifiers, won the final victory. The Cross has become the symbol of our faith and its triumph.

Man is free to conform to heredity and environment. He can compromise his moral status by yielding to the seductions of modern equivalents of "food offered to idols." He can organize his life around wrong values and purposes and to that extent abuse his God-given freedom. In fact, the worst sins have ever been the abuse of the greatest gifts. To take one example, the sex instinct is a gift. Used as the giver intended, it can give the necessary impulse to loving companionship, to happy married life, to the building of a lovely home, and to wise parenthood. It can be given expression in social service and

[4] See Arnold J. Toynbee, *A Study of History,* abridgment by D. C. Somervell (New York: Oxford University Press, 1947); Lionel Curtis, *Civitas Dei; The Commonwealth of God* (London: Macmillan & Co., 1938).

29 Conscience, I say, not thine own, but of the other: for why is my liberty judged of another *man's* conscience?

30 For if I by grace be a partaker, why am I evil spoken of for that for which I give thanks?

and for conscience' sake — 29 I mean his conscience, not yours — do not eat it.) For why should my liberty be determined by another man's scruples? 30 If I partake with thankfulness, why am I denounced because of that for which I give thanks?

29. So far the argument is clear; but who interposes the objection about liberty being determined by another man's scruples? In vss. 28-29*a* Paul has been contending that this ought to take place, that the Christian should be limited not only by his own sense of right and wrong, but also by the conscience of another. Does not then 29*b* express the objection of one of the strong? Does it not defend the point of view of the free man whom Paul proposes to limit by this stress upon love? The objector throws Paul's argument back at him. Why should he be denounced for eating any food over which a thanksgiving has been pronounced? Though love is a Christian virtue, so likewise is inner integrity. How can a man pretend, even out of a spirit of love, that an action is wrong when he knows that it is not? Understood thus, the passage would present the unresolved dialectic of the conflict of love and sincerity.

Against this interpretation two considerations are raised. One is grammatical; we would expect in that case an adversative particle instead of γάρ (for). Also it would mean that Paul made no attempt to resolve this conflict. (But how can one theoretically?) The RSV adopts a neat solution by putting vss. 28-29*a* in parentheses. The passage is treated as an aside which Paul does not develop further. Vs. 29*b* continues the thought of vs. 27. Paul is asking these rhetorical questions to defend the freedom of a dinner guest

in love of country or many other great causes. Abused, it can create unspeakable havoc in the realm of personal relationships and, of course, in the life of the individuals concerned. The same truth holds good in every aspect of life. It was said of a greatly gifted man who died, and who had held some of the highest offices in the government of his country, that "he fell far short of the achievements within his capacity because he gave little thought or time to things unseen." His life was organized on the level of materialism. Like the rich farmer of the parable (Luke 12:13-21) he made three mistakes—he mistook his body for his soul, time for eternity, and himself for God. In the end death with a simple gesture exposed the emptiness and insecurity of such a life. Yet it was his own choice. He was corrupted by the idols which he served, and the responsibility was his alone. One modern psychologist—and he finds increasing support among others—has written:

> Personal development . . . , as opposed to mere material existence, comes through the awakening of reason and conscience, and the gradual achievement of freedom, which demand that a man should stand over against the instinctive compulsions within him, commanding them in the interests of an ideal instead of being swept along by them as a mere thing.[5]

[5] W. Fearon Halliday, *Psychology and Religious Experience* (London: Hodder & Stoughton, 1929), p. 4.

(*b*) *We must each render an account to God.* This is the apostle's second underlying conviction, and it receives increasing emphasis as his thought matures (Rom. 14:12). It is clearly implied by his statement that a sin against weaker brethren is a sin against Christ. The Master made it plain in his parable of the last assize (Matt. 25:31-46). This is a moral universe: mankind is not treading a road that leads to nowhere. Spiritual forces are constantly at work among us. Moreover, Christian faith will regard this world as the terrestrial phase of an eternal purpose. This is the context in which all earthly conduct is set. Mystics like Böhme have emphasized such convictions. Somehow, somewhere, sometime the divine drama will work itself out and man will stand before the judgment seat of God. As a proverb puts it, "God does not pay on Saturdays, but in the end he pays." It is a sobering thought; Paul meant to sober those somewhat irresponsible Christians. "You sin against Christ" (8:12).

Yet it is a sustaining and encouraging thought. In the end it is better to be judged by God than by ourselves or by our benevolent friends. He sees what is hidden from them; the hidden motive, the inner conflict, the secret sorrows, the frustrations endured, the temptations resisted. His justice will far transcend that of the wisest earthly judge. He is the Christlike

31 Whether therefore ye eat, or drink, or whatsoever ye do, do all to the glory of God.

32 Give none offense, neither to the Jews, nor to the Gentiles, nor to the church of God:

33 Even as I please all *men* in all *things*, not seeking mine own profit, but the *profit* of many, that they may be saved.

31 So, whether you eat or drink, or whatever you do, do all to the glory of God.
32 Give no offense to Jews or to Greeks or
to the church of God, 33 just as I try to
please all men in everything I do, not seeking my own advantage, but that of

---

in a pagan home to eat anything set before him. The thought of vss. 25-26 is repeated in the new context. Χάρις means both "thankfulness" and "grace." The KJV leaves a strange impression by using the latter translation here.

10:31–11:1. Paul now draws his final conclusions. Eating and drinking are not in themselves enough (Luke 13:26). All of the conduct of a believer should redound **to the glory of God.** The argument is not, as in Rom. 14:6-7, that food cannot separate us from God. In both cases, however, the aim is to **give no offense** to those who are weak. It is

---

God! Love and justice are perfectly blended in him.

> Is it, if heaven the future showed,
> Is it the all-severest mode
> To see ourselves with the eyes of God?
> God rather grant, at His assize,
> He see us not with our own eyes! [6]

We shall look on him who shared our life, who made of it a divine glory, and our hearts will condemn us (John 19:37). The verdict will lie with his perfect justice and eternal love. That we may be able to withstand that day and fulfill God's purposes on earth, let these moral convictions govern our relationships and mold our character, and may these lines be our prayer:

> Spirit of purity and grace,
> Our weakness, pitying see;
> O make our hearts thy dwelling place,
> And worthier thee! [7]

31. ***The Whole of Life to Be Lived to the Glory of God.***—Paul finally expands to the whole range of everyday activities his exposition of our obligation to live blamelessly in the eyes of God and in the light of the law of love. **So, whether you eat or drink, or whatever you do, do all to the glory of God.** This is the full mandate of Jesus Christ, through his apostle, to all Christian believers. It is the clearest possible statement that Christianity is the whole of life, cleansed, illumined, dominated by the indwelling Spirit of Jesus Christ. It means that in all circumstances it is possible to live a consistent Christian life (cf. 7:17-24).

In the midst of everyday activities—this is suggested by the phrase **whether you eat or drink, or whatever you do**—Christian witness can be most effective. Someone has suggested that it is not what we do on holidays that fashions us. This is true. The major part of life is lived in the grooves of daily routine, in the home or place of business. If Christianity is to be of value and help to ordinary men and women, the fact must be reckoned with. In effect, Paul writes to the church in Corinth that it is there the witness is needed most.

In addition, we are to remember that "the soul grows, not by expanding the universe, but by deepening it." How can that be done? How can we fulfill the apostle's requirement that we **do all to the glory of God?** We can do it by cultivating the art of regarding things from a somewhat different angle. This can be a refreshing experience, for nothing is really commonplace. Only our own attitude makes it so. We can change that attitude. Surely here is at least one element in the meaning of the word "repent." After all, great art is to a large extent the transformation of common things.

> The poem hangs on the berry bush
> When comes the poet's eye;
> The street begins to masquerade
> When Shakespeare passes by.[8]

Prose is turned into poetry by the poet's use of the devices of transfiguration, concreteness, and vividness. Certainly, when a real Christian experience changes one's angle on life, the whole of life is transformed and immeasurably

[6] Francis Thompson, "Epilogue to a Judgement in Heaven." Used by permission of Burns, Oates & Washbourne.

[7] Harriet Auber, "Our blest Redeemer, ere he breathed."

[8] William Channing Gannett, "We See as We Are."

11 Be ye followers of me, even as I also *am* of Christ.

11 many, that they may be saved. 1 Be imitators of me, as I am of Christ.

noteworthy that Paul divides mankind into three groups: **Jews,** and **Greeks,** and **the church of God.** The first two had been isolated in 1:22-24; those who preached Christ crucified to the two groups were the **church of God.** Nothing could illustrate better the high consciousness that they were the elect people of God. Paul picks up once more the argument of 9:20-22 (see Rom. 15:2; Phil. 2:4). The purpose is that **many** may be saved. The last appeal is to his own example as one who endeavors to imitate **Christ.** He had shown in ch. 9 what that involved. Neither here nor elsewhere in his letters does he cite any specific acts of Jesus which he was trying to emulate (cf. Rom. 15:3). As far as the community is concerned, they are asked to imitate the Christ who dwells in Paul. In the absence of written Gospels this is quite understandable and provides no basis for a charge of egotism against Paul.

---

deepened. That particular transformation has been described by John Masefield in his marvelous lines depicting the effect of the conversion of Saul Kane, the onetime pugilist.

> O glory of the lighted mind,
> How dead I'd been, how dumb, how blind.
> The station brook, to my new eyes,
> Was babbling out of Paradise;
> The waters rushing from the rain
> Were singing Christ has risen again.
> I thought all earthly creatures knelt
> From rapture of the joy I felt.[9]

The whole of life is lighted up with the glory of God when we look on it with Christian eyes. In doing so we catch the Master's gift of looking up. To him the whole world was a sacrament that spoke of the handiwork and unfailing providence of Almighty God.

Again, we can seek to **do all to the glory of God** when we attempt life's ordinary tasks and experiences in an extraordinary spirit. Some of life's deepest inspirations may be found there. Trouble is one of the commonplace things, but many a sickroom has been a sanctuary, and many a pastor has been inspired by the shining courage manifested there.

The workshop can be transformed by the spirit of the persons who work in it. Robertson of Irvine, a Scottish divine of a bygone generation, was asked by a visitor to his church, "Who is that man who has just offered prayer?" The answer was given, "He is an elder of mine who lives in communion with God and makes shoes." Every workshop can be such a sanctuary if it is permeated by the genuinely Christian spirit. One wonders if this was one of the apostle Paul's deeper reasons for earning his living with his own hands at his trade as a tentmaker. Surely that thought must have been present to the mind of one who had taken it as his mission so to Christianize the whole of life that we might even eat and drink to the glory of God. In the end there can be no genuinely better social, national, or international order if this spirit is lacking. Everything that has its legitimate place in life must be brought into subjection to Jesus Christ.

11:1. ***Christ as Our Example.***—This lies at the back of Paul's thought. **Be imitators of me, as I am of Christ.** That life was lived out amid commonplace things and in contact with commonplace people. In his great and everlasting gospel Jesus used commonplace events and circumstances to illustrate his message. There was nothing formal about his language. Perhaps that is why the common people heard him gladly! Yet the gospel record and the N.T. documents that the gospel itself inspired have resulted in anything but a commonplace book. What is his secret, that we might follow him, and help him fulfill his purpose to redeem the world? The secret is simple. Nothing was common in his eyes, because there was no point in life where we might not meet with God. For Jesus Christ this is a sacramental universe. He invites us to follow him there, even as Paul followed; and for us, as for the great apostle, there is a "grace sufficient" that will enable us to accept and to fulfill that heavenly invitation.

11:1. ***Paul's Own Example.***—Paul ends this portion of his letter with an appeal to his readers to follow his example. He can fairly claim that he incarnates in his own life and spirit, as far as possible, conscious doubtless of many a defect and failure, the Christian faith and life that he so passionately preached. That, after all, is the irrefutable argument for the reality and greatness of the faith. One can refute an argument; one cannot refute a life. Enoch, who walked with God, although nothing

[9] *The Everlasting Mercy.* Copyright, 1911. Used by permission of The Macmillan Co., The Society of Authors, and Dr. John Masefield, O.M.

2 Now I praise you, brethren, that ye remember me in all things, and keep the ordinances, as I delivered *them* to you.

2 I commend you because you remember me in everything and maintain the traditions even as I have delivered them to

V. Christian Worship (11:2–14:40)

At this point Paul turns to a discussion of various types of disorder in the services of worship. He deals in turn with the conduct of women, with wrong attitudes at the Lord's

is added about his special gifts or services, yet left an indelible impression on the mind of one ancient chronicler and through him on subsequent generations. People took note of a significant difference in the simple fishermen of Galilee, Peter and John, as they walked through the streets of Jerusalem (Acts 4:13). Peter and John walking in the spirit of Jesus Christ, conveying his grace in life's common places, in London or New York or anywhere, would exercise a similar ministry. No believer should underestimate the significance of the service he can render to the Master. As a celebrated Scottish commentator, A. B. Davidson, once put it to his students, "An ordinary life lived well is the greatest of all deeds." And in times of testing it is not arguments but inspiring examples that carry the day. In any case, very few have been argued into accepting the Christian faith, and very few have been argued out of it. Christianity is not statements about Jesus Christ: Christianity is Jesus Christ. He is the living head and the beating heart of the church, which is his body, and which therefore is his continued incarnation in the life of the world, and the vehicle of his purposes.

Paul, as a member of that church, as the great missionary of its delivering faith to the Gentile world, was probably the first example the Corinthians had seen of a consistent Christian life. The best interpretation of the gospel is to be found precisely in such individual lives. The truth of the gospel is best transmitted through consecrated personality. Paul could well be described by Chaucer's familiar lines, so vividly descriptive of the parson in his "Prologue" to *The Canterbury Tales.*

> A bettre preest I trowe that nowher noon ys;
> He waitede after no pompe and reverence,
> Ne makèd him a spicèd conscience,
> But Christes loore, and his Apostles twelve,
> He taughte, but first he folwed it hymselve.

As Moffatt has pointed out, Paul had no wish to dominate the Corinthian church; all his desires and ideals for every church with which he was concerned—and he was a great lover of the churches—was that the members should grow in grace and in strong, sane, wholesome Christian manhood and womanhood, thus commending their faith to their fellow men. In a similar connection, dealing with similar problems in the church in Rome, he writes: "For the kingdom of God does not mean food and drink but righteousness and peace and joy in the Holy Spirit; he who thus serves Christ is acceptable to God and approved by men. Let us then pursue what makes for peace and for mutual upbuilding" (Rom. 14:17-19).

He was distressed that there should be a faction which made his name their party "watchword." It is the faith that matters, the message and not the messenger, Christ and not his instrument, save that the instrument should be adequate and entirely commendable to him who uses it. He knew very well indeed the peculiar trials and temptations and tests and pressures from their pagan environment that the members of the Christian communities had to endure, and so he sought to set before them the example of a strong, clean Christian life. He who had done and endured so much for the faith could without any hint of egotism or insincerity urge his converts to copy him; for his own consistent desire and goal was that he himself should be "complete in Christ."

No one should underestimate the power of a consistent Christian example. Often enough we may be tempted to wonder if it really exerts any influence at all. Only God can fully resolve that doubt. The probability is that its influence is far more profound and far reaching than the believer or his contemporaries could tell.

> It is an acknowledged fact that Christian faith depends often upon belief in some guide or spiritual counsellor who stands more effectively than anything for the reality of religion. Struggling aspirations may be reinforced, vague doubts may be resolved, and loyalty to the cause may be revived and purified, as men are able to see their cherished end in the personality of one to whom they have good cause to pay grateful homage.[1]

Paul, the bondslave of Jesus Christ, could and did bring to his fellow believers in Corinth and elsewhere the inspiration and driving force of authentic, consecrated leadership.

2-16. ***The Place of Women in the Church.***—This section of the epistle, dealing with the

[1] Moffatt, *I Corinthians,* pp. 147-48.

Supper, and with the unedifying exhibitions of speaking in tongues by the "spiritual." This topic calls for a wider discussion of the nature and value of spiritual gifts.

A. The Veiling of Women (11:2-16)

In this section it should be noted that Paul deals only with the conduct of women during worship—as they pray and prophesy. It is linked closely in subject matter with the description of the service of the word in ch. 14. The passage illustrates the perennial problem of the relationship of social customs to Christian morality. Paul writes out of the background of the patriarchal Jewish family. He addresses people who live in the midst of a Greek city with fixed customs. It was not easy for the apostle to draw consistent conclusions from his conviction that in Christ "there is neither male nor female" (Gal. 3:29). At least while the present age lasted, important differences remained. When respectable women were veiled outside their homes, and only courtesans were unveiled,

---

place of women in the public worship of the church, is bound to present difficulties to the modern mind. It is hard for us to understand the apostle's indignation and his obvious concern about such matters as women appearing unveiled in the congregation, or cutting their hair short. But in its context, though the views of Paul are not now generally accepted as the mind of Christ on these matters, what he has to say would be well understood, and in the main approved, by the majority of his readers. He is writing in a conservative and most rabbinical mood. The "Hebrew of the Hebrews," who was also an heir of Greek antiquity, though liberated into new dimensions of freedom through Jesus Christ, is inevitably bound to be colored in outlook and temperament by his traditions and environment. Even so he is, perhaps unknown to himself, in advance of his times. At least, while strongly and even abruptly asserting the traditional point of view as to the place of women in the church, he indicates a finer, more Christian attitude. The section should be ranked as among the least permanently valuable of Paul's writings. Its value and permanence lie almost solely in the fact that it represents his views on women, and is also a side light on the life and customs and problems of the early Christian communities.

I commend you because you remember me in everything and maintain the traditions even as I have delivered them to you. Is there a hint here of the celebrated Pauline irony? We know how deeply the apostle was perturbed by the reports he had received about various disorders in the church. The report to which he refers here is that of the church itself, a report which no doubt set down for the apostle's consideration certain problems of conduct, or rather procedure, which were common to churches in Asia Minor and in Macedonia and Greece as well. No doubt, too, its authors wished Paul to think well of them; hence their remembrances, and their assurances that in everything they are seeking to maintain the traditions they had received from him. Paul makes suitable and courteous acknowledgment of their words, but indicates at once that he does it with marked qualifications. Of what traditions is he thinking? Elsewhere he writes, "So then, brethren, stand firm and hold to the traditions which you were taught by us, either by word of mouth or by letter" (II Thess. 2:15). We can be sure that by traditions he means the preaching of the word and the administration of the sacraments; for in Pauline thought and exposition these are the twin focuses around which there swings the ellipse of the Christian gospel. "Christ crucified and risen" is central in Paul's preaching, and the remembrance of that gospel in the sacrament of the Lord's Supper is central in his doctrine of the fellowship of the church. Surely the high-minded Pharisee's sense of order and dignity in matters of worship and assembly was to find expression in the tradition of Christian fellowship. Traditions are not to be lightly regarded. Where the public worship of God is concerned, there ought always to be present, besides awe and reverence, a sense of inspiration and control. Traditions are to a church what institutions are to a state, or character to a man or woman. They provide the element of structure and coherence and stability. To be sure, their strength may be a source of weakness, as we may discern in the very passage under consideration: Paul's views on the place of women in the church have been all too influential in certain religious quarters to this very day. Traditions at their best are meant to conserve what is most valuable in the experience of men; but when conservation becomes no more than conservatism, it can erect many a barrier to progress.

Did Paul, however, include more among these "traditions" than the things already mentioned, which must be accepted as central and enduring in Christian faith and worship? It

3 But I would have you know, that the head of every man is Christ; and the head of the woman *is* the man; and the head of Christ *is* God.

you. 3 But I want you to understand that the head of every man is Christ, the head of a woman is her husband, and the head

the exercise of "freedom" could lead to gross misinterpretation. On the other hand, if the meeting of the community constituted a family circle, why should not women enjoy the freedom of their own homes?

11:2. Before beginning his criticism Paul starts with a general word of praise. He speaks as one who has transmitted **the traditions** to them. It is instructive that this should be the vocabulary of a teacher twenty years after the resurrection of Jesus. As the rabbis passed on their traditions from generation to generation, Paul passes on what he had received from the communities before him (vs. 23; II Thess. 2:15). The noun **tradition** and the verb **delivered** are from the same Greek root (see Rom. 6:17; II Thess. 3:6).

3. The apostle turns at once to a tradition which his readers were not following because they had not understood the hierarchic principle which extended through the entire universe. All do not stand on an equality, but each is subordinated to the one above. Paul begins with the middle terms in the series. The **head** is the one to whom obedience is due. A Christian man is part of the body of Christ, and **Christ** is "the head

seems that he did. Certainly he is no mere traditionalist. We have evidence in his epistles of the fierce fight he waged against the Judaizing elements in the Christian church who tried to impose Jewish rites and practices, such as circumcision and the keeping of Jewish feast days, upon pagans who had become converts to Christianity. Yet while setting aside these strictly Jewish traditions as by no means binding on his converts, there were obviously others, among them the Judaistic and rabbinical interpretation of the status of women in the religious community, by which he insists they must regulate their church order and belief.

The particular problem arose no doubt because of the practice of some of the women members of the congregation in appearing at the sessions of public worship with their heads uncovered. To us this seems a trivial matter. Perhaps no mention had been made of it in the official report sent by the church. It may have been brought to Paul's notice by the members of the household of Chloe, or by Stephanus and his companions. At any rate, the apostle is indignant and deeply concerned. Why? There is surely something to be said for the offenders, if such they are. These women probably considered themselves, being converts to Christianity, as liberated into a new order of life. In Paul's own glowing words they had become "a new creation; the old has passed away, behold, the new has come" (II Cor. 5:17). They had been set free from the inhibiting beliefs and estimates of paganism; they felt themselves to be under a very different order, and were aware of a new status and dignity as the outcome of their acceptance of it. Moreover, as the context of this and kindred passages makes plain, they were allowed to take a prominent and active part in public worship; they were permitted freely to pray and to prophesy (vs. 5). This was an advance on the practice of the Jewish synagogues. Socially it was correct procedure for a woman to keep her head covered while she traversed the streets, but once admitted to a private house it was in order for the head covering to be removed, and the church met in private houses. Besides, in some of the higher Greek cults both men and women worshiped without wearing any covering for the head. The Corinthian women appeared to have reasoned, and not without justification, that no less freedom should be the portion of those who had been initiated into a faith that sets men and women free from every kind of bondage save bondage to Jesus Christ. There is nothing to indicate, even in Paul's strong and almost violent strictures, that there was anything indecorous in their behavior. His strong protest and ruling are not based on any such charge, but on religious grounds, rabbinically interpreted. Here we have an illustration of the manner in which belief can make havoc of logic, and indeed of sensibility. The sole concession that can and ought to be made to Paul, and to those who shared his views, is that they were, at least in this respect, the children of their times. This of course is no blemish on their character; it is a reflection on the power and weight of custom and belief.

3-16. ***The Grounds of Paul's Objections.***—In these verses, as in the more primitive account of creation in the book of Genesis, Paul finds a rabbinical interpretation of the rela-

4 Every man praying or prophesying,
having *his* head covered, dishonoureth his
head.

5 But every woman that prayeth or
prophesieth with *her* head uncovered dishonoureth her head: for that is even all one
as if she were shaven.

6 For if the woman be not covered, let
her also be shorn: but if it be a shame for
a woman to be shorn or shaven, let her
be covered.

of Christ is God. 4 Any man who prays or
prophesies with his head covered dishonors
his head, 5 but any woman who prays or
prophesies with her head unveiled dishonors her head — it is the same as if her head
were shaven. 6 For if a woman will not veil
herself, then she should cut off her hair; but
if it is disgraceful for a woman to be shorn

of the body" (Eph. 1:22; 4:15; 5:23; Col. 1:18). That a wife was subordinate to **her husband** was a teaching of the law (Gen. 3:16) which Paul did not look upon as abrogated in Christ. The subordination of **Christ** to **God** is continually affirmed in this letter (3:23; 15:28). In the order of creation each is the head of the one below: **God, Christ, man,** and **woman.** As in 7:22, where Paul reminds masters of slaves that they too have a master, here also he reminds the head of the household that he too has a **head.** Though vs. 7 presents a somewhat different point of view, it is unnecessary to brand vs. 3 as a gloss.

4-6. To anyone who has attended an orthodox Jewish service this passage will be quite unintelligible. But in the first century a Jewish man did not cover **his head** for prayer. That custom, originally a sign of sorrow, arose in the fourth century (Strack and Billerbeck, *Kommentar zum N.T.*, III, 423-26). Paul's authorization of the custom of his time is still taken by some Christian bodies as a divine injunction. It must be borne in mind that Paul is dealing only with conduct during worship. We are not to think of the Moslem custom in the Near East in more recent times. Yet it was expected that a woman would cover her head outside the house, and even her face was often veiled. Two

tionship of woman to man, especially perhaps of a married woman to her husband (vss. 8, 11), and also a divine sanction for his ruling (see Exeg., vs. 3). In accordance with his purpose to retain the custom of women remaining veiled during the conduct of worship by insisting on the superiority of the man, he ignores the passage in Genesis (1:27) which implies that both man and woman were made in the "image" or "likeness" of God. In theory, in the Judaistic and Greek world, woman was considered to be man's inferior. In both worlds, as we know from various writers of antiquity, practice rose superior to theory. We have noted one instance of this in the practice of both men and women participating with bared heads in certain Greek rites. But the theory was explicitly accepted. In particular, in the Judaistic realm a woman suffered distinct and harsh social disadvantages. She could be driven away from her home and even divorced for the most trifling and humiliating reasons. Some of the sterner sayings of Jesus were directed against such manifest injustices. Religiously, she was at even greater disadvantage: she apparently ranked with slaves in having no religious privileges or duties. It is to the great apostle's credit that while he seems unquestioningly to have accepted the traditional social view of the status of women, he rejected the traditional religious view. Certainly he pays tribute elsewhere to the ministry of women in the church, and acknowledges his debt to them for the hospitality he had received in their homes (cf. Rom. 16:1-15). In rejecting these religious disabilities as applied to women it can also be set down to the apostle's credit, despite his views, that he initiated the Christian movement which has resulted in the social and religious emancipation of women in Christian lands.

For all that, Paul's point of view is less than Christian in his insistence that man made in the likeness of God reflects the glory of God, while woman made from man reflects the glory of man. The emphasis throughout is on the superior status of man as God's representative on earth; as such, he is invested with divine authority and dominion over the rest of created things, including woman. On the rabbinical view which Paul here states, Eve was created to be man's helpmeet. **(For man was not made from woman, but woman from man. Neither was man created for woman, but woman for man.)** Nothing could be more explicit or less convincing! Paul himself may have been subconsciously aware of the inconclusive nature

7 For a man indeed ought not to cover *his* head, forasmuch as he is the image and glory of God: but the woman is the glory of the man.

8 For the man is not of the woman; but the woman of the man.

9 Neither was the man created for the woman; but the woman for the man.

or shaven, let her wear a veil. 7 For a man
ought not to cover his head, since he is
the image and glory of God; but woman
is the glory of man. 8 (For man was not
made from woman, but woman from man.
9 Neither was man created for woman, but

---

different words are used by Paul for the cutting of the hair. The shaving was with a razor; the shearing, with scissors. Such a cutting of the hair was a mark of a slave or of a woman in mourning. In other words, Paul suggests that the quest of the women for emancipation and equality with men was in fact a reduction in status. It was a violation of the divine order.

7-9. That man was created in the **image . . . of God** was the teaching of Gen. 1:27. **Glory** is here used in the sense of the secondary as opposed to the original. Genesis includes both "male and female," but for Paul **woman** is the weaker copy. From the story of the creation of woman in Gen. 2:22, he infers a priority of man (cf. I Tim. 2:13). Man was not created to meet the need of woman, but she was created because man needed a

---

of his argument, for he almost immediately states the case against this conservative rabbinical interpretation—(**Nevertheless, in the Lord woman is not independent of man nor man of woman; for as woman was made from man, so man is now born of woman. And all things are from God.**) That last sentence reaches deeper and more permanent, therefore more convincing, levels. Here we begin to approximate a Christian conception of the relationship of the sexes. When we add to this more enlightened interpretation all that Paul has said about the prominent and valuable part women take in the public worship of the church, we have a point of view that inevitably means the disintegration of the conservative rabbinical position he has just stated (cf. Gal. 3:28). Great as Paul undoubtedly is, we must not expect perfection or absolute consistency. Part of the greatness of his spirit lies in the fact that he was a learner in things Christian to the end of his days. No doubt here, as in other important matters, e.g., in the modification of his earlier belief with regard to the immediate return of the Lord, he was continually revising his views as he entered more and more deeply into the mind and grace of his Master.

But perhaps the effect of custom and habit was more influential in determining the apostle's views than the rabbinical interpretation of creation in which he seeks a divine sanction for his ruling on the matter under discussion. Certainly his opinions are in complete accord with Greek sentiment that women should not appear in public save with their heads covered. The idea behind the custom is that of the inferiority of the woman, coupled with a recognition of the headship or dominion of the man. This provides the reason for the apostle's strictures on the growing practice, taken from what appears to have been an innovation in the Jewish synagogues at the time, of men keeping their heads covered while engaged in prayer. The uncovered head of the man signified his status as lord and master by divine ordinance, therefore **any man who prays or prophesies with his head covered dishonors his head.** In all circumstances he must preserve his superiority of status, **but any woman who prays or prophesies with her head unveiled dishonors her head.** That for Paul is a crowning disgrace (vs. 6). It is disgraceful on two counts: first, it contravenes the divine order of creation which he has evoked for the sanction he needs to give authority to his ruling; second, custom decreed the veil as a symbol of respectability (see Exeg., vss. 4-6, 10). It assured the status of the woman: it indicated that she was under the authority and protection of her husband or her father or a guardian, who were thus responsible for her, and to whom she in turn owed respect and submission. Only immodest women whose character and conduct could not bear examination appeared in public with their heads uncovered. The very circumstance of such an appearance proclaimed them for what they were.

Moreover, then as now—there were instances in World War II where women who had betrayed either their countrymen or their allies to an invading enemy suffered the indignity and disgrace of having their heads shaven—a shaven or cropped head in a woman was a

10 For this cause ought the woman to have power on *her* head because of the angels.

11 Nevertheless neither is the man without the woman, neither the woman without the man, in the Lord.

12 For as the woman *is* of the man, even so *is* the man also by the woman; but all things of God.

woman for man.) 10 That is why a woman
ought to have a veil[n] on her head, because
of the angels. 11 (Nevertheless, in the Lord
woman is not independent of man nor man
of woman; 12 for as woman was made from
man, so man is now born of woman. And

[n] Greek *authority* (the veil being a symbol of this).

"help meet" (Gen. 2:18). So far everything is clear regarding Paul's commentary on the O.T.; but the conclusion he would draw is decidedly obscure and appears to involve a *non sequitur*.

10. What is meant by the ἐξουσία which a woman should have on her head, and what connection has this with angels? (*a*) Some take it as a "sign of dependence." Then the angels would be mentioned because they were the protectors of the orders of creation. But against this is the fact that this **power** is something which the woman exercises. (*b*) Others take **power** in the sense of "protection." The angels are looked upon as present at the service of worship and women need defense against their lust. But did Paul use the word **angels** for evil beings? (*c*) The RSV accepts the evidence adduced by Gerhard Kittel (*Rabbinica* [Leipzig: J. C. Hinrichs, 1920], pp. 17-31) that ἐξουσία is here equivalent to **veil** (in fact, many MSS have that reading). Though we may not with Sir William Ramsay appeal to present Oriental customs and conclude that a veil is a protection (*Cities of St. Paul* [London: Hodder & Stoughton, 1907], pp. 202-3), we may recognize in it an indication that she shares in the power of her husband (or guardian). With this interpretation the angels are invoked to defend the order imposed by God in creation.

11-12. Possibly Paul feared that he had gone too far in stressing the subordination of women. At least, he adds, **man** and **woman** are **not independent** of each other.

---

mark of disgrace. Even if she had cut off her own hair the disgrace remained, and was indeed enhanced, since the act seemed to signify that she was aping man and aspiring to his status or denying his superiority. With all its exceptions in the matter of social practice, the ancient Greco-Roman world held jealously by the theory of male superiority. Many long years were to pass before women were accorded their full rights in accordance with Christian teaching and standards and spirit. Paul's thought and outlook were undoubtedly deeply dyed in the color of social custom. **For if a woman will not veil herself, then she should cut off her hair; but if it is disgraceful for a woman to be shorn or shaven, let her wear a veil.**

The argument is reinforced by an argument from nature, also unconvincing. **Judge for yourselves; is it proper for a woman to pray to God with her head uncovered? Does not nature itself teach you that for a man to wear long hair is degrading to him, but if a woman has long hair, it is her pride? For her hair is given to her for a covering.** The modern religious mind is not likely to be persuaded either by the argument from creation or by that on the grounds of natural propriety. It would be considered folly to argue, as Paul implies, that men are likely to be less spiritually sensitive or alert because their hair is worn long, or that a woman loses spiritual and social standing because her hair is short, or because she appears in public with her head uncovered. The argument would have been unconvincing, in some respects at least, even in Paul's day; for Greek heroes often wore long hair, and many ancient philosophers, as well as their modern counterparts, followed the same practice. Paul is entitled to his opinion and to his adherence to social custom. He is not entitled to make his personal opinion, or the prevalent social customs of his time, the basis of a moral law or of a categorical imperative of the Kantian order. What is permanent in all this discussion is that the conduct of church affairs, and public worship in particular, should be marked by reverence and order, by dignity and decency. Nothing should be permitted that attracts undue attention to itself.

Two final points bring the discussion to a close. There is a rabbinical note in the verse **a woman ought to have a veil on her head, because of the angels.** The reference is to good angels whom Paul, in common with his con-

13 Judge in yourselves: is it comely that a woman pray unto God uncovered?

14 Doth not even nature itself teach you, that, if a man have long hair, it is a shame unto him?

15 But if a woman have long hair, it is a glory to her: for *her* hair is given her for a covering.

16 But if any man seem to be contentious, we have no such custom, neither the churches of God.

all things are from God.)
13 Judge for yourselves; is it proper for a woman to pray to God with her head uncovered?
14 Does not nature itself teach you that for a man to wear long hair is degrading to
him, 15 but if a woman has long hair, it is her pride? For her hair is given to her
for a covering. 16 If any one is disposed to be contentious, we recognize no other practice, nor do the churches of God.

Originally **woman** was taken from the side of **man,** but now it is woman who gives birth even to men. But **all** creation is **from God.** He is the ultimate source of all life.

13-16. Paul turns from his appeal to scripture to an appeal to **nature.** It would be expected that Greeks, especially those who had been under Stoic influence, would appreciate this. But they too would be puzzled by the conclusions which the apostle seeks to draw. Many Greek men did wear long hair. The fact that Paul disapproved and thought it was **degrading** hardly served to prove that his assumption was a law of nature. Likewise, since most women did not cut their hair, but enjoyed this **covering** for their heads, it might be argued that they did not need any other covering. But Paul did not really base his conclusions on a "natural order." He was rationalizing the customs in which he believed, and in the end he admits it. He must have recognized that women would contest such deductions from scripture and from nature. He falls back finally on the assertion of his own authority. There is a **practice** found in all **the churches of God** which Corinthian women should accept. Congregational autonomy is not admitted in a matter of this kind.

This is a most revealing and instructive passage. Without knowing the exact circumstances or the inner motives of these women, we cannot judge whether Paul's decision

---

temporaries, believed to be present during the worship of God, and who were regarded as mediators and guardians of the created order (see Exeg., vs. 10). These ideas found expression in the writings of the Neoplatonist Dionysius the Areopagite of the fifth century A.D., particularly in his book *Concerning the Heavenly Hierarchy.* This book was influential in giving the medieval church its angelology. But to discuss these things would take us too far afield. Paul uses the belief to reinforce his main ruling that as angels are spectators of the scene when the church meets for public worship, nothing should be done that is an offense against decorum and order. Lastly and very curtly, as if he were uneasily conscious of the inadequacy of his arguments, he cuts the discussion short with an assertion of apostolic authority which is tinged with a dictatorial spirit and which he aligns with a reference to the catholic practice of the churches. **If anyone is disposed to be contentious, we recognize no other practice, nor do the churches of God.** In other words, "That is my opinion. I mean to stick by it and will permit no argument. Conform to the accepted practice of the churches." We must concede to Paul a genuine anxiety for the full well-being of the churches he loved so passionately and served so well. To such great love and mighty service much can be forgiven and overlooked. We have noticed that in important respects the apostle is a man of greater spirit and outlook than is indicated by his custom-bound opinions. He would always be a strong contender for the right of women to pray and to prophesy in public under the inspiration of the Spirit. To that extent he even initiates the movement which in the end undermined and helped to destroy his strongly expressed rabbinical convictions. However, inconsistent though we may deem it to be with the spirit and teaching of Jesus, to say nothing of the Christian experience of the members of the church, men and women alike in every generation, his ruling was undoubtedly accepted by the Corinthian community and apparently accorded with catholic practice. As a matter of fact, in certain quarters it endures to this day. But time and the essential spirit of the gospel message are against him. Probably today he would be well content, other things being equal, to have lost this particular fight.

17 Now in this that I declare *unto you* I praise *you* not, that ye come together not for the better, but for the worse.

17 But in the following instructions I do not commend you, because when you come together it is not for the better but for the

was altogether wise or not. We do know that it has fastened divine authority upon particular mores in a way that has confused custom and morals. It is often not easy for us to distinguish our own customary procedures from the eternal will of God.

B. The Lord's Supper (11:17-34)

In this passage we have the clearest picture of a Eucharistic celebration which we possess from the first century. Still there are many points upon which uncertainty remains. All except Albert Schweitzer and his followers agree that this account reports an evening meal. There is nothing in the chapter to indicate the day of the week. In 16:2 Paul speaks of their laying aside contributions on the first day of the week, but this does not necessarily mean that they met on that day. Yet from the later custom it is a highly probable conclusion for this time.

The meal was more than a symbolic tasting of food. It was one in which gluttony and drunkenness were possible. It may be that these dangers increased after the time of Paul and ultimately led to the detachment of the liturgical act from the common meal. This came to be known as the agape or love feast (Jude 12). But at Corinth in the decade of the fifties the liturgical act accompanied the meal.

If the whole church could eat together, presumably in the home of one of the members, we have some insight into the size of the community. Yet if factions and divisions appeared, it was not so small. The N.T. writers were not interested, however,

17-22. *Disorders at the Church Meeting.*— These verses mark an unmistakable change in Paul's letter to the Corinthian people. The level is heightened, while the emotional element is immeasurably deepened. It is as if Paul himself were aware of the difference in relative value between the subject previously discussed (vss. 2-16) and this central and sacred element of the gospel with which he had been entrusted and which he had transmitted to his converts. Here he is dealing not merely with a temporary and transient aspect of church life, but with regard to matters that will endure so long as there is a Christian church in the world. He is writing of a temporal situation, but he is concerned with eternal things. He shakes off from his feet the clogging, hampering mud of meretricious controversy and spreads his wings for a flight to the great sunlit heights of God's deepest and highest revelations to mankind. The words he here pens (one wonders if he realized it as he wrote them; perhaps, being a man of intuitive insights into spiritual things, he half glimpsed the mighty fact) were destined to become part of the best known, best loved, and most sacred tradition of the church of Jesus Christ. How often they have been repeated as the followers of Jesus have sat down together at the Communion table! We cannot be other than profoundly moved by the passages now under discussion. Here the deep in God calls to the deep in man; here the things of eternity come spilling over into time.

But like a Rembrandt portrait, these luminous, revealing truths shine out of a dark background. Strangely enough, we who read and study Paul's words, and his explanation of the Lord's Supper, are almost grateful to the Corinthians for the state of disorder in their church fellowship in so far at least as it evoked this section of Paul's letter. Perhaps the only regret we feel is that having written so much, the great apostle did not write more. But what we have is sheer gain. Part of the dark background of the passage is the disorder in the church meeting at Corinth; part of it is the apostle's breaking heart as he braces himself for the application of aseptic and astringent words with a view to healing the grievous hurt done to the Christian fellowship. And part is in preparation for his great plea on behalf of Christian love.

It would seem that the sacrament of the Lord's Supper at Corinth was associated with a common meal which could be attended by all the members of the Christian community. The sacred rite could take place either at the beginning of the meal or at its close. Further, it would seem that any of the brethren who felt moved to do so could start the meal by blessing the loaf of bread which would then be distributed among those present. After an interval a

in exact statistics. We need not hold that the factions here were on the same basis as those discussed in 1:11–4:21. There the divisions were caused by devotion to various leaders; here they are grounded in varieties of social position and in personal cliques. The members who arrived first were naturally those who could stop work early and did not need to take so long to clean up for the occasion. When a congenial group had gathered, why should they not go ahead lest their food grow cold?

How was the food procured for the meal? If everyone brought his own meal or a "covered dish," late-comers would at least be able to eat what they had brought. Does Paul mean to suggest that the poor would be humiliated in sitting down to the meager fare which they had prepared? Or were the supplies for the meal purchased from the common fund, and the best portions already gone by the time the poorer members arrived? On the whole this is the more probable hypothesis.

Nothing is said concerning who is to preside at the meal. There is no intimation that it is impossible to hold a Eucharist unless certain ordained ministers are present. Paul does not appeal to any church officials to correct the abuses which had arisen. That was a responsibility of the whole church. A half century later the church had developed a fixed practice in this regard (I Clem. 40:2-4; Ign. Smyrn. 8:1). It is highly probable that presiding at the Eucharist was an important factor in the development of monarchic episcopacy. But I Corinthians offers no definite evidence on the subject.

Paul criticizes a practice at the Lord's table which appears to go back to a very different theory concerning its nature. Many of the members were turning the meal into a joyous festivity. Paul insists that it should be a solemn commemoration. Does this difference rest solely in the careless selfishness of some in the community, or may it not be due to basic differences of interpretation? The latter conclusion has been rendered very probable by the researches of Hans Lietzmann in *Messe und Herrenmahl* (Bonn: A. Marcus & E. Weber, 1926). He holds that there were two quite different types of celebration in the primitive church. One was the Jerusalem type; the other the Pauline type. The Jerusalem type had no particular relation to the Last Supper. It afforded rather a continuation of all the tablefellowship which the disciples had enjoyed with their Master on earth, and it looked forward to their reunion at the messianic banquet so soon to come. It was the "breaking of bread . . . with glad and generous hearts" of which we read in Acts 2:46. For Paul (and we know not how many others) the meal was a com-

---

similar action took place with regard to the cup of wine. These are to be regarded as the strictly sacramental aspect of the occasion. It is also a fair inference that this was probably the procedure among most, if not all, of the Christian churches. Paul takes no exception to the order of events which is here described; his strictures are directed against certain social aspects of the common meal.[2] Ideally, the arrangement seems to have been a very fine piece of church organization, one that could have ministered to the building up of a robust fellowship. Food and drink were purchased most probably from the common fund of the church, although it is likely that individuals brought their own contributions as well. Everyone was meant to share on a basis of equal fellowship in the food that was provided. But unfortunately the mood and temper of partisanship had also invaded this aspect of the church's life. Cliques had been formed even with regard to the common meal. This in turn had an adverse effect on the sacred rite associated with the meal. Naturally the impact on the spirit of church fellowship was deadly. Little wonder that Paul cannot commend them. **It is not for the better but for the worse. For, in the first place, when you assemble as a church, I hear that there are divisions among you; and I partly believe it.** Paul is so deeply moved by this shadow that lay so heavily on the fellowship of the Corinthian church that he never got beyond "in the first place," and we are left speculating as to what other things he had in mind when he wrote, things that probably were driven from his thoughts by the intensity with which he grapples with the deadliest of them all.

The divisions to which he refers not only neutralized all the good that the common assembly might have done; those who participated were actually worse in spirit and outlook than they were before they assembled. The greatest sins have always been the abuse of the greatest blessings. One can measure the depth of Paul's

[2] See Moffatt, *I Corinthians*, pp. 157-66.

memoration of the Last Supper. The Cephas faction at Corinth was apparently leading the way toward a Jerusalem type of celebration and Paul was much concerned for what he felt to be the more correct view. Therefore he reminds them of the events which they were commemorating. To enforce his polemic against the other point of view, he inserts the words **this do in remembrance of me;** for this was the understanding of the act which he had received from the Lord.

It is difficult for a modern Christian to conceive of a celebration of the Lord's Supper without the repetition of the "words of institution." But Paul says nothing to suggest that these words were in fact repeated at every communion meal by a presiding officer. He recalls them just because they were in danger of being forgotten. He says that *he* had delivered these words to them, and that in eating the bread and drinking the cup they were proclaiming the Lord's death. He does *not* say that any official was accustomed to repeat them when he performed the liturgical act. This silence does not prove the non-existence of the later custom; yet it is important to point out that Paul does not present the words of Jesus as a necessary formula for the consecration. For him the words offer the authoritative interpretation of the meaning of the community act.

From ch. 10 we may also conclude that this was a sacrificial meal. That did not mean, however, that Christ was the victim who was in some sense consumed. For the early church the sacrifice consisted in the offering of the food to God. We should avoid confusion between the death of Christ as a sacrifice and the Lord's Supper as a sacrificial meal. The sacrifice of Christ was in its very nature unrepeatable, once for all. The Lord's Supper was repeated again and again. It is Cyprian who first connects the sacrifice in the death of Christ with the sacrifice of the Mass. In the church before him, and certainly according to the mind of Paul, the offering was of bread and wine in thanksgiving to God.

1. The Conduct of the Meal (11:17-22)

17. Against the background of these general considerations we may come to grips with the details. Paul refers to his general commendation in vs. 2, though no illustration has been given of why it was deserved. The RSV is avowedly an interpretation: the Greek contains no words for **the following.** Only from the context does it appear that Paul is not referring to what he has just said about covering the head. The **worse** results will be made more explicit in vss. 27-32.

---

concern by the very words he uses in rebuke of those whose spirit and unchristian attitude were disrupting the life of the church. How have these divisions arisen? What are the **factions** among the brethren which Paul condemns? (See Exeg., vs. 19.) Consider again the picture of the church as we must conceive it. It was composed of the poorer and humbler sections of the community; among them there were undoubtedly servants and slaves. Yet there also appears to have been a sprinkling of the more well-to-do and socially refined elements of Corinthian society. Doubtless these had their own impelling social affinities and would instinctively shrink from the rougher and more uncouth members of the congregation. A high-caste Brahman who embraced Christianity, and was cut off from his family and inheritance and all his old associations as a consequence, gladly paid that price as a token of the reality and strength of his new-found faith. But he confessed that at first when he sat down to a Christian communion service beside an out-cast Hindu Christian brother, his "stomach just turned upside down," as he put it. Perhaps in milder form this is how some of the members of the Corinthian fellowship felt toward others of their number. But that spirit has to be disciplined and exorcised if there is to be any real fellowship at all. The one institution, of the modern as of the ancient world, in which all barriers must fall, all caste fade away, all faction die a natural death, and a real and full fellowship be made manifest, is the Christian church. The whole habit and practice of worship, with its sacred rites—as Paul will insist in ch. 12—fulfills its purpose in deepening the spirit of fellowship, in lifting the members out of and above themselves and all their petty weaknesses into a status of individual dignity and value, destiny and vocation, that can achieve its full and perfect expression only in a community of love and service for Jesus Christ and for one another. As Moffatt puts it,[8] "God's living church has parts, but it has no parties."

[8] *Ibid.*, p. 159.

18 For first of all, when ye come together in the church, I hear that there be divisions among you; and I partly believe it.

worse. 18 For, in the first place, when you assemble as a church, I hear that there are divisions among you; and I partly believe

---

18. As a church would distinguish this meal from a private dinner party. At the latter a man might invite the guests he desired; but this is a table where the Lord has issued the invitations.

The "body of Christ" must be marked by the unity in diversity of all its members.

Again, such worship is meant to remind us that we belong not to one world but to two, and that the spiritual, invisible realm, in which Christ in all his fullness abides, is the much more significant and vital of the two. Compared to it this material world, which is also God's world and in which we are meant to take our place, play our part, and pull our weight, is but the terrestrial phase of holy and eternal purposes. In the worship of the church, men and women are invited to "look not to the things that are seen but to the things that are unseen; for the things that are seen are transient, but the things that are unseen are eternal" (II Cor. 4:18). Worship is intended to enable the participants to transcend all earthly considerations, and to find themselves anew in the larger, fuller environment of the love and purpose of God as revealed in Jesus Christ. It is intended to remind us of the great guiding convictions of the Christian faith, which, if believed in sincerely and put to the practical test in daily living, invest life with coherence and meaning and purpose, develop Christian character, and give to men and women, both as individuals and as social units, that "sense of direction" which is one of our deepest and most constant needs. Above all, the worship of the church in all its forms is intended to hold those who take part in it to the standards of Jesus Christ. There are capacities and elements of man's being that are never fulfilled unless they are challenged and stretched by the highest standards of life and of service. The highest standards for Christian folk are those of the great head of the church, Jesus Christ. How could any genuine experience of worship fail to dispose of all the barriers that divide men from one another, or to disperse all shadows that fall across their lives? How could it fail, if genuinely and sincerely expressed in the spirit and attitude of the worshipers, to weld them into a unity at once comprehensive and catholic, transcending anything that the world can demonstrate? The entire hope of the race, so far as its organic unity in righteousness and its prosperity and peace are concerned, is bound up with the meaning and potency and manifest destiny of the Christian fellowship. "Behold, the Lamb of God, who takes away the sin of the world!" (John 1:29.)

All this and doubtless much more is in Paul's mind as he pens his indignant remonstrance to the church in Corinth. He does not expect perfection from any of the little Christian communities. That would be expecting too much. The most that he hopes for is that their hearts will be set in the right trend, and that they will more and more approximate the great ideals and possibilities that are latent in the very conception of the Christian fellowship; **for there must be factions among you in order that those who are genuine among you may be recognized.** As ugliness in a sense draws attention to beauty, as darkness reveals light, as imperfection indicates perfection, so these factions and cliques serve a purpose, viz., they do indicate the genuine members of the fellowship whose life and witness are a rebuke to the selfishness and lovelessness of those whom the apostle condemns. It has been suggested that there is a hint of the celebrated Pauline irony in this reference to the *genuine* members of the factious community. In that case his words can be taken as a subtle rebuke to the Pharisaic spirit. But in the light of our experience in similar situations the alternative explanation may hold good. In every community, however much it fails to attain the standards of devotion and fellowship that are expected of Christians, there are those whose sincerity and genuineness reflect the spirit of the Master. Nonetheless, the situation cannot be allowed to rest at that point. The disorder must be subjected to discipline: the spirit that occasions the disorder must be eliminated. The church must fulfill its manifest destiny if it is to live.

Paul now indicates the nature of the abuse that is disrupting the spirit of fellowship. **When you meet together, it is not the Lord's supper that you eat. For in eating, each one goes ahead with his own meal, and one is hungry and another is drunk.** Not only were there divisions in the church based on the differences in social status of the various members of the community, but these were emphasized by the social

19 For there must be also heresies among you, that they which are approved may be made manifest among you.

it, 19 for there must be factions among you in order that those who are genuine among

19. Paul speaks quite ironically of the need for **factions.** He uses two different words: first, the one he had employed in 1:10 from which we get "schism"; then a different one from which we get "heresy." Originally heresies in the church were simply parties. The **genuine** were those who did not join in these social cliques.

practice of many of those who attended the so-called "common meal" or "love feast." Personal tastes and class consciousness and economic status were allowed to intervene in a particularly divisive and pernicious way. People of similar standing apparently drew instinctively together and shared their provisions with their own set to the exclusion of others. The cultured people would congregate in one group; the rougher, poorer members of the community would gather in another. Those from the slums were thus segregated from those who came, so to say, from the suburbs; the well to do were separated similarly from the poor; and the result was that a social occasion, closely associated with the sacramental rite of blessing and breaking the bread and spilling forth the wine, tore to shreds the whole idea of Christian fellowship. The very fact that the church met within the confines of a private dwelling house increased the awkwardness of the occasion.

The spirit of fellowship being riven to pieces, the situation went from bad to worse. Some were guilty of downright bad manners. In their greed they ate up all the food available, with the result that some poorer brother, perhaps a servant or even a slave, who had certain duties to perform and who could not get along to the church meeting in time, had to go hungry. Others imbibed too much wine and were well advanced in drunkenness as the meeting proceeded. Little wonder that Paul is sick in soul as well as hot with indignation as he ponders over the havoc that such behavior makes. Could paganism be worse? Such a gathering is more remote from the spirit of the Lord's Supper than the farthest star from our earth! What is there to commend in such a travesty of the idea of the common meal? How can the blessing of the bread and wine, which was undoubtedly hastily done by some individuals who were anxious to get on with their own private party or personal meal, be called a sacrament at all? **It is not the Lord's supper that you eat.** Far from it. That is where the apostle's emphasis falls. These people were treating the meal as if it were a strictly private and personal affair. This would seem to be the meaning of the word rendered **factions** in the RSV, whereas the very idea of worship is to enable such narrowly conceived individualism to transcend itself in the very spirit and essence of fellowship, and so to achieve that fullness of personality which is part of "the abundant life" and is in the gift of the Master to those who are his in spirit and in service. There can be no real Christian spirit of fellowship in any meeting which makes a humbler brother or sister feel sorry or ashamed; and that is just what happened in Corinth when late arrivals found the provisions exhausted and those in possession replete even to drunkenness. They had turned what was meant to be an expression of Christian fellowship into a private social occasion. If that is what they desire, then **What! Do you not have houses to eat and drink in? Or do you despise the church of God and humiliate those who have nothing?** They would do better to stay at home (see Exeg., vss. 20-22). Paul will not tolerate anything that violates the spirit of true fellowship in the church. **What shall I say to you? Shall I commend you in this? No, I will not.**

The essence of the message is needed in all successive generations. Would not the apostle have rebuked the social exclusiveness that sets up special pews in some of our churches for certain members to the exclusion of others? To be sure, there is a place for organization and arrangements that minister to the well-being of the congregation as a whole; but anything in any branch of the church's work that makes for social segregation or exclusion or cliques is against the spirit of Christian fellowship. Surely this is the angle from which the problem of race, both at home and in the mission field, must be approached. Of course there is place for careful thought: there is need to give consideration to every vital factor in dealing with any such problem. There may be danger in precipitate action, as in permitting a mingling of races on a Christian basis before both sides have been prepared and educated up to the idea. One must cultivate a sensitivity to the feelings and needs of the other persons in seeking to make the best Christian approach to them. Babes in the faith, and in the culture and status that go with the faith, must be dealt with

20 When ye come together therefore into one place, *this* is not to eat the Lord's supper.

21 For in eating every one taketh before *other* his own supper: and one is hungry, and another is drunken.

22 What! have ye not houses to eat and to drink in? or despise ye the church of God, and shame them that have not? What shall I say to you? shall I praise you in this? I praise *you* not.

23 For I have received of the Lord that which also I delivered unto you, That the

you may be recognized. 20 When you meet
together, it is not the Lord's supper that you
eat. 21 For in eating, each one goes ahead
with his own meal, and one is hungry and
another is drunk. 22 What! Do you not
have houses to eat and drink in? Or do you
despise the church of God and humiliate
those who have nothing? What shall I say
to you? Shall I commend you in this? No,
I will not.
23 For I received from the Lord what I

20-22. The resulting revelry was unbrotherly and a denial of the purpose for which they had met. We are not to conclude from this passage and from vs. 34 that Paul disapproved of holding an actual meal. What he opposed was the individualism which did not require waiting for the group and the inconsiderateness which would **humiliate** God's poor. Paul could find nothing to praise in this disorderly conduct.

2. The Tradition About the Last Supper (11:23-26)

23. Paul writes that he had received the tradition **from the Lord.** Obviously he had not himself been present at the Last Supper. If we insisted on taking his words literally, we would have to conclude with the "history-of-religions school" interpreters that Paul had **received** it in a vision from the risen Lord. They held that Paul was the originator of the sacrament by means of this etiological legend, and that Mark drew his account from the Pauline version. Today this point of view is almost universally rejected. The attempt to derive the Christian Eucharist from Hellenistic cult meals cannot be

---

as "babes" before they can be dealt with as adults.

But as to the ultimate goal there can be no argument. In the fellowship of the church of Jesus Christ each is a member of one great family, and in the true family each is of unique and infinite value. As in the parable of the prodigal, even an erring son is still a son, and an erring daughter is still a daughter. The circle is incomplete until each takes his place and plays his part. Our conception of the church is incomplete until it achieves the full unity in fellowship and status of all its members. Our picture of Jesus Christ is incomplete until every race and nation has added its own unique contribution. Africa can perhaps alone paint into the picture Christ's shoulders—Africa which has borne so heavy a portion of the white man's burden. India can add, perhaps, to our sense of his mystic insight into the ultimate realities of life. China and Japan and the islands of the seas have their contribution to make. It may lie in their veneration for tradition and so help to deepen the ethical values and aspects of Christian doctrine and life. The Western nations may contribute their practical abilities; the Communist lands may help enhance our sense of "community," when their desirings are baptized with the Spirit of Christ.

Similarly, in the local church there can be parts and "gifts" but no parties. All are "one" in him. The mark of the fellowship is a unity that should and can transcend anything the world can provide. Nothing must be allowed to mar or to hinder it. The world needs it, needs it desperately. Surely the function of the church, at least in part, is to demonstrate the beauty, the grace, and the power of such a spirit. When it is achieved all over the world, then that petition of the Lord's Prayer will have been fulfilled—"Thy will be done on earth, as it is in heaven." Then the kingdom will have come! For where Christian fellowship is, there is heaven! The Spirit of Christ is present. Where Christian fellowship is not, there is hell. Thucydides, the ancient historian, wrote for all competent historians when he said of history that there "the lessons of the past are set forth in their historical context to furnish a guide for future generations." But the future generations are slow to learn.

23-26. ***The Last Supper.***—Paul now turns to the consideration of the Supper which had been so grossly profaned by the pagan practices of

Lord Jesus, the *same* night in which he was betrayed, took bread:

also delivered to you, that the Lord Jesus on the night when he was betrayed took

sustained, as Lietzmann and others have shown. Paul received the tradition from the Jerusalem community and those before him in the faith. Though he was vehement in repudiating any idea that his gospel was dependent upon men (Gal. 1:12), inevitably he received his knowledge of the words of Jesus and the events of his life from the tradition. But, as has been suggested above, Paul may still be asserting that his *interpretation* of the Lord's Supper was received by him from the risen Lord.

Apparently Paul knew no other way to date the Last Supper than **on the night when he was betrayed.** We would not inquire further if it were not for the fact that Mark describes the meal as a Passover celebration, while the Gospel of John is equally clear that the Passover was still to come. Though by ingenious conjectures scholars have sought various ways to resolve this contradiction, the theories must be rejected as improbable apologetic devices. On which side of the controversy concerning the date of the death of Jesus does Paul stand? If he had believed that the meal was a Passover, it would have been easy for him to have said so. If it was only a supper eaten near that time, the language which he uses would be as explicit as he could make it. Hence, the weight of the Pauline evidence is against Mark at this point.

It is not the task of a commentary on one of the accounts to attempt a reconstruction of the most probable text of the words of Jesus at the Last Supper. All of our accounts reflect the Eucharistic practice of the communities from which they come. Matthew has no independent historical value. Luke's version has textual uncertainties, and scholars differ on whether it is a free rewriting of Mark or is based on another early source. Mark and I Corinthians give parallel versions which can be compared with profit.

some of the Corinthian Christians. We have seen what havoc these had made of the fellowship. Such a spirit and such practices were in his view a sin against Christ himself (vs. 27). Hence, it became needful to remind them of the origin, the nature, and the significance of the sacramental rite. Paul had received the traditional apostolic account of the original Supper and had passed it on to the newly formed Christian communities (see Exeg.). Nothing here can be properly interpreted as a claim that he had received the tradition at first hand from Jesus himself. He definitely indicates that it is historically based on the happenings in the upper room on the night in which the Master was betrayed.

Now follows this moving description of the Supper and its relevance for the church in every age. These verses should be read in conjunction with the reference made to the Supper in the apostle's discussion of food offered to idols on the occasion of pagan temple feasts. Together they help us apprehend more clearly what this sacred rite meant for the apostle and what he intends it to signify in the life of the church.

The use of the symbols of bread and wine verges on history and on supreme authority. These elements were used by Jesus in the original celebration, and he has given them to his church as his chosen symbols of remembrance. Nothing is older in the history of Christianity. Their place in the rite is one more link in the long chain of continuity stretching back to times before the Gospels or even the epistles were written, and strengthens, if that were needed, the historical basis of our faith. The choice of such symbols, taken as they were from among the common aspects of daily life, was a stroke of spiritual genius. Their use through the centuries has given powerful emphasis to the Master's purpose in choosing them. As Samuel Johnson once said, "It is not sufficiently considered that mankind requires oftener to be reminded than informed." For many Christians these symbols are final because they were chosen for us and given to us by the great head of the church. Their use has a deep significance (see Exeg., 10:14-22).

Both passages indicate that while the Eucharist is an acted parable and a memorial rite, it is a great deal more: it is the dramatic representation in action of the redemptive grace of God on behalf of man and the mode of its consummation in man's response (see Exeg., vss. 23-26). The sacrament is a communion service. Something more is intended to happen than the teaching or demonstration of a mighty truth. The celebration of the Supper is "symbolic" in that more ancient use of the term in which the "symbol" effects something; it conveys the

24 And when he had given thanks, he brake *it,* and said, Take, eat; this is my body, which is broken for you: this do in remembrance of me.

bread, 24 and when he had given thanks, he broke it, and said, "This is my body which is for[o] you. Do this in remembrance

[o] Other ancient authorities read *broken for.*

---

24. Paul used **given thanks** (εὐχαριστέω) instead of "bless" (εὐλογέω) which stands in Mark. This was the table blessing which every Jew pronounced as he thanked the God who gave the food. Both accounts mention specifically the breaking of the bread. At the Last Supper and again at the Lord's Supper it was a necessary preliminary to the eating. The koine text of I Corinthians refers to the body as **broken.** This may be an interpretative gloss, as most modern editors of the Greek text hold. But it does bring out the emphasis upon the symbolic significance of the breaking of the loaf in its relation to the breaking of Christ's body in his death. Mark has no word to amplify **this is my body,** but he does have the summons to eat. That is lacking in Paul, and in its place there stands a command to repeat the act in remembrance of Christ. No Gospel contains this; the long text of Luke (22:19*b*-20) is almost certainly a later insertion based on I Corinthians. When we realize the polemical purpose which Paul has in this section and the absence of the phrase in the Gospels, we can hardly contend that the words come from Jesus. This is recognized by most historical students today. Some say, however, that these words

---

thing symbolized. This point has been put clearly and germinatively by P. T. Forsyth:

> Let us at least get rid of the idea which has impoverished worship beyond measure, that the act is mainly commemoration. No Church can live on that. How can we have a mere memorial of one who is still alive, still our life, still present with us and acting in us? . . . A Sacrament is as much more than a symbol as a symbol is more than a memorial. It is quite inadequate to speak of the Sacrament as an object-lesson—as if its purpose were to convey new truth instead of the living Redeemer. It is not an hour of instruction but of communion. It is an act, not a lesson; and it is not a spectacle nor a ceremony. It does something.[4]

Those who partake, granted that they are present in the right spirit of devotion to their Master, and of fellowship with one another, are in the closest possible relationship to Jesus Christ. He is not only the giver of the feast; he is the feast itself.

Paul's emphasis on the sacrificial aspects of the death of Jesus is made clear by the words **And when he had given thanks, he broke it, and said, "This is my body which is broken for you"** (see Exeg., vs. 24). There was no word in the ancient world that might stand as the exact equivalent of "person," but there can be little doubt the reference is to the whole person of Jesus. He gave himself for man's redemption. Nor is there any need for much discussion of the word "is" (see Exeg., vs. 26). Obviously it could not be applied literally to the "body of Christ"; he was in full possession of his physical attributes even as he uttered the words. Reference to similar instances (see II Sam. 23:17) in which the word is used in scripture and in Jewish religious practices makes it plain that "is" implies "means" or "represents" or "symbolizes." If Jesus spoke in Aramaic, as doubtless he did, then the verb would not be used at all.[5] The passage might be paraphrased as follows, "This bread means my whole person which is given for you." Could Christendom agree on this, nothing of deep and abiding spiritual significance need be lost or even qualified. On the contrary, there might be wonderful gain.

The Master has given to his church for all time this simple, dignified, suggestive, and sacred rite to remind it of his willing sacrifice that his truth and his spirit should prevail despite everything that the opposing powers of evil and death did or might yet do to prevent them. It was given that his revelation of God's redemptive grace and forgiving love might forever remain among mankind; that the cross of sacrifice might be uplifted, a symbol of weakness and shame, to emphasize the fact that it is yet stronger by far than great nations or empires or races, and that it has power beyond all else to shake the human soul into contrition and repentance, and to symbolize a sacrificial way of life in which "the cross leads the generations on." It was given that, by the new faith it can and does evoke, men everywhere should be won to a greater and more glorious allegiance than they have ever known; and that they might be assured that the love and the power revealed in the Lord's sacrifice, thus

[4] *The Church and the Sacraments* (2nd ed.; London: Independent Press, 1947), p. 229. Used by permission.

[5] See C. A. Anderson Scott, *Footnotes to St. Paul* (Cambridge: Cambridge University Press, 1935), p. 115.

25 After the same manner also *he took* the cup, when he had supped, saying, This cup is the new testament in my blood: this do ye, as oft as ye drink *it,* in remembrance of me.

of me." 25 In the same way also the cup, after supper, saying, "This cup is the new covenant in my blood. Do this, as often as you drink it, in remembrance of me."

correspond to the unexpressed intention of Jesus. Of one thing we can be sure: the Christian church would have been greatly impoverished without this memorial emphasis. But it is even more impoverished when the Lord's Supper is confined to this one meaning.

25. If the cup came **after supper,** we may conclude that the liturgical act stood at the close of the meal in a Pauline celebration rather than at the opening. That might explain why those who came early began eating at once. **The same way** may imply a separate thanksgiving for the wine. Mark makes this explicit. In the word spoken in connection with the cup the accounts are farthest apart. Mark reads, "My blood of the covenant, which is poured out for many." The double genitive with "blood" is difficult. Paul seems to be more original when he identifies the cup with the covenant, a **covenant** which is **in** [his] **blood.** That does not make Jesus invite his disciples to drink blood, which to any Jew would be a most revolting thought. Paul's version makes the allusion to Exod. 24:8 more clear. When God made a solemn agreement with his people at the

symbolized, are available for them. One can readily understand why the sacrament has lovingly been named "the Eucharist," and why it has become the most sacred, most priceless element of our heritage in Christ.

25. ***The Blood of Sacrifice.***—It seems that a fairly long interval passed between the breaking of the bread and the passing of the cup (see Exeg.). Normally the bread was blessed and broken before the common meal began; but the cup was passed around **after supper.** The wine suggested blood, the blood of sacrifice. Here the sacrificial blood is given new significance. The old covenant of Sinai, which required the blood of animals slain on the altars by the priests in expiation of the sins of the people, is set aside by a **new covenant** between God and man signified and sealed by the shedding of the blood of Jesus Christ. The old covenant had failed in its purpose (Mic. 6:6-8).

> Not all the blood of beasts,
> On Jewish altars slain,
> Could give the guilty conscience peace,
> Or wash away our stain.[6]

Something more was required. Prophets of the sensitive insight and tenderness of Jeremiah looked forward with longing and hope to a new covenant (Jer. 31:31-34; see also Exeg., vs. 25). How that prophetic longing must have weighed with Jesus as he faced the hour for which he had been born into the world! His sacrificial death established the new covenant between God and man forever. "God in Christ" takes upon himself the burden and agony of man's sin, and meets it with all the power of his forgiving, cleansing grace and love, in order that man, brought to repentance by the uplifting, transforming power of vicarious sacrifice and suffering, might find available a new way of life, a new communion and fellowship with God, and greater opportunities of fulfilling himself in service for God and in the consummation of God's purposes. There are some who profess to be revolted by the idea that the sacrifice of Jesus Christ is central in God's purpose for man's salvation. Two things may be said. One is that "God in Christ" makes the sacrifice. He carries the burden of man's sin and he bears the agony. Nothing in the world is comparable to the redeeming power of such vicarious suffering. The other is that civilization has been saved at least twice in the twentieth century by those who shed their blood, and by many others who were prepared to make the same sacrifice. Such sacrificial service must rank among the greatest heights scaled by the human spirit. Can we deny in the highest degree to God what is reckoned as greatest in man?

25-26. ***Do This in Remembrance of Me.***—Surely such a work of grace must be fittingly remembered and remembered often. Even so Jesus enjoined his disciples to observe this rite (Luke 22:17-19). It was given that the disciples and their converts, and Christian believers through the ages, might recall with thankfulness, with a deep sense of indebtedness, and with unspeakable joy the Lord's sacrificial death. And throughout the centuries when this has been done, this sanctum sanctorum of Christian worship has in fact recalled him so vividly to memory that he has been known and

6 Isaac Watts, "Not All the Blood of Beasts."

time of Moses, this was ratified by the sprinkling of the blood of a sacrifice. In the death of Christ God had given a **new** dispensation or **covenant.** It too was ratified by the blood of a sacrifice, the **blood** of Christ. In giving his disciples the cup Christ extended to them the benefits of this new dispensation. The Greek word διαθήκη originally meant "last will" or **testament,** as our phrase "New Testament" shows. It had been used in the LXX to translate *berîth.* Most covenants, however, are two-sided agreements. In using the word διαθήκη the LXX translators underscored the fact that God did not make a bargain with men. He freely gave. Since God never dies, **testament** is not a figure of speech which can be applied to him literally. If we use the word **covenant,** it must be in full consciousness of all these biblical associations. Mark does not use the phrase **new covenant.** But Paul clearly had in mind Jer. 31:31-34, though in that passage there is nothing about the need for a sacrifice to ratify the new covenant.

Some interpreters propose translating "offer this" instead of **do this.** This might mean that it was the body and blood of Christ which was offered by the community instead

---

worshiped as personally present among his people even as he had promised. Thus it is that when we come to the table, we remind ourselves that it is his table and not ours; that the sacrament is his, not ours. We come to receive a presence and to have a spirit bestowed. In and through the whole experience of the sacrament our Lord offers himself. Well is it that the apostle, so marvelous an interpreter of the mind and spirit of his Lord, re-emphasizes the injunction of Jesus, that his followers are to remember him in the breaking of bread and the pouring of wine.

As often as you eat . . . and drink. To his exposition of the supper Paul adds his own emphasis, "Do it often." Yet let us beware lest mere repetition should dull our apprehension of the significance and sacredness of the rite. Familiarity can breed a spirit akin to contempt even with regard to the most sacred things of our faith. This is the Eucharist, and it will remain the Eucharist if the spirit of indebtedness, of love, of hope, and of joy is preserved.

Until he comes. The eschatological note is struck in this closing phrase (see Exeg.). The Christian church worships not a dead Christ but a living Lord. Its central symbol is a Cross, not a crucifix. The sacrament is observed not merely to recall certain historical events, not even to celebrate his memory, but to worship the living Christ, to wait upon him, and to wait for him and for his manifestation in final, complete triumph. Adequate celebration of the sacrament does at least three things. It bids us look back to a historic, redemptive sacrifice made once for all as a ransom for many; it bids us worship the ever-present Lord; and it bids his church look forward to the consummation of the purposes of God and to the second and final coming of Christ.

The effectiveness of the finished work of Jesus Christ for believers lies also in their participation (see Exeg., 10:16). The redeeming grace of God is mediated to faith. "His action inspires a spiritual response: there is something we are called upon to do." In Pauline language we participate in the body and blood of Christ (10:16). Effective participation requires repentance, faith, good will, and devotion on the part of the participant. Paul is writing with a certain situation in view and some of the implications of his simple exposition of the sacrament of the Lord's Supper will be made plain immediately (vss. 27-32). The penitence, the faith, the good will, and devotion help clear away any obstacles that would obstruct the divine grace freely offered in the sacrament and prevent it from accomplishing its perfect work. As in full obedience to our Lord's command we break the bread and pour the wine, so do we by faith receive Christ into our lives. His full redemption is not only a work done; it is a spirit offered to us. The "life abundant" which he proclaimed as God's free gift to all who would receive it is not only a standard that is set—that might be a daunting experience—but also a power "given" that will enable us, at least in a measure, to attain. The fruition of Paul's conception of the meaning and relevance of the sacrament of the Lord's Supper lies in his own great words, "I have been crucified with Christ; it is no longer I who live, but Christ who lives in me; and the life I now live in the flesh I live by faith in the Son of God, who loved me and gave himself for me" (Gal. 2:20). These words strike the sacramental note.

To maintain the tradition of this Christian experience, as expressed in and through the sacrament of the Lord's Supper, is relevant in every age which recognizes that a better world depends on better men and women. The relevance of Jesus Christ in respect of such standards of betterness lies in the historical fact that he has demonstrated once for all what a gloriously divine thing human nature can become when it is illumined in all its aspects by

26 For as often as ye eat this bread, and drink this cup, ye do show the Lord's death till he come.

26 For as often as you eat this bread and drink the cup, you proclaim the Lord's death until he comes.

---

of the food of their common meal. Linguistically it would be possible, but in the context so improbable as to be excluded. Others insist upon taking **in remembrance of me** not as "celebrating my memory," but "with a view to recalling me." No sure basis for this preference is to be found in the text.

26. The cup is used by metonomy for the contents of the cup. The community are to eat bread and drink wine, but it is clear from 10:16-22, and the verses which follow here, that this is not ordinary food. Though we may not with Luther insist that the verb "is" means an absolute equation—it would not have stood in the Aramaic at all—we must on the other hand guard against ascribing to the apostle the meaning of a "mere" symbol. For Paul it was a very realistic sacrament (see on vss. 33-34). The phrase in Mark which is absent in Paul is the eschatological word about drinking "new in the kingdom of God." It is striking that despite Paul's expectation of the Parousia in his own lifetime, he has a much weakened form of this emphasis. Yet, **until he comes** preserves the eschatological outlook.

---

his faith, and animated in all its quality and relationships by his Spirit. Further, the relevance of his finished work, his message and spirit for men, is illustrated in the lives of those who have put their faith in him. These men and women—every age has known them, respected them, admired them, and is under an immeasurable debt to them—are part of the fact and significance of Christ. Apart from him they could not be what they are. No man has ever yet increased his moral and spiritual stature by tugging at the hair of his own head. For that, a Spirit and a power above and beyond anything that he himself possesses is needed. Christianity is a gospel—good news—because it not only proclaims a way of life, but offers the means whereby those who desire it may attain it. There is the drama of man's redemption as enacted in the sacrament. That is why it is the most sacred and significant rite of the Christian church. It proclaims that highest truth which cannot be spoken; it can only be done.

Let us close this discussion by going back to the scene in the upper room, as described for us in the Fourth Gospel. The view here taken is that whatever the authorship may be, there are genuine historical elements in the record set forth by John; and moreover, that the Johannine and Pauline interpretations of the gospel have proved to be the true line of development and progress for the perpetuation and spread of the church. The sacramental note in Paul's interpretation of his experience of Christ has already been mentioned. It is also to be found in John (cf. John 13–17), and notably in the great parable of the vine and the branches (John 15). Christ is the life of his church and of his people (John 15:1-8). Soon the disciples were to know what these words meant, for soon their supreme ordeal was to be upon them, even as his supreme ordeal was upon their Lord. Realizing how imminent it was, knowing how shattering the impact would be on his followers, yet he is quiet, sure, confident, and unperturbed. From his lips fall such promises and convictions, he manifests such radiance of faith in God, as the world had never before heard or witnessed. Speaking as he did, manifesting his faith in utterance and aspect, he was even then putting into them, as they were able and willing to receive it, something of his own quiet and confident strength. He was fortifying them against the events of the coming day. But it was more than that: it was the promise and demonstration of a life and a power that was to be their portion and their inspiration throughout the experiences and years to come. These chapters (John 14–16) are the exposition of the meaning and relevance of the Lord's Supper not only for the men who took part in the original, but for the servants of the living Christ in every subsequent age. The life and the Spirit that were available then are available still. Paul is clear about this. For him Christ's redeeming presence and the gifts of his grace are ever here. His indignation against those who were guilty of unworthy conduct lies in the fact that though their Lord was sacramentally present to them, they were insensitive to him. For them the elements were mere food, and the rite mere ritual. But disciplined worship in every age of the Christian Era brings with it the assurance that the Lord's real presence is the glorious portion and experience of his people, an as-

27 Wherefore whosoever shall eat this bread, and drink *this* cup of the Lord, unworthily, shall be guilty of the body and blood of the Lord.

27 Whoever, therefore, eats the bread or drinks the cup of the Lord in an unworthy manner will be guilty of profaning the body

3. Dangers in the Celebration (11:27-34)

27-30. Having reminded his readers of the tradition, Paul returns to the disorders at Corinth. **In an unworthy manner** has been defined in vss. 18-22. The apostle was not thinking of sins in general, but the clannishness and drunkenness displayed at the Lord's

surance ratified and made vivid by the sacrament of the Lord's Supper. That Supper does not add anything to the word that is spoken: it reiterates and gives effect to it.

> Sacraments, and not socialities, make the centre of our Church life and social unity—Sacraments, and not even social beneficence. Make much of them. Clothe them with great seemliness, great earnestness, great reverence, great, but not formidable, solemnity. For it is more than the consecration of our sorrow, it is the forgiveness of our sin and our life eternal that is here held out to us and taken. And for a Church this is the thing most important of all. A Church rests not on sacred sorrow but on a holy Redemption. Christianity is not the worship of sorrow (which may be but poetic and aesthetic) but of grace. The great thing, however, is not to be sure that something was done, but to have part and lot in doing it, to have it done in our soul, to be doing it with Christ, with Him to die and with Him continually to rise.[7]

In such an exposition of the Lord's Supper Paul and Forsyth would have perfectly understood and agreed with each other.

27-34. ***A Solemn Warning.***— (See also 10:14-22.) Now comes the application of these sacred truths to the immediate situation as it had developed in Corinth. As we have seen, Paul is indignant because of the disruption caused by the selfishness of some members, and the tendency of other individuals and groups of the same or similar social caste to meet together to the exclusion of the humbler members of the community. That in his view is to be regarded as a heinous sin meriting divine judgment. It is a sin against the Lord himself because it threatens the corporate fellowship, life, and witness of the church. **Whoever, therefore, eats the bread or drinks the cup of the Lord in an unworthy manner will be guilty of profaning the body and blood of the Lord. Let a man examine himself, and so eat of the bread and drink of the cup. For any one who eats and drinks without discerning the body eats and drinks judgment upon himself.** With the exposition of these verses we should associate the relevant verse from the previous chapter, "Because there is one loaf, we who are many are one body, for we all partake of the same loaf" (10:17; see also Exeg. 11:27-30).

As is evident at a glance, two or three thoughts are involved in the context of these passages. The "body of Christ" is the company of those who have been drawn to him in faith and gratitude for his sacrificial redemption of them on the Cross, and who are bound to him and to one another by his Spirit, recognizing in one another brethren for whom the Lord died. This mystical unity of Christ and his church is signified in the one loaf which is broken, and in the participation in eating of it. Just as the one loaf is the visible symbol of the mystic unity and communion of the Lord and his church, so it is essential that when they do partake they should discern the unity of the body.

But that unity may not be discerned without also discerning the **body and blood of the Lord.** The truth here conveyed is double truth. For one to partake irreverently at the Lord's table, to insult a member of the body by excluding him from any particular social set, to leave nothing for a late-comer to eat, to be under the influence of wine, or to be disorderly in any way is in the apostle's judgment a failure to discern the body: more, it is a sin against it, and therefore against him who is its life. Nothing is more profound or more strongly represented in Paul's exposition of the nature and fellowship of the church than his insistence on the mystic unity of believers in Jesus Christ: they can and ought to say with Paul that Christ lives in them. That living communion is the vital expression of the new covenant. Therefore any offense against any member of the fellowship, whatever form it takes, is an offense against Christ. What place can there be for division, or cliques, or social exclusiveness, or selfishness, or indifference in such a fellowship? The duke must in humility and in the spirit of Christian fellowship take his place beside the ditcher.

27-28. ***The Need for Self-Discipline in Preparation for and Celebration of the Lord's Supper.***—Paul enjoins the members of the community

[7] P. T. Forsyth, *The Church and the Sacraments* (2nd ed.; London: Independent Press, 1947), p. 244. Used by permission.

28 But let a man examine himself, and
so let him eat of *that* bread, and drink of
that cup.
29 For he that eateth and drinketh unworthily, eateth and drinketh damnation
to himself, not discerning the Lord's body.
30 For this cause many *are* weak and
sickly among you, and many sleep.
31 For if we would judge ourselves, we
should not be judged.

and blood of the Lord. 28 Let a man examine himself, and so eat of the bread and
drink of the cup. 29 For any one who eats
and drinks without discerning the body
eats and drinks judgment upon himself.
30 That is why many of you are weak and
ill, and some have died.[p] 31 But if we judged
ourselves truly, we should not be judged.

[p] Greek *have fallen asleep* (as in 15. 6, 20).

---

table. He does not say that "they crucify the Son of God on their own account" (Heb. 6:6), but that they are **guilty of profaning the body and blood of the Lord.** Here he returns to the language of 10:16, which shows that he is thinking of the bread and wine and of their relation to the living Lord. That the bread was primary is shown by the fact that Paul mentions only the **body** in vs. 29. Some interpreters understand this as the mystical body, i.e., the church. They understand the apostle to mean that when a partaker does not discern that the community is the body of Christ he is condemned. It is much more probable that the two verses are parallel and that in each case there is some connection between the food and the body and blood of Christ. Yet Paul does not say "eat the flesh," as we find it in John 6:53.

---

to examine themselves lest they participate **in an unworthy manner** and so be guilty of failure to discern the body. Just as the Christian preacher ought to prepare himself before he prepares his sermon, so every worshiper should be suitably prepared for participation in this sacred rite. Paul is insistent on the need for moral preparation. No one should come to the table in the spirit of disunity or partisanship. That spells sacrilege. None should come in an unforgiving spirit. The Lord made it clear in the prayer that he taught his disciples that the forgiveness of God is contingent on man's forgiveness of his fellow man. Paul has here the mind of Christ. Nor can any participate worthily if they know that they have offended some other member of the community. Again, the Lord made that plain by his teaching in what we call the Sermon on the Mount (Matt. 5:23-24). The attitude of neither the worshiper nor the priest can add anything to the content of the Eucharist, but that does not mean that the spirit of the partaker is of no importance: it is of vital importance. The spirit of love must be in all and through all. Even so did the Lord on the night in which he was betrayed give his disciples and their followers a new commandment (John 15:12). Paul had occasion again to underline his admonition to the church in Corinth with regard to the need of participating in the Lord's Supper in the right spirit (II Cor. 13:5). As in the other aspects of Christian worship, there is here little or nothing for the casual mind. But granted that the worshipers do come in the right spirit and nothing seems to happen, yet there is gain, though it may not be immediate. It may not be beside the point to observe that there are ideals which we are induced to formulate and which flourish for a time, then wither and die. Yet even so it is not all loss. The withered ideals are like the leaves that fall in autumn; they help to fertilize the ground in which the tree itself stands, and from which it draws its life and its strength. So is it with the regular observance of the Supper. Time is required, and in time the significance of the rite will sink deeper into the consciousness and spirit of the participant, gradually conforming him into the likeness of the Lord. Therefore, **let a man examine himself, and so eat of the bread and drink of the cup.**

31-32. *A Homiletical Warning*.— (See Exeg.) On the other hand, what of those who partake unworthily, and who, according to Paul, eat and drink judgment upon themselves? This certainly does not mean that the offending parties will be eternally damned; but in Paul's view they who practice such selfishness and irreverence at the Lord's table are guilty of a flagrant sin for which they will surely be punished. He is undoubtedly influenced by his Jewish tradition and beliefs. Rightly or wrongly, he believed that divine punishment in terms of physical suffering was meted out to those who were guilty of the heinous sin of sacrilege at the Lord's table. It is a discipline which is intended to bring offenders to their senses. If they proved obdurate, then the consequences might become serious (vs. 30). Those who do prepare themselves set a good example to the

32 But when we are judged, we are chastened of the Lord, that we should not be condemned with the world.

32 But when we are judged by the Lord, we are chastened[q] so that we may not be condemned along with the world.

[q] Or *when we are judged we are being chastened by the Lord.*

Just as dire results came to the Israelites of old despite their sacraments (10:5-10), evils have followed a sinful use of the Lord's Supper on the part of Paul's readers. The Greek word (ἀνακρίνω) translated **examine** in vs. 28 is rendered **judged** in vs. 31*a*. In 31*b* Paul shifts to the simple verb (κρίνω); the judgment is here the divine condemnation. But why are they condemned? Was it because they had eaten divinity-charged food? After what Paul has said about **discerning the body** and **profaning the . . . blood of the Lord,** this might at first glance appear probable. But in ch. 10 the Israelites did not die because of the evil effects of sacred food. They died because of their sins. Likewise, Paul here concludes that because of their sins many have become sick and **some have died.** This deduction may be no more welcome to us than the other. It stops short of those passages in scripture which deny a necessary connection between sin and misfortune (John 9:3; Luke 13:1-5). Paul drew no such conclusion about his own "thorn in the flesh." In fact, he uses the observation here more as homiletical warning than as theological conclusion. As in Heb. 12:5-7, suffering is expected to have a disciplinary effect. If it brings repentance, it will save us from the final judgment against the world (I Pet. 4:17).

---

others. Thus **if we judged ourselves truly, we should not be judged** (vs. 31). Paul is quite certain that there will be a divine riposte upon those who break this spiritual law; but he points out that the chastening is a discipline and a warning intended to secure the salvation of the erring brother, for whom indeed the Lord has died (see Exeg., vss. 27-30).

We can surely agree with Paul that self-preparation, examination, and discipline are necessary if we are to participate with benefit to ourselves and others in the sacred rite. But what are we to make of his statements concerning the discipline of suffering, of sickness, and even of death that might follow upon irreverent behavior? Paul's language and strictures seem far removed from the life and experience of our times. Yet there is a sense in which he lays the emphasis on a solemn truth. There may have been, and probably were, other reasons for the sickness and death among the Corinthians. But it is at least possible, making allowance for the pagan mind of the times and its demonology, that a modern psychological explanation would meet the case. As we know from modern instances, the physical concomitants of psychological conflict can be marked and even dramatic. The new Christian faith, its requirements, its truth, and its fellowship and discipline were bound in the minds of the converts to add an inner tension to the tension that we know must already have existed in their relationship to the pagan community in which the church was set. They would constantly be subject to a pull, so to speak, from both directions. Much of that "conflict," as we know, goes on beneath the level of consciousness. Something of the sort must have existed in the mind of Peter as he dreamed his significant dream on the housetop of Joppa, a conflict between the universality of his Christian faith and gospel and the traditional exclusiveness of his Jewish upbringing. Only so can we really understand and interpret the symbolism of his dream. Fortunately in his case the conflict was resolved; when his better Christian part gained the mastery of his motives and outlook, Peter was prepared in spirit for his Gentile visitors (Acts 10). Paul himself could have added a good deal from his own personal experience. For him the tension and conflict had a dramatic climax with marked physical consequences (Acts 9:1-9). The very close relationship between the Lord's Supper, with the tradition it involved, and the common meal, might have helped to create an inner ferment in a near-pagan mind, with marked physical consequences to those who made the conflict more acute by irreverent behavior at the Supper. Surely something, or Someone, stood up in the souls of these people to make a protest. Have we not seen it happen again and again? This is fundamentally a moral and spiritual world. Just as we pay the penalty for any infringement of physical law, so are there penalties annexed to infringements of moral and spiritual law. These people had received the tradition. We can be certain that Paul left them in no doubt as to its interpretation. To offend against it, as they had done, was to invite the inevitable recoil upon them-

33 Wherefore, my brethren, when ye
come together to eat, tarry one for another.
34 And if any man hunger, let him eat
at home; that ye come not together unto

33 So then, my brethren, when you come
together to eat, wait for one another —
34 if any one is hungry, let him eat at
home — lest you come together to be con-

33-34. The final summary brings together Paul's directions. A meal which is simply to satisfy the hunger of an individual may be taken at home. The Lord's Supper is a spiritual experience in the church, and that requires the presence of the group. Paul knows nothing of a private Mass; the sacrament is a corporate fellowship at which Christ is the host.

Was the Lord's Supper for Paul a sacrament? This question has often been raised, but it cannot be answered without a clear definition of terms. Of course the Latin word *sacramentum* is never employed. Paul knew "mysteries" (μυστήρια), but he never applied the word to the Eucharist. Modern discussions too often assume that ancients distinguished "sacrament" and "symbol" as carefully as some modern theologians; also, that the question at issue is that of Hellenistic influence—though Albert Schweitzer would derive sacramental ideas from Jewish eschatology. It will be best to avoid labels and to deal directly

selves. Jesus himself, in the most solemn manner, often warned his hearers of their responsibility as such. His words, "Take heed what you hear," and his parable of the house on rock and the house on sand still remain as a warning to those who hear a truth and disregard it. Sooner or later all must face the test that will reveal the quality of their moral and spiritual foundations (Matt. 7:24-27). We can add the even more solemn warning he uttered in the great parable of the vineyard (Matt. 21:33-41). To play fast and loose with spiritual realities is not likely to pass without consequences of some kind or other. Paul's warning is salutary. We cannot set it aside: we have known too many cases of the spiritual and physical deterioration that takes place in the lives of those who are careless or casual—or worse—in their handling of sacred matters.

33-34. ***Paul's Separation of the Lord's Supper from the Common Meal and Its Consequences.***—Three other points call for brief comment. First, it must not escape notice that Paul not only rebukes those who have been guilty of abuses; he seeks to correct the abuses by making an alteration in social practice. "What! Do you not have houses to eat and drink in? Or do you despise the church of God and humiliate those who have nothing?" (See Exeg., vss. 20-22, 34.) The consequences have been remarkable, and perhaps in some ways saddening. Could these words mean that the meal should be taken at home? If so, the abuses on the social side would be eliminated. There is a certain gain in this procedure. The blessing of the bread and the cup would stand out by themselves, and the minds of those who participated would be free to concentrate on the significance of the rite. In passing, let it be said that the "blessing" was not a blessing on the elements themselves. That development seems to have come much later, and when it came it invested the elements with sacramental significance. Nothing, surely, could have been further from Paul's thoughts and wishes. For him the experience of Christ's real presence is involved in the sacramental act, and also in the fellowship of believers. The blessing was a thanksgiving born of a sense of indebtedness to him who provides the feast, and who is the feast. How different the subsequent history of the church would have been had this been clearly understood! But a full and adequate discussion of these matters would take us too far afield.[2] Here it is merely pointed out that the separation of the Lord's Supper from the common meal led to a certain concentration upon the Supper itself and later on upon the elements.

But it was not all gain. The second consequence was to formalize the Lord's Supper and to empty it of the vital social content which is also an important aspect of the fellowship of the church. Once the social aspects of the fellowship of the church were closely associated with the rite. This association underlined a truth we need often to reaffirm and to recover, viz., that Christianity has to do with life in all its relationships and aspects, indwelt by the Spirit of Christ and therefore consecrated to him. As one result of the dissociation of the Supper from the common meal, the latter has become a mere church social which is no doubt valuable in itself, yet devoid of the deeper significance such an association would give it.

Still further consequences have followed. There seems little doubt that the original Lord's Supper involved a collective act (Mark 14:23). Would we not keep closer to the procedure and

[2] See Forsyth, *Church and Sacraments,* ch. xiii.

condemnation. And the rest will I set in order when I come.

demned. About the other things I will give directions when I come.

with Paul's thought. It is clear that he ascribed no automatic virtue to the Lord's Supper any more than he did to baptism. Yet it is equally clear that he thought very realistically about the value of the community meal. It was no "mere" symbol, but a very real partnership in which the bread and wine brought actual participation in all that the life and death of Christ had brought to men. It is useless to ask how far he anticipated later theories of the church, but the apostle certainly believed in a very real presence. The sacraments did not make faith unnecessary, but Paul would not have understood an expression of Christian faith apart from a community in which the Lord's Supper was celebrated. Here there was a clear alternative—either **discerning the body,** or **profaning the body and blood of the Lord.**

We have seen that Paul relates the sacramental meal to all three phases of redemption: (*a*) It is a commemoration of the Cross and Resurrection, the crucial events in God's victory in the past. (*b*) It is a partnership with the living Lord who is now the host at his table. (*c*) It looks forward to the final victory of Christ when he comes to establish

spirit of the original Supper and at the same time discern the body in the fellowship if we were to retain the collective aspect of the act, and eat the bread and drink the cup together? Then the Lord's Supper might have retained more of its sacramental significance and acquired less of the atmosphere of a mystery cult.

A third consequence in the dissociation of the rite from the meal has been to transfer the idea of sacrifice, symbolized in bread that is "broken" and wine that is "poured out," to the sacrament itself, so that whenever the Eucharist is celebrated, the sacrifice of Christ "in the elements" is repeated again. As P. T. Forsyth points out:

> We begin rightly enough by treating the occasion as a sacrifice of praise. The εὐχαριστία was an offering of thanksgiving . . . But the transfer of the idea to the whole rite was of the most fatal import and consequence. There is no such description of it in the New Testament, though it came in soon after. It is proper enough in the Act to present before God the finished sacrifice of Christ as His gift to us, and therefore the best sacrifice we have to give. But when we re-enact the sacrifice of Christ, when we repeat the Cross instead of pleading it, we not only cause man to offer up a Christ Who alone could offer Himself (as Judas forced His hand), but we hide the ruling idea of Christ in the Church's midst, offering Himself and His finished work afresh to His own. The more the act was removed from the community to the official, so much the more deadly was its transfer to be a real sacrifice or a repetition of Christ's sacrifice, and the transfer of the administrator to be a priest. . . . The sacramental side was subordinated to the sacrificial. In the end it came to this, that, while the New Testament teaching is that Christ offered Himself, now the priest offered Him. . . . It was an absolutely unscriptural change.[3]

[3] *The Church and the Sacraments* (2nd ed.; London: Independent Press, 1947), pp. 271-72. Used by permission.

That is finely said. Note the emphasis on the finished work of Jesus Christ. The sacrifice was offered once for all and needs never to be repeated. It is difficult to escape the conclusion that if the Supper had remained in association with the common meal and other measures taken to avoid abuses, the church might have been spared divisions that are difficult to heal. There might have been less suggestion of magic and the mystification that goes with it; and the full import of the relationship of the sacramental act to the fellowship of the church, as well as to the individual member, might have been kept steadily before the community. God's love might then have been made manifest to us in concrete fashion, enhanced in a natural way by the love and fellowship of the members one with another. Perhaps to that more original form of Supper and fellowship the church of Christ will have to return before it moves on to the fulfillment of its purpose in the world. Sometimes we have to move back before we can move forward. "Back to Christ" may well be involved in any forward movement with him. To whom better can we go for the spirit and the guidance that we so desperately need in this and in all matters? Paul was a great man. He evokes the admiration and love of all who know how great is their indebtedness to him. But he was a man of impatient temperament, apt to make hasty judgments. In his anxiety to correct an undoubted abuse he may well have made an error of judgment, the ultimate consequences of which would certainly have horrified him even more than the events in Corinth. For his sake we can be thankful that he was not able to foresee them.

The section ends on a quiet note. Paul's depth of passion is an index to the depth of his

12 Now concerning spiritual *gifts,* brethren, I would not have you ignorant.

12 Now concerning spiritual gifts, brethren, I do not want you to be

the messianic kingdom. A ritual which aims to express Paul's interpretation must include all three of these aspects.

C. The Use of Spiritual Gifts (12:1–14:40)

The next item in the questionnaire of the Corinthian church concerned **spiritual gifts.** Yet we cannot be sure whether the word πνευματικῶν is masculine (2:15; 3:1; 14:37) and refers to the people who possessed the gifts, or is neuter (9:11; 14:1; 15:46) and refers to the gifts themselves. The address **brethren** frequently accompanies the taking up of a new theme (10:1; 15:1; Rom. 1:13). The discussion runs to the end of ch. 14. In ch. 12 are described the many gifts of the one Spirit; ch. 13 is a digression (but see below, p. 165) on the greatest gift of all, love; ch. 14 comes to grips with the immediate issue of the disorders in public worship. Paul attempts to solve them by exalting prophecy above tongues. Here we receive the fullest description of the service of the word. Already it was found that the **spiritual** could present as difficult problems as the worldly members.

1. Many Gifts of the One Spirit (12:1-31*a*)

a) Recognition of the Spirit of God (12:1-3)

12:1-3. Former **heathen** had experienced ecstasy in their previous forms of worship. This might come from possession by demons. In the Gospels we have the contrast between possession by evil spirits and by the Holy Spirit of God (Mark 3:22, 30). Paul did not

---

great love for the beloved community. Passion has exhausted itself. In any case, how could it remain in the ascendant after his meditation on the significance of the Lord's Supper? Once again we reflect that here is an authentic mark of an authentic letter: that it should express so many variations of mood, that what is begun with a torrent of reproaches should end with a flood of tenderness. He has high hopes for the Corinthian community: he is not forgetful of the things he can commend as well as those he must condemn. So he concludes with a calm plea and a promise, **So then, my brethren, when you come together to eat, wait for one another —if any one is hungry, let him eat at home— lest you come together to be condemned** (vss. 33-34). As for the other matters which he had in mind when he began this section of the letter (vs. 18), these can and must wait. Perhaps the question of the celebration of feast days and of vegetarianism was included among them (Rom. 14:2-6). The more urgent particulars have been attended to: the rest can be deferred until Paul pays his promised visit (4:19-21). We can be grateful that this rewarding section of Paul's letter was evoked by the serious situation in Corinth, even while we must regret the anguish it brought to his great heart.

12:1–14:40. ***Concerning Spiritual Gifts.***—Already we know a good deal about the church and the composition of its membership. Now the epistle is swung to a different plane of discussion.

We shall feel the force of Paul's admonitions, and his passionate desire that the Christian standards shall be held high, if we remember that the community included not only professing believers who had been baptized into the fellowship on their profession of faith in Jesus Christ as Lord, but also those who had become interested in the new religion and in its organized life. Perhaps interest had been aroused by the conversion of a relative or a friend. In any case, such people, interested but as yet not definitely attached, formed part of the regular life of the community. It may even be that these were among the people whom Paul had in mind in his deeply felt concern for "weaker brethren." Doubtless there was usually present another group: unbelievers who were curious about these novel religious developments, and who wanted to see what took place when the church gathered for worship. Moreover, this section of the epistle conveys the impression of a sustained and coherent piece of writing, as if Paul had suffered fewer interruptions than usual as he applied spirit, mind, and heart to the matter in hand.

Again, it helps to correct another impression that might have formed itself in our minds. All too easily could we be brought to believe that there was little which could be described as

think of the Holy Spirit as available to all men, but as given by the risen Christ under certain circumstances. Yet he grants that enthusiastic religious behavior is found elsewhere, and especially in connection with idol worship. There it is without understanding. Dumb **idols** might stimulate frenzy in worshipers, but they could not answer prayer.

---

praiseworthy, far less Christian, about these Corinthian believers. The following studies help to redress the balance and to present us with other and very different aspects of the life of the church. Paul refers to the members of the church more than once in terms of affection (10:14; 15:58). There was bound to be something more in its life and witness than the difficulties and problems with which he had to deal.

There are other matters which ought to be kept in mind. Then as now the church at Corinth and elsewhere was criticized on the ground that its members were no better than the decent people one meets elsewhere. The short answer to this attitude of mind is that the church is not meant for the superior people who feel no need of the help and inspiration and encouragement that it exists to give. The Master himself "came not to call the righteous, but sinners to repentance." Some no doubt shunned membership on the ground that they were not good enough to belong to a fellowship that existed in order to maintain and to inculcate the Spirit and standards of Jesus Christ. The short and loving answer to that attitude of mind is that such are precisely the people for whom the church of Jesus Christ does exist. Were everyone perfect there would be no need of a church at all. We need not expect to find perfection in the church of Jesus Christ, whether at Corinth or anywhere else. We expect to find imperfect people who make many mistakes, who often fall away from the best they have been taught, but among whom there is the desire for better things. That fills the situation with light and hope, and makes worth while all the passionate efforts of the apostle to foster the flame that burns still on the altar in Corinth. There, in the end, lies the hope of the world!

It must be remembered too that there was passionate enthusiasm for the cause of Christ, and a great zeal for the manifestation of the grace, and especially the power, of the Spirit of God. These people had undergone a wonderful experience. They had been liberated from the crippling shackles, the fear and the hopelessness and darkness of paganism, into new dimensions of life. The divine image in which all of us are created had been defined afresh. All the pent-up possibilities of the deeper capacities of the soul had been set free. Every power of their being had been released and vivified by their new conception of God and of the relationship in which they stood to God. The Christian conception of human life is that personality is man's capacity for God. When the personality of a man is opened to the flood tides of God's holy and indwelling Spirit, then with the opening of the sluice gates of the soul there comes a great enhancement of all his powers, physical and mental, moral and spiritual. There eventuates the experience which is described in the gospel as "life abundant."

It may be that the early rapture had partly died down; but the church in Corinth, pressed on every side by a hostile or indifferent pagan environment, and troubled in its own life by something more than mere reminiscences of the old pagan customs of the various members, could not have continued in existence but for the fire that still slumbered. This revealed itself in zeal and enthusiasm for the Christian cause, and also in a desire to manifest in their midst, and to the city of Corinth, the marks and gifts of the new spirit that possessed them. Let this passion and zeal be set down to the credit of the community.

Doubtless their motives were mixed. These volatile Corinthians had often been impressed by the ecstasies and other manifestations associated with religious rites in pagan temples. They had heard of the Delphic oracle, and of votaries who were believed to be specially possessed by the deities they served. They had heard of the prophecies, perhaps had even witnessed them, that were uttered by the priests and priestesses of the manifold pagan cults. Therefore, being children of their times, they desired among themselves such similar extraordinary manifestations of the presence of the Spirit whom they now worshiped. For them such experiences were the visible signs of his invisible presence; in the absence of such signs and manifestations they were probably haunted by the fear that they had been forsaken of God.

Paul had no fault to find with this zeal. Indeed he commends it and deals very tactfully and tenderly even with its less edifying expressions. Certainly he welcomes every sign of strength and vitality that marks the Christian witness in Corinth (1:4-8). Yet such zeal has need of correction and direction and discipline if it is to be saved from unspiritual excess. It is all too easy to indulge spiritual emotion for its own sake. When strong emotions are thus indulged, they dissipate themselves in the sands

2 Ye know that ye were Gentiles, carried away unto these dumb idols, even as ye were led.

uninformed. 2 You know that when you were heathen, you were led astray to dumb idols, however you may have been moved.

How are the two types of behavior to be distinguished? Paul affirms that the attitude toward Christ will indicate who is really moved by **the Spirit** bestowed by him. All will agree that this is a sound criterion provided a man's words are sincere. Jesus himself, however, insisted, "Not every one who says to me, 'Lord, Lord,' shall enter the kingdom of heaven" (Matt. 7:21-23). Surely Paul did not mean that simply the use of one phrase rather than another was determinative. Confession to the lordship of Jesus was primary (Rom. 10:9; Phil. 2:11), but Paul would have been the first to test this assertion by the fruit of the confessor's life. The Spirit is the Spirit of Christ (Rom. 8:9), and that Spirit does not dwell in a man who lacks moral qualities (3:1; Gal. 5:23).

Who would be saying **Jesus be cursed?** It is quite believable that Jewish opponents within the synagogues at times would make such ejaculations. But elsewhere in this section

---

of mere sentimentality; when they are directed into practical channels that are of value to the individual and to the community, they form worth-while sentiments. Sentiments are among the foundations of character itself. Sentiment is a good thing; sentimentality is a bad thing. Hence the need for a sound judgment concerning spiritual gifts, and for wise advice concerning their value and their practical application in the life of the community and in its witness to the outside world. With these general considerations in mind let us now turn to a closer examination of the text.

12:1-3. ***Now Concerning Spiritual Gifts, Brethren, I Do Not Want You to Be Uninformed.***—Presently the apostle will include a list of the gifts he has in mind, and tactfully and persuasively put them into a certain order of value. Meantime, he has something important to say about their origin and also about the channels into which the energy that these gifts possess may best be guided. It is all too easy to be led astray by uncontrolled enthusiasm: under its stress one is liable to be guided by impulse rather than by disciplined thought. In the matter of exercising spiritual gifts of various kinds this type of discipline was essential. The context bears the inference that at least some of the members of the community were concerned about the many excesses related to that exercise and had written to Paul for advice and guidance on the subject. Of course he instantly and willingly responds.

There is a realm of experience to which he can refer them for guidance and help. They were as pagans very well acquainted with the emotionalism associated with pagan rites (vs. 2), and they had learned under the teaching of Paul and those who followed him that the "dumb idols" associated with such rites stand in a very low degree of comparison to the Lord Jesus Christ whom they now worship and serve. But there were also similar emotional and indeed ecstatic experiences associated with their worship of him. And these were earnestly desired as affording evidence of the inspiring power of the Holy Spirit in the midst of the community. The practical point at issue is how to distinguish Christian from pagan inspiration, and so avoid confusion in the life of the community. How shall they discriminate the manifestation of the Spirit from that of demons? (See Exeg.) Such a problem put in such a way seems remote from our life and our times. Yet it is not so. In the field of religion, as in that of politics, especially under conditions of emotional revivalist preaching or political demagogy, it is all too easy to obtain the effects of mass emotion with its concomitant irrationalism and uncontrol. Whether one believes in "demons" or not, in the political sphere especially the results can be demonic and catastrophic. The morality of a crowd or a nation swayed by mass emotion is much lower than that of the average individual member, and excesses of various kinds are all too possible and even probable. Doubtless such reflections range far beyond the apostle's thought and purpose in his present instructions and advice to his Corinthian friends, but they are intrinsically involved in the situation and experiences with which he is dealing.

There is a simple and profound test, even if at first sight it seems rough and ready, that may be applied to the circumstances under discussion. **I want you to understand that no one speaking by the Spirit of God ever says "Jesus be cursed!" and no one can say "Jesus is Lord" except by the Holy Spirit.** Paul is anxious that the discernment of Christian believers shall be as clear and decisive as possible in all such matters. To the church in Philippi he wrote that his prayer for them—and we can believe it

3 Wherefore I give you to understand, that no man speaking by the Spirit of God calleth Jesus accursed: and *that* no man can say that Jesus is the Lord, but by the Holy Ghost.
4 Now there are diversities of gifts, but the same Spirit.

[3] Therefore I want you to understand that no one speaking by the Spirit of God ever says "Jesus be cursed!" and no one can say "Jesus is Lord" except by the Holy Spirit.
4 Now there are varieties of gifts, but

---

the apostle is dealing with disorders in Christian worship. Could it be that there were speakers with **tongues** who gave vent to their enthusiasm in this way? Paul himself did not hesitate to curse all who did not love the Lord (16:22).

b) The Manifold Gifts of the Spirit (12:4-11)

Paul is eager to say that spirituality is not one uniform experience which is separate from all other areas of life. The spiritual is not in contrast to the material and the intellectual. Manifestations of the Spirit are to be found in wide varieties of conduct, because spirituality exists wherever the living, acting God works through capacities of any type. Spirituality is not a separate compartment of life, but a divine relationship which may ennoble all aspects of experience.

4-7. Paul expresses this idea through a carefully constructed piece of rhetoric in which he uses both repetition and variation of terminology. In the first sentence he

---

included all the churches—was that their love, knowledge, and discernment might so deepen and enrich their understanding that they would approve what is excellent (Phil. 1:9-10). His practical suggestion to the Corinthian church is that they should take note how certain people refer to or speak of Jesus Christ. In similar circumstances the Master himself returned a similar answer, "By their fruits shall ye know them" (Matt. 7:16-20).

There can be little doubt that the apostle had actual instances in mind when he set down this piece of advice in his letter. We know that the opposition he encountered from some of the Jews of the synagogue was exceedingly bitter. They hated the Christian church and they hated its founder. To them it was rank blasphemy to proclaim Jesus as divine. For them the curse lay heavy on all who had been hanged on a cross. How could such a one even remotely be related to their God? We can imagine some fanatical Jew, from the synagogue situated next door to the home of Titius Justus, where the Christians met (Acts 18:7), shouting out in frenzy, "Your Jesus is an accursed impostor." None could have any doubt that such utterances were not inspired by the Holy Spirit. Or it may be that Paul also had his own experiences in mind, in the days when he too was a persecutor of the Christian church. When he was being tried before Festus and Agrippa in Caesarea, he recounted his attempts to force the Christians to blaspheme in some such manner (Acts 26:11). A third possibility is that such ejaculatory cries were associated with glossolalia or "speaking with tongues." Paul deals with this matter carefully, tenderly, and cautiously. The point will be taken up more fully in the exposition of the section itself. But it is mainly fanatical blasphemy that he has in mind. Even today one meets with it. There are still Jews of the more fanatical type like those who used to forgather at the Wailing Wall and elsewhere in Jerusalem; men whose faces must look much the same as those who so frantically cried out for the crucifixion of the Lord long years ago; whose hatred for Christ and Christians is as fierce now as then, and who say to Christians, "Take away your dead Christ; we don't want him here." Let it be set down at once that they represent a small minority. Even in the most embittered times there is a spirit of toleration which is nourished by right-thinking people of all nations. But the fanatics with their spirit-destroying hatred and prejudices are also still with us. Paul's test is good. There is all the difference in the world between utterances inspired by the spirit of righteous love and those which are born of bitterness, envy, and hatred. The spiritual quality of the person making the utterance freights the very words he uses. **No one can say "Jesus is Lord" except by the Holy Spirit.** Here as in other similar circumstances, "By their fruits shall ye know them."

4-11. ***Varieties of Gifts and Services.***—Now the apostle turns to a consideration of the various spiritual gifts and services concerning which the fellowship in Corinth was exercised. In a sense he is reverting to the points he

5 And there are differences of adminis-
trations, but the same Lord.
6 And there are diversities of operations,
but it is the same God which worketh all
in all.

the same Spirit; 5 and there are varieties
of service, but the same Lord; 6 and there
are varieties of working, but it is the same
God who inspires them all in every one.

---

repeats the word for **varieties** (διαιρέσεις) three times (RSV), though the KJV obscures this. All are **gifts;** yet at the same time they are activities involving effort on the part of those receiving them. This idea of activity is suggested first by the word **service** and then by the most general term possible—**working.** Three sources are named for these gifts: **Spirit, Lord,** and **God.** The order of the three differs from that in II Cor. 13:14 as well as from that in Matt. 28:19. The **Spirit** is put first because it is the term which Paul will use throughout the section. The emphasis of the entire paragraph is upon the fact that all gifts come from the same source and all of these activities draw their energizing stimulus from the same power. Since **Spirit, Lord,** and **God** are used successively in stating this idea, they are not entirely distinct and different sources. Paul has no formulated doctrine of the Trinity; he can use these terms quite interchangeably (Rom. 8:9-11). The gifts

---

sought to emphasize at the beginning of his letter. There he attempts to put the "instruments" into their right relationship with the message they were appointed to bear, and to stress the latter as possessing supreme value (3:5-15). His procedure here is similar. Not all gifts possess the same value. Some are more helpful than others. But there are certain aspects common to them all. These Paul is concerned to underline. **There are varieties of gifts, but the same Spirit; and there are varieties of service, but the same Lord; and there are varieties of working, but it is the same God who inspires them all in every one.** The first of Paul's two main points in these verses is recognition of the variety of the gifts. A few lines farther on he appends a long list on which brief comments will be made. Here the general fact is recognized and stated. The second point is the more important: all the gifts alike are from God. They are the gifts of his grace. His is the Spirit who inspires them in all their varieties (see Exeg., vss. 4-7). Paul is concerned that there shall be frank and glad recognition of this fact by the members of the church. Probably there was a tendency, such is human nature, for some members to rank the gift which they themselves possessed above that with which others were endowed. Men may be equal in the sight of God, but they are not equal in respect of their endowment. Some are more gifted than others. Some have ten talents, some five, and some only one. Some have greater mental ability, others have more imagination, and others have greater force of will. So it is in the Christian community. But recognition is given there to one great overriding reality that puts all variety and difference of gifts and their manifestation into due proportion and order. Recognition is given explicitly to the fact that none possesses any gift or grace that he has not received. God is the source and giver of every good gift. What we possess is not ours, it is his. Paul implies that due acknowledgment should be made of this great truth. Such acknowledgment will help to deepen and enrich the sense of fellowship one with another. In any case, the greatest of all gifts, with which he will deal almost immediately, is available to every member of the community. Let there be an earnest desire among the Christian brethren for its possession. It is said that one day Francis of Assisi found Brother Juniper in a disconsolate mood. Poor Juniper was so stupid that he could not be entrusted with even the simplest domestic tasks. He had actually attempted to cook rabbits without divesting them of their skins. He felt that he was a useless member of the band of brothers. But Francis knew better. "Cheer up, Brother Juniper! Don't you know that you possess the greatest gift of all—a loving heart?" The main points are that there is a variety of gifts, and that God is the giver of them all. Recognition of that truth should prevent any unseemly pride or boasting among those who imagine themselves more richly endowed than others. The glory belongs to God alone; **it is the same God who inspires them all in every one.**

A third point follows: **To each is given the manifestation of the Spirit for the common good.** Again Paul reveals his deep sense of the nature of the Christian fellowship. It provides him with a sure test of the value of particular instances. His test is: How do these affect the life of the fellowship? Are its life and witness thereby enriched? Almost immediately, though with great tact and gentleness, he applies this very test in the matter of the gift of tongues.

7 But the manifestation of the Spirit is given to every man to profit withal.

8 For to one is given by the Spirit the word of wisdom; to another the word of knowledge by the same Spirit;

7 To each is given the manifestation of the
Spirit for the common good. 8 To one is
given through the Spirit the utterance of
wisdom, and to another the utterance of
knowledge according to the same Spirit,

---

have not been bestowed for private enjoyment; they are to serve **the common good.** This was not always the case, as is evident from ch. 14; but such was the demand of God. The particular gift which a person receives is not of his own choosing but is determined by the Spirit. Hence, there can be no ground for pride in respect to what is entirely a matter of grace.

8-11. Nine different gifts of the Spirit are enumerated to emphasize with almost monotonous repetition the fact that they are all from the same Spirit. The first two, **wisdom** and **knowledge,** look back to the discussion of these themes in chs. 1–4. Here, however, Paul is thinking more particularly of **the utterance** of these, i.e., of the teaching ministries of the church. Capacities for thought are mentioned first in the equipment for service, just as these come first in vs. 28. It is striking that Paul calls **faith** a gift (cf. Rom. 12:3). Certainly the apostle does not conceive of the faith that justifies as a human work; it is the product of divine grace. Yet here Paul is speaking of a gift which only certain members of the community receive, so that the **faith** cannot be understood as the common faith involved in the reception of salvation, but as faith of a particular kind (cf. 13:2); it is the wonder-working faith that leads to healings (Mark 5:34; 10:52) and

---

Meantime, he is content to make a general though significant statement. In his view every manifestation of the Spirit is meant to benefit both the individual concerned and the entire community of which he is a member. Individual benefit involves something other than mere self-display or self-gratification; the benefit to the individual concerned is obviously such as will enhance his value as a member of the community. Thus Paul prepares the way for his striking exposition of the nature of the Christian community under the figure of the "body" and its "members." These points should all be kept in mind in studying the passages that follow.

Surely in these deliverances the apostle has set down guiding principles that have a continuing value for the church of Jesus Christ right up to our own time. There are diversities of gifts today, as there were in those far-off days of the dawn of the Christian church. Some have gifts of organization, others in the realm of some art. Some can teach, others can preach. Some feel that they can only stand and wait, or watch and pray, like Milton in his blindness. Let none esteem himself above any other member of the community. What does any one of us possess that we have not received? Our responsibility is to recognize that something has been given us, and that we are expected to exercise due stewardship with regard to it as those who must render an account to God. What has been given, no matter what the nature of the gift may be, is to be used for the good of the community and not for any selfish purpose. Even so do we acknowledge him who is the source of every good and perfect gift.

8. ***Wisdom and Knowledge.***—Now comes a list of some of the various gifts with which members of the community may be endowed. The first two are rather difficult to distinguish from one another. Earlier in his letter Paul contrasts the wisdom of the age with the wisdom of God (ch. 2). Here the thought is somewhat different. **To one is given through the Spirit the utterance of wisdom, and to another the utterance of knowledge according to the same Spirit.** Broadly speaking, in our own time one may distinguish between knowledge and wisdom by saying that wisdom is that deeper insight which can turn knowledge to the best advantage. It is doubtful if Paul had such a distinction in mind. One finds it difficult to resist the inference that the apostle himself had his convictions about the relative value of different gifts, and he may have recognized a difference of degree between knowledge and wisdom. Or perhaps he meant that some members of the community were able to state the facts of the gospel to their brethren, while others were better able to expound the significance of the facts in their bearing upon the spiritual development of the church and its mission in the world. There have been and doubtless are many instances of such corporate service being rendered in Christian communities. Some are able to state the facts of a situation; others are able to see the bearing of these facts. Both types can render genuine service to

9 To another faith by the same Spirit; to another the gifts of healing by the same Spirit;

9 to another faith by the same Spirit, to another gifts of healing by the one Spirit,

---

impossible exploits (Mark 9:23; 11:22; Luke 17:6). In other words, Paul speaks here of πίστις more in the sense of the Synoptic Gospels than in the sense customary with him. This leads to the next two **gifts** in the list, **healing** and **miracles.** Paul says nothing of the use of oil (cf. Jas. 5:14-15). He will return to the ministers who possess these **gifts** in vss. 28-29. The word for **miracles** is that for powers (δυνάμεις; cf. 12:28; Matt. 11:20;

---

the community as a whole. In general it may be said that those who were endowed with the gift of knowledge and those who had the gift of wisdom exercised their God-given graces in illuminating expositions of the Christian faith.

9. ***The Gift of Faith.***—In Paul's understanding and expression, **faith** is a greathearted and unquestioning trust in God, as God has made himself known to us in Jesus Christ. There are degrees of faith (see Exeg.). The faith of some is stronger, more robust, more contagious and inspiring than that of others. The faith of a few, in varying circumstances, has more than once been the living spring which has nourished the morale of the many. In some people faith is a feeble and flickering flame; in others it is a great beacon shining through the darkness of every spiritual night. Christian faith should always be at its best when things are at their worst. Its supreme expression is the filial trust in God manifested by our Lord when he was dying in agony on Calvary's Cross. That is one of the truly convincing things about the Christian gospel. Many have been convinced of its central message precisely because it is not the offspring of life's sunlit hours, but because those pallid, dying lips unfalteringly proclaimed an unassailable trust in God. "Father, into thy hands I commit my spirit!" (Luke 23:46.) There have been those who have been enthralled and held by that faith in every age and in all circumstances. They have clung to their faith at all times, and so perhaps have been unconscious towers of strength to their fellow men. They have sought to approximate the faith of him who inspired their own. Their contribution to the common good of the Christian fellowship cannot be overestimated. There lived in London some years ago an old schoolmaster, one of the pioneers of the coeducational system in England. He was a man of unorthodox religious views, but he was also a man of strong, quiet, and confident faith. His influence on his pupils was impressive. Some who are now ranked as leaders of their profession were of their number. One and all held the old schoolmaster in high esteem. When he died, it was said of him that being what he was he made it easier for others to believe in God. Despite his unorthodoxy he possessed the gift of faith.

This is the spirit in which Christian believers should seek to live. More depends on it, so far as the true progress of the race is concerned, than we are apt to realize. The consequences of unbelief can be dramatic enough. They are obvious in every age. When faith in God goes, other things take its place. The realm of the spiritual abhors a vacuum just as much as the physical realm. When faith in God is diminished or extinct, confusion, incertitude, inconsequence, wrong motives, and wrong values take its place. When faith in God goes, cultural and spiritual sickness spreads among men like an evil contagion, corrupting their moral and spiritual nature. The sole satisfying cure for little faith is not less faith but more, as Jesus in effect pointed out to Jairus who came to him requesting that his daughter might be healed of her sickness, and also to the woman who suffered from an "issue of blood." The consequences of such a growing faith, could we only realize it, would be even more dramatic than the consequences of unbelief. All sorts of mountains would be removed. Were Christian faith really to possess the hearts and minds of men, it would no doubt be saying too much to assert that every problem which torments the race would thereby be solved, but one can say that our feet would be set on the road that leads in the end to the right solution. Luther never uttered a more pregnant word than when he said that miracles happen not because they are performed but because they are believed. Let every Christian community, and not only that in Corinth, give thanks for those in its midst who bring inspiration to all the members through the strength and contagion of their own faith.

9. ***The Gift of Healing.***—This great gift of healing should be taken as a special instance of the working and power of Christian faith. In the Gospels it is made quite plain that the salvation which the Master proclaimed involved the well-being of the whole man, body, soul, and spirit. It is true that the deeper need was spiritual. It is also true that he healed the sick

10 To another the working of miracles; to another prophecy; to another discerning of spirits; to another *divers* kinds of tongues; to another the interpretation of tongues:

10 to another the working of miracles, to another prophecy, to another the ability to distinguish between spirits, to another various kinds of tongues, to another the

---

Luke 5:17) —an evidence of the work of the Holy Spirit among them. The miracle is more than simply an external marvel, though of course such marvels would have been looked on as **miracles.** The presence of the messianic time was thus witnessed by God (Gal. 3:5;

---

and the mentally deranged where he found men and women whose faith in him and whose spirit of expectancy gave him an opportunity to perform a healing work. His message was for the whole of the human personality, for its physical as well as its spiritual aspects. There seems to be no good reason for believing that he conceived of pain as an illusion existing in the mind of the sufferer. His own agonies on the Cross were terribly real. Nor is there any good and sufficient reason for thinking that he expected wholehearted acceptance of his message would enable mankind to dispense with physicians. Luke may have practiced his art as a doctor while Paul worked at his tents when they set out together on their journeys. Yet it is also indubitable that healing took place in the Christian church through faith and prayer, and that certain members of the church were endowed with gifts of healing. Some are so endowed to this day, and services of faith healing, which are meant to supplement and not to dispense with orthodox medical aid, are frequently held in churches.

We are thus recovering something that the Christian church possessed in its early days and that for long centuries was almost completely lost. Moreover, where some essential aspect of the full work and message of the church has been for some reason or other obscured, then sooner or later certain movements have developed which made the missing or lost aspect of the Christian mission its main emphasis. Christian Science may be so regarded. Its main insistence rests on the healing mission of the church. In that setting Christian Science should be regarded as a challenge to the Christian church to rediscover, preach, and practice its full gospel. Modern developments in the field of psychology, and in that scarcely explored realm of spirit that lies beyond the physical and the psychical, help to re-emphasize the old-time practices of the church. There are vast realms of psychological and spiritual realities that have an important bearing upon every healing work. Many an individual has died who physically speaking had every reason to recover from his sickness but for the fact that somehow or other he lacked faith. Faith and prayer can be, and often are, a great reinforcement to the strictly physical and physiological. The human personality is a unity of physical, mental, and spiritual elements and must be treated as such. Nor have there been lacking physicians, psychiatrists, and psychologists who have insisted on and have practiced the value of faith and prayer in their efforts on behalf of their patients. Not a few of them have made grateful acknowledgment of the sometimes astonishing results that have accrued. Attention is therefore being given again to the need for co-operation between the church and the medical profession in the treatment of the sick. Once again prayers are offered in many churches for sick members and healing services are held. There is no thought of emphasizing faith healing to the exclusion of scientific medicine, but increasingly the spiritual factors with which faith is related are being recognized, and institutions are being set up in various countries in which both faith healing and medicine combine to achieve the recovery of the patient. Such things, terminology apart, were a commonplace in the early Christian communities; and in the church in Corinth there were those who were specially endowed with gifts of healing. Let the church possess and use all its resources in God.

10. ***The Working of Miracles.***—The phrase, **to another the working of miracles,** would be more accurately expressed as "the demonstration of mighty powers" (see Exeg.). Paul does not use the word "miracles" in its modern sense. He would include the healing of various diseases as indicated in the previous section. Where the cure took on a more than usually dramatic form—recovery of sight in the case of functional blindness, or of movement in the case of functional paralysis; restoration of mental balance where there had been what was then termed demon possession, and what is now more generally described as psychoneurosis, or even multiple personality—the word miraculous in our sense might be applied. Generally speaking, **miracles** would be descriptive of healing works of the more unusual type. The difference between the gift of healing and the working of

miracles is one of degree. These three—faith, healing, and the working of miracles—form a connected section by themselves. Obviously they are interrelated. Once again the abiding inference is that given faith and expectation in relation to God, as he has revealed himself and his gracious purposes for mankind in and through his Son Jesus Christ, the consequences would be dramatic. We have scarcely begun to explore the spiritual resources open to faith and to prayer. Who can set their limits since God himself is involved?

10. ***The Gift of Prophecy.***—Those persons who were endowed with the gift of **prophecy,** the first of another group of related gifts, were the recipients of that prophetic revelation which yielded insight into the purposes of God, so far as these bore upon the existing state of affairs or indicated future developments. The prophet sees beneath the surface and clearly apprehends the inner, hidden trend of events. He sees the unity that is enmeshed in the multitudinous variety of everyday circumstance. He often has prevision of the consequences for good or ill that may eventuate if certain trends are allowed to work to fulfillment. One finds some such prescience in great statesmen. They too seem to be endowed, each in his own fashion, with a capacity for clearly envisaging the outcome of certain details of present policy in the life of a nation. With varying degrees of skill and advantage to state or party they deal with the exigencies of their time; legislate perhaps for many years to come, foreseeing as they do the trend of events, and possessing often the power to determine at least in some measure the direction of the trend.

In the deeper, more significant realm of spiritual things this is the nature and function of the prophet. An Isaiah can foresee the futility of an alliance with Egypt under the threat of an Assyrian invasion, and so can recall his nation to its true destiny in relationship to God. He can foresee the dire consequences of religious declension long before they are apparent to the ordinary man. That is why he is so fierce and urgent in his denunciations. That is why he is disregarded, even hated and often persecuted, by his contemporaries. But that is the essence of prophecy. The church has need of its prophets. The nation has need of them too. There are many preachers, and good preachers, but all too few prophets. Prophecy is a great gift: to prophets are given revelations of the mind and purpose of Almighty God. The church, despite its blemishes and defects, was not lacking in any spiritual gift. There were prophets in Corinth.

10. ***The Gift of Discernment.***—This gift might be better expressed as the power of discernment which enabled certain members of the community to sift, as it were, the wheat from the chaff in any assessment of the mind of the church on matters pertaining to its spiritual welfare. We must keep in mind what we have already noted, viz., the abounding enthusiasm and zeal—an enthusiasm and zeal often carried to excess—that seem to have been characteristic of the church. Paul is far from wanting to quench this ardor; he is, however, anxious to give it direction and moral value. Misguided enthusiasts have often enough brought perfectly good causes to the verge of disaster. More than once, and in various ways, Paul indicates that God wants his creatures to use the faculties with which he has endowed them. The use of common sense and intelligence should be ranked among such faculties. In most Christian communities there are some who are more insightful than others: they can see the bearing of some suggestions better than others. They have more experience and perhaps more wisdom. These gifts and powers are also to be used for the glory of God and for the furtherance of his purposes.

Enthusiasm and inspiration are not to be despised. On the contrary, they are to be welcomed. But in themselves they are not enough. If there is a member of the community who is able to see the strength or weakness of any suggestion or utterance, let his gift be put at the disposal of the church in making the issues plain. It should be done in a spirit of brotherliness and persuasiveness, and with a sense of responsibility to God for the well-being of the community as a whole. Such a gift may not be so striking as the gift of oratory or healing, nonetheless it is important. The member of the church who can disentangle his thoughts from his emotions and prejudices is more likely to be disinterested and to "think straight" than his more ecstatic brother. The value of his contribution to the common good may on that account be much greater. His is a gift of the same Spirit who inspires them all. Sanctified common sense is as great an asset to the Christian community as emotional preaching and may procure much more lasting results. Let the gift of discernment have its due place in the counsels of the church.

10-11. ***The Gift of Tongues and Their Interpretation.***—Paul treats with caution and tact this peculiar expression of the faith, enthusiasm, and intensity of spiritual emotion in the church. A little farther on in his letter (ch. 14) he gives further guidance as to its value to the community and suggests practical tests. These points will be discussed in due course. Some authorities distinguish the practice of speaking with various kinds of tongues from the activity recorded in the Acts, when after

11 But all these worketh that one and the selfsame Spirit, dividing to every man severally as he will.

interpretation of tongues. 11 All these are inspired by one and the same Spirit, who apportions to each one individually as he wills.

Heb. 2:4). The last four gifts belong together, **prophecy** and speaking in **tongues,** and the ability to evaluate the prophecy and to interpret the tongues. Paul regards the ability to judge true inspiration as being a work of the Spirit no less truly than the actual revelations

---

Pentecost the apostles being "filled with the Holy Spirit . . . began to speak in other tongues, as the Spirit gave them utterance" (Acts 2:4). The narrative then goes on to indicate that the multitude which gathered to listen to the apostles as they preached the gospel of the resurrection was amazed and bewildered "because each one heard them speaking in his own language" (Acts 2:6). Luke's meaning is quite plain: under the stress of spiritual emotion these men spoke intelligibly in foreign tongues and were understood by those standing around who spoke the same language.[4] The phrase **kinds of tongues** can better be interpreted as "ecstatic utterances." This is a fairly well-known phenomenon, and has been an accompaniment of all such religious revival movements as were characterized by strong emotions. Students of the psychology of religion have noted it, and describe it in terms of the release of strong emotion which cannot find satisfying expression in more normal ways. In the early Christian church it was accepted as a spiritual gift, though of inferior value and quality to the others listed by the apostle. Apparently it was used chiefly, or perhaps even exclusively, in prayer (14:2; see Exeg., 14:2-4), and Paul himself confesses that he spoke in tongues (14:18); but he was also, as we shall see, quite clear in his own mind as to the spiritual value of the gift. Other characteristics of this ecstatic experience are that the utterance was unintelligible both to the speaker and to the hearers unless another party was present who professed to be able to interpret the utterance. This was distinguished as a "gift" by itself. **To another the interpretation of tongues.** There could have been little guarantee that the interpretation bore any relationship at all to the unintelligible utterance. Yet there can be no doubt that these ecstatic utterances were treasured by the early church as signifying the presence and power of the Spirit in the midst of believers. Ecstatic utterances were probably regarded as a kind of divine frenzy, and therefore of superhuman origin. The Corinthian Christians seem to have been particularly susceptible to this emotional experience, and seem to have attached such value to it that they ranked it above some of these other gifts of the Spirit listed by the apostle. Paul applies his sanctified common sense to the situation in order that the church may be saved from the danger of confusion and lack of discipline. The tests are the same as for other gifts. Does this gift benefit the individual and the community of which he is a member? Let it be estimated accordingly.

Undoubtedly the psychological explanation already indicated is the most satisfying account of the phenomenon. Under the stress of religious emotion and excitement the mind, particularly in its subconscious reaches, becomes supercharged, and emotional release is found in these particular ecstatic experiences. To "speak with tongues" is at least an innocuous way of letting off superfluous spiritual steam. Paul's deeper intent is presently to point out a "more excellent way" (vs. 31). Meanwhile, he again stresses the point that all true and beneficial gifts are inspired by the Spirit himself. These are given in manifold variety to the church so that in every way its spiritual life may be enriched and its witness to the things of the faith be strengthened. No one is to boast that he possesses any spiritual endowment superior to that possessed by other brethren. None has any gift that has not been apportioned to him by the Spirit. Recognition of this truth will preserve a sense of balance and of humility in the life of the community, and the glory will go to him alone to whom it is due. **All these are inspired by one and the same Spirit, who apportions to each one individually as he wills.**

Once again, in studying this list of spiritual gifts as recounted by Paul, we get more than a glimpse of a Christian community which despite all its faults, failures, and other blemishes was characterized by genuine zeal and enthusiasm. In the better sense of the phrase the members were possessed by the greatness and glory of the gospel that had transformed their lives and their outlook. The tides of the Spirit were allowed free scope among them. Officialdom had not as yet succeeded in repressing the

[4] F. J. Foakes Jackson, *The Acts of the Apostles* (London: Hodder & Stoughton, 1931; "The Moffatt New Testament Commentary"), p. 11.

12 For as the body is one, and hath many members, and all the members of that one body, being many, are one body: so also *is* Christ.

12 For just as the body is one and has many members, and all the members of the body, though many, are one body, so it is

themselves. The comparative value of these last gifts will be discussed in ch. 14, but at the moment Paul is eager to affirm the divine character of them all. The possessor of any one is truly **spiritual.**

c) The Body and Its Members (12:12-26)

12. To illustrate this truth of diversity in unity Paul turns to the figure of the human body. Its several parts are quite different and yet all belong to the same organic entity. In carrying through his analogy we would expect Paul to say, "So it is with the church"; instead, he says **Christ.** For Paul this was more than a mere analogy or figure of speech. The church was in a real sense the mystical body of Christ. He does not mean to say that the church is *like* a body; it *is* the body of Christ. In Rom. 12:4-5 he will develop again the same figure, and there also in connection with the gifts of the Spirit and the ministries of the church. In Colossians a new element is added—that Christ is the "head of the

native zeal of these converts. "Abundant life" was more than a phrase to them. It is true that order and discipline are necessary to avoid confusion and dissipation of spiritual energy, and even to enhance its strength and to define its direction and to increase its impact. Niagara, harnessed, can yield more beneficial power for human well-being than Niagara picturesquely running to waste over its precipices. Yet Niagara too severely harnessed loses something of value, viz., spontaneity and loveliness and grandeur. So is it with the growth of the Christian church. Paul was well aware that ethical value could be given to the emotional exuberance of these Christian communities, and especially that in Corinth, only if a certain measure of order and discipline, and also a sense of relative values, were imposed on it. But spiritual freedom must not be lost in the process. "Abundant life" is a phrase like "living water," also beloved of the Master. "Living water" is a leaping, rippling, dancing, sparkling thing. Life is enhanced, not diminished, by Christian faith and experience. Capacities and powers are enlarged, not reduced, as the outcome of spiritual experience. There is a place for heart as well as mind in the life of the community no less than in that of the individual. So there was much in the emotional exuberance and abundant zeal of this church in Corinth that commended itself to Paul. He was very wise in his dealings with the churches. His aim was to give the fullest effect to the many-sidedness of a living Christian witness to the world, and at the same time to safeguard its essential unity, to develop its spiritual character, and to ensure that these qualities should be reflected in the life of the individual member. Unity and variety are therefore keynotes to this section of his letter, and Paul's insight has been authoritative and influential in the subsequent history of the church. In his view the fellowship was real, very real, and supremely significant. But if the adherence of the individual was intended by him to make its own addition to the life of the fellowship, so the fellowship itself was meant to give full scope and expression to the individual member who is of infinite value in the sight of God, and for whom in the end the church of Christ exists. These were matters of central importance for the life of the church. They lead on to one of the great apostle's guiding convictions.

12. ***Paul's Parable of the Body and Its Various Members.***—Paul, having prepared the way in these two paragraphs on the variety of spiritual gifts, now proceeds to strengthen his argument under the fruitful and suggestive figure of the church as "the body of Christ" (vs. 27; see Exeg., vs. 12). Let us keep in mind what has already been said about unity and variety, for this is a matter on which the apostle feels deeply, and it is one which needs to be stressed again and again in view of the spirit of partisanship in the Corinthian church. The very variety of spiritual gifts may be a menace to the unity of the fellowship. Paul now seeks to show the intimate relationship of **the members of the body** to one another and to Christ, by whom and for whom the church exists. With such a strong spirit of individualism, so characteristic of the Greek temperament, at work like a ferment in the church, it is not surprising that divisive tendencies should make their appearance. This has always been a danger, particularly in Protestant communions. The true and

body" (1:18; 2:19). In our letter all of the members, including eye and ear—parts of the head—are individuals in the church. Apparently Christ is the head in the sense of 11:3, the one in authority. Just how the crucified one, who in his resurrection body of glory is now at the right hand of God, is related to another body which is distributed in many different cities about the Mediterranean is a mystery which Paul never attempts to explain. Here is the Paul who writes to the Galatians, "It is no longer I who live, but Christ who lives in me" (Gal. 2:20). It is doubtful that the apostle thought in terms of a pantheism that would melt down all distinctions of personality. Nor is it likely that his language is to be explained simply as a parallel to demon possession. Some contemporary scholars would explain Paul's terminology by the Gnostic conception of a heavenly being or *aiōn* into which the redeemed are incorporated. It is more probable that we are to understand it from his eschatology, the oneness of Messiah and messianic community. If the church

---

most effective Christian catholicity is unity in diversity and diversity in unity. These are fundamental concepts in Paul's thought. In the opening Expos. of the apostle's strictures with regard to the spirit of partisanship that threatened the existence and witness of the church in Corinth, it was stated that Paul had in mind the world-wide unifying mission of the church. It is true, on the other hand, that he also looked forward to "the end of the ages" and felt it to be imminent. Yet while both conceptions were present in his mind, the former seems to have become stronger and more marked. In his later epistles (e.g., Romans) he seems practically to have given up any thought of the imminence of "the end of the ages." These points are helpful in considering the background against which such a mind as Paul's saw the essential unity in variety of the church. Nowhere in his correspondence do we find a more fruitful and suggestive image of it than we have in his parable of the body and its various members. **For just as the body is one and has many members, and all the members of the body, though many, are one body, so it is with Christ.**

The thought of the church as a body with its constituent members is germinative with Paul himself, and it would also strike responsive chords in Corinthian minds. The apostle had obviously given much consideration to this matter; a study of his subsequent use of the metaphor in later epistles reveals how it developed in his own mind. Various commentators have pointed out that this figure of speech was in common use in Paul's time; it was applied frequently to the body politic, and therefore would be understood and appreciated by his readers.[5] Paul took up the idea and applied it to the church. It admirably served his purpose in emphasizing the variety of the membership, and at the same time its mystical unity and its relationship to Jesus Christ. There seems to be little doubt that, as he wrote, the apostle was concerned solely with the Corinthian church. But his imagination seized hold of the idea and he extended it in his later letters to the Ephesians (1:22-23; 4:15-16) and to the Colossians (1:18; 2:19). There is still, in the present letter, a certain elasticity of conception which in itself indicates that the apostle's mind was open to the development of Christian thought. Paul was no static theologian. For him, as he makes quite clear in this very epistle, the gospel is given once for all. He conceived himself as called not to give vent to his own personal opinions, or to proffer good advice, but to preach the gospel with which he had been entrusted. But the theological and ecclesiastical implications of the gospel are constantly open to extension, to modification, and to re-examination and restatement. The apostle was alert to the "growing point" of religious insight. Hence his developing conception of the church as "the body of Christ" (vs. 27).

By the time he wrote his epistle to the Ephesians his thought of the church as "the body of Christ" had become crystallized, as though he were confirmed in the belief that this metaphor admirably fulfilled his purpose. But whereas in I Corinthians and in Romans (12:4-5) Christ is conceived as the whole body of which individual Christians are particular members, in Ephesians (4:15) and Colossians (2:19) the church is conceived as the "body" of which Christ is the "head." One can see at once that this later conception carries the apostle's thought a stage further. Doubtless it was already implicit in his thought as we have it set down in the present epistle. In these later epistles the suggestion of the dependence of the "body" on Christ, the head, is more strongly emphasized. Its very existence depends on him who is its ruler, savior, and sustainer. But there is also a complementary truth in the apostle's mind, and it covers his conception of the Christian church in all the phases of its development. The "body," too, has an important function to fulfill. Not only does this conception of a church

[5] Moffatt, *I Corinthians*, p. 183.

13 For by one Spirit are we all baptized into one body, whether *we be* Jews or Gen-

with Christ. 13 For by one Spirit we were all baptized into one body — Jews or

is the body of Christ, its members have been united with him in a living organism. Since all of the gifts of the Spirit are found in the one body of Christ, we are faced once more with the functional identity of the Spirit and the risen Christ (II Cor. 3:17-18).

13. The union in one body is effected through the sacraments. Baptism means dying and rising with Christ (Rom. 6:3-4) and incorporation into his body. Though Paul does not specifically mention faith here, we are not to conclude that he would hold to the

as a living organism akin to the human body suggest vitality and unity and variety. The implication is clear, and it underlines the apostle's writings, that the church exists to continue the propagation of the gospel to the whole world; that since it is animated by the spirit and life, the knowledge and wisdom, which find their source in its great "head," it is his continued incarnation in the world. Its supreme function is to perpetuate and to spread his spirit everywhere, until the whole of life becomes a like organism, illumined, inspired, controlled, and dominated by the Lord of all good life. The process is to go on until the sovereignty of the world passes into the sovereignty of God and his Christ; until, in effect, the whole world of humanity in all its aspects becomes a church (see 15:24-28). For this great conception of their significance in the life of the world, and of their part in the unfolding of the great purposes of God, the apostle is constantly preparing the Christian communities with which he has to deal and which he loves so dearly. Meantime, having dropped this germinative thought into the minds of his readers, he draws out the more immediate and practical implications in relation to the question under discussion, viz., the nature and value of various spiritual gifts.

13. *The Unity of the Body.*—We have noticed that Paul was apprehensive of any threat to the unity of the church arising from divisions among the members. The witness of a church can be nullified by a spirit of divisiveness, and the cause, so far as the witness of such a church is concerned, can all too easily be lost in its own neighborhood. Examples are all too frequent. It is not too much to say that the spirit of divisiveness is the spirit of Antichrist.

The apostle reinforces his point from two angles. The mystic unity of "the body" which is animated by the spirit of Christ transcends all distinctions of race or caste. Both **Jews** and **Greeks**, and doubtless representatives of many other races as well, were members of the church and found in their faith in Christ a unity that transcended all racialism or nationalism. The N.T. makes it abundantly plain that the Christian church is not a national church: the N.T. knows nothing of such a church. In so far as the church is national it cannot be Christian: in so far as it is Christian it transcends nationality. God reckons little of nationality or race or status in the fulfillment of his purposes. The leaders of Christendom, and the rank and file too, would do well to reflect deeply on these things. Nationalism ever presents a threat to Christianity; sometimes it even seems to compete with Christianity as an alternative religion. The church of Jesus Christ is not even international: it is supernational. As such, in terms of its faith, its program, and its spirit, it provides the sole indispensable spiritual basis for the genuine unity of a world in which scientific inventiveness, commercial, political, and economic developments proclaim with ever-increasing and ever more resonant insistence that all races and men are members one of another. The church of Jesus Christ has the vision, the ethos, and the mission that enable it to give to the whole world the spiritual and moral leadership which that world so desperately needs. Let it with faith draw upon the unlimited and freely proffered reservoir of spiritual power and resourcefulness which is offered in the abundant self-giving of God whom we have seen revealed in Jesus Christ.

In the same way the church of Jesus Christ transcends all differences of status; **slaves** and **free** are of equal value in the mystical unity of this body of Christ. There is little doubt, as has been suggested, that both classes were included in the membership of the Corinthian church. That is a great matter. The life of the church is vastly enriched by the peculiar contribution that every member can bring to the fellowship. The mystical insights of the East are needed as much as the practical temperament and achievements of the West. The church of Christ needs the tribute that culture can pay. He who gave so much deserves the very best that human achievement in any realm can lay at his feet. Could culture be finally divorced from his cause, then in his world, fashioned for the achievement of divine purposes, it could have no legitimate place. Culture is itself enriched and mellowed when baptized into the spirit of

tiles, whether *we be* bond or free; and have been all made to drink into one Spirit.

Greeks, slaves or free — and all were made to drink of one Spirit.

efficacy of baptism apart from faith. Baptism was the time of the bestowal of the Spirit, and the various gifts were received from the same source. The figure is that of a liquid poured out from which a person might drink. We see here how the language used of the Spirit shifts from personal to impersonal analogies (cf. Rom. 8:26). The unitary source from which believers receive their differing gifts leads Paul to a side remark concerning the human differences which are removed within the one body of Christ (Gal. 3:28;

Christ. So also are the insight and the experience of those who have borne the burden of labor, sorrow, and hardship needed for the enrichment of the Christian fellowship. In Paul's comprehensive thought every type is needed. All are invited; all are to be made welcome. Each is organic to the whole body, and the whole body manifests itself and its life in the various parts. In short, our conception of Christ and his church, and the purpose that church was divinely created to serve, cannot be fully comprehended or understood or visualized until all races, nations, and individuals take their proper places and play their proper parts. When "internationalism" and "humanitarian" concepts of brotherhood—many of them characterized by the spirit of Antichrist—press their claims upon humanity, the church of Christ has a great opportunity and a great message with which to match the opportunity. It is the sole classless society that does full justice to the whole nature of man—spiritual, mental, moral, and physical. And Christ is the living Spirit that animates the whole body; on him it entirely depends.

By one Spirit we were all baptized into one body . . . and all were made to drink of one Spirit (see Exeg.). The apostle reinforces his argument with a second point. He makes direct reference to his previous teaching on the nature of the sacrament, teaching which we examined in some detail. Both sacraments, baptism and the Lord's Supper, serve to emphasize the mystical unity of "the body of Christ." Baptism is a confession of faith in Christ and a definite break with the old sinful way of life. As such it gives distinctiveness to the Christian fellowship. In the Lord's Supper the "real presence" of Christ is discerned in the breaking of bread and the pouring of wine, and in the corporate unity of the fellowship which participates in the sacrament. The apostle's meaning is clear. Christ is the animating Spirit who gives life and unity to the church, and on whom it depends for all that is essential to its life and witness in the world. He is the fountainhead of the gifts of the Spirit, as he is the life of his church. The "body" is animated through and through by his indwelling Spirit, and its service and communion are therefore a corporate experience of which particular gifts are a special expression. None of these can dispense with any other, or with the "body" to which they severally and organically belong. In this way Paul again emphasizes the practical test he has already given, viz., how does the exercise of any gift contribute to the common good? In everything the essential unity of the church must be maintained.

More generally, and without seeking to drift too far from the anchor to which this particular section of exposition is secured, while Paul is undoubtedly thinking of the unity of the local church, the same considerations must surely apply to the church universal. This point has been stressed more than once, and it need not be elaborated here. But if divisiveness in respect of powers of organization or special characteristics or gifts is a deadly threat to a local church, the same would seem to hold good with regard to the witness of the Christian church everywhere. Unity can be no less essential in the church universal than in the local community. The Spirit cannot have one "mind" for the local church and a different "mind" for various churches scattered across the world. Surely his "mind" or purpose is the same for all. There is a definite place for variety. Temperaments are different and cannot be bridged. But variety, as Paul so intensely points out, is not incompatible with unity. It will be the unity in variety expressed in a fellowship of love—as he will be at pains to make clear presently—e.g., in the corporate experience of a gift which is offered to all and can be shared by all. This in the end may impress and win the world for Christ. Many types of organization are needed. None can exclude any other without stultifying its own witness. Little wonder that again and again we catch a hint of heartbreak in Paul's very language as he pens these urgent, tear-stained lines to a church that he had served so faithfully and at great cost. Once again we should ponder well the full implications of Paul's great conception of the church as "the body of Christ." Such the whole church of

14 For the body is not one member, but many.

15 If the foot shall say, Because I am not the hand, I am not of the body; is it therefore not of the body?

16 And if the ear shall say, Because I am not the eye, I am not of the body; is it therefore not of the body?

17 If the whole body *were* an eye, where *were* the hearing? If the whole *were* hearing, where *were* the smelling?

18 But now hath God set the members every one of them in the body, as it hath pleased him.

14 For the body does not consist of one
member but of many. 15 If the foot should
say, "Because I am not a hand, I do not
belong to the body," that would not make
it any less a part of the body. 16 And if the
ear should say, "Because I am not an eye, I
do not belong to the body," that would
not make it any less a part of the body.
17 If the whole body were an eye, where
would be the hearing? If the whole body
were an ear, where would be the sense of
smell? 18 But as it is, God arranged the
organs in the body, each one of them, as

Col. 3:11). The "drinking" may also be related to the Lord's Supper (cf. 10:3), though it may be nothing more than a figure for the reception of the Spirit (John 7:37-39).

14. A human **body** needs all of its organs; each of these serves the function for which it is designed. The whole body is weakened if any part is lost, for no other organ can completely take the place of the one that is lost. The same is true of the church and its various members. Each has an indispensable function without which the body (i.e., person) is handicapped. Therefore each member should honor the other, not in spite of varied gifts, but because of these differences. Here speaks a genuine catholicity that does not seek uniformity in the life of the church, but a unity in diversity. Though the gifts differ, there is no need to divide on the basis of these varieties. There is all the greater need to keep the members together, for each requires the complement of the other.

15-21. Foot, hand, ear, and **eye** are mentioned in succession to show that a body would be crippled by the loss of any one. A body which consisted of only one organ would not be a body at all. That Paul is thinking functionally—though he uses no word

---

Christ must in the end become if it is to fulfill its mission. Religion is the serious business of the human race. Let all who carry the Christian treasure in earthen vessels be careful how it is handled.

14-26. ***Illustration from the Human Organism.***—Further emphasis is given in these verses to the apostle's conception of the organic unity of the church. The human organism presents a unity with a variety of parts, all of them organically and vitally related to the whole and all of them in various ways serving one another. The foot serves the hand (vs. 15), and the ear serves the eye (vs. 16); so do all the other organs serve one another. God has so ordained it. **But as it is, God arranged the organs in the body, each one of them, as he chose.** How grotesque it would be if the whole body had been resolved into a single organ (vs. 19). No, the various organs and parts of the body are indissolubly related to one another and are of service to one another. Moreover, and this is important for the apostle's purpose, **The parts of the body which seem to be weaker are indispensable, and those parts of the body which we think less honorable we invest with the greater honor, and our unpresentable parts are treated with greater modesty, which our more presentable parts do not require** (see Exeg.). Paul here by implication utters his last warning in the present letter against any tendency in the church fellowship that would create disunity. Doubtless such is the frailty of human nature that some "gifts" were more highly esteemed than others. Those who, according to this attitude, were less well endowed probably felt that as relatively humble members of the community they did not greatly count, and for any major purpose would not be missed should they fall out. There may have been a tendency for those who possessed the more spectacular gifts to give themselves airs and to assume powers of authority and leadership for which they may not otherwise have been especially fitted. Certainly in giving themselves airs they demonstrated their spiritual unfitness for the posts of true leadership. They were in danger of forgetting their Master, who came to be "servant of all." Paul, in his use of this analogy, seeks to redress the balance. Every part is vital to the smooth and effective working of the human organism. As we know even better than

19 And if they were all one member, where *were* the body?

20 But now *are they* many members, yet but one body.

21 And the eye cannot say unto the hand, I have no need of thee: nor again the head to the feet, I have no need of you.

22 Nay, much more those members of the body, which seem to be more feeble, are necessary:

23 And those *members* of the body, which we think to be less honorable, upon these we bestow more abundant honor; and our uncomely *parts* have more abundant comeliness.

he chose. 19 If all were a single organ,
where would the body be? 20 As it is, there
are many parts, yet one body. 21 The eye
cannot say to the hand, "I have no need of
you," nor again the head to the feet, "I
have no need of you." 22 On the contrary,
the parts of the body which seem to be
weaker are indispensable, 23 and those parts
of the body which we think less honorable
we invest with the greater honor, and our
unpresentable parts are treated with greater

---

which could be translated by such a modern term—is seen by the fact that he speaks of **the sense of smell** instead of the nose. Though man has been exceedingly ingenious in providing substitutes for organs lost in war casualties, that provision only underscores Paul's emphasis on the indispensability of all the parts.

22-26. The organs mentioned thus far serve the most prominent functions. But Paul sees another aspect of his analogy worth stressing—the proper evaluation of the weaker and humbler members of the church. As a matter of fact, he has constructed his figure more for the sake of the application he is to make than because of any situation which would actually arise. What **foot**—if we could conceive of a foot thinking or speaking for itself—would ever imagine that it did not belong to the body because it was not a hand? Paul really has in mind to reassure those who did not possess the gift of tongues that they were not therefore outside the body of Christ. He calls attention to our use of clothing. The more attractive parts of the body, such as the face, are left unadorned. The other parts we cover with what is thought to be something more attractive. From this Paul draws the conclusion that we honor most the least spectacular. He does not

---

he knew, obscure glands do fulfill most important functions. So it is in the Christian church. It is not necessarily the greatly talented whose service will rank the highest with God. Christ sets great store by a "cup of cold water" given in his name. Such is a service that may be rendered by all. A well-known Scottish minister of a bygone generation was wont to illumine his sermons with apt illustrations. One day he recounted to his congregation one of his dreams. He had dreamed that he died, and naturally had presented himself at the pearly gates of heaven. But to his dismay Peter denied him admission until he presented his credentials. The old man told of the sermons he had preached, but Peter said that no one had heard them in heaven. He spoke of his service to his city and of his pastoral work, a work that had made him beloved by multitudes of people. Even that was unknown in heaven. As in his despair he was about to turn away from the gates, Peter said, "Stay a moment and tell me this. Are you the man who fed the sparrows?" "Yes," was the reply, "what has that to do with it?" "Come away in," said Peter, "the Master of the sparrows wants to thank you." That tale illustrates the point which holds good for our day as well as Paul's. Great services may indicate our talents and capacities, but small services indicate the depth and range of our consecration, and Christ wants that. To the church at Corinth Paul writes that none shall despise a fellow member because his gifts are of a less dramatic or striking order than those of other members of the community. Nor let such a one think less of his gift, or of himself, than he should. The least may rank the greatest in the sight of God. All the gifts are gifts of his Spirit; all are indispensable for the attainment of his purposes. There is a place in life for candles as well as stars. How dark the world's darkness would become were all the lesser lights to be quenched! Let each then esteem the other, whatever his gift; so far as the Christian community is concerned, every gift is indispensable to its life. The valuation of any gift and its use is a matter for God. **God has so adjusted the body, giving the greater honor to the in-**

24 For our comely *parts* have no need: but God hath tempered the body together, having given more abundant honor to that *part* which lacked:

25 That there should be no schism in the body; but *that* the members should have the same care one for another.

26 And whether one member suffer, all the members suffer with it; or one member be honored, all the members rejoice with it.

27 Now ye are the body of Christ, and members in particular.

modesty, 24 which our more presentable parts do not require. But God has so adjusted the body, giving the greater honor to the inferior part, 25 that there may be no discord in the body, but that the members may have the same care for one another.
26 If one member suffers, all suffer together; if one member is honored, all rejoice together.

27 Now you are the body of Christ and

---

mean that some gifts should be hidden under a bushel measure, but that the more spectacular are not on that account the more honored. By **honor** (vs. 23) Paul of course means the clothing, which indicates at the same time our **modesty. Schism** (KJV) is not a very happy rendering in vs. 25; for the apostle was not thinking of the divisions discussed earlier in the letter, but of the jealousies resulting from the overevaluation of certain gifts. Instead of jealousy and mistrust, there should be mutual respect and helpfulness within the church. This leads to the final conclusion from the analogy. An injury to one organ of the body affects the entire organism. If the church really is a body, the body of Christ, the same will be true among its members. The sorrows of one member will be the sorrows of all; the joys of one will be the joys of all. When Paul comes to discuss the offering for the Jerusalem saints (16:1-4), he will extend this beyond the local community. "Organic union" did not mean for Paul legislating for the life of others, but feeling with them so completely as to share their experience.

d) The Apostolic Ministry (12:27-31*a*)

27. After summing up the meaning of his highly elaborated analogy, Paul returns to the place of spiritual gifts in the leadership of the church. This passage gives our earliest description of the Christian ministry. Though the apostle wrote in the interest of unity, what he wrote has been subjected to divisive, confessional interpretations. His actual words are entirely clear; the differences of opinion lie in the relationship between what

---

ferior part, that there may be no discord in the body, but that the members may have the same care for one another (see Exeg., vss. 22-26).

A further attribute of the vital organic relationship of the parts to the whole is seen in the fact that **if one member** [of the body] **suffers, all suffer together; if one member is honored, all rejoice together.** How true! If an individual's digestion is out of condition, he is out of condition. If his foot suffers an injury, his consciousness is full of the pain ensuing. A threat to a part is a threat to the whole. Sickness and health concern the entire organism. So it is with the church of Christ, local and universal. Let us rejoice with any of our brethren in any spiritual triumph that they have experienced. Let us make the care of each of our churches the concern of all. True, each should play a full part. As Paul wrote to the church in Galatia: "But let each one test his own work, and then his reason to boast will be in himself alone and not in his neighbor. For each man will have to bear his own load" (Gal. 6:4-5). But he also wrote to the same church, "Bear one another's burdens, and so fulfill the law of Christ" (Gal. 6:2).

27-31*a*. *Application of the Foregoing to the Life of the Church.*—Is there a suggestion here of a rudimentary church organization in respect of the various services that members may render their community? There is as yet no mention of bishops or presbyters or deacons, yet there can be little doubt that some kind of order must have been emerging in the developing life of the church. Paul, in view of what he has just said, is certainly not setting up a hierarchy. A monarchical system seems to have no place in the N.T. conception of the church of Christ (cf. Exeg., vss. 27, 28). The impression left on the minds of the apostles by a Master who on

28 And God hath set some in the church, first apostles, secondarily prophets, thirdly teachers, after that miracles, then gifts of healings, helps, governments, diversities of tongues.

individually members of it. 28 And God has appointed in the church first apostles, second prophets, third teachers, then workers of miracles, then healers, helpers, administrators, speakers in various kinds of

---

he says here and our later information about the ministries of the church. In Rom. 12:6-8, Paul is even more functional in his discussion of these ministries, and in neither passage does he use any of the later titles for offices in the church.

28. The order in which the ministries are named is deliberate: the **apostles** have received the highest gift and the speakers in **tongues** the lowest. This gradation in rank is in formal contradiction to what has been said earlier in the chapter about the common source and equal quality of all gifts. We may also inquire how one may expect higher gifts simply by earnestly desiring them (vs. 31). If my gift is that of healing rather than of teaching, should I manifest dissatisfaction by wanting another? Paul did not have any such problem in mind. He is only indicating that speakers in tongues, instead of being excessively proud of their fluency, should desire a gift that served more directly for the upbuilding of the church. Paul mentions three types of such service: the teaching work, service to physical needs, and administration. Each of the first two types is divided into three groups; the third type is not differentiated. The N.T. evidence concerning these different ministries will be summarized briefly.

Apostles were those sent out by the risen Christ as his representatives (cf. 1:1; 9:1). The term ἀπόστολος would presumably be a natural word to designate "one sent"; but in fact it is almost never found in Greek usage before the Christian Era. Judaism recognized the practice of sending on various missions an accredited representative or *shālîaḥ*. Though this affords a certain parallel to the Christian apostles, the differences are even more important. Jewish missionaries were never called by the name *shālîaḥ,* nor was a prophet ever spoken of as *shālîaḥ* of God. It is the distinguishing mark of the apostles of Jesus that God had so designated them, not that they had been chosen by the community (as the Sanhedrin sent out their messengers). Apostles were commissioned to witness to the gospel and to win men to allegiance. They were related to the whole church and not simply to a single community. As Christ's messengers they had special authority on earth, but there is nothing in the institution of the *shālîaḥ* which provided any precedent for the idea that they could delegate their authority in turn to others.

Twelve disciples had been chosen by Jesus as an inner group and as rulers over the twelve tribes in the new age (Mark 3:13-19; Matt. 19:28). Though these made a preaching tour during the lifetime of Jesus, the term apostle referred primarily to those sent out by the risen Christ. In addition to the twelve, James (Gal. 1:19), Barnabas (I Cor. 9:6), Andronicus and Junias (Rom. 16:7), and others (II Cor. 8:23) are designated by this title. From the Didache (11:3 ff.) we know that into the second century there were wandering preachers who were called "apostles." In Acts 1–5 the term seems to be confined to the twelve and that became the later usage.

Prophets. For Judaism the Spirit was no longer given since the closing of the canon of the prophets. But within the church there was a new outburst of prophecy. In Acts we meet prophets, especially in connection with the early communities (Acts 11:27; 13:1; 15:32; 21:10). But the church at Corinth was also accustomed to this speaking in the Spirit. Though their message was often eschatological, these prophets were bearers of

---

the night in which he was betrayed girded himself with a towel and washed their feet was still too vivid for such a departure from his spirit and example. Yet every organ of the body has its own function, and no organ is meant or devised to undertake the functions of another.

For the well-being of the entire church there were bound to be diversities of gifts and therefore of functions. Recognition is to be accorded to these as such. To **apostles** is given the duty of transmitting the traditions of the faith (see 11:2). This will always be necessary and will

29 *Are* all apostles? *are* all prophets? *are* all teachers? *are* all workers of miracles?
30 Have all the gifts of healing? do all speak with tongues? do all interpret?

tongues.
29 Are all apostles? Are all prophets? Are all teachers? Do all work miracles?
30 Do all possess gifts of healing? Do all

---

divine revelation rather than soothsayers. In Did. 11:7 ff. it is shown that the order persisted into the second century, and in connection with the apostles. The revival of prophecy in the early church marked the presence of the Spirit in their midst.

Teachers are joined with prophets in Acts 13:1 and elsewhere are referred to in the primitive church (Jas. 3:1; Heb. 5:12; etc.). This term is a favorite designation of Jesus in the Synoptic tradition, and of course could be applied to anyone who gave instruction of any kind. We do not know the exact nature of the teacher's work in a congregation like the one at Corinth. Possibly he was to train members in the O.T.; possibly he was expected to transmit the tradition about Jesus; possibly he was to give other types of instruction related to the Christian message. Though he did not speak in ecstasy, the teacher was just as much a Spirit-endowed minister as those with more spectacular gifts (cf. Acts 6:10; 7:55).

It is unnecessary to elaborate further on the three groups of "social workers"—**workers of miracles, then healers, helpers.** The gospel ministered to physical health from the very beginning. After the preaching of the gospel came practical service to various human needs. This should be the order of emphasis within the church. (See the section on "Unction" in the Intro. to James, Vol. XII.)

Administrators (RSV) or **governments** (KJV) are as vague and undefined as one could imagine. In I Thess. 5:12 they are simply called "those . . . over you." Possibly the "pastor" (shepherd) in Eph. 4:11 is a more technical term for one carrying the same responsibility. Though Acts knows of elders in churches founded by Paul in Asia Minor (Acts 14:23; 20:17), the term is never used by Paul himself in any extant letter. "Bishops and deacons" are mentioned in Phil. 1:1, probably because these were finance officials. Unquestionably there were administrative responsibilities which had to be cared for from the first, but Paul does not appeal to these officials to assume authority in the disciplinary problems which he raises. He appeals directly to the church as a whole. Administrators are definitely subordinated to the teaching and serving functions of the church.

No person possessed all of these gifts, and there was no endowment in which all shared. God had provided a division of labor and a distinction of gifts. But before Paul takes up the contrast between prophecy and tongues, he turns to a theme in connection with which such a contrast does not apply: **love** is a gift which all may share. This **more**

---

carry the requisite authority. To **prophets** is given the task of revealing the deeper meanings of the traditions as these are involved in the gospel and as they are to be applied to the life and trend of the times. **Teachers** are necessary for instruction in the faith, that sound doctrine may be safeguarded from insidious heresies. The practical power of the faith is to be demonstrated through **workers of miracles** and **healers.** There are **helpers** who are also indispensable to the well-being of the community. Someone must serve tables and look after finance and attend to details of routine. As the work develops, so does the call come for those who are gifted **administrators** (cf. Exeg.). Some speak **in various kinds of tongues.** All are needed. Were there only one order of workers, what helpful purpose could they serve? Let there be among the Corinthian Christians, and in every Christian church in any age, clear recognition of the simple truth that in such a divinely appointed organism as the body of Christ, for its vitality and its effective witness, a variety of functions is required. Let each respect the gift the other brings, no matter what it is. All are essential and all are vitally necessary to each other. The keynotes must always be unity and fellowship, and a deep, abiding realization of the significant and overriding truth that "all these are inspired by one and the same Spirit, who apportions to each one individually as he wills" (vs. 11). Given the sincere and humble acknowledgment on the part of each and all Christian believers of these

31 But covet earnestly the best gifts: and yet show I unto you a more excellent way.

speak with tongues? Do all interpret? 31 But earnestly desire the higher gifts.

And I will show you a still more excellent way.

---

excellent way is open to everyone. **Love** is as supernatural as any other gift, and the one which truly builds up the community (cf. 8:1).

2. The Way of Love (12:31*b*–13:13)

This celebrated chapter is the high point in Paul's description of the Christian life. It is so perfect a literary production that many have thought it unlikely that Paul could have dictated it while writing a mere letter. He must have composed it earlier and inserted it by means of the connecting sentences, 12:31*b* and 14:1*a*. But on closer examination it is seen that almost every word in the chapter has been chosen with this particular situation at Corinth in mind. Though the passage is often referred to as a psalm of love, it is not written in meter. The mood is instructive fully as much as lyrical. Paul sets forth the **love** without which the community cannot be built up.

What did Paul mean by ἀγάπη—**charity** (KJV), **love** (RSV)? Was it man's love for God or for fellow men? Since the studies of this word by James Moffatt in *Love in the New Testament* (London: Hodder & Stoughton, 1929) and Anders Nygren in *Agape and Eros* (London: Society for Promoting Christian Knowledge, 1932), there can be no

---

sublime and sobering truths, the church of Christ will move on to the fulfillment of God's purposes in the whole world. Nothing can stop such a church. The stars in their courses are fighting for it.

31. ***But Earnestly Desire the Higher Gifts.***— Once again the apostle indicates his happiness at the rich endowment of the church with so many gifts. These are a sign of vitality, and they should be exercised within the church for the benefit of the "body" as a whole, as well as for the well-being of those who are so endowed. It is as legitimate in Paul's view to desire and to develop a gift for prophecy, or for healing, or for the interpretation of Christian truth and experience as to develop one's gift for music or art or science. One might add that it is a Christian duty to develop any power or capacity with which we have been endowed, if as a consequence the life and witness of the church are enriched. The law of atrophy through disuse applies to the more strictly spiritual qualities and powers as well as to other realms of mental and physical endowment. Let every member of the church seek to be the best he can be, to acquire the finest equipment within his power, for the sake of the cause with which he is identified. Scholarship is needed in the church of Christ. Let no one despise it or belittle it. We are invited to believe in God with all our minds as well as with all our hearts. Gifts in the realm of art are needed. Let churches be as beautiful and as much cared for as the homes in which we dwell or as other public buildings. It is a fallacy to say that buildings dedicated to the cause of Christ should be plain and barnlike because our fathers worshiped in such places. They had no choice; we have! The Master deserves the best we can bring to him. Let us **earnestly desire the higher gifts,** not for our own self-glorification, but for his sake.

And I will show you a still more excellent way (cf. Exeg., 13:1-3). Now the apostle comes to the point that he has had in mind from the very beginning of his letter. It is that none of the other gifts so greatly desired and treasured can be truly effective unless and until they are inspired and illumined by the spirit of love. This is the **more excellent way.** Nothing else can take its place; it is better than tongues, better than prophecy or philanthropy or courage; it marks that grace of Christ to which he refers in his opening salutation (1:3). It is the grace that will achieve unity of mind, heart, and spirit, and will heal all the divisions in the church. Given its full scope, it will heal all the divisions between mankind throughout the world.

12:31*b*–14:1*a*. ***The More Excellent Way.***— Here we enter upon one of the best-known and best-beloved passages of Scripture. Well has this thirteenth chapter of I Corinthians been entitled "The Hymn of Love." Incidentally, it reveals the great apostle in a somewhat new light. It has been usual to regard Paul as the preacher of faith, and John as the preacher of love. Faith is one of the key words in Paul's writings, and "justification by faith" is the

doubt what the apostle had in mind. Paul never quotes what the Gospels give as the first commandment, and rarely speaks of love for God. In fact, he rarely expresses any object for the verb. He speaks simply of ἀγάπη. In contrast, he never uses ἔρως, which expressed the love of the adorable object, or φιλία, which means essentially "friendship." Into the less common word ἀγάπη early Christian experience poured the richness of the central revelation that had come to them. God's unmerited grace had been bestowed on them in Christ. This was *love,* not affection for an adorable object, but the undeserved grace which they had received. Man could not return this to God; he could only respond to God's love by loving his fellow men in the same way.

The English rendition has had a strange history. Influenced by the Latin *caritas,* Wycliffe had used **charity** in all cases, and in this he was followed by the Roman Catholic translators. Tyndale used the Anglo-Saxon word **love,** and was followed in this by Cranmer and the Geneva Bible. Roman theological influence led to long debates through the sixteenth century. The KJV made a curious compromise. Though it retained the

---

watchword and banner he gave to the reforming movement which found its outstanding exponent in Martin Luther. Love is one of the key words of the Gospel and Epistles of John. Doubtless it is true that Paul does emphasize faith, and John does emphasize love; but neither emphasizes the one spiritual quality to the exclusion of the other. John writes, "For whatever is born of God overcomes the world; and this is the victory that overcomes the world, our faith" (I John 5:4); while Paul writes, "Love does no wrong to a neighbor; therefore love is the fulfilling of the law" (Rom. 13:10). We need not be surprised, then, that in this letter written by Paul to a dearly beloved church, beloved despite all its blemishes, we should find one of the noblest eulogies of Christian love that has ever been penned. Nor should we miss the point that the preacher of faith insists that love is supreme.

Again, we see still more clearly what Paul has had in mind from the very outset, viz., the spiritual unity and quality of the Christian fellowship in Corinth. We must keep in mind that the word used by Paul and translated "love" in this chapter is *agapē,* which was not the common name or usual word for love in those days, particularly so in Corinth. Nor is it found in classical Greek writings, although the verb is sometimes used. The fact seems to be that the common word used for love (*eros*) was associated with sensual passion. In one way it was a daring thing for Paul to write about love at all to these people, for Corinth was reckoned to be one of the most vice-ridden and sensual cities in the ancient world. The apostle therefore uses a new word to convey his meaning. The word *agapē* signifies moral love; there is a hint of austerity in it. It conveys the idea of good will, of brotherliness, of friendship. There is an element of reverence in it, as indicating what man's attitude toward God and his fellow men ought to be. The love of which the apostle writes has nothing whatever to do with the senses or the instincts; it is an intellectual, moral, and spiritual quality; and as Paul uses it in this chapter it admirably fulfills his purpose in writing the epistle (cf. Exeg., 12:31*b*–13:13).

In Paul's view all the churches can and ought to be regarded first and foremost as a new order of friends and as a great experiment in friendship. In that sense every epistle he wrote can be rightly understood only as an essay in friendship and as intended to foster the spirit of Christian friendship in the various communities. The members were to be characterized by their deep sense of the spiritual bond that united them in faith and loyalty and love to their Lord and to one another. This spirit and bond were intended to draw the Christian believer out of the loneliness and isolation of a self-centered life into a unity with Christ and with fellow believers that nothing in life or death could ever destroy (see Rom. 8:38-39). Here he is pleading, as so often before in all his contacts with the churches, for a great new order of friendship that will fufill the intention of its Founder, an order of friendship such as the world has never conceived (see John 15:12-15). He saw clearly what a glorious consummation such a church could bring to a tragic and desperately needy world, and what a marvelous mission it might sustain; and so he was deeply conscious of the tragic contrast between his Christ-inspired ideal for the churches and the actual condition with which he had to deal, not only in the world, but in the church itself. Critics of organized religion, with all their professed admiration for the so-called simplicity and directness of the gospel preached in Galilee, could have told Paul nothing. He was well aware of the defects and blemishes of the Christian communities, none more so. But unlike the critics, modern as well as ancient, he refused to stand apart from these poor parodies of churches. Instead of that, he

13 Though I speak with the tongues of men and of angels, and have not charity, I am become *as* sounding brass, or a tinkling cymbal.

13 If I speak in the tongues of men and of angels, but have not love, I am a noisy gong or a clanging cymbal.

---

noun **love** in forty-eight passages in Paul, and always used this verb, in twelve instances (half of them in this chapter) it inconsistently translated the noun as **charity.** Many Christians who would be quite surprised to hear, "Who shall separate us from the charity of Christ," still feel that **charity** is desirable in this chapter. But that obscures the unity of Paul's conception of ἀγάπη. What he is talking about is not the human quality of benevolence, but the divine graciousness revealed in Christ. It is quite true that the English word **love** has many lower associations. *Agapē* is not to be confused with sensual attraction for the opposite sex. It is much more than the sentimentality which binds together those who are kin or of kindred interests. The "mutuality" which our pragmatists recommend falls short of *agapē;* for the height of this love is love for enemies, which is anything but an experience of mutuality. *Agapē* is another kind of love which roots in the undeserved goodness men have received in Christ.

The chapter falls into three clearly defined sections: (*a*) the superiority of love, vss. 1-3; (*b*) the nature of love, vss. 4-7; (*c*) the permanence of love, vss. 8-13. In the first and last of these Paul contrasts love with tongues, prophecy, and knowledge. After vs. 1 not a single descriptive adjective is used in the Greek. Paul uses verbs, for love is dynamic and active, not static. It is natural to feel that some person must have sat for this portrait. Is it not the Christ whom they are to imitate through the revelation of his Spirit in the apostle?

a) The Superiority of Love (13:1-3)

13:1. The **tongues** are those discussed throughout ch. 14. Paul knows two kinds, those **of men** and those **of angels** (Rev. 14:2-3; II Cor. 12:4), though this may simply be

---

carried them on his heart until it broke. To the end he went on loving them, as his Master did, and to the end he proclaimed with passion the supreme gift of the Spirit in which all alike might share if they so desired. Paul knew, long before Browning, that

> . . . life, with all it yields of joy and woe,
> And hope and fear (believe the aged friend),
> Is just our chance o' the prize of learning love,
> How love might be, hath been indeed, and is.[6]

In the greater part of the epistle we see the apostle unraveling, patiently, knot after knot in the tangled skein that sundry well-meaning and well-intentioned but misguided persons had made. We must also assume that sundry mischief-makers had also been at work. We have seen how he has straightened out some of these confused issues, and how with consummate genius he uses the local circumstance to illustrate an eternal truth. Even in this marvelous eulogy of love he stops to brush firmly aside various forms of the sickly sentimentality that so often masquerades as love; the affected outlook and spirit that describes itself as love when

[6] "A Death in the Desert."

all the time it is concentrated on its own selfish ends. But at last he makes himself quite clear, though he has to fall back on negatives to do it.

> Oh could I tell ye surely would believe it!
> Oh could I only say what I have seen!
> How should I tell or how can ye receive it,
> How, till he bringeth you where I have been?[7]

Little wonder that Paul is so enraptured by his theme that his very language, exalted as it is by high emotion, falls into a certain rhythmic pattern. His thought swings between the pettiness of the members of the church who are so contentious in their partisanship and so jealous of the relative value of such gifts as they possess, and the greatness of the love he celebrates as the supreme quality and method of such a spiritual fellowship as the church was meant to be. Here is the greatest gift of all. It is the very bond of unity that makes them a church, and it is within the power of every member to share in it. Moreover, lacking this supreme gift, other virtues and gifts must inevitably fail to accomplish the spiritual purpose for which they were given. No one after perusing such a pas-

[7] F. W. H. Myers, *Saint Paul.*

a rhetorical way of saying all possible tongues. It would appear from this that those who prided themselves on speaking eloquently in **tongues** imagined that they were speaking the language of angels. Paul is not condemning "tongues" outright, but he insists that they are valueless without **love,** because in themselves they are only a jangle of sound.

---

sage should be under any misapprehension as to the nature of Christian love. The supreme idea is to practice it in all the relationships of life and especially in the Christian community itself.

13:1. *Love as the Bond of Unity.*—Paul makes it clear, as we have seen, that love will fructify the various gifts that the members of the church possess, and at the same time will deepen their fellowship one with another and with Christ, who is the life of the church. The same is true in its larger context, and surely that larger context must also have been in the mind of the greatest of all Christian missionaries. This section of the letter written to these Corinthians applies just as truly to all the nations of the world. For each nation has its own peculiar contribution to make. By its history and tradition, by its geographical location and its characteristic temperament as developed by its environment, every nation possesses its particular gift. The Hebrews had developed wonderful insight into the nature and purpose of Almighty God. This is the gift that they have brought and can still bring to the life and true progress of mankind. The Greeks have raised all the questions that tease the human mind and have suggested many of the answers; they had also supremely their sense of the beautiful, a great spiritual value, to give to the world. France too has her sense of beauty, and her characteristic capacity for clear logical thought. Rome was endowed with a marvelous sense of law and order. Great Britain has a vast store of accumulated political experience and wisdom; Russia, a sense of community which an ever-smaller world must develop if mankind is ever to learn the art of living together. The United States of America has demonstrated how various peoples gathered from every quarter of the globe can achieve, first, nationhood, and then a sense of international mission and responsibility. Every nation and race has its gift to bring. We are "members one of another." Let none covet the other's gift or despise it. All are needed. But to give full effect to the contribution that each can bring, something more is required. Long ago Paul, following closely the mind and life of his Lord, saw it clearly and set it down. It is the way of love, of true brotherhood, of co-operative fellowship and friendship. In that sense he is no impractical dreamer; he is many years ahead of our times. He was one of the greatest and most practical statesmen the world has ever had. As someone has said, "He had a massive and majestic intellect, he had a disengaged heart, he never strove for party, he had a vision that was imperial of the world." Every gift that any nation possesses will be enriched both in its value for its own people and for the whole human race when at long last the rulers of nations and their peoples realize that the way of Christ is the **more excellent way**—the way of love. There is no worth-while quality in national or individual life that will not be marvelously enhanced when it is illumined and inspired by that same spirit which is at the very Heart of reality itself—the spirit of Christian love. To cultivate talents and powers is a good thing; best of all is to cultivate the spirit of Christian love. Love succeeds where all else fails.

If I speak in the tongues of men and of angels, but have not love, I am a noisy gong or a clanging cymbal. Notice again, not for the first time, the exquisite courtesy of this greathearted Christian gentleman in the use he makes of the first person singular in these opening verses. If he is by implication to deal with certain defects of spirit and fellowship in the church, he will use himself as an illustration. There is pastoral value in Paul's method. For one thing, it disarms possible resistance on the part of the person or persons to whom his words are most likely to apply, since the reference is to the apostle himself. But even more, it illustrates his sense of unity and identity with his Christian brethren to whom the letter is addressed. His awareness of the organic unity of a body where all the members suffer with each goes very deep. That is the true pastoral touch. Congregations neither understand nor love Olympian ministers; but the pastoral touch which identifies ministers with people always tells.

Love is the antithesis of self-importance or self-display. One of the temptations—and it is a very human trait—of the Corinthians was to use certain gifts in an ostentatious manner; this gave rise to faction and jealousy. Some gifts are more spectacular and dramatic than others. Eloquence is one; speaking with tongues, as we have seen, was another. These were greatly coveted gifts. To speak with tongues, even though the speaker was unintelligible to himself and to his audience—unless someone was present who possessed the gift of interpretation—was considered a high mark of the divine presence and favor (cf. Exeg.). It is not necessary

2 And though I have *the gift of* prophecy, and understand all mysteries, and all knowledge; and though I have all faith, so

2 And if I have prophetic powers, and understand all mysteries and all knowledge,

---

For a comparison the apostle turns to the temple worship, where the **gong** and **cymbal** were struck (Ps. 150:5). The point of similarity did not lie in the loudness (though **tinkling** is an inappropriate adjective to describe the sound of a cymbal) or in the repetition. The sound of gong and cymbal is without melody; speaking in tongues is equally without meaning.

2. Seldom in the N.T. is prophecy criticized (cf. Matt. 7:22); but here we are told that in the absence of love it gives no distinction. **Mysteries** (see 2:6-16) and **knowledge**

---

to enlarge on this point, as Paul deals with it more completely later on (ch. 14). These ecstatic utterances had little value so far as the edification of the church was concerned. The more interesting point is the suggestion of eloquence in the phrase **tongues . . . of angels.** Eloquence is a great gift, and he who possesses it has great power over the mind and imagination of his fellows. By the skilled use of it he can move and inspire, can calm or arouse, persuade and convict, his hearers. Whole nations have been stirred and excited to action by eloquent speech. It can evoke the noblest and the most depraved passions of the human spirit. From the earliest times until now, history has provided illustrations of all these effects of human eloquence. The noblest eloquence of all is that which is concerned with the sacred things of religious faith. It is a great and yet a dangerous gift. Paul was well aware both of the danger and of the finer possibilities involved in its possession. He knew that it must be inspired and disciplined by the spirit of Christian love if it is to be put to its noblest use. In effect, he says that there is no real eloquence unless it is so inspired.

True eloquence cannot be taught by the schools. All that the schools of elocution can teach is the technique of good and persuasive speech. But such speech is uninspiring unless there is in it and behind it the passion and conviction of a man who is in love with his theme and who is possessed and enthralled by it. Great command of speech which lacks the fire of passion and conviction and the moving power of love may be marked by clever epigrams and finely spun sentences, but its final impact is deficient in power, dull and unconvincing. That is why many a speech replete with every literary grace yet leaves the hearers indifferent, while the far less polished utterance of a speaker impassioned by love of his subject can shake the hearts of those to whom it is uttered. Too many, even among those who speak of sacred things, convey the impression that they are the masters of their subject and have it under complete control. Great eloquence, in the sense intended here, is the mark of a speech delivered by one who is mastered by his subject, and who is its instrument in the proclamation of its truth.

The Corinthians coveted this gift of eloquence both because of its undoubted power and because of its opportunity for self-display. Paul thought such speech unworthy to deal with the great matters pertaining to the Christian faith. It was the mark of a man in love with himself rather than with his subject. It was of as little value as the booming of a gong or the clanging of a cymbal. The very words the apostle uses suggest the sound of these instruments. What is essential to great and moving speech? What was the open secret of Paul's power to move men either to conversion or to fierce antagonism? Later on he writes, "The love of Christ controls us" (II Cor. 5:14). Is not that part of the secret? Other qualities are helpful, indeed highly valuable: gifts of words, ability to state a good case, capacity for creating interest; but it is vital that those who listen should have the conviction conveyed to them that the speaker is in love with his theme.

2. ***Prophetic Powers and Faith.***—These two gifts of prophecy and faith may be taken together. Paul seemingly ranks the gift of prophecy very high (14:3-5), and it is not the idea of prediction that he has chiefly in mind. Prophecy implies insight into spiritual truth; it involves the understanding of divine mysteries, and also genuine knowledge of the traditions and principles of the Christian faith. Paul adds to prophecy so conceived the faith that can **remove mountains** (cf. Exeg.); yet he dismisses them as of little value if love is lacking in the prophet and man of faith. He is not depreciating the gifts; they are of great significance and spiritual worth. The use to which they are put may be of help and comfort to those who listen to the prophecy, and to whom the traditions and principles of the faith are taught. The faith of the prophet has its own inspiration, and may serve to strengthen other members of the fellow-

that I could remove mountains, and have not charity, I am nothing.

3 And though I bestow all my goods to feed *the poor,* and though I give my body to be burned, and have not charity, it profiteth me nothing.

and if I have all faith, so as to remove mountains, but have not love, I am nothing. 3 If I give away all I have, and if I deliver my body to be burned,[r] but have not love, I gain nothing.

[r] Other ancient authorities read *body that I may glory.*

(see 8:1-13) have already been discussed at some length; Paul asserts once more the superiority of love to them. As indicated under 12:9, the **faith** that is spoken of is not the reception of the gospel, but miracle-working trust in God. When Paul describes this in terms of moving **mountains,** it is hardly possible to deny that he is dependent on the word of Jesus (Mark 11:23; Matt. 17:20). Though faith should work wonders, unless **love** provides the motive, there is nothing but external display.

3. In his catalogue of gifts Paul has moved from verbal displays toward expressions of active good will. Like Jesus (Matt. 6:2-4), the apostle insists that almsgiving is not a virtue unless performed from the most worthy motive. The Greek verb ψωμίζω means to feed by putting little bits into the mouth. The KJV kept something of the literal figure in the translation **bestow all my goods to feed the poor.** Paul simply means getting rid of one's possessions. There is nothing actually said about doing it for the poor. What he is condemning is the ascetic attitude which exalts poverty as a virtue in itself.

In the next clause there is an important textual variant. Many of our best MSS read καυχήσομαι instead of καυθήσομαι; it is read in the margin of the ARV and the RSV, and is adopted by Goodspeed when he renders, "Even if I . . . give myself up, but do it in pride, not love." The word is usually translated "boast" and is a favorite with the apostle, occurring in his letters as a noun or verb almost fifty times. Those who adopt

ship; but if love is lacking, the prophet himself counts for nothing: **I am nothing.** Paul is underlining a sobering truth for these impulsive and sensation-loving Corinthians, viz., that gifts count little with God, while character means much. Many a gifted individual has lacked character. God cares for character. Part of an adequate understanding of this ambiguous and challenging world in which our lives are set is that God, who created it and has ordained that we shall live out our lives here, cares far more for our character than for our comfort. He is not concerned to make life easy for any of us; he is concerned to make us great. But as the apostle points out, there is no real greatness of character without love. The Corinthians were placing the highest values on the wrong things. The gift matters less than the manner of man who possesses it. If he is without love, he is nothing! Is there an echo here of one of the more somber of the sayings of Jesus? (See Matt. 7:21-23.) As someone has said, "To call Jesus 'Lord' is orthodoxy; to call him 'Lord, Lord' is piety; but if those who do so lack his spirit of love, he will disown them." "I never knew you; depart from me, you evil-doers." Loveless faith and loveless prophecy account for some of the more tragic pages in the Christian story through the ages. It has burned so-called heretics; it has stultified the sincere quest for truth; it has often been contentious and embittered; and it has often issued in the denial of Christian brotherhood to fellow believers. Character, rather than gifts, counts with God. The warning was salutary; for the Corinthian Christians were only too apt, temperamentally, to become engrossed with their own importance—as evidenced in such gifts as prophecy and the faith that could accomplish veritable wonders—forgetting the things that mattered most.

3. ***Philanthropy and Self-Sacrifice.***—Surely here is an unselfish gift. When we add Paul's own thought of a self-sacrifice that goes to the utmost length of martyrdom for the cause, surely here is a gift to be commended without qualification. **If I give away all I have.** Such charity is one of the loveliest of Christian graces, and Paul has written much in commendation of it. Toward the close of the epistle he will remind his Corinthian readers of their duty to their brethren in this respect (16:1). The same thought was in his mind when he penned his Epistle to the Romans (12:8). The liberal spirit always commended itself to the great apostle; it is one of the marks of the indwelling of him who gave himself for us and for all men. Jesus set his seal on the grace of charity in his vivid parable of the last assize (Matt. 25:31-46). But the implication in his teaching, and in that of this apostle who so intimately entered into

this reading believe that Paul refers to the extreme case of a man selling, not his possessions, but his own person into slavery. If, on the other hand, we read **burned,** the reference may be either to voluntary self-torture or to martyrdom. Paul would have in mind the three young men who were thrust into the fiery furnace (Dan. 3:19-28) and the hot caldrons used to torture the seven brothers at the time of the persecution under Antiochus Epiphanes (II Macc. 7). The latter reading may be regarded as preferable on two grounds: (*a*) Though there is no reason why a copyist should remove a favorite word of Paul's in favor of one which is not elsewhere used by him, we can readily see that an early scribe might have reversed the process, taking offense at what he regards as a criticism of martyrs. When Christians were being burned at the stake, scripture should not belittle this sacrifice. (*b*) To boast without having love would not provide a situation in any way parallel to the illustrations which have preceded. Paul has been speaking of acts which are good when the motive is good. Though Paul may at times refer to boasting in other than a bad sense (9:15; Rom. 5:2; II Cor. 12:1; Phil. 2:16), the parallel expression

---

his Master's spirit and thought, is that such generosity springs from a loving heart. True giving is Godlike. God loved and God gave is the message of John 3:16. There lies the real condemnation of those who in that parable of judgment were sent away from the Master's presence. They had no eyes to see the need of their fellows, and they had no love to supply the need they saw.

But here a deeper truth is underlined. It is quite possible for charity to be given without any love being involved. There would seem to have been a picture in the apostle's imagination of some Greek giving away with his own hands large quantities of goods, but it is done for his own self-glorification. It is marked by the spirit of ostentation. He does it not because he really cares about the people to whom he is distributing his charity, but because the action commends him in the eyes of his fellow men. It might even be done to further his own fortunes in some branch of public life. The Caesars knew how to secure the plaudits of the multitude by furnishing them with bread and circuses.

How curious are the motives of certain people in the dispensing of their charities! It looks well to have one's name on certain subscription lists. Often it is the short cut to some public honor or title. The baser sort of Pharisee was castigated by Jesus because he chose some prominent place in which to do his alms and say his prayers, even had a trumpet blown to attract the crowd (Matt. 6:1-5). Perhaps, to set over against them, Paul had in mind his friend Barnabas, who because of the love in his heart for his fellow men sold the "field which belonged to him," and made the money available for the needs of his poorer brethren (Acts 4:36-37). That is the true philanthrophy which springs from the right motive. The Corinthians were in need of this warning; they were keen to stand well in the eyes of their fellows and to secure their meed of public applause. Such giving is not the expression of thoughtful love, but of perverted selfishness. One has to be loving and thoughtful to be kind. It is the love and thoughtfulness that convert the gift into a grace, and make it a blessing both to those who receive and to those who give. It is possible to give in such a way that while the gift ministers to the recipient's body, it wounds his spirit. Love is the motive that alone commends the gift and confers on it its real value, whether it is large or small. A large gift given without love ranks small in the sight of God; a small gift given in love is in his eyes great indeed. Those who thus give stand to gain. Did not the Lord say, and is there not a reminiscence of his saying in the very words used by the apostle himself, that if a man's charity is not given in love he gains nothing? But "Whoever gives to one of these little ones even a cup of cold water because he is a disciple, truly, I say to you, he shall not lose his reward" (Matt. 10:42). The meaning is clear: the disciple of Christ is he who shares Christ's spirit.

Paul follows up his thought with a striking illustration, **And if I deliver my body to be burned, . . . I gain nothing.** Some have thought that there is a partly hidden reference here to voluntary enslavement. It appears that in the early centuries of the Christian Era there were some who sold themselves voluntarily into slavery to make funds available for the succor of the poorer brethren and for the propagation of the gospel.[8] The reference in this case might be to the branding of the slave's body with the mark of his owner. Or as Moffatt suggests, there may be a reference to an incident, of which the Corinthians would be aware, in which an Indian fanatic cast himself during the reign of Augustus into a burning pyre, preferring to perish thus rather than to endure the enfeeblement that prolongation of life might bring to

[8] Moffatt, *I Corinthians*, pp. 193-94.

4 Charity suffereth long, *and* is kind; charity envieth not; charity vaunteth not itself, is not puffed up,

4 Love is patient and kind; love is not

in vs. 2 suggests that the clause in question defines not the purpose of the action but its nature. As faith is expressed in removing mountains, so the giving up of one's body is the suffering of death by burning. The translation "boasting" would not provide such a parallel. Paul recognizes then that even martyrdom may be sought for sub-Christian motives and without genuine love.

b) The Nature of Love (13:4-7)

4. The nature of love is expressed by Paul in a series of verbs, the active character of which may not be fully indicated by the crisp adjectives in the RSV. Two affirmatives are followed by eight negatives and then finally there are four positive statements which stress the word **all.** In Col. 3:14 Paul says that love "binds everything together in perfect harmony." Love is a rope composed of many different strands. To change the figure, its

him (cf. Exeg.). Either of these types might involve no more than mere egoism or self-glorification. The true martyr does not seek his cross any more than the Master, in one sense, sought his. But when it is imposed on him for the sake of the faith that is in him, then for love of his God and his fellow men he embraces it and endures it. It is the love that is in his heart that sanctifies the self-immolation of the martyr. Mere pride, or eagerness for a martyr's honors, or bravado can never give spiritual quality to any degree of self-sacrifice, even if it is of life itself. How different is such ostentation from that love for Christ, and for his glorious gospel message to all mankind, which sent Ignatius into the arena to face the lions, enabled Polycarp to endure the flames, brought Scottish Covenanters the shame of the scaffold, death on their native heath or in the sullen waters of the Solway Firth! The very extremity of the illustration the apostle uses serves to drive home his point. It is love that gives its value to any gift of the spirit; it is love for Christ and for the brethren that sanctifies a martyr's death in the cause. If it is lacking, **I gain nothing.**

4-7. ***Love in the Fellowship.***—Now comes a paragraph, still marked by poetic rhythm, which deals with some of the practical aspects of the spirit of love as it ought to manifest itself in the Christian fellowship. We are able to infer from the very phrases Paul uses something of the situation with which he is dealing, and so we can form a fairly accurate conception of the nature and quality of this early Christian community. Every negative implies a positive. The apostle is admonishing his brethren, but at the same time he sees the greater possibilities, and it is for these he is pleading. He is anxious for them to follow the supreme way of life; the way that never fails; the way that in the end leads straight to God's predestined goal; the way of love.

Paul's tone and method of dealing with these fractious brethren should be a guide to us in dealing with like communities in our own day. After all, here was a new adventure in friendship and fellowship. Those taking part in it had been drawn together in new and strange ways. They represented differences in type, in station, in temperament, and in outlook. They were far from perfect. Yet they did provide the possibility of a fellowship which would indicate and enshrine the way of salvation for all mankind. Paul pleads with them to give Christian love a chance to prove what it can do for them. He lists some of its characteristic marks.

4*a*. ***The Excellence of Love.***—Paul's method is not to define love—he never does—but to tell his readers how it works (cf. Exeg.). **Love is patient and kind.** Perhaps no one can define love; like every other universal spiritual value it can be defined only in terms of itself. Yet much can be said about it. It is "patient." As the KJV puts it, love **suffereth long.** There were difficult people in the church at Corinth. Their uncouth and brusque ways were apt to hurt tender feelings and to put an almost intolerable strain on mutual relationships. It would have been so easy to retaliate in kind, or to nurse a grievance, or to become bitter. But none of these is the "more excellent way." Paul broadens his use of the word "patience" by adding to it the word "kind." The sense of the phrase is perhaps best covered by the term "magnanimous." This suggests a certain spaciousness and generosity and greatness of spirit. Here we have one of the characteristic marks of Jesus Christ. Often enough when we read the teachings commonly included in the Sermon on the

white light may be analyzed into the various colors of which it is composed. If the negatives are more numerous than the positives, that is because it is easier to say what love will avoid than to give prescriptions in advance. The qualities of patience and of kindness are joined together by Paul in four other passages (Rom. 2:4; II Cor. 6:6; Gal. 5:22;

Mount, we think, and think rightly, of the high demands they make upon those who desire to be true followers and disciples of Jesus. But they are also the reflection of his own mind and spirit. They are, so to speak, windows through which we catch a glimpse of the great soul of the Master himself. Greater by far than even the greatness of his words is the wonder of his life. He had the undoubted right to lay such demands upon the conscience of those who call themselves by his name, because first of all he lived his own teachings. These great demands indicate the dimensions of his own magnanimous spirit. He could require forgiveness of enemies, prayer for persecutors, generosity to people who sometimes made unreasonable demands, and love for those who do us despite, because he practiced such graces himself. All of this and much more is involved in the patient kindness of Jesus Christ.

We can be quite certain that Paul is taking his standards from the Master himself in setting down these marks of Christian love. Love is magnanimous; it will not give way to bitterness or anger; it has in it a breath of the infinite patience of God, who is love. As it approaches the perfection that is revealed and demonstrated in Jesus Christ we look at the very nature of God. This is one of the fundamental themes of Scripture itself. The story set down for us in our Bibles tells of "the long-suffering of God." We shall feel the full force of the phrase if we transpose the terms. God "suffers long." He suffers long because his nature and name is love. To that love of God, Christian love, especially among the fellowship of believers, ought to approximate. What patience God manifests to the children of Israel! Prophet and priest and psalmist tell the wonderful story. These folk for whom he did so much constantly rebelled against him; they broke his laws; they thwarted his purposes. Despite all the signal tokens they had received of his providence, despite the deliverance from Egypt and the unfailing provision made for them in all their desert wanderings, time after time they forsook him and worshiped idols. The history of the nation is again and again the history of religious declension. Yet God is patient: he will not give them up. One of the great notes struck by prophets like Isaiah and Hosea is that God's love is such that he never relinquishes those whom once he has made his own. Over the entire history of Israel from the pilgrimage of Abraham to the crucifixion of the Savior could be written the legend, **Love is patient.**

In the light of the Cross and the subsequent story of the church in the N.T. the legend bursts into letters of sacred flame. It is the face of God in Christ that gleams out through these lines as Paul, his heart on fire for Christ and with zeal for the well-being of his church, sets down the various colors of this white blaze of love. Substitute the name "Christ" for every mention of the word "love" in this thrilling chapter of the epistle and in the end we have another marvelous portrait of the Master. "Christ is patient and kind"; and those who bear his name and are members of his fellowship, organic elements in "the body," should manifest the same characteristics in their dealings and relationships one with another and with their fellow men. How patient Jesus was with his blundering disciples and followers! How patient with the multitudes that gathered around him, at first with plaudits, and at the end with execration on their lips and in their hearts. How patient he was with the sick and the poor! How patient with Pilate! And how patient with those who crucified him: "Father, forgive them; for they know not what they do." So it has been right through the long centuries of the Christian Era to this very day. In every age his church has failed him. Christians have not measured up, save in few cases, to the standards and spirit of their Master. "The greatly sanctified," says an old Scottish proverb, "are sair to seek." They are so few. Yet God has been patient. He has not swept the obstinate sons of men out of existence, nor has he cast off his faithless followers. He loves them still. Part of the "long-suffering" of God is to be found in the fact that like any good earthly parent he desires to do so much for his children, but they will not let him. In very truth, the long processes of creation itself proclaim the infinite patience of Almighty God, the God whom Jesus Christ incarnated for us.

And **love . . . is kind.** To be patient is to be Christlike in forbearance; to be kind is the more active expression of Christian love. To be patient suggests self-restraint; to be kind suggests self-expression in love to our fellow men. The two are here bound in one. Love that is patient reveals itself in kindness. The love of Christ which Paul is expounding is unlike that contemplative love which is so often emphasized

Col. 3:12). God has been long-suffering and gracious toward us; we must show the same attitude toward our fellow men. The term ζηλόω means either to strive for or to show envy or jealousy. Paul introduces (12:31*a*) and closes (14:1) the chapter with this word and in the first sense. Here he is speaking of jealousy as an attitude which cannot be

---

by some of the Christian mystics as the supreme expression of the Christian spirit. The love of Christ is not only contemplative; it is also active. Impression and expression found their perfect balance in Jesus Christ. It was because he loved that he went about doing good. The miracles of healing that he wrought were outward expression of inward love. The truth that he preached to the multitudes that hung upon every utterance was the outward expression of his inward love of truth. His prayer on the Cross for the forgiveness of those who crucified him was the outward expression of that inward yearning which only a few hours before had found its way into other words: "That they may all be one" (John 17:21). The love that endured revealed itself in kindness, a kindness that was not merely congenial: it was ethical kindness; it embodied goodness and often in turn evoked it. Scholars have suggested that one of the root meanings of the Greek word used by Paul, and translated "kind," is "respect," i.e., the patient love of which the apostle writes was meant also to be esteemed in view of the benefits it conferred. Here again is another illustration of the unique balance of Paul's thought. Here, though in different language, yet for similar people, he requires that devotion to God which also is approved by men (see Rom. 14:16-19). And here there is more than a reminiscence of Jesus himself, who celebrates the offering of a cup of cold water "in his name," which means "in his spirit."

There was need for this word of the apostle to the community in Corinth. There is need for it in every age and at all times. Our contemporary world calls for the love that is patient and kind. There is so much misery, so much heartache, so much sin, and so much sorrow. It is beyond none of us, for the love that loves us, to be patient with our fellows—beyond none to be kind. Kindness costs no money, only the effort that is required, and that discipline of spirit which holds us close to our Lord. It is as easy to go about with a smile as it is to go about with a frown, and far more useful. People could not quarrel and fight if they cultivated the art of smiling sincerely to one another. To pay a visit, to say a word of cheer or comfort, to convey friendliness by a shake of the hand, these are small tokens, perhaps, of a loving spirit, but they are symbolic of the very nature and purpose of God. Moreover, the consequences are incalculable. Such a spirit expressed in such a way sends out into the spiritual and moral atmosphere of the universe in which we live ripples that never exhaust themselves. Only God can calculate the full consequences. It is a great thing to live in that spirit of love which expresses itself in patience and kindness.

Well may we pray that in this, as in other ways, our "love may abound more and more, with knowledge and all discernment," so that we "may approve what is excellent, and may be pure and blameless for the day of Christ, filled with the fruits of righteousness which come through Jesus Christ, to the glory and praise of God" (Phil. 1:9-11). Or as an old hymn puts it,

> There are lonely hearts to cherish,
> While the days are going by;
> There are weary souls who perish,
> While the days are going by;
> If a smile we can renew,
> As our journey we pursue,
> Oh, the good we all may do,
> While the days are going by.[9]

To live like that is to walk in the spirit of Christ. His love was patient.

> And the heart of the Eternal
> Is most wonderfully kind.[1]

Kindness is the convincing evidence of Christian love.

4*b*. *Love Is Not Jealous or Boastful*.—These two thoughts may and should be taken together, for they are complementary aspects of the situation with which the apostle is dealing. Some of the members of the community were inordinately proud of their particular spiritual gift and boasted about it. More than once Paul has asked them to consider whether they had any real occasion for boasting (see also II Cor. 11:12). It seems to have been a marked weakness of this particular church. Probably, as would seem to be implied by his strictures against disorders in the church meeting and at the Lord's table, some were snobbish about their social status. Such people were apt to make a parade of themselves, so that the poorer, less fortunate members of the fellowship were humiliated (see 3:3; 11:22; II Cor. 12:20) and moved to jealousy. All of this was bound to

[9] George Cooper, "There are lonely hearts to cherish."

[1] Frederick W. Faber, "There's a wideness in God's mercy."

joined with love (3:3). The KJV translates the next verb **vaunteth not itself.** "Boast" is a more common modern synonym. The word φυσιόω has been a key term of the letter (4:6, 18, 19; 5:2; 8:1). The Corinthians have been **puffed up** (KJV) or **arrogant** (RSV). But **love** does not act in that way.

---

make havoc of the spirit of fellowship, and the sole cure for it was to inculcate the very different spirit of Christian love.

Love is not jealous. Jealousy is one of the deadly sins. Nothing can more thoroughly embitter the human spirit and poison personal relationships than the spirit of envy or jealousy. It is given pride of place in the order of vices by the writers of the O.T. According to them it was the direct cause of the first crime in the story of the human race (Gen. 4:1-8). One of its roots strikes deep down into life's obvious inequalities. Men may be and undoubtedly are equal in the sight of God. But in respect of native endowment, of position, and of success they are not equal; and even more significant, some of these inequalities, humanly speaking, seem to be irremediable. Have we not all felt the pangs of envy and jealousy as we have looked on those more splendidly endowed and circumstanced than ourselves? Here, as in other matters, the members of the Christian community in Corinth were very like their modern counterparts. This unpleasant vice of jealousy is often all too manifest in those whose profession of faith as followers, and even as ministers, of Jesus Christ should make them patterns of Christian love to their fellow men. Shakespeare, that close observer of humanity and its varying moods and passions, has written:

> The general's disdain'd
> By him one step below, he by the next,
> That next by him beneath; so every step,
> Exampled by the first pace that is sick
> Of his superior, grows to an envious fever
> Of pale and bloodless emulation.[2]

Jealousy is a scarlet thread of unholy passion that runs not only through the church in Corinth, but through all human life. He is a magnanimous man indeed who can, with patent sincerity, rejoice in the greater success of another in a sphere similar to that occupied by himself. But the trouble goes still deeper. Jealousy is a sin, and a sin is like an infected wound: the infection spreads. Jealousy is an infected wound in the soul and it breeds further infection: it begets hatred, hatred begets strife. Only Christian love is pure and strong enough to endure differences in endowment, in status and circumstance which are inevitable, just as Christian love alone is strong and pure enough to endow with graciousness those who are so privileged. Paul saw the spirit of love as the one hope of unity in the disordered Corinthian church. It disciplines one to the point of unalloyed pleasure in another's gifts or success. It develops the unquenching spirit. Perhaps Paul had in mind some exemplars of that spirit among the friends who meant so much to him. Barnabas found Paul a congenial companion on their joint missionary journeys, and so did Luke, though both must have recognized in the apostle the greater man. Or perhaps Paul thought of the relationship between Jonathan, son of that other Saul, king of Israel, and David, the shepherd-psalmist. These are examples of the love that casts out jealousy.

There are at least two marks of the love that is not jealous. The first is that its values are spiritual and not material. The latter give rise most to the spirit of envy. Later in the chapter the apostle lists some of these spiritual values. Let it suffice here to say that its standard is the spirit of Christ, and that its heart is set not on things that are temporal, but on things that are eternal. The second mark is that Christian love is generous in its appreciation of the good qualities in others. Jealousy is a selfish vice: it centers one's attention on oneself. Christian love is unselfish: it centers its attention on the object of love, which is other than oneself, and it rejoices in the wholesome success and prosperity of every worthy person or cause. Such love is not only unselfish, it is sacrificial. "Greater love has no man than this, that a man lay down his life for his friends" (John 15:13). For this unselfish and sacrificial love Paul pleads, that it might not only enrich the life of the Christian community in Corinth, but that through all such communities it might spread out into the life of the world.

Love is not . . . boastful. Some of the members of the community were only too greatly aware of their importance, at least in their own eyes, and as a consequence they were filled with conceit and pride. Pride, with its offspring conceit, is another of the deadly sins. In the Sermon on the Mount, by implication, Jesus gives it a leading place in the list of vices that must be displaced by the Christian spirit when he says, "Blessed are the poor in spirit, for theirs is the kingdom of heaven" (Matt. 5:3). The humble-minded are the teachable and receptive people in whom all conceit and pride have been slain. Once again there is an inner

[2] *Troilus and Cressida,* Act 1, scene 3.

5 Doth not behave itself unseemly, seeketh not her own, is not easily provoked,
thinketh no evil;

jealous or boastful; 5 it is not arrogant or
rude. Love does not insist on its own way;

---

5. This verse really begins in the middle of a sentence, as in the RSV. The verb rendered in the KJV as **behave . . . unseemly** occurs only here and in 7:36. Paul may be thinking of the disorders in worship mentioned in 11:2-16 or in ch. 14. **Rude** would be a

---

balance in the apostle's thought. Jealousy is an inward state of the soul: boastfulness is one of the outward expressions of this unchristian spirit. As the KJV puts it, love **vaunteth not itself.** The suggestion is that some of the Corinthian believers were apt to indulge in self-display; they loved to attract attention to themselves; they were proud of their own position and relative importance in the community. Wherever that sort of conduct is found it is always the mark of a mean and small spirit. The truly great never indulge in self-display; there is an engaging atmosphere of quiet humility about them, a humility that is oceans apart from the spirit of servility. The truly great are so sure of themselves in their humble, gentle way that they do not need to attract attention to themselves. They indulge in no self-advertisement. If they are Christians, and if they hold any position of prominence or importance in the Christian community, they are always willing and even anxious that their life and service should express not themselves but the spirit of the Master. Love's humility is its greatness. It is never boastful.

The vaunting of oneself in conceit or pride may be and often is the mark of inner uncertainty. So modern psychology would seem to teach. It is one of the characteristics of an inner feeling of inferiority. Such people seek what compensation they can find by overemphasis in respect of such gifts and qualities as they may possess. But such emphasis nullifies these gifts in the eyes of the onlooker. Boasters and conceited persons are in the end merely pathetic, deserving of pity rather than censure. Christian love must learn to treat them with firmness, but also with patience and kindness.

But the entire context of the epistle conveys the thought that Paul has in mind certain immodest and superior people who really thought more highly of themselves than they ought. They were self-assertive. They were anxious on every possible occasion to flaunt their gift in the eyes of their fellows, no matter whether it resulted in edification or not. Like the Pharisees, they were minded, as it were, to blow a trumpet and to attract attention. Their attitude was the very reverse of modesty. Paul is gently teaching these obstreperous members of the church that love is always modest: it is willing to serve. True love is content to serve even without acknowledgment, and is ever ready to perform the humblest tasks. Pride reaches up ambitiously to the heavens; it knows no limits. Love stoops to the earth, and no humble task is too lowly for its service. Paul would have these people ponder often the spectacle of One who, on the night in which he was betrayed, girded himself with a towel and washed his disciples' feet. May those who are his followers ponder it often. May they ponder it always when pride and conceit begin to stir within their hearts. Love is never jealous or boastful, precisely because it is modest and humble. When such love stirs within the human heart, and is allowed to have its way in a human life, it reminds its possessor always of his indebtedness to the love of God. The man who recognizes and acknowledges his debt is bereft of boasting. He is made fit to serve. Christ's love glorifies all true service, however humble.

> He prayeth best, who loveth best
> All things both great and small;
> For the dear God who loveth us,
> He made and loveth all.[3]

Such love is far beyond jealousy or conceit or boastfulness; it is born of "the love of Christ [which] constraineth us."

5a. It Is Not Arrogant or Rude.—It has been said that "manners makyth man," and there is truth in the saying. Just as style in the realm of literature is a revelation of the spirit of the writer, and as preaching is truth expressed through personality, so manners are an index to the inner quality of any life. And there is a place for manners, for the so-called minor virtues, in the Christian style of living. Nor is it at all difficult to imagine that as the Master himself is the Christian standard in all things, so is he in this realm our exemplar. How exquisite his courtesy and tact. These qualities are, like his indignation, a manifestation of the depth and quality of his nature. How gently he dealt with the woman who touched the hem of his garment; how tenderly and with what deep feeling he shielded the woman who

[3] Coleridge, *The Ancient Mariner.*

general characterization of either situation. In the eating of food sacrificed to idols many of his readers had been insisting on their own way (10:24, 33; cf. Phil. 2:4, 21). **Love**

---

washed his feet with her tears and anointed them with her precious ointment! How delicately and with what grace he spoke to the woman taken in adultery whom the scribes and Pharisees brought to the temple that he might either condemn her or condemn himself! Paul, as his apostle, was bound to teach his converts the whole counsel of Christ and to put before them the full style of Christian living. That he should do so had become necessary. We have already seen (ch. 11) that he was disturbed by the reports he had received of disorderly and ill-mannered conduct in the church, and particularly in the church meeting. There is a reference to these things in the phrase he now uses. Some were arrogant. They were conscious of their status as citizens, or of their wealth, and preferred to eat, even in the church meeting or at the Lord's table, either by themselves or in company with their social equals. That must have exacerbated the sensitive feelings of the humbler members of the community who often arrived too late to participate in the common meal, or who were unable to provide a contribution comparable to that of their better-circumstanced brethren.

There was also a freedom from formal styles of worship in the early Christian churches; inevitably so. Such freedom has its values, but it also has its disadvantages. When the power of the Spirit of God comes flooding with pentecostal force into the lives of such men and women as composed the community in Corinth, it is difficult for a time to confine the enhancement of mental and spiritual quality, which is one of the concomitants of such an experience, within reasonable or even reverent bounds. There is a sort of overplus of spiritual power and energy that is apt to vent itself in unusual ways. Revival movements in every age afford many illustrations. So it was in Corinth, and this was seen particularly in the matter of tongues, preaching, and prophesying. The result was not only confusion but unmannerly conduct. Some of the speakers thought that what they had to say was more important than what another brother was saying. Thus they would either sit in ill-concealed impatience until the other had finished, or make it obvious that they were not interested in what he was saying; or worse still, jump up and interrupt him with their own harangue. Feelings were bound to be hurt by such practices. Paul had to deal with the ensuing situation. How he emulates the Master as he writes that love **doth not behave itself unseemly. It is not arrogant or rude.**

Where there is true Christian love or good will or friendship, even the roughest, most uncouth gesture on the part of those who have never been taught better takes on a certain indefinable dignity or gentleness. The uncouthness is qualified by the light in the eyes or the expression on the face. How often one has seen it happen. Here is the sovereign remedy for all arrogance and unmannerliness: Let these Corinthians truly learn to love one another, and they would lose all self-assertiveness with its accompanying rudeness. They would learn to prefer their brethren before themselves, and would gently insist that the other should take prior place. Love like that begets chivalry and honor and courtesy. Where there is Christian love between the sexes, honor is safe and personality is sacred and respected. Where there is such love, homes are secure. The Christian man will always seek to be a perfect gentleman in his home as well as in his relationships with the community at large. Such love would be an antidote for the malaise of society, both national and international, for the rudeness and arrogance and ill-mannered behavior of every order where force is the final arbiter of what is right and wrong. Love is never unseemly. The loving spirit is courteous and kind and trustworthy. He who possesses it can walk at ease. His life will be a leaven amid the ferment of anxiety and fear. There is a great place for the "seemliness" of a love that is never arrogant or rude. We need Christian leaders and gentlemen in every walk of life, in public as well as in private affairs. Just by being themselves they set up a standard of judgment and a test for all who come within their ambit. That is part of the Christian mission to the world. There is much for it to do abroad; there is much for it to do at home. Many a church meeting or council or assembly would be a stimulus and inspiration in the common relationships and trend of life if the eyes of all who attend them were confronted by the text, **Love . . . is not arrogant or rude.** We can make certain that it is not by walking in close company with Christ.

5b. Love Does Not Insist on Its Own Way. —These words follow naturally on the foregoing paragraphs. The arrogant, boastful, and rude members of the community were revealing a selfish or self-centered spirit. They were apt to insist on having their own way, that others should defer to their opinion. Such self-assertiveness was bound to disturb the peace of the fellowship of Corinth, and such inconsiderateness was bound to hurt the feelings of many of

would not do that. The thought implied in παροξύνομαι is that of irritation rather than rage. In Acts 15:39 the noun is used in connection with the dispute between Paul and Barnabas. The **easily provoked** of the KJV is appropriate enough, but **thinketh no evil**

---

the other members. In *Middlemarch,* George Eliot describes one of those antique mirrors that we sometimes see in the homes of friends. It is usually a round, concave mirror of excellent reflecting quality, but polished for so many years that its surface is now covered with innumerable tiny scratches, not obvious save to the closest gaze. Were anyone to hold a lighted match or candle close to its center, the little scratches would arrange themselves in concentric circles around the reflected central flame. Is not this a parable of many a life? These people in Corinth, and their counterparts in every age, may not have been consciously selfish folk, but they were self-centered. And self-centeredness is a subtle thing; it attacks our life at many points. It gets into literature and other forms of art. It invades the religious sphere. Many prayers are self-centered in their main emphasis. So are many hymns. Instead of striking the objective note and concentrating the attention upon God who is the object of worship, they concentrate attention upon ourselves; they do it even to the extent of looking upon God as one whose main business it is to look after us and our affairs, and in particular to safeguard us from all ills. Such a spirit is to be guarded against, not only in Corinth, but in all Christian circles: it is the very antithesis of the spirit of Christ.

Christian love is never self-centered: it **does not insist on its own way.** Love lives to give, and not to get. Again the KJV puts the point in the negative, as if the positive affirmation that is implied were too great even for Paul's descriptive powers. Love **seeketh not her own**—but every man's! That addition takes us right into the presence of God. Here is the very essence of love. The progressive understanding of God's nature and God's ways has led to the realization that he is constantly giving himself—"for every man." He is "the seeking Shepherd," as C. G. Montefiore points out in his studies on Luke. In seeking to win man to himself and his purposes, God seeks not his own glory but man's good. Jesus Christ has revealed this quality of God's spirit in his own life. From Bethlehem to the garden of the Resurrection and the mount of the Ascension, his life is the supreme illustration of unselfish love. His Cross is the supreme example of it. And this thought lies at the very heart of his message to the world. To seek "first the kingdom of God" is his invitation and appeal to men to put God and not themselves at the center of their lives. That is precisely what he himself did in the garden of Gethsemane. To repent is to change one's attitude toward life. Human life is self-centered, it insists on having its own way; it seeks its own interests, and its own benefits. But it was devised to be God-centered. What other way of salvation is there for ourselves and for the whole world? Life is sure to be out of joint, and confusion is bound to be rampant, when humanity is out of touch with reality. When the Master insisted that men should seek first the kingdom of God, and added that if they did so all other things would be given unto them, he was not trying to bribe them into believing. He was making a statement about the nature of reality itself. There is bound to be confusion both in the church and in the world, as well as in individual lives, when the center is wrong. Life, to be right, must be centered in God. And God is love. As the sun is the original source from which all our forms of light are drawn, so God is the love which is the fountain of all lesser loves. His love seeks not his own glory, but fullness of life for every man; salvation lies in fellowship with him and in playing a proper part in the fulfillment of his great creative purposes. True love is ever unselfish. Where self is at the center, that is neither the way nor the spirit of love. The greatest souls our world has ever known, or ever can know, have always been those who lived for others. Paul was anxious that in Corinth the fellowship should be real and helpful, that the communion of the members with God through Christ might give to them fullness of life and a foretaste of heaven. Where love is, heaven is; for where love is, God is! God is love. And that love is revealed supremely in One who loved us and gave himself for us. To all his followers in every age, and in all the churches, he has left an example, that we should follow in his steps.

Love . . . is not irritable. The apostle now turns to the effects that every display of ill-manners and arrogance might have upon those whose susceptibilities have been hurt. How difficult it is not to feel irritated in such circumstances! Few things are more exasperating than to endure cavalier treatment that reckons little of the rights and privileges of other members of the same community. There must have been some in the Corinthian church—in fact, we know this to be true of the ascetic element—who were actuated by high ideals of Christian morality and held like ideals for the conduct of the church's worship. It irritated them to see

is definitely a mistranslation: λογίζομαι here does not mean to think, but to reckon or take account of. The most common use of the word is in numerical calculations. **Love** will not keep track of all of the wrongs received, i.e., it will not cherish resentment.

---

worship brought into confusion, and doubtless contempt, so far as interested pagans were concerned, by the bad manners of those whose very pretensions to superior status should have required them to behave better. Paul, however, pleads for the Christian endurance that is part of the spiritual fruit of Christian love. Later on he lays down certain broad rules for the conduct of public worship (ch. 14). Here he prepares the way for the dissemination of such a spirit in the community as will make it amenable to the rules. Rules may not be set aside or disregarded unless they are supported by the right spirit. Love is the sovereign remedy for irritation and resentment. Paul knew—and none better, for he had a hasty temper himself—that irritation is apt to be the outward manifestation of pride and self-love. One is irritated if one's vanity is hurt. It is not difficult to imagine some member of the community in Corinth protesting to another who has been guilty of rudeness, "You can't do that to me!" Vanity and pride are almost sure to be involved in such reaction to rudeness. Once the disciples quarreled among themselves as to the places of honor each might occupy when their Lord entered into his kingdom. In particular, they were very angry with those disciples, the sons of Zebedee, on whose behalf a special plea had been made to the Master. It is difficult to resist the inference that they were less chagrined that such a request had been made than that someone else had made it first. Their pride and vanity were hurt. So it may have been in Corinth. Some had insisted on displaying their gifts and the others felt aggrieved. Much of the irritation which often broods upon a slight, as if it were engraved on the tablets of memory, springs from such circumstances. The root trouble was self-assertiveness. It rent the spirit of fellowship into shreds. Paul pleads for the "more excellent way." Irritation, after all, springs from the minor ills of life. Even ordinary and humble people are brave to the point of heroism in the face of major ills. The petty annoyances and frustrations get us down and make us irritable. Only a finer, better spirit can cleanse that mood and restore peace of mind again. Let the love that is not centered in self, but on God, fill the hearts of all members of the community, and irritation will go into banishment with the things that give rise to it. It is the self-centered people who are apt to be supersensitive and easily annoyed. Christian love, which is not self-centered, cannot be irritable. God knows neither resentment nor irritation. And once again, "God is love, and he who abides in love abides in God, and God abides in him" (I John 4:16).

We ought to distinguish here between anger and irritability. Love cannot be irritable but it can be angered. There are several pictures in the Gospels of a fierce, angry Christ. His love and his indignation both spring from the same capacity for deep emotion. And there is a wrath of God which is directed against sin and against all unrighteousness. This is one of the dominant themes of scripture. History and individual experience can furnish many an instance of the anger of God. Love is capable of anger but not of irritability or resentment.

Nor is irritability or resentment a mere matter of temperament or disposition. It is true that some people are more choleric than others. When provoked, they are quick to flash into anger. James and John, disciples of Jesus, were said to be hasty of temper. They wanted to call down fire from heaven on the Samaritan villagers who refused to give hospitality to their Master (Luke 9:54), and were rebuked for their fiery spirit. Paul, too, had a capacity for flaming anger (Acts 23:2-3). Such people are very apt to have flashes of irritability. Irritability has been called "the vice of the virtuous." Sometimes it is condoned as a weakness rather than as a sin. To be sure, it might be going too far to term it a sin. Yet the irritable spirit has been the cause of much unhappiness and misery; it has clouded many a life; it has poisoned with bitterness many a home; it has broken many a friendship. And many other unpleasant traits are closely associated with it, such as sarcasm, sullenness, or brooding resentment. Surely only a vice can evoke so much desolation. Paul saw with horror the havoc it was making of the fellowship of the church, and pleads tenderly, yet urgently, for the substitution of a love that is patient and gentle and kind. It is a plea for hospitality to the indwelling Spirit of One who, when he was reviled, reviled not again, and met the envy and bitterness and hatred that nailed him to a Cross with a cleansing, heart-moving flood of love.

Finally, the irritable spirit will yield to discipline. John, at any rate, became known as the apostle of love. He became noted for his gentleness and gracious patience; while the picture of Paul in his old age, awaiting martyrdom in Rome, is that of a man who has brought every passion into subjection to Christ. We take

6 Rejoiceth not in iniquity, but rejoiceth in the truth;

it is not irritable or resentful; 6 it does not rejoice at wrong, but rejoices in the right.

6-7. The wrongs done to one another (6:8) cannot be the basis of any rejoicing. **Truth** (KJV) in this connection is not the opposite of error but of **iniquity;** hence the

---

on the spiritual color of the company we keep. Not only for those of quick, fiery temperament, but for all who would manifest the spirit of Jesus Christ to their fellow men, one prayer should often be uttered, "O Master, let me walk with thee." In the light of his realized presence all irritation fades away like mist in the morning sun.

Love . . . is not . . . resentful. Paul rightly associates the resentful spirit with irritability, though not all easily irritated people harbor resentment. The suggestion in the text is that those who are prone to resentment keep a careful account of the slights, fancied or real, which they have endured, and which have been so wounding to their self-esteem. They brood over that mental record until molehills assume the size of mountains. Their wrongs are stored up in the tablets of memory, and every time the record is reread the impression becomes deeper and is less easily erased. Paul pleads that love keeps no such accounts. It is the India rubber that erases the record. More, it is the spirit that forbids any original entry.

We can select our memories. We can deliberately forget the unpleasant experiences that have befallen us. To blot out from the mind the wrongs that have been inflicted on us is a Godlike thing. This is what God does when a truly contrite sinner makes confession of his sins. His forgiveness involves forgetfulness. In the prayer that the Lord taught to his disciples he makes the forgiveness of God concordant with man's forgiveness of his fellow men. Love is forgiving, and forgiveness to be real must involve forgetfulness. Someone has written that Abraham Lincoln never forgot a kindness and never remembered a wrong. That ought to be the mark of Christian people. The unforgiving spirit comes perilously near to that ultimate sin which is described as unpardonable. What place can there be in heaven, the abode of love, for the spirit that is resentful? Resentment can have no place in the heart or in the fellowship that is dominated to the full by the love of Christ.

6*a*. *It Does Not Rejoice at Wrong.*—Now the scope of love is widened as Paul turns to more general considerations. Love does not allow itself to be irritated by the petty annoyances of life, nor does it harbor memories of wrongs personally endured. Next he adds that it has no pleasure in reports either of failure on the part of others or of the wickedness that they have done. It takes no pleasure in scandal or unedifying gossip. These were probably far from being uncommon in such a community as the church in Corinth. The very city in which the church was situated offered endless opportunity for moral failure. The atmosphere was tainted with every kind of temptation. Not for nothing did Corinth achieve its reputation for vice of every description. Moffatt has given us a vivid translation of the phrase under consideration, "Love is never glad when others go wrong." This is a verse which could well be given a prominent place in all religious assemblies, for here is a weakness to which many people who profess the Christian faith are prone. There are many inside the church, though no doubt more not of its membership, who take an unseemly and unchristian pleasure in the failures and misdeeds of others. We can see that subtle temptation comes in this way. The Germans have a word for it that cannot be fully translated into English: they call it *schadenfreude,* which is a kind of malicious delight in the misfortunes of others. When such misfortune involves moral and spiritual things, *schadenfreude* is mingled with an element of moral superiority on the part of those who indulge it: they are more satisfied with themselves. They have found an excuse for practices more lightly regarded than those to which the unfortunate person has fallen victim. Paul condemns such a spirit: it is far removed from the spirit of love, which takes no delight in listening to scandal, however authentic the account may be. Should the scandal have any basis in fact, it means from the Christian angle that some personality is diminished and blemished in spiritual worth; and that is never a matter for pleasure among professing Christians. Such satisfactions may be left to the minions of hell.

Less often, professing Christians draw unseemly satisfaction from the moral excesses of others. They read literature or attend shows that pander to the baser passions. Such licentiousness has no place in Christian love; so widely distant is it from even the ordinary moral decencies of life that probably it did not even come within the purview of Paul's thought. With all debasing and soul-destroying circumstances Christian love is, or should be, engaged

7 Beareth all things, believeth all things,
hopeth all things, endureth all things.

7 Love bears all things, believes all things,
hopes all things, endures all things.

RSV renders it as **right.** The same contrast is found in Rom. 1:18 and 2:8. For Paul truth is a religious and ethical principle which cannot be united with unrighteousness. With

---

in violent and aggressive war; for they represent Antichrist.

But the persuasive thought offered thus by the apostle to his beloved brethren covers mostly what is known as gossip. Gossip need not be, and often is not, malicious. Yet it has its dangers. As the story of one incident or other is passed from lip to lip, it is apt to take on such additions or suffer such mutation as to be transformed out of all recognition. Gossip can do untold harm. There have been some "divines" who have put it on record that they would refuse to all known gossips admission to the Communion service. Three simple tests should be applied whenever there seems to be any tendency for gossip to develop, especially in the Christian community: Is it true? Is it necessary to retail this story? Is it kind? Let every bit of gossip be faced squarely with these questions put to it by those who have been baptized by faith into the spirit of Christian love, and doubtless at that point it will die an unlamented death. How can love listen with pleasure to the story of another's moral failure? Love would weep rather than rejoice. Jesus Christ is our exemplar here as in all else. Ponder the scene in the temple when they brought to him a woman caught in the act of adultery. Was it not pity for her and shame for them that made him avoid their eyes and communicate his thought to the honest dust? Over that scene a legend is written, "Love does not rejoice at wrong." At its deepest it makes atonement; and that takes the form of a Cross!

6*b*. *Love Rejoices in the Right.*—Or as Moffatt translates it, love is "always eager to believe the best." There we have the positive aspect of the matter. Love encourages goodness and is always glad to hear about it. This is the mark of a magnanimous spirit. It is one of the marks of the Lord Jesus. He was always alert to any good quality in the life of others. His eye alone saw the greater possibilities of the fishermen of Galilee whom he chose to be his followers. He marveled at a Roman centurion's faith, and immortalized it by making it the text of a lesson that abides to this very hour (Luke 7:1-10). He could see the queen in the harlot. While others regarded the wine, he regarded the water. Whenever he saw the beginnings of better things he was uplifted in spirit and encouraged them (cf. John 4:32). And he undoubtedly expected his followers in every age to be moved by the same spirit.

Every human heart hungers for such treatment. Children bloom in the sunshine of the spirit that encourages and helps them whenever they try to do well. There is a child in every heart. Long years ago when an old Scottish minister died it was beautifully said of him, "There is no one left in our village now to appreciate the triumphs of ordinary folk." That tells us all we need to know about the old minister. He was one who walked closely in the footprints left by his Master. What rich harvests a spirit like his would yield, could it be broadcast among the nations. It would increase genuine good will; it would encourage every effort in the direction of better, finer things; it would prepare the way for the solution of many a pressing problem in the realms of personal, social, and international relationships. There are in the main two groups of people in the world—"plus" people and "minus" people. The minus people diminish life's values; they are by their attitude encouragers of everything that detracts from life's finer qualities. But there are the plus people. They promote every virtue that in respect of the finer things adds to life's blessedness and true enrichment. On the one side is Antichrist; on the other side is Christ. **Love . . . rejoices in the right.**

7. *Love's Greatest Qualities.*—Now comes a series of confident, positive, and strengthening statements. With these Paul's glowing and exalted eulogy of love rises to a great and comprehensive climax. Here the apostle's soul sheds its shadows and rises into the perfect and shadowless light of God's very nature and purpose. How fond he is of that phrase **all things!** It is one of the keynotes of his mighty ministry. We have noticed already in this epistle the comprehensiveness of his thought (3:21). To the Ephesians he writes, "He has put all things under his feet and has made him the head over all things for the church, which is his body, the fullness of him who fills all in all" (Eph. 1:22-23). Yet again, "I can do all things in him who strengthens me" (Phil. 4:13). Many another passage in his letters stands in a like context. So here there is a fourfold repetition of the same phrase. It suggests the universal comprehensiveness of love, which Paul always relates

this turn to a positive description of love Paul comes to four final actions. Love **bears, believes, hopes,** and **endures.** The second and third of these anticipate the closing words of the chapter. Love **believes** the best and **hopes** for the best. The fourth term refers

to Jesus Christ. While he was in prison for Christ's sake, and therefore had time to meditate on these great matters, he thought of his beloved churches; and to the church in Ephesus he wrote a prayer in which he asks God "that Christ may dwell in your hearts through faith; that you, being rooted and grounded in love, may have power to comprehend with all the saints what is the breadth and length and height and depth, and to know the love of Christ which surpasses knowledge, that you may be filled with all the fullness of God" (Eph. 3:17-19). There can be little doubt that all things for Paul are made possible, and are summed up, in the love of God revealed through Christ Jesus. This is the climax of his soaring thought.

7a. Love Bears All Things.—For this greathearted apostle it is the ultimate answer to the wrongs and ills and challenges of life. He knew what he was writing about, for he had endured many things. His faith is strong and his ultimate convictions are unshakable because he has put them to the test. To be sure, there is a place for shrewdness and for caution and for foresight: often a time comes when strong action is required. Moral love is no weakling; nor is its purpose served in allowing itself to be treated with disdain. Love is realistic, as realistic as the very nature and creative purposes of Almighty God: love is Reality itself, and Reality has its adamantine aspects. In the moral sense perhaps the most solemn thing one can say about God is to affirm that he is love. That statement means that since "the nature of things" is summed up in God, it is a futile thing to fight against him. We cannot remind ourselves too often of this salutary truth. But there is also a persuasive gentleness and forbearance of love, and this Paul celebrates in the phrase **love bears all things.** Sometimes the words have been translated "love covereth all things" (cf. Exeg.). A picture is at once conjured up in the imagination of love casting a veil over the weakness and failings and wrongs of others. This has already been suggested in the Expos. of 4*a*. Here Paul's thought goes much deeper. It implies restraint and forbearance in the presence of wrong; but even more it implies that love carries the burden and even the blame for the wrong upon itself. Love carries on its own heart, so to speak, the sin and the sorrow and the tragedy of all the world. We can see the shadow of the Cross in this aspect of it. After all, these people had been told in plain language that the apostle had come among them proclaiming the gospel of Christ crucified. He has been insisting all through in various ways that the mark of a Christian fellowship is to manifest the mind and spirit of Jesus Christ. And his is a cross-bearing spirit. It is the spirit that "hath borne our griefs, and carried our sorrows" (Isa. 53:4). When in the days of the Master's flesh, in a confused and troubled time, men were looking everywhere for a scapegoat on which they might place the onus and burden of the sin and guilt that lie, although the sinners do not realize it, at the foundation of all spiritual and moral confusion, and when they were blaming everyone but themselves, he stepped forward to take the blame. There, as we gaze upon his Cross, we see Paul's great words break, as it were, into flame: **Love bears all things.**

Vicarious suffering is the highest expression of love; such love takes voluntarily upon itself the sins and failures of others. And when it does so it becomes the greatest power for spiritual and moral redemption in the life of the world. Mahatma Gandhi, whether one's judgment emphasizes the wisdom or otherwise of the various courses of action he took on behalf of India, has demonstrated in his fasts and self-imposed punishment for wrongdoing of his countrymen, the power of vicarious suffering to change men's attitude and to transform their spirit. There is no power equal to it for moral redemption. For us the supreme exemplar of that power is "Christ crucified." His church is his "body." It is his continued incarnation and witness to the truth of his gospel throughout the ages; and its fellowship, with regard both to the members of the community and to their witness in the world, should be animated by that same spirit.

Could his church recover that unity for which the apostle pleads, and could all its members be baptized anew into the Master's spirit of vicarious love, the redemption of the world might indeed be accomplished. Wrong is not to be condoned. It is sometimes to be exposed and condemned. But its ultimate cure depends on our carrying upon our hearts and spirits as individual Christians the sins and failures of others, and among these others especially such as have sinned against us. If the knowledge that such vicarious suffering is endured by those who have been wronged fails to move the wrongdoer, then the latter has become perilously like a lost soul. Vicarious suffering is the supreme height to which the human spirit can rise. It is the highest manifestation of Christian

to the steadfast endurance which Paul stresses over and over again (Rom. 5:3; 8:25; II Cor. 12:12; I Thess. 1:3; etc.). It is expressed by facing tribulation with courage. What additional idea, then, is carried by the first clause, **love bears all things?** The verb στέγω

---

love. It is Godlike, for there is a cross eternal in the heart of God. What Jesus Christ was in time and history, God is through all eternity. **Love bears all things.**

7b. Love Believes All Things.—In its context this means that the loving spirit is always prone to believe the best about men and women. Its constant attitude is to put the highest construction upon their motives, even if at times their conduct proves difficult to understand. The phrase might be translated rather freely, "Love is trustful of mankind." It will go to the uttermost lengths, trusting and believing in the better elements of human nature, before it is reluctantly forced to some other conclusion. That is far from asserting that love is credulous. Many a poet and many a mystic in various ways have pointed out that love, above all else, yields true insight. It was Burns's love for the simple daisy broken by his plowshare that made him describe it as a "bonnie gem." Browning in many a poem tells of the insight of love. Really to understand literature, one must love it. The same is true of music or any other art. Above all, it is true of men and women in their mutual relationships. Christ's great love for mankind enabled him to see the possibilities, hidden from all eyes but his, in those whom he called to be his disciples. Love sees beneath the surface because love is in harmony with reality. To love men in this way is to believe in their best. To believe in the best is to help to arouse and to evoke it. To be contemptuous of any person is to risk making that person worthy of contempt. Let love express itself by believing in the better possibilities of mankind and it becomes a challenge and an inspiration to men to live up to such high ideals and expectations for them. F. W. Robertson, minister of Trinity Chapel, Brighton, England, was such a man. He loved people and believed in them. His own life was a constant inspiration to those who knew him. It is said that a certain merchant kept a portrait of Robertson in his shop because, as he confessed to a friend, the very sight of it held him to honesty and decency and to all that is involved in a consistent Christian life. To love people, believing in their best, is to lift their eyes to the hills of accomplishment. What did the church in Corinth or in any place need more than this spirit?

Paul has the weaker brethren in mind as he writes, or those who have fallen. His words are thus to be taken to heart by the strong-minded who may be prone to indulge in censure. Let failings be pointed out, let faults be remedied, let wrongdoing be rebuked, but above all let those who have been dealt with thus be made to realize that they can recover their place as brothers beloved in the family circle, and that they have their contribution to make to its life. Christ's faith in God was truly wonderful, and from it came his wonderful faith in men. Knowing the weakness of Peter and the cowardice of the other apostles, prepared as he was for the treachery of Judas Iscariot, he yet went to the Cross, believing that these men, with one exception, would sustain his mission and spread his message and spirit throughout the Roman Empire, and that future generations would give that message a hearing denied to him. How marvelously his faith in man has been justified! One indispensable quality needed to attain the best is to believe in its possibility. That rehabilitates failure: it enhances every good gift and quality. **Love . . . believes all things.**

7c. Love Hopes All Things.—We shall plumb some of the depths of Paul's use of the word "all" in this phrase if we remember that love goes on hoping for the best even if for the time it can find no adequate ground for such hope. This is one of the distinctive marks of the truly Christian spirit; this is one of the marks of the Lord Jesus. His love yielded the insight into human nature which made him hopeful where others saw no hope. He saw the possibilities of the fishermen of Galilee, of Mary Magdalene, of Paul himself even when Paul was a bitter enemy of the Christian church. There is the authentic ring of personal experience in this great section of the letter to Corinth. The kindliest people, longing as they do for better things in those with whom they may be concerned, often fail to find adequate ground for hope. But because their kindliness is inspired by Christian love they go on hoping against hope. Love may not be able to give reasons for its hopefulness, but it will not relinquish its hopes. No one whom the world would account worthless is so regarded by Christian love. "What shall we do with this worthless wretch?" said a doctor, speaking in Latin to his colleagues, with regard to a victim of poverty picked up as dead and sent to them for surgical experiments. To their surprise the supposedly dead man answered in faultless Latin, "Call not him worthless for whom Christ died." The prodigal son is still a son, the erring daughter is still a daughter. There is a chair in the true home, and a place in the true parent's heart for them, until

may also mean "cover," and perhaps should be so translated here. The meaning then would be, as in I Pet. 4:8, that "love covers a multitude of sins." Moffatt is paraphrasing that idea when he uses the phrase, "slow to expose." Love will always take this attitude because it clings to the possibility that the wrongdoer will come to a true insight.

---

the day arrives when they "come to themselves" and so find the way back to complete restoration in the family circle. For long there may be no sign that justifies such optimism. Yet love goes on hoping. Love knows that there is a limit to the frustration of better things, to the loneliness that man can bear, and so it bides its time.

The reason for love's hopefulness is not difficult to find. Love is of God, for God is love. They who truly love abide in God, and God abides in them (see I John 4). This first epistle of John can profitably be read in conjunction with I Cor. 13. The love of God is marked most strongly by his longing and questing for man. He is engaged on a quest that he will sustain until he attains his purpose. Can such love ever finally be deflected? On the other hand, man is made for God: in his own way he is a seeker. There is that in his nature which can never be satisfied apart from God. In this sense God has a point of contact with man, no matter how debased he may be. The splendor of the divine image in which he was created may be a clouded splendor but it is there. Every now and then it keeps breaking through. Sometimes the most unlikely people surprise us by the height to which in an emergency they can rise. This gives the Godlike insight of love its basis for hope. No possibility should be excluded. **Love . . . hopes all things.**

The apostle pleads for this facet of the diamond he has been describing to his Corinthian friends. There were loveless and almost hopelessly unlikeable people in that church. These injected an element of bitterness and churlishness into the atmosphere of the fellowship. They were a great disappointment both to their fellow members and to the apostle himself. Their name is legion. They are to be met with in practically every Christian community; it is difficult to feel charitable toward them. They are in a truculent minority of one or two where the major decisions of the church are concerned. They will not accept the will of the majority. They will undermine if they can the status of other members of the fellowship. But they are brethren for whom Christ died. They are men and women who were made in God's image. His love seeks for them until it finds them and transforms them. It meets truculence and opposition and a fractious spirit with love that hopes steadily for better things. God's love should be reflected undiscouragedly in all who call themselves by the name of Christ; this ought to be a mark of those who are "called to be saints." To follow that calling in such circumstances can never be easy. But Jesus never promised his followers that it would be easy. If this world is meant to be a playground and its purpose pleasantness, then we may resign ourselves to despair. If it is meant to be a school for souls, then let us be prepared to deal with difficult situations and difficult people. Above all, let love prevail. Someone has said that "man has always had to climb the cataract"; but in doing it he has achieved great character. That cataract runs through the church as well as through other aspects of life. Love will go on persisting in hopefulness as it climbs. It will go on hoping when the waters are thundering past and the footholds and handholds are slippery. But as God's spirit is in it, surely one day it will reach the crest of the fall; somehow, somewhere, sometime, it may be in ways beyond our present knowledge, the love of God will triumph over every obstacle.

What holds for the church community in Corinth and elsewhere throughout the centuries holds too for social, national, and international relationships. Often enough the signs of the time seem to herald an irremediable darkness. Men speak often of the impending ruin of civilization. Yet over that scene is the love of God. Such love is the adamantine rock on which everything that denies and rejects it shall be broken. But some things are broken for the sake of their ultimate salvation and their abiding beauty. Things sometimes have to be broken in love that the beauty of holiness may be achieved. This is a work of love. A star was broken to make the planets; a rainbow in all its beauty is broken light; a bud is broken before the flower may appear; a family circle is broken that another family circle may be formed. The body and the heart of the Christ were broken on a Cross that men might be saved. These are illustrations of the work of love. Reality is love, love is reality! Who or what can ultimately resist it? Christ was the incarnate love. No matter to what depths men may fall, on the very morass of human sin love lays the foundations of its boundless hopes and its sublime optimism. Nothing can limit it. **Love . . . hopes all things.**

7d. Love Endures All Things.—This also is one of the tests of Christian love. Where there is no obvious ground for faith it continues to

8 Charity never faileth: but whether *there be* prophecies, they shall fail; whether

8 Love never ends; as for prophecy, it

c) The Permanence of Love (13:8-13)

8-11. The permanence of love is set forth in a succinct topic sentence; but some readers of the KJV miss the meaning of **faileth.** The Greek does not mean that love always succeeds

hope; where there is no apparent ground for hope it continues to endure. Love is like an army that is threatened with overwhelming defeat by superior numbers of the enemy but steadfastly refuses to give ground. In the now classic words of the British field marshal, Earl Haig, in the dark days of 1918, when it seemed as if everything was lost, and as if the exultant foe of those years was sweeping on in triumph to a resounding victory, "Our backs are to the wall." Then followed the demand for a steadfastness that would endure without giving way. Love is often called upon to do something similar. Despite the darkest midnight it looks toward the dawn. It endures.

Here also is one of the characteristic marks of strong Christian witness. Speaking to his followers and warning them of the trials and difficulties that would beset them as they pursued their Christian pilgrimage, Jesus said, "But he who endures to the end will be saved" (Matt. 10:22). And the author of the Epistle to the Hebrews, pondering the tenor of the Master's life, wrote for the strong comfort of the Hebrew Christians who were undergoing a fierce test, "Consider him who endured from sinners such hostility against himself, so that you may not grow weary or fainthearted" (Heb. 12:3). To adapt a phrase of George Herbert's, such love is like "seasoned timber": it "never gives." It stands every test. Those who walk in the spirit of Christian love have their example in One who endured the Cross and despised the shame, and is now seated at the right hand of the throne of God (Heb. 12:2).

It is so easy for those who are engaged in Christian social service, either in the Christian community itself or in the community at large, to grow weary in their well-doing. The world needs desperately to be saved. But in the main, so far as spiritual and moral well-being are concerned, it reveals little evidence of any desire for such salvation. To lift humanity to a higher plane of social living, of international righteousness or economic justice and peace, is a herculean task. One need look for little help, and perhaps even less gratitude, from those whom one would help. So easy is it in such circumstances to become embittered or cynical or soured. But the love that is inspired of Christ, the love that is lit from eternal fountains of fire, will cling to the task in every field despite reverse and disappointment. Love's back may often be against the wall, but that wall is exactly what faith in God is meant to provide—and does provide. At the heart of love is the quality of endurance. But for those who endure, the ultimate triumph comes.

8*a*. ***Love Never Ends.***—Now comes like a benediction Paul's great assurance of the finality of love. This is the last pearl in the necklace that he has been forming; or to retain a previous metaphor, it is the last facet in the diamond, and the light it reflects is full of color. Moffatt translates it, "Love never disappears," which conveys a similar thought. The KJV puts it, **Charity never faileth,** and Weymouth, "Love never fails." Perhaps these renderings get just a little closer to the apostle's meaning. The Greek phrase he actually uses can be translated with fair accuracy, love "never falls down on its job." That rendering covers both the unendingness and the unfailing nature of love. Paul's suggestion is clear: Love, if it is the real thing, never lets us down. Surely there were those in the church in Corinth to whom this needed to be said. Real love is eternal, and it is final, for it is of the very essence of God himself. Were such love to fail, it would mean that God had failed; that the situation had become too much of a burden to be sustained; that the forces ranged against him were stronger than he. How could the apostle cherish such a thought? The love of God, as revealed in Christ, is as vast and enduring as eternity. It never ends. Let us follow that thought for a time.

As we have seen, there was jealousy in the Corinthian church over the possession of different spiritual gifts, and as the outcome of a certain accepted assessment of their relative value (vs. 4*b*). Now the apostle, who has been urging the members of that church to consider the wonderful prospect that this greatest of all gifts is open to everyone, however humble, contrasts it daringly with these other gifts which were held in such high esteem. He has, indeed, been emphasizing in glorious speech the wonder of love as the supreme gift. It "bears all things, believes all things, hopes all things, endures all things." No defeats or disappointments, no trials or disillusionment, no adverse circumstance whatever can get it down. It builds an

—that it is sure to win—rather, it will never "fail" in the sense of "come to an end." The Elizabethan translators were using **fail** as the equivalent of "diminish" or "perish." Though that could not happen to love, transiency was the inevitable fate of all other gifts of the Spirit; **prophecy, tongues,** and **knowledge** have no permanence. Paul's repetitious style is abandoned by the KJV when it gives three different renderings of the same

---

edifice of glorious hopes and resplendent optimism on the least inviting foundation. Now Paul carries his claim for love a stage further. He wants to make it clear to the minds of all who will read his epistle that love has no equal as a spiritual gift. Here he adds the finishing touch to his theme. **Love never ends.**

That is always one of the distinguishing marks of genuine love: it is not evanescent. There is no end to the love that we see in Jesus Christ. It is illustrated in the relationship between Jesus and his followers. "Having loved his own who were in the world, he loved them to the end" (John 13:1). We know that he loved them beyond the end, "Lo, I am with you always, to the close of the age" (Matt. 28:20). We know only too well how they failed him, grieved him, disappointed him; how one denied him and another betrayed him; but nothing could diminish his love for them. Even at the supper table he made a gesture of love to Judas Iscariot when he offered him a piece of bread soaked in wine; and in the garden of Gethsemane he greeted Judas with the word "friend" (John 13:21, 26; Matt. 26:50). Paul, who entered so deeply into the mind and spirit of his Master, in another of his marvelous rhapsodies summons into his presence all the enemies that can daunt and defeat the human soul, looks them straight in the face and bids them "Begone," for he knows that nothing can separate him from the love of God that is in Christ Jesus (Rom. 8:38-39). These glorious convictions of the Christian faith, based on personal experience of the love of Christ, have become part of the precious heritage of the church in every age. The eternal quality of this heavenly love lies behind all the great assurances the Master gave to his fearful disciples in the upper room on the night in which he was betrayed. He knew that love was stronger than death, that it transcended death, and that it would bring Master and disciples together again (John 16:22). What radiance of assurance there has been in such a promise for those who have known great sorrow from his day to ours! It is based on this knowledge that love is eternal, and that God who is love never relinquishes those whom once he has made his own. Death can make no difference to him. He whose love gave us life has conquered death. Divine love is eternal.

This is one of the qualities of love that was bound to appeal greatly to the Corinthian Christians: it marks love at once as vastly superior to those other gifts which some so greatly coveted. Those other gifts were by their very nature evanescent; love by its very nature is permanent. Paul illustrates his point and drives it home in a series of contrasts.

8*b*. *Love Contrasted with Prophecy*.—Surely the apostle does not intend to belittle the value of prophecy. We shall see presently that he gives it a high rank in the hierarchy of gifts. But with all its great qualities it is not comparable to love. Prophecy is a "forthtelling." It is inspired insight into the purposes of God. It is a deeper reading of the trend of events. But it is conditioned by time and by circumstance: it is linked to faith. Time comes when prophecy will be fulfilled and time itself will end. This world is the terrestrial phase of God's eternal purposes. When it has fulfilled its part it will be superseded, and with it the necessity for prophecy; for prophecy has as its purpose the strengthening of our faith. In that day when we shall walk in God's presence, not "by faith" but "by sight," there will be no need for prophecy; yet love will still abide.

Similarly with prophecy regarded as preaching. That is a great vocation. To be a preacher of the gospel is the highest office to which any may attain. But by its very nature prophetic preaching is a transient thing: it presupposes an imperfect world, a world still largely unreconciled to God. So long as this is so, preaching will be necessary. But when the dawn of eternity breaks forever upon our souls, then in the realm of perfection thus revealed there can be no further place for preaching. None will need to be brought to God; none will need to be put into saving relationship by faith with Jesus Christ: for every eye shall see him and every tongue confess his name (Phil. 2:9-11; Rev. 22:3-5). But love will still remain; for in the realm of God love is his nature and his name.

8*c*. *Love Contrasted with Tongues*.—As for tongues, they will cease. We have noticed that Paul deals tenderly with those in the church who were given to ecstatic utterances; but it is obvious enough from what he has already said—and he will say more presently—that he did not hold the gift of tongues in very high esteem. Yet these people seemed to set great store upon this bizarre, dramatic, and individual gift. They rated it even above prophecy.

there be tongues, they shall cease; whether *there be* knowledge, it shall vanish away.

will pass away; as for tongues, they will cease; as for knowledge, it will pass away.

verb καταργηθήσεται, **pass away.** Our present **knowledge** is **imperfect.** This fact is obvious and Paul's appreciation of it is not surprising; but it *is* striking that he should speak of the coming of the **perfect,** not as bringing the **imperfect** to completion, but as meaning its entire abolishment. He is not thinking of the growth of scientific information,

Its one value—and that is of no great significance—may have been that it attracted unbelievers to the church. But when the church has become strong enough to dispense with such adventitious aids, then best let them die a natural death. Incidentally, the same thought might be applied to certain modern methods of attracting the attention of present-day unbelievers. There is a definite place for good taste and dignity and reticence in setting before men the message of the church. Sometimes the "end" is lost sight of in a maze of "means." The Corinthians lost sight of the greater value of love in their anxiety to possess the meretricious gift of tongues. To do so was to neglect the permanent for the transient. Speaking with tongues had no future at all. The gift could not be justified even on the ground that it edified those who spoke or those who heard. Hence, in the nature of the case, speaking with tongues was bound to vanish from the regular life and witness of the church. It has largely done so, and without spiritual loss. But love remains a permanent necessity. One imagines that the gift of tongues in the modern sense of the phrase—i.e., extensive acquaintanceship with foreign languages—will no longer be necessary in the hereafter! The human imagination simply cannot conceive what the conditions of that life will be, but it is possible to think that love will find a mode of expression which will be used and understood by all. Tongues will cease but love will remain: it never ends.

8*d*. *Love Contrasted with Knowledge*.—As for knowledge, it will pass away. The Corinthians boasted of their knowledge. There were "intellectuals" in the church who prided themselves on their superior insight into the mysteries of the faith. They had lost from view an important fact which, obvious though it is, seems to be frequently overlooked, i.e., knowledge is never final; it is ever expanding. Moreover, the more men know, if they are also wise, then the more they realize how much they still have to learn. The people who know most are invariably humble and therefore wise. Such was one of the lessons that Socrates sought to teach the Athenians in the agora, and such was the lesson Paul tried to teach his converts in Corinth. He does not disparage knowledge; that is also needed for the adequate presentation of the gospel. But he knew well that there was no finality about knowledge. Theology is constantly undergoing change; so is science; so are literary forms and their expression. Change in knowledge involves every field of human interest and endeavor. It is like the flowing stream according to Heraclitus. In respect of any kind of knowledge his followers were wont to say, "You cannot put your hand into the same river twice." The waters flow on. So it is with knowledge.

But love remains. Knowledge may become as obsolete as the scientific theories or inventions of a hundred years ago; but love is never obsolete. We outgrow the knowledge of bygone days, but we never outgrow the need for love. As Moffatt has put it, love never disappears from the scene. All else may go: riches, position, fame, even prophecy and knowledge; but love, being eternal in God, is immortal in man. We lose these other things; love is never lost. It binds the life here with the life hereafter, and assures us above prophecy or knowledge that we shall meet our loved ones again. The very pain in our hearts as we stand by an open grave is God's assurance to us that as human love is stronger than death, so his divine love is stronger still. Let all Christians then hold to love. Knowledge fades and passes away; love knows no such end.

"Love never fails" (Weymouth). Let us turn now to the second thought suggested by the phrase under discussion, viz., that "love does not fall down on its job"; it never lets one down. That is a very great claim for even Paul to make. So often love does seem to fail. It fails when those to whom it is directed are unresponsive, as in the case of Judas Iscariot. Sometimes it fails because of something lacking in those who would exercise it. If love is not tempered by judgment, it can easily degenerate into something like sentimentality, e.g., the kind of sentimentality that we observe in overindulgent parents. Yet the Christian gospel is supremely a gospel of love, and the Christian fellowship is a fellowship of love. Here we are dealing with central matters: the entire epistle, with its constant insistence on the need for unity in the things of the gospel and in the life

but of the coming of the new age. The transition from the experiences of this age to those of the age to come is compared with the transition from childhood to manhood. The "I" is not meant by Paul as personal, for what he says is true of everyone. The analogy is not free from fault. It is true that childish games and immature ideas are not

---

of the community, leads up to this section, with its strong insistence on the supremacy of love. How could it be otherwise? The gospel message is that God is love. Jesus Christ, the great revealer of God, lived a life of love. His requirement from his disciples was that they should love one another. And the mission of the church to the world is that the law of love—love to God and, as its corollary, love to man—should be the foundation of all civilization. By this gospel message, by its truth or falsity, Christianity stands or falls. In what sense can Paul say that "love never fails"?

Earlier in his letter he has written that while knowledge "puffs up," love "builds up" (8:1). There he emphasizes the constructive work of love. To be sure, in an imperfect world the sanction of force is necessary for the preservation of law and order. In the premoral stage of life, while as yet the right and good are not chosen and done for their own sake, sanctions to secure both right and good are needed. Only so can chaos be held at bay. There is such a sanction involved, e.g., in the blood-feud code. But in the long run coercion can never finally solve social and individual problems involved. Coercion has definite limits. Moral good will, or at its deepest, Christian love, is required for all truly abiding, constructive work. Love is needed to achieve fine married life, true parenthood, the building of good homes and sound national life, of character and morale. The cross of Christ itself is the ultimate expression of the failure of coercive force to gain such ends. At Calvary evil, allied to force, nailed incarnate Love to a tree. But the flag of victory refused to wave over the heads of the crucifiers. The victory remained, and throughout the long centuries continues to remain, with love. Races, nations, and empires founded on force have come into being, have endured for a time in the colorful pageant of human history, have waxed in strength, and then have faded away and perished as though they had never existed. But the Cross, symbol of sacrificial love, still leads the generations on.

Love never fails to set up a standard of judgment—a test and a goal at which to aim. How often this happens in the realm of values. One of the vital necessities of life is that humanity should achieve and hold fast to a scale of values. Beauty is such a value. Where it appears it sets up a standard and a test by which we can judge everything in its neighborhood. It may take the form of a picture, a vase, a spray of flowers, a verse of poetry, a shaft of sunlight striking a cliff or a hillside, the binding of a book, or something else; wherever it does appear it sets up this standard of value and of judgment. So love came into the world, as never before, in Jesus Christ. With his coming a new standard and test were set up. In the light of his teaching and life it is being slowly borne in upon the mind and conscience of man that, in the world God has created, his way is the only possible way for all humanity. Violence of every type has no future. The future lies with the constructive good will supremely revealed through Jesus Christ. One has only to look at the world and to read history to realize that every other way has failed. Who can doubt that if all mankind were animated by the spirit of Christ, this world would be a place of justice, peace, security, decency, and happiness for ourselves and for all humanity? Common sense and genuine good will must ever seek to keep that standard before the eyes of men. Man must strive after it, judge everything by it, and seek the grace and power of God to help him approximate it. Love never falls down in its task of setting before us such a standard.

Love never fails to achieve great results. Given its opportunity, it never fails to achieve great character. Love is a magic gift that enriches the giver as well as the person to whom it is offered. The more love one gives, the more loving in spirit one becomes. We tend to think mainly of love's effect on those to whom love is given; but there is also this profound effect on those who love. The greatest souls in the long annals of the race have been those who could sincerely say, "Write me as one who loved his fellow men." Paul was deeply concerned that these Corinthians should have a firm grasp of the constructiveness of love. By implication, bitterness, jealousy, pride, and ill-will never fail to destroy fellowship. These were threatening the very existence of the church in Corinth. The "more excellent way" never fails to build fellowship, because it is constructive in the realm of character. Jesus Christ is by far the greatest personality in human history. We still date our calendars from his day. The central secret of his greatness is that he loved the whole world and gave himself in love for its salvation. Surely the future belongs to love and not to its opposite. Love never fails, when given its opportunity, to achieve great and beneficial and

9 For we know in part, and we prophesy in part.

9 For our knowledge is imperfect and our

carried over into manhood, but there is no such discontinuity as is here indicated; our knowledge does grow from more to more. The analogy fails at another point also: **a man**

constructive aims. Wherefore let the church in Corinth and all over the world make love its aim; for love never ends and love never fails.

9-12. *Contrast of the Indirect and the Direct, the Imperfect and the Perfect.*—Paul is so concerned with making his points on love clear and strong that he buttresses his previous statements with this additional series of contrasts. Moffatt, in a very fruitful passage, draws the contrast in these verses between the knowledge that is indirect and that which is direct.[4] This suggestion is strengthened if we include the contrast that is in Paul's mind between the imperfect and the perfect. We notice in passing that there is no reference in the passage to the gift of tongues; the implication is that this much-esteemed type of ecstatic speech, in the apostle's view, has no future at all. As such it is hardly worthy of further consideration, although Paul has some final words to write concerning it (ch. 14). It is a gift of little value. But he goes on to say that the much higher and more valuable gifts of knowledge and prophecy are also to vanish in the full revelation of perfection, even as the pools left on the sea beaches among the low-lying rocks are swallowed up in the fullness of the returning tide. On this side of time, so to speak, knowledge and prophecy are in the very nature of the case bound to be indirect, partial, and fragmentary. What a wonderful piece of philosophical anticipation there is in these thoughts! Modern epistemology confirms the apostle's view. We apprehend our world in terms of sense experience, and sense experience yields power and adaptation, but provides only the initial data for genuine philosophical and scientific insight into the nature of reality both in its physical and spiritual aspects. Reality must "appear" in order to be known. But as more than one philosophical and scientific thinker has pointed out, there is a vast difference between reality as it "appears" to our senses, and as it must be conceived by scientific thought. To be sure, even in sense data we have a direct face-to-face apprehension of the world in which we live; but this bestowal yields power rather than insight. To that extent our knowledge of the world is indirect.

Plato, in his allegory of the cave, said much the same thing. Mankind apprehends only shadowy representations of the realities amid which life is set. Man must await his translation to, and acceptance by, the spiritual realm before he can feast his astonished eyes upon the perfect ideas, the pattern laid up in heaven, of which these representations are a shadowy and imperfect copy.

Maybe Paul, as a university man, had some acquaintance with the teachings of Plato. Certainly he well understands that both knowledge and prophecy, wonderful "gifts" though these undoubtedly are, no matter how both may be progressively enlarged, are nevertheless bound to be partial and fragmentary. Those who know most, and we can add those to whom the prophetic inspiration is given, are conscious of this sobering truth, e.g., the more that science investigates the mystery of the universe, a mystery of which Paul is obviously aware, the more mysterious it becomes. The greatest scholars are learners to their dying day.

Similar considerations hold good in the realm of religious experience. Had the partial and fragmentary character of our knowledge been better realized, less exclusive claims might have been made by sections of the church as to the finality and completeness of their particular aspect of Christian witness; and the spirit of brotherliness, for which Paul is pleading, might have been sustained and developed, both to the advantage of the church and to the extension of its witness in the world. Knowledge and prophecy for this great and liberal-minded apostle are valuable; they yield true insight. As such they are to be used with judgment and discretion; but they are incomplete, indirect, and therefore imperfect and never final. Man's deepest and most comprehensive knowledge, and also the insight that prophecy may bring, still leave him a child in the elementary grades of the school of religious experience and of the knowledge of God and God's ways. Paul softens any hint of asperity there might be in his allusion to childishness by reverting courteously and thoughtfully, as his wont is, to the personal pronoun. **When I was a child, I spoke like a child, I thought like a child, I reasoned like a child** (cf. Exeg., vs. 11). He makes willing and full admission of his immaturity. In the schoolrooms on earth one must pass through the infant grades before proceeding to the junior and senior grades. But with maturer judgment

[4] *I Corinthians*, pp. 200-2.

10 But when that which is perfect is come, then that which is in part shall be done away.

prophecy is imperfect; **10** but when the perfect comes, the imperfect will pass away.

---

childish thoughts must go. **When I became a man, I gave up childish ways.** Notice here that Paul never lost his childlike heart. Childlikeness and childishness are not the same thing. The childlike mind is trustful, pure, imaginative, receptive. Jesus himself commended it in memorable words (Mark 10:13-16; Luke 18:15-17; Matt. 18:2-3; 19:13-15). The childlike mind is an essential condition for entry into the kingdom of heaven. But childishness is pettiness in an adult, and implies immaturity. Some members of the community at Corinth were childish; that Paul rebukes. Childlikeness he was certain to commend. What is appropriate to the years of childhood in the sense indicated is an anachronism when one reaches adult life.

Therefore, as with growth in so-called secular knowledge there are lessons and experiences and a development appropriate to childhood, so is it in the realm of spiritual knowledge and experience. Just as in the record of Scripture itself there is the story of man's progressive knowledge and understanding of God and God's ways, so is it in human life, and so is it in the Christian church. There must be growth in understanding. Yet at their best both prophecy and knowledge are imperfect. Probably Paul has prophecy in mind rather than knowledge; or it may be he assumes that such knowledge of God and God's ways as men have, has come through prophecy (vs. 9). But the insights and revelation of the prophetic consciousness depend on dreams and visions and intuitions that well up into the conscious mind from that region of transubjective, interpretative, and inferential processes which is commonly called the "unconscious," and where, it would appear, the Spirit of the living God makes one contact with finite man. Man's knowledge of God is thus, even for the prophets, indirect and imperfect. These men whose sensitiveness to things spiritual made them available for God's revelation to their day and generation were aware of the inspiration of God, not always directly, but in the effects and consequences of his presence. Just as we know by the stirring of the leaves of the trees, or by the foam-flecked waves of the sea, or by a pressure on our faces, that the viewless wind is blowing, so are we aware of God's presence, not directly, not perfectly, but by appropriate signs that we have learned to interpret and to understand. This does not diminish the reality or the greatness or even the grandeur of the experience; but it does indicate that in the nature of the case, and in the light of our present development and experience, our knowledge of God is a dim, blurred, fragmentary, indirect, and imperfect experience.

Before we proceed further with this point let us draw at least one outstanding lesson. To realize the imperfection of both knowledge and prophecy should save Christian folk from pride and from a dogmatic spirit. Many a so-called heretic would have been saved from unchristian persecution had this imperfection and indirectness of Christian knowledge been more generally realized and acknowledged. Often enough such heretics have been the pioneers of larger spiritual truths. Jesus himself was a heretic in the eyes of the orthodox Jews of his day. There was no need at all for dogmatic assertion of any personal point of view in the church at Corinth; there was every need for a spirit of toleration and brotherliness which realized that the white light of knowledge and prophecy is made up of many colors, and is all the richer because of it. That truth still holds: it invites those who name themselves by Christ's name to practice the open mind and to realize that there is still more light and truth to break forth from God's word.

10-12. ***When the Perfect Comes, the Imperfect Will Pass Away.***—Paul reinforces his main contention, viz., the temporary nature of all imperfection, in order to make a final avowal on the permanence of love. New knowledge continually makes past knowledge obsolete, and therefore supersedes it. Prophecy never reaches finality in respect of its spiritual insight into the nature and purposes of God; but Paul looks forward with hope, and he bids the church in Corinth to do the same, to a day when like Moses—this would seem to be the thought in the background of his mind—we shall see God and speak with him face to face (see Exeg., vs. 12). In the fullness of that vision and intercourse perfection of knowledge will come and prophecy will cease. In that grand consummation all imperfection will vanish. Plato's cave dwellers will dispense with shadowy representations when at long last they gaze upon "the eternal ideas," the ultimate realities. So Christians, when they stand in the white revealing light of God's holy love, will be able to dispense with inferences based on the effect and consequences of his presence. In the beauty of the fullness of that intimate personal communion and fellowship the Christian will be living in the realm of that perfect knowledge and perfect

11 When I was a child, I spake as a child, I understood as a child, I thought as a child: but when I became a man, I put away childish things.

[11] When I was a child, I spoke like a child, I thought like a child, I reasoned like a child; when I became a man, I gave up

is presented as deliberately putting away his **childish ways.** The coming of the Parousia, however, will not depend upon any such act of human will.

understanding of God which is of the very essence of heaven. All limitations will have gone forever.

Meanwhile knowledge, though incomplete, and prophecy, though imperfect, are not to be disregarded. The apostle uses a homely, well-understood and well-chosen illustration to clarify his message. **For now we see in a mirror dimly, but then face to face. Now I know in part; then I shall understand fully, even as I have been fully understood.** Such mirrors as Paul had in mind were made of polished metal, either of silver or of bronze, and Corinth was famous for the production of such mirrors. But at their best they reflected no clear image. So is it with man's apprehension of God. He has no clear apprehension. Through the dim voices of nature he hears the voice of God suggesting that the Creator is the author and giver of law and beauty, and that man must conform to nature's laws and so adapt himself to God's purposes. But the majesty of God as thus conceived is dimmed by the problem of physical evil. The war of nature, famine and death, the widespread entail of suffering through disease and national catastrophe, things for which man is not always to blame, cast their shadows over the being of God. Man does not understand. He tries to trust and to believe that his life is set in the midst of a friendly universe. But he sees as in a mirror, dimly.

Through the strange and varied pageant of human history man seeks for God. Is contingency the law of human life? Is it all a matter of chance? Is man the product of forces that had no prevision whatever of the ends they have actually achieved, or are these strange, immortal longings that stir within his breast the intimation of his high status and destiny as a child of God? When one thinks of the trials and the sufferings of the innocent and the righteous, and of all that is involved in the problem of moral and spiritual evil, it is often difficult to believe in the omnipotence and the omnipresence and the infinite love and grace of God. Job's great exclamation is pertinent. "Oh that I knew where I might find him!" (Job 23:3.) Christian faith has to be at its best when things are at their worst, but that does not make it easy to believe in God. Man sees as in a mirror, dimly.

Through scripture God seeks to reveal himself to man; but often enough the note of uncertainty sounds even there. Psalmists and prophets saw more clearly than their fellows and tried to tell what they saw. But Paul himself, nurtured in the tradition created by lawgivers, psalmists, and prophets, acknowledges in this very letter the imperfect nature of their deepest insights. We believe that we see God most clearly in Jesus Christ. How otherwise can we account for that strange figure, and for his saving impact upon men throughout the centuries? Yet even there the reflections are not always clearly defined. The Godhead is veiled in flesh. Jesus could not explain himself to men as clearly and completely as he himself would have desired. "I have yet many things to say to you, but you cannot bear them now" (John 16:12). Despite all the subsequent revelation of God's grace and purpose which we have had throughout the centuries by the inspiration of the Holy Spirit, these words of the Master still hold good, and will hold good to the end of time. The most comprehensive knowledge and the highest prophecy will remain incomplete and to a degree obscure, like "baffling reflections in a metal mirror"; but in the fullness of God's perfect time faith will be translated into sight, and inference into a full, satisfying personal communion. Thus all imperfection of both knowledge and prophecy will end. Meantime, those who live by faith and hope and love are on the way that leads home; and the great apostle finds comfort for himself, for his converts in Corinth, and for all who read his words, in the thought that though man's understanding of God is dim and incomplete, yet God knows man and loves him. The mystery exists on man's side, not on God's. There is therefore a place for faith and hope, both of them enriched as they are illumined by the spirit of love in the individual and in the church. **Then I shall understand fully, even as I have been fully understood.**

There are wider and more suggestive implications of the phrase under discussion. More than once the apostle expresses his sense of the mystery of God's ways to the mind and spirit

12 For now we see through a glass, darkly; but then face to face: now I know in part; but then shall I know even as also I am known.

childish ways. 12 For now we see in a mirror dimly, but then face to face. Now I know in part; then I shall understand fully, even

12. Paul now turns to an entirely different figure in order to express the radical difference between the experiences of this age and the life of the age to come. Our glass **mirrors** may give a perfect reflection of an object, but that was not the case with the polished metal of the ancient world. Moffatt has paraphrased effectively in his rendering, "the baffling reflections in a mirror." This approaches the view of the letter to the Hebrews that earthly forms are only copies of the heavenly realities. **Face to face** indicates the immediacy of contact with God which Moses had enjoyed (Num. 12:8). We would expect the observation that our present knowledge is partial to be followed by the

---

of man (see 1:18-29; 2:1-14). Doubtless a similar thought is somewhere in the back of his mind as he writes of love, and also the necessity here for the exercise of faith and hope. Throughout the centuries there have always been those who have had genuine difficulty in acquiring a strong faith in God, not just the faith to which they can hold, but a faith which can support and encourage them. In fact, the supreme task of every age is to rehabilitate faith in God and love for God. Yet many, sincere seekers among them, are baffled in their quest for faith and love of God. Paul would have been kind and considerate to such people. Jesus himself respected honest inquirers and seekers who came to question him: he even taught some of them how to put their questions. Paul is aware of the imperfection of knowledge and prophecy on earth; he is conscious of these "baffling reflections" seen in the metal mirror, and he would certainly insist that it is part of the task of the church to help those who are on the quest. Some things he would be sure to say not only to the incertitude of his times but also to our own.

Hold fast even to an imperfect faith. One step is to hold to what we have, however incomplete and imperfect, against the day of fuller knowledge and greater insight. Let men and women believe as much as they can. That is at least a beginning. The implication is plain throughout his epistles, and in this letter to the church in Corinth, that the concept of God is so great, so august, and so awe-inspiring, that no human mind can fully take it in. Should we be surprised that it makes difficulties for faith? The situation is similar with regard to scientific truth. Scientists have been exploring the mystery of the physical universe, and the more deeply they penetrate that mystery, the more mysterious it becomes. Yet no scientist would be deflected from his exploration by his consciousness of deepening mystery. That consciousness would itself inspire further exploration. He would hold to what he had and make it the basis for another voyage of discovery.

Let it be so with God. We can be grateful for the dim reflections. Other great believers in every age have been overwhelmed by the greatness of the mystery. Paul had his moments of insight which he simply could not put into words (II Cor. 12:1-4). Yet he believed what he could and was always ready, as his capacity for faith grew, to receive greater illumination. Many things trouble and confuse sincere and good men in their quest for a faith that will give life stability, inner coherence, and direction. If the lamp flickers, it is better to follow a fitful flame than walk in unlighted darkness. Meantime, let hope be allied to faith. An imperfect faith is the growing point of deeper insight and surer knowledge. If we are faithful to what we can believe, then we are on the road to more perfect knowledge: it will surely come.

Imperfect faith offers direction and guidance. These Corinthians are urged to hold to their faith despite its mysteries; it at least offers clearer direction and guidance than the pagan cults from which they have been emancipated. So it is in our day; so it has ever been. If there have been difficulties in the way of faith in God and love for God, there are also grave difficulties in the way of disbelief. Faith has its difficulties: Jesus Christ never promised his followers that they would find it easy to follow in his way. A great faith has always had to carry a heavy load of doubt and uncertainty and inconclusiveness. Yet there are many things that have their place in our common experiences of life that cannot adequately be illumined and understood in any other way than by faith in God. Consider the unity and coherence and law-abidingness of the world! Think of the heights of moral heroism and self-sacrifice to which human nature can rise when the call comes! How can we account for the great and inspiring and uplifting hours of life, as when we read

13 And now abideth faith, hope, charity, these three; but the greatest of these *is* charity.

as I have been fully understood. 13 So faith, hope, love abide, these three; but the greatest of these is love.

---

assurance that our knowledge hereafter will be complete; but that is not the way in which Paul expresses his thought here. At the Parousia he will **know** as God knows him. He also shifts to another word—a fact which the KJV obscures by using **know** in both clauses. The RSV renders the new term ἐπιγινώσκω as **understand: I shall understand fully, even as I have been fully understood.** It is not unusual for Paul to emphasize the fact that we are thus "known" by God (cf. 8:2).

13. One is tempted at this point to believe that Paul is quoting from a well-known slogan, for the phrase does not fit the context very well. As a matter of fact, the entire

---

great literature, or see something strikingly beautiful, or are hauntingly transported by sublime music? What explanation can we offer for the radiant and gracious personalities we have known? How account for Jesus Christ? No secularist explanation will suffice. There are grave difficulties on the side of unbelief: in its mirror too the reflections are dim. We must accept in these scenes of earth and life and time the difficulties that are associated with the point of view we choose as our interpretation of life. The imperfections of faith are preferable to those of disbelief.

"Trouble obscures God." To this charge Christian faith may reply that trouble is to be expected in a moral universe if mankind infringes the moral law. In any case it ought to be obvious enough that God cares more for the character of man than for his comfort, and trouble can play a wonderful part in developing the finer aspects of character. If this world was meant to be a school for character, we can face life with faith and hope and courage.

"Social and political confusion obscures God." To that charge it can be replied that Christian faith should not be, and is not, surprised or dismayed by social chaos. God's world will work only in God's way. Man has known for a long time what God requires of him. In that *praeparatio evangelica* which is to be found in the Greek philosophers as well as in the Hebrew prophets there has always been the insistence that it is better to be just than to be unjust, better to be generous than mean, better to be kind than cruel, better to be a friend than an enemy, better to love than to hate. But while knowledge comes, wisdom lingers. Moreover, Jesus Christ, fully sharing the limitations of our humanity, has demonstrated the abiding glory and splendor of a life lived in the light of these things as inspired by his great faith in God and by a great love for him. The alternative is to adopt a secularist interpretation of life which involves the pessimistic conclusion that all human effort and sacrifice and achievement are doomed, and that the cemetery is the end of all civilization. Christians, despite the difficulties of faith, hope, and love, are fully aware that **now we see in a mirror dimly,** but are not credulous enough to embrace secularism. They hold fast to faith, imperfect though it is, knowing that in the fullness of God's time the perfect will be revealed. Therefore they live in hope.

Moreover, there are certain practical and valuable effects even of a fragmentary faith. It does put meaning and coherence into life and history; it finds cosmic support for the moral life; it is convinced that righteousness and truth will triumph in the end, since the universe is working out a righteous purpose; it believes that love will hold the field. Where such a faith is strongly held it inspires great leadership. More, it constantly enlarges the range of man's spiritual vision. Christian faith claims every decent, clean, and worth-while activity for Christ and his kingdom. For the God revealed in him it seeks the best of all thought and knowledge, of labor and leisure, of politics, economics, commerce, and business, of recreation, and of all social and individual life. It bids Christians believe that they are not aliens in the world, whose main and urgent purpose is to pass through and out of it until they reach the eternal haven of light and peace and security. They are rather outposts of light in the darkness. They are here to stay, to endure, to fight and to triumph, until all the ambiguity of the darkness is dissipated forever by the light of the glory of God in the face of Jesus Christ. We can celebrate a faith, though aware of its imperfection, which holds within it the inspiration of the highest service and the promise of a fullness of life and knowledge and love to come. **Now I know in part; then I shall understand fully.** So be it.

13:13–14:1*a*. ***The Vital Necessity of Love.***— The great passage comes to its fitting close on a

paragraph seems to insist that **love** alone abides. The time is coming when **faith** will be replaced by knowledge, and when **hope** will find its realization. But in the new age **love** will not be superseded, for God is love (I John 4:8). Reitzenstein suggested (see Lietzmann, *An die Korinther I-II* [2nd ed.; Tübingen: J. C. B. Mohr, 1923; "Handbuch zum

---

lovely note. **So faith, hope, love abide, these three; but the greatest of these is love. Make love your aim.** Love is the supreme virtue: the words cannot mean anything less than this (see Exeg., vs. 13). It is Paul's great criterion of value. But that does not imply that the Corinthians or any other Christians can dispense with faith and hope. Paul may conceive it possible to have faith and hope without having love. That is possible, but it is also improbable: true love is both hopeful and faithful. Poets as well as apostles have celebrated the faithfulness and the hopefulness of love. Nor does the context bear the inference (but see Exeg.) that in the hereafter faith and hope shall be superseded and that love will remain. Faith will surely remain. The more adequate interpretation is that while here on earth faith has to struggle and strive in order to flourish, hereafter that particular strain will be lifted and faith will grow both in strength and in vigor. It is a good thing to have faith in an absent friend; but faith in him is strengthened by that close proximity that confirms one's best and deepest belief. Surely life in that fuller communion with God will confirm our deepest convictions and so strengthen and enrich our faith in him.

Likewise with hope. None can imagine what the conditions of the life hereafter are likely to be. All we can confidently assert is that God who has created the conditions under which we manifest ourselves here will create the conditions under which we shall continue to manifest ourselves hereafter. Whether these will involve space and time and ratiocination none can confidently affirm. We may safely leave it with God. Our hope of immortality is assured not in any estimate of the nature of the soul, but in all that we know about God, especially as he has revealed himself in Jesus Christ. Even so, it is impossible to imagine a heaven, with all that is involved in the eternal purposes of God and in his progressive revelation of himself to man, where there is no room for hope. Part of the essence of heaven will be that with all man ever learns about the infinite Being who gave him life, and whose lovingkindness is greater than life, there will still be more to know. This is the basis of a hope that abides. Here we are reminded again of a quotation that the apostle included earlier in his letter, "God has revealed to us through the Spirit" (2:10). But the revelation is unending, even as the resources of God are inexhaustible and the riches of Christ unsearchable. We shall never come to an end of exploration into the nature and being and purpose of God. Thus hope abides. And most surely love abides. To see the highest is to love it. Love is the life of heaven, for God is love and God is life. Love is therefore eternal and supreme: it is the ultimate criterion of value, never to be defined save in terms of itself.

In the light of this supreme value all other spiritual gifts fall into their relative and subordinate position. From the first the apostle has been concerned with the unity of the church and the spirit that animates its fellowship and its service. Here is the gift in which each member can share; it is denied to none. No one possessing it has any occasion for boasting or for thinking more highly of himself than he ought. Given the true spirit of love the community will at least approximate what it should be as the "body of Christ" on earth; and other spiritual gifts, distributed as they may be among the various members, will in turn make their contribution to the spiritual welfare of all.

There can be no doubt concerning the continuing validity of the apostle's teaching for all ages of Christian witness. As we have seen, the core of the gospel is love. Jesus Christ was the incarnation of love, and his commandment to his disciples was that they should love one another. These convictions are vitally and urgently necessary. Someone has said that if Christianity had really been understood and believed and practiced, then the world in which we live would present a far more pleasing spectacle to our gaze. There is a sobering and challenging truth in the statement. Jesus himself insisted that his followers should be known by their love for him and for one another. Paul, writing as he does, is simply reiterating the Master's teaching. After all, Jesus came not to lay down rules and regulations for human behavior, but to manifest a spirit and to be the pioneer of a new way of life. He blazed the trail, set up his signposts, and invited men and women to follow him. His revelation was of a quality of life initiated, sustained, and empowered by the grace of God. Without that spirit life is bound to be incomplete and imperfect and defective. Let us consider this briefly.

Love completes and crowns every human relationship. What is neighborliness if there is no love between neighbors? Asia, Europe, the Americas are vast neighborhoods; but they manifest little of the love that would produce

Neuen Testament"], p. 69) that as against a Gnostic quartet, faith, knowledge, love, and hope, Paul set a triad, which did not include *gnōsis*. But the triad is a favorite one with Paul; it is found in his earliest preserved letter (I Thess. 1:3; 5:8), and also in one of his latest (Col. 1:4-5). In all these instances he follows the more natural order of **faith,**

as its fruit mutual co-operation, justice, peace, and security. Married life soon goes to shipwreck if it is not crowned and completed by a spirit that burns with a steadier flame than the romantic passion which brings people together. Surely love burns with that flame. Parenthood is one of the precious relationships of life, yet there is bound to be a gulf between the generations in the same family circle if it is not bridged by love. We must approximate that love in the realm of international affairs if the family spirit is to spread over a world that is steadily becoming a smaller place. The relationship between the Master and his disciples was imperfect and incomplete until it had been crowned with love. Such is the main trend of his last talk to them in the upper room (John 14–16). This comprehensive, illuminating spirit of love is a vital and urgent necessity for the world in which we live.

Love is a contribution that everyone can make. Even the meekest and humblest, in Paul's view, can take his place and play a part. It is always a temptation to think, in the face of the superior endowment of others, or in the light of the pressing problems of the times, that one's own contribution can make small difference. And, indeed, the main problems of life in the personal, national, and international fields are not only pressing but almost overwhelming. What is any individual life, in the midst of the heaving tumult of such a scene, but a fragile reed swayed and bent by the storm? Yet it is wrong to yield to such temptations. One should never underestimate the personal contribution that may be made: it is not unimportant how ordinary, humble people comport themselves in such circumstances. One bucketful of water will not quench a raging fire; but the principle is right, and many buckets of water will do it. Man's life is set amid a vast web of personal relationships in an ever more closely integrated world, and that web of relationships, in some degree or other, affects the life of all mankind. Into that system of relationships we can each pour our personal contribution of love and fellowship. To do so is like dropping a pebble into a still pool. No section of that pool is undisturbed by the ensuing movement. So it is with the spiritual contribution that Christian people can make. We, unlike the Corinthian Christians—since we stand at this vantage point in time and history—may take comfort and draw inspiration from the undoubted fact that from small beginnings great issues have come. Mighty rivers have their sources in small mountain streams and springs. The Christian cause began with the Man of Nazareth and his Galilean fishermen and their friends. On the first Good Friday when he was crucified it seemed as if he and his cause were expunged in his own blood and in dire and pitiful tragedy. But the stream of salvation rolled on. Love triumphed and triumphs still. The stream has become an ocean of love. To that vast and continuing movement individuals have given significant service. How could it have prospered or spread, apart from individual contributions of love to Christ and to men? Or, to change the metaphor, there may seem at any given time to be but few great lights in the dark firmament of human history; but consider how dark the darkness would be were all the lesser lamps quenched! Let the lamp of love shine. In the ultimate consequence there will be such a vast aggregation of constellations made up of millions of individual lights as will drive the darkness away forever. The love of Jesus Christ is the great central sun from whose energy we draw our light. In heaven itself there will be no night at all—physical, mental, or spiritual: his love will be the light thereof (Rev. 22:5).

The future belongs to love. The future belongs to love because it speaks a language that everyone can understand and that everyone can speak if he will. A loving, kindly glance, or word, or shake of the hand, a simple deed, is recognized in every land. That is one reason why Henry Drummond in his well-known little book held that love is "the greatest thing in the world." We have seen how it enriches him who gives as well as those who receive it. But even more, the future belongs to it because love is the ultimate reality. God is love. Love is the guarantee that hate and fear and falsehood, all enmity and bitterness, are doomed. They are, as the Greek philosophers would put it, surds or streaks of irrationality in the cosmic scheme of things. The resurrection of Jesus Christ signifies for all future generations not only that love is the ultimate reality, but that to it the victory belongs. In that marvelous symbolic representation of the moral and spiritual struggle throughout the ages which is set forth in the strange book of Revelation, such is the verdict. All the unspeakable energy of a spiritual and moral universe is on the side of those who have aligned their life with the love that

14 Follow after charity, and desire spiritual *gifts,* but rather that ye may prophesy.	**14** Make love your aim, and earnestly desire the spiritual gifts, especially

love, and **hope.** A life which begins in **faith** expresses itself through **love** and is sustained by the **hope** of salvation. It is easy to see why Paul reverses the last two here. **Love** is not only **the greatest** gift of the Spirit; it is the only one which abides through eternity.

3. The Service of the Word (14:1-40)

a) Contrast of Prophecy and Tongues (14:1-12)

No longer does Paul stress satisfaction with the gifts which the Corinthians have. He specifically exalts not only the love which all might share but also the special gift of prophecy. He is not content now to assure those who lack the gift of tongues that they have equal evidence of possession by the Spirit. He points to prophecy as a distinctly superior gift because it builds up the community. In this chapter the curtain is raised on

---

was incarnate in Jesus Christ. Not death itself can defeat or destroy them. Wherefore, **make love your aim.**

14:1-40. ***Directions for the Exercise of Prophecy and Tongues.***—Having set up Christian love as a criterion and standard of judgment and value, and having made it quite clear that this supreme gift of the Spirit is available to every member of the church, Paul now turns to the delicate task of relegating other gifts, notably speaking with tongues and prophesying, to their respective places in the scale of value. The whole section is marked by a refreshing common sense, deep spiritual insight, and yet a winsome and gentle tactfulness that disarms resentment and embarrassment. When occasion required, Paul had a gentle touch. One is conscious of it here. Yet nowhere else in his writings does he make it more clear that he set little value on the gift of tongues. Certainly he makes it obvious that he sets high value on prophesying. His treatment of the subject is the more interesting because the possession of the gift of tongues was held in great esteem. As in pagan rites, so in the Christian communities of those days it was regarded as a marked sign of the divine presence. One reason for the apostle's tenderness in dealing with it is due to his consciousness that at its best it was a manifestation of the emotional enthusiasm engendered by the new faith: it was a sign of spiritual fervor. As such it was apt to be contagious. A near approach to it is seen in great revivalist gatherings, where emotion can sweep across a vast audience like a breeze rippling over a field of ripening corn. Speaking in tongues, as in certain instances of the same phenomenon in our own times, might take the form of an unintelligible monologue which was conceived to be inspired by the indwelling Spirit of God. Or it might take the form of ejaculations and ecstatic utterances, some of which were intelligible, as when the name of God was pronounced, or an ascription of gratitude or praise—such as "Glory" or "Hallelujah"—was incorporated with other less intelligible sounds. There is no need, following Paul's courteous and understanding example, to treat such manifestations with disdain. Their value may be, undoubtedly is, slight. But the manifestation was not confined to the less well-educated or less intelligent members of the community. Paul keeps his Corinthian friends in countenance by confiding to them, not without a hint of satisfaction, that he himself had often spoken with tongues (vs. 18). Yet he realized better than any other the limitations of this gift of the Spirit. It had engendered jealousy among the members of the church: some who did not possess it desired it as the mark of divine approval. Those who did possess it were apt to be proud of the distinction conferred upon them. Again, the effect on the church meetings was not altogether fortunate. Under the emotional tension that must often have developed, some who possessed the gift seem to have become hysterical, others lapsed into a catalyptic trance, while still others, feeling the tension, could not forbear breaking into utterance even while other brethren were speaking, and so brought disorder into the worship of the church. This upset the more sober-minded members, and at the same time called down upon the new faith the derision of unbelievers. There can be little doubt that some of the questions submitted to Paul concerned the use of this much-coveted gift. Thus, recognizing as he does that it is a genuine manifestation of sincere religious enthusiasm, and that as such it may have a certain place in the worship of the church, yet he realizes clearly that it must be controlled and disciplined. There is a place for order and decency in everything pertaining

the worship of a Gentile church. The service has little in common with the synagogue worship which was later to influence the development of Christian liturgy, with its fixed prayers, lessons from the law and the prophets, and the interpretation of these. That would have seemed far too "High Church" for these men and women imbued with pentecostal enthusiasm. They valued spontaneity and direct revelation.

It is clear from the chapter that by **tongues** Paul means speech directed toward God and caused by the Spirit. Words and sounds which are without connection and meaning to men are uttered in ecstasy. The phenomenon is well known to students of the psychology of primitive and emotional types of religion. Such outbursts were known in the Hellenistic mystical religions of the time, and some parallels are also to be found in Judaism. The magical papyri show formulas which contained a jumble of incoherent ejaculations. There have also been secular forms of tongues. If Corinthians held that ecstatic speaking was the mark of the Spirit par excellence, it must be remembered that the author of Acts also saw in the gift of tongues proof that the Spirit had been given (Acts 10:46; 19:6). Though there may be some question about the exact nature of the event at Pentecost, there can be no possibility that Paul is speaking here of a capacity to speak in foreign languages.

Why should babbling in these meaningless syllables be described by the term γλῶσσαι? The primary reference is to the tongue as an organ of the body; but that is not applicable here. The word is also used to denote an archaic, mysterious, secret expression. Some students find that meaning here. A further meaning of γλῶσσα is language, or dialect, and other interpreters understand Paul to be referring to a heavenly, supernatural

---

to the worship of the church. Clear judgment and discernment, and a due sense of relative value, are involved in all these matters. In this part of his pastoral letter the apostle wonderfully combines a tender regard for susceptibilities with deep insight and clear thought and judgment with respect to the advice he offers.

1. ***Prophecy Is Superior to Speaking with Tongues.***—Paul commends the eagerness of those who wish, however mixed the motive, to excel in their spiritual equipment both for the upbuilding of the fellowship and for its witness to the world. It is safe to infer that the motives of those who desired such gifts, especially the gift of tongues, were rather mixed. But that need not involve condemnation; for as modern psychology teaches, the whole range of human instinct is involved in all rational conduct. It is the "end" to be achieved that moralizes the "motive." The instinct of self-display can be sublimated and the emotion of satisfaction fulfilled in the effort to achieve a good moral purpose, with respect to both the character of the recipient and the edification of the community. A born preacher has something innate in him that seeks for satisfaction; that may be the "hidden motive," as psychology puts it, in his urge to preach. But in setting the innate "urge" to a moral and spiritual task the "urge" itself is moralized. There is no call for condemnation. Christian experience and expression require the right use of our endowments, whether of nature or of grace. Paul could not have put his point in such language; but something like it is intended when he enjoins the members of the church that they should **earnestly desire the spiritual gifts.** There are occasions where the mixed motive may be justified; but in the end, as one "grows in grace," it ought to be fully sublimated into that love to Christ which issues in loving service to men.

Later on Paul will give convincing reasons for placing the gift of prophecy above glossolalia (see Exeg., vss. 1-12). We note here that preaching ranked high in the various forms of Christian witnessing to the world. Capable orators and speakers were held in great repute in those far-off days. Even today the spoken word in the mouth of one who is possessed by his subject has more power than anything else to move the hearts and minds of men. Style in speaking, as in writing, is the subtle conveyance of the personality of the speaker. Certainly no preacher should ever obtrude himself upon his message. Better to commend the Master than to commend oneself. Yet for all the perils associated with it, the preaching of the word and participation in the sacraments were, and still are, the twin focuses of the great ellipse of the gospel. By preaching, Christianity spread through Asia Minor to the continent of Europe and across the empire. The church in Corinth was founded as the outcome of preaching. Paul himself was a great preacher. In his view no service of worship could be complete without preaching that was at once intelligent, encouraging, inspiring, and comforting. He is

2 For he that speaketh in an *unknown* tongue speaketh not unto men, but unto God: for no man understandeth *him;* howbeit in the spirit he speaketh mysteries.

3 But he that prophesieth speaketh unto men *to* edification, and exhortation, and comfort.

4 He that speaketh in an *unknown* tongue edifieth himself; but he that prophesieth edifieth the church.

that you may prophesy. 2 For one who speaks in a tongue speaks not to men but to God; for no one understands him, but he utters mysteries in the Spirit. 3 On the other hand, he who prophesies speaks to men for their upbuilding and encouragement and consolation. 4 He who speaks in a tongue edifies himself, but he who prophe-

---

language. A special word in English is needed to designate the phenomenon. Some use the word from the Greek, glossolalia. Goodspeed paraphrases by "speak ecstatically." The KJV inserted "unknown" before "tongue" throughout the chapter. This is one of the biblical terms which cannot be satisfactorily translated.

14:2. Is not a worshiper addressing **God** rather than **men**? Why then should Paul complain that speaking **in a tongue** does not edify men? His answer would probably be that corporate worship is a social experience in which all must be able to join. The **mysteries** to which he refers are not those special aspects of his own message to which he alludes in 2:7 and 15:51; they are secrets in the sense that the syllables in which they are expressed are unintelligible.

3-4. Prophecy was ecstatic utterance under the guidance of the Spirit; yet this involved the use of speech that was intelligible to the human mind. The prophet speaks on behalf of God for the spiritual development of men. The **upbuilding** of the community takes place in two general directions. The word παράκλησις may mean either "consolation" or

---

anxious that the exercise of other gifts shall not encroach on this important aspect of the life and witness of the church. So he seizes the nettle firmly at the very outset: preaching is superior in value and rank to glossolalia, though preaching is subordinate to love. This theme will be developed shortly; meantime, Paul has made the preliminary point that preaching is to take supremacy over the gift of tongues. Now he proceeds to set forth the real limitations of this latter "gift."

2. *Limitations of the Gift of Tongues.*—It is unintelligible to the speaker and to the hearer. **For one who speaks in a tongue speaks not to men but to God; for no one understands him, but he utters mysteries in the Spirit.** This is the one section of the N.T. where the apostle kindly yet firmly discusses the definite limitations of the gift of tongues. His treatment is the more courageous because of the regard in which it was held, both in pagan and in Christian communities. He is ever prepared to put the highest interpretation on the actions and motives of other people, and so he indicates the possibility that those who speak in tongues may indeed be the medium of a divine monologue and thus utter **mysteries in the Spirit** (see Exeg.). But Paul immediately qualifies this high interpretation of the phenomenon by adding in effect that only the Spirit can understand the utterance. The person who speaks with tongues is speaking not to his fellows but to God. To the others who are present the utterance is unintelligible. To be sure, among the "gifts of the spirit" there was included "the interpretation of tongues" (12:10), i.e., someone might be present on such occasion who had the faculty of reading the mind of the speaker and catching the trend of his thought from such coherencies as might emerge, and who was thus able to interpret more or less adequately the message that was fermenting and creating tension in the person speaking. There is just a possibility that something of value might emerge in such circumstances, though the occasions were probably few. But unless someone in this way should interpret the utterance, nothing of value to the church could emerge (vs. 5).

4-11. *The Gift of Tongues Leads to Confusion.*—Paul gently emphasizes this point by a tactful reference to himself. Not for the first time in this letter do we get such a characteristic glimpse of a great apostle, firm and even passionate in asserting his status as an apostle, yet also a courteous, kindly, Christian gentleman. **Now, brethren, if I come to you speaking in tongues, how shall I benefit you unless I bring you some revelation or knowledge or prophecy or teaching?** The sole advantage, if

5 I would that ye all spake with tongues, but rather that ye prophesied: for greater *is* he that prophesieth than he that speaketh with tongues, except he interpret, that the church may receive edifying.

6 Now, brethren, if I come unto you speaking with tongues, what shall I profit you, except I shall speak to you either by revelation, or by knowledge, or by prophesying, or by doctrine?

7 And even things without life giving sound, whether pipe or harp, except they give a distinction in the sounds, how shall it be known what is piped or harped?

8 For if the trumpet give an uncertain sound, who shall prepare himself to the battle?

9 So likewise ye, except ye utter by the tongue words easy to be understood, how shall it be known what is spoken? for ye shall speak into the air.

sies edifies the church. 5 Now I want you all
to speak in tongues, but even more to
prophesy. He who prophesies is greater than
he who speaks in tongues, unless some one
interprets, so that the church may be edified.
6 Now, brethren, if I come to you speaking in tongues, how shall I benefit you
unless I bring you some revelation or knowledge or prophecy or teaching? 7 If even
lifeless instruments, such as the flute or
the harp, do not give distinct notes, how
will any one know what is played? 8 And
if the bugle gives an indistinct sound, who
will get ready for battle? 9 So with yourselves; if you in a tongue utter speech that
is not intelligible, how will any one know
what is said? For you will be speaking into

encouragement. Because Paul uses another word for **consolation,** the second of the two possible meanings is the natural translation here. The English term **edifies** (originally "to build," hence "edifice") has acquired the peculiar sense of "improve by religious instruction"; but that is entirely appropriate at this point.

5. Possibly Paul fears that he has gone too far in rejecting **tongues.** Hence, he makes it clear that he is not forbidding them, but is insisting on the superiority of prophecy. Since communal worship is for the growth of all, there is no place for **tongues** unless there is someone to interpret the meaning in words which all can understand.

6. The apostle proceeds to illustrate the necessity for an intelligible revelation. Paul may intend two pairings in his formulation: **revelation** and **knowledge, prophecy** and **teaching.** The prophet brings revelation; the teacher gives instruction in the Christian *gnōsis.*

7-9. If music is to convey meaning, it must be understood; without variation in tone or tempo there is no melody. In Jewish worship the singing of psalms accompanied the temple worship rather than the synagogue service. Christian worship was to continue

any, of speaking with tongues, in cases where there is no one who can interpret what is said, is that **he who speaks in a tongue edifies himself.** Such edification would amount to little more than a sense of satisfaction that the speaker had been the instrument, so he believed, of the Holy Spirit—plus some measure of release from tension that would also be a consequence of the outburst. There is no edification in such a speech. Nothing is added to the church's knowledge of the gospel or insight into spiritual things; nor are any practical inferences drawn from such teaching as they have received. Paul asks them to imagine the effect of music upon them if the instrument were played indistinctly or without regard to any set pattern. No one is stimulated to gird himself for conflict if a bugle is not used as intended—to give a clear, sharp, rousing summons to battle (vss. 7-8; see Exeg., vss. 7-9). Imagine an orchestra where the members each play what they like without reference to the conductor or even to the music set before them. The result would be unmusical confusion: it would bear no resemblance whatever to a symphonic poem or a concerto. So is it with the gift of tongues. There can be nothing but confusion if there is no clear, intelligible utterance: it is like speaking in a foreign language, or listening to it, when no one present, either speaker or hearer, knows the meaning of the words used. Both speaker and listener would be foreigners to each other (vss. 10-11). **So with yourselves; if you in a tongue utter speech**

10 There are, it may be, so many kinds of voices in the world, and none of them *is* without signification.

11 Therefore if I know not the meaning of the voice, I shall be unto him that speaketh a barbarian, and he that speaketh *shall be* a barbarian unto me.

12 Even so ye, forasmuch as ye are zealous of spiritual *gifts,* seek that ye may excel to the edifying of the church.

13 Wherefore let him that speaketh in an *unknown* tongue pray that he may interpret.

the air. 10 There are doubtless many diff-
ferent languages in the world, and none is
without meaning; 11 but if I do not know
the meaning of the language, I shall be a
foreigner to the speaker and the speaker
a foreigner to me. 12 So with yourselves;
since you are eager for manifestations of
the Spirit, strive to excel in building up
the church.

---

elements from both of these. It is assumed that fixed **bugle** calls gave specific signals. If a listener cannot tell whether it means retreat or advance, of what use is it? The application to tongues is clear and the analogies clinch the nature of the phenomenon. The Greek shifts the construction with γλῶσσαι here; but the KJV's **utter by the tongue** tends to obscure the fact that Paul is still speaking about the same ecstatic phenomenon.

10-12. Paul turns to languages for his final illustration. The much-traveled missionary had heard many different dialects spoken. He had known what it was to live in the midst of people whose language he did not understand. The word φωνή in the plural may mean **voices** (KJV); but in this connection it clearly means **languages** (RSV). To a Greek the word **barbarian** signified a person who did not speak Greek. He might be quite civilized, but the language barrier made communication impossible. **Foreigner** conveys this to us much better than a literal rendering. In vs. 12, Paul repeats the essence of the exhortation with which he had begun the chapter. He does not use the word χαρίσματα, the term usually rendered as **spiritual gifts** (KJV), but πνεύματα. Since his major contention in ch. 12 was that there is only one Spirit, what Paul has in mind is a plurality of **manifestations of the Spirit** (RSV). Not all of these build up the church.

b) The Comparative Value of These Gifts (14:13-25)

13-15. Earlier Paul had spoken of the interpretation of tongues as a separate gift. Also in vss. 27-28 it would appear that the interpreter is not the same as the one speaking

---

that is not intelligible, how will any one know what is said? For you will be speaking into the air.

12. ***The Gift of Tongues Does Not Contribute to Christian Fellowship.***—One test of the value of a gift is the contribution it makes to the building up of the church. Here is clear acknowledgment of the enthusiasm and zeal of the members of the church. These gifts are entirely commendable. Better zeal, with all the possibilities of excess, than discretion disembodied of all deep feeling. The first needs to be restricted and disciplined, the second needs to be galvanized into action by some revolutionary Christian experience. Cold formalism and overmuch control can be stultifying in their effect on Christian life and service. It is a good and commendable thing for members of the Christian church to desire to be the best they can for the sake of his cause who gave himself so utterly for them. Nor is it only the great and dramatic talents that he desires. The consecration of the so-called lesser qualities, capacities, and powers is even more precious in his sight. "A cup of cold water" given in his name is marked in heaven.

Edification is the test to be applied (see Exeg., vss. 3-4). In his wisdom the apostle gives them the controlling and disciplinary aim that provides the fullest and most satisfying expression for the gift, whatever it may be. The Corinthians are to **strive to excel in building up the church.** There is the practical test. More than that, when this test is met and satisfied, the consequence is obvious to all. None but the utterly disgruntled could criticize it. Paul develops the theme in what is one of the outstanding passages of the epistle.

13-25. ***Intelligence and Understanding Are Necessary to Edification.***—The first construc-

14 For if I pray in an *unknown* tongue, my spirit prayeth, but my understanding is unfruitful.

15 What is it then? I will pray with the spirit, and I will pray with the understanding also: I will sing with the spirit, and I will sing with the understanding also.

13 Therefore, he who speaks in a tongue
should pray for the power to interpret.
14 For if I pray in a tongue, my spirit prays
but my mind is unfruitful. 15 What am I to
do? I will pray with the spirit and I will
pray with the mind also; I will sing with
the spirit and I will sing with the mind

---

in tongues. Since there is no certainty that such a person will be present, the apostle appears to urge that speakers **in a tongue** pray for this gift as well. In vs. 14 the speech is referred to as a prayer because it is addressed to God. In 2:14-16, spirit and mind are used as synonymous terms. The distinction between them here should serve to warn against ascribing to Paul a scientifically exact psychological vocabulary. By **spirit** Paul does not mean so much a human faculty as the divine *pneuma* which dwells in the baptized believer and enables him to pray. "We do not know how to pray as we ought, but the Spirit himself intercedes for us with sighs too deep for words" (Rom. 8:26). The **mind** is an organ of moral judgment, a faculty of intelligent discrimination. Paul is not putting **spirit** and **mind** in opposition to each other. It is a case of *both-and*—the ecstasy of the Spirit should be joined with sober judgment; but this was not always the

---

tive consequence that follows from edification is that with the matter of speaking in tongues shall be associated the further gift of interpretation. Then possibly edification will follow. Again we note how gently and tactfully Paul deals with this gift. Perhaps he would allow the gift as an exercise in private devotion, though it is difficult to see what value it has for that purpose if the utterance remains unintelligible for the person concerned. Such would seem to be the implication of the passage **for if I pray in a tongue, my spirit prays** (see Exeg., vss. 13-15). One can hardly imagine the apostle himself, unless for the purely psychological relief to emotional tension such a practice may bring, expressing himself in this way. That is suggested by the addition to the above sentence **but my mind is unfruitful.** Intelligence does not come into the experience at all, either as involved in deeper understanding of God and God's ways, or as involved in the expression of the soul in prayer. Prayer, like everything else that has a proper place in public worship, should be intelligible. Paul is quite clear and concise on this matter. Speaking for himself, and by implication commending his own example to the members of the church, he writes, **What am I to do? I will pray with the spirit and I will pray with the mind also; I will sing with the spirit and I will sing with the mind also.** Understanding of what is involved, not only for the sake of the person who is leading the devotions of the community, but for the sake of the community as a whole, is required right through.

This is important in Paul's view. Although he was well aware that the call to be "saints" had come in the main to the humbler people of the great seaport, yet as a man of culture he was also aware of the great intellectual and spiritual tradition of the Greco-Roman world. That had to be won for Christ and his kingdom. He knew what store the Greeks set on reason and form in all things spiritual and cultural. How could such considerations be absent from the mind of one who was prepared to "become all things to all men, that I might by all means save some" (9:22). Paul had a deep sense of the dignity as well as of the magnificence of the gospel, and desired that good order should be maintained in the public worship of the church. Disorderly ways, all slovenliness and carelessness with regard to detail, would find small favor in the sight of Paul. Slovenliness in the conduct of worship may indicate defectiveness of character. He knew how to comport himself in the presence of king and procurator (Acts 24–26). The church of Jesus Christ must not bring itself into disrepute in the sight of the world. It is even conceivable that had they been available, the apostle might have encouraged the use of orders of service. He had himself been reared in the traditions and forms of his own faith. There must often have been a sense of contrast in his mind between the crude excesses of emotion in these early churches and the elaborate and stately ritual of the temple. Moreover, the devotional literature of what is now called the O.T., in respect of dignity of language and sublimity of expression and spirit, must have had its effect on his mind. The right use of these things is a help to order and to understanding. "For God is not a God of confusion but of peace" (vs. 33).

16 Else, when thou shalt bless with the spirit, how shall he that occupieth the room of the unlearned say Amen at thy giving of thanks, seeing he understandeth not what thou sayest?

17 For thou verily givest thanks well, but the other is not edified.

18 I thank my God, I speak with tongues more than ye all:

19 Yet in the church I had rather speak five words with my understanding, that *by my voice* I might teach others also, than ten thousand words in an *unknown* tongue.

also. 16 Otherwise, if you bless[s] with the spirit, how can any one in the position of an outsider[t] say the "Amen" to your thanksgiving when he does not know what you are saying? 17 For you may give thanks well enough, but the other man is not edified. 18 I thank God that I speak in tongues more than you all; 19 nevertheless, in church I would rather speak five words with my mind, in order to instruct others, than ten thousand words in a tongue.

[s] That is, *give thanks to God.*
[t] Or *him that is without gifts.*

case. Paul knew workings of the Spirit which did not ennoble human faculties but rather displaced them. The word **sing** anticipates the "hymn" in vs. 26. Col. 3:16 gives a much fuller description of the place of music in every Christian worship.

16-19. Bless (εὐλογέω) and **thanksgiving** (εὐχαριστία) are not to be distinguished; both are used in the Eucharistic formulations. But who is meant by the ἰδιώτης, which the KJV renders as **he that occupieth the room of the unlearned,** and the RSV as **any one in the position of an outsider?** The term is found again in vs. 23, where this person is distinguished from an unbeliever. It is apparent that he does not possess the Spirit. Possibly it was a term used to refer to unbaptized inquirers who were receiving instruction. In general, the word designates the layman in contrast to the specialist. Only the context can show the particular sense in which the word is to be understood. Lietzmann believes that it refers here to any church member who does not understand speaking in tongues, but vs. 23 would indicate the more specialized meaning above. The custom of responding to prayers by **Amen** was taken over from Judaism (Deut. 27:15-26; Ps. 106:48; Neh. 5:13). Its full acceptance in Christian worship is shown in Rev. 5:14; 7:12; 19:4. The word means "So be it." Paul was not satisfied with a prayer that was not expressed in words that could be understood; nor does he anywhere in the chapter exalt silence as a mode of

16-19. ***Participation of the Entire Community.***—(See Exeg.) The term "outsider" here seems to refer to the ordinary worshiper. One cannot imagine that a pagan, who had come from motives of curiosity, would be moved to say "Amen." The picture we must hold before ourselves is that of one of the members, enraptured by his participation in the worship, standing, swaying on his feet, while he gives vent to incoherent ecstasies. There was no point in such circumstances at which the other worshipers present could make any contact with the mind or spirit and experience of the devotee. Paul insists that in the worship of the church every member ideally should have some part. It might be a passive part, as recipient of some insight, or of an interpretation offered by another member, or it might be a more active part; but the point is that all should in some sense benefit from the worship. There is of course a great place for private devotion and prayer, but where public worship is concerned everyone should be included. Even if, while "speaking in tongues," the worshiper is pouring out his gratitude to God, as may well be the case in ecstasy, still it is true that the other worshipers are excluded by the private and unintelligible aspect of such worship and are not edified (vs. 17). Paul tactfully clinches the argument by writing that while he is thankful that he too has the gift of tongues and has often used it, doubtless in private devotions, yet **in church I would rather speak five words with my mind, in order to instruct others, than ten thousand words in a tongue.** That is the point! The other worshipers are not illumined or instructed, nor is the church built up in any way if the utterances are private to the individual and unintelligible to the others who are present. A valid principle is involved here for public worship in the churches throughout all ages. It should be devised to meet the needs af all the worshipers. None should be denied the right and the privilege of participating. If any worshiper is excluded—always assuming that he comes in the spirit that is willing to give as well as to receive—to that extent the service fails of its purpose. The order of service requires at

20 Brethren, be not children in understanding: howbeit in malice be ye children, but in understanding be men.

21 In the law it is written, With *men of* other tongues and other lips will I speak unto this people; and yet for all that will they not hear me, saith the Lord.

20 Brethren, do not be children in your thinking; be babes in evil, but in thinking be mature. 21 In the law it is written, "By men of strange tongues and by the lips of foreigners will I speak to this people, and even then they will not listen to me, says

worship. The use of a foreign language is objected to by implication: he insists that the words should be intelligible to all the worshipers. It is not God who needs our worship, but we need to worship him. True worship will build up the church. In closing, Paul wants to remind his readers that he does not take this position because of any shortcoming of his own. The gift which he is depreciating is one in which he himself excels. It may have its place in private worship, but not **in church,** where the criteria of value are social. It is hard to see why the KJV felt it necessary to supply **by my voice.**

20. A second ground for the superiority of prophecy lies in its usefulness in impressing unbelievers. This idea is introduced by a general contrast between maturity and immaturity. Paul has just insisted that the mind should be active, even in worship. Childishness belongs to the past which has been put away (13:11). **Babes** are those who have not yet reached full development. Immaturity is a proper state for a believer in regard to **evil,** but not in his **thinking.** Progress is expected in Christian living (3:2).

21-23. The O.T. shows that men will **not listen** to speech in **strange tongues.** As a matter of fact, this citation does not come from any book of the law, but from Isa. 28:11-12. Paul does not follow the LXX, which is close to the Hebrew: "With stammering lips and another tongue will he speak to this people, . . . yet they would not hear." Paul puts the

least as much thought and devotion as any of its elements of praise or prayer.

20-25. ***Speaking with Tongues Tends to Evoke the Derision of Pagan Witnesses.***— (See Exeg.) Above all, Paul wished the public services of worship in Corinth to be impressive not only for the believers who took part, but also for the pagans whose curiosity or interest brought them to such gatherings. He asks the members of the church to consider the unfortunate effect of "speaking in tongues" on such members of the congregation. **If, therefore, the whole church assembles and all speak in tongues, and outsiders or unbelievers enter, will they not say that you are mad?** "Outsiders" here would seem to include people who were genuinely interested, but not yet convinced believers in Christ, while "unbelievers" would include those who came from motives of curiosity, but whose presence nonetheless gave the members of the church a good opportunity to present the faith with convincing and converting power. It is not difficult to imagine the scene conjured up by Paul's words. Even if two or three were to indulge themselves at the same moment, as sometimes happened, the effect on the minds of inquirers and unbelievers would be, to say the least, unfortunate. It certainly would create an impression less of spiritual exaltation than of madness. The more perilous effect would be, as has happened in similar instances in more recent times, to bring the cause into disrepute, to bring ridicule on the members of the church, and perhaps even to kill the infant church itself. Paul ends his instructions as to the place the gift of tongues should have in the church on a strong note. In effect, he writes that there ought to be no more than two or three utterances at the most, so far as speaking in tongues is concerned. Even then he insists on order and discipline. Such speaking must be in sequence and not a medley in which all strive at once to be heard, none giving way to the other. Nor is any of it to be permitted unless someone is present who can interpret what is said. If these conditions cannot be fulfilled, then "if there is no one to interpret, let each of them keep silence in church and speak to himself and to God" (vs. 28). Here Paul seems to indicate that the "gift of tongues" is primarily meant for personal and private devotion. Obviously he is deeply concerned that no opportunity for convincing the unbeliever and those who are on the fringe of the fellowship shall be lost. The members of the community are to exercise mature thought in the matter of public devotion and witness to the faith (vs. 20). At best—and here Paul uses a strange argument against public indulgence in the gift of tongues—such dramatic expres-

22 Wherefore tongues are for a sign, not to them that believe, but to them that believe not: but prophesying *serveth* not for them that believe not, but for them which believe.

the Lord." 22 Thus, tongues are a sign not for believers but for unbelievers, while prophecy is not for unbelievers but for

---

verb in the first person, changes the time when "they" will not hear, and uses a term making a clearer connection with **tongues.** What support he had for these changes we have no means of knowing. By a **sign** the apostle means one that is not understood (Matt.

---

sions of the faith are more likely to foster skepticism than to induce conviction and belief. To strengthen his argument he quotes the law to show that the things of God can be brought into contempt through such unintelligible ecstasies (vs. 21). **Thus, tongues are a sign not for believers but for unbelievers.** In effect, Paul means that while there is little benefit by way of edification to the believer, there may be positive harm to the unbeliever. Some who may have come to pray remain to scoff (see Exeg., vss. 21-23).

One further inference may be made in the light of these instructions. It is that members of the church can and must exercise self-control, especially with regard to tongues. Where there is self-control and self-discipline in these and other matters, one of the conditions is fulfilled that make for the edification of all who are present on public occasions. Confusion is eliminated. Order takes its place. Peace reigns.

Meanwhile, it is quite impossible to miss the contrast that Paul is drawing all along between the gift of tongues and that of prophecy. We have noticed the definite and final arguments that he has set against the former: it stands under condemnation in that it does not edify the hearers, and not always the speaker himself. To this point we must now turn. The ultimate end in view is given in vs. 26; how prophecy contributes to it is set forth in vss. 1-4.

22-26. ***Let All Things Be Done for Edification.***—The instruction covers every aspect of public worship and public gathering. Here Paul introduces a great and important motive for Christian service. This is the standard the Corinthians are to apply to all that has a place in the life of the Christian fellowship. **Edification** is a word that has largely lost its meaning in modern forms of expression. Toward the end of the nineteenth century it fell into disrepute, mainly because it had been given a sanctimonious and unctuous flavor. Lectures and addresses that were intended to "edify" were looked at askance during the first part of the twentieth century. Yet Paul's use of the term is entirely helpful. It bears the suggestion of "constructiveness" in the best sense of that word. More than once he has referred to the need of the church to "build up" and so strengthen its life. Love helps to build up the fellowship as well as the Christian character of those who love their brethren. In this very chapter he exhorts his readers to "excel in building up the church" (vs. 12). All of this is covered by the word **edification.** It is a motive and standard for Christian life and service that has the widest range and application. Whatever is effective in fostering the growth of the community and of its individual members is edifying. The qualities that edify are those that build up the life of the entire community. This test is one that the apostle constantly has in mind, and here he presses it on the attention of the church.

Prophecy is to be preferred above glossolalia because it fulfills this test and measures up to this standard. The church is constantly in need of "upbuilding" and "encouragement." The members who really care about the life and fellowship and witness of the church will be eager to achieve depths of insight into the mind of Christ, knowledge of his teaching and its application to their own lives and the lives of others. They will seek to promote growth in grace, in holiness, in purity, and in peace. Few gifts are better fitted to secure these most desirable ends than that of prophecy. i.e., of witnessing. To witness is the prerogative of every member. Given sincerity, genuine insight and knowledge, a loving spirit, and the eloquence that is the offspring not of the schools of elocution, but of the theme which has taken possession of the speaker and made him the vehicle of its utterance, then no other gift can so move heart and mind and will of men. Such preachers can do much for the upbuilding of the spiritual life of the community. How could speaking in tongues ever begin to be compared with the exercise of this gift?

Inspired preaching or witness bearing has this too as one of its marks: it provides and stimulates moral and spiritual incentive. The brethren are encouraged to keep their testimony bright and shining as they take their place in the life of the great pagan city amid which their little Christian community is set. Those

23 If therefore the whole church be
come together into one place, and all speak
with tongues, and there come in *those that
are* unlearned, or unbelievers, will they not
say that ye are mad?

believers. 23 If, therefore, the whole church
assembles and all speak in tongues, and
outsiders or unbelievers enter, will they

12:39). Though it is said that **prophecy is for believers,** it is clear from the following verse that Paul does not deny completely its value **for unbelievers.** Yet if it does lead to their conversion, they become **believers.** Those who do not possess the Spirit get an impression of insanity from the speaking in tongues (cf. Acts 2:13).

---

who feel that their lamp of witness is weak and flickering are bidden to remember that the darkness would be the more dense were all the little lights extinguished. Those who feel that their talents bear no comparison with the talents of the more gifted members of the church are encouraged to believe that it is not unimportant how ordinary folk comport themselves, despite the trend of the times in which they live and the apparently overwhelming problems that have to be faced and mastered. They have their own unique contribution to make. Not even one-talented people are to despise the paucity of their equipment. The consecration of that one talent can make it tell in the impact of the gospel of the kingdom on the life of the world. The waverers are encouraged to take their place in the ranks and to add their strength to the advance of the cause. The inspired preacher or teacher encourages his Christian hearers to recognize that they are outposts of light in a world of darkness, and that their light is to shine until the darkness breaks forever before the brightness of Christ's cloudless love. He who prophesies encourages the brethren.

Consolation is needed too. Life and circumstance can be overwhelming and men and women need comfort; they need to be heartened as well as stimulated. They need to be assured that all the resources of a spiritual and moral universe are at their disposal, and that Christ fulfills his promise to be the companion of their way right on to journey's end. The ministry of comfort is needed by the sick and the disappointed, the frustrated ones, and those who have been bereaved. Blessed is the man or woman who is the medium through whom the strong comfort and assurance of Christ is conveyed to those in need. How could speaking in tongues ever begin to be compared with the richness and practical value of this gift of utterance? How true is it that those who speak in tongues edify themselves? They get a selfish thrill from the experience, and the mistaken belief that it marks the signal favor of God. How much better to be "a voice for God" for the upbuilding and encouragement and consolation of the saints. Through such a ministry the great and glorious convictions of the faith are renewed in their life-giving strength to those members of the community who gather together in fellowship to partake of "the bread of life." Such a ministry is to be ranked far above the meretricious gift of speaking in a tongue.

Prophecy appeals to the intelligence. As such it commands respect both in the community and from unbelievers. Prophesying may not be so dramatic in expression as glossolalia but it is infinitely more beneficial in the practical advantages it brings. In the building up of the Christian church, a fellowship in the faith of men and women who had so recently been pagans, and who were bound in a measure still to be tainted by their pagan customs and practices, to say nothing of their being subject to the pressure of their pagan environment, it was essential that there should be sound teaching and firmly based knowledge concerning the Christian faith and tradition. Earlier in the letter Paul commended them because they maintained "the traditions" he had delivered to them (11:2). But repetition, exposition, and amplification were essential if the church was to continue to be nourished in the faith. These traditions contained "the rule of faith" for the Corinthians, even as the entire Bible contains the rule of faith for the Christian church today. In our time we are grateful for all the scholarly insight, inspired interpretation, exposition, and teaching we can receive concerning the Scriptures. The need was even greater in Corinth. The gift of speaking in tongues could make no adequate contribution to meet this need. Paul writes that more attention should be given to those who possessed the gift of instruction and exposition because of their knowledge of the traditions of the faith, and perhaps even of the Hebrew scriptures, than to those who spoke in tongues. The latter may move the hearts of their hearers—Paul is not too severe on that—but the former could move both mind and heart. That is the greater and

24 But if all prophesy, and there come
in one that believeth not, or *one* unlearned,
he is convinced of all, he is judged of all:
25 And thus are the secrets of his heart
made manifest; and so falling down on *his*
face he will worship God, and report that
God is in you of a truth.

not say that you are mad? 24 But if all
prophesy, and an unbeliever or outsider
enters, he is convicted by all, he is called
to account by all, 25 the secrets of his heart
are disclosed; and so, falling on his face,
he will worship God and declare that God
is really among you.

24-25. How different is the effect of prophecy! From vss. 29-31 it is certain that Paul does not mean that **all** are to speak at once. The meeting to which he is referring is one into which an **unbeliever** might stray. This seems to prove that the service of the word was separate from the common meal. Three results of this prophetic preaching may be expected. The first is conviction of sin—cf. John 16:8, where we find the same Greek word regarding the function of the Counselor to convince the world concerning sin. The second result is that one is **judged** (KJV) or **called to account** (RSV). This verb (ἀνακρίνω) is used in 2:15, where Paul says, "The spiritual man judges all things, but is himself to be judged by no one." The third result is the disclosure of **the secrets of his heart** (cf. I Pet. 3:4); when Jesus speaks to the woman at the well of her past life, this is heralded as evidence that he is a prophet (John 4:19). It is unlikely that Paul

more necessary service. To a fine piece of exposition, to some recapitulation of the teaching of Jesus or of the main events of his life, to some flash of spiritual insight, to the application of the Christian message to the life of Christ's followers or to the human situation in which the church was set, the hearers could well add a resounding "Amen." There is intelligence both in speaking and in hearing. There is genuine edification when the speaker prays or sings or speaks intelligently: he engenders a higher kind of enthusiasm.

Throughout the centuries the need for intelligent and inspiring instruction in the elements and traditions of the faith has never diminished. It is as great today as it has ever been, both inside and outside the church. Doubtless there is in our time little that might be compared to glossolalia, but there is always room in the services of the church for expository preaching and systematic study of the Bible. Perhaps the time is ripe for a call from this flaming apostle who yet with calm dignity and sound sense requests his readers to give adequate place in the public services of the church to those who can give such instruction. It is good for preachers, and hearers also, to ponder these passages and to let them search the heart.

Prophecy may convict and convert the unbeliever (see Exeg., vss. 24-25). We have noted that one of the grave limitations of glossolalia is the unfortunate effect it might have on the interested outsider who has been attracted to the church services. How different is the effect that prophecy might have on the skeptics and critics who had come to satisfy their curiosity. **But if all prophesy, and an unbeliever or outsider enters, he is convicted by all, he is called to account by all, the secrets of his heart are disclosed; and so, falling on his face, he will worship God and declare that God is really among you.** The contrast that the apostle is drawing is very clear. Glossolalia, if not interpreted, can do little or nothing either to edify or to inspire the community, while preaching, or "prophecy," not only inspires, instructs, comforts, and edifies the assembly of believers, but also disarms the skepticism, criticism, and derision of pagans who may be present. Or it may even convince and search their hearts, and so convert them to the faith. That has been the noble function of preaching and of witness bearing in every century of the Christian Era. The preacher or any member of the Christian fellowship whose mind and spirit have been prepared by prayer and meditation (vs. 20) may speak with inspiring and moving effect to both believers and unbelievers. Great preaching pre-eminently has as its purpose the bringing of those who hear into the very presence of God. Preaching which fails to do this has failed in its essential purpose. The supreme aim of all great speaking is not primarily to commend the speaker, but the subject with which he is concerned. While there is truth in the Roman Catholic doctrine that the character of the priest does not affect the content of the gospel, it is also true that the integrity and sincerity of the speaker or preacher are involved, and that effective presentation of the gospel can to some extent be nullified by the unworthiness of the person who may be preaching it.

Where the preacher is in accord with his subject, however, definite and marked results

26 How is it then, brethren? when ye come together, every one of you hath a psalm, hath a doctrine, hath a tongue, hath a revelation, hath an interpretation. Let all things be done unto edifying.

26 What then, brethren? When you come together, each one has a hymn, a lesson, a revelation, a tongue, or an interpretation.

ascribed thought reading to the Christian prophets at Corinth. They may, however, show such evidence that God is speaking through them that strangers will recognize the fulfillment of Zech. 8:23 and will join in the worship.

c) The Corinthian Order of Worship (14:26-33)

26. The Corinthians' worship does not strike us as very formal. Nevertheless, Paul was seeking to inculcate greater orderliness in their meetings. Yet he had no thought of restricting the speaking to an ordained ministry, much less of keeping the service within any prescribed liturgy. The service resembled the Quaker form more nearly than any in existence today, not because of any stress upon silence, but because every member was free to speak as he was moved by the Spirit. There was only one restriction: everything should be done for mutual edification and nothing as private exhibitionism.

are likely to follow. A sense of awe, the kind of awe that is involved in numinous experiences, pervades the gathering. All who hear are gripped and moved to the depths of their being by the message. Consciences are made sensitive, and there is deep conviction of sin; for none can be brought into the presence of One who is of holier eyes than to behold iniquity without some awareness of the gulf that separates unworthy man from his Creator. To this is added the keen and disturbing awareness of the individual's personal responsibility in the sight of God and his accountability to God. The fact that these convictions are shared by all believers present helps to emphasize and drive home such salutary truths to the heart and conscience of the unbeliever. **He is convicted by all, he is called to account by all.** He feels that his very mind in its deepest and most secret recesses is an open book to all present, an open book that all may read. As preacher follows after preacher in exposition, in exhortation and entreaty, the effect becomes overwhelming. At last the unbeliever may be moved to repentance. That is, or should be, the final consummation of a service of public worship in which preaching or prophesying is given pre-eminence. Paul must have had many such scenes in mind as he penned these lines to his people in Corinth. They had participated in such scenes and knew from personal experience exactly what Paul meant. Where the gospel is accepted fully and wholeheartedly, where there is a real concern for the salvation of men and the building up of the fellowship of the church, where preachers are afire with the glory and power of the message and so become in the best sense of the word channels of God's utterance, then such consequences readily follow. Here are the marks of genuine religious revival; here is a moving, graphic description of the authentic fire of heaven that purifies and refines the human spirit. The great apostle is concerned that this fire should never die down on the sacred altars. When it burns, the very place itself becomes luminous with the presence and glory of God.

26-33. ***Some Directions for the Conduct of Worship.***—In all true worship order is necessary if the spirit of reverence is to be preserved. Enthusiasm must be controlled and variety of gifts must be disciplined by the unity of the fellowship itself. We have seen how great was the need in Corinth for the simple yet effective instructions that Paul now gives for the conduct of church worship. Prophesying and speaking in tongues are to be brought within certain bounds that they may be the more effective as spiritual gifts (see Exeg., vs. 26). In passing, we can be grateful to the church in Corinth for evoking from the apostle the picture that is presented by this paragraph. So far is it removed from generally accepted forms of worship that it is almost completely different from anything that falls within our common experience. The nearest approach to it would be a combination of a meeting of the Society of Friends and the testimony meeting of Methodists and certain Independents: it is completely different from the ordered forms of church worship as we know them. In Corinth each member of the congregation was free to make his own contribution to the worship as he felt moved in spirit to do. Such procedure has its own inspiration, yet it also has its dangers. There was apt to develop a certain amount of confusion that failed

27 If any man speak in an *unknown* tongue, *let it be* by two, or at the most *by* three, and *that* by course; and let one interpret.

28 But if there be no interpreter, let him keep silence in the church; and let him speak to himself, and to God.

Let all things be done for edification. 27 If any speak in a tongue, let there be only two or at most three, and each in turn; and let one interpret. 28 But if there is no one to interpret, let each of them keep silence in church and speak to himself and to God.

Five types of contribution to the service are mentioned. The list cannot be intended as exhaustive; for nothing is said about **prayer,** to which reference has been specifically made in vss. 14-15. Therefore no emphasis is to be laid on the failure to mention reading from the O.T., or from collections of the words of Jesus—if such actually existed. By a **psalm** (KJV) or **hymn** (RSV) Paul is not necessarily thinking of the O.T. psalms. The poems in Luke 1–2, the hymns in the book of Revelation, and the snatches of songs elsewhere in the N.T. (Eph. 5:14; I Tim. 3:16; etc.) indicate that the Spirit moved the early Christians to new lyrical expressions about God's mercy. From its position in the list are we to conclude that their meetings opened with song? By **a doctrine** (KJV) or **lesson** (RSV) the apostle was thinking of some exposition of Christian teaching, possibly an interpretation of the O.T. That will be expected from those whom God has appointed as teachers, just as **a revelation** will be expected from prophets.

27-29. Speaking **in a tongue** is to be permitted, but limited at three points. Persons shall speak **in turn,** and not two or three at a time; **three** is the outside limit at any one service; and there shall be no speaking at all unless someone is present to provide an interpretation. Can it be that Paul is giving here a permission on the basis of conditions which could not often be met? How could anyone know in advance that another would

---

either to edify the members of the church or to convince those who were interested but not as yet convicted of sin and of the need for repentance. Hence these simple yet helpful instructions.

What then, brethren? When you come together, each one has a hymn, a lesson, a revelation, a tongue, or an interpretation. Let all things be done for edification. . . . For God is not a God of confusion but of peace. The variety of the services of worship is obvious in the very instructions Paul gives. Apparently they began with a hymn: the note of praise is struck at the outset. This seems to have been a common practice dating back to the intimate gatherings of Jesus and his disciples (Matt. 26:30; Eph. 5:19; see Exeg., vs. 26). Probably its genesis lies in the custom of the synagogue. Praise is essential to receptiveness in public worship: praise suggests gratitude for benefits received, for grace bestowed. The first note in man's approach to God should be adoration, awe, wonder, and praise. This predisposes the worshiper for the further benefits and insights that the disciplined and continuous practice of public and indeed private worship is intended to bring. Moreover, praise engenders happiness in the best sense; for praise is the expression of gratitude—grateful people are happy people; ungrateful people lack happiness. How can the latter enter into the spirit of public worship? What contribution could they possibly make? Reading the N.T. with imagination brings to view every now and then companies of happy people. They have been brought through their acceptance of the gospel message into a wonderful experience of spiritual deliverance: Christianity swept through the empire precisely because it was a "deliverance" religion. Those who were liberated could hardly express themselves for joy. Even in that strange and inspiring book of the Revelation to John, that testament of a crucified church, almost every second text waves over the heads of the persecuted Christians a banner inscribed with the legend "Victory." One of the great undertones of its mighty music is the note of praise. "To him who loves us and has freed us from our sins by his blood and made us a kingdom, priests to his God and Father, to him be glory and dominion for ever and ever. Amen" (Rev. 1:5*b*-6). How could it be otherwise when the transport of so great an experience of the mercy and love of God filled the minds and hearts of the ardent worshipers?

Such a spirit of praise helps to keep alive the soul of a church, a community, even a nation. Over and over again in the history of the world different peoples have been subjugated by their enemies. And over and over

29 Let the prophets speak two or three, and let the other judge.

30 If *any thing* be revealed to another that sitteth by, let the first hold his peace.

31 For ye may all prophesy one by one, that all may learn, and all may be comforted.

29 Let two or three prophets speak, and
let the others weigh what is said. 30 If a
revelation is made to another sitting by,
let the first be silent. 31 For you can all
prophesy one by one, so that all may learn

---

actually have the gift of interpretation? Some meet this problem by translating, "unless he is an interpreter." Doubtless some of the "spiritual" would contend that Paul was "quenching the Spirit" (I Thess. 5:18-20). But he would probably reply that he was putting no limit on the amount of speaking in tongues between a man and God. Corporate worship, however, must be regulated in accordance with what helps the group. **Prophets** are free to speak according to their inspiration, but Paul recognizes that there are false prophets as well as true (cf. Matt. 7:15; Mark 13:22; Acts 13:6; I John 4:1). The community is to **weigh what is said** (RSV) and thus to **judge** (KJV) the source of inspiration. In O.T. times there had been false prophets; but Jeremiah had been canonized, and not Hananiah. Inspiration is always given to individuals, but it is corporately evaluated. Just because a man affirms, "Thus says the Lord," it does not follow that he is a chosen mouthpiece for the Spirit.

30-33. But even true prophets sometimes speak at inordinate length. Paul does not presuppose a moderator who would call time on a speaker. He appeals again to individual moderation rather than to administrative authority. If the others are **sitting,** we may assume that the speaker stands. Another prophet is not to begin speaking at the same time. The one Spirit of God will not be trying to find expression through two prophets

---

again, as in Poland, the poets and singers have helped to preserve the soul of the nation against the day of eventual liberation. Paul's instinct was sure and sound. Let the undoubted inspiration of the fellowship in Corinth express itself in praise to God. That exercise will direct the mind and the emotions from the worshiper to God, who is the sole object of worship; it will strike the objective note! It will prepare an atmosphere of expectation in which the living Christ will be able to visit his people with further blessing. Isaac Watts surely caught the authentic note of Christian worship in his great hymn of praise inspired by Ps. 103.

> My soul, repeat his praise
> Whose mercies are so great,
> Whose anger is so slow to rise,
> So ready to abate.
>
> . . . .
>
> High as the heavens are raised
> Above the ground we tread,
> So far the riches of his grace
> Our highest thoughts exceed.[5]

The Christian church must never lose the note of happy, grateful praise and adoration. No service can live or be inspiring without it. It furnishes the individual worshiper with the opportunity to make his own contribution. None need be excluded save by his unwilling spirit. Praise, rightly directed, wisely and intelligently chosen, can sweep the entire congregation into the realized presence of God. How sure is the touch of the great apostle in all these matters which are concerned with the spiritual vitality of the church! Where worship is, there heaven is, and true fellowship, and the inspiring presence of the great Head of his church.

Then follows **a lesson.** To be sure, Paul is not laying down a set order of service which must be invariably followed; but even so, some of these details ought to have a regular place in Christian worship. It is the supreme *teaching* function of the church to maintain and to pass on to succeeding generations the sacred heritage of the faith. After all, it was for the churches that the Gospels were written; it was to the churches these letters were indited. The very fact of the existence of the churches made it necessary that certain things should be written down, so that after the eyewitnesses and the early apostles had passed to their rest there should still be scriptures to which reference might be made as to the nature of the faith. One cannot be certain to what extent records existed when Paul wrote to the church in Cor-

[5] "My soul, repeat his praise."

32 And the spirits of the prophets are subject to the prophets.

and all be encouraged; 32 and the spirits

in the same place at the same time. The next prophet should be given the opportunity to show that he also has a revelation for the group. Paul will not listen to the protest that the prophet is helpless in the grip of a higher power than himself. Once more (vs. 32) the apostle uses the word spirit in the plural (πνεύματα). Probably Paul means that the divine Spirit within the prophet shall be subject to the rational control of the prophet's own mind (vs. 15). God's Spirit and man's will may be bound together and fused; mystical intoxication should never get beyond moral control.

The antecedent of **all** (vs. 31) shifts. Elsewhere Paul does not suggest that every believer has the gift of prophecy. The first **all** includes only the prophets, but there is no

inth, though it is likely that some did actually exist, and copies would therefore be available for the various Christian communities. The oral method, though well developed, had its aspects of weakness. Paul refers to the "traditions" of the faith which he had transmitted to the community in Corinth. Probably there were elements of the Jewish scriptures among them. In any case, he commends the teaching of a lesson, based on the tradition committed to them, as a valuable item in public worship (see Exeg.). The incorporation of a lesson will enable the church to do two things: to maintain the tradition, and to pass it on as part of its heritage to succeeding generations. It would also keep within bounds any tendency to excessive deviation from the central paths of the gospel message. Even in these early days there was a twofold pressure to be resisted: there was heresy within the church, and there was paganism without. It was good, therefore, and edifying, that a lesson should be read.

What held then holds still. So far as the responsibility for the message of the church is concerned in our modern forms of worship, it is incumbent on those mainly responsible not to express their own opinions. No man is ordained to the ministry for the expression of his individual opinions, but to preach and teach the gospel, to spread the kingdom, and to build up the saints. Naturally he will seek to do this in terms of his own age. But his task in that case is to find new molds for the old truths, and not to modify the essential message, God's revelation of himself in Christ crucified, to suit the prevailing intellectual trend of the times. The need of the age, and of every age, is not to adjust the Christian message so as to make it acceptable to a particular civilization, but to baptize civilization into the spirit and truth of Jesus Christ. Mankind still needs the great guiding convictions of the Sermon on the Mount; mankind still needs the redeeming spirit of him who died on the Cross and who rose from the dead.

A revelation has its place in public worship: it is an element in inspired and prophetic teaching. The suggestion is that of insight or illumination. Just as one sees new colors and beauties in a piece of mother-of-pearl as one turns it over in one's hand, so does new beauty or light reveal itself to the sensitive and meditative minds of those whose hearts are set on things above. Intuition has its place in dealing with the things of Christ. It may be a revelation of the bearing of his truth upon the social situation, upon some problem of interpretation, or upon some problem in the life of the community. Should such a revelation be given to any member of the congregation, let it be contributed to the church as a whole. Then other minds will be brought to bear on it, and its implications will be the most clearly seen.

A tongue, or an interpretation (see Exeg., vss. 27-29). Further comment on these gifts is not necessary here since enough has already been written to suggest their value and their limitations. What is of greater practical importance is the insistence of the apostle on the power of those who are inspired in this way to control and to discipline themselves. There is little value so far as edification is concerned if those who speak in tongues have no one to interpret for them, i.e., assuming that they are unable to interpret for themselves. Far better in that case to let their devotion run in private and personal channels (vs. 28). If there is an interpreter present, he is to speak for the two or three—no more—who the apostle suggests will quite fill the quota of those who in this fashion can offer some contribution to the inspiration of worship.

Similarly with regard to the more valuable gift of preaching or "prophecy." **Let two or three prophets speak and let the others weigh what is said.** This gift is subject to the discipline of self-control. Religious gatherings, like gatherings of a different kind, can be saturated to the point of sheer inability to absorb anything more if there is excess of prophetic illumination (see

33 For God is not *the author* of confusion, but of peace, as in all churches of the saints.

of prophets are subject to prophets. 33 For God is not a God of confusion but of peace.

member of the community who does not need to learn and to receive encouragement (vs. 3). Paul's final summary is a precious affirmation about God. **Confusion** (ἀκαταστασία) is a word which may be used either for "tumults" in a nation (Luke 21:9) or "disorders" in small groups (II Cor. 12:20; Jas. 3:16). Obviously the latter is in Paul's mind rather than a disturbance of the national peace. The God of peace is a frequent phrase in Paul (Rom. 15:33; II Cor. 13:11; Phil. 4:9; I Thess. 5:23; etc.), though it usually refers to salvation rather than to the absence of strife.

Exeg., vs. 30). Paul knew that one could be blinded with excess of light in more senses than one. There is a genuine place for proportion in preaching, even if there is only one preacher. Those who preach are apt to overlook the significant fact that they have normally a much longer time to meditate, and to prepare the matter with which they are concerned than those who come to hear them. To leave the hearers with the impression that the speaker has reserves, and that these will be available on a later appropriate occasion, is far better than any attempt to exhaust the inexhaustible riches of the gospel in one session of public worship. How wise Paul is! He pleads that the listening congregation be given an opportunity to "weigh up" what has been said. What the congregation is inspired to weigh up for itself is likely in the long run to carry more weight in effectiveness, both personal and social. The preaching that is remembered is the preaching that stimulates the hearer to preach to himself. Such preaching, like praise, will be all inclusive: it will give the members of the congregation an opportunity to realize their responsibility in hearing, just as the speaker should realize his responsibility in speaking.

Paul really feels the importance of that particular point, for he goes on to add that should one member of the church become aware that another is inspired to make some revelation (vs. 30), then the first should be content to sit in quietness. By-and-by his own turn will come. For each is to be encouraged to add his contribution of illumination, or teaching, or whatever it may be, to the common spiritual good of the church as a whole. Only so can prophets be trained to succeed prophets. The babes must be given an opportunity to walk; the church must make adequate provision for its continued witness. Here is the germ of the theological training necessary for the continuance and expansion of the church's work. Paul's vision ranges far, even in these simple instructions for order and discipline in the work and witness and worship of the church. Only so **all may learn and all be encouraged.**

Besides this, he sets down a principle of true value when he writes, **And the spirits of prophets are subject to prophets.** They are subject to prophets at least in two respects. Other prophets who have listened in reverent silence to those who have spoken have the spiritual responsibility of exercising discriminating judgment on what they have heard. This, in the context of Paul's direction, would be done in no captious or censorious spirit. There is no suggestion that there should be any debate. The idea is that, with a view to the spiritual well-being of the entire church community, the collective mind of the most spiritually mature members should be brought to bear on the high matters which have been conveyed in this way to the fellowship as a whole. The second respect in which the spirits of prophets are subject to prophets is in the matter of their personal responsibility for the use of the gift to the benefit of their fellow members. No one who has some grace or endowment of the spirit is entitled to keep it to himself. There need be no false modesty about the exercise of the gift in public for the benefit of all the brethren. Sufficient check against excess will rest on the spiritual responsibility of other prophets in the congregation. For the enrichment of the life of the church no one should hide his light under a bushel: each should express the best he knows. In so expressing it he will possess it the more strongly himself; in failing to do so he will subject it to the law of atrophy. A talent buried is a talent lost, and both the church and the one-time possessor are the poorer. All things are to be **done for edification.** This is the overriding consideration. That which truly builds up the strength and witness of the fellowship is of true spiritual value; that which fails to do so can be modified or set aside. Meantime, let eagerness be welcomed; let enthusiasm have its place: zest and fervency of spirit are ever the marks of a living church. But Niagara tamed yields power in more effective form than

34 Let your women keep silence in the
churches: for it is not permitted unto them
to speak; but *they are commanded* to be
under obedience, as also saith the law.
35 And if they will learn any thing, let
them ask their husbands at home: for it is
a shame for women to speak in the church.
36 What! came the word of God out
from you? or came it unto you only?

As in all the churches of the saints, 34 the
women should keep silence in the churches.
For they are not permitted to speak, but
should be subordinate, as even the law
says. 35 If there is anything they desire to
know, let them ask their husbands at home.
For it is shameful for a woman to speak in
church. 36 What! Did the word of God
originate with you, or are you the only ones
it has reached?

---

d) Closing Injunctions to Obstinate Groups (14:34-40)

34-36. A fourth group of attendants at the service of the word is composed of **women.** In a synagogue service they sat apart; they were not fully subject to the law. What Paul has just said about prophesying and speaking in tongues does not apply to them, for women are not to give instruction to men. Even if they wish to ask questions, they should wait until they get **home** and then inquire from **their husbands.** What did Paul expect those to do who took his advice and remained unmarried? Possibly they should put their questions to their fathers. The point of view of this passage corresponds exactly to I Tim. 2:11-12, where the later Paulinist writes: "Let a woman learn in silence with all submissiveness. I permit no woman to teach or to have authority over men; she is to keep silent." This author appeals to the law, though the genuine Paul had insisted that Christ was the end of the obligation to the law (Rom. 10:4). Though 11:2-16 falls short of a removal of all distinctions between male and female, it is assumed there that women will pray and prophesy in public. Paul sought at that point only to regulate the head covering.

Niagara tumbling in a wild, beautiful welter of waters over its precipices. So is it with the power of the Spirit, as the Spirit seeks expression through fallible human lives. God is not honored by disorder, or strife, or confusion, or unchristian competition among brethren to reveal their gift. Such do not commend their Master: in the end they do not even commend themselves. Once again, **God is not a God of confusion but of peace.**

34-36. ***Women at the Church Meeting.***— (See Exeg.) Some commentators, struck by the seeming harshness of the tone of these verses, have formed the opinion that they were not originally written by Paul, but that they were incorporated later on by someone else. One point in favor of this opinion is that previously in this same letter, and in language much more in keeping with the section of the epistle we have been considering, he has referred to the practice, apparently without taking any exception to it, that he now condemns (see 11:5). There, all that Paul is concerned with is that women should not pray or prophesy with the head uncovered. In the Expos. of that passage we noted the apostle's reasons for this direction. Textual authorities also disagree as to the position of these present verses. Certainly they do not chime in with the spirit of the section as a whole. Elsewhere in his epistles Paul refers with obvious gratitude to the ministrations of devoted Christian women. He owed much to Lydia and to Prisca and to many another.

On the other hand, in the exuberance of the great deliverance that had come to these Corinthians through their new found faith, it is probable that their initial enthusiasm had run to excess. Evidence of that excess has been apparent in the chapter we have been discussing. The female members of the church were not likely to have escaped the impact of the prevailing emotional atmosphere. Moffatt has fruitfully suggested that as Paul was drawing this portion of his letter to a close, one of the friends who had come from Corinth, probably Stephanas or Fortunatus or Achaicus, drew his attention to the disorder contributed by the women members. As in ch. 11, he quotes scripture as a kind of final court of appeal whose decisions are not to be questioned or qualified. The women members are not to be allowed to participate freely in the public meetings: they are to maintain a discreet silence, and if any questions are in their minds, they are to ask their husbands concerning them when they go home. This is a rule that is not to be challenged. In this matter the general practice of all the churches is to be their guide in Corinth. Let them conform, for there is no special dispensation of the gospel for the community in Corinth.

37 If any man think himself to be a prophet, or spiritual, let him acknowledge that the things that I write unto you are the commandments of the Lord.

38 But if any man be ignorant, let him be ignorant.

37 If any one thinks that he is a prophet, or spiritual, he should acknowledge that what I am writing to you is a command of
the Lord. 38 If any one does not recognize

How is the contradiction between these two passages to be resolved? The Bezan codex (D) and related Western MSS have vss. 34-35 at the close of the chapter—which suggests that they may have originated as a marginal gloss and were inserted into the text at different places. This is the conclusion of many commentators. Others believe that we should not seek to remove the contradiction because ch. 11 refers to small house congregations, while Paul is speaking here of the full community gathering. There is no question but that Paul believed in the definite subordination of women (Col. 3:18) and was convinced that the emancipation of women from this subjection would be a violation of the divine order. Both at the beginning and at the end of the paragraph he appeals to the uniform custom of **the churches.** The Corinthian community is not empowered to make innovations. The need for uniformity of practice is assumed.

37-40. Apparently Paul realizes that he is walking on delicate ground in demanding that regulations be imposed upon those who were themselves confident that God was giving special revelations to them. Why should a prophet take orders from Paul? Were not his own revelations as authentically divine as those of the apostle? Paul assumes that the Spirit of the Lord must agree in his communications to all persons. Since the apostle

And there we must leave it. One can hardly imagine, in the light of his own teaching, far less in that of the subsequent development of the church, that these lines could possibly represent the great apostle's final judgment on the place that devoted women should take in the life of the church.

37-40. ***Some Final Words on Spiritual Gifts.*** — (See Exeg., vss. 34-40.) This great and fruitful section of the letter comes to an end with a strong yet tender reaffirmation of Paul's apostolic authority. It is likely enough that some of the more exuberant and stubborn minded among the brethren in Corinth would be inclined to rebel against these instructions. Eagerness is difficult to keep within bounds. It is so easy to damp enthusiasm by cold, hostile criticism. Paul has avoided this. But there were some in the church who might be disposed to resist what they would scarcely hesitate to describe as his interference in matters which they claimed did not concern him. Nor would they hesitate to describe his directions as merely his private opinion. The apostle anticipates their opposition. How acute his premonition was may be realized by a reading of II Corinthians (see chs. 10–13). In words that ring out like a hammer beating on an anvil he writes, **If any one thinks that he is a prophet, or spiritual, he should acknowledge that what I am writing to you is a command of the Lord. If any one does not recognize this, he is not recognized.** Nothing could be more clear and definite. Once again the apostle makes it quite obvious that he will brook no questioning of his status or authority. He goes even further. He has written these counsels and directions under the immediate constraint of the Spirit. Thus he is sure and firm about his message. If there are those in the church who fail to recognize the authentic marks of divine inspiration in the letter that he has written for the spiritual well-being of the church, they thereby cast reflections on their own claim to be spiritually inspired. On the other hand, those in the church who are themselves truly inspired will have no difficulty in receiving and accepting the directions that he has sent. The recalcitrant are to be set firmly aside and disregarded as interfering nobodies who are unworthy of consideration. Salutary advice! There are times when the churches would be well served if such action were taken, provided that prayer and meditation and counsel among the more spiritually mature of the members preceded such action. Divine love itself exhibits adamantine qualities.

But Paul's final word, like God's, is instinct with tenderness: it is a word of loving encouragement and toleration. None are to be repressed; all are to be encouraged to exercise their gift so long as order and decency and reverence are preserved. Even speaking in tongues is not to be harshly proscribed. **So, my brethren, earnestly desire to prophesy, and do**

39 Wherefore, brethren, covet to prophesy, and forbid not to speak with tongues.
40 Let all things be done decently and in order.

15 Moreover, brethren, I declare unto you the gospel which I preached unto you, which also ye have received, and wherein ye stand;

this, he is not recognized. 39 So, my brethren, earnestly desire to prophesy, and do not forbid speaking in tongues; 40 but all things should be done decently and in order.

15 Now I would remind you, brethren, in what terms I preached to you the gospel, which you received, in which

is speaking according to the Spirit, it is nothing less than a **command of the Lord.** We feel sure that Paul was right in this case about the superiority of prophecy to tongues, and we understand what a difficult position he was in as he sought to save worship from anarchic disorders. But we can well imagine that all were not ready to agree that his best judgment actually was a **command of the Lord.** Elsewhere he draws a clear distinction between authoritative words of Jesus and his own matured convictions (7:10, 12). The KJV missed Paul's clever turn here because it was following another text, **if any man be ignorant, let him be ignorant.** Even though this reading is now supported by the earliest papyrus (p^{46}), it should be rejected. The hortatory form probably arose through a scribe's failure to perceive the original application. If anyone who thinks that he is spiritual **does not recognize** that Paul is announcing God's will, he should not be **recognized** by the church. Once more Paul repeats his advice, reminding them that he does **not forbid speaking in tongues.** He is interested only in a proper orderliness of worship.

VI. The Resurrection of the Dead (15:1-58)

Though ch. 13 is the best-known portion of this letter, ch. 15 has the greatest historical significance. It contains the earliest and most important testimony to the resurrection of Jesus and to its place in the early Christian message. Paul does not take up this question because of an inquiry in the letter he had received; as is true also of 6:12-20, the problem had been brought to his attention in some other way. It is not absolutely certain what point of view the apostle is opposing. Were there members of the church who did not believe in any form of life after death? What could the gospel have meant to them? Or were there Greeks who were offended by the Pharisaic doctrine of a

not forbid speaking in tongues; but all things should be done decently and in order. There speaks the greathearted Christian gentleman and saint. His spirit of wise toleration and kindness shines through all that he writes. He embodies the virtues he commends. He is the "man in Christ" who bears upon his loving heart a great concern for the life and well-being of all the churches. He has written this because above all he desires them to be worthy of that Christ whose portrait he has painted in his great eulogy of love (ch. 13). Where such love reigns, the rest will follow. The foundation is laid on which the superstructure can be built. In the light of that same love every difficulty and problem can be solved or transcended to the edifying of the body of Christ.

15:1-58. ***Concerning the Gospel of the Resurrection.***—Now we turn to the glorious passage in this heart-stirring letter which is mainly concerned with the gospel of the resurrection of Jesus Christ, and some of the inspiring and gladdening inferences that can be drawn from that wonderful fact. Paul addresses himself to the subject for a variety of reasons, all of which are suggested by the line he takes in dealing with it. We have had reason more than once to remind ourselves of the pagan background of those Corinthian Christians, and also of the constant pressure to which they were subject from their pagan environment. It cannot be deemed surprising in such circumstances that there were deviations from the faith, and that questions were raised by those inquisitive and speculative Greeks. There were people in Corinth who were inclined to modify the gospel message that had been preached by Paul and the others, drawn as they were by the attractiveness of some of the pagan cults which accounted for the creation of all things in terms of emana-

2 By which also ye are saved, if ye keep in memory what I preached unto you, unless ye have believed in vain.

you stand, 2 by which you are saved, if you hold it fast — unless you believed in vain.

---

resurrection (cf. Acts 17:32) and substituted for it a belief in the immortality of the soul? Or did some believe that the resurrection was past, in that it took place when believers died and rose with Christ at baptism (II Tim. 2:18)? It would be hazardous to assume that we can read between the lines a sure answer to these questions. Paul does make large concessions to those who found the thought of the revivification of the body repulsive; but he insists firmly on the primacy of belief in the resurrection.

A. The Resurrection of Jesus (15:1-19)

1. The Tradition Concerning the Fact (15:1-11)

15:1-2. Paul would remind them of the **gospel** which he **preached.** The noun is a favorite with him, being used no less than fifty times in his genuine letters. Three relationships of this gospel are enumerated: (*a*) it is a message of grace to be **received;** (*b*) it is the basis for continuing steadfastly in the Christian life; (*c*) it contains the ground of salvation. Here salvation is spoken of as present (1:18) rather than as future (3:15). The grammar of this passage, as it appears in Greek, is awkward, to say the least. This awkwardness also marks the KJV translation. **Keep in memory** is quite indequate for **hold it fast;** and a literal rendition of the next clause would be "by what speech I preached unto you." The RSV translates the word **preached** only once instead of repeating it as the Greek does, and moves up τίνι λόγῳ to the first clause, rendering **in what terms I preached**

---

tions of a divine creative wisdom. This type of philosophy reached its apex in later centuries in the teachings of Plotinus. The immediate point at issue was that such a pseudoreligious philosophy dispensed with the need of any doctrine of a resurrection.

There was, in addition, the influence exerted by the skeptical attitude of cultured people. Paul himself had felt their antagonism when he preached in Athens. Associated with this attitude was the further question as to the nature of the resurrection body and the immortality of the soul. All these matters involve central doctrines of the Christian faith, and the apostle felt the urgent need to deal fully with them. Doubtless our gratitude is linked with the gratitude of many generations of Christians in subsequent ages that the situation in Corinth should have evoked such a great reply and contribution as we have in this chapter of the epistle. It will prove to be well worth our while to examine it at some length, and we can begin with the apostle's strong affirmation of the gospel he had preached on his great missionary journeys, as the outcome of which the church in Corinth had been born.

1-4. ***The Gospel Preached by Paul to the Corinthians.***—Could any outline of the great saving message which Paul had proclaimed be given in clearer, more concise terms? With the utmost economy of words the apostle sets down the main points of the gospel he had delivered, and which they had, to their great benefit, received. More than once in this same letter he has had occasion to remind them of "the traditions" which he had transmitted to them (see Exeg., vss. 1-2). Here again a warning note is sounded. It was obviously an ancient as well as a modern tendency to break away from or to modify the foundations of the Christian faith in a spirit of accommodation to some popular cult that happened to interest and tantalize the spiritual palate for the time being. The tendency to adjust Christian convictions and doctrines and dogmas in the light of the latest scientific theory is a case in point. Paul directs attention to the foundational elements of the gospel which he will immediately insist have their bases strongly laid in history and in experience. Obviously his rather trying experience in Athens had in no way induced him to temper the directness of his language; it may even have intensified it. Without hesitation and without shame, as in his letter to the church in Rome (Rom. 1:16), he had fearlessly preached the saving gospel of the Lord who was crucified, and who being buried, rose from the dead. For Paul this is fundamental. From no other fountain could spring the quality of life and ethics that of necessity flows from it. Without it there could in his view be no gospel at all: it is, to use his own words, **of first importance** (cf. Exeg., vs. 3). His mission—as for every other to whom the revelation of the risen

3 For I delivered unto you first of all that which I also received, how that Christ died for our sins according to the Scriptures;

3 For I delivered to you as of first importance what I also received, that Christ died for our sins in accordance with the

to you the gospel. This gives a compact statement of Paul's thought. If his readers do not **hold fast** to this message, but instead reject belief in the resurrection, their faith will have been **in vain** (cf. vs. 17).

3. In the past the English tradition has taken ἐν πρώτοις in a temporal sense, but modern commentators are almost unanimous in holding that Paul means primacy in **importance** rather than priority in time. As a Pharisee, he had been taught a tradition which he should in turn transmit. That had dealt with the correct interpretation of the Torah. When he became a Christian, he had **received** a different tradition. That dealt with the saving activity of God in Christ. What follows is not given as a revelation (cf. Gal. 1:11-12). It was the tradition which he had received. Paul's statement shows that though the death of Christ does not figure in the sermons in Acts, it belonged to the earliest *kerygma* or preaching message (see C. H. Dodd, *The Apostolic Preaching and Its Developments* [Chicago: Willett, Clark & Co.], pp. 7 ff.). Paul's gospel was based on these facts of the tradition; but he did not originate the stress upon them. Nothing is said concerning the teaching of Jesus about the resurrection (Mark 12:18-27). Paul does not assert that Jesus had given more cogent arguments for the resurrection than did contemporary Pharisees. The apostle argues from events that began with the death of Christ **for our sins** (Gal. 1:4). Frequently he simply says that Christ died "for us" (11:24; Rom. 5:6; 8:3; II Cor. 5:15, 21; I Thess. 5:10). He always uses the Greek preposition meaning "on behalf of" (ὑπέρ); never does he use "instead of" (ἀντί) in this connection. Nor does

Christ had been given—is to preach, with all the power and authority which such an experience conveys, the gospel of the resurrected Lord. Moreover, this gospel is authenticated as the fulfillment of the scriptures (vss. 3-4). Here he can only refer to the O.T. teachings, particularly those in Isa. 53. We may remind ourselves how strong was the tendency even then in the early church to relate the crucifixion and resurrection of Jesus to the religious traditions of the Jewish race. Consider the story of the walk to Emmaus as described in Luke 24:13-35 (particularly vss. 25-27). There Jesus himself is depicted as expounding in a new way, and in the light of the recent events centered in himself, the religious traditions of the race. These disconsolate travelers, like so many others at that time, had high expectations of a messianic deliverance in the mode of the militant Maccabees. Their expectations had been centered in Jesus, the greatest and best friend they had ever known; and these hopes and expectations had been shattered by what seemed to be the crowning disaster of the Cross. But as he expounded to them a different way of deliverance, a way of deliverance based on a love which suffers all that man in his folly and wickedness can do, which meets such enmity and wickedness with ever more saving, forgiving love and vicarious suffering until the divine purpose has been gained, their hearts burned and glowed within them. Such, doubtless, was the interpretation of the O.T. scriptures that the apostle propounded in explication of the death and resurrection of Jesus, not only to Jewish, but also to pagan communities. There is the heart of the gospel; **Christ died for our sins in accordance with the scriptures.** God, like any true earthly parent who vicariously takes on himself in agony the wrongdoings of an erring son or daughter, "in Jesus Christ" takes upon himself the sins and follies of the men and women made in his image. He bears the blame and shame of it in himself. Jewish people, who had been nurtured in a religious tradition that provided for the sacrifices of the day of Atonement, and who understood the symbolism of the scapegoat that was driven out into the desert, would understand the language of the apostle. Greeks, who were also accustomed to the sacrificial idea of expiation in their pagan cults, would have almost as little difficulty. When both Jew and Greek grasped the thought that "the Lord of glory" had offered himself in expiation for the corporate and individual sin of mankind, the idea was imbued with immense spiritual force. Paul feels no need at this point to expound the doctrine in all the fullness of its implications. Only the urgent reminder is required. It was **for our sins** that the Master died. That was the

4 And that he was buried, and that he rose again the third day according to the Scriptures:

scriptures, 4 that he was buried, that he was raised on the third day in accordance

---

Paul have Mark's phrase, "for many" (Mark 10:45; 14:24). He does not elaborate in what way the death of Christ was **for our sins,** nor does he elsewhere give a very clear doctrine of the Atonement (Rom. 3:21-26; II Cor. 5:18-21; Gal. 3:12-14). It is not certain what scripture he had in mind here. Deut. 21:23 is the only one he actually quotes; the striking thing is that Isa. 53 is not specifically cited by Paul in connection with the death of Christ. Argument from the fulfillment of prophecy, however, clearly belonged to the Christian apologetic from the beginning.

4. The express mention of the burial, which in the case of a criminal would not be taken for granted, indicates that the story of Joseph of Arimathea was included in the passion account which Paul had received. The resurrection **on the third day** was not the unanimous primitive tradition; "after three days" is the witness in Matt. 12:40; Mark 8:31; 9:31; 10:34. It is often assumed that Paul's wording assures his knowledge of the story of the discovery of the empty tomb on the third day. But this is an unwarranted conclusion. What Paul asserts is that God **raised** Jesus **on the third day.** The failure to find a body on a particular day would not in itself indicate when the Resurrection had taken place. God's act in raising Christ from the dead is not to be identified with the discovery of this fact by any particular person. The only source of knowledge for the time of the Resurrection which Paul cites is scripture. He follows Hos. 6:2 instead of Jonah 1:17. At Pentecost Peter is represented as appealing to Ps. 16:10 (Acts 2:31). An appearance to women on the third day is totally ignored by Paul or else is rejected. He expressly states that the first appearance was **to Cephas.** The apostle names three

---

first essential step in the great spiritual deliverance which is part of the essence of the gospel.

And the weight of man's sin was carried by Jesus Christ in full. Part of the preaching of the gospel is the revelation not only of the shamefulness of sin as symbolized by the Cross, but also of the fact that the spiritual fruit of sin is death. Part of the essence of the gospel is the note of judgment (Rom. 6:23). That note had sounded in Corinthian ears. But the glad, delivering gospel was that even the judgment of death had been met: and **he was buried.** Or as Paul has put it earlier in this great epistle, the bread of life was broken and the wine poured forth when Jesus went to his cross (11:23-26). He was really dead and buried! What closer identification could there be between him and man than in the manner and reality of his death in respect of human sin? Yet the gospel is still incomplete. Were the Cross and the tomb the final terms in the great delivering revelation that Jesus Christ brought to man, what good tidings would these grim facts convey? One step more is essential for the revelation truly to become a gospel, viz., **that he was raised on the third day in accordance with the scriptures.** This insistence on the significance of the third day, apart from the actual fact itself, would help to meet Greek ideas and Jewish rabbinical conceptions (see Exeg., vs. 4).[6] There is much more to follow, and Paul goes on to expound the significance of the Resurrection as the great vindication of Jesus Christ by the power and love of God. These implications will be dealt with presently. What is essential as a starting point is that the members of the Corinthian church should be reminded of the great foundations on which their newly won faith had been built. These must not be tampered with. Even a great cathedral is no stronger than its foundations.

Here then is the gospel which Paul preached and which they received. Their new status, no longer that of "servants and slaves" but of children of God, "and if children, then heirs, heirs of God and fellow heirs with Christ, provided we suffer with him in order that we may also be glorified with him" (Rom. 8:17), was based on that gospel **which you received, in which you stand.** We can imagine with what rapture the great apostle preached to these people, some of whom were meek, lowly, and untutored, the new status available to them through faith in Jesus Christ. And we can imagine with what rapture and enthusiasm the weak and unconsidered ones would receive his message of the "unsearchable riches" so wonderfully and graciously offered to them. They were

[6] Moffatt, *I Corinthians,* pp. 237-38.

5 And that he was seen of Cephas, then
of the twelve:
6 After that, he was seen of above five
hundred brethren at once; of whom the
greater part remain unto this present, but
some are fallen asleep.

with the scriptures, 5 and that he appeared
to Ce'phas, then to the twelve. 6 Then he
appeared to more than five hundred brethren at one time, most of whom are still alive,

---

appearances to individuals and three to groups. Since he gives no hint concerning the place of these appearances, he offers no help in deciding between the Galilean tradition in Matthew and the Jerusalem tradition in Luke. The apostle's words may re-echo a creedal formulation of an early type.

5. As the first witness to the Resurrection, Cephas had a real claim to be called the rock on which the church was built (Matt. 16:18). Curiously, no Gospel reports this appearance, though it is alluded to in Luke 24:34. An appearance to Peter in Galilee is reported in John 21:7 ff., and an account probably stood in the Gospel of Peter. If the event did take place in Galilee, it must have been nearly a week after the Crucifixion. That would be entirely consonant with what Paul says. It was the act of God, not the experience of Peter, which took place **on the third day.** The aorist passive of ὁράω is regularly used not as a passive, **was seen** (KJV) but as a deponent verb, **appeared** (RSV; see Heb. 9:28; etc.). Paul was not thinking of a subjective vision (though see 9:1), but of an actual appearance of the risen Lord. The appearance to **the twelve** is reported in all Gospels except Mark (Matt. 28:16-20; Luke 24:36 ff.; John 20:19 ff.). Many early MSS change **twelve** to "eleven," recalling the defection of Judas.

6. An appearance **to more than five hundred brethren** cannot be identified with certainty. Johannes Weiss thinks that it must have taken place in Galilee, for only there

---

heirs both to great possessions and to great expectations. In that same chapter (Rom. 8) the apostle lists some of the riches that are the portion of those who put their faith in Jesus Christ. These were part of the gospel that he preached to the Corinthians, a gospel vindicated in its truth and in its power by the resurrection of Jesus Christ from the dead. Strange that so soon they should need to be reminded of their new "standing" in Christ. It would be a saving gospel only to those who held it fast. As in other walks of life, the "casual" in mind and attitude would discover that their foothold was precarious. To be a Christian was a serious matter. Already the apostle has insisted on the need for training and discipline if the believer is to be spiritually fit. But for those committed to Christ by faith, the trend of life would be in harmony with the purposes of God. That is salvation: life become "Christ-centered," based on the faith that in and through him men have the truth about the world in which they live and the life they are surely meant to live. Only sincerity and consistency are required if that salvation is to be effective. On such terms the resurrection of Jesus Christ is the guarantee of the validity of a faith in the grace of God, revealed through Jesus Christ, **by which you are saved, if you hold it fast.**

5-8. ***Various Revelations of the Risen Christ.*** —This gospel message, Paul declares, was common to all the leaders of the church in his day. Thus he can write that he delivered to them "what I also received"; but to the testimony of tradition he adds the witness of those who had actually seen the risen Lord, including as well his own experience.

Just as it was essential in Paul's view to convince the doubtful or wavering members of the church in Corinth of the reality and significance of the resurrection of Jesus, so had it been essential with regard to the disciples and other followers of Jesus in the days of his flesh. Part of the evidence is still to be found in the transformation that was wrought in them. After the crucifixion and burial of their Master they were terrified and disconsolate men, hiding fearfully behind barred doors in an upper room in some back street of Jerusalem. They trembled at every knock on the door; they feared the same fate that had befallen him. But after they had been convinced—and they were not easily assured, as the various resurrection narratives make quite clear—they were men transformed. Fear was transformed into courage, uncertainty into strong and radiant faith. Soon they were out in the open streets of the city that had dealt so brutally with their Master, proclaiming with passion and joy the great

7 After that, he was seen of James; then of all the apostles.

though some have fallen asleep. **7** Then he appeared to James, then to all the apos-

would such a number of former followers of Jesus be ready to receive such an experience. It is more likely that this is another version of what Luke reports in Acts 2. The difference in numbers will not surprise anyone who has heard popular estimates of crowds. For Paul also the Lord is the Spirit (II Cor. 3:17). That the majority should be alive about twenty-five years later is not so surprising as that Paul could presume to know that they were.

7. Though the appearance **to James** is reported in the Gospel According to the Hebrews, it is found in no canonical gospel. Since the brother of the Lord early became the leader of the church at Jerusalem, it would almost be necessary to assume such an event even if we did not possess these words from Paul. Some interpreters try to take **all the apostles** as simply recapitulating those previously mentioned. Robertson and Plummer suggest that it includes Thomas (John 20:26 ff.). But for Paul **the apostles** were a much wider company of missionaries. He does not say, as he does of the five hundred, that Christ appeared to all of them **at one time.** Every apostle had been

salvation that had been wrought through this mighty vindication of his Son by Almighty God. The implication in Paul's references to the various appearances of Christ lies in these facts. In effect, he is persuading certain elements in the church in Corinth that there could have been no gospel to preach, nor could any churches have been founded as the outcome of the preaching of that gospel, had not the first Christian disciples, apostles, and followers of Jesus been convinced beyond any doubt that he had risen from the dead. This is the main point of the various references to groups of people and to individuals to whom the experience had been granted of seeing and conversing with the resurrected Christ. Vss. 4-8 are in general accord with the narratives in the four gospels. Peter (Cephas), the leader of the apostolic band, was vouchsafed the vision and, according to John 21, received instruction for the building up of the fellowship of the resurrection faith (see Exeg., vs. 5). The mention of the twelve in vs. 5 must surely mean the eleven, as in Matt. 28:16 or in John 20:26-29, while the reference to a revelation given to over **five hundred brethren at one time** appears to have some connection with the story of Pentecost; or it may have stood in the line of a tradition that has been lost (see Exeg., vs. 6). At any rate, there was no doubt in the mind of Paul as to the authenticity of this particular experience, for he tells his readers that if they care to do so, they can verify his statements by checking them with the majority of that great multitude who were still alive (vs. 6).

Two further pieces of evidence are added to clinch the matter. **Then he appeared to James, then to all the apostles** (vs. 7). That he should appear more than once to all the apostles is in keeping with Christ's purpose of strengthening the assurance that such a revelation was bound to bring, and also is part of the process that was intended to wean the disciples away from reliance upon sense impressions and to engender a robust faith in unseen spiritual realities. But the revelation to the Lord's brother James is not only interesting and significant; it is also strangely persuasive, for almost the last people to believe in Christ's mission were those of his own household. They did their utmost, more than once no doubt, to induce him to give up his teaching and healing work and to return home; they may even have thought that he was mad (Mark 3:31-32). If so, it is an arresting fact that his brother James should have been at last won over, and that he should have become one of the leaders of the church. We may perhaps fairly conjecture that the change came through the revelation that Jesus had been vindicated by his resurrection from the dead. How otherwise was this man, so hard to win, who would have saved Jesus, as it were, from himself, converted to the faith?

More important than anything else, when one considers not only the immediate but also the far-reaching historical consequences of the event, was the dramatic conversion of Paul himself. **Last of all, as to one untimely born, he appeared also to me** (see Exeg., vss. 8-10). For all who knew anything about Paul's history as a zealous persecutor of the church, that was a clinching and final argument. He had been transformed out of all resemblance to his former self, and as the great missionary to the Gentiles, though neither he nor they knew it then, had become one of the most significant men in the Greco-Roman world. What Paul believed, despite the still strong expectancy of the almost

8 And last of all he was seen of me also,
as of one born out of due time.
9 For I am the least of the apostles, that
am not meet to be called an apostle, because I persecuted the church of God.

tles. **8** Last of all, as to one untimely born,
he appeared also to me. **9** For I am the
least of the apostles, unfit to be called an
apostle, because I persecuted the church

---

called to that ministry by the risen Christ (9:1). Paul was simply the last of these (Acts 9:3 ff.). It is clear that he knows of no event akin to an ascension (Acts 1:9), which, forty days after the Resurrection, set an end to the appearances. Though we do not know how long after the resurrection of Jesus Paul's conversion came, surely a year or more must have elapsed. Yet he makes no distinction between the other appearances and the one to himself. There is no suggestion that the resurrection body of Christ differed in one case from the other. The only difference lay in the preparation for the experience. In the events enumerated we may trace essential steps in the development of the early church. It was the risen Christ who had been the activating force.

8-10. English readers may imagine that in the phrase **untimely born** Paul was referring to the lateness of his arrival in the group of apostles. The noun ἔκτρωμα is used rather of an abortion or a premature birth. Possibly it had been a word of reproach used against him, or it may have been chosen to emphasize the suddenness with which he had been

---

immediate return of Jesus Christ—though even then we may legitimately surmise that a more mature view of this great consummation was forming itself in his fertile and far-seeing mind—was that the church held in the germ of its fellowship the true way of life for all mankind. That made both the church and the apostle of the highest significance for future ages. Some historians have not hesitated to point out that the Christian tradition, which is one of the essential elements in the civilization of the Western world, owes the fact of its pre-eminence in the main to the missionary journeys of Paul. Certainly he himself would have entered no such claim (vs. 10; Gal. 2:20).

To be sure, this great sequel could scarcely weigh with the community in Corinth; but it ought to weigh with us. Just as part of the fact of Christ in any estimation of his relevance and significance is to be found not only in himself, but also in the spirit and life and witness of those whom he has influenced in every age, so part of the significance of Paul is to be found in the effect of his life and thought on subsequent developments in the field of history. God never mistakes his man, his instrument, or his time for the initiation and development of his purposes. In that sense, Paul was not **untimely born.** He was not **untimely born** with regard to the work in Corinth or elsewhere. All seasons and all times belong to God. But these considerations apart, we can say with confidence—knowing what Paul was, and having had experience ourselves of the intense flame of his passion for Christ and for the kingdom of God—that he might well point to himself as a tangible bit of evidence for the reality of this tremendous life- and thought-changing event, the resurrection of Jesus from the dead. If personal experience in the individual, if experience as recorded on the broad canvas of immediate and subsequent history is any criterion of truth and therefore of reality, the astounding thing is not that men should believe that Jesus rose from the dead, but that they should ever harbor the least doubt. By that revelation Paul the persecutor and self-confessed "chief of sinners" was saved. Well may he point to himself as evidence of the great fact.

9-11. ***A Flash of Legitimate Pride.***—At this point there seems to have broken into his train of thought some stinging recollection of the doubts and aspersions cast on his status as an apostle by some of his malicious critics in Corinth. These had their counterpart elsewhere among the more strictly Judaizing Christians who looked askance on the mission to the Gentile world, and where Gentile converts were concerned insisted on full observance of Jewish rites and ceremonies to which Paul took strong exception. They were apt to say that he was an apostle at second hand: he had not been numbered among the original twelve. Moreover, was not his record encrimsoned with Christian blood? With a curious mixture of humility and pride—an endearing human touch, and quite consistent with the characteristics of a letter which in the nature of the case is liable to reflect swift transitions of thought and emotion—he agrees with his critics. **For I am the least of the apostles, unfit to be called an apostle, because I persecuted the church of God.** Then he turns his humble confession, tinged with pride though it may have been, or at least col-

10 But by the grace of God I am what I am: and his grace which *was bestowed* upon me was not in vain; but I labored more abundantly than they all: yet not I, but the grace of God which was with me.

of God. 10 But by the grace of God I am what I am, and his grace toward me was not in vain. On the contrary, I worked harder than any of them, though it was not I, but the grace of God which is with

thrust into his new work. He had had no preparation by contact with the earthly Jesus. He goes on to emphasize his own unworthiness to receive this commission (cf. Eph. 3:8; I Tim. 1:15). He had formerly been a persecutor of **the church of God** (Acts 8:3; Gal. 1:13; Phil. 3:6). But God's **grace** had condescended even to such a sinner (Gal. 1:15), and that **grace** had not been bestowed **in vain** (II Cor. 6:1). Since the salutation, Paul has used his favorite word χάρις only three times in the letter; now it occurs three times in this one sentence. God's unmerited goodness is not proclaimed as a boon to others; with the deepest sense of gratitude Paul acknowledges his own infinite dependence on the divine mercy. And yet, though he has continually excluded the possibility of human merit (1:31), he cannot leave unnoticed the fact that he had **worked harder** in preaching the gospel than **any** of the other apostles (II Cor. 11:23). But this was not the result of his own work; it flowed from God's unmerited favor. When Paul writes "not . . . I . . . , but sin" (Rom. 7:20), we may feel that he has stated a dangerous doctrine, capable of

ored by a dash of resentment, to spiritual gain. Like the O.T. prophets, he points away from himself to the glory and grace of God. He was not concerned to commend himself; a truly great man never is. His personality and character can safely be left to speak for themselves. Only the lesser lights feel the need to draw attention to the fact that they shine. Thereby in the end they dim their light. He turns the occasion of stinging criticism and makes it emphasize the greatness of the grace, freely given to one so undeserving, which has provided him with his commission as an apostle of Jesus Christ. That, he insists, is the open secret of such passion and inspiration and moving power as he may possess, **His grace toward me was not in vain.** Where God's grace is as freely received as it is given, it never is in vain. The sole limits are those imposed by man's capacity as an individual and as a socially conditioned being. Even if the grace of God does not always manifest itself in ways that would be most congenial to ourselves, when freely received it is still effective (see II Cor. 12:7-10).

But even more, the very contrast between what he was and what he is has made for the still greater effectiveness of his own service. **On the contrary, I worked harder than any of them, though it was not I, but the grace of God which is with me.** The phrase **worked harder** bears the sense of outdistancing or outstripping the others in all their service for the Master; although again Paul is quick to give the credit to the inspiration of God's gracious Spirit. Such an attitude keeps all Christian service in its legitimate context and perspective: it focuses the attention on the central figure of our faith. It draws the eye away from the instrument, valuable though that may be, to him who uses it. That was Paul's purpose and he gloriously sustained it to the very end. Nonetheless, he will not allow any reflection on his status as a true apostle. Let the instruments then be not overmuch in evidence. **Whether then it was I or they, so we preach and so you believed.** That is the truly important matter. Thus the passage ends as it began. To the Corinthians as a matter of "first importance" (vs. 3) this gospel of the crucified, buried, and risen Christ was preached not only by Paul but by the others. Let them keep personalities out of it (see Exeg., vs. 11). That which was preached is what the people needed to hear. Hearing, they had believed, to the satisfying and even joyful and enthusiastic transformation of their lives (vss. 1-2). Let them recall these things to mind and do it often. Was not the sacrament of the Lord's Supper itself given them for this very purpose? Centering their life and their thought in love upon these great and significant events, they will find fellowship and strength as a community of Christ. Throughout the whole passage the undertone is the apostle's insistence that they hold fast to the faith engendered by the gospel that had been preached.

There is vitality in such a message for our own times. So easy it is to distract the mind and spirit of people from the central message of the faith to the methods and instruments employed for its propagation. Many who use modern and sometimes extraordinary devices are obviously sincere. Held in true and adequate perspective, in relation to their purpose of directing people's attention to the vital things of the Christian

11 Therefore whether *it were* I or they, so we preach, and so ye believed.

12 Now if Christ be preached that he rose from the dead, how say some among you that there is no resurrection of the dead?

me. 11 Whether then it was I or they, so we preach and so you believed.

12 Now if Christ is preached as raised from the dead, how can some of you say that there is no resurrection of the dead?

---

great abuse. This is hardly the case with the complementary words, **not I, but the grace of God.** In them speaks true Christian humility.

11. But a comparison with other apostles might fan the embers of the party strife discussed in chs. 1–4. So Paul turns quickly from the human ministers to faith in the gospel which all apostles had preached. This centered in the Resurrection as God's confirmation of the messiahship of Jesus and the beginning of a new stage in God's dealings with men. The implications of the Resurrection for Christian faith were crucial.

2. The Significance of His Resurrection (15:12-19)

12-18. There can be no denial of the general belief in the **resurrection of the dead** which does not involve a rejection of the particular belief in the resurrection of Jesus.

---

faith, these strategies and expediencies may for a while enjoy a degree of success. Yet the point of full effectiveness is as a rule quickly reached. Thereafter they cease to be of any great value. But over and over again the "old, old story" reasserts itself, and where it is allowed to reassert itself in simplicity and directness, with winning sincerity, it manifests its old-time power to move the heart and to win the mind. Take from the gospel message the cross, the burial, and the resurrection of Jesus Christ, and what is there left to preach but a body of ethics? Ethics can be reduced to a series of propositions. Can one live in a saving companionship with a series of propositions, however noble? Not for long! Philosophy and theology have great things to say to us and do for us. One is grateful for profound and germinative thinking in every field. But Christian faith is based on the greatest life that has ever been lived, on the Truth and the Spirit that were incarnate in that life, and on the mighty demonstration of their victory, in death as in life, over all the fell force of the evil that was concentrated against them. That gives men a gospel; it adds to the gospel the assurance not only of great truths, but of power to live by them, and of the inspiration of a companionship that graciously conveys its spiritual quality to those who accept the friendship so freely offered. That is what people really want to hear, not opinions about a variety of interesting topics, but a gospel convincing in its power to heal, to help, to save; to save not only from sin, but also to a life of love and constructive service for God and for man. This gospel is still delivered to us all as a matter "of first importance." Let it find a living voice in a living church!

12-19. ***Doubts Concerning the Resurrection and the Ensuing Consequences.***— (See Exeg.) It was this gospel of the risen Christ that Paul, so utterly convinced himself, preached with zeal and passion to these Corinthians. He had made it plain to them that the gospel of deliverance, with its promise of eternal life, was based not on any philosophical or theological doctrine of the immortality of the soul, but on the fact of the resurrection of Jesus Christ. There is nothing in Christian belief to suggest that the soul of man is intrinsically immortal, and so by the necessities of its own being continues in existence after death. To be sure, there was a shadowy, twilight belief in the continued existence of the soul of man, both in the Hebrew idea of Sheol and in the Greek conception of the underworld. But both described an attenuated type of existence bereft of the fullness and richness of life as experienced here. From these dismal conjectures the Christian gospel of the Resurrection delivered Christian believers: it broke upon that twilight darkness like a great and radiant sun. Its assurance was that life abundant, here and hereafter, risen, glorified—not the inevitable evolution of man or the natural continuation in some form of his existence after death—was the gracious gift of God to all believers and sincere followers of his truth and Spirit and purpose as revealed in Jesus Christ. Philosophically, the Christian doctrine of the Resurrection can be expressed thus: God who has created the conditions under which we manifest ourselves here has also created the conditions under which we still continue to manifest ourselves hereafter; and the assurance has been ratified for us in the resurrection of Jesus Christ from the dead. Nothing

13 But if there be no resurrection of the dead, then is Christ not risen:

13 But if there is no resurrection of the

Since this was the crucial event for faith, what was at stake was nothing peripheral, but the entire structure of Christian faith. The resurrection of Jesus was the cornerstone of that faith (Rom. 10:9) ; six times during the next nine verses Paul uses the perfect tense of the verb **raise** (ἐγείρω) . The uniform terminology of Paul is not that Christ rose from

---

depends on the nature of man; all depends on the nature of God. As a consequence, the Christian doctrine of the life hereafter is far removed from any Asiatic conception of reincarnation, with its mechanisms or rewards and punishments, or of absorption into the infinitude of the eternal Spirit. It is, on the contrary, the enhancement and enrichment of personal life. It is based on the faith that there is no good thing which God would withhold from those who commit themselves to him. Such was the context of Paul's message. It was, therefore, almost with a gasp of incredulity that he learned of these Corinthians, so lately liberated into so great and large and rich a faith, that they were now so subject to doubts and fears as to question the whole Christian conception of the afterlife, especially the resurrection of Christ.

Yet we must not be too harsh in our judgment of them. After all, that people so hard to persuade of the fact, and therefore of the significance, of the Resurrection should become converts to the Christian faith in its fullness, is in itself strong evidence of the validity of that faith. Contrary to many shallow modern views, the first Christians did not live in an unduly credulous age. Far from it! The disciples themselves, and the immediate followers of Jesus, those who had been in his company in the days of his flesh, were very difficult to convince that he had risen. If we consult the record in all four Gospels this impression remains (see Matt. 28:17; Mark 16:9-20; Luke 24:11, 25, 41; John 20:19-29) . When Paul stood making his defense before King Agrippa in Caesarea, he told how difficult it was for him to yield himself to the truths of the gospel: he was not easily won to the Christian faith, but the resurrection of Jesus, as we have seen, was borne into his mind and heart with terrific force on the highroad to Damascus. He points out that the highest hopes of his race were based on the events that had taken place in Jerusalem and what had come of them; but declares that, despite this, people were hard of heart and slow to believe. "Why is it thought incredible by any of you that God raises the dead?" (Acts 26:8.)

The truth would seem to be that the mental atmosphere of the times by and large was against the idea that anyone could be raised from the dead. Even in those far-off days of mystic cults and practices people believed in weighing the evidence and giving play to reason before too readily accepting any such belief. Paul's experience with the philosophers in Athens indicates the difficulties he had encountered in proclaiming his faith in the risen Christ, and these philosophers represented the finest wisdom of the times. When preaching to them and reasoning with them on Mars Hill he had received courteous attention and a sympathetic hearing. They were willing to consider the novel views of this stranger who was so obviously convinced of the greatness of his message. But scorn curled their lips when he reached the climax of his argument, the resurrection of Jesus Christ (Acts 17:22-34) . Doubtless he was politely dismissed but to them the idea of the resurrection of a crucified Christ was ludicrous.

The same held true of the empire as a whole. There religion was at a low ebb; irreligion was spreading everywhere. A vicious materialism had invaded the lives and homes of the people and particularly of the ruling classes. The old wholesome though stern Roman virtues were slipping, and the empire was showing signs of decay and disruption. In such an atmosphere the preaching of a faith based on the resurrection of a crucified Jew was unlikely to get even a courteous hearing. In Jewish circles, in Palestine and abroad, the Sadducean priesthood and its adherents were all powerful. Men like Annas and Caiaphas denied the possibility, and scoffed at the very idea, of a resurrection from the dead. In fact, they attempted to pour ridicule on Jesus himself when they put their question to him about the woman who had married successively seven brothers (Matt. 22:23-28) . The incident indicates the depths of incredulity in influential Jewish circles concerning this belief.

Thus it is not to be wondered at that in such an atmosphere of skepticism and doubt some of those "weaker brethren" in the Corinthian church should have been inclined rather to adopt the ideas involved in the cults of their day than to give wholehearted acceptance to the belief that one who was dead should have been raised. Yet their doubts had to be dissipated if the faith was to survive and to spread among them. Paul felt it incumbent on him to

the dead but that he had been raised by God. The KJV obscures this by treating the passive voice as if the verb were deponent and translating as Christ **rose** and **is risen.** It

state the consequences of such doubt and of the denial that sprang from it. In effect, he writes to them, "Let us say that there is no resurrection." Then with calm, inevitable, yet relentless logic he sets forth the ensuing conclusion: **If there is no resurrection of the dead, then Christ has not been raised.** The inference is plain. Everything that Christ represented, all that he taught, and all that he lived for, were in jeopardy. What conviction could a faith like his convey to men if God, the object of that faith, had left him to die on a Cross and to rot in a tomb? Such a denouement would mean the apotheosis of the forces that combined to destroy him. It would be the victory of Antichrist; it would cast forever a dark, impenetrable shadow on the face of God. **If Christ has not been raised** there can be no faith in him as the Savior of the world. Who would care to follow a dead and defeated leader? How could the victim of death be the Lord and Giver of abundant life? If there was no resurrection of Jesus Christ, then any hope of resurrection, with all it implies for man's immortal longings, is dead as dust. It can never be more than the fantastic flight of winged illusions; it is only a silken cobweb strung across the horns of the moon. A dead Christ could never be the inspirer or object of a living faith.

One is reminded of the imaginative picture John Henry Newman once drew of a world into which one looked for some trace of God and found none. There was only a blank! He compares such an imaginary experience with that of looking into a mirror and seeing nothing! That, indeed, would be a horrifying experience. We can imagine the impact of Paul's words on the minds of these Corinthians so lately released from pagan darkness and liberated into the light of Christ's gospel of salvation and everlasting life, a gospel authenticated by the Resurrection. For them it would mean that their new-found liberty and the boundless hopes that were associated with it were a delusion and a snare. All the old haunting questions would remain. How, then, could some of their number think even for a single moment that Christ had not risen? **If Christ has not been raised** everything that conspired to destroy him and his cause is pedestaled in triumph!

What held good in their day holds good in ours. We may conjecture hopefully that what the modern idealistically inclined mind calls "spiritual values" may ultimately triumph; but it remains in the realm of conjecture. To be sure, there are good reasons, despite the protagonists of relativism and utilitarianism in morals, for the philosophic faith that universal spiritual values have a determining voice in the ordering of the universe.[7] Many thinkers are not overimpressed by the plausible arguments of those who accept the absolute validity of scientific propositions as a description of reality while assigning only pragmatic value to moral and spiritual propositions and ideals. Such thinkers have rather carelessly overlooked the plain fact that the data on which scientific propositions are based are similar in kind to those on which our moral and spiritual judgments and values are based. If the one set of propositions is valid, why not the others? If moral and spiritual judgments have only utilitarian value and yield no real insight into the nature of reality itself, does not the same argument hold good for strictly scientific judgments as well? One has to be unduly credulous to accept any other position. Surely Kant and the Neo-Kantians have shown philosophic thought the way out! One should be grateful that a philosophy of life which is idealist through and through, and all the stronger for being based on realistic premises, is convincingly possible. Christian thought should welcome such a powerful ally. But even so, the Christian belief in the resurrection of Christ from the dead injects into the idealist position that sharp thrust of historical certainty that yields a foundation of genuine assurance. Foundations are of supreme importance in the building up of life and character. When one can add personal experience, in terms of spiritual communion with that same risen Christ, not only in the individual life, but in the fellowship of a living, inspiring church, then assurance is twice assured. Could there have been, and could there be, such a church or such an experience **if Christ has not been raised?** The philosophy of relativism, and of moral pragmatism, despite what remnants of value they may possess, should purge themselves of the arrogance that would set aside well-nigh two thousand years of Christian history and experience. A gospel, authenticated by the Resurrection, that has endured such a test and is the sole hope of mankind in counteracting the secularist spirit of the age, a gospel that has commanded, and commands, the love and allegiance of such multitudes of men, and among them many who are no mean thinkers, is too well established to be thus set aside. Nor could it have been founded on a lie or a delusion. Lies

[7] Norman Kemp Smith, *Prolegomena to an Idealist Theory of Knowledge* (London: Macmillan & Co., 1924).

14 And if Christ be not risen, then *is* our preaching vain, and your faith *is* also vain.

dead, then Christ has not been raised; 14 if Christ has not been raised, then our preaching is in vain and your faith is in vain.

---

was not the act of Jesus, however, but the act of God. By raising him from the dead, God had demonstrated that Jesus was not a criminal, and that the events of the end-time had really begun. To the event itself testimony had already been given in vss. 3-8. Paul's

---

have short legs; they can achieve only short-term results. Delusions are soon exploded by the atomic force of truth and reality. Two thousand years is a long time. The testimony of millions of witnesses to this very day is impressive evidence. How can any modern mind, alert and sensitive to such evidence and experience, even harbor the thought that Christ did not rise from the dead? Once for all, in the light of such a frame of mind, Paul has drawn the inevitable conclusion, **If there is no resurrection of the dead, then Christ has not been raised.** Everything to which his truth and life and death and resurrection give significance should be laid in the tomb with him! Christian ethics divorced from the essentials of the Christian faith are the shadow of a shade; they have been eviscerated of all content and of all reality. They are the spectral remnants of a ghastly illusion and as such have no future: **if Christ has not been raised.** Modern man is still on the march, but to nowhere in particular.

14. ***Then Our Preaching Is in Vain.***—That next step follows relentlessly in the calm, severe, challenging logic of the apostle's thought. This greathearted man has never been averse to looking all his enemies, physical or spiritual, straight in the face to measure their reality and their strength. That trait makes his riposte the more overwhelming. Here he points out to those in Corinth who now question this basic conviction of their new faith that the reflection is on himself and on the other apostles and teachers who have preached the gospel of a resurrected Lord. **If Christ has not been raised,** then they who affirmed it are either lying charlatans or peddlers of fantastic illusions. Strong language; but the context bears this interpretation. Apart from other consequences, some of which we have already noticed and some of which are yet to be faced, the very sincerity of those who shared with him the preaching of this gospel is called in question. All the evidence that he had marshaled to fortify their conviction, his reference to "eyewitnesses" and to his own personal experience, is manufactured evidence, and these Corinthians who trusted the Christian preachers have been cruelly misled. Their hopes have been raised to the heights only to be dashed to the depths. All that the gospel of the Resurrestion enshrined of the power of God and of the love of God, for these are central elements in the gospel of Christ, is so much conjecture. So far from being a possibility, these great qualities of God are negated by the darkness of the Cross. The faith for time and for eternity that was built on such an illusion is founded on a quicksand that will soon engulf it, and it will perish as though it had never been. For its master light the Christian gospel has the resurrection of Christ; and if that light must be quenched in the interests of truth, nothing remains but the pagan darkness from which it had seemed to summon them. The God of love and power, whom Jesus trusted to raise him from the dead in vindication of his truth and of his spirit, either was powerless to respond to that amazing trust or chose not to do so. In either case he is no longer reliable.

Is there not a picture in the apostle's mind as he pens these blunt, almost terrifying words, a picture of God—if indeed on such an assumption there could be a God at all—watching Christ as he proclaims the gospel of a divine love and of a divine power that matches the love, so that what love promises, power can perform; watching the enmity of those who feared and then hated him, summoning their evil energies like a great, dark, tidal wave to overwhelm him; watching the huge, swelling billows crash over his devoted head; hearing the terrible, heart-rending cry of dereliction on the Cross; listening to the last quiet, peaceful, and triumphant assurances, "It is finished"; "Father, into thy hands I commit my spirit!" and doing—nothing! How could there be such a thing as faith in such a God or in any message concerning him? Granted the historical fact of Jesus Christ, of his spirit and of his teaching, what kind of a God would he be who allowed the final reflection on such a life to be, "Jesus Christ, crucified, dead, and buried"? Lesser men who in some sense have served their fellows have won from imperfect human nature a love and devotion that would far outdistance the spirit of such a God. Even on a priori grounds can we deny to the Creator of all existing things, the source and giver of every good and perfect gift, the highest qualities of love, devotion, and trustworthiness that we assign to

argument there is identical with that of Peter in Acts 2, who also appeals to scripture and to appearances of Christ to chosen witnesses. Now Paul proceeds to develop

man at his best? Moreover, if the Greek philosophical method has justified itself, and surely it has, then the lesser is conditioned by the greater. Paul knew what he was doing when he challenged the thought and aspirations of the community in Corinth, even the thought and aspirations of the doubters, with regard to the faith they had received. He was saying to them, in effect, if we may adapt some of his own vivid metaphors, **If Christ has not been raised, then** I am a runner who has no conception of any goal toward which the race tends; I am a boxer who dissipates his energies in beating the air. You may justly distrust my sincerity, and you may rightly set aside my message. We, and those who were and are associated with me, have deceived you. **Our preaching is in vain.**

14. ***Your Faith Is in Vain.***—That corollary inevitably follows. T. H. Huxley once said, "I cannot see one shadow or tittle of evidence that God is love." If he could have looked on the half century that followed, with its vast entail of tragedy and utter misery and despair, concomitants of two great world wars, he might have made that statement even more emphatically. Preoccupation with the human scene to the exclusion of higher things, tends, at least to some extent, to such a conclusion. For the Christian a different verdict is possible, even on a realistic appraisal of that human scene, if the appraisal is firmly based on the life and teaching, the cross and the resurrection of Jesus Christ. All four elements are essential to the Christian faith. The life and teaching of Jesus Christ met their decisive test in the Cross. P. T. Forsyth[8] has pointed out that the Cross is central to the Christian faith, not only because Jesus Christ who died on it was able to deal with human suffering, but because he was even more concerned to deal with sin: he endured that suffering and carried that burden of sin on himself; he was strong enough to see the world continue to suffer for the realization of moral and spiritual purposes, and to have his own creative part in the suffering, until there was borne into the consciousness of mankind the realization of the atoning victory of the redeeming love and power of God which he, Christ, revealed. There is the heart of the gospel. On the Cross all that Jesus taught about God's redemptive purpose of love and his power to achieve it; all that he taught about a providence that cared even for grass and for sparrows, and therefore "how much more" for man; all the assurances he gave in the upper room that the Giver of life would demonstrate his loving power as the conqueror of evil and death, and that therefore he would see his disciples again; all the assurance that goes with such teaching, backed by such a spirit as his, was put to its ultimate and final test. If ever the ultimate nature of reality staged a cataclysmic crisis of creation and history on this globe, it was on Golgotha nearly two thousand years ago. There the issue between God and evil itself, rather than between God and man, was joined in a life-and-death grapple for the human soul and for its at-one-ment with God. Faith in the victory of God's love and in his power to achieve his purpose lay in the outcome of that crisis of creation. In the Christian view it still lies in man's acceptance of what happened then. Christianity continues to assert its relevance because it claims to make final statements about the nature of the reality and about the meaning of history. For the very possibility of that faith, the Resurrection and convincing demonstration of the continued life of Christ are absolutely indispensable. If there was no resurrection, then evil has utterly and finally triumphed; if there is, then forever, despite all appearance to the contrary in the affairs of mankind, men can put their faith in God's triumphant adequacy. The final triumph is sure, for the victory is won! Who could go on living in such a world as ours if we were to be bereft of such a faith? Paul was writing, therefore, not only for the strengthening of the faith of the Corinthian Christians, but for all future generations, when he compelled them to face this issue. **If Christ has not been raised, . . . your faith is in vain** are words pregnant with significance for all mankind in every age. It matters tremendously what we believe concerning the death and resurrection of Jesus Christ. To such as Huxley, who in effect say that they can discern no evidence of the identity of God in suffering and in love with the world as we know it, Christianity can and does, again and again, point to the cross of Christ, or rather to him who suffered there, and says, "God *is* identified with human suffering, and God *is* love." To those who have, perhaps like Huxley, consigned themselves to a noble but cold stoicism with regard to the ultimate outcome of life, because they see no shadow of evidence that evil will be finally vanquished by good and that hate will fall victim to victorious and finally triumphant love, Christianity points to the Cross, but above all to the risen

[8] *The Cruciality of the Cross* (London: Independent Press, 1909).

15 Yea, and we are found false witnesses of God; because we have testified of God that he raised up Christ: whom he raised not up, if so be that the dead rise not.
16 For if the dead rise not, then is not Christ raised:

15 We are even found to be misrepresenting God, because we testified of God that he raised Christ, whom he did not raise if it
is true that the dead are not raised. 16 For
if the dead are not raised, then Christ has

---

what is involved in the denial. All the apostolic testimony would have to be rejected. If the resurrection of Jesus was not true, there had been no divine confirmation of his

---

Christ, and says, "We worship the victorious majesty that we see." The issues of creation, of history, of life here and hereafter, of morality and religion, of every noble idealist philosophy, of every high aspiration of the mind of man are bound up with the glorious, triumphant fact that Christ is risen from the dead and faith is not in vain.

15-19. *God Is Misrepresented.*—Paul misses no point. **We are even found to be misrepresenting God, because we testified of God that he raised Christ, whom he did not raise if it is true that the dead are not raised.** That, too, is clear. The basis falls out of the Christian conception of God. For Christians, Jesus Christ, as it were, has become the very language in which they think and speak of God. His life and spiritual quality and character have enabled us to fill up the concept of God. It has often been said that what Jesus Christ was in history, God is throughout all eternity. To be more accurate, as far as finite minds can approximate accuracy in dealing with an infinite spiritual Being, we must understand that there is more in the concept of God than is revealed in Jesus Christ; for Jesus was subject to the limitations imposed by his incarnation. Yet in Jesus Christ we have all, and more than all, the revelation we need in forming our estimate of the God in whom we are invited to put our trust. Christian faith has been based on a sublime proposition, which is founded on the life and teaching of Jesus, viz., that God in his purpose to reveal himself to man has spoken to man in a language that man can understand, i.e., through humanity itself; he has done so in such a way and so intimately that one human life perfectly, for his purpose, expressed and revealed his nature and his plans for humanity. All this God did through Jesus Christ. We have been able to affirm ever since that God is love, and is gracious, pitiful, and compassionate, universal in the range of his redemptive purposes, and all-powerful to achieve them. His spirit of truth and of love is manifest in Christ's teaching, in his deeds, and in his death; the power of God in the vindication of that truth, and of that spirit of love, is revealed in the triumph of the Resurrection with its satisfying pledges to all who put their trust in him. But **if Christ has not been raised,** what is the basis of this faith? Jesus is then no more than a good man who was deluded in respect of his ideas about God. In the supreme hour of his life, when everything he stood for with regard to his mission of introducing man to God, and of revealing God to man in a new, full, and satisfying way, was being tested, God failed him. If so, all he has demonstrated is that one can live a good life under trying circumstances; but that if goodness and love go beyond a certain point, then the contrary forces will and can combine to destroy those who are the instruments of such goodness, truth, and love. God is not merely misrepresented: he is completely ruled out! There is no value for religion or for life in a God who is not powerful enough to defend and maintain the truth concerning himself, or who is careless and indifferent about doing so. We have glimpsed some of the consequences for the religious interpretation of creation, of history, and of life, if that conclusion has to be accepted. No deity in any form of religion has continued to command the faith and allegiance of man when man has become convinced that there are other more powerful forces, or beings, to whom or to which that deity himself is subordinate. The God whose triumph was written in the resurrection of Christ has been misrepresented if that resurrection is a myth without any basis in historical fact. He can be safely set aside. Where the real issues of life are concerned he is impotent!

The consequences for the Corinthians would then be serious: they would lose their new-born faith and would, if they could, revert to the paganism from which they had been delivered. How could they possibly return to the gross materialism and superstition represented by some of those cults? Yet it is probable that this would have happened. Some, the finer sort, would embrace one of the more refined types among the mystery religions; others, grosser in nature, would probably go back to the orgiastic ceremonies associated with Diana worship or some such cult. In either case there would linger

17 And if Christ be not raised, your faith *is* vain: ye are yet in your sins.

not been raised. 17 If Christ has not been raised, your faith is futile and you are still

---

messiahship, no redemption in his death, and no assurance of the approach of the messianic time. The **preaching** of the apostles and the Corinthians' own belief were **in vain.**

---

a sense of loss. Modern man would probably relapse into some kind of vague theism; the kind of vague theism that avoids all reference to Christ and his church, that in varying forms is seeking the support of men and women everywhere. Or he might, as so many have done, give himself without much restraint to secularism. None of these alternatives, happily, were inevitable for the Corinthians; nor are they for modern man. Yet such, in some sort, are the issues and alternatives if the vindicating basis of the Christian faith is lost or surrendered. We know next to nothing about God, and are more than liable to misrepresent him, **if Christ has not been raised.** Once again Paul draws the general conclusion, **For if the dead are not raised, then Christ has not been raised.** His resurrection is the guarantee of the resurrection of all believers: the possibility and reality of resurrection are demonstrated by the fact that he rose from the dead.

17. ***Sin Remains; Forgiveness Is an Illusion.***—More than once we have noticed that Christianity had appeal for the Greco-Roman world because it was a deliverance religion. Over the Roman Empire there was settling a pall of moral decay and dissolution. Home life was going to pieces, morals were on the decline; the old Roman virtues associated with military discipline were fast disappearing; the old pagan gods were dying, and the cult of Caesar was failing to arrest the decline. In such a dark spiritual night of the race the star of Bethlehem rose, and the impact, as of a great bursting sea of light upon the slowly decaying empire, of One who was hailed as a deliverer and Savior of men from their sins, was immense. The tides have receded and again run to the full several times in the course of the centuries, and always have advanced farther than in the immediately previous onrush. They have always, likewise, receded less far than the immediately previous ebb. And the force of these tides has been in the divine assurance of forgiveness and moral regeneration, in Christ's power to cleanse the defiled image of God within each human being, and to restore it to something like its original splendor. Belief in the forgiveness of sins comes near the close of the Apostles' Creed, though not at all as afterthought: rather does it stand at the very heart of the Christian message, joining hands with the resurrection of the body, and the life everlasting.

Man's distinctiveness in the animal creation, his characteristic mark, lies in the realm of his moral sense. He knows that there is a difference between right and wrong. He knows that though the issues of right and wrong often shade into one another, yet when he reaches the point where he recognizes the difference, so that "this is right" and "that is wrong," then the gulf between the twain is absolute, and the demand of the "right" is a categorical imperative. That moral sense of man carries with it an inborn intuition of his responsibility in the sight of God. He may conceive of his responsibility in crude and superstitious ways, or with the refinement and sensitiveness of a great saint; yet from the lowest reach to the highest, the same principle is involved. There is a moral category in the "blood-feud code" of the savage tribes in their primeval jungles. At the heart of it lies a sense of responsibility with regard to the indiscriminate taking of human life, and of the responsibility devolving on the relatives of the person slain to revenge the death. There may be discerned the root that has blossomed through the years into the more carefully cultivated flowers of retributive and reformative justice; there, from earliest days, is the germ of moral responsibility to others and to oneself. This element in the moral sense has been put into clear, concise language in what is known as the "General Confession": "We have left undone those things which we ought to have done; And we have done those things which we ought not to have done." That confession touches every normal life in which a decent spark remains alive. None would honestly claim that everything good that lay within our power has been done; nor would anyone claim so perfectly to have fulfilled the moral obligations of life as to have left no room for wrongdoing. Paul's experience is that of every man (Rom. 7:7-24). In our better hours, and particularly when we realize our moral responsibility to God, we know that both in terms of omission and commission we have sinned. When man looks at the confusion and chaos, the tragedy and tears of the world, when he considers its wrecked lives, its broken homes, its shattered hopes and ideals, its crimes, its wars, its hosts of unconsidered and downtrodden people, he

Paul and the others were shown to be **false witnesses,** testifying to something which had not taken place, if the general truth were established that there was **no resurrection of the**

knows that sin in the human heart is the root cause of all the misery that afflicts mankind. Whether the garb worn is the respectable broadcloth of the suburbs or the rags and dirt of the slums, it covers the same foul spiritual disease; and the name of the disease is sin. The world of personal relationships, that closely enmeshed system in which our lives are more or less harmoniously integrated, is permeated through and through with sin. None can escape its contagion. Moreover, the sin of the world, reflected in the state of the world, has its roots and its springs in the human heart. Sin, individual and social, is one of the major facts of life. How adequately to deal with it is life's greatest practical problem. No social reform, no lasting betterment of international relationships, no genuine progress, national, social, or individual, is feasible or likely to be effective if the fact of sin is not faced and adequate remedies for the disease are not found. To deal with sin by rearranging things would be like trying to cure cancer by sprinkling scent on the sores. Drastic diseases need drastic remedies. Deep in his moral consciousness man knows where the real trouble lies. He knows that if man's spirit everywhere could be changed for the better, the world too would be changed for the better.

It was against the background of this great problem that the gospel of the risen Christ made its appeal. The Cross is the ultimate, final, and damning exposure of everything that challenges, denies, and frustrates the Christian spirit in every age. At the Cross sin seemed to be triumphant; but the garden of the Resurrection was the setting of another, better tale. The Resurrection made Christ's teaching of God's forgiving, redeeming, renewing grace and love a glad and glorious gospel. The early Christians preached with joy the forgiveness of sins.

Now all the hopes of a better life here and of a fuller life in the imminent hereafter were jeopardized; for one of the inescapable consequences of **if Christ has not been raised** was that **you are still in your sins.** These words must have fallen like a death knell upon the hearing of the Corinthian Christians. Could they possibly have thought out the full consequences of their easygoing questioning of the reality of the resurrection of Christ? One almost doubts it. Paul is determined to drive deeply home to their hearts the significance of that great event. Imagine that he is not risen, then sin remains triumphant: forgiveness is another myth that has no foundation in reality. All that was and is involved in the "saviorhood" of Jesus—the N.T. is written around his saviorhood—is to be set aside as a pathetic illusion. If the Cross was really the end of him, then sin has had the final word, and all hopes of heaven are to be forgone. He has failed to be a Savior. More than that, there are intimate personal consequences as well. Remorse remains! The newborn sense of freedom and of a glorious fresh beginning has gone, and peace of heart and mind has also gone. When, as so often happens, conscience long stifled suddenly comes to life, and the past with its bitter memories and forgotten experiences is resurrected, then there is no relief. Sin, unforgiven sin, not blotted out by the redeeming, cleansing grace of God, is like a shadow that constantly haunts the sinner: he cannot get away from it. The thought of the person wronged continually thrusts itself on the imagination; one's very dreams are disturbed. The person wronged may be separated from us by a great distance in terms of miles, yet he is ever present with us. What would not many such tormented souls give for the assurance of a forgiveness that is cleansing, renewing, and real? What can lift the weight of guilt that John Bunyan symbolized in his great allegory, *Pilgrim's Progress,* by the burden which Christian carried on his back? That was a problem for the people in Corinth; it is a problem for man in every age. Some think that modern man need not be concerned about his sins, and even less about forgiveness. The consulting rooms of doctors and psychiatrists, and the vestries of many trusted pastors and Christian workers have been the scene of a very different state of affairs. Sin, as a word, may frequently be banished from current speech; as a devastating reality that robs people of their peace of mind, of their power of concentration, of the brightness of life, it is always a present reality. What such people need, what everyone needs, for we are all poisoned by the moral miasma of the world, is the assurance of a power, far above anything that man himself possesses, by which he can be set free from the tyranny of his sins; set free of the very thought of them; set free from the crippling effects of remorse, and ushered through the open doors of a new beginning.

Such hope was evoked by the Christian message of forgiveness based upon the saviorhood of Jesus. But the saviorhood of Jesus was itself based upon the fact of his resurrection; for the Resurrection means, among other things, that the sin which nailed him to the Cross and sent him to the tomb was powerless to keep him

18 Then they also which are fallen asleep in Christ are perished.

in your sins. 18 Then those also who have

---

dead. In slightly varied phraseology the apostle repeats these assertions again and again. If this denial were true, it would mean that those who lived were **still in** their **sins,** and those who had died had experienced no real salvation (I Thess. 4:16).

---

there. The Cross itself has become the symbol of Christ's triumph. The resurrection of Jesus Christ from the dead means that there sin met its match and was defeated; that the repentant sinner who accepts the pardon which God offers through Jesus Christ is free, the sin blotted out, remembered against him no more. The Resurrection has always been the assurance of the power and love of God manifested in forgiveness to those who will accept it. More than that, the saviorhood of Jesus Christ, ratified by his resurrection from the dead, has meant from the first that man is not only saved from his sin; he is also saved to a new, different, and fuller life. The divine image in which he was created has been restored. The standard of manhood that he may attain has been set before him in Jesus Christ; and the power that will at least enable him steadily to approximate that high standard is guaranteed in the fact that Christ has risen, and is therefore able to fulfill his promise to be with his followers even "to the close of the age" (Matt. 28:20).

Surely the message of the Resurrection is relevant for the time in which we live. Many proclaim the need of a new spirit among men: the very idea suggests that there is something wrong that needs to be put right. Others plead the necessity of a new kind of political, economic, and social life. That suggests the same thought. Something must be wrong with the present order if so many people desire to see it radically changed. Some pin their hope on legislation, some on education, some on the scientific exploitation and control of physical resources and the application of them for the benefit of mankind. But there are limits to what legislation can do. One can legislate for the construction of houses; something more is required to turn them into true homes. One can legislate with certain effect against social evils, but something more is required to transform a drunkard into a sober Christian citizen. Education yields power; of itself it does not guarantee that the power so transmitted will be used for human well-being. Many of the people responsible for the ravaged state of the world before, between, and after the two great wars fought during the first half of the twentieth century were educationally competent. The same is true of science, and scientific inventiveness: power is thereby placed in human hands. Atomic energy is neutral: it can be used for the benefit of mankind or for destructive purposes. Everything depends on the spirit and outlook and motives of those who control it. If the spirit of man is right, his motives and intentions will be good. He may make mistakes, but he will seek to rectify them. If it is wrong, then his spirit must be changed. Once again, the very idea that a new order is desirable, and that a new spirit among men is urgently necessary, suggests that there is indeed something, whatever it is, that needs to be changed. Man needs to be changed. He is a sinner who cannot save himself. He needs to be saved by a power greater than anything he possesses. That power, which can and has and does change the human spirit, was signally and triumphantly manifested in the resurrection of Jesus Christ from the dead. How foolish, then, those ancient Corinthians were, and how foolish their modern counterparts, in face of such urgent and vital necessity, to question the resurrection from the dead of the Lord Jesus Christ. **If Christ has not been raised, your faith is futile and you are still in your sins.** If that is true, then good-by to mankind's highest aspirations and fairest hopes. Thank God, it is not true!

18-19. ***Death Remains—the Hope of Reunion Is an Illusion.***—The words, **then those also who have fallen asleep in Christ have perished,** read to the community in Corinth, must have rung like a bell tolling for the dead. We have seen what an attenuated existence at best was believed to be the portion of those who had died, if indeed they survived death at all. They were mere shadows of their former selves. With what gladness Paul and the others commissioned to preach the gospel of Christ had liberated their pagan converts from the dull deadliness of such a conception of the afterlife! The grace of God, mediated through Christ, proclaims life abundant and life eternal to all who believe. All such are partakers here and now of life everlasting; and the experience of life's fullness on this side of the veil of time, marvelous though it is, shows but a faint reflection of the fullness that will be revealed when at the touch of God's white-winged messenger of death the spirit of the believer is released from the trammels of the flesh and

19 If in this life only we have hope in Christ, we are of all men most miserable.

fallen asleep in Christ have perished. 19 If
in this life we who are in Christ have only hope,[u] we are of all men most to be pitied.

[u] Or *If in this life only we have hoped in Christ.*

---

19. The KJV wrongly connects the word **only** with the phrase **in this life.** In the Greek it clearly goes with **hope.** It is also probable that **in Christ** does not designate the object of the hope, but rather describes those who share in it. **In Christ** defines the status of a believer. The RSV is based on this understanding (but cf. mg.) . If there is **no resurrection**

---

translated into the place of God's presence. That experience can never be described in human language, for human language is conditioned by the necessity of thinking in terms of space and time. Yet it can confidently be affirmed, as the apostle has already done earlier in the letter, that while faith looks forward with hope and longing to that consummation of life, and while intuition and imagination soar with expectancy into realms of speculation, the highest flights of fancy will fall far short of the actual realization of "what God has prepared for those who love him" (2:9) . How could such a message have failed to thrill and fire the mind and spirit of those to whom it was first preached? Yet doubts had arisen concerning the resurrection of Christ, and Paul is constrained to point out the full consequences and implications of such doubts.

"What of those who have died?" he asks, and adds the thought-provoking words, **If in this life we who are in Christ have only hope, we are of all men most to be pitied. Hope** that held no assurance of ultimate realization meant for Paul that any prospect of a fuller life, freed from the limitations of earthly existence—still bound, as we are, by sin and the consequences of sin so graphically described elsewhere (Rom. 7:24) —or of reunion with the beloved dead, was no more than another illusion. Sooner or later such a fantasy was liable to suffer a tragic awakening. The apostle clearly recognizes and states that possibility (see Exeg., vs. 19) . Later on (vs. 32) he reverts to it and indicates its all too likely result. Meantime, it seems that the ideas involved in some of the Greek cults have had their effect on the volatile minds of these Corinthians. We know that all contact with "matter" was considered an evil thing, since for some of the Greeks "matter" was considered to be the principle of evil. This is the root idea of the Gnostic heresy so strongly contradicted in the prologue to the Fourth Gospel and elsewhere in the N.T. Those who were influenced by these cults and doctrines may have harbored some faint, wistful hopes of immortality conceived in purely spiritual terms; but as we have seen, such immortality was a pale, attenuated type of existence. For Paul the whole conception of a future life is given robust and convincing reality by the resurrection of Jesus Christ and by all that it implies. Christian belief in an afterlife is no mere adaptation of Greek ideas; even less does Christian faith share the Gnostic heresy that "matter," of which the body in part consists, is evil. The distinctive Christian doctrine is one of resurrection. This involves a full personal life with all its characteristic and distinctive marks. It was this assurance that for Paul, and for those others who had preached the good news in Corinth, filled out the Christian message and indeed made it a gospel. The apostle's strong faith in the fullness of the gospel, so far from making him **of all men most to be pitied,** inspired him to constant rejoicing. "Rejoice" is a word constantly on his lips as he preaches to those who come within range of his voice, or to whom he writes these strong yet tender and helpful pastoral letters. Now the joy with which they had received this gospel of forgiveness and redemption and resurrection has been quenched by cold doubts. It is as if a sudden black, heavy, impenetrable cloud had passed over the sun and all the warmth had gone out of the atmosphere. Take away the hopes of life's fullness hereafter, as indicated and justified by the resurrection of Jesus Christ, and his glorious gospel is reduced to a mere system of ethics; God, the God of love and power, the Father-God, as men had been taught to see him revealed in Jesus Christ, is no more, if even that, than an ethical principle necessary to give the substance of ultimate reality to the ethical life. To cut Christian ethics from the religious beliefs and implications in which they are planted, and from which they draw their nourishment, is like filling a crystal vase with lovely flowers. The flowers are beautiful and real, but they have been severed from their roots: they are under sentence of death. So is it with the Christian ethic sundered from the great spiritual implications of the Christian faith. It has no future. The great and glowing hopes that have been raised by the preaching of the gospel are under the cloud of man's mortality. These were some of the broader im-

of the dead—which is the postulate of the entire paragraph—believers possess in the only life they will enjoy nothing but a **hope** which has no chance of fulfillment. That is a more miserable situation than if there were no hope at all. But Paul is through with

---

plications of Corinthian doubt and denial. They hold good still.

To fall back on my meaner world, and feel
Like one who, dwelling 'mid some smoke-dimmed town—
In a brief pause of labour's sullen wheel—
'Scaped from the street's dead dust and factory's frown—

In stainless daylight saw the pure seas roll,
Saw mountains pillaring the perfect sky:
Then journeyed home, to carry in his soul
The torment of the difference till he die.[9]

If Christ has not been raised **then those also who have died in Christ have perished.** Naturally and inevitably, save for some ill-founded eschatological hopes, the same fate awaits those who are still alive. They may be impressed by the manifest signs of Christ's presence in the life and worship of the community, and on the basis of such experiences may harbor hopes of his spectacular return, so that those who are still alive may by supernatural power be caught up to meet him in the air (cf. I Thess. 4:17); but should they die before this takes place, then in Paul's view they share the fate of the Christian believers who have already died.

The implications are plain, and the apostle means his readers to feel their weight. It is true that he has something brighter and happier to say; but in painting his picture on the basis of what had actually taken place in the community, he is depicting the shade to accentuate the light. If Christ is not risen, then these dear departed ones are perished. If it is not possible to conceive that such a man as Christ, by the power and grace of God, was raised from the dead, why should those others survive? What guarantee is there, if Christ is not risen, that those who have put their faith in his teaching will achieve a life that is fully personal and fully immortal? Would it not be nearer the truth to opine that their life is snuffed out like a candle? Shakespeare has faced the issue in the tragedy of Macbeth.

To-morrow, and to-morrow, and to-morrow,
Creeps in this petty pace from day to day,
To the last syllable of recorded time;
And all our yesterdays have lighted fools
The way to dusty death. Out, out, brief candle! [1]

[9] Sir William Watson, "The Glimpse." Used by permission of George G. Harrap & Co., London.

[1] Act V, scene 5.

If the Cross and the tomb were the end of Jesus, if all men's hopes of life hereafter are to be founded on spiritual experiences such as have been indicated in our study of the gifts of the Spirit, is there any guarantee at all that the grave is not the end? Paul thinks not. At least the strongly historical element has been taken out of this aspect of the gospel, while all the rest—the teaching and life and death of Jesus—is founded on historical facts. The whole idea of a general resurrection, that distinctive Christian doctrine, is jeopardized if his resurrection did not take place. It means that the love in human hearts, which is stronger than death since it survives the agony of the parting, and which longs with unutterable yearning

. . . for the touch of a vanished hand,
And the sound of a voice that is still,[2]

is only another element that adds to the agony. The chasm is fixed, and none may cross it if there is no resurrection of the dead. Love and immortal longings are finished forever "if Christ has not been raised." Little wonder that Paul's written words throb with deep emotion as he faces the full implication of this doubt of the resurrection of Jesus, and as he compels his readers to do the same. Such are the consequences: the gospel is in vain, it only raises expectations that are doomed to disappoint those who harbor them; forgiveness is an illusion, remorse lingers on to the end of our earthly days; full personal immortality is a forlorn hope, and men shall never see their loved ones again. Moreover, no real trust can be founded on the character of God. This is really Paul's fundamental argument: it is the fundamental argument in any adequate discussion of immortal life, either in terms of the Christian doctrine of the Resurrection, or from any other angle worthy of consideration. No other so-called proofs, whatever their value, can really take its place. Spiritualism at its best may by some be supposed to indicate survival of the soul; but immortality is a richer, more meaningful conception than mere survival. A God of love and power, who cares for men to the extent of the cross of Christ, in which his redemptive purpose is revealed, will not let his care for them end with death. The Cross itself for that reason becomes the most profound assurance of the Resurrection, and of all that the Resurrection implies for Christian faith.

[2] Tennyson, "Break, Break, Break."

KJV	RSV
20 But now is Christ risen from the dead, *and* become the firstfruits of them that slept.	**20** But in fact Christ has been raised from the dead, the first fruits of those who have

suppositious cases. Those who are **in Christ** do not possess merely a **hope;** they enjoy a certainty.

B. The Eschatological Drama (15:20-34)

1. The Order of Events (15:20-28)

20. Νυνὶ δέ (**but in fact**) introduces some of Paul's most important affirmations (13:13; Rom. 3:21; 6:22; 7:6; Col. 1:22; etc.). It does not carry here a temporal significance, but introduces the contrast to the hypothetical situation which has been discussed in the previous paragraph. The **fact** is otherwise; **Christ has been raised.** This event has inaugu-

---

But Paul has had enough of shadows and sighs. Having clarified for his readers the somber implications involved in any doubt of a fact on which Christian faith and life are built, he now changes his colors. The great hopes inspired by the gospel will indeed fade; but they will fade like the stars in the glory of the morning sun. There is light that more than counterbalances darkness, and the sound of the apostle's jubilant trumpet now banishes tears and sighs.

20-28. ***Significance of the Resurrection of Christ.***—The words of vs. 20 reaffirm the basic conviction that God's love and power were involved in the crisis of the Cross. Evidence has already been set before the community in the very fact that this gospel has been preached to them, evidence which vindicates God's honor as well as his justice, power, and love; Paul himself, a man transformed, redeemed, and inspired by the risen Lord, had preached it: the fact of the Resurrection ought to be beyond any further doubts or questionings, and should never even for a moment be set aside in favor of some semireligious, semiphilosophical cult of immortality. Faith in God's love and power and redemptive purpose for them and for all mankind is historically based on this mighty act (see Exeg., vs. 20). As they grasp it afresh, all that it involves, not only for the life that is, but for that which is to come, is to their joy renewed. The gospel is vindicated. They need never again question the love of God. Nor need they ever again question the power of God. The Giver of life is the almighty Conqueror of death. For life and death, and for what lies beyond death, they may safely trust themselves to him.

That is a great matter. To possess and to be possessed of such a faith as this alters one's attitude to life. It colors all our thoughts and emotions. These and all our purposes and desires are set in eternal perspectives. It colors our attitude to our fellow men, to the events of history and circumstance, and to daily life; it gives us a philosophy of history based upon the redemptive purposes of a God who is actively and ceaselessly involved in the historical process. As an idealistic philosopher-historian like Arnold Toynbee might put it, there is, in any estimation of the historical process, on the basis of such a faith as this, a place for universals as well as particulars. The particulars are real: one must come to terms with them; but they are conditioned by the universals. More concretely, such a faith helps us understand that this world is not a road that leads nowhere: everything points forward to a great consummation in which God's eternal truths, his justice, his love and power will find their fullest expression. That will forever be heaven. Those who commit themselves to such a God, no matter what befalls, are in his sure and steady hands: he is equal to any emergency; they will participate in his victory.

Forgiveness is real; sin is vanquished (vs. 21). The world constantly needs to hear and to believe that message. Individual men and women need to hear it. For the cleansing away of sin on the widest, as on the most individual scale, a gospel of forgiveness is needed. For the possibility of new ways of life, richer ways of life, with all the promise and potency of a justice for all mankind, of economic plenty, of social and individual freedom, of high thinking and noble living, the prerequisite is the cleansing of the springs of human nature. Sin was defeated, and its power broken, for those who have faith to believe it, when Christ rose from the dead. Man's spirit can, if he believes, be free forever.

And again, death is vanquished (vs. 26). Saints and martyrs, and humble, loyal followers of the Christ, all who believed in him and have passed through the portals of death, are in his safekeeping. They are alive forever, more fully alive than ever before. They share the

21 For since by man *came* death, by man *came* also the resurrection of the dead.

fallen asleep. 21 For as by a man came death, by a man has come also the resurrec-

rated the drama of the end-time. There follows a concise picture of the whole series of eschatological events, the fullest which we have from the pen of Paul. But the apostle is not seeking merely to satisfy curiosity about the future; he wants to show the certainty of the resurrection of believers. His purpose calls for a preliminary presentation of the contrast between Adam and Christ (vss. 45-49; Rom. 5:12-21). The offering of the first fruits to God symbolized the dedication of the entire crop to him (Rom. 11:16). Paul uses the term **first fruits** of the first converts in a church (16:15; Rom. 16:5), or of the Spirit (Rom. 8:23), whose work is the first installment of our salvation; or as here, of Christ himself, who is "the first-born from the dead" (Col. 1:18; Rev. 1:5). Those whom Jesus had raised from the dead during the earthly life were still subject to death at a later time. The resurrection of Jesus stood on an entirely different plane; not Jairus' daughter, but Jesus himself was the **first fruits.**

21-22. As in Rom. 5:12-18, Paul contrasts Adam and Christ as regards the effects which have followed them. It is death rather than sin that results from Adam's disobedience (Gen. 3:17-19). Because of his sin Adam returned to the dust of the earth, and mortality was inherited by all his descendants. Christ is likewise called **man,** the man

resurrection life and power of their risen Lord. Love tells the truth when it still yearns for the sight and companionship of the loved one who has gone before. Men are not mocked by some devil who has put such an agony into personal relationships. The resurrection of Jesus Christ is the pledge that love will be victorious. In the upper room on the night in which he was betrayed the Master told his disciples, confidently and quietly, with superb faith, that he would see them again. That pledge will be kept for all who put their faith in him. The Resurrection was the supreme victory of the Lord of life over death: his followers share it with him. Let the Corinthian Christians hold fast to the faith delivered unto them: it is a gospel of good news with regard to the supreme issues of time and of eternity. To be possessed of such a faith, to be possessed by it, adds such zest to life as can be found nowhere else. Let modern man recover it! It will nerve him to stand on his feet and live.

We have already seen that in Paul's view the resurrection of Jesus is the guarantee of the general resurrection of all his followers. He is **the first fruits of those who have fallen asleep.** No further comment is needed here: the meaning is made clear in all that precedes this paragraph (see Exeg., vs. 20). But the principle that is involved is important. Paul has been dwelling on the fact of the Resurrection; he has also emphasized the consequences that logically follow from the denial of it. Now he draws further consequences of great importance from what for him, and doubtless for them, is the established fact.

The Resurrection does not involve only Christ himself. It has a representative meaning and value for all believers: it is the guarantee that since he was resurrected, and since resurrection is an essential element in the full gospel message, all shall rise who put their faith in him. In that representative sense he is **the first fruits of those who have fallen asleep.** The love and power of God that were operative for him will be operative for them. Without that assurance the gospel would have been incomplete; without it the gospel would scarcely have survived.

But there is a further consequence, a consequence which is closely related to one of the major themes of this epistle. We touched upon it when we considered Paul's great anxiety with regard to the spirit of partisanship that was threatening the life and witness of the church. For him that partisanship threatened other things.

The principle of race solidarity is also implied in the resurrection of Jesus Christ from the dead. Elsewhere Paul has written of the social implications of sin. Individual men and women are involved in the guilt of society: it is inescapable. By our very constitution we are social beings. Thought is itself in part a function of the social consciousness. We are susceptible to the pressure of the social environment, to the trends of the times, to all the implications, whether we are aware of them or not, of the herd instinct and of other gregarious elements in our native endowment. Our ideas and desires and purposes and habits are largely conditioned by these environmental factors. So far as the moral and spiritual blemishes of society are concerned, as well as in other ways, "we

22 For as in Adam all die, even so in
Christ shall all be made alive.
23 But every man in his own order:
Christ the firstfruits; afterward they that
are Christ's at his coming.

tion of the dead. 22 For as in Adam all die,
so also in Christ shall all be made alive.
23 But each in his own order: Christ the first
fruits, then at his coming those who be-

from heaven. This may be Paul's way of translating *bār-nāshā'*, instead of using the barbarous ὁ υἱὸς τοῦ ἀνθρώπου, lit., "the son of the man." The connection of the human race with Adam was natural and universal; all his descendants are *in* him and all are therefore mortal. Did Paul conceive the relationship to Christ as equally universal and inevitable? Did he really mean that all shall be made alive in Christ? That is the conclusion of some interpreters; but this position can hardly be reconciled with what he says elsewhere. The **all** are to be qualified by **in Christ.** Those who have become part of his body through faith and baptism will inevitably share in all his experiences. As certain as their death with Christ is their resurrection with him, because believers are a part of his body, unless cut off by sin. Here is the essential link in Paul's argument which is not perceived by those who have not understood the intensity of mystical union with Christ. Why should the fact of Christ's resurrection carry with it the guarantee of the resurrection of anyone else? There would be no demonstration except on Paul's premise that believers are members of Christ's body.

23. This interpretation is confirmed by Paul's description of the resurrection which is to follow. It is not of all men but only of those who belong to Christ. This does not take place at the death of the individual believer, but first **at his coming** (παρουσία). The word does not mean *second* coming, but simply **coming.** It is used by Paul of the arrival of persons (16:17; II Cor. 7:6; Phil. 1:26); when the word is applied to the coming of

are members one of another." That is part of our destiny. A mind so comprehensive as Paul's was sure to apprehend clearly this important truth (see also Rom. 3:23; 5:12). In the present letter he sums up in Jewish terms what may be termed his "doctrine of original sin." No doubt his meaning was clear to those who read the letter. **For as by a man came death, by a man has come also the resurrection of the dead. For as in Adam all die, so also in Christ shall all be made alive.** So does he apply the principle of race solidarity to sin and its consequences, viz., corruption and death.

Now he turns to the gospel aspect of the same principle as illumined by the fact of the Resurrection: **so also in Christ shall all be made alive.** In rising from the dead, Christ is the forerunner of a great new order of life which through faith in him has become possible for all mankind, even as Adam, who brought death into the world by sin, was the forerunner of racial corruption and death (see Exeg., vss. 21-22). We need not let the imagery be a stumbling block to our recognition of the plain sociological and religious fact. In respect of the ties of our common manhood we are involved in the corruption of the race. But the complementary gospel truth is glorious. The trend toward death, as the consequence of sin, has been arrested by the life, death, and resurrection of Jesus. A second beginning has been made. Christ demonstrated a new harmony, replacing the old that was broken by sin; demonstrated it in his own life through his faith in the redemptive love and power of God. He was perfectly at one with his Father in heaven. He was at peace with himself. His life of prayer and faith and communion with God, and his obedience to God, created within him in terms of his humanity a completely integrated personality. It was marked by his sense of unity with mankind. This is not to say that men were in unity with Christ: manifestly they were not. It was his *attitude to them* that was perfect. He had come to teach and to impart the secret of abundant life; some would not give him the opportunity to help. Nonetheless, he was the friend of all, especially of those who needed it most. And he was perfectly in harmony with the events and circumstances of life, being quite at home in God's world, and obviously living by faith in the conviction that God in everything works for good with them that love him. To live like that is truly to live. In his complete unity with God, Jesus Christ demonstrated life's fullness. He is the incarnate atonement. As such he was the forerunner, the first born of the great new order of life.

This life is God's purpose for all mankind. The race can if it will find new solidarity in

24 Then *cometh* the end, when he shall have delivered up the kingdom to God, even the Father; when he shall have put down all rule, and all authority and power.

long to Christ. 24 Then comes the end, when he delivers the kingdom to God the Father after destroying every rule and every

Christ it means his coming in messianic power at the end of the age (Matt. 24:27; I Thess. 2:19; 4:15; 5:23; etc.) in contrast to the veiling of his glory during the days of his flesh. For Paul this coming was in the very near future (vss. 51 ff.; I Thess. 4:15; Phil. 4:5).

24-28. The next two stages in the drama are mentioned in reverse order. Before the final **end** (vs. 24) there is to be a period of the rule of Christ during which he will complete the subjugation of all the opposing forces which had been defeated on the

these terms, for Christ's redemption is open to all who are willing to believe in him and to follow him. Paul sees the possibility of a redeemed humanity illustrated in the life of the Christian community; that community itself is the demonstration of a new relationship among men because of their new relationship through Christ to God (see Exeg., vss. 21-22). It would be asserting too much to say that the apostle was fully aware of all the implications of his message, or even of the understanding he had, of the mind and spirit of his Master. We have seen already that he sometimes writes as if he were expecting the imminent consummation of the age, yet in his later writings he seems to have reconciled himself to that consummation as a more remote prospect. He must have realized, at least subconsciously, that it would require time for the Christian gospel to reach all the peoples of the world and to fill that world with the sound of a name above every name. For him certainly Christ's work was to go on until the kingdom of God should be consummated, every enemy destroyed, and all things, including the Son himself, put in subjection to God (vss. 24, 26-28). All these implications are involved in the statement that **for as in Adam all die, so also in Christ shall all be made alive.**

Here is the charter for the world-wide Christian mission, for the ecumenical church, and for the race-embracing family of God. Surely this comprehensive redemption of all mankind may well fall within the august purposes of the Eternal! He who sent his Son to the Cross, and who by his mighty act raised him from the dead —will he ever be defeated by the loss, in the end, of a single soul? In this connection it is at least a curious thing that Paul says so little about the future of the wicked, or of those who fail to respond to the grace of God revealed through Christ. Is there indeed what is sometimes called the gospel of the larger hope? If so, it raises many interesting points. Certainly none can be indifferent to the greatness and glory of the vision and all that it entails. What a world it would be, what blessedness of justice, peace, and brotherliness would reign in the heart and midst of men if the great globe itself could become like the church as Paul conceived it, all the members perfectly united to God in reverence and love, and to one another in the bonds of the Spirit and in the service of their Master! In any case, nothing less than that goal, whether to be achieved in time or perhaps in the vast reaches of eternity—the goal of a redeemed humanity, and a redeemed human society—nothing less is great enough to be worthy of so great a gospel which enshrines so great a redemption achieved at so great a cost.

Before the apostle turns to the consideration of the final consummation toward which all these great events and movements are directed, he makes his own view clear that there is a divine order in such matters. Christ is **the first fruits** as the pioneer or "principal" of the new life. He it was who blazed the trail, set up the signposts, and called upon men to trust in his message and to follow him. Then at his coming, that "imminent" event of which the early Christians lived in expectation, those who had followed him, believing in him and his message, would share in the resurrection life. There he is the pioneer who must never be preceded but always followed. No doubt part of the comfort and blessedness of the gospel for the early Christians was the thought that beyond the veil they would be met and welcomed by their Master and Friend whose royal prerogatives in some degree they hoped to share. Paul seems here to be anxious to emphasize, above all such considerations, the supremacy and priority of Christ. That would seem to be a fitting corollary to the Master's own requirement that his followers should seek first God's kingdom and his righteousness. That condition fulfilled, the promise is added, "And all these things shall be yours as well" (Matt. 6:33).

24-28. ***The Final Consummation.***—Here is another of the victorious consequences of the resurrection of Christ and of all that is implied by his triumph over the supreme enemy, death.

25 For he must reign, till he hath put all enemies under his feet.

authority and power. 25 For he must reign until he has put all his enemies under his

Cross (vs. 25). Four of these are named. **Rule** and **authority** and **power** appear elsewhere in Paul's lists of angelic powers (Rom. 8:38; Col. 1:16; 2:10, 15), but **power** is omitted in Colossians. Satan is not specifically mentioned, nor is there any such warlike portrayal as in Rev. 19:19–20:3. **Death,** which is **the last enemy,** may be synonymous with Satan. Elsewhere Paul frequently personifies **death** as if he were a demon with power to rule and to separate men from God (vs. 54; 3:22; Rom. 5:14; 8:38). The Lordship of Jesus began with his resurrection (Phil. 2:11). This triumph was decisive in the conquest of the principalities and powers, but their final subjection would not be complete until the Parousia. Then the visible rule of Christ and the saints would come. The length of this rule of Christ is not specified, but it corresponds to the thousand years in Revelation. There, only the martyrs are raised to participate. For Paul all those in Christ share in the rule (6:2). This conception of an intermediate messianic kingdom before the age to come is found in the Jewish apocalypses from the period between Paul and Revelation (II Baruch 30:1; II Esdras 7:26-30). The later rabbis also distinguished the "days of the Mes-

Everything that is opposed to the creative purposes of God is to be destroyed. That is part of the work of Jesus Christ. All that is exposed and condemned in the light of the Cross, everything that conspired to erect that Cross and to nail to it God's Son, is to be utterly and finally annihilated. This is the apostle's view, and it was undoubtedly shared by the other apostles, certainly by the author of Revelation. The vast platform of history is the stage on which the moral and spiritual struggle between the purpose of God and that which is opposed to his purpose is working itself out to a final issue. That struggle rages even more deeply *in* history, amid the thoughts and emotions, the desires and instincts of the human soul. Agelong it works toward a great consummation, to be marked by the utter defeat of all evil things and the final glorious victory of Christ (see Exeg., vss. 24-28). This is a plain statement of what can be termed Paul's philosophy of history; it is the orthodox Christian view, and can be strongly supported by reference to the rise and fall of civilizations.[3] No civilization has yet endured that has, as it were, turned its back on the moral and spiritual illumination it has received in the course of its existence. Since Christianity must claim to be the truth about this mysterious reality in which humanity is set, some such consummation as that indicated in general terms by Paul and his fellows is necessarily involved. Various interpretations have been given the phrase, **then comes the end;**[4] but the most satisfying is that clearly implied by the context: since God is the author of all things that have existence, all things, whatever their intermediate course may have been, must be made completely subject to his sovereign purpose.

The last enemy to be destroyed is death. It would no doubt be true to say that Christianity has to some extent ceased to regard death as an enemy, and with good reason would now look on it rather as an episode through which believers pass into life. There are many who feel that the apostle's view was colored by the ideas of his time. Yet surely we should observe that even then some thoughtful people—the Stoics among them—regarded death in a very different light. They thought of life as something to be endured with stoical courage, and were inclined to welcome death as providing friendly release from pain and hardship. Their modern counterparts are never far to seek. "If the next life is like this one," said an old Welsh woman who had suffered great sorrows, "then I, for one, don't want it!" Were we able to put a question to millions of people who are living in conditions of almost unspeakable misery—victims of famine, of epidemics, of injustice—and ask, "Do you think that life is worth living?" they might well answer, "No." And the reaction would be understandable. Only the Christian faith, with its essential message of abundant life as the gift of God's grace to those who put their trust in Christ, may justly tend to regard death as an enemy to be destroyed, and therefore underscore its menace. The Resurrection conveys the assurance that for the believer that menace will in the final consummation of the drama of redemption be forever removed! **That God may be everything to every one.**

The apostle is clearly doing two or perhaps three things in these rather difficult passages.

[3] Arnold J. Toynbee, *A Study of History* (New York: Oxford University Press, 1934), Vols. I-VI.

[4] Moffatt, *I Corinthians,* pp. 247 ff.

26 The last enemy *that* shall be destroyed *is* death.

feet. 26 The last enemy to be destroyed is

siah" from the "age to come." Some interpreters have tried to avoid acceptance of an equivalent to the millennium of Revelation because Paul is not so explicit in teaching it elsewhere. They identify the **end** with the **coming** of Christ and hold that the reign of Christ during which he puts all his enemies under his feet is the present rule of Christ in his church. But an intermediate kingdom is implied in Col. 1:13 and cannot be explained away here. Paul's language is shaped by Ps. 110, a favorite proof text in the early church. It was believed that Jesus had appealed to it (Mark 12:36); it was used in Peter's sermon at Pentecost (Acts 2:34-35), and was a key passage for the author to the Hebrews (1:13). Paul adds to this also Ps. 8:6, He **has put all things in subjection under his feet.** This refers to the son of man (Heb. 2:6-8) and shows definitely that Paul recognized "Son of man" as a term for Christ (see Phil. 3:12 also for the subjection of all things to Christ). Vs. 27 is a somewhat pedantic digression to remove a possible—but improbable—misunderstanding. The **all things** which are subjected to the Son of man do not include God himself. The subordination of Christ to God remains true at all times; but when this conquest and rule are completed, the reign of Christ will come to an end. That brings

Throughout the epistle, as in all his writings, his strong ethical sense compels him to insist that a certain kind of life and conduct is involved in the profession of the Christian faith. This appears in his strictures against the partisan spirit, in his insistence that the member guilty of immoral conduct shall be sternly disciplined, in his advice concerning the relationship between the married and the unmarried, and in his demand for orderliness in the church meeting and in the conduct of public worship. He is always quite clear that character shall be strictly consistent with profession. Paul owes his ethical sense in part to his Jewish training, which Christ fulfilled.

Again he is insistent on his demand for devotion to Jesus Christ: his gospel message was centered on Christ crucified and risen from the dead. It was through his own intensely personal experience of Jesus Christ that he came to a new and deeper understanding of God, of God's ways with men and purposes for men. Paul himself is never lacking in devotion to the central figure of our faith, and it is plain enough in his letters that he requires a like devotion from those who have become converted to Christianity. But we must remember that he had been brought up as a strict monotheist, and so was well aware of the influence on pagan minds of the various cults with their tendencies to lead men toward a multiplicity of deities. Therefore, while he is in no doubt that God is mediated through Jesus Christ, he never fully identifies the two. God must be supreme from first to last. It is God, and God alone, who is the alpha and the omega. Whatever the relationship in terms of communion may be between the Father and the Son, they are not in the apostle's thought identical. In respect of the work of Christ among men, for man's redemption, the relationship is one of subordination to the Father. Paul goes so far as to say that while in the Father's redemptive purpose everything is predestined to be subject to the Son, yet he, God, can never be made subject (vss. 27-28); (also see Exeg.). This is Pauline and not modern language; but the apostle's purpose is plain. Without expressing himself in any final way on the ultimate relationship of the Son to the Father, he is nonetheless anxious to avoid the dichotomy that might develop, with serious consequences to the faith and witness of the church, into something like a "Christ cult." "I love Jesus, but I hate God," said a little lad who had suffered his second or third amputation for cancer, an illness that subsequently killed him, to his father, a devoted minister. The father was able to put the lad's thoughts right. In different, yet perhaps somewhat similar circumstances, the Corinthians might all too easily have drawn the same distinction to the detriment of faith and worship (see also 3:23; 11:3).

Paul is always certain that God was revealed uniquely in the life and person of our Lord; to that extent he would undoubtedly fill in his concept of God in terms of all that he knew and had experienced in Jesus Christ. All that he had realized of the grace and love of God had been mediated to him, as to all the others, through Jesus Christ. He would agree wholeheartedly with the unknown author of the Epistle to the Hebrews that "in these last days [God] has spoken to us by a Son, whom he appointed the heir of all things, through whom also he created the world. He reflects the glory of God and bears the very stamp of his nature, upholding the universe by his word of power" (Heb. 1:2-3). But the distinction of "persons"

27 For he hath put all things under his feet. But when he saith, All things are put under *him, it is* manifest that he is excepted, which did put all things under him.

death. 27 "For God[v] has put all things in subjection under his feet." But when it says, "All things are put in subjection under him," it is plain that he is excepted who

[v] Greek *he.*

---

us to the affirmation which Paul made in vs. 24. It is possible to take τὸ τέλος in a variety of ways. Some understand it to mean "finally." Note that there is no word for **comes** in Greek. Others translate it as "the rest." They think that Paul is speaking of a third group who are raised from the dead at the end of the messianic rule of Christ in a general resurrection which introduces the final judgment (Rev. 20:12-13). Paul certainly believed in such a Day of Judgment (Rom. 14:10; II Cor. 5:10), but nowhere in his letters is it asserted that there would be a resurrection of the unjust (cf. Acts 24:15). It is better therefore to translate, as do both the KJV and the RSV, **the end,** leaving quite undecided whether Paul believed that this was accompanied by a general resurrection. There is no evidence that he speculated on the fate of those who had never heard the gospel, except in so far as it affected the fate of Israel (Rom. 9–11).

---

is clearly preserved. When the rule of God is established and the last enemy, death, is destroyed, then Christ's particular work will be completed and the kingdom will be delivered to God the Father (vs. 24). **Then the Son himself will also be subjected to him who put all things under him, that God may be everything to every one** (see Exeg., vs. 28). Paul is anxious that God shall never be relegated to the background as a superior type of spiritual context for the person and work of Christ. That person and work, so far as the field of human history is concerned, and so far as man's apprehension of these things is involved, fall within the eternal scope of God's being and purpose.

We need feel no theological difficulties here, nor indulge in the outworn controversies between Unitarians and Trinitarians as to the place, relationship, and importance of Jesus Christ in our conception of the deity. Paul obviously paid divine honors to Jesus Christ: the church exists for the worship of the Father and of the Son and of the Holy Spirit. One does not worship a superior type of humanity; one respects, honors, and admires it. Jesus Christ is much more than a superior type of humanity. If that were his status we could not acknowledge his saviorhood. Moreover, we would be consigned to utter despair if he were set before us merely as an example to follow. As well expect someone who had no ear for music to emulate and equal the supreme masters of the art. But if the stress is to lie where Paul obviously wants it to lie, on "God in Christ," then we see what God can do and has done in terms of humanity, and we can put our faith in him, yield ourselves to him, and hope someday to approximate that same perfection of spirit that we see revealed in Jesus Christ.

The emphasis here, as in all that Paul has written, particularly about the resurrection of Christ from the dead, falls upon the act of God. God initiated the redemptive work in sending his Son into the world to save the world. God sustains that work in all that Jesus taught and accomplished during his life and on the Cross. God vindicated his Son, and himself, and justified man's faith in the whole work of Christ by raising him from the dead. When the redemptive process is complete, then everything will be consummated in God. Some of the mystics, notably Böhme, would have heartily agreed with this vast conspectus of the creative process. Time and history fall like a brief episode into God's measureless and eternal love. Within their little space the almighty Creator has manifested himself in ways which man can understand, but supremely and uniquely through Jesus Christ his Son. That self-disclosing was for man's redemption and deliverance from everything that thwarts God's purposes and debases the human spirit. That was the work of Jesus Christ: none other could have understood the Father's purposes so well or fulfilled them so perfectly. His work being finished, everything is consummated in the fullness of God, **that God may be everything to every one.** Here is the ultimate victory of justice, grace, love, and power. Here is eternal life. Here is heaven: to fulfill the deepest meanings of one's being in communion with that suprapersonal and eternal Deity whose nature and name and purpose have been so wonderfully revealed to man's powers of comprehension through Jesus Christ. To achieve this is to complete the work for which Christ was sent into the world. To believe this is to know something of the inspiration and thrill of an interpretation of life that

28 And when all things shall be subdued unto him, then shall the Son also himself be subject unto him that put all things under him, that God may be all in all.

29 Else what shall they do which are baptized for the dead, if the dead rise not at all? why are they then baptized for the dead?

put all things under him. 28 When all
things are subjected to him, then the Son
himself will also be subjected to him who
put all things under him, that God may
be everything to every one.
29 Otherwise, what do people mean by
being baptized on behalf of the dead? If
the dead are not raised at all, why are peo-

---

28. After the time of the rule of the Son, God will assume the direct rule and be **all in all** (KJV). What did the apostle mean by that? Though an English reader might assume that all the world of phenomena was to be absorbed into the ultimate reality of God, that certainly was not the expectation of Paul. He did not believe in the loss of individual consciousness by absorption in the world soul. We find the same phrase in Col. 3:11, where complete devotion to Christ is expressed by "Christ is all, and in all." The RSV tries to make this clear by its rendition **that God may be everything to every one.**

2. Ad Hominem Rebuttal (15:29-34)

29. After setting forth these eschatological events Paul returns once more to his argument against those who would deny the resurrection. First he points to the inconsistency of their actions in relation to their professed beliefs. Apparently when some "outsiders" died without having been baptized, living persons had been baptized on their behalf. Some modern interpreters have been unwilling to believe that such a superstitious practice could have grown up in a church founded by Paul. Schlatter has proposed that "baptize" is used here as a figure for death (Luke 12:50), and that Paul

---

exalts man, that ennobles humanity, that banishes all evil things as aliens in the commonwealth of God, and that carries with it, vindicated by the Resurrection from the dead, the unshakable assurance of Christ's final triumph. Who would not live and fight for such a Lord?

29. *Vicarious Baptism.*—The rapture of these cosmos-embracing words and vision over, Paul turns to an interesting item of church practice in Corinth, and probably elsewhere too, and uses it to reinforce his main point that God had vindicated Jesus Christ and so justified their faith in him by raising him from the dead (see Exeg.). **Otherwise, what do people mean by being baptized on behalf of the dead?** The point is that there would be no sense in the procedure if there were no resurrection. Whatever doubts some members of the church had concerning it, there were others who were such firm believers in the Resurrection that they submitted to this rite of vicarious baptism on behalf of certain of the brethren, probably catechumens, who had passed away before they had been baptized and received into the full membership of the church. Perhaps also they had a feeling, natural enough at that stage of Christian understanding among those who had so recently been pagans, that unbaptized believers at the resurrection would not be so near to their Lord as those who had undergone the rite. Or they may have done it to ensure as far as possible that nothing would be lacking in respect of the eternal bliss of the redeemed. At its best, the vicarious ceremony was a tribute to the spirit of fellowship, of unity, and of solidarity in the community, and as such it would be sure to commend itself to Paul. There are still some survivals of this ancient Christian practice, though in the main it has fallen into disuse. In a sense it might be compared with prayers offered for the dead. They too may for some signify the deep spiritual unity and solidarity of the Christian fellowship in heaven and on earth, in which all are one in Christ Jesus. Whatever the effect of such practices on the joy of the saints in heaven, they do reflect a kindly, generous, and Christian spirit on the part of those on earth in the desire for the continued and increasing well-being of those who have passed beyond the veil. Perhaps it is as well to leave the matter there. Paul is content to do so, merely pointing to this ancient rite, and incidentally giving us another glimpse into the customary procedures of the early Christian fellowship as they illustrated the truth of the Resurrection. If Christ is not raised, and if therefore there is no resurrection of the dead, what could such baptism mean?

30 And why stand we in jeopardy every hour?

31 I protest by your rejoicing which I have in Christ Jesus our Lord, I die daily.

32 If after the manner of men I have fought with beasts at Ephesus, what advantageth it me, if the dead rise not? let us eat and drink; for to-morrow we die.

ple baptized on their behalf? 30 Why am I
in peril every hour? 31 I protest, brethren,
by my pride in you which I have in Christ
Jesus our Lord, I die every day! 32 What
do I gain if, humanly speaking, I fought
with beasts at Ephesus? If the dead are not
raised, "Let us eat and drink, for tomor-

---

is conceiving of a ministry on behalf of the dead, as in I Pet. 4:6. That is very unlikely. We do not know that Paul approved of the custom, nor is it certain that he was entirely fair to the point of view attacked here and in the following verses. If these people believed in immortality despite their denial of a resurrection, their conduct would not be so absurd. The same question arises concerning Paul's following contentions. Many earnest people feel that it is unjust to say that man will not strive morally unless he has the hope of personal survival. We realize that this was certainly not true of the great prophets of the O.T., like Amos and Hosea, who had no expectation of a resurrection. Likewise, there are many noble souls today of whom the same could be said. But Paul, the former Pharisee, feels most intensely that without belief in a resurrection of the dead, life would lack an essential dimension.

30-32. He begins with his own experiences. Particularly in the Corinthian correspondence do we find an emphasis on his sufferings for the gospel (4:11-13; II Cor. 4:8-12; 11:23-29; etc.). To the reader of these passages, the words **I die every day** do not appear exaggerated. The apostle refers in this place to one particular case for illustration. Some have supposed that he was alluding to the riot in the theater, described in Acts 19:29-41. But Paul was not in any personal danger at that moment, for he was dissuaded from

---

30-32. ***Paul's Adventures and Hardships on Behalf of the Faith.***—A further reinforcement of his preceding arguments is taken from his personal experience. "Is it likely," he asks, "that one such as myself should undergo such desperate perils and hazards and suffer such penalties for a mere fantasy?" (See Exeg., vss. 30-32.) **I die every day! What do I gain if . . . the dead are not raised?** That he should willingly face such perils and endure such hardships with his faith in the Resurrection undimmed and undiminished helps to illustrate surely the strength and tenacity with which he holds to it. Paul is not indulging his imagination; he is not using metaphorical language, save perhaps in his reference to fighting **with beasts at Ephesus.** As a Roman citizen, it is unlikely that he was ever compelled to undergo the indignity of facing wild beasts in the arena. He is thinking rather of the brutish men who assailed him there when, as silversmiths, fashioning and selling for handsome profits images of Artemis, they detected in him and in his gospel a threat to their trade (Acts 19:23-41; cf. also 20:19). He had suffered more than one such murderous attack, but was ever ready to face death, daily if need be, for the sake of the Lord in whom he had put his trust and whose faithful servant he was. The inference is plain. He would never have endured these experiences had he not been utterly and finally convinced of the resurrection of Christ from the dead. Doubtless he sets his own personal example of fortitude and daring before them in the hope that it will inspire like courage and strength of belief in them. An ounce of example is worth a ton of precept. Paul never lacked the courage to back his own convictions with his life if the necessity arose. There, as in other matters, he pressed closely in the footsteps of his Lord.

32. ***What if There Is No Resurrection?***—This is a more dramatic repetition of the calmer statement made earlier in this section of the letter, "If in this life we who are in Christ have only hope, we are of all men most to be pitied" (vs. 19). Nothing matters if there is no resurrection. Everything will end in the darkness of death. All the toils and sacrifices of mankind, all the achievements of the race, no less than the pathetic faith and witness of the saints, and the still more pitiable tragedy of Jesus Christ, who put his trust in God and who perished helplessly and tragically on a Cross, will be consummated, not in God, but in the dust of the cemetery.

What then? Paul writes, **Let us eat and drink, for tomorrow we die.** To some his words might suggest that nothing is left but a hedonist or

33 Be not deceived: evil communications corrupt good manners.
34 Awake to righteousness, and sin not;
for some have not the knowledge of God:
I speak *this* to your shame.

row we die." 33 Do not be deceived: "Bad
company ruins good morals." 34 Come to
your right mind, and sin no more. For
some have no knowledge of God. I say
this to your shame.

---

going to the theater. Did he mean that he had been put in the arena with wild beasts? Were Roman citizens subjected to such an indignity? Were gladiatorial contests actually held at Ephesus? Since this is improbable, it is likely that the words are to be taken metaphorically (cf. Ign Rom. 5:1). There were opponents who fought against him with bestial ferocity. Since Paul writes **at Ephesus** instead of "here," the question arises if he was not away from that city when he dictated this chapter at least (cf. 16:8). The Epicurean conclusion that, since death ends all, life is to be enjoyed to the full, is one possible conclusion, but it is not the only one possible. Others say that since nothing lies beyond the grave, we must work with redoubled effort. The words of Isa. 22:13 found abundant re-echoing in the pagan world of the time (cf. Horace *Odes* I. 4; II. 3; IV. 7).

33-34. The quotation is from Menander's comedy "Thais." Menander was an author rich in practical wisdom, and it is not strange that Paul should know this line. It was a proverbial expression which he may have heard without ever having read the play. It is the only Greek quotation in a genuine letter. What connection did Paul have in mind? Is the "bad company" anyone who denies the resurrection, because he might lead others to join in his agnosticism and thus corrupt their moral practices? How intensely Paul felt this to be true is shown by his closing exhortations. The KJV does not quite catch his meaning with its **awake to righteousness.** He did not use a noun, but the adverb "rightly." The verb ἐκνήφω means "to become sober"; the **awake** comes from the idea of sleeping off

---

"epicurean" attitude to life. This is a possible interpretation of the phrase **let us eat and drink;** but as such it would be out of keeping with all that we know about Paul's character and temperament. Of course life must go on even if the faith and hope based on the resurrection of Jesus Christ should, after all, prove to be illusions. Other alternatives than those of hedonism are open to people of like character to that of the apostle. The Stoics did not believe in any resurrection or even in the possibility of an afterlife. Yet they achieved a dignity of character and bearing that has evoked the admiration of successive generations of cultured and thoughtful people. Again, there was a certain refinement of life among some of the Epicureans of those bygone days that has also been held in high respect. Paul must have been well aware of these possibilities. Had he been compelled to relinquish his faith there can be little doubt that though lacking the inspiration such a faith had given him, he would still have set a high standard of noble and consistent life and character before his fellow men. In view of the immediately following vss. 33-34 may we not reasonably believe that in some such terms as these we are to interpret the apostle's words?

33-34. ***Exhortation to Some to Cease from Sin.***—By his allusions to his perils, to the bestial practices of the times, and to the hedonistic alternative, the apostle has reminded the Corinthian Christians of the moral morass from which they have been delivered, and of the full and glad and liberating and ennobling conceptions which mark the Christian faith. Let them now stand firm on the solid rock of historical fact authenticated so signally in their own and in his experience: the act of God in raising Christ from the dead, together with the guarantee it carries of the general resurrection. Meanwhile, doubts that resurrection and all that it might entail by way of rendering an account of one's life to God had apparently led some members of the community into loose ways of living. So close a connection is there between doctrine and life that if men do not believe certain things, their denials have power to influence their mode of living no less than their affirmations. Their conscience loses its keen edge. Moreover, such people have a bad influence on others (see Exeg., vs. 33). Again we have a hint of Paul's strong sense of solidarity. Any member of any community is susceptible as a social being to the moral atmosphere of that community and of everything that has a part in it. Hence the apostle's warning. **Do not be deceived: "Bad company ruins good morals."** A man cannot touch pitch without being defiled; nor is he in much better case

35 But some *man* will say, How are the dead raised up? and with what body do they come?

35 But some one will ask, "How are the dead raised? With what kind of body do

a drunken stupor. What Paul wants his readers to do is to accept belief in the resurrection. There can be no such dire moral results from that! Hence, the RSV renders **Come to your right mind.** The present imperative of a Greek verb means to stop something that is now going on. **Sin no more** captures that shade of meaning. Paul does not say merely that some do not have knowledge of God (KJV). The negative does not limit the verb. The apostle used the word ἀγνωσία, from which we get "agnostic." Those who were boasting of their knowledge as a matter of fact had **no knowledge.**

C. The Resurrection Body (15:35-50)

1. Various Types of Body (15:35-41)

Having contended vigorously for the Resurrection as the form of life after death, Paul now makes important concessions concerning the nature of the resurrection body. Some Palestinian believers in the Resurrection taught the restoration of exactly the same body that was laid away. "For the earth will then assuredly restore the dead . . . making no change in their form, but as it has received, so will it restore them" (II Baruch 50:2). Paul must have been compelled many times to distinguish his belief from this crude hope. He resorts to an analogy from human experience to show how totally different the resurrection body will be. Jesus had appealed to the power of God to create entirely new conditions of life (Mark 12:24-25). Paul elaborates the idea in terms similar to the later Johannine word about a grain of wheat falling into the earth (John 12:24). Both a body and a seed are put into the ground and something entirely different comes out of it.

if the pitch should inadvertently touch him. To that extent the spiritual tone of the Christian church itself is lowered. We cannot escape the moral and psychological consequences of the fact that we are members one of another. The subtle, all-pervading influences of the total human environment affect us in every way. John Donne, the seventeenth-century metaphysical poet, and dean of St. Paul's Cathedral in London, in one of his sermons put that thought into reasonable and well-known words. "No man is an *Ilande,* intire of it selfe; every man is a peece of the *Continent,* a part of the *maine;* . . . any man's *death* diminishes *me,* because I am involved in *Mankinde;* And therefore never send to know for whom the *bell* tolls; It tolls for *thee.*"[5] That holds good of the moral situation too.

Those who give themselves, for whatever reason, to gross or loose practices inevitably lose their sensitiveness toward God. So subtle is the process that for long it may pass unnoticed: but it goes on inexorably. In the end it tends to an unnatural way of life: unnatural in the sense that as Christ is the expression and interpretation of the ultimate nature of things, and therefore of the purpose of the world, whatever runs counter to him, to his truth and to his spirit, is unnatural. Paul therefore urges the delinquents in Corinth, **Come to your right mind, and sin no more.** The core of the matter is that all in the church should hold fast by the full gospel as it was preached to them, and always let the great convictions of the faith be the formative forces of life and character and conduct.

35-50. ***The Nature of the Resurrection Body.*** —Having delivered himself on these matters of sinful doubts and practices, the apostle now turns from his consideration to the form of the resurrection and discusses some of its further implications. We may legitimately surmise that there had been, and still was, a good deal of discussion of these things in the church. Such discussions are a tribute to the liveliness of the community. Its members were keenly interested and concerned about such matters; it is hardly conceivable that some of them would have gone to the length of being baptized as proxies for believers who had passed away before they could undergo the rite for themselves (vs. 29) had there not been a deep-seated conviction regarding both the fact and the manner of the Resurrection. The very form of the words Paul uses in introducing this intensely interesting section of his letter suggests that the question of the nature of the resurrection body had actually been debated.

[5] *Devotions,* ed. John Sparrow (Cambridge: University Press, 1923), p. 92.

36 *Thou* fool, that which thou sowest is
not quickened, except it die:
37 And that which thou sowest, thou
sowest not that body that shall be, but bare
grain, it may chance of wheat, or of some
other *grain:*
38 But God giveth it a body as it hath
pleased him, and to every seed his own
body.
39 All flesh *is* not the same flesh: but
there is one *kind of* flesh of men, another
flesh of beasts, another of fishes, *and* another of birds.

they come?" 36 You foolish man! What you
sow does not come to life unless it dies.
37 And what you sow is not the body which
is to be, but a bare kernel, perhaps of
wheat or of some other grain. 38 But God
gives it a body as he has chosen, and to
each kind of seed its own body. 39 For not
all flesh is alike, but there is one kind for
men, another for animals, another for

Strictly speaking, the seed does not die if the power of germination remains. But the apostle did not mean to describe a strictly natural process. He did not believe that powers of germination were resident in a dead body from which would grow another kind of body by a process of natural development. God would raise the dead by his own miraculous power. So Paul describes what takes place in nature in such a way as to make it correspond to his belief about the Resurrection. **God gives it a body as he has chosen.** Hence, it is not legitimate to argue the same continuity between the physical body and the resurrection body that we know to exist between a seed and the plant growing from it. It is the body which **God . . . has chosen,** not one that develops naturally from the previous one. The only point of comparison which Paul makes is the complete difference between the two.

The translation **bare kernel** is not meant to suggest a connection between this discussion and that on being found "naked" (II Cor. 5:2-3) after death. Rabbi Meir (*ca.* A.D. 150) said that if a grain of wheat is buried naked and yet is raised clothed with many leaves, how much more will the pious who are buried in their clothing. But the clothing about which Paul is concerned is the "building from God" (II Cor. 5:1), his resurrection body. Until he is clothed with this he is in a state of nakedness. The problem of an intermediate state is not faced in the letter before us because the apostle expected to survive until the Parousia.

39-40. The shift from **body** to **flesh** is striking, but Paul must be using the words here as synonymous. There is great variety in God's creation of earthly beings, in form, in

---

But some one will ask, "How are the dead raised? With what kind of body do they come?" (See Exeg., vss. 35-41.) In exalted lyrical vein Paul uses a series of analogies and contrasts in making his reply clear and plain. His main contention and conviction all through this section is in complete accord with one of the central themes of the entire letter, viz., that as the gospel itself is based on God's initiative, as spiritual gifts are the endowment of God, as the resurrection of Jesus Christ with all that it implies for the general resurrection is the mighty act of God, so also the resurrection body is his gift.

36-41. ***A Series of Analogies.***—This contention is illustrated in a series of analogies in which may be traced certain aspects of rabbinical influence. Yet even though we admit rabbinical influence, Paul gives his contentions a characteristic stamp that is uniquely his own. Just as a seed must be planted in the ground and undergo certain changes before it can fulfill its function of producing a harvest of one sort or another, so is it with the body: **What you sow is not the body which is to be.** The final result is the production of something very different from the seed originally planted. As Paul puts it—for he has the Jew's inherited tradition of the universal, life-giving providence of God as manifested in all created things—**God gives it a body as he has chosen, and to each kind of seed its own body.** The ideas of transformation and survival are obviously involved in these illustrations and in the line of argument that Paul adopts. We realize, of course, how difficult it is to find a perfect analogy. Paul's illustration of the seed is imperfect in the sense that the seed which is planted does not actually die.

40 *There are* also celestial bodies, and bodies terrestrial: but the glory of the celestial *is* one, and the *glory* of the terrestrial *is* another.

41 *There is* one glory of the sun, and another glory of the moon, and another glory of the stars; for *one* star differeth from *another* star in glory.

42 So also *is* the resurrection of the dead. It is sown in corruption, it is raised in incorruption:

birds, and another for fish. 40 There are
celestial bodies and there are terrestrial
bodies; but the glory of the celestial is one,
and the glory of the terrestrial is another.
41 There is one glory of the sun, and
another glory of the moon, and another
glory of the stars; for star differs from star
in glory.
42 So is it with the resurrection of the
dead. What is sown is perishable, what is

---

color, in substance, and in shape. The apostle expresses this by enumerating types of organisms. The same variety is to be found in the heavenly world. The **celestial bodies** differ from the terrestrial on the one hand, and they likewise differ among themselves. In many passages in the O.T. the stars are looked upon as angels (I Kings 22:19; Neh. 9:6; Job 38:7; etc.), and this was assumed by Paul. They do not have bodies of **flesh** but of **glory.** Some modern translations use the word "splendor" instead of **glory** to render δόξα. The word means the aura of light surrounding God and other heavenly beings. The heavenly bodies share in this splendor in different degrees. These illustrations bear upon Paul's contention at the one central point: God has shown his power to create radically different bodies.

2. A Spiritual Body (15:42-50)

42-44. Paul is now ready to apply this principle to **the resurrection of the dead.** He uses the word **sown** in an entirely different and completely figurative sense. He is not referring to the burial of the body, but to the birth of the human individual. Four terms are used to describe man's mortal life. It is obvious that it is **perishable** and full of

---

But this is not his main point; we ought not to press the analogy too far in matters of detail, or attempt to make it carry more than the apostle had in mind. His point is that the seed lives on in a transformed but recognizable further stage of existence. So regarded, the illustration fits the case he is out to establish in his teaching concerning the resurrection body.

He adds a supplementary argument. Just as there are different kinds of seed, and just as there are differences between man and the animals, and between celestial bodies, so is there a difference between the body with which the spirit was, so to speak, clothed in this life, and that with which it is to be adorned in the Resurrection. God endows each form of created existence with a "body" or "natural substance," which is probably the idea Paul has in mind, appropriate to its type. Then the argument proceeds: as in the resurrection the conditions of existence will be different, so there will be an appropriate difference between the body as conditioned by an earthly existence and that body as conditioned by a heavenly existence (cf. Exeg., vs. 38). Or to put it in Paul's own words, a little farther along, "Just as we have borne the image of the man of dust, we shall also bear the image of the man of heaven" (vs. 49). As with **body** (vss. 37-38), so with **flesh** (vs. 39; see Exeg.); a near equivalent perhaps would be the modern concept of natural substance. The point is not important save as illustrating the sometimes free and easy habit Paul has of dealing not only with references to the O.T. in support of a particular argument, but also with such terms as "flesh" and "body." Now, having cleared the way by his series of analogies, he passes to a fuller consideration of the "spiritual body."

42-50. ***The Spiritual Body.***—The key to this section is the apostle's clear conviction that the afterlife of the Christian believer involves full personal immortality, and that this implies everything that is essential to identity and recognition. There is not a breath of suggestion of any philosophic doctrine of reincarnation or of any idea of absorption into the being of some infinite spirit. Paul's deep, traditional moral sense makes it extremely unlikely that he would ever hold to the former, in which there could be little moral value without some recollection and understanding of the circumstances and reasons that would account for the progress

43 It is sown in dishonor, it is raised in
glory: it is sown in weakness, it is raised
in power:
44 It is sown a natural body, it is raised
a spiritual body. There is a natural body,
and there is a spiritual body.

raised is imperishable. 43 It is sown in dishonor, it is raised in glory. It is sown in
weakness, it is raised in power. 44 It is sown
a physical body, it is raised a spiritual body.
If there is a physical body, there is also a

weakness, but is it necessarily something of **dishonor?** Paul is using contrasting pairs, and this stands in opposition to **glory.** One of the meanings of δόξα is "good opinion." But since Paul elsewhere (Phil. 3:21; Col. 3:4) speaks of the heavenly body as a "body of glory," it is more probable that he uses it in that sense here. In 12:23 Paul spoke of the parts of the body that are "less honorable." In the resurrection body there will be none such. The final designation is as a **physical body** (RSV). By the translation **natural body** the KJV attempts to show the connection with the "natural man" of 2:14. The Greek word is the adjective ψυχικός, which is built on the noun meaning soul—ψυχή. Paul used the word because it stood in Gen. 2:7, "man became a living soul." He wanted to draw a sharp contrast between *psyche* and *pneuma.* He does not speak of the resurrection of the body any more than he does of the resurrection of the flesh, but rather of **the resurrection of the dead.** That which is raised receives a *new* body, imperishable, a body of

or regress implied by such a doctrine. Even the Christian gospel of redemption he would have held to be incomplete unless it involved full personal immortality. In any attempt to read the apostle's mind as expressed in this part of his letter, so much at least would seem to be the inevitable implication of the message he so enthusiastically proclaimed. To this extent the mystic cults current in his time had little effect on the development of his thought.

We shall be able to put the section into its full context if we keep in mind two widely prevalent conceptions of immortality that were extant in his day. On the one hand, his Jewish contemporaries, particularly the followers of the Pharisees—for the Sadducees seem to have denied the possibility of any resurrection—held that the resurrection body was identical with the earthly body. The Greeks, on the other hand, in so far as they held any belief in immortality at all, thought of it as taking the form of disembodied spirits. Paul contradicts both views and puts forward his own unique and important contribution to the subject.

In developing the contrast between the physical body and the spiritual body we must notice the apostle's use of the phrase **a spiritual body.** Obviously he believes that the "earthly" or "fleshly" body perishes, but God endows the resurrected spirit with a spiritual body that is appropriate to its new, glorified mode of existence (see Exeg., vss. 42-44). Paul also seeks to preserve everything that appears to him to be essential for recognizable, personal identity. Probably he had in mind, as he wrote, the various resurrection accounts preserved in the Gospels of the sudden appearances and disappearances of the risen Lord. All the marks of personal identity are there. We have seen that Thomas was insistent on identifying his crucified Master by the nail prints in his hands and feet and the spear wound in his side. In the account given by John, the Master offers Thomas the opportunity to apply his own test (John 20:27). So far as these records are concerned there is no doubt that Jesus is represented as having appeared in bodily and identifiable form to the disciples. But with a significant difference. He was untrammeled by physical conditions. He could appear and disappear at will. No obstacle could keep him apart from his followers. To convince them of his bodily substantiality he once ate a piece of fish (Luke 24:36-43). In addition to all this, Paul also had the vivid recollection of his own experience, to which he had just made reference (vs. 8). True he says little about the nature of the "spiritual body"; yet it seems certain that all these aspects and recollections of the risen Christ were in his mind as he arrived at this new conception. It was in terms of his **spiritual body** that the risen Lord was recognized and identified by his own disciples. He remembered them; he could think about them and make plans for them; he was obviously freed from the limits placed upon him by physical conditions: yet though transformed in these significant ways, he was the same wonderful friend and Lord they had known when they companied with him in Galilee and Judea. All of this was the mighty work of God.

These points are reinforced by a series of contrasts throughout which it is not difficult to discern Paul's rapturous sense of the divine

45 And so it is written, The first man Adam was made a living soul; the last Adam *was made* a quickening spirit.

46 Howbeit that *was* not first which is spiritual, but that which is natural; and afterward that which is spiritual.

spiritual body. 45 Thus it is written, "The first man Adam became a living being"; the last Adam became a life-giving spirit.
46 But it is not the spiritual which is first but the physical, and then the spiritual.

glory that belongs to the Spirit. Spirit is not the substance out of which the new body is made any more than soul is the substance out of which the earthly body is formed. Our new body will be a body of glory or splendor.

45. It is one thing to describe the contrast between earthly bodies and those of a different character; it is another thing to demonstrate that there *is* an imperishable body that belongs with the divine *pneuma*. Everything really hinges on the truth of that possibility, for Paul agrees that perishable flesh and blood can have no part in the coming kingdom of God which lies beyond the resurrection (vs. 50). Once more Paul appeals to scripture: not to the literal words of the O.T., but to the implications which he believes flow from them. Gen. 2:7 is quoted with two important additions. The apostle inserts the word **first** to prepare for its opposite, the **last.** Also, he adds to the Greek word for man the Hebrew word **Adam.** This simply meant **man** but Paul reserved it for the special sense of the inaugurator of an order of humanity (vs. 22; Rom. 5:12-18). That a new series had begun with Christ was derived less from scripture than from the certainty of his own experience. That persons belonging to this order have a new body followed from the nature of the risen Christ. This second Adam was not a soul that possessed life; he was himself the Spirit (II Cor. 3:17), the one who gave life (John 6:63) through the Spirit which he bestowed (John 20:22).

46. Why should Paul digress to argue that the first Adam really was the first? It is clear that he was repudiating another type of speculation based on this same verse in Genesis. We meet with it in Philo (*On the Creation* 134; *Allegorical Interpretation* I. 31). This contemporary of Paul noted that Genesis had two accounts of the creation of man. Knowing nothing of an analysis into different documents, he drew the conclusion that in Gen. 1:26 we have the account of the creation of ideal man, the Platonic archetype. He was made in the image of God. When Gen. 2:7 tells of the forming of **man** out of the **dust** of the **earth,** it describes the creation of empirical man, the one who sins. Later rabbis indulged in similar speculations. It has been contended with some probability that this speculation roots in an Iranian conception of a primitive heavenly man through

marvel of the change from earthly to heavenly conditions of existence. In passing, we may note the ascending scale involved in his analogies. One is reminded of the doctrine of a hieratic universe which is so fruitful a thought with the Neoplatonists from Plotinus to the Pseudo-Dionysius.

Though he nowhere emphasizes the idea that the human personality enjoys a continued existence in the resurrection life, yet the thought of its immortality is clearly stated. **What is sown is perishable, what is raised is imperishable. It is sown in dishonor**—or as Moffatt translates it, "inglorious"—**it is raised in glory. It is sown in weakness, it is raised in power. It is sown a physical body, it is raised a spiritual body.** Exegetes have a certain degree of difficulty with these particular passages—and they are important for Paul's conception of immortal life—mainly because there is no adjective which corresponds to the term "soul." If there were, we could explain the matter for ourselves by saying that the contrast which he has in mind is mainly that between the "spiritual body" and the "soulish body" (see Exeg., vss. 42-44).

In speaking of **what is sown,** the apostle means to convey to his readers that he does not consider physical death to be the inevitable prelude to the Resurrection (cf. vs. 51). On the contrary, he is thinking of birth. The soul of man is planted like a seed into the mortal conditions under which it manifests itself in this life. To that extent it is subject to change and decay and all the mishaps and limitations of a merely physical existence. He underlines his point by referring to the first, or historical, Adam, as exemplifying his meaning. "And the Lord God formed man of the dust of the

47 The first man *is* of the earth, earthy: the second man *is* the Lord from heaven.

48 As *is* the earthy, such *are* they also that are earthy: and as *is* the heavenly, such *are* they also that are heavenly.

49 And as we have borne the image of the earthy, we shall also bear the image of the heavenly.

47 The first man was from the earth, a man
of dust; the second man is from heaven.
48 As was the man of dust, so are those who
are of the dust; and as is the man of heaven,
so are those who are of heaven. 49 Just as
we have borne the image of the man of
dust, we shall[w] also bear the image of the

[w] Other ancient authorities read *let us*.

---

whom the redemption of the world is to come. But Philo did not relate his speculation about the heavenly man to the messianic hope. Paul argued against the Philonic type of interpretation because he did not begin with the two accounts in Genesis but with the eschatological fact of Christ. Actually the apostle disregards Gen. 1:26 completely. He did not think in terms of heavenly originals and earthly copies as did the author to the Hebrews. He assumed a historical sequence of two different ages, each having its origin in one man. The point of view here contrasts with that of Christ as pre-existent (10:4) and the agent of creation (8:6). If the world was created through Christ, he *was* actually before Adam in time, and Adam was not the first Adam. But in this passage Paul is thinking not of cosmological relationships but of the eschatological situation. That which is related to *psyche* came first; *pneuma* comes only through the one who gives this eschatological gift.

47. Earth and **earthy** (KJV) suggest a spatial contrast to **heaven** and **heavenly,** but that is not what Paul had in mind. He was thinking of the words of Gen. 2:7, "God formed man of the dust of the ground." The man from heaven is the Son of man coming on the clouds, as found in the Synoptic tradition. When Paul applies the term **man** to Christ, it is not so much an affirmation of his simple humanity as an indication of the connection with the myth of an *Urmensch,* an essentially supernatural creature. Paul did not doubt the genuine humanity of Jesus, but that was not the significance of "man from heaven" any more than of the Synoptic phrase "Son of man."

48-49. Man of dust describes the perishable nature of the first Adam and of all those who are made in his likeness. Death came to all those who were descended from Adam. Paul did not think of man as an immortal soul, as the idealistic philosophers have believed. Nor did he draw any conclusions from the assertion in Gen. 1:26 that man is made in the image of God. Rather, men correspond to one or the other of the two Adams. All men have inevitably **borne the image of the man of dust.** Whether **we bear the image of the**

---

ground, and breathed into his nostrils the breath of life; and man became a living soul" (Gen. 2:7). For Paul the first, or historical, Adam, the "man of dust," was a personality who was born as a "soul" (see Exeg., vs. 46). It is the "soul"—the nonspiritual personality—that is sown. But it is the spiritual man, the "new creation" in Christ (II Cor. 5:17), who is to be raised at the resurrection. As such he will be endowed with an indispensable spiritual **body which** will ensure his full, continued, distinguishable personality, together with the enhancement of all its spiritual powers. All this is rather difficult to express, yet the apostle's thought is clear enough.

He is seeking to relate his conception of the **spiritual body** with the main doctrines of the gospel of Christ (see Exeg., vs. 47). Those who truly and sincerely put their faith in Christ are transformed from soulishness into spirituality. Their mode of life is radically changed because the quality of their life has been fundamentally altered. They are no longer, in Paul's words, men of dust, but **as is the man of heaven, so are those who are of heaven.** This they owe to the redeeming power of Jesus Christ. He is **the last Adam** who **became a life-giving spirit.** His work is the spiritual regeneration of the men and women, born or "sown" as souls, who accept him as Master and Lord. They are his; they belong to him. Soulishness is transformed into spirituality: habits, thoughts, desires, and actions take on a new quality of Christlikeness. Theirs are God-centered, or Christ-centered, lives, which is of the essence of the gospel. They are the spiritual beings who will be endowed in the resurrection with a spiritual body that corresponds to their new

50 Now this I say, brethren, that flesh and blood cannot inherit the kingdom of God; neither doth corruption inherit incorruption.

51 Behold, I show you a mystery; We shall not all sleep, but we shall all be changed,

man of heaven. 50 I tell you this, brethren: flesh and blood cannot inherit the kingdom of God, nor does the perishable inherit the imperishable.

51 Lo! I tell you a mystery. We shall not all sleep, but we shall all be changed,

---

man of heaven depends upon our relation to him. Those who through faith and baptism are united with him will be raised at his coming (vs. 22). At that time he "will change our lowly body to be like his glorious body" (Phil. 3:21).

50. The discussion of the nature of the resurrection body is concluded by the strongest possible assertion that the kingdom of God involves a totally different type of existence. Since even the living will be changed to a different kind of body, why not the dead? Paul speaks of **flesh and blood** in Gal. 1:16 in sharp contrast to the risen Christ who had appeared to him. The phrase describes humanity living under present earthly conditions. These are not continued in the Resurrection (Mark 12:25). **Flesh and blood** are perishable and do not endure into the age to come. Naturally the same was true of Christ's resurrection body. Paul knows nothing of an appeal to sensual experiences, such as in Luke 24:39, nor does he recognize an ascension after forty days (Acts 1:9) that divided the appearances of the risen Christ from the life of the heavenly Lord. The first-born from the dead had put on the imperishable at once.

D. The Christian's Confidence (15:51-58)

51. Paul's words rise to ever-increasing heights of exaltation. His "mysteries" are not matters to be kept secret but are truths which are mysterious in character (Rom. 11:25;

---

spiritual nature (see Exeg., vss. 48-49). It is possible that in distinguishing between soul and spirit Paul was influenced by the Greek notion of spirit as a particularly refined type of substance.

We need not take up time with bygone speculations as to the nature of **the man of heaven,** for the context of the entire passage makes it abundantly clear that Paul has in mind the risen and exalted Christ, whom he conceives as being in heaven, and whom, as we shall see immediately, he expects to come in triumph from heaven to consummate his redeeming work. This is the predestined climax. This is that

> . . . one far-off divine event,
> To which the whole creation moves.[6]

Then, in Pauline language, those who have here committed themselves to Christ will be "complete in him"; so shall they **bear the image of the man of heaven.** The passage ends with the firm statement that **flesh and blood cannot inherit the kingdom of God.**

51-58. ***Paul's Glowing Vision of the Climax.*** —Now the apostle's thought has taken wings. It soars to heavenly places, divulging one of his intuitive insights into God's secret purposes. **Lo! I tell you a mystery.** The revelation is colored by vivid apocalyptic imagery and doubtless owes much to the apocalyptic expectations of an imminent return of Christ in triumph to the earth. Yet Paul's language can be too easily misunderstood. He does not actually say that those who are alive, i.e., some of those to whom he is writing—among whom he includes himself—will never taste of death but will be invested at the sound of the **last trumpet** with an imperishable and therefore immortal nature. His real point is that whether Christian believers are alive or dead when the last trumpet sounds, they will all instantly **be changed.** Mortality will be transformed into immortality. The paragraph is really a vivid apocalyptic restatement of the points he has already made (vss. 21-23). This consummation of the redemptive process begun on earth will be the final demonstration of God's love and power and his abiding victory.

There can be no doubt that in the eyes of the apostle, and surely for the people to whom he wrote, death was a fearful calamity; it is an evening that threatens with oblivion all that we hold dear. How can it appear otherwise? What could give greater cause for rejoicing than the assurance, vindicated and justified by

[6] Tennyson, *In Memoriam,* last two lines.

52 In a moment, in the twinkling of an eye, at the last trump: for the trumpet shall sound, and the dead shall be raised incorruptible, and we shall be changed.

52 in a moment, in the twinkling of an eye, at the last trumpet. For the trumpet will sound, and the dead will be raised im-

Col. 1:26-27; 4:3). As often, **sleep** is a euphemism for die (11:30; 15:6, 18, 20; I Thess. 4:13-15). The word indicates his conception of the state of the dead. It was not a conscious existence in an intermediate state but a longer night of sleep. And yet he can say that death does not separate from the Lord (Rom. 14:9). He can say this because the coming of the Lord was so imminent that not all of his readers would experience even this short night of sleep before the resurrection of the dead. In I Thess. 4:13-18 Paul does not refer to the *changing* of the living; *here* he says nothing about those who are left until his coming being caught up in the clouds to meet the Lord in the air. Such differences in detail of expectation illustrate how fluid and undogmatic the conceptions of Paul were. He was not composing chapters on Christian eschatology, but writing to meet the issue of the moment.

52. The Greek word translated **moment** is "atom" (ἄτομος), its only occurrence in the N.T. The blowing of trumpets was a regular part of the temple cultus (Ps. 47:5; I Chr. 13:8; Ezra 3:10), but this is the eschatological trumpet of Isa. 27:13, which will

a resurrection which could only be ascribed to a God of righteousness and love and power, that death would finally be utterly vanquished? Such is the assurance that Paul is able to give as he divulges the secret that had in some mystic fashion been revealed to him. And he insists that this consummation is the gift of God whose redeeming work in Jesus Christ evokes the praise of grateful lives (vs. 57). With glowing heart the apostle apostrophizes the last great enemy of mankind. **O death, where is thy victory?** (See Exeg., vss. 54-55.) Rabbinical tradition has one final word in the comment he adds by way of reply to his own apostrophe. It is sin that is the occasion of death; and sin is reinforced by the law, which by making known God's high moral requirements to man reduced such as Paul to despair (Rom. 7:7-12), revealing the exceeding sinfulness of sin. But sin, even as revealed in its strength through the light thrown on it by the law, has been conquered by the resurrection of Jesus Christ, whose victory God permits those to share, as a gift of his grace, who have put their trust in him. So Paul ends on a great note. The members of the church are exhorted to hold fast by the convictions of the faith as these have been delivered to them. More, they are to put them into effect by practicing them in their daily life (see Exeg., vs. 58). The end may be imminent or it may be delayed. But whether imminent or delayed, those will be most ready for the sound of the trumpet, and for the instantaneous tranformation its summons will herald, who live in the spirit of the Lord, and who are doing their best to spread and to perpetuate his spirit and his message throughout the life and circumstances of their times. Convictions held fast and consistently practiced yield strong and stable character. Christian convictions expressed in service, by the grace of the indwelling Holy Spirit, begin to fashion us here for the life of fellowship and further adventure into that knowledge of God's righteousness and love which is of the very essence of the life that is eternal. Such lives, again by the inexhaustible and unmeasurable grace of God, may even lay further claims upon God! May not that consideration have been somewhere on the margin of Paul's mind when he wrote these thought-provoking words, "Just as we have borne the image of the man of dust, we shall also bear the image of the man of heaven" (vs. 49)? Having regard to what his followers may be called upon to endure for Christ's sake, may it not daringly be said that earth has a claim upon heaven and man has a claim upon God? If so, Paul makes it abundantly clear that God will honor the claim. Hence he can close this rapturous section of his letter with fortifying words of assurance and hope. **Therefore, my beloved brethren, be steadfast, immovable, always abounding in the work of the Lord, knowing that in the Lord your labor is not in vain.**

Obviously these teachings of Paul concerning the resurrection of Jesus Christ, and all that it implies for those who believe in him and who have trusted their life and destiny to him, have great and abiding significance for the spiritual and moral life of man. No exposition of these teachings would bear any adequate resemblance to completeness if some of the more important implications were not explored. It

53 For this corruptible must put on incorruption, and this mortal *must* put on immortality.

54 So when this corruptible shall have put on incorruption, and this mortal shall have put on immortality, then shall be brought to pass the saying that is written, Death is swallowed up in victory.

perishable, and we shall be changed. 53 For this perishable nature must put on the imperishable, and this mortal nature must put on immortality. 54 When the perishable puts on the imperishable, and the mortal puts on immortality, then shall come to pass the saying that is written:

"Death is swallowed up in victory."

---

call back the dispersed to the worship at Jerusalem. It is part of the apocalyptic picture in Matt. 24:31—but not in Mark—and also in I Thess. 4:16 (cf. II Esdras 6:23). The series of woes in Rev. 8–9 is introduced by the blowing of trumpets. In our letter the trumpet seems to be the signal for the twin events of the resurrection of the dead in Christ and the transformation of the living members of the church. But the relation of this to the period of messianic rule assumed in vss. 24-27 is not at all clear.

53. Paul repeats again in other language the necessity for the coming change. He reiterates the distinction between the **perishable** and the **imperishable** and then adds another word which occurs in Paul only here and in the next verse. In contrast to the mortal are those who have **put on immortality.** The term ἀθανασία was a key word in Hellenic thought. The gods were believed to be immortal (cf. I Tim. 6:16), and, according to the Platonic school, so was the soul of man. Though the craving for immortality was widespread in the ancient world, the assurance of it was not. Satisfaction was sought in the mysteries and in other forms of religion. Immortality meant not simply a continuation of life but the divinization of man. Belief in the existence of an elixir of immortality played a role in fantasy. The O.T. contains no equivalent for the word **immortality,** for Jewish thought conceived of man as essentially mortal. But in the Hellenistic-Jewish literature ἀθανασία is found (Wisd. Sol. 3:4; 15:3; IV Macc. 14:5, and often in Philo). There we see the adoption of the Greek idea of immortality. But even when Paul uses the word here it is in a quite different sense: immortality is not something which belongs to man by nature; it is **put on** when God raises him from the dead.

54-55. Two quotations illustrate what this glorious future event will bring. In each Paul departs from the original Hebrew text. This only serves to emphasize how completely different Paul's thought was from the scripture whose fulfillment he announced. In Isa. 25:8 Paul is closer to the rendering of Theod. than to that of the LXX, which did not contain the word **victory.** Since the apostle never uses the word "Hades," it is not

---

cannot be a matter of unconcern to any thoughtful person as to whether or not human history and experience, particularly in its spiritual and moral aspects, has a more than temporary meaning and value, and as to whether or not the soul of man is immortal in some afterworld that he may be able to conceive, though not to describe. Whether he admits it or not, there are "immortal longings" in man. The times come, often unexpectedly, when the thought of immortality has deep interest for him as proposal for the continuation of his own personal life. Times come when the idea is almost a necessity of the heart, as when death snatches from his side a beloved relative or friend. Certainly philosophers, from Plato's day to our own, have thought of immortality either as an inherent element in the human soul or as a postulate that is essential for the completeness of the moral life, a requisite corollary of righteousness and duty well done, and of the moral character which is the consequence of such ethical integrity.

This is not the place for a full discussion of these points. They are set down for certain reasons that will immediately be made plain. At once it can be said that there is no specific religious interest, certainly no Christian interest, in the fact that man may desire an immortal life either for the sake of his own continuing personal existence, or for the sake of ultimate reunion with his loved ones. Immortality for such reasons as these, and one would not for a moment treat them lightly, might appear desirable to an agnostic or even to an atheist. Nor do there seem to be any well-grounded and unassailable reasons for holding that the soul of man is inherently immortal. Such was Plato's

55 O death, where *is* thy sting? O grave, where *is* thy victory?
56 The sting of death *is* sin; and the strength of sin *is* the law.

55 "O death, where is thy victory?
O death, where is thy sting?"
56 The sting of death is sin, and the power

---

strange that he repeats **death.** The KJV follows the koine when it reads **grave,** correcting Paul's words to the original text of Hos. 13:14. As may be seen from modern translations, that passage contained on the lips of the prophet a terrible pronouncement of doom.

> Shall I ransom them from the power of Sheol?
> Shall I redeem them from Death?

The answer was, of course, "No."

> O Death, where are your plagues?
> O Sheol, where is your destruction?
> Compassion is hid from my eye.

Nothing could illustrate better the new confidence which had come to Paul than the entirely different tone which he has given to these words. For him death had lost its power.

56-57. Possibly we feel that Paul should have gone on with vs. 57 and made at once his triumphant affirmation of the victory over this last enemy which God had made possible through our Lord Jesus Christ. But it is entirely characteristic of the apostle (Rom. 7:25) to preface his most exultant conclusions with such a prosaic parenthesis.

---

view as expounded in various dialogues; but the validity of his reasons for holding it is open to question. It may be argued that since in large measure the soul of man seems to be endowed with the capacity to organize itself around certain interests and purposes, with an appreciable degree of disregard for its own immediate physical condition, it is therefore able to survive the dissolution of the body. But that only permits us to hold a doctrine of survival, not of immortality. Modern psychological researches into the nature of the psychophysical organism view with more than a degree of skepticism all phenomena that are regarded as warranting this inference. In the light of our present knowledge the nature of the soul is such, or so it would seem, that a psychophysical apparatus is essential to its existence in this four-dimensioned world. What then is the basis of the Christian hope of life hereafter? Paul has already made his own position clear that Christian believers are of all men most to be pitied if in this life they have only hope in Christ (see Exeg., vs. 19). For him something more definite by way of assurance was required. He found that assurance in the resurrection of Christ from the dead.

There may be those who think that even if there were no resurrection of the dead, and no afterlife of the human personality, it would still be better to live a Christian life than to live selfishly on a materialistic plane of existence. One may be sympathetic with such a view without being convinced by it. One reason for such lack of conviction might be that the Christian life involves purposes and ideas that far outrange the possible attainment of a single generation. Thus these purposes and ideas still further outrange the span of a single human life. And since each generation has to find its own moral and spiritual starting point—in the sense that apart from institutions which help to conserve the experience of the race its members must acquire moral and spiritual character by their own individual life and service—the sheer impossibility of ever consummating many of the most worth-while of these purposes and ideas would tend in many cases to destroy all zeal and enthusiasm in pursuing them. In fact, on a large scale this has happened. Many, in what was once described as Christendom, have discarded Christianity as impracticable and indeed impossible. As G. K. Chesterton put it, the religious situation is not that Christianity has been tried and has failed: it has been found difficult and has not been tried. This may be so because, despite moments when an immortal life seems desirable, very many have relinquished all hope of it. The Christian faith requires for its inspiration and fulfillment the assurance that Paul sought to convey in his letter to the church in Corinth. The very work of Christ himself in spiritualizing the soul of man by centering it upon God, and

57 But thanks *be* to God, which giveth us the victory through our Lord Jesus Christ.

of sin is the law. 57 But thanks be to God, who gives us the victory through our Lord Jesus Christ.

That sin brings death is Paul's affirmation in Rom. 5:12 and 7:13; that it is the **law** which strengthens the **power of sin** anticipates his argument in Rom. 7:8, "Apart from the law sin lies dead." The word **victory** appears only three times in Paul's letters, all of them in this one paragraph. **Sin** and **law** and **death** are among the foes who have been overcome by *Christus Victor.* Redemption has not involved appeasing God, but conquering the enemies of God.

not upon self, requires the assurance of a life hereafter for the conservation and completion of his work. On the human side what would be the reaction were man forced to realize that this new dawn, with all its potency and promise of a transformed life, having in it the spiritual quality of eternity, because centered on God and based on a continuation of fellowship with God, heralds not an undying day, but an undying night? More, what convictions could man harbor about the justice and righteousness and love and power of God? In that case it were far better that the redeeming work had never been begun: its glorious promise would only be more than dissipated by the ensuing disappointment. But the resurrection of Jesus Christ from the dead has put the great resounding note of assurance into Christian faith. It remains for us to see if it can afford a reasonable and convincing basis for man's hope of life eternal.

Christian doctrine is not one of immortality but of resurrection. We shall do well to get this point clear. As expounded by the apostle Paul, whom we believe to have entered more deeply into the mind and spirit of his Lord than any other, man's hope of survival depends not on the inherent immortality of his soul, but on the act of God. His immortality is involved in his resurrection, not his resurrection in his immortality. There is nothing in Paul's writings nor in the N.T. to suggest that the soul is inherently immortal. The one assurance of immortal life is that by finding a new center in God, and not in self, the soul is spiritualized and begins to partake of the quality of eternal life. The quality of eternal life is, of course, the quality of God as we have known and experienced him in his revelation to us through Jesus Christ. On this the Christian emphasis falls from first to last. Everything, so far as life hereafter is concerned, depends on the activity of God as that activity is made available for man through man's faith. This is precisely what is meant when we emphasize the fact that life hereafter is a specifically religious interest.[7] Immortality is the gift of God's grace in response to man's faith. Everything depends on the nature and purpose of God. His righteousness and power and love are involved. If he has begun in man, as the outcome of the redeeming work of Jesus Christ, a life of fellowship with himself in which eternity would seem to be an ever-increasing and life-enriching adventure into the infinite deeps of God's wisdom and righteousness and love, then his justice and power, no less than his love, are involved not only in inaugurating the adventure by evoking man's faith, but also in sustaining it. Otherwise there would be a fundamental contradiction in the ultimate nature of things. Surely here we have a stronger, more satisfying reason for belief in a life hereafter, a life that is immortal, than any that is precariously founded on the nature of the soul.

[7] See William Temple, *Nature, Man and God* (London: Macmillan & Co., 1934), pp. 427-51.

The Christian doctrine is one of full personality. This is a legitimate inference from Paul's exposition of the gospel to the church in Corinth and elsewhere. There is no question of rewards and punishments. All we may legitimately infer is that under the conditions that God has created, conditions which may be far removed from the type of physical reality that we experience here, the adventure and pilgrimage of fellowship with himself, the exploration of his mind and purpose as he is pleased to reveal these to us, will be continued. Already we have something more than hints and intimations of that purpose. In Pauline terms, God in Christ is working in us, spiritualizing soulishness, and in doing so investing us with the very quality and spirit of eternal life. We are being fashioned, slowly it may be, with "many a labor, many a sorrow, many a tear," into Christlikeness. We are being fashioned in "the image of the man of heaven," the greatest of all personalities. We are slowly being conformed to his likeness. Our personal life and quality, as we follow him in sincerity and truth and love, are being progressively enriched. Every faculty and power is gradually approximating completeness in him (Col. 2:10). Even now the greatest compliment that can be paid

58 Therefore, my beloved brethren, be ye steadfast, unmovable, always abounding in the work of the Lord, forasmuch as ye know that your labor is not in vain in the Lord.

58 Therefore, my beloved brethren, be steadfast, immovable, always abounding in the work of the Lord, knowing that in the Lord your labor is not in vain.

---

58. Here we see the right relationship between ethics and eschatology. There is nothing that men can do to inaugurate the drama of last things which accompanies the resurrection of the dead. That situation should not lead them to quietistic resignation; it should encourage them to steadfast devotion in the **work of the Lord** because the certainty of the coming consummation brings assurance that this work will not be **in vain** but will receive its reward (vs. 32).

---

to the character of any man is to describe it as "Christlike." If this world is what Keats described in one of his letters as "a vale of soul making," the fashioning of his followers into his own likeness is the work of Christ. That is a process which may well go on through all eternity.

We need not allow ourselves to be troubled by the thought of endlessness. What eternity is eludes our most penetrating speculations. We can be content with the thought that what God has begun he will continue until he has perfected his creative purpose. If that purpose is a deepening sense and realization of fellowship between him and ourselves, our own personality is bound to be enhanced and enriched in the process. Perhaps John has come as close as the inspired mind of man can come to describing the experience that shall be ours. "Beloved, we are God's children now; it does not yet appear what we shall be, but we know that when he appears we shall be like him, for we shall see him as he is" (I John 3:2). The same thought of a continuity of process is found in the book of Revelation. In his vision of the final issue of the spiritual and moral conflict that runs through all history and all life, the seer of Patmos sees that character, as developed here, carries its quality into the hereafter. "Let the evildoer still do evil, and the filthy still be filthy, and the righteous still do right, and the holy still be holy" (Rev. 22:11). Whatever the ultimate outcome may be in the realm of the hereafter (see vs. 28; also Rom. 14:11; Phil. 2:9-10), if words and penetrating insight mean and convey anything, it is clear that the Day of Judgment begins on earth with man's choice of the type of life he means to live. But the power of redemption is also available here and now, and the life that is to be everlastingly redeemed begins on earth its transformation. Surely this is the highroad to full, free, personal existence. The fellowship begun on earth will with still more glorious consequences in the realm of personality and character be continued in heaven. Temple writes:

> The stress in the New Testament is all laid upon the quality of the life to come and the conditions of inheriting eternal life. It does not call men to a mere survival of death while they remain very much what they were before, but to a resurrection to a new order of being, of which the chief characteristic is fellowship with God. Consequently the quality of the life to which we are called is determined by the Christian doctrine of God.[8]

One final word may be added. Paul says very little concerning those who have not fulfilled the conditions as set forth in the N.T. whereby they may receive the gift of eternal life. To be sure, he writes both to the church in Rome and to that in Corinth that we must all appear before the judgment seat of Christ (Rom. 14:10-12; II Cor. 5:10), but the context indicates that the resurrection is for those who have followed in the Christian way (cf. Phil. 3:10-11). What then can be said of those who have not walked in that way, or perhaps have even set themselves against it? Here we enter a realm of speculation, and dogmatism must be at a discount. God's justice is certainly involved. It would not be just simply to wipe out the consequences of evil-doing on the part of individual men and women whose way of life and whose spirit have made it exceedingly difficult if not impossible for them and often for others to understand and to respond to the love and grace of God. How could self-centered people enjoy any heaven of happiness in contemplation of that which is foreign to their very nature? Nor would it be just to set before such people the prospect of that fellowship with God which is the reward of those who have fixed their affections on heaven above.

On the other hand, the love and the power and the purpose of God are involved. Every soul that fails to respond to him is in a sense a defeat to his purpose. Even if the obdurate

[8] *Nature, Man and God,* pp. 464-65.

16 Now concerning the collection for the saints, as I have given order to the churches of Galatia, even so do ye.

16 Now concerning the contribution for the saints: as I directed the churches of Galatia, so you also are to do.

VII. Personal Matters (16:1-24)

A. The Contribution for the Saints (16:1-4)

16:1. The gathering of a great offering for the church at Jerusalem occupied much of the attention of Paul in A.D. 53-56. The date of Galatians is uncertain; the reference in Gal. 2:10 to his promise to "remember the poor" may be our earliest recorded mention of the enterprise. Though Galatia is not mentioned in II Cor. 8–9 or in Rom. 15:26, it is clear from this verse that according to the original plan the churches there were expected to collaborate. It may be that because of the defection of the Galatian churches they did

---

are annihilated—for it would seem that there is no doctrine of eternal punishment in the N.T.; there are references to eternal flame, but except for the doubtful passage in Matt. 25:46 not to eternal punishment—that too would be a reflection on the power and love of God. Such annihilation would mark the defeat of God's gracious purposes. We do not possess sufficient insight into the nature of God to presume to make any definite declaration of belief; but may we not say even of the most abandoned souls that there is a spark of the fire whence that soul was lighted? May we not believe that somehow, somewhere, sometime, God's great and eternal love will win its complete and final victory? May we not hope that such as Annas and Caiaphas and Judas Iscariot and Pontius Pilate, and many another who has shared their spirit and outlook, will look on the love that once they crucified and be broken and won by it? Let no one indulge in shallow and sentimental and unworthy optimism about the good nature of a God who will overlook everything and condone everything. God is not like that. His love is holy love. We must leave the answer to all such questions with him.

16:1. ***Now Concerning the Contribution for the Saints.***—The apostle Paul was nothing if not practical in his insistence that Christian truth is intended to be applied to life. He has been insisting on the unity of the local church as a fellowship of believers in Jesus Christ; he has spoken of Christian love as the distinctive spiritual quality of the Christian life; he has shown that only such a quality of life can participate in the resurrection to that life which is the gift of God. Now he writes and requires the church in Corinth to play a worthy part in applying his teaching to the life and need of the larger Christian community. Doubtless the question of making a collection for the relief of hard-pressed brethren elsewhere in Asia Minor, and particularly in Jerusalem, had been referred to the apostle for his advice and guidance (see Exeg.). This was a matter that was close to his heart. The mother church in Jerusalem was in sore distress, and Paul had pledged himself, at the request of Peter and John and James, the Lord's brother, to do his best for the succor of the brethren there. Other churches had responded generously; the church in Corinth was to emulate their example (see Rom. 15:25-29; Gal. 2:9-10). Moreover, he was concerned that his converts should grow in grace and in the knowledge of One who had loved them and given himself for them. They too, like all the others, often needed to be reminded of the words of the greatest of all teachers, "It is more blessed to give than to receive" (Acts 20:35). He wanted them to bring that blessing upon themselves, and in so doing to cement their unity with their Christian brethren elsewhere.

Surely such a contribution in such circumstances must rank high as a concrete expression of Christian love. There are times when words of sympathy are a hollow mockery unless they are accompanied by deeds. It is of little use to pray for the well-being of others if we neglect to give practical effect to our prayers—assuming of course that we are aware of their need and are able to do something about meeting it. In such circumstances he who gives quickly, gives twice. Those to whom the succor comes are immeasurably heartened by such a concrete expression of the Christian love of their brethren far away from them in terms of distance, it may be, but close by their side in terms of practical sympathy. It is one of the marvelous and unique characteristics of the catholicity and universality of the Christian church that thousands who do not know our names may yet uphold us by their faith and by their prayers, and that we are privileged to do the same service for them. Such a reflection, supported so often in the course of the centuries by such aid as Christian men and women are able to give to one another, has been a means of grace and an

2 Upon the first *day* of the week let every one of you lay by him in store, as *God* hath prospered him, that there be no gatherings when I come.

3 And when I come, whomsoever ye shall approve by *your* letters, them will I send to bring your liberality unto Jerusalem.

4 And if it be meet that I go also, they shall go with me.

2 On the first day of every week, each of
you is to put something aside and store it
up, as he may prosper, so that contributions
need not be made when I come. 3 And when
I arrive, I will send those whom you ac-
credit by letter to carry your gift to Jerusalem. 4 If it seems advisable that I should go
also, they will accompany me.

---

not continue to participate. It is improbable that this brief direction concerning the method of collection was the apostle's first mention of the project (cf. II Cor. 8:6; 9:2). Possibly one of his assistants had explained it earlier. All Christians were **saints,** but the term was especially applied to the mother community at Jerusalem (Rom. 15:25, 31; II Cor. 8:4; 9:1, 12). Here, in contrast to Rom. 15:26, Paul does not assign their poverty as a reason for the contribution.

2-4. This is our first mention of the first day of the week as carrying special significance in the early church (Matt. 28:1; Acts 20:7). Paul does not use "Lord's day" (Rev. 1:10) to parallel "Lord's supper" (11:20). He does not specifically say that there was a community meeting on this day. Something might be put aside at home by each head of a family. Paul's exhortation called for regularity in saving rather than for faithful attendance upon the assemblies. But since at the time of Justin (*Apology* I. 67. 6) contributions were received at the meetings on the first day of the week, it is probable that at Corinth they were brought each week at this time. Paul calls for proportionate giving; neither here nor in II Cor. 8–9 does he speak of tithing. Since Christ was the end of the law (Rom. 10:4), any such appeal would have been most inconsistent. **As he may prosper** suggests no one fixed percentage of income. If a worthy sum is to be raised, the effort must extend over a considerable period. The apostle does not want to spend his time in raising money

---

encouragement to faith in the experience of many who have been enduring hardship as good soldiers of Jesus Christ.

And these practical expressions of Christian love bring their own peculiar blessing to those who give as well as to those who receive. In every age there are periods when anxiety presses more heavily than at other times. Such periods are marked by a widespread spirit of uneasiness, of insecurity, and often of discontent. Victims of the concentration camps in World War II have in some cases noticed the deteriorating effect of privation on the character of many who had to endure it. Only those whose faith was strong and whose courage was great survived with their spirit unscathed. To a lesser extent, in less tragic but trying circumstances, similar hardships may have a like effect. They can dry up the springs of enthusiasm, of happiness, and of laughter. As social histories have often recorded, they may engender the spirit that seeks to get instead of that which seeks to give. One of the sources of happiness lies here. Man must recover the joy of giving: giving not only of his substance, but of himself. And Christians must show the way. To do so bring its own glow to the heart. Paul has written much about love, about the savor of eternity that it adds to life, about the unity it gives to a fellowship of Christian faith. Now he invites his beloved converts to add to their experience the joy of giving. He seems to have realized the peril that lurked near all the churches, but especially near that in Jerusalem. What uplift of spirit might come to the brethren there as they received practical tokens of the love, faith, and fellowship of those elsewhere. Christian brethren are in need! Let the Corinthian Christians demonstrate their spirit of fellowship by making their individual contributions.

2-4. *Be Businesslike in Method.*—There is a place for system and discipline in the ordering of the affairs of the church. Paul asks the Corinthians to apply the same method here. His suggestion is very practical. As God has prospered him, let each member of the church set aside, **on the first day of every week,** a day when they will call to remembrance One who gave everything for them, some contribution for the cause (see Exeg.). Such regular disciplined giving on the part of every member is the only

5 Now I will come unto you, when I shall pass through Macedonia: for I do pass through Macedonia.

6 And it may be that I will abide, yea, and winter with you, that ye may bring me on my journey whithersoever I go.

7 For I will not see you now by the way; but I trust to tarry a while with you, if the Lord permit.

8 But I will tarry at Ephesus until Pentecost.

9 For a great door and effectual is opened unto me, and *there are* many adversaries.

5 I will visit you after passing through
Mac-e-do'ni-a, for I intend to pass through
Mac-e-do'ni-a, 6 and perhaps I will stay
with you or even spend the winter, so that
you may speed me on my journey, wherever
I go. 7 For I do not want to see you now
just in passing; I hope to spend some time
with you, if the Lord permits. 8 But I will
stay in Ephesus until Pentecost, 9 for a wide
door for effective work has opened to me,
and there are many adversaries.

---

on his next visit. The Corinthians should realize that it is their own benevolence and should be carried by their own messengers accredited by letters from the community. In II Cor. 8–9 Paul shows that he was aware of the delicacy of handling such a matter; the passage amplifies our knowledge of the delegated representatives. The group named in Acts 20:4 were apparently those who accompanied Paul for this purpose, though Acts does not explain the size of the company. Vs. 4 indicates that at this early stage in the enterprise the apostle was not certain that he would accompany them.

B. Travel Plans (16:5-12)

5-9. The projected travels **through Macedonia** correspond to what is reported in Acts 19:21 and 20:1-2. But in II Cor. 1:16—written from Macedonia (II Cor. 7:5-6) on his way to Corinth (II Cor. 13:1)—Paul defends himself against the charge of vacillation because he had not come to them directly from Ephesus. Between the writing of I Corinthians and II Corinthians there must have been a sudden visit (II Cor. 2:1) induced by a new emergency. The possibility that he may **spend the winter** with them may correspond to the three months actually spent in Greece according to Acts 20:3. On the other hand, Tit. 3:12 indicates a decision to spend the winter at Nicopolis. Whether or not this belongs to a genuine Pauline fragment from this period, it reflects the belief that Paul had been this far toward Illyricum. Rom. 15 looks back upon a visit to that province and forward to his journey to Jerusalem with the contribution. Whatever the situation might be, the apostle's plans depended upon the Lord's permission (4:19). Pentecost was at this time the limit for his stay in Ephesus. Apparently the letter was written about the season of Passover (5:7). Midsummer and fall would be devoted to a preaching tour, but at the

---

means whereby a church may meet its responsibility to the poor and sustain its own Christian work. We should not be less systematic and less businesslike in our handling of the specific matters which concern the church than we would be in directing our own business affairs. System and spontaneity are not necessarily incompatible with one another. System added to spontaneity in the matter of church finance gives greater effect to the contribution. And it saves time—which can then be devoted to other matters of relatively greater importance.

5-12. ***Plans for Visiting Corinth.***—Paul was particularly anxious for economy in this matter of time because of the deterioration in the life of the church in Corinth. It is not difficult to sense his anxiety. He makes it clear that there is much to do in Ephesus (vs. 8); there are problems to be solved, dangers to be faced, and difficulties to be overcome. We can catch a glimpse of the great spirit of the man, a spirit to be imitated by all Christian workers, in the very phrases he uses. His presence is urgently needed; great opportunities have been opened to him. In his own vigorous imagery these opportunities are like a door of hope swinging widely on its hinges and beckoning his dauntless spirit to pass through, **A wide door for effective work has opened to me, and there are many adversaries** (see Exeg., vss. 5-9). It is as though he were saying that difficulty and opportunity go hand in hand. They do for those who

10 Now if Timotheus come, see that he may be with you without fear: for he worketh the work of the Lord, as I also *do*.

11 Let no man therefore despise him: but conduct him forth in peace, that he may come unto me: for I look for him with the brethren.

10 When Timothy comes, see that you put him at ease among you, for he is doing the work of the Lord, as I am. 11 So let no one despise him. Speed him on his way in peace, that he may return to me; for I am expecting him with the brethren.

moment the apostle was loath to leave the opportunity in Asia. He often used the figure of a **door** in connection with evangelistic opportunity (II Cor. 2:12; Col. 4:3; also Acts 14:27). More frequently the word has an eschatological reference to the coming judgment (Luke 13:25; Rev. 3:8, 20). The presence of adversaries is vividly illustrated by the riot scene in Acts 19:23-41. Opponents from Asia apparently were so bitter that they followed him to Jerusalem to make trouble (Acts 24:18-21).

10-11. The departure of Timothy to remind them of Paul's "ways" had been announced in 4:17. Apparently he had other missions en route and would not be expected until after the arrival of the letter. Paul had selected him as a helper even before the

know as well as he knew how to transmute difficulties into opportunities. Was he not the follower of One who made a Cross of shame the symbol of his triumph?

The situation at Corinth was also pressing for his personal attention. None of his devoted friends had really been able to cope with it. He would come to the city as soon as possible (see Exeg., vss. 5-6). Let the church have all matters concerning the contribution for the saints in readiness against the time of his coming. They could then appoint trustworthy messengers to carry their gifts to Jerusalem, and Paul himself would speed these on their way (see Exeg., vss. 2-4). Meanwhile he is sorry to disappoint those who have been urging his personal attention to church affairs in Corinth; there are other matters that require attention in Macedonia (vs. 5). In the end, however, he hopes to pay them more than a flying visit (vs. 7); he may even spend some time with them and so be enabled to deal adequately with all the matters raised in his letter, to say nothing of others which he also doubtless had in mind.

There are some scholars who think that despite the pressure of Ephesian and Macedonian affairs, Paul was forced to pay a flying visit to Corinth (see Exeg., vss. 5-9). This, it seems to them, is borne out by references in what has been called the "sorrowful letter" (II Cor. 10:1-2; see also 12:14). If so, the visit failed of its purpose: his opponents were too strong, and the evil too widespread. In that case, it is probable that a visit of Timothy (vs. 10) preceded the projected second visit of Paul to the church, and that Timothy too, despite the apostle's commendation, had to return to Ephesus reporting failure (see Exeg., vss. 10-11). Hence the "sorrowful letter" in which the heartbreak is all too evident. There is no record of this second visit in Acts, but some scholars have argued that it is required in order to give coherence to Paul's movements at this period of his life. Apparently the "sorrowful letter," together with a visit from Titus, at length brought the church in Corinth to repentance and reform, and returned it to the traditions of the faith. The community thus recovered something of its first rapture for Christ and his cause; waverers were strengthened, the mischief-makers were discomfited, and the faithful ones were comforted. Then Paul was able to write a further letter (II Cor. 1–9) in which he expressed his gratitude to God and his joy at so wonderful an outcome.

On any interpretation it is not difficult to realize that there were urgent reasons for Paul's anxiety concerning the well-being of the church, and that anxiety is the context in which the epistle must be set. It underlines his instructions for Timothy's reception in Corinth. He is not to be disregarded (vs. 11; also see Exeg.), but to be helped in every way so that soon he may return with Erastus (see Acts 19:22) and other brethren who are left unnamed (vss. 10-11).

Besides these personal references, another adds to the historicity of the epistle: the reference to Apollos. Apparently some members of the church had made inquiries about him and were asking when he would pay a return visit to them. This may have been at the instance of the Apollos party in the church. If so, Paul chooses to disregard the fact. There was nothing petty or mean about this greathearted apostle of Christ. His spirit was molded in large dimensions of friendship and generosity. His reference to the eloquent Alexandrian is al-

12 As touching *our* brother Apollos, I greatly desired him to come unto you with the brethren: but his will was not at all to come at this time; but he will come when he shall have convenient time.

13 Watch ye, stand fast in the faith, quit you like men, be strong.

14 Let all your things be done with charity.

12 As for our brother A-pol'los, I strongly urged him to visit you with the other brethren, but it was not at all God's will for him to go[x] now. He will come when he has opportunity.

13 Be watchful, stand firm in your faith, be courageous, be strong. 14 Let all that you do be done in love.

[x] Or *his will to go.*

founding of the church at Corinth (Acts 16:1). Hence, at this time he would have had at least five years of experience as an assistant. But Paul's language betrays great uncertainty about the effectiveness of the mission and the reception which he will receive. A different Greek word is used for **despise** in I Tim. 4:12. **The brethren** who were returning with him may have included Erastus (Acts 19:22), who, according to Rom. 16:23, was a Corinthian Christian. Paul's uncertainty about Timothy seems to have been well founded. Throughout II Corinthians Titus is the emissary upon whom the apostle depends. But Timothy is mentioned as coauthor, suggesting that Paul wants to assure the Corinthians of his continued faith in the young man.

12. The cordial relations between Paul and Apollos are once more indicated by the apostle's eagerness for the fellow missionary to visit Corinth again (Acts 18:24). The Greek noun **will** may refer to the decision of Apollos himself (KJV) or to the divine purpose (RSV).

C. Exhortations, Greetings, and Benediction (16:13-24)

13-14. These ethical exhortations seem very abrupt in the midst of the personal communications. Like 15:58, they emphasize the need for steadfastness in the midst of the trials through which Paul's readers must pass. To be **watchful** is particularly commended in relation to the expected Parousia (Mark 13:34 ff.; Rev. 3:2; 16:15; I Thess. 5:6). The need to **stand firm** (Gal. 5:1; II Thess. 2:15) is not to be related to a body of doctrine, for Paul does not use **faith** in that connection. What faith calls for has been illustrated over and over again in the letter. Once more **love** is given the primary place.

together friendly. He had urged Apollos to accompany **the other brethren** who were to visit Corinth, but Apollos seems to have regarded it as his duty to remain with Paul as he sustained his hopeful but difficult mission in Ephesus. Moreover, both were constrained—so it seemed to them—to bow to a still higher decision. **It was not at all God's will for him to go now. He will come when he has opportunity.**

13-14. *Be Watchful.*—These reflections are summed up in a word of advice to the church. The members are to be vigilant so that their spiritual liberty may not be endangered and so that the fine edge of their spirit may remain sharp and keen. They are to be spiritually alert, not compromising with anything in their environment, or playing with any temptations that would make them less sensitive to spiritual things. It is so easy to be clear and strong about one's central convictions, and so easy to compromise at the marginal point; yet it is often on life's margins, and not at its center, that the danger lurks. The church, therefore, is to **be watchful.** It is again enjoined to hold fast to its faith. The members have been reminded more than once of the things that are central in the Christian tradition (see Exeg., vss. 13-14). These are to be defended with vigor, with loyalty, with courage, and with strength. Otherwise what chance could there be for the deepening of the life of the fellowship or for growth in Christian character? Nothing fine or strong can possibly emerge if such matters are treated in an easygoing, casual spirit. Therefore, **stand firm in your faith, be courageous, be strong.**

With only this admonition to follow, lest any attempt to dictate or domineer be the occasion of contention: **Let all that you do be done in love.** And how indeed could he have resisted it—he who had written them of the "more excellent way" with such passionate concern; he who knew so well how the truly Christian spirit must of necessity manifest itself! **All . . . in love.** There lies the supreme test.

15 I beseech you, brethren, (ye know the house of Stephanas, that it is the firstfruits of Achaia, and *that* they have addicted themselves to the ministry of the saints,)

16 That ye submit yourselves unto such, and to every one that helpeth with *us,* and laboreth.

17 I am glad of the coming of Stephanas and Fortunatus and Achaicus: for that which was lacking on your part they have supplied.

18 For they have refreshed my spirit and yours: therefore acknowledge ye them that are such.

15 Now, brethren, you know that the
household of Steph'a-nas were the first converts in A-cha'ia, and they have devoted
themselves to the service of the saints; 16 I
urge you to be subject to such men and
to every fellow worker and laborer. 17 I
rejoice at the coming of Steph'a-nas and
For-tu-na'tus and A-cha'i-cus, because they
have made up for your absence; 18 for they
refreshed my spirit as well as yours. Give
recognition to such men.

15-18. Paul begins an exhortation (KJV) and then stops to name the church's delegates and to commend their **service.** The RSV transfers the words **I urge** to precede immediately the content of his injunction. None of the individuals is mentioned in Acts. If **first converts (firstfruits** KJV) in Achaia is to be taken literally (cf. Rom. 16:5), then Acts must be in error about there being converts in Athens (Acts 17:34). Possibly Paul at the moment was overlooking the fact that Athens was also in Achaia. If the church is **to be subject to such men,** they must have been church officials of some kind. But they are described with the same vagueness as the leaders in I Thess. 5:12, suggesting the absence at this time in the Pauline churches of fixed nomenclature for administrators. We meet the noun διακονία (ministry) in vs. 15; and the verb κοπιάω in vs. 16 appears also in I Tim. 5:17 in the description of the work of elders. The phrase **refreshed my spirit** recurs in II Cor. 7:13 (KJV) and shows how Paul can use πνεῦμα of the human factor as well as the divine. The appeal to **give recognition to such men** seems to be based on the

---

15-20. ***Some Final Words and Commendations.***—Paul has had full reason to be heavy of heart as he pondered the situation in the Corinthian church, but he has not been without his compensations. How often his spirit has been warmed by his loyal friends. These represented for him the ultimate truth about the reality of Christian grace. He rejoiced in the love and sympathy and kindness that he received from such as Prisca and Aquila, from Stephanas and his retainers, Fortunatus and Achaicus. If Christianity is a great new adventure in friendship, then its possibilities are seen in such as these. They made up for all that Paul had to suffer in his love for the churches and in his work on their behalf, and they represented the Corinthian church at its best. How could he have endured had he not been supported by the prayers and faith and lovingkindness of these good folk? So it is fitting that his letter should end with warmhearted commendation of his friends.

Stephanas and his household, who had so refreshed Paul's spirit (vss. 15-18), were well known to the community in Corinth. They were known as being among Paul's first converts (see Exeg., vss. 15-18); and they were known not only for their loyalty to him, but also for their loyalty to Jesus Christ and for their Christian integrity of character. Their judgment and spirit could be trusted. Paul therefore enjoins the church in Corinth to be guided by their counsel. **I urge you to be subject to such men and to every fellow worker and laborer. . . . Give recognition to such men.** There is always a special place in the church for the devoted servants of Christ. The church needs them; it owes much to them. They are the members in whom the Master manifestly reveals himself. Others in the fellowship do well to be subject to them (see Exeg., vss. 15-18).

From the church in Ephesus, meeting in the house of the faithful Aquila and Prisca who had so often given hospitality as well as friendship to Paul, and from the wider community of the Asian churches, greetings are sent to the church at Corinth. Such greetings are at once a reminder to it of its place in the life of a wider fellowship, and an implication of its responsibility in that connection (see Exeg., vss. 19-20). They are also an encouragement to the members to "stand firm" in their faith.

19 The churches of Asia salute you. Aquila and Priscilla salute you much in the
Lord, with the church that is in their house.
20 All the brethren greet you. Greet ye
one another with a holy kiss.
21 The salutation of *me* Paul with mine
own hand.
22 If any man love not the Lord Jesus
Christ, let him be Anathema, Maranatha.

19 The churches of Asia send greetings.
Aquila and Pris′ca, together with the
church in their house, send you hearty
greetings in the Lord. **20** All the brethren
send greetings. Greet one another with a
holy kiss.
21 I, Paul, write this greeting with my
own hand. **22** If any one has no love for
the Lord, let him be accursed. Our Lord,

---

quality of the service they have rendered rather than upon any prerogative accompanying their office. A generation later I Clement will attack the Corinthians for failure to subject themselves to the rightful elders.

19-20. From the use of the plural ἐκκλησίαι it is apparent that Paul is thinking of the separate congregations. Acts 19:10 indicates that during the more than two-year stay of Paul in Ephesus, he had worked for the evangelization of the province as a whole. Aquila and Prisca would naturally wish to send greetings, for they had rendered invaluable assistance in the founding of the church at Corinth (Acts 18:2) and had left Corinth with him (Acts 18:18). Apparently wherever they went they developed a house community (Rom. 16:5). II Tim. 4:19 assumes that the couple are again in Ephesus. If an Ephesian address for Rom. 16 is accepted, the extent of their travels is appreciably reduced. The greeting with a holy kiss is mentioned also in Rom. 16:16; II Cor. 13:12 and I Thess. 5:26. In the time of Justin Martyr (*Apology* I. 65) it had a fixed part in the ritual of worship.

21-22. It was customary for Paul to add a greeting in his own handwriting (Col. 4:18; Philem. 19). This served to authenticate the document (II Thess. 3:17). How otherwise could readers be sure that the apostle really had dictated the contents of the letter which they received in an unidentifiable hand? But to take up the calamus himself and lay the scroll across his own knees frequently seemed to stir in Paul even more violent

---

They are not alone: others are with them, thinking of them, praying for them, sharing in similar hardships, and glorying in the same great mission. **The churches . . . send you hearty greetings in the Lord. All the brethren send greetings.** And he adds, as a token of their membership in the Christian community where the spirit that binds them to their Lord and to one another is Christian love, **Greet one another with a holy kiss.** Such a greeting as between Christians was a minor sacrament of friendship.

21-24. ***Paul's Final Words.***—It would seem that Paul has dictated the letter to some amanuensis (see Exeg., vss. 21-22). Now that after many interruptions it is finished, having had it read over to him, he takes the pen into his own hand to write his own vigorous greeting. For a fleeting moment his recital of the failures of the church in Corinth to live up to his teaching and thus to honor its Lord fills him with indignation. There is one last stern word of condemnation. So utterly wholehearted in his own love and devotion to Jesus Christ, he cannot endure in professing Christians anything less. He has been insistent throughout the epistle that a great love for Christ is to be expressed in a consistent Christian life. He knew that only so would the Christian gospel commend itself to the world of his day, a world that desperately needed to hear it. That is true for every age. For this devoted apostle, whatever fell short of such allegiance was akin to treating the Lord with contempt. Inconsistency in a professing Christian would bring upon the Christian cause the derision of the pagan community it was meant to win. Such "professors" in Paul's view were "enemies of the Cross of Christ." They were to be regarded as "beyond the pale." **If any one has no love for the Lord, let him be accursed.**

Then this living torch of a man, consumed by his tremendous love for his Lord and Master, ponders all these things, as he sees in vision how glorious human life everywhere could become were it illumined by the teaching of Jesus and inspired and dominated by his faith and spirit. A prayer bursts through his lips from his very heart. **Our Lord, come!** (see Exeg., vs. 21-22). It is the same cry that broke from the lips of the seer of Patmos as he pondered the moral struggle which runs through all history and

23 The grace of our Lord Jesus Christ *be* with you.
24 My love *be* with you all in Christ Jesus. Amen.

¶ The first *epistle* to the Corinthians was written from Philippi by Stephanas, and Fortunatus, and Achaicus, and Timotheus.

come![y] 23 The grace of the Lord Jesus be
with you. 24 My love be with you all in
Christ Jesus. Amen.

[y] Greek *Maranatha.*

---

expressions than usual (Gal. 6:11). Immediately he invokes a curse, not on personal opponents, but on **any one** who had **no love for the Lord.** The KJV leaves the word **Anathema** untranslated (cf. 12:3; Rom. 9:3; and Gal. 1:8). But why should any version fail to translate such a word? By so doing it only obscures the fact that some early Christians gave little heed to the word of Jesus to "swear not at all" (Matt. 5:34). Likewise, the KJV left **Maranatha** untranslated. Here there was more justification; this was an Aramaic phrase which Paul himself included untranslated in his Greek letter. But the KJV was perpetuating the old misunderstanding that **Anathema Maranatha** was an oath formula. **Maranatha** has been interpreted in three different ways. John Chrysostom took it to refer to the Incarnation, "The Lord has come." The same division of words, *maran atha,* may be understood as "Our Lord is coming" (Phil. 4:5). The most probable meaning is *marana tha,* **Our Lord, come!** This prayer appears in Greek in Rev. 22:20. For the early church "Thy Kingdom come" is naturally turned into a petition for the coming of the King. The phrase comprises the last of the Eucharistic prayers in Did. 10:6. Here lives and prays a church for which the imminent coming of the Lord is a vital hope.

23-24. All the benedictions which close the letters in the Pauline corpus contain the prayer that the grace of God may be with Paul's readers. In three there is reference to **love.** II Cor. 13:14 has the "love of God" as the second clause in a trinitarian blessing. In Eph. 6:24 grace is commended for "all who love our Lord Jesus." Here Paul's own love is assured for all of them. After the harsh criticism at so many points in the letter, the apostle closes with the assurance of his affection for **all** who are **in Christ Jesus.**

---

all life, and especially as his imagination and heart were moved by his contemplation of the awful persecution of the Christian church, "He who testifies to these things says, 'Surely I am coming soon.'" To which the saints in their anguish and expectation respond, "Amen. Come, Lord Jesus!" (Rev. 22:20.) The ultimate hopes and expectations of his followers are based on Christ's final triumph when his work is consummated. Let Christian love still find urgent and expectant expression in Christian service that the time may be hastened. To this day sensitive hearts re-echo the cry, "Come, Lord Jesus, come!" In that great consummation there would be a speedy end to all that makes for strife and heartache and lovelessness among men. Meantime, the hope of his coming, which in the gospel message is linked with the assurance of his presence among his own throughout the intervening time, is the continual inspiration of all who are devoted to his cause.

So the epistle draws to its close on a note of tenderness and affection and with a benediction. The depth of the apostle's indignation is outfathomed by his love for those who have so sorely hurt him. As it began, so it ends with a prayer that the grace of Christ may continue to be with them. What more could a loving father in the things of Christ wish for his children in the faith? And as it is love that has dictated the letter, and as it is love that he wished to spread abroad in the midst of the community, the supreme gift of the Spirit to all who are willing to receive it, so he would assure them of his love. **My love be with you all in Christ Jesus. Amen.** Had Paul been unable to pen these words from the depths of his heart, he could never have written this letter.

The Second Epistle to the

CORINTHIANS

Introduction and Exegesis by Floyd V. Filson

Exposition by James Reid

II CORINTHIANS

INTRODUCTION

The relations of Paul with the church at Corinth are more fully known than are his dealings with any other church he founded. This, however, is not due to the book of Acts. It tells only of the visit on which Paul founded the Corinthian church (Acts 18:1-18). To be sure, Paul visited this church later, during the three months spent in Greece just before his final visit to Jerusalem (Acts 20:1-3). But Corinth is not mentioned, nor are the intervening events or the letters Paul wrote to Corinth.

This silence of Acts is due to Luke's purpose and method. He is concerned with the expansion of the Christian movement. His method is to tell how Paul came to each new center of work, began his preaching, usually with the Jews, and was forced to turn to a wider preaching among Gentiles. There then follows the story of his departure, perhaps the recounting of the specific incident which made Paul decide to move on. We may want to know the stages in the development of the church before and after Paul left the city. It also would interest us to learn how Paul kept in touch with each church by letter and messenger in order to guide its growth. But the book of Acts is consistently silent on such points—not because the author is unwilling to tell of the troubles and faults of the young, inexperienced churches, but because his purpose is to tell how the gospel spread and new churches were founded (Acts 1:8).

In order, therefore, to follow the course of events at Corinth after Paul left, we are forced to rely solely on the letters he wrote to Corinth, and on scattered clues to his movements and work which we gather from his other letters. We know that he wrote at least four letters to Corinth.[1] A "lost letter," referred to in I Cor. 5:9, included a strong demand that the Christians separate from complacently immoral men. The pastoral letter that we call I Corinthians dealt incisively with problems of faith and life which had arisen in the vigorous but unstable church. Some time later a "stern letter" sought to quell a bold rebellion against the leadership of Paul. When this letter had done its intended work, a "thankful letter" undertook to express Paul's joy at the turn of events and lead the Corinthians into full Christian loyalty.

Our task is to trace the events that followed the sending of I Corinthians and thus make clear how II Corinthians came to be written.[2]

I. Paul and the Corinthian Church

A. Paul's Leadership Challenged.—By the time Paul wrote I Corinthians (A.D. 56 or 57), three problems had appeared that were to make further trouble. The moral laxity so characteristic of life in Corinth was a threat to the church. Converts from pagan cults were slow to realize that Christian faith contained an inherent moral standard; some continued to think, as they had in the past, that religious loyalty and moral purity were not connected. A second difficulty was the combative and divisive character of the converts. This opened the way to party divisions in the church. Finally, the coming of Apollos to Corinth, and the influence

[1] Johannes Weiss, in his study of Paul's Corinthian ministry and letters to Corinth, decides that Paul wrote six letters to that city. See *The History of Primitive Christianity*, tr. Frederick C. Grant (New York: Wilson-Erickson, 1937), I, 292-94, 323-57, especially the summary, pp. 356-57. Hans Windisch, *Der zweite Korintherbrief* (Göttingen: Vandenhoeck & Ruprecht, 1924; "Meyer's Kommentar"), makes a different literary analysis, but likewise concludes that Paul wrote more than four letters to Corinth.

[2] The reconstruction of the course of events as presented above is necessarily tentative in many points. For other reconstructions see the introductions to the letter in the commentaries cited in the bibliography; see also Weiss, *op. cit.*, and Kirsopp Lake, *The Earlier Epistles of St. Paul* (London: Rivingtons, 1911), ch. iv.

that Peter exercised, either by personal visit or through friends (Acts 19:1; I Cor. 1:12), show that outside leaders could intervene in this church founded by Paul (10:14). At the time of I Corinthians the party divisions did not seriously threaten the existence of the church. Paul recognized in Apollos and Peter fully Christian leaders, and blamed their followers for the quarrelsomeness and party lines that marred the brotherhood. But the influence of these leaders showed that the Corinthians would be open to persuasive appeals by unworthy leaders who might choose to meddle in the life of their church.

Trouble soon came, though we cannot trace its origin in detail. Concerning the immediate effect of I Corinthians no direct evidence survives, except that, according to the plain statement in II Cor. 12:21, the tendency to moral laxity persisted in spite of what Paul had written in I Cor. 5–7. If Timothy reached Corinth, as Paul rather expected (I Cor. 16:10-11), after I Corinthians had been received, Paul's fears that the young man might be scorned may well have been realized. Certainly in later negotiations with Corinth Timothy played no role; Titus was Paul's able go-between. The mention of Timothy as coauthor of II Corinthians (1:1) —though Paul himself is solely responsible for the wording of the letter—may be the apostle's way of saying that he still stands by the helper whom they had rejected.

The new trouble was no mere continuation of the party strife condemned in I Corinthians. The same combativeness was present, but it was spurred on by a new occasion. Certain Jewish Christians (11:22) had arrived in Corinth, carrying glowing letters of recommendation (3:1), and claiming the right to exercise authoritative leadership in the churches (11:5). In all probability they came with the deliberate purpose of undermining the influence of Paul. In this they succeeded remarkably. Such prompt success argues not only that the newcomers had great personal ability, but also that considerable resentment against Paul existed in the Corinthian church. Leaders of parties, persons guilty of moral wrongs, participants in lawsuits, and others who felt that their position concerning marriage, food offered to idols, spiritual gifts, and the resurrection of the body had been wrongly condemned in I Corinthians were no doubt in the mood to listen to sweeping criticisms of Paul and his authority. It was a gifted, strongheaded, and unsteady church; and without clear understanding of what it was doing, it turned against its founder.

One Corinthian Christian was particularly active and so especially guilty in this revolt (2:5; 7:12). His self-assertion may have included an insult to Timothy—if the latter came to Corinth. It may have expressed itself in hostility to some other Corinthian friend or traveling representative of Paul. Or it may have come to offensive climax only when he confronted Paul himself. For Paul came to Corinth. When he wrote I Corinthians he had visited Corinth but once; no trace of a second visit occurs. But before II Cor. 2:1; 12:14; 13:1-2 were written, Paul clearly had paid a second, painful visit. From his location in Ephesus (I Cor. 16:8) direct sea transport to Cenchreae (Rom. 16:1), the eastern port of Corinth, was easily available. When Paul heard of the rebellion in Corinth, he evidently took ship there, and undertook to deal summarily with his opponents.

The effort failed. So many of the Corinthians were infected with the spirit of rebellion that Paul could do nothing effective. He could not induce them to expel the intruders who were supplanting him. The ringleader in the revolt may now have treated the apostle with such brazen contempt that no remedial action could be undertaken. There was no obedience to Paul; there was no shame concerning moral laxity (13:2). So, with a warning that soon he would return and act sternly to right matters, Paul left and went back to Ephesus.

B. The Stern Letter.—Yet he did not give up. Undoubtedly he had stanch friends at Corinth, who did not cease to press Paul's claim to respect and loyalty. There were also things Paul could do; and he was not the man to leave them undone.

First of all, Paul wrote the "stern letter" (A.D. 57). Even his opponents had to admit that he was an effective letter writer (10:10). In great agitation—so much so that he wrote in tears (2:4)—but with stern determination to compel the church to see the folly of its attitude, he wrote a militant letter intended to bring the Corinthians to their senses and renew their obedience to him (2:9). His purpose was to make them feel his love and deep concern for them (2:3-4), and at the same time to demand that they punish the open rebel who was leading the opposition (2:6). He denounced the intruders who were making so much trouble, but he could not deal directly with them. It was only through Corinthian support that they could have any influence; and whenever Paul could win back the loyalty of the church, the troublemakers would no longer endanger Paul's leadership. Moreover, the Corinthians could not punish or control such visiting leaders; they could discipline only their own members, and so Paul's demand was directed against the local leader.

This "stern letter" Paul sent from Ephesus some weeks, or more likely some months, after

I Corinthians. The bearer was Titus, who possibly had visited Corinth at an earlier time to further the collection for the relief of poor Christians in Judea (8:6). The alternative view is that Titus, while in Corinth with the "stern letter," used the occasion to promote the collection. But the strained relations at that time hardly favored the start of a financial campaign, and the reference to "a beginning" in 8:6 suggests that Titus had been at Corinth early in the history of the taking of the collection, which was already under way when I Cor. 16:1-4 was written.

It may be that Titus felt hesitation about taking the "stern letter" to Corinth. It was a critical situation, and the "anguish" and "tears" with which Paul wrote may have suggested that the letter would fail of its purpose. If Timothy had been rebuffed at an earlier time, this fact, added to the personal affront that Paul had suffered, could well make Titus feel that the task was too great for him. Yet he consented to go, and was persuaded in part by Paul's stubbornly surviving faith in the Corinthians. He assured Titus that they were not a hopeless lot, and could yet be won back (7:14-15). So Titus went, and Paul was left with the hardest task an anxious, active man can have: he had to wait.

When Paul wrote I Corinthians, he was planning to leave Ephesus for Macedonia, and from there go down to Corinth (I Cor. 16:8-9). A little later the revolt against him led him to make his second hurried visit to that city. Failing to win back the Corinthians he returned to Ephesus and, either as he was leaving or in the "stern letter" that he wrote from Ephesus, he spoke of a new plan to visit them. He promised to come first to Corinth, go north to Macedonia, and return to Corinth on his way to Judea (1:16). But as he thought further, he decided it was better not to go back to Corinth until conditions there became more favorable (1:23). So, to give the Corinthians time to come to their senses, he went back to his original plan of going first through Macedonia, and instructed Titus how to meet him. Titus was to go to Corinth, deliver the "stern letter" and seek by personal ministry to improve the situation, then travel north through Achaia and eastward through southern Macedonia. If he still had not met Paul, he was to cross over into Asia Minor and seek Paul along a prearranged route. Paul, on his part, was to move northward through western Asia Minor to Troas, and then, if he still had not met Titus, cross to Macedonia and keep to the route along which Titus was to come.

When Paul came to Troas, Titus had not yet appeared. The apostle could have remained longer at Troas; indeed, an unusually responsive hearing invited him to stay (2:12). With deep regret he withdrew from this promising situation because of his haunting concern for the Corinthian church. "My mind could not rest because I did not find my brother Titus there. So I took leave of them and went on to Macedonia" (2:13). Somewhere in Macedonia, perhaps at Philippi, he met Titus. It was not at once; for a time "our bodies had no rest" and he was disturbed not only by troubles affecting the church where he was—"fighting without"—but also by "fear within" concerning the Corinthian situation (7:5). Because of this lapse of some days or weeks, Paul may have moved on westward toward Thessalonica, but he may have been still at Philippi when Titus finally came.

The news Titus brought was heartening. The situation at Corinth had improved immensely. Paul's letter had deeply grieved the Corinthians. Its blunt speaking shocked them into awareness of their fault, and they were filled with strong regret and earnest determination to clear themselves. Perhaps even before Titus arrived in Corinth, their consciences had been troubling them. This at least is what Paul suggests when he says that they received Titus with "fear and trembling" (7:15). Certainly, once they had heard the letter read and listened to the personal appeal of Titus, their brazen rebellion gave way to "godly grief" (7:9-10). The voices of the steadfast friends of Paul now received a more favorable hearing. Others dropped their hostile attitude. The church repudiated the arrogant intruders and administered punishment to the one of their own number who had led the opposition to Paul (2:5-11).

There was no unanimous agreement as to how severe the punishment should be, but "the majority" imposed a penalty—perhaps rebuke and exclusion from the congregation—so severe that Paul feared the offender might be driven to irrevocable despair. He therefore saw the need to forgive the repentant wrongdoer and thus save him for Christ and the church; to Paul the gospel was a message of forgiveness even to one who had personally opposed him. Whether the minority favored a milder or still sterner punishment is not stated. But Paul warns against being too severe, and insists that the punishment inflicted is "enough." This suggests that some, no doubt ardent friends of Paul, were in favor of still stronger measures. If so, the Corinthian church was now entirely loyal to Paul (7:11, 16); the only difference among its members concerned the way to prove that loyalty. For Paul, the hurt spirit, the anxious concern over the welfare of his converts, and the anxiety that his letter had not been effective gave way to welcome relief and thankful joy.

C. The Thankful Letter.—Paul could now go to Corinth without fear of repudiation. Two things, however, temporarily delayed him. Both were connected with the collection that he was preparing to take to Jerusalem for destitute Christians there.[3] First of all, he was in Macedonia for what he expected to be his last visit. He was hoping to go on to Corinth shortly, sail for Palestine, and then go to Italy and Spain. So before he left the Macedonians, he must make sure that their collection was fully ready, and give them his final teaching and counsel.

In addition, Paul wanted Corinth's collection to be prepared before he arrived. He had told the Macedonians that Corinth was ready (9:2). The Corinthians had indeed begun the work, and he had assumed too hastily that it was as good as finished. But their revolt against Paul left it incomplete. It would embarrass both him and the Corinthians if Macedonians came with him to Corinth and discovered the failure. So he sent messengers ahead to see that the job was fully done before his arrival (9:3-5). This would have the added advantage of freeing Paul from suspicion of personal greed or profit. The collection suggested to some that Paul was seeking financial benefit, and Paul wanted the actual promotion of the project and the carrying of the money to be in the hands of others, so that his honesty might be plain (8:16-24; cf. I Cor. 16:3). So he stayed in Macedonia for a time, counseling with the churches, completing the collection there (8:1-5; 9:2), and waiting for Corinth to prepare its part in this great plan of Christian sharing.

In this situation, when the sting of bitter memories had been taken away by the joy of restored friendship, it was inevitable that Paul should write to Corinth. His immense relief and joy demanded immediate expression. Moreover, the energetic apostle saw the need to cement this renewed friendship by a deeper understanding of the Christian ministry and message and by a common interest in Christian giving. So Paul promptly wrote the "thankful letter," his last letter to Corinth of which we have any knowledge (A.D. 57). Under the circumstances it was inevitable that it should show deep emotion, lay bare the motives and spirit of Paul, and carry the warm note of appeal and affectionate counsel. This is the most personal of all Paul's letters, the one that most fully reveals his heart and purpose. The success of its appeal is clear from Rom. 15:25-27, which shows that the collection was soon completed.

[3] For recent studies of the collection see Paul S. Minear, "The Jerusalem Fund and Pauline Chronology," *Anglican Theological Review*, XXV (1943), 389-96; Charles H. Buck, Jr., "The Collection for the Saints," *Harvard Theological Review*, XLIII (1950), 1-29; John Knox, *Chapters in a Life of Paul* (New York and Nashville: Abingdon-Cokesbury Press, 1950), pp. 51-58, 69-72. All three studies discount the narrative of Acts, think in terms of one collection, and hold that it was taken in a relatively short time. Buck places it before the Jerusalem council, Minear and Knox after it. See also Exeg. of Rom. 15:25-33 (Vol. IX).

II. Outline of Contents

This letter falls into three main divisions: (*a*) In chs. 1–7 Paul's discussion of his recent relations with the Corinthians is split into two parts, 1:12–2:13; 6:11–7:16; between these sections is enclosed a rich presentation of Paul's apostolic ministry and message. (*b*) In chs. 8–9 Paul urges the completion of the collection for the needy Christians in Judea. (*c*) In chs. 10–13 he deals sternly with the Corinthians for their shameful acceptance of false leaders and their unrepentant attitude.

A detailed outline of the contents is as follows:

- I. Introduction (1:1-11)
  - A. Address and Christian greeting (1:1-2)
  - B. Thanksgiving for recent deliverance from death (1:3-11)
    - 1. Thanksgiving for comfort in all affliction (1:3-7)
    - 2. The recent deliverance from deadly peril (1:8-11)
- II. Recent relations with the church at Corinth (1:12–7:16)
  - A. The reason for change in travel plans (1:12–2:13)
    - 1. Paul has acted with open sincerity (1:12-14)
    - 2. Change of plans not due to fickleness (1:15-22)
    - 3. The purpose: To avoid another painful visit (1:23–2:4)
    - 4. Paul freely forgives the punished offender (2:5-11)
    - 5. Paul crosses to Macedonia to seek Titus (2:12-13)
  - B. The great parenthesis: The apostolic ministry (2:14–6:10)
    - 1. Thanks to God for using Paul in the ministry (2:14-17)
    - 2. The Corinthians are Paul's letter of recommendation (3:1-3)
    - 3. The superior ministry of the new covenant (3:4–4:6)
      - *a*) God qualifies the ministers of this covenant (3:4-6)
      - *b*) The new covenant surpasses the old in splendor (3:7-11)
      - *c*) The boldness of the risen Lord's ministers (3:12-18)
      - *d*) The ministry of light against darkness (4:1-6)
    - 4. God sustains his ministers in their wearing work (4:7-18)
      - *a*) The life of Jesus manifested in their bodies (4:7-12)

- *b*) Faith in the Resurrection sustains them (4:13-15)
- *c*) Eternal glory will follow brief affliction (4:16-18)

5. The hope of an eternal home with the Lord (5:1-10)
   - *a*) Paul hopes to receive it before physical death (5:1-5)
   - *b*) He is content to die and be with the Lord (5:6-8)
   - *c*) The main thing: Be ready always for judgment (5:9-10)
6. The ministry of reconciliation (5:11–6:10)
   - *a*) Paul seeks to serve God and the Corinthians (5:11-13)
   - *b*) In Christ God reconciled men to himself (5:14-19)
   - *c*) Paul's urgent ministry of reconciliation (5:20–6:2)
   - *d*) His diligence and suffering in this ministry (6:3-10)

C. The bond between apostle and church renewed (6:11–7:16)
1. Appeal for love between ministers and people (6:11–7:4)
   - *a*) Plea for return of Paul's affection (6:11-13)
   - *b*) Parenthesis: Shun fellowship with unbelievers (6:14–7:1)
   - *c*) Renewed, confident appeal for mutual love (7:2-4)
2. Paul's joy at the good news from Corinth (7:5-16)
   - *a*) Relief and joy at the repentance in Corinth (7:5-13*a*)
   - *b*) The joy of Titus confirms Paul's confidence (7:13*b*-16)

III. The collection for needy Christians in Jerusalem (8:1–9:15)
A. Macedonia's liberality should inspire Corinth (8:1-6)
B. Christ's example teaches generosity (8:7-15)
C. Recommendation of Titus and two other leaders (8:16-24)
D. Appeal to finish the collection before Paul comes (9:1-5)
E. God's blessings rest upon the liberal giver (9:6-15)
1. God will liberally supply the giver's needs (9:6-11)
2. Both givers and recipients will glorify God (9:12-15)

IV. Rebuke of the revolt against the apostle (10:1–13:10)
A. Defense against slanders and false leaders 10:1–11:15)
1. Persistent revolt may force Paul to stern action (10:1-6)
2. His action will be as stern as his letters (10:7-11)
3. Unlike his foes, he keeps to his own field (10:12-18)
4. The Corinthians too readily follow false leaders (11:1-6)
5. Paul's self-support unmasks the false leaders (11:7-15)

B. Paul boasts of his labors—and weakness (11:16–12:10)
1. He asks tolerance for foolish boasting (11:16-20)
2. His advantages, labors, and sufferings (11:21-29)
3. His escape from Damascus shows his weakness (11:30-33)
4. His thorn in the flesh checks pride in visions (12:1-10)

C. Paul's work merits commendation and trust (12:11-18)
1. Miracles have demonstrated his apostleship (12:11-13)
2. He has not acted and will not act in greed (12:14-18)

D. Appeal to repent before Paul comes (12:19–13:10)
1. He seeks to move the Corinthians to repent (12:19-21)
2. On his third visit he will not spare sinners (13:1-4)
3. Let them do right so that he need not be severe (13:5-10)

V. Conclusion (13:11-14)
A. Final exhortations and greetings (13:11-13)
B. Benediction (13:14)

III. The Question of Unity

From the time that II Corinthians began to circulate in the church at large it has had the form we know in our English Bibles. No manuscript divides it into two or more letters, or omits any section. If therefore we raise a question about its unity, this can be only because the contents appear to require it. The unity of each of the three main parts of the letter has been questioned.

(*a*) The section 6:14–7:1 seems a surprising intrusion into the midst of Paul's appeal for an affectionate response to his love. It sternly exhorts the Corinthians to avoid sinful ties with unbelievers and to cleanse themselves "from every defilement of body and spirit." If it is omitted, the subject of 6:11-13 continues in 7:2-4 without a break.

Because it appears to break a natural connection, a number of scholars conclude that it did not originally belong here.[4] Occasionally it is suggested that Paul did not write 6:14–7:1 at all; in support of this view is cited the use of six words found nowhere else in Paul's letters. But the rare words are due to the special content, and it is generally and rightly held that Paul is the author. Many, however, consider it a fragment of another letter, perhaps the "lost letter," warning against friendly ties with forni-

[4] For a detailed presentation of the evidence see Alfred Plummer, *A Critical and Exegetical Commentary on the Second Epistle of St. Paul to the Corinthians* (New York: Charles Scribner's Sons, 1915; "International Critical Commentary"), pp. xxiii-xxvi; Windisch, *op. cit.*, pp. 18-20, 211-20.

cators, which Paul mentions in I Cor. 5:9. While this is possible, it may be better to conclude that Paul wrote the entire passage as it now stands. The verse 7:2 does not follow 6:13 as smoothly as some have said. It reads like a resumption of an appeal after an interruption. And a connection between 6:11-13 and 6:14–7:1 can be discerned. In 6:11-13 Paul asks the Corinthians to "widen" their hearts to welcome him. Then, as a warning against being too broad and lax in friendship, he adds: But keep clear of sinful associations with unbelievers. Then in 7:2-4 he goes back to his main appeal for personal welcome from his readers.

(*b*) Ch. 9 begins as though introducing the subject of the collection for the needy Christians of Jerusalem. Yet ch. 8 has already dealt at some length with this subject.[5] For this reason some have thought that we have here two independent discussions of the collection, written either to Corinth at two separate times, or to two separate churches in Greece. The general situation, however, is the same in both chapters. Furthermore, ch. 9 has much new material; it is not a real parallel to ch. 8, but carries the appeal forward with fresh arguments for the most part. Moreover, the reference to the sending of the "brethren" in 9:3-5 is vague, contrasting strongly with the explicit recommendation of Titus and the two other "brethren" in 8:16-24. The most reasonable solution is that after a pause, Paul resumes dictating with 9:1, and refers first to the embarrassing reason why the Corinthians should promptly complete their share in the collection: Paul has told the Macedonians that Corinth has been ready for some months, and he therefore is quite anxious that they should have done their part before the Macedonians come with him to Corinth. He explains, what he has not said before, that this is his reason for sending the brethren ahead. He then gives added appeals to complete the collection.

(*c*) The most serious question as to unity concerns chs. 10–13.[6] A minor point is the question whether 11:32-33 belongs in this letter, at least at this point. In the opinion of some scholars it breaks the context and has no point. But it is either an answer to a distorted report about the way Paul fled from Damascus, or, more likely, is chosen, as an example of the humiliating weakness that characterized his life and work, to illustrate "the things that show my weakness" (11:30). The real question concerns the entire four chapters (or 10:1–13:10). There can be no doubt that Paul wrote them, but after the "thankful letter's" joy at the restoration of completely satisfactory relations and its friendly appeal to complete the collection, they give a startling blast against both the Corinthians and the false apostles. The radical change in tone cannot be obscured by saying that in chs. 1–9 Paul addresses the now reconciled majority, while in chs. 10–13 he attacks the still rebellious minority. This view has been proposed, but it breaks down under examination. There is no evidence of persistent rebellion and unrepentant immorality in chs. 1–9. Neither is there the slightest hint in chs. 10–13 that Paul is addressing only a minority; he speaks to the church of Corinth as a whole, and envisions a situation different from that described in chs. 1–9.

The vocabulary Paul uses confirms the conclusion that there is a real break at the start of ch. 10. Since both sections are by Paul, they naturally share many words, and even have rare words in common. But sometimes they use words so as to show a change of mood. For example, in chs. 1–9 the words "to boast" or "boasting" (καυχάομαι, καύχημα, καύχησις) are used in a sense favorable to the Corinthians. But in chs. 10–13 these same words are used of Paul's boasting concerning his own position, in opposition to the claims and attitude of the rebellious Corinthians. Moreover, the two sections are marked by different outstanding words. In chs. 1–9 there occur over fifty words not found in any other letter of Paul or in chs. 10–13; in chs. 10–13 are found over thirty words not found in any other letter of Paul or in chs. 1–9. Words frequent in chs. 1–9 but absent from chs. 10–13 include "glory" (δόξα) nineteen times, "comfort" (παράκλησις) eleven times, "affliction" (θλῖψις) nine times, and "joy" (χαρά) five times. Among words absent from chs. 1–9 but frequent in chs. 10–13 are "weakness" (ἀσθένεια) six times, and "to be weak" (ἀσθενέω), seven times.[7]

The break between chs. 9 and 10 is a fact. How is it to be explained? Did fresh news of new rebellion at Corinth lead Paul to add chs. 10–13? These chapters give no hint of news just received; 13:2 clearly has in mind an unsatisfactory situation of some duration. And why, if rebellion had recurred, did Paul leave chs. 1–9 unchanged? Other suggestions seek the answer in the temperament of Paul. He took the pen from his scribe at 10:1 to add a final note, was carried away by memories of the revolt, and wrote a final blast to make sure such revolt would not happen again. Or, he paused after ch. 9, and had a "sleepless night" (Lietzmann), after which he resumed dictation in a sterner tone. Or, only after some days did he complete

[5] The data for this problem are well presented in Windisch, *op. cit.*, pp. 242-43, 286-88.

[6] The able study by James Houghton Kennedy, *The Second and Third Epistles of St. Paul to the Corinthians* (London: Methuen & Co., 1900), is still important for the study of these chapters.

[7] Cf. Plummer, *op. cit.*, p. xxxiv.

the letter; by then his mood had changed, and he decided to speak more sternly. All such hypotheses fail utterly to explain why Paul left the earlier chapters unchanged. They also charge Paul with a psychological unsteadiness that borders on complete irresponsibility. In chs. 1–9 the Corinthians' repentance and zeal to defend Paul give him "perfect confidence" in them (7:16). But in chs. 10–13 they follow false leaders, refuse to defend Paul, and remain unrepentant for gross sins (11:4, 20; 12:11, 21). While Paul was emotionally vivid and vigorous in speech, we have here two radically different moods, each linked with a quite distinct situation. The hypothesis that the "thankful letter" did not include chs. 10–13 is therefore probable.

It seems unlikely that these chapters were written after the "thankful letter" (chs. 1–9).[8] In it Paul was expecting to reach Corinth soon, and according to Acts 20:1-3 did so. While in Greece, and very likely in Corinth, he wrote Romans, and the tone of the reference to the completed collection in Rom. 15:26 argues that his relations with Corinth were then good. It would be almost impossible to place a new crisis, another stern letter, further negotiations, and finally restored friendship in the short space of time between the sending of chs. 1–9 and the arrival of Paul at Corinth.

The one reasonable explanation is that chs. 10–13 formed part of the "stern letter" which Paul wrote from Ephesus after his futile visit to Corinth. It was written under great personal stress, to demand obedience to Paul, and in an effort to bring the Corinthians to repentance. On the whole, this agrees with the tone of chs. 10–13. Other arguments support this hypothesis. The reference to preaching in "lands beyond you" (10:16), a reference to Paul's desire to move westward to Italy and Spain, fits perfectly if it is part of the "stern letter" from Ephesus; in Macedonia, where chs. 1–9 were written, Italy and Spain were not "beyond" Corinth. Again, in chs. 10–13 there is long-standing rebellion and immorality, while in chs. 1–9 a new obedience and repentance have appeared. This favors the priority of chs. 10–13. The latter chapters demand obedience and are written to lead the Corinthians to reform before Paul comes (10:6; 13:10); chs. 1–9 rejoice over their new obedience and recall that it was to spare them and give them time to repent that the visit was postponed (1:23; 2:3, 9). This clearly sounds as if the delay announced in chs. 10–13 has achieved its purpose, and in chs. 1–9, written later, Paul can look back with satisfaction to the success of his strategy.

Against these strong arguments it is said that there is no manuscript evidence for the division into two letters, that chs. 10–13 contain no reference to the Corinthian ringleader whom the "stern letter" demanded should be disciplined (cf. 2:9), and that chs. 1–9 still contain self-defense by Paul against a persistently rebellious minority, who are in mind in 2:6. These arguments have some strength. If we could explain the change of mood without the hypothesis of the uniting of two letters, we should do so; but the change seems too marked. We need not assume that the two letters were joined by accident; rather, it would seem that when the two letters were first prepared for use in the church at large, the section that we call II Cor. 10–13 was taken from the "stern letter" and added to the "thankful letter," in order to preserve its picture of Paul's apostolic ministry and leadership. Other parts, of more painful nature to the Corinthians, were omitted as of no direct value for other churches. Hence no reference to the demand that the ringleader be punished was preserved. As for the view that the minority in 2:6 was still in rebellion when the "thankful letter" was written, Paul there is warning against too severe a punishment of the wrongdoer; this suggests that the minority, jealous for Paul, favored even stronger punishment, and so were not rebels who still needed denunciation.

On the whole, then, it seems best to conclude that in chs. 10–13 we have part, but not all, of the "stern letter." It was united with chs. 1–9 when copied for use outside of Corinth. If such editorial work occurred, then the same editor may have placed 6:14–7:1 where it did not originally belong, or united chs. 8 and 9, or inserted 11:32-33. But such conclusions do not necessarily follow. The argument for assigning chs. 10–13 to the "stern letter" is stronger than the argument for the other editorial changes. It may be regarded as reasonably convincing.

IV. False and True Apostles

It would help greatly if we could form a clear picture of the opponents who came to Corinth and worked against Paul. When he wrote the "stern letter," their bitter hostility was having alarming results. They charged him with being tricky and insincere; even when he pretended to be unselfish, as in taking no financial support from the Corinthians, he was scheming to get their money through his subordinates: he "got the better of you by guile" (12:16). He did not have the manifest power of a true apostle. He might write bold and threatening letters, but he was weak in personal appearance and an ineffective speaker (10:10). Indeed, he was obscure

[8] A few scholars have held this view. Windisch is the leading one.

in his preaching (cf. 4:3). This Paul, who could "speak in tongues more than you all" (I Cor. 14:18) and told of pretended visions which no one else shared or could verify (12:1; I Cor. 9:1), was, they declared, mentally unbalanced and no fit leader for the church.

Who were these traveling intruders, and what were their claims? They were Jews of pure ancestry who professed true faith in Christ (11:22-23). They asserted that they, rather than Paul, were true "apostles of Christ" (11:13). Indeed, they made so much of this claim that Paul ironically called them "super-apostles" (11:5; 12:11). He did not concede that they were Christians; he said bluntly that they were "false apostles, deceitful workmen, disguising themselves as apostles of Christ" (11:13). They came to Corinth bearing letters of recommendation from other Christians (3:1). Probably these were not from Jerusalem, and so not from the twelve or James, the brother of the Lord. Certainly the intruders showed no interest in the welfare of the needy Christians of Jerusalem, for it seems from chs. 8–9 that the collection which Paul was promoting for these needy Christians had been stopped by the agitation of the newcomers. They readily accepted financial support for themselves, and indeed insisted upon it (11:12), but showed no interest in promoting gifts for others. Their eagerness to displace Paul was a sign of self-centered life; they were "those who pride themselves on a man's position" (5:12), "who commend themselves," "measure themselves by one another, and compare themselves with one another" rather than with the standard of Christ (10:12). They "boast beyond limit, in other men's labors," and instead of bearing the trials and sufferings of establishing new churches, as Paul did, take the easy way of "boasting of work already done in another's field" (10:15-16). They lacked the pastor's heart; they were domineering, arrogant, greedy, and brutal (11:20).

What did they preach? Paul tells us amazingly little. He does assert that they preached "another Jesus than the one we preached," and "a different gospel from the one you accepted" (11:4), but he never specifies precisely wherein their message differed from his own. At times he seems to admit that they are Christians (10:7; 11:23), but elsewhere he specifically denies this and classes them as servants of Satan (11:13-15). It has often been thought from 11:22 that these men were Judaizers, like those who caused trouble in Galatia by insisting that Gentile converts must keep the Jewish law, at least in essentials. But Paul would surely have answered such a legalistic position, as he does in Galatians. Some have suggested [9] that these Jews were very "broad" in their views on moral questions, and approved laxity in physical life on the ground that the spiritual man is not injured by such actions. But had they so definitely encouraged what Paul rightly regarded as evil living, he would have spoken sternly on this point. What they taught cannot be determined, unless we conclude, on the basis of what Paul actually says about them, that their real heresy was that they preached themselves (contrast 4:5). In their persistent self-interest they were foes of the gospel, false to Christ, and a deadly threat to Christian faith and obedience.

How, then, does Paul picture himself as a true apostle? He is a reconciled sinner (5:18), a frail human being (4:7) who has neither the spiritual nor the physical resources for such a ministry. But God gives the needed grace and strength (3:5; 12:9), and only by God's will is he an apostle at all (1:1). As a minister of the new covenant in the Spirit (3:3, 6), there is given him the power to serve and to work the signs of an apostle in miracles (4:7; 12:12). As Christ's captive (2:14) and ambassador (5:20), and for Jesus' sake (4:5), he carries on a pioneer work (10:13-16) as an evangelist (5:11) and minister of reconciliation (5:18-19). He sums up his message as "Christ Jesus the Lord" (4:5). He never forgets his churches; the care of them all rests constantly upon him (11:28), for he is their servant (4:5) and counselor. Motives which move him are gratitude to God and Christ (1:3; 5:14), reverent fear of the Lord his Savior and Judge (5:10-11), and sincere love for his churches (2:4; 11:11), who are his joy and concern (2:2-3). Integrity and faithfulness mark his ministry, and the scars of wearing labor and willingly accepted suffering are the marks which identify him as a true apostle (1:12; 6:3-10; 11:23-29).

V. The Strategy of the Collection

Back of the plans and work of Paul was a sound sense of strategy. It governed his choice of centers for his missionary work. Increasingly he concentrated on the great cities of the provinces, settling where there had been no real Christian mission before, and letting the light of the gospel radiate from these central places into the surrounding regions. His collection for needy Christians in Jerusalem was likewise an expression of the same sense of strategy. This does not mean that he lacked human sympathy for those in need. It means rather that he saw a

[9] For the history of this view that the "false apostles" brought a Gnostic-libertine message to Corinth, and that such people claimed that they were truly "spiritual," cf. Lake, *Earlier Epistles of St. Paul*, pp. 219-32; Windisch, *Der zweite Korintherbrief*, pp. 23-26.

still wider purpose that the collection should fulfill. Paul had it on his heart to preserve the sense of unity between the Jerusalem Christians and his Gentile churches.

Perhaps this concern had been at least a partial motive back of the collection which Barnabas and Saul took to the Jerusalem Christians as famine relief at an earlier time (Acts 11:27-30). Certainly at the Jerusalem conference, when Paul's zeal for a united church was actively at work, he had agreed to continue this relief work (Gal. 2:10). He undertook such a collection in Galatia (I Cor. 16:1), but we do not know the outcome of it. In both I and II Corinthians and in Romans we find a record of the collection taken in Macedonia and Achaia (i.e., ancient Greece). Paul's purpose was to bind the churches together, so that the Jewish Christians in Palestine would feel and acknowledge the truly Christian faith and spirit of the Gentile Christians, and the Gentile Christians would remember with gratitude that they had received the gospel treasure from their Jewish-Christian brothers. He took this gift to Jerusalem at the risk of his life, as he knew; but the unity of the church was so important to him, and the role of the collection so hopeful a means of expressing and promoting that unity, that he refused to let danger deter him (Acts 21:4, 11; Rom. 15:30-32).

VI. Central Themes of the Letter [10]

(*a*) "The God and Father of our Lord Jesus Christ, the Father of mercies and God of all comfort" (1:3). Paul does not start from natural theology but from Christ. God, "the living God" (3:3; 6:16), is the active, self-revealing God, and he has made himself known in Christ. He is also present with power in his weak human agents (4:7; 6:7; 13:4). He therefore is to be feared (7:1), for he made this world a moral order and is active to preserve that order. Yet he is the faithful God (1:18), and this is the ground of man's assurance. He is not merely the creator; this idea appears only indirectly in 4:6. It is God's new creation in Christ that holds Paul's attention. Through Christ and the Spirit he gives life to sinful, mortal men, and sustains them in the wear and burden of their service for him (3:6; 4:10). Thus he is the God of grace, of mercies, and of love (1:2-3; 13:11, 14). "All this is from God" (5:18). The future is safe for those who trust in him (5:5).

This is true in spite of the barriers in the way of victory. The power and cleverness of Satan are not belittled. Indeed, he is even said to be "the god of this world" (4:4), and his skill in disguising himself "as an angel of light" (11:14) means that men need faith and insight to see where the lines are drawn in the moral battle of life. To this diabolic power the perverseness of human sin is added; the "trespasses" of men made necessary the work of reconciliation and the "new creation" (5:17-19). But the redeeming work of God has broken the power of evil and will completely achieve his saving purpose. In this faith Paul lives; he knows the inner peace that God gives to every believer (1:2).

(*b*) "Our Lord Jesus Christ" (1:3; cf. 4:5; 13:14). That Christ is the "image" or "likeness" of God (4:4), the Son of God (1:19), and sinless in character (5:21), Paul never doubts. Yet Paul's emphasis is not on who Christ is but on what he does. He is the "Yes" to God's promises made to Israel and recorded in scripture (1:19-20); in him the hope of Israel was fulfilled. He is thus the Christ of Israel, a fact axiomatic for Paul; with other Christians Paul can let the title "Christ" become a proper name without weakening his deep conviction that Jesus was the expected Messiah of Israel. All Jews should believe in him and live in the church as his followers (cf. 3:12-15).

He was the reconciling Christ, who willingly accepted the way of suffering to save sinful men; "Though he was rich, yet for your sake he became poor" (8:9, a clear reference to his pre-existence), in order that by his unselfish ministry and vicarious suffering he might reconcile and renew and enrich those who believe in him. But he carries forward this work as the living Christ. Raised from the dead (4:14), he is the living Lord of the church, "our Lord Jesus Christ," and also, as men will finally learn, the rightful Lord of all; at the end he will judge all men (5:10). In saving men through Christ, God does not abandon his moral order, but gives the new life and power that makes it possible for men to enter into the perfect order that will endure. It is all the doing of God (5:18), but it is *doing* and not mere make-believe. Christ changes and tests life.

(*c*) "The Holy Spirit" (13:14). The new order which God has established through Christ is marked by the work of the Spirit, who "gives life" as the written code could not do (3:6). It is often said that Paul identifies the risen Christ with the Spirit, and 3:17-18 apparently gives some support to this view. That the risen Lord is a life-giving Spirit was certainly Paul's conviction (I Cor. 15:45). But that he simply identified the Lord with the Spirit is too sweeping a statement. As 13:14 shows, the two are closely related without being completely merged.

[10] Valuable for the study of the thought of Paul, though not limiting attention to II Corinthians, are James S. Stewart, *A Man in Christ* (New York: Harper & Bros., 1935); Elias Andrews, *The Meaning of Christ for Paul* (New York and Nashville: Abingdon-Cokesbury Press, 1949); and Knox, *Chapters in a Life of Paul*, pp. 111-59.

The Spirit works in the hearts of men and produces results in the lives of men, so that the Corinthians, for example, may be read by others as "a letter from Christ delivered by us, written not with ink but with the Spirit of the living God . . . on tablets of human hearts" (3:3). The Spirit is a transforming power; he gives life (3:6). The gift of the Spirit is fellowship with God (13:14). And the gift of the Spirit is the Christian's "guarantee" that God will fulfill all his promises for the future (1:22; 5:5). Using a business term which means the down payment that binds the purchaser to pay fully the total price, Paul says that the Spirit whom God gives at the start of the Christian life is God's down payment, his first installment that obligates him to complete all that he has promised the believer. In noncommercial words this initial gift of the Holy Spirit to each believer guarantees the full bestowal of every promised gift of grace.

(*d*) The Old Testament as the church's scripture. While Paul does not often quote the Old Testament in this letter, he clearly indicates that for him it is scripture and permanently significant. It contains the promises which in Christ find their "Yes" (1:19-20). It is inferior to the ministry of Christ and the Spirit; a written code cannot be a life-giving power (3:3, 6). But it is still read, and rightly (3:14-15). Yet it must be understood aright. The Jews here make a fatal error. They do not see that to reject Christ as the key to the understanding of the Old Testament is to fail to get its true message; it is as though a veil still hindered clear reading and understanding. In other words, the Old Testament rightly understood points to Christ, and is the proper possession of the church.

(*e*) The role of suffering. II Corinthians, as indeed the New Testament in general, persistently combines weakness and suffering with power and triumph. It is the Christ who "became poor" and "died for all" who is the risen, reigning Lord of the church. "He was crucified in weakness, but lives by the power of God" (13:4). This gives the pattern of the Christian life. Man's weak and mortal body is the "earthen vessel" of the divine grace and power. As Christ's work had shown, it is precisely through suffering, holy love that redeeming power finds its one effective channel, and so the Christian minister must stand ready to accept all labors, hardships, dangers, and even death if it comes, in the faith that God's saving will is done and his "power is made perfect in weakness" (12:9). As in the gospel narrative, the way of the Cross is the way to do God's work. On this point, as so often, Paul has grasped the depths of the gospel message and let it shape his ministry.

(*f*) The Christian hope. Faith and despair are incompatible. Hope is the twin of true faith. Naturally, therefore, the note of hope is continually heard in what Paul says. He has known crises; in the very recent past he has faced a situation so ominous that he felt sure the end of his earthly life had come (1:8-9). Even though he was delivered from that crisis, he still encounters danger daily (11:26). It is a daily death, but to match it he receives the daily gift of the life of Jesus at work in his mortal body, and he always can look forward to final resurrection with Jesus and to "an eternal weight of glory" (4:10-18). In one respect his hope may have changed somewhat since the writing of I Corinthians. It is difficult to be sure of this, for in Paul's letters new teaching may only be something long held and now first mentioned, rather than the result of a change in thinking. But in I Cor. 15:52, as in I Thess. 4:17, Paul speaks as though he expects to be alive when the end of the age comes. In II Cor. 5:2-4 he still has this desire, but the following verses show that he no longer expects its fulfillment so confidently. Moreover, he has come to feel that death before this age ends would give closer fellowship with the risen Christ, and so offer actual advantage. By far the most important thing, however, is his unshaken conviction that in any event the future is secure with Christ, provided only "we make it our aim to please him" (5:9). In all the inevitable uncertainty of human life, Paul lives with the steadying support of grateful hope.

(*g*) Prayer. The letter tells little of the common worship of the church but, like all of Paul's writings, reflects the large place which prayer holds in the Christian life. Prominent in the "thankful letter" is the note of thankfulness in prayer. Paul thanks God for the mercy and comfort so recently shown in deliverance from death and in the happy solution of the Corinthian crisis (1:3-4); for God's use of himself as a minister of Christ (2:14); for putting concern for the Corinthians in the heart of Titus (8:16); and "for his inexpressible gift" (9:15), which is either the unity of the church or God's gift of Christ himself.

The "Amen" which Christians utter in worship (1:20) is their reverent answer to God's gifts of grace in fulfillment of his promises. This grace is a constant need and an ever-available resource; free, undeserved, life-giving grace and steadying peace God daily gives to sincere believers in answer to prayer (1:2). The divine grace, love, and fellowship Paul knows to be the blessing the Corinthians need (13:14). This reminds us how great a part intercessory prayer plays in Paul's life, and he asks the Corinthians to share in this great chorus of unselfish intercession for him (1:11). They know he continually prays for them that they may do no wrong (13:7), and that they may ever improve in Christian living (13:9). Paul prays for what he himself needs, and especially that his persistent, troublesome "thorn in the flesh" may be taken away. He has been answered—by strength to bear his physical ailment and by the insight that the power of God is able to do its great work through human weakness (12:7-9). Like Jesus in Gethsemane, he has learned that even one who has worked miracles of healing may not have every prayer answered precisely as he asks. But that God answers prayer, Paul had discovered even in this personal suffering.

(*h*) Christian giving. As the background of all Christian giving Paul places the immeasurable and constant gifts of God and the inspiring example of Christ's own self-giving (5:18; 8:9; 9:15). The basic gift of man is the gift of himself to the Lord (8:5); nothing can be substituted for that. All human giving is a work of God's grace bringing forth its fruits in the Christian life (8:1; 9:14). True Christian giving is voluntary (9:5, 7), eager (8:4), cheerful (8:2; 9:7), generous (8:2-3; 9:6, 11), according to means (8:11-12), without condescension, but rather with a sense of equality (8:14), out of genuine love (8:8), in faith that God will provide (9:8), and with a resolve to fulfill one's total responsibility (8:10-11). The giver may be challenged by others (8:1, 8; 9:2), and in turn will stir up others to give (9:2). The funds must be handled in an open and plainly honest way (8:20-21). Truly Christian giving builds brotherhood, understanding, and the spirit of mutual worship among the whole church of Christ (9:12-14). For the giving of which Paul here speaks is "benevolent giving," for the needy Christians in Jerusalem far away. No Christian has the right to use these passages unless his giving has the larger outreach which Paul is fostering in the Corinthian church.

VII. The Early Use of the Letter

II Corinthians was undoubtedly known and used in the church at large from about A.D. 140.[11] At that time Marcion included it in the ten letters of Paul which he combined with the Gospel of Luke to form his canon. The letter must have been known to various churches for some time before that date; there is not the slightest reason to think that the collection of the letters of Paul was initiated by Marcion. The probable use of II Corinthians by Polycarp about A.D. 115, the explicit use by Irenaeus about A.D. 185, as well as its inclusion in the Muratorian canon not far from A.D. 200, confirm the statement that the Christian church knew the letter as an authentic writing of Paul and never had the least doubt as to its genuineness.

How early was this letter known outside of the church at Corinth? When Clement of Rome wrote on behalf of the Roman church to aid in quelling a new revolt of the Corinthians against their leaders (*ca.* A.D. 96), he spoke of I Corinthians as "Paul's letter" to them, and took no notice of any other, although in a matter of rebellion against their leaders II Corinthians offered much relevant material. There is thus doubt as to whether Clement had any knowledge of a second letter of Paul to Corinth, although the phrase quoted is not by itself decisive, and a few passages in his letter resemble somewhat expressions in II Corinthians. Those who date the writing of Ephesians about A.D. 90[12] may make a stronger case for early knowledge of II Corinthians; a few passages of Ephesians suggest that its writer knew this epistle. This date for Ephesians is much disputed and falls short of being convincing. That Paul wrote Ephesians, and that the wider circulation of his letters was stimulated by his death in particular, seems more probable.

The essential facts, then, are that while acquaintance with II Corinthians by A.D. 95 cannot be proved, it is possible; and the circulation of the letter early in the second century is clearly reflected by the evidence. It always circulated in its present form, and if it now consists of portions of more than one letter, as has been argued, the joining of such parts took place before public circulation in the church at large began. No author other than Paul has ever been suggested, and there is nothing in the content of the letter to warrant any question concerning apostolic authorship. It is an authentic expression of the mind and heart and ministry of Paul.

VIII. Selected Bibliography

GOUDGE, H. L. *The Second Epistle to the Corinthians* ("Westminster Commentaries"). London: Methuen & Co., 1927. Combines critical commentary and some practical application. Stoutly defends the unity of II Corinthians.

KENNEDY, JAMES HOUGHTON. *The Second and Third Epistles of St. Paul to the Corinthians.* London: Methuen & Co., 1900. A strong argument that chs. 10–13 were part of the "stern letter."

LAKE, KIRSOPP. *The Earlier Epistles of St. Paul.* London: Rivingtons, 1911. Ch. iv is a detailed

[11] The earliest use of the letter in the ancient church can be studied in Albert E. Barnett, *Paul Becomes a Literary Influence* (Chicago: University of Chicago Press, 1941).

[12] See especially Edgar J. Goodspeed, *The Meaning of Ephesians* (Chicago: University of Chicago Press, 1933). For the view preferred above see H. E. Dana, *A Neglected Predicate in New Testament Criticism* (Chicago: Blessing Book Stores, Inc., 1934), pp. 14-21.

study of Paul's relations and correspondence with Corinth. Agrees with Kennedy.

LIETZMANN, HANS. *An die Korinther I-II* ("Handbuch zum Neuen Testament"). 4th ed. by Werner Georg Kümmel. Tübingen: J. C. B. Mohr, 1949. Outstanding compact commentary. Defends the unity of II Corinthians.

MENZIES, ALLAN. *The Second Epistle of the Apostle Paul to the Corinthians.* London: Macmillan & Co., 1912. Introduction, text, original translation, and exegetical notes. Defends the unity of II Corinthians.

PLUMMER, ALFRED. *A Critical and Exegetical Commentary on the Second Epistle of St. Paul to the Corinthians* ("International Critical Commentary"). New York: Charles Scribner's Sons, 1915. The best commentary in English. Assigns chs. 10–13 to the "stern letter."

STRACHAN, R. H. *The Second Epistle of Paul to the Corinthians* ("Moffatt New Testament Commentary"). London: Hodder & Stoughton, 1935. Outstanding popular commentary based on the English text. Assigns chs. 10–13 to the "stern letter."

WINDISCH, HANS. *Der zweite Korintherbrief* ("Meyer's Kommentar"). Göttingen: Vandenhoeck & Ruprecht, 1924. The best detailed commentary. Argues that chs. 10–13 belong to a letter later than the "thankful letter."

II CORINTHIANS

TEXT, EXEGESIS, AND EXPOSITION

1 Paul, an apostle of Jesus Christ by the will of God, and Timothy *our* brother, unto the church of God which is at Corinth, with all the saints which are in all Achaia:

1 Paul, an apostle of Christ Jesus by the will of God, and Timothy our brother,
To the church of God which is at Corinth, with all the saints who are in the whole of A-cha'ia:

I. INTRODUCTION (1:1-11)

A. ADDRESS AND CHRISTIAN GREETING (1:1-2)

1:1. In the usual Greek letter the writer gave first his own name, then that of the person addressed, and added a word of "greeting" (χαίρειν). **Paul** follows but enlarges this pattern; he describes the Christian position of both writers and recipients, and completely Christianizes the greeting (vs. 2) by making it a prayer for **grace** and **peace.** As in Galatians, the statement that he is **an apostle** is a stout defense and positive claim; it combats recent denials at Corinth of his apostolic position and power. The word **apostle** (ἀπόστολος), meaning one sent forth on a mission, was used of "messengers," as in 8:23, and of traveling missionaries, such as Paul, Silvanus, and Timothy (I Thess. 2:6), or Barnabas and Paul (Acts 14:14). This wide meaning enabled the "false apostles," as Paul calls them (11:13), to claim the title for themselves. The word, however, was used more explicitly of the pioneer witnesses whom the risen Christ had called to testify to his resurrection (I Cor. 9:1; Acts 1:22), and finally in later times was limited to the twelve (Matt. 10:2) or to the twelve and Paul. Paul did not choose this honor; it was owing to **the will** and call **of God** that he was the chosen messenger, the captive (2:14),

---

1:1. ***Paul, an Apostle.***—Paul's usual way of beginning his letters is to state his authority as an apostle. But there is special point in asserting it here, for it was this which had been challenged by his opponents in the church at Corinth. He had been called to preach the gospel. It was not a task which he had chosen on his own initiative. His call was rooted in the experience which befell him on the Damascus road. There he had been laid hold of as by an arresting hand, and commissioned to carry the gospel to the Gentiles (Acts 9:15). The conviction that he is called of God is the essential qualification of a preacher. "How can men preach unless they are sent?" (Rom. 10:15.) It was to preach that Paul felt himself called. "Christ did not send me to baptize but to preach the gospel" (I Cor. 1:17). It was a task he dared not refuse. "Woe to me if I do not preach the gospel!" (I Cor. 9:16.) The compulsion of this call does

2 Grace *be* to you, and peace, from God our Father, and *from* the Lord Jesus Christ.

2 Grace to you and peace from God our Father and the Lord Jesus Christ.

the ambassador (5:20), the minister of Christ (11:23). The word **Christ** (Χριστός) was originally an adjective, meaning, as did "Messiah" in Hebrew, "anointed." It was used with the article as a title of Jesus; he was "the anointed one" promised by God to his people as their redeemer and leader. But the word soon became, as here, a proper name equivalent to Jesus. **Timothy,** named as coauthor, had nothing to do with the actual dictation of the letter. Perhaps he is named because he had been scorned by the Corinthians (cf. I Cor. 16:10-11 and Intro., p. 266), and Paul wanted to show that he stood by his helper. **Brother** means "fellow Christian," perhaps with the added idea that he is Paul's comrade-in-service.

The letter is to be read aloud **to the church . . . at Corinth,** the local fellowship of that body of Christians whom God has reconciled to himself and called to be his people. For it is **the church of God;** it is not Paul's creation or a voluntary human association, but a divinely established brotherhood. Because Corinth (see above, pp. 3-4) was the capital city of the Roman province of **Achaia** (i.e., all of Greece south of Macedonia) and the church Paul had founded there was the center of Christian life in that region, he includes in his address the other Christians in **the whole of Achaia** (e.g., Cenchreae, Rom. 16:1; Athens, Acts 17:34). They are **saints,** as all Christians are, for the word means consecrated to God and members of the people of God, who thus are obligated to live worthily of this position. But they have their position only by God's grace, a divine gift which, as vs. 2 implies, they continually need.

2. Grace (χάρις) often means the initial act of free, undeserved favor by which God redeems and forgives the sinner and receives him into fellowship with himself. But here

not, of course, imply that he was reluctant to obey. Preaching Christ was a joyful passion, as it must be if it is to be effective. Paul was full of wonder and gratitude when he thought of what Christ had done for him. G. K. Chesterton's words, explaining the tireless labor of Francis of Assisi, are an echo of Paul's own feeling, "It is the highest and holiest of the paradoxes that the man who really knows he cannot pay his debt will be for ever paying it." [1]

Paul was conscious also that he had the one message that can meet the needs of men in their spiritual hunger, their purposeless living, their burdened consciences, their feeling of being crushed by the impersonal forces of life. These needs of the human heart are unchanging in this material world. Christ alone has the power to meet them. Those who have experienced his power feel constrained to pass on the good news, as one cured of a dire disease is eager to publish the remedy to all similar sufferers.

Behind the call Paul saw the will of God, his agelong purpose reaching down to himself to take him up into its mighty movement. This gave him confidence. It freed him from all doubt about whether or not he was the right man for the task. It freed him from all concern about his resources for the work. "Our sufficiency is from God" (3:5). It delivered him from all anxiety about results. The preacher is not responsible for the effect of his message; he is responsible only for his faithfulness in declaring it. Francis Younghusband, who was sent by the viceroy of India on a mission to Tibet, a hazardous and difficult task, describes the spirit in which he faced it.

> I had the greatest possible confidence in the Viceroy who sent me. He had himself selected me for the mission. . . . He knew what he wanted in sending me, and I knew he would support me through thick and thin in getting it. He would not abandon me at the crucial moment.[2]

2. ***Grace to You and Peace.*—Grace** and **peace** are key words in Christian experience. **Grace** is not a thing—to be conveyed from one to another as if it were a material substance. It describes an attitude and an act of the will. It means here the continuous and gracious activity of God toward us, whereby we are not only awakened to penitence, brought to surrender, and forgiven, but also daily empowered (see further on 8:9). This benediction is really an expression of Paul's own gracious attitude to the Corinthians, and of his desire that they may become conscious of God's gracious working in their hearts.

[1] *St. Francis of Assisi* (New York: Doubleday, Doran & Co., 1931), p. 117.

[2] *Within* (London: Williams & Norgate, 1912), p. 88.

it is the constant divine favor and help that daily upholds believers on their Christian way. **Peace** (εἰρήνη) is the right relationship with God and the resulting steady quiet of spirit that the grace of God gives. Both gifts are needed constantly; both are divine gifts.

Peace is the fruit of the relationship with God and with man which results from his forgiveness and his acceptance of us as his sons. It must not be confused with the absence of trouble, or of struggle against evil. There is a "foul tranquillity" like that of a stagnant pool. The peace that comes of harmony with the will of God is of the heart. It coexists with the most active conflict with evil in ourselves and in the world around us. Within the church it is the harmonious fellowship of those who have been made one in Christ Jesus through their reconciliation with God.

Grace and **peace** are therefore correlated. There can be no peace within ourselves or in our relationships with others until selfishness in all its forms has been subdued by the experience of grace, and hostility and resentment have been overcome through the consciousness of sin forgiven. There are three main elements in peace. The foundation of it is the reconciliation with God which comes through his grace. By his gracious dealings with us in Christ we are brought to judgment, in the light of which we see our sin for what it is, and are led to a true repentance. The enmity toward God which is rooted in self-will is overcome, and through his forgiving love we are restored to fellowship with him (see Expos. on 5:19). This sense of unity with God is peace—"Peace with God through our Lord Jesus Christ" (Rom. 5:1).

But peace with God cannot be complete till we are also reconciled to one another. Jesus made this clear: "If you are offering your gift at the altar, and there remember that your brother has something against you, leave your gift there before the altar and go; first be reconciled to your brother, and then come and offer your gift" (Matt. 5:23-24). The same obligation to seek reconciliation with our brother rests upon us even when it is he who has done the injury. This is important for ourselves as well as for our brother. A sense of grievance can be as disastrous to peace of mind as a sense of sin. It "works like madness in the brain," as Coleridge says. It is a burden on the spirit. There is evidence that cherished resentment is at the root of some forms of neurotic trouble, though the cause may not be recognized. It isolates us from others as well as from God. Forgiveness is healing. It can, in Shakespeare's words,

> Cleanse the stuff'd bosom of that perilous stuff
> Which weighs upon the heart.[3]

[3] *Macbeth*, Act V, scene 3.

It is pride that keeps us from confessing the wrong and so receiving forgiveness, or from overcoming the sense of injury that keeps us from forgiving. Only as we see God's forgiving grace in Christ, and are humbled by it, can we be made willing to forgive or to seek forgiveness. This is the secret of peace between us and others.

There is a third aspect of peace which is important. It is peace of mind in a threatening world—the peace that sets us free from worry and fear. It was this peace which Jesus possessed as he faced the Cross, and which he offered to his disciples. "Peace I leave with you, my peace I give to you. . . . Let not your hearts be troubled, neither let them be afraid" (John 14:27). This peace is not found in material security. Increase of wealth or power brings increase of anxiety. We are left still at the mercy of the "changes and chances" of the world. There is no assurance that we shall be protected from life's ills. Loyalty to Christ may even bring some of these ills upon us. "In the world," said Jesus, "you have tribulation: but," he added, "be of good cheer; I have overcome the world" (John 16:33).

What the Christian faith offers us is an untroubled heart in a troubled world. This also is the fruit of the grace of Christ; for in it we see a love from which nothing can separate us and which is able to make us "more than conquerors." When through reconciliation with God we are at peace with him and with one another we can confront the troubles of life in the sure knowledge that nothing can defeat or destroy the spirit. Peace has been defined as "the conscious possession of adequate resources." Paul was given the assurance, "My grace is sufficient for you" (12:9). This provides a sense of security that nothing can disturb. It is often deepest when life is darkest, because then all the frail shelters in which we hide are shattered, and we are led to rest utterly on God.

> There is a state of mind, known to religious men, but to no others, in which the will to assert ourselves and hold our own has been displaced by a willingness to close our mouths and be as nothing in the floods and waterspouts of God. In this state of mind, what we most dreaded has become the habitation of our safety.[4]

This is the "peace . . . which passes all understanding" (Phil. 4:7).

[4] William James, *The Varieties of Religious Experience* (New York: Longmans, Green & Co., 1903), p. 47.

3 Blessed *be* God, even the Father of our Lord Jesus Christ, the Father of mercies, and the God of all comfort;

3 Blessed be the God and Father of our Lord Jesus Christ, the Father of mercies

They are jointly given by **God our Father and the Lord Jesus Christ;** here, as often, Paul places Jesus Christ on God's side of the divine-human relationship. **Lord,** used of God in both O.T. and N.T., here refers to the risen Christ, the living Lord of the church, who always joins in giving the divine gifts by which that church is founded and lives.

B. Thanksgiving for Recent Deliverance from Death (1:3-11)

1. Thanksgiving for Comfort in All Affliction (1:3-7)

3. Except in Galatians, where the situation called for immediate sharp rebuke, Paul's letters to his churches follow the widespread custom of adding to the address and greeting an expression of thanksgiving. In the other letters he thanks God for the faith and Christian growth of the readers, but here, in this his most personal letter, he offers praise and thanks to God for comfort given him. The key word is **comfort,** which as verb or noun (παρακαλέω, παράκλησις) is used ten times in these five verses. Thus we feel at once the tone of relief and joy that marks the "thankful letter." Jesus Christ is "the Son of God" (vs. 19); he is **our Lord,** a title that reflects his divine position (and as is shown

The association of God the Father and the Lord Jesus Christ is part of the usual Christian benediction. God the Father is the source of grace and peace, which are conveyed to us through Christ. But Christ is no mere channel. He is the Lord Jesus Christ, himself equally with God the divine source and center of grace and peace.

3a. Blessed Be the God and Father of Our Lord Jesus Christ.—Paul begins his message with gratitude to God. Thanksgiving is always the right mood in which to face life, or to begin any enterprise. It is the starting point of prayer, the motive of service. The sense of gratitude is the most direct road to the consciousness of God. The man who is deeply grateful finds it almost inevitable to think of God. The perplexity of a grateful atheist who has no one to thank has often been remarked upon. In the face of hardship or misfortune, gratitude helps us keep the right perspective. There is always something in the most desolating situation for which we can thank God. Even for the hardship itself we can learn to thank him because of its call to courage and faith, and of the gracious possibilities inherent in it. Paul learned, in fact, to thank God in everything and for everything, and exhorts us to the same practice. "Always and for everything giving thanks" (Eph. 5:20). It is for the blessing in the heart of a grievous burden that Paul here thanks God.

His thanksgiving expands into a description of God. He is, for one thing, the **God and Father of our Lord Jesus Christ.** There is a sense, in Paul's view, in which Jesus is always subordinate to God. The position of sonship to God as Father, with its complete trust in and surrender to his will, was the only one which the man Christ Jesus could take when he came in the flesh. He "emptied himself, taking the form of a servant, being born in the likeness of men" (Phil. 2:7). Subordination to his Father in his earthly life was inherent in his self-emptying. He was the perfect Son, living in utter trust and obedience to the perfect Father. Only so could he reveal the true attitude of men to God. This he did through the whole course of his life—in his temptation, in the face of overwhelming danger, in his attitude to those who opposed and thwarted him, and last of all, in the suffering which brought him to the Cross. His perfect relationship to God determined his reaction to events and to people. It inspired all he said and did. It is the key to his life, the only way in which he can be understood. To be like Jesus is first of all to be brought by him into sonship with God. This sonship must direct all we say and do. We are to bless them which curse us, and pray for them which despitefully use us, that we may be the children of our Father which is in heaven (Matt. 5:44-45).

It is through Christ's oneness with God that he reveals God to us. His peace and joy come out of his experience of God's omnipotent care and love in final control of all events and circumstances; e.g., in the storm on the lake, where the calm of his spirit reveals the sovereignty of God. The Father's love shines in his love for all men. The only explanation of the personality of Jesus is that God was in Christ.

3b-4. Father of Mercies and God of All Comfort.—All **mercies** come from God's fatherly

4 Who comforteth us in all our tribulation, that we may be able to comfort them which are in any trouble, by the comfort wherewith we ourselves are comforted of God.

and God of all comfort, 4 who comforts us in all our affliction, so that we may be able to comfort those who are in any affliction, with the comfort with which we ourselves

---

by *Maran,* meaning "our Lord," in I Cor. 16:22, this position was ascribed to him from the very early days of the church). Yet here, since his sufferings are noted (vs. 5), the main thought is of Christ's real human life or his dependence as Son. God, as the RSV rightly translates, is **the God and Father of our Lord Jesus Christ.** The relation of sonship, dependence, and obedience even unto suffering (vs. 5) is precisely that presented in the Gospels, but it does not obscure the divine role and rank of Christ. In Paul's thought, although the holy firmness of God is not forgotten (2:15-16), his gracious goodness to men takes the central place; he is the merciful **Father,** and the richness and range of his **comfort** is expressed in vss. 3-4 by the threefold use of πᾶς **(all, all, any). Comfort** is more than consolation in sorrow or trial; it includes encouragement, and implies the divine gift of strength to meet and master life's crises.

4. Only in vs. 8 does Paul refer to a specific **affliction.** Here he stresses that God's comfort is given in **all** trials; the present tense means that God continually **comforts.** In part, Paul thinks of the comfort received from God's solution of the crisis at Corinth. But he does not wish to speak directly of this as yet; so he speaks of the larger fact of God's continual comfort in every trial. **Us** and **we** refer primarily or exclusively to Paul himself; there may be a minor reference to Timothy (vs. 1). At times, later in the letter, a reference to other apostolic leaders or helpers, or even to Christians generally, may be felt in these words. The divine purpose in God's comfort is to enable Paul to bring more

---

love. At the heart of the universe there is a never-failing fountain of mercy and **comfort.** Like a spring of fresh water on the seashore, it may be covered at times by the tide, but never cut off. This comfort Paul had lately experienced afresh. It came to him through desolating pain, pain which had passed, though the memory of it was still poignant. The comfort of God now glows in his mind, as a rainbow shines in the rain-drenched sky. The precise nature of this comfort he does not here define, but we can read between the lines and gather its content.

Comfort is a word which in modern speech has lost much of its N.T. meaning. It suggests to us a kind of sedative, a palliative for pain of body or mind. But the comfort of God is no narcotic. The word "comforter" applied to the Holy Spirit really means "strengthener" (John 14:16). It has the same root as "fortify." We comfort a sufferer when we give him courage to bear his pain or face his misfortune. Comfort is what sets him on his feet.

The **comfort** of God is rooted in his fellowship. It is found in the new access of conviction, of strength, and of understanding which comes from the entry of God upon our situation. It brought to Paul fresh insight into the love of God. The best answer to our human need is a more adequate thought of God. A missionary was teaching an Indian woman the Lord's Prayer. When he had taught her the first phrase, "Our Father," a light came into her face. "I do not need to know any more," she said. "If God is our Father that changes everything." To see the love of God alters our whole outlook. Pain and sorrow are absorbing facts. They may shut out the face of God. Yet they can be the means of illumination. Need and despair can make us sensitive to the love of God, from which the security and sufficiency of this material world may screen our eyes. Those who turn to God in their deep need find that he responds. Here is an experience which has been too frequent to be mere fancy. Apart from him this is a tragic world, without meaning, purpose, or hope. But only through what Miguel de Unamuno calls "the tragic sense of life" do we realize the wonder of God's grace. Against the background of a shattered world the love of God in Christ becomes real and radiant. It makes trouble bearable. It delivers us from the fear of this crushing universe. It fills life with hope. It takes us out of the grip of loneliness.

So this vision of God's love brings with it inner reinforcement. The picture of Christ upon the cross is one that Paul repeatedly recalls to his readers. He lifts it up like a flag in the thick of battle, and with the same effect. It reminded men of their cause and of their leader. It set free within them the hidden reserves of the spirit. To know that God was with them was like balm to a wound.

5 For as the sufferings of Christ abound in us, so our consolation also aboundeth by Christ.

are comforted by God. 5 For as we share abundantly in Christ's sufferings, so through Christ we share abundantly in comfort too.[a]

[a] Or, *For as the sufferings of Christ abound for us, so also our comfort abounds through Christ.*

---

sympathetic comfort and help to afflicted fellow men. Paul's affliction, rightly accepted, becomes a means of blessing for others.

5. **The sufferings of Christ** are the sufferings that the apostle bears in the fellowship and service of Christ. For Paul, suffering is part of the true Christian life (Rom. 8:17), and he as an apostle has to "complete what remains of Christ's afflictions" (Col. 1:24). But though the sufferings **abound** in Paul's life (cf. 11:23-29) the divine **comfort** fully meets his need. That the suffering Paul needs comfort shows that by his suffering he does not save himself; he always looks to the grace and power of God to redeem him and uphold him in his life and sufferings. But in it all he is bound to Christ in both suffering and comfort.

There are things that make suffering wholly desolating, e.g., a guilty conscience, or the knowledge that we have brought it on ourselves. The relief which God's forgiving presence brings can calm and heal the spirit and, through the spirit, the body. But God's comfort always comes to us through facing the truth about ourselves, and accepting his purpose for us in Christ; e.g., when we fear death, the only way of comfort is to face it in the knowledge that it has been overcome. The only real comfort in face of misfortune comes through accepting it in the knowledge that blight can be turned into blessing.

In addition, there is always the assurance of the power our own suffering gives us to comfort others. Suffering in which we have found for ourselves the comfort of God is an equipment for service. It puts us alongside of others. It gives us entry to their pain, making them willing to listen to us. We can speak with authority for we have been there. There are things people can take only from those who have sat where they sit (Ezek. 3:15). Against some such background as this, and nowhere else, can the mind find comfort in its outlook on experience. When affliction becomes the means of the knowledge of God and of equipment for service it finds its place in an ordered world. It is taken up into the purpose of God. It makes sense. In this context Paul can speak of sharing Christ's sufferings. We share them when we meet our own sufferings in the spirit which he imparts, allowing them to take their place in God's redeeming movement. In this way we share the comfort that supported Christ—the assurance of God's love and fellowship, and the confidence he had in the final victory which his very pain would help to bring. Thus suffering loses its power to perplex the mind by its apparent conflict with the love of God. The Christian faith harmonizes experience as no other outlook does. It gives the mind the comfort of a reasonable view, that "in everything God works for good with those who love him" (Rom. 8:28).

The comfort with which we ourselves are comforted by God is therefore the only form of comfort which is effective. Sympathy which merely assures people that we feel for them can do little. It may even increase their trouble by communicating a sense of our helplessness. It may feed their self-pity. The true comforter is one who can carry to others the strength of an experience in which God has given him the victory. This comfort is of universal application. It applies to all situations. It speaks to the hearts of people **in any affliction.** All troubles find healing in a right relationship with God, and in the opening of the mind to his message.

5. ***As We Share in Christ's Sufferings so We Share in Comfort.***—The thought that in his afflictions he was sharing in Christ's sufferings was part of Paul's comfort. This may be interpreted in two ways. It may mean simply that as Paul was suffering for his faith and through the love for his brethren which Christ had created, his sufferings were of the same kind as the sufferings of Christ. But in another passage (Col. 1:24) Paul carries this idea further. For the church, he will complete "what remains of Christ's afflictions." This does not depreciate the uniqueness of Christ's sacrifice, which was unique because Christ was unique. He came with the message and the power of reconciliation to break through the barrier which our sin had made between us and God. "For our sake he made him to be sin who knew no sin, so that in him we might become the righteousness of God" (5:21). He did for us what we cannot do for ourselves. In that sense no one can share his sufferings. No one can enter, as he did, into the full experience of human guilt which he bore on the Cross. No one

6 And whether we be afflicted, *it is* for
your consolation and salvation, which is
effectual in the enduring of the same sufferings which we also suffer: or whether we
be comforted, *it is* for your consolation and
salvation.
7 And our hope of you *is* steadfast, knowing, that as ye are partakers of the sufferings, so *shall ye be* also of the consolation.
8 For we would not, brethren, have you
ignorant of our trouble which came to us

6 If we are afflicted, it is for your comfort
and salvation; and if we are comforted, it
is for your comfort, which you experience
when you patiently endure the same sufferings that we suffer. 7 Our hope for you is
unshaken; for we know that as you share
in our sufferings, you will also share in our
comfort.
8 For we do not want you to be ignorant,

---

6. Paul lives for his Lord and his churches. In every trial and comfort he sees not merely a personal matter, but something which he can endure for the benefit of his converts, or something which blesses him in order that he may the better serve them; cf. 4:5, 15; 5:13. He pays a cost to bring them the gospel, guide their growth, and comfort them in their trials. For the Corinthians have had to face **the same sufferings.** These sufferings that Paul and the Corinthians endure are not their anguished feelings over the strained relations that have recently existed between them; that strain has passed. Paul thinks rather of the ridicule, denunciation, and mistreatment which he and his fellow Christians have to bear because they are Christ's followers (cf. I Thess. 2:14) ; the apostolic church grew not for lack of hostility and persecution, but in spite of it. The Christian life was truly, as Jesus had said (Mark 8:34) , a fellowship in suffering (cf. Rom. 5:3-5) .

7. Through the comfort he continually receives, and by reason of the Corinthians' recent change of attitude toward him, Paul is confirmed in his **hope** for them. It is no new hope; but now, in spite of their recent wavering and weakness, it remains firm, **unshaken.** This hope does not spring from confidence in human resources, but from the God-given **comfort** that Paul receives. Paul names but one condition: the readers, in faith and constancy, must **share** with him in the **sufferings** of the Christian cause. This unity of suffering and trial with comfort and triumph is found in Jesus' ministry and in Paul's career as well as in his teaching. It is no mere theory for him; he has learned its truth by his service for Christ.

2. The Recent Deliverance from Deadly Peril (1:8-11)

8. Following the general praise of God for continual help and comfort (vss. 3-7) , Paul now recalls his recent remarkable deliverance from death. The Corinthians, it

---

can offer to God the perfect penitence which comes from his insight into the depth of human sin. But there is a real sense in which Christ died that we might do for others in our degree what he did, carrying the burden of their sin, and revealing in the love that suffers the love that saves. In Christ we see that the world can be redeemed only by suffering, and that all suffering can be redemptive.

6. ***If We Are Afflicted.***—Paul has found in his passion to help others the secret of investing his own suffering with meaning. The hope he sets before them is that just as the past unhappiness need not remain a shadow on their fellowship with him, so the lot of the Christian in a hostile world, which he and they share and share alike, may become the very means by which the hurt is not only healed, but is made to strengthen and enrich their common service to Christ. The redeeming power of God is such that it can transform the whole situation and make it fruitful in the growth of the spirit.

7. ***Our Hope for You Is Unshaken.***—The only way in which the Corinthians can share in Paul's sufferings is by entering into the full bitterness and pain which their conduct has caused him. Only by so doing is it possible for them to share in his comfort. He has evidence now, with the return of Titus from his mission to Corinth, of a change of heart in the Corinthian church. He wishes to assure them that since they realize what their disloyalty has cost him they can share to the full the comfort God has given him. In this experience of God's comfort he is assured that all will be well. (Yet see Exeg.; cf. 2:3.)

8-9. ***We Do Not Want You to Be Ignorant, Brethren.***—The precise experience "in Asia" to which Paul refers is not easy to identify (see

in Asia, that we were pressed out of measure, above strength, insomuch that we despaired even of life:
9 But we had the sentence of death in ourselves, that we should not trust in ourselves, but in God which raiseth the dead:

brethren, of the affliction we experienced in Asia; for we were so utterly, unbearably crushed that we despaired of life itself.
9 Why, we felt that we had received the sentence of death; but that was to make us rely not on ourselves but on God who

---

would seem, knew of it, for he does not tell them any details; but they did not know how serious a danger it had been. In Paul's letters the expression **we do not want you to be ignorant** occurs six times to introduce a point he wishes to emphasize. The dangerous **affliction** occurred in **Asia**, the Roman province in western Asia Minor. Ephesus was its chief city, and the event may well have happened there. Paul refers not to the depressing news of the Corinthian revolt, as some have thought, but to some physical danger. A clue has been sought in Paul's word that he "fought with beasts at Ephesus" (I Cor. 15:32). But this seems to be a figurative reference to bitter hostility he had encountered, and the time of these hostile attacks by his enemies was before I Corinthians, and so earlier than the quite recent danger of which II Corinthians here tells. Nor was the **affliction** the riot described in Acts 19:21-41, unless Acts has greatly understated the danger to Paul on that occasion. Very likely it was some danger of the kind described in 11:23-26, of which no definite account has survived. But to Paul, who had faced danger often, it was unusually ominous, as he indicates by the double expression **utterly, unbearably crushed.** He thought death had come at last; he lost all hope of surviving.

9. Hope of escape gone, Paul **felt that** he **had received the sentence of death;** in his own mind he anticipated the event. In this he did wrong; he did not reckon on God. Here, as in vs. 4, he sees a divine purpose working itself out in this apparently futile suffering. In this hard way God was teaching him to **rely** not on himself (cf. 4:7; 12:9), but **on God,** who in his wisdom not only cares for his people, but also, as was said in a synagogue prayer Paul knew, **raises the dead** (4:14; Rom. 4:17). In these latter words Paul may have a twofold meaning. Prominent is the assurance that God can deliver, and recently in Paul's case has delivered, one of his people from apparently certain death. Coupled with this may be the sustaining thought that even if death should come, God is master of both life and death, as Christ's resurrection has made clear. So in every crisis Paul can stand fast and trust God; rescue may come, but in any case, he does not need to fear death.

Exeg.). It has been taken to refer to physical suffering such as had often been his lot. But it was not Paul's way to make much of his physical sufferings in the cause of Christ. Only once, when he was defending his right to speak in the name of Christ, did he lift the curtain and reveal what in another letter (Gal. 6:17) he called the "marks of the Lord Jesus." Whatever it was, the **affliction** was so deep—the defection of the church at Corinth coming on top of perhaps a physical experience—that it seemed to him like **the sentence of death**—a blow from which he could not recover. Sentence of death, however, may mean such loss of heart and hope that we are brought to a despair in which there is nothing between us and darkness except God's mercy. It may therefore be a saving experience, awakening that need of God which he is waiting to answer, and without which he cannot deliver us. Paul recognized this. His despair and helplessness forced him to rely completely upon **God who raises the dead.** The death and resurrection of Christ are more than historical facts in the story of Jesus. They reveal a divine principle which is always at work in the world of spirit as well as in the world of nature. "Unless a grain of wheat falls into the earth and dies, it remains alone; but if it dies, it bears much fruit" (John 12:24).

> For there is nothing lives but something dies,
> And there is nothing dies but something lives.[5]

The old self must die that the true self may come to life. This may happen in various ways: through a sense of moral failure, through tragic sorrow, through misfortune, in this particular

[5] "Ode to the Setting Sun," from *The Poems of Francis Thompson* (London: Burns Oates & Washbourne, 1913). Used by permission of Sir Francis Meynell, copyright owner.

10 Who delivered us from so great a
death, and doth deliver: in whom we trust
that he will yet deliver *us;*
11 Ye also helping together by prayer
for us, that for the gift *bestowed* upon us
by the means of many persons thanks may
be given by many on our behalf.
12 For our rejoicing is this, the testimony
of our conscience, that in simplicity and
godly sincerity, not with fleshly wisdom,
but by the grace of God, we have had our

raises the dead; **10** he delivered us from
so deadly a peril, and he will deliver us;
on him we have set our hope that he will
deliver us again. **11** You also must help us
by prayer, so that many will give thanks
on our behalf for the blessing granted us
in answer to many prayers.
12 For our boast is this, the testimony
of our conscience that we have behaved in

---

10. The hard-learned lesson gives Paul not only joy but hope. God had **delivered** him. We do not know how, but Paul was certain that God's power and love did it. So he will not despair. Danger will come again; Paul expects that. Death may come later; that is not his concern or worry. God can deliver him **again,** and Paul believes that **he will** do so. So Paul faces future crises with hope, but only because he can leave the issue with God.

11. Just as faith and the experienced goodness of God lead Paul to hope, so the faith and gratitude of the Corinthians must find expression in intercessory prayer. They **must help** Paul in future crises by united **prayer** for him, and when God has answered their prayers, as Paul implies God will, the blessing of deliverance **in answer to** their **many prayers** will lead **many** others to **give thanks** to God for his goodness to Paul. This seems to be the meaning of a rather involved sentence. Throughout the section (vss. 3-11) the faith, fellowship, deliverance, comfort, and service of which Paul writes are possible only through the grace and power of God. He and the readers live in God-given and God-supported freedom and assurance.

II. Recent Relations with the Church at Corinth (1:12–7:16)

A. The Reason for Change in Travel Plans (1:12–2:13)

1. Paul Has Acted with Open Sincerity (1:12-14)

12. Paul begins to defend his recent actions. Before explaining his change of travel plans (vss. 15-22), he first declares that in his actions and letters he has been honest and sincere. He can hope for God's future care and ask for the Corinthians' prayers because his conscience is clear; this is his "boasting" or **boast** (not **rejoicing** as in the KJV). Here occurs the word so characteristic of II Corinthians: "boasting" (καύχησις), used here, occurs six times, "boast" (καύχημα; used in vs. 14: "you are our boast"), three times, and

---

case perhaps through peril of death. The principle of resurrection thus came into play, and Paul's confidence in God was renewed; for in it all God was at work.

10. ***Deliverance from Peril.***—In dark moments when the light of God's presence is removed and feeling has dried up, the memory of past experiences keeps hope alive. The Bible itself is a storehouse of such recollections on which the Christian mind can feed. God can never cease to be in the future what he has been in the past. "Jesus Christ is the same yesterday and today and forever" (Heb. 13:8). But the Corinthians must help to make all this possible.

11. ***You Also Must Help Us by Prayer.***—Paul is determined to extract from every experience every fragment of blessing for others of which he is the channel. In the valley of trouble we can dig wells at which others who pass that way may drink. To this end he calls the church to prayer. The Christian strategy by which trouble may be prevented from leaving a painful scar is to pray that it may be turned into blessing. When once it comes, it is irrevocable. We cannot elude it by turning our minds from it; but God can so redeem it that it becomes a memory from which we have no desire to escape. Paul is convinced that the whole church may benefit from this and every other crisis as it sees in the issue how God has been at work.

12-14. ***For Our Boast Is This.***—One of the charges made against Paul during the estrange-

conversation in the world, and more abundantly to you-ward.
13 For we write none other things unto you, than what ye read or acknowledge; and I trust ye shall acknowledge even to the end;
14 As also ye have acknowledged us in part, that we are your rejoicing, even as ye also *are* ours in the day of the Lord Jesus.

the world, and still more toward you, with holiness and godly sincerity, not by earthly wisdom but by the grace of God.
13 For we write you nothing but what you can read and understand; I hope you will understand fully,
14 as you have understood in part, that you can be proud of us as we can be of you, on the day of the Lord Jesus.

"to boast" (καυχάομαι), twenty times. In chs. 1–9 Paul's use of these words is apologetic and friendly to the readers; in chs. 10–13 his tone is more militant and stern; the difference supports the assigning of chs. 10–13 to the "stern letter." In both cases, however, he is answering charges made against him at Corinth. He had **behaved** (this is what **had our conversation** in the KJV means) honestly; in saying **still more toward you** he does not mean that he has lacked honesty toward others, but that he has had more occasion to show the Corinthians his integrity in action. **Holiness** (ἁγιότητι), the original reading, is replaced in several less important MSS by **simplicity** (ἁπλότητι), i.e., "single-minded sincerity." The general sense of integrity is the same. **Godly, lit.,** "of God" (τοῦ θεοῦ), probably means "God-given," "prompted by God"—"God-given holiness and sincerity." It was not low, self-seeking cleverness, **earthly wisdom,** that moved Paul; **the grace of God** produced his uprightness and sincerity of act. His salvation, his ministry, his achievement are all due to God; he is the very reverse of a self-made man.

13. Since integrity marks his life, his readers may expect that his letters also will be sincere and straightforward, and indeed they are. They seem to have been attacked not as weak (cf. 10:10) or as hard to understand (cf. II Pet. 3:16), but as being deceptive or evasive. But he says what he means and thinks; "You don't have to read between the lines of my letters; you can understand them" (Moffatt). **Read** probably means "read aloud" in the Christian assembly. Paul feels sure that the Corinthians "recognize" or **understand** what he means, at least **in part,** and he hopes they **will understand** it **fully.** The Greek for **fully** (RSV) means literally, as the KJV translates, **to the end** (ἕως τέλους), which probably means here "to the fullest degree," but may include the idea that this fulfillment will come only at the last day.

14. The repentance of the Corinthians and their changed attitude toward him, as a result of the "stern letter" and Titus' appeal (7:9-16), show that they now understand and appreciate Paul **in part.** He does not mean, by saying **in part,** that their repentance

---

ment was that of insincerity. It was said that he did not mean what he wrote, that his words were capable of double meanings, that he used worldly wisdom, and was crafty and cunning in his arguments. Nothing can be more damaging to a man's reputation or influence than to call him insincere. It imputes base motives for his good actions. It suggests that he has selfish ends in view while he appears to be seeking only the good of others. This shakes confidence, undermines influence, and makes others suspect all his words and actions. No preacher or leader can hope to keep his power to help or influence others for good if his motives are suspect. All right human relations depend on mutual confidence—the assurance that words mean what they say, that promises will be kept, that each is seeking only the other's good. To kill that confidence by innuendo, or by direct charge, is like poisoning a well.

The enemies of Jesus used this weapon. They could not deny his good deeds, so they tried to discredit his motives. They suggested that he was an emissary of the prince of darkness camouflaged as an angel of light. They said that he wrought miracles by the power of Satan. The charge was easy to disprove (Mark 3:25). Christ saw in this attempt to turn his good into evil that willful blindness to the truth which is the final apostasy. It means that the light has gone out in the soul.

Perfect sincerity is not easy to achieve. Our motives are apt to be mixed. A man may do good work from a variety of motives: the love

15 And in this confidence I was minded to come unto you before, that ye might have a second benefit;	15 Because I was sure of this, I wanted to come to you first, so that you might have

is unsatisfactory, or that there is still a rebellious minority; 7:11, 16 exclude such ideas. But they still need to attain a fuller understanding of what God's grace is doing for them through Paul. The clause introduced by **that** tells what they have begun to understand. They have grasped to some degree that on the last day, when Christ returns and lays bare all hidden secrets at the judgment (5:10; I Cor. 4:5), they can **boast,** take pride, in Paul and what he has done for them; and his **boast** or pride will be their faith and growth in Christ. He anticipates that even when under judgment, unselfish love and joy in the other's gifts and achievements will be his and their great concern. So also in I Thess. 2:19-20; Phil. 2:16. Deep and strong is the tie between the apostle and his people (cf. 2:3); to know how deeply and permanently their lives are bound together will be to **understand fully** what he is and what his letters mean.

2. Change of Plans Not Due to Fickleness (1:15-22)

15. Paul's integrity, so strongly asserted in vss. 12-14, has been challenged at Corinth. Because he has changed his travel plans, he has been accused of being unreliable. He first denies in vss. 15-22 that he has been fickle, and says that in virtue of his very position as a minister of the faithful God (vs. 18) he could not be. Then in 1:23–2:4 he gives the reason for his change of plans. His first plan, announced in I Cor. 16:5-6 (cf. also Acts 19:21), was to go through Macedonia on his way to Corinth. The later crisis at Corinth, which led him to visit that church and write the "stern letter," convinced him that he should visit them as frequently as possible. Hence, while in Corinth trying to quell the revolt, or perhaps in the "stern letter," he had told them that he would visit them twice in the near future. On leaving Ephesus he would go to Corinth **first** (πρότερον, lit., "before," "formerly," probably means here, "before going on to Macedonia," and so as his

of good work, the desire to serve the community, to earn a living and support his family, to succeed, to stand well with others. All these may operate and some may be called selfish, but God knows the heart and can sift the gold from the dross. The purification of our motives is part of the process of sanctification. None of us has any right gratuitously to impugn the motives of others or to question their sincerity. We cannot see into their hearts and it is not our part to judge.

Paul's defense against the charge was twofold. For one thing, the testimony of his own conscience gave him confidence. He could look into his own heart without self-reproach. He recognized, however, that his sincerity of purpose toward the Corinthians was not his own achievement; it was the work of God's Spirit, and the gift of God's grace. There was no conscious pride in his self-respect, for the self he respected had been brought to birth by Christ.

For another thing, the Corinthians had acknowledged what they owed to him. Good work for a time may be done from bad motives, but in the end the quality of our motive will affect the quality of our work. This is most true, of course, of that which is done to influence the mind and spirit of others. Paul ends by bringing his readers and himself before the judgment seat of Christ. A man cannot do this and retain in his soul any lurking selfishness or cunning. We cannot live in the light of God's judgment and cherish grudges or animosities, or persist in uncharitableness. The secret of fellowship is walking in the light (I John 1:7).

15-17. ***Because I Was Sure of This, I Wanted to Come to You.***—Here Paul deals with another charge—that of fickleness, arising from his failure to keep to his original plan (see Exeg.). His declared intention had been to visit Corinth twice, on going to and returning from Macedonia. He changed his mind on hearing of the storm that had broken out in the Corinthian church. His confidence in their loyalty and in the pleasure his visit would give them had been shaken. It had for the time being taken the heart out of him. Had they put themselves for a moment in his place they would have understood his reluctance to go where he was not welcome. The atmosphere in which alone he could speak his message was lacking. God's message cannot be heard by ears that are full of the clamor of strife. There are times when people must be left till the needs of the soul produce

16 And to pass by you into Macedonia, and to come again out of Macedonia unto you, and of you to be brought on my way toward Judea.

17 When I therefore was thus minded, did I use lightness? or the things that I purpose, do I purpose according to the flesh, that with me there should be yea, yea, and nay, nay?

18 But *as* God *is* true, our word toward you was not yea and nay.

a double pleasure;[b] 16 I wanted to visit you on my way to Mac-e-do'ni-a, and to come back to you from Mac-e-do'ni-a and have you send me on my way to Judea. 17 Was I vacillating when I wanted to do this? Do I make my plans like a worldly man, ready to say Yes and No at once? 18 As surely as God is faithful, our word to you has not

[b] Other ancient authorities read *favor*.

---

first stop). In that way he could give them **a second benefit** (χάριν, "grace" or **benefit** [KJV]; some MSS read χαράν, "joy" or **pleasure** [RSV]), i.e., he could see them first on his way to Macedonia, and again on his way back from Macedonia to take the collection to Jerusalem (chs. 8–9; I Cor. 16:1-4; Rom. 15:25-26). Still later, however, he decided (vs. 23; 2:1) to await a better opportunity for the visit, and so changed back to the plan of I Cor. 16:5-6. At every stage his decisions were made in the **confidence** expressed in vs. 14, that he and the Corinthians were linked together then and for the future.

16. As chs. 8–9 show, the purpose of the visit was not only to give pastoral counsel, but also to make sure that the collection for the Jerusalem Christians was complete, and to take it to **Judea.**

17. The shift of plans led to two charges: (*a*) He was **vacillating;** he was not serious and responsible in statements and plans. (*b*) He planned **according to the flesh,** or as the RSV well puts it, **like a worldly man** who acts without principle and in a selfish, God-ignoring spirit. The result (the ἵνα clause seems here to express result) of such irresponsible and worldly decisions was that he said **Yes and No at once,** or more likely, said "Yes" at one time and arbitrarily changed to "No" in the next breath.

18. The charge hurts Paul so much, and is so serious, that in his reply, somewhat as in vs. 23, he puts himself on oath. He swears by the axiomatic faithfulness of God that his statements to the Corinthians have not alternated arbitrarily between **Yes and No.**

---

the void in which God's word can reach them (see also Expos. on 2:1-4).

But Paul's change of plan had given his enemies a further cause to abuse him. They called him fickle, charged him with speaking with two voices, making promises that he was ready to break when his own convenience or self-interest dictated a change of plan. Had they reflected for a moment they would have realized that one who was always ready to suffer death for the gospel would not lightly have been deflected from his purpose. When our hearts are turned against a man, everything he does is liable to be twisted into another cause of grievance.

Paul's answer to the charge lifted the whole matter to the highest level. He was concerned to defend himself, but much more to reveal the glory of Christ. A mind which has Christ for its center will not long permit itself to be occupied by things on the circumference. This explains the sudden leap in the argument from his apparent fickleness to the faithfulness of God in Christ.

18-20*a*. *As Surely as God Is Faithful.*—How could they charge with fickleness one whose gospel message had always been so affirmative? He did not speak with two voices in his proclamation of it. His tone was never muffled. The trumpet never gave an uncertain sound.

The message of the gospel is always positive, the proclamation of eternal facts, the good news in Christ of God's character and deeds. Preaching must always be positive. The keynote of the Christian message is struck in the prologue to I John: "That which . . . we have heard, which we have seen with our eyes, which we have looked upon and touched with our hands, concerning the word of life . . . we proclaim also to you" (I John 1:1, 3). These words define the nexus between preacher and hearers. He has something to tell them which he knows to be true. Real preaching is the communication of an experience. But Paul does not labor the point. He turns swiftly to bring his readers face to face with Christ. It is as if he were saying, "Forget about me and my apparent fickleness, and think about the faithfulness of God. God

19 For the Son of God, Jesus Christ, who was preached among you by us, *even* by me and Silvanus and Timotheus, was not yea and nay, but in him was yea.

been Yes and No. 19 For the Son of God, Jesus Christ, whom we preached among you, Sil-va′nus and Timothy and I, was not Yes and No; but in him it is always

19. Here Paul might have explained the good reason for his change in plans. But he postpones that until 1:23–2:4; his reference to the faithfulness of God (cf. I Cor. 1:9) leads him to speak first of God's faithfulness in fulfilling his promises in his Son. The **faithful** God, in his Son, faithfully fulfilled all his promises, found in the scriptures; and his ministers, it is implied, are likewise faithful and not fickle. It is clear from Acts 18:5 that **Silvanus and Timothy** shared Paul's work at Corinth (we may reasonably assume that Silvanus and the Silas of Acts are one and the same). This locates the writing of I Thess. 1:1 and II Thess. 1:1 at Corinth.

keeps all his promises. He has fulfilled every one of them in Jesus Christ."

What Paul means by **the promises of God** he does not need to define. The O.T. pages are studded with them as the night sky with stars. Some were prophetic visions of what God had in store for his people when the time was ripe (Isa. 2:2-4). Some were direct and simple promises of his forgiving mercy and deliverance. They all sprang from his purpose first declared to Abraham, that from his stock there would come a nation through which God would reveal himself to all men (Gen. 12:2). They corresponded to human need in all its aspects. Chief among them was the promise of a forgiveness that would restore men to fellowship with God, which through their sin they had lost. This proclamation of forgiveness echoes like music through all the stern judgments announced by the prophets. There was also the promise of a new kingdom in which God's rule would become supreme, and through which righteousness and peace would be established on the earth. After tribulation and tears a future would dawn for God's people in which all the hopes which faith had kindled in their hearts would be realized.

These promises were definite and clear to the religious mind. In the coming of Christ they were fulfilled. This is the theme of the songs recorded in the stories of the birth of Christ, the Benedictus of Zechariah (Luke 1:68-79), the Magnificat of Mary (Luke 1:46-55), and the Nunc Dimittis of Simeon (Luke 2:29-32). For all these people the promises of God, so long cherished as buds upon the tree of his unfolding purpose, had burst into flower in Christ. Peter made the same announcement after Pentecost. Explaining the meaning of the new experience in which the church was born through the coming of the Spirit, he quoted the promise made by the prophet Joel, and said, "This is that!" (Acts 2:16.)

Through Christ the love of God becomes so clear and plain that we can apprehend it. The longing to know God's care and love, which breaks like a sob from the heart of man abandoned, as he imagines, in an alien world, is satisfied. The forgiveness of God, which alone can bring peace and hope to the guilty conscience, becomes an unmistakable reality in the forgiving love of Christ, and supremely in his cross. The kingdom of God, which means God's rule, becomes established in this present world through his power in Christ to enter and rule our hearts and win our trust and obedience. The future blessedness of God's children is thus assured. In this kingdom, which they enter through Christ, death is past and time and space become irrelevant. The full victory over evil which is promised as the consummation of God's purpose is not yet accomplished. But the power to achieve it is here in Christ. It can never be exhausted or defeated. In him the kingdom of God has rooted itself in the world. Like an unconquerable invading army which has found a foothold on territory overrun by an enemy, it has established a base from which it cannot be dislodged. Through his Spirit and his resources God's final victory is sure.

These definite **promises of God** are **yea** and **Amen** in Christ Jesus. The promises of God which are made in the Bible are reflected in all the best hopes that life awakens. Hope is a natural constituent of the mind. Without it the spirit cannot be sustained through a long strain. Paul goes so far as to say that we are saved by hope (Rom. 8:24). Is this hope a mere illusion, set within us to lure us on, but not destined to be fulfilled? Does it correspond to anything real? The answer is in Christ. Hope springs from the fact that we are spiritual beings, and we cannot find complete satisfaction in a material world. When we seek the fulfillment of our hopes in material things, in money, or comfort, or freedom from trouble, we are frustrated. We do not find what we seek; or, having succeeded, we find that these material things do not satisfy. The worst kind of frustration may be an un-

20 For all the promises of God in him *are* yea, and in him Amen, unto the glory of God by us.

21 Now he which stablisheth us with you in Christ, and hath anointed us, *is* God;

Yes. 20 For all the promises of God find their Yes in him. That is why we utter the Amen through him, to the glory of God.
21 But it is God who establishes us with you in Christ, and has commissioned us;

---

20. The **promises** which Christ fulfills are those given to Israel as recorded in the O.T. Paul here implies that the O.T. contains God's message and promise, that Israel was God's people, and that Israel's mission reached its climax and fulfillment in the coming of Christ and the emergence of the church. For this fulfillment the church in worship is bound to give God praise and **glory.** The saving work is God's; man's part is grateful response, which Paul sees expressed in the **Amen** which the Christians utter. Amen, a Hebrew word meaning "so be it," was taken over into Greek as a word of reverent affirmation. It was used in Christian worship to respond in agreement to a declaration or testimony (I Cor. 14:16). Here, where Christ's fulfillment of the promises is in mind, the Amen may be the response upon hearing these promises in the scripture readings as well as in preaching. The **Amen,** like all Christian speech and action, is expressed **through** Christ. **We** here refers to the leaders, or possibly to the Christians as a group. In any case, the utterance is **to the glory of God;** it expresses grateful praise to him for what he has done.

21. In vss. 21-22 God, Christ, and the Spirit are united in the divine redemptive work, as in 13:14; I Cor. 12:4-6; Eph. 4:4-6. None of these passages is a formal statement of doctrine, but each expresses the faith and experience out of which the trinitarian doctrine came. Here, as so often, Paul is asserting that "all this is from God" (5:18). His real defense against the charge of fickleness is not that he is wise, consistent, and skillful, but that God is using him and directing his life. Only the life that God confirms and establishes

---

satisfying success. Then hope turns to cynicism or despair, both of which are the outcome of hope which is not rooted in or directed by faith. Once it was thought that a mirage in the desert was an illusion, and hope was often called by disappointed people a mirage. Now we know that a mirage is the reflection on the desert haze of some object, a green oasis, or a city, which is really there. Hope is the reflection in us of the things that God has prepared for those who love him. That reality Christ reveals. He purifies our desires. He makes us want the things God is waiting to give. He awakens the spiritual hunger which he came to satisfy. An Arctic explorer who had been subjected to eight months of slow starvation was asked whether during these months he and his companions had suffered much from the pangs of hunger. "No," he answered, "we lost them in the sense of abandonment, in the feeling that our countrymen had forgotten us and were not coming to the rescue. It was not till we were rescued and looked in human faces that we felt how hungry we were." [6] In the presence of Christ the spiritual needs and longings of the heart awaken. We learn what it is we ought to pray for, with the assurance that such prayers will be answered. We realize that life does not consist in the possession and enjoyment of material things.

This does not mean that our material hopes will not be fulfilled. Jesus promised that if we seek first the kingdom of God all that we need will be added. The material blessings of life and the peace, freedom, and happiness for which we naturally long, because we need them, are by-products. They are found in their fullness only when we cease to set our hearts upon them and seek to know and to do the will of God as Christ reveals it. In this sense also the promises of God are fulfilled through him.

20*b*. *That Is Why We Utter the Amen Through Him, to the Glory of God.*—When we know the things Christ offers they are seen so clearly to be the fulfillment of our hopes that they become the substance of our prayers. The complete fulfillment is still beyond us; but in Christ we see the road to it. We consent to all he asks and offers. We know that our life is fulfilled according as God is glorified in us.

21-22. *But It Is God Who Establishes Us with You in Christ.*—The logical connection between these words and the preceding verses is not easy to trace, but it emerges when we remember that what set Paul speaking of the faithfulness of

[6] George Adam Smith, *The Book of Isaiah* (New York: A. C. Armstrong & Son, 1902), I, 442.

22 Who hath also sealed us, and given the earnest of the Spirit in our hearts.

22 he has put his seal upon us and given us his Spirit in our hearts as a guarantee.

is stable and reliable. **In Christ,** God has established both Paul and his fellow workers, so the Corinthians should know that God directs his decisions and even his changes in plans. **Anointed** (KJV) has the same Greek root (χρίω) as the word Christ. It seems used here of the leaders, including Paul, as anointed for special service, **commissioned** (RSV); if taken of all Christians, as is the word from the same root in I John 2:27, it would mean "consecrated" (Moffatt) and empowered for Christian living.

22. The **seal** may well be here, as it was later in the church, a reference to baptism, by which the believer was marked as God's own and accepted under God's protection. At the time of baptism God gave the Christians the Holy Spirit as the **earnest** (KJV) or **guarantee** (RSV) of the full and final salvation which the loyal believer might confidently expect. The term **guarantee,** used also in 5:5, was taken from commercial life. It meant the down payment by which the purchaser bound himself to complete the payment of

God was the charge of fickleness. He is not fickle whom God establishes and directs. The apostle had experienced in his own life and spirit the fulfillment of God's promises in Christ. So had they. The certainty of salvation and of sonship is not reached by argument. We cannot climb into spiritual conviction by any ladder of logic; it is an experience born through the revelation to us of his love, as we become conscious of the beauty of a sunset or of a great poem through the impact of their loveliness. It is God himself who establishes us. It is his action through Christ upon our souls that makes us sure of him, and creates in us the steadfastness of true disciples. It is his hold of us, not ours of him, that makes us trustful and worthy of trust.

This thought of the divine hand reaching down and grasping him was to Paul as real as if it were the hold of a human arm thrown out to arrest him on some dangerous road. The grip of that hand was an unforgettable experience. In it was the assurance of a love that would never let him go. This is the ground of our confidence. In this world we are exposed to the pressure of evil forces, and to the ebb and flow of feeling in our own hearts. We may lose all sense of the love of God for a time. The great mystics have much to say about the "black night of the soul." But our lack of feeling does not affect the reality of God's love. Our grasp may slacken; his never does. If our desire to know him remains, if there remains even the sense of spiritual loss in not knowing him, we can be sure that the contact with him is unbroken. In the vision of his unfailing love the spark of faith can be rekindled. It is always God who establishes us in our sonship to him.

But God had not only established Paul in the faith; he had given him his commission as an apostle. From this Paul draws his authority, though this authority is not the mere right to impose his own ideas on his hearers, or to dictate their conduct. It is the authority of the Spirit, and the Spirit does not dictate. He persuades; he reveals the truth which brings its own conviction; he subdues by the power of goodness and love.

The Exeg. points out that the words **seal** and **guarantee** were borrowed from the phraseology of a commercial transaction; the buyer pays a deposit on the transaction as a guarantee of the bargain and of the future payment in full. R. H. Strachan suggests that involved also is the idea that the vendor guarantees the quality of the goods and stamps them to ensure their safety in transit.[7] It is possible that some such thoughts were in Paul's mind and would be familiar to his readers, accustomed as they were to commercial practice. The anointing of the **Spirit** was undoubtedly the assurance to Paul of his own apostleship. How could he know? How can any man be sure that he has been "anointed by the Spirit"? Not by any surge of emotion which takes control so that men are no longer in command of their words or actions. Paul always insists that the spirit has to be tested to make sure that it is the Spirit of Christ. These tests are ethical. The power of the Spirit is the power of goodness. The possession of the Spirit can be tested by asking if the action that suggests itself is one that Christ would have us take. Is it in line with his command or his purpose? Are we, through what we claim to be the guiding of the Spirit, becoming more like Christ? "The fruit of the Spirit is love, joy, peace . . ." (Gal. 5:22).

When Paul applied these tests to himself, he could claim the anointing of the Spirit. It was clear to him that his experience on the Damas-

[7] *The Second Epistle of Paul to the Corinthians* (London: Hodder & Stoughton, 1935; "Moffatt New Testament Commentary"), p. 59.

23 Moreover I call God for a record upon my soul, that to spare you I came not as yet unto Corinth.

23 But I call God to witness against me — it was to spare you that I refrained

the full price agreed upon. So God, in giving the Spirit at the start of the Christian life, has bound himself to give all the other blessings that belong to complete and permanent salvation (cf. Rom. 8:32). Paul here implies that since he is thus established and supported by God, he cannot justly be charged with fickleness.

3. The Purpose: To Avoid Another Painful Visit (1:23–2:4)

23. Paul now explains why he did not carry out the plan of vs. 16. Had he come as planned, it would have been another painful visit (2:1); the Corinthians were still opposing him, and strong disciplinary action would have been required. (Even that might have failed, but Paul does not consider that possibility.) By delay he gave them opportunity to repent. Thus **to spare** them he did not "come again" (neither **came not as yet** in the KJV nor **refrained from coming** in the RSV properly translates οὐκέτι ἦλθον).

cus road had changed him. Pride had been replaced by humility, intolerance by love and forbearance, and self-centered ambition by a Christ-centered passion for the souls of men. True humility does not mean denying the qualities we possess. It accepts these with gratitude as coming from God, gives him the glory, and seeks his grace to use them for him.

The final test is that of our influence on others. Does it produce in them the desire to know God, to be faithful followers of Jesus Christ? Do spiritual values become more real and the material values of less importance through our presence? Is the church we serve a living plant which is propagating its own life?

The seal or stamp was no doubt associated in Paul's mind with baptism, as the Exeg. suggests. Though baptism had profound significance, it had no magical efficacy. It was an act through which God manifested to him his grace and love, and to which it was his part to respond. As James Denney says, God had marked him as his own. It did not make the change, but it marked the change from the old life to the new, that process which Paul describes as "a new creation" (5:17). It seals God's covenant with us into an indissoluble bond.

The gift of the Spirit is also an **earnest** of more to come. It is a **guarantee** which God will implement. It is the title deed to future inheritance, the seed from which will spring the flower of an immortal life. "We have been born," says Peter, "to an inheritance which is imperishable, undefiled, and unfading" (I Peter 1:3, 4). Eternal life is not merely a life into which we are introduced by death; it is a new quality of life into which we are born through the Spirit, and which we possess here and now. This conviction with regard to the ethical quality of what we know as eternal life corrects loose views which regard the life beyond as a mere extension of the life we now know in this material world. It is little wonder that with such views many people find the prospect of life after death tedious and futile. Without the sense of divine purpose, the vision of service, the deepening of love which come through fellowship with Christ, time withers the zest for life. Without the gift of the Spirit, immortality is apt to become both incredible and undesirable.

23-24. *I Call God to Witness.*—From the mountain view Paul here returns to the matter that had provoked the charge of fickleness—his change of plans to visit Corinth. The explanation he gives reveals the outlook and spirit that lie at the center of a true pastoral relationship. It was not for his own sake primarily that he had refrained from coming to Corinth; it was to spare them pain. That this is the truth he calls **God to witness.** His conscience is open to the most penetrating light of God's judgment. Without this no man can be sure he is speaking the truth. Otherwise we may say what is pleasant, or convenient, or merely what we would like to believe or would like others to think we believe, or what is merely a reflection of mass opinion. The preacher's answer to the unspoken desire of his hearers to be told only what they want to hear must always be that of Micaiah, "As the Lord liveth, what the Lord saith unto me, that will I speak" (I Kings 22:14).

In vs. 24 we have one of those parenthetical flashes that are struck from Paul's mind like sparks from an anvil. It declares his respect for the freedom of his fellow Christians even while he is trying to convince them. He does not **lord it over** [their] **faith,** but works with them **for** [their] **joy,** because they also stand fast in the faith. This is a crucial statement. It reveals his view of the use of his authority as a teacher

24 Not for that we have dominion over your faith, but are helpers of your joy: for by faith ye stand.

from coming to Corinth. 24 Not that we lord it over your faith; we work with you for your joy, for you to stand firm in your

This delay in the visit to give time to repent is mentioned also in 13:2, 10, which probably belong to the "stern letter." The attack upon Paul's sincerity has been so strong that here again, as in 1:18, he puts himself on oath; he calls God **to witness against** him and punish him if he is lying.

24. The word **spare** in vs. 23 might sound domineering. To prevent misunderstanding, Paul promptly disclaims any power or desire to **lord it** over his readers. Their Christian life rests upon **faith,** which cannot be forced, but is free trust. The "false apostles" who came to Corinth did indeed act arrogantly (11:20), but Paul respects his converts, and he and his helpers act as fellow workers with the Corinthians, to give them **joy.** He has had to pain them in order to bring them to their senses, but his deep and ultimate purpose has always been to help them find full joy in faith. It is **by** their **faith,** not by external dictation and control, that they **stand.**

---

and a leader, his conception of the freedom of Christian men, and the method and aim of his work.

His authority cannot be used to impose either his will or his doctrine, however right and sound these may be. A Christian minister has the right to speak in the name of the church by reason of his ordination to office after his training in theology and because of his call by a congregation. All these are regarded as essential to a minister's qualifications. But the only power that can be exerted by him for the guidance of his people and for their growth in Christian character and knowledge is his own insight into truth, his own disciplined character, his own heart of love, and such grace as the Spirit of God alone can supply. To impose truth upon others instead of awakening their apprehension of it is to **lord it over** [their] **faith.** It is to treat them as things and not as persons. A truly personal relationship and attitude to those in his care is the only medium for the pastor's work. It involves the recognition of the fact that people have minds and consciences of their own. They can accept as true and right only what they themselves see to be true and right. The sole power which Jesus sought and used in his ministry was the power of truth and love. In the Temptation he deliberately rejected all the external means commonly used to influence people—the appeal to appetite, to love of sensation, and to force.

The Christian believer has his rights to freedom as a Christian man. To **stand firm in** [the] **faith** means that he has been born by faith into sonship with God. He is entitled therefore to judge of the truth which is preached or taught him, to use his own insight: in other words, to think things out for himself. It is this right of private judgment which is denied by those who find the seat of authority in an infallible church or in an infallible Book. Private judgment is liable to error, but it is a risk that must be taken for the sake of freedom; without it no one can come to maturity of mind or character. In spiritual as in political matters, authoritarian rule is fatal to the growth of personality.

The true minister co-operates with people, as Paul says, in the search for truth. He must induce them to think with him. Jesus employed this method. In reply to questions he would often give no direct answer, but would himself put a question, or would tell a story from which his hearers could draw their own conclusions. It is the same in matters of conduct. He laid down no rules; he set down principles that demanded thought and forced men to choose, even at the risk of making a mistake. It is in this co-operation that we find the joy of Christian living, just as the joy of work is found when masters and men are seeking together a common objective.

Joy is a word that constantly recurs in the N.T. It is hard to define. It can coexist with sorrow. "As sorrowful, yet always rejoicing" (6:10). It is the condition of mind in which our powers are so absorbed in some creative task that we are set free from self-concern. Craftsmen are happy when their skill is employed in making something useful or beautiful. The deepest source of joy is found through tasks in which we are one with the creative will of God, and are in tune with his Spirit. The opposite of joy is not sorrow; it is sin, which breaks the harmony between us and one another, and between us and God. Joy cannot be found by seeking it. It is a by-product of self-forgetful activity. It is a fruit of the Spirit, not an artificial compound of pleasurable excitements or sense stimuli. The church should be the center

2 But I determined this with myself,
that I would not come again to you in
heaviness.
2 For if I make you sorry, who is he then
that maketh me glad, but the same which
is made sorry by me?
3 And I wrote this same unto you, lest,
when I came, I should have sorrow from
them of whom I ought to rejoice; having
confidence in you all, that my joy is *the joy*
of you all.

2 faith. 1 For I made up my mind not to
make you another painful visit. 2 For
if I cause you pain, who is there to make
me glad but the one whom I have pained?
3 And I wrote as I did, so that when I
came I might not be pained by those who
should have made me rejoice, for I felt sure
of all of you, that my joy would be the joy

2:1. Paul delayed his visit because he did not want to visit them again "in grief." His first visit (Acts 18:1-18) was not "in grief." That long stay, though not without trials, was on the whole a very fruitful period. But when, after writing I Corinthians, he again visited Corinth to correct conditions there, he had been contemptuously treated (see Intro., p. 266). This second **painful visit** is also referred to in 12:14 and 13:1-2. At that time he had promised to return soon, before going to Macedonia. But later he decided to delay his return; this is the change of plan for which he was criticized and which he is now defending. He sent Titus to Corinth with the "stern letter," while he himself, waiting for conditions at Corinth to improve, took the long route to Corinth through Macedonia.

2. He could not face another **painful visit.** He could take no sadistic pleasure in disciplining those he loved. His joy could come only through their joy, their growth in faith and love. Should he grieve them by rebuke and discipline, there would be no one to gladden him. His life was linked with theirs in joy and sorrow.

3. When therefore he decided not to go, he **wrote** a stern letter instead. He wrote "this very thing," i.e., that to spare them he was delaying his visit (cf. 13:10). This letter caused pain to them because of the rebuke in it. It also pained him in the writing (vs. 4), but he thought this a lesser evil than to come at once. It let him avoid the grief of an

---

of the highest type of joy, which is fellowship in Christ among people fully consecrated to his purpose and responding to his love.

2:1-4. ***For I Made Up My Mind Not to Make You Another Painful Visit.***—The explanation lifts a curtain and lays bare the apostle's heart. To visit them would have given them pain, and would also have pained him. He would have had to say things which it would have hurt him to say and them to hear. It is not true that love is blind. It has penetrating insight into moral reality. Elsewhere Paul bids us speak the truth in love (Eph. 4:15). There is no other way of speaking it but in love, for there is no other way of seeing it. But it will sometimes wound him who speaks, as well as him who hears. If we find ourselves taking a secret pleasure in words that give pain, it means that we are deficient in love. Only love that feels the pain of another's wrongdoing can awaken repentance.

Those we love are part of our very selves. This is the burning core of a pastor's relationship to his people. Hence their sorrow is his sorrow, their joy is his joy. How bitter it had been to write what had been written, Paul now reveals. But he had had to write it, for the harmony which brings joy could be restored only through their recovery of a Christian mind. Appeasement is not peace. Peace can come only from a common allegiance to a Christian standard. The temptation to be content with a superficial peace must be resisted. To compromise with moral principles, to flatter those who take offense instead of opening their eyes to their pride, are the marks of the false prophet (Jer. 6:14). Genuine love cannot accept superficial solutions of troubles that disturb the church.

Paul's love for the church had nothing in it of self-interest. Love "seeketh not her own" (I Cor. 13:5). He had no mercenary motives, no love of power, no worldly ambition. He was primarily interested in people, not in ideas or in himself. The source of real authority lies very near the heart of love. Only the minister who truly cares about his people has power to help them. It was said of a minister who had small intellectual gifts, but whose preaching drew crowds, that his secret was the gift of making every member of his congregation feel his personal interest.

Love also gives confidence. Paul had faith that the Corinthians would feel what he felt. **I felt**

4 For out of much affliction and anguish
of heart I wrote unto you with many tears;
not that ye should be grieved, but that ye
might know the love which I have more
abundantly unto you.
5 But if any have caused grief, he hath
not grieved me, but in part: that I may
not overcharge you all.

of you all. 4 For I wrote you out of much
affliction and anguish of heart and with
many tears, not to cause you pain but to let
you know the abundant love that I have for
you.
5 But if any one has caused pain, he has
caused it not to me, but in some measure —
not to put it too severely — to you all.

---

unhappy meeting with those whose presence should give him a strong surge of Christian **joy.** Even as he wrote in rebuke and stern appeal, he wrote with **confidence;** he had not given up hope for their repentance and better understanding. He still expected them to realize, even though it had to come through rebuke and anguished appeal, that his **joy** was really their joy too, so that they could never find peace of soul until by their attitude they had restored to him that joy in his converts which was his deep satisfaction. This confidence back of his writing Paul also expressed to Titus, as the latter started to Corinth with the "stern letter" (7:14).

4. The **affliction, anguish of heart,** and **tears** were thus not the expression of despair, nor of mere wounded vanity, though Paul was deeply hurt. Both the sorrow and the severity in his letter expressed his **love** for his readers. Love must sometimes be stern, and this was such a time; but the love was in control. His **abundant love** for them does not mean that he loved other churches less, but that his love went out more actively and with deeper concern to meet the greater need of this immature and rebellious church.

4. Paul Freely Forgives the Punished Offender (2:5-11)

5. Only now do we get partial information concerning the trouble at Corinth. A church member, prompted by intruders hostile to Paul (11:4, 20), had led a revolt against him which the apostle interprets as an affront to the entire Corinthian church. The offender cannot have been the immoral man of I Cor. 5:1; of such a situation Paul could not have written (vs. 9) that his only interest was in obedience to himself. If the ringleader was a spokesman for the Christ party (10:7; I Cor. 1:12), the situation had changed since Paul wrote I Corinthians, for the opposition against Paul is now concentrated in one party with one outstanding opponent. All that is clear is that after writing I Corinthians, Paul was attacked and insulted by an assertive Corinthian, quite probably at the time Paul visited the church to quell the revolt. Though this undoubtedly **caused pain** to Paul, he glossed over that fact to make the readers see that the troublemaker's greatest offense had been against their own church; he had done immense damage to their Christian life, and involved them in a wrong to Paul. They have now come to feel deep regret for what had happened (7:8-11); so he speaks tactfully. But he feels he must recall

---

sure of all of you. He gives them credit for the best, and makes them feel that he expects it. This faith in people has a powerful appeal.

Love had burned in all that Paul had written. The fire of his indignation had been kindled by love. He had hoped that they might see this and read in it a message to their hearts. He speaks now of writing **out of much affliction and anguish of heart and with many tears.** This is the language of a broken heart, not of a wounded pride. His concern here was not to establish his reputation, but to recover them to fellowship with him through a real repentance. This is the love that shines from Calvary, and we can receive it only from Christ.

5. ***But If Any One Has Caused Pain, He Has Caused It Not to Me.***—The insult offered to Paul is not a personal matter, and Paul refuses to deal with it on personal grounds, however much he himself has suffered. His concern is always for the church, the body of Christ. Sin is antisocial. Like some physical disease, it does more than cause pain at one particular point; it weakens and infects the whole body. In the church the wrong that one Christian does to another cannot be circumscribed. Like a stone dropped into a pool, it sends disturbing waves through the whole mass. It creates disunity; it may divide the church into parties. Above all, it weakens the witness of the church and blocks

6 Sufficient to such a man *is* this punishment, which *was inflicted* of many.

7 So that contrariwise ye *ought* rather to forgive *him,* and comfort *him,* lest perhaps such a one should be swallowed up with overmuch sorrow.

6 For such a one this punishment by the majority is enough; 7 so you should rather turn to forgive and comfort him, or he may be overwhelmed by excessive sorrow.

---

that the ringleader has at least **in some measure** troubled **you all.** He puts it mildly (**not to put it too severely**) so as not to stir up past irritation. He does not name the offender; he and the readers both knew who it was.

6. Brought to their senses by the "stern letter" and by Titus' appeal, the church had acted vigorously to clear themselves (7:11) and had punished the rebel. **This punishment** Titus had reported; Paul does not say what it was, but cf. I Cor. 5:11; II Thess. 3:14; it was something less than I Cor. 5:5 proposed for the immoral man. **The majority** imposed it. This does not mean that a minority remained rebellious; 7:15 excludes that. Vss. 6-8 suggest rather that some, friends of Paul, favored a still more severe penalty, arguing that blatant rebellion called for extreme severity. Paul checks this move: severity has no point in itself; his interest is in the obedience of the church (vs. 9) and in the attitude of the offender. The penalty has expressed the obedience and made the offender repent; so it is **sufficient.** The welfare of others, not his own pride, is Paul's concern.

7. Now that the offender has repented, free forgiveness and brotherly encouragement are in place. The Greek expresses this strongly. It does not say that **you should . . . forgive;** it states as a fact that you do. In such a situation, where repentance has appeared, you naturally **forgive** and **comfort** (this includes encouragement). Here is the inevitable Christian response. Paul lays stress on it because he has heard through Titus that the

---

the channel through which the Holy Spirit works.

6-10*a*. *For Such a One This Punishment by the Majority Is Enough.*—Paul does not say who the offender was. This reticence is part of the forgiveness for which he now pleads. Forgiveness may not bring forgetfulness, but it takes the sting out of bitter memories. The passage describes the action of church discipline upon an offending member up to his full restoration to fellowship.

The first thing Paul observes is that the punishment meted out to the offender has been effective. The church has not only taken a moral stand, but has expressed it in a definite judgment on the offender. This judgment has produced in him an awakened conscience. It has made him aware of the reality of his offense against love. Such deep contrition has come upon him that there is danger of its passing into hopeless remorse.

Here is the effect that must always be sought in any action by the church against an offender, whatever the nature of his offense. Our judgments of others avail nothing for their reformation unless they are brought to self-judgment. This is not easily achieved. Church discipline of a formal sort is largely a thing of the past. The judgment of the church is now generally exercised by a public opinion which delegates to one or two members, or to the minister, the task of dealing with the offender, and of endeavoring to bring him to a sense of his sin. But the prerequisite for this way of handling the situation, if it is to be effective, is that it should be the expression of a sound conscience in the church. The Christian church should have a continual power of self-purification. But it can have this power only if its own conscience is so open to the full light of Christ that it maintains the spirit of contrition which delivers it from self-righteousness. Bunyan's attitude to his own judgment of others is fundamental. "I went myself in chains, to preach to them in chains; and carried that fire in my own conscience, that I persuaded them to beware of." [8] Nothing so surely produces such conviction of sin in another as the confession by us of our own sin. The self-righteous tone or spirit provokes resistance. "Judge not," said Jesus, "that you be not judged" (Matt. 7:1). All judgment to be effective must bring men face to face with Christ. If the church "lived under the Cross," formal discipline would scarcely be needed.

But conviction of sin is only the first step in redemption. The next step is the restoration to fellowship for which Paul pleads. Forgiveness in the full Christian sense has a deeper meaning than the word usually carries. It was one of the

[8] *Grace Abounding,* par. 277.

8 Wherefore I beseech you that ye would confirm *your* love toward him.

9 For to this end also did I write, that I might know the proof of you, whether ye be obedient in all things.

10 To whom ye forgive any thing, I *forgive* also: for if I forgave any thing, to whom I forgave *it,* for your sakes *forgave I it* in the person of Christ;

8 So I beg you to reaffirm your love for
him. 9 For this is why I wrote, that I might
test you and know whether you are obedient
in everything. 10 Any one whom you forgive, I also forgive. What I have forgiven,
if I have forgiven anything, has been for

---

offender, deeply grieved, is in danger of despair; the apostle wants the issue of this **sorrow** to be "repentance that leads to salvation" (7:10).

8. The actual decision to restore the offender Paul leaves to the church, but he earnestly pleads for that action. Note two points: their action is not to be merely formal, but is to spring out of real Christian **love** for the forgiven rebel; but it must have clear outward expression, so that the repentant man will plainly see that in act they **confirm,** outwardly show and express, their love for him.

9. They have shown the obedience he had asked (cf. 10:6). At the time of rebellion Paul had had to make the offender a test case; the health of the church could be restored only by their obedience to his demand that they punish the man. He **wrote** the "stern letter" to **test** them; the test case, if rightly met, would lead them to be **obedient** to him **in everything.** On this point he is now completely satisfied (7:11-16).

10. Here, as in vs. 5, Paul minimizes the offense against himself; he even speaks as if it were doubtful whether he had **anything** to **forgive.** As in vs. 8, he leaves the actual decision to the Corinthians. **For your sake,** he says, **I have forgiven** freely. Because he

---

words which Jesus used and transformed. It does not mean merely the cancellation of a debt, or the showing of kindness to one who has wronged us. It means the effort to restore to fellowship one who has broken it. Paul uses the words **forgive and comfort.** The danger of deep contrition is that a man may be **overwhelmed by excessive sorrow.** The sense of sin may turn to remorse, the hell of self-torture of which Nathaniel Hawthorne gives such a vivid picture in *The Scarlet Letter,* where he reveals the effects upon a convicted sinner of the rigid judgment of a self-righteous society. Modern psychiatry has discovered the prevalence of a morbid sense of guilt, created in some cases by living continually in the atmosphere of blame; but psychiatrists have not always known how to set people free from this without depriving them of moral standards.

The Christian fellowship has the secret. It can mediate the forgiveness of God by the love and humility with which it restores an offender to fellowship in the fullest sense of the word. There is often no other way in which the divine forgiveness can become real. The penitent who comes back to the fellowship and is received with coldness or constraint may well feel, and often does, that the gates of the kingdom have been closed against him. The timid flower of hope may be frosted and the soul be permanently overcome by cynicism or despair. The church has the key to sin's prison house. It can either open the door, or keep the door locked. This is the real meaning of Christ's words to the disciples after the Resurrection, "If you forgive the sins of any, they are forgiven; if you retain the sins of any, they are retained" (John 20:23). The forgiveness of God is revealed and becomes a redeeming power through the depth and reality of our forgiving love.

Such is the challenge which Paul puts up to the Corinthians. Will they rise to it? It will be a test of their loyalty to him, and of the extent to which his authority, the nature of which he has already described, has power to produce the response in them of free obedience. The assurance that he will forgive anyone whom they forgive does not mean that his forgiveness is dependent on theirs. It is the assurance that he has no personal resentment.

10*b*. *What I Have Forgiven Has Been for Your Sake.*—Paul will allow no grudge of his own to endanger a human soul or mar the unity of the church. But wider issues are involved than the restoration of a wrongdoer to fellowship. The power of evil is very subtle and is always seeking a loophole for attack on the Christian faith. Paul does no more than to imply

11 Lest Satan should get an advantage of us: for we are not ignorant of his devices.

12 Furthermore, when I came to Troas to *preach* Christ's gospel, and a door was opened unto me of the Lord,

your sake in the presence of Christ, [11] to keep Satan from gaining the advantage over us; for we are not ignorant of his designs.

12 When I came to Tro'as to preach the gospel of Christ, a door was opened for me

---

always acts **in the presence of Christ,** he must act in the spirit of the gracious Christ, doing nothing from caprice or petty pride.

11. Paul forgives "lest we be defrauded by Satan," i.e., by Satan's capture of the despairing brother (vs. 7). This repentant man should be forgiven; it would be a loss to the church if his regret made him despair and left him open to Satan's wiles instead of leading him to hope and new life through the forgiveness and love of his Christian comrades. The danger from Satan is real; he is clever and crafty. The Christians already know this, for **we are not ignorant of his devices** or wiles. Knowing this, they must act promptly to forestall his attempt to gain possession of the sorrowing brother.

5. Paul Crosses to Macedonia to Seek Titus (2:12-13)

12. Paul nowhere tells a connected story of his recent plans and travels. He first planned to go from Ephesus through Macedonia to Corinth (I Cor. 16:5). Then he decided, while at Corinth on the painful visit, to come back there on his way to Macedonia (1:16). Further thought, after his return to Ephesus, led him to delay his visit to Corinth, to give them time to repent of their rebellion (1:23). So he returned to his original plan, sent the "stern letter" to Corinth by Titus, and traveled north from Ephesus toward Macedonia. Titus was to travel north from Corinth and east through Macedonia, and meet Paul somewhere along a prearranged route. **Troas** (full name, Alexandria Troas), a seaport on the northwestern tip of Asia Minor, was one place where the meeting might

---

one way in which the subtle power of the tempter works in such a case as this; other ways are obvious.

A disunited church provides the enemies of Christ with a first-class argument. Lovelessness and strife in a church mean either that the members do not accept the gospel they preach, or that the gospel has no power. Christians cannot expect the world to listen to their claim that the love of Christ can overcome all barriers and unite the nations if they themselves have obviously not been united by it. Such arguments against the Christian faith may not be sincere. They are too often used to excuse men's rejection of a faith which on deeper grounds they do not want to accept. But that is not always so. Simple people judge of a tree by its fruits, and to this Christ gave his authority (Matt. 7:16).

The devil also finds room for his wiles within ourselves in such a situation. Broken fellowship in the church is like an unhealed wound; it becomes the soil for infective germs. It offers a foothold for self-righteous pride. The spirit of evil challenges our sense of duty, our respect for moral standards. It suggests that these will suffer if wrongdoers are not punished. It represents moral indignation as a noble sentiment. It insists that forgiveness must not be made cheap; or that forgiveness will do no good, will only encourage the wrongdoer to repeat his wrongdoing. Hence we may do better to expel him from the church. These suggestions are all wiles of the devil. Moral indignation can easily turn into self-righteousness. To give up the effort of reconciliation is to turn our back on the way of Christ.

But more, the unforgiving mind is an unhealthy mind. Hate and resentment are really burdens that weigh upon our spirit as surely as the sin which is unforgiven. They bring their own reactions. We are unhappy, depressed, inhibited from wholehearted service, from obedience to God's will. Modern psychiatry throws light on this condition as well as on that of guilt. The unforgiving spirit can work as much havoc as the unforgiven sin. Bitter resentment can be as dangerous to harmonious living as black remorse. Forgiveness heals both him who gives and him who receives it.

12-14. ***When I Came to Troas.***—Paul takes up again the story which he had begun. In Troas he had found much encouragement, but could not settle down to reap a harvest because of his anxiety about the trouble in Corinth. His mind

13 I had no rest in my spirit, because I found not Titus my brother; but taking my leave of them, I went from thence into Macedonia.

in the Lord; [13] but my mind could not rest because I did not find my brother Titus there. So I took leave of them and went on to Mac-e-do'ni-a.

---

have taken place. Wherever Paul went he preached the gospel; so he says that he **came to Troas** "for" (εἰς), i.e., **to preach the Gospel** of salvation through Christ. People were ready to listen; **a door was opened** (cf. Acts 14:27; I Cor. 16:9; Col. 4:3; these passages make it clear that it is God who opens the doors by providing a favorable situation and opening men's hearts and minds to listen). **In the Lord** seems to mean in his service.

13. The natural thing would have been for Paul, with his strong evangelistic fervor, to seize the opportunity and give himself wholeheartedly to building a strong church in Troas. Some of the Christian group pictured in Acts 20:7-12 were no doubt converted at this time, although Paul could have won his first converts in Troas on the earlier visit of Acts 16:8. But he was too concerned to meet Titus at the earliest possible moment to remain in Troas long. His **mind could not rest;** it found no release from the tension and anxiety that the Corinthian crisis was causing him. So he crossed **to Macedonia** to meet Titus the sooner. This persistent concern for the spiritual welfare of the Corinthians should banish from their minds the idea that Paul acted out of fickleness. He thought and prayed constantly for their welfare; his plans and movements were controlled by his love and concern for them.

At this point Paul seems ready to tell of the joyful meeting with Titus somewhere in Macedonia, and of his delight at the good news Titus brought. The outburst of thanks in vs. 14 shows that the good news came. But Paul does not tell of it until 7:5-7.

---

was divided, and at last he turned his steps toward Macedonia. His departure for Macedonia was evidence of his anxiety, not proof of his supposed vacillation (see on 7:2-7).

Titus eventually met Paul and relieved all his anxieties, though Paul does not mention the meeting till later. The relief was so great that he was overwhelmed with gratitude. The phrase translated **leads us in triumph** is capable of two meanings. That adopted in the RSV is taken from the spectacle of a Roman conqueror's triumph, where he enters Rome with his captives led behind him to give proof of his achievements. Their humiliation heightens his glory. It is God's triumph that Paul celebrates, the triumph he won through Christ. The changed atmosphere in the church at Corinth is a victory for God because it is a victory of the spirit of Christ. Freedom from resentment or bitterness is Christ's victory within us. We are made free by the mastery of his love. In the Christian life there are no victories that are not God's.

Yet God's victory, of course, is also our victory. The picture of these defeated captives dragged at the heels of some arrogant conqueror does not represent the Christian life, though there is truth in it. God's triumph in which we share is possible only through his conquest of us. It comes when we are forced to our knees in surrender to his love. That surrender comes through the judgment of God in which we see ourselves as we are, and pride and self-will are broken. This had happened to Paul. The experience of his conversion was never absent from his mind. There the pride in his own goodness which had sustained his resistance to the truth was shattered. In the light of the crucified Christ his lovelessness was laid bare. He was reduced to such despair that he fell to the ground in abject defeat and surrender, asking only, "Lord, what wilt thou have me to do?" (Acts 9:6.)

Naked I wait Thy love's uplifted stroke!
My harness piece by piece Thou hast hewn from me,
And smitten me to my knee;
I am defenceless utterly.[9]

He was a captive of Christ, as completely conquered as one in a Roman general's pageant of triumph. But in this captivity he found freedom. His real self was released in power to triumph over the evil that had once ruled his life. It is the Christian paradox that in bondage to Christ is the secret of freedom. When we yield our sword to him, we become conquerors through his love.

[9] "The Hound of Heaven," from *The Poems of Francis Thompson* (London: Burns Oates & Washbourne, 1913). Used by permission of Sir Francis Meynell, copyright owner.

14 Now thanks *be* unto God, which always causeth us to triumph in Christ, and maketh manifest the savor of his knowledge by us in every place.

14 But thanks be to God, who in Christ always leads us in triumph, and through us spreads the fragrance of the knowledge

---

The thought of how the turn of events at Corinth has vindicated him leads him to interrupt the narrative and discuss at length his ministry as Christ's apostle.

B. The Great Parenthesis: The Apostolic Ministry (2:14–6:10)

1. Thanks to God for Using Paul in the Ministry (2:14-17)

14. The good news Titus brought leads Paul to thank God (cf. 8:16) for his sovereign and gracious control of the apostle's life. In the Greek **to God** stands first, to emphasize where the credit and praise belong. **In Christ,** i.e., in union with him and in a life lived in his service, God **leads** the apostles **in triumph,** as victorious generals, parading in triumphal procession, led their captive foes chained to their chariots. So in all this missionary travel God is leading Paul, who in letter after letter gladly acknowledges that he is the prisoner (Philem. 1, 9) or servant (e.g., Rom. 1:1) of Christ his Lord. This idea that God and Christ control his life and travel is another answer to those who have thought his change of plans a sign of fickleness. But Paul's thought expands beyond the immediate situation; he is preparing to discuss his apostolic ministry in a broad way, and the words **always** and **everywhere** show he is thinking of his entire ministry. Perhaps he still thinks of the conqueror's procession, along whose route incense was released. So Paul, by his preaching, and the **knowledge** of God (or αὐτοῦ, **of him,** may mean "of Christ") which he gives by it, releases along the route of his travels the pleasant **fragrance** of tribute to God. In speaking of the fragrant smell Paul may also think of sacrificial incense and fragrance (cf. Rom. 15:16; Eph. 5:2) ; his mind often moves freely from one allusion to another as he writes. But the main thought is that his apostolic ministry has been one long triumphal procession of the victorious God, who in Christ has controlled and led him, and now has given another proof of this in the recent triumph of Paul over his foes at Corinth.

And even this is not all. Through us God **spreads the fragrance of the knowledge of him everywhere.** The surrendered life has a quality which is like the perfume that permeates the air from a flower that is crushed. This influence is hard to describe. Paul calls it a fragrance. Others have described it as a radiance. Walter Pater, picturing a congregation of early Christians in Rome, speaks of the singing:

> It was the expression not altogether of mirth, yet of some wonderful sort of happiness—the blithe self-expansion of a joyful soul in people upon whom some all-subduing experience had wrought heroically, and who still remembered, on this bland afternoon, the hour of a great deliverance. [Later he remarks on the expression on the faces of the worshipers.] As if some searching correction, a regeneration of the body of the spirit, had begun, and was already gone a great way, the countenances of men, women, and children alike had a brightness on them . . . —an amenity, a mystic amiability and unction.[1]

[1] *Marius the Epicurean* (London: Macmillan & Co., 1901), II, 72, 99-100.

This quality is found in those who are so conscious of the love of Christ that they are unconscious of themselves. It cannot be artificially produced; it is the reflection in us of God's Spirit. When Mary broke the box of costly ointment over the feet of Christ in self-effacing love "the house was filled with the fragrance of the ointment" (John 12:3). Goodness born of the love of Christ has the quality of peace and happiness which Jesus described in the Beatitudes. Robert Louis Stevenson spoke of it as "flowering piety." It appears when resignation has blossomed into the joy of accepting and doing God's will instead of merely submitting to sorrow or misfortune as fate, or when the judgment of God that lays us low becomes the means of the triumph of his grace. It is **the fragrance of the knowledge of him.** Its effect on others is to produce an experience of God. God is not revealed by argument, but by a quality of spirit which creates the capacity to feel and respond, as light awakens the eye to see. Nothing else will reach the hearts of men. Lives which lack

15 For we are unto God a sweet savor of Christ, in them that are saved, and in them that perish:
16 To the one *we are* the savor of death unto death; and to the other the savor of life unto life. And who *is* sufficient for these things?

of him everywhere.
15 For we are the aroma of Christ to God among those who are being saved and among those who are perishing,
16 to one a fragrance from death to death, to the other a fragrance from life to

15. The apostles, who preach the gospel that gives the fragrance of the knowledge of God, are here called the pleasant odor. It is the message rather than the man that gives the sweet **aroma,** and this message concerns Christ; so it is really the fragrance **of Christ.** Just as **to God** opened vs. 14, so here **of Christ** stands first with emphasis in the Greek clause; Paul continually seeks to drive home the truth that the gospel concerns the work and will of God, the saving action of Christ. It is not based on the human resources of the apostles; they point men to the divine source of redemption and moral power. In vs. 15*b* the illustration takes a startling turn. The perfume or incense of the gospel message produces quite different effects in those who hear it; vs. 16 will explain that. But now Paul states generally that the message is truly Christ's fragrance in all who hear it, whether they **are being saved** or **are perishing.** The present participles that designate these two groups (σωζομένοις, ἀπολλυμένοις) describe men who by their reaction to the gospel are shown to be on the way either to salvation or to ruin.

16. It is the same **fragrance** of Christ, the same message of his saving work; it is always an incense or tribute offered to God. But the results differ sharply. The prepositions **from**

serenity or grace have no attractive power. Only a faith which makes us happy in spite of adverse conditions can speak to the secret unhappinesss of those who are unreconciled to life or to God.

15-16*a*. *For We Are the Aroma of Christ to God.*—Like incense from an altar, **the aroma of Christ** (see Exeg.) rises to God from surrendered lives. It gives God satisfaction, as the writer to the Hebrews suggests: "Wherefore God is not ashamed to be called their God" (Heb. 11:16). In them God sees the fruit of his agelong purpose of redemption. To realize this deepens our sense of the importance of our loyalty to Christ. Christian lives are the one product in history which gives history its meaning. The value of a civilization may not properly be judged by art or architecture, or by the comfort and security it offers, but by the number and vitality of its Christian men and women. Political and social theories must be tested by the extent to which they encourage the growth of Christian character in freedom, co-operation, moral principle, and reverence for personality.

But as the aroma of incense during a triumphal procession spreads everywhere and has different effects on different people, e.g., on those who were about to die, and on those to whom victory meant life, so has the **sweet savor of Christ** varied results according to men's reaction to it. It makes good men better and bad men worse, just as light on an unhealthy eye may produce blindness, while to a healthy eye it brings greater illumination. The Christian spirit brings men to judgment. It awakens the conscience to moral realities. It brings human pride and all its superficial triumphs to the dust. Men may resist that judgment, or try to escape it, only to plunge the deeper into evil. They resist goodness and are hardened. Neglect of spiritual values, as well as deliberate rejection, dulls the spiritual sense. Charles Darwin confessed that he became insensitive to the music of Handel's *Messiah* through his absorption in science. The pursuit of money or material success has the same effect. We become blind and like the men in H. G. Wells's fantasy, "The Country of the Blind," are not aware that we are blind. This is what Paul means by death—the total loss of the spiritual sense. It is a tragic possibility. The final issue of moral choice is between life and death.

On the other hand, acceptance of God's judgment through the influence of the Christian spirit opens up to us his grace and forgiveness. The knowledge of God to those who receive it becomes a **fragrance from life to life.** Spiritual capacity grows by exercise. Vision becomes clearer by obedience. Christ becomes more and more to those who follow him. The reward of following him is thus a deeper understanding of his message and a greater freedom to obey it. The decisive point of Paul's own life was his obedience to "the heavenly vision" (Acts 26:19).

16*b*. *Who Is Sufficient for These Things?*—It is a responsible thing to be a Christian. There is no distinction between laity and clergy in this

17 For we are not as many, which corrupt the word of God: but as of sincerity, but as of God, in the sight of God speak we in Christ.

life. Who is sufficient for these things? 17 For we are not, like so many, peddlers of God's word; but as men of sincerity, as commissioned by God, in the sight of God we speak in Christ.

---

and **to** describe a process that is now confirmed and given impetus. The gospel finds one group on the way to ruin, spiritual **death;** their rejection of it sends them farther on the way. In the other group the message is welcomed, and so it helps them on the way to God's full gift of eternal **life.** Paul does not say how this happens, but only states the fact. The gospel confirms some in their sin; they reject it and become more hardened in wrongdoing. It finds in others a response that is the open door to immense blessings. That God's will and wisdom are back of this, Paul firmly believed; that men are responsible for their decision, he held equally firmly. But here he does not seek to balance the sovereignty of God, which to him is the basic fact, and man's responsibility, which is also true. He turns rather to a question which shows that to him it is a terrible responsibility to confront men with a message which either hardens them in sin or opens the way to life: How can any man dare to carry on a ministry that has such immense, eternal issues? **Who is sufficient . . . ?**

17. One might expect the answer: "No man." But Paul implies in this verse that the apostles are sufficient. Not in themselves, nor by their own resources (3:5); but Paul like every true apostle is **sufficient.** The **many,** i.e., the false apostles who have been troubling the Corinthians (11:13), are not. They are hucksters, **peddlers.** They think of personal advantage and profit (11:20); they adulterate **God's word,** the message of salvation, to suit their interests (11:4); and so Paul applies to them the figure of the unscrupulous petty tradesman or peddler who thinks only of using every tricky means to make financial profit. In contrast, the ministry of Paul and his apostolic comrades

---

matter. All need love, insight, and the power to reflect without distortion the mind of Christ. The concern of all Christians must be to make sure that no one is turned away because they misrepresent him. Our only safeguard is complete humility and utter sincerity. Of this Paul goes on to speak.

17. ***For We Are Not, Like So Many, Peddlers of God's Word.***—Peddlers are petty merchants who sell their wares from door to door. But here there is the connotation of dishonesty. The apostle is thinking of men who use cunning to persuade people to buy cheap or adulterated goods. They are not concerned either with the quality of the goods or with the real interests of their customers. Some preachers are only clever salesmen, doing good business for themselves. Their stake in the truth they preach is not the good of their hearers, but the advancement of their own reputation. Paul insists that the preacher must be sincere, without mixed motives, seeking no personal gain. He cares only for the reputation of Christ. He must be a channel of truth, not an exhibitionist who puts himself in the forefront. He will present the truth unadulterated by specious ideas of his own, by political bias, or mere patriotic enthusiasms. He will not appeal to the self-interest of his hearers, but to their interest in the kingdom of God. Robert Louis Stevenson quotes an entry from Pepys's diary and comments on it,

> "A good sermon of Mr. Gifford's at our church, upon 'Seek ye first the kingdom of heaven.' A very excellent and persuasive, good and moral sermon. He showed, like a wise man, that righteousness is a surer moral way of being rich than sin and villainy." It is thus that respectable people desire to have their Greathearts address them, telling, in mild accents, how you may make the best of both worlds, and be a moral hero without courage, kindness, or troublesome reflection; and thus the Gospel, cleared of Eastern metaphor, becomes a manual of worldly prudence, and a handy-book for Pepys and the successful merchant.[2]

Only a preacher's utter sincerity with truth will deliver him from unworthy motives, and from the self-consciousness, the timidity, the doubt and the discouragements that spring from self-concern. He must do his work **in the sight of God.** Integrity with truth can come in no other way. To know that God is looking on will keep us from "handling the word of God deceitfully" (4:2).

[2] *Familiar Studies of Men and Books* (New York: Charles Scribner's Sons, 1904), p. 300.

3 Do we begin again to commend ourselves? or need we, as some *others*, epistles of commendation to you, or *letters* of commendation from you?

2 Ye are our epistle written in our hearts, known and read of all men:

3 Are we beginning to commend ourselves again? Or do we need, as some do, letters of recommendation to you, or from you? 2 You yourselves are our letter of recommendation, written on your[c] hearts,

[c] Other ancient authorities read *our*.

---

stands the test; they can be trusted with the life-and-death issues of the gospel. (*a*) They are sincere; integrity and loyalty to God rule their motives and methods. (*b*) They are sent **by God** and have their message from him. (*c*) They give their Christian witness knowing that they speak in God's presence and so are known to him and responsible to him. (*d*) They **speak in Christ;** their lives are linked with his, and they do their work in his spirit and with the power God gives through him.

3. The Corinthians Are Paul's Letter of Recommendation (3:1-3)

3:1. In 2:17 Paul asserts his integrity in the apostolic ministry. Before going on, in 3:4-6, to further discussion of his competence for that ministry, he answers the charge that he is merely an egotistical braggart who delights to recommend himself (**we** here means Paul). Such a charge is not new; **again** indicates that previous statements of his had evoked the same accusation. This probably refers not to I Corinthians, but to the "stern letter" in which he had defended himself. If chs. 10–13 are part of that letter, as seems probable, such passages as 10:8; 11:16-29; 12:1-6 show how the charge could have arisen. We need not assert that Paul, who was but human, always kept completely free from pride. But vicious attacks on him had forced him to defend his record, as he does again in 4:2; 6:4 ff. Had he not done so, his leadership and his gospel would have been disowned, and the Corinthians, even more than he, would have been the losers. The second question of vs. 1 is a partial answer to the first. In dealing with the Corinthians, Paul, whose work and love for them they know so well, surely does not need, as outsiders do, to bring **letters of recommendation. Some,** i.e., the "many" of 2:17, who seem to be the same as the "false apostles" of 11:12-13, 22-23, evidently did bring such letters to Corinth. Being outsiders with no claim on that church, they had reason to do so, but Paul needs no such testimonials. Moreover, the traveling leaders seem to have asked for letters **from** the Corinthians to other places. Why Paul does not need such letters vs. 2 explains.

2. Instead of a written **letter of recommendation** from the church at Corinth, this active and well-known church is itself all the recommendation Paul needs. He was God's human instrument in converting the Corinthians and founding that congregation, and

---

The true preacher has a sense of being **commissioned by God.** The great prophets were reluctant to preach when God's call came to them. Moses and Jeremiah felt they had neither the power nor the capacity to declare God's word (Exod. 4:10; Jer. 1:6). Isaiah, confronted with the vision of God, felt that his lips were unclean. He was not fit to be God's messenger. Only when God had cleansed his lips with fire from the altar did he consent to his call (Isa. 6:5-8). Confidence and power come when the reluctance produced by a sense of unworthiness is overcome by the irresistible call of God.

Last of all, Paul says that he speaks **in Christ.** The phrase has the force of an adjective. It means the state of the soul which is rooted in Christ, as the plant is rooted in the soil from which it draws its life. It reflects a condition of continual dependence on Christ, and continual response to the moving of his Spirit. When Paul preaches, as when he lives, it is he himself who speaks, and yet not himself but Christ in him.

3:1-3. ***Are We Beginning to Commend Ourselves Again?***—The charge of self-commendation had already been flung at Paul by his opponents. In case they should be tempted to do this again he proceeds to forestall them. "A minister's character is the whole capital he has for carrying on his business, and . . . nothing can be more cruel and wicked than to cast suspicion on it without cause."[3] But the final commendation of his worth as a Christian minister is the quality of the lives which he has influ-

[3] James Denney, *The Second Epistle to the Corinthians* (New York: A. C. Armstrong & Son, 1899; "The Expositor's Bible"), p. 100.

3 *Forasmuch as ye are* manifestly declared to be the epistle of Christ ministered by us, written not with ink, but with the Spirit of the living God; not in tables of stone, but in fleshly tables of the heart.

to be known and read by all men; 3 and you show that you are a letter from Christ delivered by us, written not with ink but with the Spirit of the living God, not on tablets of stone but on tablets of human hearts.

---

all men, i.e., throughout the entire church, know how effective and fruitful his work was. This widespread favorable report means much more than a formal written recommendation of Paul. **Read** here continues the comparison with a letter of recommendation; actually, **known and read** means that others hear orally of Paul's work and know that the very existence and vitality of the Corinthian church are a high tribute to him. Paul never lets the demands of consistency keep him from saying what he considers important. So here he inserts **written in our hearts** (KJV), to express how deep and constant is his love and concern for the Corinthian Christians. His tie with them is not formal or transient, but personal, close, and marked by enduring love. The RSV, following a reading much less well supported by ancient MSS (ὑμῶν instead of ἡμῶν), reads **written on your hearts;** this would express the idea that the Corinthians have a deep and constant affection for Paul. But it is less likely that he is reminding them of that fact than that he is assuring them of his love for them.

3. Paul develops further his statement that the Corinthians are his **letter of recommendation.** It was **ministered by us,** i.e., by Paul primarily; throughout this passage it is doubtful whether **we** and **us** include his helpers or apostolic comrades. The Greek aorist participle which the KJV translates **ministered** (διακονηθεῖσα) centers attention on the time of the founding of the Corinthian church. The word carries out the figure of a letter by implying that Paul was the scribe who wrote down the **letter** at the dictation of **Christ,** whose letter the church really is. Possibly the word includes the idea that the letter was **delivered** (RSV) by Paul, since he brought the gospel to Corinth. But before they had believed, the Corinthians were not Christians, and so were not a letter of Christ; thus the meaning seems to be not that he brought the gospel to their city, but that in preaching and converting them Paul was the scribe or agent of Christ, who was the "author" of their salvation. That their Christian faith and position are due not to themselves, nor even to Paul, but rather to God, is expressed by the fact that they are a letter of Christ and were written by **the Spirit of the living God.** But he contrasts the Corinthians not only with letters **written . . . with ink** but also with the Mosaic **tablets of stone** containing the Commandments (Exod. 31:18). He refers to the Decalogue as the symbol of the entire law of God contained in the Scriptures. Of the law he intends to speak further, but before he closes the reference to the letters of recommendation, he points out that in contrast to the external code of the law, which was without vital power to

---

enced. Do they reveal the marks of the Christian spirit? Have people been brought out of darkness into light? The source of the Christian life is the new birth, and the real test of a minister's validity is the measure in which his ministry under God produces this miracle. This is a searching test.

Paul says that the Corinthian Christians themselves are his **letter of recommendation.** It has been written on their hearts, in the transformation which the Spirit of Christ had wrought and which was plain for all men to read (but see Exeg.). The difference Christ had made in them he describes in Gal. 5:19-24, where he contrasts the works of the flesh and the fruit of the Spirit.

He sought no other commendation. No other is valid. There is a quality in a genuinely Christian life which nothing but the power of Jesus Christ can explain. This had been revealed to Paul himself as he watched the dying of Stephen and felt the serenity and power of a forgiving spirit. Stephen's life at that point was a translation of the gospel, seen and read by Paul and resulting in his conversion.

In the case of the Corinthians it was Paul's hand which had written the epistle; but that hand was only the instrument of the Spirit. No preacher can claim to be more than a transmitter. His power depends on the measure in which he is subdued to the purpose of Christ, as the

4 And such trust have we through Christ to God-ward:

4 Such is the confidence that we have

redeem and renew life, the Spirit of the living God works in human hearts to produce not only inner renewal, but also outward obedience that other men can see. The idea of writing on the human heart goes beyond the comparison with a letter of recommendation; other men cannot see what is written on the heart. But Christian living has such deep inner roots in faith and dedication that Paul cannot neglect them. Moreover, there no doubt hovers in his thought the memory of the assuring promise of Jer. 31:33, that God would put his law "in their inward parts, and write it in their hearts." Because the Corinthians are living evidence of the fulfillment of that prophecy, they are an effective letter of recommendation for Paul.

3. The Superior Ministry of the New Covenant (3:4–4:6)

a) God Qualifies the Ministers of This Covenant (3:4-6)

4. The **confidence** Paul expresses refers primarily to the conviction just stated: since he, acting for Christ and by the power of the Spirit, has founded the church at Corinth, the very existence and vitality of this church is his letter of recommendation. But this

artistic quality of an artist depends on the measure in which his hand is the instrument of the creative spirit of beauty. But the members of the church have also their responsibility. To be a professing Christian is to offer our lives for others to read in them the message of the gospel. Every Christian life ought to be a translation of the gospel. There is no other way in which multitudes of those around us will read it. But if this is to happen, it must be written in **our hearts.**

The fact that every Christian life is itself a translation of the gospel—an epistle of Christ to be known and read—does not absolve the ordinary Christian from the duty of communicating his experience in conversation or teaching. The truth that it is the life that speaks must not be made an excuse for cowardly silence, nor for evading the responsibility which rests on all members of the church to spread the message of Christ. The church which is content to devolve its responsibility on a professional ministry is not in the full sense propagating its life and is therefore in danger of becoming sterile. E. F. Scott says:

> During the great age of expansion which followed the death of Paul we do not hear of the name of a single outstanding missionary. The real work was done by countless obscure men and women who made it their first duty to spread the message in their own circle of friends and neighbours. Along with the obligation to follow the gospel in one's own life Paul dwells on this other obligation to make it known.[4]

[4] *The Epistles of Paul to the Colossians, to Philemon and to the Ephesians* (London: Hodder & Stoughton, 1930; "Moffatt New Testament Commentary"), p. 253.

4-6. ***The Spirit Gives Life.***—A preacher must have **confidence** in the adequacy of his message and faith in its power. He cannot otherwise stand up to opposition from without and to the doubts that arise from lack of apparent results. Paul's spirit stood erect and firm, like a great tree amid drought and tempest, because his confidence was rooted in the activity of God. He was supported continually by the God who came to him through Christ. He had no confidence in himself apart from God. The qualifications for the ministry are all God-given. Natural gifts are gifts from him, and the full use of them is possible only as they are enriched and directed by the Spirit (I Cor. 12–13). The realization of our own insufficiency is the indispensable condition of the endowment. Whatever gifts we may be aware of possessing, we must realize that they are not of our merit but of his grace.

The word **covenant** belongs to the religious outlook and language of the O.T. It defined the relationship of the people of Israel with God. God and his people had made a covenant with one another in which God had taken the initiative: on his part it was a promise of guidance and protection which would lead at last to a great future for the nation in which all the earth would be blest; on Israel's part it was a pledge to obey God's commandments, which later took shape in the Jewish code. This was the old covenant which Paul had in mind when he spoke, by contrast, of the **new covenant.** It was **a written code** of laws which could be precisely understood. Obedience to it meant the fulfillment of regulations. It expressed the fact that this world is based on a moral order which is itself the expression of God's will. If that order, that will

5 Not that we are sufficient of ourselves to think any thing as of ourselves; but our sufficiency *is* of God;

6 Who also hath made us able ministers of the new testament; not of the letter, but of the spirit: for the letter killeth, but the spirit giveth life.

through Christ toward God. 5 Not that we
are sufficient of ourselves to claim anything
as coming from us; our sufficiency is from
God, 6 who has qualified us to be ministers
of a new covenant, not in a written code
but in the Spirit; for the written code kills,
but the Spirit gives life.

---

implies, as 2:16-17 suggested, that he is indeed sufficient and qualified for the apostolic ministry. To that thought he now turns, but not to boast of personal greatness. It is only **through Christ,** through what Christ has done for him and through the assurance he has as he lives in daily dependence on Christ, that he can have such confidence. The grace of Christ enables him to feel confident **toward God,** i.e., in the presence of God, to whom he is responsible and on whom he relies in all that he does.

5. What Paul implied in vs. 4 he now emphatically states. **We** (this practically means Paul here) **are sufficient** for this apostolic task, but **not . . . of ourselves,** i.e., not in our unaided human understanding and strength. We cannot consider or look upon **anything** in our Christian perception or competence **as coming from us.** The Greek in the first part of the verse is involved, but the general meaning is clear: Paul's grasp and mastery of his apostolic task find no explanation in his human resources. All the credit belongs to God. Just as in considering the origin of salvation Paul freely confesses that "all this is from God" (5:18), just as he has to acknowledge that "by the grace of God I am what I am," a forgiven sinner called to be an apostle (I Cor. 15:10), so here, in explaining his competence for his work, he must say: **Our sufficiency is from God.**

6. The idea of sufficiency, twice expressed in vs. 5, occurs again here, for the opening words, literally translated, are, "who also made us sufficient." When God called us into the Christian life and into his service as apostles, he **made us** competent and qualified to be **ministers.** His grace and gifts made us adequate for the exacting task (2:16*b*). The word **ministers** (διακόνους) does not refer to an order of officers in a constitutionally

---

of God, is flouted, we suffer. Health deteriorates, character degenerates, stamina is lost, life becomes purposeless.

But God in the O.T. is not merely a lawgiver. He is both merciful and gracious. The Psalms are full of the most tender and winsome pictures of him, e.g., Pss. 23; 103. The law was not regarded by a religious Jew as mere restraint. It captured his idealism, as the beauty of a mountain peak entrances the climber. "O how love I thy law!" is a note that echoes through the Psalms. Those who had come to know God as the great prophets reveal him felt that whatever he asked must be good, and however irksome his commands, it was a joy to accept them.

Yet the best spirits knew that complete obedience to rules was beyond them. With all their efforts they failed. In a flash of insight Jeremiah saw man's need of a new covenant in which the law would be written in the heart. This means that obedience to God would spring from insight into his will and love for him. The new covenant had been made in the coming of Christ. In it God offers a new relationship like that between father and son. It rests upon his forgiveness of us, but a forgiveness far deeper than the word usually implies. It is more than a clean sheet in which past transgressions are forgotten. It is a creative act of love. It produces repentance and surrender through which God's Spirit comes to dwell within us, giving us insight into God's will, and kindling love to him and to men. Through this love we are able to interpret and to do his will. The result is life, the liberation of the whole personality in union with him. This wholehearted service is perfect freedom because his will has become ours.

The change from the old to the new covenant is illustrated in Jesus' parable of the prodigal son (Luke 15:11-32). As a result of his self-will and disobedience, the son finds life turned against him. In loneliness and hunger he comes to himself, realizes that he is his father's son, and makes up his mind to go home. He asks for a place as a hired servant in which he can earn his living and be at peace with his father. Had the father accepted this, it would have been the old covenant, in which doing right is mere obedience to commands in return for food and shelter. But the father will not have the old covenant. That had already broken down. He proclaims a new covenant, throws his arms

organized church, but to those who serve God or act for him in response to his call. God's call gave Paul authority to act, but the church did not have as yet a formal organization or a rigidly fixed constitution. The apostles are **ministers of a new covenant** (RSV; the misleading English translation **new testament** in the KJV comes from the fact that the Greek διαθήκη, which everywhere in the N.T. except Heb. 9:16-17 means covenant, was translated into Latin by the word *testamentum,* which then was rendered into English by the word testament; our familiar phrases "Old Testament" and "New Testament" for the two parts of the Bible should be "The Old Covenant" and "The New Covenant"). A **covenant** in the Bible was not an agreement between equals. It was an arrangement offered by God for the benefit of his people, who accepted it in gratitude and promised in return to fulfill their prescribed duties. It was axiomatic that God would faithfully fulfill his promises, and that he had the right to reject or punish his people if they failed to do their part. The very making of such a covenant was an expression of God's gracious character; even behind the law is the grace of God, just as God redeemed his people from Egypt before he gave them the commandments (Exod. 20:2). But the "first covenant" (Heb. 9:18) made with Israel through Moses (Exod. 24:3-8) was not the full and final expression of God's will and purpose. It was set down in a **written code** (RSV). The KJV translation **letter** (γράμμα) is literally correct, but has often led to the quite erroneous idea that Paul here condemns the written form of teaching in contrast to free spiritual insight, or that he discards the literal meaning of scripture in favor of a free spiritual interpretation. For Paul the O.T. is scripture; he does not reject the written scripture or the literal meaning. He is speaking rather of the deadly effect of the written law, in contrast with the transforming effect of the gospel message, through which the living power of the Spirit of God acts to bring redemption and "newness of life" (Rom. 6:4) to those who believe. The written code of the Mosaic law stated man's duty and so made him answerable to God, but gave no power to obey, and so, since man was perverse and in the grip of evil desires, it alone could lead only to spiritual ruin; it **kills.** But now God has replaced the legal system of the old covenant with a **new covenant** (cf. Mark 14:24; I Cor. 11:25; Heb. 12:24). It was effectively inaugurated by the death and resurrection of Jesus Christ, and brought home to men not primarily by the preaching of the apostles, though that was necessary, but by the transforming work of **the** Holy **Spirit,** who **gives life** to believers. Note that the establishment of a new covenant means that Christ is the head of the reconstituted people of God, who accept and live under this covenant. The believer is not an isolated Christian; he lives in the people of God, in

---

around the prodigal's neck, and takes him right into the home with all the privileges of a son. In return he seeks only the son's trust and love. All the rest will follow from that relationship.

It is by his own experience of this new covenant of grace, as he elsewhere calls it, that Paul knows himself qualified of God to be a minister. He himself had been unable to keep the law. He had been impotent, broken, in despair. But the love of God in Christ that had revealed him to himself and brought his pride to ruins had come with a message of forgiveness, the free offer of God's fellowship, and a call into God's service. No man can preach the gospel who has not known that experience, however he may describe it.

Paul now elaborates the difference between the old and new relationship, the legal and the filial. It is the contrast between letter and spirit. **The written code kills, but the Spirit gives life.** This can be seen in work or in art. Mere slavish obedience to directions makes work mechanical. It turns a man into a machine, which is death. But work done from the love of it, with a mind that co-operates with the master's purpose, becomes craftsmanship in which the spirit lives and grows. If an artist is a mere copyist his work is lifeless, while he himself loses creative capacity. But if he has an eye for beauty and the passion to create it, his work is alive and his own power develops. If a man takes the words of the Bible woodenly, making no real contact with the mind of the writer, or with the truth he is expressing, Scripture becomes a dead letter, as we say, and kindles no light in the heart. Similarly, if religion is a matter of obedience to commandments and to rules, conduct becomes mechanical, without vital goodness. Conventional religion produces a blind conscience and a loveless heart. This is the nemesis of an external authority which imposes obedience, dictates beliefs, and coerces conscience. In the state it may produce

7 But if the ministration of death, written *and* engraven in stones, was glorious, so that the children of Israel could not steadfastly behold the face of Moses for the glory of his countenance; which *glory* was to be done away;

7 Now if the dispensation of death, carved in letters of stone, came with such splendor that the Israelities could not look at Moses' face because of its brightness, fad-

---

the church. For Paul, to become a Christian and to become a member of the church are one and the same thing.

b) The New Covenant Surpasses the Old in Splendor (3:7-11)

7. The contrast between the old order and the new, hinted at in vs. 3 and more clearly asserted in vs. 6, is now developed in detail. The section shows how radical a break Paul made with Pharisaic Judaism when he became a Christian. Note that by the law Paul means not merely the ceremonial features but the entire legal order of life established by the Pentateuch and embodied in Judaism.

Back of vss. 7-18 is the story in Exod. 34:29-35, according to which the face of Moses shone when he came down from Mount Sinai, so that in order to avoid frightening the people he put a veil on his face while he talked with them. This brightness soon faded from his face, as the story implies and later Jewish tradition explicitly stated. In this fact Paul sees a symbol of the truth that while the old covenant was indeed from God, it has now been superseded by the greater and permanent order of the new covenant that Christ has established. The old had its own splendor, but nothing to compare with the glory of the new, with its Spirit-led life of Christ's people.

The contrast is set forth in three parts, in vss. 7-8, 9-10, and 11. The "ministry" (διακονία), i.e., the **dispensation** or organized order of life under the law, is said to be one **of death** because, as vs. 6 has said, a "written code," without power to produce in man vital faith and obedience, "kills." As in vs. 3, the Decalogue, **carved in letters of stone**, is used as the symbol of the entire law, and indeed of the legal order of life. Back of **glorious** and **glory** in the KJV, and **splendor** and **brightness** in the RSV, is the Greek word δόξα. In the N.T. it usually means "praise," "honor," "glory," and is frequently used in reference to God. But the purity, majesty, and awful holiness of God were regarded in both the O.T. and the N.T. as expressed in brilliant, blinding, "unapproachable light" (I Tim. 6:16). So this Greek word was used in the Greek O.T. to express the "brightness," "splendor," associated with the presence of God. Angels were thought to share somewhat this brightness, and here Moses, who has talked with God, reflects that **brightness** on his face when he descends Mount Sinai; hence the people, perhaps less from blind terror than from awe because they saw in the brightness evidence of the divine presence, could

---

an ordered society, trimmed to a pattern of individual or social living; but the result is the death of human personality. It is the abolition of man.

There is more than this, however, in Paul's words, **the written code kills.** The effect of the law had been twofold. It had become an incitement to sin, suggesting or provoking the deeds which it forbade, as a thing may attract a child because it is forbidden. But its worst effect had been produced through man's inability to obey it, fastening on him a sense of guilt from which he could not find deliverance, and culminating in a sense of moral impotence which bound chains upon his soul. Paul himself had known this death-dealing experience: "Wretched man that I am! Who will deliver me from this body of death?" (Rom. 7:24.) Bunyan's pilgrim, to whom through the reading of the Bible the world has become a City of Destruction, is typical.

But the Spirit gives life. Through him we have power to become children of God (John 1:12). The soul is set free from the burden of guilt. We are brought by God himself into that right relationship with him which is the only righteousness we can ever know. The result is that we pass from death to life.

7-11. ***The Dispensation of Death.***—Paul has to admit that the dispensation under which the Israelites had lived before Christ came had its **splendor.** This is symbolized by the light which shone on the face of Moses when he came down

8 How shall not the ministration of the
spirit be rather glorious?
9 For if the ministration of condemnation *be* glory, much more doth the ministration of righteousness exceed in glory.
10 For even that which was made glorious
had no glory in this respect, by reason of
the glory that excelleth.

ing as this was, **8** why should not the dispensation of the Spirit be attended with greater
splendor? **9** For if there was splendor in the
dispensation of condemnation, the dispensation of righteousness must far exceed it
in splendor. **10** Indeed, in this case, what
once had splendor has come to have no
splendor at all, because of the splendor that

---

not look **steadfastly** at his face (ἀτενίσαι implies a steady gaze). The brightness indicates that the law was really given to Moses, and so to Israel by God; it was a divinely established order. Yet even as Moses spoke, the brightness was **fading** from his face; the present participle καταργουμένην speaks of a process going on at the very time he talked with Israel. Just so the legal **dispensation** itself had but a fading **splendor.**

8. The new order, established by the work of Christ, and vitalized by **the Spirit,** "gives life" instead of "death" (vss. 6-7). It is only natural, therefore, that it should be attended with still **greater splendor** than the old legal order had. In this verse **splendor** refers less to visible brightness (but cf. 4:6) than to the high spiritual privileges of Christian faith, worship, and life belonging to one led by the Spirit.

9. The second contrast is between the legal order and the new life in the Spirit: The old order made known God's will; it made man responsible; but it gave no power to break the grip of sin and live the life commanded; therefore it led only to **condemnation.** The new **dispensation** gives the free gift of **righteousness.** This word refers primarily to God's gracious justifying of the sinner on the basis of Christ's work; but since "the Spirit gives life" (vs. 6), there is probably the further suggestion that this righteousness is more than a legal acquittal and includes a moral vitalizing of the believer. The grace of God is also a gift of life-transforming power. Naturally so effective and beneficent a power as that of the Spirit surpasses in **splendor** the old order which ended in condemnation. Paul knew that there was grace and power in the O.T. period; but it did not come through the legal system as such. As Rom. 4 and Gal. 3:6-9 show, faith and forgiveness were the true way of life even then.

10. Literally: "For indeed that which has been given splendor has not been given splendor in this respect, by reason of the surpassing splendor"; i.e., though the old legal order had a real **splendor,** since it was given by God and reflected its divine origin, yet in comparison with the greater **splendor** of the new order, it does not seem to have any

---

from the mount with the tablets of stone on which the Ten Commandments were inscribed (Exod. 34:29). The Commandments inform the conscience and light up the moral world, so that the right road becomes visible. The moral imperative which is embodied is not subject to our changing moods. It gives us the sense of a dependable order in the universe. There is something in us that craves an authority higher than our own self-will. In that authority we would find rest. This is what gives dictators their power. The voice of duty which speaks to us through the law of God can be a welcome thing.

> Me this unchartered freedom tires;
> I feel the weight of chance-desires:
> . . . .
> I long for a repose that ever is the same.[5]

[5] William Wordsworth, "Ode to Duty."

So far as they go, the Commandments embody the will of God. Paul declares that the law is our schoolmaster to bring us to Christ. It is as essential for the full-grown man as is the training he receives in school. It creates for us the outlines of the picture of the good life which is fulfilled in Christ, and which has prepared us to recognize him. It also brings us to that condition of moral despair which makes him welcome as our Savior. The splendor of the moral law of which Paul speaks was reflected on the face of Moses, as it has been on the faces of many men of heroic character.

But if the life lived under the law had its splendor, how much more the life that comes from the indwelling Spirit! The **dispensation of condemnation** is surely outshone by the **dispensation of righteousness.** The defect of the law was that it could not make men righteous. But

11 For if that which is done away *was*
glorious, much more that which remaineth
is glorious.
12 Seeing then that we have such hope,
we use great plainness of speech:
13 And not as Moses, *which* put a veil
over his face, that the children of Israel
could not steadfastly look to the end of
that which is abolished:

surpasses it. 11 For if what faded away came
with splendor, what is permanent must
have much more splendor.
12 Since we have such a hope, we are
very bold, 13 not like Moses, who put a
veil over his face so that the Israelites
might not see the end of the fading splen-

---

splendor at all. Just as a candle seems to give no light when held in the full light of the sun, so the lesser splendor of the old legal order pales away and seems as nothing in the presence of the new Spirit-filled order of the Christian fellowship.

11. Bright **splendor** attended the giving of the law, but it "was fading away" (the present participle is used here as in vs. 7) at the very time that Moses, just returned from the mountaintop, was establishing the legal order. The fading brightness of Moses' face was a symbol of the transiency of the old order. The new order in which the Spirit is at work is **permanent** and so by that very fact superior to the old.

c) The Boldness of the Risen Lord's Ministers (3:12-18)

12. Paul and other apostolic leaders have **such a hope,** expressed in the preceding verses, that the "dispensation of the Spirit" is not only superior in "splendor" and effect but also "permanent." Naturally, then, they **are very bold** in the speech and action that mark their ministry. **Plainness of speech** in the KJV gives the root meaning of παρρησία, "bold freedom of speech"; but the word here probably refers to both speech and act.

13. Christian leaders, Paul says, are **not like Moses;** the Christian dispensation in which they minister has a "permanent" (vs. 11) and not a **fading splendor,** and so they do not have to show the caution **Moses** showed. In the story of Exod. 34:29-35, Moses **put a veil over his face** to keep **the Israelites** from seeing **the end of the fading splendor;** he did not want them to watch the splendor slowly fade. The Exodus story does not ascribe this intent to Moses; for Paul, however, purpose and effect in history are closely related, and he wishes to make the point that Moses did not let Israel see that the order he was establishing was inadequate and transient.

---

the new covenant does. By the revelation of love it brings the sinner into that condition of penitence and trust which is the essence of righteousness.

Further, the one splendor is passing, the other is **permanent.** The glory faded from the face of Moses; the glory of life in the Spirit remains. The joy does not pass. The hope of Christlikeness does not turn to disillusionment, for "God's love has been poured into our hearts" (Rom. 5:5). The effort after moral obedience may end in self-righteousness. It may produce in us the censorious temper which often condemns in others the faults from which we are not wholly free. Nothing can be more unattractive. But love to God and to men, rooted in humility and penitence, never loses its winsomeness.

12-13. ***Not Like Moses, Who Put a Veil Over His Face.***—It is difficult to explain Paul's use of the story of the **veil** (Exod. 34:33). He may have had in mind the charge made against him of being needlessly obscure in his preaching. There is no ground in Exodus for the suggestion that Moses used a veil to hide the fact that his face was losing its radiance. Allegory and fact are apt to be mixed in a mind accustomed to rabbinical methods of argument. The fact is that there is a veil over the truth when men read the O.T. without the light of Christ (but cf. Exeg.). They cannot see even the meaning of the old covenant till they have seen the new. They cannot understand the law till they see it supplanted and fulfilled by the law of love which Christ revealed. They cannot see any escape from its condemnation till they see in Christ God's free gift of forgiveness and the grace which brings us into sonship with himself. The picture of the suffering servant wounded for our transgressions (Isa. 53:5) is a mystery until the figure comes alive in the suffering Savior (see Philip's encounter with the Ethiopian eunuch, Acts 8:26-35). The O.T. is full of perplexities, defective morality, and primitive ideas of God. Only as we find in it the record of God's growing revela-

14 But their minds were blinded: for
until this day remaineth the same veil un-
taken away in the reading of the old testament; which *veil* is done away in Christ.
15 But even unto this day, when Moses
is read, the veil is upon their heart.
16 Nevertheless, when it shall turn to
the Lord, the veil shall be taken away.

dor. 14 But their minds were hardened;
for to this day, when they read the old
covenant, that same veil remains unlifted,
because only through Christ is it taken
away. 15 Yes, to this day whenever Moses
is read a veil lies over their minds; 16 but
when a man turns to the Lord the veil is

---

14. But since Israel did not see that the brightness on Moses' face was fading, and so did not understand that the Mosaic order was transient, **their minds were hardened** or dulled. Was this result the work of God, or of Satan (4:4), or of the Israelites themselves? Paul does not say; he would have seen truth in all three answers. In the word **hardened** Paul thinks first of all of the Israelites at the foot of Mount Sinai, but his thought begins to look down through the years at the later Jews who reject the Christian gospel. All through the years, and even to this day, in which the Christ is preached as the fulfillment of the promises of the **old covenant,** i.e., the O.T. scriptures, the people living under the Mosaic order have not understood the incompleteness of those scriptures nor their reference to Christ. The phrase **old covenant** (cf. vs. 6) is of Christian origin, and occurs only here in the N.T. (but cf. Gal. 4:24; Heb. 9:15). The expression underlines how great was Paul's break with Judaism and how decisive he understood God's action in Christ to have been. The **veil,** first mentioned as placed over Moses' face, Paul regards as now worn by the later Jews, i.e., he takes the veil in the story as a symbol of the veil of willful ignorance that keeps the Jews from understanding aright their scriptures and seeing their fulfillment in Christ. It is only the Christians, he clearly infers, who accurately interpret the O.T. The word **only** (RSV) is not found in the Greek. Vs. 14*b* may be translated: "The same veil remains, not being removed because" only "in Christ [i.e., through believing in Christ, which the Jews have refused to do] is it taken away." This is essentially what the RSV reads, and is preferable. Another possible but less likely translation is: "The same veil remains, it not being revealed to the unbelieving Jews that in Christ it is taken away."

15. But this escape from spiritual dusk and dullness through faith in Christ does not occur in these Jews; rather, **to this day whenever Moses** [i.e., the law] **is read** publicly in the synagogue service (cf. Acts 15:21), **a veil** of ignorance and misunderstanding lies **upon their heart.** The N.T. uses **heart** (καρδία) for the seat of intelligence, imagination, emotion, and will. The RSV translation **minds** may thus be defended (νοήματα, which clearly means **minds,** was used in vs. 14). But **heart** may express here the more complete attitude of the persons who hear the law read.

16. This verse resembles but does not quote literally Exod. 34:34, which says that "when Moses went in before the Lord to speak with him, he took the veil off." Possibly Paul here thinks of Moses, and means: "But whenever he [Moses] returns to the Lord [God to speak with him again], he takes off the veil." This to Paul would suggest that Jews should now turn in faith to the Lord Jesus Christ and thereby remove **the veil** that hinders

---

tion of himself and his will for men which culminated in Christ can we understand it. Only in Christ is the veil lifted.

14. ***But Their Minds Were Hardened.***—The more men refuse his light, the more hardened their hearts grow. The eye is blinded by its refusal to see. The heart is hardened by truth which it refuses to face.

15-16. ***When a Man Turns.***—Christ has the power to open blind eyes. This spiritual miracle is one of the central truths of the Fourth Gospel. His light has the power to awaken the capacity to see it. He can kindle insight, quicken conscience, even give to the loveless the capacity to love. If it were not so, he would not be Savior, for there would be no answer to spiritual blindness. One condition is that men fix their minds on him. The things to which we attend are those that have power over us. His one demand of us is for moral sincerity, which means surrendering

17 Now the Lord is that Spirit: and where the Spirit of the Lord *is*, there *is* liberty.

removed. 17 Now the Lord is the Spirit, and where the Spirit of the Lord is, there

their true understanding. More probably Paul is thinking primarily of the contemporary situation, and means: "But whenever it [i.e., their heart (vs. 15)], or he [i.e., one of the Jews], turns [in faith] to the Lord [Christ], the veil is taken away," the scripture is rightly understood, and the relation of the Mosaic order to the new covenant becomes clear.

17. Here and at the end of vs. 18, as in Rom. 8:9-11, **the Lord,** i.e., the risen Lord Jesus Christ, is not clearly distinguished from **the Spirit** of God. Yet it is wrong to say, as do some scholars, that they are simply identified. In this letter, especially in 13:14, Paul repeatedly speaks of each as in some sense separate, and the identity of the Lord Christ with the historical Jesus is too clear to him to permit of his identifying the Lord with the Spirit. But because the Lord is the risen Jesus, who now has a "spiritual body" and has become "a life-giving spirit" (I Cor. 15:44-45), he and the Spirit are one in nature

to him all such objections as honesty would make us realize are mere screens from a light we are unwilling to face.

17. ***Now the Lord Is the Spirit, and Where the Spirit of the Lord Is, There Is Freedom.***— The word **Lord** refers to Christ. It is not, however, to be taken as referring to Jesus in his earthly life, but to Christ as the focus of spiritual power—the power which is represented by his resurrection and ascension. This is the power of the Spirit who dwells in the heart and energizes and inspires the soul. The influence of the Spirit was revealed in ethical qualities. Paul did not exclude the phenomenon known as the gift of tongues; but he insisted that "tongues" must be tested by their power to convey a Christian message. In general, the fruits of the Spirit are all moral and spiritual. But as fruits they grow from the root of love set in the heart, not from mere obedience to commands. This is the true meaning of freedom. The restraint of commandments, both positive and negative, is replaced by the constraint of the love of Christ.

It is important to understand Paul's idea of liberty. The word is ordinarily used in various senses. Failure to realize this creates much confusion both in the political and moral spheres. By liberty most people mean freedom from external restraint, i.e., freedom from restraint on their movements, or on their right to think, speak, and act according to their beliefs or their consciences. There is another kind of freedom which many have come to crave—economic freedom. Those who are obliged to toil for long hours in order to satisfy the barest physical necessities feel that they are unable to fulfill themselves or to develop their capacities. In consequence, they have ceased to value political or religious liberty, and are willing to endure regimentation if their material wants are satisfied. Another form of liberty is freedom from the restraints imposed by religious or moral standards. Many have come to regard these as a denial of liberty, and have thrown them over in the effort to find happiness through the satisfaction of their desires.

The removal of all these external restraints, however, creates a problem. How shall we order our lives when we are free to do as we like? Walter Lippmann says, "We have come to see that Huxley was right when he said that 'a man's worst difficulties begin when he is able to do as he likes.'" He goes on to describe those who have thrown off moral restraints, but do not know what to do with the freedom they have found. "These are the prisoners who have been released. . . . The prison door is wide open. They stagger out into trackless space under a blinding sun. They find it nerve-racking."[6]

Paul's solution of this problem is found in his idea of liberty and of its purpose. True liberty is not the freedom to do as we like; it is the power to do as we ought. Through Christ, Paul had been emancipated from the restraints of the Jewish law to become a son of God. We are free only when our capacities are released through devotion to something greater than ourselves. An artist finds freedom in devotion to his art. A craftsman finds it when his powers are released by the vision of what he is seeking to create. Most of all, we find release through love for others whose welfare we seek.

Paul sees the true purpose of liberty in the service of others: "You were called to freedom, brethren; only do not use your freedom as an opportunity for the flesh, but through love be servants of one another" (Gal. 5:13). This is not only the purpose of liberty, but its safeguard. He points out that unless we use our

[6] *Preface to Morals* (New York: The Macmillan Co., 1929), pp. 6, 7.

18 But we all, with open face beholding as in a glass the glory of the Lord, are

is freedom. 18 And we all, with unveiled face, beholding[d] the glory of the Lord, are being changed into his likeness from one

[d] Or *reflecting*.

and share in the active guidance of the church. Paul neither identifies them nor clearly separates them. Here, in saying that **the Lord is the Spirit,** he means especially that as Spirit the Lord can be with his people everywhere. He gives them **freedom** from sin and condemnation—a gift the Mosaic law could not provide, for it was a "dispensation of condemnation" (vs. 9). He gives freedom of access to God in worship unafraid, and effects life-changing results, as vs. 18 now states.

18. We, which often means Paul alone and frequently refers to the Christian leaders of whom Paul is one, here seems to broaden its meaning to include **all** Christians; but his

liberty for the purpose of service, i.e., in the interests of love, we shall find ourselves in a deeper bondage, the bondage to the flesh. This reveals the fact that there is another kind of bondage than that imposed by external restraints. It is inner bondage to our own unruly passions and desires. To this many of those who boast of their liberty are subject, often unconsciously. They are slaves of fear, of lust, of pride, and of various forms of selfishness. "Do you not know that if you yield yourselves to any one as obedient slaves, you are slaves of the one whom you obey, either of sin, which leads to death, or of obedience, which leads to righteousness?" (Rom. 6:16.) In reality the only freedom we have, to begin with, is the freedom to choose our master.

The secret of liberty is found in the power of the indwelling Spirit. Through him we find both guidance as to what we ought to do and the power to do it. We are free to do as we like because Christ has enabled us to love what we ought to do. He orders "the unruly wills and affections of sinful men," so that they may love the things which he commands and desire that which he promises.[7] This is what Paul means when he says, **Where the Spirit of the Lord is, there is freedom.** He refers to himself more than once as the bondslave of Christ. Only so can we become our true selves. Only so are we set free from the selfish desires which enslave us; and all the instincts and powers of our nature are captured and united in a stream of devoted service. We experience the liberty of the sons of God.

The constraint of love which sets us free does not mean that for a Christian all restraints are abolished. Freedom is not attained at a bound. We grow into it by stages. We are here to become free. In the Accademia in Florence there are some uncouth blocks of marble on which Michelangelo had been at work. In each of them dim human forms are seen emerging from the marble, but still imprisoned in it. They seem to be waiting for the touch of the master to set them fully free. They are in fact called "The Prisoners." Like these we are still in part imprisoned in our lower nature and in our material conditions. Jesus calls us to co-operate with him in the overcoming of self, which will set us free. This is the real meaning of self-denial. External restraints will still remain. We may still be subject to necessity, to external force, to uncongenial tasks, even to suffering for conscience' sake. But we are free in the sense that through loving obedience to God in the circumstances life imposes we are able to fulfill our true nature and co-operate with him in the service of his kingdom. This is the meaning of life.

If I have freedom in my love,
And in my soul am free;
Angels alone, that soar above,
Enjoy such liberty.[8]

Jesus said to the weary and heavy laden, "Take my yoke upon you, . . . and you will find rest for your souls" (Matt. 11:29). A yoke is not a burden; it is the means by which an animal is attached to a burden so that the burden can be borne without friction or strain. If the yoke is easy, the burden will be light. The yoke Christ offers is his own. It is the yoke of love to God and the desire to do his will, whereby the hardest tasks are done in freedom and joy, and the heaviest burdens become light because we bear them in his Spirit.

Paul then describes the process by which this inner transformation is wrought.

18. *We All Are Being Changed.*—Likeness to Christ is not a human achievement. It is a growth produced by the creative power of the Spirit. "For God is at work in you, both to will and to work" (Phil. 2:13). We must work out our own salvation, of course; but all effective

[7] Book of Common Prayer, Collect for the Fourth Sunday after Easter.

[8] Richard Lovelace, "To Althea, From Prison."

changed into the same image from glory to glory, *even* as by the Spirit of the Lord.

degree of glory to another; for this comes from the Lord who is the Spirit.

special interest throughout this long section is in the apostolic leaders. Paul goes back to the story in Exod. 34:29-35. Moses alone stood before God **with unveiled face**, but **we** apostles and indeed we Christians **all** worship and live in the presence of **the Lord** Christ, **beholding** constantly his divine **glory** (or, instead of **beholding,** κατοπτριζόμενοι may mean "reflecting as does a mirror"; if so, the meaning is that the Christians, like Moses, reflect on their faces the divine **glory** that Paul, according to 4:6, had seen "in the face of Christ") . But for the Christians this is not merely external beholding (or a mere surface reflection) . It transforms the life into the very **image** or **likeness** of the Lord Christ, and it does so progressively, **from one degree of glory to another. This** amazing transformation of finite, fallible human beings is not their own doing. Yet it is intelligible when we remember that it **comes from,** is due to, **the Lord** Christ, "who is spirit" or "who sends the Spirit" (as explained under vs. 17, identification of the Lord and the Holy Spirit is not intended; hence either of these translations of πνεύματος seems better than the RSV's **who is the Spirit**).

action is a response to the creative activity of God in us. We work out what God works in. A plant grows by thrusting forth its twigs and leaves into the light. There are even, according to some scientists, traces of an elementary will. But this activity occurs as a response to the play of the sunlight and the rain to which the plant is exposed. In the soul the likeness of Christ is produced through contemplation of the glory of the Lord. This beholding or contemplation is the essence of worship, whether it takes place in church, where we gather for the purpose, or in our private devotions.

The glory of the Lord has various elements. It includes the moral beauty of Christ, which shines like light by its own perfection. He came in the flesh that we might behold his glory (John 1:14) . This glory is seen most vividly in his love and forgiveness, which reach their point of incandescent splendor on the Cross. To bring it vividly before worshipers the walls of many churches are covered with frescoes depicting scenes from his life, death, and resurrection.

But the glory of the Lord is not confined to his moral beauty. It is also revealed in his triumph over death and in his ascension to the "right hand of the throne of God." It consists in the truth that he who was dead is alive forevermore and has the keys of death and of hell (Rev. 1:18) . It is not merely his memory we recall in worship, as one recalls the memory of a departed friend. It is a living Lord who reigns and is the power of God's redeeming movement in history and in our individual souls. The best expression of **the glory of the Lord** in the hymns of the church is the *Te Deum.*

Several things are essential in the spirit of worshipers if worship is to be real. One is sincerity (John 4:24) . **With unveiled face** means that no prejudice or self-interest must be allowed to come between us and the light of Christ. All the barriers must be down. His glory will judge us. It will produce contrition. It will command us as well as comfort us. It may reveal to us some task or duty which we have neglected, or are unwilling to do. Reverence is something more than adoration. It is the "willingness to be commanded." There must also be passivity—the quiet submissiveness in which God can work. It is when we have ceased from all self-effort and are ready to let God's Spirit take command that his power is able to work. This is illustrated in the conversion experiences of Paul, Augustine, Luther, and others. In all these cases deliverance came when despair had reduced them to impotence, and faith in God had replaced all effort to earn their own salvation, or win their own spiritual victory. Bunyan's picture of the burden falling from Christian's back while he gazed at the Cross is a vivid illustration of this passivity of worship in which God acts. "Then he stood still awhile to look and wonder. . . . He looked, therefore, and looked again, even till the springs that were in his head sent the waters down his cheeks." [9]

This contemplation is transforming. We are **changed into his likeness.** It is a well-known principle that we become like what we look at. Our qualities of spirit are an unconscious reflection of those we admire in others. The inward change may even be revealed in our outward appearance. Milton makes this point:

> Till oft converse with heavenly habitants
> Begins to cast a beam on the outward shape,
> The unpolluted temple of the mind.[1]

[9] *The Pilgrim's Progress,* ch. iii.

[1] "Comus," l. 458.

4 Therefore, seeing we have this ministry, as we have received mercy, we faint not;
2 But have renounced the hidden things of dishonesty, not walking in craftiness, nor handling the word of God deceitfully; but,

4 Therefore, having this ministry by the mercy of God,[e] we do not lose heart.
2 We have renounced disgraceful, underhanded ways; we refuse to practise

[e] Greek *as we have received mercy.*

d) The Ministry of Light Against Darkness (4:1-6)

4:1. Since 2:17 Paul has been discussing his fitness and integrity in the apostolic **ministry.** It is the ministry of the "new covenant" (3:6), and so is vastly superior to the ministry of the old legal order, for the gospel of the Lord Christ gives liberty, life, and power. Paul is speaking of his task rather than official position. **We** in this chapter refers to Paul, or, at any rate, mainly to him and secondarily to his fellow workers. Since he has so essential and urgent a task to do for Christ, he does not **lose heart** or falter, but serves with alert, conscientious faithfulness. His conversion, call to service, and effective work are not to his personal credit; all this comes only **by the mercy of God** (cf. 3:5; I Cor. 15:10).

2. But Paul has made honest and diligent use of the gracious gifts of God. The reference to deception and dishonesty is not aimed at the earlier statement (3:13) that Moses, by putting a veil over his face, prevented Israel from seeing how transient was

Wordsworth also makes the same point in describing the education of his daughter:

She shall lean her ear
In many a secret place
Where rivulets dance their wayward round,
And beauty born of murmuring sound
Shall pass into her face.[2]

"Prayer makes a good face," said a young artist to his mother after a long absence, when she told him she had prayed much for him.

The worship of Christ, which exposes our souls to his glory, transforms us into his likeness. The change is unconscious. We know only that we become more conscious of him and that he becomes more and more to us. The growth in us of Christlikeness corresponds with the depth and enlargement of our vision of Christ. "We know that when he appears we shall be like him, for we shall see him as he is" (I John 3:2).

The change is gradual, **from one degree of glory to another.** The soul, like a plant, develops by imperceptible changes. The word "disciple" means "learner," and education is always by stages. The process of transformation into Christlikeness is not smooth or easy. Self-discipline is necessary if we are to keep the contact through which the Spirit can change us. The real battles of the soul are fought against the things that keep us from the "practice of the presence of God." But the result is sure, for it is produced in us by the power of the Spirit. The knowledge that the Spirit is the power of the risen Christ will keep us humble in victory and hopeful in failure and defeat.

[2] "Three Years She Grew in Sun and Shower."

4:1. *We Do Not Lose Heart.*—To **lose heart** is a temptation that comes to all, and not least to a minister. Paul's way of meeting it is to fall back on the fact that he has been called to the ministry by the mercy of God. It was neither through his own merit nor by his own choice that he became a minister. Whatever the burdens and troubles of his calling, it was always sheer wonder to him that this grace had been given to him, the "least of all saints" (Eph. 3:8). When a man has been rescued from death he will, when he remembers it, make light of the troubles and difficulties that life entails. If he recalls to his mind the mercy that saved him, he will recover his courage. If he further knows, as Paul did, that this mercy is of God, who has saved him for the purpose of saving others, he will realize that God has power to see him through. Giant Despair, says Bunyan, fell into fits on sunshiny mornings and lost for a time the use of his hands.[3] Despair cannot live in the sunlight of God's mercy. (See on vs. 16.)

2. *We Have Renounced Disgraceful, Underhanded Ways.*—This disclaimer reflects some of the charges that Paul's enemies had made against his preaching. The gist of them was that he tampered with the word of God. It is a charge not unknown today. It may sometimes be made against those who accept the help of modern scholarship in their interpretation of scripture. We need all the light upon the scriptures which scholarship can give us if the message of God which they contain is to be elucidated. We **tamper with God's word** if we twist the words of scripture to fit some idea of our own, or when in deference to current views or

[3] *The Pilgrim's Progress,* ch. vii.

by manifestation of the truth, commending
ourselves to every man's conscience in the
sight of God.
3 But if our gospel be hid, it is hid to
them that are lost:
4 In whom the god of this world hath
blinded the minds of them which believe
not, lest the light of the glorious gospel of

cunning or to tamper with God's word, but
by the open statement of the truth we
would commend ourselves to every man's
conscience in the sight of God. 3 And even
if our gospel is veiled, it is veiled only to
those who are perishing. 4 In their case the
god of this world has blinded the minds

---

the Mosaic dispensation. Paul never lingers long in the past; his thought returns rapidly to his present situation. Here he thinks of the "false apostles" (11:13) with whom he and the Corinthians have had to deal (cf. 2:17). He may also be answering a charge against him (cf. 1:17) that his actions have not been honest. He has **renounced disgraceful, underhanded ways** (more lit., "shameful hidden things"). This means he is **not walking in** cunning **craftiness** in his methods and dealings with people, nor is he tampering, adulterating, falsifying (δολοῦντες) **the word of God,** i.e., the gospel message of salvation he has been called to preach. This **word** is also called **the truth** and "the gospel" (vss. 3-4); its central content is stated in vs. 5. **Manifestation of the truth** means its outward expression to others, especially by preaching; hence the RSV translates manifestation by **open statement,** but Paul may mean manifestation in both word and act. By this faithful expression of the truth he "recommends" himself; this is the same verb used in 3:1*a*. He appeals to **every man's conscience** in the confident hope that his integrity will be clear to every honest man. Yet he is conscious that in his preaching and appeal to men he acts **in the sight of God,** who is his final judge.

3. But not all who hear Paul believe. Why? Has it been suggested that Paul is at fault, if not for deception or falsification, at least for not making the gospel clear? The failure of men to believe is not his fault; the trouble is in them. In 3:15 Paul spoke of the "veil" over the heart of Jews. Here he thinks of men in general, and uses the same figure of the veil that prevents clear vision and understanding. He does not excuse the unbelief, here or even in vs. 4; men are responsible to God for rejecting the gospel. Here he only notes the fact that some do not clearly face the gospel, and says that such men **are perishing.** The present participle (ἀπολλυμένοις) indicates that they are on the way to full and final ruin.

4. Paul sees this world as a battleground in which Satan and his hosts contend with God and his forces for the lives of men. To Paul, God is in final control and Christ by his

---

popular opinion we blunt the edge of its message, or if we take words or phrases out of their context in order to establish some particular theory or doctrine. Paul denies that he has tampered with the word of God by hiding its meaning or by making cunning use of it for his own ends. On the contrary, his effort has been to state the truth frankly and openly so that it might make its own appeal to **every man's conscience,** wherever that conscience has been open to God's light. The gospel is not a message for the spiritually elite only—for people of special intelligence or unusual insight. It does appeal to these. But it is in its essence a message for the uninstructed mind and sincere conscience of the ordinary man. It is the truth about God and man, and therefore corresponds with universal human needs and aspirations.

3. ***Even If Our Gospel Is Veiled.***—The message of the gospel may fail to find its mark for various reasons. It may be obscured by words that hide its meaning. The veil may be upon the truth as it is handled by the preacher; or the fault may be in men's consciences. They may be blinded so that they cannot recognize the truth. Paul declares that if his gospel **is veiled** it is for the latter reason. Because the soil is hard the seed cannot penetrate it (Matt. 13:19). In this case even the best seed will be sterile. There are blind spots on the conscience as well as on the eye. In some cases the conscience may be wholly dead. The spiritual eye may have gone blind.

4. ***The God of This World.***—(See Exeg.) Here is the glamour of those material things which appeal to "the lust of the flesh and the

Christ, who is the image of God, should
shine unto them.
5 For we preach not ourselves, but Christ
Jesus the Lord; and ourselves your servants
for Jesus' sake.

of the unbelievers, to keep them from seeing
the light of the gospel of the glory of
Christ, who is the likeness of God. 5 For
what we preach is not ourselves, but Jesus
Christ as Lord, with ourselves as your

---

victory over sin and death has already broken the grip of Satan on mankind. But the effect of this victory is not yet complete, and only believers know something of it. So great is the remaining power of Satan that Paul can call him **the god of this world,** or better of "the present evil age" (αἰῶνος), from which Christ has essentially redeemed believers (Gal. 1:4; cf. John 12:31; 14:30; 16:11; Eph. 2:2). Satan blinds unbelievers (though not against their will) **to keep them from seeing the light of the gospel.** The reference to the **likeness of God** and to Paul's conversion in vs. 6 indicates that he thinks of the **light** as a visible expression of the divine splendor and nature of Christ; **glory** here means both exalted nature and visible expression of it. Here, as usually, Paul's reference to Christ means the risen Christ, glorious and exalted and indeed bearing the very **likeness** (RSV) or **image** [KJV, εἰκών] **of God.** This means far more than that Christ, like all men (Gen. 1:27), was made "in the image of God"; Christ is the unique, divine Son (1:19).

5. This verse states what Paul meant in vs. 2 by the "manifestation of the truth"; it is to preach the message and live the life in which Christ is central and dominant. Paul has been charged with self-praise (3:1), and probably also with seeking personal advantage. He strongly denies this. He (or **we** may include his comrades) does not **preach** himself; he knows that men would find no redemption, no renewal, no power in what he by himself can do. He and his hearers alike must look to Christ for help. He preaches **Jesus** of Nazareth, the **Christ** who fulfilled the messianic promises of God to Israel, and who, having died for men and risen from the dead, is now the living **Lord,** in a position of authority "at the right hand of God" (Rom. 8:34; Col. 3:1). Why does Paul say that **we preach** not only Christ as Lord but also **ourselves as your servants?** Is it only a loose way of adding that "we are your servants"? Perhaps. But the gospel of the risen Lord was not complete until after the Resurrection and Ascension, and so the witness of Paul and other apostolic preachers to this total message was indispensable. Thus the apostolic witness is an inherent part of the gospel, and Acts and the epistles are a necessary part of the N.T.

---

lust of the eyes and the pride of life" (I John 2:16), and which prevent men from seeing the light of the gospel. The **unbelievers** are not the honest doubters who seek to know the truth but cannot reach religious conviction. These do not become the prey of the **god of this world.** Their honesty of mind and love of truth keep them sensitive to moral and spiritual values, which are an antidote to the corrupting power of a gross or sensual materialism. The unbeliever who becomes the victim of the **god of this world** is the man who makes deliberate choice of a godless view of life. He does not believe in God because he does not really want to believe in him. He rejects faith because the way of faith is not the way in which he has chosen to live. By a series of what appear trifling decisions God is thrust into the background and spiritual values are obscured.

The attraction of the world is a form of worship. Man must have something to adore. This must be recognized. Money, power, position, and popularity can become the object of that adoration. People reverence the rich, the powerful, the popular; mark the homage accorded to the celebrities of the screen or of sport. These fealties cannot permanently satisfy, but they make the mind impervious to the glory of Christ.

Paul describes his gospel. It is the **gospel of the glory of Christ, who is the likeness of God.** The gospel does not consist in what Christ taught, or even in what he did; it consists in what he is—the living center of power and love from which his teaching and his actions spring. His glory is explained by the fact that he is the likeness of God and reveals his nature and character. It is the person of Christ who ought to be the subject of the interpreter's message.

5. ***What We Preach Is Not Ourselves.***—Paul emphasizes the fact that it is Christ he preaches, not himself. The pulpit is not a church for

6 For God, who commanded the light to shine out of darkness, hath shined in our hearts, to *give* the light of the knowledge of the glory of God in the face of Jesus Christ.

servants[f] for Jesus' sake. 6 For it is the God who said, "Let light shine out of darkness," who has shone in our hearts to give the light of the knowledge of the glory of God in the face of Christ.

[f] Or *slaves.*

scripture. It is striking that Paul does not say "Christ's servants" but **your servants.** He is of course the grateful servant of his Lord Christ, but this means that he is likewise the willing servant of the Corinthians; he serves them in preaching, teaching, and pastoral care. He does it all **for Jesus' sake;** a service to men is obedience to Christ (cf. Matt. 25:40), who made it his lifework "to minister" (Mark 10:45).

6. The God of creation is the God who redeems men through Christ. With the light of creation which shone forth at God's command (Gen. 1:3) Paul compares the brilliant **light** which at his conversion (cf. Acts 9:3; 22:6; 26:13) he saw on **the face of** the risen **Christ.** Yet here, unlike the narrative in Acts, Paul says that God **has shone in our hearts,** just as in Gal. 1:16 he says that God was pleased to reveal his Son "in me." He evidently thinks of it as a visible brightness, for he saw the face of Christ, but it was more than external light; it also suffused his whole life and was a spiritual presence and power, not a merely physical occurrence. The illumination or light which **the knowledge of the glory of God** gave was not just for himself; as vs. 5 indicates, and as **for** at the opening of this verse implies, God shone in Paul's heart **to give** others **light** through the knowledge which the conversion experience gave him of God and his saving work. Paul thought of every spiritual blessing as given for use in his apostolic ministry.

exhibiting the preacher's gifts, but for revealing the glory of Christ. A great N.T. scholar at the end of his life said, "All through my life I have had one chief aim, to see Jesus Christ and to show him to others." The power to see Jesus and to show him to others had come to Paul from God, and was itself part of the ongoing revelation (see Exeg.).

6. *God Has Shone in Our Hearts.*—Here Paul recalls the experience of his conversion, which was the root of all he was and of all he taught. It was a creative experience produced by a divine act which he could compare only to the great moment in creation when God said, "Let there be light: and there was light" (Gen. 1:3). The picture in Paul's mind was obviously taken from Gen. 1:2, "The earth was without form, and void; and darkness was upon the face of the deep. And the Spirit of God moved upon the face of the waters." Would this not come home to Paul as a picture of his own pre-Christian condition? His life had been in chaotic darkness, without any vital purpose to give it meaning. There was no light by which he could understand himself or solve the problem of his uneasy conscience. Yet from his earliest youth the Spirit of God had brooded over him. Looking back he could see signs of this which he had not before been able to interpret. Then at last had come the light, the creative word, bursting through the primeval darkness, reducing chaos to order and bringing new life to birth within him. It is a vivid picture of the difference Christ makes; for the light was that of **the glory of God in the face of Christ.** With unveiled face that Christ had looked upon Paul's soul, scattering the darkness of pride and sin that had hidden God from him, and awaking him to his true life of sonship. Two points struck him about this experience. The first was that it was the act of God. There was nothing in it of his own effort or merit. In the living Christ God had taken the initiative. The second was that God had acted creatively. There was a "new creation" (5:17). The full force of this truth may be missed by many because they are not conscious of any revolutionary change, any violent emotional disturbance, or any sudden break with the past. In northern latitudes the dawn is slow and gradual, while at the equator it "comes up like thunder," as Kipling says. But it is the same dawn. So it is with the coming of God's light. It is the action of God, and its effect is creative. A new thing has happened. The soul has been born. To realize this truth and identify our experience with the light of God's glory in the face of Jesus Christ will bring to us the recognition of God's presence in our life and set us exploring and discovering the love of Christ.

7 But we have this treasure in earthen vessels, that the excellency of the power may be of God, and not of us.

7 But we have this treasure in earthen vessels, to show that the transcendent power

4. God Sustains His Ministers in Their Wearing Work (4:7-18)

a) The Life of Jesus Manifested in Their Bodies (4:7-12)

7. In the life-giving ministry of the new covenant, which is so vastly superior to the old Mosaic order, Paul (his thought here may include his fellow workers) has proven honest, faithful, and competent. The light of the gospel of Jesus Christ, the living Lord, has led Paul not only into the Christian life, but also into unselfish ministry for the Corinthians and others. **But** the credit for this does not belong to him. Perhaps to crush any temptation to pride, and certainly to keep his readers from misunderstanding, he confesses that **we have this treasure** of the glorious gospel in **earthen vessels,** a figure suggested perhaps by Gen. 2:7, and used to show how humble, fragile, and transient weak mortal bodies are. The idea may have come to Paul's mind partly as a result of his recent narrow escape from deadly peril in Asia (1:8); but 10:10; 11:23-29; 12:7 show that more than one experience had made the point clear to him. Paul sees a divine purpose in the fact that such humble, mortal men preach the gospel; this should make it clear to all that **the transcendent power,** superior to all difficulties and opposition which Christ's workers may meet, **belongs to God.** This is a truth that the Corinthians with their party strife and slogans (I Cor. 1:12) have constantly missed. But they need to see it; indeed, it is the very truth of the gospel story, in which, through the humble

7. *We Have This Treasure in Earthen Vessels.* —The light of the knowledge of the glory of God was a **treasure.** It was the infinitely precious thing Paul had been given to pass on through his life and message. He is humbly aware that it was contained in an earthen vessel, or as Moffatt translates it, "a frail vessel of earth," possibly a reference to the clay lamp which was commonly used to hold the light.

This and the verses which follow contain a frank acknowledgment of his weakness. Paul's physical disabilities were obvious to all. They had been flung in his teeth by his Judaizing opponents, with the probable suggestion that they were clear marks of God's contempt. His bodily presence was "weak, and his speech of no account" (10:10). He was subject to a recurrent malady—a "thorn in the flesh" (12:7)—which harassed him, and which remained despite his urgent prayer that it might be removed. No man, however strong his physique, could have come unbroken in health through all that he had suffered—shipwreck, stoning, beating with rods, etc. (11:24-27). It is an impressive list, and added to it was the mental anxiety due to his concern for the welfare of the churches he had founded. He must have been of tough fiber to have borne all this and still have been able to carry on.

Moreover, the weakness was not only physical. The apostle is conscious also of spiritual weakness, against which he has always had to strive. Mental perplexities and imperfect insight are the lot of human nature. The true saint is the last to claim sainthood. Such a claim would be a sign that he is no saint, for it would be evidence of spiritual blindness. The closer we live to Christ, the more we are conscious of our own inadequacy.

> And they who fain would love thee best
> Are conscious most of wrong within.[4]

But Paul finds, if not comfort, then understanding in the fact that the vessel which holds the treasure is of earth. The clay could not have produced what it enshrines. Clearly, **the transcendent power belongs to God.** When we look at a wayside flower, it has been remarked, we do not say that there has been great effort here; we say that there is a great power here. Eloquence, polished speech, an impressive appearance, or high intellectual attainments may actually prevent people from realizing that a preacher's power—or any other man's power—is of God. Many who have done outstanding work for the kingdom of God have had some crippling physical disability. Livingstone of Africa had a crippled arm. George Matheson, hymn writer and preacher, was blind. Others have even had defects of character which perplexed and wounded their friends. The list is legion. Handicaps can stimulate hidden capacities and give opportunity for a victory of the Spirit, as a crack in a piece of crystal causes a

[4] Henry Twells, "At even, when the sun was set," st. iv.

8 *We are* troubled on every side, yet not distressed; *we are* perplexed, but not in despair;
9 Persecuted, but not forsaken; cast down, but not destroyed;

belongs to God and not to us. 8 We are
afflicted in every way, but not crushed;
perplexed, but not driven to despair; 9 persecuted, but not forsaken; struck down,

---

earthly life and shameful death of Jesus, God did his revealing and redeeming work. The divine life and power are released precisely in the life of unselfish service and of suffering for others.

8. In a series of four contrasts Paul now declares that the constant succession of desperate crises he has had to meet have never brought him to defeat, because the power of God has been with him in even the most ominous situations. What happened in Asia (1:8-11) is what continually happens; the present participles in vss. 8-9 indicate a succession of deadly perils. Though **afflicted,** he is not "straitened" (στενοχωρούμενοι), i.e., hemmed in and hard pressed so that no escape is possible. **Perplexed, but not driven to despair** contains a wordplay in Greek: perplexed, but not perplexed to the point of complete despair (ἀπορούμενοι, ἐξαπορούμενοι).

9. "Pursued" or **persecuted,** as though in flight from the field of battle, but not **forsaken,** left behind, abandoned by the army's commanders and comrades. **Struck down,**

---

beam which shines through it to break into the colors of the rainbow. Paul is stating his own experience when he says that the power of God triumphs through our weakness. A second-century letter gives this picture of him: "A man of moderate stature, with curly [or crisp] hair and scanty; crooked legs; with blue eyes; and large knit eyebrows; long nose; and he was full of the grace and pity of the Lord, sometimes having the appearance of a man, but sometimes looking like an angel." [5] Dan Crawford, an African missionary, thus describes a fellow missionary:

> A white, fragile-looking traveller, with a Pauline gleam in his eye. "Have come to pay my debt!" said he, with a winning smile, and there you have the whole story in two words—that white fever face trying, but failing, to kill that glad smile. . . . This holy man, if you please, had drunk so deeply of God's wine of joy . . . that it kept him going at high pressure right on to the end. The new wine, in fact, was busily at work breaking up his old bottle of a body. . . . So the fragrant saint died at his post. . . . *He* had only died into glory as the stars die at sunrise.[6]

8-9. ***God's Triumph in Paul's Weakness.***—This is described in four situations. **We are afflicted in every way, but not crushed.** Moffatt translates this as "harried but not hemmed in." The situation suggested is that of frustration, from which God always provides a way out. There is no impasse on the road of God's service. The way of obedience is never a dead end. The Bible is full of instances of this, e.g., the crossing of the Red Sea and of the Jordan.

Perplexed, but not driven to despair. Perplexities may be of two kinds. There are practical perplexities for which our human wisdom is not enough. There are also perplexities of faith. Our minds are not big enough to solve all the problems which faith presents. In some ways, indeed, faith in the love of God as it meets the cruelties of life and the apparent callousness of the universe deepens perplexity. The materialist who has no room for God in his outlook has no problem of this kind. His trouble is not perplexity but despair. To be without God is to be without hope (Eph. 2:12). But faith gives us light to walk by, and the promise of the perfect day. "For now we see in a mirror dimly, but then face to face. Now I know in part; then I shall understand fully, even as I have been fully understood" (I Cor. 13:12).

Persecuted, but not forsaken. To be persecuted is to be singled out for personal attack because of one's faith or opinions. It is a lonely form of suffering, for it generally involves social ostracism. Like countless others before him, Paul had experienced this loneliness. Yet he never felt himself forsaken. Dostoevski tells how, when he was kept in solitary confinement for his political opinions, the little shutter in his cell door was opened every evening, and a mysterious voice whispered, "Courage, brother, we also suffer." In similar situations Paul was conscious of the presence of God. When he stood on trial, at his "first defense," no one was with him. "But," he writes, "the Lord stood by me" (II Tim. 4:17).

[5] Quoted in T. R. Glover, *Paul of Tarsus* (New York: Richard R. Smith, 1930), p. 172.

[6] *Thinking Black* (New York: Harper & Bros.; London: Marshall, Morgan & Scott, 1912), pp. 101-3. Used by permission.

10 Always bearing about in the body the dying of the Lord Jesus, that the life also of Jesus might be made manifest in our body.

but not destroyed; **10** always carrying in the body the death of Jesus, so that the life of Jesus may also be manifested in our bodies.

---

as in single combat with an enemy in battle, but **not destroyed,** given the final deathblow. Though the apostle's situation is always apparently desperate, it is never really hopeless; God rescues his ministers when human eye sees no hope.

10. This divine power works through the close union of the apostle with Christ his Lord. For Paul this is not merely a union in final glory, but even now, **always,** in the midst of hardship and daily service. The glory comes only to those who suffer (Rom. 8:17). "The promises of God are to those who endure," as Roger C. Cumberland wrote just before martyrdom on the mission field. The **dying** (νέκρωσιν, lit., "the putting to death") of Jesus is being re-enacted in a series of sufferings and crises the apostle must endure; the **dying** here seems to be, not as in vs. 16 a constant process, but a series of continual escapes and deliverances (Plummer; cf. Col. 1:24; Phil. 3:10-11). The **life** that comes to Paul in such sufferings is the resurrection life of the crucified but risen Jesus. United with the living Christ, Paul knows both the suffering and the decisive triumph of his Lord (cf. Gal. 2:20).

Struck down, but not destroyed implies more than physical attack. What he suffered through the disloyalty of the church at Corinth was a blow at the heart. Such an experience can sap the springs of courage. A great sorrow can have the same disabling effect. Faith is the secret of resilience. "It is a perpetually defeated thing which survives all its conquerors."[7] It gives us contact with the inexhaustible resources of God. Part of the secret of Paul's victory was the attitude toward his sufferings which faith brought.

10. ***Always Carrying in the Body the Death of Jesus.***—Paul realized that his sufferings and hardships were a kind of death. But death is more than physical decay. Its meaning depends on the purpose it serves. Christ's outlook on it was twofold. By it his Spirit would be released into full and fruitful life. The words he used before Calvary reveal this: "Unless a grain of wheat falls into the earth and dies, it remains alone; but if it dies, it bears much fruit" (John 12:24).

> For birth hath in itself the germ of death,
> But death hath in itself the germ of birth.[8]

His death was also the central act of God's redeeming movement in history. The Atonement has many aspects, but this includes them all.

Because of his union with Christ Paul saw the same process at work in his own **dying.** It was the continual laying down of the life of the body through which the life he had in Christ might be manifested and released. Through it also he shared in the same redemptive movement. This outlook shaped his attitude to his hardships and dictated the spirit in which he bore them. It enabled him to accept them rationally and calmly. They were not a fate or a misfortune. They were the operation of the law of sacrifice through which the spirit is released into fruitfulness and power. It enabled him also to dedicate them. He consecrated his hardships to the purpose of God. By opening his heart to the spirit in which Christ bore his cross he made his own suffering tributary to the stream that flowed from Calvary.

There is no theoretical solution to the problem of the suffering that prematurely destroys the body. Christ offers us none. But in his own outlook and attitude he reveals and communicates the spirit by which "death is swallowed up in victory" (I Cor. 15:54). The redemption of suffering is part of the redemption Christ brings through his cross. Even the suffering we bring on ourselves through sin or selfishness can be transformed and made to serve God's redeeming purpose. Paul's sufferings were not all free from the bitterness of self-reproach; some may have been more intense than they need have been had some defect of character not complicated the situation. But even the suffering that in part at least we bring on ourselves is not excluded. Guilty suffering can be a purifying power. It also can enable us to manifest the forgiving spirit toward others. In the confidence that the life of Jesus is being manifested in his body

[7] G. K. Chesterton, *G. F. Watts* (New York: E. P. Dutton & Co., 1904), p. 101.

[8] "Ode to the Setting Sun," from *The Poems of Francis Thompson* (London: Burns Oates & Washbourne, 1913). Used by permission of Sir Francis Meynell, copyright owner.

11 For we which live are alway delivered unto death for Jesus' sake, that the life also of Jesus might be made manifest in our mortal flesh.

12 So then death worketh in us, but life in you.

13 We having the same spirit of faith, according as it is written, I believed, and therefore have I spoken; we also believe, and therefore speak;

11 For while we live we are always being
given up to death for Jesus' sake, so that
the life of Jesus may be manifested in our
mortal flesh. 12 So death is at work in us,
but life in you.

13 Since we have the same spirit of faith
as he had who wrote, "I believed, and so I
spoke," we too believe, and so we speak,

---

11. This verse repeats and so emphasizes the thought of vs. 10. The main addition is the idea that the suffering which Paul endures he accepts **for Jesus' sake,** i.e., to serve the Jesus who suffered and died, and yet rose and now rules as Lord. Paul speaks of **Jesus** to make vivid the memory of the earthly suffering of his Lord, but here, as elsewhere, he thinks of him as risen and now in authority. We the living workers for Christ are always being led into situations so full of danger that we can speak of them as times when we are **given up to death,** but the triumphant life of Jesus is made clear in his apostles; he delivers them and makes them able to continue their service for him.

12. The thought takes a sudden turn. Paul has said that both death and life are at work in him as he lives in close union with the crucified and risen Jesus. He has said that he accepts this suffering **for Jesus' sake.** Now he adds that while **death is at work in** Christ's ministers, it is for the good of others that they suffer. The result is **life in you** Corinthians. This is not ironical; it is deep spiritual truth that one suffers for another; this truth is embodied in Jesus' cross and in the cross that the follower of Jesus takes up and carries. Only by the great cost that Christ paid and by the voluntary suffering of Paul and his fellow workers do the Corinthians have the gospel and continue in its blessings (cf. 1:6) .

b) Faith in the Resurrection Sustains Them (4:13-15)

13. It takes great **faith** to stay steady under such continual sufferings and still **speak** boldly the Christian gospel and the pastoral counsel that Paul has given the Corinthians. He has such a sturdy faith; and in vss. 13-15 he mentions four factors that uphold him in his hard and perilous work. First, he is reassured to recall the psalmist's courageous declaration in a time of trouble: **I believed, and so I spoke** (Ps. 116:10; Paul quotes as usual from LXX) . In the same spirit of steadfast faith Paul too speaks, not only in what he

---

Paul can face the long hard way of increasing physical weakness. He sees that even as a historical fact the life of Jesus is not ended. Jesus lives in and through those who suffer with him and who give their lives in his service. This is Paul's comfort.

11-12. ***Always Being Given Up to Death.***— Those who had been tempted to despise Paul for his weakness might well be ashamed. All their experience of Christ had come to them through Paul's sacrifice. There is no other way by which spiritual work can be fruitful. It may be a material sacrifice such as the abandonment of money or social position. It may demand the giving of ourselves to the point of exhaustion in the care of people and in meeting their deep spiritual needs. A minister who tries to save himself from physical or mental cost is stultifying his own power. Paul's attitude to his sufferings is the secret of turning burdens into inspirations. Samuel Rutherford, one of the saints of the Scottish Covenant, wrote of the Cross, "He that takes up that bitter Tree and carries it cannily [quietly] will find it such a burden as wings are to a bird or sails are to a boat." [9]

13-14. ***We Too Believe, and So We Speak.***— Paul, like the psalmist (116:10), speaks from conviction born of experience of God's deliverance. He returns again to the foundation on which his faith rested: the fact that Christ was raised from the dead by an act of God's power. This is the assurance that Christ **will raise** him from the grave into which by his labors he is now moving, and will bring him with the Corinthian Christians **into his presence.** Paul's

[9] *Letter LXIX,* To the Viscountess of Kenmure.

14 Knowing that he which raised up the Lord Jesus shall raise up us also by Jesus, and shall present *us* with you.

15 For all things *are* for your sakes, that the abundant grace might through the thanksgiving of many redound to the glory of God.

14 knowing that he who raised the Lord Jesus will raise us also with Jesus and bring us with you into his presence.
15 For it is all for your sake, so that as grace extends to more and more people it may increase thanksgiving, to the glory of God.

---

has said above (vss. 7-12), but in all his preaching and teaching. Paul cites the psalm passage as scripture, **according as it is written** (KJV); the RSV rendering does not make this clear.

14. The second support to Paul in his suffering is that no matter what men do to him, God **(he) will raise** him and give him full salvation. **Knowing** is a causal participle, "because we know." As in I Cor. 15:23-28, the fact that God has **raised . . . Jesus** is taken as solid ground for confidence that he **will** likewise **raise** those who believe in **the Lord Jesus.** The resurrection of Jesus is the guarantee of the resurrection of his people at the last day. **With you** does not mean "at the same time," for Jesus has already been raised; it means as a result of the resurrection of Jesus and by reason of the union of the believer with the risen Christ. Although in I Thess. 4:16-17 and I Cor. 15:51-52 Paul writes as though he expects to be alive when the last day comes, he here either ignores that question or inclines to think that he may no longer be alive at that time (cf. 5:1-8). Paul here passes over the idea of the final judgment (cf. 5:10); his confident trust is that the God who has raised Christ and offered salvation to those who believe will at the end **present us** (KJV) to Christ, or **bring us . . . into his presence** (RSV). Removing all trace of separation, he will give believers full salvation in perfect fellowship with the Lord to whom they owe their eternal life. But Paul cannot speak of this merely as a privilege which he, or he and his fellow workers, enjoy. He is too deeply bound with his churches for that. God will **raise** and **present us with you.** Paul is confident that they will share with him in the complete gift of God's grace (cf. 1:14; I Thess. 2:19-20; Phil. 4:1).

15. In the opening clause Paul explains why he added "with you" at the end of the preceding verse: **for all things,** Paul's suffering and service, and indeed all the saving work that God is now doing through the apostle and will complete at the last day, are **for your sakes.** The hard blows and wearing labor are neither enigma nor nonsense; through Paul's suffering God is working out his purpose, and Paul gladly endures it all for the benefit of his churches. Concern for them is his third support in his work. The fourth is found in the clause that states the divine purpose: "in order that the" divine "grace, abounding through the greater number" who are continually being added to the church, "may cause thanksgiving to abound, to the glory of God." The increase of converts will cause ever-increasing thanksgiving. The final and greatest word Paul has to say about this entire drama of salvation is that it all works out **to the glory of God.** This word primarily,

---

mind was dominated by the conviction that this is a passing world, and that our final home is beyond. For this translation to the life beyond they must prepare. His aim in his ministry was not merely to comfort or change a few people who would encounter one another like ships that pass in the night. It was to build a fellowship that would stand the test of death. What he planted through his gospel and his own spirit was the seed of immortality. He would meet these people again in the presence of Christ.

15. ***For Your Sake.***—All Paul had endured was for the sake of the church. His outlook was selfless. His ambition was that God's grace should extend **to more and more people.** It was always the grace of God he was concerned to magnify—the clear gift and wonder of it—never his own skill or wisdom. To kindle this wonder and gratitude in a multitude of hearts rejoicing in the glory of Christ was the only satisfying object of his ministry. **Thanksgiving** may not seem a very profound result of making God known. But deeply considered it means that the truth has come home. It has rung a bell in the heart. The experience of redemption by the sheer love and pity of God has become real. Doxology is always the characteristic note of the Christian spirit.

16 For which cause we faint not; but though our outward man perish, yet the inward *man* is renewed day by day.

17 For our light affliction, which is but for a moment, worketh for us a far more exceeding *and* eternal weight of glory;

16 So we do not lose heart. Though our outer nature is wasting away, our inner nature is being renewed every day. 17 For this slight momentary affliction is preparing for us an eternal weight of glory beyond all

---

with the welfare of his churches as a second interest, sums up Paul's purpose and joy in his ministry.

c) Eternal Glory Will Follow Brief Affliction (4:16-18)

16. So, Paul says, in view of the faith and hope expressed in vss. 13-15, **we do not lose heart.** The RSV omits **but** (ἀλλ'), which here may well be translated "rather." The following words really give another reason why Paul does not lose heart. To be sure, **our outward man,** i.e., the physical man that undergoes the wearing and continual afflictions encountered in the ministry (vss. 8-11; cf. 11:23-29), is always **wasting away.** Paul feels the drain on his physical vitality, and no wonder. But **the inward man,** the redeemed and Spirit-supported self, **is being renewed every day.** The thought is not that there is a gradual and progressive growth in the inner spiritual life, but that though the Christian leader has to endure constantly the wearing strain of trials and sufferings, yet each new day his resources of faith and courage are so restored by God that he has adequate strength to meet the tests of life. The body may wear down, but the renewing grace and power of God keep his faith, loyalty, and will to serve at high level.

17. In vs. 16 the point was that the daily wasting away of the physical life is counteracted by the daily renewal of inner spiritual life and strength. To that thought is now added the assurance that in spite of the **affliction** an increasing and eternal blessing and

---

16. ***Outer Nature, Inner Nature.***—After reviewing his experiences Paul returns to the statement with which the chapter began. He does **not lose heart** because, in spite of the frailty of the vessel in which the treasure was held, his spirit is kept equal to the strain; and through the sacrifice of his strength the life of Jesus in him has taken root in the hearts of his converts. As for himself, while the **outer nature is wasting away** the **inner nature is being renewed every day.** The flesh is decaying; but the spirit is expanding into fuller life. These two facts are vitally connected. The energy of the body, spent for Christ and the work of the kingdom, is being transformed into the energy of the living spirit. There is a corresponding process in the natural world. Physical energy is continually being changed into higher forms. The energy of the sun pouring on the earth is taken up by plants in the garden and transformed into flowers and fruit. This process is used by man for his own purposes. The energy of a river, which would otherwise be lost in running down to the sea, is changed by means of a turbine into electric power to heat and light our homes.

The physical strength of the body is gradually running down. It may be expended in futile living or even poured out in self-indulgence, in which case it is lost. On the other hand, it may be dedicated to God and poured into the channel of his purpose, so that the spirit grows day by day in Christlikeness. Physical energy is thus transformed into the beauty and power of the spirit, until the death of the body results in the full release of the spirit. This dying into life is the meaning of our existence on earth. It is also the meaning of the world process. The earth is a clock that is running down. Scientists foresee the day when it will become a frozen ball from which life will be extinct. But God's purpose for it is that the physical energy which produces and nourishes life should be transformed into the life of a community of immortal spirits—a kingdom of redeemed and developed souls—the children of God. This is that

> one far-off divine event,
> To which the whole creation moves.[1]

17. ***An Eternal Weight of Glory.***—This verse expands the same idea. **Affliction** here is transmuted into glory beyond. The humiliating sufferings of life in Christ's service are the means by which the spirit is purified, developed, and brought to blossom in the beauty of Christlikeness. The affliction is **slight** and **momentary** by comparison with the **glory** which is massive and

[1] Alfred Tennyson, *In Memoriam,* st. xxxvi.

privilege is being prepared. The afflictions are real; indeed, on occasion Paul can truthfully speak of them as heavy and almost overwhelming (1:8; cf. 11:23-29). They can be called slight only when contrasted with the even greater **glory** to which they lead. They are also to end soon; they are **for a moment,** i.e., for a short while. Instead of **far more exceeding** (KJV) or **beyond all comparison** (RSV) we may better translate, "more and more exceedingly," "in ever-increasing abundance" (καθ' ὑπερβολὴν εἰς ὑπερβολήν). For Paul and others who serve Christ in the ministry of the church, affliction, which is present and real but in view of the blessing involved light and soon to end, is working out (present tense, κατεργάζεται) an increasingly abundant and **eternal weight** or fullness **of glory.** Paul does not mean that the splendor and privilege will be an earned reward, but that the way of the cross, costly service, is the only way to the newness of life with the risen Christ. **Weight** may suggest that when the afflictions are put in one side of the scale,

---

unfading. Paul can say this because he does not look merely to "the things that are seen but to the things that are unseen" (vs. 18). Our judgment of things depends on the background against which we see them, as the background of a picture gives us perspective and qualifies the foreground. If the background is out of focus, a molehill can look like a mountain. Each of us has in the mind a background of ideas and beliefs in the light of which we make our judgments. If we have no belief in God or a future life, if we know nothing of Christ, if our view of the world is that it is merely a mechanical process without spiritual value or purpose, everything will be colored by this outlook. Trouble will be a disaster; pain will be a calamity; and sorrow a tragedy. But if we have the Christian view, the sufferings of earth will be no more than the chisel strokes of the sculptor, forgotten in the beauty of the statue which he is shaping from the marble, or even welcomed as the means of his achievement. The lost pleasures of life, the things that are denied us, will be no more than the fragments that are chipped from the stone to liberate the artistic masterpiece.

What were the unseen things which made up the background of Paul's mind, shaping his outlook and coloring his judgments? We can distinguish various elements as we scan his writings.

First of all, there was the agelong purpose of God which brought mankind into being and finally broke on the world in Christ. No background to a man's thinking is complete which does not contain the story the Bible tells. Without it our tradition of freedom is hanging in the air, and our moral standards have no solid foundation. When Paul looked at his life, he saw it always in the light of one transforming experience—the meeting with the living Christ on the Damascus road. There God laid hold of him (Phil. 3:13). His one concern thereafter was to fulfill that for which God had laid hold of him. But behind that experience Paul saw the agelong purpose of God which had pursued and found him. God "destined us in love to be his sons" (Eph. 1:5). Robert Louis Stevenson in Samoa wrote of his own past:

> The sights and thoughts of my youth pursue me; and I see like a vision the youth of my father, and of his father, and the whole stream of lives flowing down there far in the north, with the sound of laughter and tears, to cast me out in the end, as by a sudden freshet, on these ultimate islands. And I admire and bow my head before the romance of destiny.[2]

In the light of this background with all its traditions and obligations he lived out his days. Paul looked even farther back—to the foundation of the world. He saw himself laid hold of by that eternal purpose and led into the ministry. It gave him security, confidence, direction, and unconquerable fortitude.

Again, behind everything Paul saw the judgment seat of God. He preached as one who must give account, to men who must give account. Awesome and searching as it is, the thought of judgment to come is indispensable if we are to realize that life matters. To see the throne of God in the background of life gives us a fixed and final standard of judgment. For a Christian man morals are not a matter of opinion. They do not depend on climate or country. What is right in particular situations may not be easy to see; but if we live in the light of God's throne we are never in doubt that his righteousness must be our aim, not merely what is pleasant or convenient.

Finally, Paul saw the sure prospect of ultimate satisfaction for the spirit. This included the perfecting of his nature through the discipline of life, and the fulfillment of God's purpose in the victory of God's kingdom. It included all that we refer to as heaven—"the riches of his glorious inheritance in the saints" (Eph. 1:18). What this would mean he could not fully describe. "Eye hath not seen, nor ear heard, neither have entered into the heart of man, the

[2] *Catriona* (London: Cassell & Co., 1913), Dedication.

18 While we look not at the things which are seen, but at the things which are not seen: for the things which are seen *are* temporal; but the things which are not seen *are* eternal.

comparison, 18 because we look not to the things that are seen but to the things that are unseen; for the things that are seen are transient, but the things that are unseen are eternal.

---

and the **glory**, the blessings and privileges, in the other, the latter will by far outweigh the trials (cf. Rom. 8:18).

18. The opening words in Greek, lit., "we not looking," probably mean **because we look not to** (RSV) or **while we look not at** (KJV) rather than "if we look not at" **the things that are seen,** etc. By **the things . . . seen** Paul means not the beauties of nature and the conveniences of physical life, but primarily at least the physical trials and sufferings he has to endure. **The things that are unseen** (cf. Heb. 11:27) include all the

---

things which God hath prepared for them that love him" (I Cor. 2:9). "The things which God hath prepared" are waiting to be received by us as home awaits the traveler. The book of Revelation shows us what strength this prospect gave the early Christians in face of a world that threatened to crush them. Even Jesus endured his cross in the light of the joy set before him. Against this background of the future glory the trials of life and all the buffetings of circumstance appear in their true perspective. They are a **slight momentary affliction.** As Paul elsewhere says, "The sufferings of this present time are not worth comparing with the glory that is to be revealed to us" (Rom. 8:18).

18. ***Because We Look Not to the Things That Are Seen.***—The view of things unseen not only gave Paul the right perspective; it also gave him the power through which affliction could be met and mastered, like Wordsworth's "Happy Warrior,"

> Who, doomed to go in company with Pain,
> And Fear, and Bloodshed, miserable train!
> Turns his necessity to glorious gain.

The only way to look at life is to see it against the background of God's purpose in Christ and of Christ's victory over sin and death. "We do not yet see everything in subjection to him"—i.e., to man (Heb. 2:8). Evil is still unconquered. The conditions of this present world would fill us with despair if we saw nothing else. "But we see Jesus, who for a little while was made lower than the angels, crowned with glory and honor" (Heb. 2:9). Stephen, looking on the world around him in the hour of his death, saw a ring of savage men hurling stones on his prostrate body. Had he seen nothing else his spirit might well have failed him, but he looked up and saw "the glory of God, and Jesus standing at the right hand of God" (Acts 7:55), and courage and faith filled his soul. His persecutors had no power over his spirit. Their blows became like the hammer strokes which nailed Christ to his cross. His suffering was for Christ and with Christ, and his response to this situation was a prayer like Christ's for the forgiveness of his enemies.

Paul's final word, **the things that are seen are transient, but the things that are unseen are eternal,** sums up the Christian outlook with regard to the events and circumstances of this material world. Sorrow and suffering may be depressing and painful, but they belong to a world that is passing away. The triumph of evil is only temporary. So also are the honors, the material successes, and the pleasures which men value.

> The glories of our blood and state
> Are shadows, not substantial things;
> There is no armour against fate;
> Death lays his icy hand on kings.[3]

But the unseen things—the love God has for us, the triumph of Christ, the kingdom of God, the character which is the fruit of the Spirit—all these are eternal. They are not at the mercy of change or decay. They continue forever.

> When a man grows older and sees more deeply into life, he does not find, if he possesses any inner world at all, that he is advanced by the external march of things, by "the progress of civilisation." Nay, he feels himself, rather, where he was before, and forced to seek the sources of strength which his forefathers also sought. He is forced to make himself a native of the kingdom of God, the kingdom of the Eternal, the kingdom of Love; and he comes to understand that it was only of this kingdom that Jesus Christ desired to speak and to testify.[4]

[3] James Shirley, "Death the Leveller," from *The Contention of Ajax and Ulysses.*

[4] Adolf Harnack, *What Is Christianity?* tr. T. B. Saunders (2nd ed. rev.; New York: G. P. Putnam's Sons; London: Williams & Norgate, 1901), p. 131. Used by permission.

5 For we know that, if our earthly house of *this* tabernacle were dissolved, we have a building of God, a house not made with hands, eternal in the heavens.

5 For we know that if the earthly tent we live in is destroyed, we have a building from God, a house not made with hands,

realities of faith, Christian fellowship, and life in the Spirit. These are not only more real to Paul than the things of sense, but they will endure eternally. The word **eternal** does not say that these realities belong to a timeless sphere, but that they will continue everlastingly.

5. The Hope of an Eternal Home with the Lord (5:1-10)

a) Paul Hopes to Receive It Before Physical Death (5:1-5)

5:1. Already Paul has spoken confidently of the resurrection hope and of the rich and glorious eternal life that awaits the faithful servant of Christ (4:14-18). As the opening word **for** indicates, he now restates that hope of an eternal home, and then considers how he may receive that gift. When he says **we know,** i.e., know with the solid assurance of faith (cf. 4:14), he indicates that this is no new teaching which the Corinthians now hear for the first time. In this section he may be more inclined than formerly to expect his physical death before the end of the age, and more willing that this should occur (vss. 6-8), but the basic hope of a future home with the Lord is not new to him, nor is it new in his teaching. He begins by contrasting the present, fragile, temporary **earthly tent we live in,** "the tentlike body which is our earthly dwelling" (Plummer), with the more durable, **eternal** building or **house** which will come to us as a gift **from God** at the last day. The reference to the physical body as a tent dwelling brings out the inferior, insecure, and transient nature of the present life. The more permanent **building** will be a "spiritual body," **not made with** human **hands** or of human origin, but God's good gift to his people to fit them for life in the coming kingdom. When Paul says that **we have** this building, he may mean by the present tense that the spiritual body is even now prepared and waiting for us. Or more likely he simply expresses the complete certainty that we are to have it. Similarly, **in the heavens** may imply that the spiritual body is ready now in the heavens, to be given us at the appointed time. But more probably it means that the house or spiritual body will be our eternal possession for our life in the heavens, i.e., with God. In affirming that **if** our **earthly tent** or physical body **is destroyed**

5:1. ***If the Earthly Tent We Live in Is Destroyed.***—Paul has been looking at his life in the perspective of the unseen world, and seeing his afflictions in their true setting. Now he faces the fact of death. It is an experience so catastrophic and mysterious that no thoughtful man, however strong his faith, can confront it with complete equanimity. It is an adventure, a step in the dark. Vss. 1-5 describe its nature and Paul's way of meeting it. He has no doubt about the final outcome. The body is **the earthly tent we live in.** It is the temporary habitation of the spirit on this earth, where we live like desert dwellers, as "strangers and pilgrims" (Heb. 11:13). The body, like the tent, is frail and insecure; the spirit of man which inhabits it is real and abiding. Paul would have dismissed the idea that body and spirit are so related that the life of the spirit cannot exist when the body is gone. Though each has an influence on the other, the spirit survives the death of the body. This has often been the impression left on the minds of those who have been with people at the moment of death. Hugh Walpole describes how such a conviction came to him when he was working with the Red Cross on the Russian front in World War I. "It was here that I learned for the first time of the utter unimportance of the body by itself. Something seemed to me always to escape at the moment of death that was of enormous value."[5] Paul's assurance of survival, however, was an integral part of his faith. Its final basis is the love of God revealed in Christ's valuation of the individual human soul. On this, and on his own experience of it in God's love for himself, Paul's faith in immortality finally rests (Rom. 8:38).

But when this earthly tent is destroyed and we enter through death the heavenly region, we shall need—and shall receive—another home. This time it will not be feeble, unsubstantial,

[5] *Affirmations* (London: Ernest Benn, 1928), p. 20.

2 For in this we groan, earnestly desiring to be clothed upon with our house which is from heaven:
3 If so be that being clothed we shall not be found naked.

eternal in the heavens. 2 Here indeed we groan, and long to put on our heavenly dwelling, 3 so that by putting it on we may

(RSV), **dissolved** (KJV), or "pulled down" (καταλυθῇ), we have a permanent house, a spiritual body, Paul does not intend to say that every Christian receives this spiritual body at death. The permanent home will assuredly be ours, but as the following verses indicate, it will be given to all at the last day, and in one of two ways.

2. In vss. 2-4 Paul states that he hopes this age will end and he will receive his spiritual body without having to experience physical death and exist bodiless for a time until the last day comes. The word **for** indicates that he now gives a reason that supports the hope in vs. 1; that we groan for the full gift of God is evidence that the hope will be fulfilled, for such groaning is evidently thought of not as a mere human whim, but as a Spirit-guided desire (cf. vs. 5). **In this** tent, i.e., physical body, **we groan;** the verb **groan** reflects Paul's desire to be free from the afflictions and imperfections of this life, and his sense that thus far he has not received the full range of salvation (cf. Rom. 8:23). Paul still speaks of the spiritual body as a building or **dwelling,** but with the words **put on,** the figure begins to change to the idea of putting on a new garment to replace the old one, and this figure of the garment is then continued through vs. 4, except for one reference to **this tent** (vs. 4). What Paul greatly desires is to put the new garment on over the old, i.e., to receive the promised spiritual body without having to take off the old physical body by death. He wants the end of the age to come before he dies; then he will be transformed without having to die (cf. I Cor. 15:52). The new dwelling is said to be **from heaven** (ἐξ οὐρανοῦ); this may mean that it is now prepared in heaven (cf. Exeg. on vs. 1), or that it will be given us from heaven, i.e., from God.

3. This verse explains why Paul longs to receive the spiritual body as soon as possible. He does not want to die and continue for a time in a bodiless intermediate state that he

and temporary. It will be a **building from God, a house not made with hands, eternal in the heavens.** It will thus be beyond the reach of death and decay. This "spiritual body," as Paul elsewhere calls it, is incorruptible and immortal (I Cor. 15:44, 53). It will correspond to heavenly conditions and environment. Of this Paul is sure. The familiar question of whether or not we shall know one another in heaven does not even arise in his mind. It goes without saying. The survival of personality involves mutual recognition. Without the love of those who have reached the heavenly region we should not be ourselves; for the love of others is a permanent enlargement and enrichment of the self. A man with a home and family is no longer an isolated self. The wife and children whom he loves have become one with himself, and without them he could not be himself.

2-4. ***Here Indeed We Groan, and Long to Put On Our Heavenly Dwelling.***—Paul's anxiety in the face of death now begins to appear. He looks forward to being clothed with his spiritual body. But he is anxious that the change from the earthly tent to the heavenly dwelling should take place with no intermittent stage of disembodiment, which was at least one of the Jewish conceptions of the state of the dead preceding the resurrection. This may well have been the possibility which struck Paul with dismay. The coming of Christ before the hour of death arrived would prevent it. It was for this he longed, for it would mean the immediate change from the earthly tent to the spiritual body. It would have been surprising if he had not looked forward to leaving the frail and ragged tent which was his earthly body. His victory over physical handicaps was a miracle of grace, but time and again he must have chafed at the limitations these imposed. He longed for a life so full and overwhelming that what was mortal would be swallowed up by it, like trampled sand by the incoming tide. This process had already begun, as was evident by the way in which the vitality of his spirit overcame the frailty of his body. When the light of God is flooding a man's soul it shines the more through a physical envelope that is torn. God's strength is made perfect in his weakness (12:9). Death in such a case is only the final destruction of the envelope, a change physically so insignificant that it may

4 For we that are in *this* tabernacle do groan, being burdened: not for that we would be unclothed, but clothed upon, that mortality might be swallowed up of life.

5 Now he that hath wrought us for the selfsame thing *is* God, who also hath given unto us the earnest of the Spirit.

not be found naked.
4 For while we are still in this tent, we sigh with anxiety; not that we would be unclothed, but that we would be further clothed, so that what is mortal may be swallowed up by life.
5 He who has prepared us for this very thing is God, who has given us the Spirit as a guarantee.

---

describes as **naked;** if the end comes before he dies, he will escape that imperfect intermediate existence. Translated literally, with supplementary explanations, the verse says: "If indeed [εἴ γε or εἴπερ], being actually [καί] clothed" with the promised eternal spiritual body, "we shall not" have to continue for a time without any body and so "be found naked" at the last day.

4. The point of vss. 2-3 is restated in clearer form. "For indeed we who are in the tent," i.e., we who are still living in this physical body, **groan** (this verb is the same one used in vs. 2), "being burdened" by the deep sense of the afflictions and limitations of this present existence and by the strong desire to receive the spiritual body without experiencing physical death. The latter point is then explicitly stated: "For [ἐφ' ᾧ seems to mean "for" or "because"] we do not want to be unclothed" by losing our physical body at death; "but" our longing is rather "to be clothed upon," to put on the spiritual body as a new garment without first stripping off the old garment, "so that the mortal" physical body "is swallowed up" and instantly replaced "by the" perfect eternal "life" with God that those with the spiritual body will enjoy.

5. This very thing seems to refer back to the idea of the closing words of vs. 4, the final replacement of the mortal form of life in a physical body by the perfect and eternal life in the spiritual body. For this transformation God **has prepared us;** Paul here thinks not of creation, but of the renewal that God's grace has worked in him, and especially of the transforming work of the Holy Spirit in him (cf. 3:6). Indeed, the gift of **the Spirit,** who has begun the transformation of Christians, is also the promise of rich blessings to come. He is the **earnest** (KJV) or **guarantee** (RSV; cf. Exeg. on 1:22) that "he who began a good work in you will bring it to completion at the day of Jesus Christ" (Phil. 1:6). "The Spirit gives life" even now (3:6), and God's gift of the Spirit is also the pledge that he will give full and perfect life in a perfect spiritual body in the eternal kingdom. On the spiritual body, see I Cor. 15:42-53; it is the perfectly adapted organ of personal life in the perfect order into which all Christ's redeemed people will enter at the end of this age.

---

scarcely be noticed. He dies into glory as the stars die into the sunrise. Yet though the physical process of death may be as natural as falling asleep, it should be noted that death ushers in a crisis for the spirit which the N.T. takes seriously. It confronts us with the judgment; it introduces us to a world which will make demands we cannot meet save through the grace of God. It bids us ask the question

> How will the change strike me and you
> In the house not made with hands? [6]

We can meet this change with Paul's confidence only if, like him, we are in Christ and through the power of Christ's resurrection in us are clothed with newness of life. It is God who must prepare us.

5. *The Spirit as Guarantee.*—The Spirit is the pledge that the change is going on, and the **guarantee** that it will be completed. It is no victory of our own spirit over the frail and afflicted body that makes us both capable and sure of this eternal life. It is the life from above which has already invaded and possessed our spirit, and taken us up into itself. We do not fit ourselves for the future life by any spiritual gymnastic of our own, like a runner training for a race. It is the invasion of the Spirit of God, enabling us to triumph in Christ through making us captive to his love (2:14). His grasp of us, not our hold on him, is our final and invincible assurance. Our love to God is shallow and

[6] Robert Browning, "By the Fireside," st. xxvii.

6 Therefore *we are* always confident, knowing that, whilst we are at home in the body, we are absent from the Lord:	6 So we are always of good courage; we know that while we are at home in the body we are away from the Lord, 7 for we
7 (For we walk by faith, not by sight:)	

b) He Is Content to Die and Be with the Lord (5:6-8)

6. So points back to what has just been said in vs. 5; since God "has prepared us" for the gift of the spiritual body and for the enjoyment of true, full life in the perfect kingdom, and has "given us the Spirit as a guarantee" that he will fulfill all he has promised, Paul faces the afflictions of life and even the possibility of physical death with **good courage. Always** means no matter what he must undergo, and even if he must face death. It may seem to us that the prospect of physical death would drain away his courage, especially when we remember how earnestly he speaks in vss. 2-4 of his desire to receive the permanent spiritual body without dying. But Paul explains how it is that he can feel so courageous as he faces this prospect of death. He is under a great limitation as long as he lives **in the** physical **body;** he is **away from the Lord.** To be sure, he has been privileged to see "the glory of God in the face of Christ" (4:6), and in a real and vital way Christ lives in him, even in this life (Gal. 2:20); the Christians as a church are the body of Christ and so in living touch with their risen Lord (I Cor. 12:27; Col. 1:18, 27). Yet great as are these privileges, they do not give complete vision. Though Paul knows that his life is indeed "hid with Christ in God" (Col. 3:3), he looks for a day when he will see God and Christ, and all the things that in this life "no eye has seen, nor ear heard" (I Cor. 2:9); "now we see in a mirror dimly, but then face to face" (I Cor. 13:12). It is clear from this verse that in Paul's view physical death will enable the faithful servant of Christ to enter into a state of fuller vision of God and the unseen world. So even though the bodiless intermediate state is incomplete, and Paul shrinks from it, as vss. 2-4 show, yet since death will give entrance into this fuller vision, he can face death with **good courage;** if it comes, he will be **at home with the Lord** Christ (vs. 8).

7. In the Greek vs. 6 is not a complete sentence. It reads: "So, being always of good courage, and knowing that while we are at home in the body we are away from the Lord." Vs. 7 is a parenthesis interrupting the construction. Then vs. 8 resumes and completes what vs. 6 had started to say. In vs. 7 Paul explains what he means by saying that while living in this physical body we are **away from** (RSV) or **absent from** (KJV) the Lord. Here we do not clearly see the Lord and the heavenly world in which he rules; we cannot see the situation into which he will bring us. So we must **walk by** a **faith** that trusts God

inconstant, but his love to us is a power that will not let us go.

6-7. ***So We Are Always of Good Courage.***—Paul examines both conditions, the earthly and the heavenly. While the physical body, which includes the material environment, is our home, **we are away from the Lord.** Then **we walk by faith, not by sight.** This does not mean that the presence of Christ is less real in the true sense of the word. The very fact that he still lives means that his presence is independent of time and space. There are moments when the conviction that he is near is vivid. Samuel Rutherford, in prison in Aberdeen, wrote that Christ came to his cell one night and every stone in the wall shone like a ruby. But so long as we are **in the body,** his presence must largely be an article of faith. Sight is the physical vision of material things; faith is the insight which apprehends the realities of the spirit—goodness, truth, and love. But the contrast between faith and sight is not absolute. Sight and insight may both operate together as they do in looking at a picture, where we see not only the form and colors of the scene but also its beauty. Physical sight is important to us so long as we are in the body and living in a material world. Christ came to earth so that men might see him, that his physical presence might be the medium for their apprehension of his Spirit. But without the insight to see his character his physical presence would have meant no more to them than that of any ordinary man. For lack of this insight the Jews saw in him only a village carpenter. Walking by faith, however, does not mean that we walk entirely in the dark by a kind of blind trust. It means that in a material world the vision of faith must always be fitful and incomplete.

8 We are confident, *I say,* and willing rather to be absent from the body, and to be present with the Lord.

9 Wherefore we labor, that, whether present or absent, we may be accepted of him.

walk by faith, not by sight. 8 We are of good courage, and we would rather be away from the body and at home with the Lord. 9 So whether we are at home or away,

---

and obeys him even though he cannot be seen; Paul's idea is similar to that in Heb. 11:27, where it is paradoxically said of Moses that "he endured as seeing him who is invisible." In this life we do not see God as we later shall, and this for Paul is a real limitation.

8. Resuming the sentence started in vs. 6, Paul states the position to which the desire for a fuller vision of the Lord has brought him. **We are of good courage and** "think it good," or "are quite content" (εὐδοκοῦμεν), to undergo physical death, which would separate us **from the body** before the gift of the spiritual body at the last day. If death should come, we would be **at home with the Lord** in a closer union and clearer vision than is possible in this earthly life. The RSV translation **we would rather** is too strong; Paul is "quite content" to die, but he does not mean that he enthusiastically prefers it. He sees a limitation in either lot. If he remains in this body, he will not see the Lord as he would after death; if he dies, he will be without a body, and that is a state from which he shrinks. But the privilege of being at home with the Lord and seeing him more fully, even before the end of this age, is enough to enable him to overcome his shrinking and be quite content to face physical death.

c) The Main Thing: Be Ready Always for Judgment (5:9-10)

9. Wherefore (διό), since the privilege of being with the Lord is as great as has been indicated, the most important thing is to make sure that we receive it. Paul has stated his desire to live until the end of the age (vss. 2-4); he has expressed his willingness to die before that day comes, since death would bring the great privilege of more open fellowship

---

There will be times when we have to walk by the light of conviction, or by the memory of insights which were once clear to us, just as in a dark night a flash of light may reveal the path for a moment and enable us to follow it even when we cannot see it. In the heavenly world our insight will be unclouded. "Now we see through a glass, darkly; but then face to face" (I Cor. 13:12).

8. ***At Home with the Lord.***—This is the condition Paul covets. He thinks of heaven as **home.** The word suggests the place where we feel secure, where our fellowship with those we love is complete, and where we are free to be most fully ourselves. Heaven is home in the full sense of the word for those who are in fellowship with Christ. There, Paul believed, we shall enter on that unclouded fellowship with God which is not disturbed by guilt or fear, or limited by human failure and the frustrations of earth.

Because we are spiritual beings this earth can never be home in any true sense of the word. We can never feel completely at rest in it. William Watson describes this condition in his poem, "World Strangeness."[7] This lack of harmony between man and his earthly environment accounts for man's restlessness. Augustine sums up his own experience: "Thou hast made us unto thyself, and our heart finds no rest until it rests in thee."[8]

There is a sense, however, in which we can be **at home with the Lord** even here if we are at one with his purpose and walk by his light. When Jesus was on earth people who were sincere found themselves at home in his company, even publicans and sinners. His presence created an atmosphere of understanding and love in which they could begin to be their true selves. Through fellowship with him the world becomes in a real sense the Father's house. Yet at the best this world has its limitations. We remain pilgrims and strangers, always seeking a fuller life, which can be found only in heaven where our fellowship with God will be complete. This is what Paul means by being at home with the Lord. Heaven is not a place but a spiritual condition. It is the product of the heavenly mind and the heavenly fellowship.

9-10. ***Our Aim.***—Life in this world and beyond has one aim for Paul—**to please** Christ. J. S. Mill said he could conceive of no higher way of living than that a man should so act that

[7] *Selected Poems* (London: John Lane, 1903).

[8] *Confessions* I. 1.

10 For we must all appear before the judgment seat of Christ; that every one may receive the things *done* in *his* body, according to that he hath done, whether *it be* good or bad.

we make it our aim to please him. 10 For we must all appear before the judgment seat of Christ, so that each one may receive good or evil, according to what he has done in the body.

---

with the Lord (vss. 6-8). Yet these things he must leave in the hands of God. But he can and must **make it** his **aim** to be well pleasing to the Lord; the assurance of God's grace and help never leads Paul to relax his own active effort to be faithful and obedient (cf. I Cor. 9:27). The contrast, **whether we are at home** in this physical body, **or away** in the bodiless state following death, may seem to imply that Paul thinks of the intermediate state as one in which moral striving and responsibility continue. But this idea he never elsewhere suggests; the thought here is rather that it is not important whether the final day finds us **at home** in the physical body **or away,** i.e., already separated from that body by death; what counts is that while we have time we should make every effort **to please** the Lord.

10. As **for** shows, Paul now gives the reason why he must make every effort to please his Lord. **We . . . all** means all of us Christians. We **must all appear,** "be made manifest," have our life laid open for scrutiny and decision as to its quality (φανερωθῆναι, the same verb that the RSV translates "disclose" in I Cor. 4:5). We shall stand **before the judgment seat of Christ.** At times Paul says that God will judge (e.g., Rom. 2:3); at other times, as here, Christ is the judge named. There is no conflict; God judges through Christ, as Rom. 2:16 clearly states. Christ is the Lord of both the living and dead (Rom. 14:9), and will judge both groups (Acts 10:42). That he will judge is repeatedly stated, not only in the Acts and epistles, but likewise in the Gospels (Matt. 16:27; 25:31-32). That God will judge all men through Christ Paul did not doubt (cf. Rom. 2:6-8), but here he speaks

---

Jesus Christ would approve his life. But Paul has an even more exacting standard—**the judgment seat of Christ.** The certainty of final judgment was never out of the apostle's mind. It was an element in Christ's own teaching (cf. the parables of the last judgment, Matt. 25). And it has deep significance. It underscores the fact that our lives have meaning. We are responsible beings, not the playthings of fate. Without any ultimate responsibility our actions lose point, except as they promote our own temporal interests. Furthermore, the assurance that life has eternal meaning gives it zest. William James, in his discussion of the question whether life is worth living, writes:

> If this life be not a real fight, in which something is eternally gained for the universe by success, it is no better than a game of private theatricals from which one may withdraw at will. But it *feels* like a real fight,—as if there were something really wild in the universe which we, with all our idealities and faithfulnesses, are needed to redeem; and first of all to redeem our own hearts from atheisms and fears.[9]

Life is worth while because we are here to fulfill God's purpose. The optimism of the Christian faith is based in part on this assurance, and the

[9] *The Will to Believe* (New York: Longmans, Green & Co., 1917), p. 61.

symbol of it is the **judgment seat** of God. Judgment is therefore not to be dreaded by Christians, but to be accepted and even welcomed.

There are various reasons for this, apart from the fact that it gives our ordinary life moral significance. God's judgment is based on the insight of almighty love. "Man looketh on the outward appearance, but the LORD looketh on the heart" (I Sam. 16:7.) He judges us by our hidden desires and intentions, not by our imperfect performance, frustrated as that is by the weakness of the flesh and the thwarting of circumstance.

> But all, the world's coarse thumb
> And finger failed to plumb,
> So passed in making up the main account;
> All instincts immature,
> All purposes unsure,
> That weighed not as his work, yet swelled the man's
> amount.[1]

God's judgment does not spring from any desire to condemn, but from the desire so to awaken the conviction of sin that we shall be ready to turn from it. "And I beheld, and, lo, in the midst of the throne . . . stood a Lamb as it had been slain" (Rev. 5:6).

[1] Robert Browning, "Rabbi Ben Ezra," st. xxiv.

11 Knowing therefore the terror of the Lord, we persuade men; but we are made manifest unto God; and I trust also are made manifest in your consciences.

11 Therefore, knowing the fear of the Lord, we persuade men; but what we are is known to God, and I hope it is known

only of the Christians; remembering that the judgment is surely coming at the end of the age, he and all other Christians must prepare to meet it. At that time **each one** will **receive** a judgment based on and in accordance with **what he has done in the body;** he will be judged by how well or badly he has responded during his earthly life to the grace of God that opened to him the privilege of faith, fellowship, and useful living. A rather literal translation of the latter part of the verse, filled out to show how it may best be understood, is: "In order that each one may receive" the proper recompense for "the things done through [or while living in] the body, in accordance with the things that he has done [or practiced], whether" that life record is "good or bad." Paul is certain that he and all Christians owe their presence in the church entirely to the grace of God. He also knows that it is only through the daily gift of grace and power that Christians continue on their way. Indeed, he never doubts that in the end all the saved must say that their salvation is an undeserved gift. Yet for him this never cancels the urgent responsibility to obey faithfully God's will, and he expects to have to account for his record. He can hold both of these apparently contradictory truths because for him divine grace is a morally creative force which opens up great possibilities of good living.

6. The Ministry of Reconciliation (5:11–6:10)

a) Paul Seeks to Serve God and the Corinthians (5:11-13)

11. In vss. 11-13 the note of defense sounds again: Paul's ministry has been marked by devotion to God, unselfish service to the Corinthians, and manifest integrity. **Therefore** refers back to the statement in vs. 10 that he, like all Christians, must stand before Christ for judgment. **Knowing the fear of the Lord** (Christ) is to be interpreted in the same connection. **Knowing** here has the sense of "prompted by and keenly feeling." **Fear** is not **terror,** as the KJV misleadingly translates; it is the wholesome reverential awe and respect with which Paul thinks of facing the divine Lord who will judge him. This reverential fear leads him to **persuade men,** either of the truth and urgency of the gospel message with which he is entrusted, or of the integrity of his ministry and motives. But whether other men recognize this integrity or not, **what we are is** even now fully **known to God** (cf. the closing words of I Cor. 13:12). At the last day we must all be made

The Christian is one who through Christ seeks to be done with lies and self-deceit, and to live in the light of moral reality. That light will be welcomed as we welcome the light of day, even though it shames us by revealing the ugliness and failure of our own lives. A sincere man welcomes the criticism of a friend, however it may pain him, because he knows that it comes from one who loves him too well to let him go on in evil. God's judgment carries with it the prospect that we shall see him in the glory of his perfect love. This will make us ashamed and bring us to the dust in humiliation. But it will also lift us up. Christ's attitude to sinners in the world beyond will not be other than it was on earth. "For God sent the Son into the world, not to condemn the world, but that the world might be saved through him" (John 3:17). It is in the light of this final judgment that we must live here and now. The judgment is not postponed to the future. It operates continually as we keep our lives open to his cross. Through the acceptance of his judgment and our response to his forgiveness we are redeemed. As for the final judgment, the God who will judge will still be the God who is "faithful and just to forgive us our sins, and to cleanse us from all unrighteousness" (I John 1:9). The purpose of the judgment is the perfecting of the process of redemption.

11. *What We Are Is Known to God.*—In the light of the judgment seat of Christ Paul lives and preaches. The fear of the Lord is not, of course, the fear of what may follow the judgment. It is the awe that comes from the vision of God's holiness, and the inexorable demands of his righteousness. The judgment of holy love is more terrible to face than the judgment of

12 For we commend not ourselves again unto you, but give you occasion to glory on our behalf, that ye may have somewhat to *answer* them which glory in appearance, and not in heart.

13 For whether we be beside ourselves, *it is* to God: or whether we be sober, *it is* for your cause.

also to your conscience.
12 We are not commending ourselves to you again but giving you cause to be proud of us, so that you may be able to answer those who pride themselves on a man's position and not on his heart.
13 For if we are beside ourselves, it is for God; if we are in our right mind,

---

manifest, as vs. 10 states, but at every point along the way there is no hiding from God; Paul always lives and works "in the sight of God" (2:17). This to Paul is both a sobering and a reassuring thought, for he implies that God knows him and approves his work. But even this assurance is not enough; he also wants the readers to believe in him. He lives to serve his Lord and his churches, and he deeply desires his Corinthian friends to be fully assured of his sincerity and uprightness: "I hope that" what we are "has become clear also in your" individual "consciences." He has good hopes that they as Christians have sufficient sympathy and insight to sense the integrity of his life.

12. Repeatedly Paul finds it necessary to defend himself; in one sense, in order to win men's confidence and spread the gospel, he must "commend" himself (cf. 4:2; 6:4). But instantly he feels the danger in such self-commendation, and realizes that it can seem nothing but egotistical boasting. So here, as in 3:1, he denies that he is speaking just to recommend himself and gain personal advantage. The word **again,** here and in 3:1, indicates that in an earlier letter he had boasted of his work in a way that aroused criticism from unfriendly persons. If chs. 10–13 are part of the "stern letter," as seems probable, Paul is pointing back to such passages as 11:16–12:13. Paul hints that the Corinthians should take over the defense of his ministry; all he is doing now is to **give you occasion** (or "good grounds," as Plummer well suggests) "for a boast on our behalf, in order that you may have" something to say "in answer to those" critics of Paul "who boast in outward position," such as pure Jewish descent and impressive personal gifts (10:12; 11:22), "and not in the heart," the inner thoughts and intents that determine the real quality of the life. These words are directed primarily against the intruders or "false apostles" whom Paul had denounced in the "stern letter."

13. The reference in **beside ourselves** is not to the amazing zeal that marked Paul's ministry, but to the notable spiritual experiences that he had had. These may have included his spectacular conversion (4:6; Acts 9:3-9), his "visions and revelations of the Lord" (12:1-4), and his "speaking in tongues," in which he was specially gifted (I Cor. 14:18). The charge seems to have been made that he had used these experiences to impress

---

one who does not care about us. Paul preaches as one whose work God will judge to men who will also be judged. He is clear that God knows his sincerity and he hopes that his hearers also will recognize it. He appeals to the judgment of their conscience. No man can hope to convince people of the truth he declares unless they are convinced that he is sincere, that he himself is living by what he believes, and has no other object but their eternal good.

12. *We Are Not Commending Ourselves.*— Paul's motive in saying this is not self-commendation. It is that these Corinthian Christians may have just reason for being **proud** of him. The only right reason for people to be proud of their minister is his complete sincerity with truth, and his disinterested concern for their souls; it is not his eloquence, his power of intellect, or his scholarship. Here is the real answer to those who judge men by externals and not by character; and Paul has written in this way not to commend himself, but to provide that answer.

13. *If We Are Beside Ourselves.*—This must refer to a suggestion that at times Paul had been out of his mind. He does not deny that there were moments in his life when he was in an ecstatic mood, speaking with tongues, soaring in his preaching beyond the range of ordinary experience. Jesus was charged with being "beside himself" (Mark 3:21). A true Christian will sometimes be thought eccentric because the center around which his life revolves is not where worldly people assume it ought to be. Men like

14 For the love of Christ constraineth us; because we thus judge, that if one died for all, then were all dead:

it is for you. 14 For the love of Christ controls us, because we are convinced that one has died for all; therefore all have

---

people and advance his own interests. This he denies; in such privileged experiences he is concerned only **for God;** they are sacred times of precious close relationship with God. These times were rare, and he knew where his duty lay. He did not forget his ministry; he worked in a sane, unselfish, and **right mind.** His purpose was clear and steady: **it is for you** and your spiritual benefit, he says, that I am concerned and work (cf. I Cor. 14:19).

b) In Christ God Reconciled Men to Himself (5:14-19)

In these verses Paul sets forth the heart of the gospel. No passage of his letters is more important. In such passages as Rom. 3:21-26 he makes it clear that the justification God offers to sinful men is a gracious gift that they do not deserve; man owes his salvation solely to the grace of God. This insight is basic in the Christian faith. It is included here, but Paul goes past the idea of legal acquittal, which justification expresses, to say that the grace of God effects a vital personal relationship to God and an inner transformation. Outstanding similar passages are Rom. 6:1-11; Col. 3:1-4.

14. Acting in reverential fear of the Lord Christ (vs. 11), Paul combines devotion to God and faithful ministry for his churches (vs. 13). Now, with the word **for,** he (**we** may include his fellow workers) gives another explanation of his great concern for his converts. **The love** that **Christ** has shown for him, especially in dying for him, **controls** him (RSV), impels him, urges him on, or as συνέχει may mean, **constraineth** him (KJV) by holding him back from self-centered boasting and living. This powerful love of Christ for him controls him, not against his will, but **because we are convinced,** "we have decided" (κρίναντας), **that one** [viz., Christ] **has died for all. For** (ὑπέρ) means "on their behalf and for their good"; in such unselfish death is an element of substitution, as vs. 21 confirms, but the central idea is that the death was for the benefit of others. The word **all** expresses

---

Francis of Assisi are called mad because the world that judges them is mad. Its values are completely different from theirs. The early Christians were accused of turning the world upside down (Acts 17:6). The truth is that it was upside down and they were trying to put it right side up. Paul might have made some such reply. All he says is that his ecstatic moments are a matter between God and himself. They have been due to the inspiration of the Spirit and not to any mental aberration. But when, according to the view of these Corinthian Christians, he is in his right mind, he is then in all sincerity seeking their interests and not his own. That is all that need concern them.

14*a*. ***For the Love of Christ Controls Us.***— Paul's mind and heart are under the conscious control of Christ. The word translated **constraineth** in the KJV means to be impelled or driven along a course from which one cannot deviate. A great missionary describes the life of Paul as being like the river Yangtze, sometimes surging through a narrow channel, sometimes flowing through a level plain, but always irresistibly moving onward to the sea. The element of restraint involved in the control of Christ has to do only with selfish desires, or with impulses that would waste our energies in secondary aims. What controls Paul is not his love for Christ; it is Christ's love for him. Wherever Paul speaks of the love of God or the love of Christ he nearly always means God's love or Christ's love, not ours. Our love is at best a response to that of Christ. It is when we forget ourselves in the contemplation of his love for us that love to Christ is born and grows; though in comparison with the splendor of his love, ours will be so feeble that we shall be almost unaware of it. Its reality will be shown by the extent to which we cease to live to ourselves. This love of Christ for us is centered in the Cross. There lies the secret of its dynamic power. Paul goes on to define the meaning of the Cross for him and for us.

14*b*. ***Because We Are Convinced That One Has Died for All; Therefore All Have Died.***— The precise meaning of this is hard to assess. It springs from Christ's identification with all mankind. The fact that he gave himself up to death as a result of human sin means that he surrendered himself to share our condition; and the fact that he **died** means that we **all have died,** i.e., in him we are dead to sin, a death which is the condition of true life. The experience of

15 And *that* he died for all, that they
which live should not henceforth live unto
themselves, but unto him which died for
them, and rose again.

died. 15 And he died for all, that those who
live might live no longer for themselves
but for him who for their sake died and
was raised.

---

the fact that the benefit of what Christ did is open to all men of all races, but it assumes that the benefit becomes effective only through faith. Paul can say that **therefore all have died** because he thinks of Christ as the new Adam, the representative and head of the new humanity, who as members of his body, the church, are vitally linked with him in all things (cf. Rom. 5:12-21; I Cor. 15:47-49). So they died with him, and when they come to faith, they die to the old life and rise to "newness of life" (Rom. 6:1-11; Col. 3:1, 3).

15. The purpose of Christ in dying **for all** was not just to save them from sin and judgment, but to make them capable and useful servants for himself. They are to **live no longer for themselves;** rather, sharing and willingly imitating his sacrificial and unselfish spirit, they are to live **for him,** even in their present situation. This earthly life is the field of that service. The phrase **for their sake** probably goes with both **died** and **raised.** As Paul says in Rom. 4:25, Christ's work was not completed by his death, but only by

---

salvation is one in which we pass from the death which is death indeed, through death with Christ into life with him. Apart from Christ we are dead *in* sin; but in Christ we are dead *to* sin. F. W. Robertson says:

> Paul does not say that Christ died in order that men might *not* die, but exactly for this very purpose, that they *might;* and this death he represents in the next verse by an equivalent expression—the life of unselfishness: "that they which live might henceforth live not unto themselves." The "dead" of the first verse are "they that live" of the second.[2]

This radical view of man's condition makes it clear that Christ's intervention on our behalf is a vital necessity. Faith in Christ is not something added to life which makes it more livable or more gracious; it is the secret of a deliverance without which there is no hope. Christian belief is therefore not merely preferable to other forms of belief or unbelief; it is literally a matter of life or death. To see this fact and accept it is the first step to life, for it brings us face to face with the reality of sin. This is what the cross of Christ reveals to us. When we see him die as the result of sin we become aware of what sin is, just as we realize the deadly nature of some invisible bacillus by seeing the condition to which it reduces a healthy man. In the case of sin, however, it strikes home to us through the Cross that what killed Christ is our sin and that we are responsible for it. So we come to realize our true condition.

This awakening to the reality and power of sin through seeing its results on those who have to bear them, and especially on those who love us, is a familiar experience. A son goes wrong and his father, one with him in love, suffers the shame, pain, and loss which are the results of that wrongdoing. Seeing what his sin has done to his father, and the love which makes the father bear it, the son realizes its nature and his responsibility. He becomes aware of his condition. That is what happens when we see in the cross of Christ the tragic consequences of our sin borne by one who loves us. Pride, self-righteousness, respect for ourselves, and all the illusions about ourselves which blind us to our true condition are shattered. We realize that apart from Christ we are spiritually dead.

But that is only the beginning of the saving experience.

15. *That Those Who Live Might Live No Longer for Themselves.*—We die with Christ in order that we may live. Life is born when we enter by faith into the sacrifice of Christ and accept the attitude to sin and to God which made him give himself for us. A man who is being swept down to death in a raging stream may be saved in spite of himself. He may be saved after he has lost consciousness. But we cannot be saved from sin in spite of ourselves. We can be saved from the death of sin only as our souls are awakened to desire the new life and to co-operate with Christ in our salvation. Vincent Taylor says that on the Cross Christ, in his identification with us and on our behalf, offered to God obedience to his will of righteousness, submission to his judgment of sin, and the contrition of perfect penitence from which the new life springs.[3] As we enter by faith into the spirit of Christ's sacrifice we become alive,

[2] "The Sacrifice of Christ," *Sermons*, 3rd Series (Boston: Ticknor & Fields, 1859), p. 143.

[3] *Jesus and His Sacrifice* (London: Macmillan & Co., 1937), pp. 307-10.

16 Wherefore henceforth know we no man after the flesh: yea, though we have known Christ after the flesh, yet now henceforth know we *him* no more.

16 From now on, therefore, we regard no one from a human point of view; even though we once regarded Christ from a human point of view, we regard him thus

---

his triumphant resurrection, which led to his position of authority at the right hand of God, and will lead to his complete victory over all God's foes at the last day. So the benefit of Christ's vicarious and costly ministry for all comes from the combined effect of his death and resurrection.

16. **Wherefore** (ὥστε) introduces a statement that gives the result of what has just been said. What is the result when Paul, and other apostolic workers like him, are drawn into such an unselfish life with the risen Christ? He no longer looks at things or thinks of Christ as he did before conversion (vs. 16); "he is a new creation" (vs. 17). **From now on** does not mean from the moment of writing, but from the time of conversion, when Paul, realizing that Christ died for all and so for him, believed. **Know** (KJV; οἴδαμεν) here means **regard** (RSV), "consider," "estimate." To estimate persons **after the flesh** (KJV; κατὰ σάρκα) or **from a human point of view** (RSV) is to judge them

---

and as we continue to live in his fellowship this life becomes progressively more real and abundant. To be one with Christ is to live. Through this union, Taylor says:

> When [a man] comes into the presence of God, it is not as a naked soul, carrying poor gifts of his own devising; he comes as one whose gifts are transfigured and caught up into something greater. The poverty of his obedience, the weakness of his submission, and the frailty of his penitence pass into strength and power in virtue of his union with Christ by faith and love. A gratitude is created which is too deep for words, and a sense of obligation which brooks neither denial nor delay.[4]

This life in Christ reveals itself in a new objective—that we who live might live no longer to ourselves but to him who died for us and rose again. True life is life with a new motive. The self-centered motive is displaced by the Christ-centered motive. We cease to live for ourselves, our own interests, advantage, or success, and begin to live for him. Our object is to be used by him in his work of redemption, and in the fulfillment through fellowship with him of the purpose of God. It is often objected that there is no difference between Christians and non-Christians. There ought to be. Christ demanded it. He asked, "If you love those who love you, . . . what more are you doing than others?" (Matt. 5:46-47.) The difference may not show itself in outward actions or habits. The non-Christian may do his work, or care for his family, or fulfill his civic or national duty as conscientiously as the Christian. The real difference will be in motive. In the case of the non-Christian the motive may be ambition, a desire to stand well with others, a love of his family,

[4] *Ibid.*, p. 317.

a sense of duty. The motive of the Christian is the love of Christ. Whatever he does, he does for Christ. This motive will inevitably reveal itself in his spirit. It will reveal itself in decisions made perhaps at moments of crisis. It will reveal itself in the things a Christian will do which a non-Christian often will not do, e.g., forgive his enemies. In such matters he does not follow the accepted standards of the community. He will do what the love of Christ demands because he is not living for himself; he is living for Christ, which also means, of course, for those for whom Christ died. The word **might** in the RSV is translated **should** in the KJV. Both are correct. A distinction may, however, be drawn. "Should" implies more strongly a sense of obligation. "Might" implies also the power to fulfill it. The door is open to what was formerly impossible. In the love of Christ the power to abandon self and follow him is available.

He died for all: There are no exceptions. The whole world has come under the condemnation of death, but all are included in the possibility of redemption which Christ's death opened up. There is no depth to which a man may have sunk from which he cannot be restored to sonship with God. No privilege, no position we have won, no goodness we have achieved, no level of respectable conduct, can exempt us from the judgment of the Cross. But no evil we have done, whatever it is, can exclude us from the sweep and power of the everlasting mercy.

16. ***From Now On, Therefore, We Regard No One from a Human Point of View.***—This verse is in part a diversion from the main argument, yet it is relevant. The human estimate of men was abolished at the Cross. Race, nationality, birth, money, position, intellectual gifts, social status, etc.—all these standards of value disap-

by external situation and standards, without a true understanding of their worth and place in God's sight; in particular, as applied to Christ, it means to think of his lowly life and shameful crucifixion as proof that he was disowned by God and so should be rejected by men. Paul **once regarded Christ** in this way; that was before he became a

---

pear in the light of Calvary. None of them can be the basis for a Christian valuation, and must not be allowed to affect our attitude to men or our relationship with one another as children of God. The one basic fact about us all is that we are sinners whom nevertheless God loves. In the light of the Cross Paul saw through the superficial things which often conceal our real selves. Every man to him was the "brother for whom Christ died" (I Cor. 8:11). This is the real foundation of fellowship. It is the basis of that forgiveness of one another through which alone fellowship is possible. Albert Schweitzer asks, "Why do I forgive anyone?" and answers,

> I must forgive the lies directed against myself, because my own life has been so many times blotted by lies; I must forgive the lovelessness, the hatred, the slander, the fraud, the arrogance which I encounter since I myself have so often lacked love, hated, slandered, defrauded, and been arrogant.[5]

No genuine community can be created by social status, intellectual interests, nationality, race, or mere sentiment. A community united by one or another of these factors may appear to be strong, but it is subject to the disintegrating power of sin, particularly of pride. All sin is antisocial. Attempts have been made to create fellowship by imposing an artificial equality in rank or property. But the only equality which can unite us is that produced by the judgment of God, in which we are all reduced to the same level of need. "All we like sheep have gone astray" (Isa. 53:6). This brings us together also in a common sense of gratitude to Christ, who has borne "the iniquity of us all." Men should be estimated by their Christian character, which consists in their honesty of purpose in seeking righteousness and serving their fellows. This honesty is revealed in the extent to which they cease to live for themselves. The final test, as Paul makes clear, is love. If we have all the gifts of the spirit but have not love, we are nothing (I Cor. 13). It is as definite as that. Without love, through which we live in right relationship with others, we are ciphers. We have, in the real sense of the word, no personality.

When Paul goes on to say that even though he may have **once regarded Christ from a human point of view,** he does so no longer, he must not be taken as meaning more than the words convey. The RSV disposes of various speculations concerning his meaning which were left open by the KJV, **though we have known Christ after the flesh.** It disposes of the suggestion that Paul was speaking of his estimate of Christ as the Jewish Messiah. Equally impossible is the idea that Paul refers to his knowledge of the earthly life and deeds of Jesus. Whether or not he had come into contact with Jesus matters little. That he did know with accuracy the contents of what was afterward recorded in the Gospels is certain. Apart from anything else, he could scarcely have been in close company with Peter and John without hearing in detail about their Master. The man who had met the risen Christ in a transforming experience would not be satisfied till he knew all that was to be known about him. Every word would be precious.

The statement that he no longer **regarded Christ from a human point of view** means just what it says. All false ideas about him were gone. Gone were the prejudices that busied themselves with his lowly birth, his humble social position, his association with doubtful characters, his disregard of the law, his appeal to the ignorant and oppressed. These all disappeared when the scales fell from Paul's eyes and he saw "the glory of God in the face of Christ" (4:6).

But there is more. To regard Christ **from a human point of view** means to lay emphasis on externals, to think of him merely in relation to his own time, to become immersed in such personal details as are emphasized in some biographies. These may be interesting, but they do not really matter. What must emerge from the picture, if we are to know him, is the ever-living Christ who once dwelt among men that they might behold his glory, and who now dwells in the heart. Such knowledge, living, personal, is real knowledge. This does not mean, as has been suggested, that Paul was indifferent to the earthly life and teaching of Jesus, and that he depended upon the Spirit for all he knew. The guidance of the Spirit has no content for us apart from that fact in history which was the earthly life and teaching of Christ. To seek the Spirit's guidance without a study of the facts is to lay ourselves open to the suggestions of our own capricious desires, and to take these for the leading of the Spirit. Countless wrongs have been done in the name of religion which would have been impossible if those who did them had been open to the message and spirit of Christ revealed in the Gospels. It is for lack of this

[5] *Civilization and Ethics*, tr. John Naish (London: A. & C. Black, 1923), II, 260.

17 Therefore if any man *be* in Christ, *he is* a new creature: old things are passed away; behold, all things are become new.

no longer. 17 Therefore, if any one is in Christ, he is a new creation;[g] the old has passed away, behold, the new has come.

[g] Or *creature.*

Christian, when he was still sinfully persecuting Christ's followers. But **now** (νῦν), since we have become Christians, **we regard him thus no longer,** for we know that he was sent of God to save men, and that as the risen Lord he rightfully claims the full allegiance of every man.

17. Paul now presents, more positively than he did in vs. 16, what men have received from the Christ **who for their sake died and was raised** (vs. 15). **If any one is in Christ,** a Christian bound closely to Christ in vital union, he has been radically transformed from his old sinful state. **He is a new creature** (KJV; RSV mg.); or as the Greek (only καινὴ κτίσις) may mean, by the power and act of God **a new creation** (RSV) "has taken place" (cf. 4:6, where Paul, in language reminiscent of Gen. 1:3, speaks of his conversion as a new act of divine creation). **The old** state of sinfulness and perverted outlook that resulted in an all too **human point of view . . . has passed away.** With an emphatic **behold** that rings with exultation, Paul declares that in Christian faith, fellowship, and service for Christ **the new** and right relationship to God and life **has come.** The

very openness that to some Christ is still only an actor in a plan of salvation. Belief in a particular doctrine of the Atonement is made a substitute for the faith-union with him which results in wholehearted Christian discipleship. The command to follow him is as imperative as the command to have faith in him. Both demand the understanding of his message and his life. But to know him at the deepest level is to have a personal contact with him in which spirit meets with spirit. The relationship of "he and I" becomes one of "thou and I." The Moravian who talked with Wesley on the voyage to Georgia made this point when he asked, "Do you know Jesus?" Wesley replied, "I know that he is the Savior of the world." "Yes," rejoined the Moravian, "but do you know him?" The result of this union is an inner transformation.

17. *A New Creation.*—The capacity to see both our fellow men and Christ in their true light comes from this inner transformation wrought by being **in Christ.** The phrase, as we have seen, describes a mystical experience in which we live because Christ lives in us (Gal. 2:20). This mystical union in its degree is found in all intimate friendships, and need not be regarded as being beyond the experience of the ordinary man. "A man in Christ" is Paul's definition of a Christian. Nothing less is adequate, for it implies an inner change which is equivalent to a **new creation.** He is not merely improved, or reformed, or altered in any way which implies no more than an external change, however great; he is remade. He is different even from what he was at his best. The change is radical; it goes to the roots of his being. **The old has passed away, . . . the new has come.** **The old** may refer to the desires and purposes of the self-centered life, and **the new** to the desires and purposes of the Christ-centered life. The essential difference is an inner change in which our thoughts and ambitions are no longer focused on ourselves, but on Christ and on the interests of others. But such an inner change means that **all things are become new,** as the KJV puts it. The new man lives in a new world because his outlook is changed; for the world we live in depends on our outlook. When we are made new, some of the things we once valued lose their appeal. Money, pleasure, position cease to have the old attraction for us. On the other hand, love, duty, brotherhood, service, which may have counted for little in our scheme of things, become important and attractive. There is a transformation of values. Suffering, disappointment, hardship, instead of being mere doom or black misfortune, become the means of God's challenge, or of his discipline, like the tools of the potter which give the cup its shape both for use and beauty.

> Machinery just meant
> To give thy soul its bent,
> Try thee and turn thee forth, sufficiently impressed.[6]

Other things, too, the beauty of the earth, the familiar blessings of life, the affections of home, the people we meet in business or in casual contacts, all appear in a new light. John Masefield in *The Everlasting Mercy* describes the familiar world as it looked to a man after his conversion. Meaning comes back into a situation which otherwise is like a code message

[6] Robert Browning, "Rabbi Ben Ezra," st. xxviii.

18 And all things *are* of God, who hath reconciled us to himself by Jesus Christ, and hath given to us the ministry of reconciliation;

18 All this is from God, who through Christ reconciled us to himself and gave us the

---

eschatological hope of a new life in "a new heaven and a new earth" was vivid to Paul, as it was to the writer of Rev. 21:5, "Behold, I make all things new." But Paul can rejoice that the beginning of the new age has come. In Christ and what he has done for men the transformation has already begun. **The new has come.** He who believes finds that even now Christ is able "to deliver us from the present evil age" (Gal. 1:4).

18. All this redemptive work that Christ has done to help and transform men **is from God.** Men neither deserve it nor share the credit for the results. Moreover, Christ does not do it apart from God's direction and action. God did it all, **through Christ.** God **reconciled us** sinful and so undeserving men **to himself.** That in God's moral world it cost greatly to rescue men from the guilt and consequences of their sin Paul clearly saw, and he points to that truth in vs. 21 and in Rom. 3:25-26. But in spite of that cost, God himself, acting with gracious purpose to redeem men, took the initiative and through Christ did everything needed to reconcile men to himself. The word "reconcile" reminds us that God not merely removed the guilt or penalty of sin, but brought about restored personal fellowship between himself and his redeemed people.

But God's gift, Paul saw, always pointed to a task, particularly for Paul and other apostolic leaders; in speaking of **us** he thinks perhaps of this group of workers. They needed redemption as much as other men; they too had been sinners and their first need was for reconciliation with God. Once reconciled, they were given **the ministry of reconciliation.** This means that they in turn were to offer to others the same message of God's reconciling grace that had met their need. The reconciliation here in mind is not between estranged men, although that will follow when men are truly reconciled to God. Paul's work was to lead men to believe in Christ, to get them to accept the reconciliation that God had effected through Christ and now freely offered to all who would believe.

---

without the key, or a stained-glass window without the light to reveal its color and significance. No one who has not submitted himself to the experience of God in Christ is competent to make a pronouncement on the world and on human life. Such an experience not only makes the world new, but adds to the world its most vital element. The knowledge of Christ, and the experience of his love, like the acquisition of a new and transforming friendship, enrich and interpret all other experience.

18. ***All This Is from God.***—In all that Paul has been describing, God is the active agent, the central source. It was Paul's conviction that in his own experience God had taken the initiative. Paul was not the pursuer but the pursued. The activity of God in all the goodness we achieve is a fact of which we become aware whenever we look deeply into our own hearts, as Paul did into his. We realize that our best actions were due to the pressure upon us of a higher will which we could not evade without a sense of disloyalty. Everything that is good in us is of his besetting love (Ps. 139:5).

So did the message of **reconciliation** spring from Paul's experience of it. God had stepped into the apostle's life to reconcile that life to himself, and to bestow upon it **the ministry of reconciliation.** The message which every Christian minister has to preach must likewise spring from his own experience, as must every man's witness. The Christian can convince people of what God can do only if God has already done it for him. In a real sense, the proclamation of the gospel in particular is the communication of an experience. Jesus, sending his disciples forth to evangelize the world, said they were to be witnesses, i.e., of his life, death, and resurrection. These are not mere historical facts. Their meaning lies in the purpose of God for our salvation which they fulfill. Nobody who has not seen his glory can relate the story of Jesus; nobody who has not known its redeeming power can describe the cross of Christ. Calvary and Easter are experiences of the soul. "Were you there when they crucified my Lord?" is a relevant challenge to all of us. The ministry, which through this experience is committed to men, is the **ministry of reconciliation,** not of denunciation, or reformation, or exhortation, or any form of uplift. We are channels of God's reconciling love. This point Paul later elaborates. He

19 To wit, that God was in Christ, reconciling the world unto himself, not im-

ministry of reconciliation; **19** that is, God was in Christ reconciling[h] the world to him-

[h] Or *in Christ God was reconciling.*

---

19. The words **that is** (ὡς ὅτι), which introduce a restatement of the heart of the gospel given in vs. 18, imply that the **ministry** just mentioned was essentially a faithful preaching of the gospel message. The KJV wrongly puts a comma after **Christ.** Paul is not saying that **God was in Christ;** he assumes that God was vitally present and active in Christ's work. He is making a statement about what God did. The word **was** should be

---

now states the fact which is the essence of the Christian gospel.

19. ***God Was in Christ Reconciling the World to Himself.***—Reconciliation to God is man's basic need. It implies that the root of our evil condition is estrangement from him. God and we are not at one in feeling, thought, and will. The fault is ours, not God's (Isa. 53:6). The chasm has been dug from our side. But in Christ God has bridged it, because we could not bridge it ourselves. He has stepped in to heal the estrangement and reconcile us to himself. It is God who seeks us, not we who seek God. It is the shepherd in Christ's parable who goes into the wilderness to seek the sheep that is lost. We shall consider later what was involved in this search on God's part. What it means depends on our understanding of the estrangement. This takes various forms. At least four of them can be distinguished, though they merge. When the love of God in Christ unveils the heart, we find layer upon layer of moral disorder.

The most common form is indifference. God is not in all their thoughts (Ps. 10:4). He is what A. N. Whitehead calls "the Void." The indifferent are not aware of any estrangement, for they are not aware of God. This does not mean, of course, that they have no consciousness of trouble, though they may not recognize its real nature. God and they have never met in any personal encounter. This moral indifference is the fundamental reason why men drift into evil without being aware of the fact. They are carried over the brink of moral disaster without any conscious decision on their part, like a boat which is carried over a cataract because its occupants are not aware of any danger.

A second form of estrangement is a more or less definite resentment against God. "God the Void" becomes "God the Enemy." This may take the shape of resentment against life and its conditions, without attributing the blame for these to God. But the elementary religious idea that God is responsible for whatever happens in the world leads men to set down their sorrows, misfortunes, lack of success, or injustice, to God. This resentment springs from blindness to the love of God. It may be due to defective religious education, to wrong ideas of God implanted in childhood, e.g., the threat of divine punishment used as a deterrent. Or it may come, in spite of the best religious teaching, from identifying a dominating parent with God. The antagonism aroused by the parent is transferred by the child to the God in whom the parent believes. A secret estrangement may be present even when the love of God in Christ has been accepted as an article of faith, but has not been seen as the loving will which is able to make all things work together for good. In this case the divine will is regarded as a kind of fate to be endured. In what appears to be pious resignation the element of resentment or rebellion may still be unconsciously present. It cannot be resolved except by realizing that God's will is not something to be endured, but something to be done in the particular situation which confronts us; and that in doing his will and so co-operating with him the situation can be turned from loss into gain.

A third form of estrangement, or enmity toward God, is the selfishness that leads us to seek our own way in defiance of what we know to be right. Selfishness has many forms, e.g., self-will, self-indulgence, self-pity, self-complacency, self-righteousness. All such attitudes are centered in the love of self, which is enmity toward God. It is then the desire to follow God's will that is lacking. The reply of the master of Ballantrae to the question why he was such a rascal when he was so well versed in the scripture and the catechism describes the condition of many people—"the malady of not wanting." [7]

But whatever the reason, God's will and ours are in conflict, and at various levels: resulting sometimes in the definite rejection of God's will, which may be rationalized by finding excuses for doing what we secretly know to be wrong, sometimes in the sheer impotence of a will to do right which is yet not powerful enough to overcome the sinful self, as when Augustine prayed, "Give me chastity and self-control, but not just yet." [8]

[7] Robert Louis Stevenson, *The Master of Ballantrae* (London: Cassell & Co., 1914), p. 257.

[8] *Confessions* VIII. 7. 2.

puting their trespasses unto them; and hath committed unto us the word of reconciliation.

self, not counting their trespasses against them, and entrusting to us the message of

taken with **reconciling;** as the RSV mg. says, **in Christ God was reconciling the world to himself.** It was sin that made this reconciling work necessary; so Paul adds that God did not count men's **trespasses against them.** God did not keep the record of these misdeeds on the books as a debit charge; he forgave them. Vs. 21 will say that this became possible through the vicarious suffering of Christ. This message of reconciliation, which was complete only after the death and resurrection of Christ, was entrusted to Paul and

The last form of estrangement may be that produced by the sense of guilt which is involved in all conscious sin, and which may remain even when the sin has been forsaken. The sense of guilt is much more common than many suppose. Psychology has revealed how prevalent it is and often how disastrous, though it may not be recognized as a sense of sin. Donald M. Baillie says: "I should like to suggest that [the modern man] has a kind of *moralistic substitute* for the sense of sin, and that this much less wholesome substitute is the chief cause of that perennial *malaise* which surely underlies the superficial complacency of the modern mind." [9] This sense of moral failure or unworthiness may lie dormant in the mind, producing a feeling of inferiority or of moral impotence and of the futility of all ideals. Worst of all, it may come like a shadow between the soul and God, making the thought of him a source of fear, and the idea of his love unreal; for the sense of guilt becomes clearest and strongest when we come face to face with God in Christ and see ourselves as we are. Then we realize that sin is disloyalty to God, the obstruction of his purpose, rebellion against his will of holy love.

In reconciling us to himself through Christ, God overcomes all these forms of estrangement. Paul makes special mention of the fact that in so doing he deals with the guilt of sin, **not counting their trespasses against them.** This means that from God's point of view the things that men have done, however evil, are blotted out as if they had never been. "As far as the east is from the west, so far hath he removed our transgressions from us" (Ps. 103:12). This does not annul all the results of sin. A man who has ruined his health by indulgence or lost his business through slackness must accept the natural consequences. The fact also that God does not count our trespasses against us will not get rid of the sense of guilt. We are forever those who have done the wrong.

Some psychiatrists regard the sense of guilt as the product of a morbid conscience. Their technique for its removal is to get the patient to realize that he is not to blame, and need not carry the burden any longer. No doubt there are cases of morbid conscience; but the danger is that in removing the burden of responsibility, which is the root of the sense of guilt, the moral world may be destroyed, and a man may feel himself to be forever the helpless slave of his own impulses, or the plaything of circumstances. Guilt is a moral fact which we cannot argue away and still remain in a world of moral realities. In his analysis of a soul under conviction of sin Hawthorne says: "The only truth that continued to give Mr. Dimmesdale a real existence on this earth was the anguish in his inmost soul, and the undissembled expression of it in his aspect. Had he once found power to smile, and wear a face of gayety, there would have been no such man!" [1] We dare not try to remove the sense of guilt by doctrines which deny human freedom and responsibility. Neither is there deliverance by penance or by works of mercy. The burden cannot be got rid of by specious arguments, or by any labor of our own. This way of dealing with it is generally an attempt to find a reconciliation with God which will save our pride and enable us to retain our self-respect. We can receive God's forgiveness only as sinners.

The guilt does not remain as a barrier to God's love; yet the sense of it may remain in ourselves. Through our reconciliation to God, however, it is changed. Its disabling effect on the mind and will is broken. The pain and shame of past sin become both a discipline and a deterrent. We are kept humble and alert, while the sense of God's forgiveness kindles a never-failing gratitude to God which is the characteristic note of Christian doxology. The past also remains; but through our fellowship with God he comes into the situation that sin has created, to transform and redeem it. We can take the past and make a future of it as we yield ourselves to God's redeeming Spirit.

Jesus' way of dealing with the sense of guilt was not to excuse the sin but to forgive the sinner. By his own attitude to sinners he made it clear that what they had done was no barrier

[9] *God Was in Christ* (New York: Charles Scribner's Sons, 1948), p. 162.

[1] *The Scarlet Letter,* ch. xi.

20 Now then we are ambassadors for Christ, as though God did beseech *you* by us: we pray *you* in Christ's stead, be ye reconciled to God.

reconciliation. 20 So we are ambassadors for Christ, God making his appeal through us. We beseech you on behalf of Christ, be

other apostolic leaders; their witness to this total gospel is therefore an essential part of the full Christian message.

c) Paul's Urgent Ministry of Reconciliation (5:20–6:2)

20. Paul has stated the heart of the gospel of reconciliation, and recalled that he and others have been given the apostolic ministry of preaching. He now tells how earnestly he carries on this important work (5:20–6:2), and follows in 6:3-10 with a reminder of what he has done and endured in this ministry. He and the other apostolic leaders are **ambassadors.** This word describes the apostles as the representatives of a sovereign ruler, and so points to their authority and responsible position. They act **for** or on behalf of **Christ,** in his interest and to further his cause. **As though,** used in the KJV to translate ὡς, seems to express doubt whether God speaks through the apostles, and Paul certainly does not intend to suggest doubt. The RSV does not translate the word at all. It may be

to his love (John 8:11). Reconciliation is a hard thing to achieve. It involves the unveiling of our need of God, the breaking of our pride, the creation in us of the penitence that seeks forgiveness and of the willingness to surrender to God's will. "The question, How is love to God or to men possible if as a fact I do not have it? would be answered if there were, as the moving spirit of the world, an aggressive lover able and disposed to break in upon my temper of critical egoism and win my response." [2] God in Christ is the "aggressive lover" who has come to break into the citadel of our self-will and set us free from the guilt and the power of sin. This is what God has done in Christ. His whole life was an offensive of divine love, which culminated in the Cross. There it triumphed over bitterness and hate, overflowing in a forgiveness that remains a miracle of grace. The Cross is God's love at the flash point of its power. By it his love can break through to our hearts, whatever our condition, if we give it opportunity.

But the Cross is more than a revelation of love. Something was accomplished which made it possible for us to enter into fellowship with God in a union of heart and will. What that something is Paul describes in vs. 21. For the moment he returns to the fact that a man who is reconciled to God is called by that experience to be a minister of **reconciliation.** It is the task of a Christian to transmit in his life and message this reconciling love. The preacher's object must be to reconcile men with God. Nothing less will bring deliverance from sin, or give peace to the heart. The emptiness and futility of life, the resentment and fear that keep us from inward serenity in the face of life's ills, the lovelessness that fills the earth with conflict, all find their cure in our reconciliation with God. Nothing less will bridge those seas of misunderstanding across which we "shout to one another." The antagonisms that divide the world are due to our own inner conflicts. Peace is one of the by-products that come from seeking God's rule and his righteousness. God has now entrusted to us this ministry of reconciliation.

[2] W. E. Hocking, *Human Nature and Its Remaking* (New Haven: Yale University Press, 1918), p. 398.

20. ***We Are Ambassadors for Christ.***—Our task is that of building the bridge between men and God and between men and men. This does not mean apologizing for God, nor does it mean a sentimental attitude to the sins of men which regards them as a form of childishness. We shall not heal their hurt by saying, "Peace, peace; when there is no peace" (Jer. 8:11). The first effect of the preaching of the gospel may be to deepen the antagonism toward God by awakening an inward conflict, which really means that the hidden enmity has been brought into the light. This is the cause of all persecutions. Jesus endured, according to the KJV, the "contradiction of sinners against himself" (Heb. 12:3). But the work of the ministry is to dispel this antagonism by the revelation of the love of God.

The task of an ambassador is one of honor and responsibility. He must present his nation's point of view, assert her rights, and at the same time seek always to smooth out frictions and create a spirit of harmony. His handling of any situation may help or hinder right relationships. The preacher (see Expos. on 3:1-3)—and in very truth every Christian man—is Christ's ambassador. He speaks at all times in the name of his Lord. He is not responsible for the message he delivers, only for transmitting it rightly. The

21 For he hath made him *to be* sin for us, who knew no sin; that we might be made the righteousness of God in him.

reconciled to God. 21 For our sake he made him to be sin who knew no sin, so that in him we might become the righteousness of God.

---

rendered "seeing that," "inasmuch as." The apostles act as ambassadors for Christ, seeing that (or inasmuch as) they are the spokesmen through whom God makes his appeal to men to accept the gospel. Note how strongly Paul holds that God is speaking through him, and how urgent he feels so important a message from so great a Lord to be. With that sense of urgency, he cannot speak indifferently; he must **beseech** or beg (δεόμεθα) men to hear and respond, to accept the message and **be reconciled to God.** Only once (12:21) does Paul ever use the verb "repent" (μετανοέω); only three or four times does he use the corresponding noun. But the appeal to be reconciled calls men to turn from the sin that estranges them from God, and to accept in faith the redemption, forgiveness, and restoration to fellowship that God offers.

21. This verse tells how such reconciliation has been made possible. Christ never yielded to temptation and so **knew no sin** that was his own evil-doing. This conviction

---

message is God's message to men. It is the offer of reconciliation, and of the power that can make us willing to be reconciled. God does not ask from us what he does not enable us to give.

But the spirit in which the ambassador transmits the message is all important. He is one who pleads. His tones must echo the yearning love of God. He must not only lift up the cross; he must carry it. If he must warn or rebuke, he will do it as one who sorrows over sin. When he looks on the hapless, ignorant crowds he will, like Jesus, be filled with compassion (Matt. 9:36), never with superiority or contempt, for he will see their condition—weary, futile, hungry for new sensations and material satisfactions—as that of shepherdless sheep. When he is tempted to condemn the obstinate narrowmindedness or bigotry of some religious people, he will remember how Jesus longed to draw such people to himself, as a mother hen gathers her chickens under her wings (Matt. 23:37). Their blindness and self-righteousness will not plant a thorn in his side, but a cross in his heart. His reactions to what men do or say will always be dictated by love. His constant aim will be to unmask the conflict between men and God, and open the way to reconciliation. Psychological insight will help him to reveal men to themselves, to disentangle the confusions, and to uncover the insincerities with which men screen themselves against the truth. It will help him lay bare the hidden roots of fear and resentment that often run back into the forgotten past. But final healing and the integration of the personality can come only from reconciliation to God. It is therefore of him that the preacher, more than any other man, will speak. God's light must shine through all he says, whether in the pulpit or in private interviews. His aim must be to produce a personal encounter with God. His insistent appeal is, **Be reconciled to God.** Paul ends this theme by stating what God has done in the work of reconciliation through Christ.

21. ***He Made Him to Be Sin Who Knew No Sin.***—It is not enough to say that God reconciles us to himself through the effect upon us of the revelation of his love, though that is the heart of it. In the fire of his love the evil desires within us are judged and consumed, and love to God is kindled to become the motive power of a new life. We must set the crucified Christ before the eyes of men, pointing to the Cross and saying, "God loves like that."

But the Cross is more than a message; it is God's deed of reconciliation. What happened there Paul defines throughout his epistles in various ways, according to the people he has in mind. Here he says that **for our sake** God made Christ **to be sin who knew no sin.** The phrase **he made him** might suggest the compulsion of one who was unwilling, which is the last thing that would enter Paul's mind. In his death Christ was completely master of the situation. So far from being God's victim, he was not even the victim of the evil men who crucified him. He was victor, not victim. "I lay down my life, that I might take it again. No man taketh it from me, but I lay it down of myself" (John 10:17-18). There is no suggestion that he died to placate an angry God. He and God were one in the sacrifice of Calvary. As it was said of Abraham and Isaac in their journey to the altar on Mount Moriah, "They went both of them together" (Gen. 22:6). "God was in Christ reconciling the world to himself" (vs. 19).

Paul does not say that God needed to be reconciled to man. But was there nothing in the situation created by man's sin that God had to

6 We then, *as* workers together *with him,* beseech *you* also that ye receive not the grace of God in vain.

6 Working together with him, then, we entreat you not to accept the grace of

---

Paul shared with the entire apostolic church; cf. Matt. 4:1-13; John 8:46; Acts 3:14; Heb. 4:15; I Pet. 2:22; I John 3:5. The word order in the Greek stresses this point by putting it first: "Him who knew no sin, on our behalf he made to be sin, etc." Neither the KJV nor the RSV brings out this emphasis. Yet though Christ never by his own choice fell into sin, God **made him to be sin** (cf. Rom. 8:3; Gal. 3:13). The ancient custom of sending a scapegoat into the wilderness bearing the sins of Israel (Lev. 16) may provide some background for this idea, but is not deep and vital enough to be a real parallel. Christ by God's will so identified himself with sinful men that in some way, Paul senses, he became involved with their sin; he helped them not by standing aloof and giving them directions as to what they should do, but by entering so completely into their situation that he stood in their place, shared their lot, and grappled with the problem for them. Only in virtue of so vital a connection with men could the reverse working take place, in which, on the basis of what Christ did in his death and resurrection, we sinful men were enabled to **become the righteousness of God,** i.e., to receive this righteousness as a gracious gift from God. By **righteousness** Paul here means more than an externally imputed good standing before God, in which God accepts men as though they are righteous, although in fact they are still unchanged sinners. He intends to say that this gift of good standing before God includes a real transformation of life by the power of God. Thus, though man is indeed transformed, he cannot claim credit for himself; this too is God's doing and gift, a part of the rich grace that man can only gratefully receive; he can never repay.

6:1. But though grace is free and man cannot claim that he earns salvation, this never removes the need of human response and diligence. So Paul works and the hearers

---

deal with so that his love might find a way through? The wrath of God is a reality. It does not mean the anger of God. It means the nemesis which sin brings upon man in a world which is a moral order. But that nemesis is no mere automatic consequence. It happens in a world which God has created, and which is sustained and directed by his loving purpose. The suffering which comes from sin is therefore his judgment, because it is the result of his opposition to evil. It is part of the continual offensive of his righteousness, which is rooted in his love. In the Cross this opposition took the form of suffering love. Christ bore the consequences of man's sin in his own body and his own heart. There was no other way in which God could deal with it so that self-will in men might turn to penitence and the burden of guilt be removed. Christ died as the Son of God in complete union with his Father; but he also died as the representative of the whole human race, through the identifying power of sinless love. The offering which he made for our sake to God has already been described (see Expos., vs. 15). That offering was not made to a God who stood apart as one waiting to receive it. It was an offering in which God's own love and righteousness were fully expressed.

He made him to be sin is only a way of saying forcefully that Christ took on himself the whole burden of our sin, the shame, the guilt, and the judgment of God upon it. It is beyond our power to enter into the full meaning of this experience of the Son of God.

But none of the ransomed ever knew
  How deep were the waters crossed,
Nor how dark was the night that the Lord passed through,
  Ere He found His sheep that was lost.[3]

Neither can we conceive the full extent of that oneness with God which Paul describes in the phrase **become the righteousness of God.** This experience is both the root and the fruit of reconciliation. Its full meaning remains to be discovered as we grow in fellowship with God. But the essence of it is that our wills are one with his. This oneness with him is the hope set before us. But it begins when we come into that faith-union with Christ in his offering to God whereby it becomes progressively ours.

6:1. *Working Together with Him.*—As an ambassador of Christ, Paul is conscious of co-operating with God. He was a willing channel for

[3] Elizabeth C. Clephane, "The Ninety and Nine."

2 (For he saith, I have heard thee in a time accepted, and in the day of salvation have I succored thee: behold, now *is* the accepted time; behold, now *is* the day of salvation.)

God in vain. 2 For he says,
"At the acceptable time I have listened to you,
and helped you on the day of salvation."
Behold, now is the acceptable time; behold,

---

must believe. **Working together with** God (in the Greek the word "God" or "him" is not expressed, but seems implied), Paul entreats or appeals to the Corinthians, who have responded in faith to the gospel message, not to **receive** this **grace of God in vain,** to no profit. All that God has done, all the labor of the preachers, will go for nothing unless the response is sincere and continued.

2. Isa. 49:8, quoted exactly from the LXX, is cited to support Paul's plea to the readers to accept and hold fast to the gospel of reconciliation. In the O.T. the meaning

---

God's power. In a real sense all men are used by God:

> All of us alike are God's instruments. By no setting of our hearts on wickedness or doing evil with both our hands can we prevent God from using us. Our folly will serve Him, when our wisdom fails; our wrath praise Him, though our wills rebel. Yet, as God's instruments without intention and in our own despite, we generally serve God's ends only as we defeat our own. To be God's agent is quite another matter. This we are only as we learn God's will, respond to His call, work faithfully together with Him, and find our own highest ends in fulfilling His.[4]

In the full sense Paul was God's agent, comprehending his purpose, seeing his will, and with wholehearted obedience doing it. This is the true meaning of being God's fellow worker, and in it we find the true privilege and joy of life. All work which is creative or redemptive is a partnership with God; but it reaches its highest point and deepest satisfaction when we become conscious of union with God, and our work or service becomes an active partnership with him. Only through this conscious co-operation with God does the fulfillment of his purpose for the world achieve also the full development of our own personality. The question which faces every man is therefore not whether he will be used by God, but whether he will be God's unconscious tool or God's conscious partner. To know that God and we are partners is the secret of inexhaustible strength.

In this consciousness Paul follows up his account of God's reconciling work in Christ by an entreaty to his readers **not to accept the grace of God in vain.** His meaning may be variously interpreted. We accept the grace of God in vain if we are content to rest in some doctrine of atonement without opening our hearts to the love of Christ. The letter of the doctrine may take the place of our surrender to the Spirit. Orthodox belief may be substituted for effectual faith. We can own a fine library without knowing the truth or wisdom it contains. "You possess the land," said a man with an eye for beauty to the owner of an estate; "I possess the landscape." In the same way, theological knowledge may never pass into receiving the grace of God.

Again, the phrase may mean being thrilled by the love of God without living by the power of it. For ages Niagara was only a wonderful spectacle for men to admire, till engineers found the way to capture the power of its water, and to transform that power into light and energy for homes and cities. The cross of Christ can be merely a moving spectacle, producing an emotional satisfaction which passes away without subduing the will to obedience, without being transformed into the service or sacrifice that makes love real. "Why do you call me 'Lord, Lord,' and not do what I tell you?" (Luke 6:46.) Unless the Cross produces in us both the desire and the power to do God's will, we accept the grace of God in vain.

Yet again, the words may mean resting content in a real conversion experience without proceeding to explore its full meaning for our life, without allowing the Spirit of Christ to rule in every part—work, leisure, relationships with others, etc. Many Christians have never developed or proceeded to that deeper experience of the love of Christ. Their development is arrested, like that of a plant which does not flower or propagate its life. "He who ceases to be better," said Oliver Cromwell, "ceases to be good."

2. ***The Acceptable Time.***—The quotation from Isa. 49:8 helps only to introduce the idea

[4] John Oman, *The Paradox of the World* (Cambridge: Cambridge University Press, 1921), p. 30. Used by permission.

3 Giving no offense in any thing, that the ministry be not blamed:
4 But in all *things* approving ourselves as the ministers of God, in much patience, in afflictions, in necessities, in distresses,

now is the day of salvation. 3 We put no obstacle in any one's way, so that no fault may be found with our ministry, 4 but as servants of God we commend ourselves in every way: through great endurance, in

was that God had heard the plaint of the servant that his work had brought no fruit or reward (Isa. 49:4). Here Paul applies the verse to make the point that since **salvation is now** being offered, **now** is the **acceptable time** to respond. **Now** means while the gospel is being preached and before the end comes. It is a word of urgency: **now,** without delay, before it is too late.

d) His Diligence and Suffering in This Ministry (6:3-10)

3. After stating the central gospel message (5:14-19) and declaring that as Christ's ambassador he faithfully and urgently entreats men to accept it (5:20–6:2), Paul describes how untiringly and steadfastly he has fulfilled his mission in the face of hardship, privation, slander, and ill-treatment. He does not think merely of his relationships with the Corinthians; the passage is quite general, a summary of his experiences that becomes almost a hymn of tribute to the apostolic minister. In construction the participle **giving** (διδόντες) seems to belong with the subject "we" in vs. 1; vs. 2 is somewhat like a parenthesis. The apostle must always remember what a responsible position has been given him; in all his dealings he must give no occasion for anyone to take **offense in any thing;** it must be his constant care to see **that the ministry be not blamed.** This is important because if anyone takes offense at anything the apostle does, he will not only blame the minister, but also be led to reject the gospel the apostle preaches.

4. Lit., "But in everything as ministers of God commending ourselves." Paul elsewhere speaks of himself as a minister of Christ (11:23), of the church (Col. 1:25), of the gospel (Col. 1:23), of the new covenant (3:6), etc. Here he implies that God sent

of **the acceptable time.** That time is now. This is usually taken to denote a passing opportunity. "Malleable moments," as Meredith calls them, do occur when the soul is susceptible to spiritual impressions. There are tides in the emotional life when we see clearly and feel deeply, and these tides need to be caught if we would grow in God's fellowship or accomplish his will. For lack of the venture of faith in response to these moments of vision the development of the spirit may be arrested, the experience of Christ may lose reality, or faith in him may even fade out. The story of the foolish virgins is a warning. Those who were ready went in and the door was shut (Matt. 25:1-13).

But Paul means something more than this. He means that the new age is here; **the day of salvation** has dawned; God's new day for the world has come. His words are a call to realize the truth that the power of God's new creation is available. They sound a note heard constantly throughout the N.T. It rings at the heart of all the apocalyptic literature of Jew and Christian alike. It is the dominant theme of the so-called eschatological elements in gospel and epistle. Every day is filled with all the possibilities of the last day, every moment big with eternity. All in readiness. Then what? The most tragic thing in the world is to see slaves who refuse freedom, sick persons who refuse healing, and exiles in bitter need who will not see that the Father's door stands open. This is the situation that fills Paul's heart with yearning love.

3. *We Put No Obstacle in Any One's Way.*—It is a bold claim to make, and few would dare to make it. Paul means conscious obstacles, things in his life or his manner which might keep others from seeing the glory of Christ, or blind them to God's reconciling love. To be a true minister of reconciliation was his passion. Love made his life an unobstructed channel between God and man. That on the negative side; whereupon he turns to the positive.

4-10. *But as Servants of God We Commend Ourselves in Every Way.*—The recital which follows is an outpouring of Paul's heart with the one object of revealing his love through what he has endured. It begins with his physical sufferings—a striking list, repeated with more detail in 11:23-28. In these sufferings Paul rejoiced, but not through any pride in martyrdom, such as has often made the sufferings of the saints a kind of masochistic indulgence. To Paul these were "the marks of the Lord Jesus"

5 In stripes, in imprisonments, in tumults, in labors, in watchings, in fastings;

afflictions, hardships, calamities, 5 beatings, imprisonments, tumults, labors, watching,

---

him and that he labors to do God's will. Though he denies that he ever indulges in idle boasting (3:1; 5:12), he does commend himself by the honesty of his speech (4:2) and by the actions of his ministry; this latter point is in mind here, and all the description that follows in vss. 4-10 tells how he commends himself. The phrase "in everything" (ἐν παντί), which contrasts with giving offense "in nothing" (vs. 3), is explained in all the phrases that follow. In the Greek each noun down through **the power of God** in vs. 7 follows the preposition ἐν, lit., "in." The KJV translation reflects this; the RSV does not. Vss. 4*b*-5 list the hardships Paul has known in his ministry. **Endurance:** victorious steadfastness under the strain of any hardship. **Afflictions:** a general term for severe, distressing trials; cf. e.g., 1:8, where death seemed certain. **Hardships** (RSV): lit., **necessities** (KJV; ἀνάγκαις); the word describes the trials or sufferings as unavoidable: **Distresses** (στενοχωρίαις), difficulties or "straits," pictured as encountered in a narrow place from which no escape is possible.

5. Stripes (KJV): wounds from **beatings** (RSV) with rods or lash; cf. 11:23-25; Acts 16:22-23. **Imprisonments:** cf. 11:23; Acts 16:23 (the arrest in Jerusalem [Acts 21:33] came later). **Tumults:** especially such riot scenes as Acts 13:50; 14:19; 17:5; 18:12; 19:29.

(Gal. 6:17), the signs of fellowship with his Lord, the outcome and proof of his faithfulness to his Master and his message. That Paul was alive to the fact that suffering could become a source of pride and be regarded as a virtue in itself is shown in I Cor. 13:3, "If I deliver my body to be burned, but have not love, I gain nothing." Suffering for Christ's sake is never to be thought of as an end in itself, but only as a means to service when service demands it. Service can be equally devoted without necessitating such physical cost.

Next we are given a description of the qualities by which the apostle's message was accompanied. Here are the fruits and manifestations of the Spirit. They are the graces which Paul sought to cultivate, and which he regards as essential in one who would commend his ministry to others. His character was an integral part of his message. However battered his body, the spirit within was resilient. It reacted to the blows of circumstance by producing all the traits of a victorious personality. These Paul enumerates.

Purity means chastity of body and mind. Physical suffering can loosen self-control and issue in a self-pity which tempts to self-indulgence.

Knowledge means knowledge of God and of the nature of the Christian message. The experiences of life were for him a highway to ever fresh discovery of the love and purpose of God. Paul's letters are a mine of intellectual treasure; but his knowledge was not reached through what we call learning, still less through speculative philosophy. It was the knowledge of God in living personal experience, not merely knowledge about God.

Forbearance means the spirit which is tolerant of those whose conduct or speech exasperates and provokes to anger or indignation. It calls for the control both of feeling and of hasty speech. There are times when the Christian spirit demands it: when words only add fuel to the flame, and silence is the most effective reply. Such was the silence of Christ's own forbearance in the judgment hall.

Kindness needs no description; but it can easily be forgotten by those who, like Paul, are on fire with the Christian message. We can be so absorbed by the importance of the work we are doing that we are blind to the healing power of

> Little, nameless, unremembered, acts
> Of kindness and of love.[5]

Yet in this insensitive world of business, pleasure, and self-seeking, a trifling deed of thoughtful kindness may be like a well in the desert, or a beam of sunlight in a cloudy sky. It can take people out of the numbing grip of an impersonal world.

The Holy Spirit means the consciousness of a grace that was not Paul's own, working in his heart, checking faults and calming fears, and producing every virtue he possessed.

Genuine love is something more than kindness. It is the spirit that lies behind the word or deed. Kindness can be a conventional thing.

[5] Wordsworth, "Lines Composed a Few Miles Above Tintern Abbey."

6 By pureness, by knowledge, by longsuffering, by kindness, by the Holy Ghost, by love unfeigned,

hunger; 6 by purity, knowledge, forbearance, kindness, the Holy Spirit, genuine

---

Labors may include both his work as a preacher and pastor, and his labor to earn money; cf. 11:23, 27; I Thess. 2:9. **Watchings:** repeated vigils of sleeplessness due to night work or to thought and concern for his churches (11:27). **Fastings:** forced by his situation in travel and poverty (cf. 11:27; Phil. 4:12).

6. This verse and vs. 7*a* list qualities and divine gifts that mark Paul's ministry. **Purity:** not only chastity; complete integrity of life. **Knowledge:** of the gospel; cf. 2:14. **Forbearance:** patient endurance of ill-treatment without irritation or retaliation. **Kind-**

It may proceed from a habitual formal courtesy in which we have been trained. As such it is not to be despised. But genuine love means a personal interest in people, which values them as persons and seeks their good. It is what Jesus means by giving a cup of cold water in the name of a disciple (Matt. 10:42), i.e., in the spirit that values people as Jesus valued them. It was with this love that Jesus touched the leper, brought him out of the despair and misery of his outcast condition, and awakened the faith through which healing came (Mark 1:41).

Truthful speech is essential; and for none more surely than for a preacher. The primary condition of effective preaching is that people should know that the preacher's statements can be trusted. The language in which he describes the love of God must often rise into poetry. But in telling people what Christ means to him, it is important to be strictly honest. He must not exaggerate or promise results that cannot be realized in ordinary experience. Truthful speech is important to fellowship. Jesus was very emphatic about this (Matt. 12:37). The reason is that speech is the means of communication between man and man, and when speech becomes unreliable the most important channel of communication is made useless.

The power of God is the dynamic fact to which Paul always returns. Here he is thinking of it not merely as the source of all he is and is able to do, but as a fact in his own experience as an ambassador for Christ. In the results that followed his preaching and labors he saw God's power at work, with the same sense of wonder and gratitude as that with which an engineer might watch the power of electricity lighting up homes and driving machinery in districts where he had laid the supply lines. It is the sign that his work is efficiently done, and in itself is commendation of that work; but he does not for a moment imagine that he is anything more than an agent.

With the weapons of righteousness for the right hand and for the left is a military figure. The Roman soldier held a sword in his right hand for attack and a shield in his left for defense. In his conflict with evil, or with those who opposed his leadership and traduced his character, Paul had only one weapon—righteousness. When our main object is victory, any weapon may all too likely be thought permissible. Means are dissociated from ends; and however unworthy these means may be, they come to be accepted if the end we seek is good. This is the reason why in political and ecclesiastical conflicts disreputable weapons are often used. Paul sought "no victories that are not God's," and realized that God's battles must be fought by weapons that are spiritual, not carnal. His way of attack and defense was to do the right. It might lead, as did the way of Jesus, to a cross. But, like Jesus, Paul knew that the pulling down of the strongholds of evil can be accomplished on no other terms.

In all this he was subjected to the contrary winds of man's favor and disfavor; but these did not affect his course. **Honor and dishonor, . . . ill repute and good repute** were both the same to him. Both are impostors. They do not affect a man who lives in the light of God's judgment. Men's good repute will not uplift him, nor their ill repute dishearten him. He will neither resent criticism nor court popularity. The judgment of men is a very small thing (I Cor. 4:3). In illustration of the ill repute in which he has often been held he cites various jibes that had been flung at him, and along with each gives the answer of his own conscience and of his spiritual experience. Some of these are aspects of the Christian paradox.

We are treated as impostors, and yet are true: No doubt this referred to the charge that in claiming to be an apostle, Paul was sailing under false colors, since he had neither been of the original twelve, nor even one of Christ's company. But the truth of his gospel could not be denied. Neither could the sincerity of his Christian life, nor the effect of his message, be doubted.

As unknown, and yet well known: That Paul was a nobody in the eyes of many is true. He

7 By the word of truth, by the power of
God, by the armor of righteousness on the
right hand and on the left,
8 By honor and dishonor, by evil report
and good report: as deceivers, and *yet* true;

love, 7 truthful speech, and the power of
God; with the weapons of righteousness
for the right hand and for the left; 8 in
honor and dishonor, in ill repute and good
repute. We are treated as impostors, and

---

ness: to all men, friendly or hostile. **The Holy Spirit:** not the pious spirit of man, but the Spirit of God, in vital relationship with whom Paul can bear these hardships. **Love unfeigned** (KJV) : and so, **genuine** (RSV) .

7. "In a word of truth" may mean **truthful speech** (RSV) or **the word of** the gospel, which is the **truth. Power of God:** the power "in," i.e., by which, Paul is able to endure and serve. In vss. 7*b*-8 the preposition changes to διά, "through." In vs. 7*b* it means "equipped with" **the weapons** that **righteousness** supplies, for both right and left hands.

8. "Through" (διά) here means that Paul continues to serve steadfastly "through" or **in** the varying situations of "praise," **honor** (δόξης) and **dishonor,** of **evil** or slanderous **report, and good report.** He tries to avoid blame (vs. 3) , but whether he succeeds or not, he faithfully carries on his ministry for Christ. Now follow in vss. 8*b*-10 seven

---

had renounced all the things that give a man worldly prestige—birth, race, learning, position. These he counted loss for Christ (Phil. 3:4-7) . He was content to be a nobody. Yet strange as it might seem to those who judge people by the values of the world, Paul had achieved through his Christian service a reputation far wider than he could have had as a learned and honored leader of the Jews. Many obscure people have won a lasting and world-wide reputation through their contact with Christ. They became immortals when they stepped into his light, as did Mary Magdalene and Zacchaeus in the gospels. No one would have heard of Francis of Assisi had he not renounced all the things that give men prestige, and followed Christ. "God chose . . . things that are not, to bring to nothing things that are" (I Cor. 1:28) . When we discover, as Paul did, that in the light of Christ we are nobody, we are on the way to become somebody.

We feel we are nothing—for all is Thou and in Thee;
We feel we are something—*that* also has come from Thee;
We know we are nothing—but Thou wilt help us to be.
Hallowed be Thy name—Halleluiah! [6]

As dying, and behold we live: The truth of this paradox Paul had already elaborated in 4:11. His critics had suggested that he had one foot in the grave, but the truth was that he was very much alive. The most significant mark of our vitality is the creativeness which intensifies the quality of life in others.

As punished, and yet not killed: His enemies taunted him with his physical weakness, which, according to some writers, prostrated him and made him an object of contempt. They called it God's judgment on sin. Paul does not rebut the idea. He saw in his physical weakness "a messenger of Satan" sent to buffet him lest he should be too elated (12:7) . A vessel with a high superstructure needs good ballast to keep it steady in a gale. The point Paul makes is that what he had suffered had not killed his spirit. Suffering never does if we take it from the hands of God and find through it his love. To know that we cannot be separated from his love is ballast enough, and more; it is the secret of the unconquerable spirit (Rom. 8:35) .

As sorrowful, yet always rejoicing: His opponents had apparently taunted him with the fact that he often looked sad. How could he help it when his heart was open to all the sin and suffering of the world? Christ was "a man of sorrows and acquainted with grief" (Isa. 53:3) . There is a sense in which the Christian outlook makes the world a darker place to live in. The love Christ kindles makes us sensitive to the pain of others. Paul bade his readers "weep with those who weep" (Rom. 12:15) . He himself did so. The power to comfort others can reach them only through our capacity to feel their pain and need. But beneath the sorrow there is a well of joy that nothing can seal up. It springs from the knowledge of Christ's victory and from the assurance in him that sorrow and pain have their place in the fulfillment of God's purpose. Sorrow and joy in Christian experience are not opposites. They are complementary. They spring from the same root. The heart which is made sensitive to sin and suffering by the love of God can by that same sensitiveness enter into the joy of his victory. To know Christ in the fellowship of his sufferings

[6] Alfred Tennyson, "The Human Cry."

9 As unknown, and *yet* well known; as dying, and, behold, we live; as chastened, and not killed;

10 As sorrowful, yet alway rejoicing; as poor, yet making many rich; as having nothing, and *yet* possessing all things.

11 O *ye* Corinthians, our mouth is open unto you, our heart is enlarged.

yet are true; **9** as unknown, and yet well
known; as dying, and behold we live; as
punished, and yet not killed; **10** as sorrowful, yet always rejoicing; as poor, yet making many rich; as having nothing, and yet
possessing everything.
11 Our mouth is open to you, Corin-

---

contrasts, in each of which he first states his outward reputation or lot and then gives his situation before God or his personal attitude. **We are treated** (RSV) is not in the Greek; it is supplied to interpret Paul's meaning; another suggestion is, "We are regarded by the world" (cf. 4:8-12; I Cor. 4:9-10). Regarded as deliberate **deceivers** (KJV) or **impostors** (RSV), we are in fact and in God's sight **true** and sincere.

9. Though contemptuously called **unknown,** "nobodies," we are **well known** to God and those who have Christian insight; cf. 3:1; I Cor. 13:12. **Dying:** constantly facing wearing hardship and danger. **Behold** expresses the note of victory and exulting triumph that runs through these verses. **We live:** cf. 4:8-12; Ps. 118:17-18. **Chastened:** subjected to God's disciplinary correction, yet rescued from death by God's grace and power (cf. 1:10).

10. He knows sorrow, but it never quenches his Christian faith and **joy.** He is **poor** in the world's goods, **yet making many rich** by bringing them the "pearl of great price" (Matt. 13:46), the gospel. He has **nothing** in possessions or settled earthly situation, but in his Christian Lord, faith, fellowship, and task he possesses **everything.** The facts and tone of these verses answer effectively those who charge him with fickleness, insincerity, or greed.

C. The Bond Between Apostle and Church Renewed (6:11–7:16)

1. Appeal for Love Between Ministers and People (6:11–7:4)

After the long section on the apostolic ministry (2:17–6:10), Paul resumes the discussion of his relationships with the Corinthian church. He begins with an appeal for a warm return of the deep affection he has for them. This appeal, interrupted by a digression in 6:14–7:1, is completed in 7:2-4.

---

is also to know him in the power of his resurrection (Phil. 3:10).

As poor, yet making many rich: At Corinth Paul earned his bread by tentmaking, refusing to be a charge on the church. This should have been cause for admiration even to his enemies; but they twisted it into a confession that he was not sure of his right to their support. The idea dies hard that it is an indignity to work for a living, especially with one's hands, and that those who live by the labor of others are entitled to high respect. Paul admits the fact of his poverty but replies that he makes many people rich. True riches are of the mind and spirit, and the proof that we possess that kind of wealth is that we use it to enrich the lives of others.

As having nothing, and yet possessing everything: To "have" means to own; to "possess" means something deeper. It means to be master of what we own so that we can enjoy and use all that it can contribute to mind and spirit. We may own little or nothing of the material things of life; yet we may possess the beauty of earth, the treasures of wisdom, the love of many friends. Above all, we may possess God's love and find his fellowship in everything. Even the hardships and sorrows of life then become ours because they have the power of enriching the spirit and can be transformed into blessing. If we are seeking God's purpose for ourselves and others there is no experience that may not be turned to profit. It is this that makes all things ours in the true sense of the word. "All things are yours, whether . . . life or death or the present or the future, all are yours; and you are Christ's; and Christ is God's" (I Cor. 3:21-23).

11-13. ***In Return.***—On the basis of this outpouring of his heart Paul now makes an appeal for unrestricted confidence. He had let down all the barriers and showed the Corinthians his inmost self. He now asks for a like response from them. It was their lack of responsiveness

12 Ye are not straitened in us, but ye are straitened in your own bowels.
13 Now for a recompense in the same, (I speak as unto *my* children,) be ye also enlarged.
14 Be ye not unequally yoked together with unbelievers: for what fellowship hath

thians; our heart is wide. 12 You are not
restricted by us, but you are restricted in
your own affections. 13 In return — I speak
as to children — widen your hearts also.
14 Do not be mismated with unbelievers.

a) Plea for Return of Paul's Affection (6:11-13)

11. Addressing the **Corinthians** by name, the only time he does so, he assures them that **our mouth is open to you** in a frank expression of affection. The reference to his **mouth** is due to the fact that he has been dictating the letter; in what he has been saying to his scribe, his mouth has been speaking freely in warm, friendly appeal. In saying that **our heart is enlarged** (or expanded) in affectionate friendship, Paul's wording reflects somewhat the Greek form of Ps. 119:32*b*.

12. Lit., "You are not straitened in us, but you are straitened in your heart [or affections]," i.e., whatever cramping, shrinking coldness there has been or in any degree still is between us, is not due to my attitude. **In us,** in our heart, there is no reserve or restraint. Any barrier or feeling of separation is due to reserve or restraint in your own heart. The Greek word used here for heart or affections is σπλάγχνοις. It refers to the vital organs: heart, liver, lungs, etc., regarded as the seat of emotion and affection.

13. "Now" to make "the same return—I speak as to [my] children—do you also be enlarged." Let them repay his freely given affection with a like outflow of unhesitating and unstinted love. In his pastoral letter (I Corinthians) he had spoken of himself as their father, i.e., he had founded the church in Corinth (I Cor. 4:15). More than once he calls his converts his **children.** So here, in his appeal for affection, he can **speak as to** [his] **children.**

b) Parenthesis: Shun Fellowship with Unbelievers (6:14–7:1)

In 6:14–7:1 the appeal for mutual love and confidence is suddenly interrupted by a stern warning that Christians must not form close ties with pagans and must separate

which had blocked the channel between them. They had been cautious, holding back their affection. It may have been some lurking prejudice, or suspicion, or perhaps the secret consciousness of the injury they had done him. In such a case only frank confession can reopen the channel of fellowship—what John calls walking in the light (I John 1:7). Their reserve, again, may have been the result of an unwillingness to receive his message for fear of what it would demand. Some people are afraid of a religion which can move them to the depths, lest they should be led to behave in unusual ways. There is something in us that makes us shrink from having too much of God. All these things prevent the full confidence which is the only condition on which a man's ministry can be effective. This holds true also in marriage and friendship. Paul's outpouring of love is the effort to clear away all barriers. It is the ministry of reconciliation at work. What he pleads for may involve making a confession, or putting away unjust suspicion, or the resolve to be Christians out and out. But whatever it may involve, he pleads for an open door. Their restraint of affection and trust constricts their own hearts. It is a form of spiritual isolationism which will narrow and cramp their spiritual life. The door is open on his side. He has kept back nothing in his love for them. If we would help others we must, like him, be ready to give ourselves away. We may have to do it by relating some experience that was humbling to undergo and is humbling to share. We must not be afraid to expose our feelings. For Christ's sake we must sometimes wear our hearts on our sleeve. It is a risk. But results are not in our hands, and often we can break down barriers between us and others in no other way.

14-15. ***Do Not Be Mismated with Unbelievers.***—The question of marriage between Christians and non-Christians introduces a new section (see Exeg.). The position of those already married is made clear in I Cor. 7:12-16. They are to remain together unless the unbelieving partner finds the tie in the altered circumstances

righteousness with unrighteousness? and what communion hath light with darkness?

For what partnership have righteousness and iniquity? Or what fellowship has light

from any corrupting associations in which they find themselves. Some have thought that Paul did not write this paragraph; they point to the sudden change of subject and the eight words used here which appear nowhere else in Paul's letters or even in the N.T. (ἑτεροζυγοῦντες, μετοχή, συμφώνησις, βελιάρ, συγκατάθεσις, ἐμπεριπατήσω, εἰσδέξομαι, μολυσμοῦ). However, two of these words are quoted, and the others fit naturally the discussion of the topic in mind; moreover, in the series of five questions effective style called for variation of wording. Paul wrote this passage. Could it have stood originally in the "lost letter" written before I Corinthians (cf. I Cor. 5:9)? This is possible, especially if on other grounds we hold that II Corinthians is composite, since chs. 10–13 originally formed part of the "stern letter" (see Intro., pp. 270-71). But we may explain 6:14–7:1 as an original part of the section in which it now stands. Paul has urged the Corinthians to open their hearts wide in affection to him (6:11-13). But because they have so threatening a background in the paganism out of which they have come, he warns them not to let this welcome to others include the pagan influences and people that would turn them from their Christian way of life. Such harmful associations they should shun; if they find themselves involved in pagan ways of life, they must promptly and decisively break such ties.

14. Paul does not forbid necessary business relations or ordinary friendliness to other people. Indeed, to give a good witness to the gospel, Christians must take an interest in sinful people and treat them with understanding. But there is a friendship with the world that is enmity toward God (Jas. 4:4), and so Paul warns against close ties that link the Christian with **unbelievers** in pagan ways of thought and action. The reference to **defilement of body** (7:1) indicates that unlawful sex relations are included in the ties forbidden. Paul does not say, "*Stop* being unequally yoked with unbelievers," but rather,

too difficult; in that case he or she is to be allowed to leave the other for the sake of peace, and the believer should then—though there is much disagreement among interpreters at this point—remain unmarried without seeking divorce. But a Christian should not marry a pagan. Paul knew the dangers of this form of mismating. Such a marriage often leads to the Christian partner's gradually becoming detached from the Christian faith and from the Christian fellowship. It is very difficult to maintain a vital religion where the home atmosphere is unsympathetic. In experience the danger is found to be greater where the believing husband marries an unbelieving wife. The woman is generally the custodian of ideals and standards in the home. It is easier for her to keep her own convictions, and through her witness and spirit to influence her partner, than it is for a believing husband to keep his faith and influence an unbelieving wife. Christians who marry worldly partners put their Christian life in jeopardy.

There is a further reason for not mating with unbelievers. Marriage is not merely a physical union; it is a union of mind and spirit. Where the two do not share the Christian faith and the Christian standards they are not at one in the most important interests of life. There will be a subtle barrier between them, an estrangement at the deepest level, which no common interest in art, or sport, or even the love of their children, can fully overcome. Differences of view on many questions are bound to arise, even where husband and wife are united in the Christian faith. Tastes and opinions will sometimes differ. This is often inevitable if each is to be free to express his or her individuality. Fellowship in freedom is preserved when both are united in the love of God and in devotion to his will. The Christian faith is also the safeguard of love, because it keeps alive in us that reverence for the spirit of the other which is the essence of love. It is the means of unity; for it brings into the common life of husband and wife a throne of judgment where self-will is rebuked, and discords can be overcome by seeking together the will of God.

It is quite another matter when there is no harmony of faith or ideals. **For what partnership have righteousness and iniquity?** The question of marriage leads Paul almost imperceptibly to the wider subject of the contacts between believers and unbelievers. Obviously, when those who live and have all their social relationships in a pagan society become Christians, the new life presents to them many conflicting loy-

15 And what concord hath Christ with Belial? or what part hath he that believeth with an infidel?

with darkness? 15 What accord has Christ with Be'li-al?[i] Or what has a believer in

[i] Greek *Beliar.*

"Do not *become* thus yoked." They must always beware of forming such ties. Five pointed questions, the first four of which are arranged in two pairs, bring out how incongruous such a bond with pagans would be; five different words for "fellowship" are used. **What** deep **partnership** or sharing (μετοχή), can the **righteousness** of the Christian believer have with the lawlessness or **iniquity** (ἀνομία) of the pagans? **Or what fellowship has** the **light** of the gospel of Christ **with** the **darkness** of paganism? Here occurs the frequent biblical contrast between **light** as the realm of holiness and the divine Presence, and **darkness** as the region of sin, unbelief, and evil powers.

15. What accord or agreement (συμφώνησις) **has Christ with Beliar?** The latter word, which seems derived, by a change of one letter, from the Hebrew word Belial ("worthlessness"), refers to Satan, rather than to Antichrist, as Wilhelm Bousset and others have claimed. **Or what part** or portion (μέρις) **has a believer . . . with an unbeliever?** The former's life is centered in Christ and lived in the Christian fellowship, while the latter rejects the loyalty that is central to the Christian.

alties, as in the mission field today. This is so even in our own society. An employee in business who becomes a Christian may realize that some practices which he had formerly accepted as normal now offend his conscience. Or he may find that former friendships and associations have to be given up because he has now a different use for his time. He may no longer care for some of the things he once enjoyed. In certain cases a clean cut with old associates becomes necessary because the atmosphere they create makes it impossible to keep unsullied the new-found life of the spirit. A young plant needs shelter from winds and frost till it has taken firm root and can survive them. The judge in Charles Morgan's story gives this advice to his stepdaughter. "Ask yourself in what work, what company, what loyalty your own voice is clear and in what muffled. By the answer, rule your life." [7]

Two things must be avoided. One is the self-righteous attitude of the prig which makes people hate us and, because of us, the faith we profess. A real Christian does not take the view that he is better than others (I Cor. 5:12). He knows that he himself is not "good," and that the only grace he possesses has come to him as the gift of God to the undeserving. The publican who blamed no one but himself is the man Jesus commended (Luke 18:13-14). The second thing to be avoided is excessive preoccupation with the culture of our own souls. We forget ourselves into Christlikeness through caring for others—among them, the unbelievers. Jesus made friends with publicans and sinners. The true safeguard of character is not isolation; it is in caring so much about the spiritual interests of others that we shall be proof against moral infection. Jesus called his disciples "salt" —material that keeps things from corruption by its own inherent quality—but salt cannot purify anything with which it is not mixed.

These questions are raised by Paul's vehement words about fellowship between **light** and **darkness,** etc. But in point of fact he qualifies this in I Cor. 5:9-13. There he expressly says that what is in his mind is not our contacts with those outside, but with those inside the Christian community. There were some glaring cases of unjustifiable tolerance in the Corinthian church, e.g., the case of incest mentioned in I Cor. 5:1. This leads Paul to mention other obstinate sinners whose presence in the church should not be tolerated. The offender must, of course, be frankly dealt with, and strong action taken if he refuses to mend his ways. It is part of our task to strengthen one who is genuinely fighting a battle with evil habits. But there may come a point where tolerance is no longer a virtue but a danger. It may be a sign of the decay of moral standards. If persistent evildoers refuse to face the light, they have obviously no place in the Christian fellowship. They do not belong there. They dim or corrupt the Christian witness. They are salt that has lost its savor (Matt. 5:13). Paul gives the same advice that Jesus gave. An obstinate evildoer in the last resort must be treated as a heathen man and a publican (Matt. 18:15-17). To treat a man as a heathen and a publican does not, of course, mean that we refuse to treat him with love or compassion. How did Jesus treat publicans and sinners? But the church must be concerned for

[7] *The Judge's Story* (New York: The Macmillan Co., 1947), p. 183.

16 And what agreement hath the temple of God with idols? for ye are the temple of the living God; as God hath said, I will dwell in them, and walk in *them;* and I will be their God, and they shall be my people.

17 Wherefore come out from among them, and be ye separate, saith the Lord, and touch not the unclean *thing;* and I will receive you,

18 And will be a Father unto you, and ye shall be my sons and daughters, saith the Lord Almighty.

common with an unbeliever?
16 What agreement has the temple of God with idols? For we are the temple of the living God; as God said,

"I will live in them and move among them,
and I will be their God,
and they shall be my people.
17 Therefore come out from them,
and be separate from them, says the Lord,
and touch nothing unclean;
then I will welcome you,
18 and I will be a father to you,
and you shall be my sons and daughters,
says the Lord Almighty."

---

16. What agreement [συγκατάθεσις] **has the temple of God with idols?** The word for temple (ναός) refers to the sanctuary or shrine itself rather than to the entire temple area in which the building stands (ἱερόν). Paul now justifies the reference to Christians as a temple. **For we are the temple of the living God,** in contrast to the temples of lifeless and impotent idols. Another MS reading, "Ye are," would direct attention more specifically to the Corinthian church, but would not change the main idea. Paul speaks of the group of Christians as the temple; he does not mean, as in I Cor. 6:19, that the individual Christian's body is a temple shrine in which the Spirit dwells. God is present in the church and walks among its members. This idea Paul supports from the scriptures. He does not quote literally; he weaves together passages from various O.T. books, remaining true to the ideas but altering the wording to form a continuous statement of God's presence (vs. 16*b*) and promise (vss. 17*b*-18), provided man refrains from defiling acts and associations (vs. 17*a*). As usual, Paul uses the Greek O.T., the LXX. Vs. 16*b* reflects Lev. 26:11-12 and Ezek. 37:27. **In** means in the Christian group and so can be rendered "among": "I will dwell among them," in their midst, "and will walk among them." Note that for Paul the church is now the people of God.

17. This verse comes essentially from Isa. 52:11; the last line reflects Ezek. 20:34. **Therefore,** to fulfill the condition on which God will be with his people, **come out** from defiling ties with unbelievers and **be separate from them. Touch nothing unclean;** in Isaiah this seems to warn returning exiles against incurring ceremonial impurity; Paul uses it to warn against immoral associations. **Then I will receive** or **welcome you,** says God, when you break with evil and come to me in wholehearted dedication to my will.

18. The O.T. passages back of this verse are II Sam. 7:8, 14; the inclusion of the reference to **daughters** may reflect such a passage as Isa. 43:6. If the Corinthian readers break with pagan ties, a step that may even call for a break with family and home (cf. Matt. 10:34-37), God **will be a father** to them, and they will truly be his children. Since

---

its own purity as an instrument dedicated to the service of God in the world.

16. ***We Are the Temple of the Living God.***—A temple must be kept clean, not merely for its effect on those who use it or visit it, but because God dwells in it. Better a church roll purged till only those who are in earnest remain than a roll swollen with lukewarm or evil-living people.

17. ***Touch Nothing Unclean.***—That can easily become a contradiction of the Christian spirit. But there are some things with which a Christian can have no compromise, and some people with whom, because of these things, he cannot associate in the service of Christ. The separation from old friends will be painful. They may resent it and turn against him. But where loyalties conflict the Christian's first loyalty is to God.

7 Having therefore these promises, dearly beloved, let us cleanse ourselves from all filthiness of the flesh and spirit, perfecting holiness in the fear of God.
2 Receive us; we have wronged no man, we have corrupted no man, we have defrauded no man.

7 Since we have these promises, beloved, let us cleanse ourselves from every defilement of body and spirit, and make holiness perfect in the fear of God.
2 Open your hearts to us; we have wronged no one, we have corrupted no one,

---

the Lord (God) is **Almighty** (a term used in the N.T. only here and nine times in Revelation, where assurance of God's power was needed), the Christians may trust in these promises; because they are such great promises, every believer should avoid all that would exclude him from their benefits.

7:1. The word **these** stands first with emphasis in the Greek; these promises are so great and assuring that they should move one to right action. **Beloved** expresses both affection and appeal. Paul pleads for complete renunciation of evil and full consecration to God; to avoid giving offense, he includes himself among the Christians who must **cleanse** themselves **from,** i.e., resolutely put away, **every defilement of body** [lit., **flesh** as in the KJV] **and spirit.** The words **every** and **make holiness perfect** ("complete") brush aside all inclination to compromise and call for immediate and full dedication to the whole will of God. It is not only the promises that should induce the readers to do this; Paul adds **in the fear of God** to remind them that the holy God is the final judge of every Christian, and that he cannot dwell with those who persist in evil. He who values pagan ties above the promises of God excludes himself from the presence and the gifts of God.

c) Renewed, Confident Appeal for Mutual Love (7:2-4)

2. Paul has finished the warning against letting compromising ties with unbelievers lead to moral laxness. He now returns to the appeal for greater affection that he had begun in 6:11-13, and completes what he there began to say. **Open your hearts,** lit.,

---

He belongs to the household of God and must find there all the love and fellowship that are found in a true home. Jesus too had to choose between his earthly family and that wider family of those who did the will of God (Matt. 12:50).

7:1. ***Let Us Cleanse Ourselves.***—Life in God's family involves two kinds of self-discipline, negative and positive. The negative kind includes the rejection of all that defiles flesh and spirit. Paul lists the main varieties of defilement in Gal. 5:19-21. The flesh is defiled by such sins as unchastity and overindulgence in food and drink. These sins consist in the satisfaction of natural appetites in defiance of conscience or out of relation with the Christian purpose of life. They are acts of sacrilege done to the physical temple. Covetousness, pride, the unforgiving temper defile the spirit. They stain and dishonor it, and make it unfit for fellowship with God. All sin results in a maimed personality. After his moral failure the psalmist prays for a clean heart and a right spirit (Ps. 51:10).

Fitness for God's fellowship must also be positive. The old man must not only be put off; the new man must be put on. The house must not only be cleaned up; it must be occupied by a new spirit (Luke 11:24-26). The Christian must strive to **make holiness perfect.** This does not mean the encouragement of self-conscious piety. The word holiness has acquired a bad reputation through misunderstanding of its original meaning. The word is akin to wholeness and to health. It is the purity which comes from the complete consecration of ourselves to the purpose of God. This consecration is more than a state of mind; it is an active devotion of the will to God. The motive Paul mentions is **the fear of God,** which again is often misunderstood. "There is no fear in love" (I John 4:18). What is meant by fear is awe—the reverence for God's holy love which makes us willing to be commanded. If we live in his light we shall be judged, cleansed, and renewed. We shall have power to work his will into the fabric of daily living. It is to this effort that Paul's argument leads.

2-7. ***Open Your Hearts to Us.***—So Paul resumes the argument broken off at 6:13. He insists that he has **wronged no one.** This may refer to charges made during the trouble. Some of the members of the Corinthian church may have been forced unwillingly to give up shady

3 I speak not *this* to condemn *you:* for I have said before, that ye are in our hearts to die and live with *you.*

4 Great *is* my boldness of speech toward you, great *is* my glorying of you: I am filled with comfort, I am exceeding joyful in all our tribulation.

we have taken advantage of no one. 3 I do not say this to condemn you, for I said before that you are in our hearts, to die together and to live together. 4 I have great confidence in you; I have great pride in you; I am filled with comfort. With all our affliction, I am overjoyed.

"make room for us in your hearts" (χωρήσατε) ; cf. 6:13. Freely given love is not possible while the Corinthians give attention to charges made against Paul; so he emphatically denies such slanders. In the Greek each of the three statements in this series begins with **no one;** this and the aorist tense of the verbs is Paul's way of insisting that he has not been guilty of a single wrong act such as enemies have alleged. **Wronged** does not refer to any specific kind of personal or financial injury, but is quite general: "No one have we treated unjustly." Moreover, no one has he **corrupted** by bad example or teaching; of no one has he **taken advantage.** The translation **defrauded** (KJV) limits attention to dishonest financial dealings; this is included in Paul's meaning, as 12:16-18 suggests, but he here denies that in dealing with the Corinthians he has engaged in any kind of sharp practice.

3. For fear that his readers, who so recently have become reconciled with Paul, may think that he is seeking to reopen the former conflict, he hastens to assure them that in defending himself against malicious charges he does not **condemn** them. His love for them is too deep and genuine to permit him to repulse them with a hostile word. Indeed, just as his life is closely tied with Christ, so that he can say that he is "in Christ," so he is vitally and lastingly bound to them in Christian fellowship and love. The bond is so firm and enduring that he will **die together** and **live together** with them. The reference is to his death and his resurrection to be with the Lord in the age to come; even in those experiences, which may seem strictly personal, he will continue to be united with them (cf. 1:6-7, 14; 4:14) .

4. Lit., "Great is my confidence toward you"; **confidence** (RSV) rather than **boldness of speech** (KJV) is the thought in παρρησία, although the KJV rightly gives the original meaning of the word. "Great is my boasting concerning you." Cf. 1:14; but here Paul thinks of boasting in the present concerning (ὑπέρ) the faith and loyalty of the Corinthians, while 1:14 has in mind the last day. He is **filled with comfort** because the Corinthian church's rebellion has ended. **With** or amid (ἐπί) **all** the **affliction** that besets his ministry in Macedonia (cf. vs. 5) , he is **overjoyed;** lit., "I abound in joy beyond measure" or "I overflow with joy." All of the declarations of this verse have in

---

practices or businesses which were lucrative. When the light in which we have made a costly decision fades we may regret it or feel resentment against those who influenced our decision. The statement that he has **corrupted no one** may refer to the feeling some had that his doctrine of Christian liberty was an invitation to loose living. "Love God and do as you like" is dangerous counsel if the emphasis slips away from the first two words. It had also been charged against Paul by some that he had made money out of his converts, or at least that he had used his power to make large demands on them for the help of distant brethren. He rejects these charges too, but hastens to add that he does not mention them by way of condemnation. On the contrary, he tells them that in death and in life he and they are bound together. He puts death before life because in such love as has united them in fellowship, death is never the last word. The love which Christ inspires is timeless, and springs up into everlasting life.

It is in this context that the result of his appeal by Titus fills him with **confidence,** with **pride,** with **comfort,** and with joy. For Paul, whose whole life was in the ministry of reconciliation, the deepest satisfaction is to see the creative love of God at work, bringing men out of darkness and self-will into light and love. It is the joy which is found in heaven over one sinner who repents (Luke 15:7) . There is compensation in it for all his labor and pain. As if to explain this outburst of feeling, he fills in

5 For, when we were come into Macedonia, our flesh had no rest, but we were troubled on every side; without *were* fightings, within *were* fears.

6 Nevertheless God, that comforteth those that are cast down, comforted us by the coming of Titus;

7 And not by his coming only, but by the consolation wherewith he was comforted in you, when he told us your earnest desire, your mourning, your fervent mind toward me; so that I rejoiced the more.

5 For even when we came into Mac-e-
do′ni-a, our bodies had no rest but we
were afflicted at every turn — fighting without and fear within. 6 But God, who comforts the downcast, comforted us by the
coming of Titus, 7 and not only by his
coming but also by the comfort with which
he was comforted in you, as he told us of
your longing, your mourning, your zeal for

---

mind the confidence, boasting, comfort, and joy caused by the coming of Titus with good news from Corinth. Of that arrival of Titus he now speaks.

2. Paul's Joy at the Good News from Corinth (7:5-16)

a) Relief and Joy at the Repentance in Corinth (7:5-13*a*)

5. In 2:12-13 Paul was ready to tell how Titus met him in Macedonia with good news from Corinth. He turned aside, however, to thank God for his place in the ministry, and went on to discuss at length the apostolic ministry and gospel. Only now does he resume the story of Titus' coming. But he was already thinking of it in vs. 4, which reflects the comfort, joy, and new confidence that the good news brought. The news was so much the more welcome because Paul's situation in **Macedonia** was difficult. **Our bodies** (RSV), lit., **our flesh** (KJV), subject to weariness and pain, **had no rest.** We were afflicted "in every way" (ἐν παντί). From **without, fightings** or strifes beset him; these may have included both opposition to Paul in the Macedonian churches and attacks from pagan foes as well (on his earlier experiences there cf. Acts 16:23; 17:5; Phil. 1:30; I Thess. 2:2). **Within were fears,** especially haunting anxiety concerning the state of affairs at Corinth. Paul was outwardly harassed and inwardly distressed.

6. But as Paul has already said in 1:3-7, **God** brought him comfort. The repeated use of the word **comfort** in vss. 6-7 and vs. 13 emphasizes what a joy and relief the news from Corinth was. **God, who comforts the downcast, comforted us by the coming of Titus** with news that the church at Corinth was again loyal to him. The word for **coming** or arrival (παρουσία) is often used elsewhere in the N.T. to refer to the "advent" of the Lord Christ at the end of the age.

7. Evidently Titus had been in low spirits; quite possibly he had almost despaired of success on his mission to Corinth. The change of affairs at Corinth had been a real **comfort** and relief to him, as it was to Paul. The joy that Titus felt was so great and contagious that it doubled the joy of Paul; when the apostle saw how much Titus himself was gladdened by what had happened, he **rejoiced still more.** A joy shared is by that fact

---

the picture of his anxiety to which he had alluded in 2:13. He had gone to Macedonia with a great burden on his mind; but Titus was not there to meet him. The anxiety was unendurable. His whole being was full of restless tension—**fighting without and fear within.** His opponents among the Judaizers kept up their persecution. The air was full of wrangling and disputing, and all the time the fear of an adverse report gnawed at his heart. Then Titus had come and all these fears were swept away. He not only brought to Paul a message of comfort, but Titus himself had been comforted by the reception that had been given him. It was all of God, **who comforts the downcast.** The signs of his reconciling work were obvious—the longing for the breach to be healed, penitence for the trouble they had made, and zeal for Paul's welfare. These are the stages that marked the prodigal's change of heart and induced his return—longing, penitence, and willingness to co-operate with his father (Luke 15:17-19). The whole passage reveals the greatness of Paul's heart.

8 For though I made you sorry with a
letter, I do not repent, though I did repent:
for I perceive that the same epistle hath
made you sorry, though *it were* but for a
season.
9 Now I rejoice, not that ye were made
sorry, but that ye sorrowed to repentance:
for ye were made sorry after a godly manner, that ye might receive damage by us in
nothing.

me, so that I rejoiced still more. 8 For
even if I made you sorry with my letter,
I do not regret it (though I did regret it),
for I see that that letter grieved you,
though only for a while. 9 As it is, I rejoice,
not because you were grieved, but because
you were grieved into repenting; for you
felt a godly grief, so that you suffered no

---

so much the greater. In his enthusiastic report Titus told of the Corinthians' **longing** to see Paul and to re-establish cordial relations with him, of their **mourning** over the wrong they had done him and the trouble they had caused, and of their **zeal** for defending and satisfying him.

8. Possibly because Paul does not want the Corinthians to think he is exulting over their humiliation and embarrassment, he is careful here to show why he felt such joy. **For** things have finally worked out splendidly, after a time when it did not seem that they could. Paul wrote a "stern letter" (cf. 2:3-4); because he feared that it would not achieve its intended effect, he for a time regretted having sent it; it hurt or **grieved** (ἐλύπησεν) the Corinthians. The verb λυπέω, used twice in this verse, means to "hurt" or "grieve" someone; the translation **made . . . sorry** (KJV) might suggest repentance, and this idea the verb does not express. Because the **letter** did achieve the intended result, in that the grief it caused was **only for a while** (lit., "for an hour") and led the readers to a saving repentance, Paul is justified in the joy he has expressed in vs. 7. But the awkward and confused form of the sentence may reflect his fear that his exultant joy will seem unkind. Lit., vss 8-9*a* say: "Because even if I grieved you in the letter, I do not regret it, even if I was regretting it; I see that that letter, even if for an hour, grieved you; now I rejoice, not that you were grieved, but that you were grieved unto repentance."

9. Now that the Corinthians have completely changed their attitude and Paul has learned of it, he can **rejoice,** as vss. 4, 7 have said he does. That they **were grieved** gives him no joy; he regrets the necessity of that. The reason for joy is that they were **grieved into repentance,** i.e., in a way that led them to repent. The word "repentance" is rare in Paul's letters, and the verb "repent" occurs but once (12:21). Does the repentance here refer to regret that they have wronged and offended Paul, or does it mean deep sorrow for their sin against God? The latter idea is suggested by the fact that they **felt a godly grief; godly** (lit., "according to God," κατὰ θεόν) means a grief such as God wants; this implies that in their repentance the Corinthians were aware that their wrong had

---

8-9. ***For Even if I Made You Sorry with My Letter, I Do Not Regret It.***—Paul now does a daring thing. Some might call it a risky thing. He recalls the painful letter which had undoubtedly grieved them. This might have stirred up lurking germs of resentment and bitterness. The wound had healed. Why probe the scar? Would not the sensible thing be to forget the past and not to allude to it again? But Paul was an expert in spiritual healing. He knew that where there has been conflict, or where a wrong has been done, healing is not complete unless both parties can think of it, and even speak of it, without mental discomfort or any likelihood of spoiling the new relationship. Healing is complete only when the wound has been so handled that all the poison has gone out of it, so that it can never again bring a sense of strain. Only so can the wound itself take its place in the restored relationship as a means of deepening that relationship and uniting more closely those who have been at variance. "Happy are the associations . . . that have grown out of a fault and a forgiveness."[8] So Paul recalls the painful letter. He had known that the letter would grieve them and had been anxious about its effect. Most people in similar circumstances have had the same kind of anxiety. But when

8 Thornton Wilder, *The Woman of Andros* (New York: A. & C. Boni, 1930), p. 51.

10 For godly sorrow worketh repentance to salvation not to be repented of: but the sorrow of the world worketh death.

loss through us. 10 For godly grief produces a repentance that leads to salvation and brings no regret, but worldly grief pro-

been not merely against the man Paul but above all against God. By such repentance they avoided the danger that Paul might come to the unrepentant church and discipline it; this seems meant by his suggestion that, had he thus come, they would have **suffered** damage or **loss through** Paul as God's representative. He does not say what penalty would have been inflicted. He was convinced that he had the right and duty to discipline a rebellious church, but he was immensely relieved that now he did not have to do so.

10. There are two strongly contrasted kinds of grief for wrong committed. The right kind, the God-directed and beneficial kind, **godly grief,** is a deep sorrow that leads to **repentance,** and so ends in the divine gift of **salvation.** For such grief, Paul assures the repentant Corinthians, one never need feel **regret;** cf. Test. Gad 5:7 (R. H. Charles, *The Apocrypha and Pseudepigrapha of the Old Testament in English* [Oxford: Clarendon Press, 1913], II, 289-90, dates this work shortly before 100 B.C.): "For true repentance after a godly sort . . . driveth away the darkness, and enlighteneth the eyes, and giveth

Paul heard the result he was glad he had written. He was glad that they had been pained, not because of the pain, but because of the penitence the pain had produced.

The risk he had taken in writing the letter was that the inevitable pain might have taken a wrong direction. It might have produced anger against himself, or hardened their self-will into obstinacy. Or again, it might have produced only superficial regret that their relationship had been strained, without any real conviction of sin. What it had actually done was to awaken a genuine repentance. Paul then analyzes two contrasting kinds of pain or grief.

10. ***Godly Grief, Worldly Grief.***—Moffatt translates **godly grief** as "the pain God is allowed to guide." Such pain awakens the realization of sin as a wrong done not only to men but also to God. It brings us under judgment. It creates that abhorrence of the sin which makes us dissociate ourselves from it, and sets us free from its power to tempt or bemuse the mind. In true repentance the change of outlook and of spirit is followed by a surrender to the way of righteousness, and to that trust in the grace and forgiveness of God which takes the place of self-loathing and self-despair. Only when this process has been completed in us has our repentance been real, and then only does it result in **salvation and brings no regret.** Augustine could call his sin *beata culpa,* because through it, and all the misery it had caused him, he had been brought to know the saving grace of God. But there was more. This penitence had led the Corinthians to the desire for reconciliation. It had enabled them to accept Paul's rebuke in the right spirit. Instead of being directed into the channel of hurt pride and resentment, the pain had led them to seek renewal of fellowship. So all pain, instead of being resented, should be accepted and brought to God, as a sufferer applies to the doctor for diagnosis and cure. Particularly is this true when the pain is the pain of wounded pride. The only way of healing that can bring good out of evil is through the prayer of the psalmist, "Search me, O God, and know my heart: . . . and see if there be any wicked way in me, and lead me in the way everlasting" (Ps. 139:23-24).

Worldly grief is of a different order. This is the grief which is felt for the consequences of sin, such as loss of friendship, physical disability, wounded self-esteem, material losses. All these are like the pain which disease produces and which may be mistaken for the real trouble. If we are content to deal only with the pain the real disease may be masked or even aggravated. We are then dealing with symptoms instead of getting down to the root of the matter. In the case of a broken relationship, for instance, peace may be sought by an apology or by the easy promise of amendment, but without any fundamental reconciliation. In the case of other sins, if the grief is only for the physical results, or the material loss, or the wound to our self-respect, it is powerless to effect any inward change. The real question is whether the sinner hates his sin because he sees it as opposition to God's will of love, or because he dislikes the pain it has produced. If his grief is of the latter kind it will merely deepen his blindness to the real condition, and deaden his conscience. He will be concerned only to escape from the pain, instead of resolving to be a different kind of man.

Jacob's struggle in the valley the night before he was to meet Esau, whom he had wronged, gives an example of how worldly grief was

11 For behold this selfsame thing, that ye sorrowed after a godly sort, what carefulness it wrought in you, yea, *what* clearing of yourselves, yea, *what* indignation, yea, *what* fear, yea, *what* vehement desire, yea, *what* zeal, yea, *what* revenge! In all *things* ye have approved yourselves to be clear in this matter.

duces death.
11 For see what earnestness this godly grief has produced in you, what eagerness to clear yourselves, what indignation, what alarm, what longing, what zeal, what punishment! At every point you have proved yourselves guiltless in the matter.

---

knowledge to the soul, and leadeth the mind to salvation." **Worldly grief** is remorse that shrinks from the penalty of wrong action but feels no real concern over the wrong done to God and man; it may result in self-torture, but it does not drive the sinner to seek forgiveness from God, and so it leads only to spiritual **death.**

11. The **grief** the Corinthians felt was not this fatal worldly grief but the kind that God guides and approves. Its true quality is clear from the results. Paul uses seven words to emphasize the complete and commendable change of attitude in the Corinthians. Their grief expressed itself in **earnestness,** which led them to prompt and decisive action to correct conditions; in "self-vindication" (ἀπολογία), manifested not merely in words of self-defense but also in corrective actions; in **indignation,** perhaps directed mainly at the "false apostles" (11:13) and chief troublemaker (2:5) rather than simply at themselves; in **fear** of Paul's coming for stern discipline; in **longing** for the friendship and favor and return of the apostle; in **zeal** for Paul and against his accusers; in "vindication" or **punishment** inflicted on the chief opponent of Paul (2:5). **At every point** they have shown themselves **guiltless,** for they have completely dissociated themselves from the revolt against Paul. He considerately passes over the fact that previously the church as a whole had been involved in the rebellion against him. Now that they have changed their attitude, he does not want to harp on their bad record. He prefers to stress the fact that the church has acted decisively and with unanimity to vindicate him and punish those who had opposed him.

---

changed into godly grief. Jacob's uneasiness as he lay down to sleep was due to his fear of Esau. He looked on the wrong he had done his brother merely as a mistake for which he might have to pay with some of his wealth; already he had taken steps in that direction by sending on ahead large gifts. It was a businessman's way of dealing with an unfortunate situation. But an unseen antagonist began to wrestle with him. It was God bringing home to him a sense of sin. He made a fierce resistance, but was crippled and had at last to yield. Which is to say that his pride was broken as he recognized his moral failure. God had guided the fear of consequences so that it produced conviction of sin. After that he was a different man and could meet his brother in the spirit of honesty and humility.

The same process is at work in the story of the prodigal. He is hungry and realizes he has been a fool. A **worldly grief** has set him thinking of the comforts of home. But as he remembers his father a deeper feeling is awakened. Instead of seeing himself as a fool he now sees himself as a scoundrel, and his desire for food and shelter is changed into true repentance for sin. "Father, I have sinned against heaven and before you" (Luke 15:18).

The results of this **godly grief** in the Corinthians are plain.

11. ***What Earnestness, What Eagerness.***— These are the marks of a real repentance. **Earnestness** means moral purpose which makes no attempt to treat the matter as of small account. **Eagerness** to clear themselves can only mean eagerness to make clear where they stood. Righteous **indignation** would be their reaction to their having been led astray (cf. Exeg.). **Alarm** is perhaps the most hopeful sign of all, for it means the realization of the moral and spiritual results of sin, and particularly its disintegrating effect on their fellowship. The **longing** is for a new spirit, or possibly for Paul himself; the **zeal** is for a wholehearted devotion to the apostle and to the service of Christ. The **punishment** was not vindictiveness toward the offender, but the determination to be ruthless in their opposition to evil. These are the signs of spiritual renewal, and they make it possible for Paul to declare the real object he had in mind in writing the letter that had grieved them.

12 Wherefore, though I wrote unto you, *I did it* not for his cause that had done the wrong, nor for his cause that suffered wrong, but that our care for you in the sight of God might appear unto you.

13 Therefore we were comforted in your comfort: yea, and exceedingly the more joyed we for the joy of Titus, because his spirit was refreshed by you all.

12 So although I wrote to you, it was not on account of the one who did the wrong, nor on account of the one who suffered the wrong, but in order that your zeal for us might be revealed to you in the sight of
God. 13 Therefore we are comforted.

And besides our own comfort we rejoiced still more at the joy of Titus, because his mind has been set at rest by you

---

12. As in 2:9, Paul declares that his purpose in writing the "stern letter" was to lead the church to see how much it owed him and so to obey him and defend him. When they faced their duty **in the sight of God,** as responsible Christians, their **zeal for** Paul became clear to them; and that was the result he wrote to achieve. The specific form of his demand was that a wrongdoer be disciplined; probably **the one who did the wrong** was the man whom the church had punished as described in 2:5-11. (Certainly he was not the immoral man of I Cor. 5; about such a moral case Paul could not have written this verse or 2:9.) He had in some way opposed Paul. **The one who suffered the wrong** may very well be Paul himself, or at least one of his messengers (Timothy? cf. I Cor. 4:17; 16:10-11) or friends in Corinth. In some way, directly or indirectly, Paul's authority and leadership had been challenged; it was a crisis that could be solved only when the Corinthians showed their zeal for him. He had no desire for retaliation; but the Corinthians, for their own good, should realize that their welfare depended upon following Paul rather than the troublemakers who were opposing him. What role the "false apostles" who had come to Corinth played in this final crisis is not clear. Paul speaks here only of the Corinthians themselves and of the Corinthian ringleader in the revolt. But we may assume that the visiting agitators were behind the trouble in some way.

13*a*. **Therefore,** on account of this change of attitude at Corinth and all that it has led the Corinthians to do to vindicate themselves and place themselves on Paul's side once more, **we are comforted.** As vs. 6 and 1:3-4 show, the comfort is given by God. The solution of the crisis and Paul's joy in restored fellowship are God's gifts. But his gifts never take the place of man's active obedience, and Paul is grateful not only to God but also to the Corinthians who have given him such good reason to be encouraged.

b) The Joy of Titus Confirms Paul's Confidence (7:13*b*-16)

13*b*. Paul now returns to the thought of vs. 7, that his own joy was greatly increased by seeing the joy of Titus. He describes how Titus was received when he arrived in Corinth bearing the apostle's "stern letter." The tone of this section implies that Titus had been deeply concerned about the rebellious attitude of the Corinthians and doubtful whether his visit to Corinth would achieve its aim. But the result had exceeded his

---

12. ***I Wrote in Order That. . . .***—Paul was not thinking chiefly of the offender when he wrote, but of the church as a whole. His real hope was that they might reassert their loyalty to him and to what he stood for. He had always believed that at heart they were sound. Now his trust has been vindicated. He knew that the way to bring the best out of people is to expect it, and to meet them on this basis.

13-16. ***Therefore We Are Comforted.***—Paul's joy is further increased by their reception of Titus, who had shared his anxiety. Paul had doubtless confided to Titus his fears. But he had also set down the good points to be looked for in the Corinthians, had even boasted about them. None of their faults, nothing even that they had done to him, had been suffered to blind him to their better qualities, or make him lose sight of their past kindnesses. He would not deepen an estrangement by depreciating people to others behind their backs. The healing of a breach can be made infinitely harder by such depreciation, with its tendency to be repeated, and thus to widen the area of resentment and bitterness. Paul was eager only for reconciliation, not for the self-justification which is often at the root of our criticism of others. While all that he said in his letter to the Corinthians was

14 For if I have boasted any thing to him of you, I am not ashamed; but as we spake all things to you in truth, even so our boasting, which *I made* before Titus, is found a truth.

15 And his inward affection is more abundant toward you, whilst he remembereth the obedience of you all, how with fear and trembling ye received him.

all. 14 For if I have expressed to him some
pride in you, I was not put to shame; but
just as everything we said to you was true,
so our boasting before Titus has proved
true. 15 And his heart goes out all the more
to you, as he remembers the obedience of
you all, and the fear and trembling with

expectations. **His mind** [so RSV; literally, as in KJV, **spirit**] **has been set at rest by you all.** Like Paul himself (cf. vs. 16), Titus now has "perfect confidence" in the formerly rebellious church. The word **all,** combined with **everything** in vs. 14, **all** in vs. 15, and **in all things** in vs. 16, indicates that the entire church responded to Titus' appeal and is now loyal to Paul. This fact argues that chs. 10–13 do not belong to this letter, but were more likely part of the earlier "stern letter"; the rebuke of those chapters could hardly be addressed to a church whose entire membership is now as loyal as 7:4-16 says Corinth is.

14. We are now told why Paul **rejoiced still more** (vs. 13). Before Titus left for Corinth with the "stern letter," Paul had **boasted** somewhat to Titus "concerning" (or better, "on behalf of," ὑπέρ) the Corinthians. "Somewhat" (τι) tactfully reminds them that since they were then in revolt, there was not much in them of which he could be proud at the moment. Even so, he had said not only more than the situation seemed to warrant, but also more than Titus thought justified. That he had boasted "on behalf of" them at such a time could remind them that he was defending them to Titus at the very time they were not defending or supporting him. But Paul's courageous confidence in them had its reward; he **was not put to shame.** Indeed, his boasting on their behalf had not been irresponsible falsehood. His love had enabled him to see deeper than the rebellious attitude of the moment and so to see good things to say about them. Hence, just as he had always spoken honestly and truthfully to the Corinthians, so his **boasting before Titus** proved to be the deeper truth about them. For a time he was anxious as to whether this would be the result; now that his hope has proved well founded, he naturally rejoices, and Titus also has been gladdened.

15. The thought goes back from the result of Titus' visit and the joy that the good news gave Paul to the way Titus was received when he arrived in Corinth to deal with the crisis. The respectful, responsive welcome they gave Titus at Corinth still gives his joy an added intensity; **his heart** [**affection,** KJV] **goes out all the more to you, as he remembers the obedience of you all.** The form in which the obedience expressed itself is given by the following words, **how with fear and trembling ye received him.** In other words, when Titus came to Corinth, they received him with a fear that was due to a

true, what he had said to Titus in their favor was also true and had been proved so in the result. He had, in other words, always made a habit of speaking the truth both to the Corinthians themselves and about them to others. If we always spoke of a man's failings to the man himself instead of to others, our sincerity would be more clearly recognized.

In vs. 13 the apostle has described the joy which came to him through the relief and happiness which Titus felt. Because his heart was rich his own happiness was created by the happiness of others. Titus had found in Corinth what Paul had led him to expect. The Corinthians had reacted to his message with **fear and trembling** because among other things it had made them realize their Christian responsibility. They had seen afresh how great a thing it is to be entrusted with the gospel, and how important for the world is the Christian church. To be the agent of God's saving purpose in a perishing world is a responsibility and a privilege such as might make men tremble, and stir in them a new earnestness and devotion. But it might well also give them confidence and deliver them from the sense of inferiority which a small church is apt to feel when confronted by the massive powers of this world. It might lead them to value their fellowship so greatly that they would be eager to cleanse it from unworthy ele-

16 I rejoice therefore that I have confidence in you in all *things*.

8 Moreover, brethren, we do you to wit of the grace of God bestowed on the churches of Macedonia;

which you received him. 16 I rejoice, because I have perfect confidence in you.

8 We want you to know, brethren, about the grace of God which has been shown

guilty conscience. This implies that even before his arrival they had begun to see that they had been wrong to rebuff Paul and side with his opponents. As soon as Titus came, they received him with all deference, listened respectfully to the "stern letter" he had brought from Paul, and acted to quell the opposition and show their loyalty to the apostle.

16. In this closing word concerning the recent crisis Paul repeats the expression of confidence that he had made in vs. 4. He concludes with renewed assurance of the joy that the successful mission of Titus to Corinth has brought him; five times in this chapter an expression of joy occurs. **I rejoice because** [ὅτι could mean **that** (KJV), but this is not the likely meaning here] **in everything I have confidence in you.** This unqualified statement of satisfaction in the present situation repeats the assurance of vs. 11*b*, and makes it difficult to hold that chs. 10–13, which so strongly condemn the readers, are part of the same letter. The content and spirit of joy in 7:4-16 favor assigning chs. 10–13 to the "stern letter" (see Intro., pp. 270-71).

III. The Collection for Needy Christians in Jerusalem (8:1–9:15)

A. Macedonia's Liberality Should Inspire Corinth (8:1-6)

Up to this point Paul has sealed the reconciliation with the church at Corinth by a review of recent events, a restudy of the apostolic gospel and ministry, and an expression of joy at the renewed loyalty of the Corinthians to himself. Now in chs. 8–9 he urges them to complete their collection for the relief of the needy Christians in Jerusalem. This project had evidently been interrupted by the recent revolt against Paul. To resume and complete it will cement their new loyalty to Paul, deepen their Christian life, widen their horizons in the church, and help to bind Jewish and Gentile Christians together in a bond of brotherhood. The Corinthians needed to learn the blessing of giving; as far as Paul's letters tell us, they had never supported him (cf. 11:8-9; 12:13; I Cor. 9:11-12) or made any benevolent gift.

8:1. Paul first seeks to challenge them by citing the example of **the churches of Macedonia;** these would include those at Philippi, Thessalonica, and Beroea. **We want you to know** underlines the importance of what follows. **Brethren** is a friendly address

ments, and to heal its divisions. This was how the church at Corinth had reacted. Well might Paul end this part of his letter by saying that he had **perfect confidence** in them.

8:1-24. ***The Proof of Love.***—In this chapter a new section of the letter begins. The trouble in the church at Corinth has been ventilated, discussed, and ended. The confidence in the church which Paul had maintained all through has been justified. He now uses this fact to introduce the subject of **liberality,** never an easy matter to handle. Most people find it difficult to part with money for philanthropic purposes, and the knowledge of this makes it hard to approach them. Those who must do so are apt to be timid and apologetic, or they try to overcome resistance by a violent appeal to the emotions. Paul's method is to put the whole matter on a Christian basis. His object is not merely to get money from people, but to induce them to give from the right motive, so that in giving they will be fully Christian. He uses three arguments.

1-2. ***We Want You to Know, Brethren, About the Grace of God.***—There is a sound instinct at work in this opening. Paul does not start with a direct appeal; he tells them what has been done by another church. He gives them, so to speak, good news from the Christian front. The generosity he cites is an example of the grace of God at work. It takes its place in the category of the things which God has done. This becomes clear when it is seen against the background of the situation to which Paul refers.

The **churches of Macedonia** had come through **a severe test of affliction.** They had suffered persecution for their faith; in addition, Rome had impoverished the country by exacting from it most of its natural wealth, notably

2 How that in a great trial of affliction,
the abundance of their joy and their deep
poverty abounded unto the riches of their
liberality.
3 For to *their* power, I bear record, yea,
and beyond *their* power *they were* willing
of themselves;

in the churches of Mac-e-do'ni-a, 2 for in a
severe test of affliction, their abundance
of joy and their extreme poverty have overflowed in a wealth of liberality on their
part. 3 For they gave according to their
means, as I can testify, and beyond their

---

to fellow Christians. **The grace** [χάρις] **of God** is primarily the freely given, undeserved favor and forgiveness that God offers through Christ to those who will accept it in faith. It is always, as it is here said to be, something **bestowed** (δεδομένην); it is never a human achievement for which man may take credit. In this verse Paul refers to the way in which that divine grace works out in the churches of Macedonia; it is the expression of grace in active life.

2. Vss. 2-3 explain what that outworking of grace was. Paul's opening word ὅτι here means "that"; and, he says, lit., "We want you to know that in much testing of affliction the abundance of their joy and their down-to-the-depth poverty abounded to the wealth of their liberality." The Macedonian Christians have been going through a testing time of **affliction.** This does not refer simply to their **poverty,** which was nothing rare among the early Christians, but rather to ill-treatment from non-Christians. The "strifes" Paul had recently had to endure in Macedonia (7:5) may well have been from the same sources (cf. I Thess. 2:14 on persecution endured at a slightly earlier time). There are two main contrasts in this verse: (*a*) between heavy **affliction** and abundant **joy** (cf. 7:4); the N.T. basis of Christian joy is never freedom from outward difficulty; it is the superiority to hardship that faith gives; and (*b*) between an **extreme poverty,** deeper than most churches knew, and **a wealth of liberality.** How great the actual amount given was, Paul does not say; but the spirit of generosity was shown to an unusual degree. It is that spirit that Paul is seeking to arouse in the Corinthians.

3. The sentence in vss. 3-5 is awkward in style, but its meaning is clear. Paul bears witness that the giving of the Macedonians was not merely **according to their means,** i.e.,

---

its minerals and its timber. In such circumstances **liberality** becomes a spiritual miracle. But God, at work in the hearts of the Macedonian Christians, had made these very circumstances contribute to it. The suffering they had undergone for Christ had set flowing in them a fountain of joy. Through what they had endured they had discovered the reality of God's love and power. It is when faith exacts hardship or sacrifice that it reveals its hidden treasure. This joy in God's fellowship had now expressed itself. It had lifted the Macedonians to a level where they were released from the love of money.

Their extreme poverty had also its part to play. It is a curious fact that those who have little to give, and may even have a struggle to make ends meet, often surprise us most by their sacrificial giving, while those who have abundance are sometimes mean and grudging. Money tends to harden the heart. It dries up sympathy. It makes men anxious about the security of their wealth. It may even make a rich man feel superior to his poor neighbors, suggesting to him that his wealth is the reward of his industry or virtue, while their poverty is the result of some lack of energy or wisdom. John Wesley knew the temptations that come with the love of money. "When I have any money," he wrote, "I get rid of it as quickly as possible lest it should find a way into my heart." On the other hand, poverty may actually set free the springs of liberality. The poor are notably kind to neighbors who are in trouble. They know the needs of others from their own experience. Their sympathies are not deadened by abundance. Their values tend to be found in personal relationships, not in the position or comfort that money brings. This is what Paul suggests had happened in the churches of Macedonia. The joy in Christ, coming to a people who had experienced poverty, had **overflowed in a wealth of liberality.** The phrase is more than a description of their abundant giving. It describes their real wealth—which never does consist in what we have but in the love we show. A man is rich or poor according to the width of his sympathy and the depth of his love.

3-5. ***For They Gave According to Their Means, and Beyond.***—The amount was not de-

4 Praying us with much entreaty that we would receive the gift, and *take upon us* the fellowship of the ministering to the saints.
5 And *this they did,* not as we hoped, but first gave their own selves to the Lord, and unto us by the will of God.

means, of their own free will, 4 begging us earnestly for the favor of taking part in
the relief of the saints — 5 and this, not as we expected, but first they gave themselves to the Lord and to us by the will of God.

---

what might be expected of good Christians, but **beyond their means,** more than he had any right to ask or expect. It was an added joy to Paul and no doubt to the Macedonians also that they were doing this **of their own free will.** This point is emphasized in what follows.

4. Lit., "With much exhortation begging of us the grace and the fellowship of the ministry to the saints." Paul is the leader and organizer of the collection. The Macedonians learn of it and ask earnestly and insistently for the privilege of sharing in it. "Grace" here may well have the general meaning **favor.** The words that follow state the favor they ask: It is "the favor of sharing in the ministry to the saints." **Saints** means persons consecrated to God (cf. 1:1), and so is a term applicable to all Christians. Here it refers especially to the Christians in Jerusalem. The place is not mentioned. Indeed, nowhere in chs. 8–9 does Paul say where the collection is to go. But the readers knew. I Cor. 16:3 and Rom. 15:26 name Jerusalem as the destination, and for no other church or churches was a collection ever taken, as far as we learn. (The Macedonian Christians sent gifts to support Paul in his missionary work, as 11:9 and Phil. 4:15 show.) The word **fellowship** (κοινωνία) here refers to "participation" in the collection, and **ministering** (διακονία) to help given by sending money to those in need.

5. And they shared in this ministry **not as we hoped** or **expected, but** in a spirit and to a degree that went beyond what was anticipated. **First they gave themselves** in a complete, costly, sacrificial dedication **to the Lord and** in active loyalty **to us.** It was a dedication of the whole life; the gift of money was but a part of their offering. Paul does not mean that he wanted only their money and not their dedication of heart and life, for such thorough consecration was **by the will of God;** it was just what they as Christians should do. He does wish to emphasize that first in time and importance was their willing offering of the entire life in faith and active devotion to God, so that the giving of the money was an inevitable expression of their whole attitude; and he adds the point that the degree of such self-dedication was beyond what he could ever have expected. The expression **gave themselves** implies costly giving, as it does in Gal. 1:4, where the same phrase is used of Christ's death.

---

cided, as so often happens, by what their neighbors gave, or even by what they could spare without inconvenience or hardship; they gave to the point of sacrifice. Giving meant going without. Liberality like this calls for an examination of our budget in the light of our real needs and of the Christian stewardship of money.

Further, the liberality of the Macedonian churches was **of their own free will.** There had been no outside pressure. They regarded the opportunity to give as a privilege, even **begging . . . earnestly for the favor of taking part in the relief of the saints.** Giving will not be generous, spontaneous, and joyful until it is regarded not as a duty but as a privilege; and this can happen only when we are concerned more about the needs of others than we are about our own, which is the outstanding fruit of the Christian spirit. In the last resort, liberality springs from the surrender of ourselves to the Lord, so that all we have, including our money, is at God's disposal. This was what had taken place. **First they gave themselves to the Lord.** The result was that they were ready to follow Paul's direction in the use of what money they had. The root of liberality is the consecrated spirit in which the whole of life is given up to the service of God. Stinginess in the face of human needs is the symptom of an incompletely surrendered life. For a Christian there is no absolute right in property. He is a steward, a trustee (Matt. 25:14). It is his Master's money he has. An appeal for our gifts may demand a decision as to

6 Insomuch that we desired Titus, that as he had begun, so he would also finish in you the same grace also.

7 Therefore, as ye abound in every *thing, in* faith, and utterance, and knowledge, and *in* all diligence, and *in* your love to us, *see* that ye abound in this grace also.

6 Accordingly we have urged Titus that as he had already made a beginning, he should also complete among you this gracious work. 7 Now as you excel in everything — in faith, in utterance, in knowledge, in all earnestness, and in your love for us — see that you excel in this gracious work also.

---

6. In vss. 1-5 the example of the Macedonian churches has been presented as a challenge to the Corinthians. Paul now tells what resulted from the Macedonian generosity. He **urged Titus** to return to Corinth and **complete** "this grace" that he had previously begun, i.e., **this gracious work** of the collection. In vs. 10; 9:2 Paul indicates that this collection has been in progress for some months at least; cf. I Cor. 16:1-4, where he assumes that the collection project is known, if not already under way. So we must conclude that Titus began the collection in Corinth before he went there with the "stern letter" from Paul. He must then have begun the collection there either when he carried I Corinthians, if he was the bearer of that letter, or at a still earlier time. Such an earlier time seems indicated by I Cor. 16:1-4.

B. Christ's Example Teaches Generosity (8:7-15)

The central appeal in vss. 7-15 is to the example of Christ (vs. 9). But other appeals are included: Let this **gracious work** match your other spiritual gifts (vs. 7). Prove how sincere your love for us is (vs. 8). Finish what you have started (vss. 10-11). Give as much as you can afford (vss. 11-12). In brotherly spirit share your resources with fellow Christians less fortunate (vs. 14).

7. With the opening word "but" (ἀλλ') Paul turns from the good example of the Macedonians, and the news that Titus is returning to complete the collection, to direct appeal to the Corinthians. They are a gifted church; they **abound in every thing,** i.e., everything else except this giving. Their **faith** is genuine; their **earnestness** (RSV) or eager **diligence** (KJV) has never been in question; even in I Cor. 1:4-7, their gifts of **utterance** and **knowledge** were praised; their renewed loyalty shows their **love for** Paul.

---

the nature of our supreme loyalty. Jesus faced people with this decision when he saw how poverty and material insecurity filled them with anxiety. He bade them seek first the kingdom of God and his righteousness (Matt. 6:24-33). This is the choice that may confront us when we are asked to give for the needs of others or for the work of the kingdom. But giving ourselves to the Lord is more than merely the prerequisite of liberality. The result of such surrender is that our liberality becomes the means of giving ourselves to others. It is quite possible to give without giving ourselves. To give ourselves with our gift is what makes the giving effective and the gift acceptable. The gift then becomes a sacrament of Christian love. It conveys the sense of brotherhood in Christ. As Lowell puts it,

> Who gives himself with his alms feeds three—
> Himself, his hungering neighbor, and me.[9]

[9] "The Vision of Sir Launfal," Part II, st. viii.

Giving such as this in the name of Christ is gracious giving. It reveals the grace of God in action.

6-7. ***This Gracious Work.***—Liberality with love behind it is the work of grace in those who give; and it is the work of grace on those who receive. Titus had initiated the collection among the members of the church in Corinth. No doubt absorption in their own troubles had suspended it. Conflicts within ourselves and within the fellowship which Christ has established prevent our interest in those outside. Now that this conflict has been healed, the whole undertaking can be resumed. Paul's approach is full of tact. He does not condemn their lack of liberality. He mentions all their strong points and then suggests that they add this one more. The gift of faith, the power to understand and expound Christian truth, earnestness of spirit, the bonds of mutual devotion are all good; but without an interest in others the finest piety may become a stagnant pool. John declares that love of the

8 I speak not by commandment, but by occasion of the forwardness of others, and to prove the sincerity of your love.

9 For ye know the grace of our Lord Jesus Christ, that, though he was rich, yet for your sakes he became poor, that ye through his poverty might be rich.

8 I say this not as a command, but to prove by the earnestness of others that your
love also is genuine. 9 For you know the
grace of our Lord Jesus Christ, that though he was rich, yet for your sake he became poor, so that by his poverty you might be-

---

This gracious work is of course the collection; the word used to describe it (χάρις) indicates that when done it will be God who does it. Yet in will and deed they must play their active part. They must do it generously; they must **abound in this** work of **grace also.**

8. Paul urges rather than commands; a good deed is always willingly done, and the Corinthians must make the decision for themselves. "Through" or **by** [means of] **the earnestness** or diligence **of others,** i.e., of the Macedonian churches (vss. 1-5), he is "testing" (δοκιμάζων) the **sincerity** (KJV) or "genuineness" (cf. RSV) of the Corinthians' professed **love** to Paul (vs. 7). Their love to Paul will of course include love to those he loves; they will be eager to help the Jerusalem Christians, his fellow Jews. If their **love is . . . genuine,** as he hopes and expects the "testing" will prove, they will give liberally.

9. Paul might have spoken of the "love" of Christ for the Corinthians, but since it was a love for sinful, undeserving men, he uses instead the word **grace.** They **know** of that grace from the preaching of the gospel message. The full name **our Lord Jesus Christ** gives impressiveness and greater appeal to the mention of Christ. **He was rich** in his pre-existent heavenly glory (cf. I Cor. 8:6; Phil. 2:6; Col. 1:15-17). **Yet for your sake** (this phrase stands first in the Greek to make the appeal more vivid), i.e., for your salvation, **he became poor** by entering upon the lowly state of human life in the Incarnation. He was poor in comparison with his earlier heavenly position. Implied but not expressed is a reference to the entire humble and costly career of Christ, as it is described

---

brethren is the test by which we know that we have passed from death to life (I John 3:14). Paul could have bidden the Corinthians make this collection, and their attachment to him now would have led them to obey. But he will not impose his will on them.

8. ***I Say This Not as a Command.***—He rejects the use of any such pressure. As he had not lorded it over their faith (1:24), so he would not lord it over their conduct. He wanted the money for the poor saints in Jerusalem. But more than the money, he sought the development of the church in the graces of Christian character. The growth of personality is from within and can be produced only in freedom. When appealing for money, let the ambassador for Christ seek to awaken in people the imaginative sympathy and love from which liberality springs, and not induce them to give because of their personal loyalty to himself. **But to prove** the example of others is useful. What is once done opens the mind to what it is possible to do. Paul says that he cites this example in order **to prove by the earnestness of others that** [the] **love** [of the Corinthians] **also is genuine.** He has no doubt of their latent liberality. To bring it fully into action needs only the stimulus of what others have done.

9. ***For You Know the Grace of Our Lord Jesus Christ.***—Here Paul brings his second argument into play—the supreme motive. On this motive he depends. In his plea he counts on their knowledge of the **grace** of Christ, and appeals to it. He does not expect Christian virtues from those who have not had the Christian experience, and these Corinthians to whom he is writing have only just emerged from a pagan society. There is almost always a temptation to appeal to lower motives, even when the appeal is made to Christian people—motives like self-interest, reputation, the various forms of pride. But on such terms no lasting good is done. We cannot get golden conduct out of leaden motives. Paul's appeals are always based on the highest motives, on loyalty to Christ, and on gratitude for what Christ has done. It is to the grace of Christ that the Corinthians, like all Christians, owe their salvation. No Christian can ever call himself a self-made man.

Grace is one of the key words of the N.T. It is one of the attributes of Christ. He is "full of grace and truth" (John 1:14). The word as commonly used has various meanings; e.g., it is used of the help God gives us by reinforcing our strength in a conflict with evil, enabling us to conquer greed, or lust, or pride, or hate. Bun-in Phil. 2:5-8. His purpose was **that by his poverty you** [this pronoun, placed first in the Greek, is thus strongly contrasted with **his**] **might become rich** through the gift of new life with God. Such complete and costly self-giving should move the Corinthians to give liberally to the collection.

---

yan's picture of Christ in the Interpreter's house, pouring the oil of his grace into a fire which evil is trying to put out, illustrates a familiar idea of grace.[1] In reality, however, grace is not a substance which can be poured into the heart. It is rather the saving activity of Christ. As John Oman points out, the grace of God is the form of his divine succor of his children. It therefore cannot be understood apart from the human need in which God comes to their aid.[2] This need is that men should become persons in the full sense of the word, i.e., that they should do the will of God of their own free choice, because they see it to be right. God cannot coerce, even in love, without destroying that which he seeks to save. He can win man's love only by his own, persuade man's mind only by the truth, awaken man's insight and quicken his conscience only by the revelation of perfect goodness and righteousness, even though in doing so he himself must suffer the tragic results of man's blindness and self-will. This is what Paul means by saying that Christ, **though he was rich, . . . became poor.** It can be illustrated rather than described, and Paul illustrates it by the initial act which brought Christ to earth—the Incarnation. He describes this more fully in Phil. 2:5-8. The essence of it is that Christ laid aside the power, dignity, prestige, and privilege that men associate with the Godhead, and took the form of a servant, sharing the ordinary labor of men, and enduring without exemption the ills and injustices of the world in which he lived. He became poor, poor in money, in position, in power, in reputation, poor in all the things that people call wealth. This he did in order to be one with men and to win them by love and goodness from the power of evil to fellowship with God. That act of love is the grace of the Lord Jesus Christ. It is pity without patronage and succor without superiority. It is love which will not let us go, and yet will not overwhelm our will or destroy our freedom. This gracious activity of Christ, in which he "laid his glory by" and stepped onto the stage of the world, involves the fact of his pre-existence. In one sense his earthly life was only an interlude. He came from God and went back to God (John 13:3), and he was conscious of the fact. His entry into human life was a supreme act of grace.

The purpose of it was that we **by his poverty . . . might become rich.** Here again Paul emphasizes the fact that true wealth is of the spirit. It consists in faith, in love, in peace with God, and in the power of the indwelling Spirit. The grace of Christ operates to produce all these, not by infusing them into our hearts, but by so reconciling us to God that we are made one with him. We share his life and yet are most fully ourselves. "In every way you were enriched in him" (I Cor. 1:5). Part of that enrichment is the spirit of liberality.

Clearly, then, to **know the grace of . . . Christ** is more than merely to apprehend the fact. It is an experience of the soul. At least two results are produced in us as we let it work upon our hearts to change us. One is that we see other people with their needs and their failings in a new light. The grace of Christ is a mirror in which we see them reflected in their own priceless value. They are revealed as our brothers for whom Christ died. See John Masefield, *The Everlasting Mercy,* lines beginning, "I knew that Christ had given me birth." [3] The poor brethren in Jerusalem were unknown to the Corinthians, who doubtless regarded them with some suspicion as people who despised Gentiles and were unwilling to accept as Christians any who had not passed through the Jewish gate into the fold. But for these, as for themselves, Christ had died. Now in the light of the Cross they had a new value. They were brethren for whom all brethren ought to care. So does the Cross change the whole perspective in which we see humanity. All men are one in their need of Christ. This is the true equality.

The experience of the grace of God also awakens undying gratitude. We are conscious of a debt to Christ which must be paid, and can be paid only to those for whom he died. "As you did it to one of the least of these my brethren, you did it to me" (Matt. 25:40). This personal gratitude to Christ, which is born of his deliverance of us, is the supreme motive of liberality. Francis of Assisi took all men to his heart because he saw in them the Christ to whom he owed everything. Chesterton sums it all up: "It is the highest and holiest of the paradoxes that the man who really knows he cannot pay his debt will be for ever paying it. . . . He will be always throwing things away into a bottomless pit of unfathomable thanks." [4]

[1] *The Pilgrim's Progress,* "In the Interpreter's House."

[2] *Grace and Personality* (2nd ed. rev.; Cambridge: Cambridge University Press, 1919), p. 40.

[3] *Poems* (New York: The Macmillan Co., 1935), p. 118.

[4] *St. Francis of Assisi,* p. 117.

10 And herein I give *my* advice: for this is expedient for you, who have begun before, not only to do, but also to be forward a year ago.

11 Now therefore perform the doing *of it;* that as *there was* a readiness to will, so *there may be* a performance also out of that which ye have.

12 For if there be first a willing mind, *it is* accepted according to that a man hath, *and* not according to that he hath not.

come rich.
10 And in this matter I give my
advice: it is best for you now to complete
what a year ago you began not only to do
but to desire,
11 so that your readiness in
desiring it may be matched by your completing it out of what you have.
12 For if
the readiness is there, it is acceptable according to what a man has, not according

---

10. Since the RSV gives so free a translation of vss. 10-11, an expanded literal translation may help in the study of the sentence: "And [my] judgment [or advice] I give in this" matter of the collection; "for this" liberal and completed giving "is expedient [or profitable] for you, who last year [or a year ago] began, before" the others did, "not only the doing but also the willing; but now complete also the doing, in order that, as" there was "the readiness to will, so also" there may be "the completing out of the having," i.e., out of what you have. Vs. 10 makes it clear, and recalls to the Corinthians, that they willingly undertook the collection; it was not forced upon them. The preposition "before" (πρό) prefixed to the verb "began" implies that they began this project before others did, a point deserving praise if only they do not fail to complete what they began. **A year ago** is a vague term; it can mean any time in the previous year. Since the Roman year began in January, the Jewish religious year in spring (in the month Nisan), the Athenian year in midsummer, and the Jewish civil year, like the Macedonian-Syrian year, in the fall, the possibilities are many. Paul writes from Macedonia in late summer or early fall; in any case, it is clear that months before he wrote, the Corinthians had voluntarily undertaken a collection for Jerusalem Christians.

11. For a literal translation see Exeg. on vs. 10. The earlier readiness to will, i.e., the free decision to make the collection, must now be matched by the full completion of what they had undertaken. This suggests—although he nowhere explicitly says so—that Paul and the Corinthians had set some definite amount as the goal. The new point added in this verse and the next is that the giving is to be according to ability; no more is asked or expected than they can afford; in the words of vs. 3, it is to be "according to their means."

12. The basic thing is the voluntary **readiness.** Their own decision to complete the giving comes first; Paul is confident that once they renew that earlier decision, the work will be finished. Given that readiness, the gift that is **according to what a man has** is **acceptable** to God. That it will be acceptable to Paul and the recipients is true, but is not here the main point.

10-11. ***In This Matter I Give My Advice.***—The third part of Paul's appeal consists in comments on the general subject of liberality, designed to meet some objections which the Corinthians may actually have made, or which he foresaw might be in their minds. They should now complete what they had begun to do and what they had at one time intended to do. Unfinished things are nothing. They are a burden on the mind and a barrier to progress. "Tasks in hours of insight will'd"[5] should be completed even if the original impulse has faded. Fresh insight into God's will grows only through obedience to insight already given. It is generally at some point of disobedience that spiritual development is arrested.

12. ***According to What a Man Has.***—God does not ask for what we have not got. He judges our liberality in relation to the means we possess, not by the amount we actually give. The widow who put two mites into the temple treasury was commended by Jesus as an example of liberality, because though the amount was infinitesimal it was all she had (Mark 12:42-44). In this light what looks in one case a princely

[5] Matthew Arnold, "Morality," st. i.

13 For *I mean* not that other men be eased, and ye burdened:
14 But by an equality, *that* now at this time your abundance *may be a supply* for their want, that their abundance also may be *a supply* for your want; that there may be equality:

to what he has not. [13] I do not mean that others should be eased and you burdened, [14] but that as a matter of equality your abundance at the present time should supply their want, so that their abundance may supply your want, that there may be equal-

---

13. Again Paul seeks to remove any idea that too heavy a load is being placed on the Corinthians. He does not mean that others should have relief (ἄνεσις, lit., "rest") from, or **be eased** of, the strain of heavy giving **and you** Corinthians be **burdened** with (lit., have the "affliction" of) large financial obligations.

14. The next words may complete the statement of vs. 13: "but" that you should give "as a matter of equality." However, they may be taken with what follows in vs. 14; so the RSV clearly takes them. In either case vs. 14 explains what is meant by **equality:** Christians should share their resources, those who have more sharing with those who have less. It has been suggested that, as in Rom. 15:27, this verse means the Gentile-Christian-Corinthian church should give financial help to the Jerusalem Jewish Christians in return for the gift of the gospel that has come to the Gentiles from the Jewish Christians. But the return the Jewish Christians are to make is mentioned as something that will *follow* the giving of the Corinthians. So the meaning seems to be that you now, **at the present time,** are to meet their need, and at some future time, if you have need, the Jewish Christians (or other Christians) will share with you. No church can tell when its time of hardship and need may come. The reference to **your abundance** makes clear that the Corinthian Christians, though mainly from the lower classes of society (I Cor. 1:26), are financially much better off than most Christians; it is implied in the entire passage (cf. vs. 2) that they are more prosperous than the Macedonian Christians, who have had to endure persecution with its inevitable financial losses.

---

sum may be only a mite; while in another case a mite may be munificent. Liberality is always relative.

13-15. ***I Do Not Mean that Others Should Be Eased and You Burdened.***—Some Corinthians had apparently objected to the collection on the ground that they did not see why other people's burdens should be eased at their expense. Such a view takes no account of God's planned economy. The principle on which the world was meant to run is that of sharing. This applies to the economic life, as well as to the spiritual. Famine in one country and plentiful harvests in another should not be accepted as God's final appointment. God intends his world to be run on the basis that it is one community. If the fruits of production were shared as he means them to be, surplus in one region would make up for deficiency in another. Many of the problems which natural calamities create for faith would be solved if love had its way. And there is a further truth. Unshared abundance can dry up the springs of plenty for those who try to keep it for themselves. This too is an economic fact as well as a spiritual truth. It is true universally, and equally true in the more limited compass of nation, church, or family. The Corinthians at the moment had a surplus, and the saints in Jerusalem a deficiency. Should positions later be reversed, their present generosity would no doubt be balanced by a like generosity to them. Love is never a one-way traffic. The fruits of our own missionary activity are forever returning in fresh visions of truth, in examples of Christian loyalty that challenge our halfheartedness, in miracles of grace which renew our convictions of the reality of God's power. The harvest illustrates a spiritual law—"Cast thy bread upon the waters: for thou shalt find it after many days" (Eccl. 11:1).

Paul's closing reference to the manna in the desert is primarily intended to enforce "the idea of equality" (see Exeg.). The point evidently in his mind is that the grasping man who gathered more than he needed found the surplus unusable, while the man who thought only of his needs for the day found that he had enough. Those who at God's call give out of their store must do so in the faith that the needs of tomorrow will be supplied. Generous impulses ought not to be checked by faithless fear of future want. This is one application of the

15 As it is written, He that *had gathered* much had nothing over; and he that *had gathered* little had no lack.

16 But thanks *be* to God, which put the same earnest care into the heart of Titus for you.

17 For indeed he accepted the exhortation; but being more forward, of his own accord he went unto you.

ity.
15 As it is written, "He who gathered much had nothing over, and he who gathered little had no lack."

16 But thanks be to God who puts the same earnest care for you into the heart of Titus.
17 For he not only accepted our appeal, but being himself very earnest he

---

15. Paul enforces the idea of equality among Christian brothers by quoting Exod. 16:18. In that passage there is no giving to others in need, but only the statement that no matter how much manna any Israelite gathered, he had just enough—no more and no less. Paul uses the figure to show a biblical basis for his idea of economic equality among Christians; those with more than others should share.

C. Recommendation of Titus and Two Other Leaders (8:16-24)

16. Paul sends Titus and two other trusted Christian workers to complete the collection at Corinth. He adopts this method not only to keep critics from saying that he is making financial profit from the collection, but also, as he explains in 9:3-5, because he has told Macedonia that Corinth has the collection ready, and he wants it to be complete before he and his Macedonian traveling companions arrive. This section connects with vs. 6 and finishes what Paul there started to say; vss. 7-15 interrupted the account of the way the leaders were to complete the collection, perhaps because Paul felt that after all the Corinthians themselves must make the actual decision and carry it out; hence their central role must be given prominence. His elaborate argument and varied appeals indicate that they were slow to take up this work. Here he thanks God for putting **the same earnest care** that Paul has for them **into the heart of Titus.** The Greek present participle for **puts** (διδόντι) implies that God in successive situations keeps putting such zeal for the Corinthians into Titus' heart. (Some MSS read the aorist δόντι, which would confine the reference to this one occasion.)

17. This verse gives the evidence for and effect of the divine gift to Titus. He does more than accept Paul's **exhortation** (KJV) or **appeal** (RSV) to go to Corinth and lead them to complete the collection. Because he is **very earnest** (or, "more zealous" than ever) he "goes forth" of his own accord from Macedonia, where he is with Paul. The verb ἐξῆλθεν is an epistolary aorist and so should be translated in English by a present tense, "is going forth"; 7:15 shows that Titus is still with Paul when he writes. No doubt he will carry this letter to Corinth. **Of his own accord** is the same Greek word (αὐθαίρετος) that closed vs. 3; it describes the voluntary nature of truly Christian action.

---

principle which Christ laid down in relation to material anxiety, that if we seek first the kingdom of God and his righteousness all the things about whose provision we are anxious shall be added unto us (Matt. 6:33).

16-19. ***The Plan.***—Paul here announces the arrangements he has made for the expected contribution. Three of the most honored brethren would come to Corinth to receive it. Titus was a good emissary. He had as much solicitude for the church at Corinth as Paul himself had, so that Paul had evidently asked him to go on his own account. He knew the whole situation, and his experience there had given him the confidence he needed in making this new appeal. With him would go **the brother who is famous among all the churches for his preaching of the gospel.** Possibly Luke, though we cannot be sure. Whoever he was, he had this to commend him—he had been appointed by the churches to accompany Paul in the **gracious work.** The apostle's exalted way of referring to the collection lifts it above sordid associations; but it does not keep him from making the common-sense plan of associating some trusted brother or brothers with him in handling the money.

18 And we have sent with him the
brother, whose praise *is* in the gospel
throughout all the churches;
19 And not *that* only, but who was also
chosen of the churches to travel with us
with this grace, which is administered by
us to the glory of the same Lord, and
declaration of your ready mind:
20 Avoiding this, that no man should
blame us in this abundance which is administered by us:
21 Providing for honest things, not only
in the sight of the Lord, but also in the
sight of men.

is going to you of his own accord. **18** With
him we are sending the brother who is
famous among all the churches for his
preaching of the gospel; **19** and not only
that, but he has been appointed by the
churches to travel with us in this gracious
work which we are carrying on, for the
glory of the Lord and to show our good
will. **20** We intend that no one should
blame us about this liberal gift which we
are administering, **21** for we aim at what is
honorable not only in the Lord's sight but

---

18. Titus leads the delegation; two others accompany him. One **brother,** i.e., fellow Christian, whom Paul does not name and whose identity we cannot determine, receives praise, which means he is widely and favorably known, **among all the churches for his** effective **preaching of the gospel. All** may refer only to all churches sharing in the collection, but is probably a general way of saying the person referred to is everywhere known, either personally or by favorable report. That Paul is sending him and the other delegates shows that the apostle is in charge of the collection.

19. This man is not only a much-praised preacher but also an official representative of the (Macedonian?) churches. This in itself gives him no authority over Corinth, for there is no hint that they have had a part in electing him, but it shows that he is everywhere trusted, as one dealing in money matters must be. **He has been appointed by the churches to travel with us** [i.e., with Paul] **in** the promotion of **this gracious work** [lit., "grace," χάριτι] **which we are carrying on** (RSV), or as the KJV more literally translates, **which is administered by us.** The following odd phrase, introduced by πρός (lit., "toward") says that this is being done by us "to show [or promote, or further] the glory [or praise] of the Lord [Christ] and our readiness." It is being so managed by Paul that it manifests or promotes both the praise of Christ and the readiness of Paul to serve him.

20. In this carefully organized plan that provides an elected representative "to travel with us," Paul says he is **avoiding this,** viz., that anyone **should blame us in this abundance** [or bounty] **which is administered by us.** The wisdom of this precaution is clear from 12:16-18, which shows that Paul was suspected of promoting the collection in order to get the money for himself. The word **abundance,** which the RSV well interprets as **liberal gift,** assumes that the amount raised will be large and represent generous giving; it is thus an indirect appeal.

21. In his ministry, and especially in this collection, Paul aims at what is good and **honorable** in the sight not only of the Lord Christ, although that is basic and primary, but also of men. The Greek translation of Prov. 3:4 is reflected here. It recognizes that

---

20-22. ***We Intend that No One Should Blame Us.***—It seems that some people had actually hinted that Paul's interest in the collection was open to suspicion. He deals with this later in ch. 12. Here he is humble enough to take steps to safeguard his integrity. That he did not take offense and adopt a highhanded attitude is another mark of his greatness. The kingdom of God, not his own feelings, is what mattered to him first and last. But these precautions were sensible. Those who handle money in trust should be scrupulously careful, not only of the money they handle, but of their reputation for honesty in handling it. There are times when one may not be able to prevent malicious gossip, and the best reply may be silence; but it is stupid to put reputations in needless jeopardy.

With the two already mentioned Paul says that he is sending another brother, who is now quite unidentifiable.

22 And we have sent with them our brother, whom we have oftentimes proved diligent in many things, but now much more diligent, upon the great confidence which *I have* in you.

23 Whether *any do inquire* of Titus, *he is* my partner and fellow helper concerning you: or our brethren *be inquired of, they are* the messengers of the churches, *and* the glory of Christ.

24 Wherefore show ye to them, and before the churches, the proof of your love, and of our boasting on your behalf.

9 For as touching the ministering to the saints, it is superfluous for me to write to you:

also in the sight of men.
22 And with them we are sending our brother whom we have often tested and found earnest in many matters, but who is now more earnest than ever because of his great confidence in you.
23 As for Titus, he is my partner and fellow worker in your service; and as for our brethren, they are messengers[j] of the churches, the glory of Christ.
24 So give proof, before the churches, of your love and of our boasting about you to these men.

9 Now it is superfluous for me to write to you about the offering for the saints,

[j] Greek *apostles*.

---

not only the actual character, but also the reputation and apparent purpose of the Christian leader are vitally important.

22. A third **brother,** unnamed but highly recommended, is sent as subordinate to the other two men. Paul is in effect writing a "letter of recommendation" (cf. 3:1!) for these leaders. While Paul does not say here that this man also has been chosen by the churches for this work of the collection, vs. 23 implies that this is the case. He is experienced, **often tested** by Paul **and found earnest in many matters** or situations. To insure him a good reception and to renew the challenge to complete the collection, Paul reports that this brother is **more earnest than ever** as he faces the task in Corinth, because he has **great confidence** in the Christians there, and is sure they will give willingly and liberally.

23. Paul now summarily characterizes and recommends the three. **Titus,** he says, is **my partner and,** by reason of two or more previous visits to Corinth, my **fellow worker in your service.** The two unnamed **brethren** are **messengers of the churches,** to be respected and trusted because they have thus been recognized as competent leaders; they are also **the glory of Christ,** i.e., by reason of their character and work they bring praise to their Lord. **Messengers** is lit. **apostles** (RSV mg.) in the broad sense of officially delegated and responsible emissaries (see Exeg. on 1:1).

24. **So,** Paul concludes, by receiving these men whom I am sending, and by completing the collection under their leadership, **give** outward demonstration or **proof of your love** for us **and of our boasting about you to these men.** Paul spurs the readers to prompt and generous giving (*a*) by appealing to their love for him, (*b*) by recalling the confidence he has expressed to the messengers when asking them to go to Corinth, and (*c*) by reminding the Corinthians that the other churches are present in these men and will hear from them what the Corinthians have done about the collection.

D. Appeal to Finish the Collection Before Paul Comes (9:1-5)

9:1. Apart from **for** (γάρ), which suggests that a previous discussion is being continued, the opening words, "Concerning the ministry to the saints," sound as though a

---

23. *The Glory of Christ.*—These companions of Titus are not named, but their lives are a mirror in which Christ is reflected. Nothing greater can be said of any man; no one should be able to say less of any Christian. Was **the glory of Christ** so evident to Paul's mind when he thought of them that their names were irrelevant?

24. *So Give Proof.*—Not only of their love, but of all that Paul has said about them. He hopes that they will not, so to speak, let him down. Nothing more needs to be said on that score.

9:1-2. *The Offering for the Saints.*—It might appear from ch. 8 that Paul had explored the subject of liberality very thoroughly, and had

2 For I know the forwardness of your
mind, for which I boast of you to them of
Macedonia, that Achaia was ready a year
ago; and your zeal hath provoked very
many.
3 Yet have I sent the brethren, lest our
boasting of you should be in vain in this
behalf; that, as I said, ye may be ready.

2 for I know your readiness, of which I boast
about you to the people of Mac-e-do'ni-a,
saying that A-cha'ia has been ready since
last year; and your zeal has stirred up most
of them. 3 But I am sending the brethren
so that our boasting about you may not
prove vain in this case, so that you may be

---

new subject is being introduced. It has been suggested that ch. 9 is a part of another letter, to Corinth or to some other city. If only one of these chapters went to Corinth, it would be ch. 9, which mentions Achaia in vs. 2; neither could have gone to Macedonia, since both mention it as another region (vss. 2, 4; 8:1). However, the reference to "sending the brethren" in vss. 3-5 recalls 8:16-24, and the fact that this chapter presents almost entirely new material argues that it continues the discussion of ch. 8. The fresh start in vs. 1, however, implies at least a pause before the dictation of ch. 9. The fact that Paul feels impelled to extend the appeal indicates that he was by no means certain that the Corinthians would give as liberally as he had asked. This, it seems, was their basic weakness; they had not learned to give themselves and their money to serve others.

The "ministry" (διακονία) here mentioned is the collection for relief of the destitute **saints,** i.e., Christians in Jerusalem; the RSV translates freely by **offering.** The same expression, "the ministry to the saints," occurs in 8:4.

2. I need not write concerning the collection, Paul says, **for I know your readiness, of which I** keep boasting on your behalf (ὑπὲρ ὑμῶν, i.e., as your friend and in a way that honors you) to the Macedonians, i.e., to the churches there. His repeated boast is **that Achaia has been ready since last year** (cf. 8:10). **Achaia,** the Roman province including all of Greece south of Macedonia, had Corinth as its capital, and the most important Christian church in Achaia was in Corinth. There was a smaller church at Corinth's eastern seaport, Cenchreae (Rom. 16:1), a small group at Athens (Acts 17:34), and quite probably other groups elsewhere (cf. 1:1). Paul here implies that all were to share in the collection. The reported zeal of the Corinthians has stirred up to eager giving "the greater number" (τοὺς πλείονας). This phrase does not imply that some Macedonians are still unwilling to give; it says that the Corinthian example has led many more in other places, specifically in Macedonia, to take part in the collection. The beginning that Corinth made the previous year (8:10) gave some justification to Paul's report, and if in his boast his hope outran the facts he knew, his overstatement expressed a confidence in them that seems to have been vindicated at the end (Rom. 15:26).

3. In vss. 3-5 Paul explains why he sends **the** three **brethren** (cf. 8:16-24). The verb ἔπεμψα is epistolary aorist, and means **I am sending;** they are going to Corinth with this letter. The motive of avoiding suspicion (8:20) is not mentioned. The reason here given

---

laid a secure spiritual basis for generous giving. Some have thought that ch. 9 must be a fragment from another letter. But this need not be so (see Exeg.). What he now says reveals a certain uneasiness in his mind. This particular offering appeared to him of great strategic importance, not only for the spiritual progress of the Corinthians, but for cementing and deepening the fellowship of the far-flung church. Therefore, while he repeats himself at one or two points, he makes some additional suggestions.

He begins with an apology for his insistence, which is also a tactful appeal. He knows how ready they are to give. He has in fact been boasting about it in Macedonia, and the news of their readiness to give has stirred up the liberality of the Macedonians. What has already happened may be taken as an example of unconscious spiritual influence. "One loving heart sets another aflame." Faith kindles faith. This is how spiritual revival spreads. But Paul is taking no chances.

3-5. *I Am Sending the Brethren so that Our Boasting About You May Not Prove Vain.*— He is anxious that they should live up to their promise, and to the picture he has painted of them. The reason he gives in vs. 5 for sending brethren ahead to make arrangements for the

4 Lest haply if they of Macedonia come
with me, and find you unprepared, we
(that we say not, ye) should be ashamed in
this same confident boasting.
5 Therefore I thought it necessary to exhort the brethren, that they would go before unto you, and make up beforehand
your bounty, whereof ye had notice before,
that the same might be ready, as *a matter of*
bounty, and not as *of* covetousness.
6 But this *I say,* He which soweth sparingly shall reap also sparingly; and he

ready, as I said you would be; 4 lest if some
Mac-e-do'ni-ans come with me and find
that you are not ready, we be humiliated
— to say nothing of you — for being so
confident. 5 So I thought it necessary to
urge the brethren to go on to you before
me, and arrange in advance for this gift
you have promised, so that it may be ready
not as an exaction but as a willing gift.
6 The point is this: he who sows spar-

---

is that he does not want his repeated boast to **prove vain** (empty) in this respect (μέρει), i.e., as to the collection being now completed. He wants it fully **ready** when he comes. The RSV wrongly supplies **you would be;** Paul means, "as I have kept saying you were."

4. Paul is coming soon; this is another stimulus to act, for to see him will embarrass them if they have not made the collection. The coming of Macedonians with him would also embarrass them, and him, in such a case. **If** leaves it uncertain whether they will arrive when he does. He intended at that time to come from Macedonia to Corinth, and then sail to Palestine with the collection (Acts 20:3). The Macedonians carrying their collection might come to Corinth with him, or at least would come there before he left. Paul speaks chiefly of the embarrassment that the failure to complete the offering would cause him, but the readers would get the point, inserted as a parenthesis, that they too would **be humiliated** (put to shame).

5. Three times in this verse Paul uses in compound verbs the preposition "before" (πρό): "go *before*" me, "arrange [or complete] *in advance,*" "your *previously* promised bounty." This repetition emphasizes that there has already been too much delay, and that prompt completion of the work is urgently desirable. What the KJV calls a **bounty** and the RSV a **gift** and **willing gift** is literally a "blessing" (εὐλογίαν), a splendid generous benefit to the destitute Jerusalem Christians. The immense importance of cheerful, willing giving is noted here and further developed in the next section. The closing words are, lit., "As a bounty [or blessing] and not as covetousness." This last word refers primarily not to grudging, niggardly giving on the part of the Corinthians, but to the fact that if the leaders have to force the giving, it may seem that they are exacting the money in a demanding and greedy spirit.

E. God's Blessings Rest Upon the Liberal Giver (9:6-15)

1. God Will Liberally Supply the Giver's Needs (9:6-11)

6. The Corinthians evidently had not learned to give to help others. They seem to have feared that such giving might lead them to suffer want later. Paul first points out

---

collection of the money is interesting. He does not want their liberality to be done on the spur of the moment, in response to a strong appeal such as he might make if he were to visit them. He will not have money wrung out of them. There will be no emotional picking of pockets. What they should give must be thoughtfully considered in the light of what he has already said, in view of the need to be met and their own ability. Their giving must be intelligent, conscientious, and deliberate. This is the kind of liberality which sustains the income of the church and of philanthropic institutions. Exceptional donations are not, of course, excluded; the emphasis here is on calculated and systematic giving. There are times when necessity demands the exceptional; but real generosity is habitual and thoughtful, not spasmodic. It is not always lack of desire to give that makes people stingy; it is often lack of thought and imagination. Paul wants the giving of the Corinthians to be generous, as appears from his next remark.

6. *The Point Is This.*—Do we have here an appeal to self-interest, of which we are rightly

which soweth bountifully shall reap also bountifully.

7 Every man according as he purposeth in his heart, *so let him give;* not grudgingly, or of necessity: for God loveth a cheerful giver.

ingly will also reap sparingly, and he who sows bountifully will also reap bountifully.
7 Each one must do as he has made up his mind, not reluctantly or under compulsion,

---

the rich blessings of liberal, willing giving, and then assures them that God will prosper those who are generous and give them the means to continue to help others. The opening words, "now this" (τοῦτο δέ), mean "now **this I say,**" or "consider this," i.e., here is an important point to remember. The rewards of giving are in proportion to the degree of generosity. **He who sows** [i.e., gives] **sparingly will also reap sparingly;** he will get a limited benefit from it. But **he who sows** [gives] **bountifully will also reap** a rich, bountiful blessing.

7. To gain the blessing the giving must be joyous and willing. Each Christian is to give as he has decided for himself; the middle voice of the verb (προῄρηται) stresses the fact that the amount is to rest on each one's voluntary decision. He is to give "not of grief or of necessity"; he is not to be sad and reluctant at giving up the money, or forced to give by Paul and his helpers and by embarrassment. Contrast "of their own free will" (8:3). In words that reflect Prov. 22:9, Paul declares that **God loves a cheerful,** joyous **giver.**

---

suspicious? Most churches omit from modern editions of their hymnbooks the eighth verse of Christopher Wordsworth's hymn:

> Whatever, Lord, we lend to thee
> Repaid a thousandfold will be,
> Then gladly will we give to thee,
> Who givest all.[6]

Paul's statement is a statement of fact. It is a law of nature. The farmer knows that if he grudges the seed he will limit the harvest, and he takes measures accordingly. Jesus says, "The measure you give will be the measure you get" (Matt. 7:2). In some form or other it comes back to us. A loving and generous spirit will reap a harvest of love and kindness. Yet no deed of genuine love or liberality can ever be done for the sake of a return in kind. There is little more in that case than a commercial transaction, which often defeats itself. Jesus urged the giving that expects nothing in return, and the hospitality which is shown to those who cannot afford to repay it. He did not however condemn the natural expectation that sacrifice for his sake would be rewarded. When his disciples asked what they would get for what they had given up, he expressly said "a hundredfold," and "now in this time" (Mark 10:30). Even a cup of cold water in his name would not go forgotten (Matt. 10:42). The world is a moral order. The desire that justice will be done, and that things will eventually make sense, is reasonable. The rewards may not be in kind. The real rewards of goodness are in the spirit. Love's true return is not even the love of others; it is the increased capacity to love. A generous-hearted man looking back on his life remarked, "I have loved more than I have been loved, I have trusted more than I have been trusted, but the balance remains with me." The reward of generosity is the generous heart which rejoices in giving and seeks no return. But the law of returns remains. We reap what we sow.

7. ***Each One Must Do as He Has Made Up His Mind.***—Paul emphasizes again the point he has made. What each man ought to give must be thought out in the light of his own responsibility for the use of his money. Having made the decision, he ought to adhere to it. Moods change. When the time comes to make the gift, the cause itself may not seem quite so urgent; or our own needs may appear more pressing. Giving must also be wholehearted. The practical usefulness of the gift may not seem to be affected by the spirit in which it is given; but a Christian man's giving is done to God. It is the vehicle of his love and service. Hence the spirit is of supreme importance. A gift reluctantly made to a friend has no value for him; its real significance lies in its providing a channel for friendship. Offerings for the temple were to be accepted only from every man who "giveth . . . willingly with his heart" (Exod. 25:2). **God loves a cheerful giver** is another way of putting

[6] "O Lord of heaven and earth and sea."

8 And God *is* able to make all grace abound toward you; that ye, always having all sufficiency in all *things*, may abound to every good work:
9 (**As it is written, He hath dispersed abroad; he hath given to the poor: his righteousness remaineth for ever.**

for God loves a cheerful giver. 8 And God
is able to provide you with every blessing in abundance, so that you may always have enough of everything and may provide in abundance for every good work. 9 As it is
written,

"He scatters abroad, he gives to the poor;
his righteousness[k] endures for ever."

[k] Or *benevolence*.

---

8. God is able to reward and, Paul believes, will reward generous giving with abundant spiritual and material prosperity, so that the giver can give still more. **All grace** (χάρις) means every gift of divine grace, **every** spiritual and material **blessing** (RSV). This complete supply of all the generous Christian's needs is stressed by using πᾶς, "all" or "every," five times in this verse (and twice in vs. 11). The result of this complete God-given sufficiency is not selfish enjoyment, but **that ye . . . may abound to** [or **have abundance for**] **every good work.** The blessings God bestows for giving now will provide the means for still greater giving.

9. Paul enforces his words with a quotation from Ps. 112:9, which speaks of the righteous man. "He scattered," gave liberally and wherever needed; this is the opposite of "sowing sparingly." "He gave to the poor" as the Corinthians are being asked to do. **His righteousness,** which here refers to his good deeds, especially to his kindly giving, **endures for ever** (cf. Rev. 14:13). God will give him an eternal blessing for his generous giving. This blessing the Corinthians may have by similar generosity.

---

the same thing. A cheerful spirit is the fruit only of wholehearted service or generosity. It is the accompaniment of self-forgetful love which sees those we help as persons, not as cases. It is the vivid realization of that personal need which gives mission work or philanthropy its most effective appeal to our generosity. Instead of being afraid lest by our liberality we impoverish ourselves, we should rely on God to supply our need.

8. *God Is Able to Provide You with Every Blessing.*—Liberality may be limited by fear for our own security. There is always a temptation to fall back on the proverb that charity begins at home, that it is our duty to provide for ourselves and for our own future. This point of view leaves two things out of account. One is that God provides for those who trust him and in faith respond to the appeal of others' need. It is from him that wealth comes. The spring of his bounty is not dried up by drawing on it for the need of others; it is stimulated. The story of the widow who fed Elijah from her slender store, and in doing so found it replenished, is a parable. Giving to others is an act of faith to which God responds. The second thing is that God intends his provision for us to be used in supplying the needs of others. We are channels. What we possess is a trust. The problem of poverty is not merely one of economics; it is also one of love. If we all saw ourselves as trustees of what we possess, the problem would find at least some approximate solution in whatever way might prove most effective. Albert Schweitzer says:

> Regarding the question of property, the ethic of reverence for life is outspokenly individualist in the sense that goods earned or inherited are to be placed at the disposition of the community, not according to any standards whatever laid down by society, but according to the absolutely free decision of the individual. It places all its hopes on the enhancement of the feeling of responsibility in men. It defines possessions as the property of the community, of which the individual is sovereign steward.[7]

9. *He Scatters Abroad.*—The righteous man is lavish in his gifts even as God is lavish in his. The prodigality of nature is boundless. The very word **righteousness,** whether of man as here or of God, includes the grace of "kindly giving" (see Exeg.). Each of the two ideas, as James Stewart points out, includes the other.[8]

[7] *Civilization and Ethics,* II, 266.
[8] *A Man in Christ* (New York: Harper & Bros., 1935), p. 246.

10 Now he that ministereth seed to the sower both minister bread for *your* food, and multiply your seed sown, and increase the fruits of your righteousness:)

11 Being enriched in every thing to all bountifulness, which causeth through us thanksgiving to God.

12 For the administration of this service not only supplieth the want of the saints, but is abundant also by many thanksgivings unto God;

10 He who supplies seed to the sower and
bread for food will supply and multiply
your resources[l] and increase the harvest of
your righteousness.[k] **11** You will be enriched
in every way for great generosity, which
through us will produce thanksgiving to
God; **12** for the rendering of this service
not only supplies the wants of the saints
but also overflows in many thanksgivings

[l] Greek *sowing*.
[k] Or *benevolence*.

---

10. In words reminiscent of Isa. 55:10 and Hos. 10:12, Paul assures the readers that God, who gives the growth and harvest (cf. I Cor. 3:6-7) in all of man's tilling and toiling, will not only supply their need and continue their income; he will **multiply** their **seed** if they "sow bountifully" by giving liberally to the collection. His first thought is that God, by giving them what they earn in their business or work, will return to them more than they have given. So, as he said in vs. 8, they can give again, and this time still more, and thus God will **increase the harvest of your righteousness.** These closing words seem to include the idea of a spiritual **harvest** or blessing for such righteous deeds as giving to the collection for the destitute Christians in Jerusalem. Paul pictures both sides of life as advancing; increasing material prosperity leads to greater generosity, which in return yields greater spiritual benefits to the giver. The Christian's financial resources are a means for unselfish helpfulness.

11. Lit., "enriched in everything [or in every way] unto all liberality." This is a final brief statement of what has been said. If the Corinthians give generously to complete the collection, by God's grace and gift they will be enriched in every part of their life, spiritual and material, to the end that they may go on to all (or to every kind of) liberality. Paul then adds a point that will be developed in the next verses: this gift, taken to Jerusalem and interpreted to the recipients **through us,** through Paul and the others who carry it, **will produce** in those who receive it **thanksgiving to God** for the gift and the givers.

2. Both Givers and Recipients Will Glorify God (9:12-15)

12. The two results of a liberal collection are now stated. **The rendering** [lit., "ministry"] **of this service** helps to supply **the wants of the** destitute **saints** in Jerusalem; the Corinthians must not let their fellow Christians suffer want. The Greek word for **service** (λειτουργία) was often used of a special religious service undertaken voluntarily. The giving of the collection is truly a religious service. "Helps to supply" (προσαναπληροῦσα) recalls that others are sharing in this collection; the Corinthians are not carrying the entire load. **But** such generous giving as Paul is encouraging **also overflows in many thanksgivings** offered **to God,** especially by those whose wants are met.

10-12. ***He Will Supply and Multiply.***—The whole process of sowing and reaping, by which the wants of men are met, has the providence of God behind it. The sower must sow the seed if he and others are to be fed. He does not fear to put his seed grain into the earth, for he knows the power that waits in the soil to multiply it. The same law of increasing returns operates in the life of faith. To those who give, God responds by increasing their power to give. He enriches us to produce a harvest of liberality. This not only supplies the actual needs of the saints; it produces in them **thanksgivings to God.**

Paul lays great stress on thanksgiving as a result of Christian activity. He has already urged it as a motive for prayer (1:11). Here, as a motive for liberality, he insists that many people will feel impelled to give thanks to God for the generosity of Corinth. In this there is spiritual significance. Thanksgiving is the note sounded in the heart by a real experience of God's mercy. It is the inevitable reaction to the

13 While by the experiment of this ministration they glorify God for your professed subjection unto the gospel of Christ,
and for *your* liberal distribution unto
them, and unto all *men;*
14 And by their prayer for you, which
long after you for the exceeding grace of
God in you.

to God. 13 Under the test of this service,
you[m] will glorify God by your obedience
in acknowledging the gospel of Christ, and
by the generosity of your contribution for
them and for all others; 14 while they long
for you and pray for you, because of the

[m] Or *they.*

13. The participle "glorifying" may refer to the act either of the Corinthians, as the RSV implies (**you will glorify God**), or more likely of the recipients of the gift, as in the KJV (**they glorify God**). The Jerusalem Christians who receive the gift will "through the test [or proof] of this ministry" be "glorifying God for the obedience of your confession to the gospel of Christ and for the liberality of [your] fellowship toward them and toward all." This "ministry" in the collection is a "test" that, rightly passed, will give "proof" that the Corinthians sincerely believe and follow the gospel. Seeing this evidence or proof, the recipients of the gift will glorify God for two things; first, generally, for the obedience that the Corinthians have expressed in their confession of Christ in response to the gospel; and then, in particular, for the liberality shown in their helpful fellowship with the Jerusalem Christians. The closing words, "and toward all," may imply that a benefit to the Jerusalem saints serves the whole church, or that this specific gift will be matched by other acts of helpfulness to "all" other Christians as opportunities arise.

14. "While they also, with prayer for you, long for you because of the surpassing grace of God" which, as your generous gift enables them to see, rests "upon you." The word "also" reminds the readers that in addition to those who receive the gift, others, and especially Paul, will pray for them. As the Jerusalem Christians think of the gift, they will not only pray gratefully for the Corinthians, but will also **long for** them, i.e., feel

consciousness of his love. The man who is full of thankfulness to God is humble, reverent, and at rest in the assurance of God's care. He has a deeper appreciation of the gifts of life because they are the expression of that care.

13-14. ***Under the Test of This Service.***—Paul's call to the Corinthians for liberality is a test of how far the gospel has won their hearts. It is a test of their spirit, like everything else in life which makes demands on our love or on our faith. We are constantly being judged by our reactions to strain and responsibility, as a bridge is tested by the weight of the traffic that passes over it, or the strength of the tree by the gale that shakes it. But in the Christian life the test is never mere judgment, revealing the quality of our character or our progress in love or faith. It is a means of deepening and developing love and faith. It is an opportunity to make fresh advances. The apostle tells his readers that they will be glorifying God by their liberality. Those around us (see Exeg.) judge of God by the spirit they see in us as we meet the various situations of life, just as a runner in the Olympian games glorified his country by the way he ran. Every victory of love over selfishness makes God both real and lovable to others.

What Paul means by **obedience in acknowledging the gospel of Christ** is not quite clear. The most probable meaning is that liberality would be a sign of their grateful acknowledgment of the gospel. Not only would they show how deeply that gospel had won their hearts; they would show also how conscious they were of its blessings. These two things are not synonymous except on the deeper levels of experience. Many share the blessings without either being conscious of the influence of Christ upon their lives or being grateful for it. The call for some act of sacrificial generosity may well set them to thinking things out, and so be the means of opening their eyes.

But the gift will be an opportunity also for glorifying God by revealing and expressing their love for the saints. Sympathy for the needs of the saints in Jerusalem on the part of the Corinthian Christians demanded not a little of the Christian spirit. The racial barrier between Greeks and Jews was very real. It was made worse by the Judaizers who asserted that without circumcision and other requirements of the Jewish law the Christian standing of Gentiles was defective. No one is more difficult to love than a man whose ecclesiastical views make him deny the validity of the Christian experience of those who differ from him. But an act

15 Thanks *be* unto God for his unspeakable gift.

surpassing grace of God in you. 15 Thanks be to God for his inexpressible gift!

deeply the bond of Christian fellowship which binds the two groups together. This is a major interest of Paul. As the largely Gentile church of Corinth helps the Jewish church in Jerusalem, they will come to better understanding and will feel greater friendliness. In a day when the church threatened to split into two groups, Jewish and Gentile, Paul made every effort to bind the two parts of the one church of Christ together in active brotherhood. The **grace of God,** Paul hints, will be seen by its effect as it leads the Corinthians to give liberally to the collection. The word **surpassing** assumes and encourages a large contribution by the Corinthians.

15. The thought of the church bound together through the fellowship of giving and receiving leads Paul to a final exclamation of **thanks . . . to God.** He thanks God either for this unity of diverse groups which come together in such practical brotherhood or, as he considers the rich benefits of what God has given in the gospel, gives thanks for the

of love may dissolve both the antagonism and the exclusiveness.

> He drew a circle that shut me out,
> Heretic, rebel, a thing to flout.
> But Love and I had the wit to win:
> We drew a circle that took him in.[9]

It is Paul's hope that their generosity may serve to overcome these intangible prejudices and build a bridge of fellowship between them and the Jerusalem Christians. Such a result would not be produced merely by gratitude for the gifts received, but by the revelation through these gifts of the grace of God at work in the Corinthians, and of grace in an extraordinary degree. Jesus says that the reality of our Christian spirit is tested by its fruits (Matt. 7:20). The fruits of the Spirit are the final evidence of the presence of the Spirit. There is no way in which prejudices against the church can be overcome except by what men see in us of the working of his grace. It is this mention of God's **surpassing grace** that releases in Paul's heart a final wave of thanksgiving.

15. *God's Inexpressible Gift.*—All that Paul has said about liberality has been said in the consciousness of God's supreme gift in Christ. What that gift means is beyond his power to express. It is, in Charles Wesley's words,

> A vast, unfathomable sea,
> Where all our thoughts are drowned.[10]

The consciousness of it, awakening wonder, worship, and boundless gratitude, would seem to make redundant all his efforts to stimulate their giving. Adoring gratitude would flow out in an irrepressible spring of generosity. All that would be needed would be to find the right channel for giving. The thought of Christ as God's gift to men pervades the N.T.: "He gave his only begotten Son" (John 3:16). "He . . . spared not his own Son, but delivered him up for us all" (Rom. 8:32). Our goodness is not our achievement but the gift of his grace. Even the faith to receive his grace is a gift from him. "By grace are ye saved through faith; and that not of yourselves: it is the gift of God" (Eph. 2:8). This is not easy for us to realize. We are impelled by pride to try to earn our own salvation. The "wise passiveness" of which Wordsworth speaks is difficult for the practical Western mind to reach; but in the last resort it is the condition in which God is able to save us. John Wesley's conversation with the Moravian pastor on this point is illuminating. Wesley was aware that he lacked the experience of full salvation. The Moravian told him his trouble was that he sought to earn it instead of receiving it as a free gift from God. Thereafter Wesley's one desire was to find this faith. Then it came.

> In the evening I went very unwillingly to a society in Aldersgate Street, where one was reading Luther's preface to the *Epistle to the Romans.* About a quarter before nine, while he was describing the change which God works in the heart through faith in Christ, I felt my heart strangely warmed. I felt I did trust in Christ, Christ alone for salvation; and an assurance was given me that He had taken away *my* sins, even *mine,* and saved *me* from the law of sin and death.[1]

The gospel is not the proclamation of an ideal; it is the good news of God's free gift in Christ. It is also the description of that gift. The failure to realize the wonder of it often keeps us from being ready to receive it. It is like treasure hidden in a field which impels the finder to

[9] Edwin Markham, "Outwitted." Reprinted by permission.

[10] "Thy ceaseless, unexhausted love."

[1] *Wesley's Journal,* May 14, 1738.

10 Now I Paul myself beseech you by the meekness and gentleness of Christ,

10 I, Paul, myself entreat you, by the meekness and gentleness of Christ —

inexpressible gift of Christ, who is able to save all men and bring them together in one church. As the Corinthians think of what has been given to them, they too should thank God, and give generously.

IV. Rebuke of the Revolt Against the Apostle (10:1–13:10)

See Intro., pp. 270-71, for the evidence suggesting that 10:1–13:10 was not part of the "thankful letter," the fourth letter Paul wrote to Corinth, but rather a part of the "stern letter," the third letter in the series. The section 10:1–13:10 contains vigorous self-vindication, including both spirited defense and withering retort; Paul is engaged in a bitter struggle for the loyalty of the Corinthian church. In chs. 1–9 the crisis has past, and Paul is expressing his joy at the happy issue of the difficulty.

A. Defense Against Slanders and False Leaders (10:1–11:15)

1. Persistent Revolt May Force Paul to Stern Action (10:1-6)

10:1. We do not have the opening of the "stern letter." Here Paul begins his defense against the charge that he is a coward who shows courage only at a distance. The rather elaborate reference to himself, **Now I Paul myself,** gives emphasis to the statement that

sell his all to buy the field and possess the treasure (Matt. 13:44); or like a pearl of great price for which a merchant sells all his other pearls (Matt. 13:45-46). It is the invitation from a king to a wedding feast (Matt. 22:2-3). In these parables Christ describes the inexpressible treasure of the gift he had come to bring in his own person. What this gift meant to Paul his letter has already revealed. It brought light on the meaning of life, deliverance from the guilt and power of sin, a new attitude to trouble and suffering by which they became God's instruments of grace.

It was also the call to a service in which his whole personality was released into freedom and fulfillment. There is a danger that this aspect of the gospel as a gift may be so used as to eliminate an equally important truth, viz., that the gift includes a demand. H. H. Farmer says: "I do not believe that God ever comes livingly to a man or a woman without making a claim, a demand. Nor does He ever come without proffering strength and succour. The two, the demand and the succour, are inseparably one." [2]

God's gift in Christ always brings with it a demand because it lays us under a sense of obligation. It raises the psalmist's question, "What shall I render unto the Lord for all his benefits toward me?" (Ps. 116:12.) The love of Christ awakens a response of gratitude which seeks a channel in service; it also opens our eyes to the need which claims our help. But God's gift may even be itself a demand. The challenge of Christ to heroic duty and self-sacrifice may be a means of salvation. If we are apathetic and impotent under some crushing trouble or some feeling of inferiority, a call to effort can be a blessing. When Henry Fawcett, afterwards postmaster general in the British government, was blinded by a gunshot wound while still a student, friends gathered round and tried to comfort him. All their kindness could not arouse him from his depression. But his Cambridge tutor wrote him a letter in a different strain. It "exhorted him to *effort,*" and brought him therefore to feel that he was "being treated as equal to life, which to a young man of action was much better than receiving sympathy for being completely *hors de combat.*" [3] The letter included a plan for hard and systematic study. The tutor's help was a gift; but it came in the form of a demand. The best gifts of life are often its demands on our energy, and its challenges to our faith and courage. When Paul was in Damascus, broken and humbled by his meeting with the living Christ, Ananias brought him the gift of God's forgiveness; but that forgiveness assumed the form of a call to God's service that would take all his strength to fulfill (Acts 9:15-16). It brought to him the incredible privilege of being used by God in the service of his kingdom. The call was part, at least, of God's inexpressible gift.

10:1*a*. *I, Paul, Myself Entreat You.*—Whether this opens a new section in the letter, or whether it is part of a former letter written from Ephesus

[2] *The Servant of the Word* (New York: Charles Scribner's Sons, 1942), p. 67.

[3] Mary MacCarthy, *Handicaps* (New York: Longmans, Green & Co., 1936), p. 111.

who in presence *am* base among you, but being absent am bold toward you:	I who am humble when face to face with you, but bold to you when I am away!

follows; cf. a similar expression in Gal. 5:2. His basic and congenial method is to **entreat;** he can be stern, but he prefers to be gentle because that is the way of Christ, whose **meekness and gentleness** Paul well understood, even though he says little of Jesus' earthly life (cf. Phil. 2:5-8). The word **by** (or "through") gives the standard to which Paul appeals; the Corinthians should recognize and possess the spirit it presents; in particular, they should recognize it and honor it in Paul. But his use of patience and moral appeal,

---

after he had heard of the trouble at Corinth (see Exeg.), Paul is conscious that he is now going to say things that will hurt. There was evidently need for plain speaking. Those who were poisoning the life of the church must be shown up, either that they might repent, or that they might be repudiated by the general body of the people. But the spirit in which stern truth is spoken is all important. Moral indignation is a dangerous force to handle; it can easily turn to hatred and self-righteousness.

To begin with, then, Paul puts his spirit to school to learn **the meekness and gentleness of Christ.** Meekness, according to Jesus, is one of the essential qualities of the Christian spirit. "Blessed are the meek" (Matt. 5:5). It is the spirit that accepts life and seeks to learn from it, without kicking at its ills or resenting its rebuffs. It is the opposite of self-assertiveness. The meek man has ceased to think or care about himself. His pride and self-will have been crucified. He does not measure the importance of events by their relation to his personal comfort or self-esteem. He sees in everything God's purpose of love, and seeks only to serve that purpose in the situations which life imposes. This does not involve taking everything, as we say, "lying down." How the meek man will react to circumstances depends on what he discerns to be God's will for him in them. Because his mind is set on God's purpose and not on his own comfort or ambition, he will offer to evil a more implacable resistance. Jesus was meek in this sense of the word. He did not complain of his treatment at the hands of men or of life. He accepted it from God; but to evil, and to evil men, he offered an unbending opposition. The things that they did to him were never allowed to poison his spirit, or fill him with anger or petulance. Before we take strong measures with those who oppose us we must be sure it is God's purpose we are seeking, not merely our own plans or wishes.

The **gentleness of Christ** sprang from his meekness. It means consideration for others, the charitable judgment that does not transfer hatred of evil to those who do it. Freedom from self-regard is the secret of the gentle spirit toward those who wrong or insult us. A meek man will feel the wrong, and feel it bitterly, but it quickens no savage anger in his soul against the wrongdoer; for he is not thinking of himself, and is not susceptible to ruffled feelings or wounded pride. He will rather be full of pity for those who can be so blinded by the storms of hate or passion. The bitter utterance, the injustice, will only drive him back on the comfort of God's truth and love. Robert Louis Stevenson tells how, traveling in the Cévennes, he came through the district of ancient persecutions, where, when cruelty was at its height, there was one at least who, facing certain death and possible torture, could say, "My soul is like a garden full of shelter and of fountains." [4]

How gentle Christ was with those who had sinned, even with his bitterest enemies! How considerate toward the feelings of those who were bearing the indignation of the self-righteous! (John 8:11.) He bids us judge not, that we be not judged (Matt. 7:1). Sin must not be excused, but it can sometimes be explained. The questions he would have us ask before we condemn are: "Why did he do it? What hidden forces were at work within him?" The man who sins is the victim of some moral disorder which he has not found the way to overcome. Contempt or hatred for the sinner may easily blind us to the hidden spark of goodness which the gentle and considerate attitude might fan into a flame. Before we let moral indignation loose in our words or actions we must be sure that our own spirit is disarmed of hatred or self-righteousness, so that we are concerned not merely with asserting the moral order, but with the true good of the man whose actions we condemn. The spirit of forgiveness must be implicit in all we say or do. We must seek in everything to bring the man who has wronged us into the condition in which he is ready to be forgiven. It is in this spirit that Paul proceeds to deal with the offenders in Corinth.

1*b*. *Humble but Bold*.—Paul had been charged with being timid in speech but brave on paper. The word **humble** was the taunt of men who did not count humility a virtue. The

[4] *Travels with a Donkey,* "Pont de Montvert."

2 But I beseech *you,* that I may not be bold when I am present with that confidence, wherewith I think to be bold against some, which think of us as if we walked according to the flesh.

3 For though we walk in the flesh, we do not war after the flesh:

—2 I beg of you that when I am present I may not have to show boldness with such confidence as I count on showing against some who suspect us of acting in worldly fashion. 3 For though we live in the world we are not carrying on a worldly

---

rather than imperious demand and force, has been misunderstood; opponents said: Oh, he is **humble** enough **when face to face with you;** indeed, he is weak, servile, cowardly; **but** he is **bold to you when** he is far **away.** Perhaps this charge rests in part on the fact that while on his hurried visit to try to quell the revolt Paul had been dismayed and helpless in the face of general opposition, in his letters he had spoken with confidence (cf. vs. 10). Note also that on his first visit to Corinth he admittedly felt inadequate (I Cor. 2:3). The verb translated **I am bold** (θαρρῶ) here refers to Paul's bold self-assertion at a distance; in 7:16 it expresses his friendly confidence in the Corinthians. This change of meaning is characteristic of the two sections of II Corinthians; words are used with a defensive and hostile tone in chs. 10–13, but with a friendly, conciliatory tone in chs. 1–9. The latter situation seems to be the later of the two.

2. Paul declares that he can be stern if necessary. He prefers not to be so, and earnestly asks the Corinthians to change their attitude toward him so that he need not be. His words imply that he is coming to see them soon; he warns them to change while there is yet time. But even if they do change, there are **some** against whom he intends to act. Whether visitors to Corinth or resident Christians there, they have not only called Paul a coward (vs. 1), but also **think of us** as walking **according to the flesh** (KJV), i.e., their estimate of him, which they insistently spread at Corinth, is that he acts **in worldly fashion** (RSV), without consistency or principle, and without Christian character. With these charges they lead the Corinthians to disown Paul, and this will weaken the Corinthians' loyalty to the gospel he preaches.

3. This verse answers the charge in vs. 2*b*. The KJV has a clear literal translation. The word **flesh** is used in two senses; **for though we walk** [i.e., live] **in the flesh,** the physical body and the conditions of this present age, **we do not war after** [or according to] **the flesh;** we do not live under the impulse of the perverted, sinful nature of the unsaved man (cf. Rom. 7:5-6; 8:3-9; Gal. 5:19-24). With the word **war** Paul begins to use the figure of a military campaign. As so frequently in the N.T., life is regarded as a battle-

---

charge sorely misconceived his spirit. He could be **bold** just because he was humble and counted on truth and love to make their impression (cf. Exeg.). It was a humility and gentleness born of confidence in God and in his message. But this confidence could also make him bold in their sense of the word (vs. 2), as those who accused him of a worldly spirit would discover. Some of his opponents had made this charge against him, which he now rebuts. He had not stooped to the methods of men of the world in his ministry, using cunning or deceit.

3. *We Are Not Carrying On a Worldly War.* —Paul was ready to acknowledge the fact that he lived in this material world. He was subject to material conditions. He was tempted, like other men, to succumb to the appetites and weaknesses of the body. But he was not fighting for material success, for earthly power or prestige, or for the discomfiture of his opponents. He had higher ends and objectives in view, of which he never lost sight. He was aware of the temptation, because we live in this world, to aim at mere material success. Many a man has started with noble ideals for society, but has sunk in the end to fight for power, or prestige, or even for material advantage.

> Just for a handful of silver he left us,
> Just for a riband to stick in his coat.[5]

Many a nation has begun a war with spiritual watchwords such as "to make the world safe for democracy," or "a war to end war," and in the end has lost sight of these objectives in a desperate struggle for victory, or even for survival. A church may lose sight of her spiritual mission

[5] Robert Browning, "The Lost Leader."

4 (For the weapons of our warfare *are* not carnal, but mighty through God to the pulling down of strong holds;)

5 Casting down imaginations, and every high thing that exalteth itself against the knowledge of God, and bringing into captivity every thought to the obedience of Christ;

war, 4 for the weapons of our warfare are not worldly but have divine power to destroy strongholds. 5 We destroy arguments and every proud obstacle to the knowledge of God, and take every thought captive to

field; war is being waged between God and Satan, between the cause of Christ and the forces of evil. Paul is a general in this war, waging a campaign for Christ against the foes that everywhere oppose him. But he does not war "in worldly fashion"; and this the Corinthians have not really understood.

4. Paul does not use the force or methods of the world (cf. the method of Christ in vs. 1). Christ, his ministry, his cross, seem weak to the worldly man, and the ministers of Christ who serve in his spirit likewise appear impotent and ineffective (cf. I Cor. 1:18-25). But these spiritual weapons of the apostle are "mighty for God in pulling down [or destroying] strongholds" of opposition to Christ. Specifically, there is a mighty power in Paul as he wages his campaign for Christ, and it will enable him to lay siege to the opposition in Corinth and demolish the enemy stronghold.

5. He continues the illustration but also begins to apply it. He tears down the **arguments** (or better, "reasonings") of his opponents; going back to the illustration, he says he tears down **every high thing,** i.e., every fortified height that proudly and defiantly is lifted up in opposition to **the knowledge of God** that the gospel contains. He implies that the real effect of what his opponents are doing is to oppose not so much him as the

in the effort to maintain an outward prosperity, handsome buildings, large attendances, a reputation for good music, fine preaching, and social prestige. But the real issue in life is the victory or defeat of God's purpose in the world, and of his Spirit in the souls of men. It is God's victory Paul seeks in every conflict he wages.

4. ***The Weapons of Our Warfare.***—Paul does not need worldly weapons. He does not use means which appeal to human passions or lusts, as men do in a political struggle or in the competitive rivalries of business. These are useless in the warfare of the spirit. Its weapons are those of truth, and love, and righteousness, which have in them the power that alone can conquer evil where it has its root—in the hearts of men. These weapons Paul enumerates in Eph. 6, where he also counsels the Ephesians to be "strong in the Lord and in the strength of his might" (Eph. 6:10). There is no other way of being strong in the conflict against spiritual wickedness. Christian's fight with Apollyon in the Valley of Humiliation is a picturesque illustration of this. Christian was beaten to the ground, and it looked as if the end had come. But this weakness drove him into complete dependence on God. A man cannot be beaten who, when he falls, falls on his knees.

Paul is confident of the efficacy of this divine power in the warfare he is now waging. It can **destroy strongholds.** There are citadels of various kinds in which evil is established. Habit, social custom, vested interests which withstand social reform, political systems which deny freedom and reject the Christian valuation of personality: all are strongholds in which opposition to God entrenches itself. There are also strongholds in the mind: pride, prejudice, and the like.

5*a*. ***Every Proud Obstacle.***—Paul is aware that the human reason has its rights. He does not scorn the use of intelligence in the defense of the faith. He would agree with Peter, who bids us be ready to give a reason for the faith that is in us (I Pet. 3:15). The Christian faith provides an outlook on the world and on the facts of life and experience which makes sense. But it is opposed by arguments that also claim to be derived from reason. Non-Christian beliefs are supported by specious and powerful philosophies which have wide appeal. Such beliefs may come in part from faulty reasoning. But in general they spring from views of life which omit essential facts and experiences. They often give no place to the reality of moral values and to the Christian revelation of God in Christ. In many cases the arguments used to support them are forms of rationalization, the process of finding reasons to bolster a way of life or justify a course of conduct already determined on. The

6 And having in a readiness to revenge all disobedience, when your obedience is fulfilled.

obey Christ, 6 being ready to punish every disobedience, when your obedience is complete.

gospel. As a Christian general in this war, his aim is to **take every thought captive to obey Christ.** This explains why he cannot rely on external force; in his work he seeks to win the inner loyalty of men; they by their own decision must accept his message and leadership. Note that Paul wants to bring **every thought** into relation to Christ; all thinking must have a consistent unity that comes from having Christ at the center. Three times in vss. 5-6 Paul uses **every** to show how inclusive the loyalty to Christ should be.

6. Two groups are here in mind. One is the church at Corinth as a whole; it is siding with the agitators who oppose Paul, and its **obedience** to him is now far from **complete.** Since he uses spiritual methods, he cannot act against the real troublemakers until the majority take a favorable attitude toward him. As soon as they do, he can and will **punish every disobedience** of the active ringleaders. The church's obedience is here yet to come; in 2:9 and 7:15 it has already been demonstrated.

question arises, Should any man's philosophy be trusted if he has not opened his heart to the experience of Christ? He has not all the facts. Nor should his philosophy be trusted if secretly or openly he is transgressing the Christian ethic. A shrewd and experienced director of souls, whenever anyone said that he had thrown over religion, used to ask which of the Ten Commandments he was breaking!

There is only one effective way of dealing with **arguments and every proud obstacle to the knowledge of God.** Counterargument, though that may help to demolish some of the outworks—the barbed-wire fences, so to speak—is of little value. The knowledge of God cannot be reached by argument, nor can those who deny it be overcome by argument. The knowledge of God is the knowledge of a person, which is reached through the awakening of the soul and conscience to his truth and love. The power of the divine Spirit alone can open blind eyes to the fact of God. Awareness of him comes through a revelation of his quality, which like beauty can make its own impression, can even create the power to see it, and can awaken the capacity to respond to it. The only way to learn to appreciate good music or good literature is to give our minds to their appeal, however long it may take for that appeal to win us. The message of Christ, the story of what God has done in him, especially in the Cross and Resurrection, can break through the web of sophistry that screens men against the knowledge of God. The Holy Spirit, said Jesus, "will convince the world of sin and of righteousness and of judgment" (John 16:8). The obstacle to belief in some cases is not doubt, but sin. This barrier can be destroyed only by the power of God, which reduces man to his true place as a creature under judgment and in need of salvation.

5b. *Every Thought Captive.*—This does not mean cramping the mind or denying the right to think. It must not be made the excuse for a censorship of ideas, such as has often been enforced by the church. The word **thought** has been rendered "project" (Moffatt). When Christ has won the surrender of the will, our plans and purposes must become subject to his guiding. The short-term plans and purposes by which life is directed need to be taken out of the control of mere caprice or self-will and made subject to him. It is the common habit to make plans and ask God's help to carry them out. But it is the plans and projects themselves which should be directed by him. Political schemes, national policies, social ideals and programs, as well as our own personal ambitions, must all be made subject to the spirit of Christ. There is no other way in which his will can be done on earth, and in which all the capacities of our being can be released in his service.

Thought, if we take the general rendering, must mean the ideas that germinate in the mind, giving rise to desire and action. Wrong ideas of God, of man, of the people with whom we come into contact, and even of life itself, are the root of many kinds of wrong action. The disorder of the mind which comes from these cannot be overcome by force, but by the power of truth which is in Christ, by the preaching that makes him known. Those who heard Christ speak were convinced by him. His words carried their own authority; it was the authority of the voice of God (Matt. 7:29).

6. *Ready to Punish.*—All these obstacles to the knowledge of God were to be found in Paul's opponents at Corinth. He promises to deal drastically with them when the majority who are loyal have wholeheartedly accepted his authority. But he depends on first winning the

7 Do ye look on things after the outward appearance? If any man trust to himself that he is Christ's, let him of himself think this again, that, as he *is* Christ's, even so *are* we Christ's.

8 For though I should boast somewhat more of our authority, which the Lord hath

7 Look at what is before your eyes. If any one is confident that he is Christ's, let him remind himself that as he is Christ's, so are we. 8 For even if I boast a little too much of our authority, which the Lord

2. His Action Will Be as Stern as His Letters (10:7-11)

7. In vss. 1-6 Paul has spoken as an authoritative Christian leader. He now warns the readers not to let any other person's claim to recognition obscure his real authority. It was given him to enable him to help them (vs. 8), but it also gives him power that can match the sternness of his letters by the vigor of his action (vss. 8-11). The opening words (τὸ κατὰ πρόσωπον βλέπετε) can mean: **Look at what is before your eyes** (RSV), i.e., the facts are there, plain to see; look at them. But the verb may be indicative. It may then be taken as a question, "Are you looking at things according to their external appearance?" Or if a statement, "You are looking at things according to their external appearance"; that is why you accept some intruder's claim of authority instead of seeing that we have God-given authority to lead you. **Any one** is probably an outstanding example of the "false apostles" who have come to Corinth to try to supplant Paul (11:13). The intruder and his companions claim to be **Christ's.** This is not a claim to belong to a Christ party in the Corinthian church (cf. I Cor. 1:12), but is either a claim to have a special relationship to Christ, perhaps through acquaintance with his relatives or earthly companions, or a claim to fulfill a prominent and authoritative role for Christ. Such a man should "consider" or "take account of" (λογιζέσθω) this fact "for [or with reference to] himself" (ἐφ' ἑαυτοῦ), that Paul is as much Christ's as he is. Here Paul claims no superiority; he does make this claim, however, in 11:23, which expresses his full conviction.

8. Boast is a key word in chs. 10–13; it is used in a defensive tone, and not, as in chs. 1–9, in a spirit of glad confidence in the Corinthians. Paul feels that there is something

support of some who stand upon the fringe and have not so far committed themselves in wholehearted obedience to the truth. A minister can deal with a recalcitrant minority only when he has the loyal backing of a faithful group.

7. *If Anyone Is Confident that He Is Christ's.*—There were obviously some who arrogated to themselves a unique authority and position as Christians because they had known the Lord, or because they had letters of commendation from the apostles in Jerusalem. They were those who declared "I am Christ's." They had tests of their own which they sought to apply to others; but such "external" tests are quite unreal. Paul does not unchurch them, but he is determined that they will not unchurch him. He bids them look at what is before their eyes in the obvious results of his ministry—the men and women brought out of darkness into light, the conversion of people in whose lives the genuine fruits of the Spirit are manifest (but see Exeg.). No one has any right to unchurch others, to invalidate their standing as Christians, or to regard their ministry as defective, if their work and character reveal the influence of the Holy Spirit. The habit of applying ecclesiastical tests is as prevalent in our day as it was in Paul's. The divisions which appeared in the church at Corinth are in germ the same as those which have since rent the church from end to end. No healing of divisions can take place which does not start from the recognition that, as Ignatius said, "Where the Spirit of Christ is obviously present, there is the church." It is hard to understand why we ignore what is before our eyes, as Paul puts it. Can a church whose members show in their lives the fruits of the Spirit, whose zeal and effectiveness in missionary work are notable, whose teachers and preachers are honored and universally accepted as inspiring exponents of the gospel, be considered to be defective in its ministry or sacraments simply because its ministers have not undergone a particular type of ordination? Healing of divisions can come only from a sense of fellowship in Christ which is already present, and which is felt across the barriers of ecclesiastical polity wherever men of genuine faith meet together.

8. *Even If I Boast a Little Too Much.*—Paul seems to check himself here, as everyone must do who uses the argument from the fruits of

given us for edification, and not for your
destruction, I should not be ashamed:
9 That I may not seem as if I would
terrify you by letters.
10 For *his* letters, say they, *are* weighty
and powerful; but *his* bodily presence *is*
weak, and *his* speech contemptible,

gave for building you up and not for destroying you, I shall not be put to shame.
9 I would not seem to be frightening you
with letters. 10 For they say, "His letters
are weighty and strong, but his bodily
presence is weak, and his speech of no ac-

---

improper about such boasting as he now feels driven to do. More than once in chs. 10–13 he shows his embarrassment at having to assert his authority and underline his achievements. The expression **a little too much** reflects this uneasiness. The boasting in mind seems to be that which he is about to make, especially in ch. 11. But even if he boasts more than he should, he will **not be put to shame,** for he will tell the truth about his past and he will be able to do what he threatens. He inserts a statement of the purpose for which God gave him authority. It was not to destroy (cf. vs. 5) but to build up. Like Jesus, who is the stern judge of stubbornly unresponsive men, yet who came not to judge but to save, Paul can defeat opposition and punish disobedience (vss. 5-6); nevertheless his real mission is to call men to faith and salvation.

9. In saying that he will never be put to shame as a fraudulent boaster, Paul implies that he can make good on all he says. But he writes in this cautious way, he now goes on to state, **that I may not seem as if I would** utterly **terrify you by** my **letters.** He is aware, as vss. 10-11 show clearly, that he has been accused of writing far more forcefully than he acts.

10. The quotation tells what was being said about him at Corinth. **They say** (φασίν) ascribes the words to his opponents generally. However, most MSS read "he says" (φησίν); the chief opponent or critic of Paul says these words, which others then take up and repeat. If this verse is from the "stern letter," its reference to **letters** is to the "lost letter" (cf. I Cor. 5:9) and to our I Corinthians, and to any other letters, unknown to us, that he may have written up to this time. Even his critics admit that he writes letters that are impressive and forceful, but they point out that his physical appearance and impression,

---

the Spirit, by asking whether he is not claiming too much for himself. But there is nothing of which he is more confident than that Christ has called him to the apostolic ministry and will continue to authenticate the call. This authority has been given him, he says in a parenthesis, for building up the fellowship, not, as his opponents used theirs, for destroying it. The test which Paul bade Christians apply to their conduct in the church was whether it tended to build up or to destroy the body. Pride, enmity, disdain, uncharitableness, disintegrate the fellowship instead of building the members together for a habitation of God through the Spirit (Eph. 2:22). The important thing is the fellowship, the body in which Christ dwells, and through which he works. That which disintegrates it, whether by the exclusiveness of pride or by the denial of love, is sin.

9-11. ***I Would Not Seem to Be Frightening You with Letters.***—Paul disclaims any intention of blustering, as he recalls the jibe which was thrown at him, that though **his bodily presence** was **weak and his speech of no account, his letters** were **weighty.** He declares that what he says in writing when absent he will do when present. Their criticism of the impression he had made in Corinth must have been painful, for it implied that his appearance and speech had been anything but imposing. There seems to be ground for this. He had first come to Corinth straight from Athens (Acts 18:1), where his attempt to appeal to the Athenians on the intellectual level had been a failure; so that he had made up his mind to know nothing among the Corinthians but Christ and him crucified, though he realized that to the Greeks this was foolishness (I Cor. 1:23). He confesses that he faced them then "in weakness and in much fear and trembling" (I Cor. 2:3). So much was he conscious of this that a special call to courage had come to him from God (Acts 18:9-10). It is hard to think of Paul as afraid of his audience, sensitive about his competence to handle it, unsure of himself, smitten with a sense of inferiority. With such fears his work in Corinth in face of hostility and physical suffering was a miracle of grace, through which he learned how God's strength is made perfect in human weakness. The second visit was more painful still (see Intro.). But it was from such experiences of humiliation and inadequacy

11 Let such a one think this, that, such as we are in word by letters when we are absent, such *will we be* also in deed when we are present.

12 For we dare not make ourselves of the number, or compare ourselves with some that commend themselves: but they, measuring themselves by themselves, and comparing themselves among themselves, are not wise.

count." 11 Let such people understand that what we say by letter when absent, we do when present. 12 Not that we venture to class or compare ourselves with some of those who commend themselves. But when they measure themselves by one another, and compare themselves with one another, they are without understanding.

---

when he comes in person (παρουσία may mean **presence** but it usually refers to "arrival"), **is** pitifully **weak, and his speech of no account,** i.e., quite unimpressive and lacking in oratorical skill (cf. I Cor. 1:17; 2:1-5).

11. Let such a person (τοιοῦτος is singular) take this into account, that upon Paul's arrival, if revolt continues, his action will be as vigorous and forcible as is his warning given in written word by letter. He will take stern measures only if he must, but he has apostolic authority to speak and act; and his words and actions will prove to be consistent. So the Corinthians should change their attitude before he comes and acts.

3. Unlike His Foes, He Keeps to His Own Field (10:12-18)

12. In this section Paul exposes the hollow pretensions of his critics as they brazenly attempt to supplant him and assume leadership at Corinth. He speaks in irony and mock humility in the presence of such astounding claims as these men make. "For we do not dare to reckon ourselves among, or compare ourselves with, some of those who recommend themselves." Plummer (*Second Epistle of Paul to Corinthians*) brings out the Greek word play by translating, "pair or compare ourselves with" (ἐγκρῖναι ἢ συγκρῖναι). The critics are, mainly at least, the intruders who have come to Corinth claiming to be

---

that the ringing conviction came, "Our sufficiency is from God" (3:5). Like Paul, we may have to learn it through bitter experience. Most preachers who are sensitive and humble in their estimate of themselves know what it means to be cowed by their audience, or at least tempted in that direction. The cure for this timidity, which may well disable our power, is not to recall our own capacity or importance. The need is to forget ourselves, and that can be done only by thinking of the needs of the people to whom we preach, by realizing that only the gospel can meet these needs, and above all that it is not by the impressiveness or eloquence of our speech that the gospel breaks through, but by the power in it of the Spirit of God. So are we brought into a deep dependence on God in which we are willing to be nothing, if thereby Christ is exalted, and in which we rest utterly upon him. This was Paul's habit. The result was a fresh confidence which makes him say that the spirit in which he writes when he is absent will be that in which he will act when he is present. It may seem strange that he should say any such thing at all. But he is aware of a temptation which often besets a minister—to be forceful in the pulpit and weak in personal contacts, to be brave in declaring the truth from a distance, and cowardly when face to face with individuals, to demand a standard of conduct in his sermons which he fails to urge in private. The exposition of the faith may even become a substitute for living it. "One thing I do," Paul writes in Phil. 3:13. Here he says in effect, "One thing I am." To be possessed by the Spirit is the secret of an integrated personality which is not influenced by circumstances.

12. ***As Other Men Are.***—There is nothing in Paul of the Pharisee whose flattering self-approbation springs from the fact that he is not like the publican (Luke 18:11). That standard is false. To measure ourselves **by one another** is to be blind to the true standard of goodness which is found only in Christ, and which brings us all under judgment. Comparison with others may be flattering, but it is false, and the fact that we use it proclaims our blindness to reality. We can find in the best of people flaws which feed our self-esteem. Some there are therefore who boast that they do not need the help of Christ to attain a reasonable standard of goodness; they feel that they are at least as good as many who profess to be his followers. To those who are so conscious of their own goodness that

13 But we will not boast of things without *our* measure, but according to the measure of the rule which God hath distributed to us, a measure to reach even unto you.

14 For we stretch not ourselves beyond *our measure,* as though we reached not unto you; for we are come as far as to you also in *preaching* the gospel of Christ:

13 But we will not boast beyond limit, but will keep to the limits God has apportioned us, to reach even to you.
14 For we are not overextending ourselves, as though we did not reach you; we were the first to come all the way to you with

apostles (11:13) and to have the right to direct the Corinthian church; evidently they did not hesitate to speak highly of themselves. But they lacked a worthy standard by which to measure themselves. **They measure themselves by one another and compare themselves with one another.** This shows that **they are without** spiritual **understanding.** Vs. 18 will state the vital truth that they have not realized.

13. "But" in contrast to such immoderate aggression and self-approval, "we," i.e., Paul, or Paul and his helpers, "will not boast excessively," **beyond limit** (RSV) or **without . . . measure** (KJV; εἰς τὰ ἄμετρα), "but according to the measure of the standard that God imparted to us as measure, to reach unto you also." The word κανών, from which comes our English word "canon," means, lit., "reed," "rod." Here it may mean a "rule" or "standard," or a "limit," or a "province" or "assigned region." In any case, Paul's meaning is clear. God assigned him his region of work. It included not only other places, but "you also" in Corinth. Thus he had the duty to go there and preach. But the intruders, Paul implies, were not sent to Corinth; only their own presumption led them there.

14. "For not as if not reaching to you do we overextend ourselves" by coming to Corinth to preach and minister to you; "for unto you also we came [or were the first to come] in" our God-directed travels to preach "the gospel of Christ." The self-important intruders, when they came to Corinth, were going where they had not been sent by God. Not so Paul; he was not reaching too far; he went to Corinth under the guidance and direction of God. Corinth was included ("you also") in his assigned field of work. The verb ἐφθάσαμεν has as its primary meaning, "come before another does," and so may mean "we came first" to Corinth, before these intruders ever thought of coming. But

they ask what Christianity can do for them there is a simple answer. The first thing Christ does for us is to show us all that we are not as good as we think we are. The Christian ideal is a standard of judgment so far above us that it continually condemns and purifies our own ideals. The man who finds peace for his conscience in the fact that he is as good as even the best of his neighbors has never seen the glory of Christ. The true church is not a mutual admiration society. The basic note of its worship is contrition, the consciousness that our best righteousness is but filthy rags. Reinhold Niebuhr says:

> The church is not a congregation of people who can pride themselves upon their unique goodness. It is rather a congregation of people to whom the eternal God has spoken and who answer the eternal word in terms of Job's contrition: "I have uttered things too wonderful for me, which I understood not. Wherefore I abhor myself and repent in dust and ashes." [6]

[6] *Beyond Tragedy* (New York: Charles Scribner's Sons, 1937), pp. 60-61.

13. ***But We Will Not Boast Beyond Limit.***—Paul is not claiming more than he ought when he claims that God has assigned to him the task of carrying the gospel to the Corinthians. He has not taken on himself more than he should when he asserts his authority as their leader. Wesley said the whole world was his parish. Paul declares that his at least includes Corinth. He has not gone where he was not sent.

14. ***We Were the First to Come All the Way to You with the Gospel of Christ.***—Paul makes a strong point here, for he had come to Corinth as a pioneer missionary and had broken ground with the gospel. He had not come, as some of those who had opposed him had done, to gather the harvest of other men's labors (vs. 15*a*), and then boast of his success in winning them over to his point of view, as if that were a triumph for the gospel. In point of fact, he had hoped to make Corinth a Christian base from which he might press on to further conquests for Christ in the districts beyond.

15 Not boasting of things without *our* measure, *that is,* of other men's labors; but having hope, when your faith is increased, that we shall be enlarged by you according to our rule abundantly,

16 To preach the gospel in the *regions* beyond you, *and* not to boast in another man's line of things made ready to our hand.

the gospel of Christ. 15 We do not boast beyond limit, in other men's labors; but our hope is that as your faith increases, our field among you may be greatly enlarged,
16 so that we may preach the gospel in lands beyond you, without boasting of

---

here, as so often in the Greek of N.T. times, the verb may mean only "we came." **The gospel of Christ** is the good news of the salvation that God has provided through Christ's death, resurrection, and living power, and now offers to all men who will believe.

15. Lit.: "Not boasting excessively in other men's labors, but having hope, as your faith increases, of being magnified among you according to our standard [or limit, or province] unto abundance." The intruders were taking credit at Corinth for what Paul himself had done, and this injustice arouses Paul's indignation. He hints at his future plans in the latter part of the verse. They depend, however, on an increase of **faith** in the Corinthians; i.e., before Paul can do anything else, the revolt in Corinth must be settled in a way that shows in the Christians there a growth in Christian faith and understanding. Then Paul can be "magnified," i.e., have the effectiveness and sphere of his work **enlarged.** The enlargement will start **among** (ἐν) them; it will be in God's plan for him, "according to our [God-given] standard"; it will send him out to new fields, as the next verse explicitly states, and as he here indicates by the phrase "unto abundance," i.e., **abundantly** (KJV) or **greatly** (RSV).

16. Lit.: "To preach the gospel to the places beyond you, not to boast in another man's standard [or province] of things prepared." Paul gives a hint of his intention to go west to Spain to preach (cf. Rom. 15:23-29). The expression "the places beyond you" suits well the view that chs. 10–13 are part of the "stern letter" written from Ephesus; there "the places beyond" Corinth would be to the west, Italy and Spain. From Macedonia, where the "thankful letter" was written, they would be south of Corinth in Africa. He wants to go through Rome and on to Spain, where again he can do pioneer work, as he did at Corinth. He will not work in an area that God has assigned to another man, nor will he boast, as the intruders at Corinth are doing, "of things prepared," i.e., of work another has already done.

15-16. ***That We May Preach the Gospel in Lands Beyond You.***—The apostle's view of the church is that it is not a sphere for a minister to work in, but a sphere for him to work through. Here he unveils a twofold weakness frequently found in the proclamation of the gospel. One is the tendency of ministers and congregations to compete with one another for adherents drawn from each other's ranks. They are apt to be satisfied with attracting to themselves Christians from other congregations. One denomination competes with another, and measures success by its power to persuade people to change their denomination, to adopt some other method of organization, or church order, or theological emphasis, without necessarily making them better Christians. The real test of the success of a minister or congregation is the number of people brought into the church from among those who are not Christians, or have no attachment to any Christian congregation, though in private they may profess faith in Christ. The church of Christ cannot continue to live, any more than an organism can, by feeding on itself.

The other weakness is that congregations are apt to live to themselves and regard the maintenance of their own organization and fellowship as an end in itself. The Christian congregation is only a base for further operations. No army could conquer a country if it were content to settle down in some stronghold instead of using every gain as a springboard for further conquests. Without an outlet life becomes stagnant, like the Dead Sea in Palestine which receives the waters of the Jordan but has no outlet except by evaporation. Missionary work is not a side show of the church, to be sustained

17 But he that glorieth, let him glory in the Lord.

18 For not he that commendeth himself is approved, but whom the Lord commendeth.

11 Would to God ye could bear with me a little in *my* folly: and indeed bear with me.

work already done in another's field. 17 "Let him who boasts, boast of the Lord." 18 For it is not the man who commends himself that is accepted, but the man whom the Lord commends.

11 I wish you would bear with me in a little foolishness. Do bear with me!

---

17. In words already quoted in I Cor. 1:31, and reminiscent of Jer. 9:23-24, Paul enlarges this criticism of the intruders. They take credit for work that Paul has done in Corinth. No Christian ought to **boast** of work he has not done, or even claim credit for what he himself has done. **Let him . . . boast** only of his **Lord,** who has given him new life and power to do his task, and to whom therefore all credit and praise belong. **Lord** here and in vs. 18 may refer to God, as in Jeremiah, or be applied to Christ.

18. Returning to the criticism with which the section began (vs. 12), Paul warns the "false apostles" and the Corinthians that man's self-commendation has no value; indeed, it is a spiritual fault. The only verdict on Christian workers that is important is the one that the Lord gives. On his "Well done" everything depends (cf. Matt. 25:21, 23; John 5:31-32; I Cor. 4:5). Paul strongly implies that the Lord will approve his ministry at Corinth.

4. The Corinthians Too Readily Follow False Leaders (11:1-6)

11:1. Paul wavers between two convictions. He knows that human boasting has no value (10:18); indeed, it is wrong because all that man has and does is God's gift (10:17). So he repeatedly speaks in an apologetic way concerning his words in his own defense. Yet the attacks of his enemies have been so influential that to save the Corinthian church from disaster he feels driven to assert his apostolic authority and point out how honorable and effective his ministry has been. So now he asks the Corinthians to **bear with** him **in a little** bit **of foolishness,** i.e., a little foolish boasting concerning what he has done and suffered. Parenthetically, he adds that they "do indeed bear with" him. This is either

---

by the gifts of a minority who are sufficiently interested. It is the main artery which is essential to the life of the body and to the strength of the heart. Nor may this missionary activity be confined to the regions beyond. Paganism is not limited to heathen lands. It is present in every community, and may be found among those who maintain an external standard of goodness yet are pagan at heart. Conversion may need to begin within the church itself, through the renewal of a living Christian experience. But the real test of that renewal will be in the recovery of the evangelical passion. A living church must be equipped for adventurous service. Like the individual Christian, it can keep its life only by losing it.

17. ***Let Him Who Boasts, Boast of the Lord.*** —No Christian dare boast of his own efforts or success. All we have been able to do in God's service he has done in us and through us. Both the call and the power are his. This is a fundamental humility which alone can exalt us (Luke 18:14). It is our safeguard, born when we are so conscious of Christ that there is no room for self.

18. ***The Man Whom the Lord Commends.***— Paul returns, as always, to the judgment of Christ, which is the final test of character. The light of Christ is the light of reality in which all things appear as they are. His judgment will surprise both those who are conscious of virtue and those who are conscious of none (Matt. 25:31-46). What God looks for in us is what he alone can give—the desire for a goodness which is kindled and fed by the love of Christ.

There are some other things, however, which Paul feels the need to say; and he begs for their forbearance if in his earnestness he should speak foolishly.

11:1. ***I Wish You Would Bear with Me.***—The tactics of those who were damaging his work and belittling his right to leadership might well drive him to desperate measures. His opponents were intruders—the kind of people whom Christ in his parable of the sheepfold described as robbers (John 10:1). Yet he would

2 For I am jealous over you with godly jealousy: for I have espoused you to one husband, that I may present *you as* a chaste virgin to Christ.

2 I feel a divine jealousy for you, for I betrothed you to Christ to present you as a

---

an ironical reminder that at Corinth some are saying that Paul is troublesome and they have to "bear with" him, or it recalls with some confidence that they are his friends and so he is sure they are patient with him. The verb ἀνέχεσθε is thus probably indicative. But it may be imperative; then it says: "But do actually bear with me."

2. It is only in vs. 16 that Paul carries out his just expressed intention to boast. Here he turns aside to explain why he is so concerned for the Corinthians. Using the illustration of the girl's father or representative, through whom the betrothal is arranged, Paul says that he has **betrothed** the Corinthian church (**you** meant as a group) **to Christ, to present** this church to him as his bride at the last day (cf. Rev. 21:2, 9; 22:17). He is responsible for seeing that the betrothed virgin is still pure when the marriage takes place, i.e., that the Corinthians are not seduced by persons who will lead them away from their confessed faith in Christ. Such seduction, Paul clearly implies, is an imminent danger at Corinth (cf. vs. 4). In the face of this acute danger Paul is **jealous** for them with a God-given **jealousy,** or with the jealousy for them like that which God also has. The word **jealousy** does not mean a blind or unworthy passion, but a justified concern for the honor and purity of the church at Corinth.

---

hold himself under such restraint as courtesy and the gospel itself might dictate.

2. ***I Feel a Divine Jealousy for You.***—Jealousy is not an attractive quality. It is painful to experience and may lead to strife, even to crime. It is the accompaniment of love, but of a love which is possessive and therefore selfish. We are tempted to it when our friends give to others the affection we covet for ourselves, or when admiration given to others seems to detract from our own reputation. Jealousy can be a devouring passion, destroying happiness and kindling hatred. Real love is not jealous of attentions paid or love given to others, for it is never possessive (I Cor. 13:4). It seeks to give, not to get. But there is a jealousy which is right and which can be the safeguard of love. It comes into play when those we love are in danger from people who might corrupt their minds or their characters. The fear which is at the root of it is not fear of loss to ourselves, but of damage to them. This is the **divine jealousy** which, so he claims, is actuating Paul.

The O.T. speaks of the jealousy of God. The first commandment says, "Thou shalt have no other gods before me," and concludes with the explanation, "for I the LORD thy God am a jealous God." The imputation of jealousy here needs most careful interpretation. God is not concerned for his own prestige. In Christ he "made himself of no reputation" (Phil. 2:7). His concern is with the corruption of human nature and the destruction of the human soul which result from an alien worship. Augustine's saying, "Thou hast made us for thyself," does not mean that man is made for God's glorification, or to satisfy his love of power. It means that man's true happiness and fulfillment are found in fellowship with God through the gifts which his love is waiting to bestow, but which cannot be bestowed in their fullness till men are seeking first his kingdom. The jealousy of God can mean only his refusal to consent to anything which would tempt man from that relationship, and would thwart his loving purpose.

Paul claims that his jealousy too sprang from genuine love. The welfare of the church, nothing else, made him jealous of all efforts to detach its loyalty from himself and his gospel; not the loss of prestige or the mere desire to keep control of it as his own preserve. Had his opponents been preaching the true gospel and genuinely helping the church, he would have been happy even if a certain detachment of it from himself had been involved. So long as Christ was preached he did not care who did it, or even how much their motives were mixed (Phil. 1:18). It takes a very unselfish love to keep a leader free from the wrong kind of jealousy. The craving for prestige, the love of power, the conceit which makes men feel that they alone are responsible for the souls of people, create jealousies that cause friction and unhappiness, and turn the ministry into a competitive struggle.

Nothing of the kind should be possible for those who see the church as the "bride of Christ." They long to keep her pure so that she may be presented **to her one husband** when

3 But I fear, lest by any means, as the
serpent beguiled Eve through his subtilty,
so your minds should be corrupted from
the simplicity that is in Christ.
4 For if he that cometh preacheth another Jesus, whom we have not preached,
or *if* ye receive another spirit, which ye
have not received, or another gospel, which
ye have not accepted, ye might well bear
with *him.*

pure bride to her one husband. 3 But I
am afraid that as the serpent deceived Eve
by his cunning, your thoughts will be led
astray from a sincere and pure devotion to
Christ. 4 For if some one comes and preaches
another Jesus than the one we preached,
or if you receive a different spirit from the
one you received, or if you accept a different gospel from the one you accepted,

---

3. The danger of seduction Paul considers great. The Corinthians are inclined to follow false leaders, who, as this verse suggests, are inspired by Satan (cf. vss. 13-15; 2:11). The reference to **the serpent** (Satan) may have in mind the Jewish legend that in the Garden of Eden the serpent seduced **Eve,** and that Cain was their son. At least, Eve was not true to God. So the thoughts of the Corinthians are in danger of being **corrupted** (KJV), i.e., **led astray** (RSV), **from the simplicity,** the singleness of devotion that a true betrothed virgin shows, "and the purity," the chaste conduct, that they ought to show "toward Christ." The words "and the purity" are not found in some ancient MSS; they probably are genuine, but the thought is essentially the same even if they are omitted.

4. Paul here tells wherein the seduction consists. He clearly indicates that the message of the intruders is not the true gospel. It is amazing how little II Corinthians tells concerning the exact teaching of these men, but Paul definitely holds that they preach **another Jesus** than the crucified and risen Lord whom he preached when he came to Corinth; they give **another spirit** (evidently regarded as satanic; vss. 13-15) than the Holy Spirit who was God's gift to those who believed Paul's preaching; in short, they preach a **different gospel** from the one true gospel (I Cor. 15:1-11; Gal. 1:6-7) that Paul preached. The phrase **he that cometh** (to preach so false a message) either designates the outstanding leader among the false apostles, or is a generic reference to all of this group

---

he returns. So runs Christ's own desire—that she might appear "before him in splendor, without spot or wrinkle or any such thing, . . . holy and without blemish" (Eph. 5:27). In this, as in everything else, Paul is concerned about what Christ will think of the church, whether or not he will be satisfied with it. Everything is lifted out of the perspective of this world and set down *sub specie aeternitatis.* External success or failure, prosperity or adversity, mattered little in his assessment of the church. These were temporary. The final test was how it would appear in the light of eternity. Would Christ, looking on it, "see of the travail of his soul, and . . . be satisfied" (Isa. 53:11)?

3. ***I Am Afraid.***—It is not the danger of the Corinthians' being led to transfer their loyalty from himself to others that troubles Paul; it is that they may be led to transfer it from Christ. A sincere and pure devotion to the person of Christ is the secret of Christianity. Sincerity means honesty of purpose. Purity adds little to it except to emphasize that devotion should be free from mixed motives. Jesus told a crowd who had followed him that they were not seeking him because they saw the love which was revealed in his miracles, but because they "did eat of the loaves, and were filled" (John 6:26). We cannot claim to be wholly free from mixed motives in our devotion to Christ, but it is in our power to make his service our main desire. If we are honest in seeking to serve him, however faint that desire, his grace will do the rest. We can at least be willing to be made willing. Paul's fear was that wholehearted devotion might be tampered with, and that a false Christianity might supplant the true faith.

4. ***Another Jesus.***—Seduction was already at work. Interlopers had come into the church to plant their destructive ideas. They had preached a different Jesus from the Jesus Paul had preached. This was crucial and still is. The Christian faith is based on devotion to Jesus, the Son of God, who "became flesh and dwelt among us," who was crucified, who rose from the dead, and who now reigns as Lord at God's right hand. The test which Christ applied to his own ministry was the impression he had made on the disciples who had lived in his company. "Who do you say that I am?" he asked (Matt. 16:15). Peter's answer set his mind at

5 For I suppose I was not a whit behind
the very chiefest apostles.
6 But though *I be* rude in speech, yet
not in knowledge; but we have been thoroughly
made manifest among you in all
things.

you submit to it readily enough. 5 I think
that I am not in the least inferior to these
superlative apostles. 6 Even if I am unskilled
in speaking, I am not in knowledge;
in every way we have made this plain to
you in all things.

---

of intruders. With irony Paul says that whether or not the Corinthians are willing to bear with him, they "bear with" such dangerous teachers well enough. A less likely reading (ἀνείχεσθε) says, you "would bear with" them readily enough; but Paul almost certainly means that the Corinthians are actually putting up with such deadly preaching.

5. Lit.: "For I consider that I have not proved inferior in any way to the superlative apostles" (cf. 12:11). This is an understatement; Paul does not regard these men as true apostles at all; they are "false apostles" (vss. 13-15). Note that the word "apostle" (cf. Exeg. on 1:1) has a wider meaning than "one of the twelve," or it could not have been used by these traveling teachers who came to Corinth. They evidently claimed to be apostles of highest dignity; Paul ironically calls them **superlative** or "superfine" apostles, and does not concede that Christ sent them.

6. It is implied that the **superlative apostles** were able and persuasive speakers, and so appealed to the Greek love of eloquence; they or their friends were quick to point out Paul's lack in this respect. He admits it (cf. 10:10; I Cor. 1:17; 2:4), but he knows that the power of God's Spirit works through his unpretentious speech; so he is content. And he is not **unskilled in . . . knowledge,** i.e., the knowledge that counts, the knowledge of the saving truth of the gospel, which the intruders would pervert. He recalls that **in every way we have made** this knowledge, or the fact that we possess this knowledge, **plain to you in all things.**

---

rest. They had seen his glory and had only one explanation of it. "You are the Christ, the Son of the living God." On men who had this faith and the devotion which it inspired his church would be built.

A different Jesus, one who was merely a descendant of David and the head of the Jewish race, or one who was merely a teacher, or a social reformer, or the best of our human kind, is not the Jesus of the Christian faith. Any such picture of him would rob the gospel of its meaning and its power. Other results would follow. A different Jesus would create a different spirit in the church; e.g., in Corinth the Judaizers rejected Christian freedom and sought to restore the shackles of Jewish legalism. When a church, faced by materialistic civilizations, ceases to worship a Jesus who is Lord, the spirit of defeatism attacks it. Those for whom the Revelation of John was written would not have survived the crushing might of imperial Rome without a Christ who was on the throne and who had the keys of death and of hell (Rev. 1:18).

Further, a different Christ leads to a different gospel. Paul does not specify what the gospel of his opponents was. It may have been the offer of good advice instead of good news, the presentation of an ideal instead of the offer of power, the substitution of good works and legal observances for salvation by faith in Christ, who had borne for men the burden of guilt. A Christ stripped of his glory as the incarnate Son of God has no cosmic significance. He cannot answer our most perplexing questions, such as those about the meaning of life, the nature of God, and man's final destiny. Neither can he meet us in our individual lives, confronting us with his claim, kindling our personal devotion, opening for each of us the kingdom of God. In the words of Thomas Chalmers, Christianity is the "expulsive power of a new affection"—the affection for himself which Christ awakens because he lives and is Lord. Paul is both sad and scornful that the Corinthian church, or any part of it, should so readily have listened to these interlopers.

5-6. ***Not in the Least Inferior.***—The reference to his opponents as **superlative apostles** is sarcastic. This superiority had been their own claim. Paul admits that he may have been deficient in the technique of oratory, but at least he can claim knowledge. He knows the Christian faith, not merely by intellectual grasp, but through experience of the living Christ who has won his wholehearted loyalty, and has given him a gospel to preach. Whatever his imperfection of speech, he has made this clear to every-

7 Have I committed an offense in abasing myself that ye might be exalted, because I have preached to you the gospel of God freely?

8 I robbed other churches, taking wages *of them,* to do you service.

9 And when I was present with you, and wanted, I was chargeable to no man: for that which was lacking to me the brethren which came from Macedonia supplied: and in all *things* I have kept myself from being burdensome unto you, and *so* will I keep *myself.*

7 Did I commit a sin in abasing myself so that you might be exalted, because I preached God's gospel without cost to
you? 8 I robbed other churches by accepting support from them in order to serve
you. 9 And when I was with you and was in want, I did not burden any one, for my needs were supplied by the brethren who came from Mac-e-do'ni-a. So I refrained and will refrain from burdening you in

5. Paul's Self-Support Unmasks the False Leaders (11:7-15)

7. In his indignant defense against the usurpers at Corinth, Paul has charged that they do not preach the true Christian gospel and do not have the Christian spirit. In one point only has he conceded their superiority; while his speech lacked rhetorical polish, they were masters of eloquence (vs. 6). Now he reveals another point of difference. He has not asked the Corinthians to support him. Vs. 20 implies that the "false apostles" demanded and received financial support, and perhaps Apollos or other Christian workers had received similar help (I Cor. 9:12). But the Corinthians show no sign of appreciating Paul's sacrificial ministry, so he asks with withering irony: **Did I commit a sin in abasing myself so that you might be exalted, because I preached God's gospel without cost to you?** Was it wrong of me so to humble or humiliate myself by self-denial and the wearing labor (Acts 18:3; I Cor. 4:11-13) by which I supported myself? I willingly accepted such hardship that you might receive the gospel of Christ without having to bear any burden. The verse reflects Paul's feeling that it was outrageous for the Corinthians to accept so great a sacrifice without gratitude or understanding.

8. Paul let other churches support him while he preached and ministered to the Corinthians. His strong feeling expresses itself in the two exaggerated statements that he **robbed other churches,** i.e., accepted gifts from them that they could well have used, and from them received "wages" (ὀψώνιον), i.e., accepted financial support. These words are not strictly true, for the gifts were freely given; however, the poverty of the Macedonians (8:2) may have made Paul feel that in accepting gifts from them he was taking money they could hardly spare.

9. At least once during Paul's stay in Corinth, and that, it seems, early during his mission there, he had been **in want.** Evidently his work at tentmaking (Acts 18:3) did not provide adequately for his physical needs. Even then, however, he did not ask the

one. In face of every kind of frustration, and in spite of the chains that held him in prison, he triumphantly wrote, "But the word of God is not bound" (II Tim. 2:9).

Meanwhile, one circumstance had given him great satisfaction, though his opponents had used it to discredit him. He had taken no money from the Corinthians for his support while there. Had he done wrong?

7-10. ***Did I Commit a Sin Because I Preached God's Gospel Without Cost?***—It was a generous act. Paul wanted the good news to be a free gift. The association of preaching with the money which is necessary to support the preacher is always a danger. The true preacher, like the artist, does not work for money.

> He lives detachèd days;
> He serveth not for praise;
> For gold
> He is not sold.[7]

Other churches had provided for Paul's support. He declares that he had made a levy on them for this new campaign, and that when he had

[7] "To the Dead Cardinal of Westminster," from *The Poems of Francis Thompson* (London: Burns Oates & Washbourne, 1913). Used by permission of Sir Francis Meynell, copyright owner.

10 As the truth of Christ is in me, no
man shall stop me of this boasting in the
regions of Achaia.
11 Wherefore? because I love you not?
God knoweth.
12 But what I do, that I will do, that I
may cut off occasion from them which desire occasion; that wherein they glory, they
may be found even as we.

any way. **10** As the truth of Christ is in me,
this boast of mine shall not be silenced in
the regions of A-cha′ia. **11** And why? Because I do not love you? God knows I do!
12 And what I do I will continue to do,
in order to undermine the claim of those
who would like to claim that in their
boasted mission they work on the same

Corinthians for help; he **did not burden any one.** And they did not offer to help. **The brethren who came from Macedonia** supplied his lack. These men were either Silas and Timothy (Acts 18:5), who brought help sent by Macedonian Christians, or Macedonian messengers whose names we do not know. Earlier, when Paul was at Thessalonica, and later, when he was in prison, probably at Rome, the Philippians sent gifts to Paul (Phil. 4:16, 18); they sent or shared in the gift Paul here mentions. So the Corinthians have never supported him, even in part, and he declares that in the future as in the past he will not burden them **in any way.**

10. Lit.: "The truth of Christ is in me, that this boasting will not be stopped for me in the regions of Achaia." Achaia, the Roman province of which Corinth was the capital, is mentioned with reference mainly to Corinth. Just as elsewhere Paul states that he has the mind of Christ (I Cor. 2:16), and the Spirit of Christ (Rom. 8:9), so here with good conscience he can say that the truth of Christ is in him. This is a solemn assurance that what he now says is dependable; it can be rendered, **As the truth of Christ is in me** and is almost the same as "I swear by the truth of Christ which is in me; it controls my speech so that you can depend on what I now say." With this strong emphasis Paul repeats the closing thought of vs. 9. He will not accept support from the Corinthians at any future time. (He evidently did not regard the private hospitality of Gaius, extended, Rom. 16:23 implies, when he later came to Corinth, as a violation of this pledge.)

11. Refusal to accept help might suggest a cold, unfriendly spirit. So Paul explains that the reason he will never accept help from the Corinthians is not that he does not love them. To the question he answers: **God knows . . . !**—God knows whether I love you, i.e., he knows that I really do.

12. Paul now explains why he **will continue** to work in Corinth without support from the church there. He does not mention the reason he gave in I Cor. 9:16-18—that in this way he, who came into the ministry only under overwhelming divine compulsion, can feel he is doing more than God requires of his ministers, and so can ease his conscience. The reason now given is, lit., "But what I do, I also will do, that I may cut off the occasion of those who desire an occasion, that wherein they boast they may be found as we also" are. This could be understood to mean that the intruders do not accept support, and Paul also refuses it so that he will be on an equality with them. But the second purpose clause depends on the closing words of the first; the meaning, well given in the RSV, is, "But what I am doing I will continue to do, in order that I may cut off the occasion of

---

run short, brethren from Macedonia had brought supplies. Was all this wrong? His opponents questioned his motives. It only showed he was conscious that he was not a real apostle when he would not receive the hire of which Christ said the laborer was worthy. They even suggested that he did not really have much interest or care for the church at Corinth.

11-12. ***And Why? Because I Do Not Love You? God Knows I Do!***—There is almost a sob in the words. Yet Paul is determined to stand firm. And for another reason: **In order to undermine the claim of those** who, when they could not succeed in blackening his motive, would have liked to have him accept support so that his generosity might not give him an advantage over them; for it seems that they accepted some form of pay for their work. At this point Paul's contempt for them bursts out like a flame. He does not mince his words.

13 For such *are* false apostles, deceitful workers, transforming themselves into the apostles of Christ.

14 And no marvel; for Satan himself is transformed into an angel of light.

15 Therefore *it is* no great thing if his ministers also be transformed as the min-

terms as we do. 13 For such men are false
prophets, deceitful workmen, disguising
themselves as apostles of Christ. 14 And no
wonder, for even Satan disguises himself
as an angel of light. 15 So it is not strange if
his servants also disguise themselves as

those [false apostles] who seek an occasion of being found just like us in the thing of which they boast." They boast of being apostles who are entitled to support; they demand and receive it (vs. 20). They want Paul to accept support too. Then he and they will be in the same position. For him to change his policy and start accepting support at Corinth would be to give them the occasion they want to point out that they work on the same terms as he does.

13. Here Paul's real estimate of the intruders comes out clearly (vs. 23; 10:7 are not so frank). I want to keep the line between myself and them clearly drawn, he says, **for such men are false apostles.** They claim the name but have absolutely no right to it. They are **deceitful workmen,** dishonest in motives and actions, **disguising themselves,** deliberately changing their appearance, to deceive people into thinking they are **apostles of Christ,** who in fact has not sent them at all.

14. That they act with such deceit is **no** cause for **wonder.** That is the way of **Satan** and his servants. He too continually **disguises himself** with such crafty skill that he appears to be **an angel of light,** whereas he has no place in the divine realm of light and uprightness.

15. **It is not strange** but only natural that Satan's **servants** follow his deceptive methods, and **also disguise themselves** so that unwary men, even Christians, may be

13-15. *Such Men Are False Apostles.*—His opponents are disguised emissaries of Satan. They seek their own power, or the success of their own party, under the guise of being apostles of Christ. Paul again recalls the story of Eve's temptation by the serpent (vs. 3). It is the habit of evil to clothe itself in the colors of goodness. The serpent's arguments were very specious. The tree was good for food and pleasant to look at and would make her wise. The elements of every temptation are there, its appeal to "the lust of the flesh and the lust of the eyes and the pride of life" (I John 2:16). Imagination, born of desire, weaves a fancy screen around some evil thing to make it acceptable to conscience. It is a form of rationalization; e.g., illicit sexual indulgence is represented as merely the satisfaction of a natural appetite, the expression of a beautiful romantic love, or the legitimate means of enlarging experience. William James points out that the temptation to drunkenness has various specious forms of disguise:

> How many excuses does the drunkard find when each new temptation comes! It is a new brand of liquor which the interests of intellectual culture in such matters oblige him to test; moreover it is poured out and it is sin to waste it; or others are drinking and it would be churlishness to refuse; or it is but to enable him to sleep, or just to get through this job of work; . . . it is, in fact, anything you like except *being a drunkard.*[8]

In controversy, abuse of an opponent is masked as concern for the truth or the right. "The heart is deceitful above all things" (Jer. 17:9).

The Judaizers in Corinth adopted the role of apostles with a message; but their real object was their own prestige or the triumph of their party. Race or religious prejudice was the real force behind their teaching and their actions. Party loyalty, national or racial feeling, often blind men to the true nature and purpose of their actions. Variety of opinion will be found in every church; for we differ in our points of view and in our experience. If these differences are not to harden into personal quarrels or sectarian strife and so to break fellowship, two things are essential. One is that all should be honestly seeking the truth, however disconcerting it may become to their own views. They must be ready to discover they are mistaken, and to accept truth even from those they may dislike or whose views in general they oppose. The other essential is that all should respect the right of those who differ from them to hold

[8] *Principles of Psychology* (New York: Henry Holt & Co., 1893), II, 565.

isters of righteousness; whose end shall be according to their works.

16 I say again, Let no man think me a fool; if otherwise, yet as a fool receive me, that I may boast myself a little.

servants of righteousness. Their end will correspond to their deeds.

16 I repeat, let no one think me foolish; but even if you do, accept me as a fool,

---

deceived. They come in the guise of **righteousness,** pretending to be righteous and to serve God's righteous order. For a time, as at Corinth, they may seem to be on the way to triumph. But **their end,** Paul firmly believes, is sure doom. It **will correspond to their** evil **deeds;** it will be defeat, condemnation, and ruin. We may ask how fair Paul was to these men who sought to supplant him at Corinth. Because he tells us so little of their specific teaching, it is hard to answer. But if we believe, as we have good grounds for doing, that he was seeking the good of the Corinthians and that the gospel he preached was the basic, eternal gospel of God, we may hold, without claiming that Paul was perfect, that the jealousy, ambition, and hostility of the intruders brought no benefit to the church at Corinth and warranted condemnation. Also, 12:21 and 13:2 indicate that they gave no moral leadership whatever.

B. Paul Boasts of His Labors—And Weakness (11:16–12:10)

1. He Asks Tolerance for Foolish Boasting (11:16-20)

16. Returning to the request of vs. 1, Paul asks **again** that the Corinthians pardon him for boasting a little. "Boasting" is the key word in the entire section 11:16–12:10. When he says, **Let no one think me foolish,** he shows again that he shrinks from this self-defense; yet he suggests that it is not really so foolish as it appears, for he is telling the truth, protecting his apostolic ministry, working for the benefit of the Corinthians. **But even if** they think he is a fool for thus parading his record, he asks them to tolerate him: **accept me as a fool.** No matter what they think of him for doing it, he must **boast a little** to make them consider facts whose significance they have failed to appreciate.

---

their own views, and continue to treat them as brethren in Christ.

These two essentials to fellowship Paul found lacking in his opponents. They were not seeking the truth in sincerity, and they did not endeavor to maintain fellowship with Paul or give him credit for Christian experience at least as real and profound as their own. They probably did not realize what was shaping their actions. Few people do until they begin to investigate their own deeper motives. Rationalization is generally unconscious. Jesus warned his disciples that it was possible for men to commit murder and yet to think that in doing so they were serving God (John 16:2).

15*b*. *Their End Will Correspond to Their Deeds.*—Again Paul is seeing the judgment seat of Christ. He has no doubt about the final outcome of these dishonest actions. We live under a God-ordained and God-sustained moral order in which evil at the last destroys itself. An insincere life is a house built on sand; it will not stand up to bad weather. Nothing survives ultimately but what is real, and only that character is real which results from hearing the words of Christ and doing them (Matt. 7:24-27). Nothing lasts but truth.

> For death takes toll
> Of beauty, courage, youth,
> Of all but Truth.[9]

Even in this life how often are the insincere found out! John Ruskin tells of a sculptor, commissioned to carve the figures in a church in Venice, who scamped his work, leaving the concealed parts of the statues unfinished. He was not discovered then; but ten years later he was imprisoned for forgery. Unreality produces unreality. The man who is kind merely in order to be popular makes no real friends. A Spanish proverb says, "Take what you will, and pay for it." We always do. Our end corresponds to our deeds.

16-18. *Let No One Think Me Foolish.*—Paul is uneasy about all this self-justification. Even if the Corinthians do feel it is foolish of him, however, he asks their forbearance. Will they

[9] John Masefield, "Truth." Used by permission of The Macmillan Company, The Society of Authors, and John Masefield, O. M.

17 That which I speak, I speak *it* not after the Lord, but as it were foolishly, in this confidence of boasting.

18 Seeing that many glory after the flesh, I will glory also.

19 For ye suffer fools gladly, seeing ye *yourselves* are wise.

20 For ye suffer, if a man bring you into bondage, if a man devour *you,* if a man take *of you,* if a man exalt himself, if a man smite you on the face.

so that I too may boast a little. 17 (What
I am saying I say not with the Lord's authority but as a fool, in this boastful confidence; 18 since many boast of worldly
things, I too will boast.) 19 For you gladly
bear with fools, being wise yourselves! 20 For
you bear it if a man makes slaves of you, or preys upon you, or takes advantage of you, or puts on airs, or strikes you in the

17. In the boasting that will follow in vss. 23-29 he does not claim that **the Lord** Christ has directed him to speak thus. He does not mean that he is violating instructions, but that he has no express direction (cf. I Cor. 7:12, where he gives advice that does not rest on any word from Jesus). This is the best way he can find to meet the crisis at Corinth, but still it leaves him unhappy, and he does not claim that it is the perfect response to the slanders against him. He does not speak "according to the Lord" (κατὰ κύριον), i.e., according to the Lord's example or command. He speaks as (and feels like) a fool "in this matter [or **confidence** (ὑποστάσει); cf. 9:4] of boasting."

18. Others, specifically the false apostles who were misleading the Corinthians, were boasting of their rights and abilities. Paul had hinted at this in vs. 16, when he said, "That I too may boast a little." He repeats that idea more explicitly here, and notes that they boast "according to the flesh" (κατὰ σάρκα), i.e., of their Jewish descent and authoritative outward position (cf. vss. 22-23). So he says, **I too will boast** along the same line, concerning my birth, position, sufferings, and achievements. His inner regret is that he must boast of such external and personal things instead of boasting "in the Lord," i.e., concerning what God through Christ has graciously done for him (10:17).

19. With irony like that in vs. 4, Paul rebukes the Corinthian attitude of superiority and condescension. This fault of theirs was nothing new. He had already rebuked it in I Cor. 4:8-10. Here it appears again. Convinced that they are wise and superior to Paul, they look down on him. **Gladly** stands first in the Greek sentence to emphasize how ready they are to tolerate Paul's talk because they feel so certain of their own superior wisdom.

20. They think they are so wise; yet look at the outrages they endure! They are duped and imposed upon by the false apostles. "Any one" (τις), **a man,** is either a

not accord him the privilege his opponents have, and allow him to live up to his reputation of playing the fool? With this proviso: **What I am saying I say not with the Lord's authority.** For the moment, since worldly things are in question, he will meet his opponents on their own ground, where he is quite able to hold his own. But what he says in this connection must not be taken as the guiding of the Spirit. Here is revealed the scrupulous nature of Paul's conscience, especially in what he writes or says. It was his habit not only to submit what he said to the censorship of Christ, but also to let the mind of Christ control his thinking so that no defective coinage of words or ideas might pass from him into circulation. This is in line with the warning Christ gave about the use and misuse of words (Matt. 12:36). It also explains in part why Paul's letters have stood the test of centuries of critical scholarship and the clear light of the most sensitive Christian spirits. Some words are really deeds. They can set men on their feet (cf. Job 4:4 Moffatt). They can influence the "thoughts and intents of the heart." The relations of people with one another would be vastly different if our communications were in Christ's control.

19-21*a*. *For You Gladly Bear with Fools, Being Wise Yourselves!*—Sarcasm is not a safe weapon, and a Christian censorship would not permit it. It is often the weapon of the strong against the weak. It both wounds and leaves a poison in the wound. Paul must have been desperate when he used it. But it is natural

21 I speak as concerning reproach, as though we had been weak. Howbeit, whereinsoever any is bold, (I speak foolishly,) I am bold also.

22 Are they Hebrews? so *am* I. Are they Israelites? so *am* I. Are they the seed of Abraham? so *am* I.

23 Are they ministers of Christ? (I speak as a fool,) I *am* more; in labors more abundant, in stripes above measure, in prisons more frequent, in deaths oft.

face. 21 To my shame, I must say, we were too weak for that!

But whatever any one dares to boast of — I am speaking as a fool — I also dare to boast of that. 22 Are they Hebrews? So am I. Are they Israelites? So am I. Are they descendants of Abraham? So am I. 23 Are they servants of Christ? I am a better one — I am talking like a madman — with far greater labors, far more imprisonments, with countless beatings, and often near

reference to the chief intruder or a general way of referring to all such troublemakers at Corinth. This sort of leader "enslaves you" by dictatorial domineering; "devours" you by living well at your expense; "takes" you, i.e., **takes advantage of you** by imposing on you in every way; "exalts himself"; **puts on airs** in conceited pride and self-assertion; "strikes you in the face," perhaps not physically but in part at least by brazen affronts and insults. You put up with all that; so, Paul says ironically, you surely will tolerate a little boasting from me. They should not endure such treatment from the intruders, he implies, and should not make it necessary for him to defend himself as he now does.

2. His Advantages, Labors, and Sufferings (11:21-29)

21. Before turning to the boasting for which he has been preparing, Paul contrasts his attitude with that of the domineering intruders at Corinth. "I speak to [my] dishonor, as though we have been weak." Paul speaks with irony: he must confess to his shame that he has been "weak," and not brazen, bold, and dictatorial, as the "false apostles" have been at Corinth. Then protesting again, as in vs. 17, that he is **a fool** to boast as he is about to do, he repeats the thought of vs. 18, that he will now match the boasting of others. **Any one** here means any one of the "false apostles" whose actions have been described in vs. 20. Paul says, lit., "But wherein anyone dares—I speak in folly—I also dare," i.e., **dare to boast** of my position and record.

22. The boasting, repeatedly mentioned from 10:8 on, now begins. In every respect, Paul declares, he can match the Jewish standing of his opponents, who evidently had made much of their connection with Jerusalem and perhaps with the original Aramaic-speaking apostles there. **Hebrews** means Jews who speak Aramaic; cf. Acts 6:1; Phil. 3:5. The opponents evidently spoke both Aramaic and Greek, just as Paul did. **Israelites** describes Jews as members of God's covenant people (cf. Rom. 11:1). **Seed of Abraham** implies that as his descendants they are heirs of the promise (cf. Gal. 3:29).

23. In Jewish position Paul has claimed to be equal to his opponents. Now he asserts that in Christian service he far outranks them. **Ministers** here seems to mean apostles;

and perhaps even legitimate for him to show up the tactics of his opponents and the weakness of the church in bearing with them. These intruders have been overbearing, dominating, unscrupulous in the demands they have made—probably for the temple tax which Gentile Christians should not have been asked to pay. They have been pompous and have even bullied the church members. It is not a flattering picture.

21*b*-22. ***But Whatever Any One Dares to Boast of I also Dare.***—He has the same grounds for pride they have—membership of the chosen race, the people who inherited the promises of God and were God's agents in the divine purpose of self-revelation.

23*a*. ***Are They Servants of Christ? I Am a Better One.***—Such comparisons are utterly offensive to Paul. It is what he has been deprecating; but the pretensions of these interlopers are so preposterous, their influence so dangerous, and the minds of some of the Christians so gullible, that he throws off his Christian modesty and lets loose a torrent of recollections from the story of his sufferings for Christ. He exposes the marks of his loyalty.

23*b*-27. ***Far Greater Labors.***—Little mention is made of these facts either in Paul's other

24 Of the Jews five times received I forty *stripes* save one.
25 Thrice was I beaten with rods, once was I stoned, thrice I suffered shipwreck, a night and a day I have been in the deep;
26 *In* journeyings often, *in* perils of waters, *in* perils of robbers, *in* perils by *mine own* countrymen, *in* perils by the heathen, *in* perils in the city, *in* perils in the wilderness, *in* perils in the sea, *in* perils among false brethren;

death.
24 Five times I have received at the hands of the Jews the forty lashes less one.
25 Three times I have been beaten with rods; once I was stoned. Three times I have been shipwrecked; a night and a day I have been adrift at sea;
2 on frequent journeys, in danger from rivers, danger from robbers, danger from my own people, danger from Gentiles, danger in the city, danger in the wilderness, danger at sea,

---

such the foes at Corinth evidently claimed to be (vss. 5, 13), and Paul can boast that he is a **better** minister of Christ than they are. But this necessary boasting wrings from him a renewed protest that this self-praise is the talk of a **madman.** Even if Paul must now so boast to bring the Corinthians to their senses, it is extremely distasteful to him; and he thinks it hardly justified even by necessity.

Compare with the following list of hardships and sufferings those in 6:4-10; I Cor. 4:9-13. Paul bases his claim to superiority on what he has suffered for Christ, and in this he reflects the mind of Christ; cf. Rom. 8:17; Mark 8:34-38. At first Paul compares his sufferings with those of his opponents, and says that he has **more** and greater ones to show, but at the end of the verse he drops the comparison and in the rest of the section simply recounts what he has endured in Christ's service. **Labors** refers to all his work for Christ. **Imprisonments** included one at Philippi (Acts 16:23), the only known instance before the writing of II Corinthians. The **beatings** are further described in vss. 24-25. **In deaths oft** recalls the numerous narrow escapes from deadly danger, such as the one mentioned in 1:8-9 (cf. 4:8-11).

24. We have no other record of these five beatings by Jewish authorities. Since they were received in the service of Christ, they evidently happened in Gentile lands where Paul preached. This indicates that Jews had some power of discipline over their people in such areas. Deut. 25:1-3 prescribed the penalty of **forty lashes;** since the law said the number must not exceed forty, the practice arose of giving one less in order to avoid all danger of violating this rule. Paul is the earliest witness to this practice, but Josephus and later Jewish witnesses confirm it. The verse reflects persistent and bitter Jewish hostility to the apostle.

25. Beating **with rods** was a Roman punishment. Acts tells only of the beating at Philippi (Acts 16:22-23). It was not lawful to beat or scourge Roman citizens, and Paul later at Jerusalem stopped preparations to examine him by life-endangering scourging (Acts 22:24). Why Paul did not protest at earlier times we do not know; he did protest, the day after the beating, at Philippi (Acts 16:37). The three beatings by Roman officials indicate that the relation of the church to the empire was more of a problem than Acts admits. The **once** Paul was **stoned** was at Lystra (Acts 14:19). No other record survives of the three shipwrecks (the one in Acts 27 occurred after Paul wrote this letter); we here learn, however, that after one of them he spent **a night and a day** clinging to wreckage while **adrift at sea.**

26. This verse mentions dangers met on Paul's wearing and **frequent journeys.** Swollen **rivers** and murderous **robbers,** Jewish and Gentile enemies and even bitterly

---

letters or in Acts. It was no mere modesty that made him ignore them. It was just that he did not think them worth mentioning. He would have deprecated all mention of his sacrifice, like David Livingstone, who said, "There is only one sacrifice; it was offered on Calvary." But there is another reason. Paul knew that these are not the things that count in the Christian estimate of worth. It is not what we suffer, but how we bear it, and for what we suffer, that make our suffering a badge of honor. Above all, it is the depth and quality of our love to

27 In weariness and painfulness, in watchings often, in hunger and thirst, in fastings often, in cold and nakedness.

28 Beside those things that are without, that which cometh upon me daily, the care of all the churches.

29 Who is weak, and I am not weak? who is offended, and I burn not?

danger from false brethren; 27 in toil and hardship, through many a sleepless night, in hunger and thirst, often without food, in cold and exposure. 28 And, apart from other things, there is the daily pressure upon me of my anxiety for all the churches. 29 Who is weak, and I am not weak? Who is made to fall, and I am not indignant?

---

antagonistic **false brethren**—some at least urging Jewish legalism as in Gal. 2:4—plots in cities and perils encountered in travels through lonely places and on the stormy sea all combined to bring continual danger of injury or death.

27. To serve Christ meant not only to meet danger but also to endure the severe wear of daily hardship. By **toil and hardship,** a phrase found also in I Thess. 2:9 and II Thess. 3:8, Paul describes his heavy load of preaching, teaching, and manual labor. He was **in watchings often** (KJV), because of concern for his churches (vs. 28) or night work; this did not always mean an entire **sleepless night** (RSV). The **hunger and thirst** as well as the frequent **fastings** may have been suffered, at least in part, while in prison, but they no doubt included enforced privation while on hard journeys; this latter is also in mind in the mention of **cold and exposure** (literally, as in KJV, **nakedness**). **Fastings** does not refer to voluntary abstinence, but to want due to unavoidable lack of food.

28. The meaning of χωρὶς τῶν παρεκτός may be **Beside those things that are without,** i.e., the external hardships such as have been described; or it may be "Apart from the additional things"—i.e., other instances of hardship and suffering that might be mentioned. In either case, the main point is that Paul's burden does not consist merely of such personal hardships. A part of his heavy burden, which he willingly carries for Christ, is **the pressure upon me of my anxiety** [or deep concern] **for all the churches.** As his letters show, he never forgets the churches he has founded. He thinks of them, prays for them, sends messengers and letters to them, and because they are so wavering and imperfect, he continually feels anxiety for their welfare. **All** includes the church at Corinth, but is a reminder that he has many more churches demanding his thought and care (cf. 2:12-13; 7:5).

29. This verse could be understood to say that Paul has sympathy for every weak and tempted man in the world. Probably, however, he thinks mainly, if not solely, of

---

men and to God which counts (I Cor. 13:3). Paul therefore sweeps all his sufferings aside and reveals his love.

28-29. ***The Daily Pressure Upon Me.***—Paul's sufferings were not only of the body; they were of the heart as well, and were all the sufferings of selfless love. He carried a constant burden of anxiety about the spiritual welfare of the churches he had founded. The Christian faith does not take away our burdens; it changes their nature. They become the burdens of love. It does not remove our anxieties and fears; it ennobles them. Our anxiety about ourselves is supplanted by anxiety about others, and anxiety about others becomes anxiety about their spiritual welfare. Our spirit can thus be tested by the nature of our anxieties. Concern about the health or success of our children is natural, but concern about their character is much more important both for us and for them. Paul's love for the people of his churches was of the same quality as Christ's. It was self-identifying. If one of his flock was weak or ailing, Paul felt it because he was literally one with him. If any were being lured toward evil or seduced from the faith, he blazed with indignation.

The example he gives of this self-identifying love is interesting. He might have mentioned sorrow or hardship, etc. He does speak elsewhere of rejoicing with those who rejoice and weeping with those who weep (Rom. 12:15). But here it is the weakness of people, easily tempted, easily drawn back into the pit from which they have been rescued, of which he speaks. We are apt to admire the strong man—the man who is free and master of himself, to whom certain things present no temptation. The weak man, who is compelled to avoid things which are legitimate in themselves but are a temptation to a nature still incompletely

30 If I must needs glory, I will glory of
the things which concern mine infirmities.
31 The God and Father of our Lord
Jesus Christ, which is blessed for evermore,
knoweth that I lie not.

30 If I must boast, I will boast of the
things that show my weakness. 31 The God
and Father of the Lord Jesus, he who is
blessed for ever, knows that I do not lie.

---

the many **weak** and endangered Christians in the churches for which God has made him responsible. He responds with sympathy to such weak converts who face strong temptation and trial. It causes him to **burn** with indignation, or with a sense of shame and distress, whenever one of his spiritual children **is made to fall.** What happens to his converts concerns him. He is not a callous itinerant orator. He has the heart of a Christian pastor.

3. His Escape from Damascus Shows His Weakness (11:30-33)

30. Paul concludes the recital of the hardships and sufferings of the ministry by saying, **If I must boast, I will boast of the things that show my weakness.** This verse also leads on to the narrative of the incident at Damascus (vss. 32-33), which illustrates the humiliating weakness of Paul, and may have given rise to a charge that he was a coward.

31. Paul here in effect puts himself on oath; his concluded recital of his sufferings and also the other things he still intends to say are true. Perhaps the point he most fears will be challenged is his assurance that he lives in constant concern and sympathy for all his churches, especially the weak and tempted members in them (vss. 28-29). For similar expressions with regard to what he fears may be contested, cf. 1:18, 23; 11:10;

---

self-controlled, is apt to be despised. There are some to whom the smell of a liquor shop, or the sight of a pack of playing cards, is almost too much for their new-found resistance to evil. These demand our most respectful and understanding help. Paul's identification with them involves his sharing of their self-discipline.

If anyone was led into temptation by others, Paul burned with indignation. It was the crime of offending "one of these little ones" of which Jesus spoke so severely (Matt. 18:6). There is room for righteous anger in the pastoral heart. It is a legitimate form of opposition to evil. The biographer of F. W. Robertson says of him:

> The indignation . . . with which he heard of a base act was so intense that it rendered him sleepless. His wrath was terrible, and it did not evaporate in words. But it was Christ-like indignation. With those who were weak, crushed with remorse, fallen, his compassion, long-suffering and tenderness were as beautiful as they were unfailing. But falsehood, hypocrisy, the sin of the strong against the weak, stirred him to the very depths of his being. "I have seen him," writes one of his friends, "grind his teeth and clench his fists on passing a man who, he knew, was bent on destroying an innocent girl." [1]

Anger of this sort is an expression of the truest kind of love.

[1] *Life and Letters of Frederick W. Robertson*, ed. Stopford A. Brooke (Boston: Ticknor & Fields, 1865), I, 186.

30. ***If I Must Boast.***—By **weakness** Paul means his own physical weakness and the weakness which he felt in sympathy with others who were weak. In addition to this, there was the humiliation which is involved in the acceptance of suffering for Christ's sake. It is the willingness to lose reputation, to be scorned and despised in the cause of Christ. It is like "the weakness of God" shown in the Cross (I Cor. 1:25), which in the eyes of faith "is stronger than men." The Cross had transformed all Paul's values.

There is also the fact, which he had experienced and which he elaborates in ch. 12, that God's strength is made perfect in his weakness. It is not easy to believe that a man can be sincere who claims that he finds satisfaction in the things that humiliate him. Only the grace of Christ, changing our whole point of view and enabling us to "pour contempt on all our pride," can make it possible.

Paul therefore calls God to witness that his statement is true.

31. ***God Knows.***—Paul cannot mention the name of God without breaking into doxology. In this fact there can be found the difference that Christ makes. The word "God" awakens different feelings according to our outlook and experience. To some it brings only a sense of gloom or fear; to others, a sense of austere demand, accompanied by a vague feeling of guilt. The mission of Jesus was to make us see and

32 In Damascus the governor under Aretas the king kept the city of the Damascenes with a garrison, desirous to apprehend me:

33 And through a window in a basket was I let down by the wall, and escaped his hands.

32 At Damascus, the governor under King Ar'e-tas guarded the city of Damascus in order to seize me, 33 but I was let down in a basket through a window in the wall, and escaped his hands.

Rom. 9:1; Gal. 1:20. For the Jewish custom of reverently praising God when his name is mentioned cf. Rom. 9:5, where the praise probably refers to God; similar phrases are frequent in rabbinical writings. For this way of referring to God as **the God and Father of the Lord Jesus** cf. Exeg. on 1:3; also Eph. 1:3; I Pet. 1:3.

32. Acts 9:23-25 parallels vss. 32-33 here, with variations which show that the two accounts are independent. Some three years after his conversion (Gal. 1:18), Paul had to leave Damascus to save his life. According to Acts, the Jews were seeking to seize Paul; it is here indicated that they must have enlisted the help of the local representative of **Aretas,** the king of the Nabataean kingdom whose capital was at Petra.

Aretas reigned from 9 B.C. to A.D. 39. No ancient coin or other record proves that his kingdom included Damascus at this time. If his representative **at Damascus** was the **governor** in full charge of the city, this could hardly have been before late A.D. 37, when Caligula became the Roman emperor; Tiberius, emperor from A.D. 14 to 37, was hostile to Aretas and would hardly have given him control of Damascus. So if we translate ἐθνάρχης as **governor,** Paul's conversion must be dated about A.D. 35 and no earlier.

But it is at least equally possible that this Greek word means "ethnarch," a representative of a foreign people who had been given partial powers of control and discipline over this foreign group of the city's population (e.g., the Jews had an ethnarch in Alexandria). If, then, there was in Roman-controlled Damascus such an ethnarch, the Jews at Damascus may have appealed to him for help in seizing Paul and putting him out of the way. Since the kingdom of the Nabataeans extended northward to the region of Damascus, the ethnarch and his helpers were in a position to watch both the city streets and the roads leading from the gates. Thus they might capture Paul as he fled through one of the gates.

33. In this situation that resembled a siege, the Christians at Damascus were in military matters as "harmless as doves," but they were also as "wise as serpents." The Arabs guarded the gates. But there was **a window in the wall** to which the disciples had access. Through it they **let** Paul **down in a basket,** evidently at night. The act was not detected; he safely **escaped,** and went to Jerusalem. Paul tells of it, however, not in a tone of triumph, but to recall how humiliating and apparently helpless his lot as a Christian messenger has been.

---

realize that God is Father, so that his very name would awaken confidence and love. He has done his work with us only when that name thrills the soul with joy and gratitude. Paul is sure God knew that when he boasted of his weakness he was stating the truth. All he does is done in the knowledge that God is looking on. All he says is said in the knowledge that God is listening. That conviction would go far to make dishonest deeds and words next to impossible. Calling God to witness can become a mere formality, as in taking an oath upon the Bible. But to one who knows God as the God and Father of Jesus Christ, and whose heart at the very mention of his name fills with adoring gratitude, the thought that he is looking on and listening will rule out many an evil thing. A thief who entered a room to steal took all the valuables except a silver crucifix; this he left in its place, after turning the face of Christ to the wall. He had evidently found it impossible to commit his dishonesty under the eyes of that figure.

32-33. ***At Damascus.***—The mention of this incident seems out of place here. It was a most humiliating experience for a proud Pharisee; but it was an act of God's deliverance. It underlines what Paul has been saying about his weakness and God's grace. It emphasizes a cardinal truth of Paul's experience, that no man

12 It is not expedient for me doubtless
to glory. I will come to visions and
revelations of the Lord.
2 I knew a man in Christ above fourteen years ago, (whether in the body, I
cannot tell; or whether out of the body, I
cannot tell: God knoweth;) such a one
caught up to the third heaven.

12 I must boast; there is nothing to be
gained by it, but I will go on to
visions and revelations of the Lord. 2 I
know a man in Christ who fourteen years
ago was caught up to the third heaven —
whether in the body or out of the body I

4. His Thorn in the Flesh Checks Pride in Visions (12:1-10)

12:1. The theme of boasting continues to dominate in this section; the word **boast** occurs in vss. 1, 5, 6, 9. Yet Paul's regret that he must boast is plain throughout, and is stressed in vs. 1. His preference, to admit his own weakness and rely on the grace and power of the Lord, finds repeated expression (cf. vss. 5, 6, 9, 10). The Greek MSS vary regarding the second word of vs. 1. The reading, δεῖ, "it is necessary," seems best supported; so **I must boast** of the RSV is correct. When Paul says "it is not profitable" (οὐ συμφέρον), he does not mean literally that **there is nothing to be gained by it,** for he hopes by this boasting, forced upon him, to make the Corinthians see that they have been wronging him and following false leaders at Corinth. The words simply express again his distaste at the whole business of boasting, and his sense that it is a desperate and suspect emergency measure of whose value he is not certain. He feels driven by a necessity he cannot evade, so he **will go on to visions and revelations** that **the Lord** has given him. That Paul had such visions is clear not only from Acts 9:3; 16:9; 18:9; 22:17-18; 27:23 but also from Gal. 1:16; 2:2.

2. As vs. 7 shows, Paul was the **man in Christ** who had the "visions and revelations" that he reports in vss. 2-4. Because they are not his own achievement, he chooses to refer to them in this indirect way. **Fourteen years ago** was probably about A.D. 44. The mention of the date indicates how vivid his memory of the privileged experience still is. No other report of this vision has survived. Paul was convinced that he was **caught up** into **the third heaven.** Since ancient Jewish writings varied in the number of heavens pictured (three and seven were the most usual suggestions), we cannot be sure whether Paul here means that he was caught up into the highest heaven. He was so thrilled by the experience that he lost all sense of physical existence and could not tell whether his **body** was caught up or left behind. Plainly, though he confesses that only God knows precisely what happened, he considers it possible for man's spirit to be temporarily withdrawn from his

can hope for any deliverance of God which will save his pride.

12:1-4. ***Visions and Revelations of the Lord.***— Boasting of any kind is distasteful, and in his heart Paul does not believe that any good can come of it. It is especially distasteful to boast of what he has had to suffer in the ministry of Christ. He would rather speak of what God has revealed to him in a special and unusual way, entirely outside his control or co-operation. **Visions and revelations of the Lord** denote different kinds of experience. Visions are mental pictures which have definite shape and form. Revelations are truths made clear to and apprehended by the insight of the soul.

The apostle now relates an experience that befell him after he became **a man in Christ,** which is his definition of a Christian. It was some kind of ecstasy, the contents of which he cannot describe. He heard words which cannot be reported and which it would be sacrilege to repeat even if he could. Tennyson describes an experience in which the spirit seemed to leave the body, rising like a dove to fly to some distant region, and after a while returning.

Like her I go, I cannot stay;
  I leave this mortal ark behind,
  A weight of nerves without a mind,
And leave the cliffs, and haste away,

. . . .

  and back return
  To where the body sits, and learn
That I have been an hour away.[2]

It would be futile to speculate on Paul's experience. He would not have us try to penetrate his mind here. He seems even to dissociate him-

[2] *In Memoriam,* Part XII.

3 And I knew such a man, (whether in the body, or out of the body, I cannot tell: God knoweth;)

4 How that he was caught up into paradise, and heard unspeakable words, which it is not lawful for a man to utter.

5 Of such a one will I glory: yet of myself I will not glory, but in mine infirmities.

6 For though I would desire to glory, I shall not be a fool; for I will say the truth: but *now* I forbear, lest any man should think of me above that which he seeth me *to be,* or *that* he heareth of me.

do not know, God knows. 3 And I know that
this man was caught up into Paradise —
whether in the body or out of the body I
do not know, God knows — 4 and he heard
things that cannot be told, which man may
not utter. 5 On behalf of this man I will
boast, but on my own behalf I will not
boast, except of my weakness. 6 Though if
I wish to boast, I shall not be a fool, for I
shall be speaking the truth. But I refrain
from it, so that no one may think more of
me than he sees in me or hears from me.

---

body even during the continuance of physical life. This idea has parallels in Greek thought (cf. 5:6-8, where Paul assumes as possible a blessed existence of his soul with the risen Lord after death, even before the resurrection).

3. It is not certain that this verse describes a second vision. If **Paradise** (cf. Luke 23:43; Rev. 2:7) was the third heaven, or was in the third heaven, this can be the same vision described in vs. 2; in that case, Paul speaks only of one vision, as an example of the many he might recount. But it is equally possible that Paul gives two examples, of which the one in vss. 3-4 is the second. In either case, Paul is clearly conscious that he has been granted a great privilege in such visions, and he may imply that the arrogant "false apostles" at Corinth cannot match these proofs of divine blessing. The experience, as in vs. 2, was so absorbing that for its duration he had no bodily feeling and could not tell whether he was **in the body** while it happened.

4. Paul expresses with a word play what he heard: "unutterable utterances" (ἄρρητα ῥήματα). This need not mean that he could not understand them; he does not tell them because they are too sacred—they **cannot be told.** They were a personal blessing and assurance to him, but were not to be told to others.

5. Such "visions and revelations" were a great privilege and support to Paul in his hardship and suffering. They will silence criticism and scorn of him in all who have the insight to see his true position as a divinely blessed "man in Christ." Yet since they are undeserved gifts and did not happen because of any human worth in Paul, he speaks of them as though another had had them, and declines to boast on his own behalf. Of his own life he will boast only of his **weaknesses** (including illness). They have kept him from unchristian pride in his visions; they have made him ready to receive the divine grace and power by which alone he can live and work effectively for Christ. This theme he develops in vss. 7-10.

6. Paul could honestly say more; he could speak of other revelations that God has granted him. Were he to do so, he would not be a deluded **fool,** as some at Corinth have thought him to be (cf. 5:13). But though to recount further instances would be **speaking the truth,** he refrains (lit., "spares" them), so that they may judge him not by his secret visions, which could be challenged by hostile men, but by what he has done and

---

self from it. It was something that happened to him in such a way that he felt himself a mere onlooker.

5. *On Behalf of This Man Will I Boast.*—It was as if a man, receiving an ovation from his fellows, were to look on the whole scene from a detached point of view, knowing that it had no relation to his gifts or merits. Paul will not boast on any other terms.

6. *But I Refrain.*—He implies that there is a good deal more which he could say in defense of his position as an apostle, if he should adopt that line of argument. But he will not give a false impression, or ask people to judge of his authority by anything except the life he lives and the message he preaches. Nothing else will authenticate him as an ambassador for Christ. It is important that the people to whom and

7 And lest I should be exalted above measure through the abundance of the revelations, there was given to me a thorn in the flesh, the messenger of Satan to buffet me, lest I should be exalted above measure.

7 And to keep me from being too elated by the abundance of revelations, a thorn was given me in the flesh, a messenger of Satan, to harass me, to keep me from being

---

suffered. This record even his enemies cannot deny; all must admit the truth of such experiences as he has told in 11:23-27.

7. Paul sees that a divine purpose has been worked out through the physical ailment he has had to suffer. It has kept him from pride and arrogance, which he might have felt as a result of his special visions. Here, as in some other passages from Paul, one gets the impression that humility was not an easy or automatic virtue for him. He now can see that the hard and continued discipline of pain and ill health was God's way of saving him from the pride that is fatal to the Christian spirit and usefulness. The sentence structure is not clear. In the probable reading the opening words must be attached to vs. 6, and we can translate: ". . . and by reason of the abundance [or ὑπερβολή may mean "excellence"] of the revelations. Wherefore, that I might not exalt myself overmuch, there was given me a thorn [or stake] in the flesh, etc." But διό, "wherefore," is omitted in some MSS; the verse then opens: "And by reason of the abundance [or excellence] of the revelations, that I might not exalt myself overmuch, there was given me, etc."

Numerous conjectures have been made as to Paul's ailment. It was a physical illness of some kind, whether epilepsy, offensive eye trouble (cf. Gal. 4:13-14), malarial fever, or some other. Any man would feel that he could do better work for Christ if freed from such an illness; it continually tortured Paul as though **a thorn** or stake was always sticking into his flesh. The thorn or stake came from God, Paul implies, but Satan was the agent through whom the ailment came; the illness was his **messenger** (cf. I Cor. 5:5). The purpose of the buffeting, to teach Paul humility and keep him constantly reminded of the need of it, was God's purpose. The present tense of κολαφίζῃ implies that the buffeting was a continual process. It was a daily drain on body and nerves.

---

among whom a man ministers should have such respect for him as will make them ready to give him a hearing. But the respect which might be created through a reputation for scholarship or spiritual gifts cannot be sustained except through the life he lives and the message he speaks. Paul knows this, and merely gives a hint that such experiences as have come to other notable saints are not unknown to him.

At the same time, he makes it clear that these should not be regarded as a normal or essential means of the disclosure of God. God does not come to us in ecstasies in which we are withdrawn from the hard realities of daily living. It is there, in fact, that God meets us—amid frustrations, vexations, sufferings—and makes known to us his grace. This is why Paul boasts of his weaknesses, as he goes on to show in another personal experience such as is within the range of all. He had a physical handicap, which he calls "a thorn in the flesh," and he describes how it became the means of power because it was an opportunity for the grace of God.

7. ***A Thorn Was Given Me.***—What the physical ailment actually was we do not know. The description of it as **a thorn in the flesh** suggests that it was painful, crippling his enjoyment of life, and frustrating his full efficiency. It was also humiliating, for it awoke in others the pity which is sometimes mingled with contempt.

There was no morbid sentimentality in Paul's attitude toward disease. He saw in it an evil thing—a messenger of Satan sent to harass him. It is not God's design for human life that we should suffer sickness or disease. Disease is a blight on his creation, part of the opposition to his creative purpose for his children. But sickness could not come without God's permission. Paul says it **was given** to him; and the word **given** suggests that there is a loving Will behind. If it did not come directly from God's hand, it came through his hand. Jesus referred to his sufferings as "the cup which the Father has given me" (John 18:11). Obviously the cup had been prepared by human hate and lovelessness, but God had taken it and put it into his hands for him to drink. The final problem of the origin of human suffering is not solved by this explanation and is not elucidated by Jesus. But it is a comfort to know that however it has come, we may take it from

8 For this thing I besought the Lord thrice, that it might depart from me.
9 And he said unto me, My grace is sufficient for thee: for my strength is made

too elated. 8 Three times I besought the Lord about this, that it should leave me;
9 but he said to me, "My grace is sufficient

8. **Three times,** evidently with earnest and prolonged prayer, Paul asked God for release from this hampering, trying trouble. The prayer was to **the Lord;** since the answer of vs. 9 speaks of "my power," which is then called "the power of Christ," this prayer seems addressed to Christ. On prayer to the exalted Christ, cf. I Thess. 3:12-13; I Cor. 1:2; Acts 7:59. He is addressed as the risen, exalted Lord, who "intercedes for us" (Rom. 8:34; cf. Heb. 7:25).

9. Paul's specific request was not granted. But he received a better answer than the one he had wanted. Just as in all of his Christian life and service he depended on divine

the loving hands of God as a burden he calls us to bear, sure that it can be used by him for our good. We are not at the mercy of blind fate but are always in the hands of God.

Paul recognized this. The thorn in the flesh was given to keep him from the spiritual pride that might have overcome one to whom such unusual revelations had been given. Ships with a high superstructure need heavy ballast to keep them from overturning. Paul repeats the phrase **to keep me from being too elated.** All pride is perilous. Dante puts it first in his list of the seven deadly sins, because it is the worst form of self-love. Pride of success, of money, or of power is evil because it is a form of self-worship and isolates us from our fellows and from God. But the pride that comes from the contemplation of our virtues, or of our insight into spiritual things, or of the secrets God has whispered in our ear, is the worst of all, because it feeds on that which should make us humble—God's mercy and grace. Paul knew the danger; it was from this pit that he had been rescued, his feet set on the rock of utter dependence on God. Yet he prayed that God would heal him.

8. ***Three Times I Besought the Lord.***—He had no fatalistic attitude towards his pain. It was God's will that it should eventually pass away. It would disappear with the redemption of man's spirit. Therefore he might ask God, even beseech God, to be set free from it. Paul does not often pray for temporal blessings, especially for himself. But he does not exclude this kind of petition. Nor does he consider it pointless, as some people do who suggest that prayer cannot deflect the order of nature, or because, since God is good, we can rely on his giving us what is good without our asking. To Paul prayer was the means of fellowship with God—a fellowship which is fully personal, and therefore admits of asking and receiving. In any personal relationship, such as that of father and son, there is room for freedom—the son's freedom to ask what he wants and the father's freedom to give or refuse. It is the same with God and his children. There is room in our petitions for personal choice. There is even a real sense in which a father cannot give his child certain things, such as counsel or guidance, unless he asks for them; for this implies that he is willing and ready to receive them and to co-operate with his father in getting them. A celebrated violinist had a daughter who took lessons from a stranger. When asked why he was not teaching her himself, the father answered that he longed to teach her all he knew, and would have done so, but she had never asked him. In the same way there are things God cannot give us till we ask him.

Prayer from this point of view is the expression of the faith and trust to which God can respond. It is a vital part of the personal relationship between us and him. It is not, as some kinds of prayer might suggest, an impersonal force exerted by us through which other forces come into play, like moving an electric switch to turn on the power or to detonate an explosive mixture. God is not a mere impersonal power; he is our Father to whom we can go with our needs. His response is not automatic. There are both purpose and intelligence behind it. He is both wisdom and love.

9*a*. ***But He Said to Me, "My Grace Is Sufficient for You."***—God's "No" is never a blank refusal. It may appear to be so; but that only means his answer is either delayed or is unrecognized. "Who rises from Prayer a better man, his prayer is answered."[3] This is not the only answer, but it is a good answer. A Christian will be content with it, even if nothing else appears to happen; for in his prayer, whatever he asks, he will be seeking God's will, and God's will is our growth as his children. If he asks material help it will not be as an end in itself but for

[3] George Meredith, *The Ordeal of Richard Feveral* (New York: Charles Scribner's Sons, 1905), p. 75.

perfect in weakness. Most gladly therefore will I rather glory in my infirmities, that the power of Christ may rest upon me.

for you, for my power is made perfect in weakness." I will all the more gladly boast of my weaknesses, that the power of Christ

grace and power, since "our sufficiency is from God" (3:5), so in this trial he receives grace sufficient to carry the suffering and endure the strain. And this, he realizes, will be better for him and for his work. The divine power cannot help or use the self-sufficient man; but this **power is made perfect in weakness.** So, Paul says, **rather** than ask further for release from the ailment, **I will . . . boast of my weaknesses, that the power of Christ,** without which, even if I were well, I could not do my work, **may rest upon me,** to lead and support me and give effectiveness to my ministry.

the better fulfillment of God's purpose. In Paul's case God's answer was the assurance that his grace was sufficient for all his need. Was he afraid that this infirmity would hinder his effectiveness, be a barrier between him and those to whom he ministered, or prove too big a drain on his resources of courage and cheerfulness? God's grace would be sufficient for all these situations. Whatever demands life might lay on him because of this defect, God could and did make him adequate to them. There are divine compensations for every handicap in life. There are spiritual resources that can enable a man to triumph over his defect, and even to win something out of it which was not possible before.

9*b*. *Power Made Perfect in Weakness.*—The point of Paul's weakness could become the place of God's power. It could become a center through which that power could most fully radiate. Emerson says, "As no man had ever a point of pride that was not injurious to him, so no man had ever a defect that was not somewhere made useful to him." [4] The story of handicapped lives is a continuous illustration of this paradox. Many of those who have done outstanding work for their country or for their fellows have had to contend with some physical defect. Moses had a stammering tongue. Jeremiah was overwhelmed with a sense of his own deficiencies. Modern examples are almost too numerous to mention. Again and again through faith in God the defect has been transformed into a stimulus. The struggle to overcome it has developed capacities that would otherwise have lain dormant. This is part of the explanation. But there is more. The weakness or defect can bring people into the condition in which they are open to God's Spirit. We come to God through the sense of need. The feeling of inadequacy turns into prayer. Self-confidence is a good quality, provided it is based not on self-sufficiency but on a deep dependence on God. We come to that dependence only when self-sufficiency has been broken by some situation or experience that is too much for us. When self in its various forms is laid in the dust, God can fully come in. The definition of God which Robert Browning's Pompilia gives, makes him responsible for these emergencies.

> God the strong, God the beneficent,
> God ever mindful in all strife and strait,
> Who, for our own good, makes the need extreme,
> Till at the last He puts forth might and saves.[5]

The point of extreme need is the place of all conversions. Isaiah, Paul, Luther, Augustine have all been there.

It may be that God refuses to remove our weakness because he needs it. Writing of John Bunyan, W. Hale White says,

> The Creator gets the appointed task out of his servants in many ways. It is sufficient to give some of them love, sunrises and sunsets and primrose woods in spring: others have to be scourged with bloody whips or driven nearly mad by dreams . . . before they do what God has determined for them. . . . We may say of men like Bunyan that it is not their strength taken by itself which makes them remarkable and precious, but rather the conflict of strength and weakness.[6]

But all weakness can bring its compensation. "When God adds He subtracts; when He subtracts He adds." [7] Through weakness his power is released in courage to face the handicap, in the gentler graces that come with suffering like the delicate colors of flowers that grow in the shade, and most of all in a larger sympathy with other sufferers. Strength and weakness need revaluation from the Christian standpoint. It was because Paul had this standpoint that he could rejoice in God's answer.

9*c*. *All the More Gladly.*—He knew that real weakness and real strength are of the spirit, not of the body. The exaggerated cult of athleticism is due to a lopsided view of life. The test of

[4] Essay on "Compensation."

[5] *The Ring and the Book,* Bk. VII, l. 1291.

[6] *John Bunyan* (New York: Charles Scribner's Sons, 1904), pp. 25-26.

[7] *Ibid.,* p. 26.

10 Therefore I take pleasure in infirmities, in reproaches, in necessities, in persecutions, in distresses for Christ's sake: for when I am weak, then am I strong.

11 I am become a fool in glorying; ye have compelled me: for I ought to have been commended of you: for in nothing am I behind the very chiefest apostles, though I be nothing.

may rest upon me. 10 For the sake of Christ, then, I am content with weaknesses, insults, hardships, persecutions, and calamities; for when I am weak, then I am strong.

11 I have been a fool! You forced me to it, for I ought to have been commended by you. For I am not at all inferor to these superlative apostles, even though I am

---

10. Paul first repeats what he has just said, that he is **content with** the physical **weaknesses** that beset him daily. But he adds that in addition to physical illness, he is ready to accept "injuries" (**insults** in RSV might be understood as merely verbal, and the word ὕβρεσιν includes the idea of physical mistreatment and injuries), **hardships** (lit., "necessities," unavoidable hardships), **persecutions,** and **calamities** ("straits," **distresses).** He has found in his ministry that **when** he knows that he is **weak** and lacking in physical and spiritual strength, then the power of God can work through him so that in effect he is **strong.**

C. Paul's Work Merits Commendation and Trust (12:11-18)

1. Miracles Have Demonstrated His Apostleship (12:11-13)

11. Once more it comes home to Paul that boasting is not the right way for a Christian to act. He stops and admits, **I have been a fool!** But he has been driven to it by the Corinthians, who, instead of commending him and defending him against vicious attacks on his work and character, have listened to his enemies. The pronoun **you** is expressed in Greek and stands first with emphasis; his own converts have **forced** him to boast. He has had to defend himself to them when he **ought to have been commended by** them. **Ought** means that all along they have owed this to him. They have been indebted to him and have had opportunity to know the effectiveness and faithfulness of his work; hence they have owed him friendship and support against all critics. They have been misled by **these superlative apostles** (cf. 11:5, and on their attitude, 11:20). But, says Paul, **in nothing** (this word οὐδέν stands first in its clause for emphasis; he concedes no exception) was he inferior to these bold pretenders. The RSV **I am not at all inferior**

---

physical fitness is what it can contribute to the strength of the spirit.

> To man, propose this test—
> Thy body at its best,
> How far can that project thy soul on its lone way? [8]

The power of the spirit is the power that comes from the indwelling Christ. Weakness may deepen this indwelling by throwing us more completely on God, and by providing the condition in which the qualities of the Christlike spirit may be developed. God's way of answering the prayer for these qualities may be to lead us into the circumstances, or to bring us face to face with the difficulty, that calls them out. We pray for courage, and God leads us by roads that expose us to danger. We pray for patience, and we get a disagreeable neighbor. We pray for love, and life throws on us the need to care for someone who may be irksome and difficult. We pray for humility, and life brings us into circumstances that break our pride. These things can be accepted in meekness if we have the Christian valuation, confident that real strength is in the quality of Christlikeness, and if this is what we want more than anything else. Having this outlook and this desire, Paul made friends with his thorn in the flesh.

10. ***When I Am Weak, then I Am Strong.***—Although Paul does not specifically refer to it, the weakness of the church too must have been in his mind. "Not many of you were . . . powerful . . . ; God chose what is weak in the world to shame the strong, . . . so that no human being might boast in the presence of God" (I Cor. 1:26-29).

11. ***Even Though I Am Nothing.***—Paul had found the only effective way to overcome the sense of inferiority: to accept the fact that we are nothing, whatever our gifts or lack of them;

[8] Robert Browning, "Rabbi Ben Ezra," st. viii.

12 Truly the signs of an apostle were wrought among you in all patience, in signs, and wonders, and mighty deeds.

nothing. 12 The signs of a true apostle were performed among you in all patience, with

has the wrong tense; the aorist tense of ὑστέρησα refers the statement back to the time of Paul's stay in Corinth; in nothing *was* I inferior to these men. It is his way of saying that he was really superior to them. This applies to his work and faithfulness, but since all of it was due to the grace and power of God, he recalls that in his own right he is **nothing** (cf. I Cor. 3:7; 15:9).

12. What should have kept them from belittling and rejecting him were **the signs** done through him—signs that showed he was **a true apostle.** He implies that his opponents have not been able to match what the Corinthians have seen done in his ministry. Yet he does not say that he did the **mighty works.** Since they were done only by the power of God, he says rather that they **were performed among you** by the power of God working in him. **In all patience** (or endurance) implies that the **signs** happened repeatedly, in spite of the physical exhaustion or outward difficulties or lack of understanding that accompanied them. Perhaps Paul has partly in mind spiritual gifts such as preaching and other pastoral abilities, but he refers mainly to miracles performed through him. They are described in three words: **signs,** events in which faith sees spiritual significance; **wonders,** happenings of astounding and unusual character; and **mighty works,** notable acts in which the power of God is at work.

The study of the N.T. miracles may best begin with this passage, Rom. 15:19, and Gal. 3:5. Writing to churches that would have challenged him had he falsified the facts, Paul refers unhesitatingly to such miracles; he knows that even his enemies cannot deny their occurrence. In other words, the study of miracles must begin by accepting the fact that many such remarkable events happened. Moreover, this verse implies clearly that other true apostles were doing similar **mighty works.**

but that through our nothingness God's power may be made manifest. Yet he cannot help feeling a certain soreness that the church in Corinth had not taken his side against those who had despised him.

12. ***Signs of a True Apostle.***—God's power had been manifest through the very weakness which the Corinthians criticized. The real signs of the apostolate are the spiritual results that flow from it. This, not some particular method of ecclesiastical ordination, is the true test of the validity of a ministry. Paul singles out **patience** as characteristic of an apostle. It means the power to hold on amid discouragement, failure, or persecution. A better name for it might be fortitude. "I reckon fortitude's the biggest thing a man can have—just to go on enduring when there's no guts or heart left in you. . . . The head man at the job was the Apostle Paul."[9] The true apostle will not be deflected or dissuaded from his task. His heart is on fire with the love of men and the love of God; and "love never faileth." He has heard God's call and must obey (Acts 4:20; 5:29). He does not look for short-term results (see Bunyan's contrast between Passion and Patience in the Interpreter's House).[1] In true patience there is faith, love, and hope. Faith has been described as "patience with the lamp lit." The deeds which mark the work of the true apostle Paul describes in three ways—**signs and wonders and mighty works.** How far he means these to be distinguished from one another it is not easy to say. **Signs** are actions which have a spiritual meaning. Like signals from a ship they need to be interpreted. They reveal the grace of God at work. Christ described his own works as signs because they revealed this grace, not because they were exhibitions of mere power. They confirm faith only as they reveal the grace of God to the insight of the heart (John 10:25). In John's view the miracles of Christ were signs in this sense—the turning of water into wine, the feeding of the multitude, the healing of the blind. These all illustrated the spiritual change which Christ was also able to work. The apostle's deeds may not be signs of which he is conscious, but to those who can see it, the grace of Christ will reveal itself in his actions. The signs may even be clearer when those who show them are not aware of them.

Wonders are the kinds of action that startle people into thinking and make them ask the

[9] John Buchan, *Mr. Standfast* (New York: George H. Doran Co., 1919), p. 177.

[1] *The Pilgrim's Progress,* ch. ii.

13 For what is it wherein ye were inferior to other churches, except *it be* that I myself was not burdensome to you? forgive me this wrong.

14 Behold, the third time I am ready to come to you; and I will not be burdensome to you: for I seek not yours, but you: for the children ought not to lay up for the parents, but the parents for the children.

signs and wonders and mighty works. 13 For in what were you less favored than the rest of the churches, except that I myself did not burden you? Forgive me this wrong!

14 Here for the third time I am ready to come to you. And I will not be a burden, for I seek not what is yours but you; for children ought not to lay up for their

---

13. Paul can truthfully say that he has done everything for the Corinthian church that he has done for his other churches, **except** that he has never accepted support from them (cf. 11:7-11; I Cor. 9). Quite possibly some at Corinth had said that he made other churches his favorites; they may have complained that he stayed away from them to favor other churches. In saying that **I myself did not burden you** by requiring you to support me, he implies, in the strong expression **I myself,** that the "false apostles" did ask and receive support at Corinth (cf. 11:20). With irony he says, **Forgive me this wrong!** This is a way of saying that if there has been any difference, he has favored *them.* Note that Paul here speaks to the entire Corinthian church. This is true throughout chs. 10–13; these chapters cannot be taken as directed only to a rebellious minority. For this reason it is hard to see how they can be part of the letter that contains 7:11*b,* 16.

2. He Has Not Acted and Will Not Act in Greed (12:14-18)

14. The interjection **behold** is used to introduce the important announcement that Paul is ready to make a **third** visit to Corinth. The first was that of Acts 18:1; the second must have been after the writing of I Corinthians, and must have been made in an attempt to stop the revolt against Paul (see Intro., p. 266). Some have thought that this verse means only that Paul has *planned* twice before to visit Corinth, and now will really come. But 13:1 clearly shows that a third visit is meant, and 2:1 indicates that the second visit was painful because of the hostility Paul then encountered.

On the coming visit he **will not . . . burden** them by asking support, as the "false apostles" do (11:20). He is not after their possessions, but wants to win them to renewed loyalty to Christ; that loyalty will bring them back into friendly relationships with him. His unselfish interest in them fulfills a natural law of human life: **children** are not

---

questions that open the way for God. At Pentecost the change in the disciples was explained by some people as due to drunkenness. Others were forced to ask, "What does this mean?" (Acts 2:12.) They sought for an explanation of a fact that had made them wonder, and this laid them open to the truth which Peter stated and which brought some of them to God. Christian living ought to reveal qualities which make people wonder and open the way for a spiritual interpretation of life.

Mighty works may denote works of healing. There is no doubt that in the early church physical healing often accompanied spiritual healing. But the greatest of all mighty works is the change which the gospel works in the heart. This is the miracle which human power cannot accomplish, though many claim that all we need is education, improved material conditions, or the application of psychological knowledge. These are essential in the deliverance of men from the power of evil. But in themselves they cannot produce the inner change which is described as "a new creation" (5:17).

All these had resulted from Paul's ministry to the Corinthians, and he could appeal to their experience.

13-14. ***In What Were You Less Favored.***—The apostle here reverts to the subject of the support which he had refused to take from the Corinthian church. The misrepresentation of this generosity had stung him, particularly the suggestion that in refusing their money he showed he thought less of them. To refuse a gift may be an act of superiority, and the refusal may hurt. Paul may even have had the feeling this his refusal had done them a wrong; yet he does not even now purpose on his forthcoming visit to take their money for his own support. The reason he gives is **I seek not yours, but you.** The

15 And I will very gladly spend and be spent for you; though the more abundantly I love you, the less I be loved.

parents, but parents for their children. 15 I will most gladly spend and be spent for your souls. If I love you the more, am I to

expected to care for their **parents;** rather, **parents** must provide for the needs of their **children** without asking repayment. Paul does not mean that children should never do anything for their parents, but that it is natural for parents to bring up a family in the spirit of unselfish giving and not ask financial reward or support.

The rule Paul states would have prevented him from accepting help from any church, if strictly applied, but we know that he did accept gifts from other churches to support him at Corinth (11:7-9). Here he simply assures his readers that they are his children in the faith, and that he is glad to labor for their good without expecting any return in money or support. That he can call the entire church his children indicates that the great majority were his converts.

15. He is ready to go beyond the natural obligation. He says: **I** [the pronoun is expressed in Greek for emphasis, perhaps for contrast with the intruders at Corinth] **will most gladly spend and be spent for your souls,** i.e., for your spiritual good. The words **most gladly** and "be completely spent" express the eager readiness to do whatever will help the Corinthians, no matter what it costs him. **Spend** refers to Paul's manual labor to

heart of a true minister speaks in his words. He does not intend to enlist people for what they can give, or for any external advantage which he or his church may gain from them. It is their very selves he hopes to win for Christ and the kingdom. Liberality in money, instead of being a channel for wholehearted devotion to Christ, may easily become a substitute for it. Generosity has often covered a multitude of sins. It is sometimes harder to reach a man's heart with the gospel than it is to reach his pocket with an appeal for money. Moreover, because money is essential for the support of the church, fear to offend the rich may tempt a minister to trim his message; not to mention the fact that the man who can give generously may claim the right to dictate in spiritual matters. Whatever it may involve, the souls of his people are a minister's first concern. **Not yours, but you** is the principle here, as in all personal relationships. Friendships are unreal where friends are valued for what they give us, not for what they are in themselves or for what we can help to make them. The same principle is also essential in the home.

Children ought not to lay up for their parents, but parents for their children. The true parent does not think of his own future security, but of the needs of his children. He does not look for material returns, or even for gratitude. The real satisfactions of life are in what we are able to do for others. Love which "seeketh not its own" will often produce the results which possessive love seeks in vain. This selfless love is Paul's motive power.

15*a*. *Most Gladly for Your Souls.*—For that Paul will spend all his energy, even to the point of exhaustion. He will use to the utmost both mind and body. The love that would rescue the souls of men is an exhausting passion, though the love itself is never exhausted. The cross of Christ is the inevitable symbol of redemptive love. Jesus was conscious of this drain upon his spirit (Luke 8:46). The taunt of his enemies when he hung on the cross stated a truth more profound than they realized: "He saved others; he cannot save himself" (Mark 15:31). He who would save others must not attempt to save himself. He must be ready to expend time, strength, interest, and sympathy to the limit. Nothing else will reach the level of redemptive service. Moses was ready to be blotted out of God's book for the sake of his people (Exod. 32:32). Paul was possessed of the same willingness to plumb the depths of self-sacrifice (Rom. 9:3).

Yet at the heart of such love there is an imperishable joy. **Most gladly** is Paul's reference to it. Every mother who spends herself for her children, every man who gives his life for a great cause, knows this inward happiness. Love of this nature is "the top of the fullness of life," as a soldier described his feeling in the sacrificial service of his country. While Paul asks for no return he comments on the strange fact that he should be blamed for his generosity.

15*b*. *If I Love You the More, Am I to Be Loved the Less?*—Something must have been wrong with the spirit of the church if generosity produced this result. But those who give themselves for the good of others must be prepared for such a reaction. There is often a secret pride in people which makes them resent the necessity of being helped. It should make us careful lest our kindness have in it any trace of

16 But be it so, I did not burden you: nevertheless, being crafty, I caught you with guile.

17 Did I make a gain of you by any of them whom I sent unto you?

18 I desired Titus, and with *him* I sent a brother. Did Titus make a gain of you? walked we not in the same spirit? *walked we* not in the same steps?

be loved the less?
16 But granting that I myself did not burden you, I was crafty, you say, and got the better of you by guile.
17 Did I take advantage of you through any of those whom I sent to you?
18 I urged Titus to go, and sent the brother with him. Did Titus take advantage of you? Did we not act in the same spirit? Did we not take the same steps?

support himself, his faithful ministry, and the hardship he has to endure to carry on his work. The unhappy question in vs. 15*b* answers the one in 11:11, and points out how unnatural it is for the Corinthians to respond with lessening love to his continually shown and eagerly given affection for them. At the time he writes, this coldness is their attitude, but by putting it in a question he avoids blunt condemnation and leaves the way open for them to change and meet love with love.

16. In vss. 16-18 Paul denies the charge that in money matters he had been dishonest (cf. 11:20; I Cor. 16:2-4, which show that he had realized the danger of such suspicion, and was trying to avoid it). The attack seems to have been directed against Paul's intention regarding the collection. The Corinthians will have to grant that he himself **did not burden** them by directly asking support or seeking gifts for himself. But the charge was still made that he was **crafty,** resourcefully unscrupulous, and **got the better of** them **by guile,** i.e., he had them take up a collection for Jerusalem, but he intended to get at least part of it for himself. The words **you say** (RSV) are not in the Greek; they are supplied to make clear that this is a charge being made at Corinth. Perhaps it would be better to supply "they say," i.e., the opponents of Paul are saying this to the Corinthians.

17. Paul can ask with confidence concerning the honesty of his messengers; no ground for suspicion of them can be found. He did not **take advantage of** them through his messengers. The question makes it clear that he had repeatedly sent such messengers to Corinth, to carry letters and to help the young church.

18. Paul affirms the honesty of Titus and an unnamed Christian brother. Titus went more than once to Corinth. He seems to have gone there to start the collection, perhaps even before Paul wrote I Corinthians (8:6). He carried the "stern letter" (2:13; 7:6, 13-15). He will return later to lead in completing the collection (8:6, 16-24). The visit meant here is perhaps the first one, when the collection was started. The questions asked indicate that Titus is above reproach, and that the Corinthians have seen in him a quality

superiority or any suggestion that we are laying those we help under an obligation. A father who makes his son feel that in what he does for him he is bestowing a favor, will produce in the son a resentment that will spoil their relationship.

16-19. ***Did I Take Advantage of You?***—The suggestion had evidently been made that while Paul did not take the money, it came to him through others. This charge Paul dismisses. Titus and he were one in this matter, and adopted the same method. But lest they think him on the defensive, he adds, **It is in the sight of God that we have been speaking.** He has no need to argue his case before the Corinthians; he stands at God's bar of judgment, and what he has said has been said out of his consciousness of union with Christ. It is what God thinks of him that matters. Then why speak? He has done it for the sake of helping them, of restoring the broken relationship, of getting rid of the poison that has been infecting their minds and disintegrating the Christian fellowship. If in defense of our own conduct we were not concerned with self-justification but only with clearing away obstacles to that fellowship, a climate would be created in which differences might be dissolved. It might awaken a sense of shame in those who have a grudge against us. To clear away obstacles to fellowship may involve humiliation, but it is the only way of reconciliation. Paul's one desire is for a relationship in which there will be no shadows from either side. The final word, **beloved,** breaks from his heart like sunlight through clouds, and should surely have produced the atmosphere he hoped for.

19 Again, think ye that we excuse ourselves unto you? we speak before God in
Christ: but *we do* all things, dearly beloved,
for your edifying.
20 For I fear, lest, when I come, I shall
not find you such as I would, and *that* I
shall be found unto you such as ye would
not: lest *there be* debates, envyings, wraths,
strifes, backbitings, whisperings, swellings,
tumults:

19 Have you been thinking all along that
we have been defending ourselves before
you? It is in the sight of God that we have
been speaking in Christ, and all for your
upbuilding, beloved. **20** For I fear that perhaps I may come and find you not what I
wish, and that you may find me not what
you wish; that perhaps there may be quarreling, jealousy, anger, selfishness, slander,

---

of spirit and action fully in harmony with the unselfish and devoted service of Paul to them.

D. Appeal to Repent Before Paul Comes (12:19–13:10)

1. He Seeks to Move the Corinthians to Repent (12:19-21)

19. Paul now begins a series of final warnings, uttered in anticipation of his impending third visit. Vs. 19*a* may be a question or a statement; in the context it may be better to take it as a statement. "All along," Paul says (reading πάλαι; but some MSS read πάλιν, "again"), "you have been thinking that we have been defending ourselves before you." Indeed Paul *has* been defending himself. But his interest has not been in mere self-vindication; as he says at the end of the verse, he has been seeking the upbuilding of his readers in Christian faith and understanding; he has been making clear his integrity and apostolic duty in order to help the Corinthians to take the right attitude, so that he will not have to discipline them when he comes. His aim has not been merely to please their whims; rather, he has spoken **in the sight of God,** to whom, rather than to the Corinthians, he is responsible; and he has spoken **in** vital union with **Christ,** a bond that keeps him from pride, parade, and crafty guile. All that he has said has been spoken for their good, even when he has had to speak in stern rebuke. The word **beloved** reflects the love behind his sternness.

20. In this and the next verse he tells why he has spoken so earnestly. The Corinthians need upbuilding; indeed, they need more than that. They need to repent, change their spirit, drop their pride, and turn from their troublemaking and immoral practices. Paul reveals here his consciousness that he has the authority, and in crisis the duty, to exercise strong discipline. Either there must be a radical change in the Corinthians or he must come and take vigorous measures to correct conditions. He warns them that if he comes and finds they are not as he wants them to be—i.e., if they have not changed—they will find him not as they wish—i.e., they will find him stern to punish.

Paul mentions eight sins that he fears he may find: strife or **quarreling, jealousy,** outbursts of **anger,** contentions or factions, railings or evil speaking (**slander** in the RSV is probably too narrow a word for all the verbal reprisals and vicious talk meant by

---

20-21. ***I Fear that Perhaps I May Come and Find You Not What I Wish.***—Paul admits that he is afraid, but fear is not always an ignoble thing. Some fears are awakened by knowledge of the evil of the world, where the human heart is prone to temptation. A true minister will be sensitive to any signs of moral weakness among his flock and will be honest in dealing with them. Paul was a realist and called wrong things by their right names. He wants to be his best and he wants the Corinthians to be their best. But he knows what vile weeds can spring up even in a Christian fellowship where lovelessness and pride have quenched the Spirit of God. The sins he mentions are those he details as "works of the flesh" in Gal. 5:19-21. They are the weeds that spring up in the garden of the soul when it is left untended. A field cleared out of the jungle goes back to the wild when it is left uncultivated. The human heart becomes the abode of all kinds of evil when we cease to fight against sin and to cultivate the fruits of the Spirit. Jesus' picture of the house out of which the evil spirit had been cast is for warning

21 *And* lest, when I come again, my God will humble me among you, and *that* I shall bewail many which have sinned already, and have not repented of the uncleanness and fornication and lasciviousness which they have committed.

gossip, conceit, and disorder. 21 I fear that when I come again my God may humble me before you, and I may have to mourn over many of those who sinned before and have not repented of the impurity, immorality, and licentiousness which they have practiced.

καταλαλιαί), **whisperings** or furtive scandalmongering of all kinds, **swellings** with pride and a false sense of self-importance, and **tumults** or disorderly wranglings among Christians. The picture is that of a selfish, proud, arrogant, jealous, unkind, quarrelsome, and disorderly church. In a word, it lacked the mind of Christ and did not even know its lack.

21. But even yet Paul has not said the worst. There is longstanding, unrepentant, and brazen sexual immorality, which Paul describes in three overlapping words as **impurity, fornication,** and wanton **licentiousness.** This problem evidently was serious when Paul made his second visit (13:2), which was so painful and futile (cf. Exeg. on 2:1). He fears that many of these sinners will still be unrepentant when he comes; note, however, his faith that there is forgiveness for such sins if repentance is real. If they still persist in such sin when he comes on his third visit, his God will **humble** him **again** (as God did on the second visit when Paul failed to bring the church back to its senses). This does not mean merely that he will look foolish and futile in the presence of the Corinthians (**before you**), but that it will be a defeat for him if he cannot get his converts to return to the right way of life. Their ruin is his defeat. If there are still such unrepentant sinners, he will **have to mourn over** them as spiritually lost or dead. He implies that they will have to be excluded from the church. As a last resort, he will take such a decisive disciplinary step; cf. I Cor. 5:1-5.

The shocking picture of vss. 20-21, which are addressed to the entire Corinthian church, can hardly apply to the situation described in 1:24; 3:3; 7:4, 11, 15-16; 8:7. These two verses constitute one of the strongest arguments for the view that chs. 10–13 are not a part of the "thankful letter," but rather belong to the "stern letter." The attitude of Paul's opponents fostered the pride and quarrelsomeness at Corinth, and they do not seem to have condemned the astoundingly lax moral standards concerning which the Corinthians were so complacent and arrogant. These verses show clearly that Paul's leadership was precisely what this church needed.

(Matt. 12:43-45). The bitterest hatreds are often those that spring in the intimacies of friendship when a rift has been allowed to widen. Coleridge describes this.

> Alas! they had been friends in youth,
> But whispering tongues can poison truth;
> And constancy lives in realms above;
> And life is thorny and youth is vain;
> And to be wroth with one we love
> Doth work like madness in the brain.[2]

Because of the very intimacy of the Christian fellowship, the most violent quarrels can arise in a church that has become divided. Loyalty to the faith turns into contention and strife, the more intense because of this loyalty, if orthodox belief comes to be regarded as more important than Christian love. In the same way marriage creates an intimacy which is precious but also perilous, as many a broken home reveals. Because of it the marriage bond needs to be kept alive by respect and courtesy and maintained by a continuous habit of forgiveness.

The roots of broken fellowship, and the evils that spring from it, do not grow on the surface and are not produced merely by the frictions of living and working together. They spring from the flesh, from rejection of the moral standards and the fundamental loyalties of love. Paul sees that this may well happen in the case of the Corinthians. That such immoralities should find their way into the church is a possibility hard to accept. But the Christian faith does not rest on a sentimental belief in human goodness. It rests on the knowledge of the inherent sinfulness of human nature apart from redeeming grace. This fact makes the gospel both credible and necessary. Robert Browning finds in such a

[2] "Christabel," l. 408.

13 This *is* the third *time* I am coming
to you. In the mouth of two or three
witnesses shall every word be established.
2 I told you before, and foretell you, as
if I were present, the second time; and being absent now I write to them which here-
tofore have sinned, and to all other, that, if
I come again, I will not spare:
3 Since ye seek a proof of Christ speaking in me, which to you-ward is not weak,
but is mighty in you.

13 This is the third time I am coming
to you. Any charge must be sustained
by the evidence of two or three witnesses.
2 I warned those who sinned before and all
the others, and I warn them now while absent, as I did when present on my second
visit, that if I come again I will not spare
them — 3 since you desire proof that Christ
is speaking in me. He is not weak in deal-

---

2. On His Third Visit He Will Not Spare Sinners (13:1-4)

13:1. There is a crisis at Corinth. It is no mere dispute as to which good leader shall have their loyalty. The intruders who oppose Paul have been arrogant and have encouraged the Corinthians in a like arrogance. The church includes brazen sinners and is a nest of pride, quarrelsomeness, and moral disorder. They not only sin thus; they have no shame about it. Paul knows he must act sternly if they do not change. So he warns them that on his impending third visit (cf. 12:14), he will discipline unsparingly if necessary. He quotes Deut. 19:15 to warn that trials will be held, witnesses heard, and penalties imposed; as 12:21 indicates, this will mean exclusion from the church if there is no repentance (cf. I Cor. 5:1-5). Some interpreters have taken the **witnesses** to refer to Paul's two previous visits and his impending third visit, but the reference is rather to witnesses who will be heard when trials are held.

2. In 12:21 it is indicated that unashamed immorality was present when Paul made his painful **second visit** (see Exeg. on 2:1). Here he clearly confirms that fact, and adds that he then sternly **warned** the sinners. He warned also **all the others,** i.e., all the other Corinthian Christians who have been sinfully complacent and tolerant of the openly flaunted sins of these immoral people. The existence of such bold sinning and blameworthy tolerance in the church shows how hard it was for Gentile Christians to break away from the sexual laxity characteristic of their environment. It was from the O.T. and the Jews, rather than from the Greeks, that the Christian faith inherited the strong standard of pure living. Paul now, **while absent,** but preparing to **come again,** warns the sinners that if he comes again, as he plans to do soon, he **will not spare them,** but will proceed to severe discipline. He hopes that this warning will lead them to repent before he comes.

3. I will act sternly and not spare you, Paul says, **since you desire proof that Christ is speaking in me.** Evidently at Corinth it was said that he talks impressively, especially in letters (10:10), but as his failure to settle the revolt on his second visit showed, lacks power to do anything decisive. **You** refers to the Corinthian church as a whole; the hostile feeling toward him is general. This fact supports the theory that chs. 10–13 come from the "stern letter" which preceded the writing of chs. 1–9. The **proof** the church wants is

---

realistic view of human nature an argument for the Christian faith.

I still, to suppose it true, for my part,
See reasons and reasons; this, to begin:
'Tis the faith that launched point-blank her dart
At the head of a lie—taught Original Sin,
The Corruption of Man's Heart.[3]

13:1-3. ***This Is the Third Time.***—Paul had already made two visits to Corinth. He now proposes to come a third time, when he will deal drastically with the offenders but will demand witnesses before he takes disciplinary measures. This drastic action will be proof that Christ is speaking through him. The Corinthians will realize the power of the Spirit in him, to convince of sin, of righteousness, and of judgment (John 16:8). The power to unveil sin and to break its hold is part of the power of Christ. And they had already experienced it. Their lives had been transformed by the word of the gospel which Paul had preached. What they

[3] "Gold Hair," st. xxx.

4 For though he was crucified through weakness, yet he liveth by the power of God. For we also are weak in him, but we shall live with him by the power of God toward you.

ing with you, but is powerful in you. 4 For he was crucified in weakness, but lives by the power of God. For we are weak in him, but in dealing with you we shall live with him by the power of God.

some decisive action or sign; Paul indicates they will get it, and in a way they may not like, for it will come in stern discipline.

They know that Paul has spoken of Christ as present and active in him (cf. Gal. 2:20). But they see no evidence for his claim. Vs. 3*b* seems to reflect a saying at Corinth: "We see no power of Christ at work in Paul, but in us, with our spiritual gifts [cf. I Cor. 12; 14], which show divine power at work among us, Christ is plainly present and powerful." Paul refers to their talk, and probably with some irony, for as vs. 4 goes on to say, they understand neither the way God's power works through weakness nor the fact that God's power is really present in Paul.

4. The combination of weakness and power in the career of Paul has its parallel in Christ. Through a life and ministry of apparent **weakness,** and even of actual suffering that reached a climax in crucifixion, Jesus came to the Resurrection and the position of **power** at the right hand of God (cf. Rom. 1:4; I Cor. 6:14). This was the working of **the power of God** in his life, and is therefore the God-given pattern for the ministry and triumph of Christ's apostles. So Paul is content to follow this same path (cf. I Cor. 4:6-13). Outwardly regarded, and judged by men's treatment of him, Paul is **weak in him,** i.e.,

had already known of the fruits of the Spirit should be evidence that Christ was speaking in him.

4. *In Weakness the Power of God.*—Paul's confidence in the power he possesses, in spite of apparent weakness, does not rest on any flimsy foundation of self-confidence. It rests on the fact of the Cross. There Christ died through the weakness he shared with all humanity. In his flesh he had no exemption from the suffering and death to which human beings are subject in a sinful and perilous world. But through that very **weakness** there was released in him **the power of God** to conquer the sin that slew him and the death that destroyed him. The picture of his own death and of its results, which Christ had in mind as he faced the Cross, was that of a seed sown in the ground, where it is stripped of the sheath which holds the germ of life and so rises from the soil that imprisons it to find a larger life (John 12:24). It was not in spite of weakness that Christ's power was released; it was through weakness. Because Paul is in Christ the same process is at work in him. Through his surrender to Christ he died. The old self perished under the judgment of the Cross; he was there stripped of all pride in himself, in his own virtues, and of all trust in good works. But through that death the Spirit of Christ rose within him to create a new life, instinct with the power of God.

The death and resurrection of Christ were more than a drama for his contemplation or an act whose blessings he appropriated. They were a process repeated in his own experience. "We were buried therefore with him by baptism into death, so that as Christ was raised from the dead by the glory of the Father, we too might walk in newness of life" (Rom. 6:4). This is the essence of the conversion experience. It is to die because we are crucified with Christ, and through death to live because he lives in us. The repetition in us, through his indwelling, of Christ's earthly experience has been expressed in a few verses by Johann Scheffler, a seventeenth-century mystic.

> Though Christ a thousand times
>   In Bethlehem be born,
> If he's not born in thee,
>   Thy soul is still forlorn.
>
> The cross on Golgotha
>   Will never save thy soul,
> The cross in thine own heart
>   Alone can make thee whole.
>
> Christ rose not from the dead,
>   Christ still is in the grave
> If thou for whom he died
>   Art still of sin the slave.[4]

Paul is sure that this power of God, whose Spirit lives in him, will make him strong. The assurance is one result of the experience related in 12:9. In Corinth that power will come into

[4] "The Cherubic Pilgrim," Part I, sts. lxi-lxiii.

5 Examine yourselves, whether ye be in the faith; prove your own selves. Know ye not your own selves, how that Jesus Christ is in you, except ye be reprobates?	5 Examine yourselves, to see whether you are holding to your faith. Test yourselves. Do you not realize that Jesus Christ is in you? — unless indeed you fail to meet

in union of life and purpose with Christ. But in Christ, Paul has been raised from the death of sin, and now **the power of God** is effectively at work in him; when he comes to Corinth, the power of God given through the risen Christ will enable him to deal decisively with the unrepented sin and pride of this misguided church.

3. Let Them Do Right So that He Need Not Be Severe (13:5-10)

5. In this concluding discussion of the crisis Paul urges the Corinthians to test themselves. He hopes that they will pass the test; to do so, however, they must repent; and to bring about this change of attitude has been his purpose in all that he has written

---

action. The insights that came to Paul were never merely truths to be stored in his mind or used in his preaching; they were always lights by which he walked, truths by which he lived. Faith is not complete till through experiment it has become experience.

5a. Examine Yourselves.—Paul's final plea to the Corinthians is that instead of throwing about their charges against him, they should let in the light of truth on their own hearts and conduct. They must **examine** and **test** themselves. It is useless to hold standards that we do not apply. The Christian church must continually keep itself under the judgment of Christ. It is fatally easy to make the acceptance of the Christian faith a substitute for living by it. Jesus issued this warning, "Why call ye me, Lord, Lord, and do not the things which I say?" (Luke 6:46). But a man must conduct his own self-examination. We may show him where his conduct is wrong, but conviction of sin is not reached till he has seen his sin and condemned himself. Only as we are willing to bring our inmost thoughts, feelings, and daily conduct under the scrutiny of Christ can we know ourselves. Some people live in a fantasy world of self-approval. They take shelter behind the sense of their own virtues and so try to avoid the self-criticism which sincerity with truth would bring. They are insulated from the power of the truth, as a man who stands on a glass plate from the power of a live electric wire. There is always a temptation for people to live from day to day on the surface of life, reacting to the pressure of events and circumstances without ever asking what they believe, or what they value most, or what kind of persons they are becoming. Only exposure to the light of Christ, which strips away all illusions, will open the way for his healing and redeeming power.

Self-examination need not be morbid. It is not morbid for a man to take stock of his business at the end of a year, or to be examined by a physician in order to discover the state of his health. It is vital to examine ourselves, provided we do not brood upon defects but take steps to put them right.

How the Corinthians should test themselves to find out whether they were holding to the faith Paul does not say. Various tests might be applied. They might ask the question whether in reality the convictions of the Christian faith are still alive in their minds. These beliefs were not summarized in Paul's day as they are in ours —e.g., in the Apostles' Creed—but they are all in his teaching. The essential beliefs of the Christian faith all hang together and all are vital. A creed which begins with "I believe in God the Father Almighty," must end with "I believe in . . . the life everlasting," and contain all that lies between. The faith of the Corinthians may have been adulterated by beliefs that were purely Jewish, such as the necessity of obeying the Jewish law in order to be a Christian. Belief in the divinity of Christ may have been qualified by Jewish racialism, so that his universality was limited.

The loss of Christian beliefs has serious effects on moral conduct. These may be slow to appear. A certain level of Christian conduct can be sustained by habit, tradition, social conventions, or respect for the moral law. In some cases Christian values are held apart from faith in Christ; but they are like the afterglow in the sky when the sun has set. They will not endure in a pagan environment without the convictions of faith. A plant will not continue to flourish in a shallow soil where it has no roots (Matt. 13:21). Conduct must be examined to find out whether the beliefs that underlie it are themselves Christian and are vital. Our real beliefs are what we live by. Theoretical belief can exist along with practical atheism; e.g., the habit of worry discloses lack of faith in the sovereignty of God. A pupil

6 But I trust that ye shall know that we are not reprobates.
7 Now I pray to God that ye do no evil; not that ye should appear approved, but that ye should do that which is honest, though we be as reprobates.

the test! 6 I hope you will find out that we have not failed. 7 But we pray God that you may not do wrong — not that we may appear to have met the test, but that you may do what is right, though we may seem

(vs. 10). He addresses the entire church, and begins by vigorously urging: **Examine yourselves. . . . Test yourselves.** Both times the word **yourselves** stands first in the Greek; with great emphasis Paul is saying: You keep looking for faults in me; you keep suspecting my motives and belittling my work; yet it is yourselves that you had better be testing; it is your own position before Christ that is in danger. By using the present imperative (πειράζετε, δοκιμάζετε) he says: Keep examining and testing yourselves, to see **whether** you are **in the faith,** i.e., whether you are really Christians or have forfeited your position. Or **do you not realize that Jesus Christ is in you?** Here are two ways of describing a Christian. He is **in the faith,** and the risen Christ is in him and is the Lord of his life (cf. Gal. 2:20; Col. 1:27). Can the Corinthians say this? Paul still hopes that the test will result favorably; in other words, he still strongly hopes that they will repent. They will do so, **unless indeed,** as he sadly admits is possible, they **fail to meet the test.** (The words δόκιμος and ἀδόκιμος, used of metals and other substances as tested and approved or rejected, are applied in this passage to Christian lives as passing or failing to pass the test.)

6. Paul adds: But **I hope that** before I come and have to resort to discipline **you will find out,** as you have not done thus far, **that we have not** failed to pass the test. I.e., he hopes that before he arrives, they will realize that he is a minister of Christ whom God has tested and approved; if they realize this, they will repent, and he will not have to be severe with them.

7. Paul's great concern is not for his own success or reputation. It is rather that the Corinthians **may not do wrong.** Even his hope in vs. 6, that they will realize that he is an approved minister of Christ, was not a selfish one, but had their good in view. So here he says anew that he wants them to **do what is right** (καλόν), even though he may **seem to have failed.** This last clause literally reads "that you may do the good, while we may be as rejected." As in Rom. 9:3, he is so concerned for other men's good that what happens to him is unimportant. He does not mean that he has failed, nor does he think that he

in a mission school asked the missionary if he really believed that God is our Father and that he cares for each one of us. On being assured that he did, the pupil asked, "Then why do you worry so much?"

The question whether we are holding to the faith might be changed to the question whether the faith is holding us. How far do we find in ourselves the need and desire for prayer, for worship, and for the message of the Bible? The quality of our conscious needs is the test of our progress. The more knowledge we have the more we seek. The more the love of Christ grows in the heart the more we are compelled to seek his presence and commune with him. Goodness in conduct is hard to assess, and contemplation of our virtues leads to spiritual pride. The final conclusion an honest Christian will reach about his virtues is that he has none of his own and nothing good in him which is not of the grace of God. But we can discover by examining ourselves what beliefs we genuinely hold and how far they determine our attitude toward life and one another. The result may be a source of comfort.

5*b*. ***Jesus Christ Is in You.***—If a man believes that Christ is dwelling in his heart, the thought will rally his gratitude, his love, and his desire to obey the guiding of the Spirit. It will make him strong to meet difficulties; it will make him proof against temptations; e.g., he will realize that the misuse of the body in immoral conduct is sacrilege, the profanation of a temple (I Cor. 6:19).

6-7. *That You May Do What Is Right.*—The failure of which Paul speaks in vs. 6 is not the failure to hold by the truth; it is the failure to convince the Corinthians of his apostolic author-

8 For we can do nothing against the truth, but for the truth.
9 For we are glad, when we are weak, and ye are strong: and this also we wish, *even* your perfection.

to have failed. 8 For we cannot do anything against the truth, but only for the
truth. 9 For we are glad when we are weak
and you are strong. What we pray for is

must fail in order for them to gain true life; but his own lot is unimportant as compared with his love for them and his hope for their mature obedience to Christ.

8. This statement is not so general as it sounds. As used by Paul, the word **truth** refers to the gospel message that he preaches. He means that he cannot bring himself to do anything, even for personal advantage, which would hinder the acceptance and progress of the gospel. His aim is always to further the knowledge and acceptance of this message. This explains why in vs. 7 he is willing to let his own personal interests drop out of sight.

9. Paul says on other occasions that he suffers and endures weakness for the Corinthians (1:6; 4:12). If only they will take the right attitude, and grow **strong** in faith and obedience to God, so that they do not need Paul's stern disciplinary action, he will gladly accept the role in which he seems **weak** and not needed. His earnest prayer here takes up and puts in strong positive form the hope of vs. 7; he prays for their **perfection** (KJV). **Improvement** (RSV) is not strong enough to translate κατάρτισιν, which refers to the attainment of religious and moral perfection. Nothing less than this perfection is his prayer for them (cf. I Cor. 1:8; I Thess. 3:11-13).

ity. He hopes they may be convinced that his power as an apostle is such that he can exercise effective discipline. But his primary concern is that they should do the right. If they do the right he is ready to rejoice in it, even if this should leave him no opportunity to show his power; or even if they should still reject his authority, and doubt his possession of the power which the indwelling Christ bestows. As a true servant of Christ he is ready to take a back seat, even to be discredited, if Christ should be glorified. Like John the Baptist watching the crowds leaving him to gather about Jesus, Paul would have said, "He must increase, but I must decrease" (John 3:30). The suppression of self in the interests of the kingdom of God and the good of men is essential to the full power of the Christian life and of the Christian ministry. A Christian minister particularly must be prepared to welcome signs of the work of God's Spirit in the hearts of people though his own part in it is unrecognized or even explicitly denied. Christ himself refused to disown one who was not a follower, but whose work showed spiritual fruits (Mark 9:39). However humbling the fact may be, the work of the kingdom is often done by those who scorn the church. Social reform has often been brought about by the efforts of those who were indifferent or even hostile to the church. They have owed their inspiration to its teaching, though they were unconscious of the fact. God is at work through many channels, and often through those which are independent of our accredited Christian agencies. In his attitude toward the Corinthians Paul reveals the large-mindedness of faith, as well as its honesty.

8. ***For We Cannot Do Anything Against the Truth, but Only for the Truth.***—This is not intended as a statement of the fact, itself true and worth remembering, that in the end the truth will win. Here rather is the real secret of patience amid discouragements. What Paul seeks to make clear is that his one concern is for the gospel. However they may disclaim his authority, that the Corinthians should in their obedience to the truth which is in Christ take the right course is all he asks.

9. ***We Are Glad.***—Paul will even rejoice in his own apparent weakness if it should appear by their conduct that they are strong. His suppression of self reaches the point not merely of accepting humiliation but of welcoming it, if his main object is secured, which is their good. This capacity to live outside of himself in the lives of others is the final result of the process by which "a man in Christ" becomes "a new creation" (5:17). The whole of the passage which ends with this statement reveals the extent to which Christ and all that he lived and died for had become the center of Paul's life, from which his inspiration and direction were drawn. This is the secret not only of being fully used by God for the ends of his kingdom, but of becoming most fully our true selves. A man in Christ is a man who by losing himself has found himself.

10 Therefore I write these things being absent, lest being present I should use sharpness, according to the power which the Lord hath given me to edification, and not to destruction.

11 Finally, brethren, farewell. Be perfect, be of good comfort, be of one mind, live in peace; and the God of love and peace shall be with you.

your improvement. 10 I write this while I am away from you, in order that when I come I may not have to be severe in my use of the authority which the Lord has given me for building up and not for tearing down.

11 Finally, brethren, farewell. Mend your ways, heed my appeal, agree with one another, live in peace, and the God of love

---

10. This concluding sentence carries a note of authority like that in 10:2, 11; 13:2. While Paul's patience and love (and perplexity) have seemed to mark him as weak, he possesses by God's gift the power to act sternly when required. But he delays coming for a short time, and writes this "stern letter" (**this** includes all said in chs. 10–13), in an earnest effort to bring the Corinthians to repentance, so that when he arrives in Corinth he will not have to be severe and even expel some from the church. God gave him **authority,** but it was given with the primary purpose of **building up;** only as a last resort is it God's will that he use it **for tearing down,** i.e., to punish and expel unrepentant sinners (cf. 10:8).

Thus chs. 10–13, which probably belong to the "stern letter," end on a note of cautious hope. As we read 2:1-9 and 7:8-12, which are parts of the "thankful letter," we see that the "stern letter," aided by Titus' appeal, effected its purpose, and brought the Corinthians back to an active loyalty to Paul.

V. Conclusion (13:11-14)

A. Final Exhortations and Greetings (13:11-13)

11. If chs. 10–13 are part of the "stern letter," 13:11-14 may well be the conclusion of that letter. It is possible, however, that these verses concluded the "thankful letter" (chs. 1–9). The final exhortations and greetings are brief, pointed, and friendly. The address **brethren** is warm in tone and describes the readers as fellow Christians. The word translated **farewell** (χαίρετε) may equally well mean "rejoice," as it does in other N.T.

---

10. *I Write This in Order That. . . .*—By writing to them thus Paul wishes to give the Corinthians a chance to put their house in order before he comes. He is sure of his authority and is ready to use it without stint. But he hopes that the effect of his letter will be such that he will not need to use this power. Christ gave it to him **for building up, and not for tearing down.** The real work of the ministry is constructive. The plow and harrow are necessary in tilling the ground, but the harvest is the real object of the farmer's labor. John the Baptist acknowledged the limitations of his ministry. He could hew down the forest; he could not turn the cleared ground into a fruitful field. "I have baptized you with water; but he will baptize you with the Holy Spirit" (Mark 1:8). Through the indwelling Spirit a Christian minister is a channel of this constructive energy. Denunciatory preaching is tempting; it is easy and can be arresting and dramatic. A well-known preacher in London used to draw crowds each week by denouncing the sins of society, and society flocked to hear him because he tickled their appetite for sensation. The diagnosis of disease can be very interesting, but what people need is health.

The building of Christian character is a creative task. It may be slow and difficult; but it is constructive work which will last. The patient building of Christian fellowship is a vital aim of pastoral work. From it the frontiers can be extended, as the consolidation of a position in enemy territory constitutes a springboard for further advance. This fellowship is the only means by which individual Christian character can be nourished and developed.

11-12. *Finally, Brethren, Farewell.*—Paul ends his letter, as always, on a note of encouragement. If the Corinthians will mend their ways (see Exeg.) and determine to live in harmony with one another, God will be with them. Harmony is not an easy thing to achieve, either in an orchestra, in a community, or in a congregation. The problem of living together becomes acute whenever people live or work in close

12 Greet one another with a holy kiss.
13 All the saints salute you.

and peace will be with you. 12 Greet one
another with a holy kiss. 13 All the saints
greet you.

passages (cf. Phil. 4:4). If translated "farewell," it is not a mere formal word for "good-by," but means "May things go well with you." The next word (καταρτίζεσθε), a present imperative form, means (if passive) "be steadily perfected"; if in the middle voice, as it may be, it means "keep perfecting yourselves," or as Plummer translates, "work your way onwards to perfection" (*Second Epistle of Paul to Corinthians*). It says more than **mend your ways;** it urges steady positive advance to perfect living. **Heed my appeal** (lit., "be exhorted") is what παρακαλεῖσθε means if passive; if middle, "keep encouraging [exhorting] one another." **Be of one mind** is a warning against the divisive tendency so chronic at Corinth. **Live in peace** exhorts the readers to express in brotherly living the harmony of spirit that has just been urged. The word **and** implies, "and then, if you do these things constantly," **the God of love and peace will be with you.** Though Paul uses the exact phrase **the God of love** only here, the idea is frequent in his writing (cf. Rom. 5:8). He speaks of **the God of peace** elsewhere (cf. Rom. 15:33; Phil. 4:9; I Thess. 5:23). The peace here meant is the reconciliation with God and so with one another which God effects through the gift of his grace and the working of his Spirit (cf. Rom. 5:1; Eph. 2:14-18).

12. The practice of exchanging **a holy kiss** was evidently widespread in the early church (cf. Rom. 16:16; I Cor. 16:20; I Thess. 5:26; I Pet. 5:14). It was called **holy** (ἁγίῳ) because it was exchanged by the saints (ἅγιοι) during the service of worship, as a mark of brotherhood in the one faith.

13. All the saints are all the Christians in the place from which Paul is writing. This would be Ephesus if vss. 11-14 are part of the "stern letter," or Macedonia if they are part of the "thankful letter" (on **saints** as a designation for Christians see Exeg. on 1:1).

contact with one another, as in a home, a workshop, a church, a nation, and in the world itself. The difficulty of living together has been increased by the fact that modern developments and communications have made us all neighbors.

The key to the solution of this problem is found in the fellowship of the church, where people of different temperaments, classes, and nations are united by one spirit and purpose, while at the same time preserving freedom. It is part of the church's task to guard, deepen, and extend this fellowship till all the barriers that divide humanity are overcome. In the case of the Ephesians Paul could rejoice that "the middle wall of partition" between Jews and Gentiles—a very formidable barrier—had been broken down (Eph. 2:14).

The responsibility for creating harmony rests upon individual men and women and depends on their willingness to **agree with one another** and **live in peace.** Harmony demands a continual process of reconciliation, by which frictions and resentments are overcome. The fellowship of the church is the center from which in the long run the reconciling spirit flows into all human relationships. Only a united church has a vital message for a disunited world. It must present to the world the divine pattern of a free community, in which individual liberty and an integrated fellowship where the members bear one another's burdens are both preserved. God is behind this effort toward free community. He is **the God of love and peace.** Love is the motive power of his purpose, and we can fulfill that purpose only as his love becomes our motive power. The object of his love is peace—peace with him, and peace between man and man. That he is behind this effort is clear from the fact that the movement of the world is toward integration. What was like brushwood is growing into a tree. But the mass of men and nations can become a living community only in the measure in which they are rooted in faith and their efforts toward unity are directed and inspired by the Spirit of God. Obedience to his guiding is the condition of his blessing. We receive what he offers in the degree in which we are willing to do what he asks.

13. *All the Saints Greet You.*—This message would remind the church at Corinth that they belong to a wider fellowship—that of the universal church. They had been separated from the pagan community to which they belonged, like a "colony" of settlers in a foreign land. Paul uses this word about the Philippian church

14 The grace of the Lord Jesus Christ, and the love of God, and the communion of the Holy Ghost, *be* with you all. Amen.

¶ The second *epistle* to the Corinthians was written from Philippi, *a city* of Macedonia, by Titus and Lucas.

14 The grace of the Lord Jesus Christ and the love of God and the fellowship of[n] the Holy Spirit be with you all.

[n] Or *and participation in.*

B. Benediction (13:14)

14. This is the most elaborate benediction found in Paul's letters (Rom. 16:25-27 is an ascription of praise rather than a benediction). In most of the letters the closing benediction is a prayer that the grace of the risen Lord Jesus Christ may be with the readers. This common practice of Paul may explain why he mentions the grace of Christ first in this verse. Another reason, however, may be his awareness that it is through Christ's redeeming work, and its revelation of the love and saving purpose of God, that Christians come to know God's kindness.

The grace of the Lord Jesus Christ is the undeserved but freely given and powerfully effective favor of Christ, which not only opens the way to faith and new life, but also

(Phil. 3:20 Moffatt). The consciousness of this wider fellowship of the church would help to take them out of the isolation produced by a narrow environment. In such an environment people tend to lose perspective, to magnify trifles, and to get on each other's nerves. It sometimes happens to small isolated groups in the mission field. The knowledge that others are thinking of us, that our welfare matters to them, and that we have our part to play in a community that extends far beyond our immediate circle, is an encouragement and a challenge. The strength of isolated churches depends on the deepening consciousness of this universal fellowship in Christ.

14. ***Grace, Love, Fellowship.***—This is known as the apostolic benediction. It is found here in its most complete form (see Exeg.). Scholars are agreed that it should not be taken as a theological statement of the developed doctrine of the Trinity. It is the description of an experience which was the central fact of Paul's life. The order is significant.

It begins with the **grace of the Lord Jesus Christ,** in which Paul's experience was rooted. It was the grace of Christ which had sought him, found him, and forgiven him on the Damascus road. He had been pursued and captured by the "Tremendous Lover" in spite of his resistance and evasions. The grace of Jesus Christ, who was forever the Lord, remained the source of all Paul was and did. It kept alive in him the consciousness that he was a forgiven man whose burden had fallen upon Christ. It was the continual secret of penitence, humility, gratitude, and adoring love. It swept out of his soul all resentment, selfishness, and everything that would have proved a barrier between himself and others, or made him falter on the hard and discouraging road of discipleship and service. Matthew Arnold's picture of his father holds something of what it meant for Paul to think of Christ:

> We were weary, and we
> Fearful, and we in our march
> Fain to drop down and to die.
> Still thou turnedst, and still
> Beckonedst the trembler, and still
> Gavest the weary thy hand.[6]

The grace of Christ had made real to Paul **the love of God.** God was no longer mere Judge or Lawgiver, but Father, in whom holiness and love were one. There is no trace in Paul's mind of the doubts about the sovereignty of God which assail the modern mind, but after his meeting with Christ, he knew it was sovereign love that was on God's throne. D. M. Baillie says, "The most remarkable fact in the whole history of religious thought is this: that when the early Christians looked back and pondered on the dreadful thing that had happened, it made them think of the redeeming love of God. Not simply of the love of Jesus, but the love of God." [7] The experience of God's love in Christ was so vivid and compelling that perplexities could not bring despair, frustration could not limit, persecution could not make him feel an outcast, depression could not break his spirit (4:8-9). It was a love which altered his whole relationship to God and brought him into the liberty of a child of God. It was a bond that nothing could break, "neither death nor life, . . . nor things present, nor things to come,

[6] "Rugby Chapel," l. 128.
[7] *God Was in Christ,* p. 184.

continues to give the believer the daily help he needs. **The love of God** is here the outreaching, active good will by which God, who has sent Christ for man's salvation, freely gives all further gifts needed to complete his divine purpose to save men (cf. Rom. 5:8; 8:32). **The fellowship of the Holy Spirit** may mean here that fellowship with God and with the other members of Christ's church which is established and sustained in Christians by the presence and working of the Holy Spirit; or the phrase may refer to the **participation in,** the sharing in, the Holy Spirit enjoyed by all members of the church. This verse is not a formal statement of the doctrine of the Trinity, but it reflects the aspects of divine redemption and Christian experience which led the church later to formulate this doctrine as the best expression it could give to the Christian understanding of God.

In the closing words **with you all** Paul shows that he bears no grudge for any of the trials and sorrows that members of the church at Corinth have caused him. It is his closing prayer that all the rich resources of God's constant gracious presence may work with power to meet every need of all these Christians, whom he greatly loves and who deeply need divine help to live truly Christian lives.

. . . nor height, nor depth, nor anything else in all creation" (Rom. 8:38-39). The man who knows that he is loved by God can never be defeated by life.

The next experience was **the fellowship of the Holy Spirit.** This does not mean fellowship with the Spirit. It is a fellowship with God which he shares through the indwelling Spirit with those who are members of the body of Christ. The fellowship of the Holy Spirit is the true description of the church. The church is more than a social group with a common interest in religion, more than a gathering of people for worship, or an organization for the service of others. The name given to it at Pentecost was "the fellowship." It was a new divine creation, a community knit together by the Spirit. The power of the church comes through this fellowship—the power that sustains the individual Christian and takes him out of the loneliness in which he might feel that he was fighting a solitary battle and walking a solitary road. The life a Christian lives is the life in him of this indwelling Spirit, by whom also he is one with the church. It is through this fellowship that the church has power to preach the gospel and to make a Christian impact upon the world. Through it the church becomes the lips and eyes, the hands and feet and burning heart of the Lord Jesus.

From this threefold experience the doctrine of the Trinity developed. For Paul, and for the church still, the important thing is the experience; and the root of it all is expressed in John's description of the Incarnation: "The Word became flesh and dwelt among us, full of grace and truth; we have beheld his glory, glory as of the only Son from the Father. . . . And from his fullness have we all received, grace upon grace" (John 1:14, 16).

The Epistle to the

GALATIANS

Introduction and Exegesis by RAYMOND T. STAMM

Exposition by OSCAR FISHER BLACKWELDER

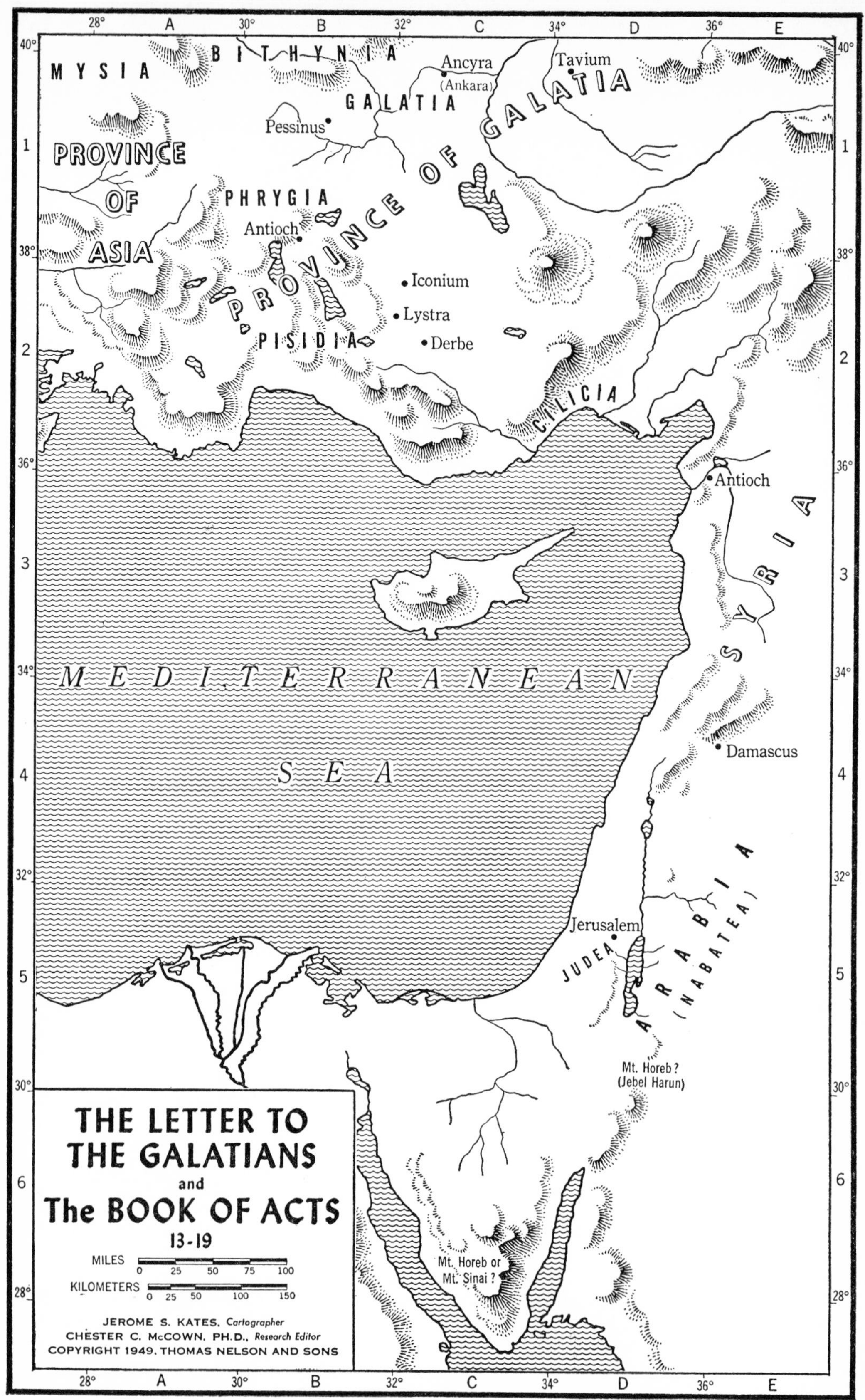

MYSIA
BITHYNIA
Ancyra
(Ankara)
Tavium
GALATIA
PROVINCE OF GALATIA
Pessinus
PROVINCE OF ASIA
PHRYGIA
Antioch
PROVINCE
Iconium
Lystra
Derbe
PISIDIA
CILICIA
Antioch
SYRIA
MEDITERRANEAN SEA
Damascus
Jerusalem
JUDEA
ARABIA
(NABATEA)
Mt. Horeb ?
(Jebel Harun)
Mt. Horeb or
Mt. Sinai ?
THE LETTER TO
THE GALATIANS
and
The BOOK OF ACTS
13-19
MILES
0 25 50 75 100
KILOMETERS
0 25 50 100 150
JEROME S. KATES, Cartographer
CHESTER C. McCOWN, PH.D., Research Editor
COPYRIGHT 1949, THOMAS NELSON AND SONS

GALATIANS

INTRODUCTION

Galatians is Paul's declaration of religious independence from men and dependence on God. It is the Magna Charta of the Christian faith, repudiating all authorities, institutions, customs, and laws that interfere with the direct access of the individual to his God. Written with no thought that it would become scripture to be read for thousands of years, this short letter speaks to the supreme need of all men in all times.

The question was: How can men, who are by nature sinful, win the favor of God, who is holy? Paul's answer was, They cannot. The only way to please God is to trust his grace and stop trying to acquire saving merit by obedience to law. God's forgiving love through Christ is the sole ground of salvation, and the only access to his eternal kingdom is by faith. The weakness of human nature foredooms all attempts at self-salvation. Rightness with God requires a new nature, and no man can remake himself. Only God through the Spirit of his Son can do that. Therefore glad acceptance of God's grace-gift of life is the only way to freedom from fear and sin, wrath and death. Where the Spirit of the Lord is—there, and there only, is liberty. But Christian liberty is not license; for although this new life in Christ is not subject to any code of law, those who live it are sons of God, with a moral character beyond the power of law to achieve. The faith which accepts God's grace is activated by his creative love to produce the fruit of the Spirit.

Galatians is therefore a most revolutionary document. Men were worshiping a God whom they had made in their own image—a Creditor, Monarch, and Judge. Taught by the Spirit of Christ, Paul sought to free men from these misconceptions, and bade them trust God as the Father who had made them his sons. Citizenship in his kingdom was not a matter of justification in a heavenly court for merits acquired in obedience to his law. Paul thus cut the ground from under the ancient system of sacrifices. No longer was it men who must appease an angry God, but a God of love who suffered in the death of his only Son to allay the wrath of men and reconcile them to himself. But this gospel seemed too good to be true—a revolution so radical that Christians ever since have been tempted, as the Galatians were, to fall back upon salvation by obedience to law.

I. Occasion and Purpose

Paul had preached in Galatia at least twice. His first visit was occasioned by a repulsive physical illness; yet the Galatians received him as an angel of God. He gave them a share in his new life in Christ, and they in turn would have plucked out their eyes if that could have helped him (4:12-15).

Among these good friends some were Jews, but most were Gentiles who had never known the true God. Their former religion consisted of special days, seasons, and sacrifices, which Paul called slavery (4:8-10). As Christian children they had to learn to make right use of their new freedom; and when they found that the way of faith was hard, they were tempted like the rebels under Moses to turn back to the old gods (4:9; 5:13).

In every sermon Paul drew a picture of the crucified Christ as plain as an emperor's notice on a bulletin board (1:3-5; 3:1). Responding with faith, the Galatians received the Spirit (3:2-5; 5:1, 16). The daily supply of this Spirit came by faith and not by law; the one essential was to become a new creation as a member of the body of Christ, in whom circumcision and all other divisive religious customs had been done away (3:26-29; 6:15). The Galatians knew God because God had first known them (4:8-9), and their willingness to suffer for Christ made Paul feel that they had got a good start in their Christian race (5:7). This explains his astonishment on hearing of their impending retreat from freedom (1:6; 5:1).

Conservative preachers were persuading the Galatians that faith was not enough to make sure of God's kingdom. Besides believing that Jesus was the Messiah, one must join the Jewish nation, observe the laws and customs of Moses, and refuse to eat with the Gentiles (2:11-14; 4:10). One must have Christ *and* Moses, faith *and* circumcision, grace *and* law. Paul insisted that it must be *either* Moses or Christ (5:2-6).

Not content with raising doubts concerning the sufficiency of Christ, the Judaizers attacked Paul's credentials. They said that he had not been one of the original apostles, and that he was distorting the gospel which Peter and John and James the Lord's brother were preaching. They declared that his proposal to abandon the law of Moses was contrary to the teaching of Jesus, and they insinuated that he had taken this radical step to please men with the specious promise of cheap admission to God's kingdom (1:10). If he were allowed to have his way, men would believe and be baptized but keep on sinning, deluding themselves that the Christian sacraments would save them. Claiming to rise above Moses and the prophets, they would debase faith into magic, liberty into license, making Christ the abettor of sin (2:17). The Judaizers were alarmed lest Paul bring down God's wrath and delay the kingdom. They had not shared the emotion of a catastrophic conversion like Paul's, and they found it hard to understand when he talked about a new power which overcame sin and brought a righteousness better than the best that the law could produce.

Another party attacked Paul from the opposite side. Influenced by the pagan notion that religion transcends ethics and is separable from morality, they wanted to abandon the Old Testament and its prophetic insights. They could not see how Paul's demand to crucify one's old sinful nature and produce the fruit of the Spirit could be anything but a new form of slavery to law (2:19-20; 5:14, 22-24). They accused him of rebuilding the old legalism, and some said that he was still preaching circumcision (2:18; 5:11). Whereas the Judaizers rejected Paul's gospel because they believed it contrary to the teaching of the original apostles, these antilegalists felt that he was so subservient to the apostles as to endanger the freedom of the Christian movement.

Actually Paul had risen above both legalism and sacramentarianism. Activated by love and lured by hope, his faith was qualitatively different from mere assent to a creed (5:6). He was living on the plateau of the Spirit, where life was so free that men needed no law to say "Thou shalt" and "Thou shalt not" (5:22-24). But this rarefied atmosphere was hard to breathe, and neither side could understand him. The conservatives were watching for moral lapses to prove that he had perverted the gospel, and the radicals blamed him for slowing the progress of Christianity by refusing to cut it loose from Judaism and its nationalistic religious imperialism. The debate was so sharp that Paul had to warn his readers against biting and devouring one another (5:15). His friends were tempted to regard him as their enemy, while he imputed selfish ambition and cowardice to those who were changing his gospel (4:16-17; 6:12-13). He can only suppose that they have been bewitched (3:1). Unless checked, the defection would spread like yeast in a batch of dough (5:9). Paul wished that he could be present in Galatia to clear up the situation (4:20), but since this was impossible he wrote a letter. In the course of his reply to his critics he gave his views on the great questions of Christian faith and life:

(*a*) The basis of man's acceptance with God.

(*b*) The supremacy and sole sufficiency of Christ.

(*c*) The validity of Paul's gospel and apostleship.

(*d*) The seat of authority in religion.

(*e*) The relation of freedom to responsibility.

(f) The unity of the church.

(*g*) The universality of the Christian mission.

Each of these items may be briefly discussed:

(*a*) Acceptance with God does not rest on law, or on law added to grace, but only on faith in Jesus Christ (2:16-17). All who rely on law are subject to its curse, which, however, is not God's curse (3:10). From the beginning it was God's will to save men through faith, and he never changed that will. This is proved by Abraham 430 years before the angels gave the law to Moses (3:17). God permitted their temporary experiment with law, in order to restrain sin, to guard spiritual minors, to convince men that they cannot save themselves, and to lead them to Christ (3:19, 21-26). But the law could not bestow the Spirit and make men sons of God, and it could not deliver them from its own curse and from slavery to the elements of the kindergarten (3:2, 13; 4:3-6). Only Christ could do that. Circumcision was not an additional guarantee; on the contrary, it cut men off from Christ and bound them to keep the whole law perfectly—which no man could do (5:2-4). Only faith was acceptable to God (3:11); and if men would live for God, they must crucify themselves with Christ (2:20). Apart from faith even obedience was transgression (2:18).

(*b*) The sole sufficiency of Christ was the issue in Paul's inexorable alternative. If justification were possible by law, Christ's death would be needless, God's grace nullified (2:21). If the inheritance promised to Abraham were by Moses through circumcision, it would not be by Christ through faith (3:18). Others—even angels—might come preaching, but their gospels were no gospels, and such preachers were accursed (1:8-9). Paul's passionate language is explained by the threat he saw to the integrity of his gospel. The world was in the market for the cheapest insurance it could get for immortality and for deliverance from the ills of this present life, but God's grace required men to be cross-bearers. When Christ's way became rough, the tempter said: "One religion is as good as another—why not lapse your policy with Christ, insure with Great Mother Cybele, and play safe with a pinch of incense at the shrine of your emperor Claudius?" In an age of mobility of populations, migrants found it easy to identify their ancestral gods with those of their new homes, and the many savior-deities who were competing for men's allegiance were losing their individuality by fusion and confusion in the minds of their worshipers. Paul's concern was to safeguard the oneness and the sole adequacy of his Lord.

(*c*) Paul's defense of his gospel and apostleship was the more difficult because he had to maintain his right to go directly to Christ without the mediation of Peter and the rest, but had to do it in such a way as not to split the church and break the continuity of his gospel with the Old Testament and the apostolic traditions about Jesus and his teaching. His call to preach Christ was a gift of God's grace, yet was not independent of men in the sense that God made no use of the apostolic brotherhood to extend it (2:7-10; Acts 13:1-4; I Cor. 15:10). He must insist that his gospel was not of human origin and that Christ had communicated it to him in person; but he must also show that the pillars of the church had recognized its truth and his right to preach it.

To this end Paul gave an account of his relations with the Jerusalem church during the seventeen years that followed his conversion (1:11–2:14). Instead of going to Jerusalem he went to Arabia, presumably to preach (1:17). After a time he returned to Damascus, and only three years later did he go to see Peter. Even then he stayed but fifteen days and saw no other apostle except James the Lord's brother (1:18-20). Then he left for Syria and Cilicia, and not until another fourteen years had passed did he visit Jerusalem again. This time it was in response to a revelation from his Lord, and not to a summons by the authorities in the Holy City.

Paul emphasizes that neither visit implied an admission that his gospel needed the apostolic stamp to make it valid. His purpose was to get the apostles to treat the uncircumcised Gentile Christians as their equals in the church (2:2). Making a test case of Titus, he won his point (2:3-5). The apostles agreed that a Gentile could join the church by faith without first becoming a member of the synagogue by circumcision. But as far as Paul's interpretation of the gospel and the genuineness of his apostleship were concerned, he says, "They . . . added nothing to me" (2:6). They did, however, recognize that his mission to the Gentiles was on the same footing as theirs to the Jews—only he was to remember the poor (2:7-10). So far was Paul from being subordinated that when Peter came to Antioch and wavered on eating with the Gentile Christians, Paul did not hesitate to rebuke him in public (2:11-14). Thus Paul vindicated his gospel of direct communication with the living Christ and won apostolic recognition of the unity of the church on the basis of the equality of all men before the grace of God (5:6; 6:15). Thereafter he could challenge his critics to show that they were more able than he to bear the marks of Jesus (6:17).

(*d*) Paul's defense of his apostolic commission involved the question: What is the seat of authority in religion? A Jewish rabbi debating the application of the kosher laws would quote the authority of Moses and the fathers in support of his views. Jewish tradition declared that God delivered the law to Moses, and Moses to Joshua, and Joshua to the elders, and the elders to the men of the Great Synagogue, and that they had handed it down through an unbroken rabbinical succession to the present. If Paul had been a Christian rabbi, he would have treated the Sermon on the Mount as a new law from a new Sinai, which God had delivered to Jesus, and Jesus to Peter, and Peter to Paul, and Paul to Timothy and Titus, and so on through an unbroken apostolic succession until the second coming of Christ. Instead of taking his problems directly to his Lord in prayer, he would ask, "What does Peter say that Jesus did and said about it?" And if Peter or the other apostles happened not to have a pronouncement from Jesus on a given subject, they would need to apply some other saying of his by reasoning from analogy. This would turn the gospel into a system of legalism, with casuistry for its guide, making Jesus a second Moses—a prophet who lived and died in a dim and distant past and left only a written code to guide the future. Jesus would not have been the living Lord, personally present in his church in every age as the daily companion of his members. That is why Paul insisted that Christ must not be confused or combined with Moses, but must be all in all. He must not be treated as a mere link in the chain of authority, so that men would ask, "What did Peter say that Jesus said that John the Baptist said that Malachi said . . . that Moses said?"

The Judaizers assumed that God had revealed to Moses all of his will, and nothing but his will, for all time, changeless and unchangeable; and that death was the penalty for tampering with it. The rest of the scriptures and the oral tradition which developed and applied them were believed to be implicit in the Pentateuch as an oak in an acorn. The first duty of the teacher was to transmit this Torah exactly as he had received it from the men of old. Only then might he give his own opinion, which must never contradict but always be validated by the authority of the past. When authorities differed, the teacher must labor to reconcile them. Elaborate rules of interpretation were devised to help decide cases not covered by specific provisions in the scripture. These rules made it possible to apply a changeless revelation to changing conditions, but they also presented a dilemma. The interpreter might modernize by reading into his Bible ideas that were not in the minds of its writers, or he might quench his own creative insights by fearing to go beyond what was written. Those who modernized the Old Testament were beset with the perils of incipient Gnosticism, while those who, like the Sadducees, accepted nothing but the written Torah could misuse it to obstruct social and religious progress.

In his daily fellowship with Jesus, Paul shifted the emphasis from religious tradition to personal religious experience. Jewish thinking had narrowed the function of the Spirit until it came to be associated almost exclusively with the inspiration of prophecy. The Spirit had once spoken through Moses and the rest of the prophets, and sometime, in the good future which God had promised, he would speak again through a prophet like unto Moses. But as for the present age, it was not worthy to have a prophet, and those who claimed the gift of prophecy were regarded as potential deceivers of the people. The Torah and its ordained interpreters were the only safe guide. In this way the Spirit was virtually imprisoned within the scriptures which he had inspired. To hear his voice one must confine oneself to reading the Bible and be guided by its authorized interpreters. Against such views Paul protested vehemently (cf. II Cor. 3:17). Associating the Spirit of prophecy with Jesus, the risen and glorified Lord, who was everywhere present, on earth as well as in heaven, the apostle in his prayer life cut straight through tradition, and was rewarded with visions and revelations of his own. As a thinker he was too original, as a personality too creative, to make another lawbook out of the teaching of Jesus.

This does not mean that Paul had no use for the Old Testament or that he by-passed the apostolic tradition and spun a gospel out of his own ideas (1:18-19). Since he preached his gospel as the fulfillment of the Jewish scriptures, he could not discard the Old Testament as some extremists wanted to do. But this fulfillment meant more than the simple fact that Jesus had been, and had done, what the Scriptures had foretold. He had revealed and made possible for men that new kind of life which the prophets had envisioned for citizens of the kingdom of God, and this fulfillment made much of the ancient revelation obsolete. Jesus opened the way for an immediate resurgence of the Spirit of prophecy as a continuing, progressive revelation which could never again be confined within the scrolls of a canonical scripture. Paul could not believe that the apostolic tradition about Jesus, fundamental as it was, had exhausted all the riches of God's revelation so that nothing was left for the individual Christian to discover through immediate personal communication with his Lord.

This issue went far beyond the immediate controversy. Paul's seat of authority was not in scripture as a dead written code but in experienced scripture. Neither did it lie in an apostolic succession through a mediating priesthood, but in the direct personal fellowship of the individual with his Lord as a member of the body of Christ, in which God continued to reveal himself. This marked the difference between a religion based on authority and a gospel based on God's grace which inspired the very faith that trusted him.

(*e*) The preaching of such a gospel runs the risk that men who are looking for an easy salvation may equate its freedom with irresponsibility and debase its liberty into license. Paul guarded against this by insisting that his gospel was not a new religion but the fulfillment of one as old as the faith of Abraham (3:8). Morally the new life which the Spirit created was more strenuous than the old slavery to the law of Moses. The difference was that in Christ one had resources to overcome the weakness of human nature and to discharge this heavier responsibility to produce the fruit of the Spirit (5:22-24). Paul had to warn that the Christian freeman must not fall below the standards and achievements of those who believed that salvation depended upon obedience to law, but must exceed them; otherwise he would be misusing Christ to encourage sin (2:17).

Paul's Christian freedom was inseparable from daily crucifixion with Christ and unbroken companionship with his Spirit (2:20; 5:24); otherwise a man was sure to fall back into the clutches of unregenerate human nature (3:3; 5:1). Negatively, this freedom refused low aims and evil desires; positively, it fulfilled the whole law through love and produced all the other fruits of God's Spirit (5:13-24). Although the Christian was so free that he needed no law, the mutuality of the Spirit made him the voluntary slave of all his fellow members (6:2, 5). Uncompelled by tithe or tax, he was a liberal giver who sowed for the Spirit, confident that he would reap eternal life (6:8-9). Christian liberty was freedom to seize every opportunity to do good to all men (6:10).

(*f*) Paul was developing the concept of the unity of all men in Christ Jesus, and of the church as Christ's instrument to incarnate and promote it. The greatest obstacle to equality in Christ was the deadly trait of men's biting and devouring one another, of competing for power, influence, and honor (5:15; 6:12-13). This sin was the more subtly corrosive because it could cloak itself in the garments of sincere, conscientious loyalty to outgrown religious ideas and customs. To submit to circumcision would have betrayed the truth of the gospel because it contradicted the principle that all is of grace and grace is for all (2:5). Perpetuated in the church of Christ, the kosher code and other Jewish customs would have destroyed the fellowship. Few things could have hurt the feelings and heaped more indignity upon the Gentiles than the spiritual snobbery of refusing to eat with them. The unity inherent in baptism and the Lord's Supper could not be maintained in the presence of a spirit of division bound to degrade the means of grace into magical sacramentarianism.

The tragedy of division was proportional to the sincerity of men's scruples. The Jews were brought up to believe that eating with Gentiles was a flagrant violation of God's revealed will which would bring down his terrible wrath. How strongly both sides felt appears in Paul's account of the stormy conference at Jerusalem and the angry dispute that followed it at Antioch (2:1-14). Paul claimed that refusal to eat with a Gentile brother would deny that the grace of Christ was sufficient to make him worthy of the kingdom. If all men were sons of God through Christ, there could be no classes, Jew or Greek, slave or free, male or female (3:26-28). What mattered was neither circumcision nor uncircumcision, but only faith and a new act of creation by the Spirit (5:6; 6:15). Without recognition of the equality of all men before the grace of God, and the right of every individual to go to him without interference by anyone, the unity of the church could be neither achieved nor maintained. The future was on the side of Paul. His success in knitting the many members into the one body of Christ was a principal factor in the victory of Christianity over its competitors.

(*g*) Church unity was essential to the success of Christian missions. Friction between Aramaic- and Greek-speaking Jewish Christians in Palestine had to be eliminated (Acts 6:1). The death of Stephen and a special vision to Peter were required to convince the conservatives of the propriety of admitting the Gentiles on an equality with the Jews; and even Peter was amazed that God had given them the same gift of the Spirit (Acts 11:1-18). This hesitation was potentially fatal to the spread of Christianity beyond Palestine. Many Gentiles had been attracted by the pure monotheism and high morality of Judaism but were not willing to break with their native culture by submitting to the painful initiatory rite and social stigma of being a Jew. Even if they were to do so, they would always be reminded that they were alien-born. Had the church kept circumcision as a requirement for membership, it could not have freed itself from Jewish nationalism. Paul opened the door of faith to all who would believe in Christ, and assured them that they were members of the true, spiritual Israel (3:29; 4:21-31). His principle of grace made illogical and senseless any attempt to compel the Gentiles to live like Jews. (On the issues between Paul and the Jerusalem church see also Vol. VII, pp. 176-186; Vol. IX, pp. 198-200, 648-51.)

II. Outline of the Letter

The following outline exhibits Paul's argument and indicates the bearing of his letter upon these problems in their modern form. It is convenient to divide it into three main parts of two chapters each: I. The Declaration; II. The Defense; and III. The Responsibility. The conventional division of all Paul's letters into "doctrinal" and "practical" sections does violence to the organic relation between faith and life which runs through everything that he ever wrote.

- I. Paul's declaration of religious independence of men and dependence on Christ (1:1–2:21)
  - A. The proclamation (1:1-5)
  - B. The circumstances which necessitated Paul's declaration (1:6-10)
  - C. Paul's commission as an apostle (1:11-17)
  - D. The recognition of Paul's apostleship by the pillar apostles in Jerusalem (1:18–2:10)
  - E. The later inconsistency of the Judean leaders (2:11-14)
  - F. The fundamental affirmation of Paul's faith (2:15-21)
    - 1. The abandonment of law (2:15-16)
    - 2. The rejection of compromise (2:17-19)
    - 3. Sole reliance upon Christ (2:20-21)
- II. The defense (3:1–4:31)
  - A. An appeal to personal experience (3:1-5)
  - B. The precedent of Abraham's faith (3:6-18)
    - 1. Preview of the gospel (3:6-9)
    - 2. Intervention of the law (3:10-14)
    - 3. The presumptuous codicil (3:15-18)
  - C. The interim function of law (3:19-25)
  - D. The new status of the men of faith (3:26–4:11)
    - 1. Freedom and equality in Christ (3:26-29)
    - 2. The end of the age of slavery (4:1-7)
      - *a*) The life of spiritual minors (4:1-3)
      - *b*) The fullness of time (4:4-7)
    - 3. The spiritual maturity required of heirs of God (4:8-11)
  - E. The personal relations between Paul and his spiritual children (4:12-20)
  - F. An allegory of freedom (4:21-31)
    - 1. The terms of the allegory (4:21-26)
    - 2. The application of the allegory (4:27-31)
- III. The responsibility (5:1–6:18)
  - A. To preserve and make right use of freedom (5:1-15)
    - 1. By resisting every proposal to return to slavery (5:1)
    - 2. By recognizing that law can add nothing to grace (5:2-6)
    - 3. By preventing interference with runners in the Christian race (5:7-12)
    - 4. By maintaining the right conception and use of freedom (5:13-15)
  - B. To serve in the war of the Spirit against the flesh (5:16-21)
  - C. To live as sons and heirs of God (5:22-24)
  - D. To join the co-operative of the Spirit (5:25–6:6)
  - E. To engage in the agriculture of the Spirit (6:7-10)
  - F. Concluding re-emphasis upon the main points of the letter (6:11-18)

III. Some Characteristics of Paul's Thinking

To understand Paul one must observe that he describes his religious experience in terms of opposites. His vision of Christ at Damascus changed him so radically that all his letters are permeated by the contrast between what belonged to the old life and the new. He "died with Christ" to all the evil powers that God was permitting to rule this present age, and he rose with Christ to begin living, right on this sin-cursed earth, the life of the new age "in Christ." Crucified with Christ, he was free from hopeless slavery to all the tyrants of the dark phase of existence—flesh, sin, law, wrath, death, and demons. Risen with Christ, he lived and moved and had his being in the realm of Spirit, where all was righteousness, freedom, grace, light, and life. Henceforth Paul aimed not only to become, but to be, what Christ had made him—a son and heir of God. His liberation from Tyrant Law did not free him magically from the powerful weakness of Tyrant Flesh, but it did give him strength to lay hold of that for which Christ had laid hold of him.

But "the law" of which Paul is speaking does not coincide with "law" in a twentieth-century state with representative government. His Greek word was νόμος, an inadequate translation of the Hebrew "Torah," which included much more than "law" as we use the term. Torah was teaching on any subject concerning the will of God as revealed in the Scriptures. Since the Jews did not divide life into two compartments labeled "religious" and "secular," their law covered both their spiritual and their civil life. Nor did Paul and his fellow Jews think in terms of "nature" and "natural law." They believed that everything that happened was God's doing, directly or by his permission. The Messiah was expected to restore the ancient theocracy with its power over both civil and religious affairs.

The Gentiles too were accustomed to state regulation of religion and priestly control of civil affairs. The Greek city-states had always managed the relations of their citizens with the gods, and Alexander the Great prepared the way for religious imperialism. When he invaded Asia, he consolidated his power by the ancient Oriental idea that the ruler was a god or a son of God. His successors, in their endless wars over the fragments of his empire, adopted the same device. Posing as "savior-gods," they liberated their victims by enslaving them. The Romans did likewise, believing that the safety of their empire depended upon correct legal relations with the gods who had founded it. The majesty of their law overshadowed all else. Each city had its temple dedicated to the emperor, and its patriotic priests to see that everyone burned incense before his statue. Having done this, the worshiper was free under Roman "tolerance" to adopt any other legal religion.

But also in the private religious associations his relation to his god was regulated by the law of the cult. Whether salvation was offered in the name of the ancient gods of the Orient, or of Greece, or of the emperor of Rome, or of Yahweh the theocratic king of the Jews, the favor of the deity was thought to depend upon obedience to his law.

One did not therefore have to be a Jew to be a legalist in religion. A Gentile brought up on the idea that he must *do* something to get right with his god and earn his salvation would miss from Paul's gospel that sense of assurance which he had formerly derived from his obedience to the law of his cult. Since Paul's first converts were drawn from Gentiles who had been attending the synagogues, it is easy to see how Gentile Christians could be as zealous to add Moses to Christ as the most conservative Jew.

This is what gave the Judaizers their hold in Galatia. The rivalry between the synagogue, which was engaged in winning men to worship the God of Moses, and the church, which was preaching the God who had revealed himself in Christ Jesus, was bound to raise the issue of legalism and stir up doubts about the sufficiency of Christ.

Gentile and Jewish Christians alike would regard Paul's preaching of salvation apart from the merit acquired by obedience to law as a violently revolutionary doctrine. Fidelity to his declaration of religious independence from all mediating rulers and priesthoods required a spiritual maturity of which most who heard his preaching were not yet capable. It was easier to have a law to tell them what to do than to decide for themselves under the guidance of the Spirit, which required the faith and daring of the pioneer. Paul's gospel has always been in danger of being stifled by those who would treat the teachings of Jesus as laws to be enforced by a hierarchy. The function of his letters to the Galatians and the Romans has been to keep the church aware of the difference between his dynamic conception of faith and pseudo-salvation by obedience to law.

IV. Address of the Letter

The main factors in the occasion, purpose, and religious message of Galatians are clear. But the letter yields no information concerning the date, place of writing, and the cities to which it was addressed. There is little in Paul's other letters to help answer these questions, and the account in Acts is fragmentary, with indefinite, summary statements at the crucial points required to fix the chronology. Attempts to reconcile Luke's account with Galatians have produced answers that vary according to the historian's estimate of the accuracy and adequacy of Acts.

The chief difficulties in dating the letter and locating its churches arise from uncertainty whether 2:1 is to be identified with Acts 11:30 or 15:2, and whether the churches were founded on the first missionary journey (Acts 13:1–14:26) or on the second (Acts 15:40–16:10). Two views of the destination of the letter have resulted. They are known as the North and South Galatia hypotheses.

In Paul's day "Galatia" might refer (*a*) to north central Asia Minor, with its principal cities, Pessinus, Ancyra, and Tavium, or (*b*) to the Roman province of Galatia, which included, besides this northern region, parts of Phrygia, Pisidia, and Lycaonia, and the southern cities of Antioch, Iconium, Lystra, and Derbe (see the map above, p. 428). The South Galatia hypothesis assumes that τῆς Γαλατίας, "of Galatia," in 1:2 refers to the Roman province, and that Paul's readers were members of the churches planted on the journey described in Acts 13–14. Those who hold the North Galatia hypothesis maintain that Paul used "Galatia" in its original sense to refer to the northern region, which was inhabited by the descendants of the Gauls who invaded Asia Minor from Europe in 278 B.C. They argue that Paul founded churches there at the beginning of his second journey (Acts 16:6), and revisited them on his third preaching tour (Acts 18:23).[1]

Protagonists of this view recognize that Luke says nothing about the founding of churches in Acts 16:6 ff., but they explain this omission as owing to his haste to get Paul to Troas and across to Europe. Traveling west, Paul and his associates headed for one of the large Asian cities on the Aegean coast; but the Holy Spirit caused them to turn northeast, and so they went through the western part of the old Gallic region. After founding some churches there, they planned to go north into Bithynia. But again the Spirit changed their course, and they passed by Mysia and went to Troas, whence they sailed for Europe. Two or three years later, at the beginning of his third journey, Paul paid these northern churches a second visit (Acts 18:23), traveling this time from east to west through Galatia and Phrygia to Ephesus. There, soon after his arrival, he heard about the troublemakers and wrote his letter to forestall them.

Advocates of the North Galatia view emphasize also that Luke does not speak of Pisidian Antioch, Iconium, Lystra, and Derbe as cities

[1] On this question see David Magee, *Roman Rule in Asia Minor to the End of the Third Century After Christ* (Princeton: Princeton University Press, 1950), I, 453-67; II, 1305-6. This work appeared after this Introduction was in proof.

in "Galatia." They infer that Acts 16:6 and 18:23 designate the northern region of the province, and they believe that the Phrygians and Lycaonians were so proud of their ancient nationalities that they would have resented being called "Galatians." They maintain that Paul referred to countries by their geographical rather than their political names (1:21; I Thess. 2:14), and conclude that he means North Galatia just as Luke does. They think that the churches in this region, being younger and less organized, would have been more susceptible to the Judaizers than the older, more settled churches to the south.

A number of other considerations have been urged in favor of the North Galatia hypothesis, but none of them has much weight. The sudden illness which turned Paul to preach in Galatia (4:13) could have occurred in the south as well as in the north, and the assertion that the natives of Lystra would not mistake a sick man for the god Hermes overlooks the fact that Luke says Paul's miracle caused them to do so. Nor does the "fickleness," which is supposed to account for the sudden defection from Paul's gospel, point especially to the Gauls in the north, for no nation has a monopoly on that trait. Paul's reference to "the marks of Jesus" (6:17) has no necessary relation to the Gallic custom of branding slaves with deep scars and cuts, for such brutal treatment was a common practice. Neither does Paul's failure in Galatians to mention the persecutions described in Acts 13–14 tell in favor of the North Galatia hypothesis, since his purpose was not to reproach the mob which had stoned him, but to retain the friends who had received him so hospitably the first time (4:13).

The main arguments for the South Galatia hypothesis are as follows: The North Galatia view has to rest its case upon two obscure passages in Acts 16:6 and 18:23. The first of these says concerning Paul and his companions, διῆλθον δὲ τὴν Φρυγίαν καὶ Γαλατικὴν χώραν, which is translated in the KJV, "Now when they had gone throughout Phrygia and the region of Galatia." But Φρυγίαν may be either a proper noun or a feminine adjective modifying χώραν. If it is an adjective, the translation is, "And they went through Phrygian and Galatian country," through frontier country inhabited by Phrygians and Galatians. But there is doubt that the feminine form of Φρύγιος was used as an adjective during the New Testament period. In Acts 18:23, Φρυγίαν is a proper noun, and Γαλατικὴν χώραν may refer to a district on the Phrygian border of western Galatia where Gaelic was spoken. The translation of Acts 16:6 would then be "through Phrygia and Galatian country." This does not differ essentially from the KJV in form; but it is important to observe that "the region of Galatia" need not cover all the territory inhabited by the descendants of the Gauls, but only the western part bordering on Phrygia.

According to this interpretation, Paul founded no churches in North Galatia. His purpose was not to preach in, but to pass through, this region (διῆλθον). In search of a new field, he intended to go down the Lycus Valley to the cities of the Aegean coastland (ἐν τῇ 'Ασίᾳ). When the Spirit prevented, he turned north through eastern Phrygia and country inhabited by Galatians, with the object of going to Bithynia. But the Spirit forbade, and he turned west again through Mysia to Troas.[2]

Defenders of the South Galatia view do not need to argue that because Paul was a Roman citizen he would employ the Roman official designations of provinces, but they hold that his use of terms for geographical and political subdivisions was not the same as Luke's. Whenever he referred to a *group* of churches, he named them by the Roman province in which they were located (I Cor. 16:19*a*; II Cor. 1:1*b*; 8:1). He spoke of the provinces of Judea, Syria, Cilicia, Asia, Macedonia, and Achaia, but not of Phrygia, Pisidia, and Lycaonia, which were merely geographical regions. "Galatia" was the only name to include all the cities which he had evangelized on his first journey. Whatever their original nationality, his readers spoke Greek. The pride of cities everywhere in being part of the Roman Empire answers the objection that the inhabitants of Pisidian Antioch, Iconium, Lystra, and Derbe would have resented being addressed as "Galatians."

Luke, contrary to his usual custom, mentions no cities in Acts 16:6-8 and 18:23. In the latter passage he says that Paul strengthened "all the disciples"; elsewhere it is *churches* that are strengthened (Acts 14:23; 15:41; 16:5). This suggests that while there may have been a few scattered Christians in that region, there were no churches such as those addressed in Paul's letter. Luke's failure to mention churches in North Galatia cannot be explained by saying that he was in haste to get Paul to Troas, where his own diary began. If he had known of such churches, it would have required only a line or two to list them. The first clear references to churches in this area are later than Paul and outside the book of Acts. It is true that Acts is not a complete account of Christian begin-

[2] See Kirsopp Lake, "Paul's Route in Asia Minor," in F. J. Foakes Jackson and Kirsopp Lake, *The Beginnings of Christianity* (London: Macmillan & Co., 1933), V, 236.

nings, and that Paul may have written to churches which Luke does not mention. But with the single exception of Colossae—not far from Ephesus—the cities to which his other letters are addressed are the very ones which bulk largest in Luke's narrative. It is more likely that Galatians was directed to Christians in Pisidian Antioch, Iconium, Lystra, and Derbe. Since Paul's main reliance was on the Spirit rather than on ecclesiastical organization to preserve the unity of his churches and the integrity of his gospel, it cannot be argued that the churches in these cities would be more probable victims of the Judaizers than the hypothetical unorganized churches in North Galatia.

A number of other arguments have been made for the South Galatia theory, but they have to be set aside. It cannot be maintained that Judaizers from Jerusalem would be more likely to visit these southern cities than the more distant ones in the north, and that Paul in seeking cities where Greek was spoken could not have found them in North Galatia where Gaelic was the dominant language; for there were Greeks and Jews in both regions. Nor is it valid to argue that Paul's reference to Barnabas (2:1, 13), without introduction to explain who he was, points to South Galatia, where Barnabas was with Paul, rather than to churches founded on the second and third journeys after the two had parted company; for in I Cor. 9:6 also Paul refers to Barnabas without introduction. Again, the fact that Timothy was a native of Lystra has been held to favor the South Galatia view, because it would explain the charge that Paul was still preaching circumcision (5:11; Acts 16:3). But Luke's report that Paul circumcised Timothy is not necessarily the basis of that charge; and even if it were, it could have circulated just as easily in North Galatia. On the other hand, the absence of representatives of North Galatia from Luke's list of delegates who helped to take the relief money to Jerusalem (Acts 20:4) need not mean that Paul had founded no churches in that region. Not all the contributing churches are mentioned in that list, and in Paul's letters there is no indication that the Galatian churches, wherever they were, actually made any contribution; he says only that he requested them to do so (I Cor. 16:1).

No argument for or against either view can be based upon its utility in harmonizing Acts with the letters of Paul. It has been argued that the events of Gal. 2:1-11 could not have occurred before Paul's second journey, because Paul would not have invited Barnabas to go with him after he had yielded to "the circumcision party" (2:12-13). Therefore, since Paul had visited Galatia more than once prior to the letter, it must have been written on the third journey; and since 4:13 implies only two visits, it cannot have been directed to South Galatia, because that would have been Paul's third time with them. But before accepting this conclusion we have to reckon with the possibility that Luke was combining two sources, one an Antiochian ("Barnabas") source, which contained what he has recorded as the "first" journey, the other a Pauline source, which included Luke's "we document" and gave an account of Paul's journey from Troas to Corinth, and later to Ephesus. In putting these sources together Luke may have made two journeys to Jerusalem out of what, according to Galatians, was only one, namely, the famine-relief journey referred to in Acts 11:30 and 12:25, and the journey to the apostolic council in Acts 15:2. Having done this, he would also have had to make two missionary tours out of what had been only one, and Acts 14:21-28 and 15:36–16:9 would be his editorial paragraphs to link them together. This explanation would obviate the need to reconcile Acts with Paul; but with the evidence at hand it cannot be proved. In any case Galatians must be treated as the primary source and not forced to conform with Acts.

Those who hold the North Galatia view do not have to resort to conjectural rearrangements of the text in order to harmonize Acts with Paul. Nevertheless their argument cannot be said to be conclusive. The South Galatia view is the better working hypothesis, although it too must be held subject to revision in the light of possible discovery of new evidence.

V. Environment of Paul's Churches in Galatia

The conclusion concerning the destination of the epistle does not involve the essentials of its religious message, but it does affect our understanding of certain passages, such as 3:1 and 4:12, 20. Moreover, the facts brought to light by archaeologists concerning the cities visited by Paul extend our knowledge of the people he was addressing, the problems they faced, the kind of salvation they were seeking, and why they were so ready to change his gospel.

The main factors in the spread of Christianity in Asia Minor were common to North and South Galatia. From the earliest times that part of the world had been swept by the cross tides of migration and struggle for empire. The third millennium found the Hittites in possession. In the second millennium the Greeks and Phrygians came spilling over from Europe, and in the first millennium the remaining power of the Hittites was swept away by Babylon and Persia. Then came the turn of the Asiatic tide into Europe, only to be swept back again by Alexander the Great. But the Greek cities with which he and his successors dotted the map of Asia were like anthills destined to be leveled by Oriental reaction.

About 278 B.C. new turmoil came with the Gauls, who were shunted from Greece and crossed into Asia to overrun Phrygia. Gradually the Greek kings succeeded in pushing them up into the central highlands, where they established themselves in the region of Ancyra. Thus located, they constituted a perpetually disturbing element, raiding the Greek cities and furnishing soldiers now to one, and now to another, of the rival kings. Then in 121 B.C. came the Romans to "set free" Galatia by making it a part of their own empire. By 40 B.C. there were three kingdoms, with capitals at Ancyra, Pisidian Antioch, and Iconium. Four years later Lycaonia and Galatia were given to Amyntas the king of Pisidia. He added Pamphylia and part of Cilicia to his kingdom. But he was killed in 25 B.C., and the Romans made his dominion into the province of Galatia, which was thus much larger than the territory inhabited by the Gauls.

More than pacification by Rome was needed to eliminate this dark heritage of bloodshed and cruelty. War and slavery, poverty, disease, and famine made life hard and uncertain. In religion and philosophy men were confused by this meeting of East and West. But man's extremity was Paul's opportunity. The soil of the centuries had been plowed and harrowed for his new, revolutionary gospel of grace and freedom.

Not all, however, were ready for this freedom. The old religions with prestige and authority seemed safer. Most Jews preferred Moses, and among the Gentiles the hold of the Great Mother Cybele of Phrygia was not easily shaken. Paul's converts, bringing their former ideas and customs with them, were all too ready to reshape his gospel into a combination of Christ with their ancient laws and rituals. The old religions were especially tenacious in the small villages, whose inhabitants spoke the native languages and were inaccessible to the Greek-speaking Paul. To this gravitational attraction of the indigenous cults was added the more sophisticated syncretism of the city dwellers, pulling Paul's churches away from his gospel when the moral demands of his faith and the responsibilities of his freedom became irksome. This was the root of the trouble in Galatia. (On the Greco-Roman environment of Paul's churches see Vol. VII, pp. 75-99.)

VI. Date and Place of Writing

The exact date and the place of writing are as difficult to determine as the address of the readers. The only certainty is that the letter must have been written after the events described in 2:1-14. The North Galatia hypothesis requires a date after the journey mentioned in Acts 18:23, since Gal. 4:13 implies that Paul visited Galatia twice before writing the letter. On this assumption the most probable place would be Ephesus "soon"—ταχέως (1:6)—after his departure from Galatia, and the approximate calendar date would be 52. This would make Galatians the third of Paul's extant letters; but the ταχέως need not be taken strictly, and Galatians may have been written after I Corinthians.

On the basis of the South Galatia hypothesis the letter can be assigned to the same period, but a number of other dates have been suggested. Some consider it the earliest of Paul's extant letters and place it in 49, just after his return to Syrian Antioch at the close of his first journey (Acts 14:26). In support of this date it is said that Paul, who had come from Perga by boat, was met by messengers from Galatia, who had taken the shorter route by land. They reported the disturbance which had arisen in his churches soon after his departure. He could not go back immediately to straighten things out in person, because he saw that he would have to settle the matter first in Jerusalem, whence the troublemakers had come. So he wrote a letter.[3]

This view would explain Paul's surprise in 1:6. By identifying his visit to Jerusalem which is described in Gal. 2:1-10 with that of Acts 11:30, it would avoid difficulty in harmonizing Acts with Paul when Galatians is dated after the apostolic council of Acts 15. Placing the letter before the council is also said to explain why it makes no reference to the agreement reported in Acts 15:28-29 as Paul's authority for not requiring the Gentiles to be circumcised.

But the reasons given for equating Gal. 2:1-10 with Acts 11:30 instead of 15:2 are not conclusive. We do not know that the trouble in Galatia was stirred up by emissaries from the church in Jerusalem (see p. 435). Moreover, this solution overlooks the crux of the issue between Paul and the legalists. His contention was that neither circumcision nor the observance of any other law was the basis of salvation,

[3] Albert E. Barnett, *The New Testament: Its Making and Meaning* (New York and Nashville: Abingdon-Cokesbury Press, 1946), pp. 29-30. See also G. S. Duncan, *The Epistle of Paul to the Galatians* (London: Hodder & Stoughton, 1934; "Moffatt New Testament Commentary"), pp. xviii-xxxii.

but only faith in God's grace through Christ. If the decrees of Acts 15:28-29 were needed anywhere, it was in Corinth; but not even in his letters to the Corinthians, which, according to Acts, were written after the Jerusalem council, did he mention them. On the matter of kosher customs, as on every other question, he directed men to the mind and Spirit of Christ, and not to law, either Mosaic or apostolic. That mind was a Spirit of edification which abstained *voluntarily* from all that defiled or offended.

This early dating encounters another difficulty. Gal. 4:13 (τὸ πρότερον) implies that Paul visited these churches at least twice prior to his letter. Identification of the second of these visits with the return to Lystra, Iconium, and Pisidian Antioch, related in Acts 14:21-23, is awkward, since Paul would have been in Derbe only once. This objection might be met by supposing that several months later Paul paid all these cities another visit, which Luke has omitted. But that would only complicate the solution with another argument from the silence of Acts. The short time indicated by οὕτως ταχέως, "so soon" (1:6), need not be measured from the founding of the churches, but rather from Paul's last visit previous to the letter; and this is true no matter whether that visit is identified with Acts 14:21-23 or 16:1-5 or 18:23. The statement that the letter to the Galatians must have been written soon after their conversion because "Paul shows no awareness that the disturbing tendencies had made their appearance during his second visit"[4] misses the point of 1:9, which indicates that he had warned them against alien gospels when he was with them. The greater Paul's previous care to guard them against error, the greater his astonishment that they were deserting his Christ; and too much emphasis need not be placed upon the time element in his surprise.

These considerations would not be fatal to the year 49 if all the other questions were satisfactorily answered. But such is not the case. If we had only Acts 11:27-30, and were to read it apart from any desire to reconcile it with Gal. 1:15–2:14, we should never suppose that the validity of Paul's gospel and the necessity of circumcision for Gentile Christians were discussed on that occasion. The only real point of contact is the reference to the famine relief, and all the rest of Gal. 2:1-10 has to be read into Acts 11:27-30. Paul's mention of the request that he remember the poor does not imply that he had been neglecting them. The poor were the concern of *every* church council. The reference to collecting money, which happens to be common to both passages, is therefore no compelling reason to identify them. Even if this equation were convincing, it would not solve all the problems of reconciling Acts with Paul, and this early date would make the relation of Galatians with Paul's other letters difficult to explain.

If Galatians is dated in 49, why do the letters to the Thessalonians, written less than a year later, bear no marks of the faith-versus-works controversy? We may say that the situation was different—that in Macedonia it was persecution from outside by Jews who were trying to prevent Paul's preaching, whereas in Galatia it was trouble inside the church created by legalistic Christians who were proposing to change his teaching; that in one case the issue was justification by faith, and in the other faithfulness while waiting for the day of the Lord. Yet as Paul wrote Romans to forestall a misunderstanding of his gospel such as had arisen in Galatia, so one would expect him to say something about the sole efficacy of grace to the Thessalonians if he had just come through the shock of battle with the Judaizers in Asia Minor. That episode was warning that sooner or later the proposal to adulterate his gospel with law would be made in every one of his churches, and it is hard to see why he did not lay specific emphasis upon it in such passages as I Thess. 5:9-10, and II Thess. 2:13-15. Conversely, there is nothing in the Thessalonian correspondence that precludes the assumption that it came prior to Galatians.

The letter to the Romans, written during the three months in Greece mentioned in Acts 20:2-3, is our earliest commentary on Galatians. In it the relation between the law and the gospel is set forth in the perspective of Paul's further experience. The brevity and storminess of Galatians gives way to a more complete and calmly reasoned presentation of his gospel. The allegories of Gal. 3:16 and 4:21-31 are replaced by a developed conception of social solidarity in relation to the death and resurrection of Christ (Rom. 15:7-12), and by hope for God's overruling of Israel's present rejection of Christ (Rom. 11:1-32). A more positive role is assigned to the law in Rom. 3:1-2 and 7:7-19 than in Gal. 3:10–4:12, and there is more compassion for those who have chosen to remain under its curse (cf. Rom. 2:10 and 11:25-36 with Gal. 1:8-9; 4:30; 5:12). Paul's answer to the fear that sole reliance upon grace may encourage sin (Gal. 2:17-21) is enlarged, and the righteousness required for acceptance with God is described more explicitly in relation to the new life in Christ (Rom. 6; 8:1-17). The assurance that the Spirit can be trusted to keep

[4] Barnett, *N.T.: Its Making and Meaning*, p. 26.

the believer from falling into the old slavery to sin (5:5, 16; 6:6-9) is expanded into a paean of victory in Rom. 8:18-39, which could hardly have failed to be reflected more fully in these Galatian passages if Romans had been written first. The same observation holds concerning the fuller statement of the reasons for abandoning the kosher laws in Rom. 14, and the more explicit description of the fulfillment of Mosaic law by Christian love in Rom. 13:8-10. These facts are best explained on the assumption that Romans was written some time after the crisis which led to the writing of Galatians had passed. How long afterward depends upon one's conclusion concerning the relation between Galatians and the letters to the Corinthians.

It has not always been recognized that Paul's correspondence with the Corinthians is just as necessary as Romans for the understanding of Galatians. As Romans supplements Galatians on grace, so the letters to Corinth throw light on Paul's concept of Christian freedom and explain more fully the attack upon his gospel and apostleship.

This does not mean that Paul had kept copies of his Corinthian and Galatian letters and consulted them when writing Romans, but that his answers to the questions dealt with in Romans were related to his own spiritual growth as a missionary of Christ. The interaction between the situation of the churches and Paul's personal religious experience determined the mood in which he wrote his letters. Since the letters to the Corinthians were written from Ephesus in the period of Acts 19:1–20:1, the question is whether the spiritual atmosphere of Galatians is sufficiently similar to warrant the conclusion that it was written at the same time. The points of comparison are (*a*) the disparagement of Paul by his enemies; (*b*) obsession with the theme of strength in weakness; (*c*) the defense of the gospel; (*d*) the attitude toward law; (*e*) the remedy for factions; and (*f*) the need to balance freedom with responsibility.

(*a*) At Corinth, as in Galatia, Paul had to defend his right to be an apostle against opponents heartless enough to turn against him the cruel belief that physical illness was a sign of God's disfavor. His bodily weakness, they said, was unbecoming to an ambassador of Christ, and they charged him with being a crafty man-pleaser peddling his gospel for money (1:10; I Cor. 4:12-13, 18-21; II Cor. 2:17; 10:1; 12:16). In reply to their demand for proof that Christ was speaking in him (II Cor. 13:3) Paul admitted his weakness and unworthiness (1:13, 23; 4:13-14; 6:17; I Cor. 15:8-9), but insisted that his commission to preach was genuine and direct from God through Christ (1:1, 11-12, 15-17; I Cor. 9:1; II Cor. 1:21-22; 3:5-6; 5:16-21; 10:4, 7-8; 11:5-6; 12:1-13). He challenged them to follow him in living so that no fault could be found with the ministry (1:24; 2:10; 4:15; 5:17; I Cor. 15:10, 30-34; II Cor. 6:3-10; 11:5, 21-29). Like him they must make themselves the slaves of all men because they were now slaves of Christ (1:10; 6:2, 5, 10; I Cor. 9:6; II Cor. 4:2-5; 5:11). Yet he insisted that each Christian must bear his own burden, and he refused to take anyone except Christ as a standard of self-measurement (6:4-5; I Cor. 4:3-5; II Cor. 5:10; 10:12, 17; 13:5-6). At times he was driven to bitter reproach of those who had disparaged him (1:7-9; 4:17; 5:10, 12; 6:12-13; I Cor. 16:22; II Cor. 11:12-15).

(*b*) Another common element in these letters is the remarkable combination of humility and self-assertion. Paul insisted that the only ground for glory was the cross of the Lord Jesus Christ and the grace of God which enabled him to commend himself to the conscience of all right thinking people (1:13-16; 6:4, 14, 17; I Cor. 1:31; 5:6-7; 9:16; II Cor. 5:12; 10:13-17; 11:16-18, 21). He rose above his disabilities by reminding himself that God's strength was perfected in man's weakness. Instead of apologizing he would boast of it, since this was the only way of glorying that would not detract from the Cross (1:5; 2:20; 4:14; 6:14, 17; II Cor. 11:30; 12:1-10). This theme is the magnificent obsession of II Cor. 10–13. One reason for this emphasis was a recent experience that caused Paul to despair of life itself (II Cor. 1:8-10). This psychological mood accounts likewise for the obtrusion of his illness into his reminder to the Galatians of their initial reception of him (4:13-15), and it suggests that these epistles were written in the same period.

(*c*) The similarities in Paul's defense of his gospel in the Corinthian letters and in Galatians also point to this conclusion. He determined to know nothing except Jesus Christ crucified; he declared it impossible for him to do anything against the truth; and he took captive every thought to obey his Lord (1:8; 2:18-21; I Cor. 2:1-2; II Cor. 10:5-6, 8). Since Christ died for all, and since Jews and Greeks, slave and free, were baptized into his one body, neither circumcision nor uncicumcision mattered (2:15-16; 3:26-28; 5:6; 6:15; I Cor. 7:17; 12:13; II Cor. 5:14). Galatians and Corinthians alike are rebuked for being so easily imposed upon by preachers of another gospel (1:6-9; 3:1-5; II Cor. 11:14), and Paul's habit of becoming all things to all men has laid him open to misunderstanding and charges of insincerity (1:10; 5:11; I Cor. 9:19-23).

(*d*) Equally striking agreements appear in Paul's treatment of the law. He substitutes the Spirit, who gives life, for the old written code, which kills (5:13-14, 18, 22-25; II Cor. 3:6). In Corinthians, as in Galatians, he allegorizes scripture to show that the old covenant is temporary (3:15-22; 4:21-31; II Cor. 3:7-16). He disparages the rulers of this age and brands as slavery the attempt to save oneself by obeying laws and customs (4:3, 8-10; I Cor. 2:8; 12:2). He exhorts his converts to put away childish things and grow up in faith, hope, and love (3:23-26; 4:1-10; I Cor. 3:1-4; 13:11; 14:20).

(*e*) Most childish of all were the factions, incipient in Galatia, and actual in Corinth. Paul attributed them to desire for recognition and status (4:17; 6:12-13; I Cor. 11:19). He called the ambitious advocates of other gospels false apostles and threatened them with a curse (1:9; 5:8-9, 12, 15; I Cor. 16:21; II Cor. 11:13). He abandoned the kosher customs and all other artificial distinctions between Jews and Gentiles and laid the emphasis where it belonged—upon the necessity for God's people to establish and maintain a higher morality and spiritual life (2:11-14; I Cor. 5:11). His aim was to give no offense and to do only what was constructive (2:18; I Cor. 3:10; II Cor. 10:8; 12:19; 13:10). He substituted a catholic spirit for partisan loyalties (1:10; 3:28; I Cor. 3:21-23; 9:22). This new way of life constituted a neighborliness and a mutuality as intimate as that between father and son (4:19; 6:2-5; I Cor. 4:14-15; 10:24, 33; II Cor. 1:6; 6:11-13; 12:14), and those who lived it were assured of reaping as they had sown (6:8-9; I Cor. 15:58; II Cor. 9:6).

(*f*) The Corinthian letters are like Galatians also in emphasizing the need to balance freedom with responsibility (5:1, 6, 13; 6:15; II Cor. 3:17–4:2; 5:17). Paul's Christian arithmetic called for the subtraction of all that was evil from human nature (5:13-15, 17-21; I Cor. 6:9-12; 15:49; II Cor. 12:20-21), and for the multiplication of the fruit of the Spirit through self-devotion to the general welfare (5:22–6:10; I Cor. 9:19; 10:31–11:1; 13:1-13).

The best explanation of the results of these comparisons is the hypothesis that Galatians was written some time during the short interval between II Cor. 10–13 and II Cor. 1–9. The exact calendar year cannot be determined, but it would fall within the limits of 53 to 55, which is the probable date of Paul's stay in Ephesus on his third tour of missionary duty (Acts 19:1–20:1). If, as some interpreters believe, Phil. 3:2–4:23 was a separate letter also written from Ephesus at this time, we have additional light upon the situation in which Paul found himself when he addressed his troubled churches in Galatia.[5]

The foregoing discussion will have made clear the difficulties of certain other dates which have been proposed. One suggestion is that the news of the trouble in Galatia came to Paul during his eighteen months in Corinth in 50-51 (Acts 18:1-18). Another dating would put Galatians at Antioch in Syria during the "some time" which Acts 18:23 says Paul spent before starting his third journey; but it is hard to see why he would write a letter if he was about to go to Galatia, since, in view of the wish expressed in 4:20, one cannot suppose that he preferred to deal with such situations by letter. Still others would date Galatians from Macedonia on the third journey (Acts 20:1-2), or from Greece, where Paul spent three months before his final trip to Jerusalem (Acts 20:3). But this was the period when Romans was written; and the more developed thought of that epistle requires us to assume that a somewhat longer time had elapsed since Galatians was composed. The same objection holds against dating Galatians from Caesarea during Paul's imprisonment there (Acts 23:23–26:32). Nothing in this letter indicates that Paul was a prisoner when he wrote it.

VII. Authorship and Attestation

If Paul wrote anything that goes under his name, it was Galatians, Romans, and the letters to Corinth. Not until the nineteenth century was their Pauline authorship denied. Then F. C. Baur and his followers tried to show that the letters ascribed to Paul were the product of a second-century conflict between a Judaist party and the liberals in the church, and that they were written by Paulinists who used his name and authority to promote their own ideas. But the contents and life situation of these letters could not have been invented without evidences of this later date being betrayed, and they fit all the facts known from other sources concerning the origin of Christianity and its history during the middle decades of the first century. The character of Paul and

[5] A more recent proposal is to date I Corinthians in the spring of 47, and Galatians, Romans, II Cor. 1–8 and II Cor. 10–13 in 47/48, or "a year or so later" (Charles H. Buck, Jr., "The Collection for the Saints," *Harvard Theological Review*, XLII [1950], 1-29). But while this would do justice to the close relationship between Galatians and the Corinthian correspondence it does not leave sufficient time between the writing of Galatians and Romans to explain the differences, and it involves a drastic hypothetical rearrangement of the chronology of Acts. See also John Knox, *Chapters in a Life of Paul* (New York and Nashville: Abingdon-Cokesbury Press, 1950), pp. 47-88.

his religious experience as they appear in Galatians are consistent with the longer letters to the Romans and the Corinthians. The rejection of Pauline authorship for Galatians has been a vagary of extremist criticism.

The earliest mention of the epistle by name occurs in the canon of the Gnostic heretic Marcion (*ca.* 144). He put it first in his list of ten letters of Paul. A generation later the orthodox Muratorian canon (*ca.* 185) listed it as the sixth of Paul's letters. Since that time it has been regarded as one of the principal sources for our knowledge of Paul and his religion. While the first explicit reference to Galatians as a letter of Paul is as late as the middle of the second century, it must not be supposed that it lay unknown and unread for a hundred years. The authors of Ephesians and the Gospel of John knew it; and Polycarp in his letter to the Philippians quoted it. Revelation, I Peter, Hebrews, I Clement, and Ignatius show acquaintance with it; and there is evidence that the writer of the Epistle of James knew Galatians, as did the authors of II Peter and the Pastoral epistles, and Justin Martyr and Athenagoras.[6]

VIII. Text and Transmission

So rich was the treasure of Paul's life in Christ that he never found it easy to put it into words, least of all in Galatians. Although the epistle was composed neither carelessly nor hastily, the anxiety and emotional stress under which Paul dictated his cascading thoughts have produced some involved and obscure sentences (2:3-5; 4:14, 24-25), and a number of abrupt transitions (1:10, 11; 4:25; 5:12; 6:7, 15). These have been a standing invitation to scribal clarification. Since Galatians circulated only as a part of the collected letters of Paul, occasional phrases from the others have crept into its text (4:17; 5:19, 21; 6:15). At 3:1 we have the later insertion of τῇ ἀληθείᾳ μὴ πείθεσθαι, "that ye should not obey the truth" (KJV), from 5:7. Paul's debate with his critics takes the form of a diatribe, which is characterized by quotations from past or anticipated objectors and rapid-fire answers to them. Paul did not use quotation marks, and this accounts for the difficulty in 2:14-15 of deciding where his speech to Peter ends. The numerous allusions to persons and places, events and teachings, with which Paul assumed his readers to be acquainted, are another source of difficulty. All these factors operated to produce the numerous variations in the text of Galatians.

The most important of these variants are discussed in the Exegesis. The reader will find it helpful to mark the passages in which the differences between the KJV and the RSV are explained by the fact that the revisers have translated a different reading of the Greek text. These are: 1:10*b*, 11, 15, 18; 2:11, 13, 14, 16; 3:1, 10, 12, 14, 17; 4:6, 7, 14, 25, 26, 28; 5:17*b*, 19, 20, 21, 24; 6:13, 15, 17. Other passages with important variants are: 1:3, 4, 6, 8, 13; 2:9, 12, 20; 3:16, 19, 21, 23, 24, 28; 4:15, 17, 19, 21, 31; 5:3, 7, 12, 13, 14, 23; 6:1, 2, 7, 10, 11, 12, 16. After 6:18 many manuscripts add ἐγράφη ἀπὸ Ῥώμης, but this designation of Rome as the place of writing was a late addition.

[6] Barnett, *N.T.: Its Making and Meaning,* p. 21. His earlier book, *Paul Becomes a Literary Influence* (Chicago: University of Chicago Press, 1941), is a thoroughly documented study of the early circulation and use of Paul's letters.

IX. Selected Bibliography

From the vast library that has been written to interpret Paul and his letters, the following modern works have been of especial value in the preparation of the present commentary.

BURTON, ERNEST DE WITT. *A Critical and Exegetical Commentary on the Epistle to the Galatians* ("The International Critical Commentary"). New York: Charles Scribner's Sons, 1920. The standard commentary in English, especially useful for its summaries of the views of previous commentators and its thorough lexical studies of important terms in Paul's vocabulary. An extended bibliography down to 1917 is given on pp. lxxxii-lxxxix.

FOAKES JACKSON, F. J., and LAKE, KIRSOPP, eds. *The Beginnings of Christianity.* London: Macmillan & Co., 1920-33. Five volumes. The following notes by Lake in Vol. V are relevant to the study of Galatians: "The Conversion of Paul and the Events Immediately Following It"; "The Apostolic Council of Jerusalem"; "Paul's Controversies"; "Paul's Route in Asia Minor"; and "The Chronology of Acts."

LIETZMANN, HANS. *An die Galater* ("Handbuch zum Neuen Testament"). 2nd ed. Tübingen: J. C. B. Mohr, 1923. A brief treatment supplemented by references to the other volumes of the same commentary series.

MOFFATT, JAMES. *An Introduction to the Literature of the New Testament* ("The Internationl Theological Library"). 3rd ed. New York: Charles Scribner's Sons, 1918. The section on Galatians (pp. 83-107) furnishes an extensive bibliography of the important works on Galatians down to 1917 and argues persuasively for the North Galatia view.

RAMSAY, W. M. *A Historical Commentary on St. Paul's Epistle to the Galatians.* New York: G. P. Putnam's Sons, 1900. The "Historical Introduction" (pp. 1-234) applies the data of the author's own archaeological explorations in the cities of Asia Minor to reconstruct the history and environment of Paul's churches in Galatia, and to challenge the North Galatia hypothesis.

ROPES, JAMES HARDY. *The Singular Problem of the Epistle to the Galatians.* Cambridge: Harvard University Press, 1929. Following a suggestion made by Wilhelm Lütgert in 1919, this stimulating study questions the usual assumption that the trouble in Galatia was caused by Jewish Christians sent from Jerusalem as part of an organized anti-Paul missionary enterprise, and attributes it to the enthusiasm for law on the part of Judaizing Gentile Christians in Galatia. The author demonstrates that Paul had to defend himself and his gospel not only against the Judaizers, but also against the radicals on the left who were proposing to discard the Old Testament.

SCHLIER, HEINRICH. *Der Brief an die Galater* ("Meyer's Kommentar"). 10th ed. Göttingen: Vandenhoeck & Ruprecht, 1949. This thoroughgoing treatment appeared after the present commentary was completed. Schlier adopts the North Galatia hypothesis. He gives an extended bibliography of works on Galatians.

STRACK, HERMANN L., and BILLERBECK, PAUL. *Kommentar zum Neuen Testament aus Talmud und Midrasch.* München: C. H. Beck, 1922-28. Four volumes. Vol. III contains the commentary on the epistles of Paul, but there are many references to the other volumes. The primary source materials from the Old Testament, the Apocrypha and Pseudepigrapha, and the Talmud and Midrash are discussed critically and applied to the understanding of the New Testament. This work is indispensable for the student of Paul's relation to his ancestral religion and for an understanding of the Jewish conception of law.

GALATIANS

TEXT, EXEGESIS, AND EXPOSITION

1 Paul, an apostle, (not of men, neither by man, but by Jesus Christ, and God the Father, who raised him from the dead;)

1 Paul an apostle — not from men nor through man, but through Jesus Christ and God the Father, who raised him from

I. Paul's Declaration of Religious Independence of Men and of Dependence on Christ (1:1–2:21)

A. The Proclamation (1:1-5)

1:1. Paul an apostle—not from men nor through man: An apostle was one who was "sent" on a mission; in this case, to preach the gospel of Christ, plant churches, and prepare men for the coming of the Lord to end this present evil age. The prepositions are ἀπό and διά, and the RSV has corrected the KJV by changing **of** to **from,** and **by** to **through.** Paul's commission came neither from a human source nor through man, but directly from and through God, and was therefore as valid as if he had been one of the twelve apostles.

Paul's gospel rested on his personal relationship with God through Christ, and he was working it out in his own creative way. The vehemence with which he insisted upon his independence from men shows how far he had shifted the emphasis from tradition to personal experience. He refused to make Christ another Moses, and he would allow no man—not even Peter and John and James the Lord's brother—to come between him

---

1:1*a. Paul an Apostle.*—Paul calls himself **an apostle;** history calls him "the apostle." More than any other, it was he who lifted the Christian fellowship from a sect within the synagogue into a world faith. "Three cubits in stature, he touched the sky" [1] was John Chrysostom's word-picture of him. "Nobody would be studying the Pauline theology if the tracks of Paul were not found all over the world." [2] "Paul was the first man in history who was really free." [3] He was "the man who understood Christ as no other

[1] See Charles E. Jefferson, *The Character of Paul* (New York: The Macmillan Co., 1923), p. 381.

[2] Lynn Harold Hough, *The Meaning of Human Experience* (New York and Nashville: Abingdon-Cokesbury Press, 1945), p. 183.

[3] Ernest F. Scott, *The Varieties of New Testament Religion* (New York: Charles Scribner's Sons, 1943), p. 113.

and his Lord. In reply to the objection that he was not a trustworthy preacher because he had not been with Jesus in the flesh, he appealed to his own face-to-face interview with Christ at Damascus. The Spirit-Christ, who now dwelt in his heart as in a temple, had become the Spirit of prophecy to inspire all his decisions and drive him to declare his religious independence. That independence was twofold: (*a*) freedom from law as a way of salvation, and (*b*) freedom from legal casuistry as a method of applying religion to life.

But through Jesus Christ and God the Father, who raised him from the dead: The preposition is διά, and therefore properly, **through** (RSV), not **by** (KJV). God and Christ jointly were both the source and agent of Paul's commission. This did not preclude God's use of men in converting and instructing him (vss. 18-20), but the essential element was Paul's daily fellowship with the risen Christ, without which all human authorization would have been futile. Paul's gospel and the exhaustless energy with which he preached it sprang from God's forgiveness and from God's mighty act in raising Christ from the dead. Apart from this Paul's faith and preaching would have been in vain (I Cor. 15:14, 17-19).

---

who has ever lived."[4] Since Galatians is the most autobiographical of Paul's letters, it is natural that in it he revealed the secret of his freedom by telling what Jesus did for him. Because he tells just that in Galatians, "Martin Luther put it to his lips as a trumpet to blow the reveillé of the Reformation."[5]

A desert way,
A burning sun,
And—Saul.
A sudden light,
A heavenly voice,
And—Paul.[6]

1*b*. ***His Credentials***.—Paul begins where every man who aspires to hold public confidence must begin: with his own credentials. In the light of what this epistle has meant to the world, his introductory reference explains how he became an apostle. Here we read both the small and large print of Paul's mind. Where did he get his vocation and his vitality? He uses prepositions that remind one of Lincoln's "of the people, by the people, for the people." Paul's apostleship was not **from men. From** reveals the origin, the seat of authority, the source from which power originates. He did not get his message, or his call to deliver it, from any group of people within or without the fellowship of the church. His election to speak and write came not **from men;** nor did it come **through man. Through** refers to the medium or means of expression. It is here that church orders could come in; however, there was no bishop, elder, or presbyter who ordained Paul. His credentials did not rest upon "tactual, apostolic succession." If that were necessary for his apostleship he was outside of it completely. If he had any human ordination it was at the hands of a layman, Ananias, against whom he had breathed threatenings during his former life under the law.

Paul uses a good portion of Galatians to tell his firsthand experience of Christ; this verse is the epitome of his essential faith, his authentic experience, his God-given apostleship. He directly contrasts Jesus with man and links him with **God the Father**. Indeed, the juxtaposition of Jesus with the Father, which pervades the Scriptures, speaks decisively for the deity of our Lord. That is classical Christianity in every age. Paul did not deny Christ's humanity; but he did not start or stop there. Christ's humanity became the vehicle of his deity. Profound religion stems from the deity of Christ; effective ethics follows upon Jesus' humanity, sustained by the grace of his deity.

1*c*. ***The Resurrection***.—There is one fact about Jesus Christ which mattered most for Paul: his resurrection. Only a living Christ could call Paul on the Damascus road; only a living Christ could draw him across the line which separated his ancient heritage from the larger fulfillment of that heritage. There are writers who portray with amazing skill the historical background of Jesus' life; there are others who deftly delineate the social setting of his ministry. But the limited and circumscribed figure they introduce, before that background and into that environment, could not make an intelligent Hebrew like Paul a Christian. Such a profound change of life as Paul experienced was and is the work of the risen Son of God.

[4] R. Newton Flew, *The Idea of Perfection in Christian Theology* (London: Oxford University Press, 1934), p. 60.

[5] G. G. Findlay, *The Epistle to the Galatians* (New York: A. C. Armstrong & Son, 1889; "The Expositor's Bible"), p. 3.

[6] Harriet Wheeler Pierson. Written especially for this commentary.

2 And all the brethren which are with me, unto the churches of Galatia:

the dead — 2 and all the brethren who are with me,
To the churches of Galatia:

---

2. **And all the brethren who are with me:** There is nothing to indicate that they took part in the dictation, but by their sympathy they helped him to reply to his critics. His reference to them would remind his readers that he was not without supporters. His declaration of independence does not mean that he needed no help from his Christian brothers.

"Brother" was Paul's name for fellow Christian. The Jews called their fellow tribesmen brothers, and the members of the Gentile mystery cults and fraternal organizations were brothers. Jesus taught that all men who did God's will were his brothers and were equal in rank (Mark 3:35; Matt. 23:8). The Christian family and the personal friendships of Christ's freedmen in each congregation were the seedbed of a fraternity which was to include every race and nation (Acts 1:8; 2:5-11). The qualifications for membership were faith, hope, and love (I Cor. 13:1-13); separation from all that defiles (I Cor. 5:11; 6:9-11); willingness to compose personal differences (I Cor. 6:1-8); to

---

Around the "actual contemporary presence of Christ"[7] the fellowship of the church gathers.

2*a. His Practice of Fellowship.*—(See also Expos. on vss. 17-23; 2:1-2, 10; 6:1.) Though the letter to the Galatians bears Paul's name, it is also a corporate letter from **all the brethren who are with me.** After Paul became a Christian he wrote out of the total of his relationships. With men like Paul salutations are more than mere words. His greetings reveal the motives behind his work. He loved people and did not work alone. Indeed, Galatians came out of fellowship—**and all the brethren who are with me.** The Pauline literature creates, enlarges, enriches, and sustains fellowship in every generation because it resulted from fellowship in the beginning.

Can a man be a Christian outside the church? The answer is "Yes" if the church is primarily an organization, an institution, a movement. If that is the church, one can do no more than tell a man outside that he is less effective than he might be within. If the church is a fellowship before it is anything else—a circle gathered around the living Christ—the answer is "No": a man cannot be a Christian away from the Fire.

Unlike some theologians, preachers, teachers, and authors, Paul was not remote, cold, and unfeeling. His brilliant mind did not blind him to the fact that ideas are less important than people; that truth is never abstract; that all truth is personal. The most seemingly objective mathematical or chemical formula has full meaning because it ultimately relates to people. Some good minds in the name of scholarship are friends of Socrates and Aristotle but are distant from living people around them. They gaze at the cup from which the hemlock has been drained while "the least of these" about them begs in the name of Christ for a cup of cold water. The technical scholar is not necessarily listening to God or the Scriptures. The world is not saved by such thinkers. The Bible speaks directly; it does not wait for the judgment of man. To say this is not to minimize scientific scholarship but rather to insist upon the primacy of human values.

2*b. The Galatians.*—The letter to the Romans is Paul's most finished book; Galatians presents the same theme, fresh and raw from Paul's heart and mind—and from God's. By speech, conference, wide acquaintance, and writing, Paul influenced men in his lifetime; and by his writing he has influenced all the centuries that have followed. Much of the world's wisdom, like unmarked graves, has been lost forever because it was never recorded in permanent form. Paul's letters, which constitute one fourth of the N.T., are a permanent testimony of the author's experience with Christ. In describing that experience to the churches of the first century Paul tested it for himself.

In Galatians he wrote to get three matters in proper focus: experience, doctrine, and conduct (or life). Indeed, experience is the place where doctrine and conduct meet. Doctrine without experience is truth without confirmation. The purest doctrine does not function automatically. One may know the Christian faith intellectually and be far from Christian living. Experience is the spark that sets doctrine into action. Conduct without experience is life apart from its beginning. There are times when morality or conduct is divorced from religion. There are other times when morality becomes one's religion. A pro-

[7] Quoted by Joseph Sittler, Jr., *The Doctrine of the Word* (Philadelphia: Board of Publication of the United Lutheran Church in America, 1948), p. 25.

3 Grace *be* to you, and peace, from God the Father, and *from* our Lord Jesus Christ,

3 Grace to you and peace from God the

refrain from all that would hurt another's conscience (I Cor. 8:11-13); to abound in the work of the Lord (I Cor. 15:58); to bear one's own and each other's burdens, and to love one's neighbor as oneself (5:13-14; 6:2). Paul's peculiar genius lay in his ability to knit into this fellowship many men of many minds and nations.

To the churches of Galatia: For a discussion of the address of the letter (τῆς Γαλατίας), see Intro., pp. 435-37.

3-5. Into the customary greeting of a Greek letter Paul has packed his whole gospel. Some authorities read **from God the Father and our Lord Jesus Christ.** Paul's usage favors "our Father and the Lord Jesus Christ" (Rom. 1:7; I Cor. 1:3; II Cor. 1:2; Phil. 1:2; Philem. 3). For Paul χάρις (**grace**) was the most beautiful word in all the tongues of men and angels: "gracefulness," "attractiveness," "graciousness," "kindness," "good will," and "thanks." Whatever pleased men was "grace." The LXX used χάρις to translate חן, which meant "favor" and "approval." Christ made the word still more beautiful by making it mean God's favor contrary to man's desert. Grace was God's gift of himself to sinful men. Before Christ came to live in him Paul had felt like an enemy alien, a guilty criminal, a bankrupt debtor, a slave without money to buy freedom, an orphan in a demon-ridden universe. In Christ all this was changed (see Intro., p. 434). Paul's very self, his past, present and future, his call to be an apostle, and even the faith

found, firsthand experience of God cuts through to the place where conduct and personal knowledge of the living Christ become one. These three—experience, doctrine, conduct—are woven into an eternal trinity in what may be regarded the epitome of Galatians—2:20.

Some of the most powerful men and intellects in history have well-nigh exhausted themselves trying to master Paul's dominant ideas. Though Paul may not always appear to be a systematic writer, he was always a systematic thinker. What he wrote and kept upon his mind moved about a central theme. This "unsystematic" writer produced the raw materials, the quarried rock, upon which giant thinkers through the Christian centuries have erected their systems. Recall the men who have built on Paul: Augustine, Thomas Aquinas, Martin Luther, John Calvin, John Wesley. Who could name more creative minds? The experiences Paul related, the profound truth he distilled from them, the life he has inspired for twenty centuries, are the truth of life and God. Indeed, he has been tested by history and has not been found wanting. By writing his experiences he has "traveled widely" across the centuries since the Damascus road.

3. ***Paul's Master Word and Key: Grace.***—With him the meaning of grace is at least fourfold: (*a*) Grace is the key to the nature of God and the personality of man (see Expos. on vs. 15). (*b*) It is the most significant word in the N.T., the summation of all that Christ does for mankind (see Expos. on 2:9). (*c*) It reaches its fullest expression in the Cross (see Expos. on 2:21). (*d*) It gathers up the faith of the Hebrew fathers into a reservoir and turns that reservoir into a fountain (see Expos. on 5:2-7).

3-5. ***How to Measure a Man's Dependability.***—When a man claims to have had the experiences Paul had and tries to set everybody else straight in their Christian faith and practice, careful minds begin to ask questions. Can they depend on this man? Or is he a neurotic visionary? Is he like those who appear to have special wiring for their prayers and yet have mental processes or social attitudes and concerns which are not impressive? Did Paul have a thorn in his mind, as he confessed he had in his body?

Centuries before psychology came on the scene Paul opened his mind and revealed its hidden places. In telling the Galatians about Christ's best gifts to mankind he wrote the confession of his own mental health and dependability—perhaps unconsciously. Concern for mental and physical health is far from the whole of religion: it is only one approach to it. In truth, it is dangerous to put all of one's religious eggs in that basket. However, mental health is surely a legitimate concern of the Christian faith. Paul indicates at least four qualities in his own mind which may be the marks of the kind of mind men can trust everywhere and which illustrate his own possession of the grace of Christ (see following Expos.).

*3a. **The Sense of Adequacy.***—Grace is the N.T. word for the divine adequacy. Paul's mind had been torn at the seams because the religion

by which he accepted God's mercy—all these were God's grace-gift, without money and without price. He prayed for the Galatians to follow him in holding fast to it.

The effect of God's grace was the "peace" (εἰρήνη) which rejoiced Paul, and which he invoked upon his fellow Christians. This was more than freedom from external strife. Paul filled it with the Hebrew *shālôm,* which meant total well-being for time and eternity. The civil war in his soul had ended, and he was at peace in Christ, assured that whatever cross-bearing he must yet endure, God had accepted him as a son and heir.

In the O.T. God was Creator of all men and Father of those who accepted his covenant. By his grace he chose the Israelites to be his sons and entrusted them with the task of making him known to the rest of the world (Deut. 32:6; Isa. 63:16; Jer. 3:4, 19; Mal. 1:6). His fatherhood was a moral and spiritual relationship with Israel his son, a conception which contrasted sharply with the Gentile idea of divine parentage through physical generation. But God could not be the Father of Israel as a nation without being the Father of the individuals who composed it. In the days of Jesus "Abba" (ὁ πατήρ) was being used more and more to describe God's relation to every righteous individual (cf. Wisd. Sol. 2:16-18). Jesus knew God as both "Father" and "Lord," but there was a filial intimacy that made "Father" his own and his disciples' characteristic name for God. God became the Father of the Christians in the special sense that he revealed himself in his Son Jesus Christ and chose them to create a fellowship of men of faith to promote the acceptance of his fatherhood among all nations. Because God was Father he was gracious, and because—but only because—men had faith in his grace, they had peace. Paul spoke of God both as "our Father" (Rom. 1:7; I Cor. 1:3; II Cor. 1:2; Phil. 1:2; Philem. 3), and as "the Father" of Christ (Rom. 15:6; II Cor. 1:3; 11:31), but this distinction does not imply that there was nothing in common between God's fatherhood of Christ and his fatherhood of men. The possession of the mind and Spirit of Christ was the essential condition of men's becoming and remaining sons of God (4:4-7; Rom. 8:15-17). Paul's conception was essentially different from the personification of the impersonal, matterbound fire deity which the Stoics called "Father."

"Jesus" means "Savior," and "Christ" is Greek for the "Messiah" who was "anointed" to rule God's people, save them from their sins, deliver them from their conquerors, and establish truth, justice, and mercy on earth. His disciples regarded his resurrection and ascension as God's mighty act which had installed him in this high office, and they looked for his immediate return to establish his kingdom on earth as it was in heaven. This was the gospel which they were to proclaim to all nations.

In their appeal to the Gentiles to repent and qualify for citizenship in the kingdom, they found that the title κύριος, "Lord," was better than "Christ," because it was free from Jewish nationalistic limitations. A "lord" was one who had control: the master was lord of his slaves, the husband of his wife and children, the landowner of his estate,

---

he had known was unable to handle his life. He who preached grace to the Galatians had grace himself which, perhaps for the first time in his life, brought him an awareness of adequacy. Inadequacy causes men to break up; fullness or adequacy holds life together. Here is where Paul got his light, his power, and the courage to handle opposition, strains, and the attacks upon him. Grace was thus the secret of his mental health.

Is a man entirely on his own or is it intelligent for him to rely on resources far beyond himself—the moral and spiritual equivalent to what air, light, and water are to his physical body? Paul's answer is emphatically clear. In his letters, preserved in the N.T., he confesses: "I can do all things through Christ which strengtheneth me" (Phil. 4:13); "My grace is sufficient for thee" (II Cor. 12:9). Paul's word is "sufficient," which means enough of fullness; the modern word is "efficient." Sufficiency means personal power to be efficient. Efficiency is playing the keyboard; sufficiency is keeping a song in one's own heart. Sufficiency means power to be skillful: it is strength to use the tools; it is power by which techniques work. Efficiency is building the boat; sufficiency is the ability of the river and sea to float it. This experience of the resources of the Eternal gave Paul mental health and made him a dependable interpreter.

3*b*. *The Sense of Peace.*—In its total meaning peace sums up a good man's life, with evidence

4 Who gave himself for our sins, that he might deliver us from this present evil world, according to the will of God and our Father:

Father and our Lord Jesus Christ, 4 who gave himself for our sins to deliver us from the present evil age, according to the will of

the emperor of his subjects, and the gods were the lords of men. In the LXX κύριος translated אדון, "owner," "master," "lord," and יהוה, the distinctive name of the God of Israel; and the Aramaic word was *mār* or *mārān*. Since the O.T. was regarded as a prophetic blueprint of the life of Jesus and his church, many passages in which κύριος stood for God could be referred to Jesus as Lord. Confronted by the lords—emperors and kings—the Christians could proclaim their glorified Master to be the Lord of Lords and King of Kings. "Jesus is Lord" was the fundamental declaration of the Christian faith (Rom. 10:9; I Cor. 12:3; II Cor. 4:5; Phil. 2:11). This was not equivalent to saying that Jesus was God, because it was God who had endowed him with his lordship (I Cor. 15:27-28; Rom. 11:36). Yet his delegated authority over men and angels was without limit (I Cor. 8:5-6; Phil. 2:9-10). As the heavenly Lord, Jesus was also the Spirit resident in the hearts of his followers, giving them peace and liberty (II Cor. 3:17-18). Although the Son of God was Lord of all, he took the form of a slave and gave the last full measure of devotion (2:20; Phil. 2:7). He died ὑπὲρ τῶν ἁμαρτιῶν ἡμῶν, **for our sins,** i.e., his concern was to set us free from them.

This freedom was not only for the individual but also a part of God's ultimate purpose to replace this **present evil age** (RSV) with his kingdom. Since Paul wrote τοῦ αἰῶνος, and not τοῦ κόσμου, **world** (KJV) is misleading. Αἰών means "lifetime," "a generation," "an indefinitely long time," "time without limit," "eternity"; and **for ever and ever** is lit., "unto the ages of ages." In the LXX αἰών translates עולם, "time without limits," "a period of indefinite duration," "age." Each age is characterized by its own culture and quality of life. The rabbis spoke of two ages, the present, which was evil and under the wicked Roman Empire, and the age to come, which would be God's golden age under his righteous Messiah.

The Christians shared this view (Mark 10:30; Matt. 12:32; Luke 16:8; 18:30). Jesus' followers expected a speedy end of this wicked age, and entertained the hope of

of sins forgiven. Peace of mind, expressed in calm and courage, reveals much of one's mental dependability. Jittery and frustrated people can help no one else. Under the personal tutelage of Christ and in the quiet of the Arabian desert the distressed, disturbed, and haunted mind of Paul found peace—a peace which he never lost through storm or shipwreck, imprisonment or persecution.

Peace may be translated "harmony." Harmony with one's self is integrity; harmony with life itself is gratitude; harmony with people is brotherhood; harmony with God is faith. All this adds up to the meaning of peace. It is the gift of Christ. To make available peace and harmony is part of his ministry of reconciliation. Mental peace is first of all a religious matter. "What are you afraid of?" is answered by "What and whom do you believe in?" This last question is the business of religion. At the center of all mental difficulties is fear. The answer to fear is faith. When Paul found that answer, or was found by Christ in terms of it, he was on the way to mental dependability.

4*a*. *The Sense of Freedom.*—Freedom for Paul meant deliverance from all that enslaves. Deliverance from evil habits that defeat, from impure and unworthy motives that depress, from sin and evil that destroy men's lives, is part of the meaning of the forgiveness of sins—the most powerful moral fact of all time. Christ's forgiveness of sins is his supreme gift to mental health and dependability. Psychiatry and psychology at best are only methods of analysis, techniques, and machinery. One service of grace is to provide power to make such machinery operate—"the enduring power, not ourselves, which makes for righteousness."[8] Too many men yearn and struggle for mental health and freedom; yearn and struggle and never find, because they have not known the profound experience of the forgiveness of their sins. If a man does not have that he cannot be truly free and dependable.

4*b*. *The Sense of Purpose.*—For a man to believe unshakenly that he is inside God's pur-

[8] Matthew Arnold, *Literature and Dogma* (New York: The Macmillan Co., 1924), p. 52.

5 To whom *be* glory for ever and ever. Amen.
6 I marvel that ye are so soon removed from him that called you into the grace of Christ unto another gospel:

our God and Father; 5 to whom be the glory for ever and ever. Amen.
6 I am astonished that you are so quickly deserting him who called you in the grace of Christ and turning to a different gospel —

his imminent second coming. This same eager longing fired Paul with missionary zeal to save men, not by deliverance from a material to a spiritual **world** (KJV), but by glorification of the physical through metamorphosis by the Spirit, which would fit them for life in the new **age** (RSV). The present age was evil, its pagan wise men fools for rejecting the Cross, its Christian fools wise beyond all human understanding for accepting it (I Cor. 1:20; 3:18). Wicked rulers were going out of business (I Cor. 2:6) because the god of this age had blinded them to the truth of the gospel (II Cor. 4:4). Christians were not to be conformed but transformed by the renewal of their minds. That would enable them to determine what was the will of God—the "good and acceptable and perfect" (Rom. 12:2), for which Jesus had given his life.

All this was the **will of God and our Father** (KJV). Here the KJV translates literally; the meaning is "of God who is our Father." God's purpose in Christ's ministry, death, and resurrection was to create persons capable of spiritual fellowship with himself. He was still the sovereign judge of all the world, but Jesus changed the emphasis when he prayed, and taught his disciples to pray, "Our Father." Life in Christ was freedom for sonship as well as freedom from sin. Paul wanted more than forgiveness because he longed for power to live without sinning, and for new life which could fulfill the purpose for which God had set him apart before he was born.

God's **glory** is seen in his character as Creator and Judge of men, but most of all in his nature as Father of Christ and of Christians. The noun δόξα is rooted in the verb δοκέω, which means "expect," "think," "suppose," and "be reputed." Not least of God's glory is what his rational creatures think of him, and the estimation, repute, and honor which they accord him. Paul's doxology is far more than singing praise to God. When he said **Amen** (אמן, "be firm") to it, he put into one word his faith in God's grace through Christ, and praised God by living a life that caused others to form right ideas about him and accept Christ for themselves. He said "Amen" with all the energy which made him God's great "expendable" in the service of the gospel.

B. The Circumstances Which Necessitated Paul's Declaration (1:6-10)

6. Paul's omission of his customary thanksgiving for the fellowship, achievements, and prospects of his churches is an index of the seriousness with which he regarded the

pose for his life—**according to the will of our God and Father**—brings a sense of direction, the assurance of belonging to the permanent scheme of things, the conviction that he is being guided not so much by what he holds but by who holds him. Without this assurance of purpose, vital living is impossible, as impossible as to expect an electric bulb to produce light when unattached to the power line. The realization that one is living inside the purpose of God for his life can be counted upon to hold, steady, enlighten, and empower him.

Christ never promises his resources outside this purpose. "That whatsoever ye shall ask of the Father in my name, he may give it you" (John 15:16). "In my name" means "inside my purpose." His promise is not that he will provide what a man wants but what a man needs to fulfill that purpose. Nothing is so impressive as the man who is doing God's will for his life. Paul could write the formula for such surety (vss. 3-5) because Christ had demonstrated it in the apostle's own life.

Underneath a word of greeting, adequacy, peace, freedom, purpose is Paul's keyboard of mental health, demonstrating his capacity to be an intelligent and reliable interpreter of life and God. He was no eccentric or neurotic. He was a dependable interpreter, a man who has been trusted, and worthy of trust, all down the years.

6-9. *In Battle for the Gospel.*—Here Paul defends what he had taught the Galatians and calls down the anathemas of God upon all who

danger of apostasy in Galatia. He begins abruptly, saying: **I am astonished that you are so quickly deserting him who called you in the grace of Christ and turning to a different gospel.** The Greek word for **deserting,** μετατίθεσθε, means "transpose," "alter," "substitute," "pervert," "change one's mind"; its participle was a "turncoat." **Are . . . removed** (KJV) is misleading because the present tense shows that they were still in the act of changing; they might yet be persuaded to remain true.

Some take ταχέως, **quickly** (RSV), to mean "rapidly," but **soon** (KJV) is equally true to Paul's usage (I Cor. 4:19; Phil. 2:19, 24). He is speaking of the shortness of time between their reception of his gospel and their proposal to change it, rather than of their speed in doing so (on the length of the interval see Intro., p. 439).

Grammatically τοῦ καλέσαντος, **him who called** (RSV), may refer to God or to Christ, but Paul generally speaks of God as the source of his call (Rom. 8:30; 9:11, 24; I Cor. 1:9; 7:15, 17). On χάρις (**grace**) see vs. 3. God calls ἐν χάριτι Χριστοῦ, **in the grace of Christ.** Here the RSV corrects the **into** of the KJV. The correction is important because, according to Paul, God's grace already surrounds men, even while they are yet sinners. The absence of the article before χάριτι gives the Greek phrase a qualitative force: it was no ordinary grace but the grace of *Christ* that the legalists were proposing to supplement by law! Four interpretations of ἐν χάριτι have been proposed: (*a*) instrumental, "by grace"; (*b*) manner, "in lovingkindness and forgiveness"; (*c*) purpose, "to live in grace"; (*d*) place, "in the sphere of grace." Paul's usage is against (*a*) and in favor of (*d*), with overtones of meanings (*b*) and (*c*). He had in mind the sphere of grace versus the sphere of law (see Intro., p. 434). This would be indicated by **into** (KJV), but the preposition is not εἰς.

The Galatians were about to leave the sphere of grace and re-enter the domain of law, which Paul says is not **another** (KJV), in the sense of a **different** (RSV), gospel, but is no gospel at all. The terms ἕτερος and ἄλλος (cf. vs. 7) were used interchangeably to mean "another" and "different"; but I Cor. 15:39-41 shows that Paul associated "difference" with ἕτερος. For the meaning of εὐαγγέλιον, **gospel,** see vss. 3-5. Εἰς denotes the direction of their impending change: they were turning toward a different gospel with an inclination to accept it (for their reasons see Intro., pp. 434-35).

Paul believed that God had a plan for all men, individually and also collectively, through membership in the church. The call to join this fellowship and produce the

---

would pervert it, water it down, minimize its significance, abuse or corrupt it. Was Paul the only man in the apostolic church who understood the gospel fully and correctly? Was he justified in his vehement defense of that gospel in his letter to the Galatians? Could he defend it by speech and writing? If so, what kind of words, as a servant of Christ, was he entitled to use in defending it? Paul stopped short only of profanity. He could have used no stronger language and have remained within the bounds of propriety.

Even assuming that he had recently passed through experiences which may have colored his diction, yet we have to acknowledge that the tremendous words he used were measured and profoundly thoughtful. He never lost his balance. He was severe because he so intended. He wrote to the Corinthians out of anguish of heart, through tears, for their failure in Christian living; he was even more severe in his letter to the Galatians, for the very core of the Christian message was at stake. Remembering that the letter to the Galatians has changed history, that all might have been different had Paul written differently, that its 149 verses altered the world, one is not surprised to find him using words that were like dynamite. They were God's words before they were Paul's.

Some advocates of extreme religious tolerance hold that what a man believes is his own business. They insist that life and work, as sure demonstrations of his belief, are the tests that matter, at least as far as the public is concerned; that every man's religion is larger than he can define; that life is more definitive than theology. Keeping brotherly is all that matters, say they. Why quibble? Be practical. Co-operate or unite for worthy service programs in the spirit of Jesus and men will be led into the truth they need to live by. Let the theologians argue, not they. Theologians, as far as they are concerned, are left to split hairs, burn the midnight oil, and live on salaries which to many laymen symbolize their worth. Not so with the drawing of sharp social distinctions. Not so with United States

7 Which is not another; but there be
some that trouble you, and would pervert
the gospel of Christ.
8 But though we, or an angel from
heaven, preach any other gospel unto you
than that which we have preached unto
you, let him be accursed.

7 not that there is another gospel, but there
are some who trouble you and want to pervert the gospel of Christ. 8 But even if we,
or an angel from heaven, should preach to
you a gospel contrary to that which we

---

fruit of the Spirit (5:22-23) was the result of God's initiative, not of man's desert by obedience to law. Man must accept it in faith, and all who did so were destined to be conformed to the character of Christ and have eternal life in him. Paul's preaching and life had been God's means of calling the Galatians. His conception of Christian responsibilities appears in vss. 15-16; Rom. 8:28-30; I Cor. 1:9; 7:15-22; I Thess. 2:12; 4:7; II Thess. 2:14-15.

7. Paul called the proposal to supplement grace by law a gospel which was not **another gospel,** but no gospel at all, adding that there were some who were agitating his converts and wanting to change the gospel of Christ. The verb translated "change" μεταστρέψαι, means "turn about," "turn round," "twist," to change for good or ill, depending on the context. Paul found neither ἕτερος, "different," nor ἄλλος, "another," admissible when speaking of the gospel which Christ had incarnated; any change could only **pervert** it. Ταράσσω (rendered **trouble**) means "stir up," "agitate physically," "disturb" mentally and spiritually, "excite" with fear; εἰσιν, **there are,** with the present participle indicates that Paul was writing while his opponents were in the very act. In 4:17 and 6:13 he ascribed to these agitators—**who trouble you**—the desire for self-glorifying leadership. The genitive τοῦ Χριστοῦ, **of Christ,** leaves the reader to decide whether Paul means "Christ's gospel" or "the gospel concerning Christ." Probably Paul meant both—the gospel which Jesus lived and taught and that which his disciples were preaching about him.

8-9. The minions of "Satan" could appear as angels of light (II Cor. 11:14-15). It was not always easy to tell whether a preacher was a minister of Christ or of Antichrist, especially when he performed miracles (Acts 8:9-24; 14:8-18). There was reason to fear lest the Serpent lead the Galatians astray by his cunning. In the LXX εὐαγγελίζομαι stands for בשר, "to bring tidings," "bring good news." In the N.T. it means to preach the glad message of God's grace in Christ. A few MSS omit ὑμῖν **(you),** suggesting that Paul's anathema rests upon preachers everywhere who denature his gospel. The Greek preposition παρά means "by the side of," "beyond," as in "parallel." The legalist "gospel"

Supreme Court lawyers, who split hairs so sharply that many of the court's most history-making decisions have been by 5-4 votes. Not so with airplane pilots, whose split-second navigation means landing safely or cracking up. Not so with the scientist, whose split-cell research in laboratory or clinic means life or death. And in high and holy fact it is not so with theology either. It is from men like Paul and books like Galatians that contenders for the significance of doctrine get their ammunition. Such men and books sharpen the church's conscience to perform its historic function of being the custodian of truth. Such men cannot understand the morals of, nor will they have fellowship with, those who are tolerant of doctrinal looseness or unconcern; because what a man in his heart believes, soon or late he begins to be and do.

Getting men to see that strong, clear doctrinal thinking essentially matters is a difficult business; for one reason, because so much of the most original, authentic, and creative Christian thought is embedded in layers of obscure wordage, cumbersome phraseology, unimaginative or overimaginative writing. It is held down by thought patterns that are unrelated to literal, demonstrable, living concerns.

For this, the scholars are in part to blame. They have so hedged the Apostle in by piles of learned rubbish that a layman can hardly get at him. Thousands of books have been written about Paul, and most of them are learned. It seems well-nigh impossible to write about him without weighting the book down with erudition.[9]

[9] Jefferson, *Character of Paul,* pp. 4-5.

9 As we said before, so say I now again, If any *man* preach any other gospel unto you than that ye have received, let him be accursed.

10 For do I now persuade men, or God? or do I seek to please men? for if I yet pleased men, I should not be the servant of Christ.

preached to you, let him be accursed. **9** As we have said before, so now I say again, If any one is preaching to you a gospel contrary to that which you received, let him be accursed.

10 Am I now seeking the favor of men, or of God? Or am I trying to please men? If I were still pleasing men, I should not be a servant[a] of Christ.

[a] Or *slave*.

is **contrary** (παρ' ὅ) in the sense that it lies on a lower plane of religious experience, where the law's curse rests upon all who do not obey perfectly. Such a "gospel" leads Paul to repeat his anathema. The phrase **now again** shows that Paul is referring to something which he had said when he was in Galatia, not to what he has just written in vs. 8. Since it is unlikely that Paul ever preached a sermon without warning his hearers to guard against all who would make specious changes in his gospel, it is better to take the **before** as a reference to his previous visits to Galatia; cf. 4:13 and Intro., p. 439. The shift from "we told you" to "I say" may imply that the former admonitions were given jointly by Paul and his associates; but the change may be merely a matter of style.

In the LXX ἀνάθεμα translated חרם, which designated a person or thing **accursed** and devoted to destruction. In Acts 23:14 it is the oath of the would-be assassins of Paul. A curse was the more terrible because it was believed that once uttered, it was beyond recall, so that not even the man who uttered it could save his intended victim from its automatic effect.

Paul's passionate single-mindedness made it hard for him to treat his critics in the spirit of I Cor. 13. In Phil. 3:2 he is equally harsh, but Phil. 1:15-18 is consistent with the mind of Christ (cf. Rom. 9:1-3). As a Jew, Paul knew that his God was "jealous" of all other gods. So too, when he became a Christian, he felt a "divine jealousy" for the Christ who was jealous of all other saviors (I Cor. 16:22; II Cor. 11:1-6). The onliness of his Lord was so vital that it required the sharpest protest against everyone who refused to trust him solely. Galatia was exposed to all sorts of quacks and peddlers of specious gospels, and the whole world was infested with religious racketeers who knew how to make money by bewitching the masses in an age of catastrophic social change and spiritual bewilderment (see Intro., pp. 437-38). Asia Minor was a home of ecstatic cults and a spawning ground of prophets of other gods. Paul tore off their masks and adjured his converts to have nothing to do with them.

10. Paul's habit of being "all things to all men" (I Cor. 9:22) exposed him to the imputation of money-making and power-seeking (I Thess. 2:1-12; I Cor. 9:12-18; II Cor.

Here is the Christian's call—to get the truth of Christ into more general circulation, so that it may influence concrete situations and the general public. Why not let the earthy style of the market place become the language of religion? That is what Luther did in translating the Bible into German. He tells us that he looked down the throats of people in the market place. Much of the world's best religious thinking, and consequently much of the world's choicest wisdom, is locked up in jeweled caskets of thought patterns and in a vocabulary so obscure and remote that folk schooled in fields other than theology pass it by; and so the world's problems are untouched by Christ's light and power, which are imperative for their wise handling. The elemental style of Jesus himself must be recovered. He used language to reveal truth, not to conceal it.

The gospel of Jesus demands and deserves exact preaching. It is infinitely more than philosophical morality, more than a series of virtues with a philosophical overtone, more than insights and disclosures. It is all that because it is far more. With Paul it centers in one gift, the grace of Christ; and in one event, his Cross, together with the other side of that Cross, the Resurrection.

10. ***The Galatian Message.***—The central concern of this book is how a man can become and

11 But I certify you, brethren, that the gospel which was preached of me is not after man.

11 For I would have you know, brethren, that the gospel which was preached by me

10:1-6; 11:7-15). By the doubled curse which he has just pronounced he makes clear that he is not trying to please men in the evil sense of his critics. Since his gospel is neither κατὰ ἄνθρωπον, "according to man," nor κατὰ σάρκα, "according to human nature," it does not please men but requires their thorough repentance. This explains the logical connection of γάρ, **for** (KJV), which the RSV has left untranslated. Paul is asking how, in view of all this, he can be charged with pleasing men.

Πείθω means "persuade," "win favor," and in a bad sense, "talk another person over," "mislead" (Matt. 28:14; Acts 12:20). **Persuade** (KJV) does not fit the reference to God as well as **seeking the favor** (RSV). Paul persuades *men* to accept Christ (II Cor. 5:11), but seeks *God's* favor. The present tense of πείθω is conative: "Am I now trying to win favor?" The revisers follow a better text than the KJV in omitting **for** in 10*b*. Δοῦλος is **slave** (RSV mg.) not **servant,** which, despite its cruel snobbery, is too genteel to convey the plight of millions in Paul's day. In Christ, Paul found the only right slavery: he was now Christ's property, subject to his will and engaged in his service; but such slavery was perfect freedom. Since Christ had been crucified for doing good, it was impossible for his slaves to please men.

Saul the good Pharisee had sought to please God and men, but from the moment he became a Christian he knew nothing else but Jesus Christ crucified. He could have pleased the Jews by preaching law observance, and the pagans by making the death of Christ a mere sacrificial transaction without the obligation to be crucified with him. Instead, he insisted on keeping the scandal of the Cross at the very heart of his gospel and taking the consequences. That was the only way to prove that he was pleasing God rather than men.

This verse, printed in the RSV as a separate paragraph, forms the transition from Paul's statement of the circumstances to his defense of his apostleship.

C. Paul's Commission as an Apostle (1:11-17)

The best explanation of the differences between Galatians and Acts is that variant reports concerning Paul's relations with the Jerusalem apostles circulated in the early church. His opponents stressed the fact that he had not known Jesus and they overemphasized his dependence upon those who, like Ananias, had been Christians before him. He himself, writing in the heat of controversy, had no time to set down all he owed to

can remain a Christian. That issue was debated all over the early Christian world. One party insisted that Gentiles, desiring to become Christians, should first become Jews through the rite of circumcision. That change made them God's chosen people. Paul and his party agreed to circumcision for the Jews, but refused to require it of Gentiles. Circumcised Gentiles were regarded by some as having an added quality and social standing which the uncircumcised did not have. But there were others, then as now, who regarded the whole question as a matter more of hygiene than of religion, claiming the issue was too trivial for so much heat. This issue, however, held the essence of the Christian movement in principle. Had Paul lost, the Christian church might have been little more than a sect within the synagogue: it would have been tied to Jewish nationalism with a limited social outlook; it would have been denied the most direct and most personal access to God for every man, which privilege is at the heart of the Christian faith; it would have made man a servant and a slave, capable only of obedience, and not even of that, in a theocracy of dead, dying, or outgrown traditions; it would have denied him the central test of personality, the right of free choice.

11-12. ***The Meaning of Revelation.***—(See Expos. on vs. 1.) Paul began where Christ began with him. His experience on the Damascus road was the secret of his call and apostleship. He was not afraid to use the personal pronoun because he was trying to explain the impact Christ had made upon his life. He had gone through an experience of earthquake propor-

12 For I neither received it of man, neither was I taught *it,* but by the revelation of Jesus Christ.

is not man's[b] gospel. 12 For I did not receive it from man, nor was I taught it, but it came through a revelation of Jesus Christ.

[b] Greek *according to* (or *after*) *man.*

previous Christians who had instructed him by word and example. He was concerned not to deny that he received the facts about the life, death, and resurrection of Jesus from others, but to defend his interpretation of those facts.

11. Not man's gospel (RSV) is clearer than **not after man** (KJV). **According to man** (RSV mg.), in the sense of "human," expresses more fully the contrast Paul had in mind. He was insisting on the divine nature as well as the divine origin of his gospel.

A gospel **according to man** would have had no Cross to scandalize the Jews and incur the ridicule of the worldly wise (I Cor. 1:18-30). A typical human gospel was that of the self-worshiping state, which proclaimed the deity and saviorhood of its Caesars. The birthday of Augustus had been celebrated by his hopeful admirers as the beginning of the gospel of peace (εὐαγγέλιον) to all the world. Men made their gods and their gospels in the image of these lords of creation, whose appetite for power, glory, and triumph required to be appeased with sacrifices, flattered with praises, and maintained with servile obedience. The Messiah of the Jewish apocalypses was expected to achieve by miracle the moral contradiction of establishing justice by breaking the teeth of sinners and ruling the Gentile nations with a rod of iron. Roman and Jewish imperialism were alike in method: all who would not submit were destined for death or slavery. That was the gospel **according to man.**

The gospel that came from God was a Cross borne by God's own Son. But the philosophers did not associate suffering with Deity, and the cults which did proclaim dying and rising savior-gods were freighted with the sacramentarianism which always springs from failure to see that religion minus morals equals magic. Although the catharsis required of their devotees was not without effect on their spiritual state, they demanded no such abhorrence of sin as Paul's "crucifixion of the flesh." They exhausted themselves in emotional participation in passion rituals and sacraments to achieve oneness of essence with their gods. Salvation by emotion was central, and moral fellowship with God by loving and serving one's fellow men was incidental. These ways of mystical union with God were attempts at self-salvation. They too were gospels according to man.

Paul's gospel was revolutionary. His God was in Christ sacrificing himself for men. The Son of God was king indeed, but a King who ruled by enslaving himself and dying for his creation. His subjects were saved not because they had never disobeyed the law—although as God's newborn sons they were now fulfilling its essential purpose—but because they had responded in faith to his grace. Their King had taught that all were his brothers who do God's will (Mark 3:31-35), and now through his church he was calling all men to join his brotherhood and be conformed to the image of the Son of God (Rom. 8:29-30). That was the gospel according to Christ.

12. The emphatic **I** (ἐγώ) stresses Paul's equal footing with the twelve apostles; he was not taught the gospel in scribal fashion (see Intro., pp. 431-32). Though the appearance of the risen Lord to him at Damascus was "last of all" to "the least of all" (I Cor.

tions which completely changed his existence. Everything which followed had its rise in those luminous moments when Christ was unveiled to his inner sight. God took the initiative, not Paul; God uncovered his face, spoke his word, and called Paul. "Revelation" to Paul meant not primarily knowledge about God but an act of God in self-revealing. God entered Paul's life and took command. That experience is basically what revelation means for any man—Christ's coming into the center of life and taking command. Paul's experience was not a matter of aspiration but of reception. It was not something he attained but something he obtained. It did not come as the result of a long search; it was rather the beginning of an endless jour-

13 For ye have heard of my conversation in time past in the Jews' religion, how that beyond measure I persecuted the church of God, and wasted it:

[13] For you have heard of my former life in Judaism, how I persecuted the church of

15:8-9), that appearance was essentially the same as to Jesus' disciples on the third day after his crucifixion in Palestine. Because of vs. 16 it is better to explain Ἰησοῦ Χριστοῦ as a reference to God's revelation of Jesus Christ to Paul than as referring to Christ as the revealer of himself. Like the Greek, both the KJV and the RSV require the reader to decide. The change from **by the revelation** (KJV) to **through a revelation** (RSV) concentrates attention upon Paul's initial vision; but since he speaks of more than one vision (II Cor. 12:1), "through revelation" is preferable.

All had to depend for the facts upon the witness of those who had accompanied Jesus during his ministry (Acts 1:21-22). Yet despite the lapse of time, Paul's fellowship with his risen Lord was as directly personal as that of the twelve. Time, space, and physical sight were not in themselves the essential factor in faith's mystical companionship. The original apostles' understanding of the mission and message of Jesus depended, even as Paul's, upon spiritual affinity and response to him. Paul, who had never seen Jesus in his earthly body, was infinitely closer to him than were Judas and Pilate. This spiritual apprehension could not be conveyed by tradition alone. Through his Spirit, Jesus became the eternal contemporary of every generation of men. His continuing self-disclosure and creative guidance of his followers could not be confined to a fixed quantum of tradition thrust once for all into the stream of history and handed down from the original disciples after the manner of the scribes who sat in Moses' seat. In this respect no man could be the intermediary, any more than the ultimate source, of Paul's gospel.

Although the full significance of the gospel was a matter of more than one revelation to Paul, he was a twice-born man who regarded his vision at Damascus as a sudden miraculous change in his relationship to God. In retrospect he could see how everything that had happened to him was part of God's eternal leading (1:15). In a flash all his pre-Christian life had concentrated like rays of light through a burning glass to fire his soul with the conviction that Jesus was the Christ and the Son of God. He never stopped to analyze this catastrophic redirection of his life: it was revelation, and that was all he needed to say. His letters rest upon the contrast *before and after,* but they do not describe how the revelation came to him. (On Paul's conversion, see Vol. VII, pp. 189-92.)

13. Note the conative imperfect ἐπόρθουν, **tried to destroy** (RSV). **Conversation** (KJV) for ἀναστροφήν is misleading; but **violently** (RSV) is not adequate for καθ' ὑπερβολήν. In I Cor. 12:31 this phrase describes Christian love as the way "beyond all com-

ney with Christ. Paul's attempt to explain what came to him confronts the reader with vast ideas. His words therefore are often difficult to analyze, interpret, or grasp; for he is writing about life's ultimates. What God does to give himself to men and to change them into Christlikeness is one of these ultimates. Out of what God gave came Paul's experience.

13. ***His Persecutions of the Christians.***—Paul persecuted violently and relentlessly the followers of that Jesus who seemed to him then the nation's chief disturber. He put Christians to death in the name of patriotism and with the protection of his government. What would he have done had he, like Pilate, been given the chance to get his own hands on Jesus? How can one account for such ruthlessness? How could a man like Paul do what he did? His conscience was at war with itself. His mad conduct may have been the rumblings of his world toppling in upon him. Men do brutal things when their consciences are disturbed. The period of his life when he persecuted the Christians may have been a kind of Gethsemane, with dark days and darker nights, because they were filled with premonitions and intimations of things to come.

His mind was torn at the seams. He had inherited and had rigorously practiced a religion of iron rules, but his growing mind was revolting against them. A religion of rules always

14 And profited in the Jews' religion above many my equals in mine own nation, being more exceedingly zealous of the traditions of my fathers.

15 But when it pleased God, who separated me from my mother's womb, and called *me* by his grace,

God violently and tried to destroy it; 14 and I advanced in Judaism beyond many of my own age among my people, so extremely zealous was I for the traditions of my fathers. 15 But when he who had set me apart before I was born, and had called me

---

parison the best." Zealous and conscientious in his study and practice of Judaism, Paul persecuted the church "beyond limit"; and, never a man to do things by halves, he carried this habit of whole-souled devotion across the bridge of conversion. He never ceased to marvel at the goodness of God, who had drawn him from the slough of conscientious fear, fanaticism, and cruelty, and set his feet upon the royal road of faith, hope, and love. In Galatians he simply mentions the fact; in I Cor. 15:9 he expressed his grief for his former conduct. He had persecuted with a good conscience, but a dangerous conscience, because uninstructed by the mind of Christ. It required conversion to make him see that the society of Jesus, consisting of both Jews and Gentiles, was the true "chosen people."

14. **Profited** and **equals** (KJV) are corrected by **advanced** and **age** (RSV). Paul's estimate of his former religion and reputation as a Pharisee appears in II Cor. 11:22; Phil. 3:5-6; Rom. 3:1-2; 9:1-5; 11:1. These passages reflect the rivalries and competitive spirit that animated his training in Judaism. As a foreign Jew from Tarsus, he had to prove equal to the best of the Palestinians. He made steady progress (προέκοπτον) in learning and doing the Torah, and he was exceptionally zealous to acquire, observe, defend, and propagate the traditions of his forefathers. By **the traditions of my fathers** he meant both the written law and its oral development and application by the scribes (see Intro., pp. 431-33). Examples appear in Mark 7:1-13 and in the tractate Aboth of the Talmud. But good as his past had been, it was not good enough in comparison with Christ.

15-16*b*. The course of Paul's argument requires "and" rather than **but** to translate δέ. He is not contrasting his persecution of the church with God's call to be one of its missionaries, but just as he had no contact with the pillars of the church in Jerusalem before his conversion, so he sought no conference with them immediately afterward. The

---

operates so that either the rules break people or people break the rules. Paul was born to be dynamic and not to be held in, as if with bit and bridle, by ancient frameworks. His mind was more like yeast than like a yardstick. He was beginning, perhaps unconsciously, to see the hopelessness of the system in which he had grown up. His furious hostility to the followers of Christ makes it look as if in excessive cruelty he were seeking release from his problems. He was committing murder in the name of patriotism because his mind was torn.

14. ***The Background He Brought to Christ.***— No one can know Paul without understanding, in broad outline at least, the background he brought to Christ in his luminous hour on the Damascus road. Perhaps that very background made his conversion experience shine more brightly, for there was no purer Hebrew heritage than his. He was of the tribe of Benjamin, with a holy flame smoldering in his blood. As such a son of Abraham, he was distinctly a man of promise. His physical ancestry gave him courage; but to share Abraham's faith was his highest ancestral prize. Israelite was the national word for privilege. It stood for God's chosen people through whom he spoke to the rest of the world; and each individual Israelite could be a miniature of the nation. Paul's heritage gave him leadership among the Pharisees, the blue bloods of the nation.

He acquired the best education of his day. He knew Judaism by heart—its laws, its traditions, its requirements. Because he believed the practice of these ensured the well-being of his nation, relentlessly he persecuted the followers of Christ.

15. ***The Meaning of Grace.***— (See Expos. on vs. 3.) Grace is the key to the nature of God and the personality of man. [He] **called me through his grace.** "By the grace of God I am what I am" (I Cor. 15:10). Grace was the secret

text of the KJV inserts the word **God;** this is a correct interpretation but the word does not belong to the original text. God had **separated** Paul in the sense of setting him apart for this missionary service before he was born; hence the position of the phrase **from my mother's womb** in the KJV is liable to misinterpretation. On the other hand,

---

of Paul's new life. He could give worth to the living of other men because he had found it for himself. He connects grace directly with the development of his own personality. Not only did grace bring to him a totally new conception of religion and God; it brought also a new conception of himself. His prolific use of the pronoun in the first person reveals either a consummate egotist or a man utterly under the control of Christ. To those who know Paul best the choice between the two is not difficult. If the forgiveness of sins through Christ is the profoundest moral fact of all time, then the grace of Christ, of which forgiveness and the gift of the Spirit are the highest expression, is the strongest moral power. Grace has changed lives among the grossly wicked; it has saved splendid, eager spirits, troubled with their sense of moral inadequacy and incompleteness. This conception of grace does not depreciate human personality but enriches it.

Consider what happened in Paul's own person when he moved over and up from abstract obedience into a life of personal companionship and living union with God, moved from a book of rules to personal attachment. Jesus lifted him to those heights. "I call you not servants"—they only take orders; "I have called you friends"—they share his creative plans and purposes (John 15:15). Paul knew the ancient scriptures which recorded the fact that Abraham was his highest ancestral possession (Isa. 41:8). Now the fact that he too could be a friend of Abraham's God stood him on tiptoe.

Paul had been caught in the mire of self-pity and defeat; his spirit was broken and his life disintegrating. That condition is what a split personality would have meant to him. What was behind it? Manifestly, his conception of God. The only God he had known was "a task-master who paid strictly for service done."[1] His idea of God was the seat of his trouble. With a soul profoundly religious by nature, he yearned for a God whom no lawbook could provide. The patriotic and racial traditions in which he gloried only aggravated his confusion. He never found his sense of worth, dignity, and adequacy until he experienced the grace of Christ. The assurance of the psalmist, "He restoreth my soul" (Ps. 23:3), was fulfilled for Paul only in Jesus.

Grace therefore brought health, gladness, courage, worth-whileness to Paul. It also brought him into proper mental focus and fellowship with the God he had so misunderstood. He found that grace, not law, revealed God's real nature. Not only was he made in the image of God but he was restored to that image through the forgiving, healing grace of Christ.

Thus the grace of Christ meant for Paul a thoroughly integrated life, and this integration saw him through to the end of his days. Many writers have not portrayed him as a well-rounded person; they have often pictured him as a hardfisted doctrinaire, always declaiming against somebody's errors, constantly correcting and arguing, as if he alone were the possessor of truth. Paul was indeed the chief defender of clean-cut, Christ-centered thinking; but he was also the answer to the proposition, how to make religion attractive. There are passages which show him as a radiant, happy, glorious Christian, filled with a sense of his own worth, reflecting the nature of God and showing the way for all men to become more Christlike.

One passage that illustrates Paul's demonstration of the attractiveness of the Christian life is I Cor. 13. This chapter is the love lyric of the N.T. It is but a reflection of the life Paul achieved in Christ. He was sharp and quick-spirited, but the grace of Christ transformed his impetuous nature into light, power, and love. In another passage, written when he was an aged man, he admonished his beloved church in Phillippi, "Whatsoever things are true, . . . honest, . . . just, . . . pure, . . . of good report: . . . think on these things" (Phil. 4:8). Grace matured Paul's life into character like that. Still another passage which shows his maturity is II Tim. 4:7, "I have fought a good fight, I have finished my course, I have kept the faith." He might have said in exact truth that he had fought a good fight and had finished his course because he had kept the faith. Better still, the faith had kept him. Grace enabled him to see life through to a majestic finish, so that his books were balanced, his soul was solvent, and his was peace at eventide. The secret lay in the commitment of his earlier years—on the Damascus road—"in Christ," and in grace.

If the grace of Christ can thus restore primal dignity to human life, what does it indicate about the being of God himself? God is surely not less than he makes possible for men. Underneath Paul's own life story—after his conversion—was his new conception of God. And what was that new conception? The picture of God

[1] Scott, *Varieties of N.T. Religion*, p. 109.

16 To reveal his Son in me, that I might preach him among the heathen; immediately I conferred not with flesh and blood:

through his grace, 16 was pleased to reveal his Son to[c] me, in order that I might preach him among the Gentiles, I did not confer

[c] Greek *in*.

in me (RSV mg.) for ἐν ἐμοί is correct; **to me** (RSV) does not express the mystical fellowship described in 2:20; cf. II Cor. 13:3. On the mode and meaning of this revelation see Exeg. on vs. 12 and on II Cor. 4:6. The Son of God had taken possession of Paul's whole inner being, and it was his greatest concern to live so that others would become fellow imitators of the Christ they saw in him.

As a Pharisee, Paul learned that life is more than an eddy of purposeless dust. The Jew was born to glorify God by doing his will. This conception of God's purpose was rooted in the O.T. prophets. Paul and Jeremiah were kindred spirits in their conception of God's call and man's task (Jer. 1:5, 10; Rom. 1:1; I Cor. 3:10; II Cor. 10:5; cf. also Isa. 49:1-3). Like Jeremiah, Paul was a wise master builder. He laid his foundation on Christ crucified and raised from the dead, and he warned the self-appointed "building inspectors" in Galatia that all other blueprints were spurious, even though they claimed the approval of the apostolic "architects" in Jerusalem. Having torn down the wreck of his past life under the law, he refused to build it up again (2:16, 18).

16*c*-17. After his trance at Damascus the natural thing would have been to consult an interpreter of dreams. The verb προσανεθέμην designated resort to soothsayers. But that is just what Paul says he did not do. We have no means of knowing exactly where

with grace as his strongest and foremost quality may be called the grace-concept of God.

Since grace is completely a personal transaction, since it is person-sourced, person-given, and person-received, obviously the grace-concept of God is that God is a person. He is at least a person: he is a person plus. Personality is the near side of God. We understand him increasingly through the vista of the personal virtues, the fruit of grace.

Some twentieth-century minds have difficulty in conceiving of God as a person. They more readily think of him in terms of force, power, process, or oversoul. The chief weakness in each of these conceptions is that it leaves the highest part of man's life untouched, unawakened, unsatisfied. And therefore man is left by his idea of God to live on a subhuman level. If God is only force or power, life is mechanical and man is like a cog in a machine; if God is but process, life loses its creativity, its highest faculty; if God is over-soul, individuality and personality are absorbed.

It is not too much to assert that the Christian religion beyond all others has adhered to and has taught belief in a personal God because of its doctrine and experience of grace. Paul was a thorough student not only of Hebrew but of Greek as well. His mind easily belongs in the best company of both cultures. His understanding, knowledge, and experience of God provided the background for his new experience on the Damascus road. Grace meant to him, and means today, resources beyond the generation of man: it means daily companionship with the God who gives this grace; it is a purely personal transaction which will not work on a mechanical, animal, subhuman level. It is in us as persons that the nature of God is revealed. "However far above purpose God may be, He is also purposeful, and however far above personality, He is also personal, and however far beyond consciousness, He is also conscious, and however far beyond fatherhood He may be He is also vitally, intimately, dependably, 'Our Father.'"[2] This was the God Paul learned to know in Christ. He was the God of all grace. Before him Paul knelt freely. Kneeling before such a God, he could stand up straight before life.

15-16. *His Conversion.*—Various descriptions of Paul's conversion should be pieced together. To the Galatians he expressed the belief that before his birth, climaxing in the Damascus roadside experience, God had been calling him through his grace, had revealed his Son to him in order that he might preach to the Gentiles.

Paul says in the book of Acts that he was stopped short, that he heard Christ call him by name, that he was blinded and had to be led into the city. Though physically blind, it was his destiny-making hour. The fact of his change is infinitely more important than the details of

[2] John Wright Buckham, *Christianity and Personality* (New York: Round Table Press, 1936), p. 132.

17 Neither went I up to Jerusalem to them which were apostles before me; but I went into Arabia, and returned again unto Damascus.

with flesh and blood, 17 nor did I go up to Jerusalem to those who were apostles before me, but I went away into Arabia; and again I returned to Damascus.

he went. It may have been into that part of Arabia which was nearest Damascus, or to some city, perhaps Petra. From his letters and Acts it is clear that he preferred cities to the country. To conclude from 4:25 that he went to Mount Sinai is sheer conjecture.

Some suppose that Paul went into Arabia to think through his shattering experience, to reconstruct his life and plan his future. They cite the examples of the O.T. prophets and Jesus, and the habit of mystics to retire for meditation. But although Paul did want to commune with God through Christ, and not with human beings—**flesh and blood**—his mysticism was of the vigorously active type, rather than purely contemplative. At once he would have to tell others about the wonderful new salvation he had found. But **immediately** (KJV) it was advisable to leave Damascus to avoid embarrassing his new Christian friends. Time was needed for his sponsors, such as Ananias, to overcome the fears of those who had suffered at his hands. His former Jewish associates, outraged by his apostasy, were ready to treat him after the pattern of his own former violence. His position immediately following his conversion was not easy.

Since Paul was never in any place very long before getting into trouble with the authorities, it is likely that his stay in Arabia was short. Why he left may be inferred from

how it came to be. Attempts to discredit it, and theories to explain it, are far less significant than the fact itself. For one thing, there is a limit to the retailing of personal experience for public consumption. Scripture seems to illustrate the Christian regard for personality by never embarrassing its heroes, by respecting private matters and personal details. Permanent values are not necessarily in personal incidents but in reproducible experiences. Men are not permitted to gaze upon but only to glimpse what matters. The curtain is lifted only for a moment. Whatever happened in his conversion had to be transcendent enough to account for the complete reversal of Paul's life.

What he had discarded, he now picked up; what he had hated, he now loved; what he had discounted, he now valued; what he had scorned, he now made central; what he had abhorred, he now adored; whom he would have killed, he now devoted his life to serving. Read his life history backward. Paul had found something and Someone greater than all he had previously defended. More than his literary skill, more than all the qualities of his mind, more than his philosophical and theological training under Gamaliel is required to explain his transformation. Instead of getting the chance to lay his hands on Christ, Christ laid his hands on Paul, and Paul's life was completely changed. In that change is the difference between Judaism and Christianity. He had found not another prophet, not a greater teacher than Gamaliel, not a wiser rabbi, but a living Presence who fulfilled, transcended, and illuminated the traditions of the fathers which he knew so well and loved so dearly.

17-23. ***The Test of Experience.***—Paul submitted his Damascus road conversion to at least five tests: (*a*) He tested it in the desert of Arabia (vs. 17; but cf. Exeg.). (*b*) He tested it in conference with Peter and James (vss. 18-19). (*c*) He tested it by sharing it with those whom he had previously persecuted (vss. 21-23). (*d*) He tested it by participating in the Jerusalem conference (2:1-2). (*e*) He tested it by conflict with Peter (2:11).

Paul tested his conversion in the loneliness of the Arabian desert. **I went away into Arabia** (vs. 17). Under what he undoubtedly believed to be the guidance of God, Paul went into the desert of Arabia, a territory stretching from Damascus to Mount Sinai, from the Red Sea to the Persian Gulf. What Paul did there and how long he stayed, no man really knows. He did not tell even Luke, his biographer and intimate friend; or if he did, Luke regarded his time of rest and reflection as a personal matter which did not belong in the record of the public ministry which is described in the book of Acts.

Could one very simple reason be at least part of the answer? Paul as a tentmaker could there support himself during his period of solitude and struggle by making tents for the nomad tribes which lived nearby. However that may be, obviously there is in the desert an awayness, an apartness rarely equaled anywhere else. There social influences are reduced to a minimum; there it is easier to cultivate the vertical awareness of God without hindrance from the

18 Then after three years I went up to Jerusalem to see Peter, and abode with him fifteen days.

18 Then after three years I went up to Jerusalem to visit Ce'phas, and remained with

what he says about Aretas in II Cor. 11:32. This was Aretas IV, king of the Nabataeans, who reigned from 9 B.C. to A.D. 40 over the territory which had been occupied in olden times by the Edomites in the region of Petra. For some reason, perhaps in consequence of preaching his new gospel, Paul incurred Aretas' hostility and returned to Damascus; then the king posted a guard outside the gates to arrest him in case he tried to leave the city. This would be the natural inference from what Paul himself says. According to Acts, the enemies who wanted to kill Paul were Jews inside the city lying in wait for him inside the gates; but it is not explained why they took this peculiar method of apprehending him.

D. The Recognition of Paul's Apostleship by the Pillar Apostles in Jerusalem (1:18–2:10)

1. Three Years Later (1:18-24)

18-20. Paul does not say whether he is counting the three years from his conversion or from his return to Damascus. Since it was customary to reckon parts of years as full years, the whole period may have been somewhat less. Paul's reason for leaving Damascus appears in II Cor. 11:32 and Acts 9:23. His purpose in going to Jerusalem was to visit Cephas. The verb ἱστορῆσαι has two sets of meanings, (*a*) "inquire," "narrate," "report," and (*b*) "visit" persons or places, a meaning which is often found in Hellenistic Greek. Instead of Κηφᾶν (Aramaic, "Rock"), many MSS substitute Πέτρον, the more familiar name of the apostle.

The tenor of Paul's argument indicates that his visit was not motivated by doubt concerning the truth of his gospel. His revelation, confirmed by three years of new life

horizontal affairs of men. A gospel which had come to Paul directly from God could be pondered and spelled out in the eternal silence of God. As the stars over the desert wastes seem so near—near enough almost for one to reach up and pluck them—so there man's spirit may be peculiarly close to the Eternal. Would this undisturbed closeness help calm and heal a mind so recently torn from its former spiritual moorings? Paul found, if he did not know before, that there is healing in this universe because there is a healing Mind at its center.

Whatever the details of the story, the desert proved a fitting place in Paul's unfolding pilgrimage. He had not easily added Jesus to his list of Hebrew prophets: his very existence had been completely altered by one who is mightier than a prophet. It took the solitariness of the desert to put his world together on Christ's larger terms and pattern. He stayed long enough away from the civilization of his day to do it. It was Christ and Paul, no others; for Paul was determined to know in more detail the One who had turned his life inside out. In the remote loneliness of the desert he found that religion in one of its aspects at least is "what the individual does with his own solitariness,"[3] what happens to a man in his solitude.

> After such a convulsion as Paul had passed through, with a whole world of new ideas and emotions pouring in upon him, he felt that he must be alone; he must get away from the voices of men. . . . He will be able to take a calmer survey of the new world into which he has been ushered, and will learn to see clearly and walk steadily in the heavenly light that at first bewildered him. . . . In Arabia one confers, not with flesh and blood, but with the mountains and with God.[4]

Some people change their life patterns readily, but not a man with the capacity of Paul. He had to go through a profound reconstruction of his total thinking. Spelled out, that meant for him not the truth of life as written in a lawbook; it was rather a present-day fellowship fresh with every morning, built upon and around "the actual contemporary presence of Christ."[5] Paul no longer looked back to Moses, not even to

[3] A. N. Whitehead, *Religion in the Making* (New York: The Macmillan Co., 1926), p. 16.

[4] Findlay, *Galatians*, p. 79.

[5] Sittler, *Doctrine of the Word*, p. 25.

in Christ, assured him that his interpretation was right. But his principle of grace for all involved a conception of the church as the one body of Christ. If this ideal was to be achieved, the leaders in Jerusalem, which was the initial center from which the church had spread, would have to be persuaded to recognize his freer and more mystical type of Christian experience as on equal footing with theirs. He had been accustomed to regard Jerusalem as his Holy City. Having decided that his work as a missionary lay in the West rather than the East, he required the Jerusalem church for a base, just as later he needed Rome when he was planning to go to Spain. The fact that he chose to visit Peter rather than any of the other apostles is an indication of the leading part this rock-apostle had taken in gathering the dismayed and scattered followers of Jesus into a church (Matt. 16:17-19).

This interview with Peter is important for understanding Paul's relation to the historical Jesus. On the basis of 2:6 and II Cor. 5:16 it has been asserted that he knew little about the details of Jesus' career prior to his crucifixion and exaltation as Christ and heavenly Lord. But this overlooks four things: (*a*) In Galatians, Paul is not declaring his independence of the original apostles for his knowledge of the facts about Jesus, but confirming the correctness of his interpretation of them. (*b*) Even though he does not quote Jesus or Peter and the rest directly, his letters are based on adequate knowledge of the things which Jesus did and taught. (*c*) He would not have persecuted the Christians so furiously if he had not known enough about Jesus and his teachings to convince him that they constituted a revolutionary threat to Judaism. (*d*) Fifteen days would be ample to get the facts about Jesus, though a lifetime was too short to work out their meaning (I Cor. 13:12).

Abraham, but forward with "the eternal Contemporary." "He was swept from all his old moorings, and left with nothing to cling to but the vision he had had of Jesus, who had somehow gotten into his heart and taken possession." [6]

Knowing Christ in the present tense keeps life filled with surprises and high enterprise. For those who have missed this central heartbeat of the Christian faith there seem to be two favorite retreats. One is to put religion into the past tense and the third person by making it a controversy over old shibboleths, prejudices, and arguments. The woman at the well tried to parry the thrust of truth into her conscience by calling up the hackneyed argument as to where the temple should be built (John 4:17-23). But Jesus was not so easily foiled. He pressed the issue until it rested in the woman's deepest mind, and there came a present tense experience for her in lieu of a past tense argument.

A second refuge for those who miss "the eternal Contemporary" is to project their religion into the future tense, thereby often running away from life's contemporary needs and present-day obligations into speculations about Christ's second coming to set up a physical government on this planet. Clearly the N.T. teaches that Christ will return in his own time to judge men and nations—but only on the basis of what men do with him in the living present.

Indeed and forever, the tense that tests is the present. Fellowship with this living, contemporary Christ makes life and religion a present tense affair. That was Paul's discovery. In that discovery he found himself, his life calling, his life message. Through the discipline of loneliness and solitariness he began to grow in the fellowship of the Christ whom he had met. He found his rainbow in the desert, and returned in possession of himself and his gospel.

He tested his experience in conference with Peter and James (vss. 18-19). It appears likely that Peter alone knew, in advance, of Paul's coming to Jerusalem; at most only Peter and James, the administrative head of the Jerusalem church. Paul's visit was to confirm his roadside experience, to which everything else was secondary. He had determined to stay away from the apostles so that his gospel and the call to spread it might be without the medium of any man, including the first apostles. They could only confirm him, but their confirmation he wanted so that there would be unity in presenting the gospel to a pagan world.

The reasons why he went so quietly to Jerusalem are clear enough. Otherwise, the rumor "Paul is here" might well have spread like a prairie fire through the Christian community, as well as among those who were still persecuting the Christians. The curious would then have

[6] Edgar J. Goodspeed, *Paul* (Philadelphia: John C. Winston Co., 1947), p. 20.

19 But other of the apostles saw I none, save James the Lord's brother.

him fifteen days. **19** But I saw none of the other apostles except James the Lord's

19. Paul did not visit the other apostles. This was probably not because they were absent from Jerusalem, nor from fear of being seen with them, but because he felt no need to consult them or secure ordination at their hands. To visit Peter was to visit the leader of the twelve, and to see James was to see the head of Jesus' family.

James the Lord's brother is mentioned in Mark 6:3. He was not one of the twelve, and he does not seem to have accepted his brother's claims until a special resurrection appearance convinced him (Mark 3:21, 31-35; John 7:5; I Cor. 15:7). But by the time Paul was presenting his claim to be included with the apostles, James was an authoritative figure in the Jerusalem church (2:9, 12; Acts 15:13; 21:18). Acts pictures him as a fair-minded conservative Christian. He kept in good standing with the Jews, having a reputation for great piety, until he was stoned to death at the instigation of Annas, a renegade high priest in A.D. 62. Tradition put him down as the first bishop of the church in Jerusalem.

Looking at the history of the apostolic age, one can see that, as in the case of Mohammed's successors, a kind of caliphate might have been formed by Jesus' family and their descendants. This was prevented partly by the slowness of Jesus' relatives to accept him, but mainly because Paul and others of like mind claimed an equal apostleship. The qualifications of an apostle are reported in Acts 1:21-22, and the lists of the twelve in Mark 3:16-19; Matt. 10:2-4; and Acts 1:13 show that while the number was fixed, tradition varied the names of the persons who comprised the apostolic group. Matthias was chosen by lot to take the place of Judas, and others of those who had accompanied Jesus during his ministry and had seen him after his resurrection were eligible to be his ἀπόστολοι, "messengers," "delegates"—to summon men to repent and prepare for the kingdom of God. But Paul sharpened the requirements for valid apostleship to one essential: to have seen the risen Lord and be filled with his mind and Spirit. Thus he grounded the Christian apostolate upon spiritual kinship with Jesus. Aspirants had to be "good" men like Barnabas, "full of the Holy Spirit and of faith" (Acts 11:24)—men with creative imagination and practical initiative, willing to risk their lives for Christ

had a field day, and the purpose of his visit would have been defeated. There were, too, in all likelihood, those who would have put him to death for changing sides.

Why did Paul choose to visit these two? He had substantial reasons; count on that! Take a look at Peter first. It was natural that Paul should talk with the man who was the spokesman of the apostolic company. If James was the administrative head of the church, Peter was the prophet. Paul's interview with Peter is frail testimony, if any at all, to the view that Peter was the first pope.

Let no Pauline enthusiast, however, discount Peter. He was a born leader, a man's man, husky and hearty, impetuous, a very gifted public speaker, a member of the fisherman's union of Galilee—at heart devoted to Jesus, even though he sometimes had difficulty understanding what Christ meant. Though lacking an educational preparation comparable to Paul's, Peter as a leader in the first-century church filled a unique place. The struggle of his days was to break through the confinements of the ancient law into full-grown freedom in Christ. At first he did not see clearly the "liberty which we have in Christ Jesus" (2:4); either he was confused or he was afraid. The battle of Peter with Paul comes later in this study of Galatians. It is sufficient now to consider Peter as a source of the firsthand personal data about the life of Jesus which Paul needed for the fuller confirmation of his Damascus road experience. Paul was in search of personal material which Peter was in a position to give. But to the point of naming the number of days he stayed with Peter, Paul is insistent on showing how ridiculous was the assumption that he got his gospel from Peter. He could hardly have taken even an orientation course in fifteen days.

What two weeks those two men must have spent together! Imagine the chief defender of Christ and the former chief persecutor walking together amid the scenes—in and about the Holy City—so dear and sacred to the Christian heart. What a visit! They must have looked

20 Now the things which I write unto you, behold, before God, I lie not.
21 Afterward I came into the regions of Syria and Cilicia;

brother. 20 (In what I am writing to you, before God, I do not lie!) 21 Then I went into

(Acts 15:26). In these respects Paul was abundantly justified in claiming that he was an apostle, even though he had not known Jesus "in the flesh."

20. The line of least resistance would have been to secure an authoritative body of tradition about Jesus and accept the twelve apostles as the only infallible interpreters of its meaning and application. Paul's refusal to do so measures the value he placed on his freedom to talk with Christ directly through the indwelling Spirit; but his difficulty in persuading his opponents of the truth of his gospel was proportional to his insistence upon his independence. The nature of the revelation at Damascus made it insusceptible of proof to those who were unwilling to give this former persecutor of the church the opportunity to prove the truth of his gospel by his life. Evidence of the way his enemies took advantage of his dilemma appears in I Thess. 2:1-12 and II Cor. 1:12–2:4; and the way he met it is illustrated in Rom. 9:1-3 and II Cor. 11:21-33, where he put himself under oath to be telling the truth.

21. Emphasizing his independence, Paul continues: **Then I went into the regions of Syria and Cilicia.** Acts tells the story so differently that no attempt to reconcile the two accounts has been successful (Acts 9:28-30; 11:19-26; see also Intro., pp. 435-37). Paul does not say where he went in Syria, nor how the fourteen years between the visit to Jerusalem mentioned in vs. 18 and that of 2:1 were divided between Syria and Cilicia; but probably the greater part of this time was spent in Syrian Antioch.

Antioch was an ideal city for this zealous missionary. The church had been founded by fugitives from the stoning of Stephen. At first they preached only to Jews, but then

deeply into each other's souls. Men of destiny! Men of God! Paul thus tested his experience, and perhaps sharpened his own insights with fresh, firsthand testimony from another of Christ's own, who though so feelingly loyal had yet to think through the meaning of his faith.

His conference with James is more difficult to describe. James was the head of the church in Jerusalem because he was the brother of Jesus. But Paul was on a much more important mission than paying ecclesiastical respects or obeying some church protocol. What was he after? What might a blood brother like James have for a spiritual son like Paul? Obviously James might possess details of Jesus' life which only a near relative could have. Such details might throw light upon Paul's inquiring mind and questions. They might add historical substance to his spiritual experience. Is it unfair and illogical to see in Paul's conference with James some possible clue to one of the church's profoundest problems: the relation of "the Jesus of history" to "the contemporary Christ" or "the Christ of experience"? James knew "the Jesus of history"; Paul knew "the contemporary Christ." How could each approach reinforce the other?

There are two facts about this Jesus of history, Jesus of Nazareth—the man about whom more is known than about any other who lived that far back in history—which throw light on the contemporary Christ. One of these facts is the quality of his character. Indeed, one of history's miracles is that in two thousand years no serious attempt has been made to attack Jesus' character. One of Jesus' words is true not only as he asked it but also in reverse: "If you cannot find fault with my life, why do ye not believe what I say?" (John 8:46). Might he not now add, "If you believe what I say, why not trust what I do, including the giving of myself as a living presence?"

The other fact about the Jesus of history that throws light upon our understanding of the contemporary Christ is the authenticity of his teaching. His teaching commands the respect, if not the allegiance, of many who decline to go further and accept him as Lord. The quality of his life and the authenticity of his teaching are evidence of Jesus' total reliability. They are norms by which to study and examine every alleged experience of the contemporary Christ. Is it too much to believe that in some manner like this Paul got help from the man who was the blood brother of our Lord, the man who certainly knew "the Jesus of history"?

Paul tested his experience by sharing it with those whom he had previously persecuted (vss.

22 And was unknown by face unto the churches of Judea which were in Christ:

the regions of Syria and Ci-li'cia. 22 And I was still not known by sight to the churches

came men from Cyprus and Cyrene preaching to the Greeks also. Soon the church made such an impact that "in Antioch the disciples were for the first time called Christians," and the city became the first great base for foreign missions (Acts 11:19-21, 26; 13:1-3).

The historical situation which favored this rapid growth throws light upon what Paul meant by "the fullness of the time" (4:4). Political and social conditions in Antioch explain why it was there rather than in Jerusalem that a fellowship which made Jew and Greek equal in Christ Jesus could take root and flourish. It was called the third city of the Roman Empire. The Romans had made it a free city and capital of Syria. The emperors beautified it, and Herod the Great paved and colonnaded one of its streets. His expenditure indicates the influence of the Jews in Antioch. They enjoyed the right of citizenship and equality of privileges with the Macedonians and Greeks who lived there (Josephus *Antiquities* XII. 3. 1). These good relations between Jews and Gentiles favored the development of the Christian ideal of oneness which transcended racial and national exclusiveness. But there were also hindrances. The blue-blooded Roman moralists, reporting facts, but also seeking scapegoats for the moral disintegration for which they too were responsible, were loud in complaint that all pestilent superstitions and immoralities were flowing from Antioch through the Orontes into the Tiber. This reputation of Antioch was a warning against the danger that a gospel of freedom from law might aggravate the growing depravity, and it helps to explain the alarm of the conservatives in Jerusalem.

22-24. The periphrastic ἤμην ἀγνοούμενος, **I was still not known** (RSV), indicates that Paul remained unknown in person—lit., **by face** (KJV)—for some time. **In**

21-24). Paul "preacheth the faith of which he once made havoc" (ASV). This preaching included, of course, public addresses, as well as personal interviews, group lessons, discussions, and conferences, especially with the most spiritually matured in the churches. By such strategy and program he showed that the Arabian retreat had had its desired effect: he now sufficiently understood his faith in Christ to be able to define and defend it. He applied to his conversion what we would call the laboratory method.

He tested himself, as well as his experience, by returning to the very places where he had been most desperately wrong, to the places where his persecution of the Christians had been most violent. He saw that the way of Christ for him was to go where he had failed, and there to demonstrate his new life and light. The reliability of his experience was tested by his willingness and ability to share his faith, especially in places where his sin had been greatest, such as **Damascus** (vs. 17) and **the regions of Syria and Cilicia** (vs. 21).

Most of all, he tested his new faith by defending it in the only way the Christian faith can be truly defended: by Christlike living. He bore his testimony by deed as well as by word. He came not primarily to debate, but to heal where he had torn down, to construct where he had been most ruthless, to redeem where he had destroyed.

22. ***Paul's Most Unique Phrase.*—In Christ** is used 164 times in Paul's letters. This phrase for him meant four profound truths. (*a*) It is the source of Christian morality (2:4). (*b*) It represents Paul's concept of what it means to be a Christian (2:16). (*c*) It illustrates the central teaching of Christ himself (2:20). (*d*) It presupposes the Cross (2:20).

Biographically for Paul, **in Christ** represented the new relationship into which his roadside experience had ushered him. Luther said a man's religion comes out in the pronouns he uses; Adolf Deissmann said it is rather in his prepositions. The latter is the story of Paul. **In Christ** is the key to all he thought and did. He uses the phrase over and over. And not alone of a personal relationship, but of a relationship in the Christian church as well: **the churches of Judea which were in Christ.** The geographical location was Judea, but the permanent locale was **in Christ.** The church spelled with a small *c* is a human organization of which a census may be taken; the church spelled with a large *C* is a divine institution which no man can number, for it includes all who love Jesus Christ. The former is the church visible; the latter is the church invisible. To be in Christ

23 But they had heard only, That he which persecuted us in times past now preacheth the faith which once he destroyed.
24 And they glorified God in me.

of Christ in Judea; 23 they only heard it said, "He who once persecuted us is now preaching the faith he once tried to destroy."
24 And they glorified God because of me.

Christ (KJV) is required for ἐν Χριστῷ, as in I Thess. 1:1; 2:14; II Thess. 1:1; Phil. 1:1, where the RSV retains the literal rendering. "Churches in Christ" are, of course, churches **of Christ,** but the latter phrase does not convey the mystical overtones of Paul's fellowship in and with Christ. **In Judea** includes Jerusalem (cf. I Thess. 2:14). In its restricted sense **Judea** comprised that part of Palestine south of Samaria and west of the Jordan, but more probably Paul used the word in its wider sense which included Samaria and Idumaea. The attempt to reconcile Acts 26:20 with Paul's statement by supposing that he had preached in Jerusalem but not in any Judean churches outside the city is far-fetched. Allowance must be made for Luke's geographical schematization which begins the Christian movement in the capital and spreads it over expanding horizons through "all Judea and Samaria and to the end of the earth" (Acts 1:8; 26:20).

23. Since πορθέω means "destroy," "ruin," the imperfect must be given a conative sense: **tried to destroy** (RSV) instead of **destroyed** (KJV). The churches in Judea kept hearing (ἀκούοντες) about Paul's miraculous change, and the **us** (ἡμᾶς) whom he persecuted refers to Christians in general. **The faith** which he had tried to break was their trust in Christ.

24. For ἐν ἐμοί the literal **in me** (KJV) should be retained, as in vs. 16. The God who was "in" Christ had shone "in" Paul's heart, germinating his word of reconciliation (II

---

is a relationship available not only for individuals but also for those same individuals as a part of the total fellowship of the church. This is the church against which the gates of hell shall not prevail. Only when the church is in Christ does it have any assurance of victory. By being in Christ the church may keep the splendor of God in the souls of men no matter how long their social hopes are frustrated or delayed.

There are those who regard the church as a kind of mold or cast into which spiritual materials may be poured. When these materials are permanently set, all the framework may be removed, since it serves only a temporary function. The church, however, is infinitely more than a scaffolding or mold, a movement, a means to an end, an association. Much of the church's organizational structure changes with the area in which it is located and with each generation; but the church as a fellowship of people in Christ antedates and outlives any other aspect of the church itself or of its mission.

The fact that a church, as well as an individual, may be **in Christ** may indicate that there is a relation in Christ only possible in group fellowship. "Where two or three are gathered together in my name, there am I in the midst of them" (Matt. 18:20). There are insights, attachments, alliances with Christ which are possible only for a man who is alone in quiet, personal devotion. There are other insights into life and experience with Christ which are possible only in association with others who, like himself, are in Christ.

23. ***The Meaning of Faith.***—(See Expos. on vss. 17-23.) Faith for Paul had at least a sixfold meaning: (*a*) faith as a capacity (3:11); (*b*) faith as response (2:20; 3:2); (*c*) faith as trust (2:16); (*d*) faith as covenant (3:15-22); (*e*) faith as belief (2:20); (*f*) faith as adventure (5:5-6).

24. ***Instrument of the Eternal.***—Checking his conversion with the fellowship never violated the sacredness of Paul's individuality. Paul was still Paul. He was not absorbed into an anonymous priesthood. He found he did not lose his identity in the fellowship. Indeed, the awareness of a splendid, definable variety of Christian experience enriches and enlarges the fellowship and every Christian within it. The Christian life is not a one-man matter; it is not for the mystic alone, or the celibate, or the specialist. Christ meets everyone where he is and in terms of his individual endowments. He walks in the dust and divinity of every path as surely as he walked on the road to Emmaus the first Easter evening, and on Paul's Damascus road.

Perhaps one reason why Christians saw God in Paul was the fact that Paul had seen the true expression of God's face in another man, a man whom he had helped to stone only a little while

Cor. 3:18; 4:6; 5:19). Paul would never say, "I am Christ," but he did conceive it to be his mission to stand as Christ before men, and that was the character in which his Galatian friends had received him (4:14). He became as Christ to others in order that they might learn "in" him what the mind of Christ was like (I Cor. 4:6). Before the Christians could glorify God in Paul, Paul had first to glorify God in himself by living among them as God's own Son had lived. In that sense every Christian was to be as Christ.

The glory of God was God's character manifested in Christ. To glorify God was to live so as to cause others to think right thoughts about him and turn to him in grateful faith in Christ Jesus. That was something greater and more difficult than to sing praises in God's honor. Since his glory was expressed in his forgiveness of sinners, the only way to glorify him was to forgive one's fellow men. In Paul's case this meant that the churches had to receive a former deadly enemy as one of themselves and to demonstrate to him and to the world the love which never fails. The stresses and strains of the Galatian controversy show how hard this was. From the standpoint of conservative Jewish Christians there was no little risk in receiving such a vigorous, restless, creative person as Paul.

---

before—Stephen, the first Christian martyr (Acts 7:58). Paul had seen a light in Stephen's face which he had seen in no other, save in that of Christ himself. How could he ever make amends for the wrong he had done? Public confessions and explanations could not bring Stephen back or heal the wounds in Paul's own soul. Perhaps there was only one way in which he could atone: he could attempt to do Stephen's work for Christ, as well as his own. Here may be one of the secrets of Paul's overfilled days. The martyr whom he had seen die became Paul's spiritual forerunner. Stephen had preached the same gospel Paul was destined to preach, a universal gospel for men beyond the limits of Judaism; and he had seen, before Paul did, the superiority of Christ over the ancient law. The way Stephen died, his praying the prayer Christ prayed on the Cross, haunted Paul to the end of his days and perhaps made him more thoroughly persuaded of the truth of Christ than any other human influence. It was his "magnificent obsession."

"Till thou hast bound me fast I am not free." Paul's desire to demonstrate his new life in Christ had the effect for which he prayed: Men glorified God on account of Paul. They saw God working through him. They saw the face of God in his face. Precisely the opposite might have happened. The Christians who had borne the brunt and burden of his persecution, and had perhaps seen their own relatives or friends die at his hands, naturally would suspect his every act, especially his desire to be taken into their fellowship. They might have thought they were taking in a Trojan horse which once admitted to their inner counsels would turn with ever increased fury upon them, as only an insider could. However, they received a former deadly enemy as one of themselves.

The amazing response to Paul from Christians of that day seems to indicate that he had become for them not a Trojan horse but a window, a voice, a hand, through which they could see God, could hear him speak, could follow his way. Thus Paul illustrated the Christian conception of vocation everywhere: always to become the body of Christ—"His eyes to see human need, His heart to feel deeply the hurt of humanity, His feet to hasten to the needy and distressed, His hands to bring succor and soothe pain, His arms to undergird the weak, His tongue to speak the words of life, His mind to guide and teach the world." [7]

Becoming by his own free choice the instrument of the Eternal, man is connected with and is the channel of something and Someone beyond himself. Life is beyond before it is within. Men can become well-organized, effective personalities only as they submit themselves to a Power greater than themselves and allow themselves to be governed by him as completely as possible. Here again is the Christian paradox. When one surrenders the control of his life to any person other than Jesus, he becomes a slave to that person. Let him surrender his life to Christ, and Christ will put him in the fullest and truest control of himself.

Paul was a pathfinder, a pathbuilder. Because men saw God in him, he was able to show thousands during his lifetime, and millions after, how to go directly to God, everyone for himself, without any intermediary institution or person to block the way. And that is as precious a possession as one may have. It is the foundation of freedom. As long as man keeps open and treads the path between his own soul and God he can never be enslaved. It is this freedom of religion which underpins every other freedom. Every other freedom depends upon one's spiritual stature. To be morally and spiritually free enables one to be the channel of political and economic freedom. Direct access to God is the

[7] *The Upper Room.*

KJV	RSV
2 Then fourteen years after I went up again to Jerusalem with Barnabas, and took Titus with *me* also.	2 Then after fourteen years I went up again to Jerusalem with Barnabas, tak-

2. Fourteen Years Later (2:1-10)

Since Paul did not regard his gospel as a new religion but as the fulfillment of an old one, he could not go to the Gentiles without persuading **those who were of repute** that faith in God's grace was sufficient. To admit that circumcision or any other Mosaic law was necessary for salvation would have fettered Christianity to Jewish nationalism and involved it in the political vicissitudes of Judaism. Yet the church of Christ must not be cut from its root in Hebrew ethical monotheism, for that would have meant the severing of the moral nerve of its spirituality and the reduction of it to the magical sacramentalism of the mystery cults. These dangers must be avoided, but in such a way that the unity of the church would be established and maintained. So Paul went to Jerusalem to get his Gentile converts recognized as true members on the basis of the equality of all who had faith in Christ Jesus.

2:1. This third ἔπειτα, **then** (cf. 1:18, 21), means that Paul is setting things down in chronological order. Since his limited contacts with Jerusalem and the length of time between his visits are essential for his proof of independence, the **fourteen years** should be counted from his visit with Cephas rather than from his conversion. **With Barnabas** might mean that it was Barnabas who suggested the journey and took Paul along; but

---

master key. Paul lived in that freedom the remainder of his days.

2:1-2. ***The Test of Experience.***—Paul tested his experience by participating in the Jerusalem conference (see Expos. on 1:17-23 for the other tests). What a trio went to Jerusalem! The line of march appears to have been Barnabas in front (he was Paul's bridge into the Jerusalem fellowship), Paul himself in the middle, and Titus last, as the one around whom the contest over circumcision gathered. In other words Paul went with Barnabas, and Titus went with Paul. Barnabas got Paul his chance. When nobody else in Jerusalem believed in Paul's conversion, Barnabas introduced him to the apostles, persuading them that he was genuine. Barnabas therefore opened the door into the Jerusalem fellowship for Paul.

Men like Barnabas are beyond price. They have the gift of wide friendships, the talent for holding men together who belong together rather than for keeping them on edge by making them suspicious and aloof. Such men have the capacity to see in each Christian the possessions that may qualify him to be a member of the communion of the saints. They are the bridgebuilders of the earth. They maintain the fellowship not on a compromise basis, or on the level of the lowest common denominator, but by seeking a higher and transcendent loyalty above the lower tests that divide those who love Jesus Christ. They inspire confidence; they earn it and dare not abuse it. It is not claimed that Barnabas was the guiding spirit in that first ecumenical conference; but he is recognized as its convener, he made it possible, he introduced the men who held it.

Paul believed he was led by Christ to go to Jerusalem after pondering, brooding, studying, preaching, teaching, and praying for fourteen years away from Jerusalem, the fountainhead of the Christian church. Think of staying away that long from the central stream of the Christian movement—or was Jerusalem not the central stream, after all? May there not have been several streams from the Source? Is there only one stream?

After fourteen years in an association largely of his own making under Christ, Paul undoubtedly yearned to know the total Christian church. The Christian life for him was always a corporate matter in spite of his intense individualism. The companionship he enjoyed with those whom he had led to Christ and had taught in his way brought him joy and strength; but he wanted to share his enrichment with the brethren in Jerusalem and with the churches which stemmed from that root. His yearning for comprehensive communion must have led to his Jerusalem visit.

Of course the Jerusalem church had heard about him. Imagine the lifted eyebrows when he walked for the first time into that apostolic company. And what a company it was! Perhaps when he arrived, representing the people and points of view that he did, "the one holy Christian and Apostolic church" gathered for its first meeting. The several traditions were there: the

2 And I went up by revelation, and communicated unto them that gospel which I preach among the Gentiles, but privately

ing Titus along with me. 2 I went up by revelation; and I laid before them (but

taking Titus along with me (RSV) shows that the translation of μετὰ Βαρναβᾶ ought to be "accompanied by Barnabas."

Paul's choice of companions was deliberate. It was Barnabas who at the critical moment had expressed faith in Paul and got him started in his lifework as an ambassador of Christ. The notices in the N.T. reveal Barnabas as a singularly attractive and effective Christian (Acts 4:36-37; 9:26-27; 11:22-26; 12:25; 15:36-41; I Cor. 9:6). His character and the esteem in which the apostles held him appear in the new name they gave him—"Barnabas, son of encouragement." His genius in discovering and inspiring others who were destined to overshadow him is seen in his recruiting of Paul and John Mark. Barnabas was a fair-minded Christian who enjoyed the confidence of both sides and was therefore best fitted to help Paul present his case in Jerusalem: "For he was a good man, full of the Holy Spirit and of faith" (Acts 11:24).

Another good man was Titus, Paul's "partner and fellow worker," a man of tact and judgment who could be entrusted with difficult tasks in desperate situations, and who more than once had been the channel of God's strength and comfort to Paul (II Cor. 2:13; 7:6-7, 13-15; 8:16-17, 23). The only fault the Judaizers could find in him was that he was a Gentile. Paul would not be embarrassed by any charge that Titus was morally inconsistent with the ideal life of the Spirit. If Titus and others like him could be as good Christians as the Jews, the argument for perpetuating Jewish separatism would fall of its own weight, and the way would be open for the Spirit to build all Christians into the one body of Christ.

2. Since this visit was not on orders from Jerusalem but in obedience to a revelation, the δέ at the beginning should be translated "but" rather than **and** (KJV). By the present

church past, present, and future was represented in the persons of James, Peter, John, Paul, and Barnabas.

Beneath Paul's yearning to know Christians everywhere lay the principal urge that took him to the Holy City. He went to that cradle of his ancestral faith to compare notes with those who had lived with Jesus, and who by that fact were leaders of the church. He went to confer and perhaps to secure additional details; but it needs to be said—as if through a trumpet—that *he did not go to Jerusalem to get instructions.* He went to confer with equals, recognizing no superiors in authentic Christian knowledge and experience. His was not a case of jealousy. There were followers who had lived with Jesus and had heard him speak; but Paul had heard the same voice. His Damascus conversion was as authentic and immediate as the experience of any apostle in Jerusalem. Damascus was as close to the living, contemporary Christ as was Jerusalem. Paul was a man of honesty as well as of tremendous capacity and, believing that he had gone through a genuine experience with Christ, he desired to share the gospel which so gripped his life with those who had lived with Christ in Palestine. He saw the Christian faith in a larger framework than did anybody else in Jerusalem. His was a universal gospel; theirs was largely limited to the house of Israel. At the heart of their gospel, however, there were facts about Jesus which he wanted for the confirmation and illustration of his own thinking. Undoubtedly the net result of his visit meant that his own faith was sharpened and reassured.

Paul's desire to test his experiences with persons who had lived with Jesus put the Christian faith where it belonged—in the laboratory. It is the language of life before it is the language of theology, except as theology may be part of the laboratory. There are some subjects which can be taught or learned only in a laboratory, e.g., chemistry, physics, botany, biology—and Christianity. Paul's resolve to compare notes in Jerusalem turned that Christian center, perhaps for the first time, into a real laboratory: it had been too much like a courtroom. Laboratories of Christian experience serve as instruments for saving men rather than as courtrooms for hearing arguments over ancient laws.

Christ himself used the laboratory method by touching a man's everyday living. The way of Jesus may be summarized in words like these: Come and see. You will find out by living, by following, by doing. Or in Christ's own terms: "Handle me, and see" (Luke 24:39). "If any

to them which were of reputation, lest by any means I should run, or had run, in vain.

privately before those who were of repute) the gospel which I preach among the Gentiles, lest somehow I should be running or

tense of κηρύσσω (**I preach**), Paul indicates that he has been preaching the same gospel ever since his conversion to Christ. He says **among** instead of "to" the Gentiles because he is preaching to all nationalities in foreign countries. The men of **repute** (RSV) are the "pillars" of vs. 9. On the assumption that there were two interviews the order of words in the sentence (αὐτοῖς before τοῖς δοκοῦσιν) would indicate that the public meeting came first; but in that case it is hard to see why a private meeting would be necessary. Since the argument rests upon Paul's consistency, we cannot suppose that he would put his gospel in one light before the public and in another in private. He knew the futility of trying to reason with a large group in which opponents could generate an explosive mixture of emotion and patriotism. There was better prospect of success in private discussion with a few of the leaders. It is more likely that there was only one meeting and that it was private.

The order of the clauses in the KJV is misleading because it suggests that this private character and not the conference itself was occasioned by Paul's fear of failure. Τρέχω, "run," is Paul's favorite metaphor for the strenuous spirituality required to reach the

man will do his will, he shall know of the doctrine" (John 7:17). "Not every one that saith unto me, Lord, Lord, shall enter into the kingdom of heaven; but he that doeth the will of my Father which is in heaven" (Matt. 7:21). "Go and show John again those things which ye do hear and see" (Matt. 11:4).

2-10. ***Paul's Difficult Dilemma.***—The first part of ch. 2 contains radiantly significant sentences, but the entire section is difficult to put together in clear logic and sequence. Understanding Paul's mind at this point is not easy. At one moment he seems to respect the authority and position of certain officials, and in the next to disregard and depreciate them. In one verse he pays them honor; in the next he challenges them. Is he writing with his tongue in his cheek? The persons **of repute** whom he consulted **privately** (vs. 2), he calls **pillars** (vs. 9); but he also says that **whatsoever they were, it maketh no matter to me** (vs. 6); and adds for reinforcement that **God accepteth no man's person.**

Paul used the strongest words in the Greek language to tell the Galatians that his experience with Christ was direct and was therefore beyond the reach of their indictment; that his message was from Christ, not from any man or any group of men, not even from the group in Jerusalem. If his message was independent of men and direct from Christ, how could he **run in vain** (vs. 2)? Paul's own firsthand experience might be confirmed, corrected, or strengthened by church officials or by any shared experience, but not falsified.

One possible explanation of what appears to be a blowing hot and cold is that Paul may have held two kinds of conferences: one with the whole congregation, fulfilling his concept of the church's responsibility to bear corporate testimony to the Christian faith; and a second with church officials from whom he desired to secure data to confirm and even to correct certain information which was not above or more important than what he had learned through his own experience, but which was outside and in addition to it.

Another partial explanation may be sought in the personal equation. Up to this time the Jerusalem leaders and Paul had differed from afar; now they were face to face. Perhaps that does something to account for the sharp exceptions that were taken on both sides, no doubt with human jealousy and suspicion. No such reason, however, can fully cover the facts. Paul's dilemma ran deeper than human relationships.

A third cause may be found in the sheer difficulty which Paul and the Jerusalem leaders had in agreeing upon the real meaning of the gospel. If interpretation is a difficult task for some minds in the twentieth century, how much more difficult was it in Paul's day, against that brief background of Christian history as compared with the centuries-old background of Jewish tradition!

Still another possibility: Do we have here the apostle's unconscious confession that his wavering, when dealing with church officials, was due to the need of grace in his own life? He acted then like an ordinary man. When he applied the gospel to himself, he arrived at high and holy levels which never failed: **they perceived the grace that was given to me** (vs. 9). When he talked and wrote about grace, he was unim-

3 But neither Titus, who was with me, being a Greek, was compelled to be circumcised:

had run in vain. 3 But even Titus, who was with me, was not compelled to be circum-

---

Christian goal (5:7; Rom. 9:16; I Cor. 9:24, 26; Phil. 2:16). He does not say how this **revelation** came to him, but in view of I Cor. 14:13-19 we may assume that his reflection upon the results and problems of seventeen years of missionary activity had much to do with his decision.

His task was difficult. To preserve his gospel and achieve the unity of the church he had to demolish the barriers between Jew and Gentile and get the Jewish Christians to see and admit that they too were being saved by grace alone. This required the neutralization of centuries of anti-Gentile prejudice which had been forged into the protective armor of the Jews by Ezra, Nehemiah, and the Maccabees. At the same time he had to answer the charge of opening the kingdom of God to Gentiles on such easy terms as to render faith in Christ morally impotent. Compromise arrayed in the sheep's clothing of "tact" would not answer; only the love of all Christians for each other in Christ could avail.

3-5. These verses constitute one long broken sentence in the Greek. The numerous variants show that it was difficult for its earliest readers. Marcion and a few others cut one knot by omitting δέ, **but,** after διά, **because of.** In vs. 5 the best-attested reading is οἶς οὐδὲ πρὸς ὥραν, "to whom not even for an hour." From this some authorities omit οἶς οὐδέ, making Paul say that he yielded for an hour. Others mend the sentence by omitting the troublesome οἶς, but if this pronoun was not written by Paul, it is hard to see why anyone created the difficulty by introducing it. The only reading consistent with the trend of the argument is "to whom not even for an hour." The translation depends upon the interpretation, and the simplest clarification is to supply after περιτμηθῆναι, **to be circumcised,** and before διά, the thought that "this was urged" or "demanded."

The KJV leaves the reader in the dark concerning what was or was not done because of the false brethren. Its wording of vs. 5 may be taken to mean that Titus was circumcised,

---

peachable. His wavering, if such an interpretation is correct, illustrated the need of grace in his own life. All other matters could take their proper place only when grace came first. The church was girded for missionary advance when grace was set in the forefront—not church protocol or worn-out traditions and rules. **Pillars** (vs. 9) in the church were pillars indeed, not in name only, when undergirded by grace. **The right hands of fellowship** (vs. 9) are genuine when the hand that grasps another is sanctified by grace. Thus Paul's dilemma seems to have been his difficulty in finding a way to get along with certain church officials without compromising the gospel. He found that way through the grace of Christ.

3. ***The Case of Titus.***—Next to Paul, it may be that Titus is the most important character in Galatians. Titus was an upright young Greek who through the guidance of Paul had committed his life to Jesus Christ and desired church membership. He had no interest, concern, or desire to go through the Jewish rite of circumcision. He was a cultural descendant of Aristotle, not of Abraham. He did not see why Moses had to come between him and Christ. He resented becoming a Jew before he could become a Christian. In this he represented the non-Jewish world. The leaders of the Jerusalem church concurred with Paul that Titus should not be **compelled to be circumcised.** With this understanding Peter preached to the Jewish world, Paul to the Gentile.

One of the strange facts of church history is the recurring difficulty of keeping the pathway open direct to Jesus for every kind, size, and height of man. It is sheer spiritual tragedy that so many impediments have blocked that path. Some church officials with their theories of ordination, virtually claiming private roads to the Lord, make the way difficult for those who cannot agree with them. Circumcision was obviously an obstacle for the first Christians. Certain forms of worship, even a liturgical service, may drive persons from the church. Some would-be Christians have blocked the path to Christ by bowing to social prestige: people who live on the wrong side of the railroad tracks have not been welcome in certain churches. Human obstacles are set while Jesus is standing, yearning,

4 And that because of false brethren unawares brought in, who came in privily to spy out our liberty which we have in Christ

cised, though he was a Greek.
4 But because of false brethren secretly brought in, who

---

but voluntarily, and not by submission to demand. The RSV takes the view that Titus was not circumcised, but this translation suggests that if the proposal had been made in good faith by true brothers, Paul might have yielded. It is unlikely that Paul made such a compromise. The tense and meaning of ἠναγκάσθη, **was . . . compelled,** and the fact that the article τῇ is used with ὑποταγῇ, imply that while pressure was brought to

---

and calling with outstretched arms, "Come unto me!" The church of Christ must serve as a highway, not a barrier.

4*a*. *Confessing the Sins of Others.*—Paul spoke of **false brethren unawares brought in, who came in privily to spy out our liberty which we have in Christ Jesus.** Instead of confessing their own sins and asking for the grace of Christ, which is the key that opens the door to any Christian gathering, those **false brethren** were brought in to bear testimony to the "heresy" of Paul and his followers. It is a decisive moment when men presume to judge others. A Christlike person is less tolerant of his own sins than of the sins of others. If it is necessary to judge at all, a Christian interprets people up—not down. He endeavors to put the most charitable constructions upon another's actions and motives. Paul's critics were bent on confessing the sins of others rather than their own; they therefore sneaked in. They feared the apostle's open and abovetable method of handling all questions. Detectives and spies do not represent the Christian way of life and liberty.

4*b*. *Freedom as Achievement.*— (See Expos. on 4:5-7 for a summary of the several meanings of freedom in Paul's letters.) The heartbeat of Galatians, as of the Christian life itself, is freedom in Christ. Such freedom is life's most sacred privilege. It gathered up all else for which Paul stood and struggled. His profound concern lest his opponents **might bring us into bondage** seems to indicate that he and his followers had already achieved much in Christian freedom.

Men begin their achievement of freedom by surrendering to Christ. They become well-organized, effective personalities only as they attach themselves to a Power greater than themselves, and allow themselves to be thus governed. One who desires beyond all else to be a free instrument of the Eternal is on his way to understanding and possessing freedom. Such freedom seems to follow a formula like this: self-surrender, self-sacrifice, self-discipline, self-control; then self-expression and self-realization. This evolution deserves concrete illustration.

A young medical student, seeing in himself the physician he would fain become, commits himself to the study of anatomy, of diseases and their treatment. A musician, in order to keep company with Bach and Mendelssohn, practices through tedious and lonely hours. A patient student of art binds himself over to line and color, that he may put on canvas the divine inspiration that floods his soul. A young woman, preparing herself to fulfill one of earth's highest experiences, prays for and strives to attain the best in motherhood. In every field of endeavor there are earnest disciples who struggle along the road that leads into the realm of the undiscovered. Perfection in professional skills, excellence in craftsmanship and in personal living, mean the achievement of truth, beauty, and goodness.

It is possible to discover, if we will, that this yearning and struggling are the result not so much of a pushing power from within as of a being laid hold on from without; e.g., an art student is in love with beauty because beauty has laid hands on him. The search for the true, the beautiful, and the good has led many to an awareness that Someone lays imperious hands on them. They realize that they are not mastering but are being mastered. As they yield and give their best, they discover a sense of freedom. They are working with Someone beyond themselves to achieve the best that life knows. They come to understand that freedom as "release" and "endowment" is a gift of God, and that freedom as "achievement" in the good life is working with the Eternal in the most rewarding kind of co-operation they have ever known.

This sense of freedom in personal achievement extends to the most significant areas of social life. One finds oneself working with Christ to set men morally free in order that they may bring political and economic freedom to mankind, and so help to complete God's unfinished world—a world in which sin, disease, slavery, injustice, and war still hold the human soul in bondage. History itself is the story of humanity's struggle against these foes. The issue may be pictured as open and closed doors. Open doors mean freedom; closed doors mean slavery. Those who labor to set others free—those who open doors—are colaborers with God. **That they**

Jesus, that they might bring us into bondage:
5 To whom we gave place by subjection, no, not for an hour; that the truth of the gospel might continue with you.

slipped in to spy out our freedom which we have in Christ Jesus, that they might bring us into bondage — 5 to them we did not yield submission even for a moment, that the truth of the gospel might be pre-

have Titus circumcised, James and Peter and John decided against the Judaizers. The case of Timothy (Acts 16:3), which is cited to show that Paul could have yielded, is not parallel with that of Titus; and even if it were, the story in Acts cannot govern the interpretation of Galatians, the primary source. If Paul had meant that Titus was circumcised, he would have had to explain that he consented for expediency and with the understanding that observance of the Jewish law was not a necessary supplement to the faith of Titus or anyone else.

Paul regarded the Judaizers as false brothers, alien from the Spirit of Christ, brought in on the side (παρεισάκτους) by those who wanted to discredit him, or sneaking in (παρεισῆλθον) on their own initiative. Their purpose was not to edify but to spy. Yet we need not suppose that all were insincere. Some were genuine patriots who believed that the gift of the law was the special mark of God's redeeming love for Israel. What Paul called slavery they considered the greatest of all blessings, and they feared that his laxity would bring down God's great wrath. The trouble was that, as happens so often in religious controversies, they adopted irreligious means to secure religious ends. To set church members spying upon one another was fatal to human fellowship. They had yet to learn the love which suffers long, is kind, and never fails.

might bring us into bondage puts all the redeemed on guard with courage and wisdom. Christ used Paul to open doors in the first century; he used Paul to open doors for Martin Luther in the sixteenth century. How appropriate that Luther nailed his ninety-five theses on the church door at Wittenberg: he too opened doors that set men free.

4c. ***The Source of Christian Morality.***—**In Christ** (see also Expos. on 1:22 for Paul's four meanings of this phrase). "The Marcionites raised the question, 'What new thing did Jesus bring?' And the answer of Irenaeus was, 'He brought all that was new, in bringing Himself.' "[8] "Being in Christ" is primal in all Pauline teaching; once grasped, the secret to Paul is discovered. It was the source of his Christian life from which all additional gifts flowed. "If any man be in Christ, he is a new creature" (II Cor. 5:17).

In the light of a man's total possibilities he is subhuman until this source of daily power is his. "Some time or other in his life every man must kneel before Christ if he is to be fully a man."[9] A man who thus kneels can stand up straight before life. **In Christ** he becomes his truest self. Christian morality for him becomes infinitely more than disclosures, insights, and precepts; **in Christ** is the wonder-working power of attachment.

Christian morality, Paul discovered, does not stem from rules or standards, or even from ideals, but from a personal relationship **in Christ.** He found through disillusion and defeat that moralism, which is obedience to precepts and rules, cannot give direction to a man's life. His conversion ushered him into a new relationship, and with it came resources which he had not known before. How else can one account for his sustained energy, his courage, his ability to bear physical as well as mental tortures? How else can one explain his years of mental strain and achievement? What made him think, write, talk, and act as he did? What were his presuppositions? In simple honesty a source must be found sufficiently large and strong to account for his new life. The answer is that he was possessed by Someone who was more than a series of truths, more than a set of morals with a philosophical overtone.

In Christ men are sons of God in a manner which is impossible by physical birth alone. An in-Christ relationship means access to the Power who can do for a man, and can enable the man to do for himself, what he could never do in his own strength. Paul possessed a Presence who acted like an inward spring of water—such as Jesus promised to the woman of Samaria at the well (John 4:14)—whose source is deep in the mountains of God. Worldly con-

[8] James S. Stewart, *A Man in Christ* (New York: Harper & Bros., 1935), p. 76.

[9] Eric Abbott, quoted in F. R. Barry, *What Has Christianity to Say?* (New York: Harper & Bros., 1938), p. 160.

6 But of those who seemed to be somewhat, (whatsoever they were, it maketh no
matter to me: God accepteth no man's person:) for they who seemed *to be somewhat*
in conference added nothing to me:
7 But contrariwise, when they saw that
the gospel of the uncircumcision was committed unto me, as *the gospel* of the circumcision *was* unto Peter;

served for you. 6 And from those who were
reputed to be something (what they were
makes no difference to me; God shows no
partiality) — those, I say, who were of repute added nothing to me; 7 but on the
contrary, when they saw that I had been
entrusted with the gospel to the uncircumcised, just as Peter had been entrusted with

---

6-9*a*. This sentence of ninety-five Greek words, strung together with relative pronouns and tumbling participles, is a typical example of Paul's headlong style. What he started to say was that James and Peter and John found nothing lacking in his conception of the gospel and recognized the equality of his apostleship by shaking hands with him. But having dictated the first six words, he interrupted with a reminder that God plays no favorites (vs. 6*b*) ; then after a fresh start he broke his sentence again to give the reason why these pillar apostles recognized him (vss. 8-9*a*) ; and finally he wrote an appendix to it (vss. 9*c*-10) to give the details of the agreement to divide the mission field and remember the poor.

Τῶν δοκούντων εἶναί τι were **those who were reputed to be something** (RSV), and ὁποῖοί ποτε ἦσαν, "what they then were," refers to their standing as leaders of the church by virtue of having been companions of Jesus in his ministry and witnesses of his resurrection and glorification. Most prominent were James the Lord's brother, Peter (Cephas), and John the son of Zebedee. Paul, who had been "last" and "least" (I Cor. 15:8-9), replied that this made no difference, since God's purpose was to save all men by his grace alone, through faith; and he reminded his detractors of an axiom of the Jewish religion that God accepts no man's "face" (πρόσωπον) and cannot be bribed (II Chr. 19:7). A man's face was his personal dignity, weight, and reputation; and spiritually it depended upon the degree of his success in being better than others. But John the Baptist warned that God was "able of these stones to raise up children unto Abraham" (Matt. 3:9) ; and Paul, strict Pharisee though he was, could not rid himself of the burden of anguish, remorse, and fearful expectation of judgment which every sinner, Jew or Gentile, had to carry (Rom. 2:8-11) until he accepted God's impartial forgiveness through Christ, who had crucified all ambitions for rank and authority. Since this true relation to God was

---

tact can never make that stream muddy or stagnant. It daily cleanses itself, and thus becomes the origin of the good life and the source of Christian morality.

7-8. *A Divided World as Christian Strategy.*— Peter and Paul divided their world for evangelistic work: Peter preached to the Jews, Paul to the Gentiles. That division only postponed the verdict on an issue which was much deeper than geography or race: Would Gentile converts have to become Jews in order to be acceptable Christians? Must Christians keep ancient Jewish customs and rules in order to be received by the Jerusalem fellowship of the church? Those questions had to be answered sooner or later.

The division of the world on racial lines in the first century, however, does hold some sound thinking. There was then, as there is now, place within the fellowship for differing groups, orders, and denominations; e.g., the religious orders of the Roman Catholic Church provide approach and expression for widely differing talents and minds that remain loyal to one church. The Franciscan mind by comparison is quite unlike the Jesuit. In like manner, Protestant denominations may be considered as Protestant orders which offer varied approaches and expressions for both clergy and laity.

"The scandal of Christianity"—defined as division within the Christian ranks—is not the most deadly of all defections, for it comes from a deeper scandal—failure in forthright commitment to Christ. Christian union may come. In Protestantism it might make possible a Protestant "pope," or board of "cardinals," to speak a common word for the Protestants around the world; but such organization would not assure

8 (For he that wrought effectually in Peter to the apostleship of the circumcision, the same was mighty in me toward the Gentiles;)
9 And when James, Cephas, and John, who seemed to be pillars, perceived the grace that was given unto me, they gave

the gospel to the circumcised
8 (for he who worked through Peter for the mission to the circumcised worked through me also for the Gentiles),
9 and when they perceived the grace that was given to me, James and Ce'phas and John, who were reputed to be

open to all impartially by faith, the particular time and circumstances of becoming an apostle were not the factors that determined the validity of Paul's Christian experience. But when Paul says that the original apostles **added nothing** to him, he does not mean that he received from them nothing essential for his gospel, but that his personal fellowship with Christ and his call to preach salvation by grace were as valid before as after the conference.

The literal translation of the genitives in **gospel of the circumcision** and **gospel of the uncircumcision** exposes the passage to the misinterpretation that there were two gospels, one for Jews, the other for Gentiles, and the substitution of **to** (RSV) for **of** (KJV) does not remove the ambiguity. There was only one gospel, and Paul was to preach it among the Gentiles, Peter to the Jews.

Challenged by Paul's consistent living and by his missionary achievements in such exemplary Christians as Titus, the "pillars" of the church could draw but one conclusion: This was God's doing! The verb ἐνεργήσας, "be active," "work," "work effectively," appears twice in this verse and should be translated in the same way each time, and not, as in the KJV, **wrought effectually** and **was mighty. He who worked** could refer either to God or to Christ, but the former is more likely. The datives Πέτρῳ and ἐμοί may be translated **in Peter . . . in me** (KJV) or **through Peter . . . through me** (RSV), the latter being preferable in view of the absence of the preposition ἐν. The RSV has clarified the KJV phrase **to the apostleship of the circumcision.** Paul does not repeat **for the mission** (εἰς ἀποστολήν) with reference to himself, but this does not mean that he was not claiming an apostleship equal to Peter's.

Luke's story of the conservative opposition to the reception of Cornelius and his family shows how hard it was for the Judaizers to grant Paul's claim and accept the

or guarantee either true greatness or the correctness of such a word. Many of the Pope's addresses, encyclicals, and pronouncements are manifestly edited so that they are little more than platitudinous, despite the number of members he represents. More than numbers is required. Significant insights, profound thinking, and spiritual power are infinitely more needed than the social and political impressiveness of church rolls. Truth often emanates from minority groups and creative thinking from small bodies within a large fellowship. One is not of course in any of this to minimize the need for unity among God's people in their testimony to a broken world. There are denominations which should unite promptly; they should perhaps never have been separated in the first place. Others, because they represent certain definite patterns of culture, should perhaps "tarry awhile" for their doctrinal uniqueness as well as for their programs of service and for their intellectual and spiritual emphases. It is imperative, however, that these Protestant "orders" should co-operate, as in the World Council of Churches.

There is no suggestion here that the Christian faith is a matter of subjective definition which may be made to conform to every man's taste or mood. Faith has to do with objective fact—and the central fact is not an open question. "Who knows Christ, knows all." To keep the path for every life open directly to him, without any intermediary institution or person, is the task of tasks. Peter, so faithful and loyal, almost blocked the path. The head is Jesus Christ, Lord and Savior; all else is subhead, method, and definition. The sacraments, to cite but a single example, are the means of grace; Jesus is grace.

9. ***A One-Word Summary.***—Grace is the one-word summary for all of Christ's work. "All is of grace and grace is for all" (see Expos. on 1:3

to me and Barnabas the right hands of fellowship; that we *should go* unto the heathen, and they unto the circumcision.

pillars, gave to me and Barnabas the right hand of fellowship, that we should go to the Gentiles and they to the circumcised;

uncircumcised Titus. Even Peter was astonished when he saw that "the Holy Spirit fell on them just as on us at the beginning" (Acts 11:15). The character produced by the Spirit in Stephen and Cornelius, Paul and Titus, and a host of other Hellenistic-Jewish and Gentile Christians was incontrovertible evidence for the impartiality of God's grace.

9*b*. Convinced that God had bestowed upon Paul an equal measure of his grace (cf. Rom. 1:5; I Cor. 3:10; 15:10), James, Cephas, and John took the only logical step. They gave Paul and Barnabas **the right hand of fellowship** in recognition of their equality and partnership, and in pledge of co-operation and support. These three apostles not only **seemed** but actually were **pillars,** persons of initiative and leadership with whom the determination of policy rested. The fact that James is mentioned first may indicate that he had most to say in matters of policy (cf. Acts 15:12-21), while Peter took the lead in the missionary work of the church (cf. Acts 10:1–11:18). Some MSS, influenced by the superior position of Peter, substituted Πέτρος for Κηφᾶς and put his name first. Note the same substitution in some authorities at 1:18 and 2:11, 14; in 2:7-8, however, Πέτρος and Πέτρῳ are the original readings. The view that Peter and Cephas were two different persons is not substantiated by the historical evidence.

9*c*. All that the Greek says is "we among the Gentiles, they among the circumcision." Some verb such as "go" or "preach" must be supplied. "Among" is better for εἰς than **unto** (KJV) or **to** (RSV), since the division of labor was not strictly along racial or territorial lines. In foreign cities Paul preached to Jews as well as Gentiles, and in Palestine, Peter baptized the Gentile Cornelius and his family. Both parties were to address both Jews and Gentiles, but Paul and Barnabas were to go to foreign lands, while Peter and the rest would concentrate on the homeland of Palestine and Syria.

Certainly Paul's understanding was that both he and they were to preach the same gospel of salvation by grace apart from law (5:6; I Cor. 7:19). The most that he could concede was that a circumcised Jew who became a Christian should not seek to remove

for a summary of the meanings of grace). "The Talmud records more than three hundred questions of law and observance on which the two schools [liberal Hillel and ultraconservative Shammai] gave conflicting rulings."[1] What was a capable, conscientious man like Paul to do? Moreover, if Paul with his superb mind and spiritual sensitivity was confused and disillusioned, how much greater must have been the confusion of the average man.

With all possible appreciation of the law, and with a realization of what Pharisaism meant to the nation, the shortcomings of that system must be understood.

> Its dogmatic assurance that the traditions of the fathers contained the whole truth and that therefore no new revelation was to be looked for, its externalizing of a man's duty to God, its glorying in good works, its legal notions of the relation subsisting between the human and the divine, its inner hardness—these things Paul could no more escape than could any other convinced and thoroughgoing Pharisee.[2]

[1] Stewart, *Man in Christ*, p. 37.
[2] *Ibid.*, p. 38.

The joy of mind and the peace of conscience which Paul could not find in the law of ancient Israel he found in the grace of Christ. He had been trying to build a ladder from earth to God, with each round in the ladder representing another rule or requirement of the law. The futility of his effort helped him to see what grace meant. It meant that God had let down the ladder to man. Paul saw that "God, to Whom he could not rise, had come to him; that the righteousness of God which he could not satisfy had been bestowed; that genuine freedom was a gift of God, and that in Jesus Christ that gift was proffered out of the initiative, the measureless and the shocking love of God."[3]

If grace sums up all Christ does for mankind, it must be the most significant word in the N.T. Not hope, or love, or even faith; grace was the watershed for Paul. The N.T. benediction indicates the place of this utterly Christian word: "The grace of our Lord Jesus Christ, and the love of God, and the fellowship of the Holy

[3] Sittler, *Doctrine of the Word*, p. 15.

10 Only *they would* that we should remember the poor; the same which I also was forward to do.

10 only they would have us remember the poor, which very thing I was eager to do.

the marks of his circumcision (I Cor. 7:18), since that would have made it a Christian *law* not to be circumcised! The subsequent actions of James and Peter indicate that they and their conservative colleagues did not agree as fully with Paul as he supposed at the conclusion of the conference. According to Galatians, that discussion had been confined to the requirement of circumcision. They had probably assented to his gospel in principle without realizing the drastic consequences of his radicalism for Jewish nationalism and *all* its peculiar customs. After further thought James and his party decided that the line would have to be drawn at eating with the Gentiles, and at Antioch, Peter and even Barnabas wavered on the issue.

10. With the agreement went the request that Paul and Barnabas should continue to remember the poor; the present tense (μνημονεύωμεν) indicates that this had been their practice. Ἐσπούδασα conveys the idea of "urgency," "earnestness," and "diligence," and σπουδή, χάρις and κοινωνία, "urgency," "grace," and "mutuality," comprise the trinity of traits which Paul the Christian always associated with giving. The Galatians knew how earnest he was in this matter (I Cor. 16:1); and II Cor. 8–9 and Rom. 15:25-28 show the importance which he attached to raising this fund, not only as an expression of gratitude and the grace of Christ in the Christian, but as a means of knitting the Gentile and Jewish members of Christ's body together in the fellowship of the Spirit.

Paul's training and practice as a Jew prepared him to comply with this request. The Pharisees taught that almsgiving, the study of the Torah, and the temple service were the three pillars on which the world stood. At home and abroad the social and economic situation of the Jews necessitated peculiar emphasis upon this expression of righteousness, justice, and mercy. The limited resources of Palestine and its perpetual political strife condemned multitudes to exist on the ragged edge of starvation, and Jerusalem, always an economic parasite, was dependent on temple revenues streaming in from abroad. One of the charges on this treasure was to support the poor and relieve the unemployed. The doom of Stephen was sealed when he declared that the temple in Jerusalem was not essential to true worship; and this economic threat to its income was a major reason for the persecution of the Christians. Continuing to remember the poor in Jerusalem would help to allay this cause of hostility to the church.

From the beginning the missionaries of Christ faced the hard fact that although man does not live by bread alone, neither does he live without bread. The gospel, both in Palestine and abroad, found its most receptive hearing among slaves and underprivileged workers. Οἱ πτωχοί, "the beggars," became the honorable title for the messianic community. They were the folk, at their wits' end materially and spiritually, whom Jesus called "blessed." He admonished the rich to sell their goods and give to the poor, and at Pentecost his Spirit produced a most joyful sharing of possessions. But the delay in his second coming led to the exhaustion of their resources at the very time when their unbelieving compatriots were expelling them from the synagogues and depriving them of their share of the relief money from the temple treasury. Likewise, on the foreign

Spirit." The grace of Christ is the key to the love of God which ushers men into fellowship with the Holy Spirit. Grace guides a man step by step into the Christian's holy of holies. It becomes the nerve of the gospel; it underlies all N.T. writing. It is by all odds the most powerful word in the N.T. It is the answer of answers. It is Christ's richest personal property.

10. *Remembering the Poor.*—(See also Expos. on vss. 1-2; 1:2, 17-23; 6:1-5.) Concern for **the poor** manifests the spirit of the early Christian church. The feeling of responsibility that the whole group had for the welfare of each individual in the group was a tie that bound the total fellowship together. Their desire to share provisions with the needy may have

mission field there was need to share one's means with the poor. To separate preaching the gospel from caring for the poor was impracticable.

Paul seized upon this project as a means of breaking the prejudice of his people against the Gentiles. He would test and see what the love of Christ could do to reconcile men to each other by setting them to work on a common task. He would not enter his almsgiving as a credit with God, but neither would he give his converts the easy comfort of a religion which takes refuge from hard tasks in cheap sentiment and in profession of faith without its fruit.

This reference to the poor is insufficient to identify Gal. 2:1-10 with Acts 11:27-30 (see Intro., pp. 438-39). Paul says he made the journey in obedience to a revelation, Luke that the Antioch church appointed him to go. There is nothing in Paul's statement to indicate that the revelation came to him through Agabus or one of the other prophets instead of directly from Christ through the Spirit. To say plainly that his second visit to Jerusalem after his conversion was by appointment to serve with Barnabas on the relief committee, and not to settle the validity of his gospel and apostleship, would have been such telling evidence for his independence that he would hardly have left it to be inferred from his use of the present tense of μνημονεύωμεν, "continue to remember." The first person singular and aorist tense ἐσπούδασα, **I was eager** (RSV), do not permit the inference that he and Barnabas were currently engaged in raising a fund for the poor.

The alternative is to identify the visit of Gal. 2:1-10 with that of Acts 15. But here too there are significant differences, which are best explained by the hypothesis that Luke was conflating sources (see Intro., pp. 438-39). Acts says that this conference was called to decide whether the Gentile converts must be circumcised, but in reporting the action of the council says nothing about circumcision. Instead, the apostolic decree is concerned with the laws governing social intercourse with non-Jews, about which Paul is silent. Acts declares that Barnabas and Paul gave their account of the Gentile mission before the whole assembly, but Paul says he presented his case privately before the men of repute (vs. 2). According to Acts, Peter takes the initiative in behalf of the Gentiles and is the uncompromising advocate of salvation "through the grace of the Lord Jesus"; but in Gal. 2:11-12 he wavers on the issue of eating with the uncircumcised. Finally, in Acts, James states, and the assembly ratifies, the conditions for admitting Gentiles; but nowhere in Paul's letters is there any appeal to this decision of the Jerusalem council. Nor does the substitution of the negative Golden Rule for "and from what is strangled" in some MSS of Acts 15:20, 29 make harmonization with Paul easier. He did abstain from all that defiled and he did live in accordance with the Golden Rule, but this was not because it was Mosaic or apostolic law, but because it was inherent in his love for Christ and Christ's love for him. Paul made no distinction between "moral" and "ceremonial," as if Christ abrogated the ceremonial law but kept salvation dependent upon merit for obedience to the moral law. He rejected all legalism in principle, and his attitude toward circumcision and social intercourse with the Gentiles grew out of his conception of grace and freedom in Christ, not out of submission to ecclesiastical authority. His differences with the Judaizers cut so deep that not even an apostolic council could reconcile them.

---

stemmed from the early communal experience of the church at Jerusalem. It is possible that the initial enthusiasm for pooling resources may have influenced some members to dispose of their property, with poverty as a result. Ministering to the poor has characterized the Christian church across the centuries. Paul found occasion to underscore his zeal for works of mercy. This was common ground on which Paul and the Jerusalem apostles could meet, despite their differences in doctrinal emphasis.

The distinctive feature of Christian service to the underprivileged, both then and now, is the spirit of love which motivates it. Therein lies the fundamental difference between the administration of social welfare by secular agencies and the "inner mission" or social welfare work of the church. To the church, physical need and spiritual need are part of the same pattern. Ministry to men's souls and ministry to their bodies flow equally from Christ's redemptive love as expressed in the lives of his followers.

11 But when Peter was come to Antioch, I withstood him to the face, because he was to be blamed.

11 But when Ce′phas came to Antioch I opposed him to his face, because he stood

The growing church was caught between two conflicting cultures, and the issue had to be wrought out of life and history. (On the whole matter of law Gal. 1:1-10 and Acts 15 should be interpreted in relation to each other. See also Vol. IX, pp. 198-200.)

E. The Later Inconsistency of the Judean Leaders (2:11-14)

11-12. Since these verses continue Paul's argument by giving another instance of his independence, "and" is better for δέ than **but. He was to be blamed** (KJV) is too weak for κατεγνωσμένος ἦν. Peter **stood condemned** (RSV) because his fear of the ultraconservatives led him to betray his own Spirit-given insight by yielding to their contention that the council had not contemplated eating with "goyim" (non-Jews). Paul rebuked him **to his face,** not behind his back like a spying false brother (vs. 4).

The agreement concerning circumcision would have been relatively easy to maintain if the liberals had gone no farther. The Jews, especially of the Dispersion, were used to having pious Gentiles at their synagogue services. But to admit that God meant to include Gentiles in his kingdom was one thing, the proposal to abandon the eating code which had been elaborated from inspired scripture (Lev. 11; Deut. 14) quite another. These customs were a product of the Hebrew struggle against absorption by paganism. Circumcision, taboos, ceremonial cleansings, and kosher observances were designed to keep God's chosen people different and faithful.

For the pious Jew, eating was not bolting one's food under pressure to do something more important. Mealtime was leisure for conversation more wholesome than alcoholic banter and persiflage. Eating together made men brothers who shared aspirations and thoughts of God. To eat without giving thanks was beastly; to partake of untithed food was to defy the Giver of every good and perfect gift; and to sit at table without

11*a*. ***Antioch as a World Capital.***—The city of **Antioch,** where the followers of Christ were first called Christians, was the forum for the Gentile-Christian world. Its cosmopolitan character helped to enlarge the narrow outlook of Judaism. Indeed, Antioch was the cradle of Gentile Christianity and of the early missionary movement of the church. How significant that Paul started each of his three missionary journeys from that center! John Chrysostom, one of the superb preachers of all the centuries, was a son of the Antioch church. Antioch offered a perfect setting for the battle to determine how binding the Jewish law should be on non-Jewish Christians. When Peter came to Antioch he stepped into an atmosphere which he had not known in Jerusalem.

11*b*. ***The Use of Power.***—The conflict between Peter and Paul is infinitely more than a personal matter, vastly more than a church debate of the first century; it is a lasting demonstration of the use of power: **I withstood him to the face.** Make no mistake, Peter used all he had, and so did Paul. Indeed, the Christian fellowship is basically a matter of power. Christ cautioned his early disciples about going out—into a world where he was largely unknown—until they had received power. The apostle John tells how to acquire power, "Abide in me, and I in you" (John 15:4). Paul wrote about the power of Christ's resurrection (Phil. 3:10). It is not too much to affirm that the essence of the N.T. idea of religion is a new kind of power, a reservoir of resources and strength. How the world today needs that power! It is Jesus Christ who makes Christianity unique, and that which makes him primarily different is not his teaching but his power, his resources and strength. While Paul here specifically refers to only one manifestation of this power, he demonstrated a threefold use of it.

(*a*) Paul had the power to stand, and he used it against Peter in Antioch. Later he admonished the Ephesians, "having done all, to stand" (Eph. 6:13). Luther demonstrated that same power when he was on trial before church and state at the Diet of Worms and cried to God and the centuries, "Here I stand. . . . God help me."

This kind of power may be illustrated by contrasting a morning-glory and an oak tree. The morning-glory is very beautiful until it wilts in the sunshine. Many well-meaning people act like that: when they are on their own

talking about the Torah was like eating food offered to idols. Participation in heathen libations was apostasy from Judaism, and no one could eat with idolaters without becoming like them. Begun with joyful thanksgiving and sanctified by conversation concerning God, a common meal became God's table, and the Jewish Christians were unwilling to risk spiritual contamination by eating with those who did not share it.

The end which these restrictions were intended to serve was worthy, but the very success of the isolationists in glorifying their God by being better than the pagans exposed them to the subtlest of all temptations. Refusal to eat with the Gentiles fostered pride and self-righteousness. The habit of obedience developed by these observances was supposed to carry over into the weightier matters of reverence for God, honesty and generosity in business, kindness, courtesy, and tact. But this was not an effect which necessarily followed, and the tendency was to substitute these observances of piety for life's difficult

---

they cannot take it. Some innately strong persons grow cynical when they have only their determination to keep them going. But look at an oak tree. Around an old Southern home there were about a dozen giant oaks. After a heavy afternoon storm, which seemed to make no difference whatsoever to those mighty oaks, an old man said to his grandson, "My boy, be a man like that." Those trees were in deep-rooted connection with the resources of the earth: no wonder they could stand during storms. So human life can stand when it begins not from within us but from beneath us and beyond us.

One evening, in the Broadway Tabernacle Church in New York, Charles E. Jefferson stepped forward into the pulpit to preach. A snowstorm had come during the afternoon, and the night was rough; but the congregation that filled the church heard a great sermon. Though he spoke about power, he lifted neither hand nor finger in gesture until the benediction. He illustrated power by telling all he could find out about electricity. And then with the quiet poise which only a man of power possesses he said, "If there is a power that can light a man's house, what kind of a world would this be if there were no power to light the man—his mind, his life, his path?" He told all he could find out about gravity and asked, "If there is a power that can hold the physical world together, sustaining a man's house and giant buildings, what kind of a world would this be if there were no equivalent power somewhere to draw and hold men?" That power, he said, is available through Christ Jesus. And Charles Jefferson was right.

When the power which is illustrated by oak trees, electricity, and gravity comes into our lives, it becomes courage. It was courage that Paul used against Peter. Courage is the power to stand up against anything that life can do or undo for us. Courage means that one can take the storms of life and say when they are over, "I have overcome the world" (John 16:33). Jesus not only declared that such power was his: he makes that same power available for those who follow in his steps.

Mark Hopkins used to say to his classes that there comes a time when a man must discover the difference between having things and being a person who counts. The difference is largely an experience in the possession and use of power. It is quite easy in an industrial civilization for men to be in control of things; but what is far more significant is the fact that they can be persons who count. When they have courage through Christ Jesus they, like Paul, have the power to stand.

(*b*) Paul found another use for this gift of power. He plainly and frankly says, **I withstood him to the face.** If the power to stand is positive and aggressive, the power to withstand is potential. Out of it, as from the subconscious mind, comes such self-control that a man is able to keep his balance, his head, and his judgment in a world like ours. After Paul received power through Christ, he never lost control.

There are at least two kinds of control. One is illustrated by the sort of mastery a man must have over his automobile. The other is the kind we have been thinking about. It is closely akin to being mastered by great music, or by a supreme idea, or by a tremendous cause. It may result in the mastery of passion, of selfish ambition, of abstract knowledge.

(*c*) Paul in his conflict with Peter demonstrated the power to stand, which means courage; the power to withstand, which means control; he further demonstrated his power to understand, which means choice. The only freedom man possesses is the freedom to choose his master. He can properly master life only when he is worthily mastered. The control Jesus holds over a man sets that man free and gives him self-control and the power to stand and withstand. Through Christ it is possible in the present to have an awareness of the Eternal which will give to life not only strength but radiance. Someone has suggested that profound religion

12 For before that certain came from James, he did eat with the Gentiles: but when they were come, he withdrew and separated himself, fearing them which were of the circumcision.

condemned. 12 For before certain men came from James, he ate with the Gentiles; but when they came he drew back and separated himself, fearing the circumcision party.

---

moral tasks. Abstention from pork and rabbits was easier than justice and mercy and honoring father and mother. To decide how much water was required for a valid ritual washing of hands before eating; to fix the precise time and formulas for the blessings over the bread and wine; to prescribe precautions when buying food in a Gentile market, and to work out the meticulous casuistry of tithing—all these were indeed evidences of a devout spirit and a sincere desire to do the will of God; but they could also become a tragic misdirection of religious energy. By themselves, all they were certain to accomplish was to make obvious that Jews were different in these respects from their pagan neighbors, in whose eyes such peculiar customs were absurd, superstitious, and downright rude. Instead of allaying hard feelings, they heightened the tension and kept alive the hatreds which rent society.

This hard shell, which had been formed to preserve Yahweh's people as a distinctive religious and cultural group, was cramping the spiritual life force that was striving to expand in the mission to the Gentiles. Jesus taught that it was not what a man ate but what he said that made him unclean, and Mark's conclusion was not only radical but logical: "Thus he declared all foods clean" (Mark 7:19). In Christ, Paul saw that obedience to all these laws was irrelevant to God's original intention to deal with all men on the basis of grace alone, and that they were obsolete in a changed and changing order of society. The separatist aim of these customs was incompatible with the ideal of Christian fellowship embodied in the Lord's Supper and expressed in the common meal which preceded it (I Cor. 10:14-30; 11:17-22).

What has been said concerning Syrian Antioch (see Exeg. on 1:21) shows that it was much easier for that church to admit Gentiles and practice equality with them than it was for the church in Jerusalem. The fact that Paul's account of the apostolic conference makes no mention of tablefellowship does not mean that previous to that meeting the Christians in Antioch had not been eating with the Gentiles. One can hardly imagine Paul refusing to eat with Titus at any time. With Peter it was different. Only slowly and with doubts and hesitations was he led to recognize the rightness of Paul's position, and before coming to Antioch he probably did not realize all its implications. Hence he

---

brings to life three major contributions: a great philosophy, a great ethic, and a great resource of power. It is the third that we are thinking about here: the power to withstand by reason of the faith, hope, and love which draw all experiences together and make life whole.

Paul could stand and withstand because he understood. He had courage and control because he had made the choice of Christ. The capacity—Paul would say "gift"—to understand, the capacity to weigh, to choose, to cleave to that which is good, gives man the courage to interpret life for himself. At every turn there are bids for our allegiance: there is the appeal of propaganda; there is the pressure of social customs. If a man becomes the captain of his own soul in this century, as Paul did in his, if he refuses to surrender to public opinion, he must have the power to understand and to interpret for himself. One of the superb gifts of Christ to mankind is the capacity to see life through. Paul stood and withstood because he understood.

11-15. ***In Conflict with Peter.***— (See Expos. on 1:17-23 for the five tests Paul gave his conversion experience.) Paul and Peter in the cosmopolitan setting of Antioch fought out the toughest problem in the early church. The two men incarnated the issue in their own personalities. Religion, education, and politics have a strange way of tying issues to personalities. Funerals are often required to settle some questions; but the issue with regard to the relation of Christians to the Jewish law could not and did not wait for any funerals. It is one thing to attack an opponent at a distance in his absence; it is quite another to come to grips with him face to face. Thus Peter and Paul proved to be the sharpest tests for each other. Men are tested

13 And the other Jews dissembled likewise with him; insomuch that Barnabas also was carried away with their dissimulation.

14 But when I saw that they walked not uprightly according to the truth of the gospel, I said unto Peter before *them* all, If thou, being a Jew, livest after the manner of Gentiles, and not as do the Jews, why compellest thou the Gentiles to live as do the Jews?

13 And with him the rest of the Jews acted
insincerely, so that even Barnabas was carried away by their insincerity.
14 But when I
saw that they were not straightforward about the truth of the gospel, I said to Ce′phas before them all, "If you, though a Jew, live like a Gentile and not like a Jew, how can you compel the Gentiles to live

---

wavered, fearing the conservatives who insisted that no one could become a good Christian without first becoming a Jew. It is easy to imagine the dismay which his unpredictable and inconsistent conduct caused in the church at Antioch.

13. By **the rest of the Jews** Paul means the Christian Jews at Antioch: they all became cohypocrites (συνυπεκρίθησαν) with Peter! **Even Barnabas** (RSV) is a correction of **Barnabas also** (KJV).

The essence of hypocrisy was to conceal one's real character, motives and purposes under the mask of something different. A bad man would pretend to be better, a good man worse, than he was. To save his face, Peter, a good man and a liberal at heart, assumed the mask of a conservative. But whether, or how far, Peter was hypocritical or insincere only Peter and Peter's God could ever know. Paul could not prove his charge without getting inside Peter's heart and knowing all his thoughts, feelings, and purposes as intimately as God knew them. The potential damage done by religious partisanship is measured by the fact that Paul was driven to make such a charge against a pillar apostle and to include Barnabas his best friend. One may infer from his statement that this, rather than the quarrel concerning John Mark (Acts 15:36-41), was the main cause of his separation from Barnabas.

14. Many MSS substitute Πέτρῳ for Κηφᾷ; some omit καὶ οὐκ Ἰουδαϊκῶς, "and not the Jewish way"; and many have τί, **why?** (KJV), instead of πῶς, "how is it that?" The verb ὀρθοποδοῦσιν does not mean "walk erect"—cf. the ambiguous **uprightly** (KJV)—but "to keep one's feet on the straight path," or in our common phrase, "to walk the chalk mark." Paul's question is, **how can you compel?** (RSV), and not **why compellest thou?** (KJV). It is not necessary to take the participle ὑπάρχων in the concessive sense of **though** (RSV).

In Judaism, "to walk" was a favorite metaphor for one's conduct and way of life. The line one had to follow was blueprinted in the Torah of Moses and continuously projected by the oral tradition into detailed directions for walking. The Christians took over the metaphor, but for Paul the blueprint was the internal "Christ in me," the mind of Christ in the Christian. That was the highest ground possible in religion, and one must walk straight ahead on the line projected by faith. To hesitate, to look back, to

---

in their depths by their attitude not toward superiors and inferiors but toward equals, e.g., John Mark was no test for Peter; he was Peter's beloved spiritual son. And Luke was no test for Paul; these two were utterly devoted to each other. But Paul and Peter met on leadership terms—Peter from the Jewish center, Paul from the Gentile. Strong men are tested by other strong men.

Obviously in many ways Peter was no match for Paul. Although limited in educational and cultural training, Peter by his native gifts of speech and leadership was the voice and prophet of the Jerusalem church (James was its administrative head). Perhaps Peter's lack of formal training was part of the personal side of the big issue. He was battling against a man of very superior mental gifts, one who had the best formal education of that day. Yet Peter had the advantage of his daily companionship with Christ, having been present at all the major events of his Savior's life. Paul was entirely

15 We *who are* Jews by nature, and not sinners of the Gentiles,

like Jews?" 15 We ourselves, who are Jews

zigzag from left to right was to lose sight of the vision of the ideal man in Christ through whom alone one could be transformed. It was to surrender freedom and be driven once more into slavery to outworn customs, fears, and motives. Paul's challenge was barbed with this implication. Peter had gone so far in giving up these nonessentials that Paul assumed him to be in agreement with his principle of salvation by grace alone. So he pressed home the logic of the new freedom in Christ by asking Peter whether he thought it was consistent to compel a Gentile to become a Jew before he could join the church. The Judaizers would reply that Peter's concessions had been mistaken in the first place, and that he was right to repudiate them.

F. The Fundamental Affirmation of Paul's Faith (2:15-21)

Since Paul employed neither paragraph breaks nor quotation marks, it is not certain whether his address to Peter ends with vs. 14 or continues through vs. 21. What he says applies both to Peter and to the Galatians, but since Peter now drops out of sight, it is better to consider Paul's rebuke as ending with vs. 14 (so RSV), and to regard vss. 15-21 as a statement of his gospel in miniature (cf. 1:1-5), directed to the situation in Galatia. Peter in Antioch knew well enough what the gospel was, without having to be told.

1. The Abandonment of Law (2:15-16)

From his own bitter defeat, and from his observation of the failure of all other men (cf. Rom. 1:16–2:29; 7:4-25), Paul concluded that credit for law observance is not the basis of right relationship with God, but this relationship is "only through faith in Christ Jesus [ἐὰν μὴ διὰ πίστεως Χριστοῦ Ἰησοῦ]." It is important to observe that in this passage νόμου is without the article: Paul does not say **the law** but "law." Here, as also in 2:19, 21; 3:2, 5, 10, 11, 18, 21, 23; 4:4, 5, 21; 5:4, 18; 6:13, both the KJV and the RSV supply the definite article. But this interpretation limits the reference to the law of Moses, whereas the whole point of Paul's letter is that there is no law of any kind, whether of Moses or of any other lawgiver, that can give life (3:21).

15. Paul's declaration of the futility of the Jewish law as a way of salvation did not include surrender of his inherited concept of Israel as God's chosen people (Rom. 3:2). Comparison with Rom. 2:27 and 11:21-24 shows that **Jews by birth** (RSV) for φύσει Ἰουδαῖοι does not convey all of Paul's meaning. It was not only birth but a nurture, a way of life, a heritage, a destiny, and a missionary task that gave the Jew a **nature** (KJV) different from sinners (ἁμαρτωλοί) of Gentile stock. Whenever anyone argued that one religion was as good as another, Paul insisted that the Gentiles were really sinners (Rom. 1:18-32). The Jews did not claim to be sinless, but they did claim to be friends and not enemies of the one God, beside whom there was no other, who was just and holy and

dependent upon the "contemporary presence"; in addition, he had been a persecutor of the church. These two strong men, so different in background, temperament, experience, and training were each other's chief tests. And what is much more important, they incarnated the issue before the church. The Galatian heresy was Peter writ large.

Peter was on the field first for **the other Jews dissembled likewise with him** (vs. 13). Even steady, liberal, trusted Barnabas was carried away. Social atmosphere or climate does affect men who are not otherwise held fast in deepest convictions. It is perhaps true that the average man is much more likely to be influenced by his environment than he ever is to change it. Many men are tempted to do in a crowd what they would never do alone. There is the problem of corporate, institutional, and social ethics. How difficult it is to break with one's family and racial traditions! Because every fact and factor played into his life and lineage, Peter was surely on the defensive. And Paul pounded into him with a bill of particulars. Men get in social jams when their fundamental thinking is at odds with truth. It would be most helpful and

16 Knowing that a man is not justified
by the works of the law, but by the faith

by birth and not Gentile sinners, 16 yet
who know that a man is not justified[d] by

[d] Or *reckoned righteous;* and so elsewhere.

---

good, and whose will they were earnestly trying to do. But because Paul took this mission with utter seriousness, he learned from sad experience that the Jews were not good enough, and that salvation by merit for obedience to law was impossible (Rom. 2:1–3:20).

16*a, d.* These two sections of this verse make the negative point: Not by works. Sections *b* and *c,* the positive: By faith. To understand Paul when he says, "for by works of law shall no flesh be justified," the modern reader must take into account the differences between **law** as he and his fellow Jews conceived it and "law" in a twentieth-century state with representative government (see Intro., pp. 434-35). The principal difference lies in the fact that the laws of a modern state have no jurisdiction over a man's relations to God, and law observance is not made the basis of God's acceptance of the citizen for life in the world to come. As a Pharisee, Paul had been taught that works of law were deeds done in obedience to the Torah, contrasted with things done according to one's own will. The object of this obedience was to render oneself acceptable to God—to "justify" oneself. Having found this impossible, Paul reinforced the evidence from his own experience by Ps. 143:2, where the sinner prays God not to enter into judgment with him because in God's sight no man living is righteous. Into this passage from the LXX Paul inserted "by works of law," and wrote σάρξ, "flesh," instead of ζῶν "one living." This quotation warns us against setting Paul's salvation by grace over against Judaism in such a way as to obscure the fact that the Jews depended also upon God's lovingkindness and tender mercies (I Kings 8:46; Job 10:14-15; 14:3-4; Prov. 20:9; Eccl. 7:20; Mal. 3:2; Dan. 9:18).

Justified is a metaphor from the law court. The Greek verb is δικαιόω, the noun δικαιοσύνη, the adjective δίκαιος. The common root is δικ as in δείκνυμι, "point out," "show." The words formed on this root point to a norm or standard to which persons and things must conform in order to be "right." The English "right" expresses the same idea, being derived from the Anglo-Saxon "richt," which means "straight," not crooked, "upright," not oblique. The verb δικαιόω means "I think it right." A man is δίκαιος, "right," when he conforms to the standard of acceptable character and conduct, and δικαιοσύνη, "righteousness," "justice," is the state or quality of this conformity. In the LXX these Greek words translate a group of Hebrew words formed on the root צדק, and in Latin the corresponding terms are *justifico, justus,* and *justificatio.* In all four languages the common idea is the norm by which persons and things are to be tested. Thus in Hebrew a wall is "righteous" when it conforms to the plumb line, a man when he does God's will.

From earliest boyhood Paul had tried to be righteous. But there came a terrible day when he said "I will covet" to the law's "Thou shalt not," and in that defiance he had fallen out of right relation to God and into the "wrath," where he "died" spiritually (Rom. 2:8-9; 7:7-24). Thenceforth all his efforts, however strenuous, to get "right" with God were thwarted by the weakness of his sinful human nature, the "flesh" (σάρξ). That experience of futility led him to say that **a man is not justified by works** "of law." His meaning becomes clear when we remember that a printer will say that a line of type

---

revealing to have Peter's actual words in this battle, for in Galatians Paul does the talking and Peter comes out in a poor light.

16*a.* ***The Faith Tremendous.***—(See Expos. on 1:17-23.) The thread that holds this section together is the charge that Peter was double-dealing. "If thou, being a Jew, livest after the manner of Gentiles, and not as do the Jews, why compellest thou the Gentiles to live as do the Jews?" (Vs. 14.) Paul goes out of his way to emphasize that he debated with Peter "before them all" (vs. 14). In the presence of everybody he was drilling into Peter's soul the dictum, "What you do talks so loud I cannot hear what you say." The climax of the indictment is the apostle's immortal, everlasting, eternal line, **a man is not justified by works of the law but through faith in Jesus Christ.**

is "justified" when its words and letters are spaced in a true and even line and made to fit the form exactly.

Paul found that there was no law that could force man's unruly nature to fit God's form. He had to admit that he was a bankrupt criminal and throw himself upon the mercy of the court. But the moment he did that a marvelous thing happened. Contrary to all expectation, God the Judge not only acquitted him but accepted him as a son and fellow heir with Christ!

Hence to be "justified" in the Pauline sense means that the sinner is "acquitted," "accepted," "set right with God," "saved," despite his crimes. In an earthly court such a scandalous verdict would impeach the judge and bring justice into contempt. But precisely that is Paul's reason for choosing this metaphor of "justification." By it he is saying that man is not saved by his merit for obedience to God the Judge, but through trust in God the Father.

In the eyes of the psalmists and rabbis this was blasphemously revolutionary. Resting on God's covenant with Abraham, they held it axiomatic that the "righteous" man who had conscientiously done his part deserved to be vindicated before a wicked world; otherwise God could not be righteous. But Paul said that no man, Jew or Gentile, had enough righteousness to dare to speak of vindication, and that if anyone was to be saved it would have to be solely by God's mercy through Christ "vindicating" sinners. In Judaism God was thought of as forgiving only repentant sinners who followed their repentance with right living; and God's righteousness was his discriminating justice which accepted those who obeyed his law and punished those who did not. Paul's faith was indeed inseparable from right living, but this living was the fruit of the Spirit and not a merit which could serve as the basis of a demand that God vindicate him on Judgment Day. The supreme manifestation of God's righteousness was his forgiveness of sinners without merit on their part.

The theological expression for this conception of salvation is "justification by faith." Unfortunately this Latin word does not make plain Paul's underlying religious experience, which was a change of status through faith from a wrong to a "right" relationship with God (see Intro., p. 430). It conceals from the English reader the fact that the Greek word also means "righteousness." The RSV retains it because it has become fixed in the language of the church, but the translators recognize the difficulty in the marginal note on 16*a* (observe also the ASV mg., "accounted righteous").

But "reckoned" and "accounted" expose Paul's thought to misinterpretation by suggesting a legal fiction which God adopted to escape the contradiction between his acceptance of sinners and his own righteousness and justice. Superficially considered, this idea might seem to be in line with Phil. 3:12-14, where Paul describes the creative power of Christ's confidence in the imperfect human beings whose feet he has set in the path that leads *finally* to the perfection which God requires. But it involves ignoring the fact that Paul so abhorred being a sinner that he wanted to be sinless now; he was not content to wait until death freed him from the tyranny of "the flesh" to *be* as righteous as God "reckoned" or "accounted" him to be.

On the other hand, Paul's term, in the passive, cannot be translated by "made righteous" without misrepresenting him. In baptism he had "died with Christ" to sin. By this definition the Christian is a person who does not sin! And yet Paul does not say that he is sinless, but that he must not sin. He never claimed perfection (Phil. 3:12), and he refused to reduce God's requirement of righteousness to the compass of his present achievement; yet he insisted that God's acceptance of him as righteous was more than a present fiction. This laid him open to a charge of self-contradiction: sinless and yet not sinless, righteous and unrighteous, just and unjust at the same time. Some interpreters have labeled it "paradox," but such a superficial dismissal of the problem is religiously barren and worse than useless. "Tension" is another proposal, but this, while expressing a truth, does not do justice to the peace which Paul says is the fruit of the Spirit (5:22-23). It suggests an impersonal force rather than the creative impulsion of a

of Jesus Christ, even we have believed in Jesus Christ, that we might be justified

works of the law but through faith in Jesus Christ, even we have believed in Christ

personal relationship with Christ. This impulsion of the love of Christ made it necessary for Paul to be—as well as to become—what he was: a new man in Christ, "perfect, as your heavenly Father is perfect."

The extreme difficulty of understanding Paul on this matter has led to a distinction between "justification" and "sanctification," which obscures Paul's urgency to be now, at this very moment, what God in accepting him says he is: a righteous man in Christ Jesus. Justification is reduced to a forensic declaration by which God acquits and accepts the guilty criminal, and sanctification is viewed as a leisurely process of becoming the kind of person posited by that declaration. This makes perfection seem far less urgent than Paul conceived it, and permits the spiritual inertia of human nature to continue its habit of separating religion from ethics. To prevent this misunderstanding it is necessary to keep in mind the root meaning of "righteousness" in δικαιόω and its cognates.

16*b*, *c*. Here we have Paul's affirmation: But by faith. How does the Christian know that God forgives and accepts him? Paul answers, διὰ πίστεως Χριστοῦ Ἰησοῦ, which the

---

16*b*. *Faith as Trust*.—The several aspects of faith proposed in the Expos. on 1:17-23 obviously interlace, for there are no arbitrary divisions. However, in an effort to see the separate facets of the one jewel it is necessary to get at faith from every possible angle. Beyond all reactions, responses, definitions, and divisions, faith as trust is the center of the Christian religion. The only way out of humanity's entanglement is faith as surrender, which means direct personal access and attachment to Jesus Christ. Not by pilgrimages to assumed holy places, or by securing forgiveness or absolution through any man, medium, or institution, but by putting one's life for time and eternity into the hands of Christ does one have faith as surrender.

Such faith means taking that Christ at his word, believing that he can and will do what the N.T. claims he can. Such faith revolves around the "whom" before the "what" of faith. The emphasis here is not on trust or faith but on Christ. For if salvation rests upon faith as an act of man's mind, what else would faith be but a way of earning or deserving salvation? Words have been called deeds of the tongue; in like manner, faith could be a deed of the mind. Trust as saving faith, therefore, emphasizes not the subject of faith (man) but the object of faith (Christ).

Faith as trust is so simple that unlettered men are able to grasp it; it is so profound that men of the most powerful intellect confess it to be one of God's mysteries. It is the way of entrance into "the universal priesthood of believers," and is available for all of whatever height or size. The one condition is unreserved trust. This is "saving faith." Many who possess it know little of the implications involved in "capacity" and "response"; but they know whom they have believed. This is the faith that is involved in the phrase, "justification by faith." To recover it was the chief end and aim of the Reformation. Could a man save himself by the good works of his life, or was salvation the direct gift of Jesus Christ in answer to unreserved trust?

Such faith, as trust and surrender, means personal attachment to Jesus Christ, so that a constant stream of righteousness flows from him to the penitent and believing heart. A man with such faith is not only declared righteous, he is made right with God and before men by his connection with Jesus Christ, the source of all righteousness. Faith therefore is not a substitute for moral righteousness but the way to secure it.

A word of Jesus illustrates this kind of trust: "Whosoever shall not receive the kingdom of God as a little child, he shall not enter therein" (Mark 10:15). To what extent can an adult be like a child? He can at least keep alive a heart that wonders, trusts, and loves. This means to be childlike, but not childish. To respond to life, men, and God, as a normal child responds to his mother, is to have childlike faith; to respond only to that which concerns one's own convenience, comfort, desires, and interests, is childish. Childlike faith is the picture Jesus paints. A child's faith is perfect; a child's reasons, imperfect and immature.

The "trust" and "response" that are described in this section are the heart and soul of the Christian life: faith which has reference to capacity, faith that changes a man's status in relation to the covenant, faith as belief, as knowledge and assent, faith as adventure, as impetus and challenge and inspiration—all

by the faith of Christ, and not by the works of the law: for by the works of the law shall no flesh be justified.

Jesus, in order to be justified by faith in Christ, and not by works of the law, because by works of the law shall no one be justi-

---

KJV brings literally into English, **by the faith of Jesus Christ,** leaving the reader to decide whether it means Christ's own faith in God, which he breathed into his disciples and transmitted to all succeeding generations of believers, or the disciples' faith in Christ as their dying and rising Savior who gave himself for their sins and made new men of them. **By faith in Christ** removes the ambiguity; but the reader must remember that Paul's faith in Christ was created by Christ's faith in God and by Christ's faith in Paul.

In Paul's life πίστις was more than "belief," "assent," or "acceptance" of a proposition about God and Christ. The Greek noun means "faith" and "faithfulness," "trust" and "trustworthiness." It is used as a "guarantee" or "pledge," a "bond" or "mortgage." The verb πιστεύω means "believe," "put confidence in," "accept as true," and "entrust" oneself and one's aims and hopes to that which is accepted as true and faithful. The Hebrew has a corresponding series of verbs which are formed on the root אמן (cf. "Amen"), which means "be firm," "lasting," "enduring." In the LXX these Greek and Hebrew streams of meaning unite in πίστις and πιστεύω.

In the Hebrew religion the basis of all human faith and faithfulness was God's trustworthiness and fidelity to his covenanted promises. It was not enough to believe that God exists, has created and cares for his world. Faith in him required personal entrustment to his will and care, and conduct in imitation of him. So too for Paul. His faith made him more than a passive, grateful recipient of God's mercy. It was intensely active, and its ingredients were trust and entrustment, belief and self-committal to the way of Christ as over against the way of Moses and all other saviors. Without faith, freedom

---

aspects of faith flow from the simple and profound concept of faith as trust.

16*c*. *Paul's Conception of What It Means to Be a Christian.*—(See also Expos. on 1:22.) Paul illustrates in his own person what it means to be a Christian. He used the phrase **in Christ** in his writing and teaching because it described his own life. The words meant for him and mean today that it is possible to be connected with the living Christ directly and intimately, with no intermediary person, law, or institution. The first question is not "What do you believe?" Rather is it "To whom do you belong?" A Christian is one who belongs to Christ; he is a "Christ-one," a status that a man does not attain; it is the gift of Christ. Faith in Christ does not bring knowledge of Christ; it brings Christ himself.

Paul wrote, "To all the saints in Christ Jesus which are at Philippi" (Phil. 1:1). A saint is one who is **in Christ,** one who belongs to Christ. Sainthood does not represent the achievement of certain virtues; that would be quite secondary. Moral and spiritual achievement is not self-generated; it comes from one's organic relationship with Christ. All we have to do, all we can do, is to keep attached to Christ, who is the Vine; the Vine will do the rest.

In Christ means that Christianity is person-centered. In that discovery Paul found the ultimate in the Christian life. It is futile to endeavor to make a case against Paul as the "complicator" of the simple gospel of Jesus. Paul had to agree with Jesus on the profoundest level, else he could not be **in Christ.** All we know of his work and life after Damascus affirms that he did agree. As Moffatt translates Phil. 1:21, "Life means Christ to me." How could such a man complicate Christ's gospel?

There are many who believe that the authority of the church is infallible: that the church is the historic interpreter of Christ and the Bible; that it speaks for Christ on matters of doctrine and morals. There are those who reply that the Christian church is only the extension of the person of Christ, that he, not the church, is the authentic voice; that the church at most only possesses the means of grace, while he is grace; that grace is greater than any means by which it may be received. They insist that the Bible is the only infallible rule of faith and practice, not a word or dictum subject to the decrees and pronouncements of church officials. They insist that the communion of saints includes all who are **in Christ,** and that no man can determine the number of saints. The church of Christ is infinitely more than a visible organization of which a census may be taken.

Others would appeal to the authority of an infallible book, the Bible. Among this group are

17 But if, while we seek to be justified by Christ, we ourselves also are found sinners, *is* therefore Christ the minister of sin? God forbid.

fied. 17 But if, in our endeavor to be justified in Christ, we ourselves also were found to be sinners, is Christ then an agent of

and the right use of freedom were impossible, and faith without moral fruitage was not faith. On the other hand, faith was not a "good work" which Paul substituted for "works of the law" as a merit to claim salvation. The very faith through which he accepted God's grace in Christ was the work of God's grace within him. To keep this clear it is better to say that men are saved by God's grace through faith in Christ than to say that they are saved by faith.

2. The Rejection of Compromise (2:17-19)

17. The Judaizers were thoroughly alarmed by Paul's teaching that all is of grace. They feared that people seeking cheap admission to God's kingdom would trifle with righteousness and sin boldly, while deluding themselves that God would accept them by mere profession of faith. It was an objection that Paul had to meet time and again (cf. Rom. 6–8). In the present passage he quotes his critics as saying in effect: "But if through seeking to be accepted as righteous in Christ we too are found to be sinners, does that not make Christ an abettor of sin?" The phrase **were found** could refer to the moment when Paul and those who sided with him gave up the law as a way of salvation and thereby classed themselves with Gentile sinners. Or it could mean that every time the Jewish Christians ate with the Gentiles, or abandoned other customs required by the law, they were sinners; in this case there would be specific reference to Peter's conduct at Antioch. But the KJV rendering, **are found sinners,** fits the trend of Paul's argument better. If a Jewish Christian should fall below the moral standard set forth in the Torah, he would be a worse sinner than the Gentiles because the law had taught him to know better (Rom. 2). This, said Paul's critics, would make Christ not a savior from sin but **the minister** (διάκονος) to promote sin and encourage lawlessness.

Paul replied with an indignant μὴ γένοιτο, lit., "Let it not be," a phrase which he was in the habit of using to reject conclusions drawn from the specious logic of his opponents. The translator has the choice of a number of phrases: "by no means," "of course not," **certainly not** (RSV). **God forbid** (KJV), while not literal, conveys more of Paul's

those who insist that the Protestant reformers substituted an infallible book for an infallible church. In truth, however, they substituted an infallible Christ for an infallible Pope: the shift was from person to Person. Luther never attempted a definition of the inspiration of the Scriptures; he assumed it. He was wiser than to undertake to define the indefinable. He proposed, however, a permanent test for any verse, passage, or book: What does it testify of Christ? In debating theories of inspiration a man may lose the gospel, or may turn the Bible into a doctrinal lawbook and the church into a debating society. Unless Jesus Christ means that "the Word was made flesh, and dwelt among us, . . . full of grace and truth" (John 1:14)—unless Christ is the living Word—the Bible is only another religious book. The presence of Christ with the Holy Spirit, as he speaks through the pages of the Bible, makes that book the Word of God. When a man hears the voice of God speaking to him through those pages, the "words" on a page utter "the Word of God" for him.

There are still others who, for their only sure footing, appeal to a trustworthy experience. The word "trustworthy" is purposely used in place of "infallible" by this school of thought, for its followers believe that the ultimate in the Christian life is one's experience with Christ, with emphasis on experience. For Paul, however, Christ himself is the first, middle, and last fact of Christian experience. He is the underlying reality which makes all experience of him genuine and authentic. Not a man's experience of Christ but Christ himself is the ultimate in Christian life, and the Bible is the norm for measuring that experience across the centuries. **In Christ** covers what Paul thought it means to be a Christian.

17-19. ***Forgiveness—An Invitation to Sin?***—The opponents of Paul accused him and his doctrine of promoting loose morality; they

18 For if I build again the things which I destroyed, I make myself a transgressor.
19 For I through the law am dead to the law, that I might live unto God.

sin? Certainly not! 18 But if I build up
again those things which I tore down, then
I prove myself a transgressor. 19 For I
through the law died to the law, that I

---

abhorrence for this suggestion. He did not want his Christians ever to think of such a thing. Yet he did not attempt a theoretical refutation. The answer to his critics had to be "written not with ink, but with the Spirit of the living God" (II Cor. 3:3). There was not then, and there never has been, any other way to prove that Paul's gospel is right than by daily living in accordance with the mind of Christ.

18. The verb συνιστάνω, "to set together," is used with the following meanings: "commend," "prove by one's action," "show by one's conduct." If a single word is wanted, **make** (KJV) is more adequate than **prove** (RSV) to express Paul's total idea here. The "if"-clause should be introduced by **for** (KJV) rather than **but** (RSV) since it gives the reason for the **God forbid.** In this passage κατέλυσα does not mean **destroyed** (KJV), but **tore down** (RSV). It represents a rabbinical expression which was used to disallow a proposed interpretation of a point of law, and its opposite was **build up** (RSV), which meant to approve the proposal.

What Paul had torn down was not merely certain statutes of the ceremonial law, but the whole law, both ceremonial and moral, considered as a necessary substructure for faith and a way of salvation by merit. In the eyes of the Judaizers that made him **a transgressor,** one who "steps across" the bound, a deliberate, highhanded violator of God's will. Paul turned the argument around. His unexpressed premise is that whatever is not of faith is sin. Obedience to the law with the intention of building up merit for salvation is what makes a man a transgressor! The Christian freeman who wavers and goes back to slavery to the law is the sinner. In his pre-Christian days Paul could not keep the law perfectly enough to win God's approval, and if he were to try it once more, he would have to fight the civil war in his soul all over again. Worse still, it would betray a lack of complete confidence in God's way of grace for the new man in the new age. That would have been the greatest of all "transgressions."

The troublemakers in Galatia cited certain concessions which Paul was making, partly by ingrained Jewish habit, and partly to win the Jews for Christ, whenever this did not compromise his principle that all is of grace. He replied that such concessions were not a rebuilding on the foundation of law, but an expression of the liberty of the Christian man.

19. The "I" here is emphatic; **am dead** expresses the truth of Paul's permanent relation to law but obscures the fact that he had in mind a particular act of disobedience which stood out in his memory as the moment when he was forced to admit that law could not save him (Rom. 7:7-12). The word **law** is in Greek without the article both times; **the law** suggests that Paul is giving up only the Mosaic law, whereas he is repudiating all kinds of legalism.

Dying to law meant ceasing to regard obedience to it as the means to secure acceptance with God. Paul continued to do, or to refrain from doing, many of the things it com-

---

maintained that he made faith and forgiveness so simple that men sin again and again, turning each time to Christ for the forgiveness which is always available. Such a setup would make **Christ a minister of sin** if it were the whole truth. But forgiveness is not that simple, and faith is not that superficial. Faith is utter commitment to Christ in one's deepest self, and though man stumbles daily, forgiveness brings daily healing, strengthening, and renewal. Forgiveness is no invitation to sin, but history's strongest deterrent. Faith is no superficial matter; it is intelligent confidence that Jesus is Savior and can do what the N.T. claims he can. Such faith brings not only knowledge of Christ, but brings Christ himself; and Christ is no invitation to sin. The movement of faith is from bondage under law to the freedom of personal

20 I am crucified with Christ: nevertheless I live; yet not I, but Christ liveth in

might live to God. **20** I have been crucified with Christ; it is no longer I who live, but

manded, but from an entirely different motive: Faith at work through love (5:6). The Pharisees taught that the Torah was the life element of the Jews; all who obeyed would live, those who did not would die (Deut. 30:11-20). But Paul found that the law, instead of enabling him to keep in right relation with God, suspended a curse over the sinner. Living to law was in reality living to self; living to God meant dying to self and bearing one another's burdens (cf. Rom. 6:10-11; 14:7-8; II Cor. 5:15).

3. Sole Reliance upon Christ (2:20-21)

20*a*. The RSV translates Χριστῷ συνεσταύρωμαι literally **I have been crucified with Christ.** The KJV brings out the continuing result expressed by the perfect tense in Greek: **I am crucified.**

In a mystical, sacramental sense Paul died in baptism and was buried with Christ; on this idea the best commentary is Rom. 6. In a spiritually creative sense Paul associated himself with Christ by taking up Christ's cross and bearing Christ's burdens; here the best commentary is Col. 1:24-25. Daily crucifixion to all that defiled and hindered was required for complete self-devotion to the work of the Spirit in Christ's body, the church (I Cor. 9:23-27).

Crucifixion with Christ means three things: (*a*) Participation in the benefits of Christ's death, including freedom from law, forgiveness for past sins, and a passionate urge never to sin again (Rom. 4:24-25; II Cor. 5:14-15; Col. 2:12-15, 20; 3:1-4). (*b*) A moral, spiritual fellowship with Christ in his death and resurrection, which takes the Christian's "I will" captive to "the mind of Christ," replacing the law as a design for living (II Cor. 10:3-6; Phil. 3:10; Rom. 6:1-11). (*c*) A partnership with Christ in his creative suffering, which requires the Christian to "complete what remains of Christ's afflictions" for the sake of his body the church (Col. 1:24-25; 3:5; Rom. 8:17).

loyalty and devotion. **I . . . died to the law, that I might live to God.** To be a son of God and no longer a servant exemplifies the theme of Galatians: freedom in Christ.

> Now the long discipline is over. The hour of release has struck. Faith resumes her ancient sway, in a larger realm. In Christ a new, universal humanity comes into existence, formed of men who by faith are grafted into Him. . . . All things are theirs for they are Christ's (I Cor. iii. 21-23). . . . He has secured for mankind and keeps in trust its glorious heritage. In Him we hold in fee the ages past and to come. The sons of God are heirs of the universe.[4]

20*a*. *In Christ: A Commentary on the Teaching of Jesus.*—"In Christ" means that **Christ liveth in me.** "Abide in me, and I in you" (John 15:4; see also Expos. on 1:22). If Paul's phrase is out of harmony with the teaching of Jesus in the Gospels, out goes the phrase and Paul has "run in vain" (vs. 2). Manifestly, however, Christ's own charge, "Abide in me," and Paul's answer, "in Christ," are wedded. "Abide in me" is a summary of the Christian faith; "in Christ" is Paul's confession of that faith. Few verses or passages of scripture belong together as one idea more than John 15:1-16 and this verse of Galatians.

Men lose their faith in God when their picture, their idea, and their consciousness of Christ are smaller than their world. It is a true principle that one must grow in the knowledge of Christ or his faith will gradually wither and eventually die. A growing faith is rooted in awareness of Christ as a living contemporary. He is not like a statue, a nostalgic memory, or only a figure in history. A man cannot maintain a living faith in a Christ who is but a childish recollection. The only God a man will never outgrow, and therefore never lose, is the God he knows in a present tense experience, a God larger than his world.

One of the names for God is the name he gave to Moses. "Thus shalt thou say unto the children of Israel, I Am hath sent me unto you" (Exod. 3:14). He is the eternal "I Am." Moses knew God as ever active, ever leading; but the children of Israel had trouble keeping the tense. Moses' difficulty was in making God's moving presence known to others. Jeremiah came to the rescue with his teaching of the "new covenant," Isaiah with his "suffering servant," Hosea with

[4] Findlay, *Galatians*, pp. 240-41.

The danger was that Paul's Gentile converts might claim freedom in Christ but reject the cross-bearing that made it possible. Lacking the momentum of moral discipline under Moses, which prepared Paul to make right use of his freedom, they might imagine that his dying and rising with Christ was a magical way of immortalizing themselves by sacramental absorption of Christ's divine substance in baptism and the Lord's Supper. The church has always been tempted to take Paul's crucifixion with Christ in a symbolic sense only, or as an experience at baptism which is sacramentally automatic. It has also been tempted to reduce Paul's "faith" to bare belief and assent to his doctrine, and to equate his "righteousness" with a fictitious imputation by a Judge made lenient by Christ's death.

Against this caricature of "justification by faith," Paul's whole life and all his letters are a standing protest. He never allows us to forget that to be crucified with Christ is to share the motives, the purposes, and the way of life that led Jesus to the Cross; to take

---

his message of yearning love, the psalmists with their vast music. But the supreme effort of God to reveal himself in the present tense was the coming of Jesus "in the fulness of the time" (4:4). Jesus came to reveal God as "the eternal Contemporary." He himself is the living Word of God, making it possible for men in every century to affirm: "He spoke to my fathers; he speaks to me. He taught my fathers; he teaches me. He saved my fathers; he saves me. He guided my fathers; he guides me." Men are concerned with Jesus not for what he is reported to have done for their spiritual ancestors but for what he is doing with them today. How can modern men get at this pearl of greatest price—this experience with Jesus in the present tense? There are three experiences that often cause multitudes to lose their awareness of his presence.

(*a*) There is the peril of loneliness (see John 15:5). Jesus looked into the heart of mankind across the centuries when he said, "Abide in me." He knew what was in the heart of man, what was not. Watch his concern for human loneliness, which weaves in and across the N.T. On that first Easter evening he joined two of his disciples on the dusty road to Emmaus, knowing their hearts were lonely and heavy. He would walk on every roadway with pilgrims who feel worthless, misunderstood, unappreciated, and with those who indulge in self-pity, which is one of the worst forms of selfishness. He offers his companionship to those who feel unloved, insecure, insignificant. Speaking through the pages of the Bible, he becomes the living Word to lonely lives. To each man whose thorn in the flesh makes him particularly lonely and unwanted, Jesus still speaks in effect as to Paul, "I cannot take it away, but you will not have to bear it alone." His real presence in the Holy Communion is his master way of keeping men "in Christ" and thereby healing their loneliness. To be in him is to be like the branch which is attached to the vine.

(*b*) There is the peril of unfruitfulness. He disciplines, corrects, prunes, and teaches so that this peril may be circumvented. "Every branch that beareth fruit, he purgeth it, that it may bring forth more fruit" (John 15:2). "The branch cannot bear fruit of itself, except it abide in the vine" (John 15:4). "Without me ye can do nothing" (John 15:5). Is that true? Nothing? A man who is not "in Christ" can readily become part of the world's problems instead of becoming part of the solutions. He may enjoy a church which others support; he may inject suspicion and a critical spirit into life instead of good will. The list adds and multiplies. Do nothing? Nothing constructive or productive. Words that were used by Arthur John Gossip in affectionate appreciation of the Scottish preacher, William M. Macgregor, could be the story of multitudes: "Apart from Christ he might have been a proud, even a ruthless, man." [5]

The mission of the church is to produce Christlike minds by instilling the mind of Christ, thereby enabling men to outthink the world; to produce Christlike character through the redemption of Christ, and in so doing enable men to outlive the world.

(*c*) There is the peril of unanswered prayers. "Whatsoever ye shall ask of the Father in my name, he may give it you" (John 15:16). "If ye abide in me, and my words abide in you, ye shall ask what ye will, and it shall be done unto you" (John 15:7). Here is the reason many do not get the answer they desire to their prayers: they are not "in Christ." They pray not "in his name," even though their prayers close with the words. They are not living and asking "inside his purpose." Only within his purpose may answers be expected, "If ye abide in me, and my words abide in you." Prayer is a movement in a life relationship; it is communion before it is petition. Only through the "wonder-working

[5] W. M. Macgregor, *The Making of a Preacher* (Philadelphia: Westminster Press, 1946), pp. 14-15.

me: and the life which I now live in the flesh I live by the faith of the Son of God, who loved me, and gave himself for me.

Christ who lives in me; and the life I now live in the flesh I live by faith in the Son of God, who loved me and gave himself for

---

up vicariously the burden of the sins of others, forgiving and loving instead of condemning them; to make oneself the slave of every man; to create unity and harmony by reconciling man to God and man to his fellow men; to pray without ceasing "Thy will be done"; to consign one's life to God, walking by faith where one cannot see; and finally to leave this earth with the prayer "Father, into thy hands I commend my spirit."

20*b*. The first δέ is continuative and should not be omitted in translation—*and* **it is no longer I. . . .** The KJV is wrong in introducing **nevertheless . . . yet not.**

Paul's crucifixion with Christ, drastic though it was, had its inner side of glory. It was a passage from darkness to light; a rescue from the vortex of rebellion in which each sin drove the sinner to some new and greater sin; and a surrender to the God and Father of the Lord Jesus Christ, who judged Paul with a mercy with which Paul's own conscience would not permit him to judge himself. Instead of death it was a new beginning in a new life (see Intro., p. 434).

Christ was now the intimate companion of Paul's soul. He does not say "I am Christ," or "Christ is Paul," but "Christ lives in me." His own individuality was not

---

power of attachment" are prayers answered. The teaching of Jesus confirms Paul's "in Christ"; Paul corroborates the teaching of his Lord.

20*b*. *Faith as Belief*.—(See also Expos. on 1:23.) The word "belief," like **faith,** has several meanings. It is used often in the sense of trust. "Believe on the Lord Jesus Christ, and thou shalt be saved" (Acts 16:31). It may stand for what one lives by, his outreach from the core of trust to a life built around it. Or it may take on a more intellectual aspect. When "faith" develops into a body of truths, convictions, and doctrines, it becomes a rational effort to explain what a Christian believes and why. Trust is first concerned with the "whom," belief with the "what." When a man begins to give the reason for his faith, and to love Christ with his mind, he is in the realm of "belief."

Paul was a pioneer in Christian thinking. Someone has suggested that those who would attempt to defend faith by attacking freedom of thought had better get out of his way. Those who would follow his lead possess the religion of living minds. He clearly states the case for mental growth and development in the Christian life: "When I was a child, I spake as a child, I understood as a child, I thought as a child: but when I became a man, I put away childish things" (I Cor. 13:11). That passage shows that he was growing in the Christian life, and that his growth was both a spiritual and an intellectual process. It is impossible for a man to face a man's world with a child's faith. It is impossible to tackle a man's battle with a child's weapons. As was Paul, so should every Christian be able to justify his faith. When a man finds himself in possession of a larger concept of life and the universe he should have a correspondingly larger concept of God, or his universe becomes his god. Larger responsibilities require a faith that knows how to tap resources that a child does not need. This explains the biblical passage, "Grow in grace, and in the knowledge of our Lord" (II Pet. 3:18). When men "lose their faith," their faith was likely the child's faith which they learned at a mother's knee or in an elementary church school. It is easy to lose what one has never possessed on any adult level.

One of the tragedies of the Christian life is the acceptance of the conclusions of others without going through the study, growth, and experiences that produced those conclusions. Many so-called convictions are like that. They are rather assertions with no understanding of the intellectual or moral content involved. A Baltimore pastor, as the leader of a student conference at Johns Hopkins University, learned one of the deepest lessons of his life. During a question period which followed his talk, a young Jewish lad with a good spirit and an open mind said: "I know you are a busy man, and I for one want to thank you for giving us your time and thought tonight. You have helped me, and I deeply respect the statement of your faith. What you have said has interested me. However, I am much more interested in *why* you believe what you do than in a statement of *what* you believe. I would stay here all night if you would tell us *why* you believe in Christ."

There are common beliefs which many churches hold necessary for the fellowship of

extinguished or absorbed in some infinite, impersonal nirvana. His capital "I" was not merged in that of Jesus. Freedom and responsibility to make his own decisions and to develop his own creative talent remained. But now it was the mind of Christ that gave content to Paul's concept of the Spirit and guided his conscience (Rom. 8:9-11). What he experienced appears in I Cor. 13 and in Phil. 2:1-11.

When Christ the Spirit came to live in Paul, Paul saw God and man through the eyes and actions of Jesus. His feelings were transfused with the emotions of Jesus, and he shared Jesus' attitude toward God's purpose for men—utter humility and self-devotion to the ends of God in human persons, which led all the way to death on the Cross. Conversing in prayer with this new Companion in his soul, receiving this new Light of his conscience, Paul was guided at each step, in each new circumstance, to answer for himself the question: What would Jesus have me do? And the answer was always this:

---

kindred minds. Some require not much more than an acceptance of the spirit and leadership of Jesus and a desire to share common causes. Others demand for active membership a clean-cut acknowledgment of Christ as Lord and Savior. Still others insist upon the acceptance of extended statements of belief and doctrine. One cannot say how far complete agreement at this point is possible. Clearly no two minds are absolutely alike. If no two fingerprints are alike, and no two leaves on a tree are alike, how can one expect to find two minds that are exactly alike? To what extent is it possible to have perfect agreement on anything? "Can two walk together, except they be agreed?" (Amos 3:3.) But agreed on what? If agreement on every minute definition is demanded, with the crossing of every *t* and the dotting of each *i*, the result would be a collection of small minds. How much difference of conviction is it morally honest to permit? How much does Christ permit?

The church on earth, among its other functions, serves as the custodian and steward of truth—the truth of God as revealed to men in the Holy Scriptures and supremely in Jesus Christ, who is the truth of God and Word of God. Certain it is that in a century of conflicting ideologies only a confessional church, knowing the reason for the truth it holds, is great enough for the hour and the task.

20*c*. *The Cross as Substitution.*— (See Expos. on 3:13.) **And** [he] **gave himself up for me.** "Our Lord Jesus Christ, who gave himself for our sins, that he might deliver us" (1:3-4). "Christ redeemed us from the curse of the law, having become a curse for us" (3:13). This concept of the Cross brings into sharp focus material that other theories do not include. There is central and profound truth embedded in it, even though distasteful to some minds. It is surely scriptural, and a nonchalant attitude toward it is unworthy. However crude certain statements in connection with the theory may be, even to the extent of unwittingly casting reflections upon the character of God, there is eternal truth in the idea of substitution.

A word of warning seems in place at this juncture for two types of mind, both of which need lessons in reverence and humility. One is the man who thinks he already has all the answers, believing that his definitions are quite complete. He often pieces together scattered scriptural verses which are historically unrelated. Such a mind forgets that God alone knows all he did on the Cross, that there is a mystery about the Cross which may belong to its deepest meaning, that the best intellects of twenty centuries have not been able to plumb its depths. All of us need to be reminded that any attempt to define the Cross completely is like trying to wrap a package with a piece of paper which is too small.

For the love of God is broader
  Than the measure of man's mind.[6]

The other type of mind that deserves a word of warning adopts a shrug-of-the-shoulder attitude toward the substitutionary theory. One would have to look widely to find modern theologians comparable with Paul, Irenaeus, Clement of Alexandria, Origen, Athanasius, or Anselm. Each of these held the substitutionary theory. There is truth here which was central in the church of the Middle Ages and which became in structure the position of classical Protestantism. Before God could forgive the sins of men, it was necessary for him to do something which only he could do. Whatever was needed he accomplished in and through the Cross.

He has come and stood in our place, under the shadow of our guilt and His own wrath, so deeply identified with our lot that—if we are willing—a mystic sharing can now take place between us, whereby His infinite goodness passes over to us, while the weight of our guilt and terror passes over

[6] Frederick W. Faber, "There's a wideness in God's Mercy."

Rely solely on God's grace through Christ, count others better than yourself, and make yourself everybody's slave after the manner of the Son of God who loved you and gave himself for you.

20c. This life of Christ in the Christian had to be lived in a human society in which evil and sin were realities, and so it had to be lived in faith.

The phrase ἐν σαρκί, which can be translated "human," means, lit., **in the flesh.** To live in the flesh was to live as a member of human society in a physical body. Someday—Paul hoped it would be soon—this would be changed into a body like that of the risen Christ, which belonged to the realm of Spirit. By faith he was sure of that, and by faith he looked forward to it. But even now for the rest of his life on earth he was living in this realm where all existence was conditioned by faith in Jesus Christ as the Son of God

---

to His strong shoulders. . . . In and through the crucifixion of Christ God has performed a hard and costly Deed which makes His love newly accessible, and makes the world permanently different for those who, coming within the radius of influence of the Deed, respond to it affirmatively. . . . If the objective atonement was only a legal fiction, invented by theologians, this might be good riddance; but if, as we have contended, the wrath of God and the alienation of man are tragic realities, then it is the height of folly to refuse to grapple with them.[7]

On the day of the Crucifixion one man understood it—at least on the surface. He was Barabbas, a prisoner who was to have been put to death. Pontius Pilate, the Roman governor, violated every semblance of legal justice when he left it to the howling rabble outside his palace to decide between Barabbas and Jesus. Inspired by the political cunning of such men as Caiaphas the high priest, they made their choice, and Barabbas was set free. As Jesus hung on the cross, Barabbas must have said over and over again, and for the remainder of his life, "He died for me; he took my place." Barabbas most likely did not understand the full meaning of Christ's death, but the unadorned raw fact he surely knew. Man will never again have to bear any experience, no matter how dark and heavy, that Jesus has not already borne. One whose son had been recently killed said to a friend: "If I had lost my son and God had not lost his, I should have had a depth of experience denied even to God himself." [8] Jesus gathered up into himself the sins of the whole world, took them with him to his cross, bore a guilt which no man can bear for himself, satisfied whatever needed to be satisfied in the justice, holiness, and love of God, and finally made possible full and complete fellowship with God for every human being in every age under every condition for all time and for eternity. In this way the fate of Jesus Christ becomes the meaning and central point of history.

Look, Father, look on his anointed face
  And only look on us as found in him.
Look not on our misusings of thy grace,
  Our prayer so languid, and our faith so dim.
For lo! between our sins and their reward
We set the passion of thy Son our Lord.[9]

According to Horace's rule of dramatic art, a god was never introduced unless the plot became so entangled that only a god could unravel it. Paul illustrated thoroughly the tangle in which conscientious men found themselves in his day. There was always the possibility of tragedy in his own life, as in every life—a power working in men which can break them, defeat them, and make a ruin out of them. Does that explain in part why many men are not willing to accept Jesus simply as a clue to God and the spiritual world, the most trustworthy guide, the mirror of the Eternal, the chief religious teacher and greatest of the prophets? The possibility of tragedy will not let them stop there. They must see and know a God who is not a remote spectator, for the world's struggle is his very life. Bethlehem, which means the entrance of the Eternal into human history, would have only a limited meaning if God did not touch life at its most difficult point, the place of tragedy. The Cross makes it possible for a man to say, "I am not alone; the Father is with me, doing for me what I could never do for myself."

Yet that scaffold sways the future, and, behind the dim unknown,
Standeth God within the shadow, keeping watch above his own.[1]

But if God suffers when man suffers, man could become very pessimistic. God suffering? Then even eternity is a vale of tears! But the Cross assures man of fellowship with a God for whom suffering is not the final word. The open

[7] Walter M. Horton, *Our Eternal Contemporary* (New York: Harper & Bros., 1942), pp. 75-76, 78. Used by permission.

[8] William E. Phifer, Jr., *The Cross and Great Living* (New York and Nashville: Abingdon-Cokesbury Press, 1943), p. 110.

[9] William Bright, "And now, O Father, mindful of the love," st. ii.

[1] James Russell Lowell, "The Present Crisis," st. viii.

21 I do not frustrate the grace of God: for if righteousness *come* by the law, then Christ is dead in vain.

me. 21 I do not nullify the grace of God; for if justification[e] were through the law, then Christ died to no purpose.

[e] Or *righteousness.*

(see Intro., p. 434). His qualification of ἐν πίστει by τῇ τοῦ υἱοῦ τοῦ θεοῦ, "faith in the Son of God," shows that, for Paul, to be "in Christ" was to be "in faith." This is the most intimate element in Paul's mysticism; to express it requires that we translate "in faith" rather than **by faith. By faith in the Son of God** (RSV) corrects **by the faith of the Son of God** (KJV); see Exeg. on vs. 16, and, for the thought, cf. Rom. 8:3, 32.

The motivation of Paul's new life in Christ was faith, hope, and love. These three are never separated in his religion. In our present passage hope (ἐλπίς) is implied by νῦν, **now,** which contrasts on the one hand with Paul's pre-Christian life, and on the other with the completion of his transformation which he expected at his Lord's second coming. For other examples of the inseparable association of faith with hope and love see Rom. 5:5; 8:37-39; I Cor. 13.

21. The verb ἀθετῶ means "set aside," "reject," hence "nullify." As in vs. 16, the RSV gives two translations of δικαιοσύνη, **justification,** and in the margin **righteousness** (with KJV). The Greek conveys both the forensic sense of acquittal and acceptance with God ("justification") and the actual righteousness required for that acceptance. No verb is expressed in the "if"-clause; KJV supplies **come,** ASV "is," and RSV **were.** The Greek word for "law" again is without the article. Paul denies that righteousness acceptable

---

tomb of Easter morning adds, "He is risen." That is why Paul always ties the Cross and the Resurrection together. The Resurrection is the other side of the Cross. Both empty cross and open tomb cry out to all struggling hearts, "He has conquered tragedy; he has overcome the world." The Christ who took Barabbas' place, and who has taken every man's place in the drama of evil, assures mankind of God's fellowship in tragedy, of his triumphant life which overcomes tragedy, of his forgiveness which heals lives that are broken by tragedy, of his power to sustain man in the good life beyond tragedy. The supreme substitution which Jesus made was the substitution of his life for man's death, his forgiveness for man's guilt. The divine tragedy belongs in a world filled with human tragedies. The cross of Christ is at home in a world filled with man's crosses.

> We may not know, we can not tell,
> What pains he had to bear;
> But we believe it was for us
> He hung and suffered there.[2]

20*d*. *In Christ: The Cross as Presupposition.* —(See Expos. on 1:22.) The order of events is clear. **I am crucified with Christ . . . I live . . . Christ liveth in me.** The Cross is central in all of Paul's teaching because it was central in his experience. A man who had been guilty of all that marred Paul's past (Acts 9:1) had to be completely changed before he could be "in Christ." He had to be cleansed, refined, healed, redirected; in one word, he had to be forgiven. He had to be brought into harmony with Christ before he could live "in Christ." His center of gravity had to be changed. This was accomplished by Jesus through the Cross. Permanent fellowship with Christ must be preceded by preparation, which always necessitates the discipline of the Cross. The Cross gets men ready to be "in Christ." The Christ who gave himself for us is the Christ who has set up the way of permanent attachment to him. "In Christ" is the redeemed man's new and permanent environment. To prepare Paul and all men for that environment is the work of the Cross.

Perhaps the most comprehensive word that ever was written about the Cross was written by Paul, "God was in Christ, reconciling the world unto himself" (II Cor. 5:19). Everything else in his thinking had to square with that. He would be "bewitched" (3:1) if he took any position or held any conception which violated that core of his experience and teaching. Take away the Cross, and "in Christ" is not Pauline; what is much more, it is not Christian.

21. *Grace Finds Its Fullest Expression in the Cross of Christ.*—(See Expos. on 1:3.) This single verse might not be so impressive if it stood alone; but grace and the Cross are wedded in all of Paul's writings. If Jesus had been only a man, the story of his death on the cross could

[2] Cecil Frances Alexander, "There is a green hill far away," st. ii.

3 O foolish Galatians, who hath bewitched you, that ye should not obey the truth, before whose eyes Jesus Christ hath been evidently set forth, crucified among you?

3 O foolish Galatians! Who has bewitched you, before whose eyes Jesus Christ was

to God can be achieved by obedience to law, whether Jewish or Roman or any other code; for if it could, then Christ died "needlessly," "for nothing," "without cause," **to no purpose.**

Paul turned the argument back upon his critics. It is not I, he says, who am nullifying the grace of God by abandoning the law which is his grace-gift to Israel, but those who insist on retaining that law in addition to the grace which he has now manifested in Christ. For if God wanted nothing more than man's obedience, law and its sanctions would have been enough. But God desired man's love, and that could not be secured by threats and force, but only by his first loving man to the extreme of sending his own Son to die for man. Otherwise there could be no satisfying explanation of why Jesus, the best of men, had suffered the worst of deaths.

In vss. 15-21, as in 1:1-5, Paul has preached his whole gospel. His next step, which covers the middle portion of his letter, is to vindicate his gospel of grace, faith, and freedom, by appeal to the facts of history and Christian experience.

II. The Defense (3:1–4:31)

A. An Appeal to Personal Experience (3:1-5)

3:1. The clause **that ye should not obey the truth** (KJV) does not belong to the text of this verse but was added under the influence of 5:7. Many MSS add ἐν ὑμῖν **among you** (KJV).

One of Paul's words for preaching was προγράφω, which meant "post a notice," e.g., on a bulletin board in the public square; "project on the screen" would convey the meaning exactly. The center of Paul's preaching was Jesus on the Cross (I Cor. 1:17, 23; II Cor. 13:3-4). As if in a picket line, he and his fellow missionaries placarded Christ crucified that all might see, not God's grievance but God's love. Every sermon and

have been told by any good newspaper reporter in a few paragraphs. He would have been no more than a martyr, and history's pages are filled with martyrs. But at every moment and in every movement of his life Jesus gave himself to men as Savior. The place where he gave himself fully and completely was the Cross. That Cross is therefore the fullest expression of his grace.

If Christ had been only God, he could not have taken upon himself our sins; if he had been only man, he would have needed all his power for himself. The Cross, the climax of what began in Bethlehem, is the supreme personal event in history. God and man meet, and meet on the deepest possible level at the Cross. There God comes to grips with the most stubborn forces that violate his love; there he draws men into full harmony with his love and with the grace that flows from it.

Not a man's hold on Christ, but Christ's mighty grasp on him is the anchor that holds and saves. God's hand of grace reaches through Christ's cross. "Christ looked at me and I looked at him and we were one forever." [3]

O to grace how great a debtor
 Daily I'm constrained to be!
Let that grace, now like a fetter,
 Bind my wandering heart to thee.[4]

The grace which comes through the cross of Christ meets life's great adventure with the great redemption. There God and man transact their most important business. Charles H. Spurgeon was at the heart of the Christian faith when he confessed, "I build my study on Mount Calvary." That was Paul's conception of the Cross.

3:1. ***Bewitched Eyes.***—Men are **bewitched,** said Paul, when they get their eyes off the Cross as the center of the Christian life. In the Cross

[3] Attributed to Charles H. Spurgeon.

[4] Robert Robinson, "Come thou Fount of every blessing," st. iv.

letter portrayed the dying and rising Christ **evidently** (KJV), **publicly** (RSV)—so clearly and openly that there should have been no mistaking God's way of salvation. Hence the Galatians were ἀνόητοι, "unthinking," "thoughtless," and therefore **foolish;** but "foolish" carries overtones of stupidity, whereas the Galatians' trouble was failure to use their power of perception, or as we say, "to put two and two together." In the passive sense ἀνόητοι means "unthinkable"; in modern Greek the word is "unreasonable." In the papyri the verb ἐβάσκανεν, "slander," "envy," "bewitch," is employed in manipulating charms against "the evil eye." Paul uses it figuratively, meaning "pervert," "confuse," "lead astray," as if man's perennial quest for cheap and easy salvation were not sufficient to victimize the Galatians without the aid of a Pied Piper of Hamelin!

The missionaries of the cross of Christ had to compete with pagan priests who paraded the images and symbols of their savior-gods in spectacular processions. There was the cult of Cybele, "the Great Mother," whose consort Attis died by self-mutilation with the decline of each year's vegetation. During his "passion week" a pine tree swathed as a corpse was carried through the streets, and three days later his devotees joyfully celebrated his "resurrection" as the guarantee of their own immortality. Another savior-god of Asia Minor was Sandan-Hercules. His symbol was a funeral pyre on which, according to the myth, he had immolated himself after performing the labors that were imposed on him. Still another was Mithra, the sun-god, who was portrayed in the act of slaying a bull, which represented the chaotic element in the universe, and which in dying was believed to give new life to the world.

---

every statement must be tested, each teaching corrected or confirmed. The Cross is an objective fact of history before it becomes a subjective fact of experience. It was always first and central with Paul, together with the other side of the Cross, the Resurrection. We know too little about God, life, and man to understand fully this supreme event of all time. "We see through a glass darkly"—but we see through, and it saves us; we see through darkly, and it challenges us. Men across the centuries, as did the Galatians, often get their eyes off the Cross and follow "contrary" gospels, especially three.

The first contrary gospel is moralism. The devotees of this school insist upon a "simple gospel," a "gospel to live by," e.g., the Golden Rule, which is not Christian in any distinctive sense. They discount heavily the importance of theology and demand practical, everyday guides for living. For them the Christian life is little more than a set of lessons to be learned, rules to be followed, qualities to be cultivated, insights to be appreciated, with a philosophical overtone for the more thoughtful—a rather big order! "Give me the Ten Commandments, the Sermon on the Mount, and the Lord's Prayer; you may keep all the rest," is the confession of some moralists—as if these three were no more than commentaries on how to live. Quite obviously they are underreading all three. Life is too subtle to be handled by a set of blueprints or a road map. It is too big to be mastered by precepts, mottoes, disclosures, and insights—and much too tragic. The fact and the power of evil throw the school of moralism into panic, for its gospel is too simple!

The second contrary gospel is humanism. This word covers a wide area. The concept of Jesus as the highest expression of the human ideal—his way of life, including his cross, as the open door to humanity's fondest hopes—stands at one end of the scale for the humanist. But from that high pinnacle other humanists descend to a position somewhat like that of a certain teacher of philosophy who maintains that we never solve many of our personal problems; that we can only live them down or master them by the logic of fatigue. Contrast this philosopher's "logic" with the following confession of a disciple of Christ:

> The brilliant materialisms, the pretentious secularisms, and the confident idealisms whose hopes have a consummation without God have had their day. They have brought bitterness and confusion and disintegration. The dark and hot voices which would go to the beast to learn the meaning of the life of man have led only to ugly frustrations of their own. The solutions in a pantheism leading to a Nirvana which is a black-out of all the distinctions that give meaning to life have an appeal only for the utterly weary who, because they have really given up the battle, try to believe that an eternal silence is better than any speech, an eternal meaninglessness is better than any meaning. They build a tomb at the end of the human enterprise and call it the ultimate peace.[5]

[5] Lynn Harold Hough, *The Christian Criticism of Life* (New York and Nashville: Abingdon-Cokesbury Press, 1941), p. 302. Used by permission.

2 This only would I learn of you, Received ye the Spirit by the works of the law, or by the hearing of faith?

publicly portrayed as crucified? 2 Let me ask you only this: Did you receive the Spirit by works of the law, or by hearing

In competition with these sensuous and often obscene observances, Paul's portrayal of the crucified Jesus suffered a disadvantage. Crucifixion was the most shameful and painful of deaths reserved for the worst of criminals, and morally the way of the cross demanded so much more than emotional pilgrimages to follow Christ's passion that many who would gladly have claimed its promise of eternal life shrank from its burden and went shopping for an easier salvation. There was always an eager audience for the purveyors of myth, magic, and miracle, who could tailor a gospel to fit their customer's spiritual size. Converts from paganism who wanted to present the Cross in terms of mystical speculation and sacramental ritual rather than of the mind of Christ could charge that Paul's demand for strenuous morality was "rebuilding" (2:18) the law of Moses. It was to prevent such demoralization of the gospel that the Judaizers wanted to keep the picture of Moses side by side with that of Christ. Paul would "project" no other "on the screen" than his crucified Lord.

2. To break the enchantment of the Galatians, Paul reminded them of God's way of bestowing his Spirit, and of their own deep joy when they first heard the gospel. **The hearing of faith** (KJV) is ambiguous: does the phrase refer to faith's hearing, or to the faith which is heard? But **hearing with faith** (RSV) is also indefinite, leaving uncertain whether **faith** is the instrument or the accompaniment of hearing. Paul has in mind a believing kind of hearing that welcomes the gospel and leads the hearer to entrust himself to Christ. In the hearing of the word which creates the faith the Spirit is received. Hearing the gospel is set over against hearing the tradition which the fathers handed down from Moses, and which required those who heard it to assume the yoke of the law.

The third contrary gospel takes the environmental approach to life. It believes that the better way, if not the only way, to produce better men is to improve the climate and order in which they live. Better housing means better families; a more just economic order means better people; freedom from fear and want provides time for the cultural pursuits. This "gospel" is also a big order, and offers much that is desirable. Nevertheless, housing, justice, and freedom from fear give men at most the opportunity, and only that, to be better people. The dark, stark fact is that so many who possess only these admit that they are neither good nor happy. Political and economic freedom comes only through men who are morally and spiritually free themselves. There remains the age-old impossibility: unchanged men trying to change the world, unclean hands trying to cleanse the political order. Social betterment strikes a mighty blow at the rim of life but not at the hub.

Paul's gospel still makes sense. The central matter is not the attainment of a catalogue of virtues or skills. The question of destiny is: To whom am I attached? Beyond all else, a man's attitude toward the Cross answers that question. Men's eyes are bewitched when they are removed from that center. The Cross is therefore the point of spiritual and social hope.

2. ***Faith as Response.***—(See Expos. on 1:17-23.) Faith as response is the answering of God's knock on a man's door. The grace of Christ is the knock, so graphically pictured in Holman Hunt's painting "The Light of the World." The latchstring must be on man's side, or he is a puppet and not a person. "Behold, I stand at the door, and knock: if any man . . . open the door, I will come in" (Rev. 3:20). In this sense faith is response.

The difference of judgment or interpretation at this point may become morally debilitating. One view holds that men do not have the power to believe in Christ; they have only the power to refuse. Even Luther's words sound as if he took that position. "I believe that I cannot by my own reason or strength believe in Jesus Christ, my Lord, or come to Him; but the Holy Ghost has called me by the Gospel, enlightened me with His gifts." [6] Is faith, then, man's act?

The perspective in which to consider this

[6] *Small Catechism*, Explanation to the Third Article of the Apostle's Creed.

The effects of the Spirit which came through Paul's preaching are described in I Thess. 1:5-6; I Cor. 12:4-11, 27-31; II Cor. 1:22; 5:5; Rom. 8:15-17, 23, 28, 37—power and joy and ecstatic revelations; a new relation of sonship to God and a partnership with his Spirit; assurance that greater things were yet to come, and that God could be trusted, despite all that was dark and doubtful, to complete the good work which he had begun in them. But this meant that Paul's converts must go forward with the Spirit and not back to Moses.

The answer Paul expected from the Galatians was therefore this: "We received the Spirit when we responded in faith as we listened to the gospel which God's grace offered to us through Christ." Receiving the Spirit was receiving Christ himself, and since Paul's idea of the Spirit was determined by what Jesus had said and done, he could receive the Spirit only through faith in Jesus as the Christ. The Spirit took the place of the Torah as the life element of the Christian.

---

problem is provided by the Christian idea of man and the Christian idea of God. Man is a person with the power and right to choose. He is either that or he is reduced to a subhuman level. The God who does the knocking will not force his hand, yet not only asks for his response but demands it. To those who hold that man has only the ability to refuse—to say "No" when God knocks—it may be replied that "No" and "Yes" are the opposite sides of the same coin or act: they are the opposing decisions of one will. God's call is universal, and the opportunity is provided for all men to decide for themselves what they believe.

Said a Christlike man to his pastor: "One of my most inspiring thoughts is to realize that the eternal Christ, with the universe on his mind and heart, has the time, and takes the time, to stand at the door of my little life and knock. He even stands and waits for me to answer. Think of the eternal Christ at my door! I must be important, significant, and worth while to him. I intend to try acting on that assumption. The least I can do is to open the door."

That same man believes the hymn writer is casting perhaps an unconscious reflection on Christ in her lines:

> Pass me not, O gentle Saviour,
> . . . .
> While on others thou art calling,
> Do not pass me by.[7]

As if Christ would! He cannot play favorites; he knocks on every door. His visit is universal; but a visit is not a trespass. He cannot be a better friend than each man permits him to be. Even Christ is limited by an attitude that declines to respond. The bestowal of Christ's righteousness waits for the faith of man: this is faith as response. "And he did not do many mighty works there, because of their unbelief" (Matt. 13:58).

[7] Fanny J. Crosby.

The supreme knock of God at the heart of humanity is the cross of Christ. More men have responded to that knock than to all the others. More men have said "Yes" to God because of the Cross than for all other reasons combined. Any church and any pulpit with a minimum place for it is generally of very slow growth. The Cross is Christ's strongest, most insistent, and most eternal knock at the door. He confessed on that Cross, "I thirst" (John 19:28)—and his greatest thirst was to be thirsted after. He yearned for those who derided him to pray to him; for the hands that crucified him to work in his kingdom.

The movement of the N.T. from the angels' chorus over the plains of Bethlehem in Matthew's Gospel to the hallelujah chorus in the Book of Revelation is along the path of God—Christ—Man! And never this order in reverse. "God so loved . . . that he gave" (John 3:16); "When the fulness of the time was come, God sent forth his Son" (4:4). It was the method of Jesus. "Come unto me" (Matt. 11:28); "I will never leave thee, nor forsake thee. So that we may boldly say, . . . I will not fear what man shall do unto me" (Heb. 13:5-6); "Lord, I believe; help thou mine unbelief" (Mark 9:24). Clearly the movement starts in God and moves through Christ to man. The mood of the N.T. is not aspiration but acceptance; not the reaching of man's hand in search for God, but the awareness of the touch of God's hand on his.

The Christian faith and life are not an attainment through a tremendous self-discipline; they are an acceptance through a complete self-surrender. Too many men, especially the strong and brilliant, have tried to attain what only God can give (see Expos. on vs. 11). The way of the law which Paul inherited offered the good life for perfect obedience; but perfect obedience man could never offer. The way of Jesus proposed what man *could* do: he could have faith, he could trust, he could respond. Response is the hearing of faith.

3 Are ye so foolish? having begun in the
Spirit, are ye now made perfect by the
flesh?
4 Have ye suffered so many things in
vain? if *it be* yet in vain.

with faith? 3 Are you so foolish? Having
begun with the Spirit, are you now ending
with the flesh? 4 Did you experience so many
things in vain? — if it really is in vain.

---

3. The Judaizers, fearing the effect of these activities of the Spirit upon the purity and perpetuation of their ancestral religion, insisted that they must be kept under strict control by the law of Moses. The logic of Paul's reply is plain. Literally translated it is: "Are you so unreasonable that having begun with Spirit, you are now ending with flesh-work?"

This antithesis of πνεῦμα, "Spirit," and σάρξ, "flesh," parallels the opposition of πίστις, "faith," and ἔργα, "works," in vs. 2. The Galatians "began" with Spirit when they accepted Paul's gospel, entrusted themselves to Christ, and allowed the Spirit to produce fruit in them (5:22-23; I Cor. 12:4-11, 27-31). But now they wanted to "end" with works done in obedience to law, which Paul calls "flesh"-works (see Exeg. on 2:16-17). The verb ἐπιτελέω ("to end") is used frequently in the sense of performing religious rites and duties. **Are ye now made perfect by the flesh?** (KJV) is not as literal as **are you now ending with the flesh?** (RSV), but it expresses exactly the legalists' contention that law must be added to faith in order to make faith mature and trustworthy as a basis of salvation.

Paul says that this would not be progress but retrogression, not perfection but a concession to human nature (σάρξ) as it was before Christian was made a new man by the Spirit. Those who cannot see this he calls "unreasonable," **foolish.** Possession by the Spirit and life under his constant personal guidance constitute the highest conceivable spiritual state. Why then be so **foolish** as to try to confirm and enrich the higher by the lower? Why seek perfection by recourse to the imperfect?

4. Knowing that his Galatians had been well satisfied with his gospel (4:8-15), Paul appealed to them to conserve the values they had found true.

Have ye suffered? (KJV) and **Did you experience?** (RSV) are interpretations of ἐπάθετε. The RSV translation is undoubtedly better. The experience may be good or evil, according to the context. Paul had in mind the joys as well as the sufferings of the

---

3-4. *The Conservation of Suffering.*—Paul's Galatian converts had dared much, had risked much, and had suffered much by becoming Christians. By dropping back into the life pattern in which they had been reared they had **suffered . . . in vain.** (But see Exeg.) By agreeing to circumcision, they were again putting the flesh, not Christ, at the center of their lives. Many twentieth-century Christians in countries like the United States, where religious liberty is constitutionally guaranteed, have difficulty understanding what the early Christians faced and endured. Those who witnessed the oppression of Christians before, during, and since World War II have seen how readily the tables can be turned. For first-century Christians the entire pattern of life was changed; becoming a Christian for them was well-nigh a cosmic event. To be free from the flesh and threadbare traditions many of them endured affliction and even death at the hands of men like Paul, the persecutor. If they fell back under the control of old laws, they lost their new freedom and so **suffered . . . in vain.** Paul saw that his Galatian converts were not holding, that they were surrendering.

> Ground we hold, whereon of old
> Fought the faithful and the bold.[8]

The abiding message of vs. 4, valid for all the centuries, is the conservation of suffering. Said a woman, "If I am doomed to be a sufferer for the remainder of my lifetime, I resolve to use that suffering to become a better person." She did not suffer **in vain.** An American clergyman did not know whether he would ever be able to preach again. When his throat was pronounced cured, his first sermon was based on the psalmist's hymn, "O Lord, open thou my lips; and my mouth shall show forth thy praise" (Ps. 51:15). He had not **suffered . . . in vain.**

[8] Justus Falckner, "Rise, ye children of salvation," tr. Emma Frances Bevan.

5 He therefore that ministereth to you the Spirit, and worketh miracles among you, *doeth he it* by the works of the law, or by the hearing of faith?

5 Does he who supplies the Spirit to you and works miracles among you do so by works of the law, or by hearing with faith?

Christian life. The term **so many** could also be "so great," but Paul's emphasis on the variety of the experiences and gifts of the Spirit favors the former (5:22-23; I Cor. 4:8-13; 9:19-23; 12:4-7, 27-31; II Cor. 4:7-12; 6:3-10; 11:21–12:10; Phil. 3:4-16; 4:8-9; Acts 14:22).

The sufferings of the Galatian Christians would include family divisions, ill-will, suspicion and persecution by relatives and former friends who were convinced, most of them sincerely, that the way of Christ would lead not to life but to apostasy from the one God whom Moses had revealed. Not least were the spiritual anguish of breaking with their ancestral religion and the doubts cast by the Judaizers upon the reality of salvation by grace alone through faith in Christ—all this in addition to the pain of daily crucifixion with Christ (for the joys of the Christians see Exeg. on vs. 2).

Paul's plea was to go forward with the Spirit, trusting the validity of the best insights of one's own past, conserving its values and pressing on to perfection. All was not yet lost in Galatia, but the issue hung in the balance, and Paul alternated from hope to fear for them. They must determine whether all that they had hitherto experienced with Christ would be in vain.

5. The unexpressed verb of this sentence must be inferred from ἐπιχορηγῶν and ἐνεργῶν. Since these participles are in the present tense, and since Paul means that the Spirit was being supplied to the Christians not only at the beginning but throughout their whole life, the present tense is required: **doeth he it?** (KJV); **does he . . . do so?** (RSV). The action is going on right under the eyes of the observer: a continuous, never-ending, ever-increasing supply of God's own Spirit.

He therefore that ministereth to you the Spirit (KJV) is misleading. The participle ὁ ἐπιχορηγῶν does not mean "he who ministers," but **he who supplies** (RSV); and it is God, and not the Christian, who supplies the Spirit that works miracles. In Phil. 1:19 the

---

5. ***Miracles in the Christian Life.***—The record of miracles has raised many of the most perplexing questions in Christian thinking. A miracle is as difficult to define as personality, which also includes visible and invisible elements. It may be only a limited or fragmentary expression of a higher order of things which is eternal. Men are inclined to label as a miracle any experience of Christ which they do not understand or which seems to violate their conception of the laws of the universe. If man understood all the physical and psychic facts of life and the world there would probably be no "miracles." The larger conception of miracles cannot violate a law-abiding and trustworthy universe.

Christ himself is the greatest possible miracle. His resurrection is history's supreme miracle. And make no mistake, if his enemies and critics could have disproved the fact of it, the entire Christian movement would have fallen. They did not because they could not. Being a miracle, it would be a miracle if he did not perform miracles. It remains to be seen what changes he may work in the lives of those who are utterly dedicated to him and his cause.

Christ's miracles mean for one thing that he has the power that moves the world. They were called "signs" of the kingdom and illustrate or signify how he is in direct connection with a higher order than our own existence. He did not need to exercise his dominion over the world of things, and yet he did just that. Miracles were one of his methods of self-revelation.

The miracles mean that Christ can help men with the physical difficulties they have to face. The gospel is not good advice, but good news. Christ performed miracles to meet specific needs, as well as to manifest his motives and purpose. He does not always remove physical difficulties—e.g., Paul's thorn—but with his help physical problems no longer mean spiritual and moral defeat for men. In his miracles he does for us what nature cannot do or undo.

The miracles mean that Christ teaches by sight as well as by insight, by seeing as well as by hearing, by example as well as by precept. Miracles are often parables in action. By performing miracles Jesus interpreted his mission and person, impressing those whom he healed as well as the onlookers with the reality of his mission and of his mastery.

6 Even as Abraham believed God, and it was accounted to him for righteousness.

6 Thus Abraham "believed God, and it

noun form of this verb indicates a supply of the Spirit so rich that no exigency of life or death can exhaust it (cf. II Cor. 9:10). Paul always thinks in terms of the grace that is more than sufficient (Rom. 5:5; 8:37), because it comes from the God who is the source of all things (4:6; I Thess. 4:8; II Cor. 1:22). The effect of this Spirit is to work miracles "in you," endowing you with power to work miracles on others. **Among** is not adequate to convey Paul's idea. He is speaking of a power resident in the heart. There is where the first and greatest "miracle" takes place; whereupon the changed and empowered life expresses itself outwardly in right conduct and miracles "among" those who observe them (on the meaning of **works of the law,** and **hearing of faith** see Exeg. on vs. 2 and on 2:15-16).

Conversions from other religions were motivated in part by the search for power to control the mysterious forces of death and life (Acts 8:18-19). Many Christians valued ability to work miracles more than any other gift of the Spirit, and especial emphasis was placed upon exorcising the demons that were believed to exist and to cause physical and mental disease. Paul's task was to keep Christians from debasing their conception of the Spirit into magic. He told them that power minus love equals zero (I Cor. 13), and admonished them to seek the greater gifts of new purposes, new goals, and new ways of living constructively as members of the body of Christ. He reminded them that God was not supplying these good gifts to individuals in isolation from the corporate fellowship, but through the togetherness of worship and mutual service. Reassured by such evidence from firsthand experience, no seeker need look for anything higher in the realm of Spirit.

B. The Precedent of Abraham's Faith (3:6-18)

1. Preview of the Gospel (3:6-9)

Having appealed to the Galatians on the basis of their own experience with Christ, Paul now turns to scripture and calls Abraham to witness for the truth of his gospel. The career of Abraham was marked by four great adventures of faith: his departure from Haran for Canaan; his acceptance of God's covenant of circumcision; his trust in God to multiply his posterity and give them the land of the Canaanites; and his willingness to give Isaac on the altar, if God had really demanded human sacrifice. Abraham was regarded as the first proselyte to the one God who had created the heavens and the earth

The miracles mean that we do not have a theoretical Christ, but one who works in concrete situations. He deals effectively with the rough facts of life. His miracles do not violate the established order of things, but instead rectify a situation that is out of order. Health and not disease, sight and not blindness, life and not death constitute the natural order designed by the Creator; the removal of all imperfections does not break the higher order.

The miracles mean that Christ is the master of the whole of life, not of just a fragment. He is Lord of all or not at all. Who can trust a master capable only of being worshiped, one who can do nothing practical for those who worship him, a master who is impotent before physical problems and the facts of everyday life? There are few heresies more devastating than that which divides life into compartments, setting aside one for religion and reserving it for Christ. Jesus cuts across the whole grain of a man's life or across none of it. The church sings, "Were the whole realm of nature mine";[9] the whole realm is his. He does not upset his own law-abiding universe. He uses it for love's sake and humanity's sake. He is the Lord of nature, of nations, of society, and of personal life. "The winds and the sea obey him" (Matt. 8:28). His miracles illustrate his personal connection with inanimate nature and with the Mind at the heart of the universe. They demonstrate the interrelation between the physical and the spiritual, and emphasize the basic truth that their oneness is to be met supremely in Christ.

6-10. ***Sons of Abraham.***—It was normal for every descendant of Abraham to desire never to lose his heritage. The conscientious Jew

[9] Isaac Watts, "When I survey the wondrous cross."

7 Know ye therefore that they which are of faith, the same are the children of Abraham.

was reckoned to him as righteousness." 7 So you see that it is men of faith who are the

---

and governed all things in justice and lovingkindness. He was looked upon as the bearer and teacher of monotheism, who gathered a multitude of other proselytes and set them an example of piety and godliness, patience in suffering, intercession for others, and hope in God for vindication in victory. Abraham was called the friend of God.

6. Paul and his Jewish opponents agreed on the character and position of Abraham, but they disagreed on which came first, his faith or his obedience. The Judaizers maintained that Abraham's faith was a good work and that it was his obedience that saved him. Paul, resting his case on Gen. 15:6, says: **Thus Abraham "believed God, and it was reckoned to him as righteousness."**

By this Paul does not mean that Abraham's faith was a good work by which he saved himself, but that his faith was the basis of his obedience. Abraham's circumcision was only a sign or seal of the righteousness which he had through faith before he ratified the covenant with God (Rom. 4:10); and so he was saved through faith 430 years before the law existed! Unfortunately the exigencies of Paul's argument caused him to employ this O.T. passage in such fashion as to endanger his fundamental principle of salvation, which makes faith itself a grace-gift of God. If he had believed that Abraham's faith was a credit set down in God's ledger rather than God's work in Abraham's soul, he would not have had the difficulty with the doctrine of predestination which appears in Rom. 9–11.

Both sides could quote scripture, and each could explain the other's "proof" in the light of his own position. The Jews believed that the Torah existed from the beginning of creation; and that, although it had not yet been written in Abraham's day, Abraham had obeyed it, being perfect in all his works and pleasing to God in righteousness all his days (Jubilees 23:10; II Baruch 57:2). To prove that Christians could not be saved without being circumcised and assuming the yoke of the Torah, the Judaizers quoted Gen. 17:14.

Paul's opponents were developing Mosaic legalism to an extreme which threatened to obliterate that strain in earlier Judaism which gave a much larger place to faith. Their tendency was to equate faith with obedience and make it a merit in God's sight. Paul was carrying the nonlegalistic strain in his ancestral religion to the opposite extreme of abandoning the law as the ground of salvation. His faith was not a pen with which to write his name and merit in God's book of life; nor was it a false entry of fictive righteousness which would naturalize him as a citizen of God's kingdom. Instead, Paul's faith was an approach, a disposition, an attitude toward God which trusted him completely, accepted his grace through Christ, and produced all manner of deeds of love as the fruit of his Spirit.

7. The law as a way of salvation was bound up with nationalistic customs; but faith was God's way for all, both Jew and Greek (Rom. 3:21-25), and its logic was plain: **It is men of faith who are the sons of Abraham.**

Since Paul is stating a case rather than making an exhortation, the indicative **so you see** (RSV) is better than **know ye therefore** (KJV). The **men of faith,** "faith people," stand over against "the men of deeds," and "the men of circumcision." Because Abraham was a man of faith, only men of faith could be his sons. Circumcision and physical descent from Abraham were irrelevant. The men of faith were those who, like Abraham (see p. 501), believed God's promises, entrusted themselves to his love and mercy, lived as his sons and friends, and so were in right relationship with him. In this sense Abraham was the faith-father of the Christians.

It was necessary to warn the Judaizers against mistaking physical descent from Abraham for a passport to Paradise. Some of them believed that on the day of Judgment God would be more lenient toward his chosen people than toward the Gentiles, provided only that they had not "cut themselves off" by repudiating their circumcision, their

8 And the Scripture, foreseeing that God
would justify the heathen through faith,
preached before the gospel unto Abraham,
saying, In thee shall all nations be blessed.

sons of Abraham. 8 And the scripture, foreseeing that God would justify the Gentiles
by faith, preached the gospel beforehand to
Abraham, saying, "In thee shall all the

monotheism, and their belief in life hereafter. Against such presumption the Hebrew prophets always inveighed. Paul was continuing this prophetic reaction to complacency when he invoked the O.T. doctrine of "the remnant" and maintained that the Christians were God's faith-people, hence the only true sons of Abraham.

In applying the remnant concept to the church, Paul viewed the history of his people as a selective process which depended not upon merit but upon faith in God's grace. The line of God's narrowing choice began with Abraham and ran through Isaac instead of Ishmael, and then through Jacob, rejecting Esau. Ten tribes fell away, leaving only Judah and Benjamin, and of these there was but a remnant in the days of Nehemiah and Ezra. Under the Maccabees men of faith and faithfulness were still fewer, and now the Pharisees and Essenes were only small groups within the indifferent mass. In every age the bearers of the orthodox religious culture of Israel followed Elijah in regarding themselves as God's faithful minority.

The Christians took over this claim. The church began in the synagogue, the main difference being the Christian affirmation of the messiahship of Jesus. But as Greek-speaking Jews and Gentiles came in, this difference in the interpretation of prophecy was widened by laxness in observing the law of Moses. The synagogue expelled the Christians, leaving them without the legal protection which Judaism enjoyed under Roman law. Enemies of the church argued that since the majority of Jesus' own people had rejected him, his gospel was false. The Christians replied that the church, though a minority, was the true Israel, and that the Jews in refusing Christ had deserted their own religion. This enabled them to assure the suspicious Roman authorities that Christianity was not a revolutionary innovation but a religion of honorable antiquity. Not only freedom from the law of Moses but the question of Christian rights under Roman law was involved when Paul declared that the **men of faith** in Christ were the true **sons of Abraham.**

So far from being an innovation and afterthought, the gospel of grace had been God's way of salvation from the beginning, revealed through faith and to faith. To prove this Paul personified scripture and represented it as having granted a preview of the gospel to Abraham two thousand years before the coming of Christ.

8. Gentiles (RSV), **heathen** (KJV), and **nations** are translations of the same **word,** τὰ ἔθνη. **The scripture** is Gen. 12:3 and 18:18. In the LXX these passages read: "All the tribes of the earth will be blessed in you," and "All the nations of the earth will be blessed in him." To adapt them to his purpose Paul writes "nations" instead of "tribes," substitutes "in you" for "in him," and omits "of the earth." Translation alone cannot bring out the full meaning of ἐν σοί, **in thee.** The Jews understood it in the sense of membership in the body politic of Abraham and his descendants, and Paul's use of ἐν Χριστῷ ("in Christ") for membership in the church as the body of Christ indicates

feared its loss perhaps beyond all other losses. In II Cor. 11:22 Paul boasts that he stands in that high succession: "Are they Hebrews? So am I. Are they Israelites? So am I. Are they descendants of Abraham? So am I." He recalls God's promise that in Abraham's seed all the nations would be blessed. To share Abraham's faith, and through it to share Abraham's life, was therefore Paul's ancestral prize. Along with faithful Jews in all centuries, he could not surrender it. Jesus provided the way by which he did not have to surrender it. The reasoning is quite clear and simple: possessing the inward presence of Christ brought to a man every worthwhile, permanent, enriching promise that any son of Abraham could possess. Paul's heritage was not discarded in Christ, but was fulfilled and illuminated; he had gained, not lost. He had everything of lasting value which a true Jew could possess, plus a sonship that Abraham

9 So then they which be of faith are blessed with faithful Abraham.

10 For as many as are of the works of the law are under the curse: for it is written, Cursed *is* every one that continueth not

nations be blessed." **9** So then, those who are men of faith are blessed with Abraham who had faith.

10 For all who rely on works of the law are under a curse; for it is written, "Cursed

---

that he had the same idea in mind. All men in all nations who are associated with Abraham by becoming men of faith will participate in his blessing. As in the LXX, Paul put the verb in the passive, "will be blessed." The middle voice, "will bless themselves," would have been closer to the original Hebrew idea. That idea was that the good life and happy state of Abraham and his posterity would become the desire of all other nations. When the ancient Hebrews wanted to wish one another the highest possible well-being, they would say, "May you be like Abraham." Thus Abraham and his descendants were to bless and be a blessing, and all mankind would acknowledge themselves beneficiaries of the overflow of their prosperity and happiness. All blessings were summed up in the belief that God's kingdom, for which the world had been created, belonged to Abraham and his heirs.

Paul, as his use of these Genesis passages will indicate, did not think of the O.T. as a vending machine for predictions and proof texts. His method was to ground all religious issues on faith, hope, and love, which were God's way for all men in all ages. He saw that history was not aimless, but God's action to produce sons and heirs in Christ. He shared the belief that scripture was the revelation of God's unbreakable will, and this belief steadied him to face the hard fact that the glorious hope of the kingdom had been deferred for two thousand years. One thing was clear: the law had failed; but it was equally plain that Gentiles like Titus were producing the fruit of the Spirit, which was the essence of the kingdom. To those who believed that non-Jews, no matter what their Christian character, would have no share in the world to come unless they were circumcised, Paul replied that Abraham lived not by law but by faith in accordance with the preview of the gospel that God granted to him.

9. The reason for changing **faithful Abraham** (KJV) to **Abraham who had faith** (RSV) lies in the dual meaning of πίστις, "faith." Although **faithful** (KJV) means lit., "full of faith," its primary meaning today is "fidelity," "reliability," so that it does not express clearly Paul's main point, which is Abraham's response in believing God. He means that all others who believe are blessed with this "believing Abraham." The RSV, however, does not bring out the element of "faithfulness" which is inseparable from Paul's "faith." A paraphrase is required: "Abraham who had faith and was faithful." Like the sun and the rain, God's blessing on such a man knows no restrictions of race or nation.

2. Intervention of the Law (3:10-14)

10. The Hebrew of Deut. 27:26 says (ASV), "Cursed be he that confirmeth not the words of this law to do them," for which the LXX has "Cursed be every man who does not abide in all the words of this law to do them." The LXX substitutes "abide in" for

---

could not give. Intelligent faith in Christ without any reservations was all that was required of a man; Christ would do the rest. The God of righteousness would constantly pour into such a man moral and spiritual power so that he could be a channel of righteousness in all his social relations. God would thus not only declare a man righteous; he would also make him righteous. Paul was saying out of his own experience that there is a "power, not ourselves, which makes for righteousness." [1] It is the source of the good life, a source not in moral precepts or legal requirements, but in a new relationship. The law demanded what it could not provide, for the law did not have the power to produce

[1] Matthew Arnold, *Literature and Dogma,* p. 52.

in all things which are written in the book of the law to do them.

11 But that no man is justified by the law in the sight of God, *it is* evident: for, The just shall live by faith.

be every one who does not abide by all things written in the book of the law, and do them." 11 Now it is evident that no man is justified before God by the law; for "He who through faith is righteous shall live";[f]

[f] Or *the righteous shall live by faith.*

"confirm" and adds "all." This addition is essential to Paul's argument that if a man is going to base his salvation upon his obedience to the law, there can be no exception, even for the least of its commandments. He must keep them all, for he will be as fatally cursed for a small as for a great infraction; it is his spirit of disobedience that condemns him (cf. Jas. 2:10).

Paul says, lit., "For as many as are of works of law are under a curse." Both νόμον ("law") and κατάραν ("curse") are without the article. To be **of the works** (KJV) of law is to **rely on works** (RSV) of law to make oneself acceptable to God. The verb which the KJV renders literally as **continueth . . . in** was a legal term meaning "comply with," **abide by** (RSV). Retention of the preposition **in** is a desirable feature of the more literal translation because the Torah was the life element "in" which the Jews lived as contrasted with Paul's "in Christ," and "in the Spirit." Τοῦ ποιῆσαι αὐτά, **to do them** (KJV), is an emphatic way of saying "and actually do them."

The range of the curse of which Paul is speaking appears in Deut. 27–30, where it occupies five times the space of the blessings. It is described in terms of the hideous torments which history inflicted upon the Hebrew people. The one word "fear" tells the story—fear of famine, disease, and death; fear of war, torture, and slavery; fear of past, present, and future. All these were punishments on earth, and death ended them. But by the time of Paul they had been projected into the hereafter, where the law's curse would pursue the soul through an eternity of torment in a hell which was conceived in the fiery imagery of Greek and Persian mythology. The dramatist of the dialogue of Ebal and Gerizim had left open one window of hope—repentance and return to God; but as for the future life, eschatology and apocalyptic had blacked out even this.

Great care is needed to understand Paul here. He does not say that the curse is God's curse. It is the curse of law, and of law misconceived as a way of salvation. His fellow rabbis reasoned that since the Scripture was God's word, the curse which it pronounced upon the disobedient was God's curse. He replied that the law was not God's way of salvation, but only a codicil which angels added through Moses the intermediary (vs. 19). That was a complete break with the synagogue. Instructed by the mind of Christ, Paul came to see that not all the things prohibited by the law were sinful, and that not all it commanded was right. The worst of its curses had fallen upon Jesus, the best of men. When Paul looked at the crucified Christ he saw a Cross, and not a curse, in the heart of God. He continued to recognize that sin invariably incurred its own inherent wrath (Rom. 1–2; cf. on Rom. 1:18), but God was in Christ reconciling all things to himself. The curse lay in thinking about God according to the law court and the countinghouse, instead of according to Christ.

11. Since the ground of salvation is grace as over against code or ledger, the axiom of Paul's gospel is: **through faith that is faithful** (cf. Rom. 1:17).

---

life. Jesus, however, offers power to achieve. He is not alone the ideal through which men live; he is not alone the end of the way: he is the way to the end.

11. ***Faith as Capacity.***—(See Expos. on 1:17-23.) Faith is "the gift of God" (Eph. 2:8). In the strictest sense Paul did not teach justification by faith, but by grace. Even faith to him was the gift of God (see Expos. on vs. 2). Without proper safeguards, definitions easily land one in a merry-go-round quandary, an almost hopeless circle, including apparently an arbitrary "choice," "election," "call," or "predestination" on God's part. If faith is the gift of God, why does God not give faith to every man? Why should he not call every life through the gospel?

The δέ is continuative, "and" rather than **but** (KJV) or **now** (RSV). Since Paul is contrasting law as part of this present wicked age with faith as the axiom of life "in" the realm of Spirit (see Intro., p. 434), "in law" is better than **by the law.** The KJV is consistent in rendering δικαιοῦται and δίκαιος by **is justified** and **the just;** the RSV obscures the root relation between the two Greek words by translating the first by the Latin **is justified,** the second by the English **is righteous.** "In God's sight" expresses παρὰ τῷ θεῷ more fully than **before God.**

Here, as in Rom. 1:17, the question is whether to construe ἐκ πίστεως, "on the basis of faith," with ὁ δίκαιος, "he who is righteous," or with ζήσεται, "will live." The RSV prefers the former interpretation and translates: **he who through faith is righteous shall live;** but in the margin it gives the ASV rendering as an alternative: **The righteous shall live by faith** (cf. the KJV). The ASV is better, because Paul's gospel includes more than this metaphor of a "justification" which assures the sinner who has faith that on the day of Judgment he will be acquitted and admitted to heaven. In this quotation from scripture Paul is indeed contrasting the future death of those who are under the law and its curse with the eternal salvation of those who live in faith, which is the life element of the Christian. But the RSV so concentrates the reader's attention on this forensic element of future acquittal and acceptance with God, regardless of actual righteousness, that he is liable to lose sight of Paul's constant insistence that the Christian's faith-life begins here and now and is inseparable from producing the fruit of the Spirit. Since Paul's life in Christ began at the very moment when he became a Christian, neither "will live," a simple future, nor **shall live,** which is directive, quite expresses his meaning. The word πίστις here means both "faith" and "faithfulness," and Paul, like Habakkuk, is speaking of a "faithful faith," i.e., faith which produces right living and holds fast to God. Consequently **the just shall live by faith** (KJV) is not an adequate translation either of Paul or of Hab. 2:4. Habakkuk's determination to be faithful rested on God's faithfulness. In its context באמונתו, "by his faithfulness," most naturally refers to the righteous man's faithfulness, but the LXX referred the pronoun to God and translated: "But the righteous man will live by my faithfulness." Although Paul has neither the "his" of the Hebrew nor the "my" of the LXX, he is at one with Habakkuk in taking for granted that man's faith must be faithful and must rest on God's faithfulness.

Habakkuk's problem arose from the fact that the "terrible and dreadful" Chaldeans, who were said by his fellow prophets to be God's broom to purge the Israelites, were

---

Why should he call one and not another? There is a further query: If faith itself is a gift of God, then until he gives it is there nothing a man can do but wait? There are sincere people who would say: "Sit down, O men of God; there is nothing you can do."

A word must be found that gathers up the essential truth of the belief that faith is the gift of God and yet is consonant with the nature of God and the personality of man. What idea of human life is big enough to justify Christ's death on the cross? The reply is the Christian idea of man. Man is no puppet; he is surely not a worm, for a worm is not made in the image of God. Man is not a tool, a machine, a serial number, an animal, or an adjective. Man was made to be a child of God on a higher level than physical birth—a son on the spiritual, moral, and intellectual level of free choice. No worm can claim that position. One must, however, guard against the other extreme. If man can make any contribution to his salvation, that contribution is the weaker or smaller part of the whole; but in clear logic the whole would depend in this sense on what man does, since no chain is stronger than its weakest link. Moreover, man is not possessed of an inward bed of coals which awaits the breath of God to start the flame. He is more empty handed and dependent than that. What word might present or contain a point of view which would correctly represent God in the salvation of man and at the same time declare Christ's own teaching about the sacredness of human choice?

The word proposed here is "capacity." Capacity for faith is part of the providence of God; it is his provision, and as such his gift. But capacity is undeveloped and unfulfilled. Among man's endowments is the possibility of using or not using this capacity; of desiring or not desiring its development. Capacity is the gift of God; its use is the privilege and responsibility of

12 And the law is not of faith: but, The man that doeth them shall live in them.

12 but the law does not rest on faith, for "He who does them shall live by them."

filthier than the house which they were supposed to clean! Perplexed but not dismayed, he climbed into his watchtower and waited. When the answer came it was this: "No matter what happens, let the righteous man hold fast to his covenant with God. Vindication will come in God's good time; meanwhile the good man will live by his faithfulness." But the prophet was not thinking of this vindication in terms of life after death; his concern was with right living in this present world. Paul laid hold of the life which is God's grace-gift in the world to come, and made it the inspiration for the present righteousness which was the first installment and guarantee of an eternal inheritance.

The translator's difficulty with this passage arises from the lack of a single English verb to express both "do right" and "be right with God"; of a noun that means both "righteousness" and "acceptance with God as righteous"; and of an adjective to describe the man who is both "righteous" and "accepted as righteous," or to use the Latin, both "just" and "justified." The resulting obscurities and inconsistencies give aid and comfort to human nature—Paul would say "the flesh"—in its habit of divorcing faith from faithfulness and justification from righteousness. The interpreter has to guard against basing "justification by faith" upon a fictive or imputed righteousness rather than presenting it as an actuality inseparable from the Christian's present life in Christ. When Paul says that the righteous man who is both just and justified is to live on the basis of faith, he is describing a way of life that is present as well as future. His faith is the determinant of action which makes righteousness actual even now.

12. Here Paul turns the law itself (Lev. 18:5) against the legalists. His argument is that since no man can obey the commandments well enough to qualify for eternal life, salvation by law is impossible. The law is not **of faith,** but belongs to the market, where men drive bargains, and to the courts, where they bring suit against one another.

---

man. At this point man is responsible. In this sense faith is man's act. Failure to use faith, even though that faith is as small as a mustard seed, may be the unpardonable sin. Lack of faith is the only sin God cannot forgive.

Such a view is in harmony with the Christian concept of man. If "grace" reveals the nature of God, the capacity for "faith" describes a son of God. The essence of personality is in the will. It is the privilege of choice that makes a man a man, and in its highest practice makes him a son of God above the level of physical creation. In the will, not in the flesh, is the seat of good and evil. What goes on in the will of man determines whether he has discovered the secret of the good life. As soon as a man's will is turned to Christ, with even his faintest move, murmur, or gesture, God's grace comes immediately to assist—with light and leading—the growth of his character around his faith in Christ. These steps are expressed in the prayer, "Lord, I believe; help thou mine unbelief" (Mark 9:24).

Many men who want to believe insist that they cannot achieve any "faith in beliefs that seem valid." Such honest seekers, aware that life is incomplete without faith, begin at the wrong end of the process. They work with subheads instead of with Roman numerals. Faith does not begin with "what," but with "who" and "whom." A study of the "what," or the content of faith, helps to put in the details and subheads after the "who" and "whom" have been determined. Faith for Paul was infinitely more than intellectual definition. It was a personal relationship: "I know whom I have believed" (II Tim. 1:12). It is a relationship before it is an intellectual definition. A man wants to account for the faith that is in him, but he cannot give a reason for what he does not possess. Faith as possession obviously precedes faith as definition. Paul may have learned the "what" during his sojourn in the Arabian desert; the "whom" he had already determined on the Damascus road. What a man can never define about Christ is what matters most. Faith in the sense of intellectual grasp accepts information about God and remains the challenge of Christian education; the initial experience of faith, however, allows God himself to enter.

Since faith is the gift of God, and since capacity for it is provided by God, faith is natural to man. It is part of his equipment to do battle in life. It is not alone the possession of queer eccentrics and spiritual experts; it is a natural act of every normal mind. Man is incurably a religious creature, but he is immature

13 Christ hath redeemed us from the curse of the law, being made a curse for us: for it is written, Cursed *is* every one that hangeth on a tree:

13 Christ redeemed us from the curse of the law, having become a curse for us — for it is written, "Cursed be every one who hangs

The men of law bargain with the Lord of the vineyard and work to earn their salvation; the men of faith accept their life as God's free gift and spend it for him in his kingdom. Since Paul has in his mind the realm of law "in" which he lived before God's grace brought him to live "in Christ," **live in them** (KJV) is better than **live by them** (RSV); see Intro., p. 434. The law coupled the promise with the command. It was a good law and a good promise, but of no avail against the evil impulse which no man unaided could conquer.

Paul's pessimism concerning law as a way of salvation was shared by the apocryphal book known as II Esdras. Saddened by the fewness of the saved, "Ezra" complained: "Our fathers received the law of life, but they did not keep it" (II Esdras 14:30). The grain of evil seed inherited from Adam multiplied and choked out the good seed of the law which God sowed in the hearts of his people at Mount Sinai (II Esdras 9:29-31). In the mass of mankind God's crop had failed. Yet the author of this work, unlike Paul, clung to the belief that life through law was possible, if only for the faithful few. The majority of Jewish teachers were optimistic. The author of the Wisdom of Solomon—a book in Paul's library of scripture—declared that obedience to the commandments was assurance of immortality (Wisd. Sol. 6:18). He equated the law with wisdom and found in it an inexhaustible treasure and means of friendship with God. He called it "the law of life and understanding," which made Israel different from all other nations. So Paul's opponents could reply that by their obedience they would prove that they too had faith in the God who had given his law to be the source of all well-being and life.

13. The pronoun **us** refers not only to Paul and his fellow Jews, who needed to be freed from slavery to the curse of the law of Moses, but also to the Gentiles of vs. 14, who

until he possesses a faith that is strong enough to master his mind and to match his total grasp of life. Faith is an everyday matter with many men of science, who begin with chosen hypotheses. Every hypothesis is a practice of faith; all science rests upon faith. In the moral and spiritual world the same process exists. The man of Christian faith takes Christ as his hypothesis, his postulate, his most glorious thesis, and affirms, "Without him, not one step; with him, anywhere." Without Christ a man is using only part of his God-given faculties. It may well be that many men of science are profound Christians, in part at least, because they are accustomed to the practice of faith in their daily work and profession. They make use of the same capacity in the moral and spiritual realm. Certainly God cannot be conceived as requiring of man what he cannot do. The central act of the Christian life is faith. And the eternal God has equipped men with the capacity for it. Faith as capacity is the gift of God.

13. ***The Principle of Redemption.***—(See Deut. 21:23.) It is a fact of profound significance that for man's highest good Jesus suffered the most terrible, the most despised, the most ignominious death. He took the cross, the ugliest way the world had of putting people to death, and made it the only way there is in that world to bring people out of death into life.

As one would expect, Paul fully grasped this principle of redemption. Perhaps his own thorn in the flesh (II Cor. 12:7), which the Lord three times over declined to remove, was the experience that enabled him to apprehend it. There are weaknesses and sicknesses which cannot be done away; but the redeeming Christ assures each sufferer who takes him seriously that he will never have to bear his pain alone. Through this Redeemer men learn that their disappointments may clear the calendar for God's appointments. Because he has the power to redeem, Christ promises that quality of life which neither poverty, disease, nor death can destroy. Through him one may experience the blessedness of being handicapped. Shortcomings and inadequacies provide openings through which the light of Christ and his redeeming grace may shine.

Paul wrote in his letter to the Ephesians, "Redeeming the time, because the days are evil" (Eph. 5:16). He was saying to them,

did not have that law but stood in equal need of the blessing of Abraham. They too were legalists in religion, and Paul regarded legalism as a curse wherever he found it.

The verb ἐξηγόρασεν means "bought out from," **redeemed** (RSV), "delivered" at the expense of one's self. The price of man's freedom was high. **Having become a curse** (RSV) is more accurate than **being made a curse** (KJV), but better still is "by becoming a curse." Paul does not imply that Christ turned himself into a curse, or that God treated him as a reprobate. It was the law's curse, not God's; observe that Paul omits ὑπὸ θεοῦ, "by God," from his quotation of Deut. 21:23 (LXX). To set men free Christ had to associate himself with all who had incurred the law's curse by disobedience. **For us** is not "in our stead," or "in our place" but "on our behalf," "for our sakes." The best commentary is II Cor. 5:14-21.

In Paul's world a curse was believed to be a living entity which generated a poisonous atmosphere all around its victim. Among the most horrible curses was that which rested upon a criminal whose body, after execution by some other mode of capital punishment, was hung on a tree for special retribution. (The Jews did not execute by hanging.) The body was not allowed to remain over night upon the tree, lest it defile the land which God had given to Israel. According to the law, the death of Jesus upon a cross delivered him into the sphere and power of God's special curse.

There had been a time when Paul believed this. Here was a messianic pretender whom Pilate executed for treason, and who was being worshiped by his blasphemous followers as the Son of God! But the more he saw of the Christian way of life the clearer it became that Jesus was not the worst, but the best of men. The forgiveness and kindness with which the friends of Jesus treated Paul became a proof to him that this crucified "criminal" was indeed the Son of God and the Christ.

"Turn evil days to good, positive, constructive account." When the world does its worst, the followers of Christ are to do their best. When the world turns out lights, Christ's disciples are to turn them on. He can make a man's failures steppingstones. He can enable anybody to take a second best, a second choice or no choice, and make a life out of it. When we have seen the things for which we gave our lives broken and crushed to earth, Christ makes it possible to stoop and build them up again, even with worn-out tools. As the world's Redeemer he can take a dream that has failed, a plan that has gone wrong, a sin that has haunted the days, and by his forgiving, healing, restoring grace shape them into a new life. In the entire Christian catalogue that fact is one of the most difficult lessons to learn and one of the most profound experiences to interpret. George Matheson grasped it, and with fading eyesight wrote:

> I trace the rainbow through the rain,
> . . . .
> I lay in dust life's glory dead,
> And from the ground there blossoms red
> Life that shall endless be.[2]

Leslie D. Weatherhead, in true Pauline tradition, was looking steadily at this principle of redemption, and most of all at the Redeemer and his cross, when he wrote:

> So the Cross, planned by hearts that hated, remains the strongest means of ending hate the world has ever seen; made by evil, it delivers from evil, made in fear, it saves from fear. The Cross was made by man, and, like a bandit's dagger, it was made to kill; but in God's hands it is as a sharp surgical knife, which, more than any other instrument, has been used to cut out hate and pride and selfishness from the heart of humanity.
>
> Surely, that *is* God's way again and again. The Kingdom of God has repeatedly been furthered by means which belong to the kingdom of evil. God doesn't move behind the clouds only: He uses the clouds too. Only so is He the Vindicator.[3]

13. ***The Cross as Redemption.***—There are at least five aspects of the Cross in Paul's Galatian letter: (*a*) The Cross as discipline (6:17); (*b*) the Cross as example (2:20; 6:17); (*c*) the Cross as redemption (3:13); (*d*) the Cross as substitution (2:20*c*); (*e*) the Cross as reconciliation (4:4-7).

Why was the Cross necessary? Why could a God of love not pardon every penitent heart directly? Why was the Cross dragged in to complicate an otherwise rather simple procedure?

[2] "O Love that wilt not let me go."

[3] *Thinking Aloud in War-Time* (London: Hodder & Stoughton; New York: The Abingdon Press, 1940), p. 105. Used by permission.

What, then, was the meaning of the death of Jesus upon the Cross? Paul illustrated it by the daily life of the Christians, many of whom were slaves under the lash of their fellow men. Death was the price which Christ had to pay to set men free from slavery to flesh, sin, law, wrath, and death, and make them citizens of God's kingdom of love and righteousness, grace and life in the Spirit. God did not curse Christ in our stead; nor was the deliverance of men from the curse of the law an irrational transaction in which Christ paid a price to God, to the law, or to Satan, forgiven sinners being merely spectators of the Cross and passive recipients of God's grace. The death of an innocent man was required to demonstrate that the law as a way of salvation was impotent and morally self-contradictory. There was indeed a curse, but the curse was inherent in each act of wrongdoing and operated in accordance with the principle of the identical harvest (6:7), rather than as a penalty imposed by a court for the violation of law.

But there was another and higher principle ingrained in human existence. This was the "law" of creative, vicarious suffering for the good of others. The death of Jesus made the problem of the innocent suffering of the righteous, which had baffled Habakkuk and Job, altogether insoluble by means of the theory of life on which the law was based. The law promised prosperity and happiness, numerous descendants, a peaceful death, a good name, and honor throughout posterity to all who obeyed it. By contrast its curse would eat away the very name of the wicked. But in the agony of history this comfortable theory was always breaking down. The good man was forever sharing the punishment of the wicked. Under stress of this painful contradiction, the Hebrew prophets developed a higher view. They reflected on how Abraham and Moses had interceded and suffered for the sake of others, and they called upon their countrymen to share the sufferings of the servant whom God had destined to bear the sins of many for their good. His task was to set justice in the earth and to cover the earth with the knowledge of God as the waters cover the sea. That required the expenditure of his life in creative suffering.

This conception of creative suffering was destined to revolutionize man's thinking about God's attitude toward sinners. From time immemorial prophets and reformers felt that it was impossible to establish God's kingdom without first purging the wicked from the earth. When all other methods failed, their last resort was to kill off the wicked.

By what logic or right must theories of the Cross come into the picture at all? The Cross is not wiped off the slate that easily. In truth, such thinking—or lack of it—is quite irrational. Whether a man desires to deal with the Cross or attempts to rule it out is not the issue at all. Students may differ in regard to its meaning, but they cannot deny it as historical fact. It is even a fact of political history: He "suffered under Pontius Pilate." The Cross is dated on man's calendar, even though conceptions of the Cross may range from the highest to the lowest. Men may call it "an irrelevant incident"; but "incident" it was, and it has to be accounted for, whether some people like it or not.

The Cross was Christ's free choice. "The good shepherd giveth his life for the sheep" (John 10:11). Only the One who was fully free could set other men free. The Cross did not overtake Jesus; he overtook the Cross. "Therefore doth my Father love me, because I lay down my life, that I might take it again. No man taketh it from me, but I lay it down of myself" (John 10:17-18). "I lay down my life for the sheep" (John 10:15).

What Christ did on the Cross is reflected in a word that is familiar to Paul's readers. That word is "redemption," and it changed Paul's total existence. The life he had been living under the ancient law of Israel showed him the law's inability to help him keep its requirements. The more he knew of those requirements the less he felt he could keep them. The sense of its impotence disillusioned the conscientious man that he was. The law at best only sharpened his awareness of his own sins and inadequacies. This was its curse. It could not and did not lift him out. It was powerless to give him power. It drove him into deeper despair. In his darkest days he must have had a haunting sense that new light was about to break through from somewhere, but from where? He must have felt that help was coming somehow, but how? He must have sensed a friendship making to his rescue, but when? Because the law affected his total existence, his experience of redemption

14 That the blessing of Abraham might come on the Gentiles through Jesus Christ; that we might receive the promise of the Spirit through faith.

on a tree" — 14 that in Christ Jesus the blessing of Abraham might come upon the Gentiles, that we might receive the promise of the Spirit through faith.

They believed that the first business of the Messiah was to break the teeth of sinners. But Jesus, when he came preaching, welcomed home and forgave God's prodigal sons. Stephen, bearing witness for Jesus, prayed for the mob that stoned him; and Barnabas, with other disciples, forgave Paul and received him with all the kindness of their Master, who set him free from the curse of the law and made a new man of him.

14. The consequence was that Paul had to delegalize and internationalize his conception of God's treatment of sinners. **The blessing of Abraham** is the blessing which Abraham possessed and enjoyed during his lifetime, together with the ever-increasing blessing promised to his descendants, and, through them, to all mankind (Gen. 12:3; 18:18; 28:4). Just as the law's curse had fallen upon all men, so Christ's inheritance was available to all. The principle of social solidarity worked both ways. **The promise of the Spirit** means "the promised Spirit" (Acts 1:4; 2:33, 39). The pronoun **we** includes all, both Jews and Gentiles. One purpose of Christ's suffering had been to remove the hindrances set up by legalism and nationalism, so that "in the last days" (Acts 2:17; Joel 2:28-32) all men might receive through faith the Spirit, which had been promised from the beginning.

---

dealt also with the whole of his life, every jot and tittle of it. Redemption releases a man from all that enslaves or imprisons him.

Christ gave his life as a "ransom" to make redemption possible. Let others continue the old debate, "To whom was the ransom paid?" The personal, practical question reads, "Are we free men because of what Jesus did?" Since he died to set men free, for those who continue a course of life and habits that enslave them, he has died in vain. From this viewpoint the Cross implements the petition of the Lord's Prayer, "Deliver us from evil." Millions of the most intelligent people, as well as unlettered peasants, have found in the cross of Christ that which releases and delivers them from the lower levels of life, from passions that consume the higher impulses, from the power of evil, from excessive selfishness, from sinfulness, from all that keeps a man from becoming what God put him on earth to be.

Men who know this release have quite naturally tried to explain whence their newly found liberty comes. Some have mumbled their secret in words like these, "Whereas I was blind, now I see" (John 9:25). The old gospel hymn sings the secret for many:

> At the cross, at the cross, where I first saw the light,
> And the burden of my heart rolled away.[4]

In *Pilgrim's Progress,* Christian, after leaving the Interpreter's House, came to a place where stood a cross, and the burden which he carried on his shoulder was loosed and fell back into the pit. He saw it no more. Millions besides Christian have also found that release.

A redeemed man confessed to his pastor: "I do not know what happened on the Cross, but I know what happened to me because of it; because Christ came down to my level, I have the power to rise toward his." The effort to try to tell how the Cross sets men free is soon "lost in wonder, love, and praise." The better way is not in definitions written on paper but in definitions written with a man's blood in daily living. Others may see what Gipsy Smith saw in one who had just led a congregation in prayer: "That man knows the way to Calvary." Or as the man himself confessed, "Even the chickens on my farm know I am a different man."

But the redemption of Christ is more than release from an evil past and haunting remorse. It means release from a baser self for the nobler self, from lower impulses for higher impulses, from lesser living for larger living. Redemption includes *for what* a man is released; it also includes the energy and power to attain. It turns confused, bewildered, defeated, disillusioned, sinful men into persons of integrity, usefulness, and courage. "He died to make us good." [5] The only really good man is the pardoned man. Such a good man deserves to be trusted. To make him that kind of man is part of the redemption of Christ; he brings to the redeemed a new level

[4] R. E. Hudson.

[5] Cecil Frances Alexander, "There is a green hill far away."

15 Brethren, I speak after the manner of men; Though *it be* but a man's covenant, yet *if it be* confirmed, no man disannulleth, or addeth thereto.

15 To give a human example, brethren: no one annuls even a man's will,[g] or adds

[g] Or *covenant* (as in verse 17).

3. THE PRESUMPTUOUS CODICIL (3:15-18)

15. Meeting the Judaizers on their own ground, Paul chooses an illustration from the law of wills. **Brethren** replaces the "unreasonable Galatians" of vs. 1, as Paul appeals over the heads of the troublemakers. The term **confirmed** (KJV), **ratified** (RSV), is common in Greek legal documents, as are Greek terms used here for **annuls** and **adds to.** Paul does not mean that no human will is ever tampered with, but that such treatment is the exception, and that those responsible are considered criminals.

The word διαθήκην, **covenant** (KJV; RSV mg.), **will** (RSV), is another of Paul's terms which cannot be translated by a single English word. It means both "testament" and "covenant," both "will" and "agreement." The context in vss. 18 and 29 and 4:1-6 shows that Paul keeps both ideas in mind, shifting from one to the other as his argument demands. He equates God's διαθήκη with God's promise, ἐπαγγελία, and likens it to a human will which disposes of a man's property after his death. He regards the law of Moses as a "codicil," attached by the angels to God's will (vs. 19). Of course, God the testator does not die; but that is just Paul's point. If the last will and testament of a mortal man must not be altered or annulled, what is to be said about the presumption of the legalists in introducing law as a way of salvation?

Paul and his readers knew quite well that a human testator had the right at any time to revoke or change his will. To be legal a Jewish will had to conform with the Mosaic law of inheritance (Num. 27:8-11); but God could do as he liked. In Christ he had chosen to include the Gentiles as equal heirs through faith. His original will had read "by faith," but the legalists dared to change it to "by works." Thus they were treating God as if he were an arbitrary human monarch. Herod the Great had made more than one will, so that his son Antipas had to decide which was valid (Josephus *Antiquities* XVII. 9. 4; *Jewish War* II. 2. 3). They entered their faith in the ledgers of their good works and brought their unauthorized codicil to court for probate. So it seemed to Paul. He was sure that the Spirit of Christ would reject it and keep God's original will inviolate.

---

of moral competence. "If any man be in Christ, he is a new creature" (II Cor. 5:17). Paul links such redemption with the Cross.

15-18. ***The Covenant and Jeremiah.***—Paul now deals with one of the most magnificent words and assurances in all religious history. Honorable men make covenants. Men in the great tradition from which and to which Paul wrote knew what such covenants meant. The very integrity of both parties is at stake in such covenants (vs. 15). Here the honor of God is at stake. The material covered in vss. 15-29 matters supremely in Hebrew-Christian history. Covenant, law, and faith had to be set forth intelligibly.

The first **covenant** was made on the basis of faith and fellowship between God and Abraham, and was never recalled. Can God deny himself and make **of none effect** his own covenant (vs. 17)? **The law, which was four hundred and thirty years after,** was introduced for an intermediary purpose, and in no sense did it **disannul** God's original covenant with Abraham. The thread which made the covenant eternal was God's promise that in the **seed** of Abraham would his covenant be fulfilled (vs. 16). That seed was Jesus Christ.

Jeremiah was the man in the long story of faith, covenant, and law who was manifestly used by God to get the nation ready for this new covenant. Jeremiah was one of those rare men whom the Eternal seems to use to transmit original and creative ideas. He has been called the one clear-eyed man of his generation. He was used by God to prophesy the new covenant. Up to Jeremiah's time God largely dealt with men on the basis of nation, race, or group. The new covenant would make it possible, said Jeremiah, for God to deal directly with individual men without any intermediary person or nation or race. "Behold, the days come, saith the LORD, that I will make a new covenant with the house of Israel, and with the house of Judah: not according to the covenant that I made with their

16 Now to Abraham and his seed were the promises made. He saith not, And to seeds, as of many; but as of one, And to thy seed, which is Christ.

17 And this I say, *that* the covenant, that was confirmed before of God in Christ, the law, which was four hundred and thirty years after, cannot disannul, that it should make the promise of none effect.

to it, once it has been ratified. **16** Now the
promises were made to Abraham and to his
offspring. It does not say, "And to off-
springs," referring to many; but, referring
to one, "And to your offspring," which is
Christ. **17** This is what I mean: the law,
which came four hundred and thirty years
afterward, does not annul a covenant previously ratified by God, so as to make the

---

16. Σπέρμα means **seed** (KJV) and is used in the sense of **offspring** (RSV), "descendant," "posterity." Paul is quoting from Gen. 22:17-18 (LXX), "Your posterity (σπέρμα) will inherit the cities of your enemies, and in your posterity (σπέρματι) all the Gentiles will be blessed" (cf. Gen. 12:2-7; 13:14-17; 15:1, 5, 18; 24:7). The apostle observes that σπέρμα is singular and argues that this makes it a promise to Christ and not to Abraham's physical descendants (plural). The subject of λέγει ("says") may be taken either as **it,** i.e., the Scripture (so RSV), or as **he** (KJV), which makes God the speaker.

This kind of "proof" from scripture by reading "spiritual" meanings into details of grammar and discovering ideas that were not within the purview of its writers was being employed more and more. Paul has relatively little of it, and when he does resort to it, his proposition has already been demonstrated on the solid ground of his own experience with Christ. His application of this method of proof in the present passage has caused him to disregard for the moment the collective meaning of σπέρμα, upon which his whole position depends, and which he recognizes elsewhere in his letters (Rom. 4:16-18; 9:6-8; I Cor. 12:12-14). He included all men of faith in all ages as joint heirs with Christ.

17. Besides the sole heirship of Christ, Paul had another reason for rejecting the law as a basis for salvation: it was 430 years later than the covenant.

Of God in Christ (KJV) translates a text which inserted εἰς Χριστόν, "in Christ," under the influence of ὅς ἐστιν Χριστός, "which is Christ," in vs. 16. Since in vs. 18 Paul is still speaking of the legacy of promise, it is better to translate διαθήκην consistently as "will" throughout vss. 15 and 17. **Does not annul** (RSV) must be taken in the sense of **cannot** (KJV). God's "will" to save men by grace was ratified before the codicil of the angels "came into existence." Consequently it could not make the original promise "ineffective" or "inoperative."

Acts 7:6, based on Gen. 15:13, reckons the period of the Israelites in Egypt as 400 years; Paul, following Exod. 12:40, finds it to be 430, beginning with the promise to Abraham. During all that time the promise of grace, and not the law of Moses, had been operative. In vs. 19 Paul explains why God permitted the angels to give the law through Moses, but throughout his letters he insists that God never intended it either to supplant or to add to faith as the sole way of salvation. If he had, he would not have waited 430 years before giving notice of his intention to change his will.

---

fathers. . . . But this shall be the covenant that I will make. . . . I will put my law in their inward parts, and write it in their hearts; and will be their God, and they shall be my people" (Jer. 31:31-33). "Come, and let us join ourselves to the LORD in a perpetual covenant that shall not be forgotten" (Jer. 50:5).

Jeremiah demonstrated his confidence in his country's future under God by accepting the proposition of his cousin, one Hanamel, who wanted him to purchase part of the old family farm (Jer. 32:9, 15), in truth only another no man's land, since Nebuchadrezzar's army was besieging Jerusalem and was fighting over it. Jeremiah put his small savings into the purchase. His only demand was that the transaction be handled in the most exact legal fashion. The proper authorities and witnesses required by law were provided. The deed to the land was put in an earthen pot and buried at a spot they would remember. Jeremiah believed in the legal processes of men because he believed in

18 For if the inheritance *be* of the law, *it is* no more of promise: but God gave *it* to Abraham by promise.

19 Wherefore then *serveth* the law? It was added because of transgressions, till the seed should come to whom the promise was made; *and it was* ordained by angels in the hand of a mediator.

promise void. 18 For if the inheritance is by the law, it is no longer by promise; but God gave it to Abraham by a promise.

19 Why then the law? It was added because of transgressions, till the offspring should come to whom the promise had been made; and it was ordained by angels

---

18. A third reason for refusing to accept the codicil lay in Paul's bitter experience that grace is irreconcilable with law. No verbs are expressed in the first clause, and the translator must supply some word such as "depends" or "rests" to clarify the phrases "from law" and "from promise," which stand in antithesis and are without the article. These phrases express more than the means **by** which the inheritance is conveyed to the legatees, and ἡ κληρονομία lays the emphasis on the right to inherit. "Then . . . not," in its inferential sense, is better for οὐκέτι than **no more** (KJV) or **no longer** (RSV). Κεχάρισται ὁ θεός is, lit., "God has grace-gifted it"; no single English word carries all the kindness, graciousness, favor, and pleasure which this Greek verb suggested. Both KJV and RSV have supplied the definite article before **law.**

God's legacy to Abraham was both material and spiritual, both for this world and for the world to come. It consisted of Palestine as the land of promise and of faith; of an ever-increasing dominion; of the privilege and task of being a perpetual blessing to all mankind (Gen. 13:14-17; 15:4-7; 17:1-8; II Chr. 6:27). The Christians denationalized it, called it the kingdom of God, and claimed it for Christ and themselves as fellow heirs with Christ (vs. 24; 5:2; Acts 20:32; Rom. 4:13-14; I Cor. 6:9-11; 15:50). The Spirit was the first installment of this inheritance, and the guarantor of the rest of it. But if the law of Moses was contrary to God's will and testament, why was it ever given? To this question Paul now addresses himself.

C. The Interim Function of Law (3:19-25)

19-20. The first answer is that the law was an expedient to cope with sin. The shorthand style of these verses requires us to fill in Paul's meaning from Rom. 4:15; 5:13, 20; 7:8, 10, 12-13; 11:32; II Cor. 3:4-18. The Galatians, who had heard his sermons, could supply the unexpressed ideas. The obscurity of the passage has produced numerous textual changes. One substitutes παραδόσεων, "traditions," for παραβάσεων, "transgressions." Another reads πράξεων, "works," and a few have ἐτέθη for προσετέθη to guard against any inference that the law was merely an addition.

Neither **because of** nor "for the sake of" can quite convey the meaning of the preposition in this passage. Paul's choice of "transgressions," instead of "sins," was determined by his belief that although sin was in the world ever since Adam's fall, it was not counted as transgression until Moses gave Israel the law. The function of this law was to turn men's sins into transgressions. It actually created transgressions by stirring man's latent sinfulness into open rebellion. This made sin "sinful beyond measure" (Rom. 7:13), and worked out wrath to the uttermost, consigning all men to

---

the moral purposes and spiritual promises of God. The best contracts of men rest for their security on the moral covenants of God. This is but one illustration of the moral theory of history.

19-21. ***The Covenant Seen by Contrast.***—The covenant was permanent; the law was temporary and provisional **till the seed should come.** The law was something **added;** it was not in God's original plan. It was limited in purpose **because of transgressions.** No matter how profoundly significant transgressions may be, the handling of them is only a part, not the whole, of Christian life. The law was foreign to the nature of God and so could not be transacted directly between him and his people. It was "mediated"

20 Now a mediator is not *a mediator* of one, but God is one.

through an intermediary. **20** Now an intermediary implies more than one; but God is one.

---

disobedience and death. Thus viewed, the purpose of the angels' expedient was not to prevent sin—a thing which the weakness of human nature made law powerless to do—but to convince men that they were so bad that nothing could save them except God's mercy through Christ. If Christ had come in the days of Moses, men would not have been ready to recognize their hopeless state. Hence the law had to be given time enough to prove its own futility as a way of salvation (4:4). Meanwhile, as the perfect tense ἐπήγγελται indicates, the promise continued in force and was never replaced by the law. One might paraphrase vs. 19*b*: "It was brought in to create transgressions until the descendant should come to whom the promise, which continued in force, had been made."

This was a clean break from the Jewish conception which held that the law was the gift of God's lovingkindness to overcome the evil impulse and prevent sin by guidance and discipline in good works. The orthodox maintained that Abraham's faith was one of these law-works. The belief that angels were present at the giving of the law was widespread (Deut. 33:2 [LXX]; Jubilees 1:27; 2:1; Acts 7:38, 53; Heb. 2:2; Josephus *Antiquities* XV. 5. 3). The presence of the angels, said the rabbis, was the measure of the law's great glory. Paul said it was a fading glory from the very beginning (II Cor. 3:13). Moreover, it was twice removed from God's own immediate action, because it was **ordained,** or "enacted," "through the agency of" angels, and even they did not communicate directly with the people, but gave the law "in the hand of a representative," i.e., Moses. **Mediator** (KJV) and **intermediary** (RSV) suggest that it was a matter of negotiation between the angels and the Israelites; hence it is better to translate μεσίτης as "representative," "agent," or "spokesman." In Greek business documents the word meant "middleman."

Here we get to the heart of Paul's religion. He wanted to call God "Father," and the Spirit of Christ taught him to do so. God's word was now in his heart, and not in the heights of heaven, whence a mediator would be required to bring it down (Rom. 10:5-10). Since God had appeared in person to Abraham, Paul believed that his way from the beginning was to communicate himself directly by his Spirit to the men of faith. But at Sinai the awe of the people kept them trembling at the foot of the mountain while Moses served as their go-between (Exod. 20:18-21). The lightning and thunder of the law got between man and his God, leaving the one in hopeless terror in the valley of sin, the other in unapproachable transcendence on the summit of his holiness. Paul reasoned that since the God who revealed himself in Christ was the one and only God, and not a plurality of gods (Rom. 11:36), he could speak directly to every human individual and had no need of a representative, whether angels, or Moses, or anyone else. The angels, being more than one, had to employ a spokesman, because they could not all speak at once. Paul would have recognized that God, although "one," could employ an agent if he chose, just as a single human person could do in arranging a business agreement. But his point is that God's original purpose was to give men his Spirit directly and without an intermediary.

(vs. 20) through angels and through Moses. The covenant, on the other hand, was God's permanent way of dealing with men: it was his direct personal approach; it was his total or comprehensive relationship with men.

God's covenant can be understood in the light of the law's essential weakness. "The law confronted man with a debt he could not pay, it threatened him with a penalty he could not bear, and set him a task he could not essay." [6] The law demanded perfection and offered little or no help in responding to such a demand. The law gave nothing and required everything. Men were not made to be forever the servants

[6] Harris E. Kirk, *The Religion of Power* (New York: George H. Doran Co., 1916), p. 229.

21 *Is* the law then against the promises of God? God forbid: for if there had been a law given which could have given life, verily righteousness should have been by the law.

22 But the Scripture hath concluded all under sin, that the promise by faith of Jesus Christ might be given to them that believe.

23 But before faith came, we were kept under the law, shut up unto the faith which should afterward be revealed.

21 Is the law then against the promises of God? Certainly not; for if a law had been given which could make alive, then righteousness would indeed be by the law.
22 But the scripture consigned all things to sin, that what was promised to faith in Jesus Christ might be given to those who believe.

23 Now before faith came, we were confined under the law, kept under restraint

---

21-22. Paul's objector is not yet satisfied. If Moses represented angels and not God, "Is the law then contrary to God's promises?" "By no means," says Paul, who adds, in effect, "For if a law had been given that could create life, certainly the righteousness required for acceptance with God would have been based on obedience to law. But the Scripture has locked up all things under sin, so that the promise may be given on the basis of faith in Jesus Christ to those who believe." **By the law** makes the noun definite, but the Greek is without the article. Paul's idea is that the righteousness which is acceptable to God does not grow out of, and is not based on, obedience to law. Neither **concluded** (KJV) nor **consigned** (RSV) preserves Paul's figure "locked up," which is carried further in vs. 23; but **all things** (RSV) is a correction of **all** (KJV) for τὰ πάντα, which is neuter. Apart from faith, all things human are locked up in the prison of sin; Rom. 3:9-18 indicates the O.T. passages on which Paul based this conclusion. The RSV clarifies **faith of Jesus Christ** (KJV) by taking Ἰησοῦ Χριστοῦ as an objective genitive, **in Jesus Christ;** but neither **promise by faith** (KJV) nor **promised to faith** (RSV) expresses exactly what Paul is saying. He did regard God's promise to Abraham as a promise to faith, but here he is thinking of the basis on which it rests. God's purpose was to keep all men dependent upon his grace. The law of Moses was a good law, and if any law could have bestowed life it would have done so. The law was not contrary to faith, but incommensurable with it; the two belonged to separate spheres, one of death, the other of life.

23-25. Since vs. 22 begins with ἀλλά, "but," and vs. 23 continues its description of the human situation before Christ, the δέ which begins vs. 23 should be translated "and" rather than **but** (KJV) or **now** (RSV). **Faith** is "the faith" which came with Christ,

---

and slaves of God, but his sons and friends. Obedience to God is less than faith and its concurrent fellowship with him.

22. ***Faith as Covenant.***—(See Expos. on 1:17-23.) Paul showed the Galatians that there were two covenants: one with Abraham and one in Christ. The common factor in both was faith, which brings the righteousness of God to men's lives. The covenant in Christ makes possible what Abraham's covenant could never accomplish. God's promise, "In thee shall all families of the earth be blessed" (Gen. 12:3), was never completely carried out till Jesus came. The covenant with Abraham was fulfilled in Christ. This new covenant made possible the entrance of all men, Jew and Gentile alike.

"It plainly lies with the Deity to dictate the terms and conditions on which He will admit man within His covenant." [7] And the condition is not difficult to find or to define. It is unreserved faith in Jesus Christ: believing that he is what he claims to be and that he can do what the N.T. claims for him. Faith thus changes a man's status. His new relationship is "Father-son."

When God comes into a man's life, he comes to stay. A man is taken into the family of God and into the Father's house.

> If a child disobeys his father and falls down the steps, he does not fall out of the house; because his body is bruised, he does not cease to be his father's

[7] B. F. Westcott, *St. Paul and Justification,* p. 38, quoted by Kirk, *op. cit.*, p. 224.

24 Wherefore the law was our schoolmaster *to bring us* unto Christ, that we might be justified by faith.
25 But after that faith is come, we are no longer under a schoolmaster.

until faith should be revealed. 24 So that
the law was our custodian until Christ came,
that we might be justified by faith. 25 But
now that faith has come, we are no longer

---

referred to in vs. 22. The omission of the definite article by KJV in the first clause, and by RSV in both clauses, makes Paul say that faith did not exist before Christ came; but his point was that Abraham was saved through faith and that faith had never been repealed by the intervening law of Moses. Paul's distinction between the Christian faith, which was faith fulfilled, and Abraham's faith, which was faith waiting, is made clear by translating τὴν πίστιν, here and in vs. 25, as "this faith." Ὑπὸ νόμον is without the article, "under law," rather than **under the law.**

Shut up unto the faith (KJV) is hopelessly obscure to the present-day reader. The meaning is "being kept in restraint while awaiting the faith that was to be revealed"; cf. **until** (RSV) for **unto** (KJV). Paul is contrasting two eras in the history of the human race, one before and one after the coming of Christ; and two phases in the life of the individual Christian, before and after the coming of the Spirit into his heart through faith.

The παιδαγωγός was not a **schoolmaster** (KJV), "tutor," or "teacher," but an "attendant," **custodian** (RSV), usually a slave who had charge of a child from six to sixteen to discipline him and keep him straight. One of his duties was to accompany the boy to school and see that he fell into no harm or mischief. Since εἰς Χριστόν is without a word to indicate time, it is better to take the phrase as purposive **to bring us unto Christ** (KJV) than as temporal **until Christ came** (RSV). Some verb such as "lead" or **bring** has to be supplied. For the meaning of **justified by faith** see Exeg. on 2:16.

Led and empowered by the Spirit of Christ, the Christian man of faith could put away childish things, including his guardian the law. But at what age could the spiritual minor be trusted with this higher freedom? Must the law not continue as the textbook for the religious education of children? Without the compulsion of sabbath customs and stated times for prayer, would the boy not be more likely to play truant with the street gangs and find it more attractive to watch the colorful procession of the pagan cults than to worship God in spirit and in truth? If all penalties were removed, would the honor of his parents and the life, property, and integrity of his neighbor's family be safe at his hands? Paul's letters give no direct answers to these questions concerning the status and education of the children of the church. But we may be sure that he believed children would be saved in the same way as their parents, by grace alone, through faith in Christ. His principle of the autonomy of the man of faith would require him to substitute inner spontaneity for the compulsion of law as early and as far as possible in the training of children. He believed that the children of Christians were "in Christ" with their parents,

---

child. And if it be objected, How about falling out of the window? my answer is that there are no windows in this house; it opens only on the eternal glories of that great upper world where God waits the home coming of His children.[8]

23-28. *The Business of the Law.*—Paul begins his analysis of the covenant with a tie-in to Abraham. God's promises to Abraham were foregleams of his future relationship with his people. The covenant anticipates a progression from law to standards to ideals to relationship: ascending steps in the dealings of God. Because his people were not ready for the final step, the law was introduced to prepare men for the coming of Christ. Paul says that faith in Christ takes up where the covenant with Abraham left off. Faith becomes the bridge between the two because it is their common factor.

The law served a threefold function until Christ came. It was a *spur* to the Galatians and others, goading them with their inability to keep the law completely and thus revealing their impotence and sinfulness. The ancient law could not bring its followers to the perfection it re-

[8] Kirk, *op. cit.*, p. 266.

26 For ye are all the children of God by faith in Christ Jesus.
27 For as many of you as have been baptized into Christ have put on Christ.

under a custodian; 26 for in Christ Jesus
you are all sons of God, through faith. 27 For
as many of you as were baptized into Christ

and this would mean bringing them up in the Spirit in such a way that they would never need to suffer the catastrophic shock of a conversion like his.

D. The New Status of the Men of Faith (3:26–4:10)

1. Freedom and Equality in Christ (3:26-29)

26. Christian freedom is grounded on right relation with God. **All,** i.e., both Jews and Gentiles. Since the context in vss. 27-28 speaks of being "in Christ," it is better to interpret vs. 26 as **in Christ Jesus . . . through faith** (RSV) than **by faith in Christ Jesus** (KJV). Christ is the Son of God, and all who are "in" him as members of his body, the church, are sons of God. Paul knew that God, by creation, was the Father of all men, but here he is speaking of sonship to God in the special sense of moral likeness and spiritual fellowship with him. To be a son of God meant to be a brother of the Christ who revealed all the elements of this sonship, particularly the humility which, unlike Satan's idea of freedom, refuses to grasp at the prerogatives of Deity and makes itself the slave of all mankind (Phil. 2:5-11). These Christian sons of God co-operate with their Father and with Christ their Elder Brother in the creative and redemptive process in which God works all things for good with those who love him.

27. To **put on Christ** was to clothe oneself with his character, to be like him. Col. 3:12-17 describes this new garment of the Christian. One way of being initiated into a mystery cult was to put on a robe symbolical of the deity, which was supposed to endow the initiate with the character, dignity, and power of his god.

Baptism, εἰς Χριστόν, **into Christ,** was more than baptism "with reference to Christ," or "calling upon the name of Christ," or "becoming a member of his body the church," although all of these ideas were included. Pronouncing the name of Christ was believed to charge the baptismal water with the celestial substance of his glorified resurrection body, which conveyed his presence. Ordinarily this body was invisible; but sometimes, as to Paul at Damascus, it was manifested in a blaze of light, and light was associated with

quired. Between Moses and Christ the law therefore served a diagnostic function: as a spur to sharpen men's sense of sin and need. It also served as *pedagogue*—not a teacher, but a truant officer—to bring pupils to the teacher and to exercise physical discipline over those who were guilty of misconduct. The law therefore could lead men to Christ and could thus prepare them for fellowship with God (the language of faith) which is a higher status than obedience to God (the language of the law).

Further, the law functioned as a method, suggestion, help, or *guide* toward an understanding of moral principles. The moral law, summed up in the Ten Commandments, is not primarily a set of rules for conduct; in it are eternal principles that are forever true and valid. They are like spokes in a wheel of which Christ is the hub. The law could not impart life, but it could lead men to Christ in whom is life abundant. In this way the law was not the enemy but the minister and servant of grace.

27. ***Baptism and the Covenant.***—Christian baptism is the entrance into the covenant. The meaning, the time, the mode have stirred some of the most heated debates in Christian history. More and more the church has learned quietly to respect the differing points of view, coming rather to center upon the meaning of baptism, whether by sprinkling, immersion, or pouring. Perhaps all would now agree that baptism is the entrance into the covenant.

Laying aside technical theological language, which we often need to do, most Christians would perhaps agree that: (*a*) Baptism means for child or adult a life dedicated to God. Those churches which baptize children would find in the rite of confirmation, or some equivalent, the opportunity and responsibility of a maturing child of God to take his stand with

28 There is neither Jew nor Greek, there is neither bond nor free, there is neither male nor female: for ye are all one in Christ Jesus.

have put on Christ. 28 There is neither Jew nor Greek, there is neither slave nor free, there is neither male nor female; for

baptism. When a convert was baptized "into" Christ, he was immersed in water permeated with Christ's spiritual "body." He could say literally, "I am in Christ and Christ is in me." Paul illustrated it by the experience of the Israelites who were in the cloud and passed through the sea in the days of Moses (I Cor. 10:1-5). It was this presence of the Spirit-Christ which made baptism a sacrament. Paul shared this realism, but he regarded the celestial body of Christ as the bearer of the mind and Spirit of Christ. He warned his fellow Christians that baptism was not a magical rite which made them immortal automatically by "regenerating" them. To be baptized into Christ was to be immersed in his character, to take up his cross, and to produce the fruit of his Spirit.

28. Where Christ is present there is unity and equality in diversity. The Greeks divided all men into two classes, Greeks and barbarians, and the Jews called all others "goyim." Even a proselyte could never be quite the Jew he might have been if he had been a blood descendant of Abraham. If he happened to be a slave, his religious duties as a Jew must not interfere with his service to his Jewish master. A wife was the property of her husband, and her status ranked with slaves and children. "In every respect woman is inferior to man," declared Josephus (*Against Apion* II. 24). When the foreigner, the proselyte, the wife, and the slave stood each in a different relation to God under the law, real spiritual unity was most difficult, if not impossible.

Paul saw that if these differences were preserved in the church, the missionary enterprise would suffer a fatal handicap. Yet he was not a radical advocating an immediate, violent revolution. The Jew in becoming a Christian did not need to become a Greek, nor the Greek a Jew. The slave might continue to serve his master, and "male" and "female" retained each its function in the ongoing stream of life. Nevertheless Paul's concept of equality and unity in Christ was an incipient revolution, the consequences of which are only now beginning to be worked out. Wherever his gospel is preached, men become uncomfortable with the age-old equation, "foreigner equals inferior"; with the incongruity of man's ancient thanksgiving that he had "not been born a woman"; and with the violation of democracy and brotherhood involved in Aristotle's definition of a slave as

Christ by his own confession of faith, to assert for himself and appropriate the dedication which his parents made for him in infancy. The child, having grown up in the Father's house, uses his privilege of choice to remain in that house or to go out. Staying in is often harder than coming in. (*b*) Baptism means that God comes into the life of child or adult as Savior, the same God having come as Creator at birth. His abiding presence is as a spring of water, assuring his daily cleansing, renewal, forgiveness, guidance, companionship. (*c*) Baptism means for child or adult that the door into the church is opened. This makes it possible for children to grow up in the Father's house. The child becomes a "little Christian"—a "Christ-one," one who is attached to or who belongs to Christ. Whatever else it may be, baptism is the way of entrance into that covenant. "John, child of the covenant, I baptize thee. . . ."

28-29. ***Faith and Personality.***—In breaking this paragraph down into words, sentences, and verses, one dares not lose sight of the theme which Paul carries forward step by step. Individual sentences must be seen in the total pattern; e.g., the race problem is but a subhead or illustration of Paul's teaching about the "covenant" and "freedom in Christ." With the most charitable handling of the ancient law, that law did not break down the partition which separated Jew and Greek, or Jew and Samaritan. In like manner, there are many in the modern world who hold that religion has been one of the chief stumbling blocks toward a realistic handling of the race issue. It was surely not so with Paul and his dealing with this profound matter.

Paul's statement sums up the conviction that in Christ human problems have a way of resolving and dissolving themselves. As Christ is the

29 And if ye *be* Christ's, then are ye Abraham's seed, and heirs according to the promise.

4 Now I say, *That* the heir, as long as he is a child, differeth nothing from a servant, though he be lord of all;

you are all one in Christ Jesus. 29 And if you are Christ's, then you are Abraham's offspring, heirs according to promise.

4 I mean that the heir, as long as he is a child, is no better than a slave, though

---

"an animated implement." No consistent Gentile Christian could participate in a pogrom or repeat the slanders that incited it; and no sincere Jewish Christian could view the Gentiles as special sinners and dogs to be excluded from the kingdom of God. Women had to be recognized as partners in preaching the gospel, and master and slave faced each other as man to man in Christ. The sin of refusing to eat with the Gentiles lay in tearing the threads of friendship that were being woven into the seamless robe of Christ.

The new suit of clothes, however, was not a uniform for those who have to march in step. When Paul says that all Christians are "one person" (εἷς, masculine) in Christ, he does not mean that they lose their individuality. Like facets of a diamond, the members are to reflect the beauty of the Christ-life, each from his own angle. The oneness of the Christians with Christ and with each other was organic and vital, and there was diversity in unity as well as unity in diversity (I Cor. 12–14). The unity of "the faith" (vs. 23) was not the crystallization of a static doctrine, nor was it a deadly sameness of emotional assent and expression. It consisted in equality of status before God and a oneness of purpose to bear the cross of Christ that expressed itself in as many ways as there were persons and circumstances in life.

29. Inheritance of God's kingdom was not dependent upon blood relationship to Abraham (cf. vss. 7, 9 and 14). All who were willing to claim the new freedom offered through Christ were assured of participation in the legacy. But this gift of God's grace required to be shared with all men, and the more it was shared, the more there was to share. The inclusiveness of grace meant the end of the law with its attendant racial prejudice and religious imperialism.

2. The End of the Age of Slavery (4:1-7)

a) The Life of Spiritual Minors (4:1-3)

4:1. This verse continues the illustration of the father's will and of the law as custodian for his minor children (3:17, 24, 29). **Slave** (RSV) corrects **servant** (KJV), but both translations of οὐδὲν διαφέρει, **differeth nothing from** (KJV), and **is no better**

---

eternal Presence, the living Contemporary, so is he the Son of man. He is infinitely more than the greatest Jew or the first Christian. If one would see what man can be, look at Jesus. All colors and races meet in him, as the rivers meet in the sea.

One's racial heritage is not the last word for a Christian; **there is neither Jew nor Greek.** One's social status, including even imprisonment, is not the last word; **there is neither bond nor free.** One's sex is not the last word; the Christian cause rests not upon gender but upon personality: **there is neither male nor female.** Paul deals with these profound problems on the deepest basis: **ye are all one in Christ Jesus.** In other words, the man who grips these matters **in Christ** is on the way to freedom.

Aristotle declared that only a comparatively few people could really live worth-while lives, and he named four classes who never could: (*a*) Slaves could not, for they are the tools of other men. (*b*) Those who die young could not, for they have not lived long enough to achieve true happiness. (*c*) Those who are diseased could not, for they are necessarily miserable. (*d*) Paupers could not, for they do not have sufficient of this world's goods. Take these four classes from society, and how many are left? But beyond Aristotle is Jesus, who bases all life upon God, and in whom the measure of time is but a segment of eternity.

4:1-3. ***Paul's Concept of Freedom.***—This chapter may appear on the surface to be the weakest part of the book. It may seem to be

2 But is under tutors and governors until the time appointed of the father.
3 Even so we, when we were children, were in bondage under the elements of the world:

he is the owner of all the estate; 2 but he is under guardians and trustees until the date set by the father. 3 So with us; when we were children, we were slaves to the ele-

---

than (RSV), are out of line with the context. Paul is not contrasting the character of a child with the character of an adult, but is comparing the child's status under guardians and trustees with the position of a slave. Whether the child is better than the slave is not the question here. The Paul who wrote Rom. 3:1-2 and 9:4-5 did not mean to say that the Jews were no different from the Gentiles, but that both were altogether dependent upon the grace of God.

2. **Guardians and trustees** (RSV) is correct, not **tutors and governors** (KJV). God in his will had set the time for the coming of Christ to end their control. Paul declared that all who had faith in Christ had come of age.

3. The word τὰ στοιχεῖα, **the elements** (KJV), meant (*a*) the letters of the alphabet, hence elementary education in any branch of knowledge; (*b*) the elements of which a thing was composed, as the fire, air, earth, and water of which the world was thought to be constituted; (*c*) the elements of the universe, the larger cosmos, including the sun, moon, planets, and stars; and (*d*) the spirits, angels, and demons which were believed to ensoul the heavenly bodies, traverse all space, and inhabit every nook and cranny of earth, particularly tombs, desert places, and demented persons. These spirits were said to be organized like human governments. In Rom. 8:38 Paul calls them "principalities" and "powers," and vss. 9 and 10 of our present chapter indicate that he has them in

---

only a summary of what the apostle has already argued in detail; but such an impression is indeed superficial. The chapter is a plateau which climaxes in Paul's statement on freedom in 5:1.

A well-nigh perfect illustration of freedom for Paul is the growth of **a child** (vs. 1). The child of the wealthiest parents on earth is no different from the child of a family of average economic status as long as the child must be cared for every moment of his existence. He must be watched, guarded, held in, and protected. It is only in growth that a child becomes free. Growth alone determines the freedom of men. But what kind of growth? Growth in one's ability and willingness to permit Christ to take control of his inward life.

The social chart of freedom conforms to the following scheme: far to the left is the group of men and women who must be held in by bit and bridle—kept in prison—the group that society knows as criminals. Their existence for a shorter or longer time must be taken over by the government. They must be held in by rules, laws, and restraints. To their right are those who are unable to carry their own load. Many of them must be supported by their families or by institutions which the government or generous citizens support. For many or most of the latter group there are no moral issues at stake. They are the victims of situations beyond their control, and so in the completest sense are not fully free. There are, however, within this large company many glorious exceptions who, though physically dependent, are morally and spiritually free. Some are shut-ins whose beds are community altars of freedom and courage, where a visitor may light his torch; their sickrooms become mounts of transfiguration. Moving farther to the right is the group who carry their own loads in society, but no more. They stand with emphasis upon their legal rights, and are quick to push those rights to the limit, even before the courts. These are the Golden Rule devotees who give little to others because they expect little in return. They regard themselves as self-made men and meet people only halfway. They practice only prudential ethics. Does society move forward upon their shoulders? Hardly; it only beats time. The best that can be expected from them is that some degree of social justice and freedom may be achieved by the clash of their self-interests. On the extreme right is the free man. He goes beyond the Golden Rule and does good to men who can never in the same degree do good to him in return. Men of this group carry their personal responsibilities with a margin, and that margin is the evidence of their freedom. "Except your righteousness shall exceed the righteousness of the scribes and Pharisees, ye shall in no case enter into the

4 But when the fulness of the time was come, God sent forth his Son, made of a woman, made under the law,

mental spirits of the universe. 4 But when the time had fully come, God sent forth his Son, born of woman, born under the

mind in vs. 3. In Col. 2:8, 20, the KJV translates, "the rudiments of the world"; the RSV is consistent in rendering these and our present passage by **the elemental spirits of the universe.**

Paul relegates the fear and worship of these spirits to the kindergarten stage of history. He includes in "the elements of the universe" all sub-Christian ideas and observances, both Jewish and Gentile. He regards these "elements" as slave drivers who frighten men with curses for not propitiating them by observance of special days and seasons, food taboos, dietary fads, and circumcision. In Christ he declared his independence of Fate, Fortune, Luck, and Chance, and from astrology, the counterfeit religion and bastard sister of astronomy, whose practitioners exploited the superstition that the stars controlled men's lives from birth to death. Whether it was the law of Moses or the law of the star-spirits, it was time, now that Christ had come, to have done with this child's play of "weak and beggarly elements" and grow up with the Spirit.

b) The Fullness of Time (4:4-7)

4-5. The four words, τὸ πλήρωμα τοῦ χρόνου, **the fulness of the time,** express a whole philosophy of history. The Hebrew prophets and Jewish apocalyptists believed that their God was the creator of the universe and arbiter of the destinies of all men and nations. Nothing could happen that was not his doing, either directly or indirectly through angels and men. He had a time for everything, and everything happened exactly on

kingdom of heaven" (Matt. 5:20). Here is the freest man of all; he is servant of all, and yet lord of all. He is above the law because he lives for much more than the law requires. He has a minimum of external restraints and a maximum of internal compulsions. "The love of Christ constraineth us" (II Cor. 5:14).

Paul pictures a child who must be held in by **guardians and trustees** until he grows up to freedom. Obviously, in all of Paul's thinking, freedom is at heart a spiritual matter. "Narrow is the way, . . . and few there be that find it" (Matt. 7:14). It is this point of view that made a modern playwright have one of his characters crying, in effect, "The very word majority is offensive to me. It is always the minority that preserves for us whatever of good there is in human life." One of the most dramatic scenes in history is that where Jesus addresses his little group of disciples—very average men—with those incredible words, "Ye are the salt of the earth. . . . Ye are the light of the world" (Matt. 5:13-14). Think of it: a little company of eleven (twelve minus Judas) were thus recognized as the spiritual aristocrats upon whom democratic movements across the centuries would depend. Freedom means growth in spiritual stature. It adds up to what a man permits Jesus Christ to do with his life. "If the Son therefore shall make you free, ye shall be free indeed" (John 8:36). Christ and freedom are wedded forever. This is the prelude to Paul's freedom (see Expos. on vss. 5-7 for detailed meanings).

4-5. *In the Fullness of Time.*—Paul worked toward definite goals; and he believed God's eternal purpose had definite objectives: that all creation moved by a divine agenda. The ultimate aim of divine grace was man's salvation through Christ, but preparation had to be made before Christ's advent. The glory in this preparation, and its triumph in completion, wells up in Paul's thrilling declaration, **When the fulness of the time was come, God sent forth his Son.**

As one tries to view these words from within the course of human events, appreciation of their content grows. What had gone on throughout the world in the interval between Malachi and Matthew—in those silent centuries between the O.T. and the N.T.? Israel had not been idle during those obscure years. Antiochus the Great had colonized Jews by the thousands in cities throughout Asia Minor, cities with names familiar to us chiefly because they figure so prominently in the book of Revelation. Antiochus the Great looked with favor on the Jews, and encouraged their religious, educational, and commercial proclivities. His successor, however, Antiochus Epiphanes, intensely hated and persecuted them, so that they were finally driven to armed rebellion. Under the leadership of Judas Maccabaeus they rose to their most glorious period of national independence. Paul, as a

time. To demonstrate his mercy as well as his power he had to work slowly, allowing good and evil all the time they needed to grow into their full harvest. A predetermined measure of wickedness had to be filled up, and a predestined number of righteous folk had to be gathered into the faithful remnant. The completion of this present age would be marked by a blood-red revolution, in which all good men and good works would be ground under the heel of the tyrant, while the wicked reigned supreme. Then suddenly God would intervene with the lightning of judgment to snatch the world from the mouth of the bottomless pit and restore it to Paradise, whence it had fallen with the sin of Adam. Sorrow and sighing would flee away, and the Messiah would reign with the perfection of a theocratic king.

At this juncture, says Paul, when the appointed period of history was "full," God sent his Son γενόμενον ἐκ γυναικός, γενόμενον ὑπὸ νόμον, "born of woman, born under law." Since Paul does not write γεννήθεντα, "born," and since the idea of birth lies in the context of γενόμενον, the second phrase is more naturally translated "subject to law." Jesus was not only born under law, but was subject to it all his life. What this involved for his childhood appears in Luke 2:21-52. The "yoke" of the Torah demanded that he observe the customs of his forefathers, such as wearing phylactery and prayer fringes, ceremonial washing of hands before eating, giving thanks at mealtime, praying at stated times, bringing tithes and sacrifices, and obeying the Ten Commandments.

Sent forth refers to God's sending of his Son from his pre-existent state in heaven (I Cor. 8:6; Phil. 2:6-8; Col. 1:15-17). Yet this Son was **born of woman.** There is nothing in these words, or elsewhere in Paul's letters, to prove or disprove that he knew the story

---

university student at Tarsus, must have reveled in this comparatively recent history.

But that was only a small segment of the fullness. Almost contemporaneously with the psalms of David were the *Iliad* and *Odyssey* of Homer. The migration of Gentile races, particularly the Indo-European races, had been going on for a long time. As far east as India cultures and religions had taken root which had their origins far to the west. Peoples in large numbers had moved hither and yon over the face of the earth. Julius Caesar, in the opening sentence of his history of the Gallic wars, says, "All Gaul is divided into three parts"; as a matter of fact, Gaul had once been divided into four parts, but the fourth part was so far removed from France that Caesar in his memoirs overlooked it altogether. The Galatians to whom Paul was writing were the fourth part.

Some two centuries before Caesar a considerable portion of the Gallic people set out to capture and colonize the Greek peninsula (see Intro., pp. 435-36). But the Greeks were too strong for them, and their conquest failed. While those defeated Gauls were wandering aimlessly in the region of the Hellespont, they received an invitation from King Nicomedes I to come over into Bithynia and help him win a war against his own brother, who was disputing his right to the throne. The Gauls accepted Nicomedes' invitation and fought successfully; Nicomedes rewarded their valor by giving them a large part of the country to the south and east of Bithynia and their area became known as Galatia. There in Asia flourished a Gentile race as Gallic as those Europeans against whom Caesar waged his historic wars. Their Galatian history is a fragment of **the fulness of the time** which was in Paul's mind as he wrote his fervent message of salvation to the Gentiles.

Persia and the Greek city-states of Asia Minor also loom large in the background. Rivalry, which eventually led to a death struggle for world supremacy, had its share in determining the religious and cultural environment of the world into which the Savior came. Even the ancient civilization of the Hittites affected the religious practices of the Greek temples in Asia, as Paul learned in his conflict with Diana of the Ephesians. Battles like Salamis and Thermopylae gave the Greek race new confidence in their military prowess. The ten thousand Greek mercenaries whom Cyrus recruited to help him wage war against Artaxerxes enjoyed victories which led to their readiness to wage war upon remote foreign soil. Xenophon's *Anabasis* is the story of the rebirth of Greek nationalism, the story of an expeditionary Greek army which conquered the world under Alexander the Great.

The Seleucid and Ptolemaic dynasties which shared the spoils of Alexander's conquests no doubt served God's purpose only in the sense that "the wrath of men shall praise" him (Ps. 76:10). Cleopatra's first meeting with Mark Antony was in Tarsus, the very city where Paul was born. Certainly life in the half century before Christ's birth was by no means

5 To redeem them that were under the law, that we might receive the adoption of sons.

law, 5 to redeem those who were under the law, so that we might receive adoption as

---

of the miraculous conception. His point here is that the Christ, although he was the pre-existent Son of God, did not come into this world with a body composed of celestial substance, but was woman-born like all other human beings. Paul's metaphor in Rom. 8:22-23 indicates how much this meant of pain for the mother and humiliation for the Son (cf. Gen. 3:16; II Cor. 8:9; Phil. 2:6-8; Luke 2:34-35). It was very different from the conception of royal sonship in Ps. 2, where the king is called God's "Son" because he has been chosen to be the Messiah. In Paul, Jesus is God's Son by nature, and his Christhood follows by virtue of this sonship. This belief was the fundamental cause of the split between the Jews and the Christians. The lowly birth, the obscurity of Nazareth, and the fact that Jesus was a common laborer, constituted a grievous scandal in the eyes of all who were expecting their Deliverer to come riding on a chariot of clouds wielding the lightning of judgment. Paul's gospel contradicts every form of hyperspirituality that fixes a gulf between God and his material world. On the other hand, his conception of the coming of Jesus was poles removed from the pagan stories of the births of heroes, savior-gods, and kings, whose legends were freighted with illicit relationships and lawless conduct like the lives of the devotees who had created them in their own image.

In neither of these verses does νόμον, **law,** have the article; in vs. 4 the reference is clearly to the law of Moses, but in vs. 5 the "we" of **that we might receive** includes Gentiles who were not under the Jewish law; hence we should read "under law," not

---

commonplace. Add to it all the Roman network of international highways over which the first Christian missionaries traveled; and to that the Greek language, which afforded such a fortunate medium for the spreading of the gospel.

Still there is more; and it is this "more" which is decisive. Perhaps it should be pointed out here that Apollos may very well have influenced Paul's concept of **the fulness of the time.** Apollos was educated at Alexandria, where Philo lived and taught, and Philo had made a scholarly attempt to prove that the principle of wisdom, which was common to many of the ancient faiths, Gentile as well as Jewish, and runs through the book of Proverbs as also through later Hebrew literature (especially Ecclesiasticus), would some day be personified in the Messiah. The Logos of John's Gospel carries the philosophy of Philo into Christian doctrine, and discloses for us part of Paul's meaning. For the rest, stress must be laid on the fact that the original Greek wording here is a perfect example of the formal use of the definite article—a delicate linguistic touch which translators have sometimes missed. Paul did not think it unimportant. Quite the contrary. To him **the time** was a very specific time, long anticipated in the providence of God. And **the fulness** was complete fullness: all things were ready for the King—the Son of God and Son of man—to enter his messianic kingdom. Is it adequate to say, **When the time had fully come?** Paul said much more than that; Paul said, **When the fulness of the time was come.** It was God's own moment for the giving of his Son to redeem the world.

5. ***The Cross as Reconciliation.***—(See Expos. on 3:13 for the several aspects under which the Cross may be viewed.) Every time the word **redeem** comes into Paul's thought or writing, the Cross is evident; with him the Cross is the means of redemption, **that we might receive adoption as sons.** "God was in Christ, reconciling the world unto himself" (II Cor. 5:19). Men who are changed from slaves to sons are reconciled. God himself took the initiative on the cross to bind the heart of mankind to himself, providing through his Son the way for men to become sons of God by **adoption** into the new covenant. This ministry of reconciliation, beginning with man's reconciliation to God, must extend across the generations: within man himself, then between races and nations, to make possible the healing of a broken world. The Cross as redemption, the Cross as example, as judgment and discipline, as substitution—all seem to funnel, focus, and point, if not climax, in the Cross as reconciliation. God is the reconciler, and he "is the same yesterday and today and forever" (Heb. 13:8). Man is the prodigal, the one to be reconciled.

The first step in reconciliation calls upon us to picture the kind of God reconciliation pre-

under the law (on the meaning of **redeem** see on 3:13). Jesus bought men free from slavery to sin and law in order that God might adopt them as his sons. It is easy to imagine the joy of a slave who was set free and adopted by his master. Although marred at times by selfishness and abuses, the growing custom of adopting children stood in bright contrast to the prevailing heartlessness of that harsh and cynical age.

Paul's illustration must not be made to say that Jesus' sonship by nature is so different from the Christian's sonship by adoption that the two have nothing in common. Paul shared the passionate faith of his nation that it was God's chosen people and therefore God's "sons" in a higher sense than the Gentiles, but he did not repudiate the conception of the relationship between the Creator and his creatures expressed in Gen. 1:26-27. In that sense all men were sons of God. They might mar his image in themselves, but that could not cancel the fact that he was their Father by creation. By failing to live

---

supposes. Up to the day of the Cross the N.T.'s best picture of God was the father of the prodigal son. That father waited daily, constantly, longingly, yearningly, prayerfully for his son's return. As evidence of these qualities in the father, the son, "when he came to himself," immediately said, "I will arise and go to my father, and will say unto him, Father, I have sinned against heaven, and before thee, and am no more worthy to be called thy son: make me as one of thy hired servants" (Luke 15:17-19). Underneath the prodigal's penitence was his conviction that he could count on his father. And so he could. The father saw the boy far down the road and rushed out to meet him. A cloak (perhaps for dignity) was put about his shoulders; shoes on his feet (perhaps for freedom, since slaves went barefoot), and a ring on his finger (perhaps for love). Dignity, freedom, and love represent God's attitude toward penitent men everywhere.

The Cross does not contradict that; it goes deeper. It demonstrates better than any verbal teaching how men may be brought back to the Father's heart. We listen to the Sermon on the Mount; we kneel at the Cross. We are edified by Christ's teaching; we are changed by his Cross. In other words, men are made new creatures by what God does. There is no higher view of God known to man than that revealed through the cross of Christ. Theories and descriptions of the Cross must be big enough to represent the true character of God. The Cross is God's deed. God did there what was necessary in order to change, redeem, make new, call home what had been lost. Make no mistake about it, Jesus did not die without good reason. The Cross is the world's completest picture of God. Men with a limited conception of the Cross have a correspondingly limited and incomplete picture of God.

But the Cross not only indicates the true character of God; it shows also God's measure of the significance of sin and evil. God had to do more than teach, reveal, and disclose what he thought about sin: for sin had not alone affected human nature, it had affected also the physical universe, so that Paul could say, "the whole creation groaneth" (Rom. 8:22). God had to do something of cosmic significance. "The suffering of Christ on the Cross is the momentary laying bare of the agelong hurt sin inflicts on the heart of God." [9]

There is, however, still another element in Paul's conception of the Cross: the Cross reflects God's estimate of man. God wants man infinitely more than man wants God. Man is worth dying for; he is worth the life of the Son of God. Reconciliation does not mean his absorption by God, so that he loses his individuality. Man and God are distinct, and yet at one. The Cross is God's best picture of himself; it is his profoundest estimate of the significance of sin and evil; and it is his definition, written in blood, of the value of man. God, sin, and man meet in the Cross. It is the place where God comes to grips with the forces that violate his love; it becomes the place where he draws men into harmony with the love and the purposes that flow from it.

Thy love unknown
Has broken every barrier down.[1]

Man reconciled to God—man at one with God, of his own free choice—is now ready to be taken into the new covenant. Paul had a fellowship with God in Christ, through **adoption as sons,** which even Abraham did not have. It is customary to refer to the Old Testament and the New Testament. A more correct phrasing would be the Old Covenant and the New Covenant. In the Old Covenant there is God's law through Moses and the prophets; in the New Covenant there is God's grace through Jesus Christ.

What else is so vital? One little word of five letters describes the world picture. That word

[9] E. D. Burton, quoted in Edwin McNeill Poteat, *The Scandal of the Cross* (New York: Harper & Bros., 1928), p. 79.

[1] Charlotte Elliott, "Just as I am, without one plea."

6 And because ye are sons, God hath sent forth the Spirit of his Son into your hearts, crying, Abba, Father.

sons. 6 And because you are sons, God has sent the Spirit of his Son into our hearts,

as sons of God (Rom. 1–2), Jews and Gentiles had orphaned themselves, and like the prodigal, had fallen into rags and starvation. Now that Christ had come, all men were summoned to clothe themselves with his righteousness and *be* sons of the God who "adopted" them.

6. Note Rom. 8:14-17. Paul shifts from "your" to "our" because he too has the Spirit in his heart, whereas it is only the doubting Galatians who require to be convinced that they are really sons and heirs of God through faith. Some MSS changed **our** (RSV), to **your** (KJV), and p^{46} reads "his [God's] Spirit," omitting "of his Son."

This statement is the foundation of Christian evidences. The members of Christ's body have only to look within their own hearts for the witness of the Spirit. But they cannot do this in isolation from the Christian fellowship (κοινωνία) in worship. From the very beginning (Acts 2:1-4) the presence of the Spirit was associated with the contagion of deep emotion generated in the Christian meetings. The O.T. promises were read and applied, and fervent prayers were offered. Visions and revelations turned men's eyes

is "split." The world is split vertically into nations; nations are split horizontally into races; races are split obliquely into classes; within classes homes are split as the increasing divorce rate indicates; within homes are what the psychologists call split personalities. With the boasted scientific skills of this century men have left out the cement which is necessary to hold life together. The reconciliation of man to man, through the reconciliation of man to God, releases the healing power of God into this anxious, broken, and bitter world. Only redeemed men can reconcile. Into the stream of human events God poured his own life in Jesus Christ, "when the fulness of the time was come" (vs. 4). Because Jesus is the judge of history, men and nations stand daily in judgment before him who is the truth. Because Jesus is guide, the wisdom of the ages is available through him for every age. Because Jesus is Savior, he literally takes into himself the evil of men and gives light and goodness in return. Fellow sinners around the cross can bridge their differences. All who would serve as reconcilers must themselves be men of integrity, who do not think in fractions and pieces but who live and work as integers, as whole numbers. How can this integration come? On the cross Christ gives himself to mankind. He is the "integrating Person" who makes inner control and mastery possible. "Peace of mind" is but the summary quality of a life that has been reconciled to God and has thereby come to terms with itself. A man healed and released in his own life can be a healer of other men.

5-7. ***Freedom as Release.***—These verses and 5:1 belong together. Paul saw freedom as release (vs. 5); as endowment (vss. 7, 31); as achievement (2:4); as sonship (vss. 6-7).

Paul had been slave on all fronts. He was mentally enslaved because the answers to his questions could not be found in his Pharisaic tradition or in the law, the flower of that tradition. Judaism just did not have the answer. He was morally enslaved, as his violent persecution of the Christians testified: persecution is not the work of normal, moral men. He was socially enslaved: his membership in the tribe of Benjamin was his world, but with every credit to that heritage it was powerless to handle him. He found that Christ alone could do for him what his Hebrew heritage could not do. More than all else, he was spiritually enslaved. His religion had meant to him only a meticulous performance of techniques. The law of God, as he had been taught, emphasized law more than God. Christ meant for Paul release from every conceivable sort of slavery. He answered Paul's questions because he answered Paul himself. Only a man who had once known slavery and had become free could write, "Stand fast therefore, . . . and be not entangled again with the yoke of bondage" (5:1). The apostle is here pleading for the very thing that makes Christianity unique, viz., the change that Christ can make in a man's life so that the man can possess and can exercise his fullest freedom. Only one who himself was free could write the Galatian letter, "the Magna Charta of the early church"; only one who had learned the meaning of freedom through hard experience. Christ—grace—Cross—faith—freedom: here is the keyboard of Christian hope. Here is freedom as release.

The controversy about circumcision may apto the future and lighted up the path of present duty. Hymns were sung, and the mighty acts and consoling words of the Savior were rehearsed. Members encouraged and admonished one another by the recital of their experiences as his disciples. The risen Lord, now present as the Spirit, bound the many into the One through his love for them and their love for him and for each other. The sacraments made his presence real, and the power to heal men's minds and bodies flowed from him to be exercised through his members. Attitudes and purposes were purified and exalted above the monotony of the commonplace, and the bleakness of life in an evil and weary world became bright with eternal meaning for the children of God. Feelings too deep for words found release in ecstatic tongues, "with groanings which cannot be uttered" (Rom. 8:26), unintelligible to outsiders, but fraught with a sense of God's purpose for the lowliest member; and interspersed through all this broken speech was the refrain **Abba! Father!** Without this revelation of God through Christ and his Spirit, the name "Father" would have been contradicted by the hard and tragic world in which his creatures had to live.

But was Paul not reasoning in a circle? How could he say that the presence of the Spirit in the hearts of men proved that they were God's sons, and in the same breath declare that God sent them his Spirit **because** (ὅτι) they were his sons? Some interpreters have felt that this is inconsistent with the doctrine of regeneration, which requires the Spirit to take the initiative in making men sons of God. They say that men are God's sons because he has first sent them his Spirit, and so they propose a different translation of the ὅτι clause: "But that you are sons—God has sent the Spirit of his Son into our hearts. . . ." But this only adds unnecessarily to the number of Paul's broken sentences, and it requires the supplying of some verb such as "to show" or "to prove"—i.e., "that you are sons."

---

pear to us like a tempest in a teapot, much ado about nothing, a matter of hygiene, of no moral or spiritual concern. But it contained in graphic form the central Christian issue: was Jesus only a new lawgiver? Was it necessary to keep the old Jewish laws in order to be a full Christian? Paul's answer came with a resounding "No."

Release had come from blind obedience into enlightened choice. Character cannot be built on unquestioning adherence to a book of rules. Either a conscientious man breaks the rules or the rules break him. When the questions of life are over the quest of life is done. It is not difficult to conceive that the man who more than all others persecuted and put the early Christians to death might well have followed the example of Judas and have gone out and hanged himself. Paul came to the place where he had to find something that blind obedience could not give. He found it in Christ. He found enlightened choice in the Christ who came into his life and took command by putting him at long last in the best control of himself. He found the freedom to be his true self. "The love of Christ constraineth us" (II Cor. 5:14). The hand that was laid on his innermost self provided him with power not only to choose but to choose the best.

Release for Paul also meant moving over from a haunted conscience to a healed and forgiven one. Nobody can suffer more acutely than a man who is keenly conscientious. Paul took his life seriously; more superficial and less capable people take theirs casually. The darkened mind of Paul was haunted by night and by day. The covenant that prophets like Hosea and Jeremiah envisioned Paul discovered personally after his conversion. "But this is the covenant which I will make with the house of Israel after those days, says the LORD: I will put my law within them and I will write it upon their hearts; and I will be their God, and they shall be my people." (Jer. 31:33.) "I will heal their backsliding, I will love them freely; for mine anger is turned away from him. I will be as the dew unto Israel; he shall grow as the lily, and cast forth his roots as Lebanon. His branches shall spread, and his beauty shall be as the olive tree, and his smell as Lebanon." (Hos. 14:4-6.) The unique contribution that Jesus makes is the forgiveness of sin. No other man has ever claimed that power. Forgiveness is the Christian's secret of freedom. Christ's forgiveness does not simply let a man go free; instead it heals his life. Forgiveness becomes the master key to mental health. It enables a man to do his part of the world's unfinished work.

Freedom as release for Paul meant moving over from impossible requirement to possible trust. The law could not be kept in every jot and tittle. But Paul discovered that his new

7 Wherefore thou art no more a servant, but a son; and if a son, then an heir of God through Christ.

crying, "Abba! Father!" 7 So through God you are no longer a slave but a son, and if a son then an heir.

Examined more closely, Paul's argument is seen to be moving not in a circle, but in an ascending spiral. It begins with faith's response to the preaching of the gospel. This believing faith then becomes the determinant of action, energizing new decisions and deeds through love, and drawing the believer onward and upward into the unknown future through hope. Whereupon these new acts of love produce a fresh increment of assurance for faith, and this in turn inspires further Christian action as the soul presses "toward the mark for the prize of the high calling of God in Christ Jesus" (Phil. 3:14).

7. This is Paul's proclamation of emancipation.

The RSV transfers διὰ θεοῦ, **through God,** to the very beginning of the sentence. This makes it mean that the believer's freedom and sonship, as well as his heirship, have their source in God and their realization through him. But while this is true to Paul's thought, it is better to keep the Greek word order and take "through God" with καὶ κληρονόμος, "also heir." This means that God makes the man who has faith in Christ an heir of the promise which he made to Abraham, including freedom and sonship to God (cf. Rom. 8:17). The bestowal of the Spirit is the first installment of this inheritance. The KJV translates a secondary reading, **heir of God through Christ.** Because it was felt

freedom in Christ asked of him what he could do, viz., trust—trust in the sense of complete surrender. That was the way out of his slavery.

7, 31. ***Freedom as Endowment.***—Paul and all others who will follow in his train inherit the riches of God: **An heir of God through Christ** (see Expos. on vs. 6). Freedom as release is but the beginning of the journey, not its end. Release from every form of slavery is the first step in the pilgrimage of Christian freedom. Freedom is not only exit, it is entrance; freedom "from" is followed by freedom "to." Too many stop with freedom as release. They illustrate the peril of the empty life—clear and set free, but empty (Matt. 12:43-45). Christ fills and feeds the life he has released.

Every item, insight, and concern that Paul touched he enlarged, including freedom. Each point of view he advocated, the varieties and facets of the Christian life that he taught, must be seen against the background of grace. Grace is always something God does to a man and for him. One fruit or gift of his grace is liberty—liberty as endowment. In this sense, "Where the Spirit of the Lord is, there is liberty" (II Cor. 3:17).

Either such considerations fit clearly into the teaching of Jesus or Paul's writing is in vain. "Tarry ye in the city of Jerusalem," said Jesus, "until ye be endued with power from on high" (Luke 24:49). "Endued with power": freedom as endowment! "Don't go out to represent me with what you have now," Jesus seems to say, "I know you too well." Another word of his sharpens our thinking: "I am the way," he taught, the path by which to walk; "I am . . . the truth," the light upon that path; "I am . . . the life," the power by which to walk it (John 14:6). There is the trilogy of the Christian life. "I can do all things through Christ which strengtheneth me" (Phil. 4:13).

The full life is the free life; the adequate life is the free life; the empowered or endowed life is the free life. Paul knew from travail of soul that the ancient law could not provide the resources to enable an honest man to keep what was required. And so he strives in all of his letters to show the difference Jesus makes; to show that what the law was powerless to perform is the business of Jesus. It is that which sets men free, and for their freedom endows them.

Charles H. Spurgeon learned of a poor woman in his London congregation who was having much difficulty paying her rent. He called at her door to pay it for her. She heard his knock but did not respond, thinking it was the rent collector, not realizing that it was Spurgeon who had come to pay her bill. Christ knocks at a man's door, and how often that door is left closed when Christ has called to bring and to give that quality of life and resource which no man can develop by himself. Paul says every man may be thus "strengthened with might by his Spirit in the inner man" (Eph. 3:16). Freedom is not the right to do whatever one pleases, but the power to do what he ought to do. Freedom is endowment.

7. ***Freedom as Sonship.***—Paul pleaded with his Galatian converts that they remain in the

8 Howbeit then, when ye knew not God, ye did service unto them which by nature are no gods.

9 But now, after that ye have known God, or rather are known of God, how

8 Formerly, when you did not know God, you were in bondage to beings that by nature are no gods; 9 but now that you have come to know God, or rather to be

that "through" was more appropriate of Christ than of God, a number of other changes were made in later MSS. One variant adds "heirs of God and fellow heirs with Christ" from Rom. 8:17.

3. The Spiritual Maturity Required of Heirs of God (4:8-11)

8. Rom. 1:18-32 and Gal. 5:19-21 give Paul's opinion of the gods of the Gentiles and the consequences of worshiping them. As a missionary for Christ, he continued the battle which the synagogue had been waging for centuries. The Jews never ceased to ridicule idols and denounce idolaters (Isa. 44:9-20; Jer. 10:1-16; Ps. 115:4-8; Wisd. Sol. 13–15). They demoted the old gods to the rank of demons and made a list of detractive names for them: angels, shepherds, princes; kings, emperors, benefactors, heroes; demons, personifications, idols, nonentities. Some were living, some dead; some were good, but were not God. Most of them were bad, and their idols were but images of "things of nought." The Lord made the stars, and all the worshipers of Fortune and Destiny were destined to the sword (Isa. 65:11-12). Idolatry was the root of all other sins and depravities.

Paul did not deny the existence of these beings whose ignorant worshipers called them gods, but he declared that they did not partake of the nature of God (I Cor. 8:4-6). God permitted them to plague mankind to punish sin, especially the sin of participating in the sacraments of the Gentile cults (I Cor. 10:19-22; 11:28-31). But Christ had conquered them and no Christian needed to fear them. There was a time of ignorance (τότε), before Paul preached the gospel to the Galatians, when his Gentile converts were in bondage to these deities falsely so called. Now they were the free sons and heirs of God, but they could not claim their inheritance if they continued to half believe in the old "gods." They must not bring into the church of Christ the old paraphernalia of magic and superstition, nor must they imagine that resort to the laws and customs of Moses would add to their assurance of salvation in Christ.

9*a*. To know God, however, one must first be known by him. The flow of Paul's thought from ἀλλά, "but" or **howbeit** in vs. 8 is smoother if δέ is translated "and" instead of **but:** "There was a time when you were slaves, and now that you know God, . . . how can you think of going back to slavery?"

One of the strong influences that led the Galatians to Christ was their quest for a knowledge of God. But there were two kinds of this knowledge and two ways of seeking it. The way of Christ was hard, requiring men to bear the cross and live in moral fellowship with God. The way of the mystic was easy, to become one with

relation of sonship instead of returning to moral bondage and spiritual slavery. If they failed to respond, he feared he had "labored over [them] in vain" (vs. 11). Belonging to the family of the Creator by physical birth is a matter with which the individual has nothing whatsoever to do; belonging to the Father's family on the level of moral and spiritual choice is conversely a matter for each man to decide. This choice is the context of being "born again" (John 3:3-4). The climb spiritually is logical, moving from release to endowment, to achievement, to sonship. The move is from laws to standards, from standards to ideals, from ideals to relationship. To be not a servant, who only takes orders, but a son, who shares in the initiative, in the creativity, in the fellowship of the family, is the joy and privilege of the Christian. The master spiritual key that still opens doors is, "To whom do you belong?" "But as many as received him, to them gave he power to become the sons of God" (John 1:12).

Such belief and faith, the optic nerve of the soul, is for many a man but a faint possibility

turn ye again to the weak and beggarly elements, whereunto ye desire again to be in bondage?

known by God, how can you turn back again to the weak and beggarly elemental spirits, whose slaves you want to be once

God by eating a sacrament, accepting a creed, obeying a law; by keeping an eye on the stars and observing lucky days and special seasons; or by climbing the mountain of speculation where one could say: "I know God; I am in tune with the Infinite; I can tap the resources of the Universe; I am God, and God is I." All this was the essence of idolatry, because it was self-worship and self-salvation. Even the law of Moses, which forbade the making of graven images, was not free of this subtlest of all idolatries; for although this law was regarded as God's revealed will, it was still the law observer who had to decide when and where it applied to him and how he would carry it out. Making this decision could easily become the equivalent of making an image of one's God in silver or gold. Both the legalist and the mystic were subject to the besetting sin of pride. When they yielded to it, they proclaimed themselves as *the* knowers—the gnostics—and destroyed human fellowship by thanking God that they knew him better than did anyone else, and by setting all others at nought.

Paul begins with a prior and more searching question: Does God know me? Inherent in the chosen people concept was the belief that God knew Israel with a peculiar intimacy not granted to any other nation. But for this very reason the prophets warned that God would hold the Israelites all the more strictly to account. God "knew" only those who responded to his merciful choice of them, who walked according to his will, and carried out the task which he had set for them. According to Paul, only the man who loves God is "known" by God (I Cor. 8:3). Being known by God is being saved by God's grace. This requires the Christian to learn to know himself as God knows him, and it leaves no room for the complacency of a static conscience which says, "I know God." Only in the future consummation will Paul be able to say that he knows as God knows him (I Cor. 13:12).

9*b*-10. Christian freedom brought the Galatians new and unsuspected hardships, dangers, and demands. Some of them, like the Israelites in the desert, forgot the slavery

at first; but if he can only whisper "Abba, Father" (vs. 6), the grace of God literally rushes to his aid with enabling power. He must respond by exercising his manhood, his free choice, his will power. If God makes the first move in tapping on his door, he must make the second by responding. For God to move further before he responds would be to violate his personality. "Lord, I believe; help thou mine unbelief" (Mark 9:24).

Membership in the family of God is not the outcome of some interminable search. God is the seeker: "After that ye have known God, or rather are known of God" (vs. 9). Not aspiration but receptivity is the movement of the Christian gospel. "Canst thou by searching find out God?" (Job 11:7.) The real question reads, "Whither shall I flee from thy presence?" (Ps. 139:7.) The task is one of realizing that presence. A more sensitive professional man confessed, "Everywhere I turn it seems that God is trying to break through into my life." He might have added, "But God will not break through until I grant him permission."

Obviously this conception of belonging to the family of God on the free terms of sonship is but a further delineation of the Christian doctrine of God and man. To have personal life and to labor with the "divinity that shapes our ends" [2] is life at its highest and fullest (see Expos. on 1:3). A lift and a light must come from somewhere to reveal the significance of man. "Man deserves to be visited by him who has ordained the stars." The Christian faith affirms that he has been so visited by Jesus Christ, whose visit makes it possible for him to be a son of God.

> Time, like an ever rolling stream,
> Bears all its sons away;
> They fly forgotten, as a dream
> Dies at the opening day.[3]

That verse, taken by itself and as it stands, is utterly unchristian; for according to it man is only an adjective to modify the stream,

[2] Shakespeare, *Hamlet*, Act I, scene 2.

[3] Isaac Watts, "O God, our help in ages past."

10 Ye observe days, and months, and
times, and years.

more? 10 You observe days, and months, and

and longed for the good old days. They were collecting **the weak and beggarly elements** of religion to make their own equivalent of Aaron's golden calf. Moses, the lawgiver, and Paul, the preacher of grace, faced the same difficulty of keeping men true to a God who is to be heard and trusted, but cannot be "seen" (Exod. 33:11, 14, 23). Men wanted images of their God, graven or mental, carried through the streets or set up in the secret places of the mind and heart. In the higher sphere of freedom, where the invisible God must be worshiped in faith, hope, and love, doubt arose; and half believers, and even sincere religious folk, sought additional guarantees on the lower, familiar, and more comfortable level, where the astrologers sold horoscopes for a price, and where men knew how to cajole and compel the gods of Fortune, Fate, and Chance, and how to manipulate all things to their advantage.

Paul could not understand how the Galatians, having had a taste of freedom, could be so keen to re-enslave themselves by going back to the kindergarten to play with these "A B C's" of their former religion. To convey his astonishment we need to translate πῶς ἐπιστρέφετε by **how can you turn?** Since the turning is not a repetition but a reversion, πάλιν is "back," not **again** (KJV) or **back again** (RSV). Ἄνωθεν, "from above," means "upper," "anew," "again," "of old," "from the beginning"; with πάλιν it is translated **once more,** expressing the desire of the Galatians to go back to the beginning and recapture their childhood at the expense of their freedom of adulthood. The present infinitive δουλεύειν, "to serve as slaves," is more likely to be original than the aorist δουλεῦσαι, which might be taken inceptively, "to become slaves."

The connection between vss. 9 and 10 becomes clear if we translate more freely, "You are beginning to observe." Paul knew that this was only a beginning, and that legalism, gaining headway, would demand more and more, with no logical stopping place

whether that stream is the race, the political state, or the economic order. Man is not a tool, a machine, a serial number, an animal, a small boat, an adjective; instead, man—made of dust and divinity—is here to weave, within the family of God and as God's son, the quality of life with which he will spend the ages. If he is to live yonder, he has found the best reason for living now. Faith in the future life rests upon the concept of God as the Father and of man as his son. God cannot deny himself and his own.

Only such sons of God are earth's genuine aristocracy. And upon them, the aristocracy of intelligence and character, all democratic institutions ultimately depend. In every generation, whether at high tide or low, such souls have sustained their own confidence and have shared it with others. Wrote a woman to such a friend, "So long as you are alive I do not entirely despair of mankind." Thomas Carlyle said of one of his heroes, "He went through this mud puddle of a world on his own terms."

Another whose sonship under God tells the story of his life and his work is Johann Sebastian Bach, perhaps the foremost creative musician of all time. He found his sense of life's worth, dignity, and destiny in the Christian faith, and set to music Paul's doctrine of justification. Many confess that Bach's music is too difficult for them to play or appreciate; but let it be remembered that Bach's eye was on no human audience when he composed. It is evident that he knew there was One listening who would understand, for at the top of his scores he wrote these words, *Soli Deo gloria* (the glory be to God alone) and *Jesu juva* (by Jesus' help). He found his inspiration, the spark for his genius, the reason for life where every man may find it, in his membership in the family of God; he was God's child and son. No wonder he could put to music the Christian doctrine of justification by faith. He looked up into the face of God, and strode through. Within the family of God there is a power not of ourselves that makes for righteousness. There God does enable a man to have a high opinion of himself; there men are justified by faith. From within it Paul bared his innermost soul to his Galatian converts, calling them to return to their freedom as sons of God.

10. ***Liturgy and Freedom.***—The Galatians were tempted to reobserve pagan "days" and the Jewish calendar but did not thus become better

11 I am afraid of you, lest I have bestowed upon you labor in vain.

seasons, and years! 11 I am afraid I have labored over you in vain.

short of works-salvation and the elimination of faith (5:9). The observances with which the Galatians were beginning were new moons, fast and feast days, and holidays such as New Year's Day. There were special months of fasting (Zech. 8:19; II Chr. 8:13), and lucky and unlucky days to do things, so that all one's undertakings had to be set for just the right times and seasons. There can be no doubt that Paul was referring especially to the Jewish calendar, with its yearly cycle of observances; but customs carried over from the Gentile cults were also included. It is not likely that the sabbatical year and the year of jubilee (Lev. 25) were observed in Galatia. If ἐνιαυτούς, **years,** referred to them, one would have to say that Paul was speaking theoretically about the application of the law of Moses, whereas his tone and urgency suggest that he was dealing with actual conditions. In the syncretic legalism which he was resisting, Jewish and Gentile customs were flowing together and mutually reinforcing their demand that Christians observe them. Paul's opinion of them appears in Col. 2:16-23.

11. While Paul was persuaded that nothing could separate him and his converts from the love of God in Christ Jesus (Rom. 8:38-39), the danger was very real that the Galatians would lose all by mistaking the shadow for the substance.

He was not **afraid of** (KJV) them but was anxious about them, knowing, as they did not, what they would lose in giving up his gospel of grace. He feared lest all the toil that he had expended for their eternal welfare, **over you,** would be in vain. What that toil was like appears in Acts 13–14, and in II Cor. 6:4-10; 11:23-29. The modern reader, accustomed to speed and comfort in travel, needs to reflect on how great was the physical and spiritual energy which Paul invested in his churches. When he left them to labor elsewhere, he never ceased to care for them. He knew that if he sowed the seed, God would give the increase; but he knew also that God in his mysterious way had left men free to make it fruitless. As their spiritual parent, he was "in travail" until Christ was fully formed in them. And so he turned to a personal appeal, urging them to conserve the life which he and they had achieved in Christ at the cost of so much toil.

persons. In like manner, the observance of the Christian calendar may result in religious servitude, with little creativity and no fresh commitment to Christ.

Historic liturgy and festivals, however, can mean enrichment for those who worship. Historic prayers which have been used through the centuries lift the preacher as well as the worshiper from the purely temporary and contemporary into the aspirations and assurances of past centuries. They warm his mind and soul with a realization of God's timelessness. The same principle operates with the truly great hymns as contrasted with religious songs. Hymns that have lived across the centuries make the worshiper conscious that "other men labored, and ye are entered into their labors" (John 4:38).

Churches that use historic liturgies sometimes unconsciously grow cold and formal. Such liturgies should be served warm and used as the vehicles of evangelistic appeal as well as for probing and sustaining the faithful. Even though the palace of Pharaoh was not a temple and not a church, the principle under consideration here is illustrated in the life of Moses, who lived in that palace as a young man. Moses saw beyond the splendor, beauty, and drapery of the palace—out to the suffering of his fellow-Israelites: so must the worshiper and the church which uses ancient liturgies and hymns. A social conscience can be and must be aroused in Christians through the use of these historic hymns, prayers, and forms of worship. There were two classical Protestant concepts of such liturgical and architectural matters. Calvin was intent on preserving whatever was *commanded* in Scripture; Luther wanted to preserve and use whatever was not *forbidden* in Scripture.

Freedom in Christian worship may be illustrated by a word from G. W. Truett, one of the granitelike personages of twentieth-century Protestantism. He was preaching in a church of another denomination than his own, which was accustomed to liturgical forms and vestments for its clergy. He said to his pastor-friend, "Do I have to wear this robe in order to keep my promise to preach for you?" "No," was the quick

12 Brethren, I beseech you, be as I *am;* for I *am* as ye *are:* ye have not injured me at all.
13 Ye know how through infirmity of the flesh I preached the gospel unto you at the first.

12 Brethren, I beseech you, become as I am, for I also have become as you are. You did me no wrong; 13 you know it was because of a bodily ailment that I preached the

E. THE PERSONAL RELATIONS BETWEEN PAUL AND HIS SPIRITUAL CHILDREN (4:12-20)

12*a*. Although a man of strong convictions and many conflicts, Paul had a genius for developing deep and lasting friendships. Between him and his spiritual children there was always reciprocity of suffering and victory (II Cor. 1:3-11). All that the Greek says is: "Become as I, because I also as you," and the meaning has to be gathered from the context in this and Paul's other letters. In 2:19-20 he has told his readers what kind of man he is, and now he asks them to become like that (cf. I Thess. 1:5-7; Phil. 2:1-5). He has a right to expect this because he too has relinquished all his special privileges as a member of God's chosen people, and has put himself on the same level as the Gentiles in respect of the grace of God (2:15-16; I Cor. 9:19-23; Phil. 3:4-11). Through faith in Christ he and they had taken their stand on common ground which required them to give up reliance upon law as a way of salvation. He proposed to maintain that ground, and he besought his Galatian brothers in Christ to do likewise. Mutuality was essential to his faith-life in Christ.

12*b*-14. Never before had the Galatians mistreated Paul, and he wanted the initial happy relationship to continue. This relationship contrasts with the hostilities described in Acts 13:45, 50; 14:4-6, 19, which would be described accurately by **injured.** But since the Christian treatment of Paul on that occasion was the exact opposite, ἠδικήσατε here covers more than physical injury. Anything that threatened the stability and hindered the progress of his churches was a **wrong** to him (I Thess. 2:17-20; 3:5; II Cor. 2:4; 11:28-29). The preachers of "another gospel" (1:7) maintained that they had a right to differ with him, and that in doing so they were not wronging him personally. Paul admitted that up to their present defection the Galatians had done him no wrong, but he implied that if they carried through their proposal to change his gospel, they would wrong not only him but the Christ who dwelt in him.

answer. "Then I will," said Truett. The privilege of choice is the badge of free men in all areas of life. This freedom is close to the center of the Christian gospel.

12-20. ***A Confession of Paul's Own Personal Freedom.***—Underneath this exceedingly personal and moving paragraph Paul discloses his personal freedom more intimately than at any other point in his entire letter. He pulls out all the stops in the organ of his soul, as he seems to say to his Galatian converts, "If you will not hear me now, I have no other way."

He revealed his deepest self to them because the very essence of the Christian movement was at stake. That movement was at the crossroads. If Peter had had his way, all would have been different. Knowing this so clearly, Paul used every argument, appealed to every historical illustration and precedent to make his case. His last appeal was to their affection for him.

His first visit and presentation of the Christian message to the Galatians must have had a startling effect. Though tempted to discredit his message because of his physical infirmity, the Galatians came to regard him as **an angel of God, even as Christ Jesus.** They were willing to pluck out their eyes and give them to him. Surely he was justified, in the light of that visit, to ask: **Am I therefore become your enemy, because I tell you the truth?** (vs. 16). He pleads that they may be zealous in the good cause, whether he is in person with them or not.

13-14. ***His Infirmity in the Flesh.***—Was this his "thorn" (II Cor. 12:7)? Whatever it may have been, he makes it the central thrust of a powerful personal appeal. He had handled it in such a Christlike manner on his first visit that it became an asset in his dealing with the Galatians. It was also at the same time one of the marks of his "freedom in Christ." He was a free

14 And my temptation which was in my flesh ye despised not, nor rejected; but received me as an angel of God, *even* as Christ Jesus.

gospel to you at first; 14 and though my condition was a trial to you, you did not scorn or despise me, but received me as

The cordial reception Paul had enjoyed on his first visit to Galatia was all the more gratifying in view of his physical illness. Since sickness was regarded as God's punishment for sins, it would have been natural for the Galatians to conclude that he was an angel, not of God, but of Satan. Paul does not tell us whether his disease was malaria, epilepsy, migraine, eye trouble, or some other malady, and the difficulty of diagnosing the case of a living patient should warn us of the futility of attempting it for one who has been dead almost nineteen hundred years. All that the meager data tell us is that Paul's affliction was chronic, very painful, repulsive, and humiliating; but not such as to disable him completely or keep him from leading an intensely active life (vs. 14; II Cor. 10:10; 12:7-10). It is more to the point to observe what Paul made of his handicap (II Cor. 1:3-11; 4:16–5:15; 12:1-10; Rom. 8:18-39).

Paul did not preach **through** (KJV), but **because of** (RSV), sickness, which made him change his plans, perhaps at the point in his first journey indicated in Acts 13:12-14. Whether the attacks recurred through the whole period of Acts 13–14, we do not know; but they were frequent enough to make a lasting impression on the Galatians. Yet they did not treat him as if he amounted to nothing (οὐκ ἐξουθενήσατε), and they did not spit in his presence (οὐδὲ ἐξεπτύσατε), as men were accustomed to do when they wanted to ward off an evil spirit. Figuratively, ἐκπτύειν, "spit out," may be translated **rejected** (KJV), or **despise** (RSV), but in view of its general use to refer to the physical act, and of the custom of applying saliva as a protection from evil, it is better to keep the literal meaning. The structure of the Greek sentence is loose and difficult. What Paul actually says is, "You did not scorn your temptation in my flesh, and you did not spit"; what he means is, "You did not scorn me and did not spit, although my physical condition was trying to you." Some MSS try to heal the sentence by changing "your temptation" to "my temptation." Paul's condition, trying as it was to himself and his friends, did not prevent the Spirit of Christ from shining in him and through him, and it allowed Christ's compassion to flow through the Galatians into his life. They treated him as Christ had treated them.

Paul refers to this occasion as τὸ πρότερον, "the first time" (ASV), **at first** (RSV). When this word indicates the first of two events, the second is stated plainly or is clearly implied. In this case Paul does not say explicitly that he was in Galatia a second time between his first visit and the writing of this letter; but this omission was presumably

man in spite of it. What matter what the infirmity was? Poor eyesight, perhaps (cf. vs. 15). Often the Scripture shows its genuineness by respecting private matters and personal rights. It is not necessary to know the details of Paul's weakness. Everybody has a thorn of some kind, and everybody is tempted to be exalted above measure.

To every saint and sinner who has prayed for the removal of some thorn, let Paul speak his word of wisdom (cf. II Cor. 12:7). He prayed three times, he tells us, for the removal of his: he thought it impaired his work. It worried him; it humiliated him. It perhaps irritated his faith and disturbed his Christian outlook. It seems that Christ did not answer, to Paul's satisfaction, his first and second prayers. Perhaps God wanted to call him closer, there to assure him that his prayer was being heard. After the third prayer, the voice spoke clearly and convincingly. The thing to do is to pray about thorns until one hears the voice speak. Such prayer makes a man brave. It may do for anyone what it did for Paul and for Jeremiah. Jeremiah has been called a pessimist only because he lets the centuries overhear him in his prayer closet; even so men heard Christ pray in Gethsemane. If complaints, defeats, pessimisms must be, let a man speak them in prayer. Should the world overhear, well enough; but let him speak courage abroad. That was the way of Paul and Jeremiah—and Christ.

Paul found the real way to courage and freedom. It was deeper than his heredity. Maybe

15 Where is then the blessedness ye spake of? for I bear you record, that, if *it had been* possible, ye would have plucked out your own eyes, and have given them to me.
16 Am I therefore become your enemy, because I tell you the truth?

an angel of God, as Christ Jesus. 15 What has become of the satisfaction you felt? For I bear you witness that, if possible, you would have plucked out your eyes and given them to me. 16 Have I then become your enemy by telling you the truth?[h]

[h] Or *by dealing truly with you.*

---

because he expected his readers to remember the course of events—vs. 16 and 1:9 point to this conclusion. Taken by itself, the Greek word does not prove that there had been two visits, but neither does it prove that there had not been. The translations **at the first** (KJV), **at first** (RSV), and "in the first place" leave the matter in doubt (for the bearing of this passage on the date and destination of the letter see Intro., p. 439).

15. Subtly Paul contrasts the initial limitless sympathy of the Galatians with what now threatens to become an evanescent satisfaction. Ὁ μακαρισμός, **blessedness** (KJV), **satisfaction** (RSV), describes the sense of total well-being which Paul's presence and preaching brought to the Galatians. In their joyful gratitude they did all they could to alleviate his condition; they would have given him their very eyes, but there was a physical limit to the range of vicarious suffering. As far as possible, he and his Galatian friends were bearing each other's burdens; but some things each had to bear for himself. (To pluck out one's eyes was a metaphor for giving up one's most precious possession, and no conclusion can be drawn from it concerning the nature of Paul's illness.) The Galatians could, however, accept and hold fast to Paul's gospel; and that was better medicine for his spirit than the removal of his "thorn in the flesh" could have been.

16. Wistfully answering his own question (vs. 15), Paul exclaims, **Have I then become your enemy by telling you the truth?** or, better, "So that in telling you the truth I have become your enemy!" He had to tell the truth even at the risk of making enemies; but this very compulsion makes the strain of religious controversy an ever present threat to Christian mutuality.

Unless counteracted, the effect of this controversy upon the fellowship would be as shattering as the religious convictions of both parties were deep and sincere. A specious tolerance might have said, "My religion is the best for me, yours is the best for you; let neither of us try to convert the other": but that would have put the Christian missionary enterprise to sleep. An equally specious intolerance would proclaim: "Since error is sin against God, religious liberty does not include freedom to err; therefore we who have the whole truth have the right and duty to prevent you from believing and propagating anything contrary to our gospel." Paul's solution was the true catholicity implied in I Cor. 3:21-23; he would test all things and hold fast to all that harmonized with his principle of salvation by grace alone through faith in Christ. But although the range of things that met this test was wide enough for eternity (Rom. 8:32), the stress of these differences of interpretation of the one gospel caused Paul to write "Anathema," and

---

his thorn was part of his inheritance; but his new courage was more vital than being an Israelite. His thorn interfered with his living a life of privilege; even his glorious ancestry through the tribe of Benjamin could not overcome it. But his experience with it became the highway to freedom. He learned to glory not in his accomplishments, sacrifices, or sufferings, but in the new fellowship which was possible only through his weaknesses, his infirmities, his thorn. He found that Christ is more concerned with the revival of the unfit than with the survival of the fittest. He learned what the law did not teach him: the blessedness of being handicapped; that man's extremity may be God's opportunity; that earth's disappointments may be heaven's appointments. There is a health that hardens, and a prosperity that makes people unkind. Defeat, illness, bankruptcy, broken friendships may be the weaknesses through which God's strength is made perfect. "My grace is sufficient for thee" (II Cor. 12:9). His grace is divine kindness in action; it is more than God's disposition, it is a disposition that acts.

17 They zealously affect you, *but* not well; yea, they would exclude you, that ye might affect them.

18 But *it is* good to be zealously affected always in *a* good *thing*, and not only when I am present with you.

17 They make much of you, but for no good purpose; they want to shut you out, that you may make much of them. 18 For a good purpose it is always good to be made much of, and not only when I am present with

---

led his spiritual children sometimes to regard him as their enemy. The Galatians, however, preserved his letter; and from that fact we may infer that the constructive love of Christ proved stronger than the corrosive effect of religious controversy.

17-20. Editors differ concerning the punctuation of these verses. Some place a period, others a comma, at the end of vs. 18. The RSV takes vs. 19 as a separate exclamatory sentence, but this, like the KJV, ignores the δέ, "and," at the beginning of vs. 20. Paul's language is so compact that a free translation is required. He says in effect: "They compete for your favor, not fairly, but because they want to exclude you from the fellowship so as to have you seek their society. Now, it is good to be sought after when the motive is good—but this is true always, and not only when I am present with you, my children, for whom I suffer birth pangs once more until Christ is formed in you; and I wish I could be with you now and change my language, for I am at a loss what to make of you."

The verb ζηλοῦσιν means "they strive zealously to win you to their side," "they compete for your favor." **Make much of** (RSV) modernizes **zealously affect** (KJV), which means "they impress themselves upon you to influence you." Paul charges his opponents with ulterior motives: they do not seek adherents καλῶς, **well** (KJV), honestly, honorably, fairly; for a **good purpose** (RSV). These would-be leaders, who want to build up a following for themselves, claim to be the only true Christians, and they exclude—"shut out"—those who disagree with them. They excommunicate men from their "true church" in order to frighten them into currying favor for readmission!

Paul grants that it is a good thing to be sought after if the motives of both seeker and sought are good, and if both are honestly serving a good cause. But in that case it ought to be **always**—not only when both parties are together, but also when one is absent. When Paul was present, the Galatians responded favorably. Now he reminds them that the same gospel is no less a joy and a blessing in his absence. He hints that if his

---

It is more than favor; it is energy. Grace is the power of God meeting a human soul and redeeming it, including the handling of its infirmities and thorns. To be in Christ is freedom and new creation.

19. ***Christmas in Galatians.*—Until Christ be formed in you** is but putting Paul's favorite and unique phrase in another pattern (see Expos. on 1:22). A man is "in Christ" when **Christ** [is] **formed** in him. This change turns B.C. into A.D., and every year of life into "the year of my Lord"; the eternal into the contemporary, the end into the beginning. It turns relations with God from a matter of history into a matter of personal experience. The word Jesus used to Nicodemus, "Ye must be born again" (John 3:7), is the possibility of every desiring heart.

Bethlehem becomes therefore not the only place where Christ may be born. Wherever he is loved, there he is born. Wherever he is welcomed, there he is cradled. Wherever he is trusted, there he is wrapped in swadding clothes. That Christ may be formed in each believing heart is, for the man who wills it, "keeping Christmas." Or in the words of an ancient liturgy, "If I love him, I shall be clean. If I touch him, I shall be refined. If I embrace him, I shall be spotless."

A colleague said of a man on his college faculty, "It does not seem to make any difference to that man whether Christ was born or not." In contrast, an English statesman was addressing the League of Nations when a reporter for the *London Times* penned this line, "That man talks like a dedicated man." Men and nations judge themselves by their response to the life that started upon this planet in Bethlehem.

This conception of the eternally contemporary Christ—formed in each believing heart—has been for millions over the centuries the deepest meaning of the Incarnation. This indwelling Christ is the revelation and disclosure of God, the unveiling of his face—surely Christ is that! He is the Jesus of history, who spoke as

19 My little children, of whom I travail
in birth again until Christ be formed in
you,

you. **19** My little children, with whom I
am again in travail until Christ be formed

---

competitors were absent, they might not care enough about the Galatians even to write letters to them.

The ancient scribe who added to vs. 17 the words from I Cor. 12:31, "but earnestly desire the better gifts" (a number of MSS have this reading), knew what Paul was driving at. Paul's challenge to the Judaizers was to imitate him in being sincere and faithful "fathers" of spiritual "children," as he called his converts. (Most MSS have τεκνία, **little children.**) In a bold figure of speech he compares his anxiety to the throes of childbirth. But as usual with his comparisons, he suddenly shifts the reference and applies it to the Galatian Christians who are about to give birth to Christ. His own "labor" now becomes the anxiety of one who is waiting until Christ is "formed" in them. He was filled with misgivings. Had his approach and language been too severe, or had he not been forthright in warning his "children"? If only he could be in Galatia! Then he could gauge the situation more accurately and control it by changing his **tone** (RSV)—**voice** (KJV), "sound," "language." Paul never spoke or wrote a harsh word that he did not speedily regret; cf. his relations with the Corinthians (II Cor. 7:5-13). His opponents attached more weight to his letters than to his person (II Cor. 10:9-11), but he himself was of a different opinion. At best, letter writing was only a partial substitute for his personal presence.

Paul's bold metaphor was realistic for his Gentile readers who were familiar with the rites of initiation into the mystery cults, where the instructor and guide of the initiate became his "father." In Judaism the rabbi was the "father" of those whom he taught, and it was natural for Paul to call himself the father of his converts (I Thess. 2:11; I Cor. 4:15-16). The difference lay in the respective patterns of fatherhood. The

---

man never spoke before, and the bringer of the most significant insights about life and God. But he is more than that; he is the One who takes up residence in willing lives that desire his presence. He whom the heavens could not contain dwells in the heart that wonders, trusts, and loves him. Put the possibilities of that splendor over against a threadbare system of rules and regulations and see the Christ who sets men free.

19. ***Seeing Christ Through Prepositions.***—A brief study in prepositions may sharpen our thinking here. Take a look at three prepositions. First, *for*. "God so loved the world, that he gave his . . . Son" (John 3:16)—a general gift available *for* all mankind. He was and is the Savior of men everywhere and at all times. His availability *for* all men, however, is not to be taken as a general truth or reduced to the level of a fact in history.

Christ is unwilling to be no more than a figure in history, or to be available for mankind only in a general sort of way. He is timeless, and moves more closely to the heart of mankind by coming *to* each man. "Behold, I stand at the door, and knock" (Rev. 3:20). He comes *to*, he stands, he knocks, he waits at the door of every life. He comes *for* all, bringing what only he can bring; but he also comes *to* each, making the gift of all he has more available by his individual call. The preposition which focuses this process is *to*.

Christ is available for all; he comes to each; and to every life that opens its door, he actually enters. His coming is so intimate, so personal, and so permanent that Paul could write about his being **formed in you.** It is possible for Christ to come to birth again in men's lives: a miracle second only to his Resurrection; a phenomenon which is the fuller meaning of the Incarnation. Christ in history is not enough. His Incarnation means his abiding presence as the living Contemporary in every life that receives him. The preposition that expresses this fuller meaning is *in*. He may be born *in* each believing heart, and when such an experience actually happens, a man is "in Christ." "I will come in" (Rev. 3:20), he has promised. Indeed, a man "in Christ" can expect certain and very definite results which affect his total existence.

Christ **formed in you** anticipates a quality of life which only the highest known adjective describes. That adjective is "Christlike." In a world built on speed, haunted with fear and uncertainty, our generation deperately needs—as did the first century—larger reasons for

20 I desire to be present with you now, and to change my voice; for I stand in doubt of you.

in you! **20** I could wish to be present with you now and to change my tone, for I am perplexed about you.

Paul who called his followers "children" was one in whom Christ lived—the Christ who revealed the true meaning of the fatherhood of God. Paul's test for a preacher who aspired to spiritual parenthood was this: Is he sincere, and does he understand the gospel rightly? Is he humble (Phil. 2:3)? Can he bear the cross of Jesus (II Cor. 6:4-10), and does he approve the things that are excellent (Phil. 4:8-9)? Above all, does he rely solely on the grace of God through Christ (2:20)? If the answer is "Yes," then it is a good thing to have such a missionary impress himself upon you and **make much of you** (RSV).

But if the man who seeks to ingratiate himself and to commend his gospel is selfish and conceited; if he desires to dominate; if he is a parasite who asks others to bear his burden while lifting not a finger to help them with theirs; if he preaches in a spirit of faction; if he claims secret knowledge and power available only to those who will join his circle of admirers; if he excludes all who will not acknowledge his word as law; in short, if he seeks followers for the purpose of having followers to seek him, he is not a father but a fraud, and he belongs to that company of exploiters of religion of whom Paul observes ironically, "There must be factions among you in order that those who are genuine among you may be recognized" (I Cor. 11:19). Paul called them "fools," but observed sadly that there were enough people who "suffer fools gladly" to make foolishness in religion a very profitable business (II Cor. 11:18-21). As for himself, he was too "weak" for that!

---

existence and fresh resources for living. As was said of that first century, so it may be said of the twentieth, "Man is about played out." Too many men in high and in humble stations are literally played out. Christlikeness grows when Christ is formed within. It manifests the permanent indwelling of the Son of God.

Formed in you challenges us to study our road maps. Because Christmas and Easter are the north and south poles of the Christian faith, they readily become fitting times for a man to get his bearings. A well-balanced life results from and out of a Christlike sense of direction—as does the sense of one's own true worth and value. If Christ is formed in us, we may put to its full use Isaiah's word: "For unto us a child is born, unto us a son is given; and the government shall be upon his shoulder: and his name shall be called Wonderful, Counselor, The mighty God, The everlasting Father, The Prince of Peace" (Isa. 9:6). When this One is formed in men, he becomes their Counselor, helping them to choose the high way instead of the low, keeping them from choosing futile ways of life that end in blind alleys instead of mountain trails. This Counselor waits to counsel us; this mighty God waits to empower us; this everlasting Father waits to show us how much he cares; this Prince of Peace waits to give peace of mind which may make each of us a channel of that peace.

Formed in you speaks of an inner shrine. When Ralph Waldo Emerson finished reading Gibbon's *History of the Decline and Fall of the Roman Empire,* it is said that he commented, "That man has no shrine."[4] Men need a shrine at the center of their lives to keep them steady, to hold in true perspective the daily job of living, with its hopes and fears, its annoyances and responsibilities. They need a shrine close to the heart of the Eternal, from which light and power can come, so that life may be loyal to great principles and not be subject to minor irritations. In this inner shrine Christ can dwell. There is his proper place of control; there he can put a man in the best control of himself. Such a shrine becomes a very "holy of holies."

Somebody has said that Jesus can give "sunshine to the blind." The man with an inward shrine can confess, "Whereas I was blind, now I see" (John 9:25). Somebody has said that Jesus turns our "sunsets into sunrises." The man with an inward shrine can reply, "He has done that for me, and he has turned my midnights into morning light." Christ is "God's nearest approach to man." The man with an inward shrine testifies quietly, surely, and confidently, "Truly this was the Son of God" (Matt. 27:54). **Formed in you** fulfills the scripture, "We are the children of God" (Rom. 8:16).

[4] Harold A. Bosley, *On Final Ground* (New York: Harper & Bros., 1946), p. 138.

21 Tell me, ye that desire to be under the law, do ye not hear the law?

22 For it is written, that Abraham had two sons, the one by a bondmaid, the other by a free woman.

23 But he *who was* of the bondwoman was born after the flesh; but he of the free woman *was* by promise.

21 Tell me, you who desire to be under
law, do you not hear the law? 22 For it is
written that Abraham had two sons, one
by a slave and one by a free woman. 23 But
the son of the slave was born according to
the flesh, the son of the free woman through

F. An Allegory of Freedom (4:21-31)

1. The Terms of the Allegory (4:21-26)

It remains for Paul to describe the new righteousness in Christ and to press home the ethical responsibilities of faith and freedom. But first he gives another illustration from the Scriptures (Gen. 16–17) to prove that man cannot save himself by obeying law.

Paul's simultaneous allegorical equations illustrate his habit of thinking in terms of opposites:

Hagar	=	slavewoman	=	Sinai	=	law	=	flesh	=	Jerusalem "now"	=	mother of slaves
Sarah	=	freewoman	=	promise	=	faith	=	Spirit	=	Jerusalem "above"	=	mother of freemen

This means that the Jews who refuse to accept Christ are slaves with Jerusalem in Palestine; whereas the Christians, Gentile as well as Jewish, are citizens of the new Jerusalem in heaven.

21. The fundamental proof of Paul's gospel of grace and freedom was the Christian experience of new life in Christ. But in appealing to Jews who did not share that experience, he had to meet his opponents on the common ground of the O.T., which they regarded as verbally inspired. So he challenged all who wanted to be **under law** to hear the law when it was read in the synagogues, and instead of losing themselves in the casuistry of the moment, to examine all the consequences of taking law instead of grace as the way of salvation.

22. To illustrate what happens to those who rely on law Paul allegorizes the case of Ishmael and Isaac, sons of Abraham (Gen. 16:15; 21:3, 9). The Scriptures represent Abraham as a pioneer of faith and obedience, who walked with God, was a friend of God, and was taken into God's confidence. But his family life was marred by the favoritism and friction of polygamy and concubinage, which were to poison the future with feuds between Israel and his neighbors. The mother of Ishmael, the oldest son, was Hagar, the slave of Sarah, the freewoman and wife, the mother of Isaac, the child of promise.

23. The son of the slavegirl, says Paul, was born **according to the flesh.** Σάρξ ("flesh") has to be translated variously according to the context; in the present case the literal "flesh" does not convey Paul's meaning. Both sons were born with normal bodies, bones and muscles, blood and nerves. But the extraordinary thing in the Genesis story is the statement that Sarah was over ninety years old when Isaac, her first and only child, was born. Paul declares that this was possible only through faith. In this sense the son of

21-31. ***The Metropolis of Christianity.***—Paul closes this section of his letter with illustrations from Hebrew history which are not easy for persons who live in another period to understand. In thorough logic, however, he is wise to bring his appeal back once more to the idea of covenant. There he stands on solid ground; for in the covenant freedom is protected, nurtured, and conserved forever (see Expos. on 3:15).

Underneath rather forbidding allegories a clear thread seems to run, a thread that marks the difference between bondage under the ancient law and liberty in Christ. The Galatian converts defined themselves as children of Abraham; but Paul reminds them that Abraham had two kinds of children, one by a **bondmaid** (Hagar), one by a **free woman** (Sarah). Those who desire to live under the law, says Paul, are

24 Which things are an allegory: for these are the two covenants; the one from the mount Sinai, which gendereth to bondage, which is Agar.
25 For this Agar is mount Sinai in Ara-

promise. 24 Now this is an allegory: these women are two covenants. One is from Mount Si′nai, bearing children for slavery; she is Hagar. 25 Now Hagar is Mount Si′nai

---

the freewoman was born **through promise.** Some MSS read "through the promise." Both readings have good support, but since Paul is contrasting "flesh" with "promise" in general terms, the reading without the article is preferable. By comparison, says Paul, Ishmael came into the world as an ordinary flesh-bound mortal, with no particular spiritual aspirations and no noteworthy contribution to make to the religious life of mankind. It was the Isaac branch of Abraham's family that accepted God's covenant, inherited Canaan, and gave Christ to the world; and all Isaac's good things, even as Ishmael's evil things, had been predetermined and promised before either was born.

24. When Paul says that these things are "allegorical utterances," he does not mean that the Genesis story is unhistorical myth, but he sees in it a religious meaning that ranges far beyond the literal history.

Allegorical interpretation rests upon the belief that every word, figure of speech, and grammatical form in scripture has a special "spiritual" significance besides its literal meaning. The theory is that the God who dictated it meant more than rests on the surface, and that while he said one thing, he also meant something else in addition to the literal sense. Paul was not the first to allegorize a sacred book. The Greeks had long since applied the method to explain away the immoral things which the gods said and did in Homer and in their other religiously authoritative poets. Then Greek-speaking Jews, like Philo Judaeus, employed it apologetically to read Greek philosophy into the O.T., proclaiming that Moses had said all these good things long before and better than Homer and Plato.

The wonder is that Paul has so little allegory. His restraint is explained partly by his training as a Pharisee. The rabbis were suspicious of any interpretation of scripture that tended to make Jews lax in their observance of the law. Jews with Gnostic leanings, and those who considered some of their ancestral customs outmoded, could resort to allegory to justify their philosophy and conduct, while maintaining that they were the spiritual superiors of the conservatives who held to the letter of the law. But it was especially the moral earnestness which the Spirit of Christ inspired in Paul that kept him from these extremes of allegorical speculation. He had been nurtured in the Hebrew regard for the actual history of his people, and when he did allegorize, it was usually because he was driven to seek common ground in scriptural authority for his defense of his gospel. His argument, however, is never strengthened by allegorical symbolism and typology, for these are convincing only to those who by imagination can find them so. Rather, as in Rom. 9–11, he introduces unnecessary complications such as the moral difficulties involved in predestination. His gospel does not rest on the quicksands of allegory, a specious method of interpreting scripture. Its interpretations are of interest to the historian not as correct representations of what the writers and first readers of the Bible had in mind, but only as source materials for understanding the life and thought of the allegorists themselves.

It was not allegorical reflection, but Paul's unsuccessful inner conflict with his own intractable nature, that drove him to conclude that all who were born "according to the flesh" were destined to **slavery.** "Hagar," their mother, came from "Sinai," where the law and its curse were at home. All who refused the new covenant of faith forfeited their claim to be Abraham's children. Their punishment was to remain slaves in the "Jerusalem" that was the home of sinful human nature.

25. The text here is uncertain. Most authorities read τὸ γὰρ Ἁγάρ, which KJV translates **for this Hagar;** some omit "Hagar"; and one omits "Sinai." The more probable text is τὸ δὲ Ἁγὰρ Σινᾶ ὄρος ἐστὶν ἐν τῇ Ἀραβίᾳ, "and Hagar is Mount Sinai in

bia, and answereth to Jerusalem which now is, and is in bondage with her children.

26 But Jerusalem which is above is free, which is the mother of us all.

in Arabia;[i] she corresponds to the present Jerusalem, for she is in slavery with her children. 26 But the Jerusalem above is free,

[i] Other ancient authorities read *For Sinai is a mountain in Arabia.*

Arabia." Since this statement is simply another link in the series of identifications begun in vs. 24, it is better to translate δέ as "and" than as **now** (RSV). Some commentators conjecture that the clause originated as a marginal note which later crept into the text. The passage reads smoothly without it, and the conjecture may be correct; but Paul's style is repetitious, and there is no compelling reason to conclude that he did not write it. The verb συστοιχεῖ, **answereth** (KJV), **corresponds** (RSV), is regularly used to draw comparisons and parallels.

26. The **Jerusalem which now is** was a most unholy "Holy City," full of injustice, violence, and murder, and subject to the cruel and wicked rulers imposed by a Gentile empire. But over against this Jerusalem of slavery lay an ideal celestial city, unseen at present, but destined soon to supersede it. Paul called it **the Jerusalem above.** Sarah, the freewoman, was the ancestress of its citizens, who were the people of faith and of freedom in Christ. **Mother of us all** (KJV) translates a text which added πάντων, "all," from Rom. 4:16.

Paul speaks of Jerusalem **above,** because this new city of freedom already exists in heaven where Christ is, where dwell the souls of those who have died in Christ. But it also exists on earth as the church, the body of Christ, whose members are colonists from heaven sent to prepare men for the full establishment of God's kingdom at Christ's second coming (Phil. 3:20; Col. 3:1-3).

The biblical root of this conception of an ideal future and heavenly Jerusalem is Isa. 54. Other descriptions appear in Ezek. 40–48; Zech. 2:1-13; Hag. 2:6-9; Tob. 13:9-18; Ecclus. 36; Pss. Sol. 17:33. Historically the expectation assumed three forms. According to the earliest hope, God would build the new Jerusalem in Palestine and make it the capital of his theocratic world government. The plan of this glorious city was graven upon the palms of his hands (Isa. 49:16). From this idea it was but a step, especially for those influenced by Greek ideas, to think of this ideal Jerusalem as already existing in heaven. According to the Apocalypse of Baruch, God had shown it to Adam in Paradise before he sinned; to Abraham on the night mentioned in Gen. 15:12-21; and to Moses on Sinai, when he gave him the heavenly pattern for an earthly tabernacle (II Baruch 4:1-6; cf. Heb. 12:22). The third conception combined these two ideas. The Jerusalem which was "above" would come down to earth to be established in Palestine in place of the city that "now is" (cf. Rev. 3:12; 21:2, 10; II Esdras 7:26; 13:36; 10:54).

So the new Jerusalem belonged to both worlds and to both ages, to heaven and earth, to the present and the future. Its constitution was the new covenant, and its citizens were the men of faith in Christ, a new kind of freemen who traced their spiritual ancestry through the line of Isaac and his mother Sarah as heirs of God's promise to Abraham. As for Ishmael and his tribe, they were the men of law, predestined to be slaves forever. Needless to say, the Judaizers found Paul's allegorical exclusion of themselves utterly unacceptable. They believed that the Torah was God's blueprint for all creation, and

---

children of Hagar, while those who live in Christ are children of Sarah. Hagar's children go back to Sinai, while Sarah's belong to the new covenant. These two women illustrate for him the old and the new covenants. Even Abraham's relation to Hagar was quite different from his relation to Sarah; therefore only the children of the new covenant will be the full heirs of their father Abraham. It would be sheer tragedy for the Galatians to go back to Hagar and surrender to the Sinai covenant.

Under an illustration even more difficult to interpret, Paul appeals to the **Jerusalem which is above** [and] **is free, which is the mother of us all** (vs. 26). That Jerusalem seems to be for him the perfect pattern of life and society. This pattern is a drawing—more like a picture than a blueprint—of the kingdom of

27 For it is written, Rejoice, thou barren that bearest not; break forth and cry, thou that travailest not: for the desolate hath many more children than she which hath a husband.

28 Now we, brethren, as Isaac was, are the children of promise.

29 But as then he that was born after the flesh persecuted him *that was born* after the Spirit, even so *it is* now.

and she is our mother. 27 For it is written,
"Rejoice, O barren one that dost not
bear;
break forth and shout, thou who art
not in travail;
for the desolate hath more children
than she who hath a husband."
28 Now we,[j] brethren, like Isaac, are children of promise. 29 But as at that time he
who was born according to the flesh persecuted him who was born according to the

[j] Other ancient authorities read *you*.

---

that it would be observed forever in the new Jerusalem. That, they said, was why God was going to purge the old city—to establish an order of life in which perfect obedience to his law would be possible.

2. The Application of the Allegory (4:27-31)

27. A telling item in the counterpropaganda of the legalists was the argument that even among the Christians only a radical fringe consisting mainly of foreign Jews, of whom Paul was one, were proposing to abandon the law of Moses. In reply Paul quoted from a chapter of expansive hope which he found in the book of Isaiah.

In one respect his quotation of Isa. 54:1 does not fit Paul's allegory. It was Sarah, the mother of freemen, who possessed the husband, and Hagar, the slave, who was the deserted woman. As usual with Paul's illustrations (cf. Rom. 7:1-4; 11:17-24), the details cannot be pressed without making them go lame; but his main point is clear. Since his contrast is between Hagar, the outcast, and Sarah, the wife, the definite article should be retained in translating τὸν ἄνδρα, "the husband."

The Isaian figure to describe the plight of Jerusalem during the Babylonian exile grew out of a common experience in Hebrew family life. Childlessness, particularly the failure to bear sons, was great grief and disgrace. Such was the sorrow of Jerusalem; but the prophet bade her look forward with courage to the time when all her scattered children would come back to her (Isa. 54:3). God was her "husband," and he would treat his faithful remnant with everlasting lovingkindness, making them more numerous than the former population and giving them a heritage of great peace and prosperity (Isa. 54:13-17). This was the promise which Paul claimed for those who accepted his gospel. The church of the new covenant was despised as an upstart religion, rejected by those who preferred the old covenant as time-tested and safe, and scorned because it had few members in comparison with other religions. Scanning the future with the eyes of faith, hope, and love, Paul assured his converts of victory and bade them rejoice because the day of rectification was at hand.

28. The Judaizers claimed that Abraham had obeyed the law of Moses by anticipation, and that God's promise was his reward. Consequently the descendants of Isaac were children of promise only if they followed Abraham's example in obeying the law. Paul turned it the other way about: the promise must be taken on faith, not as credit for obedience. Since this admonition was directed especially to Gentile Christians in Galatia who were enamored of law, it is better to read **you** (RSV mg.) than **we.** The latter may be explained as a variant produced by assimilation to vss. 26 and 31. Note the absence of the article before τέκνα, **children.**

29. According to the flesh was always at war with **according to the Spirit.** Neither phrase has the definite article in the Greek. By "according to flesh" Paul characterized Ishmael's birth and rearing as those of a human being without benefit of God's promise and the spiritual status which it conferred. But with Ishmael's flesh-bound descendants he included those of the line of Isaac who refused to accept Christ and who continued

30 Nevertheless what saith the Scripture? Cast out the bondwoman and her
son: for the son of the bondwoman shall
not be heir with the son of the free woman.

Spirit, so it is now. 30 But what does the
scripture say? "Cast out the slave and her
son; for the son of the slave shall not inherit with the son of the free woman."

---

to rely upon their Jewish upbringing and culture, which he himself had written off as a total loss compared with Christ (Phil. 3:2-11). By "according to Spirit" Paul described the birth of Isaac, the child of promise, who typified the new humanity in Christ. Included in Isaac's descendants were all, both Jews and Gentiles, who lived in the Spirit by faith. For them God had prepared what "eye hath not seen, nor ear heard, neither have entered into the heart of man" (I Cor. 2:9).

But, says Paul, all through history this Ishmael and his tribe of "flesh-men" have been persecuting Isaac and his "faith-men." A rabbinical tradition of the second century A.D. interprets the Hebrew participle מצחק (LXX παίζοντα) in Gen. 21:9 to mean that Ishmael's "playing" became so rough that Isaac's life was in danger. This son of a slave is said to have shot arrows at Isaac to kill him, and Paul's statement shows that some such tradition was current in his day. He applied it to the Judaizers who were trying to force the Christians to observe the whole law of Moses, and to the unbelieving Jews who were excommunicating the Christians and their families and getting them into trouble with the civil authorities (1:7; 4:17; 5:10; I Thess. 2:14-16).

30. The quotation is from Gen. 21:10, omitting ταύτην, "this," after παιδίσκην, "slavewoman," and substituting τῆς ἐλευθέρας, "of the free woman," for τοῦ υἱοῦ μου Ἰσαάκ, "my son Isaac," so as to make plain the parallelism of the allegory. The speaker of these words is Sarah, who is filled with rage against Hagar and Ishmael. Abraham is represented as greatly grieved, but God is said to have sanctioned the demand of the cruel and jealous wife. So Paul takes this scripture as the will of God for Isaac and Ishmael.

This story was one of the effects and one of the causes of the perpetual feud between the Israelites and the tribes that descended from Ishmael. The Hebrews were so sure that God wanted them to have Palestine that they found no moral difficulty in saying that it was God himself who had overruled Abraham's conscience (Gen. 17:18-21). They affirmed that Ishmael's character and destiny had been predetermined (Gen. 16:12). Consequently, even his circumcision at the age of thirteen could not make him a member of God's chosen people. However great this innocent victim of a family feud might become by virtue of the halfhearted blessing conceded by an uneasy conscience (Gen. 17:20-21), he and his descendants were barred forever from the higher blessing. Theirs was to submit to the religious imperialism of the most favored nation or die. Moreover, all Abraham's other sons except Isaac were barred from the promise and sent away "unto the east country" (Gen. 25:5-6). And yet while all this was said to be the Lord's doing, it was in the same breath declared to be the doing of the human actors in this drama of the nations. Sarah herself was said to have suggested that Abraham become a father by her Egyptian slave girl. Then, too, it was explained that Hagar's flight from the cruelty of her mistress was voluntary, making her, rather than the callous compliance of Abraham, responsible for her plight "in the wilderness, by the fountain in the way to Shur" (Gen. 16:7).

God. The kingdom is within men; it is among men; it is beyond men. It is a gift, a task, a hope. It is the gift of God; its impulses, power, and meanings start not with men but with him. It is a task in which those who are his work with him. It is a hope, far beyond full accomplishment on this planet. It is a hope in the sense of its partial fulfillment here but its complete fulfillment yonder. If men live and work there, they have found their best reason for living and working here. It is all part of one piece. What is true there is true here. That which can never be fully accomplished here will be fulfilled there. "Eye hath not seen, nor ear heard, neither have entered into the heart of man, the things which God hath prepared for them that love him" (I Cor. 2:9). As the earthly city of Jerusalem formed the ancient center of Judaism, so

31 So then, brethren, we are not children of the bondwoman, but of the free.

5 Stand fast therefore in the liberty wherewith Christ hath made us free, and be not entangled again with the yoke of bondage.

31 So, brethren, we are not children of the slave but of the free woman.

5 For freedom Christ has set us free; stand fast therefore, and do not submit again to a yoke of slavery.

Paul's use of Abraham's expulsion of Hagar and her child has its parallel in the equally heartless treatment of Esau which he employs in Rom. 9–11 in his longer discussion of the divine process of selection. Here too it was assumed that the hatred generated by centuries of war for the possession of Palestine lay in the heart of God. "I hated Esau," said Malachi (1:3), making God the speaker; and Rom. 9:6-13 presses it to the utmost limit of predestination. But the love of God in Christ Jesus made Paul's heart better than his inherited doctrine, and it is in the light of the conclusion of his argument in Rom. 11:25-36 that his allegory of freedom in Galatians must be judged. When the history of the struggle for the possession of "the Holy Land" is allegorized to justify a doctrine of "election" which foredooms countless souls to an eternity of torment in a future hell, it becomes as morally atrocious as it is irreconcilable with Paul's gospel.

Nevertheless Paul's allegory gives the historian an insight into Paul's mind as he wrestled with the insoluble problem of God's sovereignty and human freedom. Throughout history certain individuals and groups, particularly the Hebrews, have risen higher and been more successful than others in translating their conception of God into the good life. Pioneers in religious thought and life have always been subject to persecution by those who want to stay on a lower spiritual plane. Paul was one of these pioneers. He was forever right in his insistence that man's case is hopeless if God deals with him on the basis of obedience to law. He saw that the only sure freedom was that complete commitment to the grace of God in Christ which consists of faith, hope, and love, and balances liberty with obligation. These were the things which Paul was trying to bring home to the Galatians by means of his allegorical illustration.

31. The Greek does not have the definite article with **slave**—therefore, "of a slave." This verse states the conclusion which the Galatians are to draw from the whole argument in chs. 3–4. With it Paul writes his conclusion to his proposition that law is not, never was, and never will be God's way of salvation for man. All it could do was to prove its own frustration through the weakness of human nature. By inciting the will to rebel it multiplied transgressions and compelled men to admit defeat, and thus served as a monitor to bring them to Christ. Only the men of faith were free; all others were slaves.

III. The Responsibility (5:1–6:18)

The remainder of Paul's letter is a plea for the responsible use of freedom. Christian liberty was not license to keep on sinning. Salvation was the grace-gift of God, but it could not be appropriated by reflex action as a starving man might still his hunger. Receiving it was a process of working it out in life (Phil. 2:12-13). In removing the yoke of the law, Christ laid his cross on men's shoulders. That meant creative self-investment in the

---

this **Jerusalem which is above** is the metropolis of Christianity. What grander crescendo could Paul voice than that in 5:1, which really closes this section of his letter, "Stand fast therefore in the liberty wherewith Christ hath made us free." (But see Exeg.)

31. See Expos. on vss. 7, 31.

5:1. ***Paul's Crescendo of Freedom.***—(See Expos. on 4:5-7.) If Christ is the source of grace, freedom is the climax or ripened fruit of grace. Grace and freedom are master words with Paul; all else that he wrote is subhead and detail. This verse and 2:20 are the two highwater marks of the entire Galatian letter: "Freedom in Christ." The remainder of the letter is a plea for, a description of, and a guide into the compulsions of a free man.

1. ***Freedom Through Truth.***—The Christian faith makes men **free** because Christ is truth. "If ye continue in my word, . . . ye shall know

lives of others for his sake. Christian freedom made the believer a slave of Christ, and the only way to use it rightly, and to preserve and extend it, was continuous production of the fruit of his Spirit. Actually this freedom was harder than the way of law; hence the temptation to go back to Moses, where indecision and doubt could be resolved by the religious authorities.

A. To Preserve and Make Right Use of Freedom (5:1-15)

1. By Resisting Every Proposal to Return to Slavery (5:1)

5:1. Paul's abrupt transition from allegory to admonition has produced a series of textual complications. The reading which best explains all the others is τῇ ἐλευθερίᾳ ἡμᾶς Χριστὸς ἠλευθέρωσεν στήκετε οὖν. The RSV places the punctuation mark after ἠλευθέρωσεν and translates, **For freedom Christ has set us free; stand fast therefore.** The KJV, translating a text which inserts the relative pronoun ᾗ after ἐλευθερίᾳ, gives a very different meaning: **Stand fast therefore in the liberty wherewith Christ hath made us free.** A third variant substitutes the relative ᾗ for the article τῇ, and thereby links this verse to the last clause of 4:31, giving the following meaning: ". . . we are not children of a slave, but of the freewoman, by virtue of the freedom for which Christ has set us free." This makes στήκετε οὖν, "Stand fast, therefore," begin the new chapter. Still another possibility is that Paul wrote ἐπ' ἐλευθερίᾳ, "for freedom," in vs. 1, as he did in vs. 13, but that some primitive error replaced ἐπ', "for," by the article τῇ. It is best, however, to take this verse as the beginning of ch. 5, and to render it in some such way as does the RSV.

The expression **for freedom** (in slightly different Greek form) appears in the certificates of sacral manumission which were given to slaves who purchased their freedom. The slave would deposit the money in the temple of his god for the priest to transfer to

---

the truth, and the truth shall make you free" (John 8:31-32).

No word needs more to be singled out in our day and underscored than the word "truth." Take only its human dimensions. An increasing stock pile of lies, false witness, and half-truths has brought about a famine of truth in the land and throughout the world. Mankind cannot long survive in such a famine. The axles of God's universe turn upon truth and will not tolerate the falsehoods of men. Where truth is sought, known, proclaimed, and abided by, only there is freedom. The scientist who has a reverence and enthusiasm for the truth of the natural world, and will labor hour after hour in the laboratory to discover another tiny bit of it, brings man on toward freedom from disease, superstition, fear, and unnecessary toil. Concern for the truth in the field of education brings us on toward freedom from the bondage of ignorance, provincialism, and small-mindedness. Mental anguish is the child of misconceptions, unfounded fears, undue worry, and self-centeredness; mental health stems from the cleansing power of truth—truth about God, the world, and ourselves. No successful solution of the problem of world peace can be worked out on the basis of deceit, falsehood, intrigue, or selfish nationalism; only truth—the full truth—can set the world free from war and misery. Imperialism is not the truth. "My country right or wrong" is not the truth. National integrity, international justice and co-operation are the truth—because they square with the moral law of God's universe. And they bring us on toward freedom. Truth is freedom, liberating the human spirit from those things that press it down and enslave it, setting it on the road toward the highest reaches of human possibility.

So Christianity is a redemptive religion because it is the religion of truth; it is the truth about God, about man, and about human relationships. It is not myth. It is not a set of abstract ideas. It is not an assembling of truths to which may be added other truths. It is ultimate truth, living truth, from which all these bits of truth find their validity. As man comes to know truth, personalized and dramatized in Christ, he discovers himself and his freedom. And that freedom no man can take from him. It is freedom in the spirit that defies the circumstances of a man's earthly existence.

As Christians we have in our possession this living truth. Our faith is established upon the rock of truth. The life of Christ is real, more real than the Rock of Gibraltar. No amount of talk about legends can destroy that fact. The records of what he said and did are real, an account that is consistent in itself and consistent with other records. His words and deeds are

2 Behold, I Paul say unto you, that if ye be circumcised, Christ shall profit you nothing.	2 Now I, Paul, say to you that if you receive circumcision, Christ will be of no

his master "for freedom." He then became the slave of his god, free from his human master. The drawback was that the slave himself had to provide the money. Not so with the Christian, whose freedom was God's grace-gift through Christ. The definite article with **freedom** needs to be stressed, although to say "this freedom" would be somewhat to overtranslate it. Paul is not speaking of what non-Christians call freedom, but of a particular kind of freedom—the freedom with which his whole letter is concerned (3:23-29; 4:9, 31). Christians, and Christians alone, are destined "for this freedom"; the KJV **wherewith** overlooks this context. God had destined men for it, knowing full well the risk and the pain he might have to suffer because of man's misuse of it (3:13; 4:4).

Paul's illustration went straight home to the common life. Some of his converts had been, or still were, slaves of men. Those who gained their liberty by purchase or gift might be expected to value it so highly that they would hold fast to it. But sometimes a freedman found that liberty brought troubles and responsibilities which he had not anticipated. So too with the Christians, who being free from law had to make their own decisions under the guidance of the Spirit. Like the Israelites under Moses, some wavered and longed for the easier life of a slave. Paul pleaded with them not to think of thrusting themselves into the yoke of the Torah or any other law. If they permitted the Judaizers to fasten the yoke once more upon their shoulders, they might never get free again.

2. By Recognizing That Law Can Add Nothing to Grace (5:2-6)

2. Law and grace were mutually exclusive ways of salvation. Reception of circumcision would prove that the Galatians did not have full confidence in Christ. They would rely more and more upon their own efforts, while seeing less and less value in him. Paul

---

still unassailable. And what is more, he is living yet. The faith of millions is anchored upon that truth. It is upon such truth that Christians stake their lives. In it they find their freedom. The more Christian they are, the more free they become; the more God-centered, the less self-centered; the more spiritual, the less a slave to the things of earth, the flesh, and time.

Does it matter then that Christ is truth? The truth always matters. If God is love, then I must love my neighbor as myself; if God cares, then I must have a holy concern for my fellows; if God is righteous, then I must live righteously; if God has a plan, then I must voluntarily be part of his plan. Christian truth means nothing—it brings no freedom—until it is truth appropriated.

Luther gave clear expression to the concept of freedom through truth in his classic treatise, *The Freedom of a Christian Man.* Following the thought of Paul, he discovered this inner spiritual freedom through faith. Christ the truth, who alone can cleanse and redeem, is to be apprehended in no other way. Faith is the sole condition of justification. It is the means of moral renewal and personal victory. It lifts the believer out of the bondage to sin, law, and death. It makes possible the exchange of the righteousness of God for self-righteousness. It frees one from the delusion that the inner man can be justified by outward works. It snatches victory from the hand of death by assuring the believer of the spiritual dominion of Christ. It is no narrow word. Much of the discussion about faith and reason, as to whether they are contradictory or complementary, is missing the mark. Faith is the confident and receptive mind, humbling itself that it may be filled with truth; faith is the loyal and adoring heart, giving itself that it may find divine communion; faith is the active and obedient will, surrendering itself that it may know true righteousness.

Faith, truth, and freedom form a perfect chain in the Christian life. Knowledge of the divine truth comes by faith and sets men free. As man freely accepts the promises of God he is able more faithfully to obey the commands of God. Augustine phrased it, "Grant grace and command what thou wilt." As man responds fully to the truth of God he is delivered from the bondage to ignorance. As he lives in Christ by faith, God's victory over sin and death becomes his own victory.

In this spiritual framework Luther proclaimed the freedom of a Christian man: "A Christian man is a perfectly free lord of all,

3 For I testify again to every man that is circumcised, that he is a debtor to do the whole law.

advantage to you. [3] I testify again to every man who receives circumcision that he is

---

could not be satisfied with the legalists' view that Christ would still be the great hero of faith, the masterful teacher of the law, the good example and inspiration, the expected Messiah. Christ was either the only Savior or no savior at all. Those who were circumcised before they heard of Christ must give up all reliance upon it. This does not mean necessarily that the Gentile Christians in Galatia had already yielded to the demands of the Judaizers, but only that some of them were strongly inclined to do so. To make the matter clear the RSV has changed **if ye be circumcised** (KJV) to **if you receive circumcision** (cf. vs. 3).

3. Every man that is circumcised (KJV) is misleading. Jewish Christians who had been circumcised before they heard the gospel of Christ were not debtors to do the whole law or any part of it. The adverb **again** does not refer to what has just been said in vs. 2, or to anything else in the present epistle, but more probably to warnings which Paul had uttered on some occasion when he was in Galatia (1:9; 4:16). The sinner's debt **to do the whole law** (KJV) was so crushing that he could only declare himself bankrupt and trust solely to the mercy of his Creditor.

---

subject to none. A Christian man is a perfectly dutiful servant of all, subject to all."[5] This is the paradox of Christian freedom: that the Christian who participates in the victory of Christ by faith is lord, master over sin and death; yet in deep gratitude for his freedom, he gladly serves his fellow men. He becomes not only a lord but a priest, which is "more excellent," a servant of servants.

2-7. *Grace, the Great Conserver.*—Grace gathers up the faith of the fathers as into a reservoir and turns that reservoir into a fountain (see Expos. on 1:3). "I am not come to destroy, but to fulfil" (Matt. 5:17), said Jesus; such was also Paul's desire and spirit. The traditions of the fathers were not to be destroyed, but fulfilled. The first part of ch. 5 seems to summarize the Hebrew tradition as it comes to grips with faith in Christ and the work of grace. Paul's own life demonstrates the reservoir-fountain idea in epitome for all men. It was a reservoir into which had flowed the streams of his ancient heritage, a heritage which he never despised or depreciated. Instead, he gloried in it, as he did in his Roman citizenship. It was because his Christian gospel was rooted in Hebrew monotheism that it was kept from having any relation in fact or appearance to the mystery cults of his day. Yet even God under the law could not or did not do what he could do and has done through grace. In Christ all ages meet. In him and through him are conserved the highest hopes, the best plans, the holiest purposes, and the bravest dreams.

A concluding line in the account of the Transfiguration (Matt. 17:1-8) adds a thought that is related to this conception of grace as the conserver of the best in all the yesteryears.[6] The disciples present were Peter, James, and John. As the events and experiences of that day were coming to an end, the greatest experience of all was theirs: "And when they had lifted up their eyes, they saw no man, save Jesus only." Moses and Elijah, representing respectively the law and the prophets, laid down their commissions at Christ's feet and retired. But in their retirement the mission of the law and the prophets was not exhausted—"the bush was not consumed"—it was fulfilled and illuminated. Moses and Elijah shine afterward in the reflected light of Christ: the way to understand them is to read history backward. Their methods of fellowship with God in their day, their visions of a better world, their practical guides for living, the background they provide for Jesus, their custody of the moral law, all abide. Especially does the moral law, as climaxed in the Ten Commandments, provide ways, means, and tools for applying the spirit and grace of Christ. In Christ these ancient truths have larger and new meanings. They serve as a teaching function in the hands of grace, but are clearly secondary to grace. As moral principles they are now written on man's inward parts, and grace as power makes possible their fulfillment.

But grace was also to Paul a filter which cleanses and refines the ancient streams of life, law, and culture. It was a light to distinguish

[5] *A Treatise on Christian Liberty.*

[6] Certain selections from sermons by Oscar F. Blackwelder in H. F. Miller, ed., *Epistle Messages* (Philadelphia: United Lutheran Publication House, 1933) have been incorporated in this Exposition. Through the kindness of the publishers, permission has been granted for the use of this material.

4 Christ is become of no effect unto you, whosoever of you are justified by the law; ye are fallen from grace.
5 For we through the Spirit wait for the hope of righteousness by faith.

bound to keep the whole law. 4 You are severed from Christ, you who would be justified by the law; you have fallen away from grace. 5 For through the Spirit, by faith, we wait for the hope of righteous-

4. "You have lost effective contact with Christ—you who seek to be declared righteous in law; you have fallen away from grace." **By the law** for ἐν νόμῳ, "in law," obscures Paul's metaphor of "falling out" of the sphere of grace and back into the sphere of law (cf. Intro., p. 434), where men seek vainly to make themselves acceptable to God by selecting and obeying such of its provisions as suit their syncretic fancy. The verb in 4*b* cannot be translated by **are justified** (KJV) because Paul insisted that no man ever was, or is, or can be accepted as righteous (justified) on the basis of law. The fact that the word **grace** has the article means that Paul is thinking of the grace of God through Christ which is the subject of this epistle.

5. Christians therefore must commit themselves solely to God's grace: "For we, by a Spirit which comes through faith, wait for a righteousness for which we hope."

The KJV follows the Greek in making the **we** emphatic, contrasting the Christians as men of faith with the Judaizers as men of law. The language is so compact that Paul's

between the changing and the unchanging. It conserved the priceless and the timeless, and it separated the tradition and rules of the moment from moral principles that are eternal. It enabled a man to discern between what is necessary at a given period in history and what is permanently required. Rules are thus distinguished from principles and, what is of greater significance, both cease to be iron weights and become guides for daily living. Let it be said with every possible emphasis that the grace of Christ did not abrogate moral laws. What had been true was and is still true.

Moral law, however, performs for the Christian man a totally different function from that which it performed for Paul "before Christ." It serves as a mirror, a yardstick, and a plumb line for the Christian's daily use. It is not now in the hands of a slave overseer but in the hands of the individual himself, who in turn is controlled by the indwelling Christ. In this sense the words, so capable of abuse, can be understood, "Love Christ and do what you please." Paul, with the mind that was in Christ Jesus, took off the trammels of law and fear and set the Christian religion down firmly in the area of liberty and life.

5. *Waiting Before God.*—Men of the twentieth century dislike the word **wait.** In a generation of gadgets, when speed is made possible by timesaving and laborsaving machines, there is nothing attractive about waiting. However, educationally, psychologically, and religiously, waiting is profoundly significant and invaluable. Only by waiting are some of the choicest possessions of life attained.

Waiting is the way to renew the strength of one's soul. "The LORD is my shepherd. . . . He restoreth my soul" (Ps. 23:1, 3). Sheep and shepherds do not move about in a hurry; instead they do a great deal of waiting. When one is waiting before the Lord, or is waiting on the Lord, or is waiting upon the Lord, he moves with the calmness of a shepherd.

We are assured by a mighty word of scripture that proper waiting will bring renewed resources: "They that wait upon the LORD . . . shall mount up with wings as eagles" (Isa. 40:31). The prophet seems to say, They that wait upon the Lord soar above the emergencies of life. "They shall run, and not be weary," for they shall be ready for every extraordinary requirement. "They shall walk, and not faint," for they shall be able to handle the responsibilities of every day. We are assured that waiting upon the Lord will bring sufficient resource for all three kinds of experience—and soon or late they come to each of us.

Waiting embodies a dimension which modern man deeply needs. Quiet intervals are necessary for him if he is to secure emotional calm, to gain that inner sight which empowers the soul. The secret of life lies farther down. By work we do things; by our waiting before God we rest in him.

The people who are too busy to be in a hurry have their hand on a master clue to living. They know they cannot discharge their long list of obligations if they hurry. The only way to put an end to restlessness is to rest in the eternal calm of the Prince of Peace, the Wonderful, the Counselor. There is a very intelligent man who keeps a vacant chair in one room of his home. It is kept for a very special friend: Jesus

meaning has to be inferred from 3:14; 5:22-23; and Rom. 8:23-26. Although the article is not used here with "Spirit," the phrase refers to the Spirit of God's Son. He creates faith, hope, and love, and gives patience and strength to wait for the perfect righteousness which will come with the redemption of the body, and which will be confirmed by God's verdict of acceptance on the day of Judgment. The Spirit comes "out of" the realm of faith—ἐκ πίστεως—"into" the hearts of believers in Christ in response to their faith. Ἐλπίδα δικαιοσύνης ἀπεκδεχόμεθα means, "we wait for a hoped-for righteousness"; the verb implies intense expectation. "I hope" is the inseparable present companion of "I wait." Since the Christian already has the first installment of the righteousness of Christ, the phrase **hope of righteousness** must be explained as hope for God's acquittal and acceptance, and for the full realization of the perfection which he has promised. Here Paul is using the word δικαιοσύνη with its dual meaning of "righteousness" and "acceptance as righteous." The translation of δικαιοῦσθε in vs. 4 by **justified** and of δικαιοσύνης in vs. 5 by **righteousness** prevents the English reader from seeing the connection between the two words (see on 2:15-16).

Christ. Beside it he places his own chair. After a period of silence he quietly leans his head back, and with eyes closed, quotes words from the lips of Jesus which he has read and memorized from the Bible. Those verses help him vividly to realize the presence of his Lord. Many would say that such a procedure is utterly superficial; but the genuineness of that man's experience with Christ is reflected in his professional skill, in his wide interest in social welfare, and in his desire to lay the mind of Christ alongside this distorted earth so that men who are tortured by the difference may rise up to labor in the kingdom.

Such rest brings to mind the remark of a salesgirl in answer to a customer who wanted to buy a compass. Her reply was, "We have the kind of compass you draw circles with, but not the kind you go places with." From such rest comes a sense of direction, purpose, balance, and proportion. It is the compass to go places with.

The ability to wait before the Lord has been one of the secrets of all the truly great wayfarers on the Christian voyage. Was it David Livingstone who said, "Without him, not one step; with him, anywhere"? Those who are acquainted with Livingstone's life know that he achieved his utter confidence in Christ by no other means. His was the spirit of another who prayed, "Whatever the future holds for me, dear Lord, as long as thou art with me on my path, I have no fear." It was so with Luther. On particularly busy and fateful days he would always get up several hours earlier than usual so that he could wait upon the Lord. No wonder such people are strong, courageous, and useful. Waiting is for them the key to the day and the lock to the night. It means looking into the face of God before and after looking into the face of men. It means confession of sin, the acknowledgment of complete dependence upon God, childlike but not childish faith, and always a heart that wonders, trusts, and loves.

George L. Robinson has given us an interesting and suggestive outline of the rather stubborn little book of Jonah. Ch. 1 tells of Jonah's disobedience: his "running away from God." Ch. 2 is Jonah's prayer: his "running to God." Ch. 3 is Jonah's preaching: his "running with God." Ch. 4 voices Jonah's complaints: his "running ahead of God." [7] Waiting before the Lord turns disobedience and complaints into prayer, witness, and service.

5-6. ***Faith as Adventure.***— (See Expos. on 1:23.) **Wait for the hope of righteousness by faith . . . which worketh by love.** "I do not know how this old world is coming out, but I believe that the future belongs to those who belong to Christ." The man who said that is waiting for the dawn, but he is not busy with charts figuring out the second coming of Christ. He is, rather, alert to hope's true business. His faith is waiting for righteousness to triumph, but at the same time is working in courageous love. And that because the Christian man is more than a receiver. He refuses to sit with folded hands, leaving things to happen in God's good time. "The joy of release, the peace of conscience, the escape from condemnation, the pulsating life of freedom in Christ—all this the creative dynamic doctrine of justification should bring to the men of today as it brought it to Martin Luther." [8]

A young man planning to be married said to his pastor, "After all, marriage is a leap in the dark." The pastor replied, "It can be a leap in the light." That is the difference faith in Christ can make. Such faith turns on a light which changes all of life from a gamble in the dark

[7] *The Twelve Minor Prophets* (New York: George H. Doran Co., 1926), p. 77.

[8] John Roy Strock, "On Justification by Faith," *The Lutheran Church Quarterly*, XVII (1944), 300.

6 For in Jesus Christ neither circumcision availeth any thing, nor uncircumcision; but faith which worketh by love.

ness. 6 For in Christ Jesus neither circumcision nor uncircumcision is of any avail,

---

6. It was quite possible for those who rejected law as a way of salvation to think it meritorious in God's sight not to be circumcised. That, says Paul, would make them just as legalistic as the Judaizers (I Cor. 7:18-19). Faith was the one thing needful, and nothing added, subtracted, or substituted could set a man right with God. But this faith was active, δἰ ἀγάπης ἐνεργουμένη, "activated through love." **By love** (KJV) and **through love** (RSV) interpret the participle in the sense of faith "operative" and "effective." This makes love the instrument of faith, as if it were faith that generated the love of which Paul is speaking. But in vs. 22 faith, together with love, is a product of the Spirit of Christ. According to Paul, the Spirit produces faith, hope, and love, and the greatest of them is love (I Cor. 13:13). The most wonderful thing he can say of God is that the initiative of God's grace creates the faith by which man responds to this love. **In Christ Jesus,** i.e., in union with Christ as a member of his body the church, man's faith is activated by God's love to invest in the lives of others and reproduce itself in them.

No passage in Paul's letters is of greater importance for integral understanding of his religion and the relation of his faith to his ethics. The mutuality of faith, hope, and

---

to an adventure in the light. Faith as adventure shows Christ as "life's invincible surmise,"[9] life's most glorious thesis and postulate. People with such faith are harnessed to God by their faith; doing good is the spontaneous fruit of that faith. Men of science are constantly devising new hypotheses upon which to experiment. Advancing steps in Christian experience, strategy, and work are like that too. Life is what William James called "forced action." No one can wait to make up his mind; he is already making up his life on some kind of pattern. There is no such thing as presumptionless thinking. Every one, including every experimentalist, has his point of view. Make no mistake about it: he has his thesis, his postulate, his assumptions. A Christian with precisely the same mental processes chooses his thesis, his postulate, his assumption; he chooses Christ as his springboard into life, his reason for existence.

> Finding, following, keeping, struggling,
> Is he sure to bless?
> "Saints, apostles, prophets, martyrs,
> Answer, 'Yes.'"[1]

"Faith without works is dead" was the conclusion which James reached (Jas. 2:26); but James was not proposing to substitute works for faith. Works are the evidence of whether the faith one confesses is alive or dead. A faith that sets a man right with God must make him right with men. When Christ of free grace grants him eternal life, he is in debt all the rest of his days. He needs to do something about his existence, something that is in keeping with his possession. It is like hearing a glorious symphony, only to have the Divine Imperative tap the hearer's conscience and whisper, "Do something about it." When one reads a truly great book, sees a painting that haunts one's best self, achieves a profound friendship, shares an experience that makes all of life grander thereafter—the same Divine Imperative speaks, "Do something about it." Men who have known the great redemption can do no other than to move out into the great adventure.

Faith as adventure explains the life service of Paul. It explains the life service of Martin Luther, of John Wesley, of Wilfred Grenfell, of Albert Schweitzer. It explains the life service, perhaps unknown beyond a small community and there often misunderstood, of humble saints of God everywhere. It is the story of a man made just by faith who determines to heal and build every broken and incomplete life upon which he can lay hold.

A sign along many highways, likely painted and put there by loving hands and a heart yearning for men's salvation, reads for the passer-by, "Jesus Saves." True—everlastingly true; but Jesus saves for what? Why must only a small minority within the church fellowship of the supposedly "saved" find sufficient joy in their faith and life to adventure beyond their own comfort and convenience?

We recover ancient liturgies; but what liturgies are we writing today? We turn to classical theologians; but what growing conceptions of God and man are we confessing today as evidence that God is keeping his promise of the Holy Spirit to lead us into all truth? We turn

[9] George Santayana, "O World, Thou Choosest Not."

[1] John M. Neale, "Art thou weary, art thou troubled?" From the Greek.

7 Ye did run well; who did hinder you that ye should not obey the truth?

8 This persuasion *cometh* not of him that calleth you.

9 A little leaven leaveneth the whole lump.

but faith working through love.
7 You were
running well; who hindered you from obeying the truth? 8 This persuasion is not from
him who called you. 9 A little yeast leavens

love—a theme repeated with many variations—runs through everything he has written and forms the substance of his theology. In vs. 5 he makes hope the future tense of faith; in vs. 6 love is the present tense, and is the activator of faith and hope. For this reason Paul's religion is distorted whenever his ethics and his "good works" are made to appear as an incidental by-product of his faith rather than as one of its essential ingredients. The practice of dividing Paul's letters into "doctrinal" and "practical" sections is a serious misrepresentation of Paul's conception.

3. By Preventing Interference with Runners in the Christian Race (5:7-12)

7-8. Running is Paul's favorite word for the effort required to reach the goal of Christlikeness (2:2; Rom. 9:16; I Cor. 9:24-26; Phil. 2:16; 3:14; II Thess. 3:1). Jesus, at home in the country, likened the hindrances to God's kingdom to weeds in a wheat field; Paul, a man of the city, compared them with obstructions on the race track. Someone has distracted the Galatians' concentration by "cutting in"—ἐνέκοψεν—with an argument concerning the right way to win the prize. Paul's question, taken in connection with "whoever he is" in vs. 10 and his surprise in 1:6, shows that he did not know the trouble-makers by name. The inference from vs. 11 is that some of them were claiming his example for the additions they were proposing for his gospel. They were bent on convincing the Galatians that they ought to be running in the opposite direction, back to Moses. Paul warned them that the only way to obey **truth** was to go forward with Christ. Since he was contrasting truth with falsehood, the textual reading which omits the article with "truth" is more likely to be correct. The reference is to gospel truth as Paul was preaching it (2:5, 14). **Persuasion** is "persuasion" in the sense of "pressure," or an attempt to persuade. The pressure had not yet succeeded. The revisers change **calleth** to **called;** but the verb is really in the present tense, and it is not likely that Paul's thought was limited to the call which came with the Galatians' first hearing of the gospel. The one who "is calling" is God (cf. 1:6). It is God's continuing call which summons the runners to turn a deaf ear to the siren voices of the "persuaders" and get on with their race.

9. In the religious symbolism of Paul's day yeast was sometimes good, more often sinister. It could stand for the kingdom of God, but it could also represent the malign

to old hymns; but what tunes and poems are we composing today to make vocal the deathless aspirations of the human soul? What are the responsibilities of churchmen who believe in the Abiding Presence and the Living Word?

One title of the Pope of Rome is *Pontifex Maximus,* which may be translated "the greatest bridgebuilder." Those who are outside the Church of Rome challenge that claim; they insist that the whole church of Christ is the world's greatest bridgebuilder—building bridges between nations, bridges between races, bridges between denominations, bridges between the have's and the have-not's, bridges between the haunted heart of the world and the cross of Christ.

There is a constant flow of righteousness from Jesus Christ into the life that trusts him. It flows out to men and through men in right desires, right choices, right relations, right actions, the right quality of life, right motives, right spirit. The man who trusts Christ is not only declared righteous; he also has righteousness given to him. That man attempts something for mankind beyond his own health, success, and security. He becomes concerned not alone with what Christ gives him but also with what Christ can give to others through him because he is righteous.

9. *The Uncommon Man Is the Free Man.*—A few men started the Nazi movement; a few men started Marxian communism. Minorities can

10 I have confidence in you through the Lord, that ye will be none otherwise minded: but he that troubleth you shall bear his judgment, whosoever he be.

11 And I, brethren, if I yet preach cir-

the whole lump. 10 I have confidence in the Lord that you will take no other view than mine; and he who is troubling you will bear his judgment, whoever he is. 11 But if I, brethren, still preach circumcision, why

influence of the Herods. Paul contrasted the old Passover with the new covenant and admonished the Christians to purge out the old leaven of malice and evil, and eat nothing but the unleavened bread of sincerity and truth (I Cor. 5:7-8). The Galatians are warned against the action of a gospel adulterated with legalism—silent, pervasive, corruptive. They must purge it at once.

10. With constructive tact and a faith that will not give them up, Paul expresses hope for the majority and offers a warning for the few.

Paul says, lit., "I am confident in the Lord"—not **through the Lord**—"in respect of you, that you will have in mind not one other thing." This is not equivalent to saying **that you will take no other view than mine** (RSV). Paul is not appealing for loyalty to himself and his views, nor to ecclesiastical authority, whether his own or that of others, but to the harmonizing, bodybuilding mind of Christ (Phil. 2:1-11; I Cor. 12:12–13:13). His faith is in Christ's holding power. This is more than the confidence which one friend places in another. It is his assured expectation that the Christ who has set the Galatians free will keep them so forever by conforming them more and more to his mind and Spirit.

Thus Paul kept his appeal on the high level of freedom. In this brief letter he does not say what the **judgment** will be for those who misuse their freedom by substituting a synthetic religion of grace and law for salvation by grace. But in writing to the Corinthians he says that the end of "false apostles" and "deceitful workmen" will "correspond to their deeds" (II Cor. 11:13, 15); and as for the sincere but unskilled workman who builds on the right foundation but uses materials unsuited for an eternal temple, his work will be burned up, "though he himself will be saved, but only as through fire" (I Cor. 3:15).

11. Paul now turns abruptly to the charge made, not by the Judaizers, but by the radical anti-legalists, saying in effect, "And as for me, brothers, if it is true that I am

change the world. Paul well knew that the Christian movement in his day would be a minority movement; he craved that the Galatians be in that minority, and said to them: "You started all right. Who has hindered you? Not anybody on Christ's side" (vss. 7-8).

The farther one gets from Jesus the larger the number of people he finds. Christ's agony in the Garden of Gethsemane is a sharp illustration of that fact. Deep in the garden was Jesus alone—the smallest possible minority. Nearer the garden's edge lay Peter, James, and John asleep; but they were there. Outside the garden were the other disciples, minus Judas. On the perimeter was the crowd. One, three, eight—the crowd. The farther one gets from Jesus the larger the numbers.

Jesus took a handful of ordinary men, so ordinary that one of them was largely known for the fact that he was not somebody else (Judas not Iscariot), and another because he was short (James the Less); but Jesus lived with them, instructed them, empowered them, and said, "Ye are the salt of the earth" (Matt. 5:13). What an aristocracy! "Ye are the light of the world" (Matt. 5:14). To be like them was Paul's plea to the Galatians.

In every generation Jesus takes the average man, like the apostle Andrew, fills him with new longings, everlasting ideals, a larger spirit, a fresh consecration, opens for him infinite resources, and thus makes him into an uncommon man. And he takes the already uncommon man of superior talent and capacity, such as Paul, and Albert Schweitzer, and binds him to life with new cords, surcharges him with a profound sense of responsibility to men and accountability to God, holds him under the light of God, gives him moral and spiritual sensitivity and power—all to make him into the kind of uncommon man the world can trust. (But cf. Exeg.; see Expos., 5:13–6:10.)

11. ***The Cross as Example.***—(See Expos. on 3:13.) It is logical for Paul to turn to the Cross as he begins the closing of his letter to the Galatians. The Cross belongs in this section of

cumcision, why do I yet suffer persecution? then is the offense of the cross ceased.

am I still persecuted? In that case the stumbling-block of the cross has been re-

'still preaching the necessity of circumcision,' why am I still being persecuted? In that case the scandal of the Cross has been abolished."

Paul was not an undiscriminating, irresponsible radical. He did not think of Christianity as a new religion, but as the fulfillment of an old one. In carrying out his missionary task he continued to observe customs which did not conflict with his gospel of salvation by grace alone. He became "all things to all men" in order that he "might by all means save some" (I Cor. 9:22). But wherever there was danger that his actions might be misinterpreted as implying belief in work-salvation he was adamant. He refused to have Titus circumcised (2:3); and in view of Luke's tendency to smooth the jagged edges of Paul's controversy with the Judaizers, we cannot be certain of the report that he had circumcised Timothy (Acts 16:3-4). Although that incident might well account for the charge that Paul was still preaching circumcision, it is hard to see how he could have evaded mention and explanation of it in connection with his affirmation of emphatic refusal in the case of Titus, if it had occurred and were known to the Galatians.

The real animus of the charge lay in the doctrine of the Cross as Paul was preaching it. The great majority of both Jews and Gentiles regarded the Cross as something worse than an **offense** (KJV) or a **stumbling-block** (RSV). To express their feeling we have to keep the Greek σκάνδαλον ("scandal") in English. The belief that a messianic pretender who had been crucified for treason was the Son of God was an intolerable "scandal" to all religious imperialists, whether Jews or Romans; and the gospel of a God who could suffer by sending his Son to die for sinners instead of punishing them

the letter (5:2–6:10), which may be labeled "conduct" or "life." Not the law but the Cross is the center of Christian conduct. The Cross rules out all other motives and sources except the reclaiming and the persuasion of the Christian heart. Christian virtues form the circumference of a life which has the Cross as its hub. Christian graces derive from Christ's grace; and that means the Cross.

Paul had few if any other sharper tests of his own Christian life than his thorn in the flesh (4:14). The grace of Christ, and the Cross as the highest expression of that grace, provided the power by which Paul managed his thorn. The Cross is not only the way by which Christ redeems and sets men free from whatever enslaves them; it is also an example of the quality of life which Christ expects from those whom he has set free. This is sometimes called the "moral influence" theory of the Atonement.

The Cross has indeed profoundly influenced men both within and outside the Christian fellowship. It sets forth a kind of life and a way of dealing with opposition and handicaps which have never been excelled. On the most conservative basis one may claim that no other event in history has inspired so much sacrificial living and unselfish work as has the Cross. It is their profound loss that many people stop with that; for no matter how practical and useful this approach may prove to be, those who see the Cross only as example will never speak the profoundest words of the Christian life. With well-nigh equal emphasis it needs to be said that those who think only in terms of "substitution" and "reconciliation" are likely to lose sight of the moral and social implications of the Cross. The Cross is the supreme example of the kind of life men can have when they are Christlike.

Only a Christ who gave his all could have moved Paul to hazard his all. Paul found in the Cross the motive for risking his life and the cause that was worth risking it for. The Cross gave him a sense of destiny. No Cross of Christ —then for Paul no imprisonment, no persecutions, no lashes, no shipwreck, no daring! For Paul the Cross meant, in addition to its deeper aspects, the ideal and the spirit of his life.

A man at a community good-will dinner, thinking no doubt of anti-Semitism, said to his neighbor at the table, "We will never have genuine good will in this city until you clergymen talk less about the Cross." The clergyman replied: "I am afraid you do not understand what the Cross means and does. It has inspired more sacrificial living and has transformed more selfishness than any other single fact in history. From it flows the good will we desire in this town. The question is not, 'Who put Jesus to death?' but rather, 'What does his death mean?' "

There are several well-known ways to get

12 I would they were even cut off which trouble you.

moved. 12 I wish those who unsettle you would mutilate themselves!

was equally scandalous in the eyes of all who followed the Greek philosophical tradition that Deity and suffering were mutually exclusive ideas.

Paul could have eliminated the scandal of the Cross for the Jews by agreeing that circumcision and obedience to the law were necessary in addition to faith. On the other hand, if he had been complacent about the morals of his converts, permitting them to reduce faith in Christ to believing in salvation by sacramental transaction while keeping their ethics and religion in separate compartments, he could have avoided the charge of the radicals that he was still preaching circumcision. But because he insisted upon keeping the Cross and cross-bearing at the center of his faith in Christ as that "wisdom" and "power" of God which is "foolishness" with men, he was being persecuted. It should have been obvious that he was not preaching circumcision.

12. So deeply did Paul feel the injustice of this charge, and so great was his indignation at the disturbance in his churches, that he exclaimed: "I wish that those who are upsetting you would even emasculate themselves!" This is what Paul said and meant. The KJV gives a very different meaning, but is incorrect. For a similar outburst see Phil. 3:2-3, where the advocates of circumcision are "dogs," and by a play on words—περιτομή, κατατομήν—"circumcision" becomes "mutilation." Paul may have been thinking of the mad spectacle of the Cybele-Attis cult, whose priests in frenzied devotion used to emasculate themselves as a sacrifice to their deity. The inference would be that if salvation depended on merit for a physical operation, these pagan observers of a more drastic rite would have greater assurance than the adherents to the Jewish custom. The shock of

things done. The political way is to argue; the business way is to organize; the military way is to fight; the Christian way par excellence is to sacrifice, and if need be, to suffer. In countries such as the United States, where it is almost impossible to produce Christian martyrs because of the constitutional guarantee of freedom of conscience, the Christian way yet involves more personal sacrifice and harder work than men by and large are willing to undertake. A woman gave up her position in a business corporation and accepted a salary reduction of almost one half because she believed God wanted her to become a teacher of underprivileged children in a community welfare institution. The Cross may mean choosing like that. An honor graduate of a distinguished medical school, who might have practiced his profession with large financial returns in a city, chose rather to spend his life in a remote mountain community which had no physician, where it was necessary for him to compound his own drugs and to carry them in saddlebags on horseback over mountain trails. For forty years he gave his life to those remote and deserving people. The Cross may mean serving like that.

The temptation of many able persons, trained in political science, experienced in business and the professions, is to refuse to become candidates for public office because of the financial sacrifice election would incur. Nothing less than sacrificial courage inspires a man to stick his neck out all the way on certain public issues. The Cross means the courage to give one's self in public service through sacrifice, inconvenience, and misunderstanding. "Where were you," asks the Cross, "when the world was so filled with crucifixion causes?"

Christ's Cross teaches that crosses borne in his Spirit become keys to the abundant life. Two of Jesus' most widely quoted sayings illustrate this viewpoint. Said he, "I am come that they might have life, and that they might have it more abundantly" (John 10:10). He also said, "If any man will come after me, let him deny himself, and take up his cross, and follow me" (Matt. 16:24). He was insisting that abundant living and crosses go together. How does that make sense? He was insisting that capacity for enjoying life and capacity for suffering are the same capacity. The way in which men handle their suffering increases or decreases their capacity for life itself. It has been incorrectly suggested that the ultimate viewpoint of the O.T. is that when a righteous man suffers, he suffers in spite of his righteousness. Surely the O.T. teaches, as does Jesus himself, that a man may suffer because of his righteousness, i.e., the more he practices righteousness the greater is the likelihood of suffering. Thus Jesus could promise, "Blessed are they which are persecuted for righteousness' sake: for theirs is the kingdom

13 For, brethren, ye have been called unto liberty; only *use* not liberty for an occasion to the flesh, but by love serve one another.

13 For you were called to freedom, brethren; only do not use your freedom as an opportunity for the flesh, but through

Paul's statement to the Judaizers can be measured in the light of the prohibition in Deut. 23:1. To a devout Jew his blunt language would be as sacrilegious as a Christian would find the wish of a disbeliever in sacraments that all advocates of baptism would drown themselves. Never happy after making such denunciations (II Cor. 1:23–2:11; Phil. 3:18-19), Paul quickly changes his tone, addressing the Galatians as "brethren" (vs. 13). In 6:1 he pleads for the restoration of those who are at fault.

4. By Maintaining the Right Conception and Use of Freedom (5:13-15)

13. Throughout history God was at work on his plan to make men his freemen in Christ. By Paul's definition a Christian was one who needed no law to make him love his neighbor and refrain from biting and devouring him. But the old competitive drive, which was incompatible with liberty, was always waiting to seize the **opportunity** to reassert itself. Originally this word (ἀφορμήν) designated a point from which to launch

of heaven" (Matt. 5:10). The Cross means living like that.

Peter helps to point up this "moral influence" theory of the Cross: "Christ also suffered for us, leaving us an example, . . . who, when he was reviled, reviled not again; when he suffered, he threatened not" (I Pet. 2:21, 23). On the greatest cross that Christ ever bore, as his flesh was torn in sharpest pain, he prayed, "Father, forgive them; for they know not what they do" (Luke 23:34). Men may at least follow his example, even though they follow afar off. There are high souls who turn beds of affliction into mounts of transfiguration. In some of the most loved poetry the world is permitted to hear the story of a heart that has been broken and to discover the secret of its courage. Some of earth's grandest music gives in melody a lonely soul's search for the lost chords of life. Many a man has taken a second or third best and has made a life out of it; the first plan of his youthful days hangs on the cross of a broken dream. Christ suffered, and in his suffering leaves us an example. He would have denied all he had taught had he refused the Cross. Conversely, his choice of the Cross indicated what he lived for.

> Love so amazing, so divine,
> Demands my soul, my life, my all.

Christ draws out man's worst in penitence and humble confession; he draws out man's best in glad surrender and dedication.

5:13–6:10. ***The Compulsions of a Free Man.***— The central task of the Christian church in Galatia and across the centuries is to produce Christlike minds, and so enable men to outthink the world; to produce Christlike character, and so enable men to outlive the world. Men who outthink and outlive the world outlove and overcome the world: they are the uncommon men. To perform that task for every generation is the work of men of God and of the church of Christ. All this is but a synonym, another way of saying "freedom in Christ." The uncommon man is the free man. But now to propose one of the most difficult of all questions: "What are the compulsions of a Christ-centered man?" Chs. 5–6 are largely given to answering the question: "Where shall a man, set free from external and ancient traditions, find his compulsions? Is he utterly on his own?" A word must be found to keep a man in charge of himself, to make him adequate for freedom in Christ.

The binding character of the ancient law has found its new and permanent place by its relation to grace. What a man must do (the language of law) is supplanted by what a man delights to do (the language of grace). External legal restraints give way to internal moral constraints. The permanent values of the law are fulfilled for Paul in four "safeguards."[2] A safeguard is something of which a man may or may not avail himself. So is his freedom protected. A safeguard is not the last word, as the law is presumed to be. It is different from a legal requirement, for it is a matter of personal choice. The big concerns are not legally imposed from without; they are morally imposed from within, through one's own conscience. And these inward compulsions are eternally true in a way that no

[2] The suggestion of the word "safeguard" is given by Arthur S. Peake, *A Commentary on the Bible* (New York: Thomas Nelson & Sons, n.d.), p. 861.

an attack. In the name of liberty sin could use the weakness of human nature as a foothold from which to scale the defenses of the soul. Consequently the Christian must beware lest his freedom become an incentive to make low use of material things, and a green light on the highway to the City of Destruction (vss. 15, 19-21; Rom. 7:8-11; 8:5-8). The only road that led to the kingdom of God was the "superexcellent way" which Paul describes in I Cor. 13. The article with **freedom** requires emphasis: it is "the" freedom which constitutes the theme of the letter; **your** (RSV) is not in the Greek. No verb is expressed in the second clause, and the translation has to supply some word such as **use,** "turn," "convert," "pervert."

The persistence of translators in saying **servants** instead of "slaves" reflects the sensitiveness of the church to the charge that Paul is fostering a slave mentality. But he is speaking of a new kind of slavery in which every man and his brother are free but willingly perform the most menial tasks for each other. Neither takes advantage of the other's voluntary self-enslavement, and each treats the other as better than himself. No Christian may say to another, "I am the head; therefore you are subject to my commands," but only this: "We are equal in the sight of God; both of us are dependent on his grace, being nothing, having nothing that we have not received; therefore let us work together in his service, each using for the other's advantage whatever gifts God has given us." Thus each bore the other's burden while bearing his own (6:2, 5). Freedom from the lower was achieved by self-investment in the higher, to build up the body of Christ (I Cor. 8:7-13; 9:12-23). That was the only way to establish and maintain human freedom. Christian liberty was both God's gift and man's task. Christian freedom is liberty to love God and man.

---

law or rule of life can be true. Paul's four safeguards for the man who would be free from the control and slavery of the law are (*a*) love (5:13-15); (*b*) the Spirit (5:16-26); (*c*) the fellowship of the church (6:1-5); and (*d*) the natural law of sowing and reaping (6:7-10). Here is help day by day for the man who is controlled inwardly by the presence of Christ.

13-15. ***Love as a Safeguard of Freedom.*****—Use not liberty for an occasion to the flesh, but by love serve one another.** Love is used to label experiences ranging from the cheapest passion, which devours personality, to the noblest sacrifice, which awakens the artist and hero in man. Love as a safeguard of Christian freedom must be clearly and thoroughly defined. It safeguards freedom for the Christian because it combines discipline, guidance, and protection. As discipline, it is self-imposed. As guidance, this question must be asked, "What would love do?" So long as a man does not violate the requirements of love, he is free—and his freedom is protected. What is more, love keeps him from violating other men's freedom.

Such love is far more than mutuality: loving those who love us. It is more than prudence: loving those who are in a position to return like favors. The latter would make love a kind of lobbying process. Love as a safeguard of freedom may mean caring for the unattractive; it may mean doing good to those who oppose or dislike us. On a purely human basis such love is not possible, not even through stoic will power or sugary emotionalism—both of which are short lived. The highest love finds its roots only in the mind and Spirit of Christ. It is the quality of life that is witnessed on his Cross. It is the quality of life which Christ conveys to those who love him.

The problem that has to be faced by everybody who has been set free from rules and traditions under which he has grown to manhood is to find a moral equivalent for those rules: a higher tradition to guide his life to a level of living which he could never otherwise attain. Paul found a higher liberty than obedience to law could give. And in finding it he was protected from expressing his liberty by sinking to the level of purely physical impulses (vs. 13*b*). He found the "expulsive power of a new affection" (vs. 13*c*), an affection which gave width to his life and depth to his morals.

Love "suffereth long." In the love lyric of the N.T., I Cor. 13, the same Paul who wrote Galatians describes love more concretely than in any other of his writings. Suffering is regarded by many people as an enemy of the good life. And indeed it may be the sweat of the soul and the defeat of the spirit. Suffering, with its concurrent pain, is one of the chief causes of adult immorality. Many men turn to narcotics or drink to dull their suffering; but when their pain is gone, the habit lingers on. Jesus got into the moral problems that are so often the consequences of pain as none other has ever done; he chose the way of physical and mental suffer-

14 For all the law is fulfilled in one word, *even* in this; Thou shalt love thy neighbor as thyself.

love be servants of one another. 14 For the whole law is fulfilled in one word, "You

---

14. Jesus, who fulfilled the law by living the ideal life which it was intended to achieve, summed up its requirements as love to God and one's neighbor. Consequently Paul could not love God without loving his neighbors, who were sons and heirs of God. The quotation is from Lev. 19:18; cf. Rom. 13:8-10. The tense of the verb "fulfilled" is perfect; thus Paul says that the **whole law is fulfilled,** in the sense of "has been fulfilled" whenever one man loves another as himself. The law aimed at right relations between man and man, and these were inseparable from right relations with God. Only the love incarnated and inspired by Christ Jesus could secure them. Paul the Christian loved his neighbor not because a commandment disobeyed would bring punishment, or fulfilled would merit reward, but because it was his new nature to do so. He went beyond the law, which, to be enforceable, could prescribe only a minimum of good conduct. When the law permitted things contrary to love, Paul would not do them; when it failed to command new duties taught by new occasions, he discharged them as a debt of love; and where its provisions were made obsolete or irrelevant by the grace of Christ, he dropped them, save only when another's conscience might be hurt. He bore a cross that love could inspire but never command.

But who was Paul's **neighbor?** He was, first of all, "the one who was near," the fellow member of the society of Christ who needed help to bear life's burdens (6:2). Then, with continuously lengthening radius, Paul drew a series of concentric circles to embrace all men (6:10; I Thess. 5:15; I Cor. 9:22). Even his enemies were included, for Christ received sinners, and personal vengeance was no fruit of the Spirit (6:1; Rom. 12:20; 15:1-3). All men were Paul's neighbors, and he was in debt to love them all (Rom. 1:14). To pay this debt he had to enslave himself, and the more he paid the more he owed. But this was not bankruptcy like the old slavery to the law; because the greater the debt, the greater were his resources in Christ to meet it. He bore the burden of his neighbor's sins, and although he sometimes had to threaten them, he was never without hope for their repentance (I Cor. 5; II Cor. 12:19–13:10; II Thess. 3:14-15). He could hurl anathemas, and his friends did not always find him easy to get on with (1:8-10; I Cor. 16:22; Phil. 3:2); but the love of Christ would never permit him to contract the circle of his neighbors (Rom. 9:1-3; 10:1; II Cor. 7:5-16; 1:23–2:11).

---

ing on the Cross. He demonstrated a kind of love that is the toughest thing in the world. It is tougher even than suffering. It can keep suffering from defeating life. It is the love that "beareth all things." A man who can maintain his integrity in suffering is a free man.

Love "envieth not." Envy is obviously an enemy of the good life. It shuts more windows, pulls down more shades, and darkens more minds than this world dreams of. It awakens the baser impulses. It is destructive, never constructive: it stands in the way of all building and growing. Love can keep it from defeating life. Love "believeth all things." It believes in the privilege of every man to run his own race and to achieve his own highest development. So does love safeguard freedom.

Love "vaunteth not itself, is not puffed up, doth not behave itself unseemly, seeketh not her own." Surely false pride too is an enemy of the good life. The man who looks out upon life and sees only the reflection of his own self, who believes the illusion that he is self-made and is fully competent to bear the consequences of his own mistakes, who forgets that other men have labored and that he has only entered into their labors, is guilty of false pride. Love keeps false pride from defeating life, from destroying liberty, because love "hopeth all things." Love hopes the best for every man, not just for one's own proud self and family. Love hopes that the right man, not necessarily one's self, will win. Love "is not puffed up"—"For whosoever exalteth himself shall be abased; and he that humbleth himself shall be exalted" (Luke 14: 11). Humility is the language of freedom; love safeguards it and keeps men free.

Love "is not easily provoked." Worry is an enemy of the good life. It is not difficult to understand why some men worry, since they

There are three elements in Paul's **love** (ἀγάπη) for his neighbor: esteem for him, desire to help him, and desire for his love in return. These elements also constitute God's love for man as revealed in Christ Jesus.

God's valuation of sinners was measured by the price Christ paid for their freedom (Rom. 5:8; I Cor. 6:20; 7:23). God has an eternal purpose for men, and his will is for their consecration (Rom. 8:29; I Thess. 4:3; 5:9). Christ became poor to make men rich and call them to be God's people (4:6-9; Rom. 1:6; I Cor. 1:2; II Cor. 8:9). All who accepted him were being changed "from glory to glory" (II Cor. 3:18), and nothing could separate them from God's love (Rom. 8:35-39). That was the pattern by which the Spirit of Christ taught Paul to esteem and help his fellow men (II Cor. 8:14-15).

Paul's desire to help his neighbors led him to preach "Jesus Christ as Lord, with ourselves as your slaves for Jesus' sake" (II Cor. 4:5 RSV mg.). He no longer lived to himself, but so as to commend himself to every man's conscience (II Cor. 4:2). He was pained by the humiliation of the poor, whom he was always eager to remember (2:10; I Cor. 11:22). He became a "father" to his converts (I Thess. 2:11; I Cor. 4:14-15), boasted of them (I Thess. 2:19), sought not what was theirs but them (II Cor. 12:14), and gladly spent his life for them (II Cor. 12:15). His heart was full of them, and his way of living was to do good to all, impartially, and with brotherly affection (6:10; II Cor. 7:3; Rom. 12:10). In all things he sought his neighbors' good, and his calling was to present them faultless before his God (6:2, 5; I Cor. 10:24; Rom. 15:16). That was how Paul helped his neighbors to achieve God's plan for their lives.

God sent Christ and called Paul to be his ambassador (II Cor. 5:20). From this fact Paul concluded that God wanted man's love in return. So, in imitation of God, he was "affectionately desirous" of his converts (I Thess. 2:8), rejoicing in their reception of him and in the good news about them (I Thess. 1:9; 3:7-10). The Christ-life of his neighbors was life to him. With the ink of the Spirit he wrote himself upon their hearts to post them as his letters of recommendation to the world (II Cor. 3:1-3). He wrote to the Romans of his longing to "be mutually encouraged by each other's faith" (Rom. 1:11-12). The Philippians were his partners, and he was thankful for their gift, but more especially for the love that gave it (Phil. 1:8; 2:2; 4:14). Christian love involved reciprocity (II Cor. 8:14), and this principle applied to the love between God and man as well as to man's love for his neighbor. The God who gave his own Son loved a cheerful giver (II Cor. 9:7), and all who responded to God's love in Christ became partners with Paul in writing his immortal chapter on the love that never fails. When the responding love was not immediate, Paul's love was very patient, very kind, hoping all things, believing all things, enduring all things.

There is a hyperunselfishness which claims that the Christian ought to love his neighbor with no thought of his neighbor's love in return. For this claim there is no warrant in the letters of Paul, although certainly he would never have regarded the "return" as a condition. Like his Master, he appealed both to the altruistic and to the self-regarding motives (6:7-9; I Cor. 9:23; II Cor. 9:6-15; Phil. 2:9-11; 3:14). Paul's Christian race was inspired and enabled by God's grace through Christ, but Paul had to do the running;

---

have only broken confidences and fading strength to meet their increasingly heavy responsibilities. The background of worry is fear; the foreground is nervousness. Both reduce vitality, impair the will, and often impair man's reason. Love can keep worry from defeating life. Love "endureth all things." Hate is like a brittle reed; love is like an oak tree. By the practice of forgiveness love heals broken confidences, restores fellowship, and opens the way for renewed strength. The answer to fear is faith. Faith expressed in love "casteth out fear" (I John 4:18). Fear, the archenemy of freedom, is handled and freedom is safeguarded by love.

Love "thinketh no evil; rejoiceth not in iniquity, but rejoiceth in the truth." Evil is the enemy of the good life. A Danish queen is said to have prayed, "O God, keep me innocent; make others great." But innocence is not possible—nor is it always strength; while true greatness includes purity. The best of dispositions, if unsupported by steady habits and fixed principles, is no guarantee against degeneracy. Frequently enough we hear men say: "It is my

15 But if ye bite and devour one another, take heed that ye be not consumed one of another.

shall love your neighbor as yourself." 15 But if you bite and devour one another take heed that you are not consumed by one another.

---

and if God and Paul's neighbors had withheld the responding love for which he longed, they would have been just as selfish in withholding as Paul in desiring it. They would have loved Paul, not for what he was in himself, but for the service he could render them. The notion that love requires the willingness of the lover to annihilate himself for others is a caricature of Paul's conception (Phil. 3:8-11).

Love your neighbor as yourself, says Paul—neither more nor less. To love your neighbor less than yourself was to treat him as means to your ends, and to love him more would have made him use you as means to his ends. One way would have been as much a violation of Christian mutuality as the other. But this mutuality required every man to set the right standard for himself. Valuing himself correctly, neither in pride nor in false humility, he must love himself with a right self-love. The character of man's love for his neighbor depended upon what he desired for the neighbor, and this in turn upon his own aims and ideals. **Love your neighbor as yourself** could be the most dangerous thing in the world when applied by one engaged in producing "flesh-works" (vss. 19-21), or in fanatical defense of ancient good which time had made uncouth. Becoming all things to all men might spring from the basest of motives, and the Golden Rule adopted by one whose ideals were not on the growing edge of the Spirit was capable of infinite mischief. Only those who were "selfish" enough to desire the fruit of the Spirit for themselves (vss. 22-23), and generous enough to produce it in and for others, could apply it safely. They who would fulfill the whole law in this one word "love" must first choose for themselves whatever was true and honorable, just and lovely, and spend their thoughts to buy the excellent and the praiseworthy (Phil. 4:8). Each must rate his neighbor better than himself, and must do it neither in pious fiction nor in hypocrisy; for even when the neighbor was inferior, the Christian would hope and pray and act to make him better than himself. And all this he would do, not as a meddler in other men's affairs, but as an exemplar of Christ persuading the world to be reconciled to God. Only thus could the evil spirit of competition be exorcised.

15. The verbs used here are the action words of the jungle. Throughout its history **bite** has never changed its meaning, but neither has the penalty of trying to "eat up," "swallow," **devour** one another. The penalty was inherent in the crime (vss. 19-21; Rom. 1:24-32), and Paul did not mean that any amount of taking **heed** could prevent mutual annihilation if men kept on fighting instead of co-operating (6:7-8). They must stop the cause if they would avoid the effect. The Galatian troublemakers were applying for a license to compete, to criticize—not constructively, but with the critic's satisfaction

---

business what I do with my life. What does it matter if I do not live your way? Evil is wrong to those who think it so. As long as I do not publicly violate social laws, what I do is my own concern. There are other hungers as pure as the hunger for food. Religion is honesty and frankness; is the church either honest or frank? You Christians differ so greatly among yourselves that I reserve the right to differ from all of you. Set your own houses in order, and then make your demands upon the rest of us. I can find God in music, in nature, in my own library or work, much more easily than from a poor choir and a rasping preacher who has a hopeless philosophy. I do not wish to be classified; I ask no group to be responsible for my actions. If God is honest, he will respect my honesty. One world at a time is enough for me. Jesus Christ has a kind of haunting appeal, but my personal relationship with him is all I want."

Recitation of doctrinal platitudes will not answer that kind of conversation. Not a declaration of faith, but a careful analysis of the content of our faith must make reply. The sharp divisions between right and wrong, light and darkness, truth and propaganda, have been shaded today. Much of life is in the twilight zone. Religion must not only carry a telescope

16 *This* I say then, Walk in the Spirit, and ye shall not fulfil the lust of the flesh.
17 For the flesh lusteth against the Spirit, and the Spirit against the flesh: and these are contrary the one to the other; so that ye cannot do the things that ye would.

16 But I say, walk by the Spirit, and do not gratify the desires of the flesh. 17 For the desires of the flesh are against the Spirit, and the desires of the Spirit are against the flesh; for these are opposed to each other, to prevent you from doing what you would.

---

that he was better than his victim—to quarrel, to split into factions, each of which claimed to have the truth, the whole truth, and nothing but the truth. But that would have made the aspiration to be joint heirs with Christ just so much empty talk. Paul refused to grant the license, and threw the suit of the quarreling legatees out of court. By the Spirit of Christ he proposed to do nothing less than to change human nature and repeal the law of tooth and claw.

B. To Serve in the War of the Spirit Against the Flesh (5:16-21)

16. Some—probably most—of Paul's critics feared that his repudiation of law as a means of salvation would lead to an orgy of bad living cloaked with the pretext of a higher spirituality. So he reassured them, saying in effect, "But, I say, walk in the Spirit, and you will not give way to the evil drive in human nature." The absence of the article in the Greek with **Spirit** and **flesh** sets the two irreconcilable ways of living in sharpest contrast. Ἐπιθυμίαν (**desires**) is that upon which man's whole inner drive is set, so that he expends all his energies to obtain and enjoy it. Since **lust** (KJV) suggests primarily the sexual element, it is better to translate by **desires** (RSV), as if the Greek word were plural. The same difficulty arises when σαρκός is translated **of the flesh.** By σάρξ Paul means more than the physical body. The word connotes all the sinful tendencies, impulses, inclinations, and desires implied in the common statement, "You can't change human nature." **Do not gratify** may also be interpreted as a promise, "you will not fulfill." What the Galatians needed was assurance that if they abandoned the law and trusted their all to the Spirit, they would not go down to defeat in the civil war between their good and evil impulses. Since the Christian is one who has been transferred from the realm of "flesh" into the sphere of "Spirit," **in the Spirit** (KJV) is better than **by the Spirit** (RSV). **Walk** is the favorite biblical metaphor to describe the whole course of man's life, including his conduct toward God and his treatment of his fellow men.

17. For connects with the previous sentence to substantiate the promise of victory. At the beginning of the second clause the KJV translates a text which read δέ, **and;** the better text is γάρ, **for** (RSV), which turns the thought to the reason for the battle in the soul of the individual. **Lusteth** (KJV) is not adequate for ἐπιθυμεῖ, even where σάρξ, "flesh," is the subject, and it is quite inappropriate to speak of the Spirit lusting. The

---

by which to see the eternal hills, but must also use a microscope to study in laboratory fashion the secret chambers of men's lives. It is the way of Jesus and must be ours. To open up to men the power to safeguard their freedom through love is the work of men of Christ. Because love can do all this, love "never faileth." Love is the instrument of Christ to overcome with good the enemies of the good life. Love gathers up into itself the true, the beautiful, and the good. The forgiveness of Christ, which is love at its best, releases the power by which to make and keep life whole. He whom the heavens cannot contain dwells in the heart that loves, and in that partnership is the good life: love safeguards freedom.

16-26. ***The Spirit as a Safeguard of Freedom.*** **—Walk in the Spirit, and ye shall not fulfil the lust of the flesh.** One of the first experiences that may come to a man who gives up the binding power of rules and traditions is for his physical impulses to run riot. Perhaps that is why Paul puts strong emphasis upon **flesh** and **Spirit.** Capitalizing the word Spirit makes it refer to the Spirit of Christ in the mind of a man: the risen Christ, now present as the Spirit. That Presence became the safeguard of Paul's freedom. The source of Paul's morality no longer resided in an external authority such as a lawbook, but in an internal Presence; not in obedience to law, but in awareness of a spring of moral power. His old freedom was little more

18 But if ye be led of the Spirit, ye are not under the law.

19 Now the works of the flesh are manifest, which are *these,* Adultery, fornication, uncleanness, lasciviousness,

[18] But if you are led by the Spirit you are not under the law. [19] Now the works of the flesh are plain: immorality, impurity, licen-

---

ἵνα-clause expresses purpose, **to prevent** (RSV), rather than result, **so that** (KJV). The purpose of the evil impulse is to oppose the good; the aim of the Spirit is to eliminate the bad; and both antagonists are trying to keep man from doing what he pleases.

This is Paul's way of stating the Jewish doctrine of the "two impulses" which are at war within the heart of man. The rabbis declared that God created Adam with two inclinations, one good, the other evil, and required him to choose which to obey. He was free to follow his good impulse, but he chose the evil, and so did all his descendants. Consequently every man became the Adam of his own soul. Some maintained that the evil impulse awakened at the age of nine, others at twelve. Study with practice of the Torah was the sovereign remedy to wear it away, but Paul found this ineffective. Only the Spirit of Christ could cure the weakness of his human nature.

Paul's statement is not a denial of all freedom of will in man. According to his description of the civil war in the heart in Rom. 7, man can will, i.e., choose the good, but because of the weakness of the σάρξ, "flesh," "human nature," he cannot do the good, but only the evil which he does not will. Only when the Spirit changes him and helps him does his good will become practicable. Thus the freedom of the Christian does not consist in having no master, but in having a new master. Man is a slave willy-nilly, either to sin or to Christ, either to flesh or to Spirit. But at the moment of submission to the Spirit he becomes free. Paul's liberty is not license to do as he pleases, but is "slavery" to the good, and that is the highest conceivable freedom.

18. In this chapter Paul uses three verbs to describe the new life in the Spirit: "walk" (vs. 16), "are led" (vs. 18), and "live" (vs. 25)—conduct, guidance, companionship. Those who are led by the Spirit are free from law in the sense that they have risen above it and are living a life that needs no law because it is better than the best that law can produce. Christian freedom is not legalism in another form (cf. Rom. 8:14). Note the absence of the article from the phrase ὑπὸ νόμον, "under law."

19-21*a*. The KJV translates a text which adds **adultery** to Paul's list. The vicious **works of the flesh,** before the Spirit transforms it, are not hidden works of darkness but open and unashamed—**plain.** They flaunt themselves everywhere, obtruding and intruding, blatant, raucous, unrepentant, in arrogant defiance of God, and ruthless disregard of men.

Πορνεία is **fornication** (KJV), **immorality** (RSV). The word means "prostitution," but includes sexual vice and unfaithfulness to the marriage vow. The task of the church in creating a conscience on this matter was made doubly difficult by the practice of prostitution in the name of religion. Long before Paul, the prophets had denounced

---

than that of army privates who have received their orders from a higher officer:

> Theirs not to reason why,
> Theirs but to do and die.[3]

The new Paul who lived in Christ derived his power from the indwelling Spirit. The relation between this Spirit and his **flesh** saved him; for the Spirit is given to safeguard man from bondage to the flesh. The word "flesh" for Paul was not a synonym for the "physical body." It stood for the raw "physical stuff of human life." Man in revolt against God is fulfilling **the lust of the flesh;** man in Christ-governed obedience to God is walking **in the Spirit.**

Even a simple enumeration of the most common attitudes people take toward that "physical stuff" which Paul called **the flesh** should be enough to show how the Spirit safeguards freedom. There are at least four such attitudes.

First of all there are those who have almost a worshipful attitude toward physical hungers—

[3] Tennyson, "The Charge of the Light Brigade."

the fertility cults and made prostitution a synonym for idolatry. Conversely, idolatry was viewed as the root of sexual immorality and a host of other sins (Rom. 1:18-27). Some of Paul's churches, caught in the downward pull of their environment, were tolerant of this evil (I Cor. 5:1-13). In warning against it Paul did not cite a commandment which had to be obeyed, but he showed how it was a violation of the Christian's fellowship with Christ (I Cor. 6:13-20; 10:1-13).

'Ακαθαρσία is **uncleanness** (KJV), **impurity** (RSV), either physical or moral. Paul is not speaking of ceremonial physical uncleanness contracted from dead bodies, lepers, tabooed animals, and other things which were believed to render a person displeasing to God and unfit for the society of "clean" people. Prescriptions for getting rid of such impurity bulked large in the law of Moses; and in the mystery cults similar cleansings were demanded of the initiates. The moral effect, even where present, was only incidental to the physical rite. Paul was concerned with "moral impurity" of every kind. The Greek word is often associated with sexual vice, but its broader meaning here includes all that defiles the heart and distracts from right living.

'Ασέλγεια, **lasciviousness** (KJV), **licentiousness** (RSV), is often used of lewdness and sensuality. But its fundamental meaning is "wantonness," conduct marked by unrestrained violence and wilfulness. **Idolatry** was regarded by the Jews as the root of all other sins and penalties (Rom. 1:18-32). Typical of their relentless warfare against it was the Epistle of Jeremiah, which described idols as dusty, termite-ridden roosts for bats, birds, and cats; not gods at all, but the work of men's hands, helpless and useless as a scarecrow in a cucumber bed. The story of Bel and the dragon heaped derision and ridicule upon Aesculapius, the god of healing, having Daniel kill his serpent by feeding it a prescription of pitch, fat, and hair! Intelligent Gentiles admitted that the idol was not the deity himself, but they insisted that it represented him. The Christians replied that these so-called gods and lords were nothing but demons (I Cor. 8:4-6; 10:19-21). Idolatry was thus a "work of the flesh." By it unregenerate human nature created its god in its own image and according to its own desires, and constructed its theology to rationalize the way it was living and meant to keep on living. Throughout history its most subtle and dangerous form has been the self-worshiping state.

Φαρμακεία, **witchcraft** (KJV), **sorcery** (RSV), was the use of drugs of any kind, whether wholesome or poisonous. Since witches and sorcerers used drugs, the word came to designate witchcraft, enchantment, sorcery, and magic. The law of Moses prescribed the death penalty for it, and the prophets denounced the Egyptians, Babylonians, and Canaanites for practicing it; but this did not prevent the Jews from producing some famous practitioners (Acts 13:6-12; 19:11-20). Next to state-worship, magic was the most dangerous competitor of true religion. It was human nature's attempt to compel God to do its bidding instead of praying as Jesus did, "Thy will be done." Claiming to specialize in the impossible, it prostituted faith to superstition, and divorced religion from ethics. Yet the N.T. Christians could not deny that these magicians were successful in performing miracles. So Peter had to warn Simon Magus that possession of the Holy Spirit required a heart that was right with God (Acts 8:14-24). In Paul's spiritual arithmetic, faith plus miracles minus love amounted exactly to zero.

"Εχθραι is **hatred** (KJV), **enmity** (RSV). The word is plural, indicating many kinds and objects of hatred and feelings of hatred toward God and man. It is the opposite of φιλία, "friendship." Where love esteems, hatreds belittle and despise; where love creates and serves, hatreds enslave and destroy; and where love desires a neighbor's love in return, the man who hates is filled with perpetual fear of retaliation.

"Ερις is **variance** (KJV), **strife** (RSV). Some MSS have it in the plural. This "flesh-work" is another manifestation of the natural man's hostile-mindedness. The word designates a series of disturbances of peace and concord that grow out of the spirit and practice of competition: "rivalry," "strife for prizes," "contention," "discord," "quarreling," "fighting." The spirit of Eris is perfectly described in the words of Lewis Carroll's *Alice in Wonderland*—"ambition, distraction, uglification, and derision."

20 Idolatry, witchcraft, hatred, variance, emulations, wrath, strife, seditions, heresies,

tiousness, 20 idolatry, sorcery, enmity, strife, jealousy, anger, selfishness, dissension, party

Ζῆλος is **emulations** (KJV), **jealousy** (RSV). The KJV follows a text which reads the plural. "Emulation" would be more charitable to human nature, being closer to the usage of Plato and Aristotle, who considered ζῆλος a noble passion in contrast with φθόνος, "envy." It began with intense devotion, loyalty, and zeal, but through unreasoning anger against whatever opposed or rivaled the object of its devotion it degenerated into jealousy of everything which stood in the way of its possession and enjoyment. The jealous man was so thoroughly and passionately selfish that he became malignant, hesitating at nothing to keep his rival in his place. Poles removed from the Spirit of Christ, he had no use for Paul's counsel to look not upon his own, but each to the other's good.

Θυμοί: **wrath** (KJV), **anger** (RSV). From this point to the end of the list the nouns are in the plural. This word in the singular signifies "soul," "spirit," "heart," hence "courage," "temper," and "anger." Θυμοί are fiery-tempered flashes of hostile feeling, and of anger that is easily provoked—the panting breath of a man in a rage. Envy, competition, and jealousy constitute a mixture that awaits only a spark to explode into outbursts of anger and passion.

Ἐριθεῖαι: **strife** (KJV), **selfishness** (RSV). This "flesh-work" is not "strife," but the selfish ambitions that lead to strife. Originally the word meant "working for wages," but in the course of time it degenerated into "selfishness," "seeking office," "factiousness," and "party spirit." In Phil 2:3 it stands for everything opposed to the mind of Christ. It lies at the root of all other sins, and its outworkings in human nature are described in Rom. 1:18–2:11.

Διχοστασίαι: **seditions** (KJV), **dissension** (RSV). The more general term **dissension** is preferable. **Seditions** are political disturbances and matters of state, whereas Paul has in mind the incipient quarrels which were threatening the body of Christ. In Rom. 16:17 he warns against those who create "dissensions and difficulties" in the service, not of Christ, but of their own appetites.

Αἱρέσεις: **heresies** (KJV), **party spirit** (RSV). Since the application of this word to unorthodox doctrine is later than the N.T., the KJV translation is inappropriate. The verb αἱρέομαι means "choose," and in this sense αἵρεσις is "choice," "preference," or "free will." Applied to religion it meant a sect or party; in philosophy it designated a tendency or school. The differences of opinion might be honest and healthy, or they could become selfish and divisive, as at Corinth (I Cor. 3:3-4; 11:18-19), where the difficulty was caused not by varieties of Christian experience and interpretation, but by the rival ambitions of the climbers who wanted special recognition in the church. Paul called this party spirit childish, and prescribed a true catholicity as the remedy (I Cor. 3:22). He admonished the members to put away childish things.

Φθόνοι: **envyings** (KJV), **envy** (RSV). The plural indicates various forms of envious desires and their manifestations. The word also means "malice" and "ill will." According to Mark 15:10 and Matt. 27:18, it was this sin that caused Jesus' enemies to deliver him to Pilate.

their chief hungers being food and sex. To them these hungers are natural. Since God made nature, these hungers must be from him. A man may therefore express himself; and in expressing, enjoy himself; and by enjoying, realize himself. This attitude of worship toward the flesh results in decisions that are made on the selfish basis of physical comfort and convenience: men yield to **the lust of the flesh.** The flesh is not sinful; but to put it in command of life is sin. When the flesh determines one's direction it becomes master, not servant.

Another attitude is depreciation. This is the direct opposite of worship. It may not be as physically disastrous in moral consequences, but it is as morally deficient, especially as it is related to mental health. Some readers have interpreted this section of Galatians to mean that the flesh is the seat of evil. They believe that everything physical is unclean. Consider

21 Envyings, murders, drunkenness, revelings, and such like: of the which I tell you before, as I have also told *you* in time past, that they which do such things shall not inherit the kingdom of God.

spirit, 21 envy,[k] drunkenness, carousing, and the like. I warn you, as I warned you before, that those who do such things shall

[k] Other ancient authorities add *murder*.

Here the KJV translates a text which added **murders,** probably from Rom. 1:29, where φθόνου is followed by φόνου. Although it does not belong to the present list, murder was certainly considered a "flesh-work" by Paul. According to Genesis, envy and murder stood with man's first act of rebellion as the trinity of original sins. Whenever the cumulative consequences of all the other sins come to an impasse, the sovereign remedy of Cain-minded human nature is to kill all whom it cannot dominate.

Μέθαι: **drunkenness.** The same word means "strong drink" and "drunkenness." The plural suggests the repeated spells of the habitual drunkard. Like murder, this "flesh-work" is as old as civilization. Κῶμοι: **revelings** (KJV), **carousing** (RSV). Drunkenness and **carousing** keep company with all the other "works of darkness" (Rom. 13:13). In Paul's day, as in all times, these were socially approved forms of recreation. Then as now, alcoholism was rationalized, the difference being that what is now explained as a disease was then attributed to the influence of the gods of wine, most popular of whom was Dionysus (Bacchus). He and other deities of drink were worshiped with appropriate carousings. The age was not wanting in "Omar Khayyáms" to praise its own alcoholic befuddlement, e.g., the man of Boscoreale who inscribed κτῶ, χρῶ, "Get and use," on his drinking cup. That was the realism of the day, which relegated moral responsibility to the "opinions" of the philosophers and meddlesome "do-gooders," and debased Epicureanism into "Let us eat and drink—especially let us drink—for tomorrow we die." So freedom was identified with license to get drunk, and the churches of Christ could not escape the impact of the alcoholic environment (I Cor. 11:21). Paul's solution for alcoholism was the driving out of the spirit of Dionysus by the Spirit of Christ.

And the like: Paul's list of "flesh-works" might go on endlessly, but he has mentioned enough to show what human nature unresponsive to the Spirit of God is like (cf. also Rom. 1–2 and I Cor. 6:9-10). Human nature, he says, is not only sinful, but full of sins. Being weak, it becomes the seat and base of operations of Sin, which proliferates into countless separate sins and sinful habits, both in the individual and in society. Three things, according to Paul, are characteristic of these "flesh-works": (*a*) They all violate the love which is the constitutive principle of the kingdom of God. (*b*) They are done in the name of freedom, but they enslave those who delude themselves with such a misconception of liberty. (*c*) They cannot be eradicated by law, but only by the Spirit of God.

21*b*. Paul therefore repeated the admonition which had pervaded his sermons to the Galatians. As a missionary of Christ, his primary concern was to get men to repent of the works of the flesh. He had a horror of death, but a greater horror of the life of sin that was the sting of death. This gives his religion and ethics a peculiar relevancy to human society in every age. The fact that he expected the near return of Christ to end this present age must not be permitted to obscure the equally important fact that he regarded his own life and witness for Christ as an essential element in hastening that

what happens to the moral life if the flesh is considered evil or the source of evil. The real issue is the question of control. Who is in control, the Spirit or the flesh? The seat of evil and of good is not in the flesh, but in the will. Depreciation of the flesh violates the sacredness of personality.

There is the attitude of toleration. It was written of a certain philosopher, "He seems to be ashamed that his soul dwells in a body." From this point of view the body is only a temporary matter. Quite soon the Spirit, like the moth, will fly away and the flesh will be left as no more than an abandoned cocoon. Such unworthy conceptions lead to anemic spirituality and impotent ethics.

A fourth attitude is appreciation. This word is quite inadequate to convey the Christian

22 But the fruit of the Spirit is love, joy, peace, long-suffering, gentleness, goodness, faith,

not inherit the kingdom of God. 22 But the fruit of the Spirit is love, joy, peace, patience, kindness, goodness, faithfulness,

---

event. There were two installments in his inheritance, one heavenly and future (I Cor. 15:50-55; I Thess. 4:13-18), the other earthly and present wherever "righteousness and peace and joy in the Holy Spirit" (Rom. 14:17) dwelt in the hearts of men; and there were three elements in this kingdom-life which formed Paul's spiritual triangle: God, the individual, and the neighbor. Whether in heaven above or on the earth beneath, whether in this present evil age or hereafter in an earthly or a heavenly society cleansed of all that defiles, the essentials of this **kingdom** were the same. Paul called them "the fruit of the Spirit" and warned that without them no man could enter **the kingdom of God.**

C. To Live as Sons and Heirs of God (5:22-24)

22-23. In introducing this list of character traits of the Christian, Paul uses the singular καρπός (**fruit**), whereas in speaking of the "flesh-works" (vs. 19) he has used the plural τὰ ἔργα (**works**). This distinction grew out of his experience. Before he became a Christian, his sinful nature had been in rebellion against God and at cross-purposes with itself, splitting his life into fragmentary deeds. Then the Spirit came to integrate his life with God and men, centering it in the unifying love of Christ. Thus each fruit of the Spirit was simply love in another form, a revelation of the character of God through Christ and through the Christians who produced it.

Ἀγάπη is **love.** The best commentary is I Cor. 13. With the noun ἀγάπη we have to include the verb ἀγαπάω, which means "be fond of," "love," "desire," "be contented with." The three elements in Paul's love—esteem, devotion, and mutuality—have been explained in connection with vs. 14. Here it remains to consider the significance of calling Christian love a fruit of God's Spirit.

Since love is a personal relation it is not a matter of law, and cannot be commanded; and since it is God's own love growing as his "fruit" in the hearts of men, no one can claim it as a merit for self-salvation. But there is a further consequence of Paul's fruit metaphor which requires special emphasis today. This is the principle of the identical harvest by which each plant, animal, and spiritual being reproduces "after its kind." Paul read this in Gen. 1, and he observed that God gave "to each kind of seed its own body" (I Cor. 15:38). Accordingly, when God incarnated his Spirit in the church as the body of Christ, the love which was the fruit of that Spirit must be of the same kind as his own.

But in every age, especially in times of great pessimism, men have found it hard to see how God could have anything in common with humanity, and Christians have been tempted to make a distinction in kind between God's love and man's love. Paul's authority has been claimed for this dualistic view. Ἀγάπη is set against ἔρως. God's love is said to be ἀγάπη reaching down to save man by his grace, and ἔρως man's self-love aspiring upward to save himself. Paul's ἀγάπη is associated with justification by faith, the Greek

---

conception of the physical side of life; but it is the strongest word at hand. Appreciation protests against the utterly selfish and debilitating effects that come from worshiping the flesh; it protests with equal fervor against the idea of depreciation or toleration. What then does it assert? Everything that God made is sacred and permanently significant. "And God saw that it was good" (Gen. 1:25). A man's brain, which is "physical," is as sacred as his mind, which is "spiritual." If the brain did not exist as a physical fact, the mind could not operate as a spiritual organ. "Flesh" (organized, as Paul would have it, into "body") is as sacred as "spirit." The Creator made them all.

The condition and habits of the mind, we know, have a direct effect on physical health; i.e., the mind can assist in physical healing. But that is only half the story. As the mind helps to heal the body, so the body helps to heal the mind. One's mental health directly

ἔρως with salvation by works. Further, it is maintained that before the coming of Christ fallen man was not worth loving; that man has no value in himself, but only because Christ died for him; that God gave his Son not because he expected man's love in return, but out of the sheer overflow of his grace; and that man is commanded to love God not because God needs his love and service, but simply for man's own good and to show his gratitude. Jerusalem and the Christian faith are made to oppose Athens and human reason, and the conclusion is drawn from the history of Christianity that ἔρως, man's self-love, has always been a source of corruption of ἀγάπη, love inspired by God's grace.

This interpretation of Christian love is intended as a defense of the doctrine of justification by faith and as a means of securing scriptural support for a dualistic philosophy which aims to protect the transcendence of God against humanism. But to draw such sweeping conclusions from a word study of two Greek nouns, without adequate consideration of other related Greek words and ideas, is to oversimplify. The LXX is full of evidence that this distinction between ἀγάπη and ἔρως cannot be maintained on the basis of lexicography. The Greek O.T. uses both the noun ἀγάπη and the verb ἀγαπάω to express not only God's love for men, but man's love for God and for his fellow man. Although there is no certain evidence that the noun ἀγάπη was used by nonbiblical writers prior to Christianity, the argument from silence may be invalidated by future discoveries, and it would be precarious to conclude that ἀγάπη was a specifically Christian word.

One-sided emphasis on God's love as "unmotivated" by anything in his creatures tempts men to regard him in the light of an egotistical philanthropist who expects gratitude and praise but neither needs nor desires the mutuality that is inherent in the very nature of love (cf. Exeg., vs. 14). Not least of the marks of God's grace is the divine-human partnership proclaimed by Paul in Rom. 8:28 and in Col. 1:24-29. This means that man's response must be motivated by something that goes deeper than gratitude. Without a faith that dares humbly to believe that God needs man's love, and that he has made man's service an integral part of his infinite enterprise of creation, the Christian's conception of his high calling to be a kingdom builder is liable to reduce itself to blind obedience to commands given arbitrarily for man's good while awaiting God's eschatological fiat. Such a misconception is bound to give aid and comfort to the inclination of human nature —"the flesh"—to divorce religion from ethics.

Grave moral consequences result from such a view of Christian love. It is associated with a doctrine of predestination that makes God's choice of the objects of his salvation utterly arbitrary. But Jesus' parable of the lost son assumes that even in the "far country" the prodigal did not cease to have value to his father, who welcomed him home not out of gracious disinterestedness, but because he really needed and wanted his son's love in return. Paul's idea is that God so valued mankind that "while we were yet sinners, Christ died for us" (Rom. 5:8). The love that "never fails" sees such value in the sinner that it carries in its heart a perpetual cross to win his love in return, and the love thus created is of the same nature as God's parent love. The three elements of ἀγάπη—esteem, devotion, and mutuality—are present in this fruit of the Spirit, both in God's love for Paul and in Paul's love for God.

Χαρά, **joy,** for the Christian is inseparable from love and impossible without it. Χάρις and χαρά, "grace" and "joy," grew from the same Greek root. The joy that was the fruit of the Spirit sprang from a life that was gracious and kind, full of good will, generous to impart itself to others, glad when they accepted and rejoiced with it, but forgiving, and still singing, when men rejected and persecuted it. Every book in the N.T. is instinct with this capacity to rejoice amid the worst of circumstances, but none is more joyous than Luke-Acts, which is infused with an unconquerable gladness that no barrier can confine. Next to Paul's own letters, its contagious communication of joy makes it the best commentary on the Christian χαρά (see especially Luke 1:14, 47; 2:14, 20; 6:23, 38; 7:47; 10:5; 12:12; 13:6-9, 14-17; 15:1-32; 24:13-35; Acts 1:8; 2:24; 5:41; 8:8, 39; 11:23; 13:48; 14:17; 16:25).

Paul became the great example of one who could be sorrowful, yet always rejoicing; for he was convinced that his sufferings were God's media for blessings and materials for thanksgiving by many (II Cor. 1:11). He had learned, in whatever state he was, to be content (Phil. 4:11), provided that his Lord was glorified. This joy, which was not a pious wish but a permanent, all-pervasive characteristic of the Christian, was irrepressibly active, fraught with inward satisfaction and outgoing benediction. But it was not a possession of the individual Christian in isolation from the body of Christ. The production of this fruit of the Spirit was a mutual process involving Paul, his Lord, and his fellow Christians.

Εἰρήνη is **peace.** By the time Paul was ready to baptize this word into the Spirit of Christ, two streams of meaning had flowed into it through the LXX. From the Greek came "harmony," and from the Hebrew "shalom." This Hebrew word expressed "total well-being," "soundness," "prosperity," "success," all that rendered a person "well off" spiritually and materially, and made life good and the world safe for goodness. It required right relations with God and justice between men, and this involved more than freedom from strife.

Paul's peace was first of all with the God and source of peace (Rom. 1:7; 15:33), the original Peacemaker, whose purpose was to create free persons to live in harmony with him and with one another. To this end he sent his Son to make peace, and his Son's apostles to preach peace and plead with the world to be reconciled to him. This peace was past all understanding. God stilled Paul's inner strife, forgave his debt, made him son and heir, citizen and colaborer (Rom. 8:28), and assured him that nothing in all the universe, past, present, or future could separate him from his love (Rom. 8:38-39).

The peace which was the fruit of the Spirit was everlasting, and could be trusted to keep men's hearts and minds (Phil. 4:7), so that they need have no anxiety about anything. This explains the sublime recklessness of the Christian peacemakers. Being colaborers with God (Rom. 8:28), they were aggressors for peace. They aimed to live at peace with all men (Rom. 12:18), but fear of making enemies did not turn them from their task of producing soundness, wholeness, and harmony in a world of chaos. Their reasonable service was to test the will of God—the good, the well pleasing and the perfect (Rom. 12:1-2)—and to substitute the righteousness and peace and joy of his kingdom (Rom. 14:17) for the low aims of "the flesh," thereby creating the conditions for peace. Their ideal was to live so that quarrels could never get started.

Christian peace was therefore neither the calm of inactivity nor the mere passive enjoyment of freedom from strife. It was not the imperturbability of the Epicurean, or the apathy of the Stoic, or the contemplation of the mystic. The man who possessed it was not exempt from storm and shipwreck, but by faith he knew that he would arrive in port (Acts 27:21-25), and that all was well for him and his fellow men-of-faith for time and eternity. And so, where all else was panic, he played the man.

Μακροθυμία is **long-suffering** (KJV), **patience** (RSV). The conditions under which this fruit of the Spirit had to be produced are described in II Cor. 6:3-10. The Spirit's peacemaker had to keep his θυμός, his "temper," under control. He was to be "long-tempered," not subject to sudden outbursts of anger and rage. His task was to bear with the weakness of men and to suffer without retaliation, imitating the kindness of God,

---

affects his physical health; one's physical health affects his mental health. Body and mind are both sacred. The conception which the N.T. presents is that the body is the temple of the Spirit. Can one defend the notion that the vehicle of the eternal Spirit is unclean, that it is the source of evil? The seat of evil is not in the flesh, but in the will.

Even the Christian idea of the resurrection of the body, which is much richer than the philosophical notion of the immortality of the soul, seems to imply this view of the body. Enough will be conserved after the resurrection to establish personal identity. The resurrection of the body surely means the permanence of personality, with the assurance that the future is not a place of disembodied spirits.

Appreciation of the flesh both in its natural raw form as well as in its redeemed form is a moral safeguard for freedom. One does not give

which was intended to lead sinners to repentance (Rom. 2:3-4). But just as God's **patience** was not to be presumed upon, so the Christian's **patience** was not a spiritless good nature that would put up with things which it could not escape, or would not prevent. It was patience with a purpose, as in Paul's plea to Philemon, which contrasts so sharply with the Stoic motive for self-control (see pp. 569-70). Those who bore this fruit "turned the world upside down" (Acts 17:6), and the enemy did not know how to deal with such unheard of patience and persistence. In Col. 3:12-17 μακροθυμία is compared to a garment in the wardrobe of the Spirit, wherewith the Christian is to set a new fashion on earth.

Χρηστότης is **gentleness** (KJV), **kindness** (RSV). In I Cor. 13:4 also Paul associates patience with kindness: "Love is patient and kind." Applied to persons, χρηστότης signifies "goodness," "honesty," kindness," "excellence of character." As with all the other fruit of the Spirit, God is the source, and Christ the ideal fruit-bearer. God was rich in kindness, which he manifested throughout the ages by leading sinners to repentance (Rom. 2:4), and what most impressed Paul about Jesus was his kindness in removing the yoke of sin and law and replacing it with a yoke which, cross though it was, was "kind" (χρηστός, Matt. 11:29-30) to his shoulders. But the only way to enjoy God's kindness was to repent and allow the Spirit to bring forth the same fruit in one's own life; otherwise one would meet not with the kindness, but with the "severity" of God, and be "cut off" from his olive tree (Rom. 11:22). At Damascus Paul responded to the psalmist's invitation. He tasted God's kindness and found it good (Ps. 34:8). As food for the soul, kindness was the pleasantest fruit on the tree of life.

'Αγαθωσύνη, **goodness**, in the LXX translates Hebrew words which mean "goodness," "righteousness," "prosperity," and "kindness." Rom. 15:14 and II Thess 1:11 indicate that Paul took the word in the general sense of "goodness." The Christian was not only to be good, but to be good for something: to let his light shine, to be worthy of his call and his calling, to teach men the knowledge of God, and to bring the ideals of the Spirit into fruition in everyday life.

Πίστις, **faith** (KJV), **faithfulness** (RSV), means both "faith" and "faithfulness," but the KJV translation is better. The one was impossible apart from the other. In 3:11, where Paul quotes the LXX of Hab. 2:4, we see that he took for granted that no man could be either "just" or "justified" without putting "faith" in God's "faithfulness" and being "faithful" in word and deed.

In order of time the factors in Paul's salvation were these: God, Christ, the Spirit, the preacher, the hearing, and the faith which believed and accepted, trusted, and entrusted one's whole life to God (1:15; Rom. 3:3; 5:6-11; 10:14-17; I Cor. 15:9-11, 14, 17). Paul's faith was neither a good work nor a self-generation in his soul in isolation from all who possessed faith before him. The light had been shining long before his eyes were opened to see it (II Cor. 4:6), and his faith rested on the power of God, and on that alone (I Cor. 1:31; 2:1-5). The faith was God's creation, the decision to respond was Paul's.

Immediately with Paul's decision the Spirit thrust him into action. The first fruit of his faith was a vital, mystical-moral fellowship with Jesus. Living thus, he learned to believe, to hope, and to love, assured of immortality and empowered to share the sufferings of Christ (Col. 1:24). Herein lay the secret of his faithfulness, which was his faith acting to present himself as a living sacrifice in rational service of God. His faith made him trustworthy, truthful, and sincere, always faithful to duty. His conscientiousness permeated all his letters, and his fidelity to his missionary calling stamped itself forever on the pages of Luke-Acts (Rom. 12:3-8; I Cor. 4:2; II Cor. 6:1-10; 11:21-29; Acts 20:24-27).

This faithful faith steadied Paul in the storms of life; but it did something even better: it enabled him to walk with his Lord on the highway of love that had been built by the prior love of the God who was faithful (I Cor. 1:8; 12:31–13:13). Unfortunately not all of Paul's followers have been able or willing to grasp his conception that faith is not faith unless it is activated and acting by love. The Gospel of Matthew and the epistles of James and John contain protests against the practice of separating faith from

23 Meekness, temperance: against such there is no law.	23 gentleness, self-control; against such there

faithfulness. The Gospel of John precludes this illegitimate surgery by substituting the verb πιστεύω, "believe," for the noun πίστις, "belief," and insisting that believing without doing God's will is as impossible as fruit bearing when the branches are separated from the vine (John 13:34-35; 14:23-24; 15:1-17).

Πραΰτης is **meekness** (KJV), **gentleness** (RSV). "Modesty," "gentleness," and "courtesy" are the flavors of this fruit. In the third beatitude it is a character trait of those who are going to inherit the earth, and, in Matt. 11:29, of Christ himself. In Col. 3:12 it keeps company with lowliness and patience, and in Phil. 2:1-11 with the mind of Christ. To produce it the Christian must estimate himself soberly, count others better than himself, and treat them as graciously as Christ has treated him (Rom. 12:3; Col. 3:13).

Negatively defined, **gentleness** is everything that the "insolent, haughty, boastful" men of Rom. 1:30 are not. It is the opposite of ὕβρις, the worst of sins in the eyes of the Greeks—deliberate, arrogant defiance of the gods by overstepping the limits set for human beings. In the O.T. such men are called "sons of Belial," the turbulent, high-handed wicked, who rage against God, kill, rob, and enslave the righteous "meek," and take possession of the earth for themselves. The psalms are full of moans and complaints against this rich and powerful majority, who used religion as a means of gain and kept their consciences in flexible subservience to the exigencies of power.

The LXX describes the pious minority as πραΰς, "meek." Those who belonged to it were not necessarily poor, although usually so, because their faithfulness kept them from using unscrupulous means to get rich. In the age to come they would inherit the earth and delight themselves in abundance of peace (Ps. 37:11). Zechariah and Elizabeth, Joseph and Mary, Simeon and Anna belonged to this group. They were the people of "low degree" of the first beatitude, the "meek" of the third, whom the Messiah would exalt (Luke 1:52). They were faithful and submissive in the trials which God was permitting. They were teachable, and they stood for peace; inflexible, and ready, if need be, to suffer martyrdom. When the laws of men commanded what God forbade, they refused to obey them. Their only weapon was an unflinching faith in a just and merciful God to vindicate their "meekness." Following in their train, Paul could say, "When I am weak, then I am strong." To be meek was not easy, but his mission was to deal with men by "the gentleness and sweet reasonableness of Christ" (II Cor. 10:1; I Cor. 4:18-21).

Ἐγκράτεια is **temperance** (KJV), **self-control** (RSV). "Temperance" is only one aspect of the "self-mastery" in this word. In I Cor. 7:9 the verb refers to the control of sexual desire, and in the same letter (I Cor. 9:25) it includes all kinds of self-control required of an athlete. In our present passage the noun applies not only to drunkenness and reveling, but to all the "flesh-works" listed in vss. 19-21. Paul's freedom did not consist in giving free rein to one's impulses and desires. Even when these were lawful and not harmful, he subjected each to three tests: Is it helpful? Is it constructive? Is it to the glory of God? (I Cor. 10:23, 31.)

The Stoics had helped to prepare the soil out of which this fruit of the Spirit was to grow. They insisted that the sovereign reason could and should contol the passions. They believed in a law of nature to which they must conform, and they endeavored to maintain their inner freedom under all circumstances. But their motive was very different from Paul's, the one being devoted to the glory of the God of grace, the other to the preservation of the sovereign self-will. When the Stoic collided with things beyond his control, his inner independence turned into apathy, practicing the motto "When we can't do what we want, we want to do what we can." He took orders from his commander in chief, an impersonal God who had the power of life or death; but he did it in such a way as to make it clear to God and men that he, the Stoic, was after all the captain of his soul. He

24 And they that are Christ's have crucified the flesh with the affections and lusts.

is no law. 24 And those who belong to Christ Jesus have crucified the flesh with its passions and desires.

---

controlled his anger because he found it a nuisance to be under the power of any passion; and in his sight meekness was contemptible weakness. (On Stoicism see also Vol. VII, pp. 86-88.)

Paul exalted humility: "It is no longer I who live, but Christ who lives in me" (2:20). His self-control was not an end in itself. When he fasted and denied himself, it was because of the necessities of his missionary task. His self-discipline was the result of his spiritual experiences, rather than an undertaking to induce them; and his self-control was sane compared with the ascetic excesses of later Christian groups such as the "Encratites," who forbade marriage and followed fantastic dietary rules.

With this word Paul concludes his list of the fruit of the Spirit. (A few ancient authorities add ἁγνεία, "consecration.") He assures the Galatians that there is **no law** against producing it. But that is looking at the matter from God's point of view; with men it is different. Unrepentant sinners have no appetite for the fruit of the Spirit, and when its production and distribution require changes in the political and economic *status quo,* men do pass laws against it. Jesus was crucified for treason; Stephen was lynched for religious liberalism; the twelve apostles were arrested for doing good; and Paul was stoned at Lystra for calling men to the living God, and jeered in Athens for speaking of the resurrection of the dead. Especially in time of war these traits of Christian character have been forbidden fruit, though given for the healing of the nations. Occasionally the world, exhausted with fighting, and sick of its cynical Epicureanism, has professed a desire for the fruits of the Spirit, but on its own terms without the cross required to produce them. On the other hand, no law could compel men to produce any fruit of the Spirit.

24. Having described Christian liberty in terms of freedom to bear the fruit of the Spirit, Paul once more states its cost, the crucifixion of **the flesh with its passions and desires** (cf. 2:20; 6:14; Rom. 6:6; Col. 3:5). **The flesh** refers to all that is sinful in human nature. In classical Greek παθήματα are the "experiences" which a person has or "suffers." They may be active or passive, good or bad. The word also means "dispositions," "propensities," "impulses"; whether they are moral or immoral must be determined from the context. The same word designates the "sufferings" of Christ and for Christ (II Cor. 1:5; Rom. 8:18), and the "passions" that have to be crucified because they bear fruit for death (Rom. 7:5). Since Paul does not mean that all the **affections** (KJV) of men are bad, RSV translates παθήμασιν by **passions.** For ἐπιθυμίαις see on vs. 17; the word **lusts** (KJV) has become narrowed to apply mainly to wrong forms of sexual expression; hence the change to **desires** (RSV).

But how is man to crucify his flesh? Abstaining from every form of evil is only the negative part; on the positive side there must be newness of moral life (Rom. 6:4), testing all things and holding fast that which is good (I Thess. 5:21-22). The first step is for a man to admit that the sinful drives in human nature deserve to be crucified, and that he

---

way so easily to the command of the **flesh,** which puts a man in slavery; one surrenders to the control of the **Spirit,** which keeps a man free. **Walk in the Spirit, and ye shall not fulfil the lust of the flesh** (vs. 16). Any one who lives in the lust of the flesh has lost his freedom.

The Spirit of Christ becomes the source of virtues which operate through the body. Paul admonished people to live on this pattern so that at least nine virtues would grow in their lives. Those virtues fall into three groups. The ones that relate to God are **love, joy, peace.** Those that relate to one's fellow men are **long-suffering, kindness, goodness, faith.** In man's relation to himself are **meekness** and **temperance.** And Paul adds, **against such there is no law** (vs. 23). Persons who embody these virtues cannot be described or handled by law. They represent a quality of life that is above the law.

And how may one become a person like that?

25 If we live in the Spirit, let us also walk in the Spirit.

25 If we live by the Spirit, let us also

must have nothing more to do with them. Then he puts himself so completely under control of the love of Christ, who died and was raised from the dead (II Cor. 5:15), that he no longer lives for himself, but suffers with Christ and is thereby transformed by beholding his glory (II Cor. 3:18). He undertakes a mission for Christ and becomes so busy in the service of others that all sinful "flesh-works" die of starvation (II Cor. 4:8-10). He nourishes his new life in the Spirit by thinking about whatever is true and honorable, just and pure, gracious, excellent, and praiseworthy (Phil. 4:8). He co-operates to build the Christian society, and thereby he himself is encouraged and built up (I Thess. 5:10-11). In short, he lives and walks with the Spirit, which is the most strenuous of all ways of living.

D. To Join the Co-operative of the Spirit (5:25–6:6)

25. Paul's crucifixion of the flesh is not an end in itself, but the removal of the road block on the royal highway of freedom. In both clauses πνεύματι ("spirit") is without the article, but the reference is to the Spirit of God. The RSV translates it as a dative of means, **by the Spirit,** which may be either by the life and power which the Spirit supplies or in accordance with the life pattern set by the Spirit. Consequently **in the Spirit** (KJV) is better; cf. 2:20; 4:6; 5:6. This does justice to the mystical element in Paul's religious experience; but neither translation indicates the fact that Paul uses στοιχῶμεν, "let us walk in line," "in step," "in fellowship" with the Spirit, instead of περιπατεῖτε (vs. 16), which stresses outward conduct, or the ἄγεσθε of vs. 18, which emphasizes the leadership of the Spirit.

To walk in the Spirit is to live one's whole life in accordance with the mind of Christ. The daily question is not "What would Jesus do if he were in my place?" but "What would Jesus have me do?" For although Christ was in Paul, and Paul was in Christ, Christ was not Paul. As a pattern, the mind of Christ was a living, growing ideal which Paul had to apply in constantly changing circumstances. The task of determining the requirements of the moment was his. Christ was the foundation of the temple of the Spirit, but Paul and his fellow Christians had to make the blueprints and specifications and furnish the materials and labor for the superstructure.

The legalists wanted a building code in which all the plans and decisions were set down in black and white. They would have reduced the gospel to rules by which to walk in assurance and comfort. They argued that most men were not yet ready for Paul's freedom, and they thought that walking in the Spirit ought to be safeguarded by the directions for walking contained in the Jewish law, lest the Christian be misled by his own fallible aims and desires while imagining that he was doing the will of God. Paul saw that the surest way to "quench" the Spirit (I Thess. 5:19) was to refuse to listen to anything the Spirit had to say beyond what he had already revealed in the Scriptures.

Not by attempting to cultivate directly the virtues Paul names, but by welcoming Christ, whose coming into a man's life can bring those virtues to him. "The water that I shall give him shall be in him a well of water springing up into everlasting life" (John 4:14). When that stream begins to flow as an inward spring, a man begins to live above the law.

In man's new nature Christ's presence is a power for daily cleansing and constant renewal. And as in healthy seed planted in the ground, or yeast in bread, the power is a growing power. Christlike virtues continue to grow as the moral and spiritual life of a man develops, until power appears in his person. He becomes a man of privilege because he lives for more than the law requires. He is the free man, because the abiding Spirit safeguards his freedom and prompts him not to abuse or violate his privileges. "Where the Spirit of the Lord is, there is liberty" (II Cor. 3:17). His Spirit comes at birth; but men have nothing to do with that phenomenon. They have everything to do with welcoming him on his second visit, when they

26 Let us not be desirous of vainglory, provoking one another, envying one another.

6 Brethren, if a man be overtaken in a fault, ye which are spiritual, restore such a one in the spirit of meekness; considering thyself, lest thou also be tempted.

walk by the Spirit. 26 Let us have no self-conceit, no provoking of one another, no envy of one another.

6 Brethren, if a man is overtaken in any trespass, you who are spiritual should restore him in a spirit of gentleness. Look

---

Here the chapter and verse divisions interfere with grasping the sequence of Paul's thought. It is best to take vs. 25 as the summary conclusion of what has preceded, and an introduction to the admonitions that begin with vs. 26 and continue through 6:10.

26. Returning to his statement of the self-devouring consequence of wrong ambitions (vs. 15), Paul pleads, in effect: "Let us not glory in things that have no value, challenging one another, envying one another."

The Greek word is "vainglorious," "glorying in things that are empty." **Self-conceit** (RSV) and "vain-mindedness" are included, but the main idea is "putting false values on persons and things." Προσκαλούμενοι means **provoking** in the sense of "challenging," inciting, goading, daring one another to do things against which some had conscientious scruples, and then "calling each other down." The danger was threefold: loss of faith in Christ as the sole and sufficient Savior; dismay at the responsibilities of freedom in Christ; and an excess of radicalism which threatened the unity of the church with a conceited assertion of liberty and a divorce of love from faith (I Cor. 8; Rom. 12; Col. 2).

Some Christians were fanatically conservative, while others inclined to patronize the world's Vanity Fair. Neither group could estimate themselves "soberly" (Rom. 12:3). Professing to be experts in discerning the truth, they succeeded only in becoming windbags (ἡ γνῶσις φυσιοῖ, I Cor. 8:1). They could not build up the church because they were driven by competition, envy, and conceit, not motivated by love's esteem and helpfulness. The right stood in terror of the iconoclasm of the left, and the radicals labeled all other men reactionaries. Each denounced the other before the tribunal of his own beliefs and standards. Both sides professed to love liberty and defend it, but neither was willing to grant it to the other. Each side suffered from its own fractional view and was dissatisfied with the other in proportion as its own conduct fell short of the mind of Christ.

Lacking perspective and balance, this fractional religion treated nonessentials as matters of life and death. For one party it was the spiritually irrelevant custom of fasting, for another the side issues of special days and seasons. Even a good custom such as sabbath observance could be so exaggerated as to convince the observer that the coming of the kingdom of God depended on it alone, and that God sent sickness and war and eternal death to punish those who violated it. Some regarded idol-worship as superstition and dared their more timid neighbors to throw overboard so many time-honored customs and taboos as to wreck their faith with doubts and fears of mortal offense. Both groups became proud, the one because it was bold to cast off the old and outworn, the other because it was loyal to the customs of its ancestors. Now, says Paul, let us not lose the things that matter—the faith, the hope, and the love that abide.

6:1. Those who lived in the Spirit had to judge themselves and others, pointing out and correcting faults, and praising what was right and good. But some were doing this in a

---

are "born again." It is the Spirit of the Lord that sets them free—that leaves them in control of themselves and in organic relationship with the source of moral activity and freedom.

6:1. ***The Healing Fellowship of the Church.***—(See Expos. on 5:13.) **Brethren, if a man be overtaken in a fault, ye which are spiritual, restore such a one in the spirit of meekness; considering thyself, lest thou also be tempted.**

The obligation to heal those who fall is not alone the work of the ordained minister: he is only the servant of the fellowship which is God's instrument of healing. Luther, in his explanation to the commandment, "Thou shalt not

bitter, envious spirit, and had to be reminded how easy it was to be "taken by surprise" and get out of step with the Spirit, in some "fall by the side," **fault** (KJV) or **trespass** (RSV). By **overtaken** is meant, not being caught in the act of stepping off the path, but suddenly and unintentionally slipping out of step with the Spirit. One may have been betrayed by overconfidence, as Peter when he denied his Lord; or one might be confused by the difficulty of deciding what was right. Paul knew that the human emissaries of "Satan" could disguise themselves as ministers of light.

What was needed was not harsh condemnation but sympathetic help to get the lapsing member back into step with the Spirit. The Christian critic must be genuinely sorry for the other's plight and do all in his power to **restore** him; the other meanings of καταρτίζω—"repair," "prepare," "fit out," "perfect"—suggest what was required. This had to be done **in the spirit of meekness,** which was a fruit of the Spirit (5:23); it included kindness and **gentleness,** but also mildness of temper, patience, and the necessary self-effacement. Ἐν πνεύματι πραΰτητος may mean "gently," "meekly," but it is best to interpret it by reference to the sphere in which the restoration is accomplished—in the Spirit, in Christ, who is himself gentle and the creator of gentleness in those who walk with him. The Spirit's "repairmen" are πνευματικοί, **spiritual,** endowed with faith and tact to restore the lapsed and prevent further transgressions. There is no room in their hearts for cynicism. They do not have to fall into the ditch themselves in order to be able to help the sinner, but they do need the sympathy for him which avoids snap judgments and takes into account all the circumstances that led to his fall. Paul warns against overconfidence: the **spiritual** too must be vigilant against temptation, but in such a way as not to live in morbid fear of falling (I Cor. 10:12-13; Rom. 8:37-39).

---

bear false witness against thy neighbor," admonishes us: "We should so fear and love God as not deceitfully to belie, betray, slander, or raise injurious reports against our neighbor, but apologize for him, speak well of him, and put the most charitable construction on all his actions."[4] Here is the acid test for a Christian: What does he do with the man who falls? What is his attitude toward those who are overtaken in a fault? What is his obligation to the man who has failed? And another question must be asked: What is the responsibility of the corporate fellowship of the church?

The first answer may be tied up in the word **Brethren.** We are to feel on a level with the man who falls. We are to regard ourselves as fellow sinners. "If thou, LORD, shouldst mark iniquities, O Lord, who shall stand?" (Ps. 130:3.) This brethren consciousness means awareness of our common danger. It includes a sense of responsibility for the other man's failure. "If meat make my brother to offend, I will eat no flesh while the world standeth" (I Cor. 8:13). A man must ask: "Have I been living wrongfully? Has my unconscious influence been the reason for another man's stumbling? Have I to any degree contributed to his weakness? Am I adding to it by not expecting him to rise, or by not helping him to start anew?" Gossip is a common temptation—interpreting people down, not up. Many men are where they are because nobody expected them to be better. It is recorded even of our Lord, "And he did not do many mighty works there, because of their unbelief" (Matt. 13:58).

The second answer may be found in the words **overtaken in a fault.** Who is going to say what constitutes a fault? When one man presumes to judge another, it is a tremendous moment for both. Who or what shall be the standard for judging? Who can see the standard more clearly than others? The difficulty is to get at the hidden secrets behind all external explanations. The word **overtaken** seems to suggest that temptation comes upon us unawares. Most sin is committed not by deliberate intention or planning but in weakness and surprise, in the passion of a rash moment. And who are quickest to judge those who err? The ones who are only slightly, if any, better than the man who is recognized as fallen. People who are weak at the very same point as the fallen are often his severest critics. Indeed, warmhearted sinners are frequently closer to the Spirit of Christ than the supercilious. And who are slowest to condemn and the most charitable in judgment? Those whose ideals are highest, those who are living on higher levels themselves. The loftiest are the most considerate. The holiest are the most understanding.

The third answer may be hidden in the word **spiritual: Ye which are spiritual.** What are the marks of a spiritually minded man? He is trying at least to be constructive; he would have his

[4] *Smaller Catechism,* Explanation to the Eighth Commandment.

2 Bear ye one another's burdens, and so fulfil the law of Christ.

to yourself, lest you too be tempted. 2 Bear one another's burdens, and so fulfill the

---

The man who was crucified with Christ was dead to sin; but Paul knew that the Spirit did not turn the Christian into an automaton who could not make mistakes. For he himself did not always find it easy to deal gently with the erring. He used irony and sarcasm and the rod. He laid a curse on the Galatian errorists and wished that the troublemakers would emasculate themselves. His dealings with Peter and John, Mark and Barnabas, show that his difficulty in being meek was proportional to the depth of his convictions and his faithfulness to his gospel.

For these reasons it is important to translate the καί ("even") which the KJV and the RSV omit: the man who is living in the Spirit can be expected not to sin; but if even he makes a mistake—restore him. The indefinite **a man** refers to a fellow church member; a few MSS clarify by changing the text to "one of you," or "a man of you." But the principle of Christian gentleness applies equally to the treatment of outsiders.

2, 5. The difficulties and shortcomings, even of Christians, constitute a burden so heavy that all have to share it. The burdens of the Christian co-operatives are Christ's burden of forgiving sins and reconciling men to God and to each other; of *re*storing, *re*pairing, *re*fitting oneself and others to *re*join the Spirit, and of *fore*seeing and *pre*venting future lapses by creating an environment which will be God's answer to "Lead us not into temptation, but deliver us from evil."

This **law of Christ** is not a law in the legal sense of the word, but the life principle of all who take up his cross of creative suffering. Christian mutuality "fulfills" **it** by going far beyond the feasible minimum of good which laws dare prescribe, taking upon itself all men's diseases, to heal, to forgive, and, if need be, to die for them. The word is

---

works to be creative and redemptive. He does a minimum of talking, and that only and always with the sense of responsibility. He fears gossip; he seeks to put the most charitable construction on another man's words and deeds. This is no pollyanna technique, a sugary sweetness and light. Like Jesus, he sees in the man who is the man who could be. And he goes about restoring, **in the spirit of meekness,** remembering that he himself could easily be in a similar position, save for Christ and Christlike friends. Only such meek people, who are anything but weak people, can do restorative work. The severe, the sharp-tongued, the suspicious, the brittle, the irritable only make healing more difficult. Theirs is not the mind of Christ; theirs is not his method of love. "The Son of man is come to seek and to save that which was lost" (Luke 19:10).

This restoring process begins with Christ, who acts through certain individuals; but the process is not carried through to its end until the man who is **overtaken in a fault** is restored to the fellowship of the church. Only then is the healing circle complete. All healing involves fellowship; and so back to the word **brethren** that begins this verse. The broken brotherhood is reunited, and the man who is restored in turn becomes a restorer. The way of healing is the way of freedom. Freedom broken can be restored; and in that restoration freedom itself is safeguarded. Only the pardoned and those who pardon are free.

2, 5. ***Sharing: Principle and Paradox.***—Life is a solo: every man shall bear his own burden. But life is also a chorus: **bear ye one another's burdens.**

Written across the whole Bible, and thus planted deep in the structure of the Christian life, is this principle of sharing. It begins on the elemental level of sharing the necessities of life: food, clothing, shelter—"Your heavenly Father knoweth that ye have need of all these things" (Matt. 6:32). It climbs to highest peaks in spiritual and intellectual sharing.

Because this principle is true, the church must give mankind at least a five-point program: Worship—climaxing in the Holy Communion—education, service, fellowship, and shared experiences. The last in this list is perhaps the most difficult to achieve on a high, constructive, and Christlike level. Said one "sharer" to a rather promiscuous group, "If you think the last speaker has been guilty of terrible things, wait till you hear my story!" It is easy, though unintentional, to turn such sharing into glorified gossip sessions, which appear almost as contests to see who has been the worst. Often there seems to be a tendency to boast, instead of testifying and confessing what the Lord has

"fill up," "satisfy completely," as with "good measure, pressed down, shaken together, running over" (Luke 6:38). Some MSS make it a promise: "You will fulfill."

The other half of **the law of Christ** is stated in vs. 5. Here the verb is the same as in vs. 2, but the noun is τὸ φορτίον, **load** (RSV), which the KJV translates the same as τὰ βάρη, **burden.** There is no great difference in meaning—βάρη suggests the "weight"; φορτίον the "freight," a ship's "cargo" or a "load" for a pack animal. In Matt. 11:30 Christ's "burden" is φορτίον, and so is the "burden" of the law in Matt. 23:4 and Luke 11:46; in these cases the RSV has not changed the KJV.

Vs. 5 is neither the antithesis, the contradiction, nor the paradox of vs. 2, but the complementary half of the fundamental principle of the Christian life stated in 5:13-14. This is the love which enslaves each member to bear the burdens of all the rest and at the same time requires him to bear his own. But on both sides the "enslavement" is voluntary. Neither may say, "You exist for my sake," for that is the path of totalitarian dictatorship; but each will say, "I exist for your sake," for that is the way of freedom. In the Christian co-operative the rights and privileges are always balanced by the responsibilities and duties. These verses are concerned with the burden of failure to walk in the Spirit of Christ, and consequently the solution which Paul applies to the trouble in Galatia ranges far beyond the immediate occasion.

Paul set the example of Christian reciprocity by taking upon himself the burden of Christ, and Christ's body, the church. As he saw it, this task was to naturalize all men for citizenship in the kingdom of God, so as to present them "perfected" in faith, hope, and love on the imminent "day of the Lord." He believed that the power to establish the kingdom was God's, but he also had faith to believe that God was working through

---

done for and with sinful human life. Such sharing is melodramatic, and in place of true, clean, Christian inspiration, produces morbid and sordid stories out of which fantasies are woven.

Jesus speaks his first and also his last words to the individual; but there are disciplines, insights, and comradeships which are available only in a group. "For where two or three are gathered together in my name, there am I in the midst of them" (Matt. 18:20). What assets may result from responsible sharing?

Responsible sharing keeps life *fresh.* It keeps life in the present tense and prevents it from becoming stale, flat, and unprofitable. When the children of Israel were journeying through the wilderness toward Canaan, God provided manna for their food. It came daily and had to be eaten daily; it could not be hoarded, for it would spoil (Exod. 16:21). When rugged individualists stored up more than their share and more than they needed, they lost what they kept. Therein is the paradox. The most valuable possessions in life, like the manna of that wilderness, are lost when they are hoarded. Our faith and our courage and our reasons for both —or the secret source of both which lies far back in the mountains of God—must be shared if we would live with freshness and radiance. When we stop sharing, we stop living. Share first of all with God your questions, your pessimisms, your fears, and your doubts; then share humbly with men your faith, your courage, your love, and your victories with Christ. Such sharing keeps life fresh.

Responsible sharing keeps life *strong.* This truth is confirmed by the teaching of Jesus: "When thou art converted, strengthen thy brethren" (Luke 22:32). There is no more effective way to do this than to share with others what Christ has done for us. Speak not to begin an argument but rather to bear testimony.

There is a church that carefully records the major experiences of its members. For example, a young couple lost their child; time and God helped to heal their grief. Another young couple several years later suffered the same loss. Beyond all other aid which that church could provide, the first couple was able to help the second.

Strength comes from responsible sharing. The old story of a bundle of sticks illustrates the principle. Each separate stick could easily be broken, one by one; but as long as the entire bundle was held together by a strong wire or cord, it was well-nigh unbreakable. Even so shared experiences in a genuine fellowship can strengthen the soul. Many persons are individually whipped in the struggle of life; but when they are held to a group in Christian fellowship they can never be defeated. "Confess your faults one to another, and pray one for another, that ye may be healed" (Jas. 5:16). In unity of mind and spirit and purpose there are healing and power and strength. The story of Pentecost is the story of responsible fellowship: "And when

him to shorten the delay. Hence the principal component of his burden was to "fill up" (cf. Col. 1:24) the afflictions of Christ which still remained. He invested his life in calling men to be reconciled to God, in turning hostility into harmony, and producing all the other fruits of God's Spirit. Knowing that sinners could never make good the hurt they were causing to God and to man, and that Christ could not reconcile men to God without reconciling them to each other, he shared the burden of sin-bearing and labored to knit men's hearts together in love (Col. 2:2). Like a mother, he was in travail until Christ was formed in his children; and convinced that he had something to contribute to the understanding of the gospel which no other apostle could give, or was giving, he devoted his life to this service of God and man (4:19; Rom. 1:8-15; 15:14-21; Col. 1:28–2:5). From first to last his letters show how great was the burden he bore for others (vs. 17; I Thess. 2:17–3:13; I Cor. 5:3-5; II Cor. 2:4, 10-13; 7:5; 11:21-29).

The method of Paul's burden-bearing and the secret of his power was this: "I try to please all men in everything I do, not seeking my own advantage" (I Cor. 10:33; cf. Rom. 15:1). When men were not pleased, he kept on pleasing Christ by treating sinners as Christ had treated them. Sometimes this kept him from doing things which would not have been wrong in themselves; and again it required him to do things which were right, but which, apart from his aim "by all means to save some," he would not have done. Always, however, his doing or not doing must not compromise his gospel of grace. Nor did he permit a merely sentimental concern for men in general to substitute for obedience to stern duty in concrete particular instances. He always got down to individual cases, as we see from his concern for Onesimus, Epaphroditus, and the friends whom he greeted in Rom. 16.

At the same time Paul expected his Christian friends to help him bear his burden. He asked for their prayers (Rom. 15:30-32; II Cor. 1:11; Col. 4:3; II Thess. 3:1), pleaded with his spiritual children to open their hearts to him (II Cor. 7:2), and called upon all his churches to co-operate in breaking down the barrier between Gentiles and Jews by contributing to the famine relief for Judea. By his own restless energy he kept his co-workers always on the alert. It was this need for help from others that kept his love from becoming the subtle pride that ensnares all who would stand aloof from those they are helping, and who give but do not share. There was always the humility about his service that was willing to receive as well as to give; and to this mutuality his friends and converts responded freely (4:14-15; II Cor. 7:6-7; Rom. 16:3-4; Phil. 2:22; 4:3, 14-18;

---

the day of Pentecost was fully come, they were all with one accord in one place" (Acts 2:1). Such spiritual unity is the channel of responsible sharing, to show what life has done to us and what God has done for us.

Responsible sharing keeps life *useful*. Here again are seen the principle and paradox. In Matthew this teaching of Jesus is explained in detail. "Whosoever shall smite thee on thy right cheek, turn to him the other also. And if any man . . . take away thy coat, let him have thy cloak also. And whosoever shall compel thee to go a mile, go with him twain. Give to him that asketh thee, and from him that would borrow of thee turn not thou away" (Matt. 5:39-42). Is that a counsel of perfection? Is it really possible for man? As a standard of life can it be realized on a large scale by a group?

Underneath such seemingly impossible ideals lies this imperishable truth: He who would live must give himself away. Responsible sharing demands that one shall be useful in the most Christlike meaning of the word. E. Stanley Jones once confessed his faith in the following statement, "I do not know how this old world is coming out, but I believe the future belongs to those who belong to Christ." Written deep in the structure of this personal universe is the principle and paradox of belonging: a man who tries to keep his life to himself and for himself will lose it; if he gives himself away, he lives. Sharing keeps life useful.

2. ***Bear Ye One Another's Burdens.***—One man may help to carry another man's burden, but he can never carry that man's responsibility. Every life sooner or later has burdens to bear, frequently in the form of permanent handicaps, sometimes in obligations that appear very unfair. It seems that this world was never intended to be a place where one cannot fail, where

3 For if a man think himself to be something, when he is nothing, he deceiveth himself.
4 But let every man prove his own work, and then shall he have rejoicing in himself alone, and not in another.

law of Christ.
3 For if any one thinks he is something, when he is nothing, he deceives himself.
4 But let each one test his own work, and then his reason to boast will be in himself alone and not in his neighbor.

Col. 4:10-14). For a full list of those who helped Paul to bear his burden, one would have to consult God's "book of life" (Phil. 4:3).

Yet there was no disposition on Paul's part to escape by loading his personal burden upon the shoulders of others. He was grateful indeed to his Philippians, but he reminded them that even without their gift he could have borne his own troubles, because he had learned "to be content" (Phil. 4:11). Moreover, there was a load which Paul, and no other must bear. That was his "thorn in the flesh," and to it he resigned himself actively in order that his Lord's strength might perfect itself in his weakness (II Cor. 12:7-10).

3. Paul gives a further reason to bear with others' shortcomings instead of becoming vainglorious.

The man described here is not Christ-minded. Ignoring the danger from his own temptations, he envies others and refuses to help them become better than himself (Phil. 2:3). Instead of estimating himself sanely by the measure of faith which God has apportioned him, he overrates and boasts (Rom. 12:3), becomes puffed up (I Cor. 8:1-2), harsh, censorious, and unforgiving, lenient toward himself, severe to all others. He condemns his erring neighbor without trying to understand the how or the why of the error; and he is not sorry but glad, because the error seems to justify him in thanking God that he is not as other men. Self-conceit, says Paul, multiplied by zero equals zero plus self-deception; and its victim is not only useless as a burden-bearer, but an added load for others to carry.

4*a*. Beginning with 5:25 we have a series of imperatives, "let us also walk," "let us not become," "restore," "bear," "fulfill," of which the δέ in 6:4*a* is continuative and should be translated "and" rather than **but.** To avoid self-deception and fulfill the "law" of love each man must measure his achievements by the mind of Christ. That is his assignment in Christ's bureau of standards. Δοκιμάζω means **test,** "discriminate," "approve," "think best," "choose." In the sense of testing it has a dual meaning, **prove,** "approve," "attest."

4*b*-5. Τὸ καύχημα is not **rejoicing** (KJV), but the inner satisfaction and exultation of which rejoicing is the manifestation; and **boast** (RSV) is an outward expression of the inner "glory" which comes from true self-knowledge and consciousness of work done so well that it stands the test of time and meets the Master's approval (I Cor. 3:10-15). Justified by the data from the laboratory, this kind of "glorying" is never out of place;

---

security is guaranteed. Burdens belong in a world like this. There is always the possibility of failure in every man's life, and burdens come out of that fact. Unless there is this possibility, there can be no personal growth. Where there is no possibility of loss, there can be no moral choice. Remove the possibility of tragedy, and there can be no spiritual awareness.

This principle is observable in the fact that there are at least three kinds of burdens. There are those that come to a man because of his own limitations in life: from inherited tendencies that do much to cause poor management; from poor judgment in assuming unnecessary risks; from poor moral insights that result in the violation of the best conscience of society; from forgetting that men always reap more than they sow. These might be called man's *unnecessary burdens.*

There are also burdens that come to every life because men live in an imperfect world. These are caused by the limitations of environment, and are the consequence of human friction and the presence of evil. They often come after one has done his best and has achieved considerable personal excellence. They are the

5 For every man shall bear his own burden.

6 Let him that is taught in the word communicate unto him that teacheth in all good things.

5 For each man will have to bear his own load.

6 Let him who is taught the word share all good things with him who teaches.

---

yet the man who is entitled to it prefers to keep it to himself (II Cor. 12:1, 11), whereas "boasting" is always lacking in good manners and is never quite free from the implication of being excessive or unjustified.

Τὸν ἕτερον is, lit., **another** (KJV), but it also means **neighbor** (RSV). The preposition εἰς with ἑαυτόν means "in respect of himself," and with τὸν ἕτερον it expresses "in comparison with."

For the meaning of vs. 5, see on vs. 2. The "load" is the task of self-examination and self-correction, and no one else can carry it for us. The standard of self-measurement in the workshop of the Spirit is never one's neighbor or fellow church member, much less the non-Christian who claims to be better than those whom he calls "the hypocrites in the church." "When they measure themselves by one another, and compare themselves with one another, they are without understanding" (II Cor. 10:12). The true standard was the design for living which Christ gave to Paul: Christ's visualization of what Paul could and should be and become. He had to measure himself by the purpose for which Christ had reached down and taken hold of him (Phil. 3:12). When his work met that test, he had the right to glory, but only provided he also said, "It is no longer I who live, but Christ who lives in me" (2:20).

6. Having stated the duty of the individual to bear his own burden (vs. 5), Paul returns to the first half of the principle of Christian mutuality (vs. 2) and applies it to the church's obligation to support its teachers. The RSV makes this verse a separate paragraph and follows the KJV in leaving δέ, "but," untranslated. This tears the passage from its context and obscures the sequence of Paul's thought, which makes it an application of the dual principle set forth in vss. 2 and 5. In present-day English **communicate** (KJV) is not readily understood in the sense of "convey," "impart," **share** (RSV). The noun is κοινωνία, "fellowship," which was the binding force that held the church together. Paul conceived of the Christian enterprise as a co-operative undertaking by the Spirit and the members of Christ's body.

There is no warrant here or elsewhere in Paul's letters to restrict the connotation of **in all good things** to material things, such as gifts of money, clothing, or lodging. The Paul who did manual labor to earn money for the poor did not mean that the teacher had no obligation beyond his "spiritual" contribution to the life of the church; nor did he mean that his pupils were to give him nothing but "material" gifts. He wanted a share in their prayers, their ideals, their achievements, their very selves. The object of sharing material things was to make possible the mutuality of spiritual gifts. Paul never put himself upon a pedestal, as if he had no need of spiritual help from his converts (I Thess. 2:8, 17-19; 3:7-9; II Cor. 1:3-11; 6:11-13; 12:14-15; Rom. 1:11-12).

---

natural issue of life's experiences, for they arise out of situations over which the average man has little or no control. They are physical (like tornadoes) or personal (like unemployment), and might well be called *inevitable burdens.*

Because of these unnecessary and inevitable burdens, a man who believes he owes anything to the world besides pulling his own weight finds himself choosing another kind of burden—life's *voluntary burdens.* Thoughts like these move his conscience: **Bear ye one another's burdens:** "We then that are strong ought to bear the infirmities of the weak" (Rom. 15:1); "Inasmuch as ye have done it unto one of the least of these my brethren, ye have done it unto me" (Matt. 25:40). Indeed, anybody who in this world has no burdens to bear is missing life altogether.

A woman who had served her church for nearly twenty years asked her pastor, "Do you

7 Be not deceived; God is not mocked: for whatsoever a man soweth, that shall he also reap.

7 Do not be deceived; God is not mocked, for whatever a man sows, that he will also

Literally translated, the verse reads, "Let the catechumen share with the catechist." Instruction was probably oral. **The word** which these earliest catechists taught comprised the whole story of God's grace through faith in Christ: instruction concerning the true God and his will for man; the mission and message of Jesus; the meaning of his death and the power of his resurrection; the expectation of his imminent second coming; the need to repent and qualify through faith for citizenship in his kingdom; and demonstrations of living and walking in the Spirit.

The reason for citing this matter of sharing as an example of the Christian fellowship is clear. The world was full of mountebanks and quacks, each peddling his gospel for a price. To avoid the charge of preaching merely for money Paul continued to work at his trade. But he saw that this could not be made the general practice without depriving those who heard the gospel of their opportunity to reciprocate. Resident teachers, who could not fall under the same suspicions as the itinerant missionaries, would suffer financial loss by having to take time from their regular occupation, and part-time teaching would retard the process of religious instruction. The laborer was worthy of his hire, and Christian mutuality required receiving as well as giving.

E. To Engage in "the Agriculture of the Spirit" (6:7-10)

7-8. Paul uses the example of Christian reciprocity stated in vs. 6 to illustrate two principles which are ingrained in the universe, (*a*) mutuality and (*b*) the law of the identical harvest. To translate literally: "Do not be deceived: God is not mocked; for whatever a man sows that will he also reap, because he who sows for his own physical nature will reap decay from the physical nature, and he who sows for the Spirit will reap everlasting life from the Spirit."

A few authorities omit μή and read πλανᾶσθε, "you are being deceived." Christians who imagined that they could reap the fruit of the Spirit (5:22-23) while competing, envying, boasting, and challenging instead of bearing each other's burdens were only deceiving themselves. God was not like men who could be outwitted, and whose laws could be evaded; no man could "turn up his nose"—such is the literal meaning of μυκτηρίδεται—at him with impunity by being stingy and expecting generosity.

remember the wretched health I had when you first learned to know me, what a nervous wreck I was?" Of course he remembered. Then she added, "I have had to bear so many burdens in my family that today I am a relatively well woman." Bearing the heavier burdens of others lifted her own. Perhaps a major key to mental health can be found in deliberately assuming the burdens of others. The help given another to carry his burden is one way by which Christ gets under a man's own.

All this, said Paul, is fulfilling **the law of Christ.** Law? After the struggle he had gone through to get the law properly placed in his thinking and in his own life, after getting the Galatians free from their entanglement with the law—why on earth did Paul turn again to that word? Was it to give the Galatians a totally new conception of law? Here law undoubtedly means for him the way of Christ, the principles upon which the Christian life operates, the act itself of love, of putting into daily living all that he had written about burden-bearing and about the restoration of those who trespass (cf. vs. 16). Count on one thing: Paul never contradicted his basic teaching with regard to the freedom which is in Christ.

7-10. ***The Natural Law as a Safeguard of Freedom.***— (See Expos. on 5:13.) The kind of God a person trusts is indicated in his method of handling problems. Anxiety and worry may indicate that his God is an absentee Lord, who is remote from man's personal concerns and cares. If he harbors hatred and resentment against people, can it mean that his God is revengeful? If he plays fast and loose with his moral life, does he think of his God as whimsical and nonchalant, not the righteous God

In the beginning God established the law of the identical harvest, to hold "while the earth remaineth" (Gen. 1:11-12; 8:22); then he planted a garden "eastward in Eden," and created man "to dress it and to keep it" (Gen. 2:8, 15). That made Adam and all his race God's spiritual agriculturists. By the very nature of his being, man's every act was a sowing. There were only two kinds of seed, one good, the other evil, and only two ways to sow it, one for the body and the low aims which the sinfulness of human nature forced it to serve, the other for the higher life of man's eternal soul. In **to his flesh** and **to the Spirit,** the preposition "to" (εἰς) does not mean that the seed was dropped "into the flesh" or "into the Spirit," but that the flesh-sower's purpose in providing for his material needs was to gratify **his own** unregenerate desires, whereas the Spirit-sower employed these same material resources to make his body the temple of the Holy Spirit.

In the culture of the soil men were never so foolish as to expect grapes from thorns or figs from thistles, and they knew that tares yielded tares. But in the culture of the soul they had still to learn that enmity, competition, and hatred do not bring peace, co-operation, and love, "because" (ὅτι, **for**) the harvest is always the multiplication of the identical seed. All the "flesh-works" (5:15, 19-21, 26) bore the spores of their own "decay" (φθοράν, **corruption**), and were doomed to die even as they grew. The **due season** did not have to wait for the day of Judgment.

The same principle held when planting the fruit of the Spirit (vss. 1-6; 5:13-14, 22-23, 25), but with the opposite result in producing a character over which death had no power. The first installment of the harvest of the Spirit was simultaneous with the sowing, and the reaping was continuous through time and eternity. The promise in these verses needs especial emphasis because the initial **God is not mocked** spreads like a cloud of doom in the mind of the reader and tends to black out the promise. Translating the δέ in vs. 8 by "and" instead of **but** helps to make clear that this is a promise as well as a warning.

Sowing and reaping were social as well as individual processes. The intention of the flesh-minded man was, of course, to sow only by himself and for himself. He aimed to get all he could by all means, fair or foul, and to invest it in the enterprises described

---

in whose world men reap what they sow? Reverence for God may become the vantage point from which we look at life. All of us grow in the direction of our reverences. In this sense an American humorist is correct when he says that the way to judge a man is not to look at him in the face but to get behind him and see what he is looking at.

The law of the harvest illustrates the everlasting fact that freedom is not the right to do what we want to do but the power to do what we ought. Freedom operates only in a moral universe. The free man is the moral man. The theory that there is nothing permanent except change; that the best a man can do is to spin from within himself all the wisdom he can know, as a spider spins his web; that there is no objective truth to which each life is accountable—every such theory runs counter to the law of the harvest. The power of gravity is permanent. And we are accountable to it, whether we wish to be or not. It would be strange if there were nothing comparable in the moral world.

This natural law of sowing and reaping is a discipline, a guide, and a safeguard to the man whose inner life is controlled by Christ. It is a constant reminder that Christ-control within is related to the law which is written deep in the structure of the universe. What a man does to life, life does back to him. What a man sows, he reaps; and he reaps in kind, as he sows. The principle may be illustrated in the achievement of a trustworthy mind. Such a mind in his later years is possible for nobody unless he has paid the price in the years that have gone by. So with the achievement of reliable character: one who sows carelessness can never reap the confidence of people. One who sows supersensitiveness will not reap happiness. "Do men gather grapes of thorns, or figs of thistles?" (Matt. 7:16.) Each of us is born with a mass of helter-skelter qualities. Sacred? Yes. Worthwhile? Not yet. We are born with nothing more than the possibility of achieving worth-whileness. Soon or late men sit down to a banquet of results and consequences. Those with well-disciplined minds and dependable personalities have through the years nurtured life's best

8 For he that soweth to his flesh shall of the flesh reap corruption; but he that soweth to the Spirit shall of the Spirit reap life everlasting.

reap. 8 For he who sows to his own flesh will from the flesh reap corruption; but he who sows to the Spirit will from the Spirit

in 5:19-21. He would have nothing to do with the mutuality of the fellowship of Christ, and what he refused to share with others he withheld to spend upon himself. But however much he might boast of being a self-made man, he had to have the help of others in sowing for his own flesh. Whereupon, by the inverted reciprocity of selfishness, in corrupting his own character he contributed to the degradation of his accomplices (I Cor. 15:33; Rom. 1:18-32), and those who helped him sow were compelled to share his harvest (Rom. 2:8-9). Moreover, in accordance with the fact of social solidarity and vicarious suffering, the burden of reaping his evil fell just as heavily upon those who all the while had been pleading with him to repent and sow for the Spirit.

Sowing and reaping for the Spirit was likewise both a social and an individual process, but with this essential difference: there was joy at harvesttime. Like any sane agriculturist, the Spirit-minded man sowed because he wanted a harvest. But his sowing was a giving, a self-investment to create the mind of Christ in others and set a contagious, enthusiastic example of the "hilarious giver" (ἱλαρόν, II Cor. 9:7) whom the Lord loves. Paul expected his sowing for the Spirit to produce thanksgiving for the glory of God and to "edify" the church by knitting its members together in harmony and mutual enrichment of life (II Cor. 9:9-15). Spirit-sowing did not mean the ascetic abandonment of material things, but the substitution of a spiritual motive for producing and in using them. As Christ's freedman, Paul labored to earn his own living and have something left over to give to the poor.

Now, says Paul, a lifetime of sowing faith, hope, and love, produces a harvest which is not only simultaneous with the sowing but which the sower can take with him when he dies. The body of the flesh-man would waste away with the material things which he was misusing in its service (I Cor. 15:50; Rom. 6:19-23; 8:5-13), and even a resurrection body would do him no good, because he was cultivating no soul-resources for life in God's kingdom of righteousness and peace and joy. Not so with the Spirit-sower. Although his outer nature was "wasting away," and although at any time his body might

secrets in the give and take of discipline and freedom.

All this adds up to life as adventure and investment—not as a gamble. Some people try to gamble their way through. They make a gamble of their most sacred possessions. But life is an adventure and an investment. The parable of the talents sharpens the point (Matt. 25:14-29). One man was given five talents; he brought back five more. Another was given two talents; he brought back two more. Another man was given one; he hid his in the ground. He put his talents in a safe-deposit box. But life is not a safe-deposit box; it is an investment. In a safe-deposit box we get back precisely what we put in; but life increases or decreases. A man gets back more than he puts in, whether of good or evil. The highest returns belong to those who are in the race, not to the group in the grandstand or balcony; to those who invest their best, their lives, for something worth the risk, and in return get a destiny out of it. **God is not mocked.**

8. ***When the Physical Body Takes Over.***—The flesh is not evil; nothing God made is evil. The flesh is not the seat or center of sin; the control is in man's will. The flesh becomes sinful when it is given the upper hand. **He that soweth to his flesh shall of the flesh reap corruption.** The question is, Who is in command? When the flesh or material body is under the direction of the mind, and that mind is saturated with the mind of Christ, we are sowing **to the Spirit,** and **shall of the Spirit reap life everlasting.** When such a relationship does not exist, we are sowing to the flesh, and the harvest is corruption: life is out of order, proportion, and balance.

Consider the realm of the emotions. When the flesh gets out of hand, emotions run riot. (*a*) They may be dwarfed or stunted. Life

9 And let us not be weary in well doing: for in due season we shall reap, if we faint not.

reap eternal life. 9 And let us not grow weary in well-doing, for in due season we

be broken like a frail earthen jar, it was being consumed in the service of righteousness, while his "inner man" was transformed day by day into the image of the Lord who is the Spirit. Then at the last great harvest he would be clothed with a glorified body like that of Christ and would reap eternal life (II Cor. 3:18; 4:7–5:10).

This was a new kind of life which was the grace-gift of God and the justification and guarantee of its own immortality (Rom. 6:4; 8:2, 6). The adjective αἰώνιον means "perpetual," "indefinitely long," "everlasting." It has often been said that the important thing is the quality of this life, not its everlastingness. But Paul would never have said that. His "eternal life" meant two things: (*a*) Companionship with Christ and a personal character congruent with it; and (*b*) endless existence and continuing spiritual growth. He always kept the two together: endless duration and infinite quality; for one was meaningless apart from the other. If the persons who lived in faith and cherished hopes and loved their neighbors were to be put out of existence as persons by death, the three things that abide would be only a trinity of abstractions for mockery. The eternal life which Paul expected to reap from his sowing for the Spirit provided for the conservation of both persons and values. It was an unbroken, endless life in Christ and with Christ; and Christ was the Son of the God who was all and in all (Rom. 8:2, 6; 11:36; Col. 3:3).

9. Taking the obligation to support the teachers of the church as an example of the general requirement to do unlimited good, Paul fortifies his appeal with assurance that the men of faith have every reason to engage in the "agriculture of the Spirit." The first half of the verse is the sower's imperative: keep on doing good; the second clause is the sower's reward: life at harvesttime.

Τὸ καλόν, "the beautiful," "the noble," "the admirable," was interchangeable with τὸ ἀγαθόν, "the good" (vs. 10; Rom. 7:18, 21). Either word could stand for the fruits listed in 5:22-23. But the farmers who cultivated them for a starving world must stay on the job and **not grow weary** and "become neglectful" (cf. Luke 18:1; II Cor. 4:1, 16; II Thess. 3:13). Ἐκλυόμενοι is a participle of utter dejection, "fainting," "losing heart," "relaxing," "giving up," from failure of nerve and weariness. The "agriculture of the Spirit" required the total investment, sustained effort, and inexhaustible patience of the whole man. God had decreed a fixed period—**due season**—for the growth of good and evil in conflict with each other, and one could not hurry the Most High.

grows in the direction of its reverences, and reverences surely include what and whom one loves. A life dominated by physical desires and hungers grows in upon itself, and so is stunted or dwarfed (*b*) They may be dulled, perhaps through drink or drugs, or through unclean habits, e.g., the reading of sordid literature. Whatever impairs the tenderness and reliability of one's conscience abuses the affections, and abusing the affections takes the edge off life and the shine from existence. (*c*) They may be weakened, sometimes by the false stimulation which impairs one's power to respond normally and healthily.

And so abused affections impair one's power to *grow*. We grow in the direction in which our emotions lead. What one likes and wants to do becomes gradually what one thinks about and wills to do. The emotions in this sense are the controlling faculty, providing the headlight for life, determining what a man sees. "Set your affection on things above" (Col. 3:2). Impaired affections mean spurious growth, growth without maturity, which makes many men old in their twenties or thirties, and makes others "smart" with ideas that outrun their living.

Abused affections impair one's ability to *react*. Among the first lessons a football coach must teach his team is how to fall, i.e., how to react to opposition. A man's ability to meet the falls and bumps of life is dependent on the health of his affections and emotions. Affections in this

In the Bible men sow with tears, and joy is reserved for harvesttime. The labor with stones and thorns and sun-baked clods; the anxiety for the rains; the risk of committing precious seed to "death" in the soil, when the hungry sower and his family were tempted to eat it instead; the long winter of waiting; the choking weeds and devouring locusts; the excessive taxes; and then the armies of human locusts who descended upon the fields to consume and carry off and destroy—all this is the black shadow against which the Bible projects the joy of the farmer when his crop happened to be good and he was permitted to keep it. But one thing was certain: if a man consulted his risks and sowed sparingly he would reap sparingly (II Cor. 9:6), and if he refused to sow he would get no crop at all. The miracle was the stout persistence of the farmers, year in and year out, who defied the uncertainties and prayed to the Lord of the harvest. They were Paul's object lesson for "the farmers of the Spirit," who could always be sure of their crop. No adverse weather, no greedy landlord, no marauding enemy, could take from them the fruit of the Spirit.

Paul's expectation of an eternal harvest to be eternally enjoyed has brought an objection. It is said that men ought to sow for the Spirit, not for reward here or hereafter, but because intrinsically that is the right way to live, and because it would be selfish to love with the expectation of love in return. But the logic of this is self-refuting. The man who sought to save himself by such superunselfishness would have to have other persons selfish enough to be his beneficiaries, and hence willing to lose their souls to accommodate him! Paul, like the wise men and prophets of his people, saw deeper than that (Prov. 22:8-9; Hos. 10:12-13; Isa. 55:9-11). They recognized that the penalty for wrongdoing and the reward for right living were inherent in the act, and they believed that the righteous man could enjoy the reward of his own right character even in this world, marred as it was by the presence of the wicked (Ps. 112:9; II Cor. 9:9). But the immortality of a good name without personal survival, or as Paul called it, a resurrection from the dead, would have made as bitter mockery of the righteous man as did the hard fact of the earthly prosperity of his wicked oppressors. With an empty hope which was never to come to everlasting fruition, the Christians would have been "of all men most to be pitied" (I Cor. 15:19). "If after the manner of men I fought with beasts at Ephesus, what doth it profit me?" (I Cor. 15:32 ASV.) The atheist and the agnostic might have answered that, even without the reward of eternal life, it would be better to fight the beasts than to be like them. But Paul would reply that a God—or a universe without God—who would require men to fight a lifelong battle with "beasts" and then let them die like the animals would be of all deities most to be pitied, a moral monstrosity, worthy, not of worship, but of the contempt and derision of his ephemeral creatures. He would have considered rejection of the hope of eternal life to be at the same time a refusal to believe in the God of grace who had raised Christ Jesus from the dead. In that case, he said, one might as well be an Epicurean (I Cor. 15:32).

Paul therefore was "selfish" enough to expect a harvest of life everlasting. But this hope was neither an "opiate" nor a contradiction of his gospel of salvation by grace

---

sense become the evaluating faculty, and part at least of the secret of happiness. Healthy affections make for happiness. A man is happy when he has found the way to handle whatever happens to him. "Happiness" and "happen" are from the same root.

Abused affections impair the power to *enjoy*. People who are incapable of sustained affections get a minimum from life. Theirs is enjoyment without obligation. They forget that where one is means much less than what one is. Life is more like biography than like geography. Spiritually the perfect tense of live is love. To love with sustained obligation leads to enjoyment in life; and that situation depends mightily upon the health of one's emotions.

Quite obviously, the forgiveness of Christ belongs here. Forgiveness includes the healing and cleansing of one's emotions, and the saturation of one's mind and feelings with Christ's quality

10 As we have therefore opportunity, let us do good unto all *men,* especially unto them who are of the household of faith.

shall reap, if we do not lose heart. 10 So then, as we have opportunity, let us do good to all men, and especially to those who are of the household of faith.

alone through faith in Christ. The sun and the soil, the seed and the rain, the inspiration to sow and the strength to reap—all were the grace-gift of God, and the harvest did not come as the reward of the sower's merit. Man did not save himself by sowing for the Spirit, but in the process of being saved he sowed, produced, and enjoyed the fruit of the Spirit.

10. The field of "the farmers of the Spirit" is as wide as their incentive is urgent, as rich as their reward is sure. **So then**—i.e., in view of the law of the identical harvest and its unfailing reward for sowing the good seed of the Spirit (vss. 7-9)—the only sane way to live was to do good for all men at every **opportunity.** In vs. 9, καιρῷ is translated **season;** here it means the right, the appropriate, the appointed time, hence **opportunity.** Paul believed that the time for doing good was short, that each right deed had its own network of persons and circumstances into which it had to fit. Hence "the farmer of the Spirit" must employ each moment for its appropriate work. **Let us do:** better, "let us labor"; **good** means the intrinsically good but also the beneficial; **to all** means "toward all," "for the benefit of all." The KJV omits δέ (**and** RSV) from the second clause; it is important not to translate it by "but." Like "temple" and "body," **household** is a metaphor for the church, implying the intimate unity of all believers in the family of "the faith," i.e., the Christian faith (the term has the article in the Greek).

The field was the whole world, and there was no contradiction between doing good especially for Christ's family of faith, and loving one's neighbor who might not yet belong to it (5:13-14). The function of the church was to continue the incarnation of Christ and to serve as the Spirit's workshop where God's love could be demonstrated under

of mind, "Let this mind be in you, which was also in Christ Jesus" (Phil. 2:5). His inward dwelling is like a well of water for the daily cleansing, healing, and renewing of one's emotions and affections.

10. ***Paul's Concern for the Fellowship.***—(See also Expos. on vs. 1; 1:2, 18; 2:1, 10.) Paul, who often seemed to play lone wolf or glorious individualist, yet carried in his heart deep concern for the total fellowship of the church. It hurt him to have that fellowship bruised, broken, or divided. His concern for the brethren comes out boldly at least five times in his letter to the Galatians. In 1:2 "all the brethren who are with me" were included in his salutation. After he became a Christian, he could write only a corporate letter. In 1:18 and 2:1 it is probable that one of his reasons for going to Jerusalem was his desire to unite the whole body of Christians into one catholic or universal body, both the older group that stemmed from the Jerusalem center and the churches he had established on his missionary journeys. Is this not the occasion of vs. 6 above, as well as of vss. 7-10, which in Paul's thought follow so significantly on it? In 2:10 he expressed concern for the poor. Many members of the early church were people of limited means, who lost the little they did have when they became Christians. For Paul the church as a whole had a peculiar responsibility toward them. In 6:1 he voiced his conviction that a man overtaken in a fault was not totally restored until he was again accepted into the fellowship. In the verse here he urges the Galatians to **do good unto all men, and especially to those who are of the household of faith.**

Why should Paul with his firsthand experience of Christ and his intellectual gifts, comparable to those of the best-known Greek philosophers, be concerned with the fellowship of such average men and women as constituted the bulk of the membership of the early church? One answer is that he was more than a great brain: he was a great human being; he was a practicing Christian. He craved the human touch second only to the divine. He was more than a sharp, hair-splitting doctrinaire, out to condemn as heretics all who differed with him. Believing with all his soul that the church has primal responsibility as the custodian of Christian truth, he knew that truth can be found and

controlled conditions. Within the church this love was to flame with unique beauty and peculiar intensity, so as to set the pattern and attract men to the Christ who inspired it. The result would be, not less, but more good for outsiders. The church as the family of faith was the place for Christian love to begin and be perfected. Paul had no use for the sentimentalist who loves his neighbor a thousand miles away but cannot get on with his own household. This does not mean, of course, that the love of family came "first" and all others came "second," but that the "home" and "foreign" missionary spirit was one and inseparable. The home life of the Spirit was to be intensified in order to generate the power to preach Christ to the rest of the world.

Paul had an ulterior motive in doing good for all men. He wanted by all means to save them. The kingdom was God's free gift, but Paul saw that God's grace would be defeated if there were no preaching to persuade men to receive it. The beneficiaries of the **good** which the members of the household of faith were doing must not be allowed to become parasites by remaining outsiders. The principle of mutuality required them to learn that it was blessed to give as well as to receive, and that they could neither know nor possess God's grace except in the process of producing the fruit of the Spirit. The business of the church was to establish and maintain a differential between itself and its environment in the degree and quality of the good that was being done (Phil. 1:9-11), and Paul urged all men to become members of its better society, where they could exercise their own best powers and contribute their maximum to naturalizing mankind in the kingdom of God. That was his reason for saying "especially."

---

grasped not alone in doctrine but also through shared experiences in the Christian life. In the process of sharing, the humblest and most unlettered man may have insights that are denied to those who are mentally better equipped. "Jesus answered and said, I thank thee, O Father, Lord of heaven and earth, because thou hast hid these things from the wise and prudent, and hast revealed them unto babes" (Matt. 11:25).

Paul further knew that in the group truth is available which is not given in private: "Where two or three are gathered together in my name, there am I in the midst of them" (Matt. 18:20). The Christian life and kingdom are more a chorus than a solo. It is a matter of relationships all the way from cradle to grave—and beyond. Vertical relationship to God must be followed by horizontal relationship to people.

In addition, the apostle was thoroughly committed to the proposition of the equality of all Christians before God, "Ye are all one in Christ Jesus" (3:28). His leadership did not mean that he was closer to Christ than the others who had passed from law to faith, "Ye are all the children of God" (3:26). His profound insights did not mean that he was nearer the mind of Christ than many quiet, unassuming, unknown members of the fellowship. He knew it could well be that such men possessed a demonstrable experience with Christ which would enrich the total fellowship. Truth is democratic. It is available to all men in the communion of saints. It is not reserved to church leaders of certain height and girth.

This awareness of the worth of each individual life is manifest in Paul's constant recognition of the fellowship. Note his strictures on everything and everybody that disturbed it (vss. 12-13; 1:8). Fellowship in Christ was to him the most dependable mirror, after Christ's own person, of the Eternal. It might even be in some sense the extension of the person of Christ.

> The fellowship of kindred minds
> Is like to that above.[5]

To belong to Christ was to belong to the fellowship. To love Christ was to love the fellowship. "We know that we have passed from death unto life, because we love the brethren" (I John 3:14). The spokes in a wagon wheel are closer together the nearer they get to the hub. The nearer to Christ, the closer to each other. It is love in all its dimensions that tests the genuineness of Christian faith.

So it was that Paul, who claimed an authority from Christ which was neither of men nor through men, craved the fellowship of those who loved Christ as he did. Something within cried out for fellowship with those who like him had committed their destinies to Christ in unreserved faith. Had he pulled out, or remained in an aristocratic ivory tower aloof from the fellowship, he would have violated all that he

[5] John Fawcett, "Blest be the tie that binds."

11 Ye see how large a letter I have written unto you with mine own hand.

11 See with what large letters I am writ-

F. Concluding Re-emphasis upon the Main Points of the Letter (6:11-18)

With this appeal for patient, continuous well-doing Paul has come to the close of his letter, but he adds a few sentences in his own handwriting to make sure that those who hear it read will remember what he has said and stand firm in their new freedom in Christ.

11. The verb ἔγραψα is an epistolary aorist, **I am writing** (RSV) instead of **I have written** (KJV); and γράμμασιν, being dative plural, refers to the letters which spell the words, and not to the epistle which has just been dictated. **How large a letter** (KJV) would require the accusative singular γράμμα; but Paul's word for "letter" in that sense is ἐπιστολή. Besides, compared with Romans and I Corinthians, Galatians is short. The statement in this verse, taken with 1:2, where Paul associated others with himself in the

knew of Christ. A man may lose the divine touch in losing the human touch. The only way to serve God is to serve humanity.

11. ***With My Own Hand.***—Perhaps in **larger letters** because of his thorn in the flesh. He evidently wrote the postscript of Galatians with his own hand, without an amanuensis or secretary. So much was at stake for the Christian church that he wanted to make his letter as intimate and personal as he knew how, with his own seal on it. That is how all genuine Christian thought and life proceed in every generation: direct from God to you—the Bible is God's living word—and direct from you to somebody else. There are no ghost writers, no quotes by permission. True witness is handmade. With every credit to unconscious and indirect influence, Christian work and communication must be direct and personal. The more direct, the more Christlike. The only reproducible experiences are firsthand experiences.

Life, both in the world and in the church, can easily become depersonalized and finally impersonal. Office demands, committee meetings, organizational machinery, are often quite unintentionally allowed to exclude hungry and yearning souls from the attention and care which of all things else they need most. Even the study can become a terminus instead of a thoroughfare. Everybody we meet is carrying a heavy burden, and may be putting up a hard battle. To shepherd men **with my own hand** is the one essential obligation. The kingdom comes in this fashion long before it comes through denominational or interdenominational agencies and programs. General church work is important, but less vital than local shepherding. The local level is the highest level.

"Handmade" Christians are the church's most effective attack upon a machine-ridden civilization. There must be some institution where the queerest, the weakest, and the least socially significant are treated as human beings and as children of God. That institution should be the church. Consider some reasons for Christianity's attack on the depersonalization of life. Small business concerns of all kinds are increasingly moving over into chain and department stores. There are gigantic production lines, made possible by high-powered machinery—the one distinctly new economic fact in the twentieth century. As a result of such economic checker-playing, machine values take the field, and a man is measured not by what he is but largely by his skills. Human and moral values, if they count at all, are secondary. Even specialized education may be a form of human machinery, which fits men best to be cogs. The little concern which many professors have for their students' lives outside of class is for further illustration. Clerks and soldiers are serial numbers. Men become adjectives to modify that to which they belong, whether race, political state, or economic order. Pride in moral attainment or personal excellence gives way as pride in handmade goods vanishes. Larger pay, shorter hours, less concern for fine workmanship are the natural results when **with my own hand** is gone. In this mechanized civilization the church is bound to do battle to maintain—which means to hold by the hand—its personal touch with people, to lift their sense of worth and value, to keep a halo around the commonplace, and to give the dear familiar things a star.

Old Ebenezer Church, on the banks of the Savannah River in Georgia, was built by the freedom-loving Salzburgers during Colonial years. Deliberate fingerprints are still visible upon the bricks in its walls. They seem to say, "Build something for God with your own hand;

12 As many as desire to make a fair show in the flesh, they constrain you to be circumcised; only lest they should suffer persecution for the cross of Christ.

ing to you with my own hand. 12 It is those who want to make a good showing in the flesh that would compel you to be circumcised, and only in order that they may not

writing, makes it unlikely that he wrote the main part of the letter with his own hand. Up to this point he has been dictating; now he takes the pen and writes, probably with stiff, square letters, which contrasted with the graceful hand of a skilled penman.

Paul's reference to his penmanship has led to the supposition that his "large letters" were the result of a physical condition, perhaps nervousness or eye trouble. Others have suggested that manual labor had stiffened his fingers, or that he was making a sardonic reference to those who wanted to go back to the kindergarten and learn their "A B C's" over again. But all this is sheer conjecture. Paul was only following the custom of authenticating dictated letters by writing at the close a few sentences with his own hand (cf. I Cor. 16:21; II Thess. 3:17; Col. 4:18). His "large letters" would serve the same purpose as our underscoring, so that those who read his epistle aloud to the churches could lay especial emphasis upon this summary of his main ideas. His intense, impetuous emotion and thought, which gave him trouble enough in framing his sentences, suggest how hard it was for him to submit to the restraints imposed by the mechanics of writing.

12-13. This passage states more pointedly what Paul has already alleged in 4:17 and 5:10-12—that the motives of the Judaizers are (*a*) to play a specious role with a good outward showing; (*b*) to avoid persecution; and (*c*) to achieve leadership even at the price of inconsistency and unspirituality. Εὐπροσωπῆσαι means "to present a fair face," "make a good show," "specious" as it may be. As in vs. 13, ἐν σαρκί has primary reference to the physical body, but it connotes the pride of heredity and nationality and its attendant delusion concerning the possibility of salvation by merit for good works. 'Αναγκάδουσιν is a conative present: **would compel,** i.e., if they could.

In vs. 13 the majority of MSS have the perfect participle περιτετμημένοι; a variant reading gives the present περιτεμνόμενοι. The perfect would say that Paul charges all who have ever been circumcised with failure to keep the law. Such a charge would be

leave upon it your own mark for his all-seeing eye to read." That is every man's true destiny, and it is uniquely his. No two fingerprints are exactly alike. Even identical twins do not have identical fingerprints; therefore no two hands are alike, no two people are alike. "You are new." Individuality is the law of personal creation; it is also the way of creative living. Paul made life's central discovery, that not by keeping ancient laws and man-made traditions could he achieve his highest manhood, but only when he incarnated the living, creative presence of Christ. Christ's presence enabled him to work **with my own hand.**

12, 14, 17. ***The Cross as Discipline.***—(See Expos. on 3:13.) In the last heartbeat of his Galatian letter Paul affirms his utter dedication to the Christ of the Cross. He was not afraid of persecution for the Cross of Christ; he gloried only in the Cross; he bore in his body the marks of the Lord Jesus. These closing sentences seem to combine the moral influence theory of the Cross with the governmental or disciplinary theory.

It was the pen of Paul that was in a sense Christ's instrument to discipline the Galatians. "Bewitched" by false teachers—whom the apostle will not spare (1:8), and of whom he takes here what might be called a very dim view (vss. 12-13)—they had put the law back into the center of their lives. That pen, however, was a secondary instrument; the primary instrument was what the pen portrayed. The Cross is Christ's way of discipline for those whom he has redeemed.

The same Cross which redeems—sets loose, makes free, empowers for the Christian life—offers more than teaching and example. It offers life, by its discipline in daily guidance, correction, forgiveness, judgment, healing, making possible growth in the kind of life which it reveals. For George Tyrrell and countless other saints, "That strange Man upon his Cross . . . drives one back again and again." [6] There is the Cross as discipline.

[6] Baron F. von Hügel, "Father Tyrrell: Some Memorials of the Last Twelve Years of His Life," *Hibbert Journal,* VIII (1909), 238.

13 For neither they themselves who are circumcised keep the law; but desire to have you circumcised, that they may glory in your flesh.

14 But God forbid that I should glory, save in the cross of our Lord Jesus Christ, by whom the world is crucified unto me, and I unto the world.

be persecuted for the cross of Christ. 13 For even those who receive circumcision do not themselves keep the law, but they desire to have you circumcised that they may glory in your flesh. 14 But far be it from me to glory except in the cross of our Lord Jesus Christ, by which[l] the world has been cruci-

[l] Or *through whom.*

---

consistent with his attitude, for although he says in Phil. 3:6 that he was blameless under the law, he also says that the commandment not to covet was "death" to him (Rom. 7:9-11). His position was that no man could really "keep" the law even if he wanted to do so, to say nothing of halfhearted or hypocritical attempts to meet its demands (Rom. 2). This interpretation is required by the KJV, **they themselves who are circumcised,** and is more in line with Paul's general position. The present participle would concentrate the statement on those who have yet to **receive circumcision** (RSV), and who are on the point of yielding to the urging of the Judaizers. The legalists, at least in their initial propaganda, were not telling the Gentiles that they would have to observe all the rest of the law, but Paul saw that further demands would follow. By the RSV interpretation his charge of inconsistency and hypocrisy would fall on the Gentiles who were about to get circumcised and, with all the fervor of new converts, demand that all others do the same. Uncertainty on the part of scribes concerning Paul's reference led to the variants in the tense of the participle.

In this letter Paul does not consider the possibility that those who were changing his gospel were sincere. In the heat of the controversy he leaves out what elsewhere he recognizes full well: that God alone is the judge of men's hearts and motives, and that man's judgment, even when most accurate and sympathetic, is only an inference from outward appearances.

14. This recalls the thought in 2:19-21. The legalists may glory in their circumcision and obedience to law, but "as for me"—ἐμοί in the emphatic position—"let it not happen." For μὴ γένοιτο see on 2:17. This is Paul's answer to the charge that he too is boasting about his converts. The antecedent of δι' οὗ may be either **our Lord Jesus Christ,** or **cross;** the KJV takes the former view and translates **by whom** (RSV mg., **through whom).**

With the strongest possible emphasis it must be said that there is a universe of difference between discipline under law and discipline through the Cross. Paul's "before-Christ" life was marked by unquestioning obedience; the discipline of the Cross bore on it the signature of his own free choice and co-operation. Christ will never force himself on any life; no imposed obedience to him could ever come within sight of the highest. The ancient law "restrained" Paul; the cross of Christ "constrained" him. Under the Cross his initiative was not crushed, nor was it left to atrophy; it was utilized and made Christlike.

At first glance this type of thinking may appear to be somewhat like walking a tightrope. The Cross as discipline may even appear to some minds as another form of law. But not when we understand that it has nothing to do with any effort to earn the favor or grace of Christ. There is no "work righteousness" in it. It lays its pressure upon the man who is already a new creature in Christ, providing him with insights, methods, and the power by which to grow in the Christian life. The Cross as a fact of history becomes a daily act in life. Just as Christ destroys evil in a man without destroying the man, so there is a discipline which does not violate man's freedom but instead keeps him free by making him more Christlike. The "rule" (vs. 16) of the Cross is by consent. Those who are not cross-bearers in this sense, in the sense of discipline and judgment, are not Christians, however much they may discuss the Cross, or whatever theory of it they may hold.

The discipline which is here proposed may perhaps be illumined by the requirements which the Roman Catholic Church makes of its members. That church sees the necessity of a constant discipline which many find it impossible to ac-

By which (RSV) is preferable; if Paul had meant the pronoun to refer to Christ, he would more likely have written ἐν ᾧ. He is speaking of the cross upon which Christ died in order that the men of faith might be crucified to the evil in the world, i.e., severed from it. There is no article with κόσμος and κόσμῳ, "a world," and the perfect tense ἐσταύρωται expresses action with results continuing: "stands crucified." The same experience is described more fully in Rom. 6:4-6; cf. Luke 14:26-27.

The world from which Paul was severed by the Cross was not the physical world of material things, but a moral world which turned "cosmos" into chaos by selfish and self-glorifying misuse of God's good earth. This meant not only the world of the Epicurean but that of the Pharisee as well (Phil. 3:3-11), the best as well as the worst in human culture whenever that best led to trust in self instead of God. Paul was not crucified to wisdom and philosophy and science, but to the world's unwisdom which chose the path of competitive survival of the fittest and self-deification, and looked upon the Cross as worse than foolishness (I Cor. 1:18-31; 2:2). He continued to live in this present world and use its good things in the service of his Lord. But he was resolved to glory only in the cross of Christ, scandal though it was in the eyes of the world's glory-seekers. Before God there could be neither a self-made man nor a self-saved soul. Paul warned that boasting and unwarranted self-esteem were the ruin of human fellowship, and he found no place for them in the kingdom of God. He would glory only in the Lord, whose strength was perfected in his disciples' weakness (II Cor. 11:21-33; 12:9-10).

---

cept: reading restrictions, the rosary, set prayers, confessions, masses, food regulations. Such discipline appears to be a carry-over from the ancient law. For Luther it violated the freedom of the Christian man. It does, however, point up the need for some kind of discipline if there is to be effective Christian living. Discipline must come from somewhere. Only the spiritually matured know what they should do; the average person is incapable of self-government without specific help. Many a modern man says to his church or pastor, "Show me how"; and he has in mind much more than a list of methods. He is asking, perhaps unknowingly, for discipline. As the redemption of Christ is available for all men, so this discipline for the redeemed man is available directly from him.

It is a discipline of the *will*. Jesus' prayer before the Cross holds the secret of all the Christian life that has come after the Cross, "Not my will, but thine be done." In the will is the vantage point of the good and evil alike. Beyond what a man permits, Christ waits for what the man desires. Unconditional surrender to him means that one's will is freed, purified, renewed. It is that everyday process which is the discipline now under our study. "Nothing gripped my whole soul until I came to Golgotha"; "Have thine own way, Lord"; "Make me and mold me after thy will"; "We own thy sway." This is no mechanical slavery, or the cowardly rolling of one's responsibility over to other shoulders. It is the kind of divine-human co-operation that is imperative for growth. "Not my will, but thine." As E. H. Pruden has said: "When a man is in tune with Christ, his lips will be saying and his hands will be doing what Christ wants." Here is the highest discipline of the will.

It is a discipline of the *conscience*. The Cross is enlightenment and constraint. The Christ who gave his life does not want to be pitied: he wants to be trusted; he wants to be taken at his word. His Sermon on the Mount makes men listen; his Cross makes men kneel. To kneel at that Cross is to stand up straight before life with a conscience illumined, commissioned, enabled. "A charge to keep I have." "We kneel how weak, we rise how full of power." [7] A conscience brought into harmony with the sort of life the Cross stands for is the kind of discipline which is written all across Paul's experience. "Herein do I exercise myself, to have always a conscience void of offense toward God, and toward men" (Acts 24:16). That was Paul's defense before the governor—and before all men. His was a disciplined conscience that would not easily let go of life at its best. In his soul, as in his body, were **the marks of the Lord Jesus.** He was Christ's own.

It means the discipline of *love*. In between the sort of love Paul knew "before Christ" and the kind he describes in I Cor. 13 is the Cross. The Cross meant for him the supreme outpouring of the love of God, and it determined what and whom he would love from then on. The Cross was and is God's way of saying that each life is worth the death of his Son. It compelled Paul to extend his love as widely as the sea.

[7] Richard C. Trench, "Lord, what a change within us one short hour."

15 For in Christ Jesus neither circumcision availeth any thing, nor uncircumcision, but a new creature.

16 And as many as walk according to this rule, peace *be* on them, and mercy, and upon the Israel of God.

fied to me, and I to the world. 15 For neither circumcision counts for anything nor uncircumcision, but a new creation. 16 Peace and mercy be upon all who walk by this rule, upon the Israel of God.

---

15. This repeats and amplifies 5:6; cf. I Cor. 7:19; Rom. 2:25; II Cor. 5:17. The words **in Christ Jesus** and **availeth** (KJV) translate a textual reading which, although in most MSS, is not original, but was introduced from 5:6. Κτίσις means either **creature** (KJV) or **creation** (RSV); since it stands in contrast with the act of circumcision and refers to the man whose faith is activated by love (5:6), the second meaning, understood as a new "act of creation," is preferable.

The Judaizers maintained that circumcision must not be set aside, because it was the foundation, sign, and seal of God's covenant with Israel. But Paul had discovered that circumcision could not guarantee that a man would love his neighbor as himself (5:14), nor enable him to fulfill Christ's "law" of mutual burden-bearing (vss. 2, 5). What was needed was a new man in Christ Jesus "the second Adam." The first Adam and all his descendants had sinned; and the law, although holy and just and good, was helpless to bestow life because of the weakness of human nature. Each Christian at work producing the fruit of the Spirit was something new in the universe.

16. The prayer of 1:3 is repeated, with ἔλεος, "pity," "compassion," **mercy,** instead of χάρις, "grace." For the meaning of εἰρήνη, "peace," see on 5:22. Some MSS have the present **walk,** others, "will walk." Translated word for word in the Greek order, the verse runs thus: "And as many as by this standard walk peace upon them and mercy upon the Israel of God." Since Paul used no punctuation marks, his meaning is uncertain, and four interpretations are possible.

(*a*) The KJV inserts a comma after "them," and another after "mercy." This makes it a prayer for peace and mercy, not only upon those who walk in fellowship with the Spirit (5:25), but also upon **the Israel of God.** Unless Paul is identifying the church with the spiritual Israel, this means that he is praying for peace and pardon upon both the Christians and that portion of Israel which has not yet accepted Christ.

(*b*) The RSV makes **the Israel of God** synonymous with the Christian church, whose members walk by the Spirit. This leaves the καί, "and," which follows ἔλεος, "mercy," untranslated and assumes that Paul is here identifying the church as the true Israel. But although he did believe that the Christians constituted the true Israel (Phil. 3:3; Rom. 2:29; 9:6; I Cor. 10:1-12), he never called the church **the Israel of God,** but used the word "Israel" to designate the Jewish nation. Since he could expect his readers to take for granted that the church was God's chosen people, it is not easy to see why he would

---

That compulsion explains why he wanted to lift the Christian movement out of and far beyond the limits of the synagogue, and of the law around which that synagogue was built. The Cross disciplined the width of Paul's love.

When a man sees the Cross as the measurement of every man's value, that man's love for people awakens and grows. Loving those whom we like and who love us is no more than human: there is nothing Christlike about that. The Cross means loving the unlovely, serving the unappreciative, giving more than one can expect in return, living beyond the Golden Rule. It means the practice of sacrificial forgiveness, the only Christlike way there is for anybody to take through life. It means the discipline of getting along with people—and that is toughest realism, a realism which has its source in him "who, when he was reviled, reviled not again" (I Pet. 2:23).

15-18. ***The Final Trilogy.***—**Peace,** the summary of the Christ life; **grace,** the most unique word in the Christian vocabulary; the **new creature** has that peace because he has this grace.

Here is our faith tremendous; here is the heritage of the ages; here is the family tree

17 From henceforth let no man trouble me: for I bear in my body the marks of the Lord Jesus.	**17** Henceforth let no man trouble me; for I bear on my body the marks of Jesus.

have added the words **upon the Israel of God** to his prayer merely as a kind of lexical note calling attention to the identification.

(*c*) Another possibility is to place the comma after "them." This would make it a prayer for "peace" upon all who walk by the standard of the Spirit, and for "mercy" upon "the Israel of God." Paul would be invoking peace upon the Christians, to whom God had already granted mercy when they joined the church, but praying only for mercy upon the rest of God's Israel, who could not have peace until they accepted Christ. But again the καί which follows ἔλεος has to be omitted to avoid overtranslation.

(*d*) The best approach to this verse is to compare it with the prayer formula in Shemoneh Esreh 19, which was used in the synagogues: "Bestow peace . . . and mercy upon us, and upon thy people Israel." This means that when an individual or a group of persons were at worship, they would extend their prayers to include the same blessings upon all the rest of the Israelites who were not present at the service. So Paul, who had invoked "anathema" upon all who preached a different gospel, now prays for his fellow countrymen who have not yet accepted Christ. (Note the similar change of attitude in Rom. 11 as compared with Rom. 2.) This interpretation means that Paul is praying for both peace and mercy upon both the church and the Jewish nation.

According to Paul, God's mercy and pardon are the foundation of all peaceful relations with him and with men. The O.T. offered directions for securing and maintaining this peace and presented a code of daily conduct consistent with it. But the weakness of human nature blocked this as a path to eternal life and sent Paul on his search for an effective way of salvation. This he found in Christ. Here he calls it κανών, "canon," "standard," "principle," **rule.** The root idea in this word is "ruler" or "straightedge." In Paul's usage the word had not yet acquired the meaning of a fixed "canon" of scripture, or of a body of doctrines formulated in a creed or promulgated as ecclesiastical law. For him the "canon" was the Spirit and mind of Christ in the Christian (vs. 15; 5:25), which led him to put all his trust in the grace of God incarnated in Jesus Christ. Whatever was not of faith in Christ was sin, but where this faith was, there was the liberty of the only right relationship with God. It was the "rule" of love, and only for those who walked by it could Paul's benediction of peace come true. All other men might pray for peace, but as long as they refused to fulfill this essential condition they were continuing to thwart God's answer to their prayer.

17. In closing his letter Paul protested against the added burden which was being inflicted needlessly by some of the very people who professed to share his ideals. Κόπους means "labors," "toils," "troubles"; from the letter itself we see what they were. His opponents charged him with pleasing men and preaching a man-made gospel. Some said his gospel was not valid because he had not been recognized as an apostle by the heads of the church in Jerusalem. Others, at the opposite extreme, claimed that he was so subservient to these conservative "pillar apostles" that he was betraying the cause of Christian freedom. Some violated the first principle of the Christian fellowship by spying on his treatment of Titus. His conservative critics reproached him with preaching a gospel that encouraged sin, and they stirred up such a controversy that he rebuked Peter and split with Barnabas. When he told the Galatians the truth about themselves, they were inclined to regard him as their enemy.

All this was trouble enough. But from Acts and Paul's own list of sufferings in II Cor. 11:23-29 we see that even heavier burdens were laid upon him by the cruelty, the ingratitude, the perversity, and the misunderstanding of men. Someone was always stirring up difficulties for him, always trying to prove him an impostor and his gospel a

18 Brethren, the grace of our Lord Jesus Christ *be* with your spirit. Amen.

¶ Unto the Galatians written from Rome.

18 The grace of our Lord Jesus Christ be with your spirit, brethren. Amen.

---

fraud. In the midst of it he pleaded with his Galatian converts not to let anyone continue "making troubles" for him.

In proof of his sincerity and truthfulness Paul offered his own willingness to be marked by the cross of Jesus. He bore not only **on** (RSV) but **in** (KJV) his body the "stigmata" of Jesus (cf. II Cor. 4:10; Phil. 3:10). The KJV translates an inferior textual reading: **of the Lord Jesus;** other MSS read "of Christ"; "of the Lord Jesus Christ"; "of our Lord Jesus Christ." These variants are explained by the tendency of scribes to use the fuller forms of the titles of Jesus.

The στίγμα was a tattoo or brand such as was stamped upon slaves. Christians who had been, or still were, slaves had no trouble in understanding Paul. Moreover, the adherents of the other cults often had marks tattooed upon their bodies to signify that they belonged to a particular god or goddess. This custom was forbidden by the law of Moses. The difference between Paul's "marks" and all other "stigmata" lay in the character of Jesus and the kind of service which he inspired (vss. 2, 5; 5:14, 22-23). **The marks of Jesus** were not the artificial product of morbid concentration upon the wound prints of the Cross, but the unavoidable consequence of doing good in a world such as this. They were caused by Paul's daily self-consuming care as he bore Christ's burden of anxiety for all the churches. For although the yoke of Jesus was kind to Paul's shoulders, the burden itself was heavy; what made it seem light was the inner buoyancy which the Spirit furnished for bearing it. In Christ, Paul was not exempt from suffering, but he was strengthened to resist temptation, to labor, to cope with his critics, and to come through more than conqueror (Rom. 8:37). Literally his "marks" were scars from beatings and stonings, and figuratively they resulted from the spiritual pain which he had to suffer until Christ was formed in his converts. These marks were the proofs of his apostleship which he challenged his detractors to match (II Cor. 6:4-10). He bore the brand of the better slave of Christ (II Cor. 11:23-29), yet he knew that it was possible to undergo all these things and come out of them not with the marks of Jesus but with the stamp of Satan—if love was lacking (I Cor. 13:1-3). He warned his churches that even martyrdom, if it was not of faith and hope and love, or if it was for a bad or mistaken cause, was of no avail. To be honorable the marks of Jesus had to be the result of suffering in the right spirit, for the right Master, and for the right cause (II Cor. 6:3-10).

How Paul's Christians in Galatia reacted to the challenge of his Christ-marks we have no means of knowing. All that can be said is that some person or group among them valued him and his gospel so highly that they preserved his letter. It may be that the influence of Galatians was destined to be far greater upon the future church than upon its first readers. In either case we can be sure that Paul considered man's judgment a very small matter compared with being in right relation with God in Christ, through faith and hope and love. The Spirit and mind of Christ constituted the present portion of his eternal inheritance, and he was sure that the marks of Jesus which he bore in his frail "earthen vessel" would not be in vain (II Cor. 4:7; 5:1-5).

18. And so Paul closed as he began (1:3) with a prayer that the grace of God in the Christ to whom the Galatians owed their new life of freedom from the curse of the law might be effective in their lives. (On the appended note in the KJV, "Unto the Galatians written from Rome," see Intro., pp. 439-41.) The prayers in Phil. 4:23 and Philem. 25 are quite similar; but only in Galatians did Paul add the word "brethren" to his final benediction. He was determined not to let his differences with them break the ties of Christian brotherhood, and when he added the **Amen,** he confirmed his fervent prayer that this might not, and his faith that it would not, happen. For if the grace of Christ, who did not please himself, but loved all men and gave himself for them (2:20), dwelt in Paul and in them, there could be no question of estrangement.

The grace of Christ for which Paul prayed was the presence of the living Christ himself, and not simply the continuing influence of a leader who lived once upon a time but was now dead and buried. It was not the grace of an absentee Lord who would someday return from heaven, but the risen Jesus, the Christ who was maintaining an unbroken fellowship individually and collectively with all the members of his body the church. Of him it could be said, "He lives in me." To his grace Paul was willing to commit himself and all his converts for time and eternity, convinced that neither death, nor life, nor anything else in all the universe, could ever separate him from the love of God in Christ Jesus (Rom. 8:31-39). That—and that alone—was the way of freedom.

---

where belong all men of the great redemption. Here is the key to Christian history: to Paul, Augustine, Luther, Calvin, Wesley. Here is evangelical Christianity.

Let Paul himself close Galatians with his own favorite phrase, **in Christ.** There is the imprint of the new creation; of peace, of grace, of all the heritage and inheritors of the evangelical tradition. The best of the past is conserved there. There the present finds fulfillment, and the future is given its promise. There a man possesses all things: heir of yesterday moving in today's freedom across the threshold of a tomorrow.

Lord, now lettest Thou Thy servant depart in peace:
According to Thy word;
For mine eyes have seen Thy salvation:
Which Thou hast prepared before the face of all people;
A light to lighten the Gentiles:
And the glory of Thy people Israel.[8]

[8] Nunc Dimittis. *Common Service Book of the Lutheran Church.*

The Epistle to the

EPHESIANS

Introduction and Exegesis by FRANCIS W. BEARE

Exposition by THEODORE O. WEDEL

EPHESIANS

INTRODUCTION

I. Question of Authenticity

The Epistle "to the Ephesians" carries in the salutation to the readers the name of "Paul, an apostle of Christ Jesus"; and begins the great prayer of supplication in ch. 3 under the name of "Paul, the prisoner of Christ Jesus, on behalf of you, the Gentiles." Again, in 6:21-22, the mention of Tychicus in the very words of Col. 4:7-8 suggests that the letter was written by the author of Colossians and at the same time. In keeping with these data, the epistle has been accepted in the church from early in the second century as an authentic work of the apostle Paul, written during his imprisonment at Rome, and carried by Tychicus on the journey to Asia on which he carried also the letter to the Colossians.

Since early in the nineteenth century, however, more and more scholars have come to the conclusion that the epistle is pseudonymous. This verdict of scholarship is by no means unanimous; a number of critics of the first rank are not convinced by the arguments which have been brought against the Pauline authorship. British scholars in general have been inclined to defend the authenticity of the epistle (Hort, Westcott, Armitage Robinson, Burkitt, Dodd, Rawlinson, E. F. Scott; on the other hand, Moffatt, Streeter, and W. L. Knox have rejected it). American and Continental scholars (apart from the Erlangen school) have generally rejected it. For the strongest argument in defense in English see F. J. A. Hort, *Prolegomena to St. Paul's Epistles to the Romans and the Ephesians* (London: Macmillan & Co., 1895); and for the most complete statement of the case against the Pauline authorship see E. J. Goodspeed, *The Meaning of Ephesians* (Chicago: University of Chicago Press, 1933).

A. External Attestation.—Traces of the use of the epistle, though not of its ascription to Paul, appear very early in Christian literature. It was certainly known and used by the author of I Peter (not later than A.D. 112). In most of the Apostolic Fathers there are, if not direct citations (first unmistakably to be observed in Polycarp), at least strong reminiscences of the language of Ephesians. It was known and used by several of the heretical schools, notably by the Valentinians and by Marcion, and by several of the apologists of the second century. Irenaeus is the first to cite it under the name of Paul, but his predecessors undoubtedly knew it as part of the Pauline corpus. It is included in the Muratorian Canon and in all later lists of New Testament writings; and the authorship was never disputed in ancient times.

B. Modern Criticism.—Erasmus was the first critic to remark upon the peculiarities of the style. Doubts of its authenticity, however, were first expressed by Evanson, an English deist, in a book on the Gospels published in 1792. Modern critical investigation began with Usteri (1824) and De Wette (1826). Baur and his followers coupled it with Colossians and rejected both—and Philemon along with them—on the ground that they showed evidence of the Gnostic trends which they thought (erroneously) did not arise until the second century; they also pointed out that the doctrine of the descent into Hades was a post-Pauline development in Christology. Later writers have based their objections primarily on observations of vocabulary and style, and on the use of materials borrowed from the letters which are surely Paul's, especially from Colossians; secondarily, and perhaps less solidly, on differences of doctrinal interest, which appear to suggest the post-Apostolic age.

C. Elements of the Problem. 1. Style and Language.—All the other epistles of the Pauline corpus (Hebrews and the Pastorals are of course excluded from consideration) are immediately concerned with the pressing problems of particular churches and are full of allusions to local situations, whether difficult (as in Galatians) or encouraging (as in Philippians). Even in Romans, the most general in tone among the acknowledged epistles, the Jewish and Gentile components of the Roman church are brought clearly into view, and the arguments and misrepresentations of opponents are pungently dealt with. In Ephesians, on the other hand, there is no controversial element; the doctrinal exposition is cast largely in the form of a devotional meditation. This feature alone would compel fundamental differences of style; the sharp play and thrust of dialectic which characterizes the other epistles would be quite out of place. It is a question, however, if this is sufficient to account for all the differences. With Paul, even when he is not moved by the heat of controversy, ideas crowd in upon his mind as he writes, and are thrown out in sudden jets and flashes of brilliance. In Ephesians there is nothing of this. The thought is marshaled in long and involved sentences, with clause linked to clause and phrase to phrase, the whole constructed with deliberation and forethought. It is scarcely true to say with von Soden that the style reveals "a phlegmatic, in place of a choleric temperament";[1] but certainly it reveals a calm and ruminative mind rather than the mercurial, impetuous, sometimes torrentlike mind of Paul. In 1:3-14, 15-23; 2:1-7, 11-13, 14-18, 19-22; 3:1-19 (with the long interpolation 2-13); 4:1-6, 11-16, 17-19, 20-24; 6:14-20 we have a succession of unwieldy periods such as no other Pauline epistle can show; it is difficult not to feel that such handling of language betrays the mind of another writer. In Colossians, indeed, there is an approach to the same style, especially in ch. 1; but even there it falls far short of the sustained reverberation of the Ephesian periods.

The peculiarities of vocabulary are as striking as the differences of style. There are, to begin with, an extraordinarily large number of *hapax legomena*—eighty-two words not found elsewhere in the Pauline letters; thirty-eight not found elsewhere in the New Testament.[2] Yet there is nothing in this epistle comparable to the picking up of technical terms and catchwords from an opposing "philosophy," which we note in Colossians, to account for the introduction of so many new words in such a short letter. There is nothing liturgical about many of them, such as ἀνακεφαλαιόω, διάβολος, μεθοδεία, ἀναστρέφω, κοσμοκράτωρ. The extreme fondness for compounds with σύν, which accounts for six of them, might be attributed to the prominence of the theme of unity. Still, it must be noted that a competent modern investigator of the problem holds that this number is not sufficiently great to cast doubt upon the authenticity of the letter, and points out that the proportion is almost as great in Philippians.[3]

More significant are the numerous phrases which, while employing common Pauline words, put them together in associations not elsewhere found in Paul. Apart from the reference to "apostles and prophets" as to a collective entity (2:20; 3:5), and a number of unusual phrases containing the word αἰών (1:21; 2:2, 7; 3:21), we may note particularly the frequent pleonasms—εὐδοκίαν τοῦ θελήματος (1:5), βουλὴν τοῦ θελήματος (1:11), ἐνέργειαν τοῦ κράτους τῆς ἰσχύος (1:19), etc. This type of phrase is a very distinctive feature of the style, and it is not so attractive that we can easily imagine Paul adopting it eagerly for this one epistle, after showing no signs of such a tendency in his previous letters.

The phrase ἐν τοῖς ἐπουρανίοις, again, is used no less than five times in this letter, in astonishingly different contexts. In 1:3 it means the sphere in which God confers his spiritual blessings. In 1:20 and 2:6 it is used of the sphere of Christ's existence in his session at the right hand of God, and of our participation in the heavenly life in mystical union with him. But in 3:10 and 6:12 it means the sphere of "the principalities and powers," of "the spiritual hosts of wickedness." Again, it is hard to imagine that Paul himself, who had never used the phrase before in any context, would suddenly become so enamored of it as to use it five times in a short letter in such a variety of contexts. If it were a term of capital theological significance, the key phrase of a fresh theological speculation, we might understand its sudden spring into prominence; but in fact it is used casually, meaning little more than "in the invisible world," and for that very reason it betrays itself as the familiar language of another writer than Paul.

But none of these things tell so strongly against the authenticity of the letter as the fact that Pauline words, even when used in the same

[1] *Der Brief an die Epheser,* 2nd ed. revised (Freiburg im Breisgau: J. C. B. Mohr, 1893; "Hand-Commentar zum Neuen Testament"), p. 90.

[2] See the lists in James Moffatt, *Introduction to the Literature of the New Testament* (New York: Charles Scribner's Sons, 1911), p. 386. There are twenty-five words more which are also found in Colossians, but in no other Pauline letter.

[3] Ernst Percy, *Die Probleme der Kolosser- und Epheserbriefe* (Lund: C. W. K. Gleerup, 1946), pp. 179-80.

combinations, are given a radically different sense from that which we find in Paul. In the apostle's own writings, for instance, τὰ ἔθνη always means "the Gentiles" in the ordinary Jewish sense of "non-Jews"; but the writer of Ephesians is clearly accustomed to think of τὰ ἔθνη as "non-Christians," and feels obliged to define the word more precisely when he wants it to mean "non-Jews." He then writes τὰ ἔθνη ἐν σαρκί—*"physically* Gentiles." Compare with this: "You must no longer live as the Gentiles do" (4:17). Even such a phrase as "by grace you have been saved" (2:5, 8), which at first sight seems typically Pauline, has in fact no true parallel in Paul. Paul never uses σώζω in the perfect, but (with one exception) always in the present or future: our "salvation" is for him something that is in progress, and its perfection is awaited. The one exception confirms this; in Rom. 8:24 he uses the aorist passive—"we were saved"—but in association with *hope*. "For in this hope we were saved." The word looks back to the preceding "We wait for adoption as sons," and forward to "If we hope for what we do not see, we wait for it with patience" (Rom. 8:23, 25). We might also note the use of οἰκονομία, not in the Pauline sense of "stewardship" or "office of trust," but in the technical theological sense of a "plan" or "policy"—"as a plan for the fullness of time" (1:10); "the plan of the mystery" (3:9). There is a further difficulty in the use of the word μυστήριον ("mystery"). In Colossians the content of the "mystery" is "Christ in you, the hope of glory" (Col. 1:27); "Christ, in whom are hid all the treasures of wisdom and knowledge" (Col. 2:3). In Ephesians, it is the "plan . . . to unite all things in him" (1:10); or "how the Gentiles are fellow heirs" (3:6); and in 5:32, the writer uses the word "in its secondary Hellenistic sense of a rite with a 'mystical' meaning,"[4] a sense never found in Paul.

2. *Secondary Ideas.*—The leading ideas of the epistle are at least anticipated in the writings of Paul and may be regarded as legitimate developments of his thought. To some critics this fact seems to be of such importance as to outweigh all the objections to acceptance of the letter as authentic. For E. F. Scott "some ideas are more highly developed in this than in the other epistles, but they are always Paul's ideas, and it is difficult to see how anyone but himself could have so drawn out their deeper implications."[5] To this it may be replied that a disciple as intimately acquainted with the mind of Paul as Plato with the mind of Socrates would be quite capable of such an accomplishment, particularly if we take into account the possibility that his acquaintance with Paul may have been personal, not merely literary. The writer of Ephesians might well be one of those who was with Paul in his last years at Rome, when his mind was moving along the lines of this epistle.

But if the leading ideas are Pauline, there are a number of secondary ideas which are not to be so described, and it is precisely in these that the peculiar bent of a different mind is revealed. Here we might notice particularly four points: (*a*) the conception of the mission of Paul himself; (*b*) the doctrine of spiritual gifts; (*c*) the emergence of the doctrine of the descent into Hades; and (*d*) the conception of the function of the "holy apostles and prophets."

This writer represents Paul as entrusted with the particular revelation that the Gentiles should be "fellow heirs, members of the same body, and partakers of the promise in Christ Jesus through the gospel" (3:6). To Paul himself, however, the admission of the Gentiles was merely the corollary to the doctrine that "Christ is the end of the law, that every one who has faith may be justified" (Rom. 10:4). The fundamental insight is not that the Gentiles are now admitted to the church of God, but that the principles on which Judaism rested are now annulled. "Neither is circumcision anything, nor uncircumcision, but a new creation" (Gal. 6:15). From this fundamental religious attitude, the acceptance of Gentiles on the same terms as Jews is a natural and necessary consequence. In Ephesians the order of priority is inverted. The cardinal thing now is the admission of Gentiles and the union of humanity in a single community of worship; the annulling of "the law of commandments and ordinances" (2:15) is merely the means to this end.

Moreover, Paul was neither the only missionary to carry the gospel to the Gentiles nor even the first to do so. The beginning was made by the unnamed "men of Cyprus and Cyrene, who on coming to Antioch spoke to the Greeks also, preaching the Lord Jesus" (Acts 11:20). They did not wait until the "mystery" was made known to Paul by revelation. This conception of Paul's peculiar mission, therefore, is historically untenable and can hardly have been given expression in these terms by Paul himself.

We have difficulty also in imagining Paul himself writing the words, which in him would savor of vanity: "When you read this you can perceive my insight into the mystery of Christ" (3:4). Such a boast of the display of insight does not accord with what we know of Paul, who

[4] W. L. Knox, *St. Paul and the Church of the Gentiles*, (Cambridge: University Press, 1939), pp. 183-84.

[5] *The Epistles of Paul to the Colossians, to Philemon and to the Ephesians* (London: Hodder & Stoughton, 1930; "Moffatt New Testament Commentary"), p. 121.

feels like a fool whenever he is obliged to commend himself (II Cor. 11:1, 16, 21, 23; 12:1, 11), and prefers to boast not of his proficiency but of his sufferings and his weaknesses (II Cor. 11:30; 12:9-10). On the other hand the words are quite natural as the tribute of an admiring disciple.

In the treatment of spiritual gifts (4:7 ff.) we observe again that the whole conception differs from that of Paul. In the first place the gifts are not imparted by the Spirit (as in I Cor. 12:7 ff.) but are bestowed by the ascended Christ. More significantly, although the writer begins by saying that "grace was given to each of us according to the measure of Christ's gift" (4:7), he shows in what follows that he is not really thinking of gifts bestowed on individual Christians, but of the spiritually gifted men ("apostles, . . . pastors and teachers") as gifts bestowed upon the whole church.

Within this passage the doctrine of the descent into Hades is introduced (vss. 9-10) as implied in the Ascension, and necessary to the completion of Christ's mission—"that he might fill all things." The descent has no place in the earliest tradition, which affirms only the burial of Christ (I Cor. 15:3-4).

Finally, we may observe the use in Ephesians of the notion that "the apostles and prophets" constitute a corporate entity on which the church is founded and to which the revelation of "the mystery of Christ" was given (2:20-22; 3:4). If we compare 2:20-22 with I Cor. 3:5-17, we shall see that the differences are such as could hardly be compassed within one mind, even at a lapse of some years (see the Exegesis on the passage). For Paul, he and his fellow missionaries are not themselves the foundation, or part of the foundation, but "servants through whom you believed, as the Lord assigned to each" (I Cor. 3:5). Paul has "laid a foundation," and declares that "no other foundation can any one lay than that which is laid, which is Jesus Christ" (I Cor. 3:10-11). The conception of the apostles and prophets as an entity is itself foreign to Paul, as it is to history; he looks upon them as individuals, each doing his appointed task. It is only in the perspective of the following age that men begin to think of them as a body corporate, with a collective task.

3. Historical Situation.—This attitude toward the "holy apostles and prophets" indicates strongly that the writer looks back toward the leaders of the primitive church with the veneration of an epigonus. There are a number of other passages which confirm in greater or less degree this impression that the work belongs to the second generation.

Without too much confidence we might allege that the figure of breaking down "the middle wall of partition" (2:14) is not likely to have suggested itself to a Christian writer before the fall of Jerusalem and the destruction of the temple (A.D. 70, six years after the death of Paul). Though this wall is treated as a type of "the law of commandments contained in ordinances," the use of the figure seems to imply the *literal* destruction of the wall, so that the historic event is made a symbol of the removal of the artificial barriers to Jewish-Gentile fellowship which the law imposed.

More generally, and more definitely, the post-Apostolic period is indicated by the fact that the writer thinks of the church as predominantly composed of Gentiles. Though he represents himself in the person of Paul as a Jew, and though he probably is himself a Jew, he is no longer able to think of the Gentile believers in terms of a bough grafted like "a wild olive shoot" (Rom. 11:17) into the "olive tree" of Israel. He cannot assume that there will be any Jews among his readers; "the saints who are also faithful in Christ Jesus" (1:1) are also those who were "at one time . . . Gentiles in the flesh, called the uncircumcision" (2:11). To him "Gentiles" has come to mean not "non-Jews" but "non-Christians," as in I Peter and other post-Apostolic works. This comes out quite clearly in 4:17, where those who have been addressed as "Gentiles in the flesh" are told that they "must no longer live as the Gentiles do." The separation of Christianity and Judaism is complete and fully recognized. Jewish Christianity has ceased to be a danger. The writer fears not that his readers may fall away to Judaism, but that they may relapse into pagan practices (4:17–5:15). The great conflict which engaged Paul's energies all through his life has ended in complete victory and leaves in this epistle barely an echo.

D. Reasons for the Pseudonym.—We shall conclude, then, that the epistle is not the work of Paul. It was published under his name as a tribute of love and admiration by a disciple of great gifts, deeply imbued with the mind and spirit of the great apostle, closely acquainted with his letters, especially with the letter to the Colossians, and quite possibly acquainted with the apostle in person. If the writer had been in touch with Paul during his last imprisonment, he may well have written the letter to give expression to ideas of Christ and the church which had been developing in the apostle's mind after the writing of the letter to Colossae; in that case he would feel, like Plato in the *Apology of Socrates*, that he was no more than the vehicle of his master's thoughts and might therefore legitimately address the church in his name.

There is no justification for the statement that Ephesians "is a product of a time when the veneration attached to Apostolic authorship made it necessary to borrow a name in order to give sanction to documents, whose purpose was to expound the Christian message in a manner suited to the changing conditions of the Church." [6] It is doubtful if such a calculation affected any of the pseudepigraphic letters of the New Testament, with the exception of II Peter. Hermas, writing considerably later than the publication of Ephesians, does not hesitate to write under his own name and to claim that new revelations have been given to him; and his work was widely received and long revered in the church.

The writer appears to have been a Jew. Writing under the name of Paul, he would of course be obliged to refer to himself as Jewish, so that his identification of himself with the Jews (1:11; 2:3, 17; etc.) is not conclusive; it can be explained as merely a literary device necessitated by the pseudonym. Apart from that, however, there is a Semitic flavor to the style of the epistle which cannot be attributed, as in the Lukan writings, to a deliberate imitation of the Septuagint. The frequent occurrence of such Semitisms as "sons of disobedience," "children of wrath," "children of light," "works of darkness," etc., seems likewise to point to a Jewish rather than a Greek writer. Again, the treatment of Isa. 57:19 in 2:13-17, and of Ps. 68:18 in 4:8-9 reflects training in rabbinical methods of exegesis and even acquaintance with particular traditions of interpretation which would be most unlikely to belong to a teacher of Gentile birth and training. Above all, it seems inconceivable that anyone but a Jew could speak of "the Gentiles" in the terms used in 2:11-12.

II. Destination of the Epistle

In the oldest Greek manuscripts that have come down to us (Papyrus 46, and the fourth-century codices Sinaiticus and Vaticanus) the epistle bears the title πρὸς Ἐφεσίους—"To [the] Ephesians." The scribes of the second century gave it this title when they prepared codices of the Pauline epistles for publication; the title of all the other epistles is given in the same form—πρὸς Ρωμαίους, πρὸς Γαλάτας, etc. This form is inconceivable as the title of a single epistle circulating by itself; it is unintelligible except in relation to a collection.

The scribes who first used this title found nothing in the text of the epistle itself to guide them. All the other epistles mention the recipients directly—"the saints . . . which are at Philippi," "the church of God which is at Corinth," etc. But the epistle "to the Ephesians" was addressed in the most general way possible "to the saints who are also faithful in Christ Jesus" (1:1). There is no evidence that the words ἐν Ἐφέσῳ ("in Ephesus") were included in any Greek manuscript before the fourth century. They are clearly a scribal insertion, put into the text to bring it into conformity with the traditional title by which the epistle had been known for the preceding two centuries.[7]

It may be observed in passing that Paul at all events could not have written such a letter as this *to the church at Ephesus.* For that city had been the theater of his longest and most successful mission; he had labored there for three years and had made it his base for the evangelization of the whole province of Asia (Acts 19:10, 26; 20:31). In writing to that church Paul could not have failed to mention his personal relations with them and to name some of his old friends; but in fact the letter implies that the readers will know of him only by hearsay (3:1), and that he knows of them only by hearsay (1:15).

The title πρὸς Ἐφεσίους did not have the field to itself in the codices of the second century. The epistle was known to the heretic Marcion under the title "To the Laodiceans." This has led some scholars to suggest that it was originally addressed to Laodicea. Harnack even conjectured that the words ἐν Λαοδικείᾳ stood in the text of the salutation, and were dropped because of the bad name which the church of that city received through its denunciation in the book of Revelation (3:14-22; especially vs. 16—"I will spew thee out of my mouth"). It is more likely, however, that this title which was used in Marcion's copy was merely a scribal conjecture, based on the mention of "the letter from Laodicea" in Col. 4:16. Some modern defenders of the authenticity of the epistle have made the same conjecture. Paul was not personally known in Laodicea (Col. 2:1), so that the difficulty of the lack of concrete references would not be felt if the letter were addressed to that city.

[6] Knox, *St. Paul and Church of Gentiles,* p. 185.

[7] The evidence may be summarily indicated. The words ἐν Ἐφέσῳ are not found at all in p[46], our only second-century manuscript; in ℵ and B, the only extant codices of the fourth century, they were not written by the original scribe, but have been added by later correctors. Origen of Alexandria (early third century), though he knows the epistle by its current title, comments on the words "the saints which are" in terms which show that they were not followed by any phrase of locality in his text. Tertullian (*ca.* 200) finds fault with Marcion for using the title "To the Laodiceans," not on the ground that it contradicts the text, but solely as defying ecclesiastical tradition. Basil (*ca.* 370) tells us distinctly that the text without ἐν Ἐφέσῳ is "the way that it was handed down to us by our predecessors, and so we ourselves have found it in the old copies." Jerome (late fourth century) indirectly confirms this testimony.

The address as it stands, however, offers no difficulty once we have abandoned the attempt to ascribe the letter to Paul. For Paul, indeed, there would be no "saints" who were not "also faithful in Christ Jesus." But in the unknown author of Ephesians, it is not to be taken for granted that the expressions are altogether synonymous. When he says to his Gentile readers, "You are no longer strangers and sojourners, but you are fellow citizens with the saints" (2:19) he is evidently using "the saints" to mean the Jewish people, as the community of faith existing of old. This would be in keeping with Old Testament usage; e.g., Ps. 148:14—"the praise of all his saints; even of the children of Israel." The further definition "who are also faithful," or perhaps better in this context "who are also believers in Christ Jesus," would not therefore be an equivalent, but a necessary qualification, to "the saints."

It has frequently been suggested that in the original letter there may have been a blank after "the saints that are," to be filled with the name of each church as the letter was received and read. Thus the carrier would insert "in Laodicea" or "in Smyrna," and so forth, as he visited each city in turn. This conjecture is not so happy as it appears to be at first sight; it would be quite without parallel in ancient literature, Christian or secular. Such circular letters as have come down to us are not so addressed (I Peter, James, Galatians). The conjecture rests on the false assumption that a circular letter would be carried from place to place by a single courier; it is infinitely more probable that copies would be made for the various churches which were to receive the letter, and each copy would contain the name of a particular city. If such place names had ever been inserted, it would be more than strange—it would indeed be inconceivable—that none of them should have been transmitted in manuscripts, but that every trace of every such name should have been lost as early as the end of the second century. We should expect such a feature to leave its traces in variant readings.

The scribes of the second century who invented the title πρὸς Ἐφεσίους were undoubtedly led to do so by their recollection of II Tim. 4:12, "Tychicus have I sent to Ephesus." Von Soden rejects this simple and obvious explanation on the curious ground that "a combination of II Timothy 4:12 with Ephesians 6:21 f. would be too learned for the second century." On the contrary it is just the lack of learning that would lead a scribe to make such a combination.

The epistle is addressed, then, to the whole Christian world. The ancient title "To the Ephesians" is of no significance whatsoever. The writer is strongly possessed of the sense of the church's unity, and what he has to say concerns all alike. Local problems of administration or of discipline are not in his mind; heresies and perversions of the gospel which may be disturbing particular Christian centers are not for him to combat. He sees the church not as an association of congregations but as a world society, and he addresses it in its corporate unity, as consisting of "the saints who are also faithful in Christ Jesus."

III. Origin and Purpose of the Epistle

We have before us, then, a treatise in the form of a letter, issued under the name of Paul by an unknown Christian of the second generation, and addressed to the whole body of believers. Can we now determine more precisely the situation in the church which may have prompted the issuance of such a work, and the purpose which the unknown author had in mind?

Edgar J. Goodspeed in his book *The Meaning of Ephesians* has put forward the attractive theory that Ephesians was written by the collector of the Pauline epistles as an introduction to the collection. He reminds us that Paul wrote his letters to local churches (Philippi, Thessalonica, Rome) or to the churches of particular areas (Galatia, Achaia—II Cor. 1:1), to deal with problems of Christian life and thought which were of immediate concern to the group addressed. Each letter would be preserved by the authorities of the church which received it, but it would not be read in public worship except on its arrival, and once the matters in controversy had been settled there would be no particular reason for consulting it again. The letters would tend, like all old letters, to lie in store unused and almost forgotten. With the publication of the book of Acts (dated by Goodspeed *ca.* 90), Christians everywhere would be given a new understanding of the greatness of Paul's career and would be eager to know more about him. One Christian especially, probably a man of Asia who had long been acquainted with the letter to the Colossians and with that to Philemon, would be moved to seek out other letters of the great apostle; and the narrative of Acts would indicate to him where he might reasonably expect to find them. It would direct him to the churches of Galatia, Philippi, Thessalonica, Corinth, and Rome. If he inquired elsewhere, he was unsuccessful; but from these five churches he was able to secure copies of the letters which Paul had sent to them years before. Thus for the first time a

Christian found himself in a position to read the whole series of letters, not merely the one or two that had been sent to his local church; and as he read them all through, new and wonderful vistas of thought opened before him. He was able then to perceive the magnificent general conception of the resources of the Christian faith and of its ultimate significance which underlies Paul's treatment of the particular local problems, many of them of only temporary concern in themselves, with which each separate letter dealt. In Ephesians he has attempted to put together the elements of permanent general significance in these fugitive writings; and thus to encourage his fellow Christians to find in them not alone the echoes of bygone conflicts, but a message of great significance for their own time. As Colossians had long been in his hands and was most familiar to him, it has not unnaturally left a deeper impress than any of the other letters; but every one of them has been utilized in greater or less degree. Indeed only about 10 per cent of his work fails to show direct indebtedness, in words or in substance, to one or other of the nine genuine letters which are included in the collection. Goodspeed, then, thinks of Ephesians as a kind of Pauline *Philocalia;* an anthology of Paulinism, selected and pointed to bring out its relevance to the life of the second generation, especially to combatting the growing apathy, the failure of Christians to realize the glory of their inheritance, and the tendency to sectarianism.

Some aspects of this theory will appear fanciful and uncalled for. For one thing, the collecting of Paul's letters cannot be made to depend on the influence of Acts. The supposition that the Christian church forgot all about Paul for a generation after his death, and that only the publication of Acts saved him and his letters from oblivion, is purely gratuitous. Moreover, the whole hypothesis is worked out too exclusively within the framework of a history of literature; everything is attributed to the influence of books. The publication of Acts stimulates the search for Paul's letters; the reading of the letters gives rise to the composition of Ephesians. It is, however, scarcely possible that the influence of Paul upon the author of Ephesians is purely literary. Certainly no other writer of the early centuries shows anything remotely comparable to this man's grasp of the fundamental Pauline ideas, or a like ability to bring out their universal implications. There is a kinship of thought here that is not to be explained on less intimate grounds than those of close personal discipleship.

The theory seems also to take insufficient account of the difference between the use made of Colossians and the much more limited use made of the other epistles. It is not alone a question of the *quantity* of material from the several letters that is reflected in Ephesians. Apart altogether from the relative frequency with which reminiscences of the other letters occur, there is the fact that entire verses of Colossians recur in Ephesians with only minor alterations, while as a rule the traces of other letters amount to no more than an occasional word or phrase. Goodspeed's table of corresponding passages fails to substantiate his claim that all the letters have been employed. When we turn from the column devoted to parallel passages from Colossians to the two columns given to "other Pauline parallels," we are bound to feel that many if not most of the alleged correspondences of language do not indicate literary dependence in the slightest degree.[8] There is simply no justification for likening the occasional and slight reminiscences of passages from the other letters to the over-all and striking reuse of entire passages from Colossians; nothing to make us feel that the relation of the work to Colossians is merely an exaggerated illustration of the relation which it bears to the whole Pauline corpus. On the contrary, not only are the actual words of Colossians taken up again and again, but the cosmic theologoumena which were brought forward in Colossians to serve the needs of an apologetic against a particular form of Gnostic syncretism and asceticism are here made the heart of a system of Christian thought, conceived independently of any controversial motivation, directed simply to leading Christians themselves onward to a fuller appreciation of "the breadth and length and height and depth" of the faith in which they believe. The theological content of the other letters is not so utilized. The ideas of predestination may indeed owe something to Romans, but even in this area the doctrine of Romans does not dominate the thought in the way that the doctrine of Colossians dominates the thought of the cosmic reconciliation. It is impossible to believe that a first-class thinker writing an introduction to the collected letters of Paul would give such disproportionate weight to Colossians, the least characteristic of the whole group. Even the hypothesis of a longer acquaintance with Colossians is insufficient to account for this.

Yet with all these criticisms in detail, there remains a substantial element of truth in the Goodspeed hypothesis. Ephesians is, and is meant by the author to be, a commendation of

[8] For instance, how can τῷ γὰρ βουλήματι αὐτοῦ τίς ἀνθέστηκεν (Rom. 9:19) be put forward seriously as influencing the phrase κατὰ τὴν βουλὴν τοῦ θελήματος ἀυτοῦ (Eph. 1:11)?

Paul's theology to the church of another generation. No other intelligible construction can be put upon the opening verses of ch. 3. It is certainly not Paul who is here commending himself; but it is equally certain that he is being commended. The writer is confident that his readers can, as they read, perceive Paul's insight into the mystery of Christ (3:4). His interpretation will help them to understand Paul's writings, and to gain through them a deeper and wider comprehension of the gospel in its profoundest implications.

There is, however, nothing whatever in these words, or anywhere else in the epistle, to suggest that the readers are now being introduced to the writings of Paul for the first time. On the contrary it is assumed that they "have heard of the stewardship of God's grace that was given to [him]" and know something of "the mystery" that "was made known to [him] by revelation" (3:2-3). It is by no means inconceivable that the writer of Ephesians is the collector of the Pauline letters, but there is nothing that can properly be called evidence to justify such a conclusion; and certainly there is nothing to show that he is introducing a man and a message that have fallen into obscurity. We have the impression rather that he is seeking to bring out the permanent significance of something that is known, but not wholly understood and consequently not appreciated at its true worth.

We may agree, then, that Ephesians stands in an extraordinarily close relationship to the Pauline epistles, at least to the extent that it represents a serious effort at interpretation for the benefit of a generation to which the conflict with Judaism is no longer a living issue. The evidence does not permit us to follow Goodspeed in all the details of his attempted reconstruction of the circumstances under which it came to be written—the alleged influence of the book of Acts is not discernible; and it is not clearly shown, though it remains a possibility, that the epistle was composed as a foreword to the collected epistles of Paul.[9] It is perfectly true, however, that it cannot be submitted to close exegesis without constant reference to the Pauline writings, to a degree that is not required in dealing with any of the authentic epistles. Many expressions of great theological importance are left unexplained in their context in Ephesians, and are seen in their true significance only when they are set in the light of the passages in which the great apostle originally hammered out the ideas. But this again seems to argue that we are not dealing with an introduction to writings that have long lain in obscurity to a public which has no acquaintance with them, but rather that we have before us an attempt to reinterpret well-known writings which no longer seem relevant and are perhaps even being employed in a distorted sense by rival sects.

The Epistle to the Ephesians is a very ambitious undertaking by a writer of great originality and power. The book is more than a summary of Pauline doctrine; more even than a commentary on the Pauline letters. It is an attempt to formulate a philosophy of religion, which is at the same time a philosophy of history, out of Pauline materials. The writer is a great theologian in his own right. Less gifted than Paul in some respects—less capable of penetrating to the heart of a situation with a sure grasp of the issue at stake, and setting it in the light of the gospel—he is at the same time a far more systematic thinker; and he has attempted, as Paul never did, to reduce Paul's bold and brilliant ideas to a system, to correlate them one with another, to bring them under the dominion of a single ruling theme—the eternal purpose of God to unite all things in heaven and on earth in Christ; and so to demonstrate their significance, not alone for the particular social situation which first called forth their expression, but for the life of the church in all ages.

We may now see why the Epistle to the Colossians is drawn on so extensively in his work. In Colossians, as in no other epistle, Paul had been forced to face the rivalry of the syncretizing paganism of the age and to combat its attempt to incorporate Christ into its system. Unlike the struggle with Judaism, this was still a living issue in the church; the struggle with Gnosticism, represented in one of its manifold varieties in the Colossian heresy, was to occupy the energies of the church for two or three generations. The controversy at Colossae had led Paul to expound the absolute significance of Christ, not as one among many mediators, but as the bearer of the whole fullness of deity, the mediator of creation and of redemption for all beings. The doctrine of Colossians, extracted from its local references and its immediate apologetic aim, was capable of serving as the nucleus

[9] While admitting the possibility, one should not regard it as a probability. The comparison of the text of the epistles in early manuscripts (especially the Beatty papyrus) and in early versions seems to show that they have passed through a period of textual transmission, during which they were copied individually on separate rolls before they entered the much longer period of a joint textual history, during which they were copied as a corpus on one or two large rolls or in a codex. Ephesians seems, like the others, to have had its own period of separate transmission. But a serious examination of this type of evidence would be both too technical and too long for a commentary of this character. This passing suggestion must suffice.

of a complete doctrine of history and of human destiny. To the author of Ephesians, therefore, this epistle seemed to be the crown of all Paul's thought, and to provide the fundamental ruling idea in the light of which all the rest of his theology could be interpreted. Not the accident of a longer acquaintance with this letter, but a sound appreciation of the compass of its thinking led to its preponderance over all the other epistles in the composition of Ephesians.

It is impossible to reconstruct the particular circumstances under which such an essay may have been composed and published. But if we can get it thoroughly into our minds that it is an essay put into the general stream of circulation, not a letter addressed to a definite group of recipients, we shall not find it necessary to seek for a special occasion for its publication. When a man's thinking has ripened to the point at which he feels that he can make a serious contribution to the enlightenment of his fellows, he does not need an occasion; he sets his thoughts down in writing and publishes them. All he needs is a reading public and—nowadays—a publisher; in the ancient world he could be his own publisher, could engage his own scribes, and multiply and distribute as many copies as he wished or could afford to have made. We know very little of the conditions under which Christian literature was distributed at this period, and we have no means of knowing where such a work as this would first be put in circulation or how it would be carried from place to place. The ordinary channels of the commercial book trade are of course out of the question. We must suppose that one of the leading churches, possibly Ephesus or Rome, sponsored the epistle and communicated it to the others; more than this we cannot say.

In such a treatise, likewise, we cannot expect to discern the immediate concrete purpose which a true letter seeks to serve. The purpose is simply to lay before others the thoughts which have been ripening in the author's mind as he has been studying and meditating upon the letters of Paul, in the hope that he may help others to find in the writings of the apostle the same enlightenment, the same vision of the scope of the gospel, the same conception of the wonder of the church, in which Christ finds his continuing incarnation and in which the ultimate cosmic purpose of God is beginning to be realized. The author hopes to show that the faith of Christ is worthy to—and is destined to—command the allegiance of all mankind; he presents Christ and the church as the center of all history and the key to the fulfillment of the divine purpose. There is no concrete indication that he feels that apathy has set in, that Christians have ceased to appreciate the glory of their calling, or that sectarian tendencies are endangering the church; his one warning is directed against the danger of relapsing into an acceptance of pagan moral standards (4:17–5:18). His principal aim is to confirm his brethren in their faith, to enlarge their horizons, and to draw still closer the bonds of brotherhood which already unite them; teaching them that the highest experiences and the loftiest thoughts are to be found within the body to which they all belong; and that in their unity lies the pledge of the unity of all mankind, and indeed of the whole creation, in Christ.

IV. Theology of the Epistle

The Epistle to the Ephesians occupies a place of supreme importance in the history of Christian theology. It could almost be said that through the centuries the influence of Paul has been felt primarily through this epistle in much the same sense as the influence of Tertullian has been transmitted through Cyprian. Certainly the Augustinian-Calvinist line of interpretation owes its strong emphasis on predestination largely to the way in which this doctrine is expressed in Ephesians; and in all schools the whole conception of the church—of its essential nature as the body of Christ, and of its mission to unite all races and nations in a single brotherhood of worship and love—has been shaped and governed by the exposition which it receives in this epistle.

Nor is the interest in it solely or even primarily historical. No book in the Bible is more pertinent to the life of our own times, when mankind faces the challenge now presented to it with compelling urgency: *Unite or perish.* It assures us that it is not the will of the God who made this universe that it should be perpetually divided against itself, but that it is his gracious purpose to bring all things in "the fullness of time" (1:10) into harmonious unity in Christ. The pledge of this ultimate unity of all things created is given in the union of Jews and Gentiles in the one church of Christ (2:15*b*, 16). It reminds us also that the unity among men which we so desperately need is and can be only the fruit of a rightly oriented life of the spirit. The unity toward which all things move is a unity *in Christ;* and the tragic divisions of mankind are healed only when men cease to be alienated from God and from the community that lives by faith in him—when we are "made . . . alive together with Christ" and lifted together to a new plane of life "in the heavenly places in Christ Jesus" (2:5-6), where we all "have access in one Spirit to the Father" (2:18).

The central theme of the epistle, then, is the movement of all things created toward an ultimate unity in Christ, and the place of the church in the attainment of that consummation. But the source and motive of unity among men and in the universe are not found in the needs of men or in the mechanical processes of nature, but in the mind and will of God. All things move to their appointed end in accordance with a purpose of love formed by God before the creation, and are governed in their movement by his wisdom and power: their chief end is to tell "the praise of his glory" (1:6, 12, 14), and to make known his "manifold wisdom" (3:10). In its beginning, in its process, and in its consummation the whole creation depends upon the God who made it, and in whom its destiny has remained hidden until it has pleased him to make it known to and through the church (3:5, 9).

God is known to us as "our Father" (1:2), who loves us with a great love, and causes us to "sit with him in the heavenly places" (2:4, 5). But in the mind of this writer "fatherhood" is not simply a metaphorical description of the relationship of God to men: it is somehow expressive of his essential nature as God. Thus he is called, absolutely, "the Father" (2:18), and "the Father of glory" (1:17); and is regarded as the prototype of all fatherhood, the reality of which all other fatherhoods are but reflections in limited orders of existence—he is "the Father [πατήρ], from whom every family [πατρία] in heaven and on earth is named" (3:14-15). In the eternal relationships of the Godhead he is the "Father of our Lord Jesus Christ" (1:3). And his universal fatherhood is the basis of the unity of the church and of the unity of the creation which the church foreshadows and initiates—he is the "one God and Father of all, who is above all, and through all, and in all." It is, then, no blind and inscrutable Fate or impersonal Necessity that governs the motions of the universe and fixes the destiny of man. It is the will of one whose whole nature is to be Father; who "destined us in love to be his sons" (1:5), who has "lavished" upon us "the riches of his grace" (1:8, 7), and "has made known to us . . . the mystery of his will" (1:9). Neither are his secrets written in the stars, to be unveiled by the skill of the astrologer. It is "in Christ" that his purpose is "set forth" (1:9); it is no longer "hidden . . . in God" (3:9), but "has now been revealed to his holy apostles and prophets by the Spirit" (3:5), and it is to be inwardly apprehended by those who are enlightened and strengthened by the same Spirit (1:17-18), and who are "rooted and grounded in love" (3:16-19).

The divine purpose is accomplished in the universe by the mighty acts of God in Christ (1:19–2:7). These words "in Christ" or "in Christ Jesus" are repeated again and again in the epistle; and it is clear that the writer uses "Christ" in the full consciousness of its primary sense, as the title "Messiah." He who was the object of Israel's hope (1:12) is now the object of the church's faith (1:13). Christ is not only the agent of God, but the spiritual locus of all the divine blessings and of all spiritual life. It is "in Christ" that God bestows all his gifts upon men (1:3); choosing us to be his own, holy and blameless (1:4), destining us to be his sons (1:5), freely bestowing on us his glorious grace (1:6), forgiving our trespasses (1:7), revealing to us the secret of his purpose in nature and in history (1:9-10), and granting us his Holy Spirit as the earnest of the inheritance which is to be ours (1:13-14). Above all, it is "according to the working of his great might which he accomplished in Christ" (1:19-20) that he has made his purpose of salvation effective. For he has raised Christ from the dead, exalted him to his own right hand in the heavenly places, and given him supreme authority in the universe (1:19-22).

Again, the death of Christ on the cross is significant as the sacrifice by which the old enmities between men are done away, by which the barriers which separate Jew from Gentile are broken down, and by which all alike are reconciled to God and brought into the unity of a common life (1:13-16). The traditional interpretation of Christ's death as an expiation for our sins is mentioned by the writer only in passing (1:7); it is not an integral part of his doctrine. Nor does he ever make use of Paul's conception of a mystical participation in Christ's death on the part of the believer. The death from which God raises us is not the death of the self in being "crucified with Christ" (Gal. 2:20; Rom. 6:5; Col. 2:20; etc.); it is the natural state of mankind, whether Jew or Gentile, as "dead in trespasses and sins" (2:1-5). This writer thinks of the death of Christ as a sacrifice which brings those to whom its benefits extend into fellowship with God and into fellowship with one another. It is therefore the key to the unifying of humanity in "one new man" (2:15), which is the harbinger of the ultimate unity of the whole creation. The roots of this conception lie not in the expiatory sacrifices of the Old Testament, but in the covenant-sacrifice (Exod. 24:5-8; cf. I Cor. 11:25) by which God and his people are linked in the mystical bond of a shared life.

The most distinctive feature in the teaching of this epistle, however, is the doctrine of the church. In the great design of God to "gather together in one all things in Christ" (1:10) the church represents the primary stage in accomplishment—the gathering of a divided humanity in one; it is the token and the earnest, as it were, of the work of redemption which is ultimately to embrace the entire cosmos, when "the creation itself will be set free from its bondage to decay and obtain the glorious liberty of the children of God" (Rom. 8:21). The mission of the church, that is to say, is even wider than humanity, for through it even the mighty angels which inhabit the spheres are brought to know "the manifold wisdom of God" (3:10). Thus does the writer's imagination soar into contemplation of the transcendental significance of the church; but the center of his interest lies in the reconciliation of man with man, and the elevation of a united humanity into communion with God. For him the fundamental division within humanity has been the division between Jew and Gentile. Social and political divisions do not concern him; he thinks only of the *religious* "wall of partition" which has excluded the entire Gentile world from any share in "the commonwealth of Israel." Until Christ came and broke down that wall of partition, all Gentiles were "strangers from the covenants of promise, having no hope, and without God in the world" (2:12). Only Israel has been "near" to God; the Gentiles have been "far off" (2:13). The great work of Christ has been the healing of this fundamental division: those who were "far off" have now been "made nigh by the blood of Christ"; he has "slain the enmity" by his cross, and reconciled Jew and Gentile "in one body" to God (2:13-16). In him a united humanity has "access by one Spirit unto the Father" (2:18) and is constituted a living temple "for a habitation of God through the Spirit" (2:21-22). There is in this the pledge of a unity that is destined to grow until it brings the whole human race into the one family of God—"till we all come into the unity of the faith, and of the knowledge of the Son of God, unto a perfect man, unto the measure of the stature of the fullness of Christ" (4:13).

The church, then, is Christ's "body, the fullness of him who is being wholly filled" (1:23). Christ and the church together constitute a single corporate personality which is complete only in the union of the two as head and body; Christ is "filled" (or "fulfilled") as the church which is the body grows to its full stature, in the mature perfection of faith and knowledge, fostered by love and truth. Christ as the head determines the nature of the body which depends upon him as the directing intelligence and will, and the source of all its vital forces. "We are to grow up . . . into him"; and from him "the whole body, joined and knit together . . . makes bodily growth and upbuilds itself in love" (4:15-16). A common life, derived from the head, runs through the whole; and each member has its own contribution to make; and the ministers of every kind—apostles, prophets, evangelists, pastors, teachers (4:11)—are the gifts which Christ bestows upon his church to promote its growth and to fit its several members for the "work of service" (4:12) which each is called to perform.

Again, the relation of the church to Christ is set forth in terms of a mystic, archetypal bridal, which is symbolized by the relation of man and wife in marriage and is the model to which Christian marriage should conform (5:22-23). The words which accompany the institution of marriage in the story of Adam and Eve (Gen. 2:24) are taken by the writer to apply primarily to the union of Christ and the church (5:31-32). The consecration of the church by baptism is the preparation of the bride, in purity and splendor, for marriage with her heavenly bridegroom (5:26-27). She and Christ are made one, as man and wife are made one in marriage.

In effect the epistle offers a Christian gnosis of redemption—a revealed knowledge of the ultimate meaning of the universe and of human destiny, and of the significance of Christ and the church in relation to the sum of things. The primitive eschatology is wholly abandoned: the thought of an imminent catastrophic end of the age and of the appearance of Christ in glory to execute judgment and to establish the kingdom of God upon earth is not so much as mentioned, and would indeed be utterly foreign to the writer's central doctrine. Our Lord is called "the Messiah," as the fulfillment of Israel's ancient hope (1:12; 2:12; etc.); but the office of messiahship is no longer conceived in terms of one who shall come in the clouds of heaven to judge and to rule as king. As Messiah, our Lord is the integrating power of the universe—the living center of all history and of all nature, to which all things are even now being gathered into one in keeping with the divine purpose in creation. And human society, despite the powerful forces of evil that are at work within it (2:2) and are ranged in mortal combat against the followers of Christ (6:12), is not doomed to end in apocalyptic destruction; it is destined to be incorporated into "the Christ that is to be," and to be made tributary to his fullness. In this sense the epistle is the first manifesto of Christian imperialism, exhibiting the church as the spiritual empire which must grow until it unites all mankind under the glorious sovereignty of Christ the Lord.

V. Construction and Contents

The Epistle to the Ephesians is a letter only in form. In substance it is a treatise on the significance of Christ and the church in relation to the divine plan for the universe, followed by exhortation and instruction in the life that befits those who are called into God's high service as members of the church. Thus it falls into two main divisions: chs. 1–3, in which the doctrine is expounded; and chs. 4–6, in which it is applied to the life of the Christian believer in the world.

The doctrinal portion is cast largely in the form of prayer or devotional meditation, couched in a measured liturgical style which rises at times to the sublime. The salutation (1:1-2) marks it as addressed in the name of Paul to the whole company of Christian believers everywhere in the world, and prepares us for the exposition of a doctrine of universal significance. A magnificent hymn of adoration (1:3-14), recounting the spiritual blessings which God bestows upon his people in Christ, culminates in the introduction of the central theme—the revelation of God's purpose to "gather together in one all things in Christ" (1:10); and points to the progressive realization of that purpose in the Jews (1:11-12), who now find their hope of Messiah fulfilled, and in the Gentiles (1:13-14), who hear the gospel of salvation and receive the gift of the Holy Spirit.

This is followed by a prayer that the readers may be granted spiritual enlightenment, that they may be enabled to understand all that is involved in this revelation. They are invited to contemplate the mighty acts of God in Christ as the manifestation of his saving power, exhibited in raising Christ from the dead and exalting him to supreme dignity and power—acts which are paralleled in their own spiritual experience, in that God has raised them from the death of sin and exalted them to share the heavenly life and the high estate of Christ himself (1:15–2:10).

The readers are now summoned to remember their past condition as Gentiles and to compare it with their present status and privileges as members of the household of God. This transformation has been effected through Christ's sacrifice of himself on the Cross and his proclamation of a universal gospel of peace; and it issues in the creation of a community of worship which is the true temple of God, incorporating Jews and Gentiles in a new humanity centering in Christ (2:11-22).

A new prayer for the spiritual progress of the readers now commences (3:1), but is interrupted at once by a long parenthesis (3:2-13), which claims for Paul a pre-eminent mission as the appointed herald of salvation to the Gentiles and interpreter of the mystery of the divine will. His sufferings in this cause are the glory of the church to which he has done such great services (3:13). The prayer is then resumed (3:14-19) in a series of petitions of surpassing beauty, asking that the readers of the epistle may attain the full perfection of life in God. This prayer, and with it the first main division of the epistle, closes with a splendid doxology (3:20-21).

The second main division is devoted chiefly to moral instruction and exhortation, keynoted by the opening words of ch. 4: "I . . . beg you to lead a life worthy of the calling to which you have been called," and supported by further expositions of the relationship between Christ and the church, and of the nature and function of the Christian ministry. There are four main bodies of exhortation. The first deals with the Christian life in relation to the church, and emphasizes the spirit of unity which must rule (4:1-16). In the second the Christian life is set in the sharpest contrast with paganism (4:17–5:20), with stern warnings against the consequences of relapse into the evil practices of pagan society (5:3-14). The third represents the application of the doctrine to the Christian's family relationships (5:21–6:9), with particular attention to marriage, which is treated as a symbol of the mystic bridal of Christ and the church (5:22-23). The fourth depicts the Christian in conflict with the spiritual forces of evil in the universe, exhorting him to fight manfully, in the strength of Christ, equipped with the spiritual arms of God himself, for defense and for attack (6:10-20).

The epistle is concluded with a commendation of the messenger, borrowed almost word for word from Colossians (6:21-22=Col. 4:7-8); and a benediction (6:23-24).

VI. State of the Greek Text

The text of Ephesians has been transmitted with exceptional fidelity. There are few variants of importance, and practically no instance in which the true text is in doubt.

In 1:1 the evidence of our earliest authorities shows unmistakably that the words rendered "at Ephesus" (KJV) are not original (see above, p. 601).

In 1:15 the phrase τὴν ἀγάπην (the "love"—rendered in both our versions) is omitted in the Beatty papyrus (p^{46}—our earliest witness) and in all three of our best Greek manuscripts, viz., Vaticanus (B), the first hand of Sinaiticus (א), Alexandrinus (A). Its insertion in other witnesses is undoubtedly a scribal corruption made in an attempt to simplify a difficult expression.

In 3:1 Codex Claromontanus (D) adds at the end of the verse the verb πρεσβεύω ("I am an ambassador") to overcome the harshness of the long parenthesis which separates the verb (κάμπτω—3:14) from the subject of the sentence.

In 3:9 the Nestle text omits πάντας ("all men"); but the manuscript evidence is overwhelmingly in favor of its retention. The phrase rendered "by Jesus Christ" (KJV) is found only in late and inferior manuscripts.

In 3:14 the addition "of our Lord Jesus Christ" (KJV) is an assimilation to more familiar phraseology. Here, however, the Byzantine text has the support of the Latin and Syriac versions and of Codex Claromontanus.

In 3:21 the omission of καί, which leads to the rendering of "by Christ Jesus" (KJV) instead of "and in Christ Jesus" (RSV) is not supported by any manuscript of the first rank.

In 4:9 Codex Vaticanus lends its powerful support to the retention of πρῶτον ("first" KJV); but it is omitted in p^{46} and in all the other primary uncials.

In 4:17 the Byzantine text adds λοιπά ("other" KJV) before ἔθνη. This is again a scribal insertion made to get around the difficulty that the readers are themselves called Gentiles earlier in the epistle.

In 4:23, 24 the infinitive ending -σθαι is replaced by the imperative ending -σθε in the governing verbs in some of the best witnesses. This is a common itacism, and it is not possible to decide between the two forms on the basis of manuscript evidence alone. A good style would favor the infinitive in both places, in parallelism with the infinitive ἀποθέσθαι of 4:22. The meaning is not practically affected.

In 5:9 the variant πνεύματος ("of the Spirit" KJV) in place of φωτός ("of light" RSV), formerly attested only by late and inferior manuscripts (Byzantine) is now supported by p^{46}. It is clear, however, that the context calls for φωτός, and that the substitution of πνεύματος is an assimilation to the more familiar expression of Gal. 5:22.

In 5:14 the last line of the citation is given in Codex Claromontanus (D), as ἐπιψαύσεις τοῦ Χριστοῦ—"thou shalt touch the Christ." There is some Latin support for this reading, and Chrysostom indicates that he had found it in some Greek manuscripts (not in any known to us except D).

In 5:15 there is a variation in the position of ἀκριβῶς ("carefully" RSV; "circumspectly" KJV) which is reflected in the different placing of the adverb in the two versions. The rendering of RSV rests upon the weightier authorities.

In 5:19 the adjective rendered "spiritual" is omitted in p^{46} and B, and in some good Latin witnesses. Its insertion may quite well be an error, due to the presence of the word in the parallel passage of Col. 3:16.

The tendency to treat 5:21 as the conclusion of the preceding paragraph (note the punctuation in KJV), failing to perceive that it is really the heading of the table of household duties which follows, left 5:22 apparently without any semblance of a verb. To complete the sense the imperative of ὑποτάσσομαι has been supplied, sometimes in the third person, sometimes in the second, in nearly all our extant witnesses. The true text, which allows the injunction to wives to depend on the sense of the preceding participle, is found only in p^{46} and B, with indications of other support from Origen and Chrysostom.

In 6:12 the Byzantine text adds τοῦ αἰῶνος after σκότους, giving "the darkness of this world" (KJV) instead of "this present darkness" (RSV). This addition is not supported by any witness of the first rank.

It is clear that none of these variants—and these are the only ones worth noticing—has any effect upon the interpretation of the epistle, apart from the addition of the name of the city in 1:1.

VII. Outline of the Epistle

I. Doctrinal (1:1–3:21)
  - A. The salutation (1:1-2)
  - B. An act of thanksgiving (1:3-14)
  - C. Prayer for the enlightenment of the readers (1:15–2:10)
  - D. Further exposition of the spiritual unity of mankind in the church (2:11-22)
  - E. On the mission and message of Paul as Apostle to the Gentiles (3:1-13)
  - F. Prayer for the advance of the readers to spiritual fulfillment (3:14-19)
  - G. Doxology (3:20-21)

II. Hortatory (4:1–6:24)
  - A. First exhortation: To promote the unity of the church (4:1-16)
    1. The need for consecration (4:1-6)
    2. Unity served, not impaired, by diversity of gifts (4:7-16)
  - B. Second exhortation: To have done with pagan ways (4:17–5:20)
    1. A general appeal (4:17-24)
    2. Some special injunctions (4:25–5:2)
    3. Light against darkness (5:3-14)
    4. A brief summary (5:15-20)
  - C. Third exhortation: To mutual subordination in the Christian household (5:21–6:9)
    1. Husbands and wives—marriage as a symbol of Christ's relationship with the church (5:21-23)

2. Children and parents (6:1-4)
3. Slaves and masters (6:5-9)

D. Fourth exhortation: To put on God's armor (6:10-18)
E. An appeal for prayers (6:19-20)
F. Commendation of the bearer of the epistle (6:21-22)
G. Benediction (6:23-24)

VIII. Selected Bibliography

ABBOTT, THOMAS KINGSMILL. *A Critical and Exegetical Commentary on the Epistles to the Ephesians and to the Colossians* ("International Critical Commentary"). New York: Charles Scribner's Sons, 1897.

DIBELIUS, MARTIN. *An die Kolosser, Epheser, an Philemon* ("Handbuch zum Neuen Testament"). 2d ed. rev. Tübingen: J. C. B. Mohr, 1927.

GOODSPEED, EDGAR J. *The Meaning of Ephesians*. Chicago: University of Chicago Press, 1933.

HORT, FENTON JOHN ANTHONY. *Prolegomena to St. Paul's Epistles to the Romans and the Ephesians*. London: Macmillan & Co., 1895.

KNOX, WILFRED LAWRENCE. *St. Paul and the Church of the Gentiles*. Ch. IX, "The Ephesian Continuator." Cambridge: Cambridge University Press, 1939.

LOCK, WALTER. *St. Paul's Epistle to the Ephesians* ("Westminster Commentaries"). London: Methuen & Co., 1929.

MITTON, CHARLES LESLIE. *The Epistle to the Ephesians: Its Authorship, Origin, and Purpose*. Oxford: Clarendon Press, 1951.

ROBINSON, J. ARMITAGE. *St. Paul's Epistle to the Ephesians*. London: Macmillan & Co., 1903.

SCOTT, ERNEST FINDLAY. *The Epistles of Paul to the Colossians, to Philemon and to the Ephesians* ("The Moffatt New Testament Commentary"). London: Hodder & Stoughton, 1930.

WESTCOTT, BROOKE FOSS. *Saint Paul's Epistle to the Ephesians*. London: Macmillan & Co., 1906.

EPHESIANS

TEXT, EXEGESIS, AND EXPOSITION

1 Paul, an apostle of Jesus Christ by the will of God, to the saints which are at Ephesus, and to the faithful in Christ Jesus:

1 Paul, an apostle of Christ Jesus by the will of God,
To the saints who are also faithful[a] in Christ Jesus:

[a] Other ancient authorities read *who are at Ephesus and faithful.*

I. DOCTRINAL (1:1–3:21)

A. THE SALUTATION (1:1-2)

1:1. In the first section of the Intro. it has been argued that the apostle Paul, though he is thus named in the salutation, cannot in fact have been the author of this epistle. The writer has chosen to issue his work under the name of the great apostle, not in the hope of giving it an authority to which its own merits would not entitle it, but in recognition of his indebtedness to Paul as the teacher who had inspired and guided him. It is the way that he takes of honoring the memory of the man who led him to

1:1. *Introductory Note.*—"One of the divinest compositions of man"—so Coleridge described the Epistle to the Ephesians. In this judgment commentators ancient and modern agree. A recent expositor speaks of it as "at once the most 'modern' in many ways, of all the books of the New Testament and the richest record of Christian experience." [1] Or to quote another of the many interpreters who have honored this N.T. classic in recent times:

> It is beautiful in expression, but more beautiful in thought, carrying us to the highest pinnacles of Christian speculation with a daring that is matched only by its reverence and humility, and wins our allegiance by its perfect reasonableness. Its language and imagery have passed into the richest treasures of the church, and on them have been founded her finest hymns and most immortal allegories—from the glorious songs of Prudentius and Bernard to

[1] F. R. Barry, *St. Paul and Social Psychology. An Introduction to the Epistle to the Ephesians* (Oxford: University Press, 1923), p. 8.

appreciate "the breadth and length and height and depth" of the revelation of God in Christ.

To the saints who are also faithful: The words **at Ephesus** (KJV) are not represented in the best authorities (see Intro., p. 601) and are certainly a gloss derived from the title (πρὸς Ἐφεσίους—"to Ephesians") which was set at the head of this letter by early editors of the Pauline corpus. The letter is not addressed to Ephesus or to any other congregation or regional group, but to the universal church. For this writer the word **saints** appears to mean "members of the holy community," once confined to Israel (2:19) but now embracing Gentiles also. The **saints** of the present age are **also faithful in Christ Jesus;** or, πιστός being given the active sense, they are "believers" in Christ Jesus. Those of earlier ages *"hoped* in Christ" (note the distinction in vss. 11-12). On the double meaning of πιστός see on Col. 1:2.

"The Church's one Foundation" of our own day; and the quaint homilies of the Middle Ages, no less than the marvellous works of the Puritan Bunyan, owe their suggestion to the picture of the Christian warrior.[2]

One outstanding characteristic of the Epistle to the Ephesians alone may bring it into special prominence in contemporary Christian history—its central theme of unity. The word unity is the theme song of many dreams and longings. Christendom is being driven to thoughts of unity by rival gospels which also promise fellowship—and produce it, of a kind. The disciples of Karl Marx gather themselves together under the banner of Communism. The very word is gospel—good news—to a world hungry for community. We have grown tired of loneliness and individualism, even of the grandeur of Christian individualism. Hence secular "churches" emerge as challenges to the disunity of the people of God. Christian insight may readily point to the fallacious foundations upon which these rival religions of unity are built. But millions in the modern world are ignorant of the Christian faith. Consequently, the lure of these rival religions of unity is difficult to escape. They come with promises of salvation, a meeting of a desperate need. They arrive on the historical scene at a time when the Christian gospel of unity in Christ has been a gospel often neglected by Christians themselves, a gospel sinned against by a disunited church. To our scattered Christian flocks can come the cry: "To your tents, O Israel." Back to unity and fellowship. Back to the Epistle to the Ephesians!

1. ***The Christian as a Saint.***—The epistle has been known in Christian history as a church epistle. An important N.T. interpretation of what it means to be a member of the Christian church meets us at the outset. To call all church members saints strikes a modern Christian as quite strange. The word saint has suffered a sea change since the days of the early church. In our time it connotes a figure in stained glass, wearing archaic clothes, and commemorated in liturgical prayers. At its simplest it designates in modern speech the extraordinary Christian, the hero, the martyr. It would not occur to a modern utterly unheroic church member to call himself a saint.

Yet one of the important clues to a recovery of the N.T. idea of the church lies in this very word. Every Christian a saint! What could that mean? As commonly used in the epistles of Paul (cf. Rom. 1:7; I Cor. 1:2; Col. 1:2), the word is a transference from the old dispensation to the new. The people of God of the O.T. were a chosen race, and therefore a holy people (Exod. 19:6; Deut. 7:6; Dan. 7:18; I Macc. 10:39; I Pet. 2:9). The holiness consisted in the call—a vocation which might or might not meet with worthy response. In fact the chosen people frequently groaned under the burden of having been singled out by God and of being compelled to live under his demanding covenant. They envied on occasion the "lesser breeds without the law." Job cries out to God: "Let me alone. . . . What is man, that thou shouldest magnify him? and that thou shouldest set thine heart upon him?" (Job 7:16, 17.) But every Jew knew quite well that he had been made a member of a holy people, a nation of "saints," upon whom God had showered blessings, but whom he had also burdened with demands.

The writers of the N.T. transferred this view of a holy people to the new Israel. Church and nation, it is true, were no longer identical. But entrance into the church by baptism corresponded to circumcision in the old covenant. Baptism, when administered to adults, implied voluntary joining. But once a member of the people of God, no escape was any longer possible from the vocation to sainthood. The story of Ananias and Sapphira (Acts 5:1-11) strikingly illustrates this paradox. The new covenant under the gospel, in the vivid picture of one of the parables of Jesus, was "like unto a net, that

[2] G. C. Martin, *Ephesians, Colossians, Philemon, and Philippians* (Edinburgh: T. C. & E. C. Jack, 1902; "The New-Century Bible"), p. 23.

2 Grace *be* to you, and peace, from God our Father, and *from* the Lord Jesus Christ.	2 Grace to you and peace from God our Father and the Lord Jesus Christ.

2. The formula **grace to you and peace,** found in all the Pauline letters, was probably framed by the apostle himself. In it the ancient Semitic greeting of **peace** is combined with the word χάρις—**grace**—to recall the common Greek wish for the reader's joy—χαίρειν. **Grace** means, of course, much more than joy (χαρά); it has in it the thought of that beauty which brings delight to the beholder. In Christian usage it means above all the favor which God bestows of his own goodness, far exceeding the best that man can achieve or deserve. In the thought of Paul, here taken up by the author of Ephesians, Christ and God are named in the one breath as the source of these blessings; all that comes to us **from God our Father** is likewise the gift of **the Lord Jesus Christ.**

The repetition of the name of Christ in each of the three parts of the salutation foreshadows the manner in which the whole epistle will bring out the central significance of Christ for the life of the church in all its aspects. Christ commissions the apostle; he is the sphere of faith for the saints; and in unison with the Father he confers upon believers the divine gifts of grace and peace.

---

was cast into the sea, and gathered of every kind" (Matt. 13:47). A net is not a natural product of sea life. It implies captivity as well as rescue.

Every Christian a saint! The concept can be fruitful of much profitable preaching and teaching. No Christian can deny his vocation to a life of holiness. This is fixed and cannot be evaded except by sinful denial. Among church members there will be those, as our text has it, **who are also faithful in Christ Jesus.** There will be those (see Acts 5:1-11; I Cor. 11:27-30) who will be unfaithful. The O.T. could be described as a story of a people far more unfaithful than obedient. The history of the Christian church is not entirely dissimilar. Either way, however, the people of God are throughout "a chosen generation, a royal priesthood, a holy nation, a peculiar people; that ye should show forth the praises of him who hath called you out of darkness into his marvelous light" (I Pet. 2:9).

In Christ Jesus. The phrase "in Christ," which occurs 164 times in the Pauline literature of the N.T.,[3] can be called the key to Pauline theology. It is, accordingly, rich in clues for the preacher and the teacher, particularly if one can transcend the modern tendency to interpret the phrase as describing a mystical and individualistic personal union with the Jesus of pietistic devotion. A Jew thought in corporate terms. In the O.T. the Messiah could be equated with Israel (see Pss. 20:6; 28:8; 89:38). In the N.T., Christ can similarly represent the new Israel. Perhaps the clearest use of the term "in Christ" with this corporate meaning is in Gal. 5:6: "In Christ Jesus neither circumcision availeth any thing, nor uncircumcision." The term "in Christ," as used in our epistle, cannot, of course, always be simply equated with the community, but the overtones of such significance should never be neglected. No one can be a Christian by himself. We meet Christ in the fellowship. Denial of fellowship is to be no longer "in Christ." To be a Christian is a socially demanding way of life. It means love of Christ as he lives in the fellowship of the church—be the members black or white, cultured or uncultured, singing majestic chorales or crude gospel hymns. To the twentieth century, this corporate meaning of "in Christ" is again presenting great appeal. The reign of individualistic evangelicalism, though it brought great riches in its train, is giving way to a rediscovery of Christ in the fellowship of the Holy Spirit. Few modern hymns have so quickly appealed to Christian conscience as John Oxenham's "In Christ there is no East or West."

2. ***Grace and Peace.***—This salutation, common in Paul's epistles, has been echoed so frequently in the church's liturgical speech that it is in danger of becoming commonplace. It was, however, once fresh coinage. For millions of men, in our time of global tragedy and of iron rule of power, words like grace and peace are no longer cheap. The gospel of grace and peace was born in "the fullness of time," a fullness not of peace but of wars and the trampling of armies. We need the perspective of history to see that gospel as literal good news. One needs merely to dip into honest history books, even of the times surrounding the N.T., to gain a new appreciation of the hunger for peace which must have made the gospel message full of meaning.

Anthony Trollope, the famous novelist, in a

[3] See G. Adolf Deissmann's thorough monograph *Die neutestamentliche Formel "in Christo Jesu"* (Marburg: N. G. Elwert, 1892), p. 3.

3 Blessed *be* the God and Father of our Lord Jesus Christ, who hath blessed us with all spiritual blessings in heavenly *places* in Christ:

3 Blessed be the God and Father of our Lord Jesus Christ, who has blessed us in Christ with every spiritual blessing in the

B. An Act of Thanksgiving (1:3-14)

Unlike the Pauline thanksgivings, which always bear direct reference to particular circumstances either of the apostle or of his readers, this passage has not the slightest *personal* application. It contemplates the magnitude and comprehensiveness of the salvation brought to the world through Christ, not in any contingent manifestation, but in the perspective of eternity. The blessings of God which are here recounted are transcendental in their nature (**in the heavenly places**), bestowed in accordance with a purpose formed **before the foundation of the world** as part of a grand design which embraces the whole of God's creation, visible and invisible—**to unite all things in him, things in heaven and things on earth.** This design is unfolded in the formation of a holy community which finds its vital principle and its bond of unity in its relationship to Christ, and the end of its existence in the praise of the God who has so gloriously manifested his nature and his will—**destined and appointed to live for the praise of his glory** (vs. 12; cf. vss. 6, 14).

3. The opening words of blessing are taken directly from II Corinthians, where Paul is expressing the deep emotion to which he was stirred by the happy outcome of a prolonged and bitter conflict with hostile elements in the Corinthian church. The form of expression goes back to Jewish liturgical usage: εὐλογητός is regularly used in the LXX to translate the Hebrew *bārûkh* (Ps. 68:20, etc), and is frequently followed by a participial clause to specify the cause for which men bless him. Here God is blessed as the author of all the blessings which he bestows on us **in Christ.**

God is known to us as **the God and Father of our Lord Jesus Christ.** The words indicate first the relation in which Christ himself stands to God, and second, the character in which Christ reveals him to us. God and Christ stand to one another in personal

little known book on Julius Caesar, gives a vivid picture of the age just preceding the Christian Era. Referring to Caesar's own commentaries, Trollope points out that nearly all the men whom Caesar mentioned died violent deaths.

> The bloody catalogue is so complete . . . that it strikes the reader with almost comic horror. But when we come to the slaughter of whole towns, the devastation of country effected purposely that men and women might starve, to the abandonment of the old, the young, and the tender, that they might perish on the hillsides, to the mutilation of crowds of men, to the burning of cities told us in a passing word, to the drowning of many thousands—mentioned as we should mention the destruction of a brood of rats—the comedy is all over, and the heart becomes sick.[4]

3. ***The God and Father of Our Lord Jesus Christ, Who Has Blessed Us.***—Belief in God, or gods, is no monopoly of the religion of the Bible. In the ancient world there were "gods many, and lords many" (I Cor. 8:5). Nor did the pagan world lack analogies to the biblical stories of a covenant between the gods and their chosen peoples. Myths and legends abounded in which gods descended and talked with men. But the Hellenistic world, under the guidance of its philosophers, had emptied these myths of literal meaning. Plato even turned upon them the scorn of a moral conscience. These myths were not history—happily so for the enlightened Greek. A "god of the philosophers" could replace the gods of crude mythmongering. The Jewish-Christian Bible, however, came with a God of history of whom the believer need not be ashamed. He was for the Jew the "God of Abraham, of Isaac, and of Jacob" (Exod. 3:16). He was for the Christian the **Father of our Lord Jesus Christ**—a Jesus who was contemporary history. To be a Christian meant covenant relationship with this God of history. To be a Christian means this today.

It is comparatively easy for a modern man to believe in a "God of the philosophers." Even the disciples of Karl Marx believe in a kind of philosophical deity. But a philosophical belief in God is worlds removed from faith in the God of the biblical drama. The God of the Bible

[4] *The Commentaries of Caesar* (Edinburgh: W. Blackwood & Sons, 1870), p. 27.

relationships; Christ himself worships God as God and loves and obeys him as Father, and teaches us to approach him in the same attitude of adoration, love, and obedience. The God thus revealed is not a philosophical abstraction like the "Unmoved Mover" of Aristotle or the "Idea of the Good" of Plato, but a Person who blesses and is blessed; and he is known and apprehended by us in this his true nature only as we see him in Jesus Christ.

Every spiritual blessing: The two adjectives suggest respectively the *comprehensiveness* and the *character* of the divine gifts. God's blessings are not partial or limited (cf. Rom. 8:32; I Cor. 3:21-22); he withholds nothing that could enrich our lives. They are called **spiritual,** not as given by the Spirit or experienced in the human spirit (though these thoughts are not excluded), but as belonging in their essential character to the realm of the imperishable, the eternal, the divine. Temporal blessings also come from God and call forth our grateful thanks; but his supreme gifts are **spiritual** and promote the highest aspects of our inward life. **Blessing** is here used concretely of the gifts by which God manifests his gracious goodness to us.

In the heavenly places: This phrase is used five times in this epistle, though it is never employed by Paul himself or by any other N.T. writer. It is not unlikely that it has been borrowed from the vocabulary of some astrological doctrine of redemption, with a tacit rejection of the sense in which astrology employed it. Astrology taught an ascent of the soul from sphere to sphere, with the highest spiritual blessing experienced only when the soul had attained to the heavenly realm above the spheres; the Christian teacher affirms that in Christ the life of believers is already transferred into the presence of God and permitted to enjoy the blessedness of heaven. The literal local sense, still important for astrology, has lost all real significance in the light of the Christian conviction that Christ has brought the atmosphere of heaven into the life of earth.

---

cannot be relegated to a world of ideas. A God of history confronts us in our history here and now. He does not content himself with being an object of philosophic theory. He acts and he speaks; he judges, and hence can also save.

"The God of Christians," so reads a famous "thought" of Pascal,

> is not a God who is simply the author of mathematical truths, or of the order of the elements, as is the god of the heathen and of Epicureans. Nor is he merely a God who providentially disposes the life and fortunes of men, to crown his worshippers with length of happy years. . . . But the God of Abraham, the God of Isaac, the God of Jacob, the God of Christians, is a God of love and consolation, a God who fills the souls and hearts of his own, a God who makes them feel their inward wretchedness, and his infinite mercy, who unites himself to their inmost spirit, filling it with humility and joy, with confidence and love, rendering them incapable of any end other than himself.[5]

Every spiritual blessing in the heavenly places. What are "spiritual" blessings? Where are "heavenly places"—or, as the literal Greek has it, simply "the heavenlies"? The word "spiritual" has certainly been wrung dry in the history of Christian preaching and Christian piety. If left undefined, we all know something of what it means, as we do also of such a phrase as "in the heavenlies." Christian experience does lift us out of the "gloomy aisles of this wailful world" into regions of the spirit where we have foretastes of heaven. Nevertheless, we need warnings as we use the word "spiritual." If it connotes merely a contrast with the material or the "bodily," it is dangerously ambiguous. The devil is a very "spiritual" being. Our epistle (6:12) speaks of "spiritual wickedness in high places." An atheistic artist, to cite a human example, could be said to be quite "spiritual." Beauty—as also truth or even goodness—is certainly of a higher realm than mere materialistic ends.

Yet there are, indeed, **spiritual blessings** which are gifts of God. The O.T. needed correction on this matter of blessings. The ancient psalmists almost broke their hearts over the problem of the rewards, in material terms, which came to the ungodly. The sufferings of Paul could rouse suspicions in Jewish minds that he was possibly not blessed of God (Col. 1:24). Spiritual blessings, however, can be, as Paul frequently points out, very concrete, and can come to Christians in the midst of physical suffering. Nor are they merely inner states of mind. They can come in the form of covenants, of relationships. A husband and wife, united in Christ, can enjoy indescribable blessings in the midst of tragedy.

[5] *The Thoughts of Blaise Pascal*, tr. M. Auguste Molinier (London: George Bell & Sons, 1890), p. 93.

4 According as he hath chosen us in him before the foundation of the world, that we should be holy and without blame before him in love:

heavenly places, 4 even as he chose us in him before the foundation of the world, that we should be holy and blameless before

In Christ: This phrase is the keynote of the whole epistle, occurring (with its equivalents "in him" and "in whom") more than thirty times. It is associated with the initiation, the working out in history, and the final consummation of God's great design in the creation and with every spiritual experience of the Christian believer. On the Godward side it expresses the sphere in which God makes his purpose known and his will effective; on the manward side it brings out the thought of the mystical unity between Christ and the whole body of Christian believers, which he fills with his presence and power. We are **in Christ** as sharing his glorious life, deriving from him all the elements of our spiritual being.

4. The writer insists strongly upon the thought that the spiritual blessings which we enjoy in Christ are not in any sense contingent, but are the fulfillment of an eternal divine purpose. God **chose us . . . before the foundation of the world.** The words suggest that the salvation of men through Christ is *prior* to the physical creation and the historical process, not an afterthought of the Creator or an accident of evolution; the universe

A story may illustrate both the phrases **spiritual blessings** and **in heavenly places.** A millionaire in his later years was asked by a friend, "What was the happiest time you can remember in your life?" After a little thought he replied, "A period of three weeks when I lay in a hospital in a strange city ill of typhoid fever." His friend registered amazement. "Yes," said the millionaire, "the answer may well surprise you. But the facts were these. There were many ill in that hospital. It was crowded and short of nurses, and we patients were a demanding and grumbling lot. But there was one nurse on our floor who, though overworked and tired, took our complaints with a smile, serving us as if we were royalty. She never entered my room without bringing peace and love with her. It was like being in heaven."

4-5. ***He Hath Chosen Us in Him . . . Having Predestinated Us.***—

How odd
Of God
To choose
The Jews.[6]

Yes, it was odd. Why did he not choose the civilized Egyptians or the gifted Greeks? Why are you and I Christians today when there may be far more worthy men and women in heathen lands who have never so much as heard of the gospel? God, however, is like the director of a drama. He chooses one actor for a role here, another for a role there. And a multitude may still stand in the wings, apparently not chosen at all. What does it all mean? Christian thought has tortured itself to penetrate the mystery—Paul in his Epistle to the Romans, Calvin in his *Institutes,* and many a maker of sermons since.

Two observations may be ventured. In the first place, an actor who has been chosen must trust the director. He may, indeed, rejoice and give thanks. But woe unto him if pride and gloating over his fellows accompanies his joy. His vocation is worthy response to the choosing. The director may have an equally important place in the future for someone apparently neglected now. Or that other has already denied his vocation, or may be given another chance (see Rom. 9:11, and above all, Rom. 11:28; Paul occasionally approximates the iron logic of Calvinism, but here clearly stops short of it). The one chosen may be found unworthy and a change may occur in the roster of players. This happened to the Jews at the time of Christ (cf. Acts 13:46). We, as our same verse puts it, have been chosen **that we should be holy and blameless before him.** The Jews were to be "a light to lighten the Gentiles." We are to be "the salt of the earth." Election and predestination are not privilege only.

Again, as a recent commentator on this very passage points out,[7] the opposite of "elected to salvation" is not merely "elected to damnation." Two verbs can be contrasted as well as two nouns, as in the phrase "rewarded with salvation." The Pauline doctrine of predestination does undoubtedly cover the fearful doom of the

[6] W. N. Ewer, in Lewis Browne, *How Odd of God* (New York: The Macmillan Co., 1934), title page.

[7] F. C. Synge, *St. Paul's Epistle to the Ephesians* (London: Society for Promoting Christian Knowledge, 1941), p. 4.

5 Having predestinated us unto the adoption of children by Jesus Christ to himself, according to the good pleasure of his will,
6 To the praise of the glory of his grace, wherein he hath made us accepted in the beloved:

him. 5 He destined us in love[b] to be his
sons through Jesus Christ, according to the
purpose of his will, 6 to the praise of his
glorious grace which he freely bestowed on

[b] Or *before him in love, having destined us.*

---

was brought into being as a theater wherein God might manifest his power and his love in the development of beings fit to sing his praise—**holy and blameless.** It is clearly implied also that his blessings are not in any sense a reward for our merits, but are altogether due to his unconditioned choice of us as the recipients of his bounty. Our fitness is the consequence, not the condition, of his choice.

5. In this verse we have the triumphant Christian response to man's inquiry concerning his destiny. Here we have no Vergil, "majestic in [his] sadness at the doubtful doom of human kind"; no victim of the prevailing astrology of the age, looking upon men as the pawns of a Fate whose blind and purposeless decrees were recorded irrevocably in the stars. This writer indulges in no general theory of human destiny, but he is filled with the glad conviction that the destiny of the Christian believer is in the hands of the God whom he has come to know in Jesus Christ, and that it is fulfilled **according to the purpose of his will.** This destiny for which God has ordained us is glorious beyond all imagination: It is that we should attain sonship to God himself. **In love to be his sons through Jesus Christ:** In these three phrases the writer sets before us our destiny under God, the spirit in which it is appointed for us, and the agent through whom it is accomplished.

6. To the praise of the glory of his grace: The highest function of the life that God has blessed is that it should sound forth the praise of him to whom it owes its blessedness.

---

unrepentant as well as the glory of the redeemed. A consistent monotheism must maintain that even the eternally lost are under the sovereign control of the one God. God has no eternal rival in his universe. But when Paul, and later John Calvin, astonish and even occasionally repel us by such daring glimpses into the mysteries of divine power, we must recall that these speculations were only the obverse side of a positive and overwhelming experience of divine grace. Their first wonder sprang from the fact that salvation was a free gift of God. We do not earn it even by keeping the law. No one earns it. In our human logic this seems arbitrary, as the giving and receiving of gifts always involves an apparently arbitrary choice of both gift and recipient. "Those who were not my people I will call 'my people,' and her who was not beloved I will call 'my beloved' " (Rom. 9:25; cf. Hos. 2:23). How tempting to penetrate the mystery, to fathom the counsels of God! The author of Ephesians, however, is wise. He does not attempt a further plunge into the involvements once so bafflingly presented by Paul in Romans. He contents himself with praise and thanksgiving. Our being adopted as children by God was not a result of our doing. No orphan child earns adoption. Our being adopted was by **the good pleasure of his will.**

We modern Christians often find this doctrine of election, which runs through the whole Bible, hard to understand. We are not humble enough. We have not been sufficiently disciplined by the righteousness of God. We are unmindful inheritors of eighteen centuries of Christian grace. We forget that we are "adopted" orphans. By nature we are not sons of God at all. We are simply sinners. We think of God as servant and not Lord. Have we not all the right to demand that the universe serve *us?* Even the godless citizen of a democracy never questions his right to be dealt with as a being of infinite worth whom society must respect. The "infinite worth of an individual soul" is, indeed, a distinguishing mark of democracy. But it is a gift from the Christian faith of democratic man's Christian ancestors. Totalitarian societies are quite logical in tossing this dogma out of the window. Unless God gives us status in the universe, **according as he hath chosen us . . . before the foundation of the world,** we are mere creatures of an hour and of the dust of the earth.

6. ***To the Praise of His Glorious Grace.***—This is the vocation to which we have been "predestined." The Christian life is, or ought to be, motivated by praise and thanksgiving. It is the one form of giving which can be a return for a gift which has not been earned. Yet as we all

7 In whom we have redemption through his blood, the forgiveness of sins, according to the riches of his grace;

us in the Beloved.
7 In him we have redemption through his blood, the forgiveness of our trespasses, according to the riches

---

The words remind us of I Pet. 2:9, which may be rendered: "You are . . . a people for God's own possession, that you may proclaim the mighty deeds of him who called you out of darkness into his marvelous light" (cf. Isa. 43:21). The verb ἐχαρίτωσεν (**freely bestowed**) is formed on the stem of the noun χάρις (**grace**), as if to mean "the grace that grace has given." It is as if the writer were so enraptured with the word that he can hardly bear to let it go; he is absorbed in the thought that God's grace overflows in grace to us, lavishes grace upon us. **The Beloved** is of course a title of Christ with messianic connotations. It recalls to us the voice from heaven, which declared to him at his baptism "Thou art my Son, the Beloved" (Mark 1:11); here, however, the perfect participle ἠγαπημένος is used instead of the verbal ἀγάπητος of the Marcan passage. The participle marks more definitely the thought that Christ is the primary and supreme object of God's love; the divine grace that is lavished on us is a manifestation of that love which we share as being "in him."

7. The sequence here is derived from Col. 1:13-14 (see *ad loc.*), but the thought is attached now to the character of Christ as **the Beloved,** not to his essential nature as Son. Being eternally God's **Beloved,** he becomes the supreme object of our love also in that he brings to us **redemption,** here defined under the aspect of **forgiveness of sins.** Thus the thought develops that Christ is **the Beloved** alike to God and to man; the eternal purpose of God is fulfilled in One whose whole nature is to be loved. And we are reminded that we love him because he first loved us and laid down his life for us; **we have redemption through his blood.**

Redemption in N.T. usage has almost wholly lost its primary sense of regaining through purchase, and has come to mean deliverance by an act of divine power—the deliverance of Christians from sin and death as prefigured in the deliverance of Israel from slavery in Egypt and from captivity in Babylon. Similarly **the blood** of Christ is not

---

know from experience, thankfulness is a volatile state of mind. It evaporates very quickly in our selfish human hearts. A cynic once defined gratitude as "a very vivid sense of benefits *to come*." Alas, how true!

We would have a more vivid sense of thanksgiving toward God if we did not take his graciousness so utterly for granted. Of course he will be gracious, so we say. Are we not his children, those for whom his world was created? Are we not predestined? We forget that there is an opposite to grace. The word "grace," in fact, has become shopworn in our sermons. It is instructive to use on occasion the word "disgrace" (dis-grace). Vivid meaning still attaches to such phrases as "I am in disgrace" or "I am disgraced." The Bible takes the "dis-grace" of God quite as seriously as his grace. The Bible calls it "the wrath of God." "By nature," so says our epistle (2:3), we are actually "the children of wrath." Only when we realize this awesome fact can we catch a vision of **glorious grace.** "Note then," says Paul, "the kindness and the severity of God: severity toward those who have fallen, but God's kindness to you, provided you continue in his kindness" (Rom. 11:22). What is desperately needed in our sentimentalized Christianity is a rediscovery of the righteousness of God. We need the O.T. as background for the N.T., as it was for Christ himself and for the early church. Until we slough off our optimistic view of man without grace, and under the wrath of God, the N.T. will remain for us a closed book. A story is told of a Sunday-school teacher who asked a class of boys, "What must I do to secure the forgiveness of sins?" One of his boys replied, "Well, first you must sin." To a juvenile mind it might seem natural that the word sin connoted merely some violent crime or an occasional moral lapse. But such an optimistic view of human nature is today not limited to the young. Modern man generally does not see himself as a sinner. Until he does, **glorious grace** will mean little or nothing.

7-8. ***The Costingness of Grace.***—We have been exploring the meaning of the word grace. The author of Ephesians explores it here also, giving concrete meaning to what is so easily a mere rote word or an abstraction. Grace involves a giving, a gift. On the part of the one who receives, this giving can be thanks-giving. When we say grace at a meal, we give such thanks. A

8 Wherein he hath abounded toward us in all wisdom and prudence;
9 Having made known unto us the mystery of his will, according to his good pleasure which he hath purposed in himself:

of his grace 8 which he lavished upon us.
9 For he has made known to us in all wisdom and insight the mystery of his will, according to his purpose which he set forth

---

a price paid to the enslaving power, but a symbol deriving from ancient conceptions of the efficacy of sacrifice, of the life force set free through death that it may be effective for the benefit of others, whether for the expiation of the sins of the community or for communicating the divine blessing to men. The thought is not of price but of power—a power of life which becomes available only when it is offered in sacrifice.

The idea of redemption is not so appropriate to the context here as in Col. 1:14, where it sustains the figure of the preceding verse. The pupil lacks the free creative power of his great teacher, and repeats his phrase somewhat mechanically. In the Colossians passage the equation of "redemption" with "the forgiveness of sins" is made simply to elucidate the metaphor and to set aside any more speculative and fanciful interpretations of the word which may have been given by the Colossian theosophists. Here there is no particular reason for making the equation, or for introducing the technical term "redemption" at all. The primary thought is of the forgiveness, which is treated as the first concrete manifestation in our experience of the grace of God in Christ, and no elucidation is given by the equation with "redemption."

8-9. The forgiveness of our sins is the beginning of our experience of the spiritual blessings which God has designed from all eternity to bestow upon us in Christ. Our admission to the knowledge of the secret counsels of God is the crowning privilege conferred by his grace—the fuller manifestation of its overflowing abundance.

In all wisdom and insight: It seems better to take this phrase with the verb ἐπερίσσευσεν (as in KJV) rather than with the participle γνωρίσας. We would thus translate: "He caused his grace to overflow toward us in all wisdom and insight." The participle

---

real gift is never earned by the recipient. It is the giver who pays. The grace of God comes to us in the form of a very costly giving, viz., a *for*-giving (contrast with *thanks*-giving). The cost of God's forgiveness is the blood of Christ. **In him we have redemption through his blood.** The N.T. writers ring endless changes on this, the heart of their message of good news. Our author cannot refrain from reminding his readers of it, even though the allusion constitutes a kind of parenthesis.

Why should forgiveness cost so much? Why is it sheer grace? The clue to the doctrine of the Atonement lies in the revelation of the O.T. God is first of all a righteous and holy God. Forgiveness for him cannot consist in overlooking evil. Forgiveness, from a strictly legal point of view, is immoral—as it appears to this day to a Hindu brought up on the strict concept of an inviolable moral law. God is holy. And yet he forgives. How is the paradox possible? The answer is the **blood of Christ.** Paul exhausts the imagery of the ancient world to suggest, even faintly, what this means.

Christian experience helps to fathom the mystery. A husband sins against the love of a wife. He repents. She forgives. The gift of forgiveness will be a costly gift just to the extent to which the moral standard of the marriage was lofty. Can we not visualize the cost? She must love what is not really worth loving. She must "ransom." She must "redeem." She must endure the memory of a great shame, the indignity of a broken covenant. She must carry a broken heart, and yet love the heartbreaker. She must enter into the husband's shame and share it, yet without surrender of her own purity. True forgiveness, even on the human plane, involves a cross-bearing. How much more when a righteous God forgives. Forgiveness is grace.

9-10. ***The Mystery of His Will, . . . Purpose, . . . the Fullness of Time, to Unite All Things.***—The audacity of such phrases can astonish us. Here is a Christian seer not afraid of cosmic visions. Christ to him is the answer to all questions man can ask. For ask them man does and must.

Many of us may have stood on the edge of the Grand Canyon of the Colorado River. The observer looks down upon rocks which geologists tell us are a billion and five hundred million years old! The very word time almost loses

10 That in the dispensation of the fulness of times he might gather together in one all things in Christ, both which are in heaven, and which are on earth; *even* in him:

in Christ 10 as a plan for the fullness of time, to unite all things in him, things in heaven and things on earth.

---

will then have epexegetic force—"in that" **he has made known to us,** etc. On the meaning of the two nouns see Exeg. on Col. 1:9; they combine the ideas of a true apprehension of first principles (σοφία) and of the practical capacity to frame conduct in accordance with them (φρόνησις). It is the **wisdom and insight** given through our knowledge of the end toward which God is working that make possible our free co-operation with him. The general thought is closely paralleled in John 15:15, which may be rendered: "I no longer call you slaves, for the slave does not know what his master is doing; but I have called you friends, for I have made known [ἐγνώρισα] to you all that I have heard from my Father."

According to his good pleasure: The ancient phrase recaptures the flavor of the original better than the **purpose** of the RSV. Εὐδοκία **(good pleasure)** suggests both the absolute sovereignty of God and his benevolence. It is the word of the angels' song: "On earth peace, good will [εὐδοκία] toward men" (Luke 2:14). More frequently we find the cognate verb εὐδοκέω in the sense "God willed," "God was pleased," always in the sense of a *gracious* decree, as in Gal. 1:15-16, "It pleased God . . . to reveal his Son in me." The phrase may be taken in dependence either on what precedes or on what follows. Both connections give a good sense—the one, that the revelation was made in accordance with God's good pleasure; the other, that his will as made known is that, in accordance with his good pleasure declared in Christ, he will unite all things in him.

10. As a plan for the fullness of time: The word οἰκονομία, here translated **plan (dispensation** KJV), has a wide range of meaning. Its primary sense is "household management" or "the office of the household manager, the steward." From the latter it is extended metaphorically to any office of trust ("stewardship"); and this is the usual sense of the word in Pauline usage, as in Col. 1:25: "According to the divine office which was given to me for you." From the former ("household management") it is likewise extended in this case to include the management of an army or of a state (whence "political *economy*"), and at length to the making of any kind of arrangements or dispositions, and even to the execution of a project previously determined upon. This last sense is the most appropriate to the context here; we might then interpret somewhat as follows: "He made known to us the mystery of his will . . . with a view to giving it effect in the fullness of the times."

The thought is of the highest significance. The writer has previously laid stress on the *eternal* counsel of God for our salvation; now he takes care to insist that it is worked

---

human meaning. The phrase **fullness of time,** in turn, assumes gigantic connotations. Did all that ocean of years contain a purpose? And was that purpose a carpenter of Nazareth in an obscure corner in a now-vanished empire, whom his contemporaries nailed to a criminal's cross? And are you and I, if we are Christians, members of a body, the church, which shares in this purposed end of all things? The Epistle to the Ephesians answers "Yes."

It does us good to set the Christian faith against the background of cosmic ultimates. And **the fullness of time** is only one of these. The fullness of space could be another. Inconceivable distances, billions of light-years, meet us there also. "The eternal silence of these infinite spaces alarms me," said Pascal. And well it might, except as faith in the God of the Bible came to Pascal's aid. It is no little thing to be a Christian and to accept the Christian faith. Let those who refuse to consider it seriously at least know what they are ignoring.

For a choice confronts us. Either a **mystery** has been revealed and a **purpose** made known, or we are lost beings in **the fullness of time.** The gospel of the N.T. beckons on the one hand. Is there an honest alternative other than acceptance of a purposeless abyss, on the brink of which man stands in stoic defiance, or from which he flees in epicurean despair? As a con-

out not in some supramundane drama, but in time and in history. In Christian thinking history has significance, for it is the sphere of the saving activity of God; it is not merely a passing show, nor are its events merely symbolical. In the Incarnation the divine enters history not as a spectator and controller, but as an active participant in the historical process itself. All the events of history are therefore viewed as somehow relevant to the acts of Christ in his historical manifestation, and are seen as ripening to their destined culmination in him. Thus it was "when the fulness of the time was come" that "God sent forth his Son . . . to redeem" (Gal. 4:4-5); and likewise the **plan . . . to unite all things in him** is to be accomplished in **the fullness of time.**

Time: More accurately "the times" (τῶν καιρῶν). The abstract notion of "time" as a continuous entity, "an everflowing stream," is scarcely to be found in the N.T. We have instead the idea of a succession of seasons or world periods, each marked by decisive events which determine its character, and each contributing to the succeeding age and to the final issue. From this point of view the N.T. writers represent the Christian Era as the last in the series of ages, inaugurated by the saving acts of Christ—Incarnation, Passion, Exaltation—and consummated in his manifestation in glory.

This consummation is here defined in terms of the achievement of a universal harmony. The final purpose of God, not to be penetrated by the natural intelligence of man and therefore termed a **mystery,** is now revealed as a grand design to **gather together in one all things in Christ.** The multiple strands of life, the entire manifold of nature and of history, and all the particular blessings of God lead to one universal goal. In the light of this purpose all things fall into place in a single gigantic pattern centered in Christ.

The infinitive ἀνακεφαλαιώσασθαι, **to unite** (RSV); **to gather together in one** (KJV), is epexegetic, defining the content of **the mystery of his will.** It is difficult to bring out the full force of this verb by any translation. In mathematics it means "to sum up" a column of figures; and in rhetoric, "to sum up" an argument, or more generally, to present a complex of ideas in a single phrase. Thus Paul tells us that all the commandments are "summed up in this sentence, 'You shall love your neighbor as yourself' " (Rom. 13:9). Here, however, the thought of *summarizing* is not appropriate. The mathematical sense might be extended to give the meaning that all the vital forces of the universe are added together and made one in Christ. But the best sense in this passage seems to be that all things are *brought to a focus* in Christ. He is the focal point

---

trast to the Epistle to the Ephesians stand such somber words as those of the agnostic Bertrand Russell: "Brief and powerless is Man's life; on him and all his race the slow, sure doom falls pitiless and dark." So to Bertrand Russell, man is in the midst of a relentless universe which, except for himself, is blind to good or evil, and he can only "sustain alone, a weary but unyielding Atlas, the world that his own ideals have fashioned despite the trampling march of unconscious power." [8]

To unite all things (RSV) or **gather together in one all things** (KJV). The Greek word used here, if translated literally, contains fascinating suggestions for popular teaching. The root of the Greek word is "head." We use the same root in such a phrase as "to head up." The Greek can also mean "to sum up."

Let us play a bit with the mathematical analogy "to sum up." Though (see Exeg.) it is not a fully accurate analogy, it can prove fruitful. The study of arithmetic in school begins with addition. A child "does sums." What is the object of adding one number to another? Is it merely the adding itself, an endless process of one number after another? There must be an end to the treadmill somewhere—the sum. The sum is the end to which the adding process is directed. The sum heads it up. Without such an end or "head" the whole business becomes meaningless.

> To-morrow, and to-morrow, and to-morrow,
> Creeps in this petty pace from day to day,
> . . . .
> it is a tale
> Told by an idiot, full of sound and fury,
> Signifying nothing.[9]

Many a man lives his life as if it were a problem in addition without an end. He never sums up. He ignores any sight of an end. "Make me

[8] "A Free Man's Worship," in *Mysticism and Logic* (New York: W. W. Norton & Co., 1929), pp. 56-57.

[9] Shakespeare, *Macbeth*, Act V, scene 5.

11 In whom also we have obtained an inheritance, being predestinated according to the purpose of him who worketh all things after the counsel of his own will:

11 In him, according to the purpose of him who accomplishes all things according

---

of the universe, of all history, and of all being; all things, as they are brought into their true relation to him, are also brought into their true relation to one another and so into an all-embracing harmony. This is the destined issue of creation, the end for which the universe was brought forth; in this the mind of God is at last revealed and his glory manifested in the grace which planned and is carrying out so great a design.

This purpose of God embraces in its scope not only the life of this planet but all spheres of being—**things in heaven and things on earth.** This is not merely a flight of the poetic fancy, as the words of Thomas K. Abbott suggest: "To the spiritual as to the poetic eye all nature seems to share in what strictly and literally belongs only to intelligent beings" (*Ephesians,* p. 19). Abbott himself adds, "Nor is it hard to see that there is a profound truth in such a view." In Colossians, Paul had declared that the creative and redemptive work of Christ embraces "all things, whether on earth or in heaven" (Col. 1:20); and in fact it belongs to the whole biblical conception of man as part of the creation to hold that his fate and the fate of the universe are inextricably associated. This may lead us to see man as helplessly involved in his environment, the pawn of a necessity which he cannot comprehend; otherwise it leads to the doctrine consistently held by the N.T. writers—that man's total environment, i.e., the universe in all its parts, shares in his salvation in the manner appropriate to its mode of existence. If we believe that in Christ there is incarnate the Logos through whom all things were made, we must also hold that all things, and not sentient beings alone, find their true home in him.

This doctrine of the final unity of the whole creation in Christ provides the philosophical groundwork of the epistle. The final issue of all things, it is now suggested, is exemplified and the manner of its outworking is illustrated in the unity of Jews and Gentiles in the church. This is the particular aspect of the universal design which is to receive extended treatment; it is briefly indicated in the closing verses of the opening act of thanksgiving. Vss. 11-12 speak of the experience of the Jews, vss. 13-14 of the participation of the Gentiles in the divine blessing.

11-12. When he speaks of "we" and "us" in the preceding verses, the writer clearly includes all Christian believers. Here, however, the first person applies only to the people of Israel, with whom he identifies himself, in distinction from the Gentile believers (**you also**) to whom he turns in vs. 13.

The ancient privilege accorded to Israel is now seen to be an integral part of God's purpose of universal blessing. Israel was "made God's portion" (ἐκληρώθημεν). The rendering **we have obtained an inheritance** (KJV) arises from a confusion of *klēros*

---

to know mine end," says the psalmist (Ps. 39:4). "What is a man profited, if he shall gain the whole world, and lose his own soul?" (Matt. 16:26) says Jesus. Clearly it is the end, the "sum," that gives meaning to all that goes before.

If this lesson is vivid in personal experience, it applies also on the larger scene—even, as our author sees it, on the cosmic plane. Can we find purpose in the universe? What is its "end," that which will make a "sum" out of the "years that are told"? For the N.T. this sum is Christ, both for **things in heaven and things on earth.** To the phrase **in him** give social meaning, including those who are "in Christ," and we get, as the end of all things, the kingdom of heaven of our Lord's teaching.

11-12. ***The Old and the New Israel.***—As an example of how in Christ God has given and is giving meaning to the story of time, the author of the epistle now turns to the history of his people, both the old and the new Israel. It is not easy for us in our day of widespread anti-Semitism, when the Jew-Gentile problem confronts us in reverse, to see how once *our* inclusion in the promised blessings of God was a difficult act of faith. All through Christian history the temptation has faced the church to belittle its Jewish inheritance. The church leader Marcion, in the second century, once

12 That we should be to the praise of his glory, who first trusted in Christ.

to the counsel of his will, 12 we who first hoped in Christ have been destined and appointed to live for the praise of his

("lot, portion") with *klēronomia* ("inheritance"). The RSV fails to bring out the peculiar significance of the verb. The description of Israel as God's "portion" goes back to the O.T., e.g., in Deut. 32:9-10: "The Lord's portion is his people; Jacob is the lot of his inheritance. He found him in a desert land, and in the waste howling wilderness; he led him about, he instructed him, he kept him as the apple of his eye."

This divine choice of Israel is related first to Christ, **in whom** the nation was made God's portion; and then to God's universal sovereignty—**according to the purpose of him who worketh all things.** The priority of Israel, then, is not absolute or final; it is a stage in the fulfillment of a divine purpose which embraces all things.

Being predestinated: The participle is to be taken closely with the main verb, so that the meaning is, "We were made God's portion by predestination"; thus is emphasized again the thought of vss. 3-4, that all the stages leading to the final consummation were planned in eternity.

We who first hoped in Christ: lit., "in *the* Christ." The article indicates that the name is here used in its primary sense of "the Messiah." The messianic hope was itself a sign that the experience of Israel was to be consummated in something yet more glorious; those who in former ages hoped now respond with praise to the glory of God revealed in the fulfillment of his promise. More widely, the spectacle of Israel, in hope awakened by promise and rewarded by fulfillment, calls forth the praise of God's glory from us and from all his creation.

boldly dropped the O.T. out of his Christian Bible. The heresy of Marcionism, as it came to be called, was conquered officially, but has it ever been fully exorcised? One can meet preachers today for whom the O.T. is a neglected portion of Scripture: "It is only about a lot of old Jews." Paul, however, although the Apostle to the Gentiles and the champion to the uttermost of their equality in the church, never ignores the priority of God's revelation to the old Israel. When we read our N.T., we should never forget that to the early Christians Scripture meant what for us is the *Old* Testament—and nothing else! They probably had scarcely an inkling that there would one day be a body of writings called the N.T., which would actually rank on an equality with the O.T. Gentile Christians read the O.T. just as faithfully as did the Jews. They merely had a fresh clue to its meaning. Every Christian had, in a sense, to become a good Jew (ceremonial laws apart) before he could become a Christian. He certainly had to know the moral law. He had to see history through the eyes of the prophets. The Christian church was an extension of Israel—new, yes, but also as old as the covenant with Abraham. Gentile Christianity was, as Paul so vividly pictures it (Rom. 11:17), a graft into the original people of God.

We who first hoped in Christ; we being predestinated according to the purpose of him who worketh all things. These words about the Jews are not spoken lightly. Could there, indeed, have been a "fullness of time" without the revelation to the ancient people of God? Our neglect of this story of the law and the prophets is the cause of much of our sentimentalized Christianity. "Jesus came to tell us that God is no longer angry." What a tragic misreading of the gospel of Christ! We need the O.T. creed as well as that of the N.T. Why has the God of history so strangely permitted Judaism to continue all these centuries? He has blotted out other nations by the score. Yet the Jews survive. In the twentieth century, as in the days of ancient exiles, they have been a suffering people, a victim, so it seems, of their own purpose in history. Have they still a lesson to teach us Christians which we have never fully taken to heart—the holiness of God, and the inexorable majesty of the law? Have we presumed upon the love of God so as to cheapen it, and have we thereby blasphemed the divine holiness?

"The one nation in all the world," so Scott Holland once described the people of the O.T.,

> which discovered a permanent purpose of God in history; the one nation which succeeded in finding a path through its own disasters, so that its own ruin only threw into clearer light the principles of God's ordained fulfilment—this unique nation pronounced that this fulfilment, this justifying pur-

13 In whom ye also *trusted,* after that ye heard the word of truth, the gospel of your salvation: in whom also, after that ye believed, ye were sealed with that Holy Spirit of promise,

glory. 13 In him you also, who have heard the word of truth, the gospel of your salvation, and have believed in him, were sealed

13-14. Gentile believers were not prepared by generations of hope for the coming of the Messiah; nevertheless, through the hearing of the gospel they have come to put their faith in him and have been sealed for God's possession by the gift of the Holy Spirit, which is the token of their participation in the fullness of the divine blessing.

The construction here is capable of two interpretations. In the Greek there are two relative clauses, both introduced by ἐν ᾧ—**in whom.** In the KJV these are taken as parallel, and the verb **trusted** is supplied with the first; in the RSV the second is taken to be resumptive and is simply omitted in translation. It seems preferable to take them as parallel, but in that case the verb of the first clause should be supplied from vs. 11, to read: "In him you too were made God's portion, through hearing the word of truth." The Gentiles are now admitted to the same high privilege as the Jews; the instrument of their admission is the gospel.

The word of truth, the gospel of your salvation: Again an echo of the language of Colossians (1:5) without the same aptness to its context. In Colossians the truth of the gospel is affirmed in contrast with the error of the doctrine of angelic mediators; here there is no such antithesis to give point to the phrase. **Salvation** and its cognates in Paul always have a future reference; sometimes they refer to preservation from the divine judgment which is to overwhelm the world ("the wrath of God," "the wrath to come," or just "the wrath"); sometimes to the consummation of Christ's work in us by translation from our present state of weakness into a glorious condition resembling his own (Rom. 5:9-10; Phil. 3:20-21; etc.). In this passage, however, the word has no eschatological connotation; it means simply the totality of the divine blessings offered in the gospel. The phrase is unique; elsewhere the gospel is defined in relation to God rather than to man; as "the gospel of the grace of God" (Acts 20:24), "the gospel of the glory of Christ" (II Cor. 4:4), or simply "the gospel of God" (I Thess. 2:9).

Believed in him: It is probable that Christ is here designated as the sphere, not as the object, of their faith. The participle πιστεύσαντες would then be construed absolutely, with ingressive force to mean: "In him [i.e., by virtue of your incorporation in his being] you came to have faith; and with the awakening of faith you were sealed with the Holy Spirit." The awakening of faith was their response to the gospel which they heard (cf. Rom. 10:17); and the gift of the Holy Spirit was God's seal set upon their faith.

The imagery of sealing reflects the Oriental custom of marking upon the skin of a devotee the symbol of his god as a token of entire consecration. Circumcision was viewed by Jewish teachers as the seal of consecration to the one living and true God. From this Jewish usage the term passed over into Christianity, where it was applied to baptism, somewhat less appropriately, seeing that the Christian rite left no visible mark. The writer here undoubtedly has baptism in mind; the seal for him is not indeed a visible mark, but the invisible presence of the Holy Spirit, which was imparted to the believer when he was made a member of the Christian community. He was thereby marked inwardly as one consecrated to God and accepted by God as his own. Note the manifest literary dependence on the language of Paul in II Cor. 1:21-22; a writer of strong original genius like Paul would not be apt thus to look back over his old correspondence to find a fitting phrase.

The earnest of our inheritance (KJV): The **earnest** is more than a **guarantee** (RSV); it is a partial payment which binds the bargain and obliges both buyer and seller to complete the transaction. This common business term is here applied to the dealings of God with his people; the gift of the Holy Spirit is the first installment, as it were, of the infinite treasure that God plans to bestow upon us; it is in this sense also the

14 Which is the earnest of our inheritance until the redemption of the purchased possession, unto the praise of his glory.

with the promised Holy Spirit, 14 which is the guarantee of our inheritance until we acquire possession of it, to the praise of his glory.

guarantee of the final entry into possession of the whole **inheritance**—the inestimable patrimony that the Father has reserved for his sons.

The phrase which follows is obscure. The RSV gives an interpretative paraphrase—**until we acquire possession of it.** The KJV translates literally, leaving the meaning as obscure as it is in the Greek—**until the redemption of the purchased possession. Redemption** is employed with a future reference by Paul in Rom. 8:23: "We ourselves, who have

pose, was to be found in *holiness of spirit,* the union of man with God, Whose image he is. Accept this as man's end, and no destruction appals, no despair overwhelms; for this is the higher life, which is worth all the deaths that the lower can die; this is the new birth, which would make all the anguish of the travailing be remembered no more. . . . But to know the secret was one thing; to achieve its fulfilment another. . . . The one possible end—the achievement of holiness—was itself become impossible to the only people who recognized it as their end.[1]

14-15. *The Gospel of Unity.*—The writer of Ephesians, having described the majestic purpose of God in the history of his own Jewish people, sees that purpose revealed at a further stage in the birth of the church in which Gentiles are included. To a Jew—even an early Jewish Christian—this inclusion must have come as an overwhelming shock. The epistles of Paul register continued surprise that such a thing was possible. By inheritance Paul was a religious snob. He could boast, "I am a Pharisee, the son of a Pharisee" (Acts 23:6) or "After the most straitest sect of our religion I lived a Pharisee" (Acts 26:5). To be a good Jew was not exactly easy. Salvation for a Jew involved hard work. Salvation had to be earned. Was not God a holy God? Could any except a righteous man have communion with the divine? Righteousness surely was not attained in a day. God's Holy Spirit, when mentioned in the O.T., had been a rare gift to a few superior prophets. Yet this new religion of Christ had appeared with miraculous powers. The Holy Spirit was being poured out "upon all flesh" (Acts 2:17). Gentiles, who had scarcely so much as heard of the intricate law of Moses, were recipients of the Holy Spirit which even the most strenuous Pharisee never dreamed of possessing. Repentance—utterly simple repentance—and faith had replaced performance as entrance requirements to the people of God. "Repent, and believe in the gospel" (Mark 1:15) had been the message of Christianity's founder. "Repent, and be baptized every one of you in the name of Jesus Christ for the forgiveness of your sins; and you shall receive the gift of the Holy Spirit," so Peter had extended an invitation to membership in the new Israel on the day of Pentecost (Acts 2:38). When the Epistle to the Ephesians was being written, this marvel was no longer a novelty, but it was still a marvel. In Christ (note the corporate overtone, as if Christ equaled the fellowship) Gentiles had **heard the word of truth,** had **believed in him,** had been **sealed with the promised Holy Spirit.**

The legalistic snobbery of many Pharisees has, so we often assume, vanished into history. But has it? Are Christian churches today ready to accept repentance in place of moral respectability and performance as the sufficient entrance requirement to membership? We are, in our turn, the new Israel. "Gentiles" to us are the "lesser breeds without the law," the uncivilized, the uncultured, the dwellers in the slums or on the wrong side of the railroad tracks. Is there no "color line" in the Christian church? We too are astonished, as were Peter (Acts 10) and Paul, that these "Gentiles" should be **sealed with that Holy Spirit of promise.** To the writer of Ephesians no "unity of all things" in Christ would have been conceivable without inclusion of Gentiles. Dare we think that it is possible today? The gospel of unity of the Epistle to the Ephesians may be for the church of the twentieth century rediscovered gospel. But first it may be awesome judgment.

14. ***Christianity and Secularism.***—Christianity has often been accused of diverting attention from the kingdom of God on earth to the kingdom in an afterlife. "Pie in the sky by-and-by." "The opiate of the people." The secular reformers of our age—the disciples of Karl Marx in particular—base much of their scorn of Christianity upon its otherworldliness. Lead people to expect justice in an afterlife and you can cheat them out of justice here and now. The master classes, so the argument runs, have utilized the Christian hope for their own selfish

[1] *Logic and Life* (New York: Charles Scribner's Sons, 1882), pp. 91-92.

the first fruits of the Spirit, groan inwardly as we wait for adoption as sons, the redemption of our bodies." It is probable that this passage is in the writer's mind here. His thought would then be that the presence of the Spirit within us issues in this **redemption;** the gift was given in order to prepare us for the fullness of life that is still to come. **Possession,** then, will be a reference to our lives as God's possession, not to our entering into possession of the inheritance; cf. I Pet. 2:9, where the same word is used: "You are . . . a people for God's possession."

The prelude of thanksgiving ends with a repetition of the note of praise which has been sounded at intervals before—**to the praise of his glory.** God's glory is revealed ever more clearly as his purpose of grace unfolds in ever-widening channels of blessing, and each stage in the development calls forth a renewal of the song of praise.

This splendid prelude, then, sets before us in solemn majesty the spectacle of all nature and of all time, and reveals to us the secret of its ultimate significance. It invites us to look upon the procession of the universe, including the spiritual pilgrimage of the human race, as the movement of all things toward an appointed goal. It begins, continues, and ends in Christ "the Beloved"; it is governed in all its parts by the will of God, in absolute sovereignty and yet in gracious love; and it so manifests his eternal glory as to issue in universal adoration of "him who worketh all things after the counsel of his own will" (vs. 11).

---

ends. They have encouraged contentedness with poverty and economic serfdom by their support of the church, which preached hope in an otherworldly righting of wrongs. Hence, in the name of justice, religions of otherworldliness must be smashed. Five-year plans must take the place of plans for distant and mythical eternities.

Is there truth in the accusation? Yes, if the critic of Christianity limits his view to a fraction of its ignoble camp followers. Religion has been a cloak for egotism from the dawn of time. *Corruptio optimi pessima est:* The corruption of the best turns into the worst.

But the tables can be turned upon the secular atheist, even with all his worthy passion for social justice here and now. Christianity's replies can be many. Has the secular utopian an answer to the problem of death? Granted a utopia on the earthly scene, will it satisfy the heart of man? Might not such utopianism prove a vanity of vanities? The book of Ecclesiastes in the O.T. can become a very contemporary classic. What if a five-year plan or a dozen five-year plans fail of success? Limit your horizon for the attainment of a kingdom of heaven to this our earth, and you will have to furnish what you promise or the very people for whom religion was supposedly an opiate will call your gospel opiate also—a gospel without hope. "If in this life only we have hope . . . , we are of all men most miserable" (I Cor. 15:19), says Paul.

These are a few of the many answers a Christian can make to the secularist. The subject tempts one to long argument. We must content ourselves with another reply to which our text can point. Otherworldliness, the fear of judgment to come, the hope of heaven—these are deeply anchored in the N.T. gospel, and nowhere more than in the writings of Paul. But it is simply *not* true that the here and now is neglected, and that "pie in the sky by-and-by" is the gospel's bribe to blind and lazy endurance of earthly injustice. Hope for eternity looks like a belittling of hopes for this world. The result, however, is the opposite of this. Eternity can give a meaning to time which even the noblest secular philosophy cannot give. The paradox meets us on almost every page of the Bible. The Bible—O.T. and N.T.—does not begin with the problem of utopia. It begins with the problem of God. And that is a problem of the here and now, desperately contemporary, one which will involve social and every other kind of justice.

The Christian, as our epistle pictures him, is one who, by "the forgiveness of our trespasses, according to the riches of his grace" (1:7), has made things right with God. He has become a member of Christ, and has been "sealed with the promised Holy Spirit" (1:13). As later chapters of the epistle will show, this life in Christ brings with it ethical demands, personal and social. It is precisely this life, here and now, which our text calls **the guarantee of our inheritance until we acquire possession.** It is not "pie in the sky by-and-by" which motivates Christian morality. The problem of reconciliation with God comes first. Solve this, and then there may be, indeed, hope of heaven. It is the joy and peace of life in Christ which constitutes a foretaste or a pledge of there ever being a heaven worthy of man's hope at all.

15 Wherefore I also, after I heard of your faith in the Lord Jesus, and love unto all the saints,

15 For this reason, because I have heard of your faith in the Lord Jesus and your

C. Prayer for the Enlightenment of the Readers (1:15–2:10)

The second main division of the epistle introduces the thought of the church as the body of Christ, in which the ultimate purpose of universal unity in him is already being fulfilled. It begins with a prayer that the readers may be given a deeper comprehension of the redeeming will and power of God. With vs. 20, however, the form of prayer is practically abandoned for a straightforward exposition of how God's power, overwhelmingly manifested in the resurrection and exaltation of Christ, continues to be exhibited in the raising to new life of Christian believers. These, whether Jews or Gentiles, were once sunk in spiritual death through sins, but are now by divine grace lifted to the heavenly plane to share in the exalted life of Christ, and are thus prepared to fulfill the functions allotted to them in the providence of God.

15. The words **your love** are not supported by any good Greek MS authority and should unquestionably be omitted. The true text is certainly τὴν εἰς πάντας τοὺς ἁγίους. This is the reading of the Beatty papyrus (p46), and of the primary uncials ℵ B and A; it is supported by 33, the "queen of the cursives," and by the secondary (ninth-century) uncial P; by the Bohairic version, and by a certain amount of patristic evidence (Origen, Cyril, Jerome, Augustine). All the evidence for the addition τὴν ἀγάπην is secondary. The whole phrase is most unusual. Literally it runs: "The faith which prevails among you [καθ' ὑμᾶς], which rests in the Lord Jesus and is shown toward all the saints." It is not easy to see in what sense their **faith** is said to be placed in **all the saints.** Perhaps the expression reflects the writer's strong sense of the solidarity between Christ and Christian

15-16. *Wherefore I . . . Cease Not to Give Thanks for You.*—It is a great thing to be a Christian—something to call forth nothing so much as thanksgiving. At any rate, that is the first note struck over and over again in the Pauline epistles (cf. Rom. 1:8, 9; Phil. 1:3, 4; Col. 1:3, 4; I Thess. 1:2, 3; Philem. 4). Is it the first thought that comes to *our* minds when we think of our Christian heritage? May it be that the wonder and glory of the gospel have grown stale for many of us? Have we become blasé Christians? Did we require the shock of seeing a civilization turned against Christianity, like the Hitler tyranny of godlessness, to arouse us out of our thankless lethargy? Or is even that monstrous episode in modern history in danger of being forgotten? Or, to think of another possibility, have we grown weary of our blessings in the Father's household? Are we like the elder brother in the great parable, at bottom envious of the younger who has dared to waste "his substance with riotous living"? We hear the Father's voice, "Son, thou art ever with me, and all that I have is thine," but the thrill of home seems to have vanished.

The causes of our lethargy may be many. One of the more obvious is quite possibly that God's love has become cheap for us. And not only God's love, but the love of neighbor for neighbor, which derives from this primary gift of divine grace. We have enjoyed the benefits of Christianity in all its gracious forms for many generations. But we may be wasting our capital reserves. A **love toward all the saints** is still being exhibited in our half-Christian homes, in the remnant courtesies of the highway and the market place, and in the church fellowships to which we may still belong. But we are tempted to take all these blessings for granted. To cite a fanciful illustration: Ask a fish to define water. The fish might not know what you were talking about. Water? What is water to a fish? A fish knows nothing else. We thankless Christians may resemble fish for whom water is so commonplace that gratitude for it is unknown.

Is the cure a plunge into godlessness, a taste of the far country from which we can then return in grateful mood? Surely that would be ingratitude heightened to blasphemy. "Shall we continue in sin, that grace may abound?" asks Paul. "God forbid," he replies (Rom. 6:1, 2). As a matter of fact, we may in very truth resemble the elder brother. We are lost sons also, as was the elder brother, only he did not know it. If we misuse or presume upon the grace of God, sooner or later we shall taste his wrath. History will assuredly discipline us. Our era of a "taken-for-granted" Christianity may soon be over. Thousands of once nominal Chris-

16 Cease not to give thanks for you, making mention of you in my prayers;
17 That the God of our Lord Jesus
Christ, the Father of glory, may give unto

love[c] toward all the saints, **16** I do not cease
to give thanks for you, remembering you in
my prayers, **17** that the God of our Lord

[c] Other ancient authorities omit *and your love.*

---

believers, so that the faith which rests in him overflows, as it were, in faith in all his followers. A somewhat similar phrase is found in Philem. 5, which says, lit., "The love and the faith which you have toward [πρός] the Lord Jesus and toward [εἰς] all the saints"; but there the zeugma with "love" removes or at least lessens the difficulty which is felt here in Ephesians. In both passages there is a change of preposition to indicate that the attitude of faith in respect of Jesus is not altogether parallel to that which extends toward all the saints.

I have heard . . . : The words belong to the literary fiction by which the epistle is represented as a message from Paul. Nothing is said of the bearer of the report, and its substance could hardly be less specific—Paul has heard that "the saints who are also faithful" (vs. 1) have faith! The phrasing is obviously borrowed from Col. 1:9, where Paul is referring to the report brought by Epaphras concerning the situation at Colossae. There was genuine substance in such a report to call forth a letter; here the words lack pertinence.

16. Remembering is better rendered "asking." The phrase μνείαν ποιεῖσθαι (lit., "to make remembrance") seems to have been extended in usage to include the thought of intercession. Such a sense is required by the following clause **that . . . God . . . may give . . .**—which is certainly the object of a request, not the matter of a recollection.

17. The God of our Lord Jesus Christ, the Father of glory is an expansion of the title of God as given in vs. 3. He is now invoked in prayer as the God whom our Lord

---

tians, living under the heel of reigns of power, are nominal no longer. They are either singing hymns of grateful penitence or are apostate.

Remembering you in my prayers. Intercessory prayers present a problem to the rationalizing inquirer. How can it help my fellow Christians, or non-Christians, to ask favors for them of God, or to thank him in their behalf when they may be ungrateful? Is not God omniscient and all-wise, knowing what we have need of before we ask? And may not our asking be unwise and ignorant? "We know not what we should pray for as we ought" (Rom. 8:26). "Ye ask, and receive not, because ye ask amiss" (Jas. 4:3). Had not prayer therefore best be limited to praise and penitence, which are certain to be acceptable to God? Might we not leave the governance of others to him?

Prayer can indeed be ambiguous and even dangerous. Prayer can be quite unchristian. We sometimes forget that prayer was not invented by Christianity. Pagans prayed. Heathen savages pray. Prayers have been directed to monstrous deities and have asked for utterly unholy things. Christian prayer is prayer directed to God "through Jesus Christ our Lord," and that implies a sifting of petitions and a subjecting of prayer to the judgment of Christ himself.

Prayer can be merely the voicing of the selfish desires of the human heart. Prayer is often called "the soul's sincere desire." It all depends upon what the heart desires. Yet the greatest corrective for egotistic prayer is intercessory prayer. We are not likely to desire good for our fellow men, at least when we are addressing God, which enhances merely our own isolated happiness. Above all is this true of thankful remembrance, such as our text describes. The N.T. pictures the church as a united society of prayer, all for each and each for all. What must it have meant to many a humble convert to enter into a fellowship in which he was daily remembered by a great body of fellow believers, by the great Paul, who had founded his congregation, by Christians in distant Rome or Antioch! A corporate strength, which is incomparable, derives from the mutual intercessory prayers of Christians. We all hunger for remembrance, for escape from the loneliness of our human lot. Men build majestic tombs and gigantic pyramids in order to be remembered even after death. The Christian church is a fellowship of mutual remembrance in which remembering is part of the church's very life. Here it costs nothing. Remembrance is freely bestowed upon the humblest as upon the greatest. Being remembered is one of a Christian's rewards.

17. ***A Spirit of Wisdom and of Revelation in the Knowledge of Him.***—The phrase (see

you the spirit of wisdom and revelation in the knowledge of him:

Jesus Christ, the Father of glory, may give you a spirit of wisdom and of revelation

worships, calling him "my God" (John 20:17), and addressing to him his own prayers (Luke 10:21=Matt. 11:25; John 17; etc.); and as the God whom our Lord reveals as the Father in heaven who will not fail to "give good things to those who ask him" (Matt. 7:11; the parallel in Luke 11:13 promises specifically that he will give the Holy Spirit). **Glory** conveys the thought of God's essential nature as manifested in majesty and splendor. The name **Father of glory** invites us at once to approach him with the simple confidence and affection of a child, and to adore him as the sum and source of all perfections—"The blessed and only Sovereign, . . . who alone has immortality and dwells in unapproachable light" (I Tim. 6:15).

A spirit of wisdom and of revelation, i.e., a receptive spirit, an inward disposition of eagerness to enter into the truth which God has to reveal. It is also possible to interpret the words as referring again to the gift of the Holy Spirit in a particular application; the prayer would then be that the Holy Spirit which we received in our baptism, with which we "were sealed" (vs. 13), may be in us as a *teaching* Spirit, imparting wisdom and revealing divine truth. This ambiguity is often found in N.T. references to the Spirit; it points in its own way to the correlation between the Spirit of God, which reveals, and the spirit of man, which reaches out after and apprehends the revelation. The operations of the Spirit are not conducted within us as some force foreign to us, as in a spiritually inert or passive medium, but as in deep and vital integration with that which is most fundamental in our own personality, by the quickening of our own spirits in fellowship with and understanding of the divine.

In the knowledge of him, i.e., of God; this is the substance of the **wisdom and revelation.** Aspects and corollaries of this knowledge are mentioned in concrete detail in the following verses; but the sum of knowledge for the Christian believer is the knowledge

---

Exeg.) is slightly puzzling. Yet, as the succeeding verses prove, the author has something very definite in mind. He wishes for his readers the rich heritage of insight of the Christian gospel. Many Christians of N.T. times had been only recently introduced to the Christian faith. They were still "babes in Christ" (I Cor. 3:1). The author wishes for them something more than milk for babes. He is about to give them a strong dose of theology. **Knowledge of him** means knowledge of God. Knowledge of God is theology.

The very word theology, however, arouses suspicions, particularly among modern lay folk. It has come to connote something technical and scholastic, a branch of study belonging to a university with its professorial specialists, not to the simple meetinghouse or Sunday school. Christianity, so many a layman argues, must be something simpler than "theology," or else only graduates in divinity could be Christians. Unfortunately there is some truth in the popular impression that theology is a scholastic by-product of Christian faith and not the real thing. There were those in Paul's day who wanted to turn knowledge of divine things into esoteric learning, in which only the advanced student could rise to full Christian rank, Christianity to consist of a graded series of philosophical disciplines similar to mathematics or astronomy. Paul wrote much of his Epistle to the Colossians to smash such a notion. It needs smashing today. Its victory would have destroyed the power of the Christian gospel as a gospel for all men.

It would require a book to confute the wrong interpretation of theology as an intellectual monopoly. There exists, of course, a theology of the schools, with its encyclopedias and technical volumes on divinity. But this is by-product only. There is another theology which is the birthright of every Christian, lettered or unlettered. This is the knowledge of God as a person, not as a textbook subject—a knowledge and wisdom which come from life in Christ, a knowledge in which the simplest peasant can be superior to the professor of divinity.

Yet this personal knowledge of God is founded upon a revelation. And this revelation needs to be known. A Christian does need to know something. Theology is an essential to a full Christian life. We do not possess knowledge of a person until we see him in action. We shall not have a faith in God until we trust him and obey him. And such trust is based upon knowledge of how he has acted in the past. A little

18 The eyes of your understanding being enlightened; that ye may know what is

in the knowledge of him, 18 having the
eyes of your hearts enlightened, that you

of God, which always means the knowledge of him *as* God, living and true, and the source of all life and truth—a personal knowledge which involves communion, adoration, and obedience in love.

18. Having the eyes of your heart enlightened: The grammar is obscure and the connection uncertain. The participle πεφωτισμένους **(enlightened)** would most naturally be taken as modifying the prepositional indirect object ὑμῖν **(you)** above; we should then have a somewhat difficult anacoluthon in the change from the dative to the accusative, occasioned perhaps by the intervening accusative πνεῦμα **(spirit).** Ὀφθαλμούς **(eyes)** would then be an accusative of respect—"enlightened with respect to the eyes." If, however, the participle is taken in agreement with ὀφθαλμούς, either the whole phrase must be treated as an accusative absolute (seldom if ever found except with impersonals), or it may be taken in apposition with the πνεῦμα-phrase, as another way of describing the gift of the **spirit of wisdom and revelation.** The gift of such a spirit means inward enlightenment.

The figure of inward **eyes** as the instrument of insight into ultimate truth, the organ of spiritual vision, is used by classical as well as by biblical writers. Both Plato and Aristotle speak of "the eye of the soul," and similar phrases recur in most of the Hellenistic writers. The Greek men of letters, however, generally speak of the mind (νοῦς) or the soul (ψυχή) as the part of man's nature by which he apprehends the truth which lies behind appearances; the reference to the heart (καρδία) in this sense is Hebraic. In the O.T. the heart of man is not the seat of the emotions but of the will, the moral understanding, the essential inward being; it is the sphere of good and evil, of sinful resolve and of repentance, of communion with God and of rejection of God. Occasionally "the heart" and "the spirit" are coupled in poetic parallelism (Ps. 51:10, 17). This usage passes over into the N.T. It is "the pure in heart" that "shall see God" (Matt. 5:8); "with the heart man believeth unto righteousness" (Rom. 10:10). Conversely, Simon, the magician of Samaria, is told that his "heart is not right before God" (Acts 8:21); and of the Gentiles who failed to glorify God, it is said that "their foolish heart was darkened"

child trusts a mother because the child "knows" mother—knows her from her actions, her nursing when ill, her care, and her discipline.

So with the Christian's knowledge of God. This too is based upon seeing God's actions in history. Knowledge of God for the Christian rests upon the Bible. The Bible is not a textbook in the ordinary sense. It is a storybook. It portrays a majestic drama. The climax of the drama is the story of God coming down from heaven, dying for love of men, rising again from a grave, returning to the heavenlies, and leaving behind him a people of God now endowed with **knowledge of him.**

This knowledge, possible for the simplest Christian, *is* theology. All technical, so-called theology is quite, quite secondary. Whenever the Christian gospel is interpreted as something essentially other than the drama of the Bible, it is no longer theology as the N.T. conceives this. But there should be no mistake here. This theology, the knowledge of God through the story of salvation of the Bible, is an essential for the Christian life. This must be known. This must be taught. Without this there can be no true faith in God. For faith means trust in obedience. Trust is based upon knowledge of the person trusted.

18. *Having the Eyes of Your Hearts Enlightened.*—Comment on this verse could well tie in with what has been said about the knowledge of God. "The heart has its reasons, which reason knows not." This famous saying of Pascal throws light on much in the Bible. An enlightened intellect is a precious thing. Nor does the Bible belittle intellectual gifts. But mental endowments are not equally distributed among men. If our salvation depended upon educational acquirements, the majority of mankind would run the danger of being lost. But the intellect is not the center of our real selves. For that citadel of the soul which stands guard over love and hate, loyalty and treachery, trust and mistrust, we still have no better word than heart. And in matters which pertain to this essential endowment of our being, true democracy reigns. The most unlettered can outrank the most learned in love and faith and in the understand-the hope of his calling, and what the riches of the glory of his inheritance in the saints,

may know what is the hope to which he has called you, what are the riches of his glo-

(Rom. 1:21). So here the enlightenment of the heart is not a mere intellectual acuteness, but a flooding of the whole inward being with the light of divine truth; it is the gift of sight to the spiritually blind; and it issues in the apprehension of the realities of divine grace in application to ourselves.

It must also be observed that the idea of a *progressive* enlightenment, however true in itself, is not to be found in this passage. The participle is a perfect, conveying the thought of a *state* of enlightenment.

18-19. His calling, . . . his inheritance, . . . his power: Three aspects of the knowledge of God are now brought forward in crescendo; the whole prayer moves toward the exposition of the third of these aspects—**the immeasurable greatness of his power in us who believe.**

What is the hope of his calling: The content of this **hope** is not expounded, nor is it clear from the context in what sense the writer would conceive the Christian hope. The general tenor of his thought would lead us to attribute to these words some such meaning as "the infinite possibilities of spiritual attainment which God holds before you in calling you to himself." He is not actively concerned with eschatology in this epistle, except in a *cosmic* context—in relation to the consummation of the divine purpose to "gather together in one all things in Christ" (vs. 10). He makes no reference to the Second Coming, or to an ending of the present age in apocalyptic catastrophe; such a way of thinking is indeed hardly compatible with his doctrine of the gathering up of all things in Christ, which really involves an affirmation of the *positive* significance of the historical process. The hope to which God calls us must therefore be interpreted, consistently with his dominant conceptions, in terms of the fulfillment of the good work already begun in us—the attainment of full spiritual development; cf. 3:19, the climax of his prayer in the words "that ye might be filled with all the fulness of God."

It is perhaps better, however, to take the words **his calling** in a wider sense, not limited to Christian believers but extending to the whole creation. The **calling,** i.e., would

ing of the mysteries of life and of God. Here the first can be last and the last first. God deals with the heart of man. It is his heart which man must yield to God in order that man may be in covenant relationship with God. Few words in the Bible unlock more of its meaning than the word heart. A glance into a concordance can yield a rich harvest—"Blessed are the pure in heart" (Matt. 5:8); "Out of the heart of men proceed evil thoughts" (Mark 7:21); "The LORD looketh on the heart" (I Sam. 16:7); "The hidden man of the heart" (I Pet. 3:4); and scores more.

Do these eyes of the heart need to be **enlightened?** Surely nothing needs light more. Scientific pedagogy can be utterly baffled by the task. Children can be taught almost anything, if time and patience prevail. But to enlighten a soul darkened by hate or blinded by unlawful desires—this requires a divine pedagogy. Only God can give to man a new heart. Hence the Bible is full of words like rebirth, repentance, salvation, grace. Homer speaks of wrath as "smoky wrath." The epithet describes a state of the soul when light is shut out. A man giving way to wrath simply does not see things aright. He must be cured of his anger before full sight is returned to him.

When the heart has been touched by God's judgment and grace, enlightenment results. Christian faith has been said to be a substitute for formal education and even for genius. It gives insight. A simple Christian can frequently see issues in the economic and political life of men which the technical expert has missed. A simple Christian can still exercise the gift which the N.T. fellowships possessed—that of prophecy. An enlightened heart is worth more than mere intellectual brilliance. There are rewards which accrue to being a Christian believer. These rewards should not be minimized. In the world of education, as in that of the market place, it is still true: "Seek ye first the kingdom of God, and his righteousness; and all these things shall be added unto you" (Matt. 6:33).

18-19. ***Witnessing to the Christian Faith.***—The author here enumerates some of the promised insights which knowledge of God (vs. 17) bestows upon the Christian—**the hope to which he has called you, . . . his glorious in-**

19 And what *is* the exceeding greatness of his power to us-ward who believe, according to the working of his mighty power,

rious inheritance in the saints, 19 and what is the immeasurable greatness of his power in us who believe, according to the work-

mean here the implementing of God's universal purpose in Christ, as the calling of every Christian is the implementing of God's eternal purpose of grace toward him; cf. Rom. 8:30, "Those whom he predestined he also called." The import of the prayer would then be that the readers may be enabled to share, by their own spiritual enlightenment, in the writer's splendid vision of the movement of all created things toward the ultimate goal of universal harmony in Christ (cf. Rom. 8:19-25).

The riches of the glory of his inheritance in the saints: Here we have a striking instance of the extreme fondness shown by this writer for a redundant fullness of expression which does not make for clarity. It is difficult (and perhaps oversubtle) to discern the precise force of every element in the combination. The center of the expression is certainly the phrase **his inheritance in the saints.** This probably means "the inheritance to which he admits us, among the hosts of holy beings who surround his throne"; the resemblance to the phrasing of Col. 1:12, which is certainly in the writer's mind, makes it almost certain that this is the true interpretation. In itself the phrase could also mean "the heritage which God is claiming for himself among his sanctified people" (cf. on vs. 11). The whole expression could then be paraphrased: "How abundantly the glory of God is manifested in the church, his heritage." **Glory** is in any case to be taken with **riches,** not with **inheritance**—"the glorious riches" or "the abounding glory."

Theodore of Mopsuestia (*On the Minor Epistles of St. Paul,* ed. H. B. Swete [Cambridge: University Press, 1880], I, 137) interprets: "How great will be the fruition of good things for the saints of God in the age to come. Well does he speak of 'the glory of his inheritance,' seeing that we shall then be clothed with glory; and he says 'the riches of the glory,' that he may mention the overwhelming abundance of God's gifts."

19. The interpretation of this verse depends on the precise relationship of the κατά-clause (**according to the working . . .**), which has been much debated. Some com-

heritance in the saints, . . . the immeasurable greatness of his power in us who believe. Like a symphony working up to a great crescendo, these phrases point ahead to the climactic theme of the epistle, the exalted Christ as head of his church (vss. 20-23). The author begins, however, with what lies within the experience of the Christians themselves whom he is tutoring in the wonders of the gospel.

To a modern Christian the epistles of the N.T. can present surprises. Judging by our contemporary methods of instruction in the Christian faith, one would expect a N.T. writer to dwell, as we are wont to do, upon the story of the earthly Jesus. Surely this is where we should begin in describing the wonder of the gospel. It comes as a shock to find that Paul and other N.T. writers pay so little attention to the Sermon on the Mount, or the parables, or the miracle stories, or the other moving scenes pictured by the evangelists. When they want to point to the most impressive fact which Christianity connoted to that first Christian age, they point to themselves. They do not start with past history. They start with the picture of present power. When they appeal for conversion to the new faith, they witness first of all to what Christ has done for them in their own lives. The key word in this whole passage (see Exeg. on vs. 19) is the word "power." Christ as present power, rather than Christ as an admired person in history, was for the early Christians the paramount miracle. Not that the "historical Jesus" was forgotten. The stories of him told in our gospels were treasured and became oral tradition. The present power of Christ could find no explanation except by way of the great drama of the Incarnation. Yet it was his living power and presence, not his memory, which amazed the early converts most—**the immeasurable greatness of his power in us who believe.** The later chapters of the epistle will enter upon concrete descriptions of what Christ had done for those converted. Here the author only alludes to the miraculous fact.

Has the N.T. method of witnessing to the Christian faith something to teach us in our age when it is once more an alien in surroundings that grow increasingly pagan? Should we too witness to the power of Christ first, and then tell his story? Is the call to the church today to become a dynamic church before it will have

mentators have taken it closely with the infinitive εἰδέναι ("know"—vs. 18); many have attached it to the participle πιστεύοντας ("believe"); and some have held that it is associated with all three of the τίς-clauses—the hope, the inheritance, and the power are all communicated to us **according to the working of** [God's] **mighty power, which he wrought in Christ.** The last is by far the best of these views; but it seems more natural to connect the phrase primarily with the thought of **his power in us who believe,** i.e., with the conception neither of **his power** alone, nor of our believing, but with the whole idea of the divine power as put forth in the life of believers.

The immeasurable greatness of his power in us who believe is the foundation of the glorious work of grace which God is accomplishing in the created universe. The mention of "the hope of his calling" and of "the glory of his inheritance" leads on to adoring contemplation of the infinite **power** which alone could accomplish so great a design. The crown of the knowledge which is given to the enlightened heart is the realization of the nature and the full scope of the power which believers have experienced in the relatively tiny field of their own lives. This power cannot be fully measured by its manifestation in ourselves. The tide will lift a rowboat, but the lifting of the rowboat is no true indication of the tide's power; and the man who sees no farther than the edge of his own dock will hardly be aware of the full power of the tide, which lifts with equal ease the navies of the world and whatsoever else floats upon the oceans. Likewise the Christian believer, whose life has been lifted into the heavenly places in Christ, will not know **the immeasurable greatness** of the divine power which has lifted him until he sees it as an instance of **the working of** [God's] **great might which he accomplished in Christ.**

In this verse the writer uses four different words to express his thought of God's power. In **his power in us who believe** the word is *dynamis;* then we have the threefold phrase, literally translated, "according to the working [*energeia*] of the power [*kratos*] of his might [*ischys*]"—another instance of the heaping together of words similar in significance, if not altogether synonymous, which we have noticed to be a feature of the style of this epistle. *Dynamis* is the more general word, embracing the content of the other three; in itself it suggests *ability* to accomplish what one has taken in hand (the cognate verb is *dynamai*—"I am able"); in *energeia* the thought of *activity* is primary, of power at work (cf. Col. 1:29, "According to his working, which worketh in me mightily"). In *kratos* the thought is of power that subdues or rules, of victory or of dominion, of *power over others;* while *ischys* means inherent *strength* or *might,* which is always the property of the possessor whether he puts it forth or not.

---

influence again as a teaching and preaching church? "Dynamic" means "power-endowed." The Greek word for power in our very verse is *dynamis.* It is very much easier to preach the gospel than to exhibit its power in life and work. Yet the early apologists for Christianity made much of its "mighty works." They proclaimed its power to heal the sick and drive out demons. They pointed to Christ alive in his church.

A wise observer of twentieth-century Christianity voices a plea for precisely such a return to the gospel as power if Christianity is again to move an indifferent society. Rival gospels in the twentieth century are dynamic gospels—communism, for example. They are church-gospels, community-faiths. Christianity will not stand up under competition unless it too appears again as a community of power, as a church, as the fellowship of the Holy Spirit.

"If the Christian message," so this observer contends,

> is to have any meaning in the conditions of today, it is necessary to offer men a more recognizable total community life. . . . Something new must enter into their experience before they can understand the Christian message. They must find in our churches in their hedge-hog positions a more recognizable total witness. But not only in our churches. Christians must play their part in helping men to experience fellowship in the communities where they already are. When they have learned something of community life, and discover how easily and quickly natural community breaks down and suffers defeat, the door is open to reveal Christ as the way of reconciliation and the revealer of God the Creator and of His purpose.[2]

[2] George McLeod, *The Christian News Letter,* March 6, 1946, pp. 2-3.

20 Which he wrought in Christ, when he raised him from the dead, and set *him* at his own right hand in the heavenly *places*,

ing of his great might 20 which he accomplished in Christ when he raised him from the dead and made him sit at his right hand

20. The supreme manifestation of this divine power is seen in what God has **accomplished in Christ.** This is now set forth in three phases—resurrection, exaltation, and the gift of universal dominion. God **raised him from the dead and made him sit at his right hand . . . ; and he has put all things under his feet** (vs. 22). His relation to the church is then viewed in the light of this universal dominion, which also imparts to the church its cosmic significance.

The verb ἐνήργηκεν (**wrought**) is the cognate of the noun ἐνέργεια (**working**) above. The true reading gives it in the perfect; in most of the witnesses this has been altered to the aorist through the influence of the following aorist participle (ἐγείρας). The perfect lays the emphasis not upon the act of God in itself, but upon its completion; it points to the raising of Christ from the dead not as an isolated event of past history, but as a divine accomplishment which is a present guarantee of God's life-giving power.

In Christ: Again (as in vss. 10 and 12) the article is used—"in the Christ"—marking this as a reference to the messianic office of our Lord, his function in relation to his

20-22. *The Ascension and Exaltation of Christ.*—Nowhere else in the N.T. is the exalted Christ, **head over all things for the church,** so gloriously portrayed. The passage may deserve extended treatment.

What does the modern church make of the ascension of Christ? Very little, one might well confess. Published sermons on the Ascension are hard to find. Yet in the thought of the early church the Ascension occupied a position of crucial importance.

A concrete visualization of the Ascension (Mark 16:19; Acts 1:11) is admittedly difficult. But the record is clear on one issue. A time arrived when the resurrection appearances, incomparably precious as they must have been, were definitely over. Jesus departed to "the heavenlies." The early Christians indulged in no spiritualistic seances to bring him back to the earthly scene. No repetitions of resurrection visions were expected. Jesus from henceforth was the exalted Christ, who, in the words of the Apostles' Creed, "Sitteth on the right hand of God the Father Almighty; From thence he shall come to judge the quick and the dead."

Modern Christianity does not find it easy to see the event of the Ascension in the perspective of the N.T. We are inclined to concentrate our attention upon the preresurrected, the preascended Christ. Much of our contemporary Christianity could be called preascension Christianity. It may need correction.

Look at the N.T. as a whole, and it does seem to divide itself into two quite distinct parts. On the one side we have the gospel story. On the other we have the epistles with their "theology," the Acts of the Apostles constituting a strange link between the two sections. How simple, comparatively speaking, is the gospel story. How difficult the epistle-commentary. Since the latter looks like mere commentary, must it not be of secondary importance? Can the heart of the Christian faith be anything except the "Gospels"? Is not this the story upon which Christianity has been built?

The Christians in the humble little churches of apostolic days were not ignorant of the stories about Jesus recorded by our evangelists. They treasured them with amazing scrupulosity. They wrote them down. But when they expressed their communal faith, as we find this in the almost casual letters which they exchanged with each other, how little of the story as told by the evangelists figures in their speech. When later the faith of the early church crystallized itself in the creeds, the life of Jesus between birth and crucifixion is condensed into a comma or a colon. The Apostles' Creed takes a leap from "Born of the Virgin Mary" to "Suffered under Pontius Pilate." What is the meaning of this apparent blank?

The simplest answer is that the Christians whom we meet in the N.T. were postascension Christians. They had a keen sense of the time sequence in the great drama of salvation of which the gospel story was the partial record. It was a drama in several acts. In the earlier acts of the drama Jesus appeared simply as the human Jesus, a rabbi, a master, a friend, a teacher. Only a later act of the drama revealed who he really was, Son of the living God. The Resurrection and the Ascension marked the great unveiling of the divine incognito.

The early Christians were postresurrection and postascension Christians. Ignorance of an incognito was over. "Therefore let all the house

21 Far above all principality, and power, and might, and dominion, and every name that is named, not only in this world, but also in that which is to come:

in the heavenly places, 21 far above all rule and authority and power and dominion, and above every name that is named, not only in this age but also in that which is

people. It is because he is the Messiah that his resurrection and exaltation are significant not only for himself, but for all mankind.

Made him sit at his right hand: The words go back to Ps. 110:1, "Sit thou at my right hand, until I make thine enemies thy footstool." This passage appears to have shaped Christian thinking about Christ almost from the beginning; it provided the language in which his exaltation to heavenly glory was proclaimed, and carried the promise of his ultimate triumph. The imagery was originally drawn from statuary which represented the king as enthroned on the right of his tutelary deity, symbolizing not only honor and dignity, but delegated power. It is a figurative way of expressing the same thought as "All power is given unto me in heaven and in earth" (Matt. 28:18).

In the heavenly places, i.e., in the invisible world, in the sphere of the eternal. It is local only in the sense that God's "right hand" is local. Limited as we are, not only by language but by the necessary forms in which our imagination moves, we use such words as "upward" and "in heaven" when we speak of the presence of God, although we believe that he is everywhere. "We look upward in order to look away from visible things" (Abbott, *Ephesians, ad loc.*).

21. Far above all rule and authority and power and dominion . . . : It would be better to replace **all** by "every." There is no thought here of earthly rulers. These are the designations of various classes of angelic beings—exalted spirits, sometimes regarded as beneficent, sometimes as tyrannous—who were believed to hold sway over different departments of the universe. In Col. 1:16 they are classified as "thrones, dominions, principalities, authorities." In some of the religious systems of the time great importance was attributed to these beings in the shaping of human destiny; the teaching which Paul combats in his letter to the Colossians centered about a cult devoted to such beings (see Intro. to Colossians

of Israel know assuredly, that God hath made that same Jesus, whom ye have crucified, both Lord and Christ" (Acts 2:36). So Peter tells the amazing news in the first recorded Christian sermon. The curtain had gone up on a new act of the drama, the story of Pentecost and of the Christian church. The Jesus of the gospel story had returned to the Father. As Second Person of the Trinity (to use later explanatory language) Jesus had departed from the human scene. God was now present as Third Person, as Comforter, as Holy Spirit. He would come again, but not as the carpenter and rabbi of Nazareth. He would come to judge the quick and the dead.

And, as in a drama, there was no going back. Nostalgic memory? There is scarcely a touch of this in the N.T. Did any of the N.T. writers try to usher the early Christians into a relationship with the preresurrected Jesus such as the disciples had once enjoyed? Was the record of the disciples in the master-disciple relationship a wholly enviable one? They had, almost to a man, turned traitors. They would have been the last to attempt a turning back of the clock. Before the Ascension and Pentecost they had been Jews. Now they were Christians. They had been transformed from timid disciples into apostles and martyrs. "Though we have known Christ after the flesh, yet now henceforth know we him no more" (II Cor. 5:16). Paul, one might suppose, is prepared to mourn the inexorable fact. But not at all. His next verse is one of rejoicing, "Therefore if any man be in Christ, he is a new creature: old things are passed away; behold, all things are become new" (II Cor. 5:17).

The early Christians knew themselves to be actors in the great cosmic drama. As actors they had a vivid sense of a *now*. The remembered Jesus of the gospel story had once been a baby in a mother's arms, but he was not that *now*. He had once been master, rabbi, companion, teacher, but he was not that *now*. He had once hung upon a cross, but he was not suffering there *now*. He was now ascended Lord. He had even received a new name, and was addressed in a new manner. God had **raised him from the dead, and set him at his own right hand in the heavenly places, far above all principality, and power, and might, and dominion, and every name that is named, not only in this world, but**

22 And hath put all *things* under his feet, and gave him *to be* the head over all *things* to the church,

to come; 22 and he has put all things under his feet and has made him the head over

in Vol. XI of this Commentary). Like Paul, this writer is not seriously interested in them; a certain mockery of the whole elaborate classification is apparent in the words, **every name that is named,** as if he were to say, "Whatever else anyone likes to call them." He is only concerned to affirm that there is no spiritual power in the universe remotely comparable in honor and dignity to the risen and exalted Christ, nor will there be in any future age.

This age . . . that which is to come: Simply "the present . . . the future"; the phrasing formally reflects the Jewish apocalyptic contrast of the two ages, but this distinction is not significantly present in the thinking of the writer of Ephesians, as it is in Paul. He speaks with equal readiness of "the ages to come" (2:7), meaning really "through all eternity."

22. Has put all things under his feet: The thought of *conquest* is added to the thought of exaltation. Christ not only holds a higher station before God than all other powers in the universe, but all are made subject to his authority. Here the words are taken from Ps. 8:6, from a paean on the glory of man as the crown of creation. As in Heb. 2:6-9, the words of the psalm are applied to Christ, who as man fulfills the destiny for which man was created.

Has made him the head . . . for the church: The verb is ἔδωκεν—lit., "he gave." Possibly this is used in the sense of the Hebrew נתן ("to give," then [frequently] "to appoint"). It is more likely, however, that the verb has its proper and common Greek sense, and that the thought is that Christ is God's *gift* to the church. For the headship is

also in that which is to come. A preresurrection relationship with him was not now possible. Many of our modern hymns to Jesus would surely have struck the Christians whom we meet in the epistles as sentimental anachronisms, if not close to denials of the ascension faith.

The Epistle to the Ephesians has been called the "Epistle of the Ascension." Here we meet the exalted Christ. But this epistle is also known as the great church epistle. Nowhere in the N.T. is the church presented in such lofty terms. This bringing together of the exaltation of Christ and of the doctrine of the church is no accident. If Christ as Second Person of the Trinity had been taken from the scene, this did not mean his absence. He was present as Third Person, as Holy Spirit. The community was actually his body and he its living head. In modern times of critical historical scholarship we speak commonly of the "historical" Jesus—meaning, of course, the Jesus of the days of Herod and of Pontius Pilate—and we contrast this historical Christ with the Christ of the church's faith. Might not the early Christians have almost reversed this contrast? Would they not have accepted the departure from the historical scene of the Jesus of Galilee, but have witnessed to his re-entrance into history through the coming of the Holy Ghost? The continuing "historical" Christ is the Christ alive in the community. Nor can we, so the N.T. would assert, meet him "historically" today anywhere else.

The Gospels? Yes, they have their place in the record and in the church's faith. But this is, in one sense, secondary. Scott Holland rightly says:

> We are drawn, as all men are, back to the immortal story of Jesus Christ on earth. Back to it we press, that we may get behind all the wranglings and the tangles of theology. Back to it we turn, that we may find in it yet again, in elemental simplicity, that which we so sorely need to sustain and guide our weary spirit. Yes, that is all right! But the difficulty is that in order to win from the Life that which it has to give us, we must carry to it the interpretation of it which gave it of old its quickening force. Those who wrote it and those who read it believed in the living Christ—alive from the dead—before they wrote and before they read. They were living themselves in the experience of His salvation. . . . Only through actual experience of what He has become through death, can the record of what He once was on earth become a revelation of what He is now in heaven. [The Gospels] were written not to create faith, but to feed it.[3]

22-23. *Christ as Head of the Church.*—Few passages in the N.T. can be called more daring than this one. The exaltation of Christ is a

[3] *Facts of the Faith* (London: Longmans, Green & Co., 1919), pp. 292-93. Used by permission.

23 Which is his body, the fulness of him that filleth all in all.

all things for the church, 23 which is his body, the fullness of him who fills all in all.

not here set forth in terms of mere authority, but in terms of vital union. Christ and the church are one; she is the body of which he is the head. He indeed rules her, as he rules all things; but more than that, he imparts to her his fullness, and she is in a sense necessary to his completeness. The thought is not really an extension of the doctrine of Christ's exaltation—that as he is exalted above the angels, so he is exalted to supremacy in the church—but turns rather to the glory conferred upon the church in the gift of such a head, one who is seated at the right hand of God, far above every conceivable form of created existence. The exaltation of the head involves of necessity the exaltation of the body also.

23. Which is his body: The compound relative has its proper qualitative or generic force—not simply "which is," but "which in its nature is," or "in that it is." The function of Christ is not an arbitrary appointment to sovereignty, which might be exercised even over alien existences; it is appropriate and necessary to the nature of the church, which belongs to him and cannot exist or have meaning apart from him.

The fullness of him who fills all in all: In Colossians, Paul had spoken of the "fullness of deity" dwelling in Christ (Col. 2:9; cf. Col. 1:19), in refutation of the heretical doctrine recently introduced, which conceived the powers and attributes of deity to be distributed among a host of cosmic spirits. Here the thought may be that the fullness of Christ, in an analogous sense, dwells in the church; this interpretation, however, falls short of what is said in our text—that the church, his body, *is* his fullness.

Some commentators insist on the passive sense of the word πλήρωμα, and take it to mean "that which is filled by Christ." This is in itself an acceptable idea: that Christ fills the church with himself, as he is filled with God; that Christ is the whole essential content of the church. But such an interpretation is not in keeping with the metaphor. The head cannot be said to "fill" the body; yet the sudden abandonment of the metaphor at this point would be impossibly violent.

breathtaking concept in itself. A human being who was once a carpenter of Nazareth, who once wore a crown of thorns, is now Ruler of the universe, Prince of all the kings of the earth and of such powers as may rule in the sky, and is to be worshiped as God! But that is not all. He has not left our mortal earthly scene in order to escape. He has left a complement of himself on earth, and dwells there too. The church is his **body,** his **fullness.** The Christ whom the Father God set "at his own right hand in the heavenly places" (vs. 20) is at the same time head of the church. In fact the exaltation of Christ had the complementary exaltation of the church for a purpose. The phrase **for the church** is startling. "For the church the world was made," says one of the earliest documents of Christian literature (Herm. Vis. I. 6).

The phrase defining the church as Christ's **body, the fullness of him who fills all in all,** has caused commentators much trouble. Can it really mean what it says? Does Christ stand in need of the church to be Christ in **fullness?** Yet why may we not take the apostolic writer's insight as valid? The creation of man, in the first place, presents something of a similar daring thought. Why, with all his foreknowledge of man's fall, should God have risked the great adventure of creating man in his own image, a being who could, if he would, rebel against him? Creation is a mystery. And the church stands at the other end of God's predestinating will. He had us in mind from the first. Another N.T. writer speaks of the things revealed to the church as "things into which angels long to look" (I Pet. 1:12).

The concept of the church as the body of Christ, complementing or fulfilling Christ himself, is endlessly rich in suggestiveness. Paul develops it more exhaustively in his first letter to the Corinthians (I Cor. 12), as does our author in his later chapters. Here only a few observations need be made.

First, the danger should be avoided of exalting the church, particularly the institutional church, to an equality with Christ. Christ remains **head over all things,** the church included. The phrase "Christ is head of the church" connotes Christ's position as Lord and ruler and judge. The bride-and-bridegroom and husband-and-wife metaphors have similar implications. The church dare not presume. When a ministry

The best sense of the word in this context, therefore, seems to be "complement; that which makes complete." Christ and the church together form an organic unity; the body is the complement of the head. At first sight this thought seems incompatible with the divine nature of Christ; certainly the Son of God is not dependent for his existence and nature upon the church as the church is dependent upon him. But the context has to do with him, not in the absoluteness of his divine nature, but in the contingent manifestation of him in his function as Messiah. The Messiah, regardless of his nature, cannot function as Messiah in the void; he must have as his counterpart the people which he is to deliver and rule. In this contingent sense the church is necessary to his completion, that he may be not merely a potential but an actual Messiah; it is the sphere in which he exercises his messianic functions; it is the organ by which he manifests his presence and his power, and brings to fulfillment the divine purpose "to unite all things in him" (vs. 10).

Christ is now spoken of as **him who fills all in all;** better "who is being wholly filled" or "fulfilled." The Greek commentators (Origen, Theodore of Mopsuestia, Chrysostom) have no doubt that the participle is in the passive voice; they start their interpretation from the observation that it is not said that "he *fills* all things," but that "he is himself being filled." The Latin versions likewise render by the passive (*adimpletur*). It may indeed be said of Christ that he "fills all things," as in 4:10—"He who descended is he who also ascended far above all the heavens, that he might fill all things"; but there the active is used. Here we have the converse thought, that all created things contribute to the fullness of Christ. "He himself finds His fulness in the sum of all that He brings into living union with Himself" (Brooke Foss Westcott, *Saint Paul's Epistle to the Ephesians* [London: Macmillan & Co., 1906], *ad loc.*). The present tense of the participle indicates that this filling or fulfillment of Christ is progressive; it points to the continuous movement of all things to their goal in him. "Wherefore Christ is fulfilled in all that come unto Him, whereas He is still lacking in respect of them before they have come" (Origen, tr. J. A. Robinson, *Ephesians,* p. 45).

Clearly the thought of the church as Christ's **fullness** is related to the thought that the whole created universe is tributary to him and will ultimately be gathered to him. In the church the ultimate cosmic unity is realized in nucleus and in anticipation; it is, as it were, "the microcosm of what all existence will finally be" (Scott, *Epistles of Paul to Colossians, Philemon, Ephesians,* p. 160).

---

within the church presumes to call one of its members the Vicar of Christ on earth, it is, to say the least, unscriptural. The church in Roman Catholic theology is frequently defined as "the extension of the Incarnation." It is an appealing doctrine, but great care needs to be exercised in its use. The Incarnation was sinless. The church is not sinless.

Second, the church, when defined as the body of Christ, must remember that it is body and not itself pure spirit. We have Paul's own account in Rom. 7 of how body and spirit can war against each other. The church is endowed with the Holy Spirit. Christ does make his home in her midst, sinful though she may be. This is great glory and joyous comfort. But the church as body can stand under severe judgment. The book of Revelation pictures a church to which God has to say, "I will spew thee out of my mouth" (Rev. 3:16). It has always been tempting to hide behind church membership as an insurance against judgment, and to substitute loyalty to institutional legalism for personal relationship with God. This is admittedly a danger within Roman Catholicism, though there are plenty of small "catholicisms" in the Protestant world also. John said to the Jews of his day, "Bring forth therefore fruits worthy of repentance, and begin not to say within yourselves, We have Abraham to our father" (Luke 3:8). The same could be said to members of Christian churches.

Third, however, the majestic glory of the church as Christ's body, while it must be guarded against presumption, is real. Sinful church that she is, the body of Christ furnishes bodily hands and feet for her exalted Lord. Spirit without body was inconceivable to the Hebraic mind. Christ as Comforter constitutes the Spirit of the body of Christ. But if he wishes to act incarnationally in history, he must act through the church. In her "the kingdom of God is at hand" (Mark 1:15). The church is the "colony of heaven" (Phil. 3:20 Moffatt), the

2 And you *hath he quickened,* who were dead in trespasses and sins;

2 And you he made alive, when you were dead through the trespasses and sins

2:1-3. The chapter division is arbitrary; there is no break in the thought at this point. **The working of** [God's] **mighty power** (1:19) is still the theme. As it wrought in Christ the head, raising him from the dead and seating him at God's right hand (1:20), so it works in all the members of the body—raising them from the death of sinful self-indulgence and seating them with Christ in the heavenly places.

The contrast of **you** (vss. 1, 2) with **we all** (vs. 3) again refers to the distinction between Jews and Gentiles, only to nullify it. Both are shown to have been alike guilty and equally in need of God's mercy. Then with vs. 4 they are grouped together (**us . . . we**) as the objects of God's great love and the beneficiaries of his saving grace.

1. You he made alive: In the Greek text this verb is not introduced until vs. 5; in the meantime the accusative (i.e., **you**) is left hanging, while the sinful condition of mankind without Christ is elaborated in a parenthesis; the thought is resumed and completed then, in vss. 5 ff. The whole passage is an expansion of the words of Paul in Col. 2:13, "You, who were dead in trespasses and the uncircumcision of your flesh, God made alive together with him." In the old life they might properly be described as **dead,** because they were cut off from God, the source of all true life, **through** [their] **trespasses**

one concrete, bodily manifestation of the eternal end of all things within time. Whenever the church is tempted to belittle her bodily existence on earth and seeks to escape into purely spiritual pieties or mysticism, she is denying her vocation. She is *body.* She is not expected to be a ghostly phantom of a disembodied heaven. The material is not the spiritual. But the material must precede the spiritual and become vehicle for the spiritual. There must be something bodily, as in the creation story, into which God can breathe his spirit. If Catholicism has been in danger of divinizing the institutional church, Evangelicalism has often erred on the other side in trying to escape the harsh historical realities of institutional church life altogether.

Even as through the body the Saviour used to speak and heal, so aforetime through the prophets and now through the apostles and teachers. For the Church subserves the mighty working of the Lord. Whence both at that time He took upon Him man, that through him He might subserve the Father's will; and at all times in His love to man God clothes Himself with man for the salvation of men, aforetime with the prophets, now with the Church.[4]

2:1. *You . . . , Who Were Dead in Trespasses and Sins.*—We are inclined to pass over such a verse as this lightly. "It applies to ancient heathen, and probably means little more than that they were morally pretty crumby folk and needed Christian ethics. To be 'dead in sins' cannot be intended literally." But a mild interpretation of the text is mistaken. The whole Bible takes the subject of death very seriously, as seriously as it takes sin. Sin and death go together. "The wages of sin is death," says Paul (Rom. 6:23). And death to Paul, as to the O.T. and the Hebraic mind generally, was literally death. Just death! The idea of an immortality of the soul as the natural birthright of every human being is foreign to the Bible. No Jew could think of disembodied life. A ghost world would have been for him no desirable or even possible heaven. The biblical answer to the problem of death is resurrection. And resurrection requires an act of God as climactic as was the creation described in Genesis. Hence, since only God could resurrect, man's fate in any world beyond death depended entirely upon how man stood before God. Sin cuts man off before the holiness of God. Therefore sin means death.

A Platonic doctrine of immortality has for so long captured Christian thought and imagination, replacing that of resurrection, that it is desperately difficult for us to see the realistic biblical view in its stark grandeur, a grandeur both of terror and of joy. But contrast the two for a moment. If I am immortal by reason of my simply being a man, and if immortality connotes blessedness, why do I need to take the problem of sin very seriously? Or, for that matter, the problem of God? There may indeed be levels of life in the immortal state, as there are here. There may be a kind of judgment and growth in the good life. But most of us manage to get by here. Why not there? Begin with stating the problem of life as one of existence and survival and hold to a doctrine of immortality as an answer, and then religion becomes a mat-

[4] Quoted from Clement of Alexandria, in J. Armitage Robinson, *St. Paul's Epistle to the Ephesians* (London: Macmillan & Co., 1903), p. 140.

2 Wherein in time past ye walked according to the course of this world, according to the prince of the power of the air, the spirit that now worketh in the children of disobedience:

2 in which you once walked, following the course of this world, following the prince of the power of the air, the spirit that is now at work in the sons of disobedience.

---

and sins. As Christ was raised from physical death, so they were in a condition of spiritual death, from which they were to be raised by the life-giving power of the "God who raises the dead" (II Cor. 1:9).

2. Walked, i.e., "lived," in respect of moral behavior. **Walked,** like the Greek word which it renders literally, is a Hebraism. In origin it is doubtless associated with the figure of life as a path which we are to tread, but in N.T. usage the metaphorical sense is seldom in evidence. The verb always retains, however, its reference to the moral and spiritual quality of life.

The old way of life, marked by **trespasses and sins,** is now said to have been subject to a demonic power of evil, conceived in terms of a personal spirit who rules over a kingdom of evil in the atmosphere which surrounds us. Originating in Persia, in the dualistic doctrine of the great prophet Zoroaster, the figure of a malevolent rival to the supreme god of light and truth had impressed itself widely upon the religious imagination of the Hellenistic age, not least effectively in the later Judaism. Among the Jews this master spirit of evil had been identified with "the Satan" (lit., "the accuser")—a comparatively inconspicuous figure of the earlier Hebrew mythology; he does not appear at all in the older strata of the O.T. The idea of a personal devil is all but unimaginable to the mind of our own times, and is capable of interpretation only as a personification of the external forces of evil which play upon human life.

---

ter of culture, of ethics, of philosophy, but not an issue of life and death, or of heaven and hell. No ultimate, desperate decisions are involved.

But turn to the Bible. All here is an issue of desperate, ultimate decision. All is a matter of life or death. The central problem is that of settling things between a holy God and sinful men. The O.T. practically never gets beyond this. And in a way why should it have done so? "Whom have I in heaven but thee? and there is none upon earth that I desire besides thee," says the psalmist (Ps. 73:25). Even in the N.T., in which the horizon has become enlarged to include eternity, the "end" to which everything points is not survival, but the judgment. God's judgment—both here and now and ultimately final. Even resurrection, a divine creative act as compared with immortality, is in the N.T. made subsidiary to judgment. All points to the interview between man and God. "Marvel not at this: for the hour is coming, in the which all that are in the graves shall hear his voice, and shall come forth; they that have done good, unto resurrection of life; and they that have done evil, unto the resurrection of damnation" (John 5:28-29). "It is appointed unto men once to die, but after this the judgment" (Heb. 9:27). Passages of similar import could be cited copiously.

Indeed, if the issue of death as judgment is kept steadily in mind, a Christian preacher may find use for the conception of immortality. But it is at best a slippery concept. Kierkegaard once preached a sermon on immortality which can serve as a model:

> We can speak rightly about immortality only when we speak of the Judgement; and naturally when we speak of the Judgement we speak of immortality. . . . Immortality is the Judgement. There is not a word more to be said about immortality. He who says one word more, or a word which has another slant, let him beware of the Judgement.[5]

Kierkegaard's warning could apply to many a sentimental Easter sermon.

The author of Ephesians does not speak in our verse of the eschatological problem of death. This can be another surprise of the realism of the Bible. If the central issues of man's life are God and sin, and sin equals death, the resurrection from the one equals resurrection from the other. Resurrection can be a present reality. The epistle addresses Christians as those whom God has already **made alive—You hath he quickened who were dead in trespasses and sins.**

2. *The Powers of Evil.*—What shall we make in the Christian pulpit or classroom of the

[5] *Christian Discourses* (tr. Walter Lowrie; London: Oxford University Press, 1939), p. 213.

The course of this world, better "the spirit of this world," i.e., the evil being, the false god whom the world worships, or to whom authority over the world is temporarily committed; it is equivalent to Paul's expression, "the god of this world" (II Cor. 4:4). The word is αἰών, which elsewhere in the N.T. always means "age"; here alone it has the personal sense in which it was used by the later Gnostic teachers—"eon" or "emanation." This sense is required by the parallel terms used in apposition with it—**prince** and **spirit.**

The power of the air: Power (ἐξουσία) is used in the sense of "area of dominion." The idea that **the air** is the realm of Satan's authority is obviously connected with the current astrology; it presupposes that the several areas of the universe have each its spirit-ruler, and assigns **the air** (ἀήρ, the lower atmosphere, as contrasted with αἰθήρ, the sky) to Satan. As the latter has just been called "the eon of the cosmos," the writer can hardly have intended to *limit* his activities to the air; the point must be rather to emphasize how closely the power of evil crowds in upon human life, impregnating the very atmosphere. This thought is intensified in the following phrase, which speaks of him as **the spirit that is now at work in the sons of disobedience**—not only filling the air about them, but active within them. **Sons of disobedience** is a Hebraism, meaning simply "the disobedient," i.e., the unbelieving.

A strict adherence to grammar would require us to construe **spirit** in apposition with **power,** not with **prince;** but this would impose a very involved interpretation. The anacoluthon (ἄρχοντα . . . πνεύματος) is easily explained by the intervention of the double genitive ἐξουσίας τοῦ ἀέρος.

Satan-mythology of the N.T.? When our epistle speaks of **the prince of the power of the air,** or in a later chapter (6:12) of "spiritual wickedness in high places," or of evil as a **spirit that . . . worketh** in the hearts and lives of **men,** readers would certainly have pictured such forces quite concretely. They were, for people of N.T. times, personal. They were devils—Satan, Beelzebub, or in Jesus' words, "the prince of this world" (John 14:30).

As the Exeg. suggests, such personalization of evil is alien to the modern mind. But should it be? Has not our scientific era lulled us to sleep by robbing evil of its living terror? God is in danger of being depersonalized, becoming an ideal, or a force (as if he were a dynamo) or merely a big pantheistic ALL (as if he were a kind of gas). As for the powers of evil, we depersonalize these also into psychological complexes, or sociological determinisms, or biological urges. The problem of evil is not explained away, but evil loses its frightening personal reality. The challenge of battle resolves itself into educational evolution or social progress or psychiatric therapeutics. In the N.T., on the other hand, the struggle is plain war. There is even "war in heaven" (Rev. 12:7). And the battle is with a personal, spiritual force, with "him who has the power of death, that is, the devil" (Heb. 2:14).

The most modern science is growing more humble, acknowledging ignorances. Are we as certain as once we were that phenomena which we call "personal" are limited to our human sphere? Personal, even anthropomorphic, analogies are the best we have even for God. It is surely better for a child to picture God as "an old man with a beard" than as a dynamo or a gas. Why should we not boldly use personal analogies for the forces of evil? These forces perform their deadly work in persons. They empower corporate bodies to do evil, as the Holy Spirit empowers the church to perform miracles of healing and of driving out demons. Dangers come with crude mythologizing, it is true. Yet myths and mythology are the language of religion. Christianity itself would wither without them. They speak to and from experience, as abstractions can never speak. The success of the little classic of C. S. Lewis, *The Screwtape Letters,* in which living devils appear, argues for a return to the language and the conceptual world of the Bible. Even sober theologians are again wrestling openly with the problem of the "demonic," a term describing the very thing our author calls **the course of this world** and **the spirit that now worketh in the children of disobedience.**[6]

Boldness in recovering biblical vocabulary can be recommended to the preacher and teacher of today. It comes, by contrast with the abstractions of science, as a novelty once more. But the hearts of men intuitively understand it. The devil has been far from exorcised from the ordinary speech of men. Simple folk are often better theologians than the learned of the schools.

[6] See the chapter "The Demonic" in Paul Tillich, *The Interpretation of History* (New York: Charles Scribner's Sons, 1936), pp. 77-122.

3 Among whom also we all had our conversation in times past in the lusts of our flesh, fulfilling the desires of the flesh and of the mind; and were by nature the children of wrath, even as others.

3 Among these we all once lived in the passions of our flesh, following the desires of body and mind, and so we were by nature children of wrath, like the rest of

---

3. The Jews, for all their privileges, cannot boast that their moral and spiritual condition had been superior to that of the Gentiles. Goodspeed (*Meaning of Ephesians,* p. 32) finds here an indication that the writer of the epistle is himself a Greek, since unlike Paul he fails to make a real distinction between the moral background of Jew and Gentile. Such a conclusion is not justified; for Paul himself sums up his discussion of the relative moral conditions of the Jewish and the Gentile worlds (Rom. 1:18–2:29) in the words: "There is no difference: for all have sinned, and come short of the glory of God" (Rom. 3:22-23); cf. Rom. 10:12, "There is no difference between the Jew and the Greek." This writer does not say that the Jews, like the Gentiles, governed their conduct **according to . . . the prince of the power of the air;** it is in the field of moral conduct, not of spiritual allegiance, that he equates Jews and Gentiles.

Lived (RSV)—**had our conversation** (KJV)—in this passage translates a verb (ἀναστρέφεσθαι) which always refers to life in association with others, in the everyday intercourse of society. The thought is that the Jews easily fell into the moral habits of their heathen neighbors.

The flesh (σάρξ) has here the same *ethical* sense as in the vocabulary of Paul. It does not mean "the physical nature," as if that were evil in itself; but the whole moral temperament, as predisposed to evil and hostile to the leadings of the Spirit of God (cf. Gal. 5:16-24; Rom. 8:5-13). **Passions** (RSV) or **lusts** (KJV)—properly "desires." The thought is not of gross physical sins, but of conduct swayed by irrational impulses, lacking any consistent governing principle. This thought of instability is intensified in the following phrase—**fulfilling the desires of the flesh and of the mind. Desires** here means "things willed"; the whole phrase pictures a life subject to self-will, and the plural

---

3. *By Nature the Children of Wrath.*—The pessimism, or supposed pessimism, of the Bible is a frequent surprise and offense to the modern mind. We often react with the comment that it cannot have been meant quite seriously, or that it describes humanity at a stage of barbarian culture which has been outgrown. A belief in the automatic progress of humanity has done much to emasculate the language of the Bible. The Bible gives little hope of an inevitable utopia in world history. It speaks instead of conversion, rebirth, repentance, and judgment, and eventually of a decision for eternity between heaven and hell. These may indeed lead to progress. But there is nothing automatic about them. The last generation on earth could as easily fail of salvation as the first.

To call the biblical view pessimistic, however, is to oversimplify. Take this verse. It has become classic in Christian theology. The sentence does not mean "deserving of wrath from the moment of birth." **By nature** signifies "by ourselves." But we are not meant to remain by ourselves. To point out our need of God is not necessarily pessimism at all. It is diagnosis, which can lead to hope and to salvation.

Furthermore, we need to grasp the full meaning of the word **wrath.** It occurs frequently in Paul's epistles, as, of course, all through the Bible. It describes the attitude of God toward man when man is in rebellion and violates the divine demand for holiness. Wrath and the law belong together. But neither wrath nor law are opposites of love. To interpret them thus is to miss the whole meaning of the Bible. Wrath implies love. Only love can really show wrath. God cares enough for mortal man to punish. Only a responsible being, created in the image of God, could possibly be the subject of wrath. We are not angry with a tree for being faulty, or with an irresponsible machine. We can exhibit wrath only against the gardener or the machinist. And our anger is a token of a gardener's or a machinist's dignity of status. More can be expected of them. If God should ever halt his wrath against us as sinners, he would cease to care. He would degrade us to the level of animals or machines. Even in our human relationships wrath has great meaning. Let us suppose that I do a shameful thing against a friend. If he should come to me and say, "Oh, I don't care; it is what I expected of you any-

4 But God, who is rich in mercy, for his great love wherewith he loved us,

mankind. 4 But God, who is rich in mercy, out of the great love with which he loved

suggests the lack of a *settled* will. The irrational self wills one thing today and another tomorrow, and the life is swayed this way and that, without moral direction or continuity. The plural διανοιῶν (**mind**), which cannot be given effect in any translation, reinforces this thought of inward unsettlement; the man is not of one mind but of many. **Children of wrath** is another Hebraism, meaning "deserving of wrath."

4-7. The **you** of vs. 1 is now at last taken up again, but with the inclusion of the Jewish Christians—as **us.** The perversity of our nature, which made us "dead through trespasses" and "children of wrath," is now set in the sharpest contrast with the grace of God which has not requited us according to our deserving, but has blessed us with the highest spiritual blessings. We observe again how the *abundance* of God's goodness is dwelt upon: he is **rich in mercy;** he acts out of his **great love** (vs. 4) ; the future will show **the immeasurable riches of his grace** (vs. 7) .

4. The ground of our redemption lies wholly in the mercy and love of God, who forgives the **trespasses and sins** that alienate us from him, and overcomes their deadly effects by the gift of new life in Christ.

way," I should suffer a final degradation. Far better a friend's blazing wrath. It leaves my dignity as a man unimpaired. It can lead to confession and restoration of friendship. "Hell begins," so someone has said, "where God stops punishing."

The paradox involved in the biblical concept of the wrath of God and of our being **children of wrath** is of great importance. It runs all through those puzzling but profound chapters in Paul's epistles (Rom. 5–8; Gal. 2–4) in which he wrestles with the similar paradox of the law. The law is the objectification of the wrath of God. All men are under the law. And the law is not salvation. By nature we are **children of wrath.** By ourselves we do not keep the law. But here the paradox begins. Paul does not mean that the law is useless or evil, or that the law argues against the love of God. Without the law we should be hopeless. "I was alive without the law once," says Paul (Rom. 7:9) , describing a state in which God had not even come upon the scene as yet. Such a state is the worst of all. "When the commandment came," so Paul describes the next stage, "sin revived, and I died" (Rom. 7:9) . The law of God and the wrath of God revealed to him who and where he was. Such a revelation could lead to repentance. And then the drama of the love of God could take on meaning.

By nature the children of wrath. The phrase and the concept are crucial to all theology true to the Bible. If this is pessimism, Christians must make the most of it. It is part of the inescapable scandal of the gospel of Christ. The gospel, however, is always good news. But this good news does not begin by merely making us feel good. It is not a philosophical and optimistic description of man as he is. It comes instead in the form of a drama—a drama wrought out in history once by God himself, but a drama which we must live through also. The drama begins with man fallen and lost, and under the wrath of God. But the drama does not end there. The phrase **children of wrath** has scarcely left our author's pen before he bursts out into the glorious description of what can follow for the Christian believer.

4-5. ***The Essence of the Gospel.***—The church of the N.T. had as yet no formal creeds. Yet it never wearied of repeating—as a creed does in more stylized mold—the essence of the gospel. Always this is in the form of drama. Christian faith is based upon a story, an epic. It is verb-theology, not a series of abstract propositions. Something has happened—a resurrection from the dead. In an earlier passage (1:20-22) the story of Christ's resurrection and ascension had been summarized. Here the same drama is pictured as an event in the lives of believers. In terms of a time sequence the drama of the days of Pontius Pilate came first, repeated then in the believers. In terms of experience, however, the new life in Christ frequently preceded understanding of the drama in history. Death and resurrection were present, not past, events. The church was a resurrection society. Men saw the miracle at firsthand. On the basis of this ever-recurring miracle it was easy to believe the story of a Jesus rising again on the third day, of an open tomb, and of an ascension into heaven. The early church did not waste much time in marshaling theological or historical proofs of Christ's divinity. The church pointed to itself. Death, Cross, Resurrection—here they are. Come and see.

5 Even when we were dead in sins, hath quickened us together with Christ, (by grace ye are saved;)

6 And hath raised *us* up together, and made *us* sit together in heavenly *places* in Christ Jesus:

7 That in the ages to come he might show the exceeding riches of his grace, in *his* kindness toward us, through Christ Jesus.

us, 5 even when we were dead through our
trespasses, made us alive together with
Christ (by grace you have been saved),
6 and raised us up with him, and made us
sit with him in the heavenly places in Christ
Jesus, 7 that in the coming ages he might
show the immeasurable riches of his grace in

---

5. The best comment on this verse is found in Rom. 6:23, "For the wages of sin is death, but the free gift of God is eternal life in Christ Jesus our Lord." The wages are earned; the free gift is all of grace.

6. The experience of Christ is repeated in the Christian believer—the communication of new life, and resurrection from the state of death caused by sin, is followed by exaltation to the heavenly places. The thought is not expressed in terms of a future expectation, but of a spiritual transformation already made effective. The three verbs—"made alive," "raised up," "made sit"—are all compounded with the preposition σύν ("with," "together with"), to bring out the thought that these are *shared* experiences, shared both with Christ and with all other Christians; the members of the mystical body share in the exalted life and glory of the head.

7. In the ages to come: Eternity is represented in analogy with the way in which time is conceived (see on 1:10), not as an undifferentiated infinity, but as a succession of ages. "For ever and ever" in Greek is lit., "unto the ages of ages" (Phil. 4:20; and

---

Later generations in the church may have been at fault in not remaining always in the N.T. tradition. The resurrection of a man called Jesus—what does it mean to me if it is merely an event in the distant past? I must see it in history now. Then the past event will have meaning. The early Christians, so A. E. Taylor, a discerning writer of the twentieth century reminds us, believed in the lordship of Christ

> because they were first convinced that they had in themselves the actual experience of a new kind of life with God as its centre, and that this life had begun with the Pentecostal "giving of the Spirit." They did not infer the transcendent significance of Christ from an antecedent belief in the moral perfection of his character. [And Taylor adds the startling assertion:] One may fairly doubt whether, in later days, any man has ever really been converted to the Christian faith simply by the impression made on him either by the story of Christ's life or by the reports of his moral teaching.[7]

If this observation is true, it can offer correction to whole areas of Christian apologetics and pedagogic effort. Become a church of the Resurrection first. Then tell us the story which explains your miraculous power.

As a matter of fact, the Christian church, even at its weakest, is still a resurrection society. It is this, or it is nothing at all, or an anti-Christ church. The church has always been a sinning, imperfect church, as was the church of the O.T. But men and women down through the ages have found in the church a new life with God. This new life has come by way of repentance and forgiveness, by way of assurances of the eternal majesties of right over wrong, by way of assurances also of God's love and care, by way of conversion, and a score of other life experiences. It is in the church that men still encounter the living God. Where else can he be found except among his own people? And whenever men and women have thus come into communion with holy Deity, no term short of resurrection adequately describes what happens.

A pastor in a great city tells that in the course of an afternoon of calling he met, in a shabby boardinghouse, a retired nurse. She was old. She had neither family nor friends. She had lost contact even with her church. The minister induced some laywomen to call on her and to bring her into the warm fellowship of a Christian group and back to worship in the sanctuary. Life returned to a lost soul. "It was," says the minister, "a literal resurrection from the dead."

6. *And Made Us Sit with Him in the Heavenly Places.*—This is a bold figure of speech. The temptation comes to leave it in the rarefied

[7] *The Faith of a Moralist* (London: Macmillan & Co., 1930), II, 130.

8 For by grace are ye saved through faith; and that not of yourselves: *it is* the gift of God:

kindness toward us in Christ Jesus. 8 For by grace you have been saved through faith; and this is not your own doing, it is the

frequently), or "unto all the ages" (Jude 25). As God's purpose of blessing was formed "before the foundation of the world" (1:4), so its effects are manifested to all eternity; cf. Ps. 103:17, "The mercy of the Lord is from everlasting to everlasting upon them that fear him." And it is reiterated that to the end, as in the beginning, his **kindness toward us** is shown **in Christ Jesus.**

8-9. The brief parenthesis of vs. 5—**by grace you have been saved**—is now taken up and amplified. The thought of Rom. 1–5 is here summarized, and in a measure generalized. The controversy over the obligations of the law does not concern this writer as it concerned Paul; he speaks, therefore, not of "the works of the law" but of "works" in general—as of self-directed human effort of every kind—by which men might seek to win salvation. Salvation is not to be gained by our own efforts toward goodness—**this is not your own doing, it is the gift of God.** The author of Ephesians has grasped clearly the simple yet bold and radical doctrine of Paul, which utterly denies to man anything of which he may **boast** (cf. Rom. 3:27–4:1; Gal. 6:14). Man can do nothing to earn the favor of God; he can only receive **through faith** that which is freely given.

atmosphere of pious rhetoric. Not only are Christians risen with Christ, but they are even ascended and are with Christ in the heavenlies now! A hope of a future life of bliss beyond death comes naturally to many religions. Eschatological promises are relatively easy. A heaven in the present tense is more difficult to make real. How many of us Christians today are convinced that we are *now* in heaven?

Taking the Bible as a norm of faith is not always pleasant. The Bible judges us so severely. Yet surely we are meant to place the Christianity of any age under the judgment of the Christianity of the N.T. Something is missing in our faith or our Christian life if we cannot share the experience of a heaven *now*.

Think of Paul. "Thrice was I beaten with rods, once was I stoned, thrice I suffered shipwreck, a night and a day I have been in the deep. In journeyings often, in perils of waters, in perils of robbers, in perils by mine own countrymen. . . ." (II Cor. 11:25, 26.) The catalog of sufferings goes on and on. It rivals a modern adventure story. By any mundane standard it describes the opposite of heaven. Yet Paul would agree fully with our author. He does not belittle a heaven beyond the grave. In a remarkable passage (Phil. 1:18-26) he sets forth a dramatic dialogue between heaven now and in the beyond, and finds little to choose. "I am in a strait betwixt the two." "For to me to live is Christ, and to die is gain." (Phil. 1:23, 21.)

This *now* of the N.T. is of great importance. It should refute once and for all the accusation against the Christian gospel that it is mere "opiate of the people," mere promises of rewards in an afterlife. This *now* can disclose the error in much "second advent" or "millenarian" Christianity also. By all means let Christianity retain the eschatological concept of a second coming of Christ. But overemphasis upon it can dangerously distort the gospel.

To the author of Ephesians heaven *now* is the church, the new life "in Christ." And from his day to this, wherever the church has been truly the church, Christian experience has validated his insight. Life is relationships. Give us a home and friends, even on the human plane, and their value will outweigh wealth and pleasure and achieved ambition. The church is a society of reborn relationship, with God and with men. It is a holy home. It is the final miracle of history. It is a heaven *now,* a foretaste of the perfect home of eternity.

8-9. ***Grace, Faith, and Works.***—Controversy has swirled for centuries around texts like these. A companion text such as Rom. 3:28—"A man is justified by faith without the deeds of the law"—even became the occasion for the Reformation break with Rome. Luther's enlarged translation of the latter verse, "Justification by faith *alone,*" has been ever since the Reformation the battle cry of evangelical Christianity as over against Catholicism's emphasis upon merit and works. It might be said incidentally that the author of Ephesians, obviously summarizing Paul's teaching, shows his genius in his slightly variant version. Salvation by grace through faith "unto good works" (vs. 10) avoids some at least of the misunderstandings to which the phrase "Justification by faith *alone*" has led. Grace, though a complex concept, has objective connotations. Faith invites subjective interpreta-

9 Not of works, lest any man should boast.

gift of God — 9 not because of works, lest

Quite un-Pauline, however, is the use of the *perfect,* in speaking of salvation—**you have been saved.** Paul uniformly speaks of salvation as a process continuing throughout life (I Cor. 1:18, "to us who are being saved"), or as the final issue of the process (Rom. 5:9, "we shall be saved"); so also in I Pet. 1:5, "guarded through faith for a salvation ready to be revealed in the last time"; and I Pet. 2:2, "that . . . you may grow up to salvation." Paul would say "you have been justified," or "you have been reconciled to God," but not "you have been saved"; rather "you await salvation" ("await a Savior," Phil: 3:20). The use of the perfect in this context is, however, in keeping with the attitude to eschatology consistently shown by the writer of Ephesians (see on 1:18); and with his declaration that God "made us sit with [Christ] in the heavenly places." The man who wrote those words could never have written: "My desire is to depart and be with Christ, for that is far better" (Phil. 1:23), nor yet: "While we are at home in the body we are away from

tions. Both are needed. Reformation theology might profit from enlargement at this point.

The basic issue with which our text deals, however, is crucial for a biblical Christianity. The layman listening to a doctrinal sermon may think that the issue should be left to ivory tower theologians. The doctrine of grace is not easy for him. Salvation by works (good works of course) is simple and clear. If grace means help in producing good works, the average Christian can see value in it. But the test according to which a man is or is not declared a Christian is surely "works" and not some hypothetical psychological action called faith, or some even more distant thing called grace. God, so moral reason could say, is not going to welcome a sinner until he has ceased to be one, or at least has tried his very best not to be one. Forgiveness is involved, of course, but this must be a plus added by God to an imperfect performance, much as a student with a grade of C receives a diploma though he has not equaled in attainment the student with a grade of A.

Nor is the naïve "works Christian" wholly wrong. Life under God must begin with taking the demands of God seriously and trying to fulfill them. The O.T. is still very much a part of our Bible, and the O.T. emphasizes the revelation of God's demands, God's law. But if a man stops with fear of the law, he still stands outside the gate leading to the Christian gospel. He is at best a Jew, and perhaps only a Jew who is in danger of becoming a Pharisee.

Any man who thinks that he has earned a good grade before God, even a passing grade, has not really come into the presence of the real God of the Bible at all. He has not yet seen the Lord "high and lifted up" (Isa. 6:1). He has not yet recognized himself for what he is in the sight of God, a sinner. He has not yet cried out, "Woe is me! for I am undone; because I am a man of unclean lips" (Isa. 6:5). Such a vision of what we are before the holiness of God becomes climactic in the N.T. Listen to the demands of God as Jesus defines them: "Whoever shall smite thee on thy right cheek, turn to him the other also. . . . Give to him that asketh thee, and from him that would borrow of thee turn not thou away" (Matt. 5:39, 42). Which of us fulfills such a law? A grace said before many a meal could take the form, "O God, forgive us for feasting while others starve." All of us could confess that the closer we come to visions of God, the more we realize our unholiness. A conviction that we have achieved a passing grade in God's classroom simply indicates that we have reduced God's stature to that of an idol of our own making. I see, let us suppose, a beggar at my door, or hear tales of starvation in some suffering part of the world. Do I obey the demands of the Sermon on the Mount? I do not, even if I perform notable deeds of charity. My conscience never gives me a final passing grade. Hence I am tempted to ease my conscience by reducing God's holiness somewhere nearer my own level of performance. I also turn my eyes away from him and begin to compare myself with my neighbors. I can generally find neighbors who perform even less than I do and can accordingly start boasting, "God, I thank thee, that I am not as other men are" (Luke 18:11). I become a Pharisee, committing the sin of pride, and this breaks my communion with God even more than if I approached God as a self-confessed disreputable publican! Salvation by works looks simple at first. It turns out, if honestly dealt with, to be impossible. The more I try to fulfill God's demands, the larger grows the vision of my failure.

Are good works, therefore, proved wrong? No. The paradox of the gospel is not quite as simple as that. Jesus did not mean by his parable of

10 For we are his workmanship, created in Christ Jesus unto good works, which

any man should boast. 10 For we are his workmanship, created in Christ Jesus for

the Lord, . . . we would rather be away from the body and at home with the Lord" (II Cor. 5:6-8). Paul is "in Christ" now and hopes to be "with Christ" in heaven; this writer feels that the Christian is both "in Christ" and "with him in the heavenly places" here and now. In this respect he stands less close to Paul than to the author of the Fourth Gospel; cf. John 5:24, "He that heareth my word, and believeth on him that sent me, hath everlasting life, and . . . is passed from death unto life."

10. This verse is the positive counterpart to vs. 9; **for good works** is the obverse to **not because of works.** The Christian life is not morally indifferent; it is made to issue in

the Pharisee and the publican that we should all go out and become disreputable citizens in order to be right with God. We must try the pathway of "works" in order to see that we must try something else. A good teacher often leads pupils to a wrong answer first in order to make a right answer stand out in bold relief later on. Only the man who has seriously tried to obey the demands of God can see himself as one in need of grace. Only then can he see what repentance means.

The good news of the gospel is the news that there is another way out of the maze of a troubled conscience. This is the news of forgiveness. Not forgiveness as a nice plus added to an already flattering reward for performance, but forgiveness as a wholly unearned gift—a gift freely extended to a worthless prodigal son, or to a disreputable publican, or to a thief on a cross, or to you, or to me. Such forgiveness can bring salvation, as good works, if they are a pretense that forgiveness is not yet needed, can never produce.

This paradox of the Christian gospel is inexhaustible in content. Later verses in our epistle expound it further. Here there is space for only one suggestive analogy. The doctrine of grace is at first mysterious and puzzling. The very word grace has an academic sound. Yet our human experience is full of analogies for the understanding of grace. These analogies crowd one upon another when we turn to the problems of personal relationships. Consider friendship, to say nothing of the higher realms of human love. Is not friendship always grace? We speak of the gift of friends. No one can earn the love of a friend. If the relationship has been established over a bargain counter, even that of a mutual exchange of good works, it is not true friendship. Particularly is this true when friendship bridges a chasm of social status, or of age, or of wealth, or of guilt. One of the parties extends the gift of a friendly handclasp in trouble, or of a kindly act in danger. It is an act of faith, and of an as yet unearned trust. A response is evoked, and the miracle of friendship happens. True friendship is never yielded on demand, a diploma for an earned grade in an examination. What the N.T. means by salvation is the birth of a covenant of friendship between the holy God and a sinner. Grace is a shorthand word for this stupendous love story. **For by grace are ye saved through faith; and that not of yourselves: it is the gift of God; not of works, lest any man should boast.**

10. *Grace and Works.*—This verse is necessary as a completion of the author's summary of the gospel of God's grace. He is not finished with the problem of good works. He apparently had read them out of court in the drama of salvation. But here they appear again. Good works are, so it seems, both belittled and exalted in the N.T. Many of the writers of the N.T. play a kind of game of hide-and-seek with the concepts of grace and good works. It is small wonder that some readers of the N.T. are thoroughly puzzled. Certain portions of the N.T. are such plain sailing: the Sermon on the Mount, the parables when moralistically interpreted, and the Epistle of James, to cite obvious examples. But the Pauline epistles, with their tortuous arguments on law and faith and grace and justification, are seemingly beyond the simple Bible reader's grasp. The Christian preacher is only little less puzzled when he faces the task of explaining the mysteries of the N.T. faith. Even the good news of forgiveness is not obviously simple. Every informed Christian teacher knows that in such words as grace and forgiveness lies the heart of the gospel message. Yet how to preach this gospel without giving the impression that good works do not really matter? "Forgiveness of sins," so Luther once remarked, "ought to make thee rejoice; this is the very heart of Christianity, and yet it is a mighty dangerous thing to preach." [8]

Several popular misconceptions have done much to obscure the understanding of the Christian doctrines concerning grace and works. One

[8] Translated from Luther's *Table Talk,* in J. S. Whale, *Christian Doctrine* (New York: The Macmillan Co., 1942), p. 79.

God hath before ordained that we should walk in them.

good works, which God prepared beforehand, that we should walk in them.

goodness; but the good works are the outcome, not the cause, of salvation. There is a further point in the reciprocal ideas that God has prepared us for his service and has also prepared a particular sphere in which we may serve—has given us tasks which are designed for us, as we are designed for them. Both versions are far too literal here. The play on words suggested by **works** and **workmanship** is not found in the Greek. **That we should walk in them** is an atrocious Hebraism, tolerable only because of its familiarity to us. The ἵνα-clause is not *final* ("in order that"), but *epexegetic,* defining the range of the noun—"duties [**good works**] for us to perform."

of these is that Christian morality is a simple affair while the doctrinal framework of Christian thought is complex, that the former is practical while the latter is academic. In actual fact and in Christian experience the reverse is almost true. A child can experience forgiveness, repentance, and the futility of mere good works. A child's relationship to father and mother is clearly founded on parental grace and on a personal love relationship which is not commensurate with a child's earnings by way of good conduct. When it comes to ethical problems, on the other hand, these can be frighteningly complex to a child. In the world of experience any Christian worthy of the name similarly knows subconsciously the mysteries of the gospel. These are not academic. We are merely tempted to call them academic because they make great demands on pride. "Verily I say unto you, Whosoever shall not receive the kingdom of God as a little child, he shall not enter therein" (Mark 10:15). We rebel against the simplicities of the gospel in terms of a personal encounter with God. Hence we try other less personal means of settling matters between ourselves and the Deity. Morality is relatively impersonal, so we turn to the world of ethics. If a little goodness, goodness defined in terms of being better than some of our neighbors, will do the trick, we are ready for such a way out. When we relinquish a personal relationship with God—prayer, repentance, faith—we do not immediately lose all our moral virtues. These may in fact become a substitute for a personal relationship with God. We fall from grace, not first of all into gross sin, but under the law (Gal. 5:4).

Another misconception of the N.T. gospel of grace and forgiveness is the opposite of the one just described. There have been those who have grasped the truth that a relationship with God is never earned, but comes as a gift. Hence, they say, morality does not really matter. We can forget about good works. All we need is faith, the justifying faith so endlessly emphasized by Paul. If we can hold to the faith in God's infinite forgiveness, we can take literally the apparent belittling of the law in the epistles of the N.T. We no longer need moral precepts. We can ignore ethics. Theologians call this kind of false grace religion "antinomianism" (*nomos* means law; hence, antilaw religion). In the Reformation period, when Luther had rediscovered the bold paradox of Paul, justification by faith, antinomianism was a real danger. In fact it remains a danger whenever Christians forget half of the paradox of forgiveness.. Forgiveness from God's side *is* sheer grace. We do not earn God's love. Nor does he ask us to do so. But forgiveness implies forgiven-ness on our side. And the state of being a forgiven sinner brings with it great moral demands.

Our text is a wise corrective to many misconceptions of the doctrine of grace. **We are his workmanship,** i.e., grace. **Created in Christ Jesus unto good works,** i.e., Christian ethics. **Which God hath before ordained that we should walk in them**—clearly it is precisely **good works** which are the end product God had in mind from the start. The moral life of Christians is not belittled. It is instead highly exalted in the drama of salvation. A great deal depends, however, on where it appears in the drama and how it is motivated.

The ambiguities involved in being or doing good have often intrigued the student of morals. I perform, let us suppose, a virtuous act. Why did I do it? I may have been moved by a passing impulse of pity. I may have eased my conscience when it was uneasy because of overindulgence in luxuries. I may have wanted my name to appear on a list of contributors. I may have been bullied by a solicitor, and a gift was the easiest way to end an uncomfortable interview. My motives were probably mixed. But in so far as self-regarding calculations entered into the action, it was not rightly **workmanship, created in Christ Jesus unto good works.** It was not a fully "gracious" act, viz., a gift flowing inevitably out of my being a self-giving person. God is pictured in Jesus' teachings as gracious in his very nature. "For he maketh his sun to rise on the

11 Wherefore remember, that ye *being* in time past Gentiles in the flesh, who are called Uncircumcision by that which is

11 Therefore remember that at one time you Gentiles in the flesh, called the un-

A question arises as to whether **workmanship** and **created** apply to the "new creation" (II Cor. 5:17), the regenerated life of the believer; or whether the thought is that the purpose for which we were first created is now fulfilled in us. The original creation, of us and of all the cosmos, was also "in him" (Col. 1:16).

D. Further Exposition of the Spiritual Unity of Mankind in the Church (2:11-22)

This passage throws further light on the writer's great conception of the significance of the church as "the fullness of him who is being wholly filled" (1:23). The ultimate

evil and on the good, and sendeth rain on the just and on the unjust" (Matt. 5:45). My virtue at its best was not divine like that. In so far as it was this side of truly Christian grace, it was at most an act performed in obedience to a law. This does not prove it worthless in the human social scene. The law of God has great meaning. But the act was not yet an act transformed by grace and **created in Christ Jesus.**

Nevertheless there exists a morality which is thus transformed. It is dangerous for us to search for it in ourselves. The moment we become conscious of it we shall boast of it, at least to ourselves, and thus destroy its standing before God through pride. But we can see such morality in others, a goodness springing from a transformed heart. A villager once described a truly Christian neighbor in the phrase, "She does good mechanical." Good works are inevitable in a life of forgiven-ness. They are no longer calculated. They are no longer deeds done "in order to" secure a reward, but deeds done "because of" a gift already received. The prodigal son, on the day after his father's gracious reception, surely did **good works** on the parental farm. But they must have differed in kind from those performed by his calculating brother, or those he may himself have performed in the days before his leaving home when his motive may have been merely that of obedience to a compulsory law. A miraculous change had been wrought in his inner life. A new covenant or relationship had been established between himself and his father. He had experienced the gift of unearned forgiveness. The response of forgiven-ness must have been little short of inevitable. To resist such grace would have been blasphemy, or a violation of the basic nature of man.

There are then, on the moral and ethical plane, two kinds of **good works.** They may look alike to the observer, but they differ in essence. The one is legal, obedient to a law or a rational principle or an ideal. It requires compulsion and effort to perform. The other springs from a changed heart. The one is response to an *ought;* the other is response to an *is.*

To be reborn **unto good works** is the miracle brought about by what the Bible calls conversion. A Christian is not a Christian unless his life is directed **unto good works.** "By their fruits ye shall know them" (Matt. 7:20), said Jesus. "Faith without works is dead" (Jas. 2:20), said James, and he is right, even though his epistle lacks the genius of Paul in penetrating to the heart of the Christian paradox. Our text in the Epistle to the Ephesians harmonizes Paul and James better than many commentators.

The same paradox runs all through the ethical teachings of Jesus, particularly through the parables. One of the most strikingly pertinent to our theme, though often misinterpreted, is the parable of the good Samaritan. The point of the parable lies in the contrast between the two questions with which the parable begins and ends. The lawyer, representing Jewish legalism, wants to obey the law. He knows he ought to love his neighbor. Hence he asks, "Who is my neighbor?" (Luke 10:29.) He wants a legal definition. *Then* he will regulate his conduct accordingly. Jesus ends his parable with a question also. But this is a revolutionary question, "Which now of these three, thinkest thou, *was neighbor* unto him that fell among the thieves?" (Luke 10:36.) The Samaritan had not asked the lawyer's question. He simply *was* a neighborly person. He was "gracious" inside. His grace resembled the grace of God which gives freely without legal defining or bargaining. His **good works** differed in kind from those at which the lawyer was aiming. A Christian **created in Christ Jesus unto good works** will resemble the Samaritan and not the lawyer.

11. ***Jew and Gentile United in the Church.***— We might as well admit at the outset of this whole section of our epistle that, in its literal

called the Circumcision in the flesh made by hands;

circumcision by what is called the circumcision, which is made in the flesh by hands

divine purpose to bring the whole created universe into an all-embracing unity is foreshadowed, and indeed is actually begun, in the church, where a divided humanity is brought together as Jew and Gentile are united in a single worshiping community. In Christ all the disabilities of an inheritance of heathendom are overcome, and all the privileges of access to himself which God had accorded to his ancient people of Israel are granted freely and fully to Gentile believers. The church is now depicted under the figure of a living temple, in which Jewish and Gentile elements are built together—a universal house of worship, inhabited by the Spirit of God.

11-12. At the beginning of the chapter the writer has spoken of the *moral* condition of the Gentile believers before they experienced the saving power of God in Christ—they were "dead in trespasses and sins" (vs. 1). Now he calls to remembrance their former state in terms of their *religious* condition as seen from a Jewish point of view, in contrast with the religious privileges of Israel. The distinction made by the Jews between themselves and the rest of mankind was in part artificial—**the circumcision . . . made in the flesh by hands**—but in part it was real. The Gentiles had no expectation of Messiah to light the future, no part in the holy community to which God vouchsafed his presence, no interest in the promises of divine blessing, no hope of a life to come, no knowledge of the one living and true God who had revealed himself to Israel.

11. The exhortation to **remember** undoubtedly suggests that the readers are in the main Gentile Christians of the second generation: it is an appeal to their background in religious history, not to their own religious experience. It is made not to any particular group, but to the **Gentiles in the flesh** as a class. The article (τὰ ἔθνη—*the* Gentiles) is not noticed in either of our versions, but its presence is highly important, as *generalizing* the address—"you, the Gentiles"; not simply **you Gentiles** (RSV), much less **ye being in**

historical setting, it no longer makes much of an appeal to a modern Christian reader. To Paul and his contemporaries the union of Jew and Gentile was the outstanding event of their time. To us it is a story of long ago. It is hard for us to realize that the victory which Paul won for his Gentile converts was one of the most important in all human history. For a time Paul fought the battle singlehanded. Even Peter and Barnabas went into retreat (Gal. 2:11-21). Would the church be one or would it be a church in schism? Would the new Christian religion be split into a Jewish Christianity and a Gentile Christianity? The church has seen many schisms in its later course through the centuries. It can, however, look back to this momentous victory of unity, on an issue more threatening than any which it has faced since.

These verses, and those to follow, can, of course, be made applicable to the problem of Christian unity as we face it today and as we shall face it for some generations to come. We need not limit their meaning to a particular issue now long outgrown. But before turning to more modern parallels, we might well try, even in contemporary appreciation of our epistle, to reconstruct the original historical conflict. It has much to teach us. The issue narrowed itself down to one of sacramental unity. Could a Gentile become a Christian without being circumcised? Could circumcised and uncircumcised have tablefellowship in the Lord's Supper? Schisms in the Christian church throughout its history have involved analogous sacramental issues. The outstanding symbol of disunity among Christians today is the fact that they do not sit down together at a supper.

The analogy must, to be sure, be carefully handled. Nor would we all agree as to how the story of this first threatened schism throws light upon our later disunity problems. Clearly, however, it was not an issue between a sacramental Christianity and one with no sacramental rites at all. The problem of a nonsacramental Quakerism had not yet appeared upon the scene. Gentile Christians as well as Jewish Christians could not easily have conceived of a church without a definite entrance sacrament, such as baptism, or the fellowship meal instituted by the church's Lord. The issue was one of race as well as religious rite. Color of skin was not the problem, but the taboos to be conquered in maintaining unity resembled those which today attach to the color line.

Disunity within Christendom has two forms today. One is that of sectarianism. Another is

time past Gentiles (KJV). They are still as much **Gentiles in the flesh** as they ever were; only **in time past** they were **without Christ . . . and without God in the world** (vs. 12), but are **now in Christ Jesus** (vs. 13).

Called the uncircumcision . . . called the circumcision: The implication is that both terms are used improperly: the physical circumcision of which the Jew boasted is of no significance. "Real circumcision is a matter of the heart, spiritual and not literal" (Rom. 2:29); cf. Gal. 5:6, "In Jesus Christ neither circumcision availeth any thing, nor uncircumcision; but faith which worketh by love." The Gentile Christians were not uncircumcised in any sense that mattered: they were "circumcised with a circumcision made without hands, by putting off the body of the flesh" (Col. 2:11; cf. Phil. 3:3). **Made in the flesh by hands,** outward, visible, and therefore significant only as a symbol of spiritual reality, of something beyond itself; contrasted implicitly with that which is made without hands—the reality to which the symbol points us. The same word (χειροποίητος) is applied to earthly places of worship as contrasted with the invisible place of God's true presence in Heb. 9:24, "Christ has entered, not into a sanctuary made with hands, a copy [better "a symbol"] of the true one, but into heaven itself, now to appear in the presence of God" (cf. Heb. 9:11; Mark 14:58; Acts 7:48; 17:24).

---

that of race. For the latter the analogy furnished by the struggle in the early church is particularly pertinent. Tablefellowship—this is our issue today in this area of conflict. It meets us on the secular social scene as well as in the church. In the church, in fact, it is partially being resolved. At the Lord's Supper white man's Christianity and black or yellow man's Christianity are beginning to be one. Before the victory can be complete, however, the pattern of the Lord's Supper must become the pattern of social supper table also. White man cannot meet black man as brother in Christ on Sunday without meeting him as brother on Monday as well. If he sins against unity in Christ on either day, he endangers the salvation of his soul. Differentiations of race remain as facts, of course, as differences continued to exist in the early church between Jewish Christians and Gentile Christians. Brotherliness, however, is a quite recognizable attitude. Violation of oneness in Christ is defined by Paul as "not discerning the Lord's body" (I Cor. 11:29). By "body" Paul means the fellowship of the church. He goes on to say that breaking of church fellowship explains "why many of you are weak and ill, and some have died" (I Cor. 11:30). The passage is one which white man's Christianity may some day understand in awe, and even terror! Does sinning against the church lead to a punishment like that once suffered by Ananias and Sapphira? If we are ever puzzled as to why Mohammedanism and Communism (there are similarities between them) are such stubborn rivals to Christianity, one explanation may be discovered in the fact that in both racial disunity has been abolished.

Something, to be sure, can be said in defense of Christianity in comparison with its rivals. Christian culture has to confess that it has not solved completely the problem of racial unity in its common life. It can plead, however, that it is slowly proceeding toward a solution on a deeper level than that envisaged in rival social orders. Equality as between the races may be achieved on the secular plane and yet leave the ultimate chasm unbridged. Even egalitarian justice does not yet mean brotherhood. A parallel can be pointed out between the problem of racial equality and that encountered in the institution of slavery. Christianity moved slowly also in destroying the institution of slavery. It created brotherhood in Christ first. The fires of Christian love, kindled in the fellowship of the church, undermined the institution from within. The cure, once set to work, was radical. It could heal not only the disease of slavery, but all breaches of unity between man and man. The weakness of all solutions of the problems of disunity in society, short of Christian love, is that they may cure institutional symptoms, but not the disease itself. The problem of race is not quite so simple as the humanitarian reformer supposes. Mere legal equality will not remove a fundamental fact of creation. Short of brotherhood in Christ *across* the walls of still recognized, and even gladly accepted, difference, no solution will endure the test of time.

No apologies for Christianity, however, are valid if they remove the sting of conscience in our hearts for our sins of disunity. Christians, as they confront their task of making real in action the brotherhood which they confess with their lips, may well stand in awe of the warning of the church's Lord: "For I say unto you, That except your righteousness shall exceed the righteousness of the scribes and Pharisees [secular

12 That at that time ye were without Christ, being aliens from the commonwealth of Israel, and strangers from the

— 12 remember that you were at that time separated from Christ, alienated from the

---

12. **Without Christ** is the negative counterpart of **in Christ.** The great act of thanksgiving (1:3-14) recounts the blessings which come to man **in Christ;** here the writer gives a summary of the disabilities of man **without Christ.** The four predicates which follow give, as it were, an outline in detail of what this separation involved.

Alienated from the commonwealth of Israel: The participle is used in a peculiar sense. Those who had never been members of the commonwealth could not be "alienated" from it. Yet it would not be sufficient to say that they were "outside" the sacred community; there was indeed a condition of spiritual maladjustment involved. The writer has in mind the words of Paul, "You, that were sometime alienated and enemies in your mind by wicked works" (Col. 1:21), which likewise describe the state of Gentile believers before they were reconciled to God. His thought is that before Christ came there was no communion of man with God except within the fold of the nation which he had made peculiarly his own. The rest of mankind, being alienated from him, was likewise alienated from the community of his worshipers.

The covenants of promise are the constitutive basis of the **commonwealth,** which rests primarily on God's promises of blessing, secondarily on Israel's response in the covenanted pledge of obedience. The **covenants** (the plural is used by Paul in Rom. 9:4) were made with Abraham, for him and his descendants (Gen. 15:8-21; 17:1-21); and with the national community under the leadership of Moses (Exod. 24:1-11); and the later prophets speak of the making of "a new covenant" (Jer. 31:31-34) and of "an everlasting covenant" (Isa. 55:3; Jer. 32:40; Ezek. 37:26). As **strangers** (ξένοι, "foreigners"), not members of the community which lived under **the covenants,** the Gentiles were entitled to none of the privileges, present or prospective, which were pledged to Israel under this divine constitution.

Having no hope: The same words are used of the non-Christian world, in specific reference to the hope of immortality, in I Thess. 4:13, where, translated literally, Paul

---

prophets of equality], ye shall in no case enter into the kingdom of heaven" (Matt. 5:20).

12. ***Being Aliens from the Commonwealth of Israel.***—No Christian of the apostolic age, even when he was a Gentile convert, could ever quite conquer a feeling that Jewish Christianity had certain priority rights. This inferiority feeling vanished rapidly, and it probably is nonexistent today. Yet its total disappearance may have been to Christianity's hurt. The problem of anti-Semitism in Christendom might have been more wisely handled. It is still acutely with us. Of the Jews might still be said what Paul—using the *present* tense—declares: "To them belong the sonship, the glory, . . . the worship, and the promises; to them belong the patriarchs, and of their race, according to the flesh, is the Christ. God who is over all be blessed forever. Amen" (Rom. 9:4-5). He shortly adds, to be sure, "that they have a zeal for God, but it is not enlightened" (Rom. 10:2). Or again, "Through their transgression salvation has come to the Gentiles, so as to make Israel jealous" (Rom. 11:11). But he adds, "If their failure means riches for the Gentiles, how much more will their full inclusion mean!" (Rom. 11:12). What light this could throw on our Jew-Gentile problem today!

Judaism presents a real problem to Christians. Sentimental solutions, mere appeals to democratic egalitarianism, are not enough. A chasm between two religions, with their inevitable differences of ethical codes, is not bridged by naïve preaching of secular brotherhood. Undoubtedly, however, the first step toward an understanding should be taken by Christians. They were, in very fact, as Gentiles, once **aliens from the commonwealth of Israel.** They became the new Israel by the grace of God. The indebtedness of Christians to the Jews is incalculable. Gratitude should prompt to much forbearance.

12. ***Having No Hope, and Without God in the World.***—Here we meet one of the great phrases of the Bible. Our author uses it to describe the state of his Gentile converts before they had been reborn into the new life with God. The phrase, however, is of universal ap-

covenants of promise, having no hope, and without God in the world:

commonwealth of Israel, and strangers to the covenants of promise, having no hope

says, "We want you to know the truth, brethren, concerning those that sleep in death, that you may not grieve as do the rest of mankind [οἱ λοιποί], who have no hope." Here the same thought is included, but the reference is more general. It may be felt that the despair of the Gentile mind is painted too blackly; for in the mystery cults initiates were promised immortality. But in fact the inscriptions on the graves and the uniform pessimism of the literature of the age provide alike unimpeachable evidence that people of all classes looked to the future without hope either for themselves or for the world. Men bade an eternal farewell to their loved ones when they laid them in the tomb; they had no hope that death, "the last enemy," should ever be "destroyed" or "swallowed up in victory" (I Cor. 15:26, 54). Any dream of a good life to come, as distinguished from a cheerless survival in the dark abode of Hades, amounted to no more than a wistful longing that it might be so; there was nothing resembling the firm Christian confidence, which was rooted in faith in the God who raises the dead. Ancient paganism knew many myths of gods (Attis, Adonis, Osiris) who died and were restored to life by some form of higher magic; but in general it may be said that it knew no god to whom belonged the power to raise from the dead whomsoever he willed. (Zoroastrianism should be mentioned as a remarkable exception; the followers of Ahura Mazda were taught to look forward to the final triumph of the kingdom of light and truth and goodness over the powers of Angra Mainyu, which opposed it, to a universal judgment of the living and the dead, and to a future life of blessedness for faithful Mazdaists. This religion had great influence on the thought of Judaism after the Exile, and so indirectly on early Christian ideas; but it is doubtful if it was as yet itself a living religion in the Mediterranean area. In

plication to all in any age who are outside the covenants of biblical faith. In the twentieth century, when lusty atheisms are sweeping the gods of many historic religions of mankind off the board, this verse leaps into life.

What is human existence like when the gods are dethroned? Few disciplines are more helpful to the preacher than journeys of the imagination into the thought world of those to whom the gospel comes as a strange new thing. We too are sent "to seek and to save that which was lost" (Luke 19:10).

Glimpses into contemporary godlessness probably come ready to hand and need not be pictured here. But a few examples from the age when the N.T. gospel was a novelty may show how our text must have been understood by its first readers. The phrase **having no hope,** whatever may be said of theoretical atheism today, is certainly the epitaph which could be written over most of that ancient, outwardly brilliant, Roman imperial world. Our examples are, at the same time, strangely modern—or will be when our secular utopian dreams finally meet mature reality.

Listen to Sophocles, most classic perhaps of ancient dramatists. Every schoolboy in the Hellenistic centuries memorized words like these and saw life through the eyes of the tragic dramas which they summarize:

> For the long days lay up full many things nearer unto grief than joy; but as for thy delights, their place shall know them no more, when a man's life hath lapsed beyond the fitting term; and the Deliverer comes at the last to all alike,—when the doom of Hades is suddenly revealed, without marriage-song, or lyre, or dance,—even Death at the last.
>
> Not to be born is, past all prizing, best; but, when a man hath seen the light, this is next best by far, that with all speed he should go thither, whence he hath come.[9]

Or, again, turn to Rome and read one of the most perfect of its poems. Catullus, its author, shared with Vergil and Horace the highest fame which the imperial age could bestow. Those who have enjoyed a classical education will attest the fact that more hauntingly beautiful, yet more hopeless, lines have perhaps never been penned by man:

> Soles occidere et redire possunt:
> Nobis cum semel occidit brevis lux,
> Nox est perpetua una dormienda.

[9] *Oedipus Coloneus* (tr. R. J. Jebb; Cambridge: University Press, 1885), pp. 191-93, ll. 1216-29.

the third century it spread widely throughout the empire, in its later form of Mithraism, being especially popular in the camps of the army.)

Nor was there any hope of a better future for the community, to compensate for the lack of hope for personal immortality; there was nothing corresponding in any way to Israel's hope of the kingdom of God. For the ancient world the golden age lay in the past, not in the future; and men looked forward with dread to what should come after them. Even the ablest emperors were sadly conscious that they were administering the affairs of a society in the throes of dissolution, and they hoped for little more than to stave off its collapse.

Without God: The phrase translates the single word ἄθεοι, "atheists" or "godless." This is the only N.T. occurrence, but it is found frequently in classical writers and in the later Christian literature. The Christians were commonly termed ἄθεοι by hostile pagans because they refused to worship the gods of their neighbors, who were also the gods of their ancestors. When Polycarp, the aged bishop of Smyrna, was led into the arena before a howling multitude clamoring for his death, the Roman procurator took pity on his gray hairs and invited him to save his life by renouncing Christ and saying "Away with the ἄθεοι." So he styled the Christians. But Polycarp waved his hand toward the bloodthirsty throngs in the arena, and cried, "Away with the ἄθεοι," turning the word back upon those who used it. The pagans were not "atheists," for they worshiped a multitude of divinities, high and low; but "we know that an idol is nothing in the world, and that there is none other God but one" (I Cor. 8:4). Their worship of these empty creations of the human imagination could not be considered in any sense as a living communion with God. There is no thought that God had forsaken them or left himself without a witness among them; but they had no fellowship with him in love. **In the world,** i.e., obliged to face the overwhelming mystery of the sum of things, the

---

Two stanzas of the poem, in a noble translation, read:

> Lesbia, live to love and pleasure,
> Careless what the grave may say:
> When each moment is a treasure
> Why should lovers lose a day?
>
> Setting suns shall rise in glory,
> But when little life is o'er,
> There's an end of all the story—
> We shall sleep, and wake no more.[1]

Or, still again, let the noblest of all pagan moralists speak, Marcus Aurelius, emperor, Stoic saint, a character rightly honored as almost a Christian. Here is paganism at its realistic best, life seen steadily, though without the Christian gospel. It would be a profitable discipline for modern men and women to learn from these honest ancients. For this *is* human life **having no hope, and without God in the world.** All modern secularism, one may safely prophesy, must come to this in the end, when it has squandered its own store of romantic illusions. Is it any wonder that the classics of Greece and Rome remained down to a generation ago the mainstay of the liberal education fostered by the church? They furnished a realistic backdrop for the gospel.

"Bethink thee often," so Marcus Aurelius meditates,

> of the swiftness with which the things that are, or are even now coming to be, are swept past thee: that the very substance of them is but the perpetual motion of water: that there is almost nothing which continueth: of that bottomless depth of time, so close at thy side. Folly! to be lifted up, or sorrowful, or anxious by reason of things like these! Think of infinite matter, and thy portion—how tiny a particle, of it! of infinite time, and thine own brief point there. . . . Consider, one after another, as it were the sepulchral inscriptions of all peoples and times, according to one pattern.—What multitudes, after their utmost striving—a little afterwards! were dissolved again into their dust.[2]

The Bible is an ancient book. Imagination is at times needed to make it come alive. Imaginative reconstruction of history is a great part of the preacher's task. But given this help, the Bible is not ivory tower literature. It throbs with contemporary experience. If we could open eyes and unlock ears, modern men and women might again flock to hear the good news of the

[1] Catullus, "To Lesbia," *The Oxford Book of Latin Verse* (Oxford: Clarendon Press, 1912), pp. 74, 455-56.

[2] Walter Pater, *Marius the Epicurean* (New York: The Macmillan Co., 1926), pp. 143-44.

13 But now, in Christ Jesus, ye who sometime were far off are made nigh by the blood of Christ.

and without God in the world. 13 But now in Christ Jesus you who once were far off have been brought near in the blood of

difficulties and dangers of an unfriendly environment, without the sustaining power of faith in the God who made the world.

13. In time past the Gentiles were **without Christ** (vss. 11-12); **now** they are **in Christ Jesus.** The difference resulting from this change of spiritual status is set forth in the immediately following verses in terms of their admission to communion with God—they now **have access . . . to the Father** (vs. 18). Formerly they **were far off** from him; now they **have been brought near.** This nearness to God has been made possible through the offering of Christ's life in sacrifice—**in the blood of Christ.** As a result of his work as Messiah, there is now one gospel for Jew and Gentile alike—**peace to you who were far off and peace to those who were near** (vs. 17).

All through this passage (vss. 13-18) the writer expounds his theme by making a Christian application of the words of Isa. 57:18-19, which in the LXX run as follows: "I gave them true consolation, peace upon peace, to those that are far off and to those that are near." Vss. 14-18 are a kind of parenthesis, in which he expounds the reconciling work of Christ in terms borrowed from this passage, which he has introduced in a preliminary way in vs. 13, in the anthithesis of **far off** (of the Gentiles) and **near** (of the Jews); then, with vs. 19 he returns to the "political" phraseology of vs. 12, to express the effects of their new condition **in Christ Jesus** in terms of their full standing in the worshiping community.

Far off . . . near: In the Isaiah passage the words have no bearing on differences of race, but refer to Jews of the Dispersion, who may live near Jerusalem or far off. Their application to Jew and Gentile, however, is not an exegetical fancy of the author of Ephesians; it appears to have been a current midrashic interpretation. A midrash on Esth. 3:9 runs: "No nation is near to God save Israel"; another, on Num. 5:6 comments: "To make known that God draws to himself those that are far off, and rejoices over them even as over those that are near"; on the latter Isa. 57:19 is cited in illustration (see Dibelius, *ad loc.*). Possibly the figure of the temple is already in the writer's mind, with the prohibition against the entry of the Gentiles into the inner court (see below).

Have been brought near: The verb is not a perfect, but an aorist; suggesting the final, decisive act of admission to the divine presence—"the ideal redemption . . . once for all accomplished by Christ's victorious Passion" (Westcott, *ad loc.*).

gospel. For to live without Christ is to live today, as in the time of the N.T. Gentiles, **having no hope, and without God in the world.**

13-14. ***Unity in Christ.***—The power of the Christian gospel to unify and to break down **the dividing wall of hostility** between alien groups is amazing. We have lived so long in a period of Christian history when the gospel seemed, first of all, a divisive force that we forget its uniting genius. The Christian church may someday look back upon the recent centuries of sectarian strife as a strange by-pass along its predestined course.

This unifying power of the gospel cannot be ultimately thwarted. Nowhere can this be more clearly seen than on the mission fields. A greater gulf between human beings can hardly be imagined than that between a cultured graduate of Oxford, let us say, and a Solomon Islands head-hunter. Yet the Christian gospel can produce a oneness across this chasm which is deeper than that existing between two Oxford graduates, the one a Christian and the other not. As with individuals, so with groups—and, wonder of wonders, even with churches!

A missionary, shortly after a great ecumenical conference, wrote a book with the title *Then and Now.*[3] Its theme is the parallel between the power of the gospel of N.T. times and its power on the mission field today. The Epistle to the Ephesians is frequently quoted. Our younger Christians of the mission lands can understand the unifying genius of the Christian church better than do the members of the older churches. What can the quarrels of the sects of the sixteenth and seventeenth centuries mean to these new converts out of heathenism? The

[3] John Foster. New York: Harper & Bros., 1942.

14 For he is our peace, who hath made both one, and hath broken down the middle wall of partition *between us;*

Christ. 14 For he is our peace, who has made us both one, and has broken down

In the blood of Christ: Again the article is used—*the* Christ; indicating that the name is used with its full messianic significance. It is because he is the Messiah that his **blood**—i.e., his life offered in sacrifice (cf. 1:7)—is efficacious as the channel of communion with God. Throughout the epistle the messianic office of our Lord is viewed as having universal significance; he is not Messiah for Israel alone (cf. 1:10, 20). So, too, the effects of his death extend beyond the redemption of the people which had been taught to look for him; cf. John 11:51-52, "He prophesied that Jesus should die for the nation, and not for the nation only, but to gather into one the children of God who are scattered abroad."

14. He is our peace: The phrase has a greater fullness of meaning than would be conveyed by saying, "He is the author of our peace." The pronoun is emphatic (αὐτός—*ipse*); and the verb is not a mere copula, but an expression of essential being (cf. on Col. 1:17). The bond of **peace** is not a doctrine or a philosophy or any kind of abstraction, but a Person.

The meaning of Christ as **our peace** is now unfolded in a series of vivid images. **Both**—Jew and Gentile; cf. Gal. 3:28: "There is neither Jew nor Greek . . . ; for you are all one in Christ Jesus." **Broken down the middle wall of partition** is a reference to the wall which divided the inner court of the temple, open only to Jews, from the outer court to which Gentile visitors were admitted; "the sanctuary" included the inner court, which was therefore open only to those who were sanctified by membership in the holy community. Josephus tells us (*Jewish War* V. 5. 2) that there were bilingual inscriptions (Greek and Latin) at regular intervals along this wall, warning Gentiles on pain of death not to enter the inner court. One of these inscriptions (in Greek only) was discovered during excavation on the site of the temple in 1871, and is now in Constantinople. It reads: "No man of another race is to proceed within the partition and enclosing wall about the sanctuary; and anyone arrested there will have himself to blame for the penalty of death which will be imposed as a consequence." The destruction of the temple in A.D. 70 carried with it the destruction of this wall; spiritually, it had already been removed as a barrier to Jewish and Gentile fellowship in religious life by the death of Christ. It is improbable, however, that the figure would have occurred to any Christian writer while the wall itself was still standing; the expression therefore points to a post-Apostolic dating for the epistle.

The RSV construes ἔχθραν (vs. 15) in apposition with μεσότοιχον, and so renders **wall of hostility.** It seems best, however, to follow the KJV in construing ἔχθραν as the

writings of the N.T., on the contrary, leap into living and contemporary significance. As the older and the younger churches meet, they can experience visible affirmation of our texts. They can say to each other, applying to our age words once descriptive of very different and yet not wholly dissimilar times: **Now in Christ Jesus you who once were far off have been brought near in the blood of Christ. For he is our peace, who has made us both one, and has broken down the dividing wall of hostility.**

And if the story of our modern mission fields illustrates our texts, older chapters of church history illustrate them also. We can turn to the so-called Dark Ages, for example. The Roman Empire had crumbled. Barbarians roamed over the continent of Europe. Illiteracy swamped the culture of an entire millennium of civilized life. But there had been planted in the midst of chaos little cells of the kingdom of Christ, as similar cells dot our chaotic world today. The church, with its little "churches," stood fast in the hurricanes of disaster. The church became the foster mother of a new European unity—not perfect, nor without having within it seeds of new disunities, but to the historian still the pattern of what such a word as Christendom can mean. The word Christendom is no longer clearly applicable to the inheritors of the medieval world today. We dream of a world uniting under more secular sanctions. Yet all forms of union short of a new Christendom may fail us.

15 Having abolished in his flesh the enmity, *even* the law of commandments *contained* in ordinances; for to make in himself of twain one new man, *so* making peace;

the dividing wall of hostility, 15 by abolishing in his flesh the law of commandments and ordinances, that he might create in himself one new man in place of the two,

---

object of the following participle καταργήσας, with νόμον in apposition: "nullifying the hostility . . . , i.e., the law with its commandments. . . ."

15. The wall of partition in the temple was merely a token of the whole system of legal observances which constituted a barrier to fellowship between Jew and Gentile. The breaking of the wall, therefore, meant the abolishing of all the external customs and taboos of Judaism, which created and perpetuated a state of **enmity** between Jew and Gentile. This **enmity** was felt on both sides; the practice of circumcision and the food taboos provoked anti-Semitism among Gentiles, and tended to develop a sense of superiority on the part of the Jews, with an accompanying scorn for their Gentile neighbors.

The participle καταργήσας—**having abolished** (KJV); **by abolishing** (RSV)—has rather the sense of "nullifying" or "invalidating," and applies better to **the law** than to **the enmity.** There is a kind of telescoping in the expression—**the enmity** is removed by the nullifying of **the law** which occasioned it. The doctrine that Christ has nullified the law is introduced as something familiar which does not require explanation; this assumes that the readers will have some knowledge of the argument of Galatians and Romans.

On the fundamental thought of this passage see also the illuminating discussion of L. S. Thornton in *The Common Life in the Body of Christ* (Westminster: Dacre Press, n.d.), pp. 10-11.

The drama of death and resurrection may have to repeat itself. The Christian churches, **far off** and **near,** minority fellowships in the nations dotting the globe, may become again the "saving remnants" of world history.

15. ***The Commandments and the Ordinances.*** —We modern Christians can no longer see much meaning for our times in this ancient conflict concerning the Jewish legal system. Large sections of the O.T. have become for us simply obsolete. The freedom from that particular legal enslavement was won for us once for all in the days of the N.T. Ours is, in Luther's phrase, "the liberty of the Christian man," or in the famous words of Paul, "the glorious liberty of the children of God" (Rom. 8:21).

But the problem of the law and of legalism—is not this still with us? Legalism is a recurring phenomenon in the histories of all religions. Men find it so much easier to set up a code of rules, and then to submit to them, than to undergo a rebirth, by way of repentance, into a personal relationship with the Author of all laws. To the Protestant the cult legalism of Roman Catholicism is a rock of offense. To the Catholic, in turn, the legalism of Protestant puritanism looks just as unchristian.

Nor does the discovery, so gloriously announced by Paul, of liberation from the law through faith in Christ, quite settle the matter. Legalism may be recognized as a danger. But legalism is not all there is to the law. The strange dietary rules of the O.T. may be one thing. The Ten Commandments are something else. The N.T., no less than the O.T., is full of the severest of ethical demands. "If thou wilt enter into life, keep the commandments," said Jesus (Matt. 19:17). Paul echoes his words, "Wherefore the law is holy, and the commandment holy, and just, and good" (Rom. 7:12).

The profound problem of the law, as this appears in the N.T. and in later Christian thought, can here receive only brief attention. Few studies can be more recommended to a reader of the Bible than to trace the relationship between the law and the gospel. Wrote Martin Luther:

> It is the opinion of St. Paul that in Christendom both by preachers and Christians a certain difference should be taught and understood between the Law and faith, between the Command and the Gospel. . . . For this is the highest art in Christendom, which we ought to know, and where one does not know this thou canst not be thoroughly sure of the difference between a Christian and a pagan or a Jew. For everything hangs upon this difference.[4]

By way of specific comment on our verse, one observation must suffice. The author rejoices in

[4] *Werke* (WA) XXXVI, 9. Quoted in Emil Brunner, *Man in Revolt* (New York: Charles Scribner's Sons, 1939), p. 516.

16 And that he might reconcile both unto God in one body by the cross, having slain the enmity thereby:

so making peace, **16** and might reconcile us both to God in one body through the cross, thereby bringing the hostility to an end.

In his flesh: Not through his death alone, but by his participation in the life of humanity; cf. Gal. 4:4, "Born of woman, born under the law, to redeem those who were under the law"; Heb. 2:14, "Since therefore the children share in flesh and blood, he himself likewise partook of the same nature." The climax of his life among men, however, was his offering of himself in sacrifice upon the Cross; so that in the following verse the reconciliation of man to God and the destroying of the enmity between man and his brother man can both be said to be effected "through the Cross."

The effect of Christ's work in breaking down barriers is twofold: first, the creation of a new humanity—**one new man**—in which the ancient divisions of race and religion are surmounted; and second (from vs. 16), the reconciliation of the once divided humanity—now no longer mutually hostile fragments, but **one body**—to God. The same gospel of peace (vs. 17) is preached to all alike; and humanity united finds an **access . . . to the Father** (vs. 18) which was not granted to any part of it in isolation from the rest. The atmosphere of hostility in human relationships was itself a barrier to full communion with God; the problem of **making peace** between man and his brother man was inseparable from the same problem as between man and God. When Christ broke down "the middle wall of partition" which barred the Gentile from fellowship with the Jew within the pale of the sanctuary, he also removed the curtain over the Holy of Holies which barred both from the final chamber of access to the divine presence; cf. Heb. 9:1-14; 10:19-20; and for a similar association of ideas in the teaching of Jesus see Matt. 5:23-24.

That he might create . . . one new man . . . , so making peace. This is the first purpose accomplished by the incarnation of our Lord—the creation of a new humanity, not by the victory of one part over another, by the conversion of the Gentile world to

the fact that Christ abolished **in his flesh the law of commandments and ordinances.** But he does not read the Jewish Christians, who still clung to the **ordinances,** out of the church. The law still is "just and good" (Rom. 7:12). Even legalisms can have a permissive and even useful place in Christian life. No Christian grouping has probably yet appeared in Christian history without developing a legal framework for its common life. But Christ remains Lord of his church. **Commandments and ordinances,** if man-made, dare not become fences which destroy fellowship in Christ. Unity in the Spirit comes first. Our epistle defines this as **one new man in place of the two.** Here is a clue to the solution of many a problem of legalism in Christianity today. The puritanical asceticisms of our forefathers, for example, are by no means as outmoded as younger generations often suppose. They were once bulwarks against flood tides of paganism. They may become necessary again in times of threatening worldliness. But to absolutize historically conditioned disciplines can become idolatry of the law. From this the gospel sets us free.

16. *One Body Through the Cross.*—This phrase could be a valued definition of the church. **One body**—yes, all Christians of every name assert that the church is this, or should be this. The word church rarely occurs in Christian prayers or creeds without the adjective "one" attached to it. And how desperately we try at times to make the church one. Christian history is strewn with synods and councils, with ecumenical conferences and commissions on church unions. We try new unifying confessions and new constitutions, and endless adjustments between clashing legal systems. Nor are such pathways toward unity wrong. The church on earth must submit to historical realities.

But in the final act unity must come from above. It can come only through the cross of Christ. We shall not achieve salvation through our merits, not even the merits of achieving unity. It is an awesome realization that whenever Christians of even the most varied name share this conviction of helplessness before the grace of Christ, unity *is* a fact. When we "truly and earnestly repent" us of our sins, do our differences greatly matter? Roman Catholic sinner kneeling before his priest in the confessional, Protestant sinner singing, "Just as I am, without one plea"—is there a great distinction in their state before the cross of Christ? Both

17 And came and preached peace to you which were afar off, and to them that were nigh.

17 And he came and preached peace to you who were far off and peace to those who

Judaism, but by the harmonious union of the warring elements into something altogether new. For Christianity is not merely a historical development within Judaism, an extension or universalizing of Judaism, as the language of the writer sometimes suggests. Judaism is only a part of its inheritance, which includes also the treasures of the Gentile world. The creative power of Christ makes "the two . . . into one new man" (τοὺς δύο . . . εἰς ἕνα καινὸν ἄνθρωπον), **so making peace.** This is indeed a "peace without victory." The Gentiles, who were "alienated from the commonwealth of Israel," are not beaten into submission to the religion of Israel, but are given an equal part in the making of the **new man.** The words really involve an attribution of positive value to non-Jewish cultures, implying that they are capable of contributing in the same sense, if not in the same measure, as Judaism, to the new synthesis in Christ. It will be observed that this conception of the union of the two apparently irreconcilable segments of humanity in the church is integrally related to the writer's interpretation of the end of all history—the divine purpose to "gather together in one all things in Christ" (1:10).

The foundations of the writer's thought are again seen to be laid in Paulinism, but the Pauline ideas are given a fresh shaping. Paul speaks of the work of Christ as "a new creation" (Gal. 6:15; II Cor. 5:17); and of the Christian as having "put on the new nature [lit., "the new man"], which is being renewed in knowledge after the image of its creator" (Col. 3:10); but both these terms are applied to the transformation in the inward life of the individual believer. Here the **new man** which Christ creates is not the Christian, but the church in its corporate personality. Moreover, the self-consciousness of the church as a commonwealth of man has emerged here with a degree of clarity which it never attains in Paul.

Having slain the enmity thereby, i.e., by the Cross. The aorist of the participle expresses coincidence with the action of the main verb; the sacrifice which was the means

---

are simply sinners seeking forgiveness. Both will someday be at one in death. They are at one, this side of the grave, in the dying to self of repentance.

Conviction concerning this *is*-ness of unity among all who confess Christ crucified does not, of course, solve the tangled problems of unity on the plane of ecclesiastical institutionalism. But such conviction could bring Christian charity on the scene. Shared repentance and shared forgiveness through the cross of Christ are the ultimate gifts of God. Other forms of unity must be declared secondary.

17. *The Far Off and the Near.*—In their context these words still describe the Jew-Gentile chasm. Have we a right to tear them out of their context and to apply them to modern conditions? These vivid phrases are surely too valuable to be left in a museum of outgrown history. At least two obvious applications readily come to mind.

The first is to the history of Christian missions, particularly to the missionary story of the nineteenth and twentieth centuries. This story already served to illustrate previous verses, e.g., vs. 13, but can serve again. The outward bulwarks of civilization may be crumbling in our era. But a city of God is meanwhile being built by God himself in the midst of rubble and chaos. It is easy for us to misread the signs of our times. We have lived long in a world which had a geographically localized Christendom. We could speak of Christian nations, Christian "rulers and magistrates." This may soon be a possibility no longer. Our post-Constantine era of Christian history may have come to an end. The church may be once more, as it was in its youth, a scattered people of God, a diffused Christendom. But should diffusion as such lead to discouragement? It could lead to the contrary reaction. At last the missionary march of the gospel has circled the globe. "Colonies of heaven" (Phil. 3:20 Moffatt) are today planted in every continent and island. One wonders what Paul would have said if he could have foreseen the miracle of the cross of Christ raised in lands of which even the philosophers of Athens and Alexandria had never so much as heard. We who have witnessed this **far off** and **near** of the missionary epic of our time could see in this story a fulfillment of our Lord's prophecy: "Blessed are the eyes which

18 For through him we both have access by one Spirit unto the Father.

were near; 18 for through him we both have

of reconciling man to God was at the same time the means of ending the enmity among men. There is a point in ἀποκτείνας (**having slain**) which is missed in the RSV (**bringing . . . to an end**); he who himself was slain is represented as slaying. He was crucified by human hatred; but in his dying, hatred itself was slain; cf. Heb. 2:14, "That through death he might destroy him that had the power of death."

18. To the **one body** (vs. 16) corresponds the **one Spirit.** The unity of Christians in **one body** is not mechanical or external; it proceeds from the participation of all the members in the **one Spirit,** which is the Spirit of Christ.

"The unity of the Body is a living unity created and sustained by the one Spirit. . . . The unity of the Church is in two directions, horizontal and vertical; fellowship with man involves and implies fellowship with God, and both depend upon participation in the gift of the Spirit" (Thornton, *Common Life in the Body of Christ,* p. 94).

Through him . . . in one Spirit to the Father: A striking illustration of the manner in which the doctrine of the Trinity corresponds to the facts of Christian experience in redemption and worship. **Access** (προσαγωγή) is a word of great weight and dignity, suggesting the high privilege of admission to the presence of a glorious monarch. Christ brings us into the throne room of the King of Kings; and causes us to know him in the fullness of his glory as **the Father.**

see what you see! For I tell you that many prophets and kings desired to see what you see, and did not see it, and to hear what you hear, and did not hear it" (Luke 10:24).

A second application of **far off** and **near** can take us to the thought world of psychology. Geographical distance is not all that divides men. Modern technology is rapidly unifying our world geographically. But the chasms resulting from hate and distrust and injustice—these are not subject to technological cures. Two men can be together in the same room and yet as distant from each other in heart and mind as if a universe of space had built a chasm between them. Rational means of building a bridge may be tried. But there are rifts between men which a thousand philosophies cannot heal. Only Christian grace can bring peace. Let repentance and forgiveness, however, come upon the scene, and no chasm between man and man is unbridgeable. The Christian gospel is rightly called "the word of reconciliation" (II Cor. 5:19).

18. ***Unity in the Holy Spirit.***—Few words in the N.T. are more frequent and at the same time more difficult to interpret than the word "spirit." This verse marks the fourth appearance of "spirit" in our epistle. Once it was used (1:13) with the adjective "Holy," and received in our translated version a capital letter. Twice it appeared (1:17 and 2:2) without capitalization and with corresponding neutral meaning. In our particular verse it connotes again clearly the Holy Spirit.

The ambiguities in the use of the word can lead, and indeed have led, to much puzzlement. Yet these ambiguities also can be of help. The phrase Holy Spirit—or simply Spirit when capitalized—refers in the N.T. epistles to a concrete historical event, and even a Person. When thus used, the story of Pentecost with its historical results was in the writer's mind. Whatever may be the meaning of Holy Spirit in the O.T. and in the pre-Pentecost acts of the biblical drama, *after* Pentecost Holy Spirit virtually meant "Christ present in his church." Nomenclature could easily become confused. John may have been mindful of this when he coined a new name for "Holy Spirit in the church," viz., the Comforter (Counselor, in the RSV). The pentecostal event brought the Holy Spirit as Comforter to the church. Before Pentecost, distinctly says John, "the Holy Ghost was not yet given; because that Jesus was not yet glorified" (John 7:39). Our modern notion that the Holy Spirit is merely synonymous with the voice of conscience which speaks in the hearts of all men, or with the innate divine working common to pagan and Christian alike, is not found in the N.T. The church alone had been endowed with the pentecostal gift. The gift was a corporate fact and a corporate possession.

"Spirit" as a corporate fact has many analogies in ordinary human life. A school is possessed of a school spirit. A regiment of soldiers develops an *esprit de corps.* The analogy is a bit startling here—"spirit of the body." Whenever spirit is thus thought of as corporate its unifying power is one of its main character-

19 Now therefore ye are no more strangers and foreigners, but fellow citizens with the saints, and of the household of God;

access in one Spirit to the Father. 19 So then you are no longer strangers and sojourners, but you are fellow citizens with the saints and members of the household of

19-20. In speaking of the church, the writer has employed first of all a *physiological* metaphor, "the body" (1:23). Now, as he returns to the new status of the Gentiles, after the parenthetical passage (vss. 14-18) on the reconciling work of Christ which is the foundation of the change, he employs the language of a *political* analogy, which was suggested to him by the mention above of **the commonwealth of Israel.** The Gentiles are **no longer strangers and sojourners**—in the position neither of foreign visitors with no rights in the community (ξένοι), nor of aliens enjoying temporary and limited rights as residents (πάροικοι)—but **fellow citizens with the saints,** no whit inferior in status to the members of the historic community of God's people. This new citizenship, however, is not conceived as a relation to **the commonwealth of Israel,** but as membership in the family of God—they are οἰκεῖοι ("kinsmen") of God. But the word οἶκος, from which οἰκεῖοι is derived, means primarily "house" in the sense of "dwelling place," and only secondarily "household" or "clan" or "family" (as in "the house of David," or in a modern setting, "the house of Hapsburg"). The word οἰκεῖοι, then, easily gives rise to

istics. Men find "spiritual" unity in corporate life—in a labor union, in a communist cell, in lodge membership, or in any one of the multitudinous groupings of social existence.

In one Spirit, so our author says, Christians are united under God. *This* Spirit is, however, not the mere product of another natural gregariousness. It is the *Holy* Spirit—Christ himself. There are many "spirits" abroad in the world, some of them dangerously deceiving, as if they too were "holy." "Believe not every spirit, but try the spirits whether they are of God" (I John 4:1). Christians find unity in Christ. This means concretely in the church. For the Holy Spirit, thought of as historically imparted to the church at Pentecost, is that "spirit" which gives life to the body of Christ. Holy Spirit and church are inseparable in the N.T.

19-20. ***Fellow Citizens with the Saints.***—These verses contain phrases which have become sacred in the liturgical vocabulary of the Christian church—**fellow citizens with the saints . . . the household of God, . . . the foundation of the apostles and prophets, Jesus Christ himself being the chief cornerstone,** and a "holy temple in the Lord" (vs. 21). The Epistle to the Ephesians can be called a liturgical epistle. It marks a stage in the life of the Christian community when tradition has begun to create a formalized community language. The hymnology of later centuries, down to modern times, has garnered rich treasures from this N.T. document.

Sermon literature also has happily utilized these chapters and verses for textual jewels of phrase. Generally these have been boldly applied to later contemporary scenes. Nor need we condemn such modernizing. As the Gentiles were once grafted into the chosen race, long thought of as limited to the Jews, so children of every race under heaven—**strangers and foreigners**—are today becoming one with the Christians of the older European tradition. The first apostolic band once stood amazed at the enlargement of the covenant so jealously guarded through thousands of years of Hebrew history. Despised Gentiles **fellow citizens with the saints!** If we of the older Christian churches could see jointly gathered with us in our decorous assemblies representatives of the mission churches around the globe, might not the thrill, and perhaps the shock, of the unifying power of Christ amaze us also? Missionary activity has been for many of us a formalized extra in our churchly loyalties. At times it has been a merely sentimental enthusiasm, its realistic products kept at a safe geographical distance. Converts out of heathen barbarism—Fiji Island Christians with strange coiffures, black Pygmy Basutoland Christians, Indian outcaste Christians, not to speak of the rival sectarian Christians in our own neighborhood—all are to be **no more strangers and foreigners.**

Yet as we modernize these textual phrases, their original meaning should not be forgotten. **Fellow citizens with the saints** carries O.T. overtones. The Christian church was new. But it was also old. It was the inheritor of Israel's promises, its peculiar privileges and burdens. "For thou art a holy people unto the LORD thy God, and the LORD hath chosen thee to be a peculiar people unto himself, above all the nations that are upon the earth" (Deut. 14:2). This ancient definition of the people of God

20 And are built upon the foundation of the apostles and prophets, Jesus Christ himself being the chief corner *stone;*

God, 20 built upon the foundation of the apostles and prophets, Christ Jesus himself

---

the use of yet a third metaphor, which might be called *architectural;* so that the church can now be described as **a holy temple** in process of erection, framed **for a dwelling place of God in the Spirit.**

20. In I Cor. 3:10-16, Paul speaks of the church as a temple; but in his use of the imagery the apostles are not the foundation but are builders who help to erect the structure. It is not easy to imagine the man who once declared, "No other foundation can any one lay than that which is laid, which is Jesus Christ" (I Cor. 3:11), now ranking himself and his fellow **apostles and prophets** as the foundation itself. The **prophets,** of course, are the Christian prophets (cf. 4:11; I Cor. 14:1-5, 24 ff.; Acts 11:27 ff.). This bracketing of prophets with apostles has no real parallel in the genuine epistles. It might be observed that as early as Polycarp, the office of prophet in the church has fallen so completely into desuetude that the martyr bishop can use the word only of the O.T. prophets, "The apostles who preached the gospel to us, and the prophets who proclaimed in advance the coming of the Lord" (Polyc. Phil. 6:3); and all the Greek commentators give it that sense in interpreting this passage.

Chief corner stone: Chief is superfluous; it is a legacy of the Vulg. (*summus angularis lapis*). Here, however, the ἀκρογωνιαῖος is not the foundation stone on which the building rests, but the stone placed at the summit of the edifice as its crown and completion. Test. Sol. 22:7 speaks of "a great corner stone [λίθος ἀκρογωνιαῖος] which I willed to set at the head of the corner to complete the temple of God." In this verse, then, the figure represents the temple as already completed from foundation to copestone; in the following the figure changes and the temple is pictured as "growing," as the readers are being **built into it.** Notice the change of tense—**built** (aorist, vs. 20); **are built** (present, vs. 22). For another treatment of the figure, cf. I Pet. 2:4-8.

---

is not altered in the N.T. (cf. Tit. 2:14; I Pet. 2:9). Nor should we soften down too much the sense of privilege which this covenanted relationship with God implied. The words "above all the nations that are upon the earth" meant what they said. The memory of being of God's chosen people sustained the Jew through centuries of persecution. Although transformed by the Cross into a paradoxical pride of slavery to Christ, a sense of privilege ought to be a possession of Christians also. The waning of an awareness of corporate chosen sainthood, of destiny under God unto worlds without end, is ever a grievous loss among Christians. We are "kings and priests: and we shall reign on the earth" (Rev. 5:10), so the author of the closing book of the Bible heartens his persecuted brethren. There may have been less danger then than in some later centuries of misinterpreting such a boast. Those early Christians, like minority Christian flocks in heathen lands, or like remnant churches in days of totalitarian flood tides, had little enough to nurture their worldly pride. They had only the promises of the chosen people of God. Listen to a contemporary's sneer at their humble status: "Workers in wool and leather, laundrymen, and persons of the most uneducated and rustic character, who would not venture to utter a word in the presence of their elders or of their wiser masters." And then he ridicules their pretensions of belonging to a superior religion or race: "They get hold of young people and certain women as ignorant as themselves. They pour out wonderful statements. . . . 'Come with the women and your playmates to the women's apartments, or the leather shop, or the laundry. There you may attain to the perfect life!' With such words they win them over."[5] Yet any missionary can attest that the good news of God's people of promise has not lost its power today.

The household of God. This phrase may deserve separate comment. It is one of the many metaphoric definitions of the church in the N.T. Less frequently employed than the phrase "body of Christ," it yet contains rich significance. A household, a family, is a peculiar sociological entity. It is scarcely a model of egalitarian democracy. Parents and children and servants are not equal in status or function. Rule is not by majority vote. Nor is justice maintained by way

[5] Celsus, in Origen *Against Celsus* III. 55. Quoted in John Foster, *Then and Now,* p. 66; cf. pp. 77-78.

21 In whom all the building fitly framed together groweth unto a holy temple in the Lord:

being the chief cornerstone, 21 in whom the whole structure is joined together and

---

21. The whole structure . . . grows: The words suggest the growth of a living organism. **Joined together:** The same participle is used, with the same main verb, in Col. 2:19, of the articulation of "the whole body . . . knit together through its joints and ligaments" (RSV) ; the passage is clearly laid under contribution here. Christ gives life to the structure and is the principle of its unity.

It is questionable whether πᾶσα οἰκοδομή can mean **the whole structure;** to justify this rendering the article would be necessary. As it stands, the phrase should mean "every structure" (sometimes interpreted in the sense that every local church contributes to the making of the one catholic church) ; or "all building"—"all that is builded." The latter is difficult to express in English, and its significance is not altogether clear. It must mean something wider than the lives of Christian believers—the καὶ ὑμεῖς **(you also)** of vs. 22. Possibly it means "all that God is shaping to his purpose"—a restatement of the movement of all things toward a final unity in Christ (1:10), with the further thought that all God's handiwork is growing harmoniously into a temple. Within this universal movement Christian believers have their appointed place (vs. 22)—**you also are** [being] **built into it.**

---

of bargaining rights. Mother does not strike for an eight-hour day, nor does father monopolize the income he earns. Yet a household could be a model for any society. Justice and law are there, but they are transformed into grace by family oneness. Love fulfills the law. Need, not earned right, determines privilege. A child in a cradle can be the focus of communal attention. The church of Christ, too, is such a paradoxical social fact. It resembles a household more than a politically legalized state. The church's democracy is that of equality before God, but not necessarily equality of status on the purely human social plane. In the early church a slave was brother-in-Christ to his master, but he might remain a slave, though in time the brotherhood of the people of God educated the external social order up to its own pattern. As in a household, the natural hierarchical orderings of society were accepted—father and children, rich and poor, educated and uneducated—but inequalities were robbed of their divisive power. In the long history of man the struggle for equality has been a noble one, yet full of the blood of revolutions and of recurring heartbreak. It has shared in the cruelty of most attempts to realize utopian dreams. Inequalities are facts of nature and of society. Is there, indeed, a solution for the problem of inequality except in **the household of God?**

21-22. *The Church a Temple.*—The word temple has much tradition behind it. It is still familiar to us today. Any sizable city still boasts of a Masonic temple, or a Mormon temple, or Jewish synagogue honored by this ancient name. Christian houses of worship are frequently referred to liturgically as temples. The earliest Christians, themselves continuing Jewish worship practices, nurtured the memory of centuries when they thought of the temple towering over the city of David and symbolizing the religion of their fathers.

A striking change, however, must have occurred in the connotation of the word temple among the Gentile-Christian groups. They possessed no houses of worship. During the space of three hundred years, until the era of Constantine, Christians worshiped in private houses. The word temple became, perforce, a metaphor. "The Most High dwelleth not in temples made with hands" (Acts 7:48). This truth became vivid experience. The Christian congregation itself was now God's temple. He had no other habitation. Not that the Christian gospel demands the *absence* of architectural expression, even though certain groups of Christians in the later history of the church have approached such asceticism. The great era of church building, following upon the centuries of persecution, was, we must assume, not wholly a mistake. The grace of communal worship deserves outward and visible signs. Even the plainest Quaker meetinghouse is still architecture sacramentalized.

Yet the paradox of the church as a people-temple needs recovery in every age. What does the word church, for example, mean to the average man today? Does he not think first of the house of worship on the neighboring street rather than of the congregation which worships in that house? The word church rightly denotes both. But the ranking of connotations should be reversed—people of God first, and then the architectural symbol. "Know ye not that ye are

22 In whom ye also are builded together for a habitation of God through the Spirit.

3 For this cause I Paul, the prisoner of Jesus Christ for you Gentiles,

grows into a holy temple in the Lord; 22 in whom you also are built into it for a dwelling place of God in the Spirit.

3 For this reason I, Paul, a prisoner for Christ Jesus on behalf of you Gentiles

In the Lord: Not only do the life and unity of the work derive from him, but the completed structure is hallowed by his encompassing presence.

22. A dwelling place of God in the Spirit: God "does not dwell in houses made with hands" (Acts 7:48) ; his true habitation is the community of the redeemed.

E. On the Mission and Message of Paul as Apostle to the Gentiles (3:1-13)

In form ch. 3 is a prayer of supplication for the readers, interrupted by a long parenthesis (vss. 2-13) which commends Paul's **insight into the mystery of Christ** (vs. 4) and describes in new and still more exalted terms the cosmic significance of the church as the appointed instrument for revealing the purposes of God to the spirit-beings who rule the higher spheres (vs. 10). The prayer is broken at the end of vs. 2 to admit this parenthesis, and is only resumed in vs. 14, where its opening words (τούτου χάριν, "for this reason") are repeated and made to lead up to the great petition that the readers may be inwardly strengthened, and so attain to the highest spiritual enlightenment and the fullness of life in God (vss. 16-19). The prayer is followed by a doxology (vss. 20-21), which likewise marks the end of the first (doctrinal) main division of the epistle.

3:1. I, Paul: This nominative is left hanging until vs. 14, where at last it finds its verb —"I bow my knees." Codex Bezae (supported by the fourth-century monk Hilary, called Ambrosiaster) simplifies the construction by inserting the verb πρεσβεύω ("I am an ambassador") at the end of the verse.

the temple of God, and that the Spirit of God dwelleth in you?" (I Cor. 3:16.) The church of Christ is first of all a social and not an architectural creation. It is a people-body, a hard, and sometimes harsh and unpleasing thing, human, sinful, made up of men and women whom we may not like. But such a group of Christians is literally **a habitation of God through the Spirit.** It is a **holy temple in the Lord.** We may not enjoy the paradox. Indeed, it is easier to attach our loyalty to an adorned shrine than to the often disillusioning fellowship within that shrine. Beautification of the shrine is fully blessed only when beautification of the "household of God" (vs. 19) has preceded. It is the household and not the shrine which is the body of Christ. The Holy Spirit is a gift to a people and not to a collection of bricks and stones.

The Holy Spirit, given opportunity, can fashion a household of God worthy of the name of temple. We stand in awe before a medieval cathedral. But the glory even of Chartres cannot compare with the wonder of a company of Christians joining in an act of repentance and forgiveness in a shabby cottage parlor. Unredeemed man can build towers of Babel, the pyramids of Egypt, the skyscrapers of New York, and any and all temples made with hands. But only the Holy Spirit can build a Christian church. A relationship founded on forgiveness is supernatural. It is miracle. Two or three gathered together in the name of Christ, knit together by the bond of forgiving love, are an "architectural" wonder before which even the angels of heaven stand in awe.

3:1. *Paul, the Prisoner of Jesus Christ.*—The picture of the apostle Paul as prisoner must have impressed itself deeply upon his contemporaries. The age of large-scale persecutions was yet to come. How were Christians to meet it? Paul's intrepid acceptance of his bonds could foreshadow the courage of the martyrs. He wears his chains as a soldier proudly wears a medal. To be in outward bonds to Caesar was a small thing compared with being **the prisoner of Jesus Christ.**

The symbol of the cross as a sign of victory is familiar to us. The rhetoric and pictorial art of the Christian centuries have made crosses commonplace. Yet the cross, both as event and as symbol, was once "unto the Jews a stumbling-block, and unto the Greeks foolishness" (I Cor. 1:23). If the universe is ruled by a God of justice and right, should not the good man receive a reward, "So that a man shall say, Verily

2 If ye have heard of the dispensation of the grace of God which is given me to you-ward:

—2 assuming that you have heard of the stewardship of God's grace that was given

The next phrase is not satisfactorily rendered in either of our versions. It runs lit., "the prisoner of the Christ [even] Jesus, on behalf of you, the Gentiles." Paul speaks twice of himself as "a prisoner of Christ Jesus" (Philem. 1, 9). This phrase has been adopted here, but the introduction of the two articles is not fortuitous. Paul is not one prisoner among many, but *the* prisoner par excellence—the one known to all the Christian world, who has made even his bonds testify to the gospel. Though he might seem to be helpless in the hands of his Roman custodians, it is "the Christ, Jesus"—Jesus in his capacity as Messiah—who has made him prisoner; in prison he is helping to fulfill the messianic task of bringing unity to a divided humanity. He is therefore called "the prisoner of the Christ . . . on behalf of you, the Gentiles." Again, as in 2:11, we have the extraordinary phrase "you, the Gentiles," which cannot apply to any conceivable body of readers, but conjures up before the imagination an ideal public for the letter, as if Paul were addressing from his prison the entire Gentile world. It is impossible to insist too strongly that this cannot be a real mode of address; it is in itself sufficient to show that the epistolary form is a literary fiction and nothing more. What possible group of Christian congregations could be addressed as "you, the Gentiles"? The omission of the article in translation conceals the significance of the expression.

Again, while Paul elsewhere speaks of his sufferings as having a vicarious character (Col. 1:24, "My sufferings for your sake, . . . for the sake of his body, that is, the church"; cf. II Cor. 1:5-6; 4:12; etc.), he never suggests that they are of benefit peculiarly to "the Gentiles," or destined to promote their unity with the Jews in the church.

2. The section, vss. 2-13, although in form a parenthesis within the prayer of supplication, is in substance one of the most important passages of the entire epistle, both in the soaring flights of its thought and in the corresponding magnificence of its expression. It is also decisive for the question of authorship, if only because it assumes that Paul's letters will be read and reread, not for their help in the solution of occasional problems that have arisen in a particular church, but for the illumination which they throw upon **the mystery of Christ** (vss. 3-4). The passage is really a panegyric upon Paul and his interpretation of the gospel. Paul is depicted as the universal teacher; it has been granted to him **to make all men see** the full scope and intention of the divine plan in creation and redemption; above all, to bring out the overwhelming significance of the

there is a reward for the righteous: verily he is a God that judgeth in the earth" (Ps. 58:11)? The reward might be delayed and hence faith was required. But to see in suffering itself a sign of God's election and grace—this, though hinted at in the O.T. prophecies, was new in the Christian gospel.

"We preach Christ crucified," declares Paul (I Cor. 1:23). And he lived his gospel. The paradox of the Cross as joy became personal experience. Suffering, borne for the sake of Christ, turned out to be "the power of God, and the wisdom of God" (I Cor. 1:24). "I would ye should understand, brethren, that the things which happened unto me have fallen out rather unto the furtherance of the gospel; so that my bonds in Christ are manifest in all the palace, and in all other places; and many of the brethren in the Lord, waxing confident by my bonds, are much more bold to speak the word without fear" (Phil. 1:12-14).

All of us are prisoners of something, if only of our egotistic ambitions, let alone our lusts, or the "prince of this world." The Christian is, like Paul, **the prisoner of Jesus Christ.** Imprisonment and bonds may be his lot. But the reward may be the conversion of Gentiles. Paul speaks of his being a prisoner as full of meaning. It had a design **for you Gentiles.** Meaningless suffering is the fate of the majority of mankind. The gospel of Christ transforms meaninglessness into divine purpose and into good news.

2. ***The Stewardship of God's Grace.***—This fresh translation of a difficult verse has given us a phrase which can be fruitfully utilized. It throws light upon the problem of predestination and election with which our epistle has already wrestled (1:4-12). If divine grace were

3 How that by revelation he made known unto me the mystery; (as I wrote afore in few words;

to me for you, 3 how the mystery was made known to me by revelation, as I have writ-

---

church as the medium through which God reveals his purpose not only to mankind, but to the mighty beings who inhabit the higher regions of the universe (vs. 10). The fundamental thought of the epistle is here given a fresh exposition and carried to new heights.

Assuming that you have heard: The εἴγε-clause is rightly taken as expressing an assumption, not a condition; it is a more modest way of saying: "For you must have heard." The implication is that Paul is addressing readers to whom he is personally unknown; it can, however, be taken for granted that they know something about his mission among the Gentiles. Obviously he could never have written such words to the Christians of Ephesus; but is it not also inconceivable that he could in his own lifetime, or would in any case in writing to strangers, lay claim to such world-wide renown as is here claimed for him? The words are far more readily comprehensible as coming from the pen of an admiring disciple.

The participial phrase τῆς δοθείσης agrees formally with χάριτος (the **grace that was given**), not with οἰκονομίαν **(stewardship)**. In substance, however, it modifies the whole expression, its case being determined by the nearer noun. If we insist on the formal grammar, the words can only mean "how I dealt with the mercy [**grace**] of God that was given me" (Goodspeed). It is not, however, the manner of Paul's administration of his gift that is in question, but the fact of it. Two Pauline phrases are here combined: "the divine office [οἰκονομίαν] which was given to me for you" (Col. 1:25*b*), and "the grace that was given to me" (Gal. 2:9). Here **stewardship** and **grace** are virtually equivalent: **God's grace that was given** to Paul was given for communication to others **(for you)**, given in trust. **Grace** here has the concrete sense—not the favor of God, but that which God out of his grace has bestowed; here, as the sequel shows, it means specifically Paul's knowledge, given **by revelation, of the mystery . . . how the Gentiles are fellow heirs . . . and partakers of the promise in Christ Jesus** (vs. 6).

---

merely privilege, its apparently arbitrary distribution might argue divine injustice. But the reception of grace implies stewardship. To be chosen implies costingness. It can be a burden. Paul, as he accepted his stewardship, might have echoed on occasion the words of Moses: "Wherefore hast thou afflicted thy servant? and wherefore have I not found favor in thy sight, that thou layest the burden of all this people upon me?" (Num. 11:11.)

Every minister of the gospel, as indeed every Christian trying to live up to his vocation, knows how grace brings with it the burden of stewardship. We are all "the prisoners of Christ Jesus" (vs. 1). All men hunger for love, yet when love comes, they rebel against its inevitable demands. A bride and a bridegroom live among the stars during a honeymoon. It is for them a garden of grace and a foretaste of the kingdom of heaven. But how soon they face the problem of the stewardship of grace. And then mere human resources fail. Election to the grace of the marriage bond turns into trial and even judgment, and frequently into the tragedy of grace refused. So it is with the grace of God. The joy of conversion to Christ is beyond compare. Our gospel hymns do not exaggerate when they describe the wonder of salvation. But conversion resembles a honeymoon. Stewardship of grace remains as a burden and a demand. Paul knew himself as one chosen. But he knew also that the choosing had a purpose attached to it. He speaks of it as a stewardship "for" the Gentiles. The key to the word predestination is *destiny*. Every Christian is chosen "for" a purpose. The "for" is as important as the grace of being chosen.

3-4. ***The Gospel as a Mystery Revealed.***—We are familiar in modern thought with the law of cause and effect. It has an almost tyrannical hold over us. We explain effects by analyzing causes. If life has a purpose, we try to find this in the causal chain—in the germ cell or the atom, or in the evolutionary ladder descriptive of life's upward thrust.

The Bible presents a mode of thinking almost the reverse of this. Purpose here comes first, a faith in *pre*-destiny. When purpose is revealed, all falls into place. The N.T. explains the O.T., not the other way around. Heaven explains

4 Whereby, when ye read, ye may understand my knowledge in the mystery of Christ,)

ten briefly. 4 When you read this you can perceive my insight into the mystery of

By revelation: No particular doctrine of the mode of revelation is implied; from the language of 1:17-18, we may conclude that the use of the human intelligence is not precluded, even though the immediate thought is of some direct communication. It is not, however, the natural intelligence rising by its own powers to the height of such a discovery; but the intelligence illuminated by the Spirit of God, and provided with the facts of the gospel story.

As I have written briefly: To what writing of the apostle is the reader referred? Προέγραψα **(I wrote afore)** may be used either of something mentioned previously in the same letter, or as a reference to an earlier letter. Goodspeed argues strongly for the latter sense: "Chrysostom was certainly right in thinking that the reference is to some other writing of Paul's. The language unmistakably points to a *later* reading of an *earlier* writing of Paul's. And what could be more natural, if the collected Pauline letters followed? It is to them that the writer refers the interested reader." (*Meaning of Ephesians,* pp. 42-43.) But what are we then to make of **briefly** (ἐν ὀλίγῳ)? The implication is surely that he is about to speak more fully of something which he has expressed in summary form before. Almost certainly he is referring to the summary statement of the content of **the mystery** which he had given in 1:9-10; and the prefixed προ means "above"—"in keeping with what I stated briefly above."

4. **Whereby, when ye read** is an unusual and difficult phrase. The participle ἀναγινώσκοντες is used absolutely, without an object expressed. The force of the prepositional phrase πρὸς ὅ is obscure—perhaps "in the light of this," or "looking to what I have written." What is it, then, that is to be read? F. J. A. Hort (*Prolegomena to St. Paul's Epistles to the Romans and the Ephesians* [London: Macmillan & Co., 1895], pp. 150-51) recognizes that "there is something unusual and obscure in the language used if . . . the 'reading' [ἀναγινώσκοντες] anticipated for the recipients of the Epistle means reading of the Epistle itself, or of some part of it." He proposes, therefore, to attribute to the verb the semitechnical sense of "reading the holy scriptures" (i.e., the O.T.); as if Paul were inviting them to compare his presentation of Christian truth with the testimony of the O.T. prophets. "The recipients of the Epistle were to perceive St. Paul's understanding in the mystery of Christ not simply by reading his exposition, but by keeping it in mind when they read ancient prophecy, comparing the one with the other."

This is a fantastic interpretation, but it at least shows that Hort was sensible of the existence of a problem. His solution is incompatible with the statement in vs. 5, just below, that this mystery **was not made known to the sons of men in other generations.** Coming from so acute a critic, it reveals the straits to which a defender of the authenticity of the letter is driven when he really perceives the difficulties which confront his hypothesis.

earth; God explains man. The church explains secular social orderings. Hence the importance in the Bible of revelation. Revelation discloses the purpose of God. When this is once seen, the key to the mystery of existence is unlocked. Only by revelation can history find meaning. Without revelation, history is left to chance, or at best to an inexorable law of cause and effect. History becomes Hindu karma, or the meaningless "eternal recurrence" of Greek philosophy.

Our author repeatedly expresses the thrill of the early Christians as they saw the majestic purpose of God in history. Revelation of purpose gave meaning to everything. Life might be tragic, but life was no longer mere "doubtful doom." These Christians resembled lovers who suddenly see their meaningless past transformed into a purposeful future. "We were made for each other," they say. Now at last they discern, as in a flash of supernal light, a pattern in the changes and chances of preceding lonely years. Christians united to Christ in the church can also say, "We were made for one another." The mystery has been revealed. Now "we know that

5 Which in other ages was not made known unto the sons of men, as it is now revealed unto his holy apostles and prophets by the Spirit;

Christ, 5 which was not made known to the sons of men in other generations as it has now been revealed to his holy apostles and

Whether there is a reference to other epistles here or not, the words clearly imply that the writer expects this letter at least to be read as theological literature, for meditation and enlightenment, and that he looks upon it as an introduction to Pauline Christianity. The reference cannot be to *reading aloud in church,* as in Col. 4:16; but to reading for study—private reading, with time to weigh what is read. It is an invitation to read and read again, pondering on the significance of what is written. Moreover, he is sure that as they read, they will be able to **perceive** [Paul's] **insight into the mystery of Christ**—to appreciate his greatness as an expositor of the ultimate significance of the gospel, and to apprehend in increasing measure his fundamental ideas.

5. To the sons of men is a Hebraism; the meaning is simply "to men." It is worth noting that no distinction is made in favor of Israel; no suggestion is made that the Jewish people were granted an anticipation of the universality of the gospel. The essential *newness* of the Christian revelation is stressed in contrast with the ignorance of mankind as a whole **in other generations.**

Revealed to his holy apostles and prophets: In vs. 3, Paul alone is mentioned as the recipient of the revelation; here it is implied that he is representative of the larger group of inspired leaders of the first generation. On the grouping of **apostles and prophets** as a collegiate entity see on 2:20. The comparison with the parallel expression in Col. 1:26 ("hidden for ages and generations but now made manifest to his saints") is instructive. First, it shows that the author of Ephesians interpreted "ages and generations" of *time,* not of *beings* ("angels and men"). More important is the substitution of **holy apostles and prophets** for "saints"—an indication of the tendency in a later generation to think of the apostolic age in terms of its gifted leaders.

all things work together for good to them that love God, to them who are the called according to his purpose. For whom he did foreknow, he also did predestinate to be conformed to the image of his Son" (Rom. 8:28-29).

5-6. ***The Novelty of the Gospel.***—Our text describes this novelty as a mystery **which in other ages was not made known unto the sons of men, as it is now revealed.**

Novelty is always appealing. The daily newspaper receives far more attention than do the classics. For men of N.T. times the gospel had the novelty of the newspaper. Rightly apprehended, the gospel is news in every age.

Just what was novel about it? Men had known about God for many centuries. Nor were they ignorant of the moral law. If ethical instruction, or appeals to a good life, were the gospel, a Socrates might have been a Messiah. In our days, also, if Christianity is presented as merely a summary of moral ideals, or Jesus as merely a super-Socrates, it is hard to see why its gospel should be good news. It is not news to learn that we ought to be good. We know that from conscience and human experience. Nor are we helped much by having such ought-ness presented in a superlative key. Even the figure of the Christ when set before us as ethical model can lead to despair instead of successful performance. The gospel as ought-ness, as an imperative, can be sad news, a *dys-angelion* in place of an *eu-angelion.*

The authentic gospel of Christ is good news because it is first of all not an imperative, but an indicative. It is the news that God loves us even *before* we present ethical achievements. "While we were yet sinners, Christ died for us" (Rom. 5:8). It is the news of justification by grace, not by works. It is the good news of the Cross, of divine forgiveness *before* we have so much as said "thank you." It is the story of a father welcoming a prodigal son even before the son has had opportunity to blurt out a confession of unworthiness. It is good news, not good advice. It begins with an *is* and not an *ought.* It is news in any age to men who see themselves for what they are, sinners hopelessly in debt to a holy God. Hence it is seen as news by publicans but not by Pharisees.

To Pharisees—and most men, both Jews and Gentiles, when touched by moral idealism, begin as Pharisees—such news is shocking. In our verses, the epistle dwells once more, as in previous chapters, on the amazement of the Jew

6 That the Gentiles should be fellow heirs, and of the same body, and partakers of his promise in Christ by the gospel:
7 Whereof I was made a minister, according to the gift of the grace of God given unto me by the effectual working of his power.

prophets by the Spirit; 6 that is, how the Gentiles are fellow heirs, members of the same body, and partakers of the promise in Christ Jesus through the gospel.
7 Of this gospel I was made a minister according to the gift of God's grace which was given me by the working of his power.

By the Spirit: Ἐν πνεύματι has the ambiguous, or rather double, reference to the Spirit of God which communicates and the spirit of man which receives the revelation. Under both aspects **Spirit** is the realm in which revelation takes place, "the Spirit himself bearing witness with our spirit" (Rom. 8:16). "The general idea of the phrase is that it presents the concentration of man's powers in the highest part of his nature by which he holds fellowship with God, so that, when this fellowship is realized, he is himself in the Holy Spirit and the Holy Spirit is in him" (Westcott, *ad loc.*).

6. There is a paronomasia in the Greek (συνκληρονόμα, σύνσωμα, συνμέτοχα) which is hard to reproduce in translation ("co-heirs, companions, and co-partners"—Moffatt), but which emphasizes strongly the *community* of Jew and Gentile in the church. The Gentiles are one with the Jews; in principle, i.e., all mankind is one—one in the inheritance with its "riches of the glory" (1:18), one in the life of the body of Christ, one in participation in the realized promise of the Holy Spirit (1:13). This new fellowship, in which the ancient and bitter divisions of mankind are transcended, is the center of reconciliation about which all elements of the universe will gather to be made one in Christ. It is the key to the execution of God's "plan for the fullness of time, to unite all things in him, things in heaven and things on earth" (1:10); cf. Rom. 8:19-21: "The creation waits with eager longing for the revealing of the sons of God; . . . because the creation itself will be set free from its bondage to decay and obtain the glorious liberty of the children of God." The goal of the entire cosmos will be reached when man attains his spiritual destiny.

7. According to the gift of God's grace . . . by the working of his power: Both these phrases are introduced by κατὰ, and it is better to take them as parallel, attaching both

---

to find Gentiles united with Jews in the church. The amazement becomes intelligible when we recall that the Jew had been taught for centuries that salvation consisted in good works. The Jew lived by keeping the law. Gentiles might enter into relationship with Israel's God, but only *after* they had achieved righteousness under the law. Justification was a reward, not an unearned gift. To see Gentiles, who had never pretended to earn their way into the covenant with God, welcomed as Christians in full standing in the church was unbelievable. It was a mystery. It was news **which in other ages was not made known unto the sons of men.** It is still news—unbelievable news to publicans and harlots, and to any man who knows himself as a sinner. Yet it is the "mystery of Christ" (vs. 4). It is the gospel.

7-8. ***Paul's Ministry.***—Among the wonders of the gospel Paul—or in this epistle a spokesman in his name—counted himself. He frequently turns to autobiography to illustrate the drama of God's grace. Here he calls himself **less than the least of all saints.** In one of the Corinthian letters he describes himself as "the least of the apostles, that am not meet to be called an apostle, because I persecuted the church of God" (I Cor. 15:9). Yet in the same context he does not hesitate to voice the objective comparison with the other apostles, "I labored more abundantly than they all" (I Cor. 15:10).

Why should Paul, rather than one of the other apostles, have become the great Apostle to the Gentiles? His power of presenting **the unsearchable riches of Christ** was no doubt owing, in part at least, to the fact that his conversion had been dramatic. It was as if a leading persecutor of Christians in our century of martyrdoms—a member of Hitler's Gestapo, for example—had been transformed into the church's most aggressive missionary. Paul would have been the last to have desired his violent experience of God's grace to be thought normative. "Shall we continue in sin, that grace may abound? God forbid. How shall we, that are dead to sin, live any longer therein?" (Rom. 6:1-2.) Vocations differ in the church. The greatest saints are not always the greatest teach-

8 Unto me, who am less than the least of all saints, is this grace given, that I should preach among the Gentiles the unsearchable riches of Christ;

9 And to make all *men* see what *is* the fellowship of the mystery, which from the beginning of the world hath been hid in God, who created all things by Jesus Christ:

8 To me, though I am the very least of all the saints, this grace was given, to preach to the Gentiles the unsearchable riches of Christ, 9 and to make all men see what is the plan of the mystery hidden for ages in[d]

[d] Or *by*.

---

to διάκονος. Paul's ministry in the gospel was not self-chosen, but was **the gift of God's grace;** its efficacy was dependent not on his own natural capacities, but on **the working of** [God's] **power.**

8. Less than the least of all saints: 'Ελαχιστότερος is a curious form, the comparative ending being added to a superlative; this is not without parallels in the Greek of the period. The depreciatory description of Paul is perhaps the most serious hurdle which confronts those who deny the authenticity of the epistle. There are, however, some striking expressions of self-depreciation in Paul's own writings to serve as models (I Cor. 15:9: "I am the least of the apostles, unfit to be called an apostle"; II Cor. 12:11).

Grace here is used in a concrete sense, of the mission entrusted to Paul. The thought as developed in this and the following verses is a restatement of Col. 1:25-27.

To preach to the Gentiles the unsearchable riches of [the] **Christ:** The article with Χριστοῦ should be translated; the whole point is that the Messiah who was promised to Israel is now proclaimed to the Gentiles as their Savior also. The **grace** given to Paul is not simply that he should be a foreign missionary, but that he should open the hope of Israel to all mankind.

Unsearchable: The word means lit., "trackless, inexplorable," not in the sense that any part is inaccessible, but that the whole is too vast to be mapped out and measured. It suggests a treasure house of grace, vast beyond all conceiving, so that no matter how far we penetrate there are rooms and corridors opening out in endless vistas, far beyond our capacity of apprehension or of vision. But as our vision widens, the limitless treasures which unfold themselves to us are always the **riches of Christ.** He himself is the treasure house, and "from his fullness have we all received, grace upon grace" (John 1:16). It might be observed that the adjective ἀνεξιχνίαστος (**unsearchable**) is used by Paul in Rom. 11:33, but with the meaning "inscrutable."

9. To make all men see: lit., "to illuminate all men." The infinitive φωτίσαι governs a second object, in zeugma with the first; for this we must give it a slightly

---

ers of the faith. The best instructors in the art of singing, to cite an analogy, are not always the best singers. The pedagogic gift is often best exemplified in those who have had to struggle hardest, and who therefore possess insight into the learner's ignorance and difficulties. In the parable of the prodigal son there is no implication that the elder brother missed the meaning of grace *because* he stayed at home. Yet the younger brother could witness to the power of a father's love in ways denied to other members of the family. God could use Paul, **the least of all saints,** to break through the wall of legalism which still sheltered and thwarted the gospel in its Jewish-Christian form. Even today the most moving evangelists are frequently adult converts to the faith. Every parish minister should make use of the teaching gifts latent in his flock—a Saul turned into a Paul. If the conversion experience has been genuine, self-glorying will be safely absent. Indeed every Christian is in final depth a Saul turned into a Paul. Every truly Christian minister, lay or ordained, will confess, **I was made a minister, according to the gift of the grace of God given unto me by the effectual working of his power.** Nothing can take the place of personal witness to the wonder of the gospel. Evangelism is not a teaching of abstract truths like mathematics. It is personal confession of what has happened to actual men and women. Even autobiographical witnessing can be wholly humble.

9. *The Gospel a Hidden Mystery.*—Why was the **plan of the mystery** of the gospel **hidden for ages in God?** Why could the full drama of salvation not have been revealed to Adam and

10 To the intent that now unto the principalities and powers in heavenly *places*

God who created all things; **10** that through the church the manifold wisdom of God

different rendering—"to cast light upon," or "to bring to light" **the plan of the mystery.** Paul has been presented to the readers first as a missionary (vs. 8) ; now he is commended as the theologian who brings out the profoundest implications of the gospel and enlightens the whole church. History has amply justified this appraisal of his significance; the man who was able to make it in the first place, before the end of the first century, must have possessed exceptional powers of discrimination.

Hidden . . . in God who created all things: Although it has only now been revealed, **the plan of the mystery** is inherent in the creation. "God, as the Creator of all things, includes in the one creative thought all the issues of finite things" (Westcott, *ad loc.*). The reference to God's creative activity is not, then, irrelevant. It is in keeping with the writer's consistent association of creation and redemption, and his emphasis on the cosmic aspect of the saving work of Christ.

For ages: lit., "from the eons." The phrase may be interpreted in the personal sense; cf. I Cor. 2:7-8, "We speak the wisdom of God in a mystery, even the hidden wisdom, . . . which none of the princes of this world knew." "Eons" would then be taken as equivalent to the **principalities and powers** mentioned in vs. 10, the spiritual essences who rule the spheres.

10. The mission of the church, like the work of its exalted head, is not confined to earth; its field is the whole cosmos. It has already been emphasized by the writer that the reunion of a divided humanity in the church is in itself the token and the initiation of

Eve, or to the heathen during the long centuries before Christ, or even to the Jews? These may be naïve questions, but they are natural to our human minds as we look at "the hidden wisdom" of God (I Cor. 2:7) . During a war the high command of an army labels its plans "top secret." They remain hidden until the day of battle. Then the reasons for many of the previous moves and countermarches are revealed. So God once dealt with his great design of redemption. The early church thrilled to the realization that now all was clear—the reason for the law, for the story of Abraham, Isaac, and Jacob, for the hard words of the prophets pronouncing doom upon Israel, for the Exile, and all the rest. Perhaps also for the tortuous history of other nations, blundering in ignorance and sins, yet reaching for the secret of salvation.

No blame attaches to a soldier who is as yet ignorant of his commander's plans. No blame for ignorance as such can fall upon the millions of human souls who have never heard the gospel. Their faithfulness in seeking for God may receive a greater reward than will come to us who possess the revelation and yet fail to respond to its gifts.

The revelation of God is an answer to life's questions. But men have to ask questions before answers can mean anything. Textbooks in arithmetic frequently print in the back of the book answers to the problems which the student is expected to solve. Memorizing the answers, however, will not produce a mathematician. He must first work the problems. God, as the great schoolmaster, had to lead his people through the discipline of the law and the prophets before Christ as the answer could mean anything.

Many a Christian teacher could learn pedagogic wisdom from God's **plan of the mystery.** Merely to memorize creeds or confessions of faith does not make a Christian. This may be like reciting the answers in the back of an arithmetic book. We must learn to see the problems to which the gospel is the answer. "Seek, and ye shall find." We must first seek. We too must repeat the experience of the children of Israel trembling before Mount Sinai, or of the sinful nation in exile crying for redemption. We too must learn to ask with the prophet: "Wherewith shall I come before the LORD, and bow myself before the high God? . . . shall I give my firstborn for my transgression, the fruit of my body for the sin of my soul?" (Mic. 6:6, 7.) Having understood the seeking, we shall understand the finding. Then we too can join in the thrill of the answer to man's questions, seeing for ourselves **what is the plan of the mystery hidden for ages in God.**

10-11. ***The Wonder of the Church.***—As in an earlier passage of the epistle (2:5-7) , the author expresses marvel at the creation of the Christian church. Even angels (cf. I Cor. 4:9; I Pet. 1:12)

might be known by the church the manifold wisdom of God,

might now be made known to the principalities and powers in the heavenly places.

the ultimate union of all things in heaven and on earth in Christ. We have now the further thought that the revelation of God's ultimate purpose in creation is made **through the church . . . to the principalities and powers in the heavenly places.**

These **principalities and powers** are the mighty angels who rule the spheres. They are not, as might be imagined, superior to men in their powers of insight into the counsels of God. On the contrary, the climactic events of the divine plan of redemption—the Incarnation, the Passion, the Resurrection, the Ascension—take place in the realm of mankind (cf. Heb. 2:16) and their significance is revealed first of all to the apostles and to the church, and then **through the church** to whatever other forms of spiritual life are to be found in the other regions of the cosmos. The powerful rulers of the spheres see the church forming, observe how it gathers into one the hostile segments of humanity, and so learn for the first time **the manifold wisdom of God.**

The form in which the thought is cast seems nothing short of fantastic to us. That is because it employs the framework of a science which is long since dead. The science of the Hellenistic world conceived the universe to consist of a series of spheres, solid but transparent, with the earth at the center. The spheres revolved about the earth with a fixed motion; the sun, the moon, and the stars were upon the spheres and moved with them; the "wandering stars," i.e., the planets, alone moved with freedom. This picture of the heavens was as firmly established and as universally accepted as is the Copernican theory in our own times. All educated men, Christian as well as pagan, thought of the universe in terms of this general description.

Against this background of contemporary science there was a widely diffused belief that the spheres, like the earth, were inhabited by sentient beings: the sun, the moon, the planets, and the stars each had its "angel." The planets had a place of particular importance in this scheme of things. Seven planets were known to the ancient world, and the comparative freedom with which they moved in different parts of the firmament led to the belief that they were the sovereign rulers of the spheres—**principalities and powers in the heavenly places.** The number of the planets likewise was taken to indicate the number of the spheres—seven. All these were of course in the heavens; but the highest heaven, the abode of God and the true home of the soul, was above and beyond the spheres.

In a universe so conceived the problem of salvation necessarily presented itself in terms of an ascent of the soul through the spheres. In its passage the soul might be aided or hampered by the angelic rulers; it might find them friendly or hostile. Almost all the religion of the time had in it a large element of astrological doctrine, which taught the

could stand in awe before this mightiest of the mighty acts of God.

If we look at the church merely as an institution, with its checkered history, with its sins and even its wars, such glorification seems extravagant. Yet look within, and the marvel can indeed not be exaggerated. At the heart of the church's life exists a covenant, a "testament" as the familiar title pages of our Bibles clearly tell us. God, as we see him in the drama of the Bible, is a majestic creator. To create heaven and earth was in itself a wonder. It was a further marvel to create man as a rational being —a being who is free to turn into a rebel against his creator. But then to woo such a rebel back to a relationship of love and obedience, to create a people who live mutually in a similar relationship of repentance and forgiveness—this is marvel indeed. Man by himself has had dreams of a covenant of justice as his high goal of social relationship. And here and there even pagan man has achieved a measure of justice. But the covenant upon which the church is founded is as far above a covenant of justice, even if perfectly achieved, as the divine is above the human. Justice cannot create forgiveness. Justice cannot create love. Justice cannot take sinners out of the gutter and turn them into saints. In the eyes of justice, repentance and forgiveness must, as a matter of fact, seem foolishness. To love a sinner *before* he has earned the status of deserving love? To forgive evil, not merely once or twice as a king might on occasion grant an amnesty, but "until

secret of securing passage. Sometimes the angels of the spheres were to be propitiated by sacrifices and prayers; sometimes they were to be overcome with the help of magic.

Christian teachers in general did not deny the reality of these **principalities and powers;** as a rule they are regarded as the enemies of the soul, seeking to retard it on its upward flight to God. They are "the world rulers of this present darkness" and the Christian must contend against them far more than "against flesh and blood" (6:12). But the Christian had no need to resort to magic or to seek means of propitiation, either to secure their aid or to avert their hostility. For Christ had overcome them, and was exalted above them all. When he ascended into heaven and took his seat at the right hand of God, "angels and authorities and powers" were "made subject unto him" (I Pet. 3:22); or in the words of our own writer, God "made him sit at his right hand in the heavenly places, far above all [better "every"] rule and authority and power and dominion, and above every name that is named" (1:20-21).

It is not clear whether Paul thinks of these spirit-beings as themselves capable of redemption or destined to benefit by the revelation which is communicated to them **through the church;** it would seem, however, that they must be included among "all things . . . , things in heaven" (1:10), which are to be gathered into the encompassing unity of Christ's rule. The point here, however, is that they have nothing to contribute to the Christian's higher life, and have certainly no power to frustrate his ascent to God. The danger of attributing to them such power over Christians is clearly shown by the Epistle to the Colossians, which is wholly occupied with the refutation of a doctrine of this kind.

It is not necessary or even possible for us to return to this ancient way of thinking about the spiritual forces of evil that inhabit our universe any more than to think of disease or madness as occasioned by the entrance of demons into our bodies. The obsolete form in which the thought is cast should not, however, blind us to its sublimity. The soaring imagination of our writer here attains the pinnacle of its flight as he sees the church rising triumphantly with Christ into the presence of God, victorious over all that might oppose it, demonstrating in its glorious life **the manifold wisdom of God.** In all the vastness of the universe there is nothing so significant as the spiritual elevation of mankind in Christ; there is no form of spiritual existence which so clearly reveals the mind of God in creation as does man when he has attained the true destiny for which God brought him forth. The world was created for spiritual ends, and these ends are realized in the church.

The manifold wisdom of God is **made known** in the farthest reaches of the universe as these ends come into view. The process of history is in itself bewildering; even **the principalities and powers in the heavenly places** have not been able to perceive the pattern in it, let alone **the sons of men in other generations** (vs. 5). In the church all the strands of history are gathered together and woven into the inheritance of Christ as all the nations bring their treasures to lay them at his feet. The meaning of the long

---

seventy times seven"? This, if not actually immoral, is, humanly speaking, surely impossible. It seemed impossible, and was impossible, even to a Jew under the old covenant of the law. But it is possible in the Christian church. The new relationship—or covenant—between man and man **realized in Christ Jesus our Lord** is precisely a covenant transcending the most extravagant dreams of earthly justice. It takes a God to produce it. Christian love, as Paul describes it in his famous chapter (I Cor. 13), is a divine miracle. We who live in a still Christian world may have become familiar with this miraculous manifestation of the divine in our social life and may not always trace it to its source. We do not realize that the love of sinners was an unheard of marvel in the ancient world. It is a marvel today in heathen lands which know only religions of law and justice.

Can it have been a marvel, as our author suggests, even to **the principalities and powers in the heavenly places?** The thought may strike us as mythological speculation, yet it expresses a deep insight. Man the sinner, a prodigal son forgiven and returned to a father's arms, knows a love of God which even angels may not share.

11 According to the eternal purpose which he purposed in Christ Jesus our Lord:

12 In whom we have boldness and access with confidence by the faith of him.

[11] This was according to the eternal purpose which he has realized in Christ Jesus our Lord, [12] in whom we have boldness and confidence of access through our faith

---

and complex experience of the human race is now revealed, and it is seen that all has contributed in its own measure to the one divine purpose. **Manifold** (πολυποίκιλος) suggests infinite diversity and beauty.

11-12. According to the eternal purpose: lit., "purpose of the ages," i.e., a purpose to which all the periods of history have made their contribution. The plural suggests not only the length, but still more the multiplicity of human experience and of God's dealings with man—the "many and various ways" (Heb. 1:1) in which God worked toward the accomplishment of his purpose. The parts are now seen in the light of the whole. God **has realized** this purpose **in Christ Jesus our Lord, in whom we have boldness. . . .** The writer now links the glorious revelation of the ultimate divine purpose in creation to our human experience of communion with God in Christ. The Christ through whom God brings to pass the fulfillment of the purpose to which all the ages contribute is none other than the Jesus whom Christians own as Lord, and in whom they **have boldness and access with confidence**—freedom to speak to God in prayer, freedom to approach him in love and faith. "The same Lord Who is the stay of our faith and hope is also the crown of the whole development of the world" (Westcott, *ad loc.*). This thought is of the utmost importance for the understanding of Christianity; it reminds us that our faith is not a private matter, nor a mere adornment of life, but is integrally related to the design of the universe itself.

A familiar children's hymn expresses this truth. It speaks of the song which Christians sing,

> A song which even angels
> Can never, never sing;
> They know not Christ as Saviour,
> But worship Him as King.[6]

12. *Coming into Judgment.*—Do we stand in need of the gift of "boldness" as we approach God? The Bible certainly thinks so. Any man who takes the presence of God lightly may not be dealing with the right God. Only through the reconciling blood of Christ, so the N.T. would say, can man come boldly before the throne of the holy Deity. The more seriously we deal with the God of the Bible, the more we shall appreciate the marvel of Christ's work in giving us confidence as we come into judgment. "It is a fearful thing to fall into the hands of the living God," says the Epistle to the Hebrews (10:31). And another N.T. writer pleads for acceptance of the gospel of God's love "that we may have boldness in the day of judgment" (I John 4:17).

Psychiatrists can testify to the enormous resistance of the average man to even a small amount of self-realization. We all shrink from seeing ourselves as we really are. We are frightened of coming into judgment. And psychological self-realization is a mild form of coming into judgment as compared with the full impact upon our guilt feeling of the presence of a holy God. We need courage. We need assurance that the one who sees us as we really are, with all our inner lusts and envyings and pride, will be able to endure the sight. We cannot endure the sight ourselves. Hence escape from self-realization, and even more from the penetrating eyes of the holy Deity, is the normal state of natural man. It is said of Adam and Eve that when God looked for them "in the cool of the day," they "hid themselves from the presence of the LORD God amongst the trees of the garden" (Gen. 3:8). All men thus hide.

The good news of the gospel of Christ is that God's love is equal to the sight of man's sin. He will look and judge, far more penetratingly than any human eye can judge, but will not turn his face away. He forgives all who repent. And repentance may mean precisely courage to face God. God in Christ is the great psychiatrist. He can do what no medical expert can do. He can give repentance and forgiveness. Only in Christ can a sinner receive the gift of courage to come first "to himself" (Luke 15:17), and then boldly to the Father. For in Christ **we have boldness and confidence of access through our faith in him.**

[6] Albert Midlane, "There's a Friend for little children."

13 Wherefore I desire that ye faint not at my tribulations for you, which is your glory.

14 For this cause I bow my knees unto the Father of our Lord Jesus Christ,

in him. 13 So I ask you not to[e] lose heart over what I am suffering for you, which is your glory.

14 For this reason I bow my knees before

[e] Or *I ask that I may not.*

---

13. The connection of this prayer with its context is not evident. Certainly it must be included within the parenthesis which began with vs. 2, for it is not until the following verse that the formula of vs. 1 is resumed; but there has been nothing to prepare us for the thought that the sufferings of the apostle have anything to do with the scope of his mission. There is, of course, an obvious reference back to the claim of vs. 1 that Paul's imprisonment is in some sense vicarious, being endured "for you, the Gentiles." The interpretation is in any case dubious. As neither the object of αἰτοῦμαι nor the subject of ἐνκακεῖν is expressed, the sentence is capable of being understood in different ways, viz., **I ask you not to lose heart** (RSV) ; or "I pray God that you may not lose heart"; or **I ask** [God] **that I may not lose heart** (RSV mg.). The last of these is certainly the natural rendering of the Greek as it stands. But if the grammar appears to impose this interpretation, the whole tenor of the passage seems to render it pointless. On the other hand, there is real significance in a prayer that the readers may not be discouraged by the sufferings of the apostle. The writer would be teaching his readers that the sufferings of the martyrs are the **glory** of the church, not a cause for losing heart but a source of renewed courage. Robinson (*ad loc.*) conjectures that ὑμᾶς ("you") has fallen out by homoeoteleuton after αἰτοῦμαι, noting that in Gal. 4:11 a number of MSS have dropped ὑμᾶς after φοβοῦμαι.

F. Prayer for the Advance of the Readers to Spiritual Fulfillment (3:14-19)

The nominative of vs. 1 **(I Paul)** now at last finds its verb **(I bow my knees)**, from which it is separated by the long parenthesis on the mission and message of the great apostle. Just as the exordium of thanksgiving (1:3-14) was followed by a prayer for the enlightenment of the readers (1:15 ff.), so now the exposition of the gospel of the unity of all creation in Christ is followed by a prayer that the readers may be given strength to comprehend all that is involved in God's great design; and above all that they may make love the foundation of their life, and **know the love of Christ which surpasses knowledge** (vs. 19).

The heart of the prayer really lies in this emphasis on **love** as better than **knowledge.** The writer has been consciously offering a Christian gnosis—a revealed knowledge of God, man, and the world, which he regards as the final result of the Pauline theology.

---

13. ***Christian Courtesy.***—In asking his readers **not to lose heart** because of his own sufferings, Paul gives an example of Christian trust in churchly fellowship. It is natural to beg for sympathy when we are in trouble, even when we know we may count on friendly concern. Here Paul simply takes such sympathy for granted, and aims at lessening his readers' concern. It is an exquisite touch—an example of how Christianity can add grace to natural virtues. Courtesy is not limited to Christians. Yet Christian courtesy can differ in kind from the politeness of the world. It springs from the heart. It is the fruit of true Christian love, which "doth not behave itself unseemly, seeketh not her own, is not easily provoked, thinketh no evil" (I Cor. 13:5).

14-15. ***The Family of God.***—The N.T. often presents the Christian faith as an exclusive religion. Of Christ it can say, "There is none other name under heaven given among men, whereby we must be saved" (Acts 4:12). The impression is at times given that peoples of the earth not beneficiaries of the biblical revelation had been left ignorant of God. Our verse, however, echoes another strain also found in the N.T. The uniqueness of salvation in Christ is not minimized, but God's revelation to all men is also acknowledged. Every people in the world's long history is a family of God, deriving

Undoubtedly he was meeting a demand of the Christian mind of the times. Greeks, when they became Christians, continued to "seek after wisdom" (I Cor. 1:22); they required—and in the last analysis it was a legitimate and necessary requirement—that religion should offer an intelligible explanation of the whole of reality. Paul had discouraged this quest because he feared that the substance of religion might be lost in profitless speculation; yet he hints that he had a full and sufficient answer to the riddle of the universe for those who were ready to receive it—"Howbeit we speak wisdom among them that are perfect: yet not the wisdom of this world . . . but . . . the wisdom of God in a mystery, even the hidden wisdom, which God ordained before the world unto our glory" (I Cor. 2:6-7). He found himself obliged in his Epistle to the Colossians to set forth something of this "wisdom" in order to counter the attractions of a non-Christian or sub-Christian cult which threatened to make inroads in the ranks of immature converts for whom he felt responsible (Col. 2:1-5). The writer of Ephesians now felt the need of expounding more fully and more systematically the fundamental ideas which Paul had thus brought forward; to provide Christianity with a gnosis of its own, which should satisfy the demand for a comprehensive theory of the destiny of man and of the cosmos, and at the same time remain true to the gospel of Christ and to the essential genius of the Christian fellowship of faith and love. Yet he makes it clear that while such **knowledge** is worth while in itself, and is a real enrichment of life, it is not to be compared with love. Men must be **rooted and grounded in love** if they are to **have power to comprehend** the truth in its fullness; and the knowledge most to be desired is that they should **know the love of Christ which surpasses knowledge** (vss. 17-19). "The writer has thus established the plain Pauline system of the love of God as manifested in Jesus as the supreme mystery and the highest Gnosis" (Knox, *St. Paul and Church of the Gentiles,* p. 193).

14. I bow my knees: Nearly all N.T. references to prayer suggest that standing was the usual attitude (e.g., Mark 11:25, "Whenever you stand praying," etc.). The phrase here contributes to the solemnity and stateliness of the prayer, which is cast in the loftiest language throughout. **To the Father:** The addition **of our Lord Jesus Christ** (KJV) rests upon late and inferior MS evidence, and should certainly be rejected. As in 2:18, the title **the Father** is used absolutely, as the name by which God is invoked in prayer; the influence of the Lord's Prayer on Christian usage is manifest. It belongs to the nature of God as Father that he should hear the prayers of his children and grant their requests (Matt. 7:11).

---

its life from the one **Father, from whom every family in heaven and on earth is named.** The verse finds parallels in several other of Paul's sayings. Like a wise evangelist, Paul knew how to make contact with pagan candidates for conversion. To a heathen audience in Lystra he speaks of God, "who in past times suffered all nations to walk in their own ways. Nevertheless he left not himself without witness, in that he did good" (Acts 14:16-17). In similar vein he preaches to the sophisticated philosophers of Athens: "From one forefather he has created every nation of mankind, and made them live all over the face of the earth, fixing their appointed times and the limits of their lands, so that they might search for God, and perhaps grope for him and find him, though he is never far from any of us. For it is through union with him that we live and move and exist" (Acts 17:26-28 Goodspeed).

Passages like these can have great meaning for the modern missionary. To present Christianity as merely one more world religion, differing from its rivals only as being relatively on a higher plane, would be to betray the gospel of Christ. But betrayal is not necessary in order to accord value to God's dealings with alien human families. All have lived by God's grace. Even the most barbarous of cannibal tribes is in a covenant relationship with the God of the Christian faith. All peoples have the divine law "written on their hearts" (Rom. 2:15), all have experienced the saving and preserving power of divine care. The full gospel covenant is for Christians a mystery revealed. For this revelation there is no substitute. But the disclosure of a mystery does not mean that the mystery had not previously existed, or that other peoples had not lived by its grace—in ignorance, yes, but yet in fact. Scientific "revelations" can hint at an analogy. A schoolboy's blunder can say: "Harvey invented the circulation of the blood."

15 Of whom the whole family in heaven
and earth is named,
16 That he would grant you, according
to the riches of his glory, to be strengthened with might by his Spirit in the inner
man;

the Father, 15 from whom every family in
heaven and on earth is named, 16 that according to the riches of his glory he may
grant you to be strengthened with might

---

15. Family (πατριά) means a group such as a clan or tribe, or even a nation, which claims descent from a common ancestor (father). The thought here is not that God is the Father of all, but rather that he is the prototype of all fatherhood. His relation to his children is the pattern of all other social relationships. The fellowship of race or nation or of natural kin in any grouping is but the shadow, under the limited conditions inherent in any form of created existence, of the eternal fellowship of the children of God with the one Father of them all, and with one another. "The name of 'Father' has not gone up from us, but has come to us from above; for it is manifest that God is Father by nature and not only in name" (Severian, *ad loc.*, cited in Greek in Robinson, *ad loc.*). The earthly families which the writer has in mind are the nations, which commonly ascribed their unity to descent from a common ancestor, as the Jews from Judah the son of Jacob, and the Greeks from Hellen the son of Deucalion. Somewhat loosely the term is extended to the angelic hierarchies, as "families" **in heaven;** probably with the thought that a social order of some kind prevails among them, though the idea of a common paternity is lacking. "He Who is the Father of men is also the source of fellowship and unity in all the orders of finite being" (Westcott, *ad loc.*).

16. According to the riches of his glory: The thought, which is reinforced in vs. 20, is that there is no limit to the resources from which God can supply our wants. Our prayers should be based not upon our poverty of attainment, but upon the infinite **riches** of God. Note that in the prayer of 1:17 also God is entreated as "the Father of glory" to grant inward enlightenment. Something of his own glory is imparted to our lives in the reception of his gifts.

Strengthened with might through his Spirit: The prayer of 1:17 ff. was for spiritual enlightenment, leading to knowledge of God's power; here it is for spiritual power,

---

Harvey, of course, invented nothing. He merely discovered what had been there all the time. Revelation in the Bible, too, is revelation of eternal fact—"the Lamb slain from the foundation of the world" (Rev. 13:8), the eternal fatherhood of God, the eternal election of God, "who will have all men to be saved, and to come unto the knowledge of the truth" (I Tim. 2:4).

16-17. *The Holy Spirit.*—A simple reader does not find verses like these easy reading. They seem to belong to that realm of religious mysticism which the plain man leaves to the experts. The concept of the Holy Spirit is at best vague in popular understanding. Even theologians can still be puzzled by it and by such phrases as **strengthened with might through his Spirit.** "With respect to the HOLY SPIRIT, however," so the great Augustine once confessed, "there has not been as yet, on the part of learned and distinguished investigators of the Scriptures, a discussion of the subject full enough or careful enough to make it possible for us to obtain an intelligent conception of . . . His special individuality." [7] And the expression **that Christ may dwell in your hearts** can be equally puzzling. Has not our epistle repeatedly emphasized the fact that Christ is the ascended Lord? How can he now at the same time dwell in our hearts? And are Christ and the Holy Spirit in this context the same? Can these mystical ideas receive practical down-to-earth interpretations?

The plain man reading these verses should, however, not despair. The early Christians were not experts in mysticism either. The clue to their experience of the Spirit and of the continuing presence of Christ they found in the fellowship of the church (see Expos. on 2:18). Christ was indeed exalted Lord. But he was not absent. John, writing at the close of the N.T. period, describes the paradox quite literally and in some detail. Jesus tells his disciples that he must depart, but adds, "It is expedient for you that I go away: for if I go not away, the Comforter will not come unto you" (John

[7] *A Treatise on Faith and the Creed* IX. 19.

granted to ourselves, leading to enlightenment. Notice again the "trinitarian" character of the prayer (cf. 2:18)—**the Father** strengthens us inwardly **through his Spirit** and (vs. 17) sends **Christ** his Son to **dwell in** [our] **hearts.** The mutual relations within the Trinity are not discussed by any N.T. writer; there is no approach to metaphysics; but the foundations of the doctrine are laid in the consistent apprehension of the work of the three Persons in and for mankind.

The inner man is, according to Pauline usage which the writer follows, the highest part of our nature, by which we "delight in the law of God" (Rom. 7:22); it "is renewed day by day . . . while we look not at the things which are seen, but at the things which are not seen" (II Cor. 4:16, 18). It is contrasted with "our outward man," which goes its inevitable way to dissolution. **The inner man,** then, is not equivalent to "the new man, which after God is created in righteousness and true holiness" (4:24), but is that part of our nature as men by which we are able to apprehend eternal things and to acknowledge the goodness of that which is good, even when we lack power to act upon it.

In an earlier part of the epistle the writer has taught that God's power acts upon us, as it were, from without: he raises us up together with Christ when we are dead in sins (2:5-6). This prayer suggests the complementary truth: that **through his Spirit** our inward nature is **strengthened;** God's power is not merely exercised upon us, but is also imparted to us in such wise that we ourselves are made strong.

16:7). The Comforter—or as the RSV calls him, the Counselor—is John's name for the Holy Spirit (John 14:26). A further clue to the experiential fact of the Spirit lies in the very word Comforter, the traditional English translation of the N.T. Greek. Comforter, in the English of the sixteenth century, meant "Strengthener." The very name suggests that Christians, through him, could be **strengthened with might.**

"Where two or three are gathered together in my name, there am I in the midst of them" (Matt. 18:20), said Jesus. This has been the experience of Christians ever since the day of Pentecost. The Holy Spirit was Christ alive in the fellowship. Since he was at the same time ascended Lord, sitting "at the right hand of God," nomenclature had to adjust itself to both facts. Hence the name Holy Spirit, or John's even more clarifying term—Comforter, Strengthener.

As the Christian flocks in the days of the N.T. met in their house-churches, or in days of martyrdom in catacombs and caves, the gift of strength **with might through his Spirit in the inner man** was vivid fact. Corporate uniting always imparts strength. Analogies crowd upon the imagination. Men hunger for belonging to a group, or at most a crowd, or at best a church. They hunger for a corporate faith, for unity with their fellows in a cause, or for a marching in an army under a leader. Weakness then gives way to strength. Listlessness yields to enthusiasm. The word enthusiasm, in fact, carries the literal meaning of "being inspired—inspirited—by a god."

Think what it must have meant to the early Christians to enter a fellowship in which they were inspired by the God of the biblical revelation. A Holy Spirit could "inspirit" their weakness. Sinners could walk upright in the fellowship of repentance and forgiveness. A slave could receive the dignity of being brother-in-Christ to his master. Only in such life of fellowship could Christ as Comforter be found. Yet this fellowship, unlike a demon-driven mob or a mere secular sociality, did not submerge the individual in a tyrannical mass. The individual flowered. To be fully a person implies receiving status and importance. In the Christian church the humblest received rank, the poorest could enjoy the untold wealth of brotherly love. Christ could dwell in the heart—the Christ whom the believer met as Holy Spirit in the church. The presence of Christ when two or three forgiven sinners gather under the cross of Christ is a mystery, but it is also unquestioned fact. And this presence penetrates to the inner man and dwells in the heart. No Christian can receive the gift of the Spirit by himself. There are no Christians rightly so called outside the strengthening presence of Christ in the church. But this does not rob the individual of his dignity or his transcendent status before God. Just the opposite is true. It is precisely in the fellowship of the Holy Spirit that the individual receives the freedom to be fully a person.

But a condition attaches to the presence of Christ in the church—the condition of unity. A broken fellowship loses its strength. God is one God. God the Holy Spirit cannot be split into fragments. Hence the theme of unity will

17 That Christ may dwell in your hearts by faith; that ye, being rooted and grounded in love,

through his Spirit in the inner man, 17 and that Christ may dwell in your hearts through faith; that you, being rooted and

17. That Christ may dwell in your hearts: Parallel in construction to the foregoing **to be strengthened,** a second object of the verb **grant** (δῷ . . . κραταιωθῆναι . . . , κατοικῆσαι), though one would expect a connecting "and." The indwelling of Christ is not "a further definition" of the inward strengthening (so Abbott; similarly Westcott), but a second means of preparing us inwardly for the increase of knowledge and love. God is asked to strengthen us through his Spirit, and to keep us in such communion with Christ that he may be said to **dwell** [κατοικῆσαι, "make permanent abode"] **in** [our] **hearts** as we are said to be "in him." The two are inseparable: if we are to **have power to comprehend** the full scope of God's purpose, we need both the inward strengthening which he imparts **through his Spirit** and the uninterrupted communion with our Lord which is expressed in the thought that he makes his home in our hearts. This abiding presence of Christ is the gift of the Father; on our part it is received, like all God's gifts, **through faith.**

Rooted and grounded in love: The syntax of these two participles is not clear. They do not stand within the ἵνα-clause **(that you . . . may have power);** and if they are attached to it, rather than to what precedes, it cannot be as dependent upon the verb but as *governing* the clause. On the whole, this is the simplest and most natural way to construe; the participles will then be taken as standing irregularly in the nominative, resuming the general thought of the objects of the prayer expressed in the two preceding infinitives. The inward power imparted by the Spirit and the abiding presence of Christ in the heart result in a life **rooted and grounded in love;** and this love gives **power to comprehend . . . the breadth and length. . . .** Goodspeed, however, appears to take the participles as imperatives, as if the form of prayer were suddenly abandoned for exhortation: "Your roots must be deep and your foundations strong, so that you . . . may be strong enough to grasp. . . ." In this rendering the words **in love** are attached no longer to

shortly occupy the attention of our author as he continues his portrayal of Christ in his church.

17-19. ***Faith, Love, Knowledge.***—The author plays with these words in these verses. The culminating phrase is in vs. 19—**to know the love of Christ, which passeth knowledge.**

Christianity, from N.T. times to our own, has been beset by the danger of being interpreted as a system of intellectual truths, in other words, as a science—which is the Latin word for knowledge, as *gnōsis* is the same word in Greek. Paul spent much of his energy as a theologian in combating this error. He summarized his conviction in one swift phrase: "Knowledge [science] puffeth up, but charity edifieth" (I Cor. 8:1). The Christian gospel can be put into words. It is a story. But memorizing a story, or building a philosophical superstructure upon the story, is not the gospel itself.

Paul should not be quoted as if he opposed scientific forms of knowledge as such. The modern warfare between science and religion is not quite what he had in mind, though the N.T. view of faith bears upon our contemporary debate. Paul was concerned, however, with destroying the intellectualist illusion of what Christianity itself really is. Christian knowledge begins with **being rooted and grounded in love** —Christ's love, not ours. Only by this gateway can men enter the realm of faith and have **power to comprehend with all the saints what is the breadth and length and height and depth** of truly Christian "science."

The Christian faith is based upon a personal relationship between God and man. God is a "Thou" and not an "It." To know something as an "it" [8] is one thing. To know a person as a "thou" in a love relationship is very different. Illustrations of this simple distinction lie all about us. A psychiatrist, in so far at least as he is scientist and not also friend, may deal with a patient as an "it." The relationship is impersonal. The Christian minister and the Christian fellowship deal with the same patient as

[8] Contemporary theology has learned much from the remarkable analysis of the contrast between "Thou" and "It" in Martin Buber *Ich und Du* (Leipzig: Insel, 1923). This has been translated as *I and Thou* by Ronald Gregor Smith (Edinburgh: T. & T. Clark, 1937). See also J. H. Oldham's paraphrase of Buber in *Real Life Is Meeting* (London: Society for Promoting Christian Knowledge, 1942).

18 May be able to comprehend with all saints what *is* the breadth, and length, and depth, and height;
19 And to know the love of Christ, which passeth knowledge, that ye might be filled with all the fulness of God.

grounded in love, 18 may have power to comprehend with all the saints what is the breadth and length and height and depth,
19 and to know the love of Christ which surpasses knowledge, that you may be filled with all the fullness of God.

---

the participles but to the preceding infinitive clause—"to let Christ in his love make his home in your hearts." The position of ἐν ἀγάπῃ makes this grammatically possible; the participles are then taken absolutely, as emphasizing in the most general way the depth and stability of the Christian life. But surely some mention is needed of the *soil* in which the life is rooted, of the *character* of its foundations. Goodspeed himself feels the need of this and therefore supplies the adjectives "deep" and "strong," which have no equivalent in Greek. It is preferable, then, to construe **in love** with the participles; cf. Col. 2:7, "rooted and built up in him." Every life has some kind of roots and foundations: the distinctive thing about the Christian life is that it is **rooted and grounded in love.**

18. To comprehend with all the saints: The highest knowledge of God and of his truth is not an individual attainment, nor a privilege reserved for a few. It is given to the community of Christian believers, and it can be appropriated by an individual only as he shares in the life of the community. We are accustomed to think of plans which cannot be carried out except by the co-operative effort of our community; here the thought is that the heights of truth can be scaled only by an effort in which all share. **The breadth and length and height and depth,** i.e., the full scope of the divine purpose; the redemptive activity of God in all its dimensions. An unreal difficulty has been found in the intrusion of a fourth dimension; W. L. Knox has felt obliged to attribute it to a slavish imitation of Paul: "His reason for the insertion was that he found both 'height' and 'depth' in Rom. 8. 39 and did not understand their meaning; after all the Pauline circle was not really interested in astrology" (*St. Paul and Church of the Gentiles,* p. 191). But in fact the writer is not thinking in mathematical terms, nor employing technical language, whether of mathematics or of astrology. He is simply trying to express with rhetorical fullness the magnitude of the vision which opens before Christian faith as it seeks to comprehend the ways of God: there is no region of the universe that is not embraced in his purpose and governed by his love.

19. To know the love of Christ which surpasses knowledge: As we advance to comprehend the full dimensions of the realm of light which God opens before us, we find that it is wholly occupied by love—**the love of Christ.** But here our knowledge must always fall short of its object: **the love of Christ** exceeds our capacity of comprehension.

---

a person—one to be forgiven and loved. An anthropologist living in the midst of an African tribe can become an expert in scientific knowledge of primitive life, yet remain a cold, unloving scholar. A neighboring missionary, with only a hundredth part of the anthropologist's scientific learning but with the love of Christ in his heart, may nevertheless come to comprehend and to "know" his people better than the omniscient scientist. Indeed the contrast between the two forms of knowing is infinite. They belong to different worlds of experience.

A paradox runs through the covenant story of the Bible. God places himself at a great disadvantage as compared with the objects of knowledge which science can explore. He cannot be known as an "It," or as an impersonal being. He must be met as a "Thou." Hence science, if it will, can ignore him. Faith in God is not a compulsory belief, as is a rational truth. If a man once comprehends that two and two equal four, denial of that truth becomes impossible. But the opposite of faith in God is quite possible. The opposite of obedience and trust and love is not only easily possible, but is an hourly temptation even for the saint.

All personal "I-Thou" relationships are different in kind from "I-It" relationships. The "I" is no longer master. No person can be manipulated as can a piece of matter or a rational idea. A personal relationship involves either love or hate, either trust or distrust, either committal or withdrawal. The dimensions of experience in a love relationship become in-

20 Now unto him that is able to do exceeding abundantly above all that we ask or think, according to the power that worketh in us,

20 Now to him who by the power at work within us is able to do far more abundantly than all that we ask or think,

This is, however, only part of the meaning of the phrase. The verb **surpasses** (ὑπερβάλλουσαν) joins the thought that the love of Christ exceeds the scope of our knowledge with the thought that it is *better* than knowledge. Among the Greek churches there was from the first a temptation to exalt knowledge (*gnōsis*) above everything else in religion; Paul's letters show that he found it necessary to warn his converts against this misplaced emphasis (I Cor. 8:1-3). Now the writer of Ephesians has been offering a Christian *gnōsis,* and has encouraged his readers, and prayed for them, that they may have power to make it their own; yet for him also the crowning thing in life is not knowledge but love.

That you may be filled with [lit., "unto"] **all the fullness of God:** This is the culminating petition of the prayer, the final issue of all the gifts which the writer has desired for his readers. Its substance is that their life should advance in all respects from the partial to the complete, that they should attain to the completeness which belongs to God and which God imparts through Christ. In principle this fullness is already granted to Christian believers; in their union with Christ the fullness of God which dwells in him is shared by them (Col. 2:9-10, "For in him dwells the whole fullness of deity bodily, and you have come to fullness of life in him"). Yet the gift has still to be realized in experience through spiritual growth; by a kind of paradox, which applies in nearly all realms of Christian experience, what God gives us in present possession remains a goal to be attained. Under the conditions of this life **the fullness of God** can be appropriated by us only in part; though God withholds nothing, we are able to receive only in the measure of our spiritual capacity. Thus the inward strength imparted through the Spirit, the abiding presence of Christ in our hearts, the rooting and grounding of our lives in love, and the deepening knowledge of the scope of God's design in creation and in redemption are aspects of our progress toward the ultimate goal of our life—that we should **be filled with all the fullness of God.**

G. Doxology (3:20-21)

20-21. The doxology is related both to the prayer and to the noble delineation of the work which God is accomplishing in gathering together in one all things in Christ. Great as is the vision of the cosmic purpose which has been unfolded to us, bold as are our petitions for grace, they still fall short of God's power—he **is able to do far more**

finite. A husband and wife can walk hand in hand through a lifetime and not exhaust the limits of personal knowing. And a love relationship on the human plane is only a foretaste of knowing **the love of Christ.** To know Christ is impossible unless it is **with all the saints.** Christ dwells in his church. To establish relationship with the Christ means relationship with the other members of his body also. Our epistle exhausts spatial imagery in attempting to describe the limitless compass of knowing **the love of Christ,** its **breadth and length and height and depth.**

20-21. ***Progress in Christianity.***—This benediction has been liturgically much honored. It brings fittingly to a close the prayer-hymn of these opening chapters of the epistle.

The modern world has become familiar with the thought of limitless progress in knowledge. We set no bounds to the envisaged forward march of science and technology. Christianity, indeed, looks like a static faith by contrast. The gospel has not changed for nineteen hundred years—"Jesus Christ the same yesterday, and to-day, and for ever" (Heb. 13:8). But the comparison is an illusion. There may indeed be progress in science. But it is a progress eventually toward death—the death, first of all, of the scientist, and then the death of the material world which he has omnisciently explored, to say nothing of the possible death of the scientist's soul in the very midst of his search for knowledge. The progress of science may lead even to man's corporate suicide.

The Christian gospel by contrast offers a vision of progress **throughout all ages, world**

21 Unto him *be* glory in the church by Christ Jesus throughout all ages, world without end. Amen.

4 I therefore, the prisoner of the Lord, beseech you that ye walk worthy of the vocation wherewith ye are called,

21 to him be glory in the church and in Christ Jesus to all generations, for ever and ever. Amen.

4 I therefore, a prisoner for the Lord, beg you to lead a life worthy of the calling

---

abundantly than all that we ask or think. Yet the manner of his working is constant, however much its scope exceeds our imagination and our desires; it is **according to the power that worketh in us** (KJV); this is the proper sense of κατὰ; not **by the power,** as in the RSV. Our experience of his power, as it is brought to bear within us, is a limited but true index to the nature of the power that governs the universe and brings all things to their appointed end.

In the church and in Christ Jesus: This striking and difficult expression undoubtedly renders the true text; **by Christ Jesus** (KJV) represents an inferior, simplified text. The double phrase is to be understood only in the light of the thought that Christ and his church are complementary parts of one organism, as head and body; together they form the sphere in which the glory of God is manifested, and the medium through which the praises of the creation are rendered to the Creator. There seems to be, however, a certain widening of the thought as it moves from **in the church** to **in Christ Jesus**—a suggestion, as it were, that the glorifying of God **in Christ Jesus** is wider than the glory which is given him **in the church.** It is of the nature of Christ that he should glorify the Father, and that the Father should glorify him (cf. John 17:1-4), with a glory which is not limited to this creation.

II. Hortatory (4:1–6:24)

Although cast in the form of a series of prayers and breathing the air of devotional meditation, chs. 1–3 have been given in substance to an exposition of a comprehensive doctrine of God's ultimate purpose in creation and the significance of the church in that purpose. Now, in chs. 4–6, the writer turns to exhortation, seeking to bring out the ethical implications of his doctrine and to urge his readers to give effect to them in their lives. The hortatory strain, however, is not maintained throughout, but new aspects

---

without end. The Christian hope of life with God beyond our historical existence has often been neglected in modern preaching. Visions of new discoveries in physics or biology have thrilled us more than old-fashioned visions of heaven. Hence Christianity felt compelled to rival scientific progress in producing results which even the scientist would have to respect. All well and good. But when the author of our epistle speaks of **him who . . . is able to do far more abundantly than all that we ask or think,** he is not envisaging "treasures upon earth, where moth and rust doth corrupt" (Matt. 6:19). He is describing a realm of experience in which progress can be limitless. Nor is this a world differing from that of material progress merely by extension in time beyond death. It differs in kind. Can there be limits to progress in a love relationship when love is Christian love? It is limitless in time. But it is limitless in depth also. Time and space are irrelevant.

The promise of these verses ought to thrill the Christian people of God. We do not realize a fraction of the adventurous possibilities of life in Christ. Our epistle speaks of **glory in the church** and equates this with glory **in Christ Jesus.** To us could be addressed our Lord's words, "O ye of little faith" (Matt. 6:30). The church is a community of sinners reconciled through forgiveness with the God of the universe. A personal relationship with the forgiving God is the privilege of each member. We can "come boldly unto the throne of grace" (Heb. 4:16). But we can come "boldly" into relationship with one another also. No pagan has ever experienced friendship as has a Christian in a true church. The church is the society of limitless brotherhood in Christ. The glory of life in the church will be the theme of our author in succeeding chapters.

4:1. ***Therefore.***—The word **therefore** is a humble word, a mere adverb and conjunction. But few words in the Bible are more important. The whole difference between Christianity and every other religion which the world has ever known is symbolized in this single word.

of doctrine are introduced and expounded in support of the appeals for Christian conduct.

A. First Exhortation: To Promote the Unity of the Church (4:1-16)

In this first section of his exhortation the writer begins with an appeal to his readers to make their lives conform to the high ends which the church is appointed to serve in relation to God's design of universal unity (vss. 1-6). This plea is supported with a reminder that Christ has endowed all his followers with distinctive spiritual gifts so that each may make his particular contribution to the good of the whole (vss. 7-16).

An alternative way of analyzing this section would be: (*a*) the plea for unity (vss. 1-3); (*b*) the foundations of unity (vss. 4-6); and (*c*) the means given for achieving unity (vss. 7-16).

1. The Need for Consecration (4:1-6)

4:1. Neither **of the Lord** (KJV) nor **for the Lord** (RSV) is a true rendering of ἐν κυρίῳ—"in the Lord." Like the more frequent "in Christ," the phrase expresses the mystical union of the Christian with Christ. Even in prison the bond of fellowship remains unbroken; "in the Lord," the apostle and his readers continue to share in the same stream of life with Christ and are bound together in the one field of spiritual service. By its position in the sentence the phrase may be taken with **prisoner,** as in both our versions, or with the verb, "I beseech you . . . in the Lord"; i.e., "I make my plea on the basis of our common life which we share with Christ."

The calling to which you have been called: The words mean simply "the estate to which you have been called." Here it might be paraphrased "the place which God has appointed for you in his plan of the ages." The repetition of the cognate words, common in Greek, is not idiomatic in English and should not be reproduced in translation; the writer is not laying a double stress on the idea of the divine "call." The relative ἧς (**to which** [RSV]; **wherewith** [KJV]) is the direct object of the verb ἐκλήθητε, standing for the accusative ἥν, which has been attracted into the case of its antecedent κλήσεως.

Our author, with the word **therefore,** turns to exhortation, to Christian ethics. But he did not begin with the moral demands of the Christian life. He has devoted three chapters to a memorial of God's acts, God's drama of salvation. Only after the story of grace has been told —"by grace you have been saved" (2:5)—does he venture to voice the obligations of response. A notable parallel is the similar order in the Epistle to the Romans. Eleven chapters in that epistle are devoted to "theology." At last Paul comes to "I beseech you *therefore,* brethren, by the mercies of God . . ." (Rom. 12:1).

Christianity has no monopoly on ethical teachings or moral ideals. Christian ethics differs radically, however, in the motives which it calls into play. Christian moral goodness is thanksgiving goodness; it is **therefore** goodness. God's saving actions precede God's demands. This is what theologians call "prevenient grace" —divine lovingkindness "going before" the divine call to response in obedience. Even in the O.T. the law comes after an act of saving. The Ten Commandments, like the ethical chapters of the N.T. epistles, are introduced by a "therefore"—implied, though not expressed. No sentence of the Ten Commandments is more important than the introduction "I am the Lord thy God, which have brought thee out of the land of Egypt, out of the house of bondage. [Therefore] thou shalt have no other gods before me" (Exod. 20:2-3).

The doctrine of grace in the Bible is hard for men to take. It assaults human pride at its roots. Men do not want to think of themselves as helpless and in need of salvation *before* they have earned merit and praise. They want salvation as a prize and not as a gift. The Pharisee in the famous parable is morally superior to the publican. He is convinced that "therefore" he deserves God's blessing. Justification by faith—by a mere confession of unworthiness, such as the publican expresses in his cry for mercy—is a shock to the Pharisee's pride.

The temptation to substitute the "therefore" of earned merit for the **therefore** of unearned grace besets all religion. Historic Christianity has yielded to the temptation again and again. The Reformation protest against medieval Catholicism was on this issue. Much of medieval

2 With all lowliness and meekness, with long-suffering, forbearing one another in love;

to which you have been called, 2 with all lowliness and meekness, with patience, for-

Calling (κλῆσις) is used concretely of the estate or function which Christians occupy through the call of God. The background of the word in this sense is Hebraic; it stems from the use of καλέω ("I call") in the LXX to render the Hebrew קרא. God is said to "call" men when he redeems them from bondage (Hos. 11:1; Isa. 43:1; etc.), or when he appoints them to fulfill a given task (Isa. 44:7; 45:3-4; Jer. 1:15; etc.). The thought here is that Christians are **called** to have part in the fulfilling of God's vast design for the universe; in their unity the ultimate unity of all things created is prefigured—and not only prefigured, but given its inception. The life of the Christian, alike in its outward expression and in the zeal which moves it, must correspond to this end which it is meant to serve in relation to the final purpose of God: it must cultivate the qualities which make for harmony among men.

2. These qualities are now explicitly indicated. **Lowliness and meekness** are closely joined together as related virtues. **Lowliness** (the word is frequently rendered "humility") is opposed to pride or haughtiness of spirit; **meekness,** to self-assertion. **Long-suffering** (KJV) is a better rendering of μακροθυμία than **patience** (RSV); the word implies not merely patient endurance in the face of provocation, but a refusal to give up hope for improvement in the disturbed relationship (cf. Rom. 4:3; I Pet. 3:20; and especially II Pet. 3:9, "The Lord . . . is long-suffering to us-ward, not willing that any should perish, but that all should come to repentance"). **Forbearing one another:** The shift from the accusative (in agreement with "you" of vs. 1) to the nominative gives the participle the force of the imperative and brings it into close relationship with the participle ("endeavoring," KJV) which begins vs. 3. **In love:** The climax of the series of virtues, given emphasis by its place at the end, and introducing a positive content into qualities which in themselves consist rather in abnegation. Gentleness, patience, and forbearance may be the result of mere indolence or of indifference; sometimes even of

Christianity had become a religion of earning salvation. Multiplying Masses, asceticism as a higher form of the Christian life, purchasing forgiveness by money payments—these were all attempts to avoid the humiliating confession that we are sinners with no standing before the holiness of God. They prompted Luther's great revolt. Unfortunately post-Reformation Christianity has been beset by the same danger of turning the gospel upside down. Evangelical piety and the observance of puritanical legalisms can become poisoned by pride as can the Romanist's system of merits.

True Christian good works are performed *because* the Christian has been forgiven, not *in order to* secure forgiveness. Christian ethics is grateful penitence. When it is not this, it may preach much moral excellence, but it is not portraying the gospel of the N.T.

2. ***Christian Humility.***—The virtues of humility—**lowliness and meekness, with long-suffering**—must strike the secular mind as examples of that escape from real life which symbolizes Christianity to the worldling. It is "opiate for the people" persuading them to accept social injustice. It is moral pacifism. Meekness is not easy to explain to a schoolboy. He understands such virtues as courage or self-control or fair play—but meekness?

Yet where would the schoolboy be if he had not been the beneficiary of the virtues of Christian humility? For these are the virtues of his parental home. A mother's and a father's love is long-suffering, or it is not love. **Lowliness and meekness** are the virtues, if we dare use the term, of our heavenly Father also. Where would any of us be if the universe dealt with us only on our merits and deserts? The drama of the Cross, on which Christian faith rests, is a story of God himself submitting to **lowliness and meekness with patience.**

The Christian virtue of humility does not mean a lowering of the standards of justice or of right and wrong. It is *not* moral pacifism. Humility may be accompanied by war to the death against evil. The humble Christian is, however, one who directs this warfare first of all against the evil in his own heart. He is a repentant sinner. This state of repentance alters radically his relations with his fellows. A sinner forgiven must be forgiving. This is **meekness.** This is **forbearing one another in love.** How a

3 Endeavoring to keep the unity of the Spirit in the bond of peace.

bearing one another in love, 3 eager to maintain the unity of the Spirit in the bond

pride—"I strove with none, for none was worth my strife" (Walter Savage Landor, "Dying Speech of an Old Philosopher"); in the Christian context it is love for one's brethren which gives rise to all these attitudes. In the context the whole exhortation bears primarily upon relations within the Christian fellowship, not upon Christian behavior toward men in general. There is a tacit recognition here that personal differences and strains are constantly making themselves felt even within the community whose very essence is the transcending of conflicts between man and man. The harmony within the fellowship, which is the harbinger of universal harmony, can be maintained only in the measure that all Christians practice the virtues here mentioned.

3. Our writer has indicated the qualities which must characterize life if it is to be worthy of the function which God has appointed for Christians; he now speaks more particularly of the motive which must govern our relations with our brethren in the faith. As the sublime function allotted to the church is that it should advance God's "plan for the fullness of time, to unite all things in [Christ]" (1:10), it is clear that any impairment of unity among Christians themselves is an impairment of the church's usefulness for the fulfillment of this function. Therefore we must be possessed with the burning desire **to maintain the unity of the Spirit.** The participle σπουδάζοντες—**endeavoring** (KJV); **eager** (RSV)—suggests a blazing zeal (σπουδή) for the cause of unity among Christians, which should be served with no lesser earnestness than that which we devote to the pursuit of truth.

Unity (ἑνότης): The word occurs in the N.T. only here and in vs. 13 ("the unity of the faith and of the knowledge of the Son of God"). Τηρεῖν, **to keep** (KJV) means primarily "to watch"; then "to keep guard over." It conveys the thought of a vigilant care not only to avoid troubling **the unity of the Spirit** ourselves, but also to resolve difficulties and dissensions which threaten from any source. **The unity of the Spirit** is not to be understood as if it meant an inward unity, contrasted with an external unity. No such

Christian may be called upon to act when evil takes on forms which can be conquered only by force is another problem. But it matters greatly whether or not a policeman or a judge or a soldier is at the same time a Christian. Lincoln's Second Inaugural was written in the midst of war by the commander-in-chief of a million soldiers. Yet the Christian virtues of **lowliness and meekness, . . . forbearing one another in love** have rarely found more noble expression. Lincoln was a humble ruler of men. Power conjoined with humility redeems. It participates in the love of God for sinners.

3. ***The Unity of the Church.***—The theme of unity has run through the previous chapters of the epistle. Here, however, it breaks forth into the open.

Let us translate Spirit as "Christ in his church" (see Expos. on 2:18; 3:16). Under the figure of the church as the body of Christ, the pentecostal gift, then, is the Spirit which gives life to that body. Or if we use the metaphor of the family—"the household of God" of 2:19—the Holy Spirit becomes, as it were, the soul of the family of God. And the Holy Spirit is the Comforter promised by Jesus himself. John reports Jesus as saying, "If I depart, I will send him unto you. . . . He shall receive of mine, and shall show it unto you" (John 16:7, 14).

Modern thought has so long accustomed us to think of personality in terms of individualism that it is difficult to recapture the sense of personality when applied to a corporate fact like a people or a family or a church. Contemporary history, however, is re-educating us so that we again take a corporate "spirit" and corporate personality seriously. Think of the demonic "spirit" which ruled Germany in the days of Hitler, or the "spirit" which can seize upon any nation gripped by totalitarian rule. Indeed, we speak quite familiarly of the spirit of America or of modern culture. There are a multitude of spirits. They wield power. They take possession of individuals or of groups. They mold individual personalities. They can transform rational men into beasts, as the Holy Spirit can transform sinners into saints. They are the great creators of unity among men, whether the unity is good or evil. When we read the story of Pentecost, the picture is one of a group, united in a confession of faith, and then empowered by the "Spirit" of the risen Christ, now no longer

4 *There is* one body, and one Spirit, even as ye are called in one hope of your calling;

of peace. 4 There is one body and one Spirit, just as you were called to the one

false antithesis is envisaged. The meaning is "the unity which the Spirit creates," or "the unity which is consequent upon the gift of the Spirit as the common possession of Christians." Naturally this is a true inward unity; but it does not occur to the writer to imagine that it may not find outward expression; and indeed external divisions in the church mark a lack of inward unity. The phrase may also be interpreted, in keeping with a long tradition in the Western church (Ambrosiaster, Anselm, Calvin, and others), of the unity which is created in the sphere of the human spirit. "In the end the two thoughts are coincident; for the unity which rules man's spirit cannot but be a gift of the Spirit of God" (Westcott, *ad loc.*).

In the bond of peace: The phrase is parallel, in the rhetorical structure of the sentence, to **in love** at the end of vs. 2, but its precise force is hard to determine. In Col. 3:14, Paul speaks of love itself as "the bond of perfectness." Clearly this expression is in the writer's mind here; and many good exegetes take **the bond of peace** to be a paraphrase for "love." More frequently, and more simply, εἰρήνης is taken as a genitive of apposition or equivalence—**peace** *is* **the bond** which links us in unity.

4-6. The sevenfold formula relates the unity of the church to the unity of Christ and of God. It has a background in formulas framed by Hellenistic Judaism to link in a similar way the unity of people, temple, and law with the unity of God. The simple formula of the Shema—"Hear, O Israel: the LORD our God, the LORD is one" (Deut. 6:4) —was the point of departure for a number of more elaborate affirmations. In Zech. 14:9, an oracle belonging to the Greek period, it is declared that the unity of God must issue in the unity of religion: "The LORD shall be King over all the earth: in that day shall there be one LORD, and his name one." Josephus, in a great apologia for Judaism, affirms that "there is but one temple of the one God (for the like is ever dear to all), common to all as God is common to all" (*Against Apion* II. 193). Philo holds that "since God

present in his resurrection body, but present nevertheless in a new personal form. The record reads, "They were all filled with the Holy Ghost, and began to speak with other tongues" (Acts 2:4). Christ absent, but also Christ present—this was the paradox of the experience of the early church. The dogma of the Trinity, so puzzling to anyone looking at it from outside the experience of the Christian fellowship, is simply an abstract shorthand symbol for a historical fact—a fact which can be tested over and over again whenever two or three are gathered together in the name of Christ. Whenever this corporate body of Christ appears, the pentecostal gift is repeated. He, the Christ, is "in the midst of them" (Matt. 18:20).

And where Christ is, there is unity. No conviction is more deeply rooted in the O.T. than that of the unity of God. "Hear, O Israel: The LORD our God is one LORD" (Deut. 6:4). Every Jew, every early Christian, recited this awesome creed. All early Christianity simply took it for granted. No N.T. had as yet outdated the O.T. as Holy Scripture.

As modern Christianity faces up to its tragic fact of disunity, it might well return to this basic creed of the people of God of the Bible. Such a return would have momentous consequences. The **unity of the Spirit in the bond of peace** is the O.T. creed in N.T. language.

4-6. ***One . . . One . . . One. . . .***—The word is repeated seven times, each time attached to a noun: **body . . . Spirit . . . hope . . . Lord . . . faith . . . baptism . . . God.** As the Christian churches of the twentieth century wrestle with the problem of unity, these verses can be a charter and a guide. Our century is being called, so it plainly appears, to great unifying adventures.

Does the history of Christianity still testify to an underlying unity in the midst of the sad story of the broken body of Christ? Clearly, yes. All Christians of whatever name still worship the same God. They unite in confessing Jesus as Lord. They join in one hope of salvation, and in the vision of the chorus of unity before the throne of Christ in heaven. The pentecostal gift is still vouchsafed to the two or three gathered together at a Romanist Mass, or a Greek Orthodox Eucharist, or in an unadorned Calvinist meetinghouse, or in the silence of a Quaker assembly.

5 One Lord, one faith, one baptism,
6 One God and Father of all, who *is*
above all, and through all, and in you all.

hope that belongs to your call, 5 one Lord,
one faith, one baptism, 6 one God and
Father of us all, who is above all and

is one, there should be only one temple" (*On Special Laws* I. 67) ; and the Apocalypse of Baruch (tr. Charles), in affirming the claims of Judaism against Christianity, proudly claims

> We are all one celebrated people,
> Who have received one law from One.

More directly, however, the writer is indebted to certain Pauline formulations, especially to Paul's linking of the unity of Christ, as the one Lord of Christian worship, with the unity of God (I Cor. 8:6, "For us there is one God, the Father . . . and one Lord, Jesus Christ . . .") ; there is also a clear dependence on the language of I Cor. 12:12-13. The greater elaboration of the formula and the rhetorical structure are probably due to pagan literary influence; Stoicism especially delighted in the creation of multiple expressions of the unity of all aspects of life, arguing from the unity of the cosmos to the unity of God, of Being, of Law, of Logos, and of Truth (as in a sentence from Marcus Aurelius, cited by Dibelius, *ad loc.*) . In the unstable, fissiparous society of the Roman Empire the quest for a principle of unity was pursued with a truly desperate earnestness on all levels, theoretical and practical alike. Unlike the pagan philosophies, however, the Christian teaching did not proceed from an unsubstantial faith in the unity of the cosmos to an inference of the unity of God; on the contrary, it started from the conviction that God is one, and made all other aspects of unity, present and prospective, to rest upon the foundation of the unity of God. The church is one in body and in spirit and in the goal on which its hope is set because it owes allegiance to one Lord and worships one God. Its unity is of the same order as the unity of Christ and of God; as there cannot be other gods or other lords, so there cannot be other churches.

5. One Lord, one faith, one baptism: Faith is the inward disposition of the heart, **baptism** the outward sign, by which we are joined to the **one Lord.**

6. The play of prepositions is another favorite device of Hellenistic rhetoric. **Above all**—of the transcendence of God; **through all**—of his omnipresence; **in all**—of his

---

It is when we come to the more "bodily" marks of unity—**one body, one baptism,** and concrete confessions of the **one faith**—that disunity raises its ugly head. The church of the N.T. fought for preservation of its unity in this area of Christian experience also. Tablefellowship of Jew and Gentile was the problem then, a problem of **one body** as over against a divided **body.** This is still the problem today.

A clue to an answer to this problem may lie hidden in the concept of "body" itself. The Bible is a very "bodily" book. Spirit divorced from body was unthinkable to the Hebrew mind. But this did not mean idealization of the body. Paul can speak freely of the carnal body warring against the spirit. "Who shall deliver me," he cries, "from the *body* of this death?" (Rom. 7:24.) This dualism can apply to the body of Christ also. Without a body, no Spirit. Biblical writers were accustomed to that view. A purely "spiritual" religion would have seemed to the men and women of the O.T. no religion at all. The chosen people of the old covenant was a very concrete, historical fact. To be a Jew meant circumcision and participation in the bodily ritual acts of the Jewish community. But being a people of God did not mean sinlessness.

The physical always precedes the spiritual. Even God as Creator "formed man of the dust of the ground" (Gen. 2:7) . The church of the N.T. is a body. To be a Christian means baptism and participation in the ritual act of unity, the tablefellowship of the Lord's Supper. Any later Christian view of the church which has attempted to circumvent these bodily expressions of church life has departed from the biblical norm. This has been the temptation of some Protestant communions. Unity in Christ is unity in **one body** and **one baptism.** To get rid of all forms of institutional unity in Christianity is to get rid of unity of the Spirit also.

The opposite error, however, is equally prominent in Christian history. The bodily

7 But unto every one of us is given grace according to the measure of the gift of Christ.

through all and in all. 7 But grace was given to each of us according to the measure

immanence. The pronouns (πᾶσιν, πάντων) may be taken either as masculines or as neuters; the ambiguity is perhaps deliberate. In the context it is God's relationship to his worshipers that is primarily in view; even so, the thought seems to embrace his relation to the entire universe, and we should probably render **Father of all** (KJV) and **in all** (RSV), not inserting the personal pronoun at any point. The fatherhood of God is not limited to his relations with humanity (cf. 3:15).

2. Unity Served, Not Impaired, by Diversities of Gifts (4:7-16)

The nature of the unity of the church is further expounded. It does not consist in uniformity, with the suppression of individual differences, but in the distribution of the needed gifts in such wise that every believer is fitted to make his own peculiar contribution to the welfare of the whole. The various ministries in the church are the agencies which Christ has provided to maintain the effective functioning of the body in all its parts till it attains its destined perfection, the fullness of its corporate life—"till we all come . . . unto a perfect man, unto the measure of the stature of the fulness of Christ" (vs. 13). This is achieved through the healthy growth which takes place in the body "when each part is working properly" (vs. 16), so that each member fulfills the function which belongs to it in the economy of the whole.

7. Unto every one of us: Stress is laid on the place of the individual in relation to the whole: each Christian severally has his particular endowment. Paul has again provided the foundations of the thought (cf. I Cor. 12:4-11); it is remarkable, however, that in Ephesians the gifts of grace are not attributed to the Spirit—they are **the gift of Christ. According to the measure:** The phrase suggests the limitations set upon the gifts for service which are accorded to any one individual; the gifts of each require to be supple-

precedes the spiritual. It is not identical with the spiritual. The temptation of the Catholic tradition has been to forget that the body can war against the spirit. A body can become a corpse. The church is the body of Christ. But the church is not sinless. The church is not, in any proper theological sense, the "extension of the Incarnation." It is not God in the flesh. Nor would the bodily unity of the church be as such proof of unity in the Spirit. The other unities stand in judgment over oneness of body—**one hope, one Lord, one faith, one Spirit.**

We may not like this dualism of body *and* Spirit. The church of the N.T. did not *like* it either. It would have been easy in the days of Paul to have launched denominational Christianity. Paul would have been spared half at least of his lifework. But O.T. monotheism was too deeply rooted in Christian faith for this to happen. If there was **one God and Father of all,** and Christ **one Lord,** there simply could be only one people of God. There could be only **one body and one Spirit.**

This monotheism of the Bible stands in judgment over disunited Christianity today. Are we worshiping one God, or are we worshiping a multitude of Baals? The comparison may sound a bit shocking. Yet it may not be altogether wrong. Yahweh won no easy victory in the drama of the O.T. Christ as **one Lord** of the church will win no easy victory today. Nor is he the Lord merely of the church. He is Lord of secular history also. He is the Lord of culture, of the state, of creation itself. Can we of the twentieth century rediscover this basic monotheism of the Bible? We must then acknowledge and serve the ascended Christ as King, as the one whom the Father has set at his own right hand, and "gave him to be the head over all things to the church" (1:22).

7. *Diversity in Unity.*—The **but** with which the verse opens is important. Unity has often been misinterpreted to mean uniformity. Paul was astonished by the fact of unity in Christ which the new covenant made possible. He was equally astonished by the variety of gifts which flowered in this unifying corporateness of the church. Christianity is full of paradox. It destroys egotism. It is inescapably communal. Yet nowhere has the individual as a person in his own right such freedom. The ancient problem of the individual as against society here finds solution.

8 Wherefore he saith, When he ascended up on high, he led captivity captive, and gave gifts unto men.

9 (Now that he ascended, what is it but that he also descended first into the lower parts of the earth?

of Christ's gift.
8 Therefore it is said,
"When he ascended on high he led a host of captives,
and he gave gifts to men."
9 (In saying, "He ascended," what does it
mean but that he had also descended into

---

mented by the gifts of all, that we may "all attain . . . to the measure of the stature of the fullness of Christ" (vs. 13). **Was given** (ἐδόθη): The aorist is gnomic, expressing a general truth, but fixing attention upon the actual bestowal of the gift rather than upon the continuing provision, which would require the present tense.

8. The scripture here cited (Ps. 68:18) was applied to Moses in a well-established tradition of rabbinical interpretation, and referred to his ascension of Mount Sinai to receive the law (Exod. 19). The form of the citation corresponds neither to the Hebrew of the M.T. nor to the LXX, which runs: "Thou didst ascend on high, thou leddest captivity captive, thou didst receive gifts among men" (ἐν ἀνθρώπῳ—a literal rendering of the Hebrew באדם). The change from the second to the third person is of no significance, but the use of ἔδωκεν (**gave**) in place of ἔλαβες ("received") is the very point of the reference. The writer is not citing carelessly out of a faulty memory, but is following a rabbinical exegesis. The rabbis again and again interpret in the sense that Moses, when he "went up" into the mountain, "received gifts *for* men," i.e., received the Torah, that he might give it to mankind; and one of the Targums actually uses the rendering "gave gifts to men" (Hermann Strack and Paul Billerbeck, *Kommentar zum Neuen Testament aus Talmud und Midrasch, III: Die Briefe des Neuen Testaments* [Munich: C. H. Beck, 1926], p. 596). It is clear from this that our author had been trained in the rabbinical schools; he first adopts a form of the text which was current among them, and then follows it by an arbitrary midrashic interpretation, transferring the interpretation from Moses to Christ. The true sense of the psalm, which celebrates the triumph of God over the enemies of his people, is completely disregarded; the writer is only concerned to affirm that the victory over the hostile spirits, wrongly ascribed to Moses by the Jewish interpreters, has in fact been won by Christ.

9-10. The midrash on ἀνέβη—**he ascended**—has no bearing on the immediate theme; it is introduced as a polemic "aside" to combat the accepted rabbinical interpretation of the psalm by showing that the words apply accurately only to Christ. The argument is that an ascent implies a descent; the ἀνά of ἀνέβη implies the correlative κατά. The psalm, since it affirms that **he ascended,** can apply only to one who **had also descended into the lower parts of the earth,** i.e., to a heavenly Redeemer. Strange and

---

We modern Christians are fond of verses like this and those which shortly follow. Diversity is familiar to us in our denominational church life. We even make it a cloak for disunity itself. We need warnings. Yet in the days when the one Lord shall again have unified his church, the times of the scattered flock may receive redemption through the bringing to the one body diversities of gifts which even a Paul could not have envisaged.

8-10. ***Creeds, and Life After Death.***—What we call "asides" in dramatic dialogue can be very revealing. Our author here (see Exeg.) is reinterpreting an O.T. passage so as to apply it to Christ. The drama of the Incarnation is vivid background for all N.T. thought. Readers are reminded of it even in a parenthesis.

Note the verbs. Here is drama, not abstract doctrine. When the church later wrote its creeds, verbs became central in them also, particularly these same verbs denoting descent and ascent. Christ in the historic creeds is the chief actor in a story of a divine descent. He is the Son of God, "who for us men and for our salvation came *down* from heaven."

The creedal development in the history of Christianity has often caused offense. If a creed is thought of as a series of abstract propositions about God or Christ which a Christian must accept whether he understands them or not, a creed can become a symbol of tyranny over the intellect. Many confessions of faith in Christian history have been used in this way. But the earliest Christian creeds were drama and not

10 He that descended is the same also that ascended up far above all heavens, that he might fill all things.)

the lower parts of the earth? 10 He who
descended is he who also ascended far above all the heavens, that he might fill all

unconvincing as the argument appears to the modern reader, it is typical midrash. Vs. 10, then, states the conclusion: that descent and ascent were both necessary to the work of the Redeemer, **that he might fill all things.** For a similar thought cf. John 3:13, "No one has ascended into heaven but he who descended from heaven, the Son of man." All this language is related to the pattern of the universe as it was conceived by ancient astrology. The descent of the Redeemer is a descent through the spheres; the ascent is his triumphant return through the same spheres, with the overthrow of the opposition offered by their angelic rulers, and the opening of the way into the true home of the soul, the realm of light and glory above the spheres—**he . . . ascended far above all the heavens.** (On the whole subject see Knox, *St. Paul and Church of the Gentiles,* pp. 220-26.)

The psalm was traditionally associated with Pentecost. In later Judaism, though not in the O.T., this festival was celebrated as the day of the giving of the Torah; the rabbinical application of its words to Moses arose naturally enough out of this association. As Christianity had come to associate the festival with the descent of the Holy Spirit (Acts 2), it was equally natural that a Christian interpreter should transfer the application of the Pentecostal psalm to Christ, the giver of the Spirit.

The lower parts of the earth: The phrase cannot mean simply the earth as lower than the heavens. It is certainly a reference—the earliest in Christian literature—to the descent of Christ into Hades. It is introduced here as included in the idea of the universal sovereignty of Christ. There is no suggestion of a preaching of the gospel to the dead, as in I Pet. 3:19; 4:6; but the "harrowing of Hell" would doubtless be in the writer's mind, in view of the words of the psalm which he has just cited, "He led a host of captives" (on the sense of this captivity see on Col. 2:15). Christ is said to **fill all things,** not in the

metaphysics or abstract doctrine. They simply summarized the story which alone explained the new life "in Christ" which Christians knew in experience. The Apostles' Creed, for example, can best be understood as a scenario of the drama of the divine descent. A scenario is a condensation in a kind of verbal shorthand of the chief events of a story. Reciting a creed, accordingly, assures remembrance of the "old, old story of Jesus and his love." No Christianity is conceivable unless it remains based upon the story of a "coming down," a rising again, and a further descent by way of the gift of the Holy Spirit, **that he might fill all things.** Is it any wonder that little creeds appear in all sorts of places in the N.T.? Readers were to be reminded that Christianity is not a mere heightened moral ideal, though it is this; nor a new philosophy, though it could lead to a new philosophy; but good news about a fact in history. God was no longer a mere Idea or a First Principle whom men might seek after or worship at a respectful distance. He was a God who had **descended.** The very notion of a descending God was a shock to both Jew and Greek. Such a God seemed soiled by our mortality and sin. Yet it was this "foolishness" of a descending God which constituted the gospel of power preached by the early church. Nothing could now be thought of as outside the care of the Deity—not mortality, nor sin, nor weakness, nor even the dreaded ghost world beyond death.

The N.T. is reticent about life after death. What has happened, so we still wonder, to the millions of souls on the other side of the veil who have never so much as heard of Christianity? The faith of the N.T. in the kingship of Christ, now **ascended up far above all heavens, that he might fill all things,** was not afraid to penetrate even this mystery. It was inconceivable that the lordship of Christ should know *any* limitations. If the Son of God could descend to our pitiful sin-stained level, he would surely include in his visitation those whom a later N.T. writer describes as "the spirits in prison" (I Pet. 3:19). The clause of the Apostles' Creed, "He descended into hell," describes an event in the descent drama which is not as clearly portrayed in Scripture as we might wish. Yet it is not inconsistent with the rest of the amazing story. It has brought comfort to many a Christian soul, tortured by thoughts of loved ones who in this life had not met the real Christ in the way. The picture of the lordship of Christ in our epistle as "head over all things" (1:22) is a great treasure of Christian faith.

11 And he gave some, apostles; and some, prophets; and some, evangelists; and some, pastors and teachers;

things.) 11 And his gifts were that some should be apostles, some prophets, some

---

sense of pervading all the regions of the universe with his presence, but as bringing all into subjection to himself by his redeeming power.

11. Vss. 9-10, then, are an "aside," justifying the application of the words of the psalm to Christ. The writer now repeats the ἔδωκεν **(gave)** of the citation, and explains that the "gifts" there mentioned are the various ministries—**some, apostles; and some, prophets; and some, evangelists; . . .** It must be observed that while in vs. 7 he has appeared to put forward the truly Pauline conception that spiritual endowments are bestowed upon every Christian to fit him for his own particular function in the organic life of the church, he now defines the gifts of Christ as the ministers whom he gives to the church to foster its corporate life. Ἔδωκεν here has its normal Greek sense (cf. on 1:22) of **gave.** As God gave Christ to the church to be its head, so Christ has given ministers to the church to serve it in various functions.

It is clear that the writer begins his classification of the ministries which are exercised in the church with I Cor. 12:28 in mind: "God has appointed in the church first apostles, second prophets, third teachers, then workers of miracles, then healers, helpers, administrators, speakers in various kinds of tongues." The changes which he makes are of the greatest significance, involving a transformation in the whole conception of the ministry. In detail we observe that while **apostles** and **prophets** still hold the first two places, a new category, entitled **evangelists,** has now been accorded the third place. The function of this group is not specifically indicated, but the title suggests that they were missionaries to the unconverted. The previous usage of the writer shows that he thinks of the apostles and prophets as a closed corporation of unique significance—the honored leaders of the first generation who constitute "the foundation" of the church (2:20) and were the

---

11-12. *The Christian Ministry.*—We are familiar with the words ministry and minister in church life. They have come to designate a professional class within the Christian community. Nor was such a ministerial caste absent in N.T. days. The church, as early as the day of Pentecost, had within it the apostolate, a group set apart for specialized functions. The church, both Catholic and Protestant, has had an order of the ministry ever since. To define the meaning and functions of this order, especially after it became solidly institutionalized, has caused the church much agony. Divisiveness in Christendom has been symbolized by nothing so clearly as by differences in the theory of the ministry.

Some at least of the sad chapters in Christian history, however, might have been avoided if the original meaning of ministry had been kept in mind. The beautiful phrase of our very passage, **the work of ministry,** has deep significance. A literal translation of the Greek word for ministry is "deaconing," and corresponds to our English word "to serve." "Deaconing" is the normal N.T. word for serving. Jesus once said, "Whosoever will be great among you, shall be your minister [lit., "deacon"]: and whosoever of you will be the chiefest, shall be servant [lit., "slave"] of all" (Mark 10:43-44). It is surely a paradox that the humblest of the professional ministerial orders in Christian history, that of deacon, should carry the functional name which ought to characterize all Christian service. If the later story of the ministry in the church had always been one of true "deaconing," or true "slavery," most of the revolts against ecclesiastical tyranny would never have happened.

We are familiar in our day with the "gospel of service." We use the phrase all too freely, and even commercialize it. Think of what the words "service station" mean as we see them on our highways. The concept of service can be degraded by ignoble motive. A satirist once coined the slogan "It pays to serve." Indeed, it does. "The children of this world are in their generation wiser than the children of light" (Luke 16:8). Despite all vulgarizations, however, mutual service remains as one of the chief marks of Christian community life. The world of commerce has merely been a beneficiary of Christian grace.

Fully Christian **work of ministry,** however, seeks no reward except being accepted by God as a "sacrifice of praise and thanksgiving." It is motivated by gratitude. Christian morality

12 For the perfecting of the saints, for the work of the ministry, for the edifying of the body of Christ:

evangelists, some pastors and teachers, 12 for the equipment of the saints, for the work of ministry, for building up the body of

original recipients of the revelation (3:5); by their very nature these offices could not belong to the permanent structure of the church. We are justified in inferring that the **evangelists,** on the contrary, are the missionaries of his own generation, who do not serve any one congregation or area, but move from place to place as they find openings for the proclamation of the gospel. The **pastors and teachers** are mentioned in a way that sets them apart from the former three categories; the form of the phrase might be taken to mean that these are dual titles for a single office—reflecting the twofold task of the settled ministry, with its duties of pastoral care and instruction; or it may simply mark them out as representatives of two different offices, linked together as sharing the care of established congregations, in distinction from the three former classes, who bring new congregations into being. Ποιμήν (pastor, shepherd) as the title of an office occurs only here in the N.T.; but its use is implied in the title ἀρχιποίμην ("chief Shepherd"—I Pet. 5:4) given to Christ, and in the clearly technical use of the cognate verb ποιμαίνω (Acts 20:28; John 21:16).

More important than such departures from Paul in the usage of particular titles is the fact that Ephesians mentions only stated offices; the nonofficial functions which Paul suggests rather than enumerates—"miracles, . . . gifts of healings, helps, governments, diversities of tongues" (I Cor. 12:28)—are not given any place among the ministries here. Evidently the church has gone a long way toward the development of a ministry of established office in place of the ministry of function which alone was known to Paul. It is significant, however, that the writer of this epistle, in complete accord with Paul, looks upon all the ministries as *given* to the church.

The fact that neither bishops nor elders are mentioned is an indication that we are still some distance removed from the developed organization that we find around the turn of the first century (Clement of Rome, Ignatius).

12-13. The purpose for which these ministries are given is now defined; it is noteworthy that the definition bears exclusively upon the *internal* economy of the church—no mention is made of the mission to the world outside, which Paul certainly conceived to be his primary duty (Rom. 15:20; I Cor. 9:19-22; etc.). The words would apply most fitly to the work of pastors and teachers, and are perhaps meant to be so taken. The three phrases of vs. 12 are not parallel, as the thrice-repeated **for** of our versions would suggest; in Greek there is a change of preposition (πρός, εἰς, εἰς). It seems best to take the first two phrases together—"in order to fit his people for the work of service" (Goodspeed).

could be generally defined as "grateful penitence." It differs in kind from all merit morality. That is why even the highest expressions of secular ethical idealism cannot be equated with Christian love. Paganism produced many noble ethical philosophies. But examine the motivations to which they appeal and a great gulf still separates their power from that which lies behind the Christian gospel of service. Non-Christian moral ideals can at best call into play only human strength. They beckon to the pursuit of virtue and even to the achievement of the divine in mortal garments. Non-Christian virtues are very conscious virtues, the result of strenuous striving. God will deal with them in his own way. But the true Christian life is the resultant not of striving, though striving is not absent, but of response to an undeserved gift. At its highest it is not even conscious of being good. "When did we see thee hungry and feed thee, or thirsty and give thee drink?" (Matt. 25:37.) A humility which results from repentance, for example, will be conscious of repentance, not of its accompanying humility. A true lover buying a ring for a loved one is not conscious of the virtue of sacrifice. He is conscious only of the unworthiness of the gift.

And a true church is a company of true lovers —lovers of God in Christ. Response to the gift of forgiveness produces grateful penitence. A new social order, undreamed of in pagan philosophies, is born. Ministry, service, becomes the

13 Till we all come in the unity of the faith, and of the knowledge of the Son of God, unto a perfect man, unto the measure of the stature of the fulness of Christ:

Christ, 13 until we all attain to the unity of the faith and of the knowledge of the Son of God, to mature manhood, to the measure of the stature of the fullness of

The third phrase—**for building up the body of Christ**—is then to be taken as the ultimate end for which the gifts of Christ are bestowed; to this end "the preparation of the saints for a work of service" is the appointed means.

Vss. 13-16 are an exposition of this last phrase; they set forth under a succession of figures all that is involved in **building up the body of Christ.**

13. Until: The conjunction here has virtually a final force, but conveys the additional thought (not given by ἵνα) that time is needed for the attainment of the end. **We all**—the use of the article (οἱ πάντες) makes the expression *collective:* not "all of us, individually" but "all of us, in the fellowship of our common life." The thinking is corporate; the fullness of spiritual achievement is not to be attained by the individual in isolation, just as one part of the body cannot reach its mature development except as the whole body continues its healthy growth.

Note that **the unity** is here presented as the goal toward which we strive, whereas in vs. 3 it is a possession to be guarded. The two aspects are complementary. That which is given us by God must be made our own by progressive appropriation (cf. the remarks of L. S. Thornton on the "double polarity" of Christian teaching [*Common Life in the Body of Christ,* pp. 57-65, and *passim*]). What was before described objectively as **the unity of the Spirit,** in terms of its source and sphere, is now described subjectively, in terms of its content of thought and experience—**of the faith and of the knowledge of the Son of God.** The title **Son of God,** rarely used by Paul, is employed here to remind us that on the highest plane both **faith** and **knowledge** apprehend Christ in his eternal relationship with the Father.

To mature manhood: The corporate nature of the thought must still be kept in mind; the reference is to the maturity of the church, not of its members as individuals.

bond of fellowship. Ministry itself is a gift and not a work looking toward a reward. It is cumulative, **building up the body of Christ.** A true church is today as much a miracle as was the fellowship of Pentecost.

13. ***Unity of the Faith.***—This phrase has often been misinterpreted in Christian preaching and teaching. It is tempting to make it mean the exclusiveness of orthodoxy, a unity of a fractional group of Christians subscribing to a common formulation of a theological confession.

We need not belittle orthodoxy. It means "right belief." Christian faith requires right belief, and even right, not wrong, intellectual formulations of the gospel. Heresy was and is, as our epistle will shortly tell us (vs. 14), a constant danger to the church.

Unity of the faith clearly means here, however, the unity demanded *by the faith* in Christ. Faith itself is not, first of all, an intellectual assent to an intellectual system. Christianity is not mathematics or a system of philosophy like Platonism. It is not mental gymnastics. Faith, as the Bible understands the concept, is a personal act. It has been well defined as "trust in obedience." The unity of the people of God must consist above all in common trust, common obedience, common listening to the words of the Lord. The specific commands of the Lord, like his gifts, may vary endlessly as they come to Christian individuals or groups. The unity can consist in the shared listening and in the shared trust.

As with faith, so with **knowledge of the Son of God.** This, too, should be thought of in personalized terms. Where can Christ be personally known? Not in systems or formulas, but in the thousands of fellowships where Christ is personally present in the Spirit. **Knowledge of the Son of God** comes in large part through unity itself, through the common life in the body of Christ. The corporate setting of this whole passage is important. Modern individualistic pietism may not find such social knowledge of Christ altogether congenial.

Individualistic interpretations may obscure also the full meaning of the further phrases in this verse, **mature manhood, . . . the stature of the fullness of Christ.** Later passages in our epistle will be addressed to the individual ("every one" of vs. 25 ff.). Here the subject is "we." The apostolic writer is thinking of the

14 That we *henceforth* be no more children, tossed to and fro, and carried about with every wind of doctrine, by the sleight of men, *and* cunning craftiness, whereby they lie in wait to deceive;

Christ; 14 so that we may no longer be children, tossed to and fro and carried about with every wind of doctrine, by the cunning of men, by their craftiness in de-

In relation to contemporary movements of Christian unity, it may be observed that our writer equates the attainment of **the unity of the faith** with the attainment of **mature manhood,** and this again with attainment **to the measure of the stature of the fullness of Christ.** It is a mark of incompleteness, of spiritual immaturity, that we are still disunited; and the remedy is by no means to be found in a *reduced* Christianity, in a lowest common denominator of agreement; but in advance to the higher levels where the fullness of truth will overcome all our deficiencies. "For our knowledge is imperfect . . . ; but when the perfect comes, the imperfect will pass away" (I Cor. 13:9-10).

14. The faults and weaknesses which impair Christian unity are here set forth as those of immaturity and instability. **Children**—not, as in Paul, typifying incapacity to receive the deeper teaching (I Cor. 3:1-3; cf. Heb. 5:13), but as symbolizing an unsettled, flighty temperament—the converse of **mature manhood.** The sudden shift to the metaphor of a ship which bobs up and down on the waves and veers with every gust of wind is somewhat disconcerting, and suggests that the metaphor of childishness is not really vivid to the writer. The erratic course of the ship does not suggest so much the rivalry of sects as the tendency to seize eagerly upon every new notion that is advanced in any quarter. It is an eccentric individualism, rather than sectarianism, that is attacked. **Sleight:** Another abrupt change of metaphor, this time to dice playing. It is generally taken to mean the cheating which commonly accompanies gambling; but it is perhaps better to understand it of the fickleness of the dice. **Sleight of men** would not, then, involve a reference to trickery attributed to teachers of heresy, but means rather "the fickleness of men." The Christian who is easily swayed into accepting novel doctrines is falling back into the fickleness of mind of the non-Christian

church. Every Christian should, of course, be an exemplar of Christ. But can he attain to this high vocation except as he shares in the **fullness of Christ** in the fellowship? The fellowship has powers of Holy Spirit which transcend any individual gifts. The body of Christ can forgive sins. It can absolve and take a sinner back into fellowship. Let the body of Christ become mature and attain to full stature. The individual Christian will partake of that maturity.

The church of Christ in its N.T. grandeur has been obscured in both Catholic and Protestant history. In Catholicism full Christian stature has been ascribed to the hierarchy or to the monk and the nun; in Protestantism, to the individual. Where in either tradition has the "whole body [of Christ], joined and knit together" (vs. 16) received full recognition? The Orthodox churches of the East may have preserved this note of the N.T. concept of the **fullness of Christ** better than the West.

14-15. ***Christian Maturity.***—The virtues of childhood, in contrast with the virtues of maturity, have rarely been better evaluated than in Paul's words to the Corinthians, "In malice be ye children, but in understanding be men" (I Cor. 14:20). The Christian gospel must be guarded against misinterpretation on two sides. It is not a "professor" religion. The childlike heart is needed for its appreciation. But this does not mean that Christians should cultivate childishness and immaturity. "When I became a man, I put away childish things" (I Cor. 13:11), says Paul in his chapter on Christian love. The setting of this famous phrase is important. Love demands maturity for its full flowering. Colloquial speech points to a real truth when it calls an untested, merely romantic relationship between man and woman "puppy love."

The illusion that Christianity is a religion for children and not for grown men and women is disastrous. It is widespread. A few memories of Sunday school are *not* enough for the storms of later life. Ignorance of Bible and creed and Christian doctrine—blameworthy ignorance, one may add—exposes thousands of men and women to **every wind of doctrine,** or to the **sleight of men,** or to **cunning craftiness.** The Christian faith is not like a first lesson in geometry, which, once learned, can be forgotten or taken for granted. It sometimes looks that

15 But speaking the truth in love, may grow up into him in all things, which is the head, *even* Christ:

16 From whom the whole body fitly joined together and compacted by that which every joint supplieth, according to

ceitful wiles. 15 Rather, speaking the truth in love, we are to grow up in every way into him who is the head, into Christ, 16 from whom the whole body, joined and knit together by every joint with which it

who has no firm principles to guide him. **Craftiness in deceitful wiles** (RSV): Goodspeed's rendering is more accurate here: "ingenuity in inventing error." Πανουργία always has a bad connotation; but it suggests rather undisciplined naughtiness than **craftiness.** Πλάνη again means "error" rather than "deceit"; it is frequently set in contrast with ἀλήθεια (truth), as darkness with light. The whole expression appears to be a warning about the proneness of the human heart to wander from the truth, rather than an accusation of bad faith against the teachers of heresy.

Speaking the truth: The meaning of ἀληθεύω is wider than this; it includes such senses as "apprehending the truth," "living by the truth," "being true," not only in speech but even more in the whole inward disposition.

15. May grow up into him in all things: The way of truth and love, which leads to spiritual maturity, brings us more and more deeply into the unity of a common life with Christ as we are progressively assimilated in our whole being to the nature of our Lord. To be "in Christ" and to **grow up into him in all things**—these are complementary aspects of our life; for our union with Christ is not a mechanical attachment which remains static, but participation in a dynamic, growing life.

Who is the head, Christ: A supplementary thought, not completing the preceding clause, but effecting the transition to the complex figure of vs. 16. The total effect would be clearer if we began a new sentence at this point, rendering: "For he is the head, from whom. . . ."

16. The physiological metaphor which Paul had employed in Col. 2:19 is now taken up and applied in a further direction. Paul had sought to illustrate the single thought

way. Boil Christian doctrine down to a few ethical precepts and no great demand for study or understanding appears essential. But the mature Christian needs much more than this. Paul preached a very simple faith in the Cross and the Resurrection. But that simple faith has dimensions of height and depth; it is not milk for babes. Paul's epistles are not easy reading. Yet the mature Christians of all the ages, even if they only heard the N.T. in lesson or sermon, have fed their souls on Paul's insights. Christianity, like Judaism, is the religion of a book. A Christian without daily, or at least weekly, contact with Holy Scripture, and without continuous growth in understanding of its meaning, will soon find his faith withering away. He will be open to the wiles of error.

Our verses, furthermore, envisage Christian maturity in a social sense. The plural "we" is important. The writer thinks of maturity as a mark of unity in the church. We grow into Christ by **speaking the truth in love.** Individualism and egotism are destroyers of unity. They are signs of childishness. As pure individualists we cannot become full-grown men, but the body of Christ can grow into the "fullness of Christ" (vs. 13). Nothing matures us as Christians so effectively as full sharing in the common life of the Christian fellowship. Think of such a concrete ideal as **speaking the truth.** It is not easy to "tell the truth." Only in a fellowship of repentance can hearts be open and lips unsealed. Only in a community of forgiveness can envy be exorcised and hatreds exposed and transformed. In a society untouched by the grace of forgiving love we do not dare to approach open communion of person with person. A famous "thought" of Pascal reads: "If all men knew what each said of the other, there would not be four friends in the world." A terrifying, even though exaggerated truth! We are accordingly locked up in our separate cells of self-hiding. Only in the church can our mutual sharing of forgiveness transform us corporately into the mature body of Christ. There we can **grow up in every way into him who is the head, into Christ.**

16. ***The Church as Community.***—Modern man has lived under the illusion that to establish community life is relatively easy. Bring people near to each other and the trick is done. Contiguity, annihilation of distance, a seating

the effectual working in the measure of every part, maketh increase of the body unto the edifying of itself in love.

is supplied, when each part is working properly, makes bodily growth and upbuilds itself in love.

of the dependence of the whole creation on Christ, who as head imparts cohesion and vital energy to the whole. Here, though much of the same language is used, the ruling thought is quite different. It sets out indeed from the affirmation that Christ as head imparts cohesion and the vital power that makes for growth—**Christ, from whom the whole body, joined and knit together . . . makes bodily growth.** But now **the whole body** no longer figures the created universe, but the church; and the ruling thought is no longer the dependence of the whole frame of things upon the head, but the interdependence of the members in contributing to and through one another the vital forces which derive ultimately from the head. The new emphasis is given through two difficult phrases: **by every joint with which it is supplied** and **when each part is working properly.** The meaning of both these phrases has been much debated. In the first of them ἁφή **(joint)** is better taken in the more general sense of "contact" (see Abbott's note, *ad loc.*); the literal rendering would then be "through every contact of the supply," suggesting the way in which the vital forces make their way through the body by an endless succession of "contacts." "The supply" can only mean "that which Christ supplies," the essential nourishment of the body; it takes up the participle "nourished" (RSV) from the Colossians passage. The thought is not merely that every part of the body shares in the life which emanates from the head, as in the comment of Ecumenius (cited by Abbott, *ad loc.*): "The spiritual power which descends from Christ taking hold upon [ἁπτομένη] each several members of him"; but that every part is a channel which receives and passes on the life. This general idea is emphasized in the accompanying phrase, **when each part is working properly. Properly** here renders ἐν μέτρῳ, lit., "in measure," and this takes up the κατὰ τὸ μέτρον of vs. 7 ("according to the measure of

around a conference table—these in themselves will produce brotherliness. Hence our naïve faith in leagues of nations or other unitings in assembly halls, in the telephone or the telegraph or the airplane, as instruments of unity. Experience is teaching us hard lessons. A bringing of people close to each other may mean merely a greater knowledge of mutual faults, or an intolerable clashing of egotisms. Distance, rather than contiguity, may be a preserver of peace. Neighborliness may be helped rather than hindered by a border wall. The appalling rise of divorce statistics casts a lurid light upon the problem of creating communion. Here is a relationship buttressed by sexual instinct, custom and law, by vows of "true love," and the memory of romance, yet how easily it turns into bitter hatred and a broken home. Well may we be afraid that our unitings between larger human groupings, between social classes and nations, may produce divorcings in place of households of love. We might conceivably re-enact in the twentieth century the drama of the Tower of Babel.

The ancient world was more realistic than the twentieth century. That is why the church appeared to the contemporaries of Paul as a great miracle. To create fellowship is simply *not* easy. It calls for divine grace. Every man is by nature a little god to himself. This is part of the truth involved in his being created in the image of God, and in the story of the Fall. Unconverted human society resembles a battlefield of rival gods. The establishing of true community between clashing egotisms, as in a marriage, means a resigning of thrones. It involves a dying to self. The N.T. does not hesitate to call it a dying.

The church is a fellowship of repentant and forgiven sinners. Repentance is equivalent to a kind of dying. Forgiveness, in turn, means a rising again. "Reckon ye also yourselves," says Paul, "to be dead indeed unto sin, but alive unto God through Jesus Christ our Lord" (Rom. 6:11).

A community of the dead and risen—that is the church. Only such a community can speak of true unity. Only such a fellowship can risk honest togetherness. The church in the story of the Bible stands over against the Tower of Babel. Only such a body, as it **upbuilds itself in love,** can bring true fellowship onto the stage of history.

And as the church lives in a world which is attempting unification on the secular plane, its vocation is breath-taking. It can be the one

17 This I say therefore, and testify in the Lord, that ye henceforth walk not as other Gentiles walk, in the vanity of their mind,

17 Now this I affirm and testify in the Lord, that you must no longer live as the Gentiles do, in the futility of their minds;

Christ's gift"). We might paraphrase, "through the working of every several part in its appointed measure."

B. Second Exhortation: To Have Done with Pagan Ways (4:17–5:20)

In this relatively long passage the writer sets forth the transformation in the moral life which must result from the knowledge of Christ and from incorporation into his body, the church. It falls into four main sections: (*a*) a general appeal to his readers to abandon heathen ways, which are the consequence of spiritual ignorance and alienation from God, issuing in vileness and self-assertion; and to cultivate the way of life which follows from what they have learned of Christ; (*b*) a series of specific injunctions, representing the application of the general appeal to the abandonment of particular vices and the practice of particular virtues; the whole summed up as an imitation of God as his nature is revealed in the sacrificial love of Christ; (*c*) a warning against the gross sins of appetite, followed by an exposition of the contrast between the old life and the new in terms of darkness and light; and (*d*) a final summary, gathering up the whole series of appeals and warnings in a brief injunction to wisdom, sobriety, and thankfulness.

1. A General Appeal (4:17-24)

17*a*. I . . . testify in the Lord: The moral appeal, as truly as the doctrinal instruction, is a matter of testimony; the teacher bears witness to the truth that has been committed to him **in the Lord,** i.e., in the mystical unity of life with Christ.

As the Gentiles do: The readers have previously been addressed as "you, the Gentiles" (3:1; cf. on 2:11), and as such have been distinguished from the Jews among the people of God (1:12-13; 2:13 ff.). Here, however, **the Gentiles** clearly means "pagans." To get around this variation in the use of the word later scribes added λοιπά—**other** (Gentiles). The phrase in its proper form reveals that this writer thinks of the church as no longer composed of a mixture of Jews and Gentiles, but of converts from heathenism. As converts they are no longer "Gentiles" except in an external sense, in the superficial usage of "the so-called circumcision" (2:11).

17*b*-19. The description of the moral condition of the pagan world is practically a summary of what Paul says on the same subject in Rom. 1:21-32; this in turn rests upon

agent on earth producing true community. It knows the secret of the one true bond between the warring wills of men and of nations, the bond of repentance and forgiveness. It can take into itself the poisons of unredeemed society. It can be the cross-bearer of the world. Corporately, as also by way of each of its members, the church can obey the command of her Lord, "Whosoever will come after me, let him deny himself, and take up his cross, and follow me" (Mark 8:34).

17-19. *Paganism.*—The best commentary on these verses is the opening chapter of the Epistle to the Romans (vss. 18-32). There, as here, Pauline eyes describe, in words which our decorous translations soften down, the morass of vice, sexual vice in particular, which characterized the ancient pagan world. Paganism is much broader than merely sexual license. Yet it is noteworthy that even in modern speech the word pagan connotes a relaxing of moral restraint in the area of bodily appetite.

Simply to equate sin with sexual immorality is, of course, not Christian. Sin is, in essence, of the spirit and not of the body. In a hierarchy of sins, such as Dante employs as a framework for his pictures of hell and purgatory, sins of the body are not treated as harshly as are sins of the mind, and, above all, sins of the will. A lapse in the morality of sex may mean weakness of character rather than willful evil. Iago, in Shakespeare's *Othello,* is an embodiment of evil on a far deeper level than is his rival Cassio, though it is Cassio and not Iago who is

18 Having the understanding darkened, being alienated from the life of God through the ignorance that is in them, because of the blindness of their heart:

19 Who being past feeling have given themselves over unto lasciviousness, to work all uncleanness with greediness.

18 they are darkened in their understanding, alienated from the life of God because of the ignorance that is in them, due to their hardness of heart; 19 they have become callous and have given themselves up to licentiousness, greedy to practice every

---

commonplaces of Jewish polemic. **Vanity** is often associated with idol worship (Acts 14:15); it suggests that apart from the knowledge of the true God human life has no meaning or direction. **Darkened in their understanding:** The inward darkness caused by unbelief, contrasted with the inward illumination which God grants to believers ("having the eyes of your hearts enlightened," 1:18). **Alienated from the life of God:** It is implied that the heathen life is a deviation from the true nature of man, an alien development. Conversion is thus a "reconciliation," the restoration of a relationship unnaturally broken (cf. on Col. 1:20).

This futility, darkness, and alienation have a twofold root in **ignorance** and insensibility **(hardness of heart).** The **ignorance** might be pardonable (ἄγνοια usually means an ignorance due to circumstances which may be overlooked, as in Acts 17:30; contrasted with ἀγνωσία, culpable ignorance, "the ignorance of foolish men," I Pet. 2:15); but "the hardening of their hearts" suggests a deliberate steeling of the will against every good impulse until men become **past feeling.** Our versions both convey the impression that the second phrase is subordinate to the first—the ignorance is caused by the hardness of heart; in Greek both phrases are introduced by the same preposition (διά) and are co-ordinate.

The heart that has been so hardened as to become **calloused** offers no restraint to the worst excesses of evil conduct; as in Paul's description of Gentile degeneration, with its particular references to the horrible prevalence of sexual, especially homosexual, vice (Rom. 1:24, 26-27), the issues of pagan life are here summed up as **licentiousness** and **uncleanness;** and the whole atmosphere in which it moves is **greediness.** The word is πλεονεξία, sometimes rendered "covetousness" (Col. 3:5; cf. Eph. 5:5); and in the N.T. writings it generally has the specific connotation of "adultery," as covetousness of a neighbor's wife. The basic meaning, however, is more general. Πλεονεξία is the vice of self-assertion, ruthless in trampling on the rights of others, concerned with nothing but the satisfaction of its own impulses. It is the key to the whole viciousness of pagan life, as love is the key to the whole goodness of the Christian life.

---

guilty of fleshly sins. Nevertheless, sexual vice is a sure symptom of the breakdown of religious and moral sanctions in an individual and in society. The common moral sense of mankind, to say nothing of the Christian conscience, has not been wrong in singling out the sexual life of men and women as requiring very special restraints. Man cannot treat himself as if he were an innocent animal. Sex in man is either sin or sacrament.

In the ancient world sexual vices had indeed taken on forms which to a moral Jew like Paul must have seemed incomprehensible except in terms of an **understanding darkened,** blindness, and a **hardness of heart** which had gone **past feeling.** If we translate the closing phrase of vs. 19 **(with greediness)** bluntly by what the author had in mind, the rendering would be "with ritual fornication." It describes the state of affairs in pagan religion in which temple worship was inseparable from religious prostitution. A religion which actually brought vice into the sanctuary of its gods must have been in Paul's eyes little short of monstrous. Our modern pagan societies have also begun to be **callous and have given themselves up to licentiousness, greedy to practice every kind of uncleanness,** as any observer of moral laxness in our time can testify. Sex has become for some of its devotees —think of writers like D. H. Lawrence or Marcel Proust—almost a religion in its own right. Sociologists are beginning to deal with sexual morality by substituting a standard of statistics for the traditional standards of monogamous restraint.

20 But ye have not so learned Christ;
21 If so be that ye have heard him, and have been taught by him, as the truth is in Jesus:
22 That ye put off concerning the former conversation the old man, which is corrupt according to the deceitful lusts;

kind of uncleanness. **20** You did not so
learn Christ! — **21** assuming that you have
heard about him and were taught in him,
as the truth is in Jesus. **22** Put off your old
nature which belongs to your former manner of life and is corrupt through deceitful

---

20-24. The general construction of the paragraph is difficult. Vs. 21 is parenthetical, and the infinitives of vss. 22-24 (**put off . . . be renewed . . . put on**) are loosely dependent on the opening phrase **learned Christ,** which requires a complement (there is no other instance in Greek of the use of this verb with a personal object). But there is an ellipsis, for the infinitives can be taken to depend only on a *positive* affirmation, which must be supplied as the converse of the negative statement **you did not so learn Christ.** The completed thought would thus be: "You have not so learned Christ as to continue to live like the pagans; you have so learned him as to put off the old nature. . . ."

This analysis treats the three infinitives as epexegetic. If it is felt that they have imperative force (as in RSV), we must attribute this to a recollection of the verbs of exhortation which stand at the beginning of the paragraph: "I affirm and testify" (vs. 17). Upon this the infinitives of vss. 22-24 would follow readily enough, parallel in structure with the infinitive of vs. 17 ("walk"). But this simple balance has been lost through the substitution of the clause **you did not so learn Christ** for a repetition of the governing verbs **affirm and testify.**

The parenthesis of vs. 21 is of course an assumption, not a condition. The clause **as the truth is in Jesus,** for all its familiarity (especially in the misquotation "the truth as it is in Jesus"), is extraordinarily difficult to interpret with precision. In the Greek the noun (**truth**) has no article; and it is difficult if not impossible to discover any meaning in the clause if **truth** is the subject. It is possible, however, to take **truth** as the predicate—"as he [i.e., Christ] is truth in Jesus," the reference being to the manifestation of the messianic office and nature in the human personality of Jesus. The interpretation must at all events take account of the introduction of the name "Jesus" in place of the "Christ" of the preceding verse; this can be understood only as a reminder that the voice of "the Christ" is heard and his teaching received in the historical "Jesus." There may be beneath the words a shaft of polemic directed against some doctrine which represented "the Christ" as a heavenly aeon, essentially distinct from the man Jesus; this would be an anticipation of a doctrine which we know to have been put forward a generation or two later in some of the Gnostic schools.

20-24. ***So Learn Christ.***—The phrase is striking, as indeed is the general use throughout the Pauline writings of the word Christ in place of the word Jesus. This substitution need not imply ignorance of the human biography of the church's Lord. The employment, unusual though it is, of the gospel name—**as the truth is in Jesus**—in this very passage must mean a reference back to the preresurrected Christ. To know that he is now in heaven and in the church we return in remembrance to the great story of Galilee and Jerusalem.

Nevertheless, it remains true that our modern familiarity of use of the simple name Jesus finds little authority in apostolic custom. Jesus had become "the Christ" by the Resurrection and Ascension. His very name now connoted a series of events and a status in Christian faith of which the gospel companions had been perforce ignorant. Christians, by the return of Christ as Comforter or Holy Spirit, could now be "in Christ." They could **learn Christ.** They had not merely **heard about him,** but had been **taught in him.** As with the phrase "in Christ," the locus of his presence in the fellowship becomes a clue to the rich meaning of these verses. **You did not so learn Christ!** Pagans, turned Christians, were in a new world, a new covenant, a new social environment, with a **new nature, created after the likeness of God.** The very word Christ connoted this inexhaustible complex of experience. Much modern Christianity, by limiting its knowledge of Christianity's Founder so largely to the human biography

23 And be renewed in the spirit of your mind;
24 And that ye put on the new man, which after God is created in righteousness and true holiness.
25 Wherefore putting away lying, speak every man truth with his neighbor: for we are members one of another.

lusts, 23 and be renewed in the spirit of
your minds, 24 and put on the new nature, created after the likeness of God in true righteousness and holiness.
25 Therefore, putting away falsehood, let every one speak the truth with his neighbor, for we are members one of another.

The infinitives will then be taken as specifying what this true Christian instruction means: the new doctrine must issue in a new life. **Put off** (vs. 22) and **put on** (vs. 24): The literal sense of these verbs, which has to do with the change of clothing, is extended metaphorically to signify a change of character. Both these infinitives are aorists, referring to a change that is made once for all; **be renewed,** on the other hand, renders a present infinitive denoting a continuing process (cf. II Cor. 4:16, "Our inner nature is being renewed day by day").

Your old nature . . . is corrupt: lit., "is perishing": the present participle suggests a progressive decay, the consequence of a governing principle of decay, **the deceitful lusts.**

The spirit of your mind: The phrase indicates that **the spirit** of man, the faculty by which he holds communion with God, is conceived to be intimately related to his faculties of thought and reason—to be, in some sense, a function of mind. Religion, then, calls for the highest exercise of the intelligence, not for its abnegation.

The new nature, created after the likeness of God: This rendering introduces into the text, perhaps justifiably, the idea of "the image" (**likeness**) of God; this is expressed in Col. 3:10, which serves as model, but is not repeated here. The phrase "according to God" (or **after the likeness of God**) seems here to suggest the *immortality* of the new life, in contrast with the transience of the old, which "is perishing." **True** balances **deceitful** in vs. 22; this observation is the key to its meaning. The desires which ruled the old self were **deceitful,** and brought life to ruin; the **righteousness and holiness** of the new life are **true,** and bring life to its true fulfillment.

2. Some Special Injunctions (4:25–5:2)

The effects of this transformation of the whole inward nature are now set forth in particulars of conduct. Once the tree is made good, it must bring forth good fruit (Matt. 12:33, 35). Here the writer deals first with the vices which are incompatible with genuine fellowship, and the virtues which essentially belong to the corporate unity of Christian believers. **For we are members one of another** is the fundamental principle which gives force to all his injunctions. **Falsehood** (vs. 25), **anger** (vss. 26-27), thieving (vs. 28), and foul language (vs. 29) are all offenses against fellowship. Conversely, truthfulness, placability, honest toil, gracious language, and readiness to forgive (vs. 32) are the virtues that reflect the reality of our fellowship and are the proper and necessary evidence of our respect for the personality of those who share with us in the common life in Christ.

25-27. Putting away falsehood: The same verb is used as in vs. 22, "Put off your old nature." **Speak every man truth with his neighbor** is cited from Zech. 8:16, where the

---

of Jesus, has tragically impoverished the N.T. faith. Such sentimental return is in fact impossible. A remembered Jesus by all means! The reading of the gospel story in the historic liturgies of the church has rightly been often surrounded with awesome ceremonial. But the Christ in his church, Christ *now,* is the rock upon which Christian faith and experience must finally rest. To **learn Christ** means life in the fellowship, rebirth into a new world, a putting off and a putting on, a literal revolution of human status. No mere acquaintance with the gospels as biographical memoirs, no "imitation of Christ" limited to an ethical reduplication of his transcendent human stature, can serve as a substitute for what the N.T. really presents as the new life in Christ and as *the* gospel.

25-27. ***Repentance and Forgiveness.***—Do we as Christians still need the discipline of the

26 Be ye angry, and sin not: let not the
sun go down upon your wrath:
27 Neither give place to the devil.
28 Let him that stole steal no more: but
rather let him labor, working with *his*
hands the thing which is good, that he may
have to give to him that needeth.

26 Be angry but do not sin; do not let the
sun go down on your anger, 27 and give no
opportunity to the devil. 28 Let the thief
no longer steal, but rather let him labor,
doing honest work with his hands, so that
he may be able to give to those in need.

---

motive given is the Lord's hatred of evil; here the motive is found in the mutual relationships which are involved in membership in the one body. **Do not let the sun go down on your anger:** This is a Pythagorean saying; and it gives the writer's interpretation of the enigmatic injunction of Ps. 4:5: **Be angry but do not sin.** This is the LXX rendering of the text; the Targum interprets it as meaning, "Tremble [before God] and you will not fall into sin" (so KJV, "Stand in awe, and sin not"). The Hebrew lends itself to either interpretation, and the rabbinical commentators generally give it the sense which we find here. The comment of our writer does not, as is often alleged, suggest that anger may sometimes be justified. His one point is that we must expel it from our hearts before the day is out; we must **give no opportunity to the devil** by "nursing our wrath to keep it warm." Justifiable indignation aroused by cruelty or vileness is not in question; if anger is righteous, it ought to be sustained until the evil which called it forth has been removed.

28. Let the thief no longer steal: We are bound to be struck by the implications of this injunction. The church was welcoming into her fellowship members of the criminal classes, to whom theft was the ordinary means of livelihood, which must now be replaced by honest toil. We have here a reminder that the gospel of Christ is not for the righteous who need no repentance, nor is the church a club for the respectable.

Ten Commandments? Yes, we do. A new life has begun for the Christian. He is a forgiven sinner. Even as a liar and a thief he can come through repentance into the fellowship of unearned grace. A new motive—a **therefore**—has been born in his heart. But this new motive of gratitude and of finding himself a member of a community of forgiveness has strengthened, not lessened, the call for moral response.

Our passage begins with warnings against lying and anger. These look like obvious social faults, which even a society of atheists would have to preach against. But a non-Christian society has little to offer by way of power to conquer these sins. It is not exactly easy for a man to **speak the truth with his neighbor.** Eugene O'Neill has written a play, *Strange Interlude,* in which a double dialogue is reported—first the dialogue actually spoken by the characters, and then the dialogue of the unspoken thoughts which are held back in the hearts of the speakers. And the two dialogues do not agree.

Why is **putting away falsehood** a difficult virtue? To reveal oneself to another human being involves opening windows into secret chambers. We are prevented from self-revelation, which is involved in speaking truth, by pride and shame. Nor is even the Christian asked to unveil his soul fully except before God. But the Christian, thanks to his faith, is free to **speak the truth,** as the pagan is not. He has "denied himself," and no longer needs to protect his egotism with lies. He can surrender his fortress of pride and can confess his faults. "Confess your faults one to another," pleads the Epistle of James (5:16). What mountains of snobbery and sham, of heartbreak, masking behind worldly pretense, would melt if by the grace of Christian love the truth could set us free.

It is only in a fellowship of repentance and forgiveness that truthtelling becomes fully possible. This is indeed one of the glories of Christian community life. Christians can "tell the truth." Why? Because they can trust one another to understand and to forgive. Anger can be resolved into a mutual laying bare of differences and of smothered resentments. Christians will become angry. But no Christian need let anger break fellowship with a brother Christian, **for we are members one of another.** A Christian can obey the ancient precept, "Let the day of your anger be the day of your reconciliation."

28. ***On Stealing.***—The sin of stealing is not limited to pickpockets and burglars. It can disguise itself in respectabilities which may go undetected in church pews. The moral sanctions

29 Let no corrupt communication proceed out of your mouth, but that which is good to the use of edifying, that it may minister grace unto the hearers.

30 And grieve not the Holy Spirit of God, whereby ye are sealed unto the day of redemption.

31 Let all bitterness, and wrath, and anger, and clamor, and evil speaking, be put away from you, with all malice:

29 Let no evil talk come out of your mouths,
but only such as is good for edifying, as
fits the occasion, that it may impart grace to
those who hear. 30 And do not grieve the
Holy Spirit of God, in whom you were
sealed for the day of redemption. 31 Let all
bitterness and wrath and anger and clamor
and slander be put away from you, with all

---

30. Do not grieve the Holy Spirit of God: These sins against brotherhood are also an offense against the divine Spirit which inhabits the body of believers. **Sealed:** On the imagery of "sealing" in relation to the Holy Spirit see on 1:13. The phrase here emphasizes the obligation laid upon us to revere the Spirit as the pledge of our glorious destiny; our present conduct must be worthy of the inheritance upon which we have begun to enter.

31-32. The traits of the old nature and the new are now summed up and set in contrast: on the one hand **bitterness** and every mark of a harsh, quarrelsome, malicious

---

of even a purely secular society can perhaps curb the more obvious crimes of avarice. Christian motivation, however, can penetrate to the root of this deep-seated sin. "We are members one of another." Christian love is derivative of the love of God, seeking not its own. Like the love of God, it is prepared **to give to those in need.**

It is significant that this verse recommends to the thief **honest work with his hands.** Modern psychology would applaud. The humble toilers of earth know something of the costliness of civilization's stores which then are enjoyed, and all too often wantonly squandered, by idle hands. The defection from the churches of the workingman of modern times may call, by way of remedy, for a rediscovery of Christian vocations in the world of shared manual labor. "We labor, working with our own hands" (I Cor. 4:12), says Paul of himself and his apostolic band. Christians may well look with fear upon a life of idle wealth. It might at the Judgment stand under the condemnation of the Eighth Commandment.

29-30. ***Christian Speech.***—The Holy Spirit **in whom** Christians **were sealed for the day of redemption** has imparted to the church the gift of tongues. Christian speech has been hallowed by this act. Christians, accordingly, are to witness to their new life in Christ even by their conversation.

Talk, we say, is cheap. But is it? Homer speaks of "winged words." Words do fly like darts. They can wound. "I tell you," said Jesus, "on the day of judgment men will render account for every careless word they utter" (Matt. 12:36).

As we of the Christian flock again enter an increasingly pagan environment, the contrast between Christian and pagan social behavior will become correspondingly important. Christian conversation can differ profoundly from that which has been untouched by the grace of the gospel. Not that Christian talk need be pious or outwardly always devout. Someone has said that one sign of a Christian is that he can listen. He listens to God, as the godless are afraid to do. But he also listens to his human brother. True listening implies selflessness. A "thou" becomes important as well as the ever-present "I." Observe conversation in a group of worldlings. Does it not often turn into a chaos of self-assertive monologues? Godless sociality is symbolized by the dispersion of tongues of the Tower of Babel. It is **corrupt communication.**

Every meeting of a man with his neighbor presents an occasion for imparting **grace to those who hear.** It can exhibit Christian love, a love which "is patient and kind," which "does not insist on its own way," which "is not irritable or resentful" (I Cor. 13:4-5), which **is good for edifying, as fits the occasion.**

31-32. ***The Ethical Teaching of Christianity.***—Christianity has no monopoly of ethical ideals. The classic literary deposit of the ages can furnish more than one "five-foot shelf" of books of lofty morality. China has its Confucius; India its *Bhagavad-Gita.* And the Greco-Roman world had a plethora of philosophers of the good life, from Plato and Aristotle to Marcus Aurelius. All could have joined with Paul in picturing a moral world in which **bitterness and wrath and anger and clamor and slander** might have been denounced as unworthy of a man's true nature or society's welfare.

32 And be ye kind one to another, tender-hearted, forgiving one another, even as God for Christ's sake hath forgiven you.

malice, 32 and be kind to one another, tenderhearted, forgiving one another, as God in Christ forgave you.

disposition; on the other, mutual kindness, tenderness of heart, readiness to forgive. **Forgiving one another, as God in Christ forgave you:** Here again the requirements of brotherhood are given a higher sanction in the transcendent realm of our relationship with God.

Yet between Christianity and the world's non-Christian moralists, not belittling the noblest, there is a great gulf fixed. Even the descriptions of moral excellence differ. Plato's list of "cardinal virtues" is still memorized in every classroom in ethics: fortitude, wisdom, temperance, justice. Aristotle added his "doctrine of the mean," and his resplendent picture of magnanimity—the "great-souled" man. But it would be difficult to find in pagan moralists anything quite approaching the loftiness of the closing verse of our chapter: **Be kind to one another, tenderhearted, forgiving one another.** Somehow even a Plato or Aristotle, or Stoic saint like Marcus Aurelius, might have shied away from picturing man as capable of such self-surrender as words like **tenderhearted** or **forgiving** imply. Aristotle's "great-souled" man would be ready to bear insults without striking back. Greatness of character can mean precisely an ignoring of the littleness of malice. Julius Caesar, giant among pygmies as a magnanimous man, produced astonishment among his contemporaries in more than one scene of "forgiveness" of enemies. But it was not real forgiveness. The virtue of the pagan sprang from a motive totally unlike that which traces back to Christian love. It sprang from the motive of pride. Pride can indeed rival in outward effect many of the marks of the Christian character.

The contrast needs emphasis. Great dangers beset the teaching of moral ideals divorced from a right theology. We may say that ethical precepts are of value, whatever the background of basic faith. Up to a point this may be true. Plato and Aristotle in medieval Catholicism became grafted into the Christian systems of dogma. Ideals of ethical excellence remain ideals, regardless of whether a Plato or a Paul commends them. But the danger line of stepping outside the thought world of the Bible is very great. A morally perfect pagan would still be far from being a Christian.

Look at the ethical teaching of the Bible, and, above all, of the N.T. Is it not noteworthy how seldom the word virtue appears? (A concordance can tell the story.) And as for the word ideal, it does not appear at all! What nonbiblical moralists call virtues and ideals are in the Bible called commandments of a living God or fruits of the Holy Spirit.

What constitutes the difference between these two contrasted categories? Clearly, the difference must be sought in the realm of motive, in the answer to the question "Why?" Many a reader of the gospels must have noted how little Jesus seems to be interested in whether the men and women he meets are good or bad. But Jesus was intensely interested in *why* they were good or bad, and in what relationship they stood with himself and with the Father. They called him "a friend of publicans and sinners" (Matt. 11:19). To the pious citizens of Jerusalem he could say, "The publicans and the harlots go into the kingdom of God before you" (Matt. 21:31).

The *why* of morality is the important question. Men can be outwardly virtuous, and even pious, for many reasons. The motive may be fear, or love of fame, or emulation of beautiful ideals, or, above all, pride. God will be the judge. And we may be certain that no seeking after the divine, however blind or mistaken, or ignorant of the gospel, will be lost in God's final kingdom. But this cannot lessen the glory of the good news of Christ, or the contrast between the ethics of the gospel and pagan virtues.

Revelation of the love of God is the *why* of Christian morality. It is a morality of response and not, first of all, of human achievement. It is the fruit of a divine gift and not the product of man's attempt to rival the Deity. The *why* of Christian morality accordingly speaks little of virtues—these being but outward signs—but says much of the reborn heart.

As God in Christ forgave you. Here is the "therefore" (vs. 25) of Christian ethics, the mighty act of the Cross. This one single fact, apprehended in repentance, can outweigh a hundred textbooks on virtues or ideals. It can evoke the ethics of forgiveness, of which even a Plato could not dream. It can make human hearts "tender" and not merely "great." It can produce the miracle of Christian love.

We frequently speak of Christian love as a virtue. Warnings are proper regarding such designation. There is undoubtedly a love of neighbor which can spring from motives short

5 Be ye therefore followers of God, as
dear children;
2 And walk in love, as Christ also hath
loved us, and hath given himself for us an

5 Therefore be imitators of God, as beloved children. 2 And walk in love, as

---

5:1-2. The last clause—**as God . . . forgave you**—now becomes the point of departure for a wider thought: that God, in his character as made known to us in Christ, is the model for our imitation. **Be imitators of God, as beloved children:** The imitation of God is the natural consequence of our knowledge of him as Father. So Jesus again and again

---

of that which is the product of the gift of the Holy Spirit. Even non-Christians can achieve fair play, just dealings between man and man, and notable deeds of charity. Generosity, for example, was a trait of character much prized among the ancients. But charity as a virtue, self-achieved, or motivated by anything short of the "therefore" of **as God in Christ forgave you** is not, in final analysis, *Christian* love.[9] It remains precisely a high pagan "virtue," not to be despised, but yet not to be confused with the real thing. When Paul, in his famous chapter on charity, describes himself as quite possibly bestowing all his goods to feed the poor, and giving his body to be burned, and yet not having "charity," he means what he says. "It profiteth me nothing" (I Cor. 13:3). The "charity" of that familiar chapter, the reader should be warned, is not a virtue in the usual ethical meaning of the word virtue at all. It is a gift of the Holy Spirit. Paul coins for it a new word, *agapē*. Much has been gained in modern theological writing by the frank employment of the somewhat technical Greek word *agapē* to designate love or charity in this full Christian sense. *Agapē* is not a possibility for unaided human nature. The Holy Spirit alone can produce it. Only in the experience of "sinner forgiven" does Christian *agapē* ever fully appear.

5:1. ***The Imitation of God.***—The phrase **imitators of God** is very striking, and even unique. We are familiar in modern Christian homilies with the variant phrase, "the imitation of Christ," or more frequently with the phrase "the imitation of Jesus." And by such imitation is usually meant the taking of the historical Jesus of the gospel narratives as ethical example. "What would Jesus do?" Jesus has in such presentations become a biographical model. Imitation is a legitimate and powerful motive in human behavior. Children imitate parents, or a beloved teacher, or an appealing figure in a history book. National traditions perpetuate themselves best by way of imitation of a nation's great men. Think of the power over the young which has been exercised by memory of Nelson or Wellington in England, or Washington, Lincoln, or Lee in the United States. Similarly, the transcendent stature of Jesus has for generations become central in much Christian nurture in our church schools—Jesus presented for imitative moral effort on the analogy of other hero-biographies. The "discipleship of Jesus" has become almost synonymous with Christianity. And by discipleship is again meant imitation of the human figure central in the Gospels.

It comes as something of a shock, therefore, to anyone reading the N.T. with fresh eyes, to find that such an appeal to the imitation of Jesus is almost totally absent from postresurrection Christianity. From the Acts of the Apostles to Revelation, where do you plainly find it? A few passages approach it (Phil. 2:5-12; I Pet. 2:21; I John 2:6). But when examined, they resemble our verse. They are appeals for the imitation of God, or of Christ as the divine mediator, not as ethical hero. It is noteworthy that the words disciple and discipleship do not occur in any of the N.T. epistles. Nor, in the KJV, is the word imitation found. Clearly, the imitation of Christ—the phrase itself classic in the title of Thomas à Kempis' famous devotional volume—needs re-examination.

We meet here, as when we saw the importance of the Ascension in the faith of the N.T. (see Expos. on 1:20), the simple fact that for the early church Jesus had become "the Christ." He was now Lord, "far above all principality, and power, and might, and dominion, and every name that is named, not only in this world, but also in that which is to come" (1:21). Imitation of Christ was now equivalent to imitation of God, whatever that could then mean. Plainly, however, it did not mean simple ethical copying of a human hero-biography. The imitation of Christ which the Christian was asked to show forth in his walk before men was the descent-drama of the Son of God, an act of prevenient love. *Agapē,* in other words, is imitation of God. But *agapē* is a gift of the Holy Spirit, not a self-engendered achievement.

[9] For a full treatment of this central N.T. paradox see Anders Nygren, *Agape and Eros* (tr. Philips Watson; London: Society for Promoting Christian Knowledge, 1932-39).

moves us to the love of all men by the example of God, teaching us that the only conduct befitting children of such a Father is that they should manifest his universal love. Jesus, however, lays the emphasis on the extending of our love beyond the circle of those that love us, even to our enemies (Matt. 5:43-48; Luke 6:32-36); it is indeed precisely in this that we show ourselves "sons of the Most High; for he is kind to the ungrateful

"Let this mind be in you," so Paul elsewhere pictures this imitation of God, "which was also in Christ Jesus: who . . . did not count equality with God a thing to be grasped, but emptied himself, taking the form of a slave" (Phil. 2:5-7). To paraphrase this somewhat boldly, Christians are to imitate the "biography of God." This is the biography or drama summarized in the church's historic creeds—God in Christ coming down for love of men from heaven, dying, and rising again. Such imitation of God or of Christ is not quite identical with mere moralistic hero-discipleship. The challenge is not a call to a kind of postgraduate moralism or to the achievement of legal righteousness, but to a realistic death and resurrection. Discipleship equals in a sense what the early church thought baptism to be. Paul describes baptism as a dying, and the new moral life of Christians as a resurrection. "Know ye not, that so many of us as were baptized into Jesus Christ were baptized into his death? Therefore we are buried with him by baptism into death: that like as Christ was raised up from the dead by the glory of the Father, even so we also should walk in newness of life" (Rom. 6:3-4). The ethical equivalent of death in baptism—though the use of the word ethical is something of a falsification—is repentance, and the equivalent of resurrection is the life under forgiveness. The publican in the familiar parable was "imitating" Christ better than the Pharisee!

Imitation of Jesus, if the words are given their obvious human meaning, was a natural attitude toward him in the days of his earthly "descent." Hence his followers were called disciples. They saw in him the great Master and Rabbi. His teaching portrayed before them a moral perfection which to a Jew must have seemed—as indeed it still is—unattainable. It asked for a fulfillment of the law, the Sermon on the Mount climaxing Deuteronomy. "Unless your righteousness *exceeds* that of the scribes and Pharisees, you will never enter the kingdom of heaven" (Matt. 5:20). Discipleship, accordingly, in terms of ethical performance, landed the disciple group in an insoluble dilemma. What, as a matter of historical fact, did it do for them? Even after three years of incomparable training in moral "imitation," they failed their Master in the end.

But look at that disciple group after the Resurrection. The master-disciple relationship could give place now to a new covenant, a new relationship *in* Christ. The demand for perfection could be allowed to do its work. It now could kill (Rom. 7:9-10). There could be a new imitation of Christ, radically different from human imitation of an impossible example, an imitation of the Lord's death and resurrection. The disciples became Christians, and even apostles and martyrs.

May not our modern emphasis on the "imitation of Jesus" need on occasion some correction by way of a rediscovery of the true N.T. picture? Which Jesus shall we imitate, the Nazarene rabbi or the Christ of the salvation drama of Christian faith? The choice may mean a decision as between virtually two religions. It is significant that as late as 1901 a theologian could say, "Every single great life of Christ since the Gospels is the product of the last sixty-five years."[1] The rediscovery of what we have come to call "the historical Jesus" has no doubt brought gain as well as loss. But it must make its peace, as must our modern discipleship Christianity, with the Christianity of the apostolic age. "In the writings of St. Paul," so says a contemporary scholar, "no trace can be found of an 'historical Christ' as we today fondly use the term."[2]

R. W. Dale, that profound commentator on the Epistle to the Ephesians, has a wise word on this important topic of imitation of Christ. He refers to the opinion of those for whom the doctrine of the divinity of Christ is a problem, since it seemingly destroys the value of his example. "But it is precisely because Christ is Divine," says Dale, "that I have the courage to make His life the law of mine." This paradox is then explained by a pointing to the fact that it is the living Christ who imparts to Christians the energy to live the new life *in* Christ. We are but branches revealing the life which is in the vine.

2. *Walk in Love.*—Here is another striking phrase which could be taken as a definition of what the imitation of Christ means to Paul. "No one can follow Christ's example," says a profound interpreter of Christian ethics, "except he who by faith has found Christ as Mediator and

[1] Henry Churchill King, *Reconstruction in Theology* (New York: The Macmillan Co., 1901), p. 186.

[2] Deissmann, *Die neutestamentliche Formel "in Christo Jesu,"* p. 80.

offering and a sacrifice to God for a sweet-smelling savor.

3 But fornication, and all uncleanness, or covetousness, let it not be once named among you, as becometh saints;

Christ loved us and gave himself up for us, a fragrant offering and sacrifice to God.

3 But immorality and all impurity or covetousness must not even be named

---

and the selfish" (Luke 6:35). Our writer, on the other hand, applying the thought within his immediate context, is thinking only of the mutual relations of Christians.

The thought of the imitation of God has been introduced in relation to the plea for a forgiving spirit: we are to forgive as God in Christ forgave us. The writer realizes, however, that forgiveness is but a single aspect of the manifestation of love, and he now broadens his exhortation, calling upon us to **walk in love,** to make love the ruling principle of all our life. The scope and quality of **love** are then illustrated by the example of **Christ** [who] **loved us and gave himself up for us** (cf. I John 3:16, "By this we know love, that he laid down his life for us; and we ought to lay down our lives for the brethren"). **A fragrant offering and sacrifice to God:** The effect of Christ's sacrifice as an atonement for sin is not in view; the thought bears solely upon the perfection of love which is therein manifested, and upon the pattern of self-sacrificing love which Christ thus presents. The phrase **for a sweetsmelling savor** is used in the O.T. only of burnt offerings (Lev. 1; etc.); here it is of course used metaphorically, to express the beauty of a sacrifice that withholds nothing but gives all, even life itself, to God as a tribute of absolute devotion (cf. Rom. 12:1).

3. Light Against Darkness (5:3-14)

The theme is still the difference between pagan and Christian morality, especially in the attitude toward the sins of the body, which is expounded as the contrast of darkness and light. It is stressed that physical impurity is not to be taken lightly, but is to be regarded as utterly abhorrent. The argument indicates that the writer has in view not the ordinary tolerance of sexual offenses and even of unnatural vice which prevailed in pagan society, but the actual defense of such immorality on the ground that the spirit is not touched by the deeds of the body—that the spiritual life is indifferent to the

---

Redeemer, and by His saving grace is armed with power to set forth on the pilgrimage after His example."[3] Love is quite literally the fulfillment of the law. Christian preaching uses this Pauline idea freely, and rightly so. Christianity is a love ethic. What is *not* understood by many Christians, however, is that love in the Christian sense cannot, in its turn, be treated simply as a new law—a law merely more "inward" than the Ten Commandments. Christian love is not produced in the same way as a virtue based upon the fear of legal punishment or the acceptance of an ideal: "Christian character is a lovely thing; therefore I shall produce it." Christian love is not a product of ethical self-culture, but a response to an act of God—**Christ loved us and gave himself up for us.** This is what theologians call prevenient grace. The Christian love ethic, as the N.T. understands it, is the result of a love story. The chief actor in that story is God and not man.

[3] H. Martensen, *Christian Ethics* (tr. C. Spence; Edinburgh: T. & T. Clark, 1873), pp. 293-94.

The astounding effect upon ethical behavior of prevenient grace can receive illustration by many analogies in our ordinary social experience. A lover woos a loved one and receives the gift of a love vow in return. Response is spontaneous. Such response is an analogy of the response of the Christian to the love gift of Christ—who **loved us and gave himself up for us.** A new ethics is born, no longer one of law, but of grace. It is, to refer to the preceding verse, an "imitation of God" ethics. "Herein is love," so John repeats the thought of our own text in his classic summary of the N.T. gospel, "not that we loved God, but that he loved us" (I John 4:10), and "sent his . . . Son into the world, that we might live through him" (I John 4:9).

3-5. *Christianity and Moral Decay.*—As the Exeg. makes clear, the sins which the author here enumerates center about the prevalent sexual vices of the ancient world. Many imperfections in moral behavior can be patiently dealt with in Christian pastoral care. But in

4 Neither filthiness, nor foolish talking, nor jesting, which are not convenient: but rather giving of thanks.

among you, as is fitting among saints. 4 Let there be no filthiness, nor silly talk, nor levity, which are not fitting; but instead

physical, and that the one is not affected by the other. This type of unhealthy dualism was not without influence in Christian circles; the author of I John also knows of men who profess to have fellowship with Christ while they walk in darkness (I John 1:6), and in the second century some of the Gnostic teachers even made a virtue of licentiousness. "There seems . . . no reason to doubt that some of the heretics believed themselves to be so far above good and evil that their conduct scandalized even the easy-going censors of Roman society" (C. H. Dodd, *The Johannine Epistles* [London: Hodder & Stoughton, 1946], p. xx. See also his notes on I John 1:8). Such a perversion of the Christian position calls forth the most earnest and vehement warnings of the entire epistle: indulgence in these practices bars men from any part **in the kingdom of Christ and of God** (vs. 5), and brings down upon them **the wrath of God** (vs. 6). These things belong to the **darkness** from which they have emerged; now that they are **light in the Lord,** they must **take no part in the unfruitful works of darkness** (vss. 8, 11).

In the preceding section the sins of deceit, dishonesty, bad temper, and filthy talk were rebuked as offenses against our fellows in the Christian community. In this section the sins of impurity are viewed as offenses against God and against the status (**saints,** vs. 3) and the nature (**light,** with its **fruit . . . in all that is good and right and true,** vss. 8-9) which we have received from him.

3. Covetousness: On πλεονεξία see on 4:19. In this context the word must certainly be given the specific connotation of "adultery" (cf. I Thess. 4:6, where "defraud" of KJV renders the cognate verb); or more generally, "sensual self-indulgence," which gratifies self at whatever cost to others. The thought of avarice is foreign to the whole passage. **Must not even be named among you,** let alone be practiced; there is not even room for discussion of whether such things are permissible for Christians. **Saints:** Primarily a religious word meaning "consecrated people," it here visibly takes on the moral sense; consecration to God ("holiness") requires purity of life.

4. Levity: Clearly in the sense of "ribaldry"; an instance of a good word which has become perverted to a low sense in popular usage. The writer is not objecting to good clean merriment, but to the habit of making a joke of indecency. **Thanksgiving** is sug-

this area of conduct a clean break with pagan mores is called for. The apostolic writer does not go so far as to say such sins cannot be forgiven. But he is sure that they must mark the doer as one outside **the kingdom of Christ and of God.**

The Christian church, both Catholic and Protestant, has frequently been criticized for its overly severe moral standards, particularly in the matter of sexual purity. Puritanism presents problems, one may grant. There is a notion abroad that for Christians "sin equals sex" and nothing much else. This needs correction. There certainly are six *other* deadly sins besides lust.

Nevertheless, the church of the apostolic age, and in its more healthy states later, has been right in setting strict bounds to leniency of judgment in matters of sex. There are sexual vices which are not merely non-Christian, but which fall below the level of the human. They are simply bestial. Moral revulsion is the only possible Christian attitude. They **must not even be named among you.** Or as vs. 12 phrases the same imperative, "It is a shame even to speak of the things that they do in secret."

It is fashionable in modern times to make light of the asceticisms of the Middle Ages and to praise the liberations of the Renaissance and the Reformation. The "liberty of the Christian man," rediscovered by the Reformers, is indeed a precious good. But neither Protestantism nor modern secularism is as aware as it should be of the debt which we owe to our ancestors in the faith who, in their revolt against pagan Rome, went into caves and the desert, or undertook monastic disciplines. There is a human **filthiness** which goes not out but by fasting and prayer. G. K. Chesterton, in his notable book on Francis of Assisi, gives a vivid picture of the sexual pollutions which poisoned the ancient world. He alludes to the associations of gracious

5 For this ye know, that no whore-
monger, nor unclean person, nor covetous man, who is an idolater, hath any inheritance in the kingdom of Christ and of God.
6 Let no man deceive you with vain
words: for because of these things cometh

let there be thanksgiving. 5 Be sure of this,
that no immoral or impure man, or one who is covetous (that is, an idolater), has any inheritance in the kingdom of Christ and of God. 6 Let no one deceive you with

---

gested as that which should give the tone to the conversation of Christians, who can never be unmindful of the goodness of God which has been lavished upon them; this remembrance is the impenetrable barrier to **filthiness** of every kind.

5. One who is covetous (that is, an idolater): Covetous is again to be taken in the sense given to the corresponding noun in vs. 3—"adulterous" or "sensual." The equation with idolatry probably goes back to the language of the O.T. prophets who speak of Israel's worship of false gods as adultery (Hos. 2:5; Ezek. 23:37; etc.); here the figure is reversed. In later Judaism, when literal idol worship had ceased to be a temptation, the rabbis applied the O.T. warnings against idolatry to other sins which seemed to them to be equally serious. A pertinent saying of Rabbi Jannai (*ca.* A.D. 225) may be quoted: "He who listens to his evil impulse is like an idolater. What is the ground of this in Scripture? Thou shalt not have in thee any strange god (Ps. 81:9) . . . you must not make the strange god within you (i.e., your evil impulse) a king over you" (Strack and Billerbeck, *Kommentar zum N.T.*, III, 607).

The kingdom of Christ and of God: The expression is unique in the N.T., which elsewhere speaks of "the kingdom of God" ("of heaven," in Matthew), except for the one occurrence of "the kingdom of the Son of his love" in Col. 1:13. The coupling of the names of Christ and of God here is in keeping with the conception of the messianic office which runs through the epistle: the messiahship is the ordained means of bringing all things into the unity which is the end of creation, i.e., in the older terminology to which the writer here reverts, "the kingdom of God." The association of the two names under a single article (lit., "of the Christ and God") indicates that he makes no effective distinction between the rule of Christ over the kingdom and the rule of God: the notion once put forward by Paul, that Christ's rule is dispensational and temporary, and that at the end "he delivers the kingdom to God the Father" (I Cor. 15:23-24) is abandoned.

6. Let no one deceive you with empty words: This warning clearly implies that specious arguments were being advanced in some quarters to justify immorality, or to

---

beauty which surround the phrase "a garden." "Then," he adds, picturing paganism by contrast, "let any one who knows a little Latin poetry recall suddenly what would once have stood in place of the sun-dial or the fountain, obscene and monstrous in the sun; and of what sort was the god of their gardens. Nothing could purge this obsession but a religion that was literally unearthly."[4] Medieval asceticism purged the world, Chesterton concludes, of this polluted naturalism. A Francis could again see the stars as cleansed of devils, and trees as other than the haunt of pagan gods. We have been beneficiaries of this cleansed world ever since. No schoolboy today dreams of taking classical mythology, with its deified immoralities, literally. But that ancient mythology was once serious religion.

[4] *St. Francis of Assisi* (New York: George H. Doran Co., 1924), pp. 42-43.

Is our day of *Christianized* naturalism coming in its turn to a close? Are the ancient gods, including Pan and Venus, returning to their thrones? Are our Broadways and our Hollywoods reverting to the unrestrained worship of the lusts of the flesh, free divorce making of marriage licensed fornication, and professors of sociology substituting statistics of animalism for the law of God? A reading of the signs of the times in our day of moral decay should be full of warnings. Christians may indeed be called upon once more to take literally the counsel of Paul, "Wherefore, come out from among them, and be ye separate, saith the Lord, and touch not the unclean thing" (II Cor. 6:17).

6-7. *God's Wrath and God's Love.*—The author, as the Exeg. points out, had in mind a very definite danger in the early church, viz., a wrong interpretation of Christian freedom. Revolt against the strict moral demands of religion

the wrath of God upon the children of disobedience.

7 Be not ye therefore partakers with them.

empty words, for it is because of these things that the wrath of God comes upon the sons of disobedience. 7 Therefore do

persuade Christians that licentious living had no significant relation to the life of the spirit. The position of the words **because of these things** gives them emphasis: These are the very sins which even now are visited with God's judgment. **The wrath of God:** Always in the N.T. in the concrete sense of the punishment which God inflicts on sin; partly with an eschatological reference ("the day of wrath when God's righteous judgment will be revealed," Rom. 2:5), partly with an immediate reference to the penalties which are visited upon sin and disobedience as they occur. **Sons of disobedience:** A Hebraism meaning simply "disobedient men."

7. With them: More correctly "in them"; the pronoun, in the genitive, is used of the deeds in which part is taken; the dative is used of the persons with whom the doer is associated.

has been a frequent fact of history. In the ancient world it took common form in a "spirituality" which thought of matters pertaining to the body as indifferent. Hence laxness in sexual morality could be condoned as bodily indulgence which need not touch "spiritual" attainments. We probably have the ethical earnestness of the Protestant Reformation—paralleled, in part at least, in the Counter-Reformation in Romanism—to thank for a lessening of the danger of such immoral spirituality in more modern times. Yet it has not wholly vanished. Think, for example, of how frequently artistic genius is exempted, in popular and even responsible Christian judgment, from moral standards. The very word artist connotes—unjustly in many instances, one should add—the life of Bohemia, not merely as symbolic of unconventionality in dress or culinary habits, but in ethical behavior as well. And all is excused on the ground that art is, of course, itself already a thing of the "spirit" and not of the body, and lives accordingly in a divine realm of its own, and is freed from the restraints proper to ordinary men and women. This illustration—and others could be cited—can indicate how dangerous the words "spirit" and "spiritual" are if loosely employed. The contrast between spirit and body, when the former is ranked higher than the latter, is derivative of Greek philosophy and not of the thought world of the Bible. The Bible knows nothing of "spiritual" religion in the Greek sense. That is one reason why the "body realism" of the Bible is so often shocking to us. The Bible does not accept the worship of beauty, or of truth, or of goodness as a substitute for the worship of a personal God of righteousness and holiness. Neither artist nor ascetic scientist nor supermoral Pharisee is, in the Bible, excused from the humbling appearance before God as a sinner. Our epistle allows of no deception in moral matters. There is no evasion. **It is because of these things that the wrath of God comes upon the sons of disobedience.**

The wrath of God (see Expos. on 2:3) is not a very popular theme in modern preaching. The N.T. itself is often interpreted as picturing a kind of "new" God who can be contrasted with the God of the O.T. The "old" God was a God of wrath. But the new God, the God revealed by Jesus, is a God of love. Jesus came for the purpose of bringing to men the good news that God is no longer angry!

Such a view of God and his love is, however, sheer sentimentalism. It abolishes the wrath of God by robbing God of his righteousness. Here, as often in reading our N.T., we must remember that no apostolic writer ever dreamed of repudiating the O.T. There is indeed something new in the N.T. God's sacrificial love, as revealed in the Cross, does solve the otherwise insoluble problem of divine wrath. But the solution is not the lessening of God's holiness or of his inexorable demands.

We would do well, whenever we speak of God's love, to prefix to the noun the adjective "holy." God's love is "holy love." Forgiveness is so costly precisely because it dare not be immoral. Acquittal before God does not mean that we as sinners have become innocent. We are still guilty sinners. Wrong has not been turned into right. Nor have God's standards of righteousness been lowered to a level where divine wrath no longer applies. The wrath against evil remains. Forgiveness is a gift across the chasm of violated holiness. Repentance on man's side makes the giving of the gift possible. But where there is no repentance, **the wrath of God comes upon the sons of disobedience.**

8 For ye were sometime darkness, but now *are ye* light in the Lord: walk as children of light;
9 (For the fruit of the Spirit *is* in all goodness and righteousness and truth;)
10 Proving what is acceptable unto the Lord.

not associate with them, 8 for once you
were darkness, but now you are light in
the Lord; walk as children of light 9 (for
the fruit of light is found in all that is good
and right and true), 10 and try to learn

8. Once . . . but now, cf. the contrast "at one time . . . but now" of 2:11, 13. In the former passage the contrast between the past and the present condition of the readers was stated in terms of their relationship to God and to the community of God's people; here it is stated in terms of character and social influence. **You were darkness: darkness** was not merely their environment; they themselves shared the nature of the evil world which surrounded them. Conversely, **you are light,** not merely "enlightened," but partaking of the nature of the light which now surrounds them, and so giving light to others (cf. Matt. 5:14; Phil. 2:15). **Walk as children of light:** Live as befits your nature; let your light shine (cf. Matt. 5:16). The idiom is again Hebraic; **walk,** of the whole tenor of the moral life; **children of light,** men whose essential nature is **light.**

9. The fruit of [the] **light:** The variant **of the Spirit** (KJV) is an assimilation to Gal. 5:22. **Goodness and righteousness and truth:** The writer is insisting on the moral significance of **light,** against false mystical interpretations, or any boast of "enlightenment" which was barren of moral effect. There are clear parallels in the Johannine writings (John 3:19-21; I John 1:5-7; 2:8-11).

10. Note Rom. 12:2, "That you may prove what is the will of God, what is good and acceptable and perfect." **Proving:** The Greek verb has two senses: (*a*) "test, assay" (of the quality of metals, fine materials, wines, etc.); and (*b*) "approve." Here we have an extension of the first sense. The thought is that we are called to exercise intelligent discrimination in the sphere of moral action, not taking for granted the standards that are commonly accepted in the society around us, but putting all our actions to the test of acceptability **to the Lord,** i.e., to Christ. **Acceptable** is nearly always used of a sacrificial offering, as in Rom. 12:2 (cf. Phil. 4:18, "a sacrifice acceptable and pleasing to God"). So here it suggests the thought that the life of the Christian is ever laid upon the altar. All our actions are to be an offering to God (here, **to the Lord;** an indication of the high

8-14. ***Darkness and Light.***—This entire section employs the metaphors of light and darkness to paint a contrast between paganism and Christianity. The metaphor is fairly obvious. Light, indeed, has been in the history of religions one of the commonest of symbols. "It has certainly been one of the things in the physical environment of man which, from the earliest times we know of, has peculiarly impressed him and been most closely associated with his thoughts of the Divine." [5]

This passage contains vivid, and sometimes unique, phrasing—**you are light in the Lord, children of light, fruit of light**—viz., **all that is good and right and true.** Commentators have exercised their ingenuity in dissecting these images. More profitable, perhaps, is it to lay emphasis upon the ethical burden of these verses. The author is not commending the gospel as a form of intellectual enlightenment, though that (see Expos. on 4:18) may be a by-product. The important verb in this passage is **walk.** Christians, as **children of light,** are to **walk** in the light. Immorality and **things that** men **do in secret** and darkness go together. The Bible knows human nature. "Stolen waters are sweet, and bread eaten in secret is pleasant" (Prov. 9:17). "For they that sleep sleep in the night; and they that be drunken are drunken in the night" (I Thess. 5:7). God, however, also is "in secret," and "sees in secret" (Matt. 6:18).

No observer of human life can fail to note how desperate for most men and women is the fear of exposure. We wear masks to hide our real selves. For the saint the mask may be one of humility. He wishes to give his alms and to say his prayers in secret, so that they may not be seen of men but of God alone. But this is not

[5] Edwyn Bevan, *Symbolism and Belief* (New York: The Macmillan Co., 1938), p. 125.

11 And have no fellowship with the unfruitful works of darkness, but rather reprove *them.*

12 For it is a shame even to speak of those things which are done of them in secret.

what is pleasing to the Lord. 11 Take no part
in the unfruitful works of darkness, but instead expose them. 12 For it is a shame even
to speak of the things that they do in secret;

Christology of the author), and we must therefore take care that they are **acceptable** to him.

11. Have no fellowship: The warning is not only against the committing of such sins, but also against the toleration of them, against any continuing in **fellowship** with those who commit them. The **works of darkness** are called **unfruitful** in the sense that they contribute nothing of lasting good to life. **Expose them:** The thought is not of denunciation, but of setting evil in the light of truth, so that every attempt to justify or palliate it is made transparent, and it is seen in its true nature. A negative attitude of abstention from evil is not sufficient; the Christian must bring the light of his own nature (vs. 8) to bear upon them.

12-14. The further thought is now advanced that such exposure to the light puts an end to the works of darkness and leads to the conversion of those who have relapsed into these gross pagan sins. The expression is obscure and difficult in detail, but the general idea is fairly clear.

12. The things that they do in secret: The reference seems to be to rites of religion which are practiced secretly, not to the misconduct of individuals. In the context the writer can hardly be attacking the pagan mysteries, though the secrecy with which they were celebrated was frequently a ground for suspicion that the ritual involved such abominations that it could not be practiced openly. He appears to have in mind professedly Christian groups which were imitating the secrecy of the pagan mysteries; and he holds that their secrecy cannot be adopted for any good purpose—it can only be a cover for shameful deeds. "The whole warning is important as evidence of the existence of sects which practised rites of such a character that they can, rightly or wrongly, be accused of the vilest secret vices, although they cannot be accused simply of idolatry" (Knox, *St. Paul and Church of Gentiles,* p. 199). The writer's words suggest that he has no certain knowledge of what actually goes on in such gatherings, and we have no means of knowing whether his suspicions were justified; the catholic church itself incurred widespread popular suspicion not many years later, without any justification, on the same grounds. The writer is opposed to secrecy in any case; like the Fourth Evangelist, he is

---

the motive for hiding of the worldling. He hides because he must. Exposure would bring danger or shame. The criminal fears betrayal. The adulterer fears the retaliation of jealousy. And all men, even the worst, nurture a sanctuary of the soul which is ashamed to reveal all. Confucius once said, "The sense of shame is of great importance to man." As indeed it is. Hence the wearing of disguises. Hence also the enormous amount of self-delusion in the hearts of men. The medical psychiatrist finds his vocation in helping people to tear off masks and to permit the light of reason—but usually not the light of Christ—to penetrate the buried memories of shunned experience.

The Christian, by contrast, is one who has exposed himself to the light. This light brought judgment and revealed ugly things. "For every one that doeth evil hateth the light, neither cometh to the light, lest his deeds should be reproved. But he that doeth truth cometh to the light, that his deeds may be made manifest" (John 3:20-21). But judgment is the very thing which the Christian has learned to accept as the gateway into his new life in Christ. Repentance can be joyous acceptance of the searching light of God's holiness. The grace of Christian repentance—for repentance too is a gift of God—can bring with it a shaking off of burdens. Masks can be thrown away. Christians walking in the light can taste "the glorious liberty of the children of God" (Rom. 8:21). Not that morbid exhibitionism of sins is a proper form of exposure. A forgiven sinful past is in God's hands and need not be paraded before men. Christians tempted to indulge in unseemly autobiography

13 But all things that are reproved are made manifest by the light: for whatsoever doth make manifest is light.

14 Wherefore he saith, Awake thou that sleepest, and arise from the dead, and Christ shall give thee light.

13 but when anything is exposed by the light it becomes visible, for anything that becomes visible is light. 14 Therefore it is said,

"Awake, O sleeper, and arise from the dead,
and Christ shall give you light."

persuaded that "he who does what is true comes to the light, that it may be clearly seen that his deeds have been wrought in God" (John 3:21), and that it is only the evildoer who "hates the light, and does not come to the light, lest his deeds should be exposed" (John 3:20). He insists that everything in Christianity must be open and aboveboard. Certainly he is aware of a serious danger, which was unquestionably present, that everything distinctive in Christianity should be swallowed up in the complex syncretism of the age.

13. This verse is particularly obscure. Render, "Whatever is exposed is made manifest by the light, for everything that is made manifest is light." It does not seem possible to give the participle φανερούμενον the middle sense, as in both our versions—**becomes visible** (RSV); **doth make manifest** (KJV). Like the immediately preceding φανεροῦται—**is exposed** (RSV); **are made manifest** (KJV)—it must be passive. But in what sense can it be said that "everything that is made manifest is light"? The underlying thought appears to be that darkness cannot live in the presence of light; therefore when light is let in upon the evil of these rites, they are not only revealed in their true nature, but are destroyed—they cannot maintain themselves once the veil of secrecy is pierced. The power of the light not only reveals, but penetrates and transforms into its own likeness whatever it illumines.

14. The phrase **wherefore he saith** elsewhere always introduces a scriptural citation (so 4:8), and it is possible that through error or forgetfulness the writer has taken this fragment of a Christian hymn to be a verse from the O.T.; he might be misled by a vague reminiscence of certain passages of the book of Isaiah (60:1; 9:2; etc.). The inexactitude of the early Christians in quoting scripture would facilitate such a mistake.

The fragment quoted is not known to us from other sources; it probably comes from a Christian baptismal hymn. As it is meant to reinforce what has just been said, it helps us to realize that when the writer has spoken of "the light," he has not been wholly taken up with the physical metaphor, nor has he thought of light solely as a symbol of purity; in his mind he has all along kept equating it with Christ himself (cf. John 1:4-9, especially vs. 9, "the true light that enlightens every man"). Sleep and death are figures

might well heed the counsel of our very epistle. **It is a shame even to speak of the things** that some of us have in our life's record.

Yet the joyousness of walking **as children of light** cannot be overrated. The testimonials of alcoholics who have found salvation in the fellowship of Alcoholics Anonymous can vividly illustrate this truth. At last the secret is out and the fact exposed: "I am an alcoholic." (Not *was* but *am*.) "I am helpless by myself." The psychological effect of this honest exposure is itself half of the cure. Light has come into darkness. The self-delusion is over. The victim of alcohol has discovered the truth of the psalmist's confession, "If I say, Peradventure the darkness shall cover me; then shall my night be turned to day" (Ps. 139:10 Coverdale). And light, as one of our verses by mixing metaphors quaintly has it, bears **fruit—the fruit of light is found in all that is good and right and true.**

Exposure of the darkness within the soul of a repentant Christian can lead also to courage in exposing darkness in the world. **Take no part in the unfruitful works of darkness, but instead expose them,** says one of our verses. Much evangelism could gain in effectiveness if, in place of premature moral exhortation, it boldly ventured upon simple exposure of **works of darkness.** We might help the victims of the "prince of this world" to see what life without God realistically means. Many a worldling could be led to confess that his creed amounts to "I believe in the lust of the flesh and in the loneliness of the soul." **Unfruitful,** surely!

15 See then that ye walk circumspectly, not as fools, but as wise,	**15** Look carefully then how you walk,

which symbolize the condition of the soul apart from Christ; both belong to the realm of "darkness."

4. A Brief Summary (5:15-20)

A brief paragraph sums up what has been said about the distinctive elements of the Christian life.

15. Look carefully: The MS evidence is evenly balanced; the transfer of the adverb to the object clause **that ye walk circumspectly** is supported by a diversity of witnesses (including all the main codices of the "Western" group, and also the Codex Alexandrinus and the Latin and Syriac versions), and these are hardly outweighed even by the agreement of Vaticanus and Sinaiticus and Papyrus 46 in attaching it to the governing imperative. The general sense is not greatly affected whichever variant is preferred: the verse is a warning against laxity in moral action. The enlightenment received from God

---

Seen in its true light, such a life, "having no hope, and without God in the world" (2:12), might lead to recoil and even revulsion. And these in turn are the gateways to the acceptance of the light of Christ in repentance.

15. *Christian Wisdom.*—Many a philosopher and moralist has pleaded for the cultivation of wisdom. The very word has become a symbol in civilized societies for the most precious of man's corporate possessions. "How much better is it to get wisdom than gold!" (Prov. 16:16.) A whole section of the O.T. bears the customary title "Wisdom Literature."

But there is wisdom and wisdom. Paul can praise wisdom when it flows from Christian faith, and can at the same time denounce it when it is mere "wisdom of this world." In a notable passage (I Cor. 1:17-29) he presses home the paradox that the "foolishness of God is wiser than men. . . . God hath chosen the foolish things of the world to confound the wise; and God hath chosen the weak things of the world to confound the things which are mighty."

An analysis of the contrast between the wisdom which can thus be called "foolishness" and the wisdom of this world could carry us far. In the days when the Christian gospel was first confronting the Greco-Roman world, it faced no greater rival than the wisdom schools of Athens and Alexandria, and the philosophies and theosophies which had captured the loyalties of the best minds of the empire. We still sit at the feet of Plato and Aristotle and admire the lofty moral precepts of a Stoic moralist like Epictetus. Such baptizing of Greek thought into fellowship with Christian wisdom does not, however, lessen the basic difference. For the Greek, religion was man's climb upward to the realm of the divine. For the Christian, the gospel was the drama of a divine descent. That God would forgive sinners was unknown to a Plato. Yet Christian wisdom must begin with acceptance of this "foolishness" of the Cross.

Nevertheless, when this basic difference has once been acknowledged, Christians are under as great an obligation as any pagan ever felt himself to be to live **not as fools, but as wise.** The Christian faith gives no license to laziness in the use of God-given intelligence. "Be ye therefore wise as serpents" (Matt. 10:16), advises Jesus. Obedience to this precept can correct much mistaken Christian piety. Christians are not exempt from the history of their own age and time. The reading of the daily newspaper may be, for many Christian vocations, almost as important as a reading of the Bible. The verbs in our verse are **look** and **walk.** Christians buy and sell in the market as do non-Christians. They **walk** the ordinary highways of secular life. They are to witness to their faith where they are. Their faith is not to be an opiate of escape from the world, but power to overcome the world. Clearly, this means a knowledge of the world as well as a knowledge of the gospel. Every Christian—with possibly some vocational exceptions—ought to be, if the phrase is rightly understood, a man of the world. Paul was this, and to an astonishing degree so was Jesus. "I have become all things to all men, that I might by all means save some" (I Cor. 9:22), boasts Paul. Paul's biography is a beautiful illustration of what **look carefully then how you walk** can mean in practice. As we read the thrilling story of Paul's last missionary journey, with its account of tempest and shipwreck and of his assumption of virtual captaincy of a pagan crew of sailors, we certainly get a picture of a Christian apostle as anything except a pallid, impractical "saint," withdraw-

16 Redeeming the time, because the days are evil.
17 Wherefore be ye not unwise, but understanding what the will of the Lord *is.*

not as unwise men but as wise, 16 making the most of the time, because the days are evil. 17 Therefore do not be foolish, but understand what the will of the Lord is.

---

does not justify heedlessness in the midst of an evil environment. **Wise:** The practical wisdom that makes conduct consistent with faith.

16. Redeeming the time, i.e., putting to profit the fleeting occasions that are given you (see on Col. 4:5). In both passages we have the interpretation of wisdom in conduct as consisting in the profitable use of opportunities. Here the injunction bears generally upon the whole of the moral life; in Colossians it is applied specifically to relations with non-Christians ("them that are without"). **Because the days are evil,** i.e., conditions often unfavorable for Christian witness. The debasement of contemporary society is not an excuse for relaxation on our part, or for acquiescence in lower standards; it is a motive for added earnestness in maintaining the Christian ideal unsullied.

17. See vs. 10. Notice again the high Christology which is implied: **the will of the Lord** is used almost unconsciously as equivalent to the more usual expression "the will of God."

---

ing from the rough-and-tumble of life. His example could give encouragement to many a Christian layman who is doubtful whether his immersion in practical life prevents his witnessing fully to his faith.

16-17. ***Redeeming the Time.***—The metaphor may on occasion need explaining, but our treasure of biblical jewels of phrase would be impoverished by its loss. It is one of the precious N.T. texts which disprove the charge that Christianity is a religion of escapism from history.

The Christian faith is both a sanctuary and a battle station, a fortress against the world and an outpost of God's reign squarely within the world. A tension must be accepted as between the two. Mere withdrawal is not the Christianity of the N.T. At no time in Christian history would escape from history have seemed more plausible than in apostolic times. The end of history was momentarily expected. The Thessalonian letters of Paul evidence a temptation to idleness as current in Christian circles. This receives strenuous warnings. Catholic mysticism and Protestant individualist pietism are not exactly idleness. Both have contributed to enrich Christian experience. Both, however, are in part deflections from the historical realism of the Bible. It would be difficult to find in the N.T. any "flight of the alone to the alone," or the ideal—Aristotelian in origin—of contemplation as the highest good. Both of these were exalted in medieval and postmedieval piety. Christians are to redeem the time, not to escape from it.

Nor is the call to the strenuous life lessened by a pessimistic view of the age. One would expect the second clause of our text to read, "despite the fact" that **the days are evil.** The word **because** accordingly heightens the imperative. There is little if any optimism about secular history in the N.T. Perhaps later Christian experience can moderate the pessimism of the days of Tiberius and Nero and Caligula. Yet it is a disastrous mistake on the part of Christians to identify Christian hope, and consequent willingness to work for the kingdom of heaven, with secular progress. We must beware of the dangers of an age when Christians become secular-minded and declare the days "good" instead of **evil.** Any feeling that the church must always be up to date in the eyes of the world should be guarded against. Our epistle would call such languorous easing of strains foolish. A Christian's duty is to look to the **will of the Lord** for a motive to redeem the time and to participate in the present tasks of history. Proofs of success or progress may or may not be forthcoming. God's grace is prevenient grace. "While we were yet sinners, Christ died for us" (Rom. 5:8). Imitation of God means similar activity of gracious service of men *before* its value may have been statistically validated. Nor is the **will of the Lord** limited to a call to practices which can be labeled strictly "religious." The **will of the Lord** applies to each one of us where we are—in every business transaction, in the theater, on the golf course, or in the little courtesies of the street corner. No occasion is too insignificant for **redeeming the time.** Time is precious. God takes it very seriously.

Is it not a tragic misreading of the Christian faith that all of us are inclined to relegate "religion" to special hours or seasons and to ap-

18 And be not drunk with wine, wherein is excess; but be filled with the Spirit;
19 Speaking to yourselves in psalms and
hymns and spiritual songs, singing and
making melody in your heart to the Lord;

18 And do not get drunk with wine, for
that is debauchery; but be filled with the
Spirit, 19 addressing one another in psalms
and hymns and spiritual songs, singing and
making melody to the Lord with all your

Do not get drunk with wine: The words are cited from Prov. 23:31 (the LXX according to Codex A). The warning is meant literally, but there is an overtone of reference to the use of wine in the cult of Dionysus and possibly in other mysteries, and to wine-induced frenzies of religious exaltation. Christian devotion calls for a clear spirit, not for maudlin ecstasies. **Debauchery:** The word ἀσωτία is a negative formation from a root closely related to σωτηρία ("salvation"); it denotes the ruin of life in dissolute living of every kind. The thought is that drunkenness is the gateway to profligacy. **But be filled with the Spirit,** probably better, "be filled in spirit"; there seems to be no instance of the construction πληρόω ἐν in the sense "fill with." The antithesis is not between **wine** and **spirit** but between the two states—intoxication with its degrading effects on the one hand; and a progressive fulfillment of the spiritual life on the other. These two are mutually incompatible.

19-20. Spiritual fullness comes to expression in joyful fellowship, in song, in perpetual thanksgiving. The Christian's whole life, when it is given its true direction, moves in the atmosphere of worship. In the context the words cannot refer to the meetings for public worship alone or even primarily, but to everyday social intercourse. The whole expression is modeled on Col. 3:16-17; but **addressing one another** suggests the general relationships of life over a broader area than the "teaching and admonishing" of the Colossians passage. Note that the singing is done **to the Lord,** i.e., to Christ; in Colossians, it is "singing . . . to God" (according to the true text). The alteration is certainly not deliberate, but is an unconscious reflection of how completely Christians had become accustomed "to

---

pointed pieties? Churchgoing and prayer hours are a necessity for the Christian life. Woe unto us if we neglect them. They are the times for listening to the word of God which will clarify for us his will. But the doing of his will is both costing and rewarding in the *now* of every day. It is reported of William Temple, Archbishop of Canterbury, that he was fond of saying, "God is not primarily interested in religion." The paradox is worth pondering. God, truly, is *not* interested in establishing a kingdom of escape from history, a history which has him for its Creator and Sustainer. Every reader of the Gospels must be impressed by the fact that Jesus himself was not conspicuously pious in the sense of limiting his activity to the synagogue or the temple. He walked roads, and sat in fishing boats, and was "a friend of publicans and sinners" (Matt. 11:19). His apparent secularism shocked his contemporaries. We, his followers, have not his full powers of resisting secular temptations. But we too are to witness to the love of God *in* the world.

18-20. ***Christian Joyfulness.***—Christian conscience, particularly in recent times, has been divided over the fitting solution for the problem of alcohol. Shall this be "Prohibition," both in the moral code of Christians and on a nation's statute books? Or at least the former? Or can temperance suffice? On one Christian precept all are agreed: **Do not get drunk with wine, for that is debauchery.**

These verses are of particular importance in dealing with this problem—whatever the legal solution—in that they present a positive alternative to the enticements, and even the rewards, of strong drink. The weakness of all merely negative prohibitions is that they do not go to the root of the difficulty. Why do men and women indulge or overindulge in alcohol? The motive is not primarily a matter of taste sensation. Many an alcoholic abhors the "taste" of the whisky which he craves. The lure of alcohol lies in what it gives by way of rewards. Men find in it a "release from troubles and a surcease from care." It offers an escape from "the sorrow of the world" (II Cor. 7:10). On the positive side, particularly when alcoholic delights are part of companioning, it produces sociality. The cocktail bar becomes a secular substitute for a church. A "spirit" is engendered in the fellowship of the wine bottle. It is not a mere verbal accident that the words spirit and spirits jostle each other in the dictionary. All men are hun-

20 Giving thanks always for all things
unto God and the Father in the name of
our Lord Jesus Christ;

heart, 20 always and for everything giving
thanks in the name of our Lord Jesus
Christ to God the Father.

---

think about Jesus Christ as about God" (II Clem. 1:1), and to find him always present with them in their joyful gatherings. On the practice of singing to Christ cf. Pliny's report on the results of his inquiry into the tenets of the Christianity of his time in Pontus (A.D. 112): he found that the Christians "were accustomed on a fixed day to gather before daybreak and to sing antiphonally a hymn to Christ as to a god" (*Letters* X. 96).

Always and for everything giving thanks: The thought of adversity is not to be found in the context, so we cannot follow the long line of commentators who read into the words, "Give thanks even for your tribulations." The thought is simply that as all life moves in the atmosphere of worship, so all worship is suffused with thanksgiving.

In the name of our Lord Jesus Christ, i.e., as his disciples, living under his authority and owing our access to God to his mediation.

---

gry for "spirit." They crave enthusiasm. The word enthusiasm, like the word spirit, has religious overtones. It means, lit., "possessed by a god." When the first Christian fellowship at Pentecost broke out into enthusiasms by speaking in tongues, observers equated the effect with drunkenness, "These men are full of new wine" (Acts 2:13). The Holy Spirit, too, as we have noted more than once, has analogies with "spirits" on the secular plane.

And when men stand outside the fellowship of the Holy Spirit, is it any wonder that substitutes are sought? Man does not live by bread alone. The enormous and alarming increase in alcoholic indulgence in our age is a symptom of the breakdown of our Christian culture. It is, however, also still a symbol of a deep hunger in the hearts of men and women for that which only the fellowship life of Christians can supply. We who are custodians of this God-given substitute for strong drink—our common life in the body of Christ—should understand before we condemn. Above all, we should clarify our witness by visible testimonials of what Christian joy and Christian enthusiasm and Christian Spirit-filled sociality can be. By our fruits they shall know us. **Be filled with the Spirit,** pleads our text, **singing and making melody to the Lord with all your heart.**

Enthusiasm comparable to that commonly experienced among devotees of the pagan god of alcohol is not too popular in Christian circles in our sophisticated age. We have grown decorous and restrained. Some of us are a bit shocked when we come in contact with Holy Rollers or humble Pentecostal groups who reduplicate the unrestrained joy of N.T. church life literally. And we are probably right in deploring such excesses. The sanctuary needs guarding as the dwelling place of the Most High. Even Paul dealt severely with his Corinthian flock as they practiced an unchecked "Pentecostalism."

But here, as so often, we make the mistake of limiting the concept of church and religion to their architectural expression in a house of God or to our Sunday worship. Have we not also parish halls and cottage parlors and a common life of Christian fellowship on weekdays? Must Christian **singing and making melody** be restricted to our rightly decorous worship hours? And as for **giving thanks always for all things unto God**—this can surely find social expression in games and picnics and singing around a campfire.

Thousands of Christian laymen and laywomen would be willing to testify that social life in our villages and suburbs, not to speak of our great cities with their pagan Broadways, cries aloud for renewed contact with Christian grace. We are hungry for Christian standards once more in our young peoples' parties, in our men's clubs, and in our amusements generally. Pagan resources for fellowship life are soon exhausted. Alcohol is a tempting recourse. But those who can recall, or can still experience, the joy of social sharing in a truly Christian home or in a community still untouched by secular world-weariness will witness to its incomparable rewards. One of the most powerful tools of Christian evangelism in the twentieth century may turn out to be a Christian supper table or a Christian conversation around a fire.

Singing and making melody. Our verses make much of the ministry of music in the Christian life. They embody a profound insight. Music, according to Aristotle, is the most "moral" of all the arts. It affects character most directly. A martial mood can be produced by a march; a mood of awe by a noble chorale; a pagan relaxa-

21 Submitting yourselves one to another in the fear of God.

21 Be subject to one another out of rev-

C. Third Exhortation: To Mutual Subordination in the Christian Household (5:21–6:9)

From the theme of the contrast between Christian and pagan morality the writer now turns to the application of Christian principles to all the personal relations of domestic life. A single phrase serves to define the fundamental attitude: mutual subjection, based on reverence for Christ (5:21). He then treats successively of the reciprocal duties and responsibilities of wives and husbands (5:22-33), of children and parents (6:1-4), and of slaves and masters (6:5-9). In this arrangement of material he is following a conventional pattern of Hellenistic philosophical literature, which frequently concluded the exposition of the doctrine with a brief social code dealing with man's duties toward the gods, toward his country and its rulers, and toward the members of his own household. His immediate model, however, is the brief "table of household duties" framed by Paul in his letter to the Colossians (3:18–4:1; see introductory note to that passage); but there is a notable change in the center of interest. Paul had been much concerned with the case of the slave Onesimus at the time that he wrote Colossians, and the other items in the table are mentioned only incidentally to the teaching on the duties of slaves and masters. This writer, on the other hand, lays his main emphasis on the section concerning the duties of wives and husbands; not because he has any external reason for stressing the marital relation at the time, but because he sees in it a reflection and a symbol of the relationship between Christ and the church. We feel, indeed, that he has recourse to this familiar literary form primarily because it affords a convenient vehicle for the exposition of this new aspect of his doctrine of the church.

1. Husbands and Wives—Marriage as a Symbol of Christ's Relationship with the Church (5:21-33)

21. In KJV this verse is taken as the conclusion of the preceding paragraph, the participle **submitting** being construed in parallelism with "giving thanks" above (vs.

tion of restraints by a saxophonic croon. A vigilant church will stand critical guard over its music.

Corporate song is akin to alcohol in imparting "spirit." It creates enthusiasm. When communal singing becomes a neglected custom, this is always a sign of a decadent corporate life. This has already happened on much of our modern social scene. Many a secular "religion" has won its way into the loyalties of men on the wings of song. One recalls the "Marseillaise" of the French Revolution, or the "Internationale" of communism, or the "Horst Wessel" of Hitler's Germany, or the "Battle Hymn of the Republic" of America's Civil War.

One man with a dream, at pleasure,
  Shall go forth and conquer a crown;
And three with a song's new measure
  Can trample an empire down.[6]

[6] Arthur William Edgar O'Shaughnessy, "Ode," *The Oxford Book of English Verse* (Oxford: University Press, 1912).

Christian enthusiasm has fed itself through all the centuries on the O.T. psalms. And the later hymnody of the church is merely psalmody brought up to date. A Christian flock **singing and making melody** is without any further stimulus **filled with the Spirit.** A hymn-sing as a substitute for alcohol? The remedy sounds naïve. But whenever tried, it proves itself. At the very least, our churches could lay more stress upon the ministry of music. Protestantism in particular has in its rich hymnody—richer by far than that which current Romanism can boast—a much-neglected treasure. We have quite possibly been deluded by the ideal of musical perfectionism. Choir and soloist have robbed the people of their corporate rights. Christian song should not be directed to critics of music, but **in your heart to the Lord.**

21. ***Submitting Yourselves.***—The virtue of submission is not popular in modern times. The ideals of democracy have pretty well broken the hold over the minds of men which rank and degree once possessed. "All men are created

20). Some of the older commentators seek—not too successfully—to interpret it in that connection; Westcott, for instance, remarks: "In mutual subjection all realise the joy of fellowship. Such harmonious subjection of one to another is the social expression of the personal feeling of thankfulness." There can be no doubt, however, that the RSV is correct in treating the participle as an imperative—**be subject**—and in putting the phrase at the head of the section which follows. The same participle is used in precisely the same way elsewhere in the N.T. (I Pet. 2:18; 3:1); and—the decisive point—this imperative is required to complete the thought of vs. 22, which in Greek contains no verb at all.

Out of reverence for Christ; lit., "in the fear of Christ." The KJV rendering, **fear of God**, reflects an assimilation to the more familiar expression. In II Cor. 5:11 Paul speaks of "the fear of the Lord," but in a context of reference to our appearance "before the judgment seat of Christ" (II Cor. 5:10); elsewhere he always writes "the fear of God." We may therefore look upon the expression "fear of Christ" (or **reverence for Christ**) here, where the thought of his function as judge is not in view, as another unconscious indication of the writer's high Christology: the attitude of awe with which we come before God belongs also to our approach to Christ. We may observe, however, that though this phrase is not used, the injunction to subjection which recurs in the social codes of the N.T. writers is generally based on our duty to Christ—"Be subject for the Lord's sake to every human institution" (I Pet. 2:13); "as is fitting in the Lord" (Col. 3:18); etc.

The spirit of mutual subjection is cardinal to the whole Christian conception of social relations. It is the antithesis of the spirit of self-assertion, of jealous insistence on

---

free and equal." This today is dogma almost throughout the world. It accounts for the revolutionary movements which are changing our social orderings around the globe.

The Christianity, also, is committed to the doctrine of human equality, in a deeper sense even than the secularist. This epistle, in the next chapter (6:9), asserts that with God there is no "respect of persons." In the Christian fellowship there can be no high or low, as the words are used in our social scene. The democracy of Judgment Day is an ultimate democracy, one in which even the hierarchical rankings of the church herself vanish. Our democratic centuries look back upon the Middle Ages with some contempt because of medieval caste systems. We are inclined to forget that the medieval world, with its feudal contrasts between lord and serf, lived under a vivid eschatological faith. Dante's *Divine Comedy*, in picturing the eternal realm surrounding the temporal, has no hesitation in assigning to his *Inferno* emperors and kings and bishops and even popes. An otherworldly framework for human life does mitigate the rigors of social caste.

No modern Christian, one may assume, would wish to belittle the blessings of secularist democracy. Human slavery, somehow accepted as normal even in the N.T., has now been outlawed by humanist and Christian conscience alike. Nevertheless, Christian insight brings criticism to bear upon the doctrine of democratic equalitarianism in its turn. Abolish inequality of inherited rank or status or caste, and you may merely have substituted for it the inequality of wealth. Abolish the inequality of wealth, and you may have left the inequality of power. And when this becomes institutionalized, the whole cycle of liberation may have to begin all over again. A communist utopia turns into a slave state! Such a realistic view of the human social problem need not lead to the conclusion that all overturnings of encrusted injustice are wrong. "It must needs be that offenses come"—even the offense of revolution. But no Christian, familiar with the wisdom of the Bible, should be fooled into confusing an era of judgment in history with utopia or the kingdom of God.

Bring the justice of human equality as up to date as you please, inequalities remain: the inequalities of talent, of power, of every social ordering from that of the family to that of the state and of the church. If "two men ride of a horse, one must ride behind." The homely truth of this Shakespearean proverb[7] is undeniable. Inequalities need the justification of useful social function. But a doctrinaire dream of a society without inequalities is dangerous. "It is not the possessions but the desires of mankind which require to be equalized," said Aristotle.[8] Would that some secular social reformers could see the problem of equality with

[7] *Much Ado About Nothing*, Act III, scene 5.
[8] *Politics* 1266*b*.

one's rights, which generally characterizes the men of the world. In substance it rests upon the example and precept of Christ, who "did not count equality with God a thing to be grasped, but emptied himself, taking the form of a servant" (Phil. 2:6-7; cf. Matt. 20:25-28).

It must be observed, however, that the principle of mutual subordination is not so applied as to destroy the complementary principle of authority, without which there can be no ordered social life among men. The head of the household, whether in his capacity of husband, father, or master of slaves, cannot be subject to his wife, his children, and his slaves, as they to him. Yet he may not wield authority as a domestic tyrant, in self-assertion or without full respect for those who are entrusted to his guidance and protection. Toward his wife he is charged to exhibit the self-sacrificing love that Christ bestows upon the church; toward his children, to care for their nurture in the things of the spirit; toward his slaves—the anomaly of the relationship is not recognized—he is to show a reciprocity of good will, and his whole attitude is to be determined by the recollection that in the highest of all relationships he himself is a slave to Christ. He is to be the kind of master to others that Christ is to him.

The particular provisions of such a code are obviously not of eternal and universal application; they are of necessity related to the sociological situation of the time. In a society which knows not the institution of slavery the admonitions to slaves and masters have no relevance; and where the social and economic position of women is fundamentally different from that which was the rule in the ancient world, the relation of wives and husbands can no longer be defined as simply subjection on the one hand and self-sacrificing devotion on the other (cf. the remarks of Edward Gordon Selwyn on the "subordinationist" ethic taught in I Peter: "It is plain that for St. Peter the 'subordination,' which the Apostle enjoins upon wives, is a matter of practical adjustment rather than of ethical principle. . . . Further, being a rule of adjustment rather than a principle of ethics, the

---

this maxim as a guide. Indeed, one could go further. Inequalities, and even rank and degree, are needed in society. Freedom requires disciplines and needs the restraints of order. Society generally, like an army, must have sergeants and captains and generals as well as privates. Liberty and equality, when emancipated from controls, can turn into the chaos of the lust for power.

> Take but degree away, untune that string,
> And, hark! what discord follows! each thing meets
> In mere oppugnancy:
> . . . .
> Then everything includes itself in power,
> Power into will, will into appetite.[9]

We thus come back to the problem of submission. In secular society submission, accepted willingly or unwillingly, is a necessity. Hierarchy of power or authority is simply a fact. We all live under some master. Even a dictator fears the people.

Is submission to power, then, enjoined upon a Christian regardless of the nature of that power? The N.T. seems at times to say this. "Let every soul be subject unto the higher powers. For there is no power but of God," says Paul (Rom. 13:1). "Submit yourselves to every ordinance of man for the Lord's sake," says a later epistle written in a time of persecutions (I Pet. 2:13). Meekness and endurance of wrong *is* enjoined upon the Christian. And if such a precept is "opiate for the people," the Christian must make the best of that fact. Submission, to be sure, has its limits. "We ought to obey God rather than men" (Acts 5:29), boldly declares Peter as he confronts the high priest of Jerusalem. Submission may lead to martyrdom. "For even hereunto were ye called: because Christ also suffered for us, leaving us an example" (I Pet. 2:21). And the power of submission to convert even the hearts of tyrants has been validated in history many times. So powerful is this weapon of submission that Gandhi and his followers could use it as itself a weapon of power.

But the involvement of the Christian in political life is not the announced theme of our passage. It has in mind submission *within* the Christian fellowship. The church is to be the pattern for all social orderings. In the fellowship a new factor is part of the picture. Here

[9] Shakespeare, *Troilus and Cressida*, Act I, scene 3.

22 Wives, submit yourselves unto your own husbands, as unto the Lord.

erence for Christ. 22 Wives, be subject to

---

command to the wife to 'obey' is changeable with changing circumstances" [*The First Epistle of St. Peter* (London: Macmillan & Co., 1946), p. 106]). All the more widely does the fundamental doctrine of *mutual* subordination come to its entire application as it is expressed in the golden words of Paul: "Let nothing be done through strife or vainglory; but in lowliness of mind let each esteem other better than themselves" (Phil. 2:3).

22. As to the Lord: The words are probably not meant to be any stronger than Paul's phrase, "as is fitting in the Lord" (Col. 3:18); the writer has allowed himself to be carried a step too far in pressing the analogy between the marriage relationship and the relationship between Christ and the church. Certainly the wife's subjection to her husband is not unconditional, as is her subjection to the Lord; it is conditioned by the fact that he, unlike Christ, is a sinful and fallible human being like herself. It may be noted that the writer assumes that both husband and wife are Christians; the counsel to wives in I Pet.

---

submission becomes mutual—**one to another,** or **to one another.** What this means in practical forms we see in ensuing verses.

22. ***Husband and Wife.***—Is it significant that the word **submit** is used here in an address to **wives,** while merely "love" is enjoined upon husbands three verses later (vs. 25)? There can be no doubt that our author had the patriarchal family order as a backdrop to his thinking. He knew no other. An orthodox male Jew, even to this day, thanks God that he is not a woman. The marvel of Christian fellowship within the church must have been so powerful, however, even in Paul's day, that the difference in forms of submission was assuredly more verbal than actual. In a truly Christian marriage, throughout Christian history, subjection has been mutual. "Be subject to one another" (vs. 21) is the inclusive command. Not that distinctions in forms of subjection as between the sexes have been abolished through what we know as the emancipation of womanhood. A Christian husband still exercises an authority which the wife must forgo. Many a modern marriage has been wrecked by unwillingness on the part of the wife to accept the sacrifices involved in the husband's choice of a profession or of a geographical location. In this area of conflict—with rare exceptions—the primary submission must perforce still devolve upon the wife. But corresponding calls for submission are laid upon the husband. Even the most patriarchal father, if love of wife was in his heart, has submitted to many an "unlordly" service in kitchen and nursery. And modern family life places demands upon mutuality of subjection greater than ever before. One could wish that the N.T. writers could have envisaged Christian family life as the N.T. itself, in the course of time, molded it into a garden of grace. But whenever masculine pride has cited the N.T. as excuse for the withholding of rights owing to womanhood, it has been guilty of a moralistic literalism which the N.T. itself repudiates.

Under the gospel of Christ mutual subjection is inseparable from true love. Love of another means accepting that other as a person, as a "thou" and not an "it." A person is never a mere object. A person is one created in the image of God, with powers of self-determination, free to say "Yes" and to say "No." A love union involves an "I will" on both sides. A free "Yes" is never produced by tyrannical power. It comes only by wooing and by grace. And wooing is again a form of submission. The "I" has to commit a temporary suicide. Even listening—truly Christian listening—demands submission. A complete egotist cannot listen. A "thou" has to become sufficiently important so that the ego of the listener is silenced in behalf of the concerns of the other.

Such, and many more, are the sacrifices which become demands if a marriage is to be a Christian marriage. Is it any wonder that purely human resources fail in the marriage bond? Modern readers of the literature of the ancients are almost universally shocked to see how happy mutuality in marriage, taken for granted as an ideal today even by the secularist, is there practically never found. What did the word "wife" mean to the noblest of the Greek philosophers, Socrates? The picture is not pretty. But the modern secularist, retaining the vision of Christian marriage as an ideal, is undergoing tragic disillusionments as he tries to actualize it without the help of divine grace. The contrast between Christian marriage and pagan marriage is becoming increasingly visible on any city or village street. In a pagan marriage two clashing egotisms try to form a union

23 For the husband is the head of the wife, even as Christ is the head of the church: and he is the saviour of the body.

your husbands, as to the Lord.
23 For the husband is the head of the wife as Christ is the head of the church, his body, and is

3 presupposes that the husband is not a Christian, and gives as a motive for subjection the hope that the husband may be won by "the reverent and chaste behavior" (I Pet. 3:2) of his Christian wife.

23. The writer here lays the foundation of his analogy, taking as his starting point a saying of Paul's in I Cor. 11:3, "I want you to understand that the head of every man is Christ, the head of a woman is her husband, and the head of Christ is God." In the application only the second of Paul's links in this ascending chain of authority is employed directly; in place of the first the writer falls back upon his own doctrine that **Christ is the head of the church** (cf. 1:22). He sees in the marriage relationship, then, a type of the unity in a common life which is God's ultimate purpose in creation, and which is realized in its absolute form in the union of Christ with his church. Headship, in the context, denotes primarily controlling authority and the right to obedience; but the control is exercised and the obedience rendered not in any external fashion, but within a living organism where the two parts are complementary each to the other. **He is the saviour of the body:** Not an aspect of the analogy—the husband is not the "savior" of his wife—but a reminder that the analogy is not perfect; the marriage relationship cannot *wholly* typify the relation of Christ to his church. The title **saviour** is not often used in the N.T. (only once in the Synoptics, Luke 2:11; once in John, 4:42; and once in

—mutual subjection unknown, repentance unknown, forgiveness unknown. The bond of sexual *eros*—indispensable in all marriage—can play its part. Custom and the remnants of legal restraint in an age of free divorce can be further props. Children too can bind together father and mother. Monogamous marriage, in fact, is so clearly an order of creation that pagan societies as well as Christian must perforce preserve it despite its many breakdowns. But no graces of nature or culture suffice to continue the pattern as post-Christian man himself accepts it as norm. Hence the Christian witness can perhaps be made visible in a pagan age by no better symbol than by placing the joy and glory of Christian marriage once more in bold relief. Here is one of Christianity's rewards. It may woo men into a search for the grace which makes it possible. "Ho, every one that thirsteth, come ye to the waters, . . . without money and without price" (Isa. 55:1).

23-25. *The Doctrine of the Church.*—Readers of books in which the scholarly ritual of footnotes is employed frequently discover that the notes are more interesting than the text. In the text proper the author is bound by the rigors of his argument. In the footnotes he can "let himself go." The author of our epistle, in these closing verses of this chapter, is annotating his instructions to the married. He uses as illustration the relationship of Christ to his church. The illustration becomes more important than the instruction. The ethical precepts on marriage are important also, but not exactly novel. But the doctrine of the church which is expressed in the illustration has rightly been considered by the later church as one of the most significant in the entire N.T.

Marriage, viewed as symbol of the relationship between God and his people, runs all through the Bible. The nuptial analogy is almost from the first implied in the very idea of a covenant, and the word covenant is itself a summary of the theme of the Bible. The prophetic movement of the eighth century before Christ began in part with Hosea's matchless picture of God as a husband and Israel as erring wife. Hosea's daring can still bring amazement to the historian. Was he not employing as symbol the sex life of man which in its degradations connoted the heathenism against which biblical religion waged its ceaseless battle? But Hosea does employ it—and so do his successors. The discourses of Jesus are full of nuptial analogies. They appear again, realistically and boldly, in the epistles of Paul. And in the last chapter of the N.T. the church is still a "bride."

It is all the more noteworthy, therefore, to observe how little modern theology makes of this symbol of the marriage. The church as the body of Christ is still a familiar figure of speech. But of the church as bride, or as spouse, or more simply and boldly still, as "wife," we hear

24 Therefore as the church is subject unto Christ, so *let* the wives *be* to their own husbands in every thing.

25 Husbands, love your wives, even as Christ also loved the church, and gave himself for it;

himself its Savior. 24 As the church is subject to Christ, so let wives also be subject in everything to their husbands. 25 Husbands, love your wives, as Christ loved the church

Paul, Phil. 3:20; a little more frequently in the deutero-Pauline literature); it is not a primary title for Christ, but a borrowing of pagan terminology. Here it appears to be used not as a title, but as describing the function of Christ in protecting and preserving the church **(the body)** from the disintegrating effects of sin and the assaults of her spiritual foes (6:12).

24. Therefore as, properly "but as." The "but" refers to the limitation on the analogy which has just been mentioned; though the husband is not a "savior" to his wife as Christ is to the church, his headship is sufficiently analogous to that of Christ to call forth his wife's subjection to him "in everything" (cf. on vs. 22).

25. As Christ loved the church and gave himself up for her: The phrasing is adapted from Gal. 2:20. The church's subjection to Christ is the pattern of the wife's attitude to her husband; the husband is now enjoined to take Christ's love for the church as the pattern of his own attitude to his wife. His part is not self-assertion, but self-sacrifice; the converse to obedience is not primarily rule, but devotion. Chrysostom nobly comments: "Wouldst thou that thy wife should obey thee as the church obeys Christ? Do thou then care for her, as Christ for the church, even if thou must lay down thy life for her—shrink not, shouldst thou suffer even this. Thou hast not yet matched at all that which Christ hath done. For thou doest this after thou hast already won her, but he sacrificed himself for her that turned away from him and hated him; and when she was thus disposed, he brought her to his feet, not by threats or insults or terror or any such

little. Can it be that the neglect of a full N.T. doctrine of the church is the result of such avoidance? We might well heed a recent historian of the marriage theology of the Bible. Contrasting our comparative familiarity with other N.T. symbols—particularly those connected with atonement sacrifices and with the church as body—he comments: "The loss of the Nuptial Idea is the loss of that system in which the other great symbols find their place. . . . It is the key to the treasure-house of the Church." He then points to the strange fact that sacrificial ideas are still vivid in Christian literature and hymnody while the nuptial symbols have been largely unused. Yet animal sacrifices are utterly foreign to modern life. Everybody attends weddings. "How strange it is that we miss this contact provided for us between ordinary life and the mysteries of God!"[1]

Is the symbol of the marriage too realistic for us, as are so many of the "bodily" symbols of the Bible? Are we, even since the Reformation, victims of the asceticism and mysticism of medieval piety, which distorted the biblical nuptial idea almost beyond recognition? It would seem so. Obvious dangers surround a literalizing of the marriage analogy. Yet there it is, in the loftiest flights of prophecy of the O.T., in the discourses of Jesus, in the majestic church theology of Paul. Our epistle does not hesitate to employ "fleshly" symbolism—the story of the creation of Adam and Eve. As Adam can say of Eve, "This is now bone of my bones, and flesh of my flesh" (Gen. 2:23), so Christ cherishes the church. "Because we are members of his body, . . . and the two shall become one" (vss. 30, 31). The N.T. symbol of the church as body of Christ quite possibly has its biblical rootage—whatever may be its Platonic derivation also—in the nuptial analogy.

The N.T. idea of the church has probably been shouldered into obscurity more tragically than any other major N.T. doctrine. What indeed has not happened to it by way of neglect and distortion? Examine, for example, the traditional scholastic definition of the church as the "mystical body of Christ." The phrase is not in the N.T., nor can the use of the word "mystery" (vs. 32) be cited as an equivalent. There is nothing "mystical" about the figure of Eve in Genesis, nor about Paul's realistic application of the concept of body to the sinning,

[1] Claude Chavasse, *The Bride of Christ* (London: Faber & Faber, 1940), pp. 17-18.

26 That he might sanctify and cleanse it with the washing of water by the word,

and gave himself up for her, 26 that he might sanctify her, having cleansed her by the

thing, but by his great solicitude. So do thou conduct thyself toward that wife of thine. . . . Her that is the partner of thy life, the mother of thy children, the spring of all thy joy, thou must not bind by terror and threats, but by love and gentleness" (translated from Chrysostom, *In Ephes.* Hom. xx. 144B-E [*Chrysostomi Opera,* ed. Bernard de Montfaucon, 2d ed. rev. (Paris: Gaume Fratres, 1838), XI, 165]). The entire homily should be read, both as one of the finest utterances of the "golden mouth" of the great Greek preacher, and as one of the noblest expositions ever framed of the Christian ideal of marriage. (Eng. tr. in *The Nicene and Post-Nicene Fathers,* ed. Philip Schaff [New York: Christian Literature Co., 1889], XIII, 143-52.)

26-27. The writer again departs from the lines of his analogy to expound under a new figure the work of Christ for the church. The figure is suggested by the bath of the bride before marriage, her being clothed in beautiful garments, and her presentation to her husband; this is represented, in the mystic bridal of Christ and the church, by Christian baptism. The writer goes beyond the analogy in representing Christ himself as

yet redeemed, flocks of Christians in Ephesus or Corinth. Connect the symbol of body with that of bride. Our epistle can well say, "This is a great mystery" (vs. 32). But the adjective "mystical" is canceled out. The bride of Christ is the historic reality which we meet in the N.T. and in the disillusioning pages of church history and in an adorned or unadorned Christian meetinghouse on our village streets today. Christ is the Bridegroom of this bodily, historical *ecclēsia.* This is the church which **Christ loved . . . and gave himself up for her.**

From heaven he came and sought her,
To be his holy bride;
With his own blood he bought her,
And for her life he died.[2]

The history of the nuptial symbol in the later church throws much light upon the difficulty modern theology encounters in rediscovering its N.T. glory (see Chavasse, *Bride of Christ,* for a full account). In briefest summary the story is this: Augustine is almost the last theologian for whom the idea of the bride of Christ was a vivid and meaningful concept. In medieval piety the bride became either the individual soul or the Blessed Virgin.[3] The majestic marriage theme of the Bible as symbol of the covenant between God and his people had been atomized. The "soul bride" had become the norm. The rapid development of monasticism contributed to this drastic revolution. For who could more dramatically typify the soul bride than the nun? The amalgamation of bride and Virgin Mother was a further natural consequence. The monk, too, of course could participate, though not with such obvious clarity, in the soul marriage with Christ. Nor was this individualistic piety overthrown completely in the overturn of the Reformation. Protestantism no longer retained the nun, but the Christian soul was left. The nuptial symbol could continue to be individualistically exploited. We still sing:

Jesus, lover of my soul,
Let me to thy bosom fly.

We rarely if ever realize that while the symbols of lover and beloved are profoundly biblical, the soul bride symbol is ultimately *not* biblical. Paul might have been shocked had he met such a distortion. Modern Christianity, blessed with an "opened" Bible, such as no previous generation of Christians since N.T. days has known, has before it a gigantic task as it reinstates in its thought and life a truly biblical doctrine of the church.

26-28. ***The Sanctification of the Church.***—Is our author in these verses picturing a perfect church with the expectation that such an ideal can be realized? The words seem clear enough. The church as bride, baptized **by the washing of water with the word,** is, like a bride on her wedding night, to **be presented before** her heavenly Bridegroom **in splendor, without spot or wrinkle or any such thing.** Is this sheer theological romanticism?

Doctrines of sanctification have caused much controversy in church history. Some at least of the problems which the idea of sanctification raises find clarification when the figure of the

[2] Samuel J. Stone, "The church's one foundation."

[3] The article "Marriage, Mystical" in the *Catholic Encyclopaedia* (New York: Robert Appleton, 1910), IX, 703-7, is disturbingly instructive.

27 That he might present it to himself a glorious church, not having spot, or wrinkle, or any such thing; but that it should be holy and without blemish.

washing of water with the word, 27 that the church might be presented before him in splendor, without spot or wrinkle or any such thing, that she might be holy and

administering to his church the sacramental cleansing of baptism, adorning her with spotless beauty, and presenting her to himself in the glory which he has shed upon her.

Having cleansed, better rendered "by cleansing"; the aorist expresses coincidental action. The aorist is used in preference to the present because the thought bears upon the definitive "cleansing" of baptism, not upon the progressive purification of the soul. **The washing of water with the word** refers, to use the later terminology, to the "matter" and "form" of the sacrament. The **word** may be understood either of the formula pronounced over the candidate (so the Greek commentators) or of the confession of faith made by him. Though modern commentators generally prefer the latter interpretation, the former is more in keeping with the context, which has to do with the work of Christ as the minister of baptism (cf. also John 15:3, "Now ye are clean through the word which I have spoken unto you").

In this language the thought of a corporate baptism of the church by Christ himself is superimposed, in a kind of "double exposure," on the imagery of individual baptism. The church in her totality passed with Christ through the baptism of death which he endured on her behalf; and the Christian sacrament in its repeated administration is the effectual sign of the believer's incorporation in the community so baptized. The background of this thinking lies in Jesus' own reference to his death as "a baptism" which his followers are to share (Mark 10:38-39); and in Paul's teaching that "all of us who have been baptized into Christ Jesus were baptized into his death" (Rom. 6:3). On the multiple imagery of the passage see especially L. S. Thornton, *Common Life in Body of Christ,* pp. 221-28.

27. The KJV is correct here in keeping the active voice—**present it to himself.** Again we have a multiple image: Christ is at once the bridegroom who receives the bride, and

bride as the corporate people of God is kept in mind, and when the O.T. nuptial imagery is recalled. The people of God of the old covenant were anything but a perfect people—as neither were the "saints" of the new Israel. Hosea's drama of the marriage between God and Israel opens with Israel an adulteress. Hosea's prophecy is in fact one of judgment. But the drama does not end there. An atonement follows. And then we read, as if the vision of our epistle were foreseen: "I will betroth thee unto me forever. . . . I will even betroth thee unto me in faithfulness; and thou shalt know the LORD. . . . As the bridegroom rejoiceth over the bride, so shall thy God rejoice over thee" (Hos. 2:19-20; Isa. 62:5). Our epistle is in the tradition of the prophets. It too is uttering the poetry of eschatology. The N.T. church, like the people of God of the O.T., is perfect only in hope and faith.

The bride-bridegroom symbol offers correction to any presumption on the part of the church. It is here that a return to vs. 23 is important. As the "husband is the head of the wife," so "Christ is the head of the church." And vs. 24 has the sharp sentence, "The church is subject to Christ." The fact that the patriarchal family pattern is background for our author's marriage symbol is doctrinally very important. A bride stands under subjection and under judgment. The doctrine of the church in the history of theological thought has grievously suffered because the nuptial analogy fell into neglect. Such a later definition of the church as "the extension of the Incarnation" might never have arisen. The "Word made flesh" was sinless. The church is not sinless. No "Vicar of Christ" is part of N.T. prophecy. The new covenant in Christ is not one of a divinely infused substance, but one of a redeemed relationship. The bride of Christ is not an incarnation of God. A bride can become an adulteress. In fact, the people of God was once an adulteress who required ransom. The concept of the church as "the extension of the Incarnation" appears like a logical corollary of the idea of the church as body of Christ. Isolate the idea of body from its nuptial context and it is capable of metaphysical interpretations. But the symbol of body of Christ

28 So ought men to love their wives as their own bodies. He that loveth his wife loveth himself.

without blemish. 28 Even so husbands should love their wives as their own bodies.

the one who prepares and presents her. **Glorious,** however, ought to be rendered as a predicate in keeping with the Greek word order: he presents her to himself clothed with the glory that he has given her. **Without spot or wrinkle:** "Without one trace of defilement or one mark of age" (Westcott, *ad loc.*). **Holy and without blemish:** The language of sacrifice is now used, bringing out the thought that the church is separated from the sphere of the profane and the worldly, and dedicated to the service of God.

28. So: The adverb is retrospective—"with such a love as this of Christ for the church." **As their own bodies,** not "as they love their own bodies," but "as being their own bodies," as part of their total self, not as another being external to them. The measure of the husband's love for his wife is not his care for himself but Christ's care for the church. The thought that the wife is the husband's "body" is correlative to the thought that the husband is the "head" of the wife, and is parallel with the thought that

as interpreted by the primary symbol of bride of Christ remains personalist and biblical.

A word more, however, can be said on the topic of sanctification. When we apply a standard of perfection to the individual Christian, difficulties abound. In what shall he be perfect? In moral behavior? That may mean merely legal pharisaism. In the faith that justifies? Who shall even attempt to measure penitence? Apply standards of sanctification to the church and difficulties appear also. The church as institution in history has been a woefully sinning church. Yet alive within the institutional church is another "church," the covenant, the marriage relationship between Christ and his spouse, his body.

A paradox meets us here—one as yet too little explored by Christian imagination. The perfection of a relationship cannot be measured by merely moralistic yardsticks. The love between a mother and her child may be a thing of beauty, yet neither mother nor child, judged moralistically, perfect at all. A marriage relationship may be foretaste of the kingdom of heaven, yet husband and wife each grievous sinners, discovering the glory of the nuptial covenant precisely in mutual repentance and forgiveness. Members of "Alcoholics Anonymous," to cite another illustration, may as individuals be simply "alcoholics," repudiating any claims to perfection. The fellowship of alcoholics itself, however, may be literally a miracle of redeeming power and deserve adjectives of superlative praise. Not that the individuals composing the fellowship fail to exhibit the grace flowing from the corporate group. They may protest that they owe their very lives to the fellowship. But it is the fellowship and not the individuals which is the marvel.

So with the covenant of the fellowship in Christ. Individually judged, members of a Christian group may be guilty publicans and prodigal sons, but as a church, gathered for worship, penitent, accepting forgiveness by faith, and "for everything giving thanks" (vs. 20)—such a fellowship *can* be the bride of Christ, **presented before him in splendor.**

The church is not an association of worshipers, but a *body* which worships. Hence the prayers of the church are acceptable unto God. "We," as individuals, so might read a paraphrase of Paul, "know not what we should pray for as we ought: but the Spirit [Christ in his church] itself maketh intercession for us" (Rom. 8:26). Normal Christian prayer is the prayer of the church—common prayer. Prayer, so runs a familiar definition, is "the soul's sincere desire." But who, as a lone individual, dares to trust his life of desire as voicing petitions not poisoned by egotism? Only the fellowship of the Holy Spirit can thus trust itself to pray aright. For fellowship in Christ consists in a visible relationship of repentance and forgiveness. "As we forgive those who trespass against us," so God can forgive us also. If the good news of the gospel is precisely the news of a new testament—covenant or relationship—a private Christianity becomes something of a contradiction. Relationship means sociality. So with prayer. "When thou art most alone thou must still, if thou wouldest pray, be in the midst of a family; thou must call upon a Father; thou must not dare to say *my,* but *our.*"[4] In other words, if you will pray a fully Christian prayer, you must pray as a member of the church.

[4] F. D. Maurice, *The Kingdom of Christ* (London: J. M. Dent, n.d.), II, 26.

29 For no man ever yet hateth his own flesh; but nourisheth and cherisheth it, even as the Lord the church:
30 For we are members of his body, of his flesh, and of his bones.

He who loves his wife loves himself. 29 For no man ever hates his own flesh, but nourishes and cherishes it, as Christ does the church, 30 because we are members of his

---

the church is Christ's body. Husband and wife together are complementary parts of one personality; therefore it can be said that **he who loves his wife loves himself.**

29. The change from "body" to **flesh** is made in anticipation of the citation from Gen. 2 which is about to be introduced (vs. 31). **Nourishes and cherishes:** The verbs belong to the thought of the husband's care for his wife, not to his care for his own skin and bones. There is a certain compression in the way that the thought is expressed; to clarify it we should have to fill it out in a paraphrase: "He who has learned to think of his wife as his own flesh (as he ought) will nourish and cherish her as Christ does the church."

30. Members of his body: The phrase prepares the way for the introduction of the reference to the story of the primal human marriage; in the background is the story of the making of Eve from a rib of Adam. **Of his flesh, and of his bones:** This addition is reasonably well attested; if accepted as authentic, it makes the reference of the initial

---

29-31. *A Reinterpretation of Piety.*—As already indicated, a stylistic confusion between illustration and original ethical precept runs through this entire passage. These verses accordingly are repetitive of themes already dealt with. Further comment can be only supplementary.

We are members of his body. Does the privilege of church membership mean to us modern Christians what it once did to the Christians of N.T. times? An honest answer might embarrass us. The individualization of the concept of the covenant with Christ, an inheritance of medieval distortions, has robbed the corporate church of much of its meaning. The covenant is thought of as one between God and the soul, and only secondarily as one between God and a people. The mystic's private cultivation of oneness with deity may have its place in Christian experience. But to present the *solus cum solo* relationship with God as the norm, or at least the crown, of the covenant brought to us in the gospel is a tragic misreading of the biblical revelation.[5] The liturgical movement in Roman Catholicism itself, in which mysticism has taken firmest root, is today trying to correct the errors of centuries. In Protestantism, in which the cultivation of subjective pieties has created corresponding loss of corporateness, a return to N.T. *church*manship may be equally called for.

If the Christianity of the twentieth century could relearn the lesson of the nuptial symbol of the Epistle to the Ephesians, we might again see a church presented as a bride of Christ "in splendor." The success of the ecumenical movement may depend upon such a recovery of a major biblical doctrine. The word "piety" is today under a cloud. It has come to connote a subjective, solitary, and, at times, even esoteric spirituality. Many a lay member of the church, living his Christian life in the world, thinks of piety as something a little morbid. Yet the inherited ideals of evangelical piety still give him a bad conscience. But let the concept of piety be reinterpreted as participation in the corporate life of the Christian fellowship—our common life in the body of Christ—and the layman "in the world" might be the first to see worth and glory in it. Courtesy over a sales counter, generosity to the needy, and, above all, the social miracles wrought by repentance and forgiveness in our daily and hourly relationships—these are among the true tokens of Christian piety when fellowship in Christ is given its central importance. Nor will the prayer and worship life of the church suffer. Give this, in its turn, social, corporate setting, and gone will be the impression so often held that only those especially endowed with mystical gifts can properly participate. Are unusual gifts of spirituality demanded of those who are guests at a marriage feast? Proper "wedding garments" are demanded, to be sure, and in the parable-symbolism of the gospels, lamps filled with oil. But the marriage feast of the King is for all. As it is written: "So those servants went out into the highways, and gathered together all as many as they found, both bad and good: and the wedding was furnished with guests" (Matt.

[5] For a searching criticism of mysticism see Anders Nygren, *Agape and Eros*.

31 For this cause shall a man leave his father and mother, and shall be joined unto his wife, and they two shall be one flesh.
32 This is a great mystery: but I speak concerning Christ and the church.

body. 31 "For this reason a man shall leave his father and mother and be joined to his wife, and the two shall become one." 32 This is a great mystery, and I take it to mean

---

phrase to the Genesis story unmistakable (Gen. 2:23, "This is now bone of my bones, and flesh of my flesh").

31. The citation (Gen. 2:24—LXX) is introduced to confirm the conception of the unity of man and wife in the marriage relationship as it has just been expounded, especially the thought that the wife is the husband's "own flesh" (vs. 29), "own bodies" (vs. 28), and to justify the writer's boldness in comparing it with the unity of Christ and the church. The last clause—**they two shall be one flesh**—is the only point that is utilized. Many commentators feel that the first clause—**a man shall leave his father and mother**—is also meant to suggest an analogy with Christ's forsaking of his heavenly home in order to win his bride; but this is quite unacceptable. There is no sense in which Christ's union with the church could be conceived as closer than his unity with the Father.

32. This is a great mystery: An unfortunate mistranslation; the adjective is the predicate. Render, "This mystery is great," i.e., "is of profound significance." The thought is not in the least that "this is a very mysterious matter," as if admitting that the subject is hard to understand. A "mystery" is not an enigma, but a revelation of spiritual truth made to those who are prepared to receive it. Here the "mystery" is the revelation of the nature of human marriage, the union of two persons into **one flesh,** as declared in the story of its institution; and the writer tells us that in his view it is realized fully and perfectly only in the union of Christ and the church. This is the ἱερὸς γάμος—the transcendental bridal of which human marriage is a shadow and an allegory.

22:10). The invitation to the feast may even today be the simple phrase: "Ye who do truly and earnestly repent you of your sins, and are in love and charity with your neighbours; . . . Draw near."

The Lord's Supper a marriage feast? Why not? The nuptial symbol does not exhaust the meaning of the Christian Eucharist, but its neglect has impoverished understanding of it. "Let us kepe a ioyfull and holy feast with the Lorde," so reads a beautiful invitation in the earliest version of the Book of Common Prayer, unfortunately omitted in later recensions.[6] The consecration formula, "This is my body," clearly has connections with the corporate body, the church; and this, in turn, with the even more basic symbol of the bride. The interweaving of this complex of symbols in the Gospels and Epistles of the N.T.—including those of the marriage itself: friends of the bridegroom, the waiting virgins, and others—invites to a fascinating study. When our author says, **We are members of his body,** Eucharistic overtones may well have been in his mind. Paul, when he speaks of "discerning the Lord's body" (I Cor. 11:29), must have recalled the nuptial symbol.

The body is the bride. We who come to the Lord's Supper are the bride and the body. The sacrament of the Eucharist is the sacrament of the unity of the body. It is the bride "adorned." "If then," says Augustine, "you are the body and members of Christ, your mystery is placed on the Lord's table, you receive your mystery. . . . Eat what you see and receive what you are!"[7]

The nuptial symbol of the church, if rediscovered in its pristine glory, could serve the church as a protection against many an error of the past. False clericalism could not maintain itself. The minister is the "friend of the bridegroom" (cf. Paul's assumption of this role in II Cor. 11:2). The bride is the whole body of Christ, who offers herself, her soul and body, as an offering to the Lord she loves. Churchmanship means membership in that body. To sin against the fellowship—willful absence is such a sin—breaks the body of Christ and defiles the bride.

32. *This Is a Great Mystery.*—Readers of our epistle can surely share with its author a feeling of awe and wonder as we contemplate the analogy between the deepest mystery of our

[6] *The First and Second Prayer Books of King Edward the Sixth* (London: J. M. Dent, n.d.), p. 224.

[7] Quoted in Massey H. Shepherd, *The Living Liturgy* (New York: Oxford University Press, 1946), p. 76.

In the Vulg. "mystery" is translated *sacramentum*, and the use of the word in this passage was the starting point of the doctrine that marriage is a sacrament. The great Roman Catholic exegetes, however, recognize the impropriety of this interpretation.

The language here implies that the interpretation of the Genesis story as a myth of the "sacred marriage" is a commonplace, and that the writer knows of other applications which he does not repudiate but does not feel called to discuss. The emphatic personal pronoun ἐγώ ("I for my part") indicates that the view here presented is not the only possible one. One might paraphrase: "The mystery of the union of man and wife into one flesh is of far-reaching importance and clearly points beyond itself toward some transcendental, eternal reality. I for my part take it to be a symbol of the union of Christ and the church."

The "sacred marriage" was a familiar theme of mythology and speculation in both Jewish and pagan circles. The starting point of the doctrine of the mystic bridal as it is expounded in Ephesians is undoubtedly the conception of Israel as the wife of Yahweh, so frequently employed by the prophets of the O.T. (Isa. 54:5, "Thy Maker is thine husband; The LORD of hosts is his name"; Hos. 2:16; Jer. 3:14, 20; etc.). There are anticipations of the doctrine also in Paul, as in II Cor. 11:2, "I have espoused you to one husband, that I may present you as a chaste virgin to Christ"; and in the references to Christ as the "bridegroom," in the Gospels (Mark 2:19-20 and parallels; though here the followers of Christ are "the children of the bridechamber," i.e., the bridegroom's attendant friends, not the bride). There seems to be no indication, however, that Jewish interpreters ever treated the Genesis story as an allegory of the marriage between Yahweh

---

biological inheritance and the climax of God's drama of redemption, the church. The sex life of man has always invited to exploration, both to blessedness and to damnation. Sex knowledge, in the ancient story of Genesis, is clearly connected with the forbidden fruit, "desired to make one wise" (Gen. 3:6). As it is written: "And the eyes of them both were opened, and they knew that they were naked; and they sewed fig leaves together, and made themselves aprons" (Gen. 3:7). The sex union between man and woman, when lawless, has been perhaps the most demonic disruptive force in the social history of mankind. Yet it is this biological "covenant" which the biblical revelation employs as its boldest symbol for the covenant between God and his people!

Which of the two relationships is type and which antitype? Our epistle opens with a picture of God as having in Christ "chosen us in him"—as a lover chooses his bride—"before the foundation of the world" (1:4). For the church the world was made. Was the human family, then, designed by God, the great Pedagogue, as a living parable of the kingdom of heaven? There is cosmic audacity in the thought.

Whether the mystery is fully explicable or not, certain is the fact that a human family can be a parable of the kingdom of God. Someone has called the Christian family "the little church." A Christian family can represent the great covenant between Christ and his church in miniature.

The full meaning of the analogy is of course enlarged by the inclusion of the relationship between parents and children. But the husband-wife relationship, even by itself, is rich in analogical suggestions. The Bible is not a textbook in metaphysics. The central problem with which it deals is not the problem of "being," but the problem of relationships. The title page of the Bible defines its theme. It is a book about "covenants." Real life in the Bible is *meeting*.[8] And where is a meeting of an "I" with a "thou" more clearly experienced on the human plane than in the marriage bond? Almost all of the great verbs and nouns of the theological vocabulary of the Bible find vivid illustration in a home. Love is an obvious example, already discussed. Repentance and forgiveness are equally important. The list could long continue. One can think of the word "ransom," as Hosea's marital drama gives it a meaning which can throw light even on Paul's use of the word in his deep wrestling with the idea of the Atonement through Christ's sacrifice on the Cross. Or the word "grace," along with the more elaborated concept of "prevenient grace." The marriage relationship gives a clue also to more than one of the profound paradoxes of the gospel—judgment as inseparable from grace or wrath, and judgment as a counterpart of love. Who is a severer judge of a husband than a loving wife? The various forms of sacrifice, again, can receive illustration. A

[8] See J. H. Oldham, *Real Life Is Meeting.*

33 Nevertheless, let every one of you in particular so love his wife even as himself; and the wife *see* that she reverence *her* husband.

Christ and the church; 33 however, let each one of you love his wife as himself, and let the wife see that she respects her husband.

---

and Israel, which is related rather to the Exodus and the Covenant of Sinai (Jer. 2:2; Ezek. 16).

On the other hand, Jewish interpreters of the Hellenistic Age treated the marriages of the patriarchs as allegories of a mystic marriage between God and the virtues, especially between God and Wisdom, with the Logos as the child of the union (Knox, *St. Paul and Church of the Gentiles,* pp. 85-87). In this they were applying to the O.T. the methods used by the Stoics in allegorizing the myths of the loves of the gods. But the theme of the mystic marriage enters into so many of the cults of the time, and finds such a variety of exposition in the philosophers that it would be impossible to offer a full discussion in this place. In no case does it appear to be applied to the relation between the divine lord of the cult and the community of his devotees, as here; but it certainly forms part of the general framework of religious speculation which lies behind our writer's exposition.

33. Nevertheless, i.e., "not to pursue these high speculations any further." However the "mystery" is interpreted, the plain duty of husband and wife remains—the husband to **love his wife as himself;** the wife to **reverence** [lit., "fear"] **her husband.** We must feel that the injunction to "fear" is another overpressing of the analogy with the church's attitude to Christ; the element of religious awe does indeed enter into the latter but not into the wife's attitude to her husband. We may again turn to Chrysostom for a discerning comment: "When thou hearest of 'fear,' demand that fear which becomes a free woman, not as though thou wert exacting it of a slave. . . . And of what nature is this 'fear'? It is that she should not gainsay thee, or set herself against thee, or love the

---

broken marriage covenant—can it be healed by propitiatory sacrifices on the part of the guilty? Must there not be, in the story of reconciliation, a "mediator," and a cross-bearing, and a descent drama as in the Christian creed? And when the broken covenant is restored, are there not then sacrifices of "praise and thanksgiving" on the part of the forgiven? A Eucharistic banquet may be expected and a new life in a reborn covenant relationship. There has been a dying and a resurrection.

The theology of the church, almost from the first, carried a heavy burden as it tried to adjust itself to the categories of Greek thought. The church of the early centuries is not to blame for this. It had to evangelize the ancient world as history had fashioned it. The Christian creeds, as a matter of fact, were victories for the covenant theology of the Bible. But the vivid personal symbols of the Bible were overlaid by the metaphysical categories of Greek philosophy—those of being and substance (transubstantiation, for example), and many others. The Reformation witnessed a great liberation. But it is only in our present age of biblical rediscoveries that the personal symbols of our Bible have a chance to be fully revived. Modern psychology and sociology can be great aids in this crucial task.

33. ***Marriage Under Divine Commandments.*** —In this closing verse of the chapter the author returns to ethical advice. If the nuptial analogy can unlock the mystery of the body of Christ, the converse is true also. Christian marriage must model itself upon the picture of Christ and his church. Marriage as an order of creation is, even as such, full of meaning. But in a fallen world it too needs redemption.

Catholic theology makes of marriage a church sacrament. Protestant theology usually refuses to grant marriage quite this status, but approves a service of vow-taking in the church. The Anglican Book of Common Prayer entitles this a "Solemnization of Matrimony." Christians are at least agreed on the need in Christian marriage of both God's law and God's grace. Marriage stands under divine commandments. Our text makes the mutual relationship of the patriarchal family pattern mandatory. The husband is to **love his wife as himself.** The wife is to respect or **reverence** or even "fear" (ASV) her husband. The Christian fellowship has felt free in later centuries to mitigate, somewhat at least, the subservient status of the wife as the

6 Children, obey your parents in the Lord: for this is right.
2 Honor thy father and mother; which is the first commandment with promise;

6 Children, obey your parents in the Lord, for this is right. 2 "Honor your father and mother" (this is the first com-

pre-eminence; if fear govern to this extent, it is enough. But if thou lovest her, as thou art commanded, thou wilt achieve more than this; nay rather, thou wilt achieve this no longer by fear, but love itself will have its own effect." (*In Ephes.*, Hom. xx. 150C.)

2. Children and Parents (6:1-4)

The short section which deals with the duties of children and parents is again an expansion of the brief and surprisingly meager sentences devoted to this theme by Paul in his table of household duties in Col. 3:20-21. The additions, though less elaborate than in the section on marital relationships, are none the less striking.

6:1. In the Lord: As always, the phrase suggests the mystical union of the Christian with Christ. In this highest of all privileges the children of Christian parents also share, and this spiritual relationship is the supreme factor in determining their conduct in the family circle. The words are omitted in Codex Vaticanus and a few other good MSS, but their presence in Papyrus 46 is a strong confirmation of their genuineness. They are to be taken with the whole thought of the sentence, not with "parents" alone; and they do not qualify the duty of obedience—as if to say, "Obey them insofar as their commands are compatible with your duty to Christ"—but refer to the whole spirit in which obedience is to be given. It is assumed that the parents are Christian, and it cannot be imagined that the children are made responsible for deciding how far their parents' commands are in keeping with the mind of Christ.

Right: Of moral obligation; preparing the way for the citation of the commandment, which shows that the specific "righteousness" required of children is obedience to their parents.

2. The first commandment with a promise: If the Ten Commandments are in mind, this is the *only* commandment with a promise. **First,** however, may be taken in the sense

N.T. still knew her. But such social relativities have not shaken Christian conviction that marriage is really itself only when it mirrors the inclusive grace of that love which is the supreme gift of the Holy Spirit.

6:1-3. ***The Christian Home.***—Modern psychological science has probably no triumphs to its credit more valuable than the explorations of the mental and emotional life of the child. Christian nurture, if wise, will avail itself of this new knowledge, though it will subject it to the criticism of the gospel. Pedagogic science in our time has much to say of the rights of a child. A child is not an adult. Hence psychologists may well plead for the liberation of childhood from many stupid parental and schoolroom tyrannies once accepted as normal by earlier generations.

But to absolutize child freedom is in its turn dangerous. If adult human nature is not angelic and therefore not to be trusted with tyrannical powers over the child, is not the converse even greater folly? A child is not an angel either. A child merely exhibits our human inheritance of original sin—think of the egotism of desire—in pygmy size. A lion's cub can be a pet and be given freedom as the adult "king of beasts" cannot. But the difference is one of weakness and strength, not of nature.

Christian insight knows that both adult and child need the restraint of law. The non-Christian psychologist knows this also, though the fact turns into something of an embarrassment. What law? In a society emancipated from the law of God, the commandment **Honor thy father and mother** can merely mean that pagan children are asked to accept the pagan standards of their parents! Freeing a child appears like a relative good, because obedience has lost transcendent meanings. Not even a society of atheists, of course, can exist without some of the Ten Commandments. Furthermore, other religions besides Christianity have made much of family solidarity. Confucianism in China is a conspicuous example, as also the pietas of ancient Roman society, when at its best. But

3 That it may be well with thee, and thou mayest live long on the earth.

mandment with a promise), 3 "that it may be well with you and that you may live

of "most important" (cf. Matt. 22:37-38: "Which is the great commandment in the law? . . . This is the great and first commandment") rather than of its place in the table; **with a promise** would then be taken not as a qualification of **first,** but as introducing a further thought: "and it has a promise attached." The commandment would be **first** in importance so far as children are concerned, not absolutely.

3. The "promise" is abbreviated by the omission of the words "which the LORD thy God giveth thee" (Exod. 20:12; Deut. 5:16; the citation combines the phrasing of the two passages as they are rendered in the LXX). This abbreviation makes it possible to take the words ἐπὶ τῆς γῆς in the sense of **on the earth,** instead of "in the land," i.e., Promised Land, to which the original text makes specific reference. It may be observed that the promise of a long life on earth is irrelevant to the primitive Christian eschatology, and is not held before Christians in any other N.T. passage. Chrysostom suggests that the parent should have a higher aim for his child: "Seek not that he should live a long life here, but that he may have a boundless and endless life hereafter" (*In Ephes.,* Hom. xxi. 161A).

such pre-Christian moral codes still have an anchorage in a "fear of the gods" shared by parents and children alike. It is in our post-Christian paganism that the problem of obedience in the parent-child relationship has become peculiarly acute. With no God to give meaning to the law, and no overarching fear of eternal commandments, obedience has no final sanctions except superior parental power. Moral chaos besets the family as it does the state. Nor will all the child psychologies of a hundred learned professors solve that dilemma.

Obedience in a Christian family, however, does have meaning. Obedience here can be **in the Lord.** Children in a Christian family soon become conscious of the fact that the obedience asked of them is not based upon arbitrary power, but upon a higher law to which the parents themselves are subject. The law is a gift handed on as a treasure, as well as a demand, from father to sons. "For ever, O LORD, thy word is settled in heaven. Thy faithfulness is unto all generations. . . . O how love I thy law!" sings the psalmist (Ps. 119:89-90, 97).

A child hungers for a solid moral universe under its feet as well as for a stable physical home. Even punishment for disobedience is not long resented if the child comes to see that its own welfare is at stake. An illuminating story is told of a little girl whose day was a tale of one misbehavior after another, with interspersed scoldings by the mother. She finally set herself firmly in an armchair with the words, "I wish father would come home and *make* me behave!" A household in which moral chaos rules is tragedy for a child. Adjustment to adult life—education being a kind of hastening of maturity—is never easy. And if such adjustment means little more than discovering protective tricks to be used against the willful and arbitrary dictates of adult power, a cancer of insecurity is implanted in the very heart. A child has been cheated of its conscience.

Can a greater blessing come to a child than to see father and mother in penitent prayer? Father and mother themselves sinners! Father and mother confessing, "We have left undone those things which we ought to have done; And we have done those things which we ought not to have done." Penitence on the parents' side will not rob the demand on the child for obedience of its sanctions. It will instead place obedience within a larger framework of security.

Nor is the reward promised in the commandment **Honor your father and mother** without significance. It is quoted in full in our verses—**that you may live long on the earth.** Modern psychology has much to say on the subject of security. The inwardly insecure are handicapped in life from the start. The ability to accept life's demands, to endure its tensions and its tragedy, to submit to the inexorable laws of a moral universe, is a priceless possession. It represents the virtue of obedience on the plane of maturity, as does **obey your parents in the Lord** on the level of childhood. Long life as a reward? Yes, that and much besides. We are a little afraid in modern Christian times to stress the rewards of godliness so frequently presented in the Bible. Selling religion over a bargain counter seems little short of blasphemous. Rather let us promise sweat, blood, and tears—or at most purely "spiritual" gains. And there is no doubt that bargain counter

4 And, ye fathers, provoke not your children to wrath: but bring them up in the nurture and admonition of the Lord.

long on the earth." 4 Fathers, do not provoke your children to anger, but bring them up in the discipline and instruction of the Lord.

Do not provoke your children to anger: A recognition that the relations which ought to obtain between parent and child may be destroyed as readily by parental harshness as by unfilial disobedience.

The nurture and admonition of the Lord: If the words are interpreted in strict relation to their immediate context, they will be taken as defining the spirit in which parental discipline should be administered, i.e., not with a harshness or unfairness which will arouse resentment in the child, but in a way appropriate to followers of **the Lord.** Such an interpretation is suggested by the rendering of the RSV, **discipline and instruction,** which might be distinguished as physical punishment and oral rebuke. In the LXX παιδεία almost always has the specific sense of "chastisement" (so also in Heb. 12:11); and Paul uses the cognate verb παιδεύω in the sense of "chastise" (I Cor. 11:32; II Cor. 6:9). Biblical usage generally, therefore, would support such an interpretation here: the father is to chastise his child and administer necessary rebuke (νουθεσία) as befits a Christian. This injunction circumscribes the absolute dominion accorded to the head of the family in Roman law (the *patria potestas*), which entitled him to expose an unwanted infant, to sell a grown child into slavery, to disinherit him, to scourge or imprison him, or even to put him to death (see A. H. J. Greenidge, *Roman Public Life* [London: Macmillan & Co., 1901], pp. 18-20). Some slight restraints were put upon this absolutism by statute and custom; but as late as A.D. 7, Augustus could banish his adulterous daughter Julia to an island in the Adriatic and cause her infant child to be put to death.

It is possible, however, to give the words a more positive content. Παιδεία appears to be used in the narrow sense of "chastisement" only in the LXX and in writings which are influenced by it. In general literature it commonly means "education" in the widest sense, embracing everything that is directed toward developing the mind and character. The verb ἐκτρέφω ("bring up"), again, can hardly be limited to the exercise of disciplinary functions; just a few verses above (5:29) we find it used in association with θάλπω ("nourishes and cherishes"), where the thought is not in the least of discipline but rather of the tenderness of the care. There is much to be said, therefore, for Goodspeed's insistence that "in this commonplace verse in Ephesians we have the first sign of Christian

Christianity has led to horrible abuses. Yet the realism of the Bible is more honest than a sentimental reading of it may indicate. "Your reward shall be great" (Luke 6:35) is a phrase more than once on the lips of Jesus. There simply *are* rewards that come to the godly—nonmaterial, if rightly seen, but no less humanly concrete. The promises of blessedness in the Beatitudes mean what they say. The promise of reward in our verses—**that it may be well with you**—has been validated countless times in Christian experience. The meaning of that promise and its dependence upon obedience in the home is a lesson wisdom can teach her children.

4. *Admonition of the Lord.*—Parental misuse of power has received allusion in the previous note. Power corrupts. Few generalizations of human experience are more sure. And where is the temptation to the misuse of power more insidious than in the parent-child relationship? Here even "Mr. Milquetoast," as father, can exercise lordly rule. Discipline dictated by selfish adult whim or convenience, exploitation of juvenile talent for parental gain, the cruelty of neglect, the equal cruelty of depersonalizing solicitude, the spoiling of a child because restraint demands time and care—any father or mother, with even a little self-criticism, could lengthen the catalogue of parental egotisms almost endlessly. The results, if not redeemed by corresponding insights of penitence, can be disastrous. They **provoke . . . to anger.** It may be worth while noting that our epistle phrases

5 Servants, be obedient to them that are *your* masters according to the flesh, with fear and trembling, in singleness of your heart, as unto Christ;

5 Slaves, be obedient to those who are your earthly masters, with fear and trembling, in singleness of heart, as to Christ;

education in the home" (*Meaning of Ephesians,* pp. 64-65). Far from relying on sternness, which may do more harm than good, the Christian father is urged to instill into his children the principles of the faith, to teach them the doctrines and duties of their religion. Certainly the whole sermon of Chrysostom on the text is based on this understanding of its significance. "Is it not utterly absurd," he writes," to send them into trades, or to school, and to do anything and everything for the sake of this, and not to bring the children up in the training and instruction of the Lord? . . . Let us give them a pattern, making them devote themselves from the earliest age to the reading of the scriptures. . . . If your child learns to be a lover of wisdom from the beginning of his life, he has acquired wealth greater than all wealth, and a mightier glory. . . . Give him the great things, not the little things" (*In Ephes.* Hom. xxi. 160A, B, 161A). There is, of course, an established background for religious education in the home, in the long-standing custom of Judaism (Deut. 6:7; etc.); Paul finds it natural to compare his training of his converts with a father's care for the spiritual welfare of his children, as he had doubtless known it in his own home: "You know how, like a father with his children, we exhorted each one of you and encouraged you and charged you to lead a life worthy of God" (I Thess. 2:11-12).

3. Slaves and Masters (6:5-9)

The injunctions addressed to **slaves** (vss. 5-8) and to **masters** (vs. 9) do not imply either approval or condemnation of the institution of slavery in itself, but are based upon the matter-of-fact recognition that it constituted the sociological framework within which many members of the Christian community found their lives actually cast. No one who is at all acquainted with the economic conditions of ancient society will find it strange that the early church did not make a frontal attack on this evil institution or even require Christian masters to free their slaves. The one would have been a quixotic tilting at windmills on the part of scattered groups of people quite without political or social influence; the other would not often have been in the best interests of the slave himself, since there was almost no market for free labor and the church was incapable

the result in terms of child psychology. A child has a vivid sense of justice. To be nurtured **in the discipline and instruction of the Lord,** like all schooling in childhood and youth, may produce moods of rebellion or desire to escape. But the mood is on the surface. A child expects maturity. A youth is an amateur adult. To be cheated of instruction—with all the discipline and even punishment necessarily involved—can produce a lifelong **anger.**

Nor will secular education suffice. There must be **admonition of the Lord.** Modern society is in no great danger of undervaluing utilitarian learning. In medieval society the church was the imposing architectural symbol of the communal concern of a village or town. Today it is the school. Many a youth of our time thanks his parents for the sacrifices which gave him his educational start in life. But will his gratitude stand final tests if parental care has paid no attention to **nurture and admonition of the Lord?** Our secularized twentieth century may soon be a time of harvest for a generation cheated in home and school of its Christian heritage. Wanderers in the deserts of unbelief and loneliness of soul may yet curse the generation of their fathers for having given them a stone of worldly success in place of the bread of life. "They shall wander from sea to sea, and from the north even to the east, they shall run to and fro to seek the word of the Lord, and shall not find it" (Amos 8:12).

5-8. ***The Gospel and Social Reform.***—Modern readers of the N.T. are often more than a little shocked over the fact that Paul and the early church as a whole did not make a frontal attack

6 Not with eyeservice, as menpleasers; but as the servants of Christ, doing the will of God from the heart;
7 With good will doing service, as to the Lord, and not to men:

6 not in the way of eyeservice, as menpleasers, but as servants[f] of Christ, doing
the will of God from the heart, 7 rendering
service with a good will as to the Lord and

[f] Or *slaves.*

of creating one, even for its own adherents. At the very least, any dissatisfaction that we may feel at the failure of the church to perceive the anomaly of holding in bondage a brother in Christ should not blind us to the significance of what actually was achieved. A. H. J. Greenidge writes: "Slavery may at all periods of the history of Rome be defined as an absence of personality. The slave was a thing (*res*) and belonged to that more valuable class of chattels which the Romans called *res mancipi,* and which included land and beasts of burden" (*Roman Public Life,* p. 24). But among the early Christians the slave was treated no longer as a chattel but as a person, and was held capable of the highest spiritual development; the inferiority of his civil status laid him under no disabilities within the fellowship of the church; and he was taught to make even his servitude the means of fulfilling his daily duty toward Christ and toward God (see also the Exeg. on the corresponding section in Col. 3:22-25).

5. **Masters according to the flesh:** A reminder that the superior position of the master holds only within the sphere of **the flesh,** i.e., under the superficial conditions of earthly society; it does not convey any spiritual advantage whatever. Nevertheless, within its own sphere it confers an authority which the slave must recognize ungrudgingly by sincere and generous obedience. **With fear and trembling:** This phrase can hardly be taken as advice to the slave to cringe before his master. It is to be taken in close relationship with the words **as to Christ.** This is the **fear and trembling** which is inseparable from all serious effort to fulfill the will of God in moral action (Phil. 2:12). The Christian walks on holy ground and is filled with awe; his conduct is not governed by external rules but by the presence of God within and about him. **In singleness of heart,** i.e., without deception or divided loyalty.

upon slavery. Historical considerations (see Exeg.) explain much in regard to this apparent moral obtuseness. Yet a certain "offense" to modern humanitarianism remains stubbornly in the N.T. The Christian crusades for social reform of later Christian history are themselves products of the gospel of Christ. The abolition of slavery as an institution, for example, owes its main impetus to Christian conscience. Yet the fact cannot be explained away that the attack of the N.T. gospel on the sins of the social order was not an attack, first of all, upon institutions or upon environmental evils. Its method was strangely paradoxical. Modern social reformers, both Christian and secular, may on occasions still find it an "offense."

When Jesus, for example, said "Blessed are you poor" (Luke 6:20), or "How hard it will be for those who have riches to enter the kingdom of God" (Mark 10:23), he may have meant what he said. If so, why should the abolition of poverty be a great concern? Or if, as in our text, the apostolic church solved the problem of slavery by creating merely "good" slaves and "good" masters, why should the institution itself not be left permanently intact? Such logic is no doubt somewhat fallacious. Yet it cannot altogether be ignored.

The truth must simply be accepted that the gospel of the N.T., in so far as it is a revolutionary social gospel, goes about reform in strange ways. It attacks a social evil first from within. This does not mean that the N.T. presents only an individualist program and ignores social concerns. The N.T. is "social" through and through. It is "covenant religion." But it does present the demands of the kingdom of God as prior to those of a utopian kingdom of this world. The pattern of the kingdom of God will inevitably, if given opportunity, remold even secular society. Yet love of God is still the first and great commandment, love of neighbor second. When ideals of social reform reverse the order, they stand under the judgment of the "offense" of the gospel.

Kierkegaard, in one of his flashes of insight, describes this "offense" vividly. The fact that Jesus himself had nothing apparently to do with

8 Knowing that whatsoever good thing any man doeth, the same shall he receive of the Lord, whether *he be* bond or free.

not to men, 8 knowing that whatever good any one does, he will receive the same again from the Lord, whether he is a slave or free.

As to Christ, not "as though it were to Christ" (Goodspeed); but "viewing it as service done to Christ." When we carry out our daily duties, in whatever capacity or under whatever authority, we are serving Christ and following his will for our lives. This thought is developed further in vss. 6-7, which follow. The human master may be deceived by service which is good only as long as his eye is upon it (**eyeservice**); but it is not he whom we must seek to please, but Christ, whom we cannot hope to please except by **doing the will of God from the heart.** This principle obviously applies as much to free service as to bond service. **Good will** was particularly appreciated in a slave. Among the Oxyrhynchus papyri there was found a will, dated A.D. 157, by which the testator grants freedom to five of his slaves "because of their good will and affection" toward him (*The Oxyrhynchus Papyri,* Part III, ed. Bernard P. Grenfell and Arthur S. Hunt [London: Egypt Exploration Fund, 1903], No. 494, *ll.* 5-6. Cited by Dibelius, *ad loc.*).

8. Conscientious service is not done in vain, whether the earthly master mark and reward it or not. It will receive its just reward **from the Lord** in heaven, who makes no distinction between slave and free.

politics must have appeared to his contemporaries as treason against his suffering nation. His people were in earthly misery, their very existence was at stake. Yet Jesus displays God's kingdom as over against the earthly.

> The contrast could not be more glaring. In a happy land in time of peace the contrast between the eternal and the earthly is not so striking. To say to a rich man, Thou shalt first seek God's kingdom, is a mild thing, in contrast with this hard saying, this (humanly) shocking thing, of saying to a hungry man, Thou shalt first seek God's kingdom.[9]

Similarly to say to a slave "Be a good slave" *before* denouncing the institution of slavery itself seems a shocking thing. Yet it is the hard way of the gospel. One does not belittle our modern passion for what we call the "social gospel" by pointing out that however noble its ideals, these must make their peace with the prior claims of God himself. The church has in her history, both Catholic and Protestant, more than once yielded to the temptation originally faced by the church's Lord, "Command that these stones be made bread" (Matt. 4:3). Dostoevski's picture of "The Grand Inquisitor"[1] ought to be uncomfortable reading for all churches even today.

But the paradox of the **obedient** slave, **rendering service with a good will as to the Lord,** does not end with demands. It also pictures a reward —a reward, first of all, in the form of an assurance that **whatever good any one does, he will receive the same again from the Lord.** This apparently otherworldly reward, however, has strange foreshadowings on the earthly scene. To those who seek first the kingdom of God comes the promise, almost startling in the words of Christ himself, that "all these [earthly] things shall be yours as well" (Matt. 6:33). Christian slaves were asked to serve **from the heart** even before gratitude for liberation might be a rational motive for such voluntary giving of self. They are to imitate Christ in the "scandal" of cross-bearing. "While we were *yet sinners* Christ died for us" (Rom. 5:8). But it is precisely this *before* which is the power of the gospel. It has worked the miracles of Christian grace in history, among these the abolition of slavery itself. It breaks hearts of stone. It evokes the response of gratitude; and gratitude in turn can revolutionize social relationships.

The paradox of the gospel, thus applied to social reform, is not always easy to grasp. Nor does it necessarily rule out a Christian's duty to employ other means in behalf of justice—those of government power, for example. Yet the paradox stands. G. K. Chesterton, in a discussion of Charles Dickens as a social reformer, points to the fact that secular humanitarianism appeals largely to the motive of pity. It pictures the despair of the poor, its motto being in effect, "Cursed are the poor." The success of Dickens as a social reformer rested, says Chesterton, upon exactly the opposite assertion, the N.T. beatitude, "Blessed are the poor." "He

[9] Sören Kierkegaard, *The Present Age* (tr. Alexander Dru and Walter Lowrie; London: Oxford University Press, 1940), p. 93.

[1] *The Grand Inquisitor* (tr. Constance Garnett; New York: The Association Press, 1948).

9 And, ye masters, do the same things unto them, forbearing threatening: knowing that your Master also is in heaven; neither is there respect of persons with him.

9 Masters, do the same to them, and forbear threatening, knowing that he who is both their Master and yours is in heaven, and that there is no partiality with him.

---

9. Masters, do the same to them: In civil law, the slave had no rights as against his master, but under Christianity the obligations are reciprocal. "Give them the same good will, love, and loyalty that you hope to receive from them." The master's attitude, like the slave's, is to be determined not by the transitory conditions of earthly life with its inequalities of status, but by the abiding relationship to Christ in which master and slave stand on the same footing.

---

described their happiness, and men rushed to remove their sorrow. He described them as human, and men resented the insults to their humanity." [2]

The basic Christian motive for social reform flows from the Christian creed. A human mother once bore a baby who was the Son of God. Then every child born of woman is related to the King of Kings. Our hearts can burn over every indignity suffered by lord or serf alike. It was the indignity of slavery, far more than its cruelty, which moved Christian conscience to abolish it.

To ask a slave to be a good slave turns out, accordingly, to be a program of social reform of incomparable power. A slave becomes worthy of freedom first. In the fellowship of the church he is already accorded "the glorious liberty of the children of God" (Rom. 8:21). Although this appears at first sight to be indifference to outward status—and is such indifference—it can lead to a radical reordering of society of which the secular reformer cannot even dream.

9. *The Christian Foundation for Democracy.* —The appeal to **masters** to be kind to slaves does not present any startling paradox. The ideal of *noblesse oblige* is no longer novel. Yet the precept of kindness to the underprivileged is never out of date. We cannot foresee a time when inequalities of talent or circumstance will not exist in the human family and when the misuse of power will not be the commonest of man's sins.

Nor will a mere preaching of human brotherhood abolish the sins of inequality. Cain was brother of Abel, yet brotherhood led to murder. Our verse cites as a sanction for mutual **forbearing** something far transcending frail bonds of nature. It recalls the democracy of Judgment Day. There is **no respect of persons** with God. Before any final testing we are all sinners—sinners in need of a like salvation. We "all have sinned, and come short of the glory of God" (Rom. 3:23).

The motive of "fear of God" is not much stressed in contemporary preaching. Yet it plays a great role in the Bible. It is plainly not the final motive for Christian action. Gratitude for redemption can replace fear of the law. But the inexorable law of God has in no sense been canceled. Nowhere is sanction of a wholesome fear of God more needed than in human relationships which involve inequality of status. It is easy even for a Christian master to presume. Has not privilege perhaps come to him as a reward for piety? The misuse of power is so insidious a poison that it can infect the household of God itself. As indeed it often does.

The dogma of democracy is frequently phrased as "One man is as good as another." But a deep-going fallacy lurks in such a slogan. The Christian foundation for democracy would rather read, "One man is as sinful as another." Rule of man over man, accordingly, requires restraints—the restraint, in any final appeal, of the overarching laws of a divine supreme court. It is not often fully realized that the American democratic form of government rests squarely upon acceptance of this profound insight. Its Constitution is a system of checks and balances. Its designers had a vivid sense of the sinfulness of human nature. Power in mortal hands cannot be trusted. Destroy this radically Christian foundation of democracy, and it can overnight transform itself into a warfare of power. Equalitarian democracy is a much frailer flower of modern culture than most of us who have thoughtlessly enjoyed its blessings can easily conceive. It can exist only when deep down in its heart it accepts the precept of our text, and addresses its governors: **Masters,** know ye **that your Master also is in heaven; neither is there respect of persons with him.**

[2] *Charles Dickens* (New York: Dodd, Mead & Co., 1906), p. 279.

10 Finally, my brethren, be strong in the Lord, and in the power of his might.
11 Put on the whole armor of God, that ye may be able to stand against the wiles of the devil.

10 Finally, be strong in the Lord and in the strength of his might. 11 Put on the whole armor of God, that you may be able

D. Fourth Exhortation: To Put on God's Armor (6:10-18)

10. Finally, or perhaps better "henceforth" (Goodspeed; cf. Westcott, *ad loc.*, "in the future"); this is certainly the sense that must be given to the phrase in the only other N.T. occurrence (Gal. 6:17). **Be strong:** The verb is better taken as a passive: "be made powerful." The means of this strengthening are to be found in the vital energy which comes from union with Christ (**in the Lord**) and in the **power** which he makes available to us out of his limitless resources of **might.** On the distinctive senses of **power** (κράτος), **might** (ἰσχύς), and **strength** (δύναμις) see on 1:19.

11. "Put on God's armour" (Moffatt; so also Goodspeed); πανοπλία ("panoply") is the collective term for "armor" and is not substantially different in sense from "arms" (ὅπλα). The needless insertion of the adjective **whole** serves only to distract attention from the real point of emphasis, which is that **the armor** which we are to **put on** is **the armor of God.** In the passage which provides the starting point for the picture it is God himself who wears the armor: "He put on righteousness as his breastplate and set the helm of salvation upon his head" (Isa. 59:17—LXX). The Christian warrior is invited to employ the spiritual armor in which God himself is clothed when he goes forth to overthrow his enemies. The genitive is therefore to be taken in the first instance as possessive, but it is also subjective—"the armor which God supplies."

10-12. *The Christian's Battle.*—The symbols of warfare have always fascinated Christian imagination. The fact need not be an argument against what we know technically as "pacifism." It can indicate, however, that Christianity is far other than a peaceful "opiate for the people." It is not withdrawal from struggle. The symbols of rest and peace have their place in Christian imagery also. But those of battle take priority.

A traditional phrase describing the Christian's battle is "spiritual warfare." The ambiguities lurking behind the word "spiritual" present a danger here. The impression is widespread that the basic conflict which the Christian experiences is that of spirit against matter. The enemy is materialism. Sin is equated with "sins of the flesh." Some form of asceticism, therefore, means Christian victory. The history of Christianity has contributed to crystallize such a conception.

Nor is this version of Christian warfare wholly mistaken. There are bodily sins in abundance against which the Christian must wage ceaseless battle. The emphasis on the ascetic ideal in Catholic tradition and the corresponding emergence of puritanic legalisms in Protestant tradition are both expressions of a basic cleavage between church and world.

Yet the error in such a simplification of Christian warfare needs even greater emphasis. Our text is important. It corrects misconceptions as to the content of the word **spiritual.** If the Christian life is to be equated with "spiritual" conquest over body or matter, what can be the meaning of **spiritual wickedness in high places?** The phrase (see Exeg.) no doubt had a mythological significance in N.T. times which it has lost today. We no longer honor or fear angels and demons in the stars, though the recurrence even in our enlightened age of astrological superstitions indicates how modern even this ancient belief still is. Regardless of a changed cosmology, however, **spiritual wickedness** is still a fact today.

The sin of pride, for example, is acknowledged by almost all biblical theologians as "the beginning of all sin." [3] It was the sin of Lucifer, or Satan, a perfect example in biblical imagery, of precisely **spiritual wickedness in high places.** Clearly, pride cannot be equated simply with sensuality. One could imagine asceticism carried to an extreme—all the world in monasteries, the laws of poverty, chastity, and obedience universally enforced—yet the sins of pride and envy turning such a monastic paradise into a hell. Sin itself is a "spiritual" fact. It may express itself in acts of **flesh and blood,** of

[3] Augustine *City of God* XII. 13. Quoted in a masterly treatment of the sin of pride, Reinhold Niebuhr, *The Nature and Destiny of Man* (New York: Charles Scribner's Sons, 1941) I, 186.

12 For we wrestle not against flesh and blood, but against principalities, against powers, against the rulers of the darkness

to stand against the wiles of the devil. 12 For we are not contending against flesh and blood, but against the principalities, against the powers, against the world rulers of this

---

The wiles of the devil: Neither of these nouns is used by Paul; each occurs twice in this epistle (4:14, 27). In place of "the devil" Paul always uses the personal name "Satan."

In the second century Christians thought of **the wiles of the devil** as exhibited especially in the many forms of torture which were inflicted upon the martyrs. So the church of Smyrna in its account of the sufferings endured by many of its members writes: "The devil tried many devices against them. But thanks be to God, his might did not prevail over any" (Mart. Polyc. 2:4–3:1). The churches of Lyons and Vienne, again, in telling of the persecution which had recently been raging among them, speak of "the greatness of the tribulation in this region, and the fury of the heathen against the saints . . . ," and proceed to ascribe the driving force behind it all to the devil. "For with all his might the adversary fell upon us, giving us a foretaste of his unbridled activity at his future coming. . . . But the grace of God led the conflict against him, and delivered the weak, and set them as firm pillars, able through patience to endure all the wrath of the Evil One" (Eusebius *Church History* V. 1 [tr. Henry Melville Gwatkin, *Selections from Early Christian Writers;* London: Macmillan & Co., 1914, p. 67]). The reference here is more general; there is nothing to indicate that persecution is either active or threatening. Accordingly, **the wiles of the devil** will mean the manifold temptations to unbelief, to sin, to conformity with the surrounding pagan world, which beset the Christian at all times.

12. We wrestle not against flesh and blood: The language is again compressed. The "wrestling" against a human opponent in the arena would not require any kind of armor. Besides the expressed contrast in the nature of the opponents (**flesh and blood,** on the one hand; **principalities, . . . powers, . . . spiritual hosts,** on the other), there is also a contrast in the nature of the conflict, in the one case "wrestling"; in the other, a warfare which we cannot undertake without the necessary spiritual armor for defense and for

---

course. But its roots go down far below the surface. It is the will of man which cries out for redemption—his life of desire. Sin is not mere ignorance, or weakness, or a yielding to temptations of the senses. Christian warfare is warfare against spirits of evil as well as against manageable matter. Science may become master of our material universe and yet fall victim to **principalities** or to **the rulers of the darkness of this world.** The mood of humility which is discernible among scientists the world over is one of the most hopeful signs of our time. Our age is learning through tragedy and pain the lesson that the powers of evil are far more formidable than recent proud centuries of enlightenment had supposed. **Spiritual hosts of wickedness** require spiritual forces to oppose them. No powers will suffice short of those wielded by the Holy Spirit himself. As our eyes are being opened to the real warfare being waged on the battlefields of world history we may again see Christians singing, with reborn enthusiasm, their ancient hymns of battle.

These verses of our epistle raise the question of dualism in the spiritual world. Must Christian faith return to a belief in the devil? The entire concept of "the demonic" (see Expos. on 2:2) has become well-nigh obsolete in modern theology. A reaction was no doubt proper against the unwholesome, and at times even abominable, use of the idea of the demonic in the Middle Ages and in orthodox Protestantism. The Enlightenment thought it had outgrown devils and demons. Our age is rediscovering their age-old power. Fear of the dark is once more disturbing our pagan calm. Depth psychology is opening up long-forgotten caverns of demon-haunted evil. And on the social scene we know that spiritual forces of literally bestial nature can bring whole nations under their control.

A logical criticism of the mythology of the demonic is easy. If the warfare between good and evil is one between God and the devil, how are we mortal men anything more than spectators or victims? We are not responsible for a "war

of this world, against spiritual wickedness in high *places*.

present darkness, against the spiritual hosts of wickedness in the heavenly places.

attack. This is no mere sport in which we try our own strength against a human opponent; it is a deadly battle in which we are pitted against spiritual forces of evil which would overwhelm us if we met them without the protection of "God's armor."

Flesh and blood: The Greek has the words in the reverse order: "blood and flesh." Elsewhere in the N.T. this order is found only in Heb. 2:14; Paul himself always writes "flesh and blood." **Principalities** and **powers** are two of the orders of spirits (angels or demons) which in the astrological thinking of the time were held to have dominion over human life (cf. 1:21; Col. 1:16; 2:10; I Pet. 3:22). To these are now added a third class—**the world rulers of this present darkness.** The title "world ruler" (κοσμοκράτωρ) is applied to a number of the savior-gods of antiquity—Serapis, Isis, Mithras, Mercury, Zeus, and others. Under this title the god appears to be identified with Helios, the sun; a sphere, representing the sun, is the symbol corresponding to this title (see the article "Serapis ΚΟΣΜΟΚΡΑΤΩΡ et Isis ΚΟΣΜΟΚΡΑΤΕΙΡΑ," by Pierre Hombert, in *Antiquité Classique,* XIV [1946], 319-29). The gods **of the Roman** Empire, then, are here regarded not as "dumb idols" (I Cor. 12:2), but as **malignant spirits of** great power. This association of the κοσμοκράτορες with the solar cult is so broadly represented—being found in such common objects as terra cotta lamps—that we are entitled to see an oxymoron in the coupling of them with "this darkness." These sun-gods, though men worship them as **world rulers,** are powerless to dispel the **darkness** which enshrouds human life apart from Christ. The word **present** is not represented in the true text of the Greek; it reflects the influence of the later addition τοῦ αἰῶνος, which has given us the phrase **of this world** in the KJV (more correctly "of this age"). There is in fact no thought of the contrast of ages here; "this darkness" means simply the moral and intellectual climate of a pagan world—"the realm of darkness" (Col. 1:13) which stands over against the kingdom of God, which is the realm of light (cf. 5:8).

The spiritual hosts of wickedness in the heavenly places: A comprehensive designation for all the classes of hostile spirits with whom the Christian must contend. The language (as in 1:21; 3:10; and 4:10) clearly belongs to the contemporary astrology, which thinks of the heavenly bodies as the abodes of spirits which hold human life in thrall. Paganism could only bid men be good soldiers of fate, accepting as unalterable the destiny which was written in the stars; the Christian teacher bids each man grapple with his evil star, summoning him to do battle against the mighty rulers of the spheres as a free soldier of Christ, clothed in the divine armor which will give him the victory. The whole conception must be transposed into the setting of an entirely different view of the universe before it can be made relevant to our own problems; but we can perceive

in heaven" (Rev. 12:7). But such escape from responsibility is not the effect which belief in the demonic has had in biblical faith. There it marks instead a recognition of the dread and inescapable power of evil. The symbols of the demonic cannot be uprooted from the soil of the N.T. without doing violence to its moral structure. And this moral structure is in the N.T. clearly more important than giving satisfaction to the philosophers who look for a solution to the problem of dualism. God in the Bible remains sovereign. But there *is* a "prince of this world." Christian experience must make the best of the paradox. And it is precisely Christian experience which still needs the symbols and the concept of the demonic. To quote F. C. Synge, a contemporary commentator on our verse:

> We can avoid Dualism by minimizing the gravity of Sin, or we can take Sin so seriously that we are pushed to the verge of Dualism. If we would follow Paul, our horror of Sin must be greater than our horror of Dualism. We may leave it to the philosophers to wrestle with Dualism, only insisting that they must not regard escape from Dualism as of more importance than a true estimate of the dreadful power of Sin.[4]

[4] *St. Paul's Epistle to the Ephesians,* pp. 55-56.

13 Wherefore take unto you the whole armor of God, that ye may be able to withstand in the evil day, and having done all, to stand.

13 Therefore take the whole armor of God, that you may be able to withstand in the evil day, and having done all, to stand.

how Christianity set men free from the bondage of this astrological fatalism by teaching them that the power of God is greater than any fate or any astral spirits who might be thought to ordain human destiny apart from human will. It encouraged men to regard themselves no longer as the puppets of necessity but as free moral agents, enabled by divinely given strength to rise to the high estate of sons of God, for which they were created.

13. **In the evil day:** This phrase is commonly interpreted, in relation to the primitive eschatology, as referring to the final mustering of the powers of evil for the decisive conflict which precedes the establishment of the kingdom of God upon earth (II Thess. 2:8-10; Rev. 16:12-16; 20:7-8; etc.) . Such a meaning is, however, quite alien to the context as well as to the general thought of this writer; the Christian is here urged to arm himself for immediate battle, not for Armageddon. We must suppose, then, either that the phrase is violently transposed from an eschatological setting into a new context to which it is not really relevant, or that it belongs to the vocabulary of the astrology which the writer is combatting. **The evil day** may then be taken to mean the time which the horoscope has designated as dangerous, when the "unlucky star" is in the ascendant; and the Christian is taught not to face such a season in the spirit of helpless resignation which would possess the pagan victim of astrological lore, but to stand up and fight like a man. It is not necessary to suppose that the writer takes horoscopes and astrology in general seriously; it is sufficient that he appreciates the paralyzing hold which such superstitions may still exercise over the minds of his readers, not wholly liberated from the influences of their pagan upbringing and environment.

13-15. ***The Whole Armor of God.***—This whole section on the panoply of a soldier of Christ has been a favorite scripture passage for liturgical use. It reads well aloud, and has the emotional overtones of a military "order of the day." Whether it is worth while to expend extended ingenuity on the exact details of the analogy may be doubted. Later commentators might have heeded John Calvin's dry advice on these verses. "Nothing," he says, "can be more idle than the extraordinary pains which some have taken to discover the reason why righteousness is made a *breastplate* instead of a *girdle.* Paul's design was to touch briefly on the most important points required in a Christian, and to adapt them to the [military] comparison he had already used." [5] Detailed analysis could show perhaps how in the armoring of a soldier a girding of the loins is a first step in the change from relaxation to readiness for battle, and how this can symbolize the Christian's need of firm conviction (**girt about with truth**) before he in his turn is prepared for the fray. Or again, how **feet shod with the preparation of the gospel of peace** is a neatly fitting picture of the Christian as evangelist. Faith symbolized by a shield has also a useful suggestiveness. But Calvin is surely right that the analogy is general and not meticulously detailed. The author weaves into his battle hymn a catalog of the great weapons in the Christian's armory—faith itself, truth, righteousness, salvation, the Spirit, the word of God.

Each of these concepts has rich connotations. Equally important is the generic concept which embraces them all—**the whole armor of God.**

The insufficiency of man to cope with the powers of evil is a fact hard for our modern age to relearn. Since the Renaissance modern man has thought of the human situation in terms of individualism. Acts of evil were man's acts, determined by his own free decisions. Evil as a power outside himself, beyond the control of conscious personality, was held an outmoded concept. Hence resources for the conquest of evil were thought to lie within man's conscious self also. He required instruction, persuasion, and the help of a good environment. Religion became a resource for self-help. Given good will and the tools of a good life, man could achieve salvation on the human plane. And all men surely were basically of good will. This merely

[5] Quoted in R. W. Dale, *The Epistle to the Ephesians* (London: Hodder & Stoughton, 1882), p. 426.

14 Stand therefore, having your loins girt about with truth, and having on the breastplate of righteousness;

14 Stand therefore, having girded your loins with truth, and having put on the

---

14. The arming of the Christian with "God's panoply" is now described in detail. With this we may compare the account which Polybius gives us of the heavy armor carried by the Roman spearman (*hastatus*): "The Roman panoply consists first of a shield with a convex surface two and a half feet wide and four feet high; at the rim, its thickness is a palm's breadth. . . . Along with the shield, there is a sword; this they carry on the right thigh, and call it a Spanish sword. It permits a powerful thrust, and a mighty cut with either edge, for the blade is strong and firm. Besides these, they carry two javelins, a bronze helmet, and greaves. . . . Most of them wear also a bronze plate of a span's breadth each way, which they place over the breasts—they call it a heart-protector; those who are worth over ten thousand drachmas wear instead of the heart-protector a breastcoat of chain mail" (*History* VI. 23). Our writer omits the javelins from his description and adds girdle and footwear.

---

needed release from outward restrictions. Freedom was the word: freedom in education, in politics, in psychological enfranchisement from complexes and fears and anxiety.

In other words, no "devil and all his works"! The thought world of the Bible, with its concept of evil as a gigantic objective fact, even personalized, before which man in his puny strength might stand helpless, has been alien to our centuries of enlightenment. And as the idea of structural evil faded into obscurity, so did the concept of objective grace. Modern man found the word "grace" in his traditional textbooks, but did not know quite what to do with it. What, indeed, can it mean to an age which sees the autonomous individual alone as the protagonist in the struggle for the good?

Hence, to return to our text, the picture of man requiring **armor** against evil is not vividly apprehended. As rhetoric, it is of course appealing. But what does it mean in life?

Experience is still the great teacher. The world wars of the twentieth century have torn veils from the demonic forces of evil. We see these again in their ancient dread grandeur. When a nation gives itself over to bestial cruelties, or when despots sit on thrones heeding no longer the laws of God or of civilized humanity, warfare between good and evil assumes corporate forms. Armies are called for, not mere autonomous individuals. Enlightenment, education, science, ideals—all may be tried, but turn out to be weapons made of straw. The structures of evil of our age are in fact products and beneficiaries of enlightenment. One is reminded of the picture in the N.T. of Satan quoting Holy Scripture for devilish, not godly, ends (cf. the Temptation story). The biblical words describing evil—"principalities," "powers," "rulers of the darkness"—are no longer rhetoric. They are stark realities. They threaten the very citadels of human existence.

In the calm days of the "gospel of progress" the symbols of our text—**armor, to withstand in the evil day**—must have seemed mere outlived negatives. Civilization was on the march. Standing still (**having done all, to stand**) would have been judged treachery. The cry was not for holding a line, but for brave advance. Today, however, and for probably many a day to come, the symbols of progress will have to give way to the symbols of the fortress. Distress signals are being unfurled from our citadels of Western culture. Someone has well said that before an army can march it may have to learn how to halt. More than one famous battle of military history—Waterloo, for an example—has been won by obedience to the precept of our text, **to withstand in the evil day, and having done all, to stand.**

Modern man, enlightened, educated, and even of good will, is seeing himself unequal to the tasks of the twentieth century. Rallying the forces of good within autonomous individuals no longer avails. He is caught in nets of evil from which there is no escape. Will and desire are themselves infected. "O wretched man that I am! who shall deliver me from the body of this death?" (Rom. 7:24.) Modern man accordingly may learn again how to pray for grace and to find objective meaning in the word. Salvation must come from outside himself. Salvation may require a drama of rescue in which the chief actor is God and not man—the drama of the Christian creed, for example. Modern man has long trusted ideals as the prime agents of salvation. But ideals are not objective grace.

15 And your feet shod with the preparation of the gospel of peace;

breastplate of righteousness, 15 and having shod your feet with the equipment of the

Truth and **righteousness** are mentioned together as girding the Davidic king of the coming golden age, "He shall be girt about the loins with righteousness, and enclosed about the sides with truth" (Isa. 11:5—LXX). **Truth** here has the sense of "faithfulness," as in the Hebrew which lies behind it (for studies of the words "righteousness" and "truth" see C. H. Dodd, *The Bible and the Greeks* [London: Hodder & Stoughton, 1935], pp. 42-59, 65-75). The figure of **righteousness** as the **breastplate** is taken from Isa. 59:17.

15. The footwear of the Christian soldier is suggested by Isa. 52:7, "How beautiful . . . are the feet of him that bringeth good tidings, that publisheth peace," though our writer probably has in mind Paul's citation of the verse in Rom. 10:15. **The gospel of peace** (genitive of apposition or equivalence) is itself **the equipment** which the warrior wears. There is something paradoxical in presenting the warrior in the midst of battle equipped with **the gospel of peace.** To establish the peace of God in the universe, which is our ultimate aim, we must do battle against the spiritual evil which disturbs that peace.

Nor are they **armor** against demons. Ideals are man-made and can be mere idols.

The rediscovery of objective structures of grace in place of subjective ideals will mark a major revolution in modern thinking. These concepts may sound technical, but they are the very stuff of life. Even Plato, without the help of the drama revealed in the Bible, saw this issue as central in human experience. To what do you or I submit our wills and our desires? Are we obeying subjectively created ideals or eternal laws written in heaven? No decision is more crucial. In the Bible, what Plato knows as impersonal laws (ideas) receive a further sanction. They are now commandments of a living God. Even ideals, though tokens of man's highest dreams, here stand under judgment.

The issue may be clarified if one looks at the illustrations of the **armor of God** of our text.

Truth. The word is familiar to the point of being commonplace. Modern man may not have worshiped God in recent centuries, but he has worshiped **truth.** Nor dare we belittle the triumphs of our age of enlightenment. The concept of **truth** has retained an objective meaning. The authentic scientist submits to something outside himself. Autonomy is surrendered. How little even the modern scientist, however, has been aware of the fact that he has been the beneficiary of Christian faith. Submission to **truth** implies a prior submission to the God of truth. Remove the divine sanction and mere idols of truth can reign in truth's stead. Truth in final analysis is a frail flower. Unredeemed man's will and desire can trample it into the mud. Truth in politics, truth in economics, truth in the realm of biblical scholarship—how long do they maintain themselves when they are confronted by the interests of power? Natural science, as we traditionally know it, has apparently remained safe. It has thus far, by fortunate circumstance, proved useful in the march of utilitarian progress. Yet ominous signs are on the horizon that truth even in the impersonal kingdom of natural science is no longer immune. It thought itself above and apart from the world of human relationships and assumed that it could escape the judgments both of Christian conscience and of the tyranny of power. We see today that such escape is illusion. It may have to choose between one or the other master, as indeed the pursuit of truth has had to choose more than once in the past. It is folly to think that the passion and the pride of man will refrain from laying violent hands even upon the priests of science.

When our text speaks of the Christian as **having girded** his **loins with truth,** it has in mind, of course, God's truth as revealed in Christ. Yet surely the larger connotations of the concept of **truth** are legitimate expansions of its meaning. In a world in which demonic forces are winning back their ancient patrimonies, only Christians may be left to guard the sacred shrine of **truth.** Even science may owe its preservation, as once it owed its origin, to Christian truth. Submission to the truth ultimately involves a dying to self. Christian history has sins against the truth on its conscience. The story of Galileo is known to every schoolboy. On the issue of submission to truth the Protestant principle is in conflict with Catholicism, though Protestantism too cannot boast of a clear record. Yet the full biblical faith in God, however obscured by the weakness of Christians, is still the only ultimate fortress for truth-

16 Above all, taking the shield of faith, wherewith ye shall be able to quench all the fiery darts of the wicked.

gospel of peace;
16 above all taking the shield of faith, with which you can quench

---

16. Above all: This translation cannot be justified; render "besides all these" (Goodspeed). **The shield** here meant is the great oblong described by Polybius, which gave shelter to the soldier's whole frame. It consisted of two layers of wood, covered with canvas and then with hide. **Flaming darts**—arrows or light spears, tipped with pitch and set ablaze—would burn themselves out against the hide-covered shield without harming the man behind it. **Faith,** then, is represented as **the shield** which will ward off the fiercest temptations, pictured as **flaming darts** hurled by Satan.

---

seeking and truthtelling in this our sinful world. Only the Christian has the final gift of courage to listen to the word of God as it resounds throughout his universe—in science, in history, and in man's heart.

16. ***The Shield of Faith.***—Is there a word in the Christian's vocabulary which is at the same time more rich in meaning and yet more vague in concrete connotation than the word **faith?** What does it designate when we glibly use it—that which is believed, or that by which we do the believing; belief *in* (as in a person), or belief *that* (as when we assert a logical truth)? Is it an act of reason or an act of the will? Is it mere assent or is it costly trust and obedience? A phalanx of questions can confront us. Nor is it idle conversation to ask them.

In this context it may suffice to deal with this inexhaustible concept as it illustrates the more general theme of the "armor of God" and of the demonic evil against which the Christian's weapons are to be used. **Faith** can be a shield to **quench all the flaming darts of the evil one.** And we may take **faith** to mean here, what basically it designates in the Bible, an act of will even more than of reason—in a word, "trust in obedience."

How do most men of good will combat evil? The ways are many. Yet none, we may assume, is more often tried than direct moral attack. We face it in naked encounter. A temptation is escaped. A sin is labeled ugly. A social crime is denounced. We call upon our reserves of moral strength. Simple fear of consequence plays a part, even if it is no more than the dread of a bad conscience when we go to bed at night. The moralist and the preacher in their turn appeal to the sanctions of ethical wisdom, of example, of precept and ideal. In the Christian pulpit Jesus is brought upon the scene as model and as ultimate moralist, the Sermon on the Mount serving as ethical blueprint of the perfection to be attained.

All, perhaps, well and good. But if conscious strength and precept and ideal fail, what then? Possibly they ought to be presented on a higher key? This may, however, in practice, merely reveal failure in more glaring light. And there comes a time when all moralisms become impotent, even the highest. To an alcoholic the Sermon on the Mount must sound like the message of doom.

Moralistic Christianity—we have seen much of it in recent generations—has run into a tragic law of diminishing returns. Paul could tell what is wrong with it. Is it not a gospel (?) of salvation by works? The majestic faith-Christianity of the N.T. has vanished from the scene. Paul could well ask whether he had written his epistles in vain.

Orthodox Christianity is right in its bold assertion that the root of sin is not weakness but unbelief. Faith is the only real cure. The Reformers were right also in confronting all works-religion with a return to the good news of "justification by faith." Rehearsal of the great Reformation argument cannot be attempted here. The relevance of the concept, even in its most general form, to the problem of Christian ethics cries out for rediscovery.

The deeper problem raised by human sinfulness is not the *what,* but the *why*. Why does the alcoholic yield to drunkenness? Why is the Pharisee proud? Why are all of us victims of **the flaming darts of the evil one?** Is not the ultimate answer lack of faith in God? Modern depth psychology can come to the aid here of Christian analysis. Alcoholism traces back to insecurity and fear and guilt. It offers an escape from the demands of the divine-human interview. And escape in turn is a symptom of want of faith. It takes courage to come into judgment and face even one's own self. Only trust in a God of love—a prodigal's trust in a father—can overcome the cowardice of unbelief. And alcoholism is merely a relatively clear illustration of the larger truth. Envy and pride, for example, spring from the same root of faithlessness. Jesus addressed his parable of the Pharisee and the publican "unto certain which *trusted in themselves*" (Luke 18:9). No more vivid proof text is needed. Substitute self-

17 And take the helmet of salvation, and the sword of the Spirit, which is the word of God:

all the flaming darts of the evil one. 17 And take the helmet of salvation, and the sword of the Spirit, which is the word of God.

17. Take, more exactly "receive" (δέξασθε). The change of verb adds to the vividness of the picture. In vs. 11 we had the general verb ἐνδύσασθε, "put on"; in vs. 13, the verb was ἀναλάβετε (resumed in its participle in vs. 16), with its proper sense of "take up," the armor being thought of as laid on the ground at the soldier's feet until he is ready to take it up piece by piece and put it on for battle. But **the helmet** and **the sword** are not "taken up" from the ground by the soldier, now clad in his coat of mail; he "receives" them from his attendant or armor-bearer. The verb is appropriate also to that which **helmet** and **sword** represent in the figure, i.e., **salvation** and **the word of God** respectively.

The helmet of salvation: In its original context (Isa. 59:17) the phrase is used of the helmet which God wears when he goes forth to war against the enemies of his people; the thought is not that it protects him, but that it symbolizes his power and readiness to save others. Here the words have a different sense. **Salvation** is itself **the helmet** which the Christian soldier is bidden to receive; it is now the symbol, not of power to save others, but of the divine protection which safeguards the wearer. In Paul's own use of the phrase he altered it to "the hope of salvation" (I Thess. 5:8), in keeping with his conception of "salvation" as the *future* consummation of the Christian life (see on 2:8).

The sword of the Spirit: Goodspeed construes this phrase in parallelism with those which precede it: "Take . . . for your sword the Spirit, which is the voice of God." It is better, however, to take the genitive here as possessive—"the sword which is the property of the Spirit"; "the sword which the Spirit Himself wields." Nor is there any-

trust for faith in God and pride is a necessary result. Self, though a moralistically perfect self, has been made "god." This "god" must be protected against attack, above all, the attack of loss of self-esteem. Hence pride. Faith in God will mean self-surrender. It will mean, even on the part of the moral aristocrat, the joining in the publican's prayer, "God be merciful to me a sinner."

Again, as with pride, so with any further catalogue of sins. The Christian church could perform no greater service to men of our disturbed and despairing time than to extend to them once again the grace of **faith. Faith** is itself a gift. No works-gospel can produce it. **Faith** requires the mediation of a structure of faith, a fellowship of trust in obedience. Only in the fellowship of faith is it safe to dethrone the false gods of autonomous man. Idolbreaking is dangerous business. **Faith** is the supreme treasure entrusted to the people of God, the church.

17. ***Further Christian Resources.***—This verse, like others in this section of our epistle, is not technical theology but the rhetoric of Christian faith. Helmet and sword need not be too scrupulously allegorized. The author, under his military analogy, is describing further resources of the Christian. The Christian is protected against evil by being in a state of **salvation.** He can use **the word of God** as a **sword.** The concepts are simply named and are not analyzed.

The word **salvation,** like the word faith, is commonplace in Christian vocabulary. It has become so comprehensive in its meaning as to be vague. It can cover the whole range of the drama of the mighty acts of the God of Christian faith and also the personal appropriation of those saving acts in experience.

In what sense can a Christian be said to "be saved"? "Are you saved?" is a question still often heard in Salvation Army or gospel tabernacle meetings. The answer hoped for is a testimonial of a conversion experience. The difficulty which many Christians run into in framing a reply is that no catastrophic conversion story is remembered, yet a sense of being saved is nevertheless a present possession. A confusion exists between the concept of salvation as an objective fact and a subjective witness to that fact. Does "being saved" imply proof of sanctification as well? If so, a positive boast is impossible for most of us. It would look like spiritual pride. A Roman Catholic might find the question embarrassing also, though he would reply with a witness to the institutional church. Saved? Yes, if what is meant is a state of grace in the sacramental system administered by the priestly hierarchy.

Does not the N.T., however, furnish us with helps toward untangling these involvements?

thing to indicate that ῥῆμα (**word**) here means "voice." The relative clause certainly depends on μάχαιραν (**sword**); the relative itself is in the neuter, not as marking attachment to πνεῦμα (**Spirit**), but by attraction into the gender of its complement ῥῆμα.

The word of God is never used in the N.T. of "the Holy Scriptures" generally. It means "the word which God gives us to speak," especially in times of crisis (cf. Matt. 10:19); sometimes used specifically of the gospel message, as in I Pet. 1:25, "That word is the good news which was preached to you"; or combining the gospel and the confession of faith in Jesus as Lord, as in Rom. 10:8-9.

The figure under which **the word of God** is represented as a **sword** has its background in rabbinical interpretations of a number of O.T. passages. For instance, a midrash on Ps. 45:3 ("Gird thy sword upon thy thigh, O most Mighty") runs, "This refers to Moses, who received the Torah, which is like a sword"; Rabbi Judah (*ca.* A.D. 150), dealing with Ps. 149:6 ("a two-edged sword") comments, "This is the Torah, written and oral"

Christian faith, if it means anything, must mean trust in a God of forgiving love. God himself, and the drama of forgiveness in the cross of Christ, are objective facts. The Christian can know, as faith "knows," that he is a forgiven sinner, justified, as our epistle has it in its matchlessly accurate phrase, *"By* grace . . . *through* faith" (2:8). The Christian can witness joyously and without the guilt of pride to this objective truth. A minister in a rural community, in which emotional revivalism is still a norm of church life, is accustomed to answer the question "Are you saved?" with the reply "Yes, and I can name the day and the hour. The day was Good Friday, and the hour three o'clock in the afternoon." The Atonement was "event." Hence salvation is "event" also.

The difficulty comes on the subjective side. The Christian is a forgiven sinner. Still a sinner? The weight of N.T. testimony clearly says "Yes," though Christian theologians of many centuries have attempted to minimize this hard doctrine. Catholicism, both of the East and of the West, has tended to limit the need of justification and forgiveness to sins of a prebaptismal past. Protestant sects which are tempted to narrow the status of "sinner" to preconversion guilt resolve the N.T. paradox in similar too easy fashion. It is the glory of the Reformation, particularly of Luther, to have re-established the paradox in its stark N.T. grandeur. Always forgiven, yet always still a sinner. This is the life of the Christian. The picture of the early church as we see it in the N.T. furnishes overwhelming proof that such is the Christian's paradoxical "state of salvation."

Yet this does not mean that the Christian as still sinner, though forgiven, is no different in moral behavior from those not in a state of salvation. Christians experience grace in two ways, "grace as power and grace as pardon." [6]

[6] See Reinhold Niebuhr, *Nature and Destiny of Man*, II, 135.

"Shall we continue in sin, that grace may abound? God forbid," says Paul (Rom. 6:1-2). Sanctification, the new life in Christ, comes as a gift of promise. One of the parables of Jesus tells the story: "For the earth bringeth forth fruit of herself; first the blade, then the ear, after that the full corn in the ear" (Mark 4:28).

Every Christian who has honestly experienced forgiveness through the cross of Christ, whether by catastrophic conversion or by the grace of a Christian environment, knows that he has a weapon against evil of incomparable power. He can begin each day and each hour with a conscience washed clean through repentance. Conscience will again become soiled. Guilt will again accumulate. But the mountains of guilt which the unrepentant bear have been taken from the Christian's shoulders. A freedom and a joy can accompany the Christian as he meets the tasks of the daily round. He is "in Christ" as in a fortress.

And besides the **helmet of salvation,** the Christian carries **the sword of the Spirit, which is the word of God. Spirit** and **word** are again concepts of wide meaning. In concrete terms the Christian has as helpers in his warfare the church and the Bible. (But see Exeg.) He returns, as the next verse tells us, to the fellowship of the Spirit, the household of prayer. He must return also to the foundation of his faith, the drama of salvation, and its record in the Bible. Trust in God is never easy. It demands death to self. Yet the self even of the Christian never remains surrendered long. It reasserts itself. The act of faith, submission in repentance, must be endlessly repeated. There is no demobilization in the Christian life. Memory of grace can never fade into forgetfulness without dire results. The experience of the centuries overwhelmingly proves that neglect of church and Bible can undermine in briefest time even the faith of saints. The flaw in much so-called "revivalist Christianity" is that it does not face realistically this demand in the Christian life

18 Praying always with all prayer and supplication in the Spirit, and watching thereunto with all perseverance and supplication for all saints;

18 Pray at all times in the Spirit, with all prayer and supplication. To that end keep alert with all perseverance, making suppli-

(Strack and Billerbeck, *Kommentar zum N.T.*, III, 618, 688); cf. also Isa. 11:4, "He shall smite the earth with the rod ["with the word"—LXX] of his mouth, and with the breath [or "spirit"] of his lips shall he slay the wicked"; together with its application in II Thess. 2:8, "The Lord Jesus will slay him with the breath of his mouth." See the further use of the figure in Heb. 4:12 and Rev. 1:16; 2:16; 19:15, 21.

18. With all prayer and supplication: The language still bears upon the stand of the Christian warrior who can hold firm against his spiritual foes only as he remains always in prayer, beseeching the aid of God. Though he is armed cap-a-pie with God's own

for repetition. It is not an accident that the later writings of the N.T. lay such stress upon perseverance and endurance. The words "beware" and "watch" were often on the lips of our Lord. The Christian life is one of disciplined remembrance. The church with its Bible can partly be defined as a fellowship of remembering. The Passover in Judaism and the Eucharist in Christianity are a "making memorial" of the biblical drama. Without such repetitive reminder, though it runs the danger of "vain repetitions" (Matt. 6:7), even the most thoroughly twice-born Christian loses contact with his God and the "due sense of all [his] mercies."

18. *The Church as an Army.*—The preceding description of the Christian soldier can apply to the individual. Here we are reminded that we are members of an army. The "spirit" needed for battle can come to the Christian only derivatively from the Holy Spirit. And the Holy Spirit resides in the fellowship of Pentecost, the church. No army can so much as march if composed of individual stragglers, each for himself. Nor will an army achieve victories without the help of a powerful "spiritual" bond of unity. The familiar French phrase *esprit de corps* expresses this in a striking metaphor. The "spirit" of the body of Christ, to apply the metaphor to the church, is the Holy Spirit.

Christians of earlier centuries of church history must have felt the meaning of corporateness more vividly than do we of the ages of divided Christendom. In the great "catholic" era of the church a massive unity was largely taken for granted. It was simply there, and called for little theoretical explication. Hence at the Reformation breakup of the medieval system the loss of *this* mark of the church of the N.T. was at first not clearly felt. Issues of basic faith were for the moment more important.

The story of how the sense of the corporateness of the people of God was lost in the journey from the early Middle Ages to modern times is complicated. The inroads of individualist misconception of the Bible go far back. The concept of the Holy Spirit became transformed from a corporate fact to one of vague spirituality and of a purely inward phenomenon of universal human consciousness. The symbol of the bride of Christ was transferred from the church to the Christian soul (cf. Expos. on 5:23). All the churches of our day suffer grievously from the obscuration of the N.T. idea of the church as a people and a nation and a household—in short, the church as Christ's unified body. Roman Catholicism still witnesses before the world to a corporate universality. This witness of Romanism can stand in judgment over Protestant divisiveness. But the great church of the papacy can maintain her claim to catholicity only by presumptuous exclusions. Nor has the Roman Church escaped the disease of individualism. Viewed with the test of congregational corporateness in mind, Rome has lost the note of "body" even more strikingly than have the churches of the Reformation. At a Roman Catholic Mass there is very little expression of fellowship across the barriers of separateness in worship and prayer. "All have sinned, and come short of the glory of God" (Rom. 3:23).

Pray at all times in the Spirit, and make **supplication for all the saints,** admonishes our text. One of the names given to the Holy Spirit in the N.T. is that of Strengthener or Comforter. The word can be brought into imaginative connection with the military analogies of our passage. Prayer is a universal practice in religion. One could assert that all men pray, if only to monstrous heathen idols, or like the Pharisee in the temple, a man by "himself" (Luke 18:11). We pray individually. But special promises are made to the church at prayer. "Where two or three are gathered together in my name, there am I in the midst of them" (Matt. 18:20). Church prayer is "common prayer." In the ages when church corporateness was more clearly known, common prayer was rated by Christian theologians as having a clear

19 And for me, that utterance may be given unto me, that I may open my mouth

cation for all the saints, 19 and also for me,

panoply, he is strong only as he maintains communion with God **in the Spirit.** The military figure is sustained through the next phrase—**watching . . . with all perseverance:** the soldier must never allow himself to be caught off guard. **Perseverance** is to be taken closely with **supplication for all saints;** the unsleeping alertness of the Christian is to be shown especially in persevering intercession on behalf of all his comrades in the fight. We are not engaged in single combat with the powers of evil, but are members of an army; and we must be concerned for the welfare of all who fight alongside us.

E. An Appeal for Prayers (6:19-20)

19-20. Here the writer paraphrases the appeal made by Paul in Col. 4:3. He seems to have interpreted "door of utterance" as "mouth."

precedence over individualist prayer. The growth of liturgies in the church was a natural development. Says Richard Hooker, echoing a traditional conviction:

> When we publicly make our prayers, it cannot be but that we do it with much more comfort than in private, for that the things we ask publicly are approved as needful and good in the judgment of all, we hear them sought for and desired with common consent. Again, thus much help and furtherance is more yielded, in that if so be our zeal and devotion to Godward be slack, the alacrity and fervor of others serveth as a present spur. "For even prayer itself (saith Saint Basil) when it hath not the consort of many voices to strengthen it, is not itself." [7]

The strengthening effect of fellowship is a commonplace experience. No lone Christian can retain "spirit" strength long by himself. Even when separated by force of circumstance from communion with his church group, the fellowship itself must be maintained. Individualistic Christianity is, according to N.T. standards, a contradiction in terms. Christianity, it is true, is intensely personal. The Reformation was in the right as it revolted against a church system in which the very concept of grace had become dangerously impersonal. Forgiveness bought over a counter in the form of indulgences makes mockery of the love of God. But a tragic confusion results when "personal" is confused with "individualistic." Protestantism has been a victim of such a confusion in much of its history.

Supplication for all the saints describes the mutual intercessory prayer of Christians. Has there ever been in the long experience of the Christian centuries a time when weakness has not been transformed into strength by remembrance in prayer? As the soldier in line of battle would faint were it not for the knowledge that comrades are fighting at his side, so the individual Christian lives on the Spirit-empowered faith and trust of the brotherhood of Christ. How desperately as Christian soldiers we need the fellowship of the Holy Spirit, our storm-tossed era will show. The pride of individual combat against demonic evil will soon be a thing of the past. For secular demonic power also is individualistic no longer. Christianity is being confronted in the twentieth century by secular "churches." And "the children of this world are in their generation wiser than the children of light" (Luke 16:8). No disciple of Karl Marx would dream of espousing a gospel of individualistic communism. The phrase itself is an obvious contradiction in terms —as the individualistic concept of the new covenant in Christ ought to be for the Christian. The communist knows—as some Christians apparently do not yet know—that a war of conflicting gospels is *class* war. It is war between great social structures. And these structures, demonic or holy, possess group personalities, or more accurately, are possessed by personalized spiritual forces. We witness again a battle between gods as well as men—war in heaven. Enlistment in an army must accordingly replace single combat. Neutrality will become impossible. We shall be members either of the church of Christ or of the "church" of Antichrist. Churchless Christianity will be revealed as impotent. We shall see meaning once more in an ancient invitation to enlistment voiced at Pentecost, "Repent, and be baptized every one of you in the name of Jesus Christ for the remission of sins, and ye shall receive the gift of the Holy Ghost" (Acts 2:38).

19-20. ***Bearing Witness to the Gospel.***—A lack of courage is not a characteristic which a reader of the N.T. would ascribe to Paul. The

[7] *Ecclesiastical Polity* V. 24. 2 (ed. John Keble; Oxford: Clarendon Press, 1888).

boldly, to make known the mystery of the gospel,
20 For which I am an ambassador in bonds; that therein I may speak boldly, as I ought to speak.
21 But that ye also may know my affairs, *and* how I do, Tychicus, a beloved brother and faithful minister in the Lord, shall make known to you all things:

that utterance may be given me in opening my mouth boldly to proclaim the mystery of the gospel, 20 for which I am an ambassador in chains; that I may declare it boldly, as I ought to speak.
21 Now that you also may know how I am and what I am doing, Tych'i-cus the beloved brother and faithful minister in

---

20. An ambassador in chains: The singular ἁλύσει ("fetter") is used, as in Acts 28:20. It refers specifically to the leg iron which bound Paul to the soldier who guarded him. Goodspeed (*Meaning of Ephesians,* p. 69) points out that the combination of the idea of imprisonment with Paul's function as **ambassador** is derived from Philem. 9 ("an ambassador and now a prisoner also for Christ Jesus"). Several of the ancient commentators draw attention to the anomaly of such treatment of an **ambassador,** whose person was inviolable in the law of all nations. Hort notes that "the writer has in mind not the mere general thought of being in bonds, but the visual image of an ambassador standing up to plead his sovereign's cause and wearing, strangest of contradictions, a fetter by way of official adornment" (*Prolegomena to St. Paul's Epistles to Romans and Ephesians,* p. 156).

F. Commendation of the Bearer of the Epistle (6:21-22)

21-22. These verses are taken almost word for word from Col. 4:7-8, and were certainly set down with that passage before the writer's eyes. It is hardly conceivable that Paul

---

picture of the apostle in these verses, therefore, conveys a hint of pathos. Even the greatest **ambassador** of the **mystery of the gospel** known to Christian history confesses to human frailty and possibly even to the sin of sloth. He may have recalled the precept of Jesus that "men ought always to pray, and not to faint" (Luke 18:1).

Mutual confessions of weakness, by way of a paradox, often produce corporate courage. The bravery of a company of soldiers is frequently paralleled by confessed cowardice on the part of the individuals who compose the group. Paul might have been powerless had he not received strength from the prayers of the brave Christian flocks of which he was the shepherd. As our verses commend "supplication for all saints" (vs. 18), there follows the plea, **and also for me.**

Does it require boldness to witness to the gospel? No preacher standing in his pulpit or layman testifying to his faith before his fellows will ever belittle the virtue of Christian courage. Salesmanship even in the secular business world calls for a kind of bravery. The audacity of the proverbial book canvasser astonishes many of us. We are familiar with a commercial phrase like "sales resistance." Profitable analogies can be drawn between the characteristics exhibited by the merchant and those needed by the Christian evangelist.

Peculiar temptations to silence, however, beset witnessing to the gospel. How shall a mere man give utterance to the words of God? The most penetrating of the words of the Lord are heard only in the secret chamber of conscience. There "the word of God is quick, and powerful, and sharper than any two-edged sword, . . . and is a discerner of the thoughts and intents of the heart" (Heb. 4:12). How shall a mere mortal penetrate behind the veil God himself may have drawn to hide his presence? A man-to-man conversation is no substitute for the divine-human interview. Religion, so we are taught in a current phrase, is what a man does with his solitariness—and there is much truth in the definition. Self-surrender is a lone act. No one can repent for another. Religion, therefore, so we are tempted to conclude, is a man's own affair. The Christian can witness moralistically, of course, by charity and social service. But Paul in our verse asks for strength to witness verbally. He prays that his **mouth** may be opened. Few of us are courageous enough to pray quite this prayer. Even the preacher in the pulpit finds it easier to utter moral homilies or sermons on topics of the times than to speak forth the deep and disturbing **mystery of the gospel.**

Reticence in matters pertaining to the intimacies of the soul's dialogue with God are proper. Public confessions of unseemly sins,

22 Whom I have sent unto you for the same purpose, that ye might know our affairs, and *that* he might comfort your hearts.
23 Peace *be* to the brethren, and love with faith, from God the Father and the Lord Jesus Christ.

the Lord will tell you everything. 22 I have sent him to you for this very purpose, that you may know how we are, and that he may encourage your hearts.
23 Peace be to the brethren, and love with faith, from God the Father and the

---

would find it necessary to repeat himself so meticulously, especially in a commendation of his messenger, where the form in which the words are cast is of no significance.

G. Benedictions (6:23-24)

23-24. The form of the benedictions reflects the encyclical character of the letter. Unlike the Pauline benedictions, they are in the third person, and are pronounced upon the whole Christian fellowship. The prayer for the blessing of **peace** recalls the fundamental theme of the writer's thought—the peace between Jew and Gentile which is the first fruits of the cosmic peace in which the work of Christ is to have its ultimate issue. **Love with faith** recalls the great phrase of Gal. 5:6, "In Jesus Christ neither circumcision availeth any thing, nor uncircumcision; but faith which worketh by love."

The concluding phrase offers some difficulty. In the KJV it is taken in the sense which is favored by most of the fathers—**in sincerity.** The noun ἀφθαρσία (lit., "incorruption") does not seem to be used of *moral* quality anywhere else, but always of "that which is not liable to decay"; in most instances it means simply "immortality." Accordingly, the phrase is rendered in the RSV by the adjective **undying.** It is doubtful, however, that it ought to be construed in such close dependence on the participle

---

even when the testimony is meant to glorify the good news of forgiveness, violate the sense of decorum which has rightly become part of Christian culture. All this and more can be set forth as reasons why witnessing to the Christian faith by bold speech requires safeguards. Yet when any of us marshal such arguments for silence, are we not conscious of guilt as well? Verbal **utterance** calls for proper times and seasons. But who of us has a clear conscience that he has heeded the call of God to **speak boldly, as I ought to speak?**

Evangelism has always implied speech. In witnessing there is no final substitute for the *word.* Judgment needs to be *voiced.* The church has prophetic duties toward the state and society. As the prophet Nathan once appeared before his king with bold words of rebuke, so the church has a commission to address the secular social order. The church may not have superior wisdom in legislative or governmental details, but the church is guardian of the law. She can utter boldly the "Thou shalt not" of the ancient decalogue. The relations between church and state present complex problems for the Christian. May it not be, however, that in this area of witness the guidance of the N.T. needs supplementation from the O.T.? The "church" of the Jewish nation is a closer parallel to the position which Christians occupy in modern society than is the picture of the embryo flocks of the days of Paul.

Leaving this large topic of corporate witness, however, we are on sure ground when we apply our text to more intimate human relationships. **That . . . I may speak boldly, as I ought to speak** is a prayer every Christian needs to repeat daily. Opportunities for a courageous word crowd upon us—a word of judgment, perhaps, but even more words of hope and of faith and of love. Here, as in much modern Christianity, we are hampered by the moralistic fallacy. Few of us can point to our sanctification as proof of the glory of the gospel. None of us ought to. One of our greatest witnessing tasks, indeed, is to interpret the gospel of Christ once again as the good news of salvation by grace and faith in place of the sad news of salvation by works. If the gospel were the latter, silence could be our only recourse. Yet it is a tragic fact that the popular conception of Christianity today—and this applies to many within the church—is that of a religion of impossible ideals. And if performance does not equal the ideals, pursuit of them is left to the pious. The gospel has been understood as good advice instead of as good news.

No Christian, humble before God, can witness to the gospel as salvation by works. His own failures would be exhibit A. A few publicans might

24 Grace *be* with all them that love our Lord Jesus Christ in sincerity. Amen.

¶ Written from Rome unto the Ephesians by Tychicus.

Lord Jesus Christ. 24 Grace be with all who love our Lord Jesus Christ with love undying.

ἀγαπώντων (**love**); there is no suggestion of a distinction between those **who love our Lord . . . with love undying** and others who love him with a transient love. It seems better, therefore, to take the words in a more general connection with the whole benediction, "Grace be with them all forever."

conceivably be turned into Pharisees. But that is all. Paul spent his apostleship in combating this antithesis to the good news in Christ. What the Christian can witness to is his faith, and the objective drama of salvation upon which his faith rests. "Tell me the old, old story," we sing in a familiar gospel hymn. Telling the story has been, down through the centuries, the making known of the **mystery of the gospel.** Hymns have told it in song. Liturgies have enshrined it in commemorative action. God is the actor in that story, not man. We can repeat it, therefore, without committing the sin of pride—a sin which we do commit when we make ourselves the center of the drama. The Christian can witness also to his personal faith. Autobiography is not ruled out. Testimonials to the miracles of repentance and forgiveness are not boasting. The Christian, speaking however boldly, is not a judge of his fellows. He is a sinner, forgiven and rejoicing, but for that very reason going forth in love to win publican and harlot. "Judge not, that ye be not judged" is the touchstone of his relations with his fellows. Like Paul he is **an ambassador in bonds**—the bonds of the love of Christ.

PALESTINE in New Testament Times

Joppa

Bethlehem
2550'

Jerusalem
2593'

Jericho
820 FEET BELOW SEA LEVEL

DEAD SEA
1292 FEET BELOW SEA LEVEL

Jord